I0813955

Christopher Ansberry is to be congratulated on a wonderful and insightful addition to the acclaimed Zondervan Exegetical Commentary series. Already known to a scholarly audience as a Proverbs expert, here Ansberry deepens and refines his ideas in a thorough engagement with this enigmatic text. He shows how Proverbs, with its rich world of characters, is a transformative text for its readers, pedagogically shaping their moral and theological discourse in carefully crafted stages. Scholars, pastors, and teachers will benefit from Ansberry's fresh translation and exegetical analyses, from his close attention to literary and structural issues and his emphasis on canonical and theological significance which showcases its relevance to Christian life and discipleship today. A tour de force of a commentary which takes its rightful place amongst the best scholarship on Proverbs in the present day.

—KATHARINE DELL, professor of Old Testament literature and theology,
University of Cambridge

Christopher Ansberry takes his readers on a journey full of clarity and insight through the "Wisdom and Virtue" of the book of Proverbs, one based on both a deep knowledge of the book's internal logic and the Hebrew text itself. Ansberry masterfully demonstrates how the different parts of the book of Proverbs form a greater unit with a clear pedagogical and theological agenda. Anyone interested in a fresh approach to this important biblical book, which has spent far too long being taken as an "outsider" within the Hebrew Bible, will find much to stimulate their own thinking.

—BERND U. SCHIPPER, professor of Hebrew Bible,
Humboldt-University of Berlin

The book of Proverbs is not dry, mundane, or irrelevant. Rather—as Christopher Ansberry shows in this masterful commentary—Proverbs offers potent resources for the (trans)formation of character through wisdom and righteousness. After providing a fresh and nuanced translation of the Hebrew, Ansberry draws out the complexity and profundity of the book's curriculum for wise living. Ansberry's writing is reasoned and judicious without losing boldness and clout; it pays attention to detail without getting lost in the detail; it remains accessible and engaging without obscuring the complexity of scholarly debates. Ansberry highlights, not only the significance of the book in its original historical context, but its potential implications for the contemporary world. Himself a masterful teacher, Ansberry equips his readers with the skills and knowledge they need to dig into Proverbs' wisdom for themselves.

—SUZANNA MILLAR, lecturer in Hebrew Bible/Old Testament,
University of Edinburgh

Ansberry's great accomplishment is to offer a full-length critical commentary on Proverbs that refuses to characterize Proverbs's moral vision as a simple guide to success and instead recognizes the heart of the book's ethics to be its concern with character formation and virtue. But more than simply pointing to this fact, through careful attention to the book's linguistic and rhetorical structures Ansberry shows readers of his commentary how Proverbs inculcates wisdom in its readers/hearers! For anyone interested in the rhetoric and pragmatics of Proverbs—how Proverbs carries out its moral vision—Ansberry's work is a must read. A keen concern for the theological dimensions of Proverbs, and how the book's discourse is refracted in later texts, including the New Testament, means Ansberry's book will be especially valuable for Christian interpreters—whether established scholars or serious lay students. It is a most welcome addition to the world of Proverbs commentaries!

—TIMOTHY SANDOVAL, associate dean and associate professor of Old Testament, Texas Christian University

In this formidable commentary, Ansberry skillfully guides readers through the imaginative world of Proverbs and the paths, poetic forms, images, and tropes that form its terrain in order to show how the book as a whole achieves its aim of cultivating wisdom and virtue. An effective pedagogue himself, Ansberry invites audiences to "take the course" offered by Proverbs with precision, depth, creativity, and wisdom. This work will be a vital resource for all students of Proverbs and seekers of biblical wisdom.

—PATRICIA VESELY, associate professor of Hebrew Bible and Christian ethics, Memphis Theological Seminary

Christopher Ansberry's commentary on Proverbs proves invaluable for navigating this intriguing book. Ansberry's meticulous and well-researched approach offers both a scholarly examination of the text and a theological understanding of Proverbs. Whether you're a scholar, pastor, or curious layperson, Ansberry's work on Proverbs deserves a place on your shelf for its engaging insights into ancient and literary contexts, and for highlighting the relevance of the book of Proverbs for modern readers.

— DOMINICK HERNANDEZ, director of de Talbot en Español and associate professor of Old Testament and Semitics, Biola University

Ansberry has capitalized on the priorities of the Zondervan Exegetical Commentary series to produce a compelling interpretation of Proverbs. His attention to wisdom's ubiquity, the concept-oriented and perspectival connections between sayings, and robust use of scholarly literature will make an abiding contribution. While Proverbs is not a book straightforwardly taken as a whole, Ansberry has written a coherent, creative, and level-headed commentary that should mark a new generation of scholarship.

—ARTHUR KEEFER, research associate, Divinity University and associate pastor, The Scot's Church, Melbourne

PROVERBS

PROVERBS

The (Trans)formation of Character in accord with Wisdom and Virtue

ZONDERVAN

Exegetical Commentary

ON THE

Old Testament

A DISCOURSE ANALYSIS OF THE HEBREW BIBLE

CHRISTOPHER B. ANSBERRY

DANIEL I. BLOCK
General Editor

The Hebrew text is from Deut 31:11–13, which highlights the importance of "hearing" the voice of Scripture:

> When all Israel comes to appear before יהוה your God at the place he will choose, you shall read this *Torah* before them in their hearing. Assemble the people—men, women and children, and the foreigners residing in your towns—so they can *listen* and learn to fear יהוה your God and follow carefully all the words of this *Torah*. Their children, who do not know this *Torah*, must *hear* it and learn to fear יהוה your God as long as you live in the land you are crossing the Jordan to possess. (NIV, modified)

ZONDERVAN ACADEMIC

Proverbs

Published in Grand Rapids, Michigan, by Zondervan. Zondervan is a registered trademark of The Zondervan Corporation, L.L.C., a wholly owned subsidiary of HarperCollins Christian Publishing, Inc.

Requests for information should be addressed to customercare@harpercollins.com.

Zondervan titles may be purchased in bulk for educational, business, fundraising, or sales promotional use. For information, please email SpecialMarkets@Zondervan.com.

Library of Congress Cataloging-in-Publication Data

Names: Ansberry, Christopher B., author.
Title: Proverbs : a discourse analysis of the hebrew bible / Christopher B.Ansberry.
Description: Grand Rapids, Michigan : Zondervan, [2024] | Series: Zondervanexegetical commentary on the Old Testament : a discourse analysis of theHebrew bible | Includes bibliographical references and index.
Identifiers: LCCN 2024011395 | ISBN 9780310942306 (hardcover)
Subjects: LCSH: Bible. Proverbs--Commentaries. | BISAC: RELIGION / BiblicalCommentary / Old Testament / Poetry & Wisdom Literature | RELIGION /Biblical Commentary / General
Classification: LCC BS1465.53 .A67 2024 | DDC 223/.7077--dc23/eng/20240505
LC record available at https://lccn.loc.gov/2024011395

Cover design: Tammy Johnson
Interior design: Beth Shagene

Printed in the United States of America

---

24 25 26 27 28 29 30 31 32 33 34 35 36 37 38 /TRM/ 19 18 17 16 15 14 13 12 11 10 9 8 7 6 5 4 3 2 1

In memory of
Dawn Marie van Wingerden (1951–2022)
and
Rev. Dr. Michael J. Ovey (1958–2017)
"The memory of the righteous, for a blessing" (Prov 10:7a)

Contents

Series Introduction

Prospectus

Modern audiences are often taken in by the oratorical skill and creativity of preachers and teachers. However, they tend to forget that the authority of proclamation is directly related to the correspondence of the key points of the sermon to the message the biblical authors were trying to communicate. Since we confess that "all Scripture [including the entirety of the OT] is God-breathed and useful for teaching, rebuking, correcting and training in righteousness, so that [all God's people] may be thoroughly equipped for every good work" (2 Tim 3:16–17 NIV), it seems essential that those who proclaim its message should pay close attention to the rhetorical agendas of biblical authors. Too often modern readers, including preachers, are either baffled by OT texts, or they simply get out of them that for which they are looking. Many commentaries available to pastors and teachers try to resolve the dilemma either through word-by-word and verse-by-verse analysis or synthetic theological reflections on the text without careful attention to the flow and argument of that text.

The commentators in this series recognize that too little attention has been paid to biblical authors as rhetoricians, to their larger rhetorical and theological agendas, and especially to the means by which they tried to achieve their goals. Like effective communicators in every age, biblical authors were driven by a passion to communicate a message. So, we must inquire not only what that message was, but also what strategies they used to impress their message on their hearers' ears. This reference to "hearers" rather than to readers is intentional, since the biblical texts were written to be heard. Not only were the Hebrew and Christian Scriptures composed to be heard in the public gathering of God's people, but also before the invention of moveable type few would have had access to their own copies of the Scriptures. While the contributors to this series acknowledge with Paul that every Scripture—that is, every passage in the Hebrew Bible—is God-breathed, we also recognize that the inspired authors possessed a vast repertoire of rhetorical and literary strategies. These included not only the special use of words and figures of speech, but also the deliberate selection, arrangement, and shaping of ideas.

The primary goal of this commentary series is to help serious students of Scripture, as well as those charged with preaching and teaching the Word of God, to hear the messages of Scripture as biblical authors intended them to be heard. While we recognize the timelessness of the biblical message, the validity of our interpretation and the authority with which we teach the Scriptures are related directly to the extent to which we have grasped the message intended by the author in the first place. Accordingly, when dealing with specific texts, the authors of the commentaries in this series are concerned with three principal questions: (1) What are the principal theological points the biblical writers are making? (2) How do biblical writers make those points? (3) What significance does the message of the present text have for understanding the message of the biblical book within which it is embedded and the message of the Scriptures as a whole? The achievement of these goals requires careful attention to the way ideas are expressed in the OT, including the selection and arrangement of materials and the syntactical shaping of the text.

To most readers syntax operates primarily at the sentence level. But recent developments in biblical study, particularly advances in rhetorical and discourse analysis, have alerted us to the fact that syntax operates also at the levels of the paragraph, the literary unit being analyzed, and the composition as a whole. Discourse analysis, also called macro syntax, studies the text beyond the level of the sentence (sentence syntax), where the paragraph serves as the basic unit of thought. Those contributing to this series recognize that this type of study may be pursued in a variety of ways. Some will prefer a more bottom-up approach, where clause connectors and transitional features play a dominant role in analysis. Others will pursue a more top-down approach, where genre or literary form begins the discussion. However, we all understand that both approaches are required to understand fully the method and the message of the text. For this reason, the ultimate value of discourse analysis is that it allows the text to set the agenda in biblical interpretation.

One of the distinctive goals for this series is to engage the biblical text using some form of discourse analysis to understand not only what the text says, but also how it says it. While attention to words or phrases is still essential, contributors to this commentary series will concentrate on the flow of thought in the biblical writings, both at the macroscopic level of entire compositions and at the microscopic level of individual text units. In so doing, we hope to help other readers of Scripture grasp both the message and the rhetorical force of Old Testament texts. When we hear the message of Scripture, we gain access to the mind of God.

Format of the Commentary

The format of this series is designed to achieve the goals summarized above. Accordingly, each volume in the series will begin with an introduction to the book being explored. In addition to answering the usual questions of date, authorship, and provenance of the composition, commentators will highlight what they consider to be the main theological themes of the book and then discuss broadly how the style and structure of the book develop those themes. This discussion will include a coherent outline of the contents of the book that demonstrates the contribution each part makes to the development of the principal themes.

The commentaries on individual text units that follow will repeat this process in greater detail. Although complex literary units will be broken down further, the commentators will address the following issues.

1. **Main Idea of the Passage:** A one- or two-sentence summary of the key ideas the biblical author seeks to communicate.
2. **Literary Context:** A brief discussion of the relationship of the specific text to the book as a whole and to its place within the broader arguments.
3. **Translation and Exegetical Outline:** Commentators will provide their own translations of each text, formatted to highlight the discourse structure of the text and accompanied by a coherent outline that reflects the flow and argument of the text.
4. **Structure and Literary Form:** An introductory survey of the literary structure and rhetorical style adopted by the biblical author, highlighting how these features contribute to the communication of the main idea of the passage.
5. **Explanation of the Text:** A detailed commentary on the passage, paying particular attention to how the biblical authors select and arrange their materials and how they work with words, phrases, and syntax to communicate their messages. This will take up the bulk of most commentaries.
6. **Canonical and Theological Significance:** The commentary on each unit will conclude by building bridges between the world of the biblical author and other biblical authors and with reflections on the contribution made by this unit to the development of broader issues in biblical theology—particularly on how later OT and NT authors have adapted and reused the motifs in question. The discussion will also include brief reflections on the significance of the message of the passage for readers today.

The way in which this series treats biblical books will be uneven. Commentators on smaller books will have sufficient scope to answer fully each of the issues listed above on each unit of text. However, limitations of space preclude full treatment of every text for the larger books. Instead, commentators will guide readers through ## 1–4 and 6 for every literary unit, but Explanation of the Text (#5) will be selective, generally limited to twelve to fifteen literary units deemed most critical for hearing the message of the book.

In addition to these general introductory comments, we should alert readers of this series to several conventions that we follow. First, the divine name in the Old Testament is presented as YHWH. The form of the name—represented by the Tetragrammaton, יהוה—is a particular problem for scholars. The practice of rendering the divine name in Greek as κύριος (=Heb. אֲדֹנָי, "Adonay") is carried over into English translations as "LORD," which represents Hebrew יהוה and distinguishes it from "Lord," which represents Hebrew אֲדֹנָי. But this creates interpretive problems, for the connotations and implications of referring to someone by name or by title are quite different. When rendered as a name, English translations have traditionally vocalized יהוה as "Jehovah," which combines the consonants of יהוה with the vowels of אֲדֹנָי. However, today non-Jewish scholars often render the name as "Yahweh," recognizing that "Jehovah" is an artificial construct.

Second, frequently the verse numbers in the Hebrew Bible differ from those in our English translations. Since the commentaries in this series are based on the Hebrew text, the Hebrew numbers will be the default numbers. Where the English numbers differ, they will be provided in square brackets (e.g., Joel 4:12[3:12]).

Third, when discussing specific biblical words or phrases, these will be represented both in Hebrew font and in translation, except where the transliterated form is used in place of an English term, either because no single English expression captures the Hebrew word's wide range meaning (e.g., *ḥesed* for חֶסֶד, rather than "lovingkindness"), or when it functions as a title or technical expression not readily captured in English (e.g., *gōʾēl* for גֹּאֵל, rather than "kinsman redeemer").

Daniel I. Block, general editor

Author's Preface and Acknowledgments

The book of Proverbs is many things. Among them, characterizations like banal, dogmatic, or secular have never crossed my mind. Proverbs is a pedagogical masterpiece; its poetic forms are designed to cultivate wisdom and virtue in readers. I've had the privilege of studying Proverbs for many years. My study began with my MA at Wheaton College (IL), when Dr. Hassell Bullock allowed me to join a PhD seminar on wisdom literature. Like the processing of harvested grapes, it was crushed and pressed under the guidance of my PhD supervisor, Dr. Daniel I. Block. It fermented through my interaction with many guides, each of whom readers will find in the footnotes of this volume. And it clarified and aged through my interaction with colleagues and students, especially at Oak Hill Theological College (London, UK). I cannot adequately express my gratitude to Dr. Block, whose trust and confidence in me to write something helpful on Proverbs is terrifying. And I cannot adequately express my gratitude to the many people at Oak Hill Theological College. Among my many friends at Oak Hill, I would like to thank my former colleagues, with whom I had the privilege of sharing an unusual camaraderie. And I would like to thank the many students who had the courage to take my wisdom literature module. With you, this commentary is far better than it would otherwise have been.

It has been a delight to serve not only at Oak Hill but also at Grove City College. I would like to thank Peter Frank, Paul Kemeny, and Seulgi Byun, each of whom created the conditions for me to find my feet back in the States and to complete this commentary. And special thanks are due to the students in my senior seminar course. Your creativity and engagement with Proverbs oxygenated my life and work.

I am grateful to the ZECOT editors and the editorial team at Zondervan for their meticulous and painstaking work, especially Hélène Dallaire and Lee Fields. And I am indebted to the libraries at Oak Hill Theological College, Tyndale House, and the British Library. I would be remiss if I did not extend a special thanks to Evelyn Cornell, the former librarian at Oak Hill. She saved me countless trips to London and Cambridge, chasing down and securing much needed resources.

My wife Carolyn and our four children have been a constant source of support across continents in the production of this volume. In different ways, they have created an atmosphere of rest, love, and laughter that places the demands of ministry and academic scholarship in proper perspective. And Carolyn has proven to be a constant illustration of the embodiment of wisdom and virtue.

The same is true of my mother-in-law, Dawn Marie van Wingerden, and my former principal, Rev. Dr. Michael J. Ovey. Both were taken home by the Lord earlier than all had wished. But both left a legacy. They showed me what godly wisdom and virtue look like through their form of life. This volume is dedicated in memory of them.

Abbreviations

AB	Anchor Bible
ABD	*Anchor Bible Dictionary*. Edited by David Noel Freedman. 6 vols. New York: Doubleday. 1992
ABRL	Anchor Bible Reference Library
ABS	Archaeology and Biblical Studies
AcBib	Academia Biblica
AEL	*Ancient Egyptian Literature*. Miriam Lichtheim. 3 vols. Berkeley: University of California Press, 1971–1980
AIL	Ancient Israel and Its Literature
AnBib	Analecta Biblica
ANEM	Ancient Near East Monographs/Monografías sobre el Antiguo Cercano Oriente
AOTC	Abingdon Old Testament Commentaries
ATD	Das Alte Testament Deutsch
b.	Babylonian Talmud
BBR	*Bulletin for Biblical Research*
BBRSup	*Bulletin for Biblical Research, Supplements*
BCOTWP	Baker Commentary on the Old Testament Wisdom and Psalms
BETL	Bibliotheca Ephemeridum Theologicarum Lovaniensium
BHQ	*Biblia Hebraica Quinta*. Edited by Adrian Schenker et al. Stuttgart: Deutsche Bibelgesellschaft, 2004–
BHRG	*A Biblical Hebrew Reference Grammar*. C. H. J. van der Merwe, J. A. Naudé, and J. H. Kroeze. 2nd ed. London: Bloomsbury T&T Clark, 2017
BHS	*Biblia Hebraica Stuttgartensia*. Edited by Karl Elliger and Wilhelm Rudolph. Stuttgart: Deutsche Bibelgesellschaft, 1983
BHT	Beiträge zur historischen Theologie
Bib	*Biblica*
BibInt	*Biblical Interpretation*
BibInt	Biblical Interpretation Series
BKAT	Biblischer Kommentar, Altes Testament

BLS	Bible and Literature Series
BSac	*Bibliotheca Sacra*
BTB	*Biblical Theology Bulletin*
BWA(N)T	Beiträge zur Wissenschaft vom Alten (und Neuen) Testament
BWL	*Babylonian Wisdom Literature*. Wilfred G. Lambert. Oxford: Clarendon, 1960
BZ	*Biblische Zeitschrift*
BZAW	Beihefte zur Zeitschrift für die alttestamentliche Wissenschaft
CBQ	*Catholic Biblical Quarterly*
CBQMS	Catholic Biblical Quarterly Monograph Series
ConBOT	Coniectanea Biblica: Old Testament Series
COS	*The Context of Scripture*. Edited by William W. Hallo. 3 vols. Leiden: Brill, 1997–2002
CSR	*Christian Scholar's Review*
CurBS	*Currents in Research: Biblical Studies*
DDD	*Dictionary of Deities and Demons in the Bible*. Edited by Karel van der Toorn, Bob Becking, and Pieter W. van der Horst. Leiden: Brill, 1995. 2nd rev. ed. Grand Rapids: Eerdmans, 1999
FAT	Forschungen zum Alten Testament
FB	Forschung zur Bibel
FOTL	Forms of the Old Testament Literature
Gen. Rab.	Genesis Rabbah
GKC	*Gesenius' Hebrew Grammar*. Edited by Emil Kautzsch. Translated by Arthur E. Cowley. 2nd ed. Oxford: Clarendon, 1910
HALOT	*The Hebrew and Aramaic Lexicon of the Old Testament*. Ludwig Koehler, Walter Baumgartner, and Johann J. Stamm. Translated and edited under the supervision of Mervyn E. J. Richardson. 4 vols. Leiden: Brill, 1994–1999
HAT	Handbuch zum Alten Testament
HBAI	*Hebrew Bible and Ancient Israel*
HCOT	Historical Commentary on the Old Testament
HS	*Hebrew Studies*
HSS	Harvard Semitic Studies
HTR	*Harvard Theological Review*
HUCA	*Hebrew Union College Annual*
IBHS	*An Introduction to Biblical Hebrew Syntax*. Bruce K. Waltke and Michael O'Connor. Winona Lake, IN: Eisenbrauns, 1990
IBC	Interpretation: A Bible Commentary for Teaching and Preaching
ICC	International Critical Commentary
IJST	*International Journal of Systematic Theology*

Int	*Interpretation*
JANES	*Journal of the Ancient Near Eastern Society*
JAOS	*Journal of the American Oriental Society*
JBL	*Journal of Biblical Literature*
JETS	*Journal of the Evangelical Theological Society*
JNES	*Journal of Near Eastern Studies*
Joüon	Joüon, Paul. *A Grammar of Biblical Hebrew*. Translated and revised by T. Muraoka. 2 vols. Rome: Pontifical Biblical Institute, 1991
JQR	*Jewish Quarterly Review*
JSJSup	Supplements to the Journal for the Study of Judaism
JSNTSup	Journal for the Study of the New Testament Supplement Series
JSOT	*Journal for the Study of the Old Testament*
JSOTSup	Journal for the Study of the Old Testament Supplement Series
JTI	*Journal of Theological Interpretation*
JTS	*Journal of Theological Studies*
LAI	Library of Ancient Israel
LHBOTS	The Library of Hebrew Bible/Old Testament Studies
LSAWS	*Linguistic Studies in Ancient West Semitic*
LUÅ	Lunds universitets årsskrift
LXX	The Septuagint
MT	Masoretic Text
NAC	New American Commentary
NCB	New Century Bible
NIB	*The New Interpreter's Bible*. Edited by Leander E. Keck. 12 vols. Nashville: Abingdon, 1994–2004
NICOT	New International Commentary on the Old Testament
NIDOTTE	*New International Dictionary of Old Testament Theology and Exegesis*. Edited by Willem A. VanGemeren. 5 vols. Grand Rapids: Zondervan, 1997
OBO	Orbis Biblicus et Orientalis
Or	*Orientalia (NS)*
OTL	Old Testament Library
OTP	*Old Testament Pseudepigrapha*. Edited by James H. Charlesworth. 2 vols. New York: Doubleday, 1983, 1985
Presb	*Presbyterion*
ProEccl	*Pro Ecclesia*
Q	*qere*
RB	*Revue biblique*
SBLDS	Society of Biblical Literature Dissertation Series
SBS	Stuttgarter Bibelstudien

SBT	Studies in Biblical Theology
Semeia	*Semeia*
SJT	*Scottish Journal of Theology*
SOTSMS	Society for Old Testament Studies Monograph Series
SPAW	Sitzungsberichte der preussischen Akademie der Wissenschaften
SubBi	Subsidia Biblica
SymS	Symposium Series
TLOT	*Theological Lexicon of the Old Testament*. Edited by Ernst Jenni, with assistance from Claus Westermann. Translated by Mark E. Biddle. 3 vols. Peabody, MA: Hendrickson, 1997
TynBul	*Tyndale Bulletin*
VT	*Vetus Testamentum*
VTSup	Supplements to Vetus Testamentum
WBC	Word Biblical Commentary
WC	Westminster Commentaries
WMANT	Wissenschaftliche Monographien zum Alten und Neuen Testament
WO	*Die Welt des Orients*
ZAW	*Zeitschrift für die alttestamentliche Wissenschaft*
ZBK	Zürcher Bibelkommentare

Select Bibliography

Aletti, J. N. "Seduction et parole en Proverbes I–IX." *VT* 27 (1977): 129–44.

Baumann, G. *Die Weisheitsgestalt in Proverbien 1–9*. FAT 16. Tübingen: Mohr Siebeck, 1996.

Berlin, Adele. *The Dynamics of Biblical Parallelism*. Rev. and enl. ed. Grand Rapids: Eerdmans, 2008.

Boström, Lennart. *The God of the Sages: The Portrayal of God in the Book of Proverbs*. ConBOT 29. Stockholm: Almqvist & Wiksell International, 1990.

Brown, William P. "The Pedagogy of Proverbs 10:1–31:9." Pages 150–82 in *Character and Scripture: Moral Formation, Community, and Biblical Interpretation*. Edited by William P. Brown. Grand Rapids: Eerdmans, 2002.

———. *Wisdom's Wonder: Character, Creation, and Crisis in the Bible's Wisdom Literature*. Grand Rapids: Eerdmans, 2014.

Bryce, Glendon E. "Another Wisdom-'Book' in Proverbs." *JBL* 91 (1972): 145–57.

Camp, Claudia V. *Wisdom and the Feminine in the Book of Proverbs*. BLS 11. Sheffield: Almond Press, 1985.

———. "Woman Wisdom as Root Metaphor: A Theological Consideration." Pages 45–76 in *The Listening Heart: Essays in Wisdom and the Psalms in Honor of Roland E. Murphy, O. Carm*. Edited by K. G. Hoglund, E. F. Huwiler, J. T. Glass, and R. W. Lee. Sheffield: Sheffield Academic, 1987.

Carr, David M. *Writing on the Tablet of the Heart: Origins of Scripture and Literature*. Oxford: Oxford University Press, 2005.

Clifford, Richard J. *Proverbs*. OTL. Louisville: Westminster John Knox, 1999.

Crenshaw, James L. *Education in Ancient Israel: Across the Deadening Silence*. ABRL. New York: Doubleday, 1998.

Davis, Ellen F. *Proverbs, Ecclesiastes, and the Song of Songs*. Louisville: Westminster John Knox, 2000.

Delitzsch, Franz. "The Book of Proverbs." *Commentary on the Old Testament*. 5th ed. Translated by M. G. Easton. 2 vols. 1874. Repr., Peabody, MA: Hendrickson, 1996.

Dell, Katharine J. *The Book of Proverbs in Social and Theological Context*. Cambridge: Cambridge University Press, 2006.

Emerton, John A. "The Teaching of Amenemope and Proverbs XXII 17–XXIV 22: Reflections of a Long-Standing Problem." *VT* 51 (2001): 431–65.

Fontaine, Carole R. *Traditional Sayings in the Old Testament*. BLS 5. Sheffield: Almond Press, 1982.

Forti, Tova L. *Animal Imagery in the Book of Proverbs*. VTSup 118. Leiden: Brill, 2008.

Fox, Michael V. "*ʾAmon* Again." *JBL* 125 (1996): 699–702.

———. "The Epistemology of the Book of Proverbs." *JBL* 126 (2007): 669–84.

———. *Proverbs 1–9: A New Translation with Introduction and Commentary*. AB 18A. New York: Doubleday, 2000.

———. *Proverbs 10–31: A New Translation with Introduction and Commentary*. AB 18B. New Haven: Yale University Press, 2009.

———. "The Rhetoric of Disjointed Proverbs." *JSOT* 29 (2004): 165–77.

———. "Who Can Learn? A Dispute in Ancient Pedagogy." Pages 62–77 in *Wisdom, You Are My Sister: Studies in Honor of Roland E. Murphy, O. Carm., on the Occasion of His Eightieth Birthday*. Edited by M. L. Barré. CBQMS 29. Washington, DC: Catholic Biblical Association of America, 1997.

———. "World Order and Maᶜat: A Crooked Parallel." *JNES* 23 (1995): 37–48.

Franklyn, Paul. "The Sayings of Agur in Proverbs 30: Piety or Scepticism?" *ZAW* 95 (1983): 238–52.

Frydrych, Tomás. *Living under the Sun: Examination of Proverbs and Qoheleth*. VTSup 90. Leiden: Brill, 2002.

Garrett, Duane A. *Proverbs, Ecclesiastes, Song of Songs*. NAC 14. Nashville: Broadman & Holman, 1993.

Gemser, Berend. *Sprüche Salomos*. HAT 16. Tübingen: Mohr Siebeck, 1963.

Gianto, Agustinus. "On יֵשׁ of Reflection in the Book of Proverbs." Pages 157–62 in *"When the Morning Stars Sang": Essays in Honor of Choon Leong Seow on the Occasion of his Sixty-Fifth Birthday*. Edited by Scott C. Jones and Christine Roy Yoder. BZAW 500. Berlin: de Gruyter, 2018.

Goldingay, John. "The Arrangement of Sayings in Proverbs 10–15." *JSOT* 61 (1994): 75–83.

Habel, Norman C. "The Symbolism of Wisdom in Proverbs 1–9." *Int* 26 (1972): 131–57.

Hatton, Peter H. T. *Contradiction in the Book of Proverbs: The Deep Waters of Counsel*. SOTSMS. Burlington, VT: Ashgate, 2008.

Heim, Knut M. *Like Grapes of Gold Set in Silver: An Interpretation of Proverbial Clusters in Proverbs 10:1–22:16*. BZAW 273. Berlin: de Gruyter, 2001.

———. *Poetic Imagination in Proverbs: Variant Repetitions and the Nature of Poetry*. BBRSup 4. Winona Lake, IN: Eisenbrauns: 2013.

Hildebrandt, Ted. "Motivation and Antithetical Parallelism in Proverbs 10–15." *JETS* 35 (1992): 433–44.

———. "Proverbial Pairs: Compositional Units in Proverbs 10–29." *JBL* 107 (1988): 207–24.

Jindo, Job Y. "On the Biblical Notion of the 'Fear of God' as a Condition for Human Existence." *BibInt* 19 (2011): 433–53.

Johnson, Mark. *Moral Imagination: Implications of Cognitive Science for Ethics*. Chicago: University of Chicago Press, 1993.

Keefer, Arthur Jan. *The Book of Proverbs and Virtue Ethics: Integrating the Biblical and Philosophical Traditions*. Cambridge: Cambridge University Press, 2021.

———. *Proverbs 1–9 as an Introduction to the Book of Proverbs*. LHBOTS 701. London: T&T Clark, 2020.

———. "A Shift in Perspective: The Intended Audience and a Coherent Reading of Proverbs 1:1–7." *JBL* 136 (2017): 103–16.

Kugel, James L. *The Idea of Biblical Poetry: Parallelism and Its History*. Baltimore: Johns Hopkins University Press, 1981.

Kynes, Will. *An Obituary for "Wisdom Literature": The Birth, Death, and Intertextual Reintegration of a Biblical Corpus*. Oxford: Oxford University Press, 2019.

Lakoff, George, and Mark Johnson. *Metaphors We Live By*. Chicago: University of Chicago Press, 1980.

———. *Philosophy in the Flesh: The Embodied Mind and Its Challenge to Western Thought*. New York: Basic Books, 1999.

Lichtenstein, Murray H. "Chiasm and Symmetry in Proverbs 31." *CBQ* 44 (1982): 202–11.

Loader, James A. *Proverbs 1–9*. HCOT. Leuven: Peeters, 2014.

Longman, Tremper, III. *Proverbs*. BCOTWP. Grand Rapids: Baker Academic, 2006.

Luc, Alex. "The Titles and Structure of Proverbs." *ZAW* 112 (2000): 252–55.

Lyu, Sun Myung. *Righteousness in the Book of Proverbs*. FAT II/55. Tübingen: Mohr Siebeck, 2012.

Malchow, Bruce. V. "A Manual for Future Monarchs: Proverbs 27:23–29:27." *CBQ* 47 (1985): 238–45.

McCreesh, Thomas P. *Biblical Sound and Sense: Poetic Sound Patterns in Proverbs 10–29*. JSOTSup 128. Sheffield: Sheffield Academic, 1991.

———. "Wisdom as Wife: Proverbs 31:10–31." *RB* 92 (1985): 25–46.

McKane, William. *Proverbs: A New Approach*. OTL. Philadelphia: Westminster, 1970.

Meinhold, A. *Die Sprüche, Teil 1: Sprüche Kapitel 1–15*. ZBK 16.1. Zürich: Theologischer Verlag, 1991.

———. *Die Sprüche, Teil 2: Sprüche Kapitel 16–31*. ZBK 16.2. Zürich: Theologischer Verlag, 1991.

Mieder, Wolfgang. "The Essence of Literary Proverb Study." *Proverbium* 23 (1974): 888–94.

Millar, Suzanna R. *Genre and Openness in Proverbs 10:1–22:16*. AIL 39. Atlanta: SBL Press, 2020.

———. "When a Straight Road becomes a Garden Path: The 'False Lead' as a Pedagogical Strategy in the Book of Proverbs." *JSOT* 43 (2018): 67–82.

Moore, Rick D. "A Home for the Alien: Worldly Wisdom and Covenantal Confession in Proverbs 30,1–9." *ZAW* 106 (1994): 96–107.

Murphy, Roland. *Proverbs*. WBC 22. Nashville: Thomas Nelson, 1998.

———. "Wisdom—Theses and Hypotheses." Pages 35–42 in *Israelite Wisdom: Theological and Literary Essays in Honor of Samuel Terrien*. Edited by W. A. Brueggemann, J. G. Gammie, W. L. Humphreys, and J. M. Ward. Missoula, MT: Scholars Press, 1978.

Newsom, Carol A. "Woman and the Discourse of Patriarchal Wisdom: A Study of Proverbs 1–9." Pages 142–60 in *Gender and Difference in Ancient Israel*. Edited by P. L. Day. Minneapolis: Fortress, 1989.

Perdue, Leo G. "Liminality as a Social Setting for Wisdom Instructions." *ZAW* 93 (1981): 114–26.

———. *Wisdom and Creation: The Theology of Wisdom Literature*. Nashville: Abingdon, 1994. Repr., Eugene, OR: Wipf & Stock, 2008.

Petrany, Catherine. "Fathers, Mothers, Sons, and Silence: Rhetorical Reconfiguration in Proverbs." *BTB* 50 (2020): 154–60.

Sæbø, Magne. *Sprüche*. ATD 16,1. Göttingen: Vandenhoeck & Ruprecht, 2012.

Sandoval, Timothy J. *The Discourse of Wealth and Poverty in the Book of Proverbs*. BibInt 77. Leiden: Brill, 2006.

———. "Revisiting the Prologue of Proverbs." *JBL* 126 (2007): 455–73.

Schipper, Bernd U. *Proverbs 1–15*. Hermeneia. Minneapolis: Fortress, 2019.

Schwáb, Zoltán S. *Toward an Interpretation of the Book of Proverbs: Selfishness and Secularity Reconsidered*. Journal of Theological Interpretation Supplement 7. Winona Lake, IN: Eisenbrauns, 2013.

Shupak, Nili. "The Instruction of Amenemope and Proverbs 22:17–24:22 from the Perspective of Contemporary Research." Pages 203–20 in *Seeking out the Wisdom of the Ancients: Essays Offered to Honor Michael V. Fox on the Occasion of His Sixty-Fifth Birthday*. Edited by R. L. Troxel, K. G. Friebel, and D. R. Magary. Winona Lake, IN: Eisenbrauns, 2005.

Skehan, Patrick. *Studies in Israelite Poetry and Wisdom*. CBQMS 1. Washington, DC: Catholic Biblical Association of America, 1971.

Sneed, Mark R. "Inspired Sages: *Massa'* and the Confluence of Wisdom and Prophecy." Pages 15–32 in *Scribes as Sages and Prophets: Scribal Traditions in Biblical Wisdom Literature and in the Book of the Twelve*. Edited by Jutta Krispenz. BZAW 496. Berlin: de Gruyter, 2021.

———. "Is the 'Wisdom Tradition' a Tradition?" *CBQ* 73 (2011): 50–71.

———, ed. *Was There a Wisdom Tradition? New Prospects in Israelite Wisdom Studies*. AIL 23. Atlanta: SBL Press, 2015.

Snell, Daniel C. *Twice-Told Proverbs and the Composition of the Book of Proverbs*. Winona Lake, IN: Eisenbrauns, 1993.

Stewart, Anne W. *Poetic Ethics in Proverbs: Wisdom Literature and the Shaping of the Moral Self*. Cambridge: Cambridge University Press, 2016.

———. "Wisdom's Imagination: Moral Reasoning and the Book of Proverbs." *JSOT* 40 (2016): 351–72.

Szlos, M. Beth. "Body Parts as Metaphor and the Value of a Cognitive Approach: A Study of the Female Figures in Proverbs via Metaphor." Pages 185–95 in *Metaphor in the Hebrew Bible*. Edited by P. van Hecke. BETL 187. Leuven: Leuven University Press, 2005.

Tilford, Nicole L. *Sensing World, Sensing Wisdom: The Cognitive Foundation of Biblical Metaphors*. AIL 31. Atlanta: SBL Press, 2017.

Toy, C. H. *The Book of Proverbs*. ICC. Edinburgh: T&T Clark, 1899.

Treier, Daniel J. *Proverbs and Ecclesiastes*. Brazos Theological Commentary on the Bible. Grand Rapids: Brazos, 2011.

Van Leeuwen, Raymond C. "The Book of Proverbs: Introduction, Commentary, and Reflections." Pages 19–264 in vol. 5 of *NIB*. Nashville: Abingdon, 1997.

———. *Context and Meaning in Proverbs 25–27*. SBLDS 96. Atlanta: Scholars Press, 1988.

———. "Cosmos, Temple, House: Building and Wisdom in Mesopotamia and Israel." Pages 67–90 in *Wisdom Literature in Mesopotamia and Israel*. Edited by Richard J. Clifford. SymS 36. Atlanta: SBL Press, 2007.

———. "Liminality and Worldview in Proverbs 1–9." *Semeia* 50 (1990): 111–44.

———. "Proverbs 30:21–23 and the Biblical World Upside Down." *JBL* 105 (1986): 599–610.

———. "Wealth and Poverty: System and Contradiction in Proverbs." *HS* 33 (1992): 25–36.

Vayntrub, Jacqueline. "Beauty, Wisdom, and Handiwork in Proverbs 31:10–31." *HTR* 113 (2020): 45–62.

———. *Beyond Orality: Biblical Poetry on Its Own Terms*. The Ancient Word. London: Routledge, 2019.

Von Rad, Gerhard. *Wisdom in Israel*. Translated by J. D. Martin. London: SCM, 1972.

Waltke, Bruce K. *The Book of Proverbs: Chapters 1–15*. NICOT. Grand Rapids: Eerdmans, 2004.

———. *The Book of Proverbs: Chapters 15–31*. NICOT. Grand Rapids: Eerdmans, 2005.

Webster, Brian L. "The Perfect Verb and the Perfect Woman in Proverbs." Pages 263–74 in *Windows to the Ancient World of the Hebrew Bible: Essays in Honor of Samuel Greengus*. Edited by Bill T. Arnold, Nancy L. Erickson, and John H. Walton. Winona Lake, IN: Eisenbrauns, 2014.

Weeks, Stuart. "The Context and Meaning of Proverbs 8:30a." *JBL* 125 (2006): 433–42.

———. *Instruction and Imagery in Proverbs 1–9*. Oxford: Oxford University Press, 2007.

Whybray, R. Norman. *The Composition of the Book of Proverbs*. JSOTSup 168. Sheffield: Sheffield Academic, 1994.

———. *Wealth and Poverty in the Book of Proverbs*. JSOTSup 99. Sheffield: Sheffield Academic, 1990.

———. "YHWH-Sayings and Their Contexts in Proverbs 10,1–22,16." Pages 153–65 in *La Sagesse de l'Ancien Testament*. Edited by M. Gilbert. Leuven: Leuven University Press, 1990.

Yoder, Christine Roy. "Forming 'Fearers of Yahweh': Repetition and Contradiction as Pedagogy in Proverbs." Pages 167–83 in *Seeking out the Wisdom of the Ancients: Essays Offered to Honor Michael V. Fox on the Occasion of His Sixty-Fifth Birthday*. Edited by K. G. Friebel, R. L. Troxel, and D. R. Magary. Winona Lake, IN: Eisenbrauns, 2005.

———. *Proverbs*. AOTC. Nashville: Abingdon, 2009.

———. *Wisdom as a Woman of Substance: A Socioeconomic Reading of Proverbs 1–9 and 31:10–31*. BZAW 304. Berlin: de Gruyter, 2001.

Translation of Proverbs

Proverbs 1

[1]The proverbs of Solomon,
son of David, king of Israel.
[2]For learning wisdom and instruction,
for understanding insightful words,
[3]for acquiring instruction in prudent living:
righteousness, justice, and uprightness,
[4]for giving to the uncommitted shrewdness
to the young, knowledge and discretion,
[5]so the wise may hear and increase instruction,
and one with understanding may acquire guidance,
[6]for understanding a proverb and an allusive saying,
the words of the wise and their riddles.
[7]The fear of YHWH is the beginning of knowledge;
wisdom and instruction fools despise.
[8]Hear, my son, your father's instruction,
and do not neglect your mother's teaching,
[9]for they are a beautiful garland for your head,
and a necklace for your throat.
[10]My son, if sinners entice you,
do not accede.
[11]If they say, "Come with us, let's lurk for blood,
let's ambush the innocent without cause;
[12]let's swallow them alive like Sheol,
the blameless like those who go down into the Pit.
[13]We'll find all sorts of precious wealth;
we'll fill our houses with spoil.
[14]Throw in your lot with us;
we'll all share one purse."

15My son, do not go on this way with them;
hold back your foot from their path,
16for their feet run to evil,
and they hurry to shed blood.
17For spreading out the net is useless
in the sight of any bird.
18But they lurk for their own blood;
they ambush their own lives.
19Thus are the ways of all who profit from unjust gain;
it takes away the life of its possessors.
20Wisdom shouts in the street,
in the open plazas she raises her voice;
21at the busiest intersection she cries out
at the entrance of the city gates she speaks her words.
22"How long, uncommitted ones, will you love simplicity,
and scoffers desire scoffing,
and fools hate knowledge?
23Turn to my reproof;
look, I want to pour out my spirit on you;
I want to enlighten you with my words.
24Because I called and you refused,
I extended my hand and no one paid attention;
25you ignored all my advice,
and my reproof you did not accept,
26I, on my part, will laugh in your disaster;
I will mock when your moment of dread comes,
27when your moment of dread comes like a storm,
and your disaster comes like a whirlwind,
when distress and anguish come upon you.

28Then they will call for me, but I will not answer;
they will seek me, but not find me,

29because they hated knowledge,
and the fear of YHWH they did not choose,
30they did not accept my advice;
they spurned all my reproof.
31So they will eat the fruit of their way,
and from their counsels they will be satisfied.
32Indeed, the turning away of the uncommitted will kill them,

and the complacency of fools will destroy them.
33But the one who listens to me will dwell securely
and be at ease from dread of disaster.

Proverbs 2

1My son, if you receive my words,
and store up my commands within you,

2by making your ear attentive to wisdom,
inclining your heart to understanding;
3indeed, if you cry out for insight,
raise your voice for understanding;
4if you seek it as silver,
and as hidden treasures search for it,
5then you will understand the fear of YHWH,
and you will find the knowledge of God;
6for YHWH grants wisdom;
from his mouth comes knowledge and understanding;
7he stores up resourcefulness for the upright;
a shield for those who walk with integrity,
8in order to protect the paths of justice,
guard the way of his faithful ones;
9then you will understand righteousness, justice, and uprightness—
every good path,
10for wisdom will infiltrate your heart,
and knowledge will be pleasant to your soul,
11discretion will guard you,
understanding will protect you,
12in order to deliver you from the way of the evildoer,
from the person who speaks perversely.

13Those who forsake the paths of uprightness
to walk in ways of darkness,
14who delight in doing evil,
rejoice in the perversity of evil,
15whose paths are crooked,
and who are devious in their ways;
16in order to deliver you from the strange woman,

from the outsider with her smooth words
[17]who forsakes the companion of her youth,
and forgets the covenant of her God,
[18]for her house sinks down to death,
and her ways to the deceased;
[19]all who come to her will never return,
nor will they reach the paths of life;
[20]so that you may walk in the way of the good,
and keep the paths of the righteous.

[21]For the upright will dwell in the land,
and the blameless will remain in it;
[22]but the wicked will be cut off from the land,
and the treacherous will be uprooted from it.

Proverbs 3

[1]My son, do not forget my teaching,
and let your heart keep my commands;
[2]for length of days and years of life,
and peace will increase for you.
[3]Do not let kindness and faithfulness leave you;
bind them around your neck,
write them on the tablet of your heart,
[4]then you will find favor and good repute
in the sight of God and humans.
[5]Trust in YHWH with all your heart,
and do not depend on your own understanding.
[6]In all your ways know him,
then he himself will make your paths smooth.
[7]Do not be wise in your own eyes;
fear YHWH, and turn away from evil;
[8]then it will be healing to your body
and nourishment for your bones.
[9]Honor YHWH from your wealth
and from the firstfruits of all your produce;
[10]then your storehouses will overflow with abundance,
and your vats will burst with new wine.
[11]YHWH's discipline, my son, do not reject,

and do not loathe his reproof,
[12]for the one whom YHWH loves he will reprove,
even as a father the son in whom he delights.

[13]Blessed is the person who has found wisdom,
and the person who gains understanding,
[14]for her profit is better than the profit of silver,
and her yield is better than gold;
[15]she is more precious than corals,
everything desirable cannot compare with her;
[16]long life is in her right hand,
in her left, riches and honor;
[17]her ways are pleasant ways,
and all her paths are peace;
[18]she is a tree of life to those who embrace her,
and those who hold fast to her are blessed.
[19]YHWH founded the earth by wisdom,
he established the heavens by understanding;
[20]by his knowledge the deeps burst open,
and the clouds drip dew.
[21]My son, do not let these escape from your sight;
protect resourcefulness and discretion;
[22]then they will be life for your soul,
and adornment for your neck;
[23]then you will walk on your way securely,
and your foot will not stumble.
[24]When you lie down, you will not be afraid,
when you lie down, your sleep will be pleasant.
[25]Do not fear sudden terror,
or the devastation of the wicked when it comes,
[26]for YHWH will be your confidence,
and keep your foot from capture.
[27]Do not withhold good from those to whom it is due,
when you have the power to do it.
[28]Do not say to your neighbor, "Go and return;
and I will give it tomorrow," when you have it with you.
[29]Do not plan evil against your neighbor,
while he is living confidently with you.
[30]Do not accuse a person without cause,
if he has done you no wrong.

31 Do not envy a violent person,
and do not choose any of his ways,
32 for the crooked person is an abomination to YHWH,
but with the upright is his counsel.
33 The curse of YHWH is on the house of the wicked,
but he blesses the dwelling of the righteous.
34 If it is a matter of mockers, he himself mocks,
but if it is a matter of the humble, he bestows favor.
35 The wise will inherit honor,
but fools will acquire disgrace.

Proverbs 4

1 Hear, sons, a father's instruction,
pay attention, so that you might know understanding;
2 because I give you good instruction,
do not forsake my teaching.
3 When I was a son to my father,
tender and the only one before my mother,
4 he taught me and said to me:
"Let your heart hold on to my words,
keep my commandments and you will live.
5 Get wisdom! Get understanding!
Do not forget, and do not turn aside from the words of my mouth.
6 Do not leave her, and she will keep you;
love her, and she will protect you.
7 The beginning of wisdom: get wisdom!
With all you possess get understanding!
8 Cherish her and she will exalt you;
she will honor you, if you embrace her.
9 She will place a beautiful garland on your head;
she will grant you a splendid crown."
10 Hear, my son, and take my words,
so that years of life may increase for you.
11 In the way of wisdom, I instruct you,
I lead you in upright paths.

12 When you walk, your step will not be hampered;
and if you run, you will not stumble.

13Take hold of instruction, do not let go,
guard it, for it is your life.
14On the way of the wicked, do not enter,
and do not tread on the way of evildoers.
15Avoid it; do not pass through it;
turn away from it; and pass on,
16for they cannot sleep unless they do harm,
they are robbed of sleep if they cause no stumbling;
17for they eat the bread of wickedness,
and drink the wine of violence.
18Now the way of the righteous is like the shining light,
growing brighter until the day is established.
19The way of the wicked is like darkness;
they do not know what they stumble over.
20My son, listen attentively to my words,
incline your ear to my sayings;
21they must not escape from your eyes,
keep them within your heart;
22for they are life to those who find them,
and healing to the whole of one's body.
23More than anything to be protected, guard your heart,
for from it flow the sources of life.
24Keep a crooked mouth away from yourself,
and remove devious lips far from you.
25Let your eyes look straight ahead,
and let your pupils look straight in front of you.
26Watch the path of your feet,
so that all your ways may be sure.
27Do not turn aside to the right or to the left;
keep your foot away from evil.

Proverbs 5

1My son, listen attentively to my wisdom;
incline your ear to my understanding,
2so that you may keep discretion,
and your lips may guard knowledge.
3For the lips of the strange woman drip honey,
and her palate is smoother than oil.

[4]But her aftertaste is bitter as wormwood,
sharp as a two-edged sword.
[5]Her feet descend to death,
her steps cling to Sheol;
[6]so that she does not watch the path of life,
her ways wander; she does not know.
[7]So now, sons, listen to me,
and do not depart from the words of my mouth.
[8]Keep your way far from her,
and do not come near to the door of her house,
[9]lest you give your splendor to others
and your honor to the ruthless;
[10]lest strangers be filled with your strength
and your toil end up in the house of an alien;
[11]and at your end you groan,
when your body and flesh languish
[12]and you say, "How I hated discipline,
and my heart despised reproof.
[13]I did not listen to the voice of my teachers;
nor incline my ear to my instructors.
[14]I have come to the brink of sheer calamity
in the assembly and congregation."
[15]Drink water from your own cistern,
and running water from your well.
[16]Should your springs flow about,
water channels in the squares?
[17]Let them be yours alone,
and not for strangers with you.
[18]Let your fountain be blessed,
and take pleasure from the wife of your youth,
[19]a lovely hind, a graceful doe;
her breasts should always satisfy you;
may you be intoxicated always by her love.
[20]Why should you be intoxicated, my son, by a strange woman
or embrace the bosom of an adulteress?
[21]For a man's ways are before the eyes of YHWH,
and he observes all his paths.
[22]His iniquities will ensnare him,
and in the chords of his sin he will be caught.

23 He will die for lack of discipline,
and in the abundance of his folly he will stray.

Proverbs 6

1 My son, if you have given surety to your neighbor,
shaken hands for a stranger,
2 ensnared yourself by the words of your mouth,
trapped yourself by the words of your mouth,
3 do this then, my son, in order to save yourself,
for you have come into your neighbor's power:
Go, humble yourself, and hassle your neighbor;
4 do not give sleep to your eyes,
nor slumber to your eyelids;
5 save yourself like a gazelle from someone's hand,
and like a bird from the fowler's hand.
6 Go to the ant, you sluggard,
observe its ways, and become wise.
7 Although it has no leader, overseer, or ruler,
8 it prepares its food in summer,
it gathers its fare during the harvest.
9 How long, you sluggard, will you lie down?
When will you rise from your sleep?
10 A little sleep, a little slumber,
a little folding of the hands to rest,
11 and poverty will come upon you like a vagabond,
and need like an armed warrior.
12 A scoundrel is a vile person,
who goes around with a crooked mouth,
13 who winks with his eyes, who shuffles with his feet,
who signals with his fingers,
14 perversions are in his heart,
he constantly plans evil,
he stirs up strife.
15 Therefore his ruin will come suddenly;
he will be broken unexpectedly and without a remedy.

16 There are six things that YHWH hates,

even seven that are an abomination to him:
[17]haughty eyes, a lying tongue,
and hands that shed innocent blood,
[18]a heart that plans vile schemes,
feet that hasten to run to evil,
[19]a lying witness who blows out deceits,
and one who stirs up strife between brothers.
[20]Keep, my son, your father's commandment,
and do not neglect your mother's teaching.
[21]Bind them upon your heart always,
tie them around your neck.
[22]When you walk about, she will lead you;
when you lie down, she will watch over you;
and when you awake, she will teach you.
[23]For the commandment is a lamp and the teaching a light,
and corrective reproofs are the way of life
[24]to guard you from the wife of another,
from the smooth tongue of the strange woman.
[25]Do not desire her beauty in your heart,
and do not let her capture you with her eyelashes,
[26]for a prostitute's fee is just a loaf of bread,
but the wife of another man hunts for precious life.
[27]Can a man carry fire in his bosom,
without his clothes being burnt?
[28]Can a person walk on burning embers,
without his feet being scorched?
[29]So is he who enters his neighbor's wife,
none who touches her remains unpunished.
[30]People do not despise a thief if he steals
to satisfy his desire when hungry.
[31]But if caught, he must repay sevenfold,
all the wealth of his house he must give.
[32]One who commits adultery with a woman lacks sense;
one who destroys his own life, he is the one who does this.
[33]He will find affliction and shame,
and his reproach will not be removed.
[34]For jealousy is a man's wrath,
and he will not show compassion on the day of vengeance.
[35]He shall not accept any ransom,
nor be satisfied though you increase the bribe.

Proverbs 7

1My son, keep my words,
and store my commandments within you;
2keep my commandments so that you may live,
and my teaching as the pupil of your eye;
3bind them on your fingers,
write them on the tablet of your heart.
4Say to Wisdom, "You are my sister,"
and call Understanding, "companion,"
5so that they may keep you from a strange woman,
an outsider who makes her words smooth.

6When, at the window of my house,
I looked down through my lattice,
7then I saw among the uncommitted,
perceived among the youths, a lad lacking sense,
8passing through the street by her corner,
striding along the way of her house
9at dusk, in the evening,
in the black of night and darkness.
10And look—a woman meets him,
in a harlot's garment, with hidden intent.
11She is turbulent and defiant,
her feet do not stay in her house;
12a foot in the street, a foot in the squares,
and beside every corner she lurks.
13Then she seized him and kissed him,
with a brazen face she said to him:
14"I had to make peace offerings.
Today I paid my vows!
15Therefore, I came out to meet you,
to seek your face, and I found you!
16I've prepared my couch with coverings,
embroidered cloth, Egyptian linen.
17I've perfumed my bed—
myrrh, aloes, and cinnamon.
18Come, let's drink lovemaking until morning,
let's indulge ourselves in love;

19for the man is not at home,
he's gone on a far journey.
20He took a bag of money in his hand,
he will return to his house at the full moon."
21She seduces him with her powerful instruction,
with her smooth lips she tempts him.
22He follows her at once,
like an ox goes to slaughter,
and like a stag skipping into a trap,
23until an arrow pierces his liver,
as a bird rushing to a trap,
so he does not know that his life is the cost.
24So now, sons, listen to me,
and pay attention to the words of my mouth.
25Do not let your heart turn aside to her ways,
do not wander into her paths.
26for many are the slain she has toppled,
and numerous all those killed by her.
27The ways of Sheol [run through] her house,
descending to the chambers of death.

Proverbs 8

1Is not Wisdom calling,
and Understanding raising her voice?
2On top of the heights, beside the way,
at the crossroads she takes her stand;
3beside the gates at the city entrance,
at the entry of the portal she cries aloud:
4"To you, men, I call out,
my voice goes out to humankind.
5Learn shrewdness, you uncommitted!
Learn sense, you fools!
6Listen, for I speak straightforward things,
and the opening of my lips contains integrity.
7Indeed, my palate utters truth,
and wickedness is an abomination to my lips.
8All the words of my mouth are in accord with righteousness;
nothing in them is twisted or perverse.

[9]All of them are straight to the one who understands
and right to those who find knowledge.
[10]Take my instruction instead of silver,
and knowledge rather than choice gold;
[11]for wisdom is better than corals,
and nothing delightful can compare with it.
[12]I, Wisdom, inhabit shrewdness,
and knowledge of discretion I find.
[13]The fear of YHWH is hating evil.
Pride and arrogance and the way of evil
and perverse speech I hate.
[14]Mine are counsel and resourcefulness;
I am Understanding; strength is mine.
[15]By me kings reign,
and rulers decree justice.
[16]By me princes rule,
and nobles, all judges of justice.
[17]I love those who love me,
and those who seek me find me.
[18]Riches and honor are with me,
enduring wealth and righteousness.
[19]My fruit is better than gold, even fine gold,
and my produce than choice silver.
[20]I walk on the way of righteousness,
in the midst of the paths of justice,
[21]to cause those who love me to inherit wealth,
and I will fill their treasuries.
[22]YHWH begat me at the beginning of his way,
the earliest of his works from that time.
[23]In the distant past I was formed,
at the beginning, at the earliest times of the earth.
[24]When there were no deeps, I was brought forth,
when there were no springs abounding with water.
[25]Before the mountains were founded,
before the hills, I was brought forth,
[26]before he made the earth and the open fields,
or the world's first lumps of soil.
[27]When he established the heavens, I was there—
when he inscribed a circle on the face of the deep,
[28]when he made firm the clouds above,

when he fixed the fountains of the deep,
29when he set for the sea its limit,
so that the waters do not transgress his command,
when he marked out the foundations of the earth.
30And I have been beside him faithfully,
and I have been delighting before him day after day,
rejoicing before him always,
31rejoicing in his inhabitable world,
and delighting in humankind.
32So now, sons, listen to me,
for blessed are those who keep my ways.
33Listen to discipline so that you become wise,
and do not neglect it.
34Blessed is the person who listens to me,
by keeping vigil at my doors day after day,
by watching the posts of my doorways;
35for the one who finds me finds life
and gains favor from YHWH;
36but the one who offends me harms himself;
all who hate me love death."

Proverbs 9

1Wisdom—having built her house,
set up her seven pillars,
2prepared her meat, mixed her wine,
then arranged her table,
3having sent out her maidservants—calls out
at the tops of the city's heights:
4"Whoever is uncommitted, let him turn aside here!"
"Whoever lacks sense"—she says to him:
5"Come, eat of my food,
and drink of the wine I have mixed.
6Abandon agnosticism, so that you may live;
and tread on the way of understanding!"
7Whoever disciplines a scoffer receives an insult,
and whoever reproves a wicked person receives a blemish.
8Do not reprove a scoffer lest he hate you;
reprove a wise person and he will love you.

9 Give [reproof] to the wise person, and he will become even wiser;
instruct the righteous person and he will maximize learning.
10 The beginning of wisdom is the fear of YHWH,
and knowledge of the Holy One is understanding.
11 "Surely through me your days will be many,
and years of life will be added to you."
12 If you are wise, you are wise for yourself;
but if you scoff, you will bear it alone.
13 Woman Folly is turbulent—
imprudence itself—and she knows nothing.
14 And she sits at the door of her house,
on a throne at the city's heights,
15 calling out to those passing by,
those going straight on their way,
16 "Whoever is uncommitted, let him turn aside here!"
"And whoever lacks sense"—she says to him:
17 "Stolen water is sweet,
and food taken secretly is a delight!"
18 But he does not know that the dead are there,
in the depths of Sheol are her guests.

Proverbs 10

1 The Proverbs of Solomon
A wise son gladdens the father;
but a foolish son, the grief of his mother.
2 Treasures of wickedness will not profit;
but righteousness delivers from death.
3 YHWH will not let the righteous person starve;
but he will push away the desire of the wicked.
4 A slack palm produces poverty;
but the hand of the diligent brings riches.
5 One who gathers in the summer, a perceptive son;
one who sleeps in the harvest, a disgraceful son.
6 Blessings for the head of the righteous;
but the mouth of the wicked conceals violence.
7 The memory of the righteous, for a blessing;
but the name of the wicked rots.
8 The wise of heart receives commands,

but one with foolish lips will be ruined.
[9]One who walks uprightly walks securely;
but one who twists his ways will be discovered.
[10]One who winks the eye brings grief,
and one with foolish lips will be ruined.
[11]A fount of life—the mouth of the righteous;
but the mouth of the wicked conceals violence.
[12]Hate awakens conflict;
but love covers all offenses.
[13]On the lips of the discerning wisdom is found;
and a rod for the back of the senseless.
[14]The wise store knowledge;
but the mouth of the fool, impending ruin.
[15]The wealth of the rich, his fortified city;
the ruin of the poor, their poverty.
[16]The wages of the righteous, for life;
the produce of the wicked, for sin.
[17]One who observes instruction, a path to life;
but one who rejects reproof leads astray.
[18]One who conceals hatred, lying lips;
and one who spreads slander is a fool.
[19]In a multitude of words, offense will not cease;
but one who restrains his lips is prudent.
[20]The tongue of the righteous, choice silver;
the heart of the wicked, of little value.
[21]The lips of the righteous nourish many;
but fools die through senselessness.
[22]The blessing of YHWH, it brings riches;
and strenuous work adds nothing to it.
[23]Lewd behavior is like pleasure for a fool;
but wisdom for a person of understanding.
[24]What the wicked fears, it will come upon him;
but what the righteous desire he will grant.
[25]When the whirlwind passes, the wicked is no more;
but the righteous, an enduring foundation.
[26]Like vinegar to the teeth and smoke to the eyes,
so the sluggard to those who send him.
[27]The fear of YHWH increases days;
but the years of the wicked are shortened.
[28]The expectation of the righteous, joy;

but the hope of the wicked perishes.
29 A stronghold for the upright, the way of YHWH;
but ruin for those who commit iniquity.
30 The righteous will never be shaken;
and the wicked will not dwell in the land.
31 The mouth of the righteous produces wisdom;
but the tongue of the perverse is cut off.
32 The lips of the righteous know what is pleasing;
but the mouth of the wicked, perversity.

Proverbs 11

1 Fraudulent scales, an abomination to YHWH;
but an accurate weight, his delight.
2 Arrogance comes, then shame comes;
but with the humble, wisdom.
3 The integrity of the upright guides them;
but the perversity of the treacherous destroys them.
4 Wealth is no benefit on the day of wrath;
but righteousness delivers from death.
5 The righteousness of the blameless makes his way straight;
but the wicked falls through his wickedness.
6 The righteousness of the upright delivers them;
but the treacherous are caught by desire.
7 When a wicked person dies, hope perishes;
and the expectation of power perishes.
8 The righteous is delivered from trouble;
and the wicked takes his place.
9 With the mouth the impious destroys his neighbor;
but through knowledge the righteous are delivered.
10 When the righteous prosper, a city rejoices;
and when the wicked perish, jubilation.
11 By the blessing of the upright a city is exalted;
but by the mouth of the wicked it is ruined.
12 The senseless despises his neighbor;
but a discerning person keeps silent.
13 A slanderer reveals secrets;
but a reliable spirit covers a matter.
14 Without guidance, a people fall;

but in a multitude of counselors, victory.
15One will be harmed severely when one goes surety for a stranger;
but one who hates agreements is secure.
16A gracious woman grasps honor;
but violent men grasp wealth.
17A merciful person benefits himself;
but the cruel harms himself.
18The wicked makes a deceitful wage;
but one who sows righteousness, a true reward.
19So righteousness [heads] to life;
and one who pursues evil, to death.
20An abomination to YHWH, those crooked of heart;
but his delight, those whose way is blameless.
21Be assured, the evil will not go unpunished;
but the descendants of the righteous will escape.
22A gold ring in a pig's snout—
a beautiful woman who lacks discretion.
23The desire of the righteous, only good;
the hope of the wicked, wrath.
24There is this: one who gives freely and gets more;
and one who withholds what is right, only to lack.
25One who blesses will be satisfied;
and one who refreshes will himself be refreshed.
26One who withholds grain—people will curse him;
but blessing for the head of one who sells it.
27One who diligently seeks good seeks favor;
but one who seeks evil, it will come upon him.
28One who trusts in his wealth—he will fall;
but the righteous will sprout like foliage.
29One who troubles his house will inherit wind;
and a fool will be a servant to the wise of heart.
30The fruit of the righteous, a tree of life;
and one who takes lives is wise.
31The righteous is repaid on the earth,
how much more the wicked and the sinner!

Proverbs 12

1One who loves discipline loves knowledge;

but one who hates reproof is a brute.
2A good man receives favor from YHWH;
but the schemer he condemns.
3No one is established through wickedness;
but the root of the righteous will never totter.
4A virtuous woman, the crown of her husband;
but a disgraceful one, like rot in his bones.
5The plans of the righteous, just;
the guidance of the wicked, deceptive.
6The words of the wicked, a murderous ambush;
but the mouth of the upright delivers them.
7Overturn the wicked and they are no more;
but the house of the righteous stands.
8A person is praised according to his intelligence;
but the perverse of heart will be despised.
9Better the lightly regarded who has a servant,
than one who honors himself and lacks food.
10The righteous knows the desire of his livestock;
but the compassion of the wicked is cruel.
11One who works his land will be satisfied with food;
but one who pursues worthless things lacks sense.
12The wicked desires a snare for evil things;
but the root of the righteous gives forth.
13In the transgression of lips, an evil snare;
but the righteous escapes from trouble.
14From the fruit of his mouth, one is satisfied with good things,
and the work of one's hands returns to him.
15A fool's way, upright in his eyes;
but one who listens to counsel is wise.
16A fool makes known his anger at once;
but the shrewd conceals an insult.
17A faithful witness declares what is right;
but a lying witness, deceit.
18There is this: one who chatters like a sword's stabs;
but the tongue of the wise, healing.
19Truthful lips endure forever;
but a lying tongue is only for a moment.
20Deceit is in the heart of those who devise evil;
but those who advise peace have joy.
21No calamity will befall the righteous;

but the wicked are filled with evil.
22An abomination to YHWH, lying lips;
but one who acts honestly, his delight.
23A shrewd person covers knowledge;
but the heart of fools proclaims folly.
24The hand of the diligent rules;
but the slack will be put to forced labor.
25Anxiety in a person's heart weighs it down;
but a good word makes it merry.
26The righteous shows the way to his companion;
but the way of the wicked leads them astray.
27A slacker will not roast his game;
but the precious wealth of a person, diligence.
28In the path of righteousness, life;
and along that way, no death.

Proverbs 13

1A wise son—a father's discipline;
but a scoffer does not listen to reproof.
2From the fruit of his mouth, one eats good things;
but the throat of the treacherous, violence.
3One who guards his mouth protects his life;
one who opens wide his lips—ruin is his.
4It craves but has nothing: the appetite of the sluggard;
but the appetite of the diligent is satisfied.
5The righteous hates a false word;
but the wicked bring shame and disgrace.
6Righteousness guards the way of the upright;
but wickedness ruins the sinner.
7There is this: one who pretends to be rich and has nothing;
one who pretends to be poor and has great wealth.
8The ransom of a person's life, his wealth;
but the poor does not listen to reproof.
9The light of the righteous rejoices;
but the lamp of the wicked is extinguished.
10Indeed, arrogance produces strife;
but those who accept advice, wisdom.
11Wealth in haste dwindles;

but one who gathers by hand increases.
12A drawn-out hope makes the heart sick;
but a tree of life is a desire fulfilled.
13One who despises a word, it will go badly for him;
but one who fears a commandment, he will be rewarded.
14The teaching of the wise, a fount of life
for avoiding the snares of death.
15Good sense produces favor;
but the way of the treacherous is their ruin.
16Every shrewd person acts with knowledge;
but a fool spreads folly.
17A wicked messenger falls into evil;
but a faithful envoy brings healing.
18Poverty and shame: one who neglects discipline;
but one who listens to reproof will be honored.
19A desire realized is sweet to a person;
and an abomination of fools: turning away from evil.
20One who walks with the wise becomes wise;
but the companion of fools suffers harm.
21Evil pursues sinners;
but the righteous will be rewarded with good.
22A good person leaves an inheritance to grandchildren;
but stored up for the righteous: the wealth of the sinner.
23An abundance of food—the fallow ground of the poor;
but the reality is this: it is swept away without justice.
24One who spares the rod hates his son;
but one who loves him disciplines him consistently.
25The righteous eats to satisfy his appetite;
but the stomach of the wicked is empty.

Proverbs 14

1The wisdom of women builds her house;
but folly tears hers down with her own hands.
2One who walks uprightly fears YHWH;
but one whose ways are twisted despises him.
3In the mouth of the fool, a sprig of pride;
but the lips of the wise guard them.
4Without oxen, the manger has grain;

but abundant produce, by the bull's strength.
5A trustworthy witness does not deceive;
but a false witness breathes lies.
6The scoffer seeks wisdom, but nothing;
while knowledge comes easy for the discerning.
7Go before a fool,
and you will not know knowledgeable lips.
8The wisdom of the shrewd: understanding his way;
but the folly of fools, deceit.
9Fools mock at guilt;
but among the upright, favor.
10The heart knows its own bitterness;
and a stranger cannot share in its joy.
11The house of the wicked will be destroyed;
but the tent of the upright will blossom.
12There is this: a way that is straight before a person;
but its end, ways to death.
13Even in laughter the heart may hurt;
and the end of joy, grief.
14The wayward of heart will be satisfied from his ways;
and a good person, from his.
15The simple believes anything;
but the shrewd considers his step.
16The wise fears and turns away from evil;
but the fool, quick-tempered and overconfident.
17A short-tempered person commits folly;
and a schemer is hated.
18The simple inherit folly;
but the shrewd are crowned with knowledge.
19The evil bow before the good;
and the wicked at the gates of the righteous.
20Even by his neighbor the poor is hated;
but those who love the rich, many.
21One who despises his neighbor, a sinner;
but one who is gracious to the poor, blessed is he.
22Do not devisers of evil go astray,
while devisers of good, loyalty and faithfulness?
23In all hard work there is profit;
but mere talk, only to deprivation.
24The crown of the wise, their wealth;

the folly of fools, folly.
25 A reliable witness saves lives;
but a deceiver breathes lies.
26 In the fear of YHWH, strong confidence;
and for his children it will be a refuge.

27 The fear of YHWH, a fountain of life
for avoiding the snares of death.
28 In a multitude of people, a king's splendor;
but in a lack of a nation, a ruler's ruin.
29 Slow to anger, great understanding;
but the short-tempered exalts folly.
30 The life of the body, a gentle heart;
but rot in the bones, jealousy.
31 One who oppresses the poor insults his maker,
but one who is kind to the needy honors him.
32 The wicked is thrust down by his evil;
but the righteous finds refuge in his death.
33 Wisdom rests in the heart of the discerning;
and in the midst of fools she makes herself known.
34 Righteousness exalts a nation;
but the disgrace of peoples, sin.
35 The king favors a competent servant;
but his wrath is for a disgraceful one.

Proverbs 15

1 A soft answer turns away wrath;
but a harsh word provokes anger.
2 The tongue of the wise adorns knowledge;
but the mouth of fools pours out folly.
3 In every place, the eyes of YHWH,
observing the evil and the good.
4 A soothing tongue, a tree of life;
but perversion in it breaks the spirit.
5 A fool despises his father's discipline;
but one who observes reproof is shrewd.
6 The house of the righteous, much wealth;
but in the produce of the wicked, ruin.

7The lips of the wise disperse knowledge;
but the heart of fools, not so.
8The sacrifice of the wicked, an abomination to YHWH;
but the prayer of the upright, his delight.
9An abomination to YHWH, the way of the wicked;
but one who pursues righteousness he loves.
10Severe discipline for one who abandons the way;
one who hates reproof will die.
11Sheol and Abaddon are before YHWH—
how much more human hearts!
12A scoffer does not love being reproved;
to the wise he will not go.
13A joyful heart brightens the face;
but in a troubled heart, a broken spirit.
14The heart of the discerning seeks knowledge;
but the mouth of fools feeds on folly.
15All the days of the poor, bad;
but a cheerful heart, a continual feast.
16Better a little with the fear of YHWH,
than great treasure and turmoil with it.
17Better a portion of greens with love,
than a fattened ox with hatred.
18A hothead provokes strife;
but the patient quiets disputes.
19The way of the sluggard, like a hedge of thorns;
but the path of the upright, a highway.
20A wise son brings joy to a father;
but a foolish person despises his mother.
21Folly, joy to the senseless;
but a person of understanding walks straight.
22Plans are thwarted without counsel;
but with many counselors they succeed.
23A person takes delight in the answer of his mouth;
and a word in its time, how good!
24The way of life, upward for the prudent,
that he might turn aside from Sheol below.
25YHWH tears down the house of the proud;
and he establishes the boundary of the widow.
26An abomination to YHWH, plans of the evil;
but pleasant words are pure.

[27]One who troubles his house: one who profits from unjust gain;
but one who hates bribes will live.
[28]The heart of the righteous reflects before answering;
but the mouth of the wicked pours out evil things.
[29]YHWH is far from the wicked;
but the prayer of the righteous he hears.
[30]The light of the eyes brings joy to the heart;
a good report fattens the bones.
[31]The ear that listens to the reproof of life
dwells among the wise.
[32]One who neglects discipline despises his life;
but one who listens to reproof acquires sense.
[33]The fear of YHWH, instruction in wisdom;
and before honor, humility.

Proverbs 16

[1]The reflections of the heart belong to humans;
but the answer of the tongue, from YHWH.
[2]All the ways of a person, pure in his eyes;
but YHWH weighs motives.
[3]Commit your works to YHWH,
and your plans will succeed.
[4]YHWH made everything for its purpose—
even the wicked for an evil day.
[5]An abomination to YHWH, every proud heart;
be assured: it will not go unpunished.
[6]By loyalty and faithfulness iniquity is atoned for;
and by the fear of YHWH, a turning away from evil.
[7]When YHWH favors a person's ways,
he makes even his enemies at peace with him.
[8]Better a little with righteousness,
than abundant produce without justice.
[9]A person's heart plans his way,
but YHWH directs his step.
[10]An oracle on the king's lips;
in judgment his mouth is not unfaithful.
[11]A just balance and scales belong to YHWH;
his work, all the weights of the bag.

[12]An abomination to kings, doing wicked deeds,
for a throne is established by righteousness.
[13]Righteous lips, the delight of kings,
and one who speaks uprightly he loves.
[14]The king's wrath, a messenger of death,
but a wise person appeases it.
[15]In the light of the king's face, life,
and his favor, like a cloud of spring rain.
[16]Acquiring wisdom—how much better than gold!
And acquiring understanding, preferable to silver.
[17]The highway of the upright, turning aside from evil;
one who watches his way guards his life.
[18]Before destruction, pride;
and before stumbling, a haughty spirit.
[19]Better a humble spirit with the oppressed
than to divide spoil with the proud.
[20]One prudent in a matter finds good,
and one who trusts in YHWH, blessed is he.
[21]The wise of heart is called discerning,
and sweetness of lips increases learning.
[22]Insight, a fountain of life for its possessor,
but the instruction of fools, folly.
[23]The heart of the wise makes his mouth insightful,
and enhances instruction on his lips.
[24]Pleasant words, a honeycomb—
sweet to the throat and healing to the bones.
[25]There is this: a way that is straight before a person;
but its end, ways to death.
[26]The appetite of the worker works for him,
because his mouth compels him.
[27]A scoundrel, one who mines evil,
and on his lips, like a scorching fire.
[28]A perverse person spreads strife,
and a slanderer separates friends.
[29]A violent person entices his neighbor
and leads him on a way not good.
[30]One who winks his eyes, to plan perversities,
one who pinches his lips has accomplished evil.
[31]A splendid crown, grey hair;

it is found on the way of the righteous.
32Better the patient than the mighty,
and one who controls his spirit than one who captures a city.
33The lot is cast in the bosom,
but from YHWH, its every judgment.

Proverbs 17

1Better a dry crust and tranquility with it,
than a house full of contentious feasting.
2A competent servant will rule over a disgraceful son,
and divide an inheritance among brothers.
3A crucible for silver and a furnace for gold,
but the one who tests hearts, YHWH.
4An evildoer, one who listens to iniquitous lips;
a liar, one who heeds a destructive tongue.
5One who mocks the poor insults his maker,
and one who rejoices at disaster will not go unpunished.
6The crown of the aged, grandchildren,
and the splendor of children, their fathers.
7An excessive lip, not fitting for a fool;
how much more lying lips for a noble.
8A bribe, a beautiful charm in the eyes of its possessor;
wherever he turns he succeeds.
9One who seeks love covers an offense,
but one who repeats a matter separates friends.
10A rebuke goes deeper into the discerning
than a hundred blows on a fool.
11The evil seek only rebellion,
and a cruel messenger will be sent against him.
12Encounter a bear bereft of her young by a man,
but not a fool in his folly.
13One who returns evil for good—
evil will never depart from his house.
14Releasing water, the beginning of strife,
so before the conflict breaks out, leave!
15One who acquits the wicked and condemns the righteous—
an abomination to YHWH, both of them.

16Why is it that a payment is in the fool's hand
to buy wisdom, when there is no brain?
17A friend loves at all times,
and a brother is born for adversity.
18A senseless person shakes hands,
going surety for his neighbor.
19One who loves an offense loves strife,
and one who makes his door high seeks destruction.
20One with a perverted heart never finds good,
and one with a twisted tongue falls into evil.
21One who begets a fool has grief;
and the father of a fool never rejoices.
22A joyful heart enhances healing,
but a broken spirit dries up the bones.
23The wicked takes a bribe from the bosom
to divert the paths of justice.
24Before the face of the discerning, wisdom;
but the eyes of the fool, on the ends of the earth.
25A foolish son, a vexation to his father
and bitterness to the one who bore him.
26Surely, punishing the righteous, not good—
striking noble people for uprightness.
27One who restrains words, a knowledgeable person,
and the calm, a person of understanding.
28Even a fool who keeps silent is regarded wise;
one who closes his lips, discerning.

Proverbs 18

1A loner seeks his own desire;
he breaks out against all sound wisdom.
2A fool does not delight in understanding,
but only in disclosing his heart.
3When the wicked enters, contempt enters too,
and with shame, reproach.
4The words of a person's mouth, deep waters,
a flowing stream, a fountain of wisdom.
5Showing the wicked favor, not good,

thrusting aside the righteous in judgment.
6A fool's lips bring strife,
and his mouth calls for blows.
7A fool's mouth, his ruin,
and his lips, a snare for his life.
8The words of a slanderer, like delicacies,
and they descend into one's innermost being.
9Even one slack in his work—
he is a brother to a destroyer.
10The name of YHWH, a strong tower;
into it the righteous runs and is secure.
11The wealth of the rich, his fortified city;
and like a high wall, in his imagination.
12Before destruction one's heart is haughty,
but before honor, humility.
13One who replies before listening—
it is folly to him, and shame.
14A person's spirit can endure his sickness,
but a broken spirit—who can bear it?
15The heart of the discerning acquires knowledge,
and the ear of the wise seeks knowledge.
16A person's gift makes room for him,
and leads him before the great.
17The first in his case, right,
until his neighbor comes and examines him.
18The lot stops quarrels,
and separates the powerful.
19An offended brother, like a strong city,
and quarrels, like the bar of a palace.
20From the fruit of his mouth one's belly is satisfied;
he is satisfied by the produce of his lips.
21Death and life, in the power of the tongue;
those who love it eat its fruit.
22One who has found a wife has found good,
and receives favor from YHWH.
23The poor speak entreaties;
but the rich answer harshly.
24There are friends to associate with,
but the reality is this: a true friend sticks closer than a brother.

Proverbs 19

1 Better the poor who walks in his integrity
than one with perverted lips who is a fool.
2 Indeed, without knowledge, desire, not good,
and one who hurries with his feet sins.
3 A person's folly leads him astray,
but his heart rages against YHWH.
4 Wealth adds many friends,
but the poor is separated from his friend.
5 A false witness will not go unpunished,
and one who tells lies will not escape.
6 Many seek the favor of the noble,
and everyone is a friend to the gift giver.
7 All the poor person's brothers hate him.
How much more do his friends avoid him!
Pursuing words—they are not there.
8 One who acquires a heart loves himself,
one who guards understanding, to find good.
9 A false witness will not go unpunished,
and one who tells lies will perish.
10 Not fitting for a fool, luxury.
How much more for a servant to rule over princes!
11 A person's insight makes him patient,
and his splendor, overlooking an offense.
12 Like a lion's growl, a king's wrath,
but his favor, like dew on the grass.
13 A disaster to his father, a foolish son,
and a constant dripping, a quarrelsome wife.
14 House and wealth, an inheritance from fathers,
but a prudent wife, from YHWH.
15 Laziness induces a deep sleep,
and the slacker goes hungry.
16 One who keeps a commandment keeps his life,
but one who despises his ways will die.
17 One who is gracious to the poor lends to YHWH,
and he will repay him for his deed.
18 Discipline your son, for there is hope,
and do not direct your desire to his death.

19The hothead bears a penalty,
for if you deliver him, you must do so again.
20Listen to counsel and receive discipline,
that you may be wise in the future.
21Many plans are in a person's heart,
but the counsel of YHWH, it stands.
22A person's desire, his kindness,
so better a poor person than a liar.
23The fear of YHWH, for life,
that one spends the night content, undisturbed by evil.
24The sluggard has buried his hand in the bowl;
he will not even bring it back to his mouth.
25Strike a scoffer and the simple becomes shrewd,
but rebuke the discerning, he will gain knowledge.
26One who mistreats a father and drives away a mother,
a shameful and disgraceful son.
27Cease, my son, to listen to instruction,
to stray from words of knowledge!
28A worthless witness mocks justice,
and the mouth of the wicked swallows iniquity.
29Judgments are prepared for scoffers,
and blows for the back of fools.

Proverbs 20

1Wine, a mocker; beer, a brawler,
and whoever is intoxicated by them will never be wise.
2Like a lion's growl, the dread of a king;
one who provokes his anger forfeits his life.
3Abstaining from strife, to a person's honor,
but every fool quarrels.
4From the winter, the sluggard does not plow.
At the harvest, he inquires, but nothing!
5The counsel in a person's heart, deep waters,
but an understanding person draws it up.
6Many people—each one proclaims his own loyalty,
but a trustworthy person, who can find?
7One who goes about in his integrity, the righteous.
Blessed are his children after him!

8A king sits on the throne of judgment
scattering all evil with his eyes.
9Who can say, "I have made my heart pure,
I am cleansed from my sin?"
10Variant weights, variant measures,
an abomination to YHWH, both of them.
11Even by his actions a youth makes himself known,
whether his conduct is pure and upright.
12A hearing ear and a seeing eye,
YHWH has made both of them.
13Do not love sleep lest you become impoverished.
Open your eyes; be satisfied with food!
14"Bad, bad," says the buyer,
but when he goes away, he boasts.
15There is this: gold and an abundance of corals,
but a precious ornament, knowledgeable lips.
16Take his garment, for he has gone surety for a stranger!
And for outsiders, impound it.
17Sweet to a person, the bread of deceit,
but afterward his mouth is filled with gravel.
18Plans are established by counsel,
so wage war with guidance.
19A slanderer reveals secrets,
so do not mix with a big-mouth.
20One who curses his father or his mother,
his lamp will be extinguished in deep darkness.
21An inheritance quickly gained at first,
in the end will not be blessed.
22Do not say, "I will repay evil."
Wait for YHWH, and he will save you.
23An abomination to YHWH, variant weights,
and fraudulent scales are not good.
24One's steps, from YHWH,
and a person—how can he understand his way?
25A trap for a person to say rashly, "Holy,"
and after vows to appraise.
26A wise king scatters the wicked,
and rolls the wheel over them.
27The human life-breath, the lamp of YHWH,
searching all the innermost parts.

[28]Kindness and faithfulness protect the king,
and he supports his throne by kindness.
[29]The splendor of the young, their strength,
and the adornment of the aged, grey hair.
[30]Bruised wounds clean away evil,
and blows, the innermost parts.

Proverbs 21

[1]Water channels, the heart of the king in YHWH's hand;
he guides it wherever he desires.
[2]A person's every way, upright in his eyes,
but the one who examines hearts, YHWH.
[3]Doing righteousness and justice,
more preferable to YHWH than sacrifice.
[4]Haughty eyes and an arrogant heart—
the lamp of the wicked, sin.
[5]The plans of the diligent, only for profit,
but all haste, only to poverty.
[6]Acquiring treasures by a deceitful tongue—
the fleeting vapor of those pursuing death.
[7]The violence of the wicked drags them away,
for they refuse to do justice.
[8]The way of the guilty person, crooked,
but the pure, his conduct is straight.
[9]Better to dwell on the corner of a roof
than a shared house with a quarrelsome woman.
[10]The soul of the wicked desires evil;
his neighbor finds no favor in his eyes.
[11]When a scoffer is punished, the simple become wise;
and when the wise is instructed, he receives knowledge.
[12]The righteous attends to the house of the wicked,
turning the wicked to ruin.
[13]One who shuts his ear from the outcry of the poor—
he too will cry out and not be answered.
[14]A gift in secret averts anger,
and a bribe in the bosom, fierce wrath.
[15]Doing justice, joy for the righteous,
but ruin for evildoers.

16A person who wanders from the way of insight
will rest in the community of the dead.
17One who loves pleasure, a needy person;
one who loves wine and oil will never grow rich.
18A ransom for the righteous, the wicked,
and the treacherous in the place of the upright.
19Better to dwell in a desert land
than with a contentious and vexing wife.
20Desirable treasure and oil in the dwelling of the wise,
but a foolish person swallows it up.
21One who pursues righteousness and kindness
finds life, righteousness, and honor.
22A wise person went up against a city of the mighty
and brought down the stronghold of its reliance.
23One who guards his mouth and his tongue
guards himself from troubles.
24Proud, arrogant—scoffer, his name;
who acts in the rage of insolence.
25The sluggard's desire kills him,
for his hands refuse to work.
26All day he longs longings,
but the righteous gives without restraint.
27The sacrifice of the wicked, an abomination;
how much more when he brings it with evil intent.
28A false witness will perish,
but the person who listens will speak successfully.
29The wicked person puts on a strong face,
but the upright, he discerns his way.
30There is no wisdom, and no understanding,
and no counsel before YHWH.
31The horse is prepared for the day of battle,
but victory belongs to YHWH.

Proverbs 22

1A name, preferable to great wealth,
and graciousness, better than silver and gold.
2The rich and the poor meet together;
YHWH, the maker of both.

[3]The shrewd sees evil and hides,
but the simple pass on and are punished.
[4]The reward of humility, the fear of YHWH,
wealth and honor and life.
[5]Thorns, snares, in the way of the perverse,
one who guards his life stays far from them.
[6]Train a youth according to his way,
even when he becomes old he will not depart from it.
[7]The rich rules over the poor,
and the borrower, a slave to the lender.
[8]One who sows iniquity reaps disaster,
and the rod of his wrath will fail.
[9]The generous person, he will be blessed,
for he shares his food with the poor.
[10]Drive out the scoffer and strife departs,
even quarreling and shame cease.
[11]One who loves purity of heart—
his lips, gracious; the king, his friend.
[12]The eyes of YHWH guard knowledge,
but he subverts the words of the treacherous.
[13]The sluggard says, "A lion outside,
in the squares I'll be killed!"
[14]A deep pit, the mouth of strange women;
one cursed by YHWH falls into it.
[15]Folly is bound in a youth's heart;
the rod of discipline drives it far from him.
[16]One who oppresses the poor, to enrich him;
one who gives to the rich, only to lack.
[17]Incline your ear and hear the words of the wise,
and direct your heart to my knowledge;
[18]for it will be pleasant if you keep them in your belly,
if all of them are secured on your lips.
[19]In order that your trust may be in YHWH,
I teach you today—even you.
[20]Have I not written for you thirty sayings
as counsel and knowledge
[21]to teach you truth, words of truth,
so as to bring back true reports to those who send you?
[22]Do not rob the poor because they are poor,
and do not crush the needy at the gate;

[23]for YHWH will contest their case
and will snatch the life of those who snatch from them.
[24]Do not befriend an angry person,
and with a hothead do not go;
[25]lest you learn his ways,
and get yourself ensnared.
[26]Do not be among those who seal a deal,
among those who guarantee a loan,
[27]if you do not have the means to pay,
why should he take your bed from beneath you?
[28]Do not displace an ancient boundary
which your ancestors made.
[29]Have you seen a person skilled in his work?
He will stand before kings.
He will not stand before the obscure.

Proverbs 23

[1]When you sit to dine with a ruler,
look carefully at what is before you,
[2]and put a knife to your throat,
if you are an insatiable person.
[3]Do not desire his delicacies,
for they are deceptive food.
[4]Do not struggle to get rich.
Desist from your own understanding!
[5]Will you let your eyes fly to it? It is no more!
for it will surely grow wings for itself,
and fly to the sky like an eagle.
[6]Do not eat the food of a stingy person,
nor desire his delicacies.
[7]For like one who calculates within himself, thus is he:
"Eat and drink," he says to you,
but his heart, not with you.
[8]You eat your morsel, you will vomit it up,
and you will waste your pleasant words.
[9]Do not speak in the ears of a fool,
for he will despise the insight of your words.
[10]Do not displace an ancient boundary,

nor encroach on the fields of orphans,
11for their redeemer is strong;
he will contest their case with you.
12Apply your heart to discipline,
and your ear to words of knowledge.
13Do not withhold discipline from a youth;
if you strike him with a rod, he shall not die.
14Strike him with a rod,
and you will deliver his life from Sheol.
15My son, if your heart becomes wise,
my heart, too, will rejoice,
16and my kidneys will exalt,
when your lips speak what is upright.
17Let not your heart envy sinners,
but rather those who fear YHWH every day.
18Surely, there is a future,
and your hope shall not be cut off.
19You yourself listen, my son, and become wise,
and stride in the way of your heart.
20Do not be among winebibbers,
among those who overindulge on meat,
21for the inebriated and the glutton will be impoverished,
and stupor will clothe them in rags.
22Listen to your father, who begot you,
and do not despise your mother when she grows old.
23Buy truth, and do not sell it;
wisdom and discipline and understanding.
24The father of a righteous son will greatly exult;
one who begets a wise son will rejoice in him.
25Your father and your mother will rejoice,
and she who bore you will exult.
26Give me, my son, your heart,
and let your eyes observe my ways,
27for a deep pit, a harlot,
and a narrow well, a strange woman.
28Surely, she lies in wait like a bandit,
and increases traitors among men.
29Who cries "Alas"? Who cries "Woe"?
Who has strife? Who has complaints?
Who has wounds for no reason?

Who has bloodshot eyes?
30Those who linger over wine,
those who come to taste mixed wine.
31Do not look at wine when it sparkles red,
when it shines in the cup,
going down smoothly.
32In the end, it bites like a serpent,
and it stings like an adder.
33Your eyes will see strange things,
and your heart will utter perverse things.
34And you will be like one who lies down in the heart of the sea,
even like one who lies at the top of a mast.
35"They struck me—I feel no pain,
they beat me—I did not know it.
When shall I awake?
I'll continue seeking it."

Proverbs 24

1Do not envy evil people,
nor desire to be with them,
2for their heart ponders destruction,
and their lips speak mischief.
3By wisdom a house is built,
and by understanding it is established;
4and by knowledge rooms are filled
with all wealth, precious and pleasant.
5A wise man—strength,
and a person of knowledge grows in power.
6For by guidance you should wage war,
and with many counselors, victory.
7Wisdom, too high for a fool;
at the gate he cannot open his mouth.
8The one who plans to do evil—
he will be called a master of schemes.
9Foolish scheming, sin;
and an abomination to a person, a scoffer.
10If you show yourself lax in the day of distress,
your strength, meager.

11Deliver those who are being taken away to death,
and those stumbling to slaughter do not refrain from sparing.
12If you say, "We did not know about this,"
does not he who weighs hearts perceive it?
Does not he who guards your life know?
And will he not repay a person according to his deed?
13Eat honey, my son, because it is good,
and honeycomb, sweet upon your palate.
14So know wisdom is such for your life.
If you find it, there is a future,
and your hope shall not be cut off.
15Do not lie in wait as a wicked person against the dwelling of the righteous;
do not destroy his resting place;
16though the righteous may fall seven times, he will rise;
while the wicked will stumble in evil.
17When your enemy falls, do not rejoice,
and when he stumbles, do not let your heart exult;
18lest YHWH see and it will be evil in his sight,
and turn his anger away from him.
19Do not fret at evildoers,
nor envy the wicked,
20for there is no future for the evil,
the lamp of the wicked will be extinguished.
21Fear YHWH, my son, and the king.
Do not disobey either of them.
22For their ruin will arise suddenly,
and the destruction of them both—who knows?
23These also are of the wise.
Showing partiality in judgment, not good.
24The one who says to the guilty, "You are innocent"—
peoples will curse him, nations will condemn him.
25But for those who rebuke, it will be pleasant,
on them shall come a blessing of good.
26He kisses lips—
the one who returns honest words.
27Prepare your outside work,
and ready it in the field for yourself.
Afterwards build your house.
28Do not be a witness against your neighbor without cause,
or would you deceive with your lips?

[29]Do not say, "Just as he did to me, so I will do to him;
I will repay the man according to his deed."
[30]I passed by the field of a sluggard,
by the vineyard of a man lacking sense.
[31]And look—all of it was overgrown with thorns,
the ground was covered with nettles,
and its stone wall was broken down.
[32]And I looked; I took it to heart;
I saw; I received instruction:
[33]A little sleep, a little slumber,
a little folding of the hands to rest,
[34]and poverty will come upon you like a vagabond,
and need like an armed warrior.

Proverbs 25

[1]These also are proverbs of Solomon,
which the men of Hezekiah, king of Judah, transcribed.
[2]The glory of God, to conceal a matter,
and the glory of kings, to examine a matter.
[3]The heavens for height and the earth for depth,
and the heart of kings, unsearchable.
[4]Remove dross from silver,
and a vessel comes forth for the refiner.
[5]Remove the wicked from before a king,
so that his throne will be established by righteousness.
[6]Do not honor yourself before a king,
and do not stand in the place of the great,
[7]for better that one say to you, "Come up here,"
than one humiliate you before a nobleman.

What your eyes have seen,
[8]do not bring hastily to argue,
lest—what will you do afterwards,
when your neighbor puts you to shame?
[9]Contest your case with your neighbor,
but do not reveal the secret of another,
[10]lest one who hears revile you,
and the slander against you never ceases.

11 Apples of gold in settings of silver:
a word spoken in a fitting fashion.
12 A ring of gold and an ornament of fine gold:
a wise person rebuking a listening ear.
13 Like the cold of snow on a day of harvest,
a trustworthy envoy to those who send them;
they refresh the life of their masters.
14 Clouds and wind but no rain,
a man who boasts of a deceitful gift.
15 By patience a ruler can be persuaded,
and a soft tongue breaks a bone.
16 If you find honey, eat what you require,
lest you become sated and vomit it up.
17 Rarely visit your neighbor's house,
lest he become sated with you and hate you.
18 A club and a sword and a sharpened arrow,
a person who testifies against his neighbor as a false witness.
19 A broken tooth and a shaky foot,
trusting a treacherous person in a day of trouble.
20 One who removes a garment on a cold day,
vinegar on a wound,
and one who sings songs to a troubled heart.
21 If your enemy is hungry, feed him food;
and if he is thirsty, give him water to drink.
22 For you will heap burning coals on his head,
and YHWH will reward you.
23 The north wind brings rain,
and a secretive tongue, angry faces.
24 Better to dwell on the corner of a roof,
than a shared house with a quarrelsome woman.
25 Cold water for a thirsty throat,
and a good report from a distant land.
26 A muddied spring and a polluted fountain,
a righteous person tottering before the wicked.
27 Eating much honey, not good,
and searching out difficult things is without glory.
28 A breached city without a wall:
a person whose spirit is unrestrained.

Proverbs 26

1Like snow in summer and like rain at harvest,
so honor is not fitting for a fool.
2As a bird for wandering, as a swallow for flying,
so a curse without cause never arrives.
3A whip for the horse, a bridle for the donkey,
and a rod for the back of fools.
4Do not answer a fool according to his folly,
lest you become like him, even you!
5Answer a fool according to his folly
lest he be wise in his own eyes.
6Cutting off one's feet, drinking violence:
one who sends word by the hand of a fool.
7Legs dangle from the lame,
and a proverb in the mouth of fools.
8Like one who binds a stone in a sling,
so is one who gives honor to a fool.
9A thornbush coming into the hand of a drunk,
and a proverb in the mouth of a fool.
10An archer who pierces everyone,
and one who hires a fool and one who hires a passerby.
11Like a dog returning to its vomit,
a fool repeating his folly.
12Have you seen a person wise in his own eyes?
There is more hope for a fool than for him.
13The sluggard says, "A lion in the street!
A lion in the squares!"
14The door turns on its hinge,
and the sluggard on his bed.
15The sluggard buries his hand in the bowl,
he is too weary to bring it back to his mouth.
16The sluggard is wiser in his own eyes
than seven who answer with discernment.
17One who seizes the ears of a passing dog,
one who meddles in a dispute not his own.
18Like a madman shooting
firebrands, arrows, and death,
19so is a person who deceives his neighbor

and says, “Was I not joking?”
20Without wood, a fire dies out,
and when there is no slanderer, strife calms down.
21Charcoal for burning embers and wood for fire
and a contentious man for kindling strife.
22The words of a slanderer, like delicacies,
and they descend into the chambers of the belly.
23Silver gloss glazed upon earthenware:
burning lips and an evil heart.
24An enemy disguises himself in his speech,
while he harbors deceit within.
25Though he makes his voice gracious, do not trust him,
for seven abominations are in his heart.
26Hatred is covered by deceit,
his evil will be exposed in the assembly.
27One who digs a pit will fall into it,
and one who rolls a stone—it will come back on him.
28A lying tongue hates those it afflicts,
and a smooth mouth works ruin.

Proverbs 27

1Do not boast about tomorrow,
for you do not know what a day may bear.
2Let a stranger praise you, and not your own mouth,
an outsider, and not your own lips.
3The weight of stone and the burden of sand,
but the vexation of a fool is heavier than both.
4The cruelty of wrath and a flood of anger,
but who can stand before jealousy?
5Better open rebuke than hidden love.
6Faithful, the wounds of a friend,
but profuse, the kisses of an enemy.
7A sated appetite tramples on honey,
but a hungry appetite, everything bitter is sweet.
8Like a bird wandering from its nest,
so is a person who wanders from his place.
9Oil and incense make the heart glad,
and the sweetness of one’s friend more than his own counsel.

10Do not forsake your friend or your father's friend,
and do not enter your brother's house on the day of your calamity.
Better a close neighbor than a distant brother.
11Be wise, my son, and make my heart glad,
so that I may answer the one who reproaches me.
12The shrewd perceives danger—he hides;
the immature pass on—they pay for it.
13Take his garment, for he has gone surety for a stranger;
and for a foreign woman, impound it!
14One who blesses his neighbor with a loud voice early in the morning—
it will be reckoned to him as a curse.
15A continual dripping on a rainy day
and a contentious woman are alike.
16Whoever hides her, hides wind,
and oil meets his right hand.
17Iron sharpens iron,
and a person sharpens the face of his neighbor.
18One who tends a fig tree will eat its fruit,
and one who keeps his master will be honored.
19As water, a face to a face,
so a heart of a person to a person.
20Sheol and Abaddon are never satisfied,
and the eyes of humans are never satisfied.
21A crucible for silver and a furnace for gold,
and a person by the mouth of one who praises him.
22Though you crush the fool in a mortar,
with a pestle among the grains,
his folly will not depart from him.
23Know well the face of your flock,
pay attention to your herds.
24For wealth is not forever,
and surely not a crown from generation to generation.
25When the grass disappears and new growth appears,
and the vegetation of the mountains is gathered,
26lambs will provide for your clothing,
and goats, the price of a field;
27and enough goat's milk for your food,
for the food of your house,
and sustenance for your maidservants.

Proverbs 28

1The wicked flee, though no one pursues,
while the righteous are as confident as a lion.
2Because of the transgression of a land—many are its princes,
but because of an intelligent person, one who knows, right endures.
3A person who is poor and oppresses the lowly:
a rain that washes away and leaves no food.
4Those who forsake instruction praise the wicked,
but those who observe instruction strive against them.
5Evil people do not understand justice,
but those who seek YHWH understand everything.
6Better a poor person who walks in his integrity
than one of twisted ways who is rich.
7A discerning son keeps instruction,
while one who associates with gluttons shames his father.
8One who increases his wealth by interest and usury—
gathers it for one who is kind to the poor.
9One who turns aside his ear from listening to instruction—
even his prayer, an abomination.
10One who misleads the upright into an evil path—
he will fall into his own pit,
but the blameless will inherit good.
11A rich person, wise in his own eyes,
but a discerning poor person sees through him.
12When the righteous rejoice, great glory,
but when the wicked arise, people hide.
13One who conceals his transgressions shall not prosper,
while one who confesses and abandons them will receive mercy.
14Blessed is the person who fears continually,
while the one who hardens his heart will fall into trouble.
15A growling lion and a charging bear:
a wicked ruler over a poor people.
16A prince lacking understanding and abundant in oppressions—
one who hates unjust gain will prolong days.
17A person who oppresses by bloodshed
will flee to a pit—let no one lay hold of him.
18One who walks blamelessly will be saved,

while one of twisted ways will fall into one.
[19]One who works his land will be satisfied with food,
while one who pursues worthless things will be filled with poverty.
[20]A faithful person, many blessings,
but one who hastens to get rich shall not go unpunished.
[21]Showing partiality, not good;
and even for a piece of bread a person may transgress.
[22]A greedy person hastens after wealth,
but he is unaware that loss will come upon him.
[23]One who reproves a person finds favor afterward
more than one who is smooth-tongued.
[24]One who robs his father and mother and says,
"There is no crime,"
he is a companion to a destroyer.
[25]The greedy stir up strife,
but the one who trusts in YHWH will be refreshed.
[26]The one who trusts in his own heart—he is a fool;
but the one who walks in wisdom—he will be delivered.
[27]One who gives to the poor lacks nothing,
while the one who closes his eyes, abundant curses.
[28]When the wicked rise, people hide,
and when they perish, the righteous increase.

Proverbs 29

[1]A person reproved who stiffens his neck
will suddenly be broken and without remedy.
[2]When the righteous increase, the people rejoice,
but when the wicked rule, people groan.
[3]A person who loves wisdom makes his father glad,
but one who associates with prostitutes destroys wealth.
[4]By justice a king brings stability to a land,
but a person who exacts contributions tears it down.
[5]A person who flatters his neighbor,
spreading a net for his feet.
[6]In the transgression of an evil person, a snare,
but the righteous will sing and rejoice.
[7]The righteous know the rights of the poor,
but the wicked do not understand knowledge.

8Scoffers inflame a city,
while the wise turn away anger.
9A wise person disputes with a foolish person,
and he rages and laughs, but there is no rest.
10Men of blood hate the blameless,
but the upright seeks his life.
11A fool lets out all of his spirit,
while the wise quiet it down.
12A ruler who listens to a deceptive word—
all his officials, wicked.
13A poor man and an oppressor meet:
YHWH is the one who gives light to the eyes of both.
14A king who judges the poor in truth,
his throne will be established forever.
15The rod and reproof give wisdom,
while a youth set loose shames his mother.
16When the wicked increase, transgression increases,
but the righteous will see their downfall.
17Discipline your son so that he may bring you comfort,
and give delight to your life.
18When there is no vision, a people cast off restraint,
but the one who keeps instruction, blessed is he!
19A servant is not disciplined by words;
though he understands, there is no response.
20Have you seen a man hasty with his words?
There is more hope for a fool than for him.
21One who pampers his servant from youth—
afterward he will be insolent.
22An angry man provokes strife,
and a hothead, abundant transgression.
23A person's pride will bring him low,
but a lowly spirit will hold honor.
24One who partners with a thief hates his life.
He hears a curse, but he will not testify.
25Fear of people lays a snare,
but one who trusts in YHWH will be protected.
26Many are those who seek the face of a ruler,
but from YHWH, a person's judgment.
27An unjust person, an abomination to the righteous,
while one whose way is upright, an abomination to the wicked.

Proverbs 30

1The words of Agur, son of Yaqeh,
the burden, the oracle of the man:
"I am weary, God, I am weary, God, but I will overcome.
2Indeed, I am more beast than human,
that is, I do not have human understanding.
3I have not learned wisdom,
but knowledge of the Holy One I will know.
4Who has gone up to heaven and come down?
Who has gathered the wind in the hollow of his hands?
Who has wrapped the waters in a garment?
Who has established all the ends of the earth?
What is his name? And what is the name of his son?
Surely, you know!
5Every word of God, refined;
he is a shield to those who take refuge in him.
6Do not add to his words,
lest he reprove you and you be proved a liar.
7Two things I have asked from you;
do not withhold them from me before I die:
8Falsehood and deceit keep far from me.
Poverty or wealth do not give to me;
provide me my apportioned food,
9lest I become sated and disavow,
and say, 'Who is YHWH?'
and lest I become impoverished and steal,
and desecrate the name of my God."
10Do not slander a servant to his master,
lest he curse you and you be held guilty.
11A generation—it curses its father,
and does not bless its mother.
12A generation—pure in its own eyes,
and not cleansed of its filth.
13A generation—how lofty are its eyes
and haughty are its eyelids.
14A generation—its teeth are swords,
and its fangs are knives
to devour the poor from the earth

and the destitute from humankind.
15The leech has two daughters: "Give," "Give."
Three things are never satisfied,
four never say, "Enough":
16Sheol, a barren womb,
the earth not quenched with water,
and fire, never saying, "Enough!"
17An eye that mocks a father,
and despises obedience to a mother—
the ravens of the valley will pluck it out,
and the brood of eagles will devour it.
18Three things are too wonderful for me,
and four I do not understand:
19the way of the eagle in the sky,
the way of a serpent on a rock,
the way of a ship in the heart of the sea,
and the way of a man with a maiden.
20This is the way of an adulterous woman:
she eats and wipes her mouth,
and says: "I have not done wrong."
21Under three things the earth quakes,
and under four it cannot endure:
22under a servant, when he becomes king,
and a fool, when sated with food;
23under a scorned woman, when she is married,
and a maidservant, when she displaces her mistress.
24Four things—they are smallest on earth,
yet they are inherently wise:
25Ants, a people not strong,
but they prepare their food in the summer.
26Badgers, a people not powerful,
but they set their homes in the rock.
27Locusts have no king,
but they all go forth in ranks.
28Lizards—you can seize them by the hand,
yet they are in the palaces of kings.
29Three things are stately of stride,
and four are stately of gait:
30A lion, mighty among the beasts,
and never retreats before anything.

31 A strutting rooster or a he-goat,
and a king no one can resist.
32 If you have acted foolishly by exalting yourself,
or if you have schemed,
hand over your mouth!
33 For pressing milk produces curds,
and pressing the nose produces blood,
and pressing anger produces strife.

Proverbs 31

1 The words of Lemuel, a king;
a burden, which his mother taught him:

2 "What, my son? What, son of my womb?
What, son of my vows?
3 Do not give your strength to women,
nor your ways to those who destroy kings.
4 Not for kings, Lemuel,
not for kings to drink wine,
nor for rulers strong drink;
5 lest he drink and forget what has been decreed,
and change the verdict of any of the afflicted.
6 Give strong drink to one who is perishing,
and wine to the bitter of spirit,
7 so that he may drink and forget his poverty,
and no longer remember his misery.
8 Open your mouth for the mute,
for the rights of those passing away.
9 Open your mouth, judge righteously,
and defend the rights of the poor and needy."
10 A valiant woman, who can find?
Her value, beyond corals.
11 The heart of her husband trusted in her,
and he had no lack of plunder.
12 She showed him good and not evil
all the days of her life.
13 She sought out wool and flax,
and she worked with delight with her hands.

[14]She was like merchant ships;
she would bring her food from afar;
[15]and she rose while it was still night,
and gave prey to her household,
and a portion to her maids.
[16]She considered a field and took it,
from the fruit of her hands she planted a vineyard.
[17]She girded her loins with strength,
and made strong her arms.
[18]She tasted that her wares were good;
her lamp did not go out at night.
[19]She stretched out her hands to the double spindle,
and her palms grasped the spindle.
[20]She opened her palm to the poor,
and stretched out her hands to the needy.
[21]She did not fear for her household because of snow,
for all her household were clothed in scarlet.
[22]She made for herself coverings,
linen and purple, her clothing.
[23]Her husband was known in the gates,
when he sat with the elders of the land.
[24]She made a linen garment and sold it,
and provided girdles to the merchant.
[25]Strength and majesty, her clothing;
and she laughed at the future.
[26]She opened her mouth in wisdom,
and loyal instruction was on her tongue.
[27]She watched over the ways of her household,
and the bread of idleness she did not eat.
[28]Her children rose up and blessed her;
her husband praised her:
[29]"Many daughters have done valiantly,
but you have surpassed them all."
[30]Charm, deceitful—and beauty, fleeting,
a woman who fears YHWH, she is to be praised.
[31]Give to her from the fruit of her hands,
so that her works praise her in the gates.

Introduction to Proverbs

Wisdom leads us back to childhood.
Except ye become as little children.
—Pascal, *Pensées*, 5.82
(trans. A. J. Krailsheimer, 1995;
repr. Garden City, NY: Dover, 2018)

The book of Proverbs is an unusual document. In light of the prominence of clichés and sound bites in contemporary discourse, the forms and terse expressions within the anthology are familiar sights and sounds. Among these familiar sounds, some of the sayings represent well-known melodies in the Christian community's life, common tunes that shape the believer's thinking and conduct (e.g., Prov 1:7; 3:5–6; 22:6; 31:10–31). And when these common tunes are heard as just another popular score concerned with self-improvement, Proverbs appears to be ordinary at best and superfluous at worst.

The book of Proverbs attends to the ordinary, but it is far from ordinary within the canon of Scripture. In fact, from a literary perspective, it is an anomaly. The generic distinctiveness of the anthology illuminates the unusual nature of the document as well as the interpretive difficulties that confront the reader of this enigmatic work. How should one read the book of Proverbs? How do the diverse materials in the document function? Is the book of Proverbs a haphazard collection of traditional sayings, a veritable graveyard of dead aphorisms that must be revived through appropriate application in specific life circumstances? Or is the book a coherent document, an anthology that has been carefully configured to serve a particular pedagogical and theological agenda?

This commentary seeks to answer these questions. In preparation for its formal investigation, it is necessary to set the interpretive stage by addressing six issues: the historical setting of the book, its discourse setting, the arrangement of the materials in the central collections, the document's distinctive literary features, its major theological themes, and its theology.

Historical Setting

While the historical context of a work plays a formative role in discerning its occasion and agenda, it is difficult to determine the setting and compositional history of Proverbs. Similar to Job and Ecclesiastes, the materials in Proverbs transcend specific historical circumstances and address issues common to all people at all times. And similar to Job and Ecclesiastes, Proverbs evinces a lack of concern with history in general and the major events of Israel's history in particular. Historical context may inform the reading of a document, but this principle does not serve as the interpretive key for unlocking Proverbs.

The ambiguity of Proverbs's historical context, however, does not serve as an invitation to read the document in a vacuum. While the book exhibits a lack of concern with specific historical events, the titles that punctuate the anthology serve as a window into its compositional history. Taken at face value, these titles attribute the discrete collections to various individuals: Solomon (1:1; 10:1), the wise (22:17; 24:23), Hezekiah's scribes who transcribed Solomonic proverbs (25:1), Agur (30:1), and King Lemuel (31:1). At minimum, these attributions indicate that the collections within the book were produced and incorporated in the anthology at different times. In this respect, the compositional history of Proverbs is comparable to the compositional history of the Psalter: it was a growing, fluid book throughout the canonical period.

In addition to sketching the compositional history of the anthology, the titles associate the collections with the name and biography of particular people.[1] But the contributions of these attributions to the setting of the collections is contested. Other factors frame and fund the contextual contributions of certain titles. The relationship between "the words of the wise" and the Instruction of Amenemope, for example, intimates that Prov 22:17–24:22 was composed between the ninth to the sixth centuries BC.[2] In light of the observation that ancient Israel experienced something of a textual revolution in seventh century BC,[3] the mention of Hezekiah's scribes places the composition of Prov 25:1–29:27 in the late eighth or early seventh century BC. And linguistic evidence, combined with the socioeconomic activities

1. Eva Mroczek, *The Literary Imagination in Jewish Antiquity* (New York: Oxford University Press, 2016), 51–85.

2. Kenneth A. Kitchen, "Proverbs and Wisdom Books of the Ancient Near East: The Factual History of a Literary Form," *TynBul* 28 (1977): 68–114; Bruce K. Waltke, *The Book of Proverbs: Chapters 15–31*, NICOT (Grand Rapids, Eerdmans, 2005), 217–18n106; Michael V. Fox, *Proverbs 10–31: A New Translation with Introduction and Commentary*, AB 18B (New Haven: Yale University Press, 2009), 706; Michael V. Fox, "From Amenemope to Proverbs: Editorial Art in Proverbs 22,17–23,11," *ZAW* 126 (2014): 76–91.

3. William M. Schniedewind, *How the Bible Became a Book: The Textualization of Ancient Israel* (Cambridge: Cambridge University Press, 2004), 91–117.

of the woman in 31:10–31, has prompted many to situate Prov 30 and 31 within the postexilic period.[4]

In contrast to these collections, the compendia attributed to Solomon have a checkered history of interpretation (1:1; 10:1). For some, the Solomonic attributions identify the author of the materials in the collections or bear witness to the intellectual tradition that emerged during the wise king's tenure.[5] For others, the similarities between these attributions and pseudepigraphic titles within instructional texts elsewhere in the ancient world indicate that the anonymous sages responsible for composing the collections attributed them to the wise king to legitimize their work and endow the materials with authority.[6] The historical and contextual value of the Solomonic titles is disputed. And neither the canonical witness (1 Kgs 3:6–28; 4:29–34) nor the content and literary architecture of ancient Near Eastern instructional texts have resolved the dilemma.[7]

The contextual contributions of the Solomonic titles have reached something of an impasse. But there appears to be an alternative to the extremes, a *via media* position that accounts for the nature of the materials in the collections and their association with Solomon. Whether or not the materials in the Solomonic collections are compositional duplicates or developments of originally oral sayings, the authority of a proverb is rooted in the general truth it communicates. To be specific, the authority of a proverb derives from its time-tested validity as well as its acceptance and use by a community, rather than from its creation by a particular author. The anonymity of the vast majority of proverbs in contemporary discourse bears witness to this reality. The locus of a proverb's authority provides a framework through which to understand the attributions to Solomon within the titles of Proverbs. While these titles may suggest that Solomon composed the individual sayings in the collections that bear his name, they need not be interpreted in such a narrow fashion, for they do not specify the nature of Solomon's activities. At minimum, the titles associate Solomon with the performance of "proverbs" (1:1; 10:1; 25:1; 1 Kgs 4:32[5:12]).

4. Christine Roy Yoder, *Wisdom as a Woman of Substance: A Socioeconomic Reading of Proverbs 1–9 and 31:10–31*, BZAW 304 (Berlin: de Gruyter, 2001); Bruce K. Waltke, *The Book of Proverbs: Chapters 1–15*, NICOT (Grand Rapids: Eerdmans, 2004), 36–37.

5. For Solomonic authorship, see Kitchen, "Proverbs and Wisdom Books of the Ancient Near East," 68–114; Waltke, *Proverbs: Chapters 1–15*, 31–36, among others. For the notion of a Solomonic enlightenment as well as the contention that the Solomonic titles indicate the materials serve as an extension of the intellectual enterprise that commenced during his reign, see Gerhard von Rad, "The Beginnings of Historical Writing in Ancient Israel," in *The Problem of the Hexateuch and Other Essays* (Edinburgh: Oliver & Boyd, 1966), 166–204; Walter A. Brueggemann, "The Social Significance of Solomon as a Patron of Wisdom," in *The Sage in Israel and the Ancient Near East*, ed. J. G. Gammie and L. G. Perdue (Winona Lake, IN: Eisenbrauns, 1990), 117–32, respectively.

6. Leo G. Perdue, "Wisdom Theology and Social History in Proverbs 1–9," in *Wisdom, You Are My Sister: Studies in Honor of Roland E. Murphy, O. Carm., on the Occasion of His Eightieth Birthday*, ed. Michael L. Barré, CBQMS 29 (Washington, DC: Catholic Biblical Association of America, 1997), 92–101.

7. Kitchen, "Proverbs and Wisdom Books of the Ancient Near East," 84–87; Stuart Weeks, *Early Israelite Wisdom* (Oxford: Oxford University Press, 1994), 13; Waltke, *Proverbs: Chapters 1–15*, 32–36; Yoder, *Wisdom as a Woman of Substance*, 19–38.

In light of the fact that some of the materials in the book are not proverbs (Prov 1:1), the titles seem to link the materials with Solomon's famed wisdom. And in light of the authority of a proverb and ancient Near Eastern perceptions of authorship,[8] the titles may indicate that the materials are consonant with Solomonic wisdom. They invite the reader to associate the materials with the wisdom and biography of Israel's quintessential wise man.[9]

The titles within Proverbs signal the dynamic nature of the anthology's compositional history and the extent of its historical setting. If nothing else, these titles indicate that the historical setting of the document is not determinative for its interpretation. Rather than searching for a historical context within which to read the book, it seems best to interpret the material within the world of the text, that is, the discourse setting of the anthology.

Discourse Setting

The discourse setting or performance context of Proverbs is significant, for this setting delineates the social and dialogical context in which the diverse materials within the anthology may be read. Since proverbs are situationally oriented, open-ended sayings that transcend social barriers and remain relevant to a wide variety people,[10] the meaning of a proverb is made clear only when it is cast in a performance context, where the communicative situation orients one to the function and significance of the saying.[11] Folklorists and paroemiologists (those who study proverbs) consider the distinctive aspects of a saying's performance context to discern the illocutionary act performed by a proverb. And the components of this communicative situation serve as a heuristic guide to understand the *literary* performance context of Proverbs. Although the materials in Proverbs have been removed from their oral context of use and grafted into a collection, their recontextualization into an anthology creates a new performance context: the *Sitz im Buch*, the discourse setting of the document. The discourse setting of Proverbs is constructed through three basic

8. From an ancient Near Eastern perspective, the author or scribe functioned as a representative of a group rather than as an independent, literary artisan within a context concerned with intellectual property. For discussion, see Karel van der Toorn, *Scribal Culture and the Making of the Hebrew Bible* (Cambridge: Harvard University Press, 2007), 27–49; John H. Walton and D. Brent Sandy, *The Lost World of Scripture: Ancient Literary Culture and Biblical Authority* (Downers Grove, IL: IVP Academic, 2013), 24–28, 60–74.

9. Mroczek, *The Literary Imagination in Jewish Antiquity*, 51–85.

10. Roland E. Murphy, "Form Criticism and Wisdom Literature," *CBQ* 31 (1969): 483; William P. Brown, *Character in Crisis: A Fresh Approach to the Wisdom Literature of the Old Testament* (Grand Rapids: Eerdmans, 1996), 14.

11. Peter Seitel, "Proverbs: A Social Use of Metaphor," in *Folklore Genres*, ed. D. Ben-Amos (Austin: University of Texas Press, 1976), 125–43; Barbara Kirshenblatt-Gimblett, "Toward a Theory of Proverb Meaning," in *The Wisdom of Many: Essays on the Proverb*, ed. W. Mieder and A. Dundes (New York: Garland, 1981), 111–21; Carole R. Fontaine, *Traditional Sayings in the Old Testament: A Contextual Study*, BLS 5 (Sheffield: Almond Press, 1982), 54–63, 67–70.

elements: the speaker(s) within the book, the addressee(s) of the piece, and the social setting of the material. These elements are delineated in the preamble (1:1–7) as well as the prologue to the anthology (1:8–9:18), which coalesce to form the dialogical context through which to read the material.

Whereas ancient Near Eastern instructional texts tend to cast their didactic discourses "as the quoted speech of named and famed individuals," Proverbs resists this performance frame.[12] The title of the anthology names Solomon (1:1), but it does not frame the materials as the quoted speech of Solomon.[13] The title does not stage the performance context of the anthology. This performance context is constructed through literary and pragmatic means.

From a literary perspective, the performance frames of the speeches within Prov 1–9 outline the general contours of the book's discourse setting. These frames indicate the speeches are delivered by a father (and mother) to a son or sons. The prologue of Proverbs contains a chorus of voices: the father (1:8–21; 2:1–22; 3:1–35; 4:1–27; 5:1–23; 6:1–35; 7:1–27; 8:1–3; 9:1–3, 7–15, 18), the grandfather (4:4–9), sinners (1:11–14), Lady Wisdom (1:22–33; 8:4–36; 9:4–6), the strange woman (7:14–20), and Woman Folly (9:16–17). But these voices are delivered through a single voice. The father's voice governs the discourses across the prologue; he not only delivers specific instructions to his son, but he also serves as the instrument through which the sinners, Lady Wisdom, the strange woman, and Woman Folly speak.[14]

The father conveys and interprets the speech of different figures for the benefit of his son as well as future generations. The son represents the *primary* addressee of the discourses. And this addressee is construed in different ways. The preamble identifies the uncommitted youth as the principal addressee of the anthology (1:4),[15] while the discourses in the prologue identify the son(s) as the principal addressee(s). The terms are distinct, but these addressees are not mutually exclusive. These discrete designations refer to the same type of person: the son is an uncommitted youth, and the uncommitted youth is depicted as a late adolescent preparing to enter the community as an independent adult. The coreferential relationship between the uncommitted youth and the son(s) finds support in Wisdom's speeches (1:20–33; 8:1–36). These speeches imitate the rhetoric of the parental instructions, address the uncommitted youth (1:22, 32; 8:5), and associate the uncommitted with the son(s) (8:5, 32).

The identity of the speaker and addressee contribute to an understanding of the social setting of Proverbs's performance context. This setting is disclosed through the

12. Jacqueline Vayntrub, *Beyond Orality: Biblical Poetry on its Own Terms*, The Ancient Word (New York: Routledge, 2019), 184–85.

13. Vayntrub, *Beyond Orality*, 186–204.

14. Carol A. Newsom, "Woman and the Discourse of Patriarchal Wisdom: A Study of Proverbs 1–9," in *Gender and Difference in Ancient Israel*, ed. Peggy L. Day (Minneapolis: Fortress, 1989), 142–60.

15. While the preamble includes the wise as addressees of the document (1:5), the uncommitted youth represents the primary audience of the piece. For further discussion, see the exposition of 1:4–5.

father-son idiom. While the idiom may be interpreted as a cipher for a teacher-pupil relationship,[16] it appears to indicate a familial relationship.[17] The biological relationship between a father and a son in a didactic setting is evident in several ancient Near Eastern instructional works. And the inclusion of the mother within certain discourses of the prologue intimates a familial setting (1:8; 6:20), for it assumes a relational dimension that transcends the teacher-pupil relationship.

The performance frames of the discourses within Prov 1–9 cast the materials in a particular setting: as the instructions of a father (and mother) to a son or sons within a domestic context. This setting is constructed through textual frames and literary means. And this setting creates a framework through which to discern the pragmatic means of speech performance in Proverbs. On the surface, the father and son represent generic, stereotypical figures—any father and any son.[18] But in light of the fact that linguistic, conceptual, and pragmatic matters are inseparable in any act of communication,[19] this father is not any father, and this son is not any son. These designations are placeholders, or better, they are subject positions.[20] The reader is invited to assume the position of the son so as to receive instruction in wisdom and virtue; and in assuming this subject position, the reader is invited to envision a parent offering authorized and authoritative guidance in wisdom and virtue. The performance context of Proverbs creates subject positions that the reader assumes and fills. As Beth Currier notes, readers "will mentally picture this actual communicative exchange differently."[21] This communicative exchange will remain asynchronous rather than the quoted speech or direct address of another.[22] Nonetheless, the performance context of Proverbs, the dynamics of its communicative exchange, and the way in which it involves the reader not only furnish the framework through which to read and receive the materials in the anthology; they also create the conditions necessary for the (trans)formation and maturation of character in accord with wisdom and virtue.

16. For discussion, see E. W. Heaton, *The School Tradition of the Old Testament: The Bampton Lectures for 1994* (Oxford: Oxford University Press, 1994); G. I. Davies, "Were There Schools in Ancient Israel?," in *Wisdom in Ancient Israel: Essays in Honour of J. A. Emerton*, ed. R. P. Gordon et al. (Cambridge: Cambridge University Press, 1995), 199–211; James L. Crenshaw, *Education in Ancient Israel: Across the Deadening Silence*, ABRL (New York: Doubleday, 1998); David M. Carr, *Writing on the Tablet of the Heart: Origins of Scripture and Literature* (Oxford: Oxford University Press, 2005).

17. Weeks, *Early Israelite Wisdom*, 15; Michael V. Fox, "The Social Location of the Book of Proverbs," in *Texts, Temples, and Traditions: A Tribute to Menahem Haran*, ed. M. V. Fox (Winona Lake, IN: Eisenbrauns, 1996), 231–32; Roland E. Murphy, *Proverbs*, WBC 22 (Nashville: Thomas Nelson, 1998), xxi; Richard J. Clifford, *Proverbs*, OTL (Louisville: Westminster John Knox, 1999), 7–8; Carr, *Writing on the Tablet*, 130; Katharine J. Dell, *The Book of Proverbs in Social and Theological Context* (Cambridge: Cambridge University Press, 2006), 30.

18. Vayntrub, *Beyond Orality*, 203–4.

19. Elizabeth Currier, "Decontextualized Instruction or Disembodied Reading? Performance Context and Speech Performance in Proverbs," *VT* (2022): 16, doi:10.1163/15685330-BJA10120.

20. Newsom, "Woman and the Discourse of Patriarchal Wisdom," 143.

21. Currier, "Decontextualized Instruction," 19.

22. Currier, "Decontextualized Instruction," 13–19.

The Central Collections (10:1–29:27): Chaos or Coherence?

As noted above, the discourse setting delineated in Prov 1–9 plays a significant role in the anthology, for it provides the communicative situation through which to read the variegated materials within the document (10:1–29:27). The interpretive value of the prologue's performance context is reinforced by the concluding discourses in the book (Prov 30–31), which recycle terms, expressions, images, and the setting of domestic instruction from Prov 1–9 to create a literary envelope around the central collections.[23] This envelope situates the diverse materials in Prov 10–29 within a particular communicative situation. And this communicative situation orients one to the nature and didactic function of the material in Prov 10–29.[24]

The discourses across Prov 1–9 offer simple, rudimentary instruction. The father rarely enumerates the substance of his teaching, and Lady Wisdom does not offer a thick description of the virtues she embodies and dispenses to her devotees.[25] These discourses are not designed to plumb the depths of wisdom and virtue. They acclimate one to different character types and accentuate the value of wisdom and virtue.[26] The central collections, by contrast, offer the reader a kaleidoscopic and paradigmatic portrait of wisdom and virtue, folly and vice.[27] The sayings that populate these collections probe the characteristics of the wise, the fool, the righteous, and the wicked—archetypes who are introduced in the prologue but remain flat or one-dimensional personages.[28] They profile the defining features of these personages, identifying particular virtues, qualities, desires, and acts embodied in certain character types. In so doing, the aphorisms across the central collections present a multidimensional portrait of various literary characters to shape the moral character of the addressee.

The central collections extend and enhance the pedagogical program of Prov 1–9. But the manner in which they participate in Proverbs's project of education for character formation is debated. While the central collections contain several coherent units (e.g., 16:1–9, 10–15; 26:1–12, 13–16), considerable disagreement remains

23. Among others, see Claudia V. Camp, *Wisdom and the Feminine in the Book of Proverbs*, BLS 11 (Sheffield: Almond Press, 1985), 186–208.

24. Cf. Arthur Jan Keefer, *Proverbs 1–9 as an Introduction to the Book of Proverbs*, LHBOTS 701 (London: T&T Clark, 2020).

25. Tomás Frydrych, *Living under the Sun: Examination of Proverbs and Qoheleth*, VTSup 90 (Leiden: Brill, 2002), 61; Timothy J. Sandoval, "Proverbs," in *Dictionary of Scripture and Ethics*, ed. Joel B. Green et al. (Grand Rapids: Baker Academic, 2011), 642.

26. Richard J. Clifford, *The Wisdom Literature* (Nashville: Abingdon, 1998), 51.

27. Frydrych, *Living Under the Sun*, 40–41.

28. Roland E. Murphy, *Wisdom Literature: Job, Proverbs, Ruth, Canticles, Ecclesiastes, and Esther*, FOTL 13 (Grand Rapids: Eerdmans, 1981), 65. For a discussion of characterization, see Meir Sternberg, *The Poetics of Biblical Narrative* (Bloomington: Indiana University Press, 1987), 321–64.

over whether the proverbs within these collections are a haphazard collection of independent sayings or the product of deliberate arrangement into distinct "pairs" or "clusters."[29] Each approach recognizes that the individual sayings are independent, self-contained entities that communicate a message(s). And each approach offers insightful observations concerning the rhetorical significance of the arrangement of the material. The purpose of the present discussion is not to lobby for a particular approach. The coherence of specific units within the central collections must be evaluated on an individual basis. Rather than choosing between chaos or coherence among these materials at the microlevel, an exploration of their arrangement at the macrolevel may reveal the literary, rhetorical, and pedagogical significance of the sayings within Prov 10:1–29:27.

William Brown's work on the "overarching editorial arrangement and pedagogical movement" of Proverbs in general and the central collections in particular is quite helpful in this respect.[30] From a bird's-eye perspective, Brown investigates the formal and thematic development among the subcollections in Prov 10–29. In light of the variety and complexity of poetic forms within latter collections and their nuanced development of particular themes, Brown contends that the discrete collections within Prov 10–29 are deliberately arranged to form the character and shape the moral vision of the reader.[31] The formal and thematic development among the materials in these subcollections illuminates their pedagogical function: they move from the "basic staple" to "more advanced, variegated fare" to develop the character of readers in a progressive fashion.[32] In this respect, the arrangement of these subcollections is comparable to modern educational curricula;[33] they move from elementary wisdom (10:1–15:33), to intermediate wisdom (16:1–22:16), to vocational wisdom (22:17–24:34), to advanced wisdom (25:1–29:27).[34] This progressive pedagogical scheme sets the stage for the final collections, which sketch the limits of human wisdom (30:1–33) and the embodiment of wisdom and virtue (31:1–31).[35] Whether the individual materials in the central collections are characterized by chaos

29. For a discussion and defense of coherent "pairs" or "clusters" in the sentence literature and their significance for interpretation, see Ted Hildebrandt, "Proverbial Pairs: Compositional Units in Proverbs 10–29," *JBL* 107 (1988): 207–24; Raymond C. Van Leeuwen, *Context and Meaning in Proverbs 25–27*, SBLDS 96 (Atlanta: Scholars Press, 1988), 3; Knut M. Heim, *Like Grapes of Gold Set in Silver: An Interpretation of Proverbial Clusters in Proverbs 10:1–22:16*, BZAW 273 (Berlin: de Gruyter, 2001). For discussion on the lack of coherence among the materials in the sentence literature and/or the interpretive insignificance of these purported units, see William McKane, *Proverbs: A New Approach*, OTL (Philadelphia: Westminster, 1970), 10, 413; Weeks, *Early Israelite Wisdom*, 20–40; Tremper Longman III, *Proverbs*, BCOTWP (Grand Rapids: Baker Academic, 2006), 38–42. For a *via media* approach, see Fox, *Proverbs 10–31*, 477–83.

30. William P. Brown, "The Pedagogy of Proverbs 10:1–31:9," in *Character and Scripture: Moral Formation, Community, and Biblical Interpretation*, ed. W. P. Brown (Grand Rapids: Eerdmans, 2002), 150–182, esp. 152.

31. Brown, "The Pedagogy of Proverbs 10:1–31:9," 182.

32. Brown, "The Pedagogy of Proverbs 10:1–31:9," 181.

33. Brown, "The Pedagogy of Proverbs 10:1–31:9," 158.

34. Christopher B. Ansberry, *Be Wise, My Son, and Make My Heart Glad: An Exploration of the Courtly Nature of the Book of Proverbs*, BZAW 422 (Berlin: de Gruyter, 2011), 71–161.

35. Ansberry, *Be Wise, My Son*, 162–83.

or coherence at the microlevel, at the macrolevel it appears the subcollections exhibit a "didactic movement."[36] This movement mirrors the progressive (trans)formation of the reader and contributes to the fundamental agenda of Proverbs, namely, the cultivation of character through the inculcation of wisdom and virtue.

Distinctive Literary Features

Various literary features fund the pedagogical agenda of Proverbs. Among these literary features, the nature of poetry in general and Hebrew poetry in particular, the genre of Proverbs, and the literary forms within the piece may be the most significant.

1. Poetry

Poetry is a unique, powerful form of discourse. In the words of Jill Peláez Baumgaertner,

> It does what no other art form can do. It compresses experience; it intensifies language; it uses words to say the unsayable. . . . Poetry cracks open our everyday lives, the mundane worlds in which we spend so much unconscious time, and it releases the extraordinary, bringing us to a different level of attentiveness.[37]

This description indicates that poetry is not a science; it is a form of art. And this description moves beyond what poetry is to capture what poetry does; it is a medium that awakens the senses, arouses the emotions, stimulates the mind, and inspires the imagination.[38] As a form of art that illuminates the extraordinary nature of the ordinary, poetry is an instrument of action, or better, an instrument of *responsible action*.[39] Through the imaginative use of language, the poet conveys certain actions and intentions; and by receiving these actions and intentions, the reader is challenged to think about and act within the world in particular ways.[40] Far from inviting the reader into a Kantian world of disinterested contemplation, poetry prepares one for concrete action within the world.[41] It accomplishes what simple, straightforward

36. Brown, "The Pedagogy of Proverbs 10:1–31:9," 164–65 et passim.

37. Jill Peláez Baumgaertner, "'Silver Catching Midday Sun': Poetry and the Beauty of God," in *The Beauty of God: Theology and the Arts*, ed. Daniel J. Treier, Mark Husbands, and Roger Lundin (Downers Grove, IL: IVP Academic, 2007), 147.

38. Baumgaertner, "'Silver Catching Midday Sun,'" 147.

39. Nicholas Wolterstorff, *Art in Action: Toward a Christian Aesthetic* (Grand Rapids: Eerdmans, 1980; repr., Carlisle: Solway, 1997), 3–11, 78–79.

40. Wolterstorff, *Art in Action*, 4–5.

41. Wolterstorff, *Art in Action*, 3–18; Craig G. Bartholomew and Ryan P. O'Dowd, *Old Testament Wisdom Literature: A Theological Introduction* (Downers Grove, IL: IVP Academic, 2011), 50–55.

commands cannot: it moves one to virtuous action.[42] In this respect, it is a literary form uniquely qualified to shape the character, sharpen the intellect, hone the desires, form the feelings, and construct the worldview of its readers in accordance with wisdom and virtue.[43]

Among the various ways the poet conveys and performs actions, "world-projection" may be the most significant.[44] Through the power of envisagement, the poet projects a world that is true in many respects; and the reader is invited not only to enter and assess this world but also to consider the way in which the world created by the poet evaluates their life within and their view of the actual world.[45] Entrance into these worlds created by artists and poets requires imagination. As Luis Alonso Schökel advised in his discussion of reading biblical poetry, "What has been written with imagination, must also be read with imagination, provided the individual has imagination and it is in working order."[46] And entrance into these imaginative worlds demands that readers move beyond Plato's conception of art as a mere representation or imitation of the real world. Works of art in general and poetry in particular are not simply a photocopy of what is real or visible; they are creative works that symbolize and interpret reality in discrete ways. In this respect, poetry not only requires imagination and the power of envisagement; it also demands that one read a poetic piece in the same way that the poet crafted the work. That is, it demands that one read poetry "cartoonfully."[47] Just as the artist or poet presents meaning cartoonfully, so also one must read a poetic piece cartoonfully, with a recognition of its symbolic dimensions and pregnant features.

This is no easy task. But it is a fruitful task. An awareness of the nature of poetry and the imagination necessary to read poetry prepares one to harvest the fruits of wisdom within the distinct sections of Proverbs. Such awareness and imagination equip the reader to enter into the world of temptation within the prologue (1:8–9:18), to hear the diverse voices vying for their allegiance,[48] to feel the characters arousing their deepest desires, and to smell the spoils promised by the sinners (1:13–14) and the adulterous woman's perfume (7:17), as well as the fare at Lady Wisdom's banquet (9:5). They enable the reader to see the different ways, women, and houses[49] and to understand the value of wisdom as well as the fate that awaits those who choose a

42. Philip Sydney, *A Defence of Poetry*, ed. J. A. Van Dorsten (New York: Oxford University Press, 1966).

43. Bartholomew and O'Dowd, *Old Testament Wisdom Literature*, 57.

44. Wolterstorff, *Art in Action*, 122; Bartholomew and O'Dowd, *Old Testament Wisdom Literature*, 55–56.

45. Wolterstorff, *Art in Action*, 123–44; Bartholomew and O'Dowd, *Old Testament Wisdom Literature*, 56.

46. Luis Alonso Schökel, *A Manual of Hebrew Poetics*, SubBi 11 (Rome: Editrice Pontificio Istituto Biblico, 2000), 104.

47. Calvin Seerveld, *Rainbows for the Fallen World: Aesthetic Life and the Artistic Task* (Toronto: Tuppence, 1980; repr., Exeter: Stride, 1988), 84.

48. J. N. Aletti, "Seduction et parole en Proverbes I–IX," *VT* 27 (1977): 129–44.

49. Raymond C. Van Leeuwen, "Liminality and Worldview in Proverbs 1–9," *Semeia* 50 (1990): 111–44.

life of folly. They allow the reader to discern the strange new world projected by the proverbs within the central collections of the anthology, to observe the wise person's perspective on life, and to discover the way in which the symmetry of the sayings reflects the beauty and goodness of life lived in right relation to God, others, and the natural world. And a recognition of the function of poetry as well as the value of the imagination helps one to grasp the limitations of human wisdom (30:1–9), to acknowledge the mystery and wonder of God's wisdom (30:4–6), to comprehend the value of proper boundaries (30:10–33), and to perceive the incarnation of wisdom in the diverse activities of everyday life (31:1–9, 10–31).

In short, the nature and function of poetry enables one to hear the clichés within Proverbs afresh and (re)capture a vision of the beauty of the wise life. That is, an awareness of the nature and function of poetry provides the reader with a means to enter the world of the text and hear its voice, cultivate its sanctioned desires, see its perspective on the world, and discover its message. As Flannery O'Connor observed, "It is from the kind of world the writer creates, from the kind of character and detail he invests it with, that a reader can find the intellectual meaning of a book."[50] The nature and function of poetry supplies the reader with a compass to enter the world of Proverbs and find its message. And an understanding of the basic aspects of poetry provides a backdrop against which to explore the conventions of Hebrew poetry. Hebrew poetry contains several conventions. Among these conventions, three features serve as the defining characteristics of Hebrew poetry.

a. Terseness

The first is terseness.[51] The short clauses and succinct, elliptical nature of poetic discourse distinguish the materials in Proverbs from ordinary forms of discourse.[52] While the distinction between poetry and prose may not be as sharp as once thought,[53] the brevity of poetic lines and the condensed nature of poetic discourse remain a hallmark of the genre. This characteristic of Hebrew poetry provides a rationale for the paucity of conjunctions within poetic material as well as the prominence of parallelism, imagery, and figures of speech. And this mark of dense language and internal richness illuminates the importance of the imagination for actualizing the pedagogical agenda of Proverbs. The poetry of Proverbs is designed to sharpen one's thinking and cultivate discernment. Its short lines, elliptical expression, and intensive use of language are the instruments through which it fosters imaginative reflection and develops perception.

50. Flannery O'Connor, *Mystery and Manners* (New York: Straus and Giroux, 1969), 75.

51. James L. Kugel, *The Idea of Biblical Poetry: Parallelism and Its History* (New Haven: Yale University Press, 1981), 87–94.

52. Kugel, *The Idea of Biblical Poetry*, 87.

53. Robert Alter, *The Art of Biblical Poetry* (New York: Basic Books, 1985), 6–7.

b. Parallelism

The second defining characteristic of Hebrew poetry is parallelism.[54] By definition, parallelism refers to the relationship between the components within a poetic line as well as the correspondence between the syntactical elements within two or more poetic lines that are juxtaposed to one another. While there are many different permutations, classifications, and categories of parallelism in discussions devoted to the subject, Knut Heim's general taxonomy may offer the best heuristic guide for understanding the different forms of parallelism in Proverbs.[55] Building on the work of Wilfred Watson, Robert Alter, and Dennis Pardee,[56] Heim identifies four levels of parallelism.

Semilinear Parallelism

The first is "semilinear parallelism" or "internal parallelism," which considers the relationship between the component parts within a single poetic line.[57] As the most basic level of parallelism, semilinear parallelism accounts for the correspondence between words or phrases within a partial line or colon. This form of parallelism may be illustrated through Prov 3:2 and 6:23, respectively.

For length of days and years of life,
  and peace will increase for you.

For the commandment is a lamp and the teaching a light,
  and corrective reproofs are the way of life.

The initial line of each text may be divided into two equal parts; and these parts or half-lines are cast in parallel relationship with one another. Whether or not the corresponding half-lines are abbreviated forms of what were once full poetic lines,[58] semilinear parallelism demonstrates that parallelism is not restricted to the relationship between the components within two or more lines; rather, it is a poetic technique that may be employed at the ground level, that is, *within* a single line.

54. For a history of interpretation on parallelism in biblical poetry, see J. Kenneth Kuntz, "Biblical Hebrew Poetry in Recent Research, Part I," *CurBS* 6 (1998): 31–64; idem, "Biblical Hebrew Poetry in Recent Research, Part II," *CurBS* 7 (1999): 35–79; Knut M. Heim, *Poetic Imagination in Proverbs: Variant Repetitions and the Nature of Poetry*, BBRSup 4 (Winona Lake, IN: Eisenbrauns, 2013), 19–29.

55. Heim, *Poetic Imagination*, 3–35, esp. 29–32.

56. Wilfred G. E. Watson, *Classical Hebrew Poetry: A Guide to Its Techniques*, JSOTSup 26 (Sheffield: JSOT Press, 1984); idem, *Traditional Techniques in Classical Hebrew Verse*, JSOTSup 170 (Sheffield: Sheffield Academic, 1994); Alter, *The Art of Biblical Poetry*; Dennis Pardee, *Ugaritic and Hebrew Poetic Parallelism: A Trial Cut ('nt I and Proverbs 2)*, VTSup 39 (Leiden: Brill, 1988).

57. Watson, *Traditional Techniques*, 104–91; Heim, *Poetic Imagination*, 24–25, 30–31.

58. Heim, *Poetic Imagination*, 31.

Intralinear Parallelism

The second level of parallelism is "intralinear parallelism."[59] This is the focus of attention in most discussions of poetic parallelism, for it considers the corresponding syntactical elements within two or more poetic lines. In light of the relationship between these elements, scholars have identified various types of intralinear parallelism. Among these types, three are especially significant for interpreting the materials within Proverbs.

Antithetical Sayings

The first is antithetical sayings. As the designation suggests, this type of intralinear parallelism is characterized by opposing concepts between parallel lines. These types of sayings pervade Prov 10–15. In fact, the initial saying of the collection is a classic example of antithetic parallelism (10:1bc):

> A wise son gladdens the father;
> but a foolish son, the grief of his mother.

Antithetical sayings play a significant pedagogical role in the book of Proverbs. They illuminate the nature, dispositions, desires, and activities of various character types in order to cultivate virtue, shape the desires of readers, and provide one with a vision of how the wise person views the world.

Better-than Sayings

The second type of intralinear parallelism is better-than sayings. Similar to antithetical sayings, these poetic forms draw a contrast. Their concern with specific virtues or dispositions suggests that they seek to illuminate the relative value of wealth and the surpassing value of moral character. This rhetorical function is apparent in Prov 16:8:

> Better a little with righteousness,
> than abundant produce without justice.

By attending to the limited value of wealth and the indispensable value of virtue, better-than sayings qualify those antithetical sayings that seem to suggest wealth is the inevitable reward for moral character. In so doing, they offer a nuanced perspective of the world and prove things are not always what they seem, for appearances aren't everything.

59. Heim, *Poetic Imagination*, 31.

Numerical Sayings

The third prominent form of intralinear parallelism in Proverbs is numerical sayings. These sayings punctuate the introductory and concluding collections within the anthology (6:16–19; 30:11–16, 18–31; cf. Amos 1:3–2:16).[60] They open with a conventional formula (X + 1) and systematize various phenomena that share a common denominator to achieve a particular purpose.[61] The rhetorical function of these sayings varies, since they can operate on several different levels. Within Proverbs, it appears that the numerical sayings appeal to certain activities or attitudes within the human, animal, and natural world in order to investigate human behavior and social organization.[62] This is clear in the final or climactic element within the numerical saying, which unites the diverse phenomena around a central theme and provides a framework through which to understand the saying.[63] The nature and function of these numerical sayings may be illustrated through Prov 30:18–19.

> Three things are too wonderful for me,
>   and four I do not understand:
> The way of the eagle in the sky,
>   the way of a serpent on a rock,
> The way of a ship in the heart of the sea,
>   and the way of a man with a maiden.

This numerical saying incorporates various phenomena from the animal, natural, and human world. And the final element serves as an interpretive lens through which to understand the saying as a whole. The saying expresses astonishment at the inexplicable wonder occasioned by the "way" of four creatures or things within the created order (30:18–19). The saying's amazement is not necessarily directed toward the mysterious movement of these creatures but toward their irrecoverable course of action.[64] They elude human calculation. Just as one cannot trace the trajectory of a soaring eagle, plot the motion of the gliding serpent, or chart the passage of a ship

60. For the form and function of numerical sayings in both the ancient Near East and the Old Testament, see Wolfgang M. W. Roth, "The Numerical Sequence x/x + 1 in the Old Testament," *VT* 12 (1962): 300–311; idem, *Numerical Sayings in the Old Testament: A Form-Critical Study*, VTSup 13 (Leiden: Brill, 1965), 5–9 et passim; Riad A. Kassis, *The Book of Proverbs and Arabic Proverbial Works*, VTSup 74 (Leiden: Brill, 1999), 234–41.

61. Tova L. Forti, *Animal Imagery in the Book of Proverbs*, VTSup 118 (Leiden: Brill, 2008), 120. In addition to these graded numerical sayings, the central collections of the book include several simple numerical sayings. See 17:15; 20:10, 12; 29:13.

62. Arndt Meinhold, *Die Sprüche, Teil 2: Sprüche Kapitel 16–31*, ZBK 16.2 (Zürich: TVZ, 1991), 506; Forti, *Animal Imagery in the Book of Proverbs*, 131.

63. Menahem Haran, "The Graded Numerical Sequence and the Phenomenon of 'Automatism' in Biblical Poetry," *VT* 22 (1972): 261–67; Andrew E. Steinmann, "Three Things . . . Four Things . . . Seven Things: The Coherence of Proverbs 30:11–33 and the Unity of Proverbs 30," *HS* 42 (2001): 63–65.

64. Murphy, *Proverbs*, 235. For a discussion of several other proposals concerning the enigmatic way of these phenomena, see Fox, *Proverbs 10–31*, 870–72.

slicing through the seas, so one cannot explain the magnetic attraction of erotic love. Love is a mystery; it is a gift. And this mysterious gift is expressed through numerical parallelism.

Several other forms of intralinear parallelism could be mentioned. While many works provide helpful designations or classifications for distinct types of intralinear parallelism, the desire for classification should not overshadow attention to the levels of parallelism, for these levels can account for the dynamic relationship between elements within and among poetic lines when parallelism at the intralinear level is absent or defies strict classification.[65] This commentary will employ the standard classifications delineated above to describe different types of intralinear parallelism within Proverbs. But these classifications will be applied through specific attention to the levels of parallelism.

Interlinear Parallelism

The third level of parallelism is "interlinear parallelism," which considers the relationship between contiguous poetic lines.[66] In the event that no parallelism exists at the intralinear level, the relationship between parallel lines and those within the adjacent saying are assessed. While Proverbs contains several examples of interlinear parallelism, Prov 26:4–5 may be the most familiar:

> Do not answer a fool according to his folly,
> lest you become like him, even you!
> Answer a fool according to his folly
> lest he be wise in his own eyes.

Since the poetic lines within the first saying defy classification at the intralinear level, their interlinear relationship is examined. And this examination bears fruit; the relationship between the poetic lines is not at the intralinear level (26:4a//26:4b); rather, it exists at the interlinear level (26:4a//26:5a; 26:4b//26:5b). This demands that the sayings be read together, not as separate proverbs pertaining to different circumstances.

Translinear Parallelism

The fourth level of parallelism is "translinear parallelism."[67] This level may be the most unusual, but it is also the most significant within Proverbs, for it considers the

65. Heim, *Poetic Imagination*, 31. Also see Michael Fox's excellent discussion of "disjointed proverbs," that is, sayings that violate the rules of parallelism, in "The Rhetoric of Disjointed Proverbs," *JSOT* 29 (2004): 165–77; Fox, *Proverbs 10–31*, 494–98.

66. Heim, *Poetic Imagination*, 27, 31; cf., Alter, *The Art of Biblical Poetry*, 14.

67. Heim, *Poetic Imagination*, 31–32.

correspondence between poetic lines that are separated by a contextual distance. Some might consider this level of parallelism repetition or even refrain since the proverbs under consideration are virtual reiterations of one another. But, in view of the nature of the anthology, it may be considered a form of parallelism. This may be the most significant contribution of Knut Heim. The central collections of Proverbs are not a haphazard collection of sayings concerning wisdom and virtue; rather, they are a deliberately crafted collection of materials. Attention to translinear parallelism accounts for the editorial arrangement of the material as well as the dialogical relationship among twice-told proverbs.[68] Within Heim's ascending levels of parallelism, this level moves beyond the poetic line and its adjacent lines to reflect on the way in which a saying corresponds with its variant counterparts elsewhere in the anthology.

As noted above, these levels of parallelism will serve as a heuristic guide through which to understand specific permutations and classifications of parallel lines within Proverbs. Parallelism is a defining feature of Hebrew poetry. And, similar to terseness, its forms illuminate the necessity of the imagination for reading poetry.

c. Imagery

The third defining characteristic of Hebrew poetry is imagery. This is not surprising, for imagery contributes to the terseness of poetry; it represents an essential element within poetry's literary register, a means of comprehension, and an instrument through which the poet evokes imaginative reflection.[69] In this respect, verbal images are comparable to concrete images in art. They depict a tangible object or action and, in so doing, conjure up mental images that re-present the object or action and initiate the generative process of contemplation, discernment, and synthesis.[70] This process is imperative, since imagery tends to operate at the level of comparison; it represents one thing by means of another.[71] The strange woman, for example, is sharper than a double-edged sword (5:4), the seduced youth is an ox marching to slaughter (7:22), and the sluggard is bolted to his bed in the same way that a door is fastened to its hinges (26:14).

As a technique that thrives on comparison, imagery is intimately related to metaphor and simile. In fact, metaphor and simile are considered the basic vehicles of figurative language. If an image is "a picture made out of words,"[72] then metaphor and simile function as the primary colors within the portrait. The former is an implied

68. For the dynamic dialogue produced by twice-told proverbs as well as sayings devoted to common motifs across the anthology, see Peter T. H. Hatton, *Contradiction in the Book of Proverbs: The Deep Waters of Counsel*, SOTSMS (Burlington, VT: Ashgate, 2008).

69. Schökel, *A Manual of Hebrew Poetics*, 95.

70. William P. Brown, *Seeing the Psalms: A Theology of Metaphor* (Louisville: Westminster John Knox, 2002), 7.

71. Mary Oliver, *A Poetry Handbook* (San Diego: Harcourt Brace, 1994), 92.

72. C. Day Lewis, *The Poetic Image* (New York: Oxford University Press, 1947), 17–18. Also see Leland Ryken, James Wilhoit, and Tremper Longman III, eds., *Dictionary of Biblical Imagery* (Downers Grove, IL: IVP Academic, 1998), xiii.

comparison between two things, whereas the latter incorporates the term "like" or "as" to indicate an explicit comparison. Far from functioning as mere literary ornaments, metaphor and simile provide a new way of seeing, thinking about, and understanding reality.[73] They combine things that differ in several respects, sending the reader into a state of "semantic shock" and forcing them to discern their common features, conceptual relationship, and figurative meaning.[74] As with terseness and parallelism, the imagistic nature of poetry illuminates the necessity of the imagination. Without it, the reader is unable to enter the world or "sign-context" of the poet,[75] visualize the image, experience its connotations,[76] receive its effect,[77] and perceive the way in which the writer has worked the miracle of King Midas, transforming the ordinary into the extraordinary.

Together, terseness, parallelism, and imagery are the most common characteristics of Hebrew poetry. While familiarity with and sensitivity to these conventions is necessary for interpreting the materials in Proverbs, it is important to recognize that poetry is not read by applying a strict set of rules. Poetry does not operate under the normal rules for discourse. Certain rules may serve as a guide for reading poetry. But, again, these rules must be applied with imagination. To be specific, they must be applied with "*truthful* imagination,"[78] which serves as the instrument through which one is able to look at the poetic piece, perceive its pregnant features, and discern its message(s).[79]

2. The Genre of Proverbs

In essence, the book of Proverbs is a collection of collections; that is, it is an anthology. This repository of traditional Israelite wisdom contains a variety of literary forms, ranging from extended instructions and encomiums to admonitions and pithy aphorisms. But if one steps back from the individual literary forms within the book and observes the generic forest for the trees, how might one describe the genre of Proverbs?

While the document may be classified as a collection of proverbs (1:1; 10:1; 25:1),

73. Paul Ricoeur, "Biblical Hermeneutics," *Semeia* 4 (1975): 75; idem, *Interpretation Theory: Discourse and the Surplus of Meaning* (Fort Worth: Texas Christian University Press, 1976), 53; Leland Ryken, *Words of Delight: A Literary Introduction to the Bible* (Grand Rapids: Baker, 1987), 169; Brown, *Seeing the Psalms*, 5.

74. For Ricoeur's expression "semantic shock" with reference to metaphor, see Richard F. Kearney, *On Paul Ricoeur: The Owl of Minerva*, Transcending Boundaries in Philosophy and Theology (New York: Routledge, 2017), 40.

75. For this context, see Max Black, *Models and Metaphors: Studies in Language and Philosophy* (Ithaca, NY: Cornell University Press, 1962); Brent A. Strawn, *What is Stronger Than a Lion? Leonine Image and Metaphor in the Hebrew Bible and Ancient Near East*, OBO 212 (Göttingen: Vandenhoeck & Ruprecht, 2005), 12–20.

76. Ryken, Wilhoit, and Longman, *Dictionary of Biblical Imagery*, xiv.

77. Janet M. Soskice, *Metaphor and Religious Language* (Oxford: Clarendon, 1985), 108–9.

78. Ellen F. Davis, *Proverbs, Ecclesiastes, and the Song of Songs* (Louisville: Westminster John Knox, 2000), 19, italics original.

79. Brown, *Seeing the Psalms*, 9.

this designation is unhelpful, for it fails to account for the diverse materials within the piece as well as the function of the anthology. The same is true of the classification "wisdom literature." Similar to Job and Ecclesiastes, Proverbs reflects a distinctive "mode of discourse."[80] This mode, however, illuminates the document's posture, interests, and style, rather than its genre per se.[81] From a literary perspective, the genre of Proverbs is a riddle; it is incomparable to any other book in the Protestant canon.[82]

Proverbs may be a literary anomaly in the Protestant canon, but it is by no means unique when it is read within the wider cognitive environment of the ancient world. Despite its distinctive characteristics, Proverbs is comparable to Egyptian and Mesopotamian instructional texts. These instructional texts provide a lens through which to perceive the form and function of the anthology. Put differently, their family resemblance to Proverbs creates the comparative conditions necessary to discern the nature of the anthology and its "horizon of expectations."[83] Since the instructional tradition is rather stable throughout the ancient world, a brief discussion of its fundamental characteristics and the ways in which these texts functioned in their respective social environments may provide a backdrop against which to assess the form and function of Proverbs.[84]

In general, ancient Near Eastern instructional texts share several common characteristics, three in particular. The first is a conventional discourse setting. Similar to Proverbs, ancient Near Eastern instructional texts tend to be cast in the context of a father transmitting advice to a son.[85] This performance context represents the dominant setting of these instructional texts and a defining feature of the genre.[86]

Second, the form or style of ancient Near Eastern instructional texts is comparable to the form or style of Proverbs. Similar to Proverbs, these texts possess a distinctly hortatory or didactic tone. In addition, they include a variety of discrete literary forms, ranging from extended instructions and autobiographical reflections

80. Stuart Weeks, *An Introduction to the Study of Wisdom Literature*, T&T Clark Approaches to Biblical Studies (London: T&T Clark, 2010), 126, 143–44; Mark R. Sneed, "Is the 'Wisdom Tradition' a Tradition?," *CBQ* 73 (2011): 57.

81. C. L. Seow, *Job 1–21: Interpretation and Commentary*, Illuminations (Grand Rapids: Eerdmans, 2013), 61.

82. It is important to note that Proverbs is comparable to Ben Sira or Ecclesiasticus, which is included in the Roman Catholic, Eastern Orthodox, and Ethiopian Orthodox canons.

83. Will Kynes, *An Obituary for "Wisdom Literature": The Birth, Death, and Intertextual Reintegration of a Biblical Corpus* (Oxford: Oxford University Press, 2019), 111, 115. As Kynes notes, "the significance of any given text depends on its perceived relationship with other texts. . . . Genre features do not exist *in* texts as much as *between* them and therefore not in their authorial creation but in their readerly comparison" (*An Obituary*, 115, italics original).

84. For an extended discussion of the content of these ancient Near Eastern instructional texts, see McKane, *Proverbs*, 51–182; Ansberry, *Be Wise, My Son*, 11–35.

85. See Prov 1:8, 10, 15; 2:1; 3:1, 11, 21; 4:1, 10, 20; 5:1, 7, 20; 6:1, 3, 20; 7:1, 24; 8:32; 19:27; 23:15, 19, 26; 24:13, 21; 27:11; 31:2. For this setting in ancient Near Eastern instructional literature, see the following representative texts: "The Instruction of Prince Hardjedef" (*AEL* [Berkeley: University of California Press, 1976], 1:58–59); "The Instruction of Ptahhotep" (*AEL* 1:61–80); "The Instruction Addressed to King Merikare" (*AEL* 1:97–109); "The Satire of the Trades" (*AEL* 1:184–92); "The Instruction of Amenemope" (*AEL* 2:146–63); "Shuruppak," trans. B. Alster (*COS* 1.176:569–70); "Ahiqar," trans. J. M. Lindenberger (*OTP* 2:479–508).

86. Stuart Weeks, *Instruction and Imagery in Proverbs 1–9* (Oxford: Oxford University Press, 2007), 12.

to admonitions and pithy sayings.[87] The tone, pastiche of forms, and generic flexibility of these ancient Near Eastern exemplars mirror the style and manifest diversity of the literary forms within Proverbs.

Third, the content or subject matter of ancient Near Eastern instructional texts resembles the substance of Proverbs. Similar to Proverbs, these documents address issues pertaining to proper speech, communal relations, treatment of the destitute, the administration of justice, and social order, just to name a few.[88] These striking similarities in content suggest that Proverbs not only attends to issues that are common to all people, but it also participates in an international conversation concerning the good life.

Together, the formal and thematic similarities between Proverbs and ancient Near Eastern instructional literature suggest that the anthology may be classified as an instructional text.[89] Similar to its ancient Near Eastern counterparts, Proverbs is a didactic text cast in a traditional discourse setting that addresses a variety of conventional matters pertaining to everyday life. Ancient Near Eastern instructional texts clarify the nature, genre, and formal characteristics of Proverbs. The clarity offered by these texts, however, does not entail that those responsible for the diverse materials in Proverbs borrowed the instructional genre or its distinctive modes of discourse from their ancient Near Eastern counterparts. Rather than reconstructing a possible, albeit hypothetical, process of textual transmission and influence, it seems best to attribute these formal and thematic similarities to Israel's participation in a "common cognitive environment"—an environment in which the ancients shared common cultural concepts and literary conventions.[90] The genre and substance of Proverbs bears witness to Israel's involvement in and contribution to the international tradition of instructional literature. But her participation in this literary tradition does not indicate she swallowed the genre hook, line, and sinker.

Proverbs differs from its ancient Near Eastern counterparts in several respects.[91]

87. For these diverse literary forms within ancient Near Eastern instructional tradition, see the following representative texts: "The Instruction of Ptahhotep" (*AEL* 1:61–80); "The Instruction of Ankhsheshonq" (*AEL* 3:159–84); "Shuruppak" (*COS* 1.176:569–70); "Ahiqar" (*OTP* 2:479–508).

88. For these common motifs, see "The Instruction of Ptahhotep" (*AEL* 1:61–80). Since the topics addressed by Ptahhotep are reiterated and adapted by later Egyptian instructional texts, the substance of the work is representative of the issues treated in Egyptian instructional tradition. For Mesopotamia, see "Shuruppak" (*COS* 1.176:569–70); "Ahiqar" (*OTP* 2:479–508).

89. Murphy, *Proverbs*, xxii. This classification is comparable to Weeks's broader designation "advice literature" (Weeks, *Introduction*, 25).

90. John H. Walton, *Ancient Near Eastern Thought and the Old Testament: Introducing the Conceptual World of the Hebrew Bible* (Grand Rapids: Baker Academic, 2006), 21–27 et passim.

91. For example, Proverbs invokes the authority of the mother alongside the father in certain instructions (1:8; 6:20; cf. 31:1 and "The Satire of the Trades" [*AEL* 1:191]); Lady Wisdom is presented as a distinct, autonomous figure in the discourse; the document does not specify or name the addressee of the discourse; and the anthology is not staged as the quoted speech of a famed individual. For discussion of these differences, see Carole R. Fontaine, "The Sage in the Family and Tribe," in Gammie and Perdue, *The Sage in Israel and the Ancient Near East*, ed. J. G. Gammie and L. G. Perdue (Winona Lake, IN: Eisenbrauns, 1990), 161; Franz-Josef Steiert, *Die Weisheit Israels—ein Fremdkörper im Alten Testament?: Eine Untersuchung zum Buch der Sprüche auf dem Hintergrund der ägyptischen Weisheitslehren*, Freiburger Theologische Studien 143 (Freiburg in Breisgau: Herder, 1990), 215–19; Vayntrub, *Beyond Orality*, 183–206.

It participates in the instructional genre; but it also integrates and invokes features characteristic of other genres, such as love poetry.[92] Proverbs may be classified as an instructional text, but it is important to recognize that the sages adapted the genre and its corresponding content in distinctive ways to reinforce their distinctive theological worldview and to achieve their distinctive pedagogical agenda.

This conclusion finds support in the apparent function of Proverbs. As an instructional text, Proverbs possesses a didactic tone and ethos. But the didactic function of the piece is shaped by the cultural context and theological worldview in which it operates. This is the case with Egyptian and Mesopotamian instructional texts. In Egypt, instructional texts served as the media through which members of the official class were taught to act in conformity with Maat—the principle of "truth" and "justice" that represented the pristine condition of the primordial order by which the gods and humanity were to live.[93] As a repository of social values, these instructional texts served as a written deposit of key cultural traditions that were used to socialize members of the ruling class and orient them to the Egyptian worldview.[94] In so doing, these documents attempted to inculcate the concept of Maat within the elite and thus maintain the order of social life.

The same is true of Mesopotamian instructional texts. Similar to Egypt, Mesopotamian instructional texts functioned within the wider project of education-enculturation in order to ensure the maintenance of cosmic and social order. According to Mesopotamian tradition, the fundamental principles of civilization instituted by the gods were preserved by a group of postdiluvian "scholars" (*ummanu*) and disseminated through literature to align the individual with the proper pattern of social order.[95] Among these forms of literature, instructional texts played a formative role in scribal education.[96] Far from functioning as simple grammatical or vocational guides, these texts attempted to cultivate proper ethical and cultural values into their addressees. In so doing, they provided members of the official class

92. For this description of genre, see Carol A. Newsom, "Spying out the Land: A Report from Genology," in *Seeking out the Wisdom of the Ancients: Essays Offered to Honor Michael V. Fox on the Occasion of His Sixty-Fifth Birthday*, ed. R. L. Troxel, K. G. Friebel, and D. R. Magary (Winona Lake, IN: Eisenbrauns, 2005), 439.

93. Erik Hornung, *Conceptions of God in Ancient Egypt: The One and the Many*, trans. J. Baines (Ithaca, NY: Cornell University Press, 1982), 213–16; Erik Hornung, *Idea into Image: Essays on Ancient Egyptian Thought*, trans. E. Bredeck (New York: Timken, 1992), 136–38; Jan Assmann, *Maât, l'Egypte pharaonique et l'idée de justice sociale*, Conférences, essais et leçons du Collége de France (Paris: Julliard, 1989), 35; Miriam Lichtheim, *Maat in Egyptian Autobiographies and Related Studies*, OBO 120 (Göttingen: Vandenhoech & Ruprecht, 1992), 18–19.

94. Jan Assmann, "Kulturelle und literarische Texte," in *Ancient Egyptian Literature: History and Forms*, ed. Antonio Loprieno, Probleme der Ägyptologie 10 (Leiden: Brill, 1996), 60–82; Carr, *Writing on the Tablet*, 77; Weeks, *Instruction and Imagery*, 16–32.

95. Benjamin R. Foster, "Wisdom and the Gods in Ancient Mesopotamia," *Or* 43 (1976): 344–54; Sara Denning-Bolle, *Wisdom in Akkadian Literature: Expression, Instruction, Dialogue*, Mededelingen en verhandelingen van het Vooraziatisch-Egyptisch Genootschap "Ex Oriente Lux" 28 (Leiden: Ex Oriente Lux, 1992), 48–56.

96. Samuel N. Kramer, "The Sage in Sumerian Literature: A Composite Portrait," in *The Sage in Israel and the Ancient Near East*, eds. J. G. Gammie and L. G. Perdue (Winona Lake, IN: Eisenbrauns, 1990); 32; Niek Veldhuis, "Sumerian Proverbs in Their Curricular Context," *JAOS* 120 (2000): 383–99; Carr, *Writing on the Tablet*, 31.

with guideposts to perform their bureaucratic functions and establish harmony in the social realm.

In a certain sense, Proverbs participates in this program of education and enculturation. Similar to its ancient Near Eastern counterparts, Proverbs addresses a variety of issues pertaining to everyday life to orient its addressees to the social world, inculcate key cultural values, and provide a compass to navigate through life and negotiate diverse circumstances. The social function of Proverbs, however, is subservient to its primary function: the (trans)formation of character through the cultivation of wisdom and virtue. Whereas character and virtue appear to be subservient to a utilitarian ethic in ancient Near Eastern instructional literature, practical strategies for coping with life appear to be subservient to the cultivation of character and virtue in Proverbs. The social orientation of ancient Near Eastern instructional literature suggests that practical wisdom is the fundamental goal. The theological orientation of Proverbs, by contrast, indicates that character and virtue are the fundamental goal, for without a moral disposition wisdom is left without a guide for virtuous activity.[97]

In this respect, it appears that Proverbs integrates various topics and traditions to form an inclusive moral vision. While the work serves as a sort of cultural primer that seeks to inculcate proper ethical values and cultivate a sense of what is fitting in the socioreligious realm, in the main, the piece seeks to shape the character, sharpen the intellect, form the feelings, and construct the worldview of its addressees in accordance with wisdom and virtue.

3. Literary Forms within Proverbs

At the macrolevel, Proverbs may be classified as an instructional text. But on the microlevel the anthology includes a variety of literary forms, three of which deserve specific comment.

a. The Proverb

The first is the proverb. By definition, a proverb is a concise, memorable utterance in popular use that communicates a traditional truth. While the precise nature of a "proverb" (מָשָׁל) is notoriously difficult to define in the Old Testament,[98] this definition provides a framework within which to understand the nature of the materials in the central collections (10:1–29:27). Similar to modern proverbs, the sayings within

97. Christopher B. Ansberry, "What Does Jerusalem Have to Do with Athens? The Moral Vision of the Book of Proverbs and Aristotle's *Nicomachean Ethics*," *HS* 51 (2010): 157–73.

98. Within the Old Testament, מָשָׁל is used in reference to a variety of different literary forms, ranging from similitudes, literary aphorisms, and popular sayings to taunt songs, bywords, allegories, and general discourses. In fact, מָשָׁל is used in the titles of Proverbs (1:1; 10:1; 25:1) with reference to sentences, admonitions, numerical sayings, better-than sayings, and epigrams, among others. Murphy, *Proverbs*, xxii; James L. Crenshaw, *Old Testament Wisdom: An Introduction*, rev. and enl. ed. (Louisville: Westminster John Knox, 1998), 56.

the central collections are short, poetic speech acts that that convey a basic truth. And similar to modern proverbs, the truth expressed by these aphorisms is limited and situational. Proverbs do not communicate a universal, hard-and-fast truth; rather, the general truth of a proverb is discovered in conversation with other sayings and through imaginative application in appropriate circumstances. This is the case with modern aphorisms as well as the sayings in the book of Proverbs. "Many hands" may "make light work," but "too many cooks" also "spoil the broth." In the same way, while plans succeed with a multitude of counselors (15:22b), despite human planning, it is YHWH's counsel that will stand (21:30). Each of these proverbs communicates a truth, but its truth is limited and contextual; it must be qualified by other sayings and applied with discernment and imagination to particular situations.

As poetic instruments that inspire the imagination, proverbs provoke reflection on one's character, one's conduct, one's situation, and one's view of the world.[99] The aphorisms in Proverbs share several features with modern sayings. Nonetheless, it is important to note that these aphorisms differ from modern proverbs in certain respects. In contrast to modern proverbs, the materials in the central collections of the anthology are cast in poetic parallelism rather than as single-lined sayings. And in contrast to modern proverbs, these materials have been removed from their live cultural and dialogical context and assembled into a collection. In light of their form, many suggest that the aphorisms within the book are the product of formal and theological development; they grew from single-lined sayings to parallel sayings and developed from secular aphorisms to theological aphorisms.[100] And in light of their integration into an anthology, some assume that the materials in the central collections are a veritable graveyard of dead aphorisms that must be revived through application in specific circumstances.[101]

While these proposals shaped the discussion of the Israelite proverbs in the past, their voice has faded. Ancient Near Eastern instructions have called into question the formal and theological development of the aphorisms in Proverbs. These texts do not evince a linear development in poetic form.[102] And they integrate religious elements with "mundane" matters, demonstrating the notion of theological development is rooted in a "modern conceptual distinction" between the religious and the secular, a distinction that is foreign to both the ancient world and the Old Testament.[103]

99. A. S. Herbert, "The Parable (*MĀŠĀL*) in the Old Testament," *SJT* 7 (1954): 180–96. Also see, Vayntrub, *Beyond Orality*, 70–90; Suzanna R. Millar, *Genre and Openness in Proverbs 10:1–22:16*, AIL 39 (Atlanta: SBL Press, 2020), 17–44.

100. Otto Eissfeldt, *Der Maschal im Alten Testament*, BZAW 24 (Giessen: Töpelmann, 1913), 12–25; W. O. E. Oesterley, *The Book of Proverbs*, WC (London: Methuen, 1929), xii–xviii; John M. Thompson, *The Form and Function of Proverbs in Ancient Israel* (Paris: Mouton, 1974), 66–67; McKane, *Proverbs*, 10–22.

101. Wolfgang Mieder, "The Essence of Literary Proverb Study," *Proverbium* 23 (1974): 892.

102. Berend Gemser, "The Instructions of 'Onchsheshonqy and Biblical Wisdom Literature," *SJT* 7 (1960): 102–28; Miriam Lichtheim, *Late Egyptian Wisdom Literature in the International Context: A Study of Demotic Instructions*, OBO 52 (Göttingen: Vandenhoeck & Ruprecht, 1983), 6–12.

103. Roland E. Murphy, "Wisdom—Theses and Hypotheses," in *Israelite Wisdom: Theological and Literary Essays in*

The aphorisms in the central collections lack a live performance context, but they are situated in a literary performance context, viz., the discourse setting of the anthology.[104] And they are open to application in a variety of circumstances.

The sayings in Proverbs are similar to and different from modern aphorisms. The same is true with respect to their function. Similar to modern aphorisms, the sayings in Proverbs serve as a conceptual vehicle that stimulate the imagination and inculcate discernment.[105] They articulate a story about the way the "world wags" in a condensed, concentrated form in order to achieve a particular goal in specific social situations.[106] As noted above, however, the aphorisms in Proverbs have been grafted into a collection and detached from specific social situations. While one may cherry-pick from these sayings and apply them in particular situations through the powers of perception and discernment, on the whole, the proverbs in the central section of the anthology function in a different way. They coalesce to form a mosaic of the wise life. This mosaic not only evokes contemplation; it also seeks to cultivate wisdom and virtue. To be specific, it attempts to shape the character, form the feelings, hone the desires, and sharpen the worldview of readers in accordance with wisdom and virtue so they might live rightly in relation to God, others, and the created world.

b. Instructions or "Lectures"[107]

The function of the aphorisms in Proverbs is comparable to the function of the second major genre within the anthology: instructions or lectures.[108] These didactic poems frame the document (1:8–9:18; 31:1–9) and mark off the personalized commands in "the words of the wise" (22:17–24:34). The parental lectures in Prov 1–9 and 31:1–9 give particular attention to the value of wisdom; they focus on instrumental virtues and address the issue of seduction from different perspectives and through distinct rhetorical strategies.[109] The same is true of the admonitions within

Honor of Samuel Terrien, ed. W. A. Brueggemann et al. (Missoula, MT: Scholars Press, 1978), 40; Lennart Boström, *The God of the Sages: The Portrayal of God in the Book of Proverbs*, ConBOT 29 (Stockholm: Almqvist & Wiksell, 1990), 36–38.

104. Van Leeuwen, *Context and Meaning*, 2; Heim, *Like Grapes of Gold*, 24; Michael V. Fox, "Wisdom and the Self-Presentation of Wisdom Literature," in *Reading from Right to Left: Essays on the Hebrew Bible in Honour of David J. A. Clines*, ed. J. C. Exum and H. G. M. Williamson (Sheffield: Sheffield Academic, 2003), 153–54; Timothy J. Sandoval, *The Discourse of Wealth and Poverty in the Book of Proverbs*, BibInt 77 (Leiden: Brill, 2006), 37.

105. James G. Williams, *Those Who Ponder Proverbs: Aphoristic Thinking and Biblical Literature*, BLS (Sheffield: Almond Press, 1981), 87.

106. William A. Beardslee, "Use of the Proverb in the Synoptic Gospels," *Int* 24 (1970): 65; R. B. Y. Scott, *The Way of Wisdom in the Old Testament* (New York: Macmillan, 1971), 52; Claus Westermann, *Roots of Wisdom: The Oldest Proverbs of Israel and Other Peoples*, trans. J. D. Charles (Louisville: Westminster John Knox, 1995), 13, 61.

107. The designation "lectures" is taken from Michael V. Fox, *Proverbs 1–9: A New Translation with Introduction and Commentary*, AB 18A (New York: Doubleday, 2000), 45.

108. While these instructions share several features with the wisdom "interludes" in the prologue (1:20–33; 3:13–20; 8:1–36; 9:1–18), they also exhibit several conceptual and literary differences. Since each "interlude" is distinct, attention to the form and function of these discourses will be examined in the commentary proper. For a discussion of the distinctive nature of these "interludes," see Fox, *Proverbs 1–9*, 326–29.

109. William P. Brown, *Wisdom's Wonder: Character, Creation, and Crisis in the Bible's Wisdom Literature* (Grand Rapids: Eerdmans, 2014), 41–48. Together with the wisdom interludes,

Prov 22:17–24:34. These brief prescriptions attend to practical virtues in order to inculcate perception and provide concrete council on how to interpret or deal with diverse people in particular situations. While the literary texture and content of these instructional forms differ in several respects, it appears that they are employed to achieve a particular didactic purpose: to (trans)form one's character through the inculcation of wisdom, virtue, and trust in YHWH (22:19–21). They outline the (im)moral contours of various character types, interpret the speech of diverse voices, illuminate the value of wisdom, cultivate discernment, shape the desires of the reader, and (trans)form their disposition by inspiring a lifelong pursuit of wisdom and virtue nurtured by faith in YHWH.

c. Autobiographical Stylization[110]

The third literary form is autobiographical stylization. This form of discourse is intimately related to the instructions delineated above; it allows the wise to move beyond strict admonitions and to convey their advice through personal experiences or discoveries. While this mode of discourse plays a prominent role in the friends' speeches within Job, as well as Qoheleth's quest, it is limited to a handful of texts within Proverbs (e.g., 7:6–27; 24:30–34). The relative insignificance of autobiographical stylization within Proverbs may call into question the value of discussing the literary form. This discussion is necessary, however, for the autobiographical cast of certain materials has led many to conclude that Proverbs operates under an empirical epistemology.

While certain texts within Proverbs are cast in autobiographical form and appear to be based on personal or sensory experience, the discoveries delineated in these passages are not empirical observations; rather, they are "statements of faith" shaped in accordance with specific ethical, theological, and cultural assumptions.[111] The purported observation or experience serves as the literary, rhetorical, and imaginative medium through which an axiomatic belief is taught.[112] Put differently, the personal experiences or autobiographical observations within Proverbs do not produce knowledge; rather, these observations and experiences reinforce the sage's values

the parental instructions in Prov 1–9 constitute a continuous, uninterrupted discourse, rather than a series of isolated instructions. Though these materials may have been produced as independent speeches, they are cast as a progressive program of instruction bound together by a series of archetypal personages and root metaphors. Weeks, *Instruction and Imagery*, 44; Scott L. Harris, *Proverbs 1–9: A Study of Inner-Biblical Interpretation*, SBLDS 150 (Atlanta: Scholars Press, 1995), 160–62.

110. This designation is taken from Gerhard von Rad, *Wisdom in Israel*, trans. J. D. Martin (Harrisburg: Trinity Press International, 1972), 37. In contrast to this designation, Estes uses the expression "fictional" or "imaginative" literature. Daniel J. Estes, "Fiction and Truth in Old Testament Wisdom Literature," *Themelios* 35 (2010): 387–99.

111. Michael V. Fox, "The Epistemology of the Book of Proverbs," *JBL* 126 (2007): 670–84, esp. 670–76. Also see von Rad, *Wisdom in Israel*, 64; Christopher B. Ansberry, "From Philosophical Theories to Phenomenological Description: Evaluating the Epistemology of Proverbs 10:1–22:16," *HBAI* (2022): forthcoming.

112. Fox, "The Epistemology of the Book of Proverbs," 673.

and assumptions.[113] They are pedagogical, not epistemological.[114] Far from offering wisdom and practical advice through mere sensory experience, the autobiographical materials in Proverbs communicate fundamental assumptions, truths, and values under the guise of experience. And this experiential guise performs an important function: it awakens the imagination, draws the reader into the psychological and emotional dynamics of the account, shapes their character, hones their desires, and cultivates perception.[115]

As noted above, Proverbs includes a variety of literary forms. Among these forms, the most significant may be proverbs, instructions or lectures, and autobiographical stylization. The characteristic features and function of these genres will serve as a backdrop against which this commentary will treat particular texts. Those texts that do not relate to these generic designations will receive specific attention in the commentary proper.

Major Theological Themes

Similar to the literary forms within the anthology, Proverbs contains a variety of prominent theological themes. These themes are woven throughout the discrete collections of the document. And they exist in dynamic, dialogical relationship with one another. Among these themes, the "motto" of Proverbs, the characters within the piece, and its root or nuclear metaphor deserve specific comment.

1. The "Motto" and Prerequisite

As the "motto" of the anthology and the prerequisite for the acquisition of wisdom and virtue, the fear of YHWH may represent the most significant theological motif in the anthology. The acquisition of wisdom is contingent on fear. Put differently, the pedagogy of Proverbs hinges on a posture of fear seeking wisdom and understanding.[116] The fear of YHWH is a well-known expression within the Old Testament.[117] The concept is employed in the discrete corpora of the canon to refer to the complex emotions associated with fear in relation to YHWH, viz., dread, trembling, awe, and wonder (Exod 20:19–21; 2 Sam 6:6–11; Hab 3:2; Ps 22:23). This range of emotions is encapsulated in Proverbs's use of the expression. And this spectrum of emotions

113. Fox, "The Epistemology of the Book of Proverbs," 673.

114. Fox, "The Epistemology of the Book of Proverbs," 674.

115. Von Rad, *Wisdom in Israel*, 38; Shimon Bar-Efrat, *Narrative Art in the Bible*, BLS 17 (Sheffield: Almond Press, 1989), 47; Fox, "The Epistemology of the Book of Proverbs," 681; Estes, "Fiction and Truth," 393–94.

116. Brown, *Wisdom's Wonder*, 19–20, 24.

117. For an extensive discussion of the expression, see Joachim Becker, *Gottesfurcht im Alten Testament*, AnBib 25 (Rome: Pontifical Biblical Institute, 1965).

serves as a window into the multifaceted nature of the posture or mode of being that this prerequisite forms within YHWH-fearers.

The mode of being produced by the fear of YHWH encompasses the ontological and epistemological dimensions of the self. This is not surprising, for the fear of YHWH assumes a particular ontology and epistemology. The ontological and epistemological dimensions of the motto are clarified by Job Jindo.[118] According to Jindo, fear and knowledge are inextricably linked in the Bible. In fact, "fear of God" and "knowledge of God" are virtually identical (Prov 2:5). The connection between fear and knowledge reflects the connection between the ontological and epistemological aspects of the "fear of YHWH." As Jindo notes, there is a certain kind of knowledge that precedes fear and creates a particular ontology or mode of being. That knowledge is perspectival rather than propositional; it is a way of thinking or seeing, a particular mode of cognition, rather than a descriptive knowledge of things.[119] When one internalizes this perspectival knowledge and adopts a particular mode of cognition, then one sees the self and experiences the world in a particular way. Put in terms of Proverbs, one perceives one's status in the cosmos in relation to YHWH. This epistemological insight leads to a state of fear, to an ontological state, which Jindo regards as "a basic norm that constitutes the normative mode of human existence."[120] On this account, epistemology determines the ontology of the self. Perspectival knowledge of one's place in the cosmos in relation to YHWH creates a state of fear, an ontology of the self that "validates one's mode of being and living as human."[121]

Jindo's description of the mode of being presumed by the "fear of YHWH" captures the epistemological and ontological dimensions of the self who seeks to acquire wisdom and virtue in Proverbs. This vision of the self indicates that the "fear of YHWH" is not a virtue, but a mode of being. It is not the conscience, but a consciousness of one's place in the cosmos in relation to God.[122] In Jindo's words, the fear of God is the fundamental norm for human being; and it serves as this norm because it situates the human agent in their divinely designed place within the cosmos.[123] This conception of the fear of YHWH and the ontology of the self explains why one may grow in one's understanding of the fear of YHWH (Prov 2:5). The magnitude of one's

118. Job Y. Jindo, "On the Biblical Notion of the 'Fear of God' as a Condition for Human Existence," *BibInt* 19 (2011): 433–53.

119. Jindo, "On the Biblical Notion," 438.

120. Jindo, "On the Biblical Notion," 435, 449.

121. Jindo, "On the Biblical Notion," 450n33.

122. Jindo, "On the Biblical Notion," 450. Also see Michael C. Legaspi, *Wisdom in Classical and Biblical Tradition* (New York: Oxford University Press, 2018), 63, who observes, "Despite the similar roles played by a general notion of conscience and the 'fear of YHWH,' there are important differences. To describe a moral life based on fear of YHWH is to emphasize the relational context that exists between the judge and the one who stands under judgment. It is also to suggest that wisdom is rooted in something more fundamental even than wonder, curiosity, or reason. Wisdom begins with metaphysical vulnerability."

123. Jindo, "On the Biblical Notion," 450.

fear is proportional to the quality of one's knowledge of God.[124] And this ontology of the self may explain the problem with certain character types who populate Proverbs, such as the fool, the wicked, the scoffer, and the lazy. If "the fear of YHWH" refers to a mode of being engendered by a certain type of perspectival knowledge, then the problem with these aberrant character types is not their ignorance or lack of propositional knowledge; it is their lack of perspectival knowledge, a knowledge that would allow them to see things through a particular mode of cognition. This is seen most clearly through the terminal condition of "one who is wise in his own eyes" (26:12, 16). As Raymond Van Leeuwen rightly notes, this type of individual engages "in a fatal act of self-perception. . . . It is finally the *failure of self-knowledge* that defines the fool. Because such a person does not know himself, he is prone to seeking glory beyond his limits."[125] The failure of self-knowledge leads to a mode of being that lacks ontological validation as being human.[126] No wonder these sorts of characters cannot learn. They know neither their place in the cosmos nor themselves.

As the motto of Proverbs and the prerequisite for achieving its goal, the fear of YHWH is much more than a distillation of Israelite epistemology.[127] It is an ontological posture produced by a recognition of one's contingency, responsibilities, and place within the cosmos in relation to YHWH (Prov 9:10; cf. 30:1–6). It is a disposition characterized by a love for what is good and a hatred for what is evil (Prov 8:13; 16:6; Job 28:28). And it is a mode of being that motivates the moral life and manifests itself through concrete activities performed through wisdom, in accordance with the will of YHWH, and for the sake of the other (31:10–31; cf. Deut 10:12–16). Put simply, the fear of YHWH is Proverbs's expression for faith.[128] This form of faith serves as the seedbed within which wisdom and virtue may develop and flourish. From this theological and epistemological frame of reference, Proverbs contends that a fearful faith is the key to genuine knowledge, for it places knowledge in proper relationship, in proper perspective, and within proper boundaries.

In addition to the way in which the fear of YHWH contributes to the pedagogy and goal of the anthology, the motif plays an important role in the literary architecture of Proverbs. As the crescendo of the preamble (1:7a), the fear of YHWH serves as the entryway into the anthology; it is the requisite posture for achieving its goal. As the hinge between Wisdom and Folly's invitations at the conclusion of the prologue (9:10), the fear of YHWH is associated with knowledge of God; both determine which woman, way, house, and banquet one will choose (cf. 1:29; 2:5). As instruction in wisdom (15:33; cf. 22:4), the fear of YHWH is situated at the center of

124. Jindo, "On the Biblical Notion," 448.

125. Van Leeuwen, *Context and Meaning*, 105 emphasis mine.

126. Jindo, "On the Biblical Notion," 435.

127. Von Rad, *Wisdom in Israel*, 67.

128. Daniel J. Treier, *Proverbs and Ecclesiastes*, Brazos Theological Commentary on the Bible (Grand Rapids: Brazos, 2011), 12.

the anthology; it is the underlying subject matter that binds together the initial half of the first Solomonic collection (10:1–15:32) with the second (16:1–22:16).[129] And as the cardinal virtue of the valiant woman (31:30), the fear of YHWH is situated at the conclusion of the anthology, where it is an embodied form of life that exercises power for the benefit of the other. The repetition of the fear of YHWH at key junctures within Proverbs illuminates the epistemological, ontological, pedagogical, and theological significance of this mode of being. Without it, one cannot realize the goal of the book and acquire wisdom and virtue.

2. Characters and Characterization

Under its motto and fundamental prerequisite, Proverbs inculcates wisdom and virtue through graphic "characterizations of character."[130] The discrete collections within the anthology focus on a specific cast of character types. And these character types are profiled in particular ways to cultivate a perspectival perspective of the world attuned to wisdom and virtue.[131] The characterizations provide prototypical models of ideal and flawed character types. Ideal character types epitomize the multifaceted dimensions of normative character. Flawed character types, by contrast, cultivate normative character by describing the way in which one should not think, feel, or act. Together, these characterizations project a way of being-in-the-world as well as a way of seeing the world. They offer patterns or molds for the formation of moral character, and they serve as a lens through which to view and evaluate different people and activities from a virtuous perspective. This perspective not only shapes the reader's vision of life in accordance with wisdom and virtue; it also shapes their character.

Among the various character types within the anthology, the wise, the fool, the righteous, the wicked, and the uncommitted may be the most significant. The wise and the fool are mirror images of one another. The "wise" (חָכָם) are those who are teachable and discerning, who accept correction and internalize knowledge (2:1; 9:8; 10:8, 14; 12:15; 13:1; 15:31). They possess the powers of perception and discretion; that is, they have the intellectual ability to interpret people, evaluate specific situations, consider the consequences associated with particular actions, and live in accordance with the divine order. As the archetype of intellectual virtue, the wise are not static characters that simply exemplify certain cognitive abilities; rather, they are dynamic characters that typify these intellectual abilities through an embodied way of life.[132]

129. Raymond C. Van Leeuwen, "The Book of Proverbs," *NIB* 5:152; Waltke, *Proverbs: Chapters 1–15*, 16.

130. Brown, *Character in Crisis*, 19.

131. Frydrych, *Living Under the Sun*, 40–41.

132. Frydrych, *Living Under the Sun*, 26.

In contrast to the wise, fools are distinguished by their indifference to knowledge. In fact, the apathy of the fool is portrayed through a variety of terms and expressions, each of which illuminate the intellectual dimensions of their character. The "fool" (כְּסִיל) is self-centered and bent on evil (13:19; 18:2). As the epitome of intellectual vice, the fool despises wisdom, lacks self-control, and is inclined to immoderation because of their inability to assess particular situations (1:22; 10:18; 12:23). In this respect, it is not surprising that the fool is closely associated with the "ignorant" (בַּעַר) and the "imbecile" (חֲסַר־לֵב), who hate correction and do not possess the intellectual capacity to perceive the consequences of their actions (6:32; 12:1). Whereas the wise are teachable and discerning, the fool is indifferent to knowledge and unable to weigh the apparent magnitude of their decisions against the consequences that await their actions.[133]

The intellectual polarity between the wise and the fool is comparable to the moral polarity between the "righteous" (צַדִּיק) and the "wicked" (רָשָׁע). Similar to the wise and the fool, Proverbs does not offer abstract definitions of these prototypes. Instead, it describes the nature of these personages by focusing on what they do, what they love, and what happens to them.[134] The characterization of the righteous intimates that this character type is *the* prototypical character within Proverbs, "the sages' chosen exemplar of the ethical and pious life" who induces desire "*by showing what is desirable*."[135] As a character representing a group that is profiled through its role within and contribution to the community, the righteous are described in relation to others. They are those characterized by the proper administration of justice (17:15, 16; 18:5, 17; 24:24; 25:26), loyalty (12:5), generosity (21:26), mercy (12:10; 29:7), reliability (12:7; 18:10; 28:1), and honesty (10:11; 13:5). And as the embodiment of all that is virtuous within the anthology, they exemplify attitudes and activities that please God (3:33; 15:28), nourish the community, and lead to life (10:16; 11:19, 30; 12:28; 21:21). Not so the wicked! In contrast to the righteous, the wicked are depicted as antisocial individuals characterized by greed (10:3), violence (10:6), deceit (12:5), perverse speech (10:32; 11:11; 15:28), and cruelty (12:10). In this respect, they are intimately related to the "fool" (אֱוִיל) and the "scoffer" (לֵץ); the former is a morally incorrigible individual (12:15)[136] who despises discipline and correction (15:5), delights in evil conduct (10:23), and lacks self-control (12:16), while the latter is the embodiment of hubris. Their arrogance and resistance to chastisement prevents them from acquiring wisdom, even if they choose to seek it (14:6).[137]

133. Fox, *Proverbs 10–31*, 940–41.

134. David J. Reimer, "צדק," *NIDOTTE* 3.757; Ansberry, "What Does Jerusalem Have to Do with Athens?," 163.

135. Sun Myung Lyu, *Righteousness in the Book of Proverbs*, FAT II/55 (Tübingen: Mohr Siebeck, 2012), 62, italics original.

136. Fox, *Proverbs 1–9*, 40.

137. Fox, *Proverbs 1–9*, 42.

While these moral and intellectual characterizations, their synonyms and equivalent phrases, overlap in certain instances (10:16–17, 31; 11:9, 30), it is important to note that the antithetical sets are not interchangeable.[138] The wise//fool and the righteous//wicked designate different semantic fields: the former presents an intellectual evaluation, while the latter provides a moral evaluation.[139] These two sets of appellations are not synonymous, but their relationship may be described as coreferential; that is, the antitheses do not have the same meaning or sense, but they refer to the same reality, the same referent in a given context.[140] The righteous/wise, the wicked/fool, and related vocabulary in either semantic field describe the positive and negative, the (im)moral and intellectual character traits of the same type of person. These moral and intellectual polarities present alternative ways of life that divide individuals into two general classes: the righteous/wise and the wicked/fool.

In light of the intimate relationship between these character types, it seems that Proverbs refuses to separate wisdom from virtue, the life of the mind from an embodied form of life. The coreferential relationship between the classes of character, combined with the intellectual and moral virtues representative of their nature, illuminate the mutual dependence of wisdom and virtue in Proverbs's pedagogical agenda: the acquisition of wisdom is dependent upon a virtuous disposition, while virtuous activity is dependent upon the acquisition of wisdom.[141]

Proverbs paints an impressionistic portrait of normative, ethical character.[142] The characters within the document typify what is desirable and undesirable; they embody either wisdom and virtue or folly and vice. In so doing, they serve as a model for how one should and should not think, feel, see, desire, and act. And these models, to borrow from Athanasius's theological approach to the Psalter, create an ethical pattern on which readers may *form* their character.[143] By outlining the fundamental contours of normative character through various "characterizations of character," Proverbs attempts to shape the character and worldview of the reader by providing them within a vision of life rooted in the fear of YHWH and marked by wisdom, which is inseparable from virtue. In this respect, the portrayals of these basic classes of character are not merely descriptive; they are also transformative. They are pre-

138. R. B. Y. Scott, "Wise and Foolish, Righteous and Wicked," *VT* 23 (1972): 146–65; repr. in *Studies in the Religion of Ancient Israel*, ed. G. W. Anderson et al., VTSup 23 (Leiden: Brill, 1972), 146–65, esp. 153; Westermann, *Roots of Wisdom*, 84; Murphy, *Proverbs*, 267–68.

139. Nili Shupak, *Where Can Wisdom Be Found? The Sage's Language in the Bible and in Ancient Egyptian Literature*, OBO 130 (Göttingen: Vandenhoeck & Ruprecht, 1993), 265–67; Heim, *Like Grapes of Gold*, 85–101.

140. Peter Cotterell and Max Turner, *Linguistics & Biblical Interpretation* (London: SPCK, 1979), 160–61; Heim, *Like Grapes of Gold*, 81–101; Frydrych, *Living Under the Sun*, 25; Waltke, *Proverbs: Chapters 1–15*, 93.

141. Ansberry, "What Does Jerusalem Have to Do with Athens?," 171–73.

142. Brown, *Wisdom's Wonder*, 15–16.

143. Athanasius, *The Life of Antony and the Letter to Marcellinus*, trans. R. C. Gregg, Classics of Western Spirituality (London: SPCK, 1980), 108, §10.

sented to form one's desires, sharpen one's thinking, pinpoint one's vices, cultivate virtue, and offer a wise perspective on life so that one may flourish in relation to God, self, and others.

In contrast to Proverbs's intellectual and moral polarities, the "uncommitted" (פֶּתִי) defy strict classification in the anthology's rendering of character. As the designation "uncommitted" suggests, this personage is situated in a liminal state, a moral twilight zone. They are neither wise nor foolish, neither righteous nor wicked. Nonetheless, they possess particular traits characteristic of the fool. Similar to the fool, the uncommitted lack sense (7:7; 9:4, 16; cf. 10:21; 15:21). And their association with fools and scoffers suggests they are morally culpable individuals whose waywardness and gullibility may lead to death (1:22, 32). The uncommitted may be comparable to the fool, but they are also comparable to the wise. Whereas the fool is unable to learn, the uncommitted are open, malleable, and capable of acquiring wisdom (9:4, 16; 19:25; 21:11).[144] This condition may explain why the uncommitted are identified as the principal addressees of Proverbs (1:4). Just as the various character types profiled in the anthology are designed to shape the reader's character in accord with wisdom and virtue, so also these vignettes seek to transform the predilection of the uncommitted, free them from their liminal state, and move them to acquire wisdom.

The fuzzy characterization of the uncommitted is representative of the fuzzy characterization of the character types across Proverbs. As intimated above, character types possess certain characteristics or defining qualities. This does not mean that character types are abstract, stale, closed categories within Proverbs. To the contrary, the categories of character are porous.[145] And the porous nature of these categories is evinced through many sayings. The righteous, for example, may fall (24:6). In fact, the righteous may totter before the wicked (25:26; cf. 12:3). The wise or discerning require rebuke (17:10). The fool may demonstrate reticence (17:28). And the wicked may possess wealth (10:2). These examples represent the tip of the iceberg. Many more will be mentioned in the commentary below. Proverbs's characterization of character types is central to its pedagogy and the realization of its goal. But this characterization of characters is by no means simplistic.[146] Like the character types across Proverbs, human character is fuzzy, porous, inconsistent, and yet tethered to certain defining qualities. This reality is reflected in Proverbs and this reality funds the pedagogical agenda of the book.

144. Waltke, *Proverbs: Chapters 1–15*, 111.

145. For an excellent discussion of prototype theory and the openness of character categories in Proverbs, see Anne W. Stewart, *Poetic Ethics in Proverbs: Wisdom Literature and the Shaping of the Moral Self* (Cambridge: Cambridge University Press, 2016), 170–200; Millar, *Genre and Openness*, 89–110.

146. Anne W. Stewart, "Wisdom's Imagination: Moral Reasoning and the Book of Proverbs," *JSOT* 40 (2016): 351–72.

3. The Root Metaphor and Its "Satellite Images"[147]

Together with the common cast of characters woven throughout the fabric of Proverbs, a root metaphor punctuates the collections within the anthology. This metaphor offers a way of seeing the world and provides a framework through which to understand other images within the discourse.[148] What's more, this root metaphor structures one's moral reasoning and funds the pedagogical agenda of the document. The root metaphor and satellite images of Proverbs are illustrated through the following diagram:

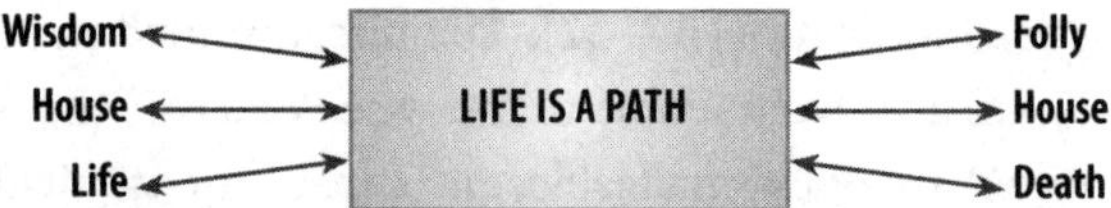

Life is a path is a prominent conceptual metaphor within Proverbs in general and the prologue in particular (1:8–9:18).[149] This metaphor serves as a window into a larger metaphoric system that includes the concepts of wisdom and folly, life and death.[150] For Proverbs, the way of wisdom and life is straight, clear, and open (3:23; 4:11–12, 18; 11:5).[151] The way of folly and death, by contrast, is crooked, dark, and dangerous (2:12–15; 4:19; 21:8; 22:5). The intimate relationship between the metaphor and these concepts suggests that the way or path is much more than a lifestyle or course of life; it also concerns one's character, kinesthetic movements, and the consequences associated with one's behavior.[152] Similar to Aristotle's ethical theory, it appears that wisdom and character determine the path or direction one travels through life: character determines the goal or direction of one's behavior, while wisdom identifies the means for achieving that goal in specific situations.[153] And, together, character and wisdom participate in a teleological activity to achieve a particular end: life or death.

Despite the common images and concepts used to describe these distinct paths, it is important to note that Proverbs does not envision two specific motorways in

147. Norman C. Habel, "The Symbolism of Wisdom in Proverbs 1–9," *Int* 26 (1972): 131–57.

148. Fox, *Proverbs 1–9*, 128–29. Fox uses the expression "*ground metaphor*," which is comparable to root metaphor.

149. Proverbs uses four basic terms to designate a "way" or "path": דֶּרֶךְ, נְתִיבָה, אֹרַח, and מַעְגָּל. Following the practice of George Lakoff and Mark Johnson, conceptual metaphors are cast in the form of small capitals. George Lakoff and Mark Johnson, *Metaphors We Live By* (Chicago: University of Chicago Press, 1980).

150. See Van Leeuwen, "Liminality and Worldview," 111, who also includes the polarity of good/pseudo-good with those mentioned above and views these as the component parts of a larger metaphoric system concerned with boundaries or limits established by YHWH within the created order.

151. For discussion of the way of life in Egyptian wisdom literature, see Fox, *Proverbs 1–9*, 130; Weeks, *Instruction and Imagery*, 148–49.

152. Waltke, *Proverbs: Chapters 1–15*, 194.

153. Ansberry, "What Does Jerusalem Have to Do with Athens?," 165–66.

life. The wise and the fool may travel on several "paths" (1:19; 2:19, 20; 3:6, 17; 4:26; 5:6; 8:32). These paths appear to capture forms of behavior or choices that may be characterized as wise or foolish, that lead to life or death. Similar to the choices and experiences of everyday life, the network of these paths is complex, like the web of a big city's streets rather than the single road that passes through a small rural town. Following Stuart Weeks, it seems that these paths "are not preordained routes"; rather, they represent "the directions that individuals take: footprints, as it were, rather than footpaths."[154] The use of the plural "paths" intimates that the metaphor does not refer to a predetermined, established way; it refers to the direction or orientation of one's life: toward wisdom and life or folly and death. As noted above, this direction is determined by character and actualized through wisdom, each of which are shaped and cultivated by the materials within Proverbs.

The metaphor of the way and its related concepts is congruent with the women and their respective houses within Proverbs. Similar to the conceptual metaphor LIFE IS A PATH, these women traverse ways that lead to distinct destinations: "Lady Wisdom" (חָכְמָה) to life (8:35; 9:6), the "strange woman" (אִשָּׁה זָרָה and נָכְרִיָּה) and "Woman Folly" (אֵשֶׁת כְּסִילוּת) to death (2:18; 5:5–6; 9:18). In fact, their homes are depicted as the gateways to these destinations (2:18; 7:27; 8:34–35; 9:13–18). And similar to the path metaphor, these women are distinguished by particular virtues or vices: one is marked by wisdom, righteousness, and justice (8:8, 14, 20), the others by seduction, deception, and folly (2:16; 5:3; 6:24; 7:5, 21; 9:13). The intimate relationship between the path metaphor and the women as well as their respective homes suggests that "the way" functions as a nuclear symbol, a governing metaphor through which to understand the "satellite images" of women and houses, life and death.[155] Together, the metaphor and its satellite images exist in dialogical relationship with one another, illuminating the multifaceted dimensions of the symbol through the discrete contexts or "zones" in which it functions.[156]

While the path metaphor is implicit in the speeches of the women and the description of their homes, the concept plays a formative role in the characterization of these figures and their domiciles. The way or path is present in the discourses of these women but cast in a different form than the parental lectures.[157] Rather than projecting a road that symbolizes the direction or orientation of one's life, the direction or orientation of one's life is incarnated through the character and speech of the women.

154. Weeks, *Instruction and Imagery*, 75.

155. Habel, "The Symbolism of Wisdom in Proverbs 1–9," 133–34.

156. Habel, "The Symbolism of Wisdom in Proverbs 1–9," 133–34. In contrast to Habel, this study does not explore the metaphor of the way and its satellite symbols through the zones of "'old' international wisdom," Israel's "covenant context," and "the cosmic field of theological reflection." This scheme assumes an evolutionary development that is at odds with the ancient Near Eastern worldview in general and the instructional tradition in particular. See the discussion above under "The Proverb" as well as Murphy, "Wisdom—Theses and Hypotheses," 40; Weeks, *Early Israelite Wisdom*, 57–73.

157. Weeks, *Instruction and Imagery*, 78.

The discourses of the women are delivered in the public thoroughfares: in the streets and at the intersections or thresholds of life (1:20–21; 7:8, 12; 8:2–3; 9:3, 14–15). Those who fall prey to the seductive rhetoric and pseudo-promises of the strange woman are characterized as those who "turn aside to her ways" (יֵשְׂטְ אֶל־דְּרָכֶיהָ; 7:25), which stands in sharp contrast to the father's command to "turn aside" (שְׂטֵה; 4:15) from the path of the wicked. Whereas those who delight in evil travel on "crooked paths" (אָרְחֹתֵיהֶם עִקְּשִׁים; 2:15), Lady Wisdom's speech is marked by righteousness; none of her words are "crooked" (עִקֵּשׁ; 8:8). And whereas Wisdom calls the uncommitted to "walk straight in the path of understanding" (אִשְׁרוּ בְּדֶרֶךְ בִּינָה; 9:6b; cf. 4:14),[158] Woman Folly attempts to divert "those who make their ways straight" (הַמְיַשְּׁרִים אֹרְחוֹתָם; 9:15b). Far from remaining an abstract metaphor concerning the direction of one's life, the female characters embody the nature of these directions (wisdom and folly) and illustrate their telos (life and death). Their discourses move away from a discussion of the orientation of one's life to the way in which character and wisdom (or the lack thereof) manifest themselves in an embodied way of life.[159]

Together, the nuclear metaphor of the way and the satellite images of women and houses, life and death illuminate the coherence of the prologue's instruction and capture the essence of its pedagogical agenda. The dialogical relationship between the path metaphor and the women within the prologue links the parental lectures and their concern with "the way" to the discourses of the women and their embodiment of different ways. The former provides instruction in the home. The latter deliver their speeches in streets and invite the uncommitted into their homes (7:14–20; 9:1–6, 13–18). The father uses conventional language to highlight the value of wisdom, to interpret the seductive rhetoric of diverse characters, and to diagnose the ways on which they walk.[160] The discourses of the women mimic one another and the figures incarnate particular ways, inviting the uncommitted to interpret their speech, to decipher the consequences of their actions, and to choose a mate, a banquet, a house, and fate.[161] The ways, women, and houses within the prologue, combined with the shared rhetoric and language among the speeches, suggest that these images are employed to shape the character, desires, and worldview of the addressee.[162] The father forms the intellect and cultivates instrumental virtues by describing the value of wisdom and the way in which it enables one to interpret people, determine the consequences of one's choices, and proceed down the way of life.[163] The women,

158. Fox, *Proverbs 1–9*, 299.

159. Weeks, *Instruction and Imagery*, 78–79.

160. Aletti, "Seduction et parole en Proverbes I–IX," 129–44; Weeks, *Instruction and Imagery*, 79–82.

161. For discussion of the complex metaphorical construction of the female figures and their shared language or "Lady Tongue," see Claudia V. Camp, "Woman Wisdom as Root Metaphor: A Theological Consideration," in *The Listening Heart: Essays in Wisdom and the Psalms in Honor of Roland E. Murphy, O. Carm.*, ed. K. G. Hoglund et al., JSOTSup 58 (Sheffield: JSOT Press, 1987), 51–58.

162. Van Leeuwen, "Liminality and Worldview in Proverbs 1–9," 116.

163. Brown, *Wisdom's Wonder*, 41–48.

by contrast, cultivate desire, either for what is good and leads to life or for what is evil and leads to death.[164] In so doing, they create a world marked by different ways that lead to different fates.[165] And the direction one chooses as well as the fate one receives is determined by one's character, desires, and response to the invitation to acquire wisdom.

Proverbs and Theology[166]

Theological reflection on the book of Proverbs has a checkered past.[167] Classical commentaries on the document are scarce.[168] And, in light of its distinctive interests as well as its lack of concern with Israel's history in general and the covenant in particular, many contend that Proverbs is among those documents that dwell in a canonical twilight zone. As a member of the category "wisdom literature," Proverbs has been labeled an "errant child,"[169] an "alien body,"[170] and "an orphan in the biblical household."[171] And as a work "near the pagan source of wisdom,"[172] some maintain that its universalistic, humanistic, and eudemonistic ethos contributed to the rationalization and demystification of Israelite religion.[173] On this account, it is not surprising that many stress the anthropocentric or humanistic character of the material in the anthology. And it is not surprising that Proverbs is deemed theologically inferior at best and downright secular wisdom at worst.

Despite its checkered past, many throughout the history of interpretation have recognized the abiding theological value of Proverbs.[174] As intimated throughout this introduction, Proverbs seeks to (trans)form one's character through the inculcation of wisdom and virtue. To be more precise, the anthology seeks to shape the character, sharpen the intellect, hone the desires, form the feelings, and construct the worldview of readers in accord with wisdom and virtue so that they might live rightly in relation

164. Brown, *Wisdom's Wonder*, 48–55.

165. Van Leeuwen, "Liminality and Worldview in Proverbs 1–9," 117–32.

166. Portions of this section are adapted from Christopher B. Ansberry, "Wisdom and Biblical Theology," in *Exploring Old Testament Wisdom: Literature and Themes*, ed. David G. Firth and Lindsay Wilson (Leicester: Apollos, 2016), 174–93.

167. For an excellent discussion of the history of interpretation of Proverbs in the last two hundred years, see Zoltán S. Schwáb, *Toward an Interpretation of the Book of Proverbs: Selfishness and Secularity Reconsidered*, Journal of Theological Interpretation Supplements 7 (Winona Lake, IN: Eisenbrauns, 2013), 4–61.

168. Treier, *Proverbs and Ecclesiastes*, 3.

169. R. E. Clements, "Wisdom and Old Testament Theology," in John Day and Robert P. Gordon, eds., *Wisdom in Ancient Israel* (Cambridge: Cambridge University Press, 1995), 271.

170. Harmut Gese, *Lehre und Wirklichkeit in der alten Weisheit* (Tübingen: J. C. B. Mohr, 1958), 2.

171. James L. Crenshaw, "Prolegomenon," in *Studies in Ancient Israelite Wisdom*, ed. James L. Crenshaw (New York: Ktav, 1976), 1.

172. G. Ernest Wright, *God Who Acts: Biblical Theology as Recital*, SBT 8 (London: SCM, 1952), 104.

173. Clements, "Wisdom and Old Testament Theology," 274–75.

174. Christopher B. Ansberry, "Proverbs," in *The Cambridge Companion to Biblical Wisdom Literature*, ed. Katharine J. Dell, Suzanna R. Millar, and Arthur Jan Keefer (Cambridge: Cambridge University Press, 2022), 137–51.

to God, others, and the created world. The pedagogical agenda of Proverbs provides ample food for theological thought. While many things could be mentioned concerning the theology of Proverbs, at least four matters deserve specific attention: ethics, creation, wisdom and the limits of wisdom, and wisdom and the New Testament.

1. Wisdom and Life: Ethics

In a certain sense, the book of Proverbs is a collage of virtues and vices. The variegated materials within the anthology outline the contours and characteristics of the moral life through a cast of characters that traverse distinct "ways" and embody diverse values. The extended discourses and pithy aphorisms give expression to discrete moral visions, to different ways of seeing and being in the world. And the document addresses matters of moral agency by attending to virtues that span the ethical spectrum and mark the structures that shape character (i.e., the family and the community). Proverbs is a work concerned with ethics and the moral life; it is a piece that profiles the qualities and dimensions of normative character through literary characterization.[175] This profile of normative character, however, is not rooted in eudemonism nor driven by pragmatism. Rather, it is rooted in "fear" (1:7)—in relationship with YHWH and knowledge of his will—driven by moral obligation to God and the other, and oriented toward a telos: life.

This theological grounding of normative character and the moral life shapes the multifaceted ethical vision of Proverbs. To be specific, it funds Proverbs's vision of those qualities, decisions, and actions that either form or deform character, divine-human and interpersonal relations, and the structures of family and community. The theological framework of Proverbs's moral vision informs its conception of speech ethics (6:16–19; 10:11, 21; 11:11; 12:14, 18; 13:2, 14; 17:20; 18:21), wealth ethics (3:9–10; 11:4, 18; 23:4–5; 30:7–9), business ethics (11:1, 24–26; 15:27; 16:11), justice (15:25; 17:15; 21:7; 23:10–11; 29:26), familial and communal relations (10:1; 17:25; 19:26; 28:12; 29:2), authority (20:8, 26; 21:1; 29:4, 12, 14), and work (10:4–5; 18:9; 22:29; 27:23–27), just to name a few. The moral agent within Proverbs exists in a highly dynamic relationship with their environment.[176] The disposition of the moral agent and the actions or decisions that proceed from their character are viewed in relation. And these relations carry implicit moral obligations. One's character, decisions, and actions affect not only oneself but also the ethos of the household, the fabric of the community and, ultimately, one's relationship with YHWH (15:8, 29).

This theological perspective on moral agency is supported by two basic pillars in Proverbs's ethical vision: YHWH's rule over the cosmos as well as the inherent

175. Brown, *Wisdom's Wonder*, 15.

176. Von Rad, *Wisdom in Israel*, 301.

dignity of humans. The character-consequence nexus articulated by the materials in the anthology bears witness to YHWH's providential governance over all human activities: he is the one who rewards and punishes in accordance with his inscrutable timetable.[177] And the fact that all human beings, irrespective of their social standing, have a dignity that derives from their common Creator forms the theological basis for Proverbs's social ethics (14:31; 17:5; 22:2; 29:13). This vision of self-in-relation within God's world and under God's governance underlies Proverbs's worldview as well as its conception of virtue and moral obligation—the stuff that constitutes moral agency and the moral life. And this vision of self-in-relation mirrors the paradigm inherent in the structure of the Decalogue and summarized through the two greatest commandments: love God and love your neighbor (Mark 12:29–31).

Against this relational backdrop, it is not surprising that the ethical principles promoted in Proverbs reverberate throughout the canon. For example, the virtues of reverence for God (Prov 1:7; 1 Pet 2:17), respect for parents and the elderly (Prov 15:20; 20:29; 23:22; Exod 20:12; Lev 19:3; Rom 13:7; Eph 6:1; Col 3:20; 1 Tim 5:1), loving the other (Prov 10:12; 15:17; 25:21–22; Lev 19:18; Rom 12:20–21; Gal 5:14), generosity (Prov 11:24–26; 2 Cor 9:6–7), humility (Prov 3:34, 18:12; 22:4; Jas 4:6; 1 Pet 5:5), and integrity in business (Prov 20:10, 14, 23; 1 Tim 3:2; Titus 1:7, 11; 1 Pet 5:2) as well as the vices of lying, deceit and false oaths (Prov 6:19; 12:17, 20; 14:5; 19:5; Exod 20:16; Lev 19:11; Matt 5:33–37; Rom 13:9; 1 Tim 1:10; Jas 3:5–12; 5:12), slander (Prov 10:18; 16:28; 20:19; Lev 19:16; 2 Cor 12:20; Eph 4:31; 2 Tim 3:3), and judicial partiality (Prov 17:15, 23; 18:5; 1 Tim 5:21; Jas 2:9) are among many principles that mark the moral vision of Proverbs and the Christian life. Proverbs articulates and contextualizes its moral vision in a distinctive way. The distinctive nature of its discourse, however, does not suggest that Proverbs is a brand of ancient self-help literature. It is not a book primarily concerned with social success or personal happiness. It is a book concerned with wisdom and virtue that enables one to live rightly in relation to God, others, and the created order. In this respect, it provides the reader with the moral vision as well as the moral capacity to fulfill the creation mandate (Gen 1:26–28) by accurately representing or imaging God's wisdom and character within his creation.

177. Character-consequence is a more accurate designation than act-consequence in Proverbs, for the materials generally link consequences to character traits, attitudes, and lifestyles rather than to individual actions. While some argue that these consequences are built into the order of creation or the actions themselves, this mechanistic view of reward and punishment is unconvincing, for it fails to account for nature and function of a proverb, YHWH's intimate involvement in the process, and his inscrutable timing in the execution of retribution and reward. The sayings link character traits and lifestyles with particular consequences; however, they do not specify how or when these consequences will be carried out. Within the broader theological worldview of Proverbs, YHWH's governance of human activities and response to characters provides a framework in which to understand his fundamental role in retribution-reward. Boström, *The God of the Sages*, 90–133; Raymond C. Van Leeuwen, "Wealth and Poverty: System and Contradiction in Proverbs," *HS* 33 (1992): 25–36.

2. Wisdom and Creation

Creation is the arena of human activity as well as the overarching horizon of instruction in Proverbs. The order and symmetry woven into the fabric of the created world is valuable and instructive, for it reflects YHWH's wisdom (3:19–20). Together with humanity, creation is the object of Lady Wisdom's delight (8:31). And the distinct views of the world promoted by the various characters within the anthology model different ways of seeing and being in creation.[178] Cosmology and anthropology, creation and character are inextricably linked in Proverbs. Creation and its order serve as the necessary context and condition for the cultivation of moral character.[179] For the sages, creation is the classroom in which character is shaped, patterns of conduct and their consequences are revealed, and wisdom may be perceived.[180] The wise are those who observe the patterns within the natural and social order and seek to align their lives with those patterns in order to live in accordance with the grain of creation, to achieve some measure of success, and to flourish in relation to God, self, and others *within the world.*

The dance between cosmology and anthropology within Proverbs is delicate. Both are integral to the world projected in the anthology. And both are necessary for formulating a comprehensive view of the wise life within the world. The methodological danger is that one will play second fiddle to the other, that cosmology or anthropology will be subsumed under the other to the extent that the discrete tunes of one are muffled or even silenced by its counterpart.[181] Nonetheless, this danger should not detract from the theological payoff of the dialectic. The intimate relationship between cosmology and anthropology, creation and human experience within Proverbs reflects the intimate relationship between revelation and reason. Proverbs refuses to distinguish the sacred from the secular; it promotes an inclusive view of life that recognizes the goodness of the created world as well as the theological significance of ordinary human activities. This sentiment is captured by Gerhard von Rad:

"The experiences of the world were for [Israel] always divine experiences as well, and the experiences of God were for her experiences of the world."[182] YHWH and

178. Brown, *Wisdom's Wonder*, 16.

179. Oliver O'Donovan, *Resurrection and Moral Order: An Outline for Evangelical Ethics*, 2nd ed. (Grand Rapids: Eerdmans, 1994), 31–38.

180. Brown, *Wisdom's Wonder*, 5.

181. For an emphasis on the cosmology, see, e.g., Gese, *Lehre und Wirklichkeit*; Hans H. Schmid, *Gerechtigkeit als Weltordnung: Hintergrund und Geschichte des alttestamentlichen Gerechtigkeitsbegriffs*, BHT 40 (Tübingen: J. C. B. Mohr, 1968). For an emphasis on anthropology, see, e.g., Walther A. Zimmerli, "Concerning the Structure of Old Testament Wisdom," in *Studies in Ancient Israelite Wisdom*, ed. James L. Crenshaw; trans. B. W. Kovacs (New York: Ktav, 1976), 175–207; Walter Brueggemann, *In Man We Trust* (Atlanta: John Knox, 1972). For an attempt to balance the dialectic, see Leo G. Perdue, *Wisdom and Creation: The Theology of Wisdom Literature* (Nashville: Abingdon, 1994).

182. Von Rad, *Wisdom in Israel*, 62.

the world are not identical. As humans live within the world, however, they partake in creation, and, by implication, live in relation to YHWH. The delicate relationship between cosmology and anthropology in Proverbs situates all human conduct in the presence of the Creator. In this context, humans are not only invited to live wisely in relation to God, others, and the creatures but also to collaborate with creation and participate in the expansion of the kingdom as they anticipate the dawn of the new creation.

3. Wisdom and the Limits of Wisdom

From this ethical, theological, and creational perspective, it is necessary to reflect on wisdom and the limitations of human wisdom. Wisdom is a difficult term to define. Elsewhere in the Old Testament it refers to the skill of an artisan, that is, expertise in a particular craft (e.g., Exod 35:30–35; Jer 9:17; Ezek 27:8–9). While this definition looms in the semantic field of "wisdom" (חָכְמָה) in Proverbs, the meaning of the concept is much broader in the document. According to Proverbs, wisdom is both an intellectual as well as a moral quality;[183] it is an embodied skill, acquired and developed through interpersonal instruction and correction. As an embodied skill, wisdom is "cognitive *and* emotional *and* aesthetic";[184] it is knowledge of right living that emanates from a virtuous disposition and manifests itself through concrete actions. It encompasses the entirety of one's being: the mind, imagination, perception, affections, attitudes, tastes, actions, and speech. In view of its use within the anthology as well as its relation to the constellation of values within the preamble (1:2–7), wisdom may be defined as the "substance of virtue-osity."[185] It includes skill, knowledge, ability, and actions; but it is much more than the sum of these semantic parts.[186] It is the epitome of virtue and the moral life.

This general definition of wisdom provides a framework through which to understand its use within the anthology as well as its intimate relationship to virtue. But this definition represents only half of Proverb's story. Wisdom is available; wisdom is accessible (1:20–21; 8:1–6); wisdom is to be the pursued and acquired at all costs (2:4; 4:7). Nonetheless, human wisdom is insufficient; it is finite and limited. While this notion is foregrounded in Job and Qoheleth, it is acknowledged in Proverbs (cf. 16:1–2; 20:24; 27:1):

> There is this: a way that is straight before a person;
> but its end, ways to death. (14:12)

183. Fox, *Proverbs 1–9*, 32.
184. Fox, "The Epistemology of the Book of Proverbs," 684.
185. Brown, *Wisdom's Wonder*, 36.
186. Brown, *Wisdom's Wonder*, 36.

A person's heart plans his way,
but YHWH directs his step. (16:9)

Many plans are in a person's heart,
but the counsel of YHWH, it stands. (19:21)

There is no wisdom, and no understanding,
and no counsel before YHWH. (21:30)

These representative sayings describe the boundaries of human wisdom through the recognition of mortal limits, an awareness of inevitable contingencies, and a realization of the omnipotence, omniscience, and inscrutability of the divine. Wisdom is valuable; it is indispensable for the moral life. But human wisdom, by virtue of human finitude, is limited. This does not preclude humans from searching the wondrous wisdom of the divine. But it does prepare them to recognize that absolute knowledge is too wonderful; it's above humanity's pay grade. This should not evoke a sense of despair; rather, it should produce trust in YHWH and engender a renewed realization of one's creatureliness. After all, "creatureliness and finitude are constitutive of human being."[187] In fact, they serve as the ontological and epistemological conditions for relational dependence on the divine expressed through the fear of YHWH.

4. Wisdom, Jesus, and the New Testament

It is important to note that creatureliness and the wisdom of God merge in a profound way through the incarnation of Christ. As Paul declared, Jesus is "the wisdom of God" (1 Cor 1:24, cf. 1:30; Col 2:3), the human embodiment of God's wisdom as well as the key to unlocking the mystery of God's redemption and kingdom order. As the Gospels bear witness to Jesus's teaching, they reveal much more than a prophet, priest, and king. They depict a rabbi, or better, a wise man who employs aphoristic speech to undermine the traditional wisdom of his opponents and to communicate the eschatological realities that have broken into the present age and anticipate the new order to come.[188] As Paul reflects on the protological identity of Jesus, he incorporates expressions and attributes reminiscent of personified Wisdom (Prov 8:22–31), describing the Son as "the image of the invisible God"

187. Frances Young, *God's Presence: A Contemporary Recapitulation of Early Christianity*, Current Issues in Theology (Cambridge: Cambridge University Press, 2013), 136.

188. Ben Witherington III, *Jesus the Sage: The Pilgrimage of Wisdom* (Minneapolis: Fortress, 1994), 155–83; Stephen C. Barton, "Gospel Wisdom," in *Where Shall Wisdom Be Found?: Wisdom in the Bible, the Church and the Contemporary World*, ed. S. C. Barton (Edinburgh: T&T Clark, 1999), 93–110. Also, for James's use of particular wisdom forms, see Richard Bauckham, *James: Wisdom of James, Disciple of Jesus the Sage* (New York: Routledge, 1999), 35–56.

(Col 1:15a), "the firstborn of all creation" (Col 1:15b), "the beginning" (Col 1:18; cf. John 1:1–2), the one through whom "all things were created" (Col 1:16; cf. John 1:3), and the dwelling place of "all the fullness of God" (Col 1:19).[189] And as the epistles reflect on the wisdom of God's redemptive work and its implications for the church's life, the writers not only pray that God would grant members of these communities "wisdom," "understanding," and "knowledge" to comprehend the cosmic scope of Christ's redemption and animate their cruciform lives (Eph 1:17; 3:10; Phil 1:9; Col 1:9–10, 28; 2:2–3, 23; 3:16; Phlm 6);[190] they also call Christians to a life of obedience and wholeness that mirrors the ethical vision of Proverbs (Jas 1:2–4; 22–26; 2:12–13; 3:13–18, 17; 4:11–12; 5:7–11, 16, 19–20).[191]

The New Testament presents Jesus as the epitome of God's wisdom. Wisdom provided the New Testament writers with a theological category through which to describe the identity and deity of Jesus, the nature of his redemptive work, and its implications for the church's life. That is, Proverbs provided the New Testament writers with terms and concepts to describe Jesus as the quintessential wise man, his redemptive work as the climactic expression of God's wisdom, the cross as "the key to understanding reality in God's new eschatological age,"[192] and the proper response of communities and individuals to the crucified Christ.

Wisdom in general and the wisdom of Proverbs in particular play an important role in New Testament conceptions of Jesus's identity and the nature of the gospel, as well as kingdom ethics. These observations represent only the tip of the theological iceberg. Nonetheless, this tip provides a point of reference from which to explore the size and scope of the theological riches that lie beneath the surface of Proverbs and contribute to the Christian's understanding of the Messiah, themselves, wisdom, virtue, and human flourishing in God's good world.

A Brief Note on Discourse Linguistics

The book of Proverbs inculcates wisdom and virtue through diverse poetic forms. In light of the intimate relationship between pedagogy and poetic form in Proverbs, the commentary that follows will employ an approach that attends to the linguistic features of each discourse unit. That is, this commentary will focus on the

189. For the way in which Prov 8 fueled the Arian controversy and was used in early discussions of Christology, see Jaroslav Pelikan, *The Christian Tradition: A History of the Development of Doctrine, Volume 1: The Emergence of the Catholic Tradition (100–600)* (Chicago: University of Chicago Press, 1971), 186–97; Treier, *Proverbs and Ecclesiastes*, 51–57.

190. Bartholomew and O'Dowd, *Old Testament Wisdom Literature*, 250–51.

191. Bauckham, *James*, 177–85, 203–5; Bartholomew and O'Dowd, *Old Testament Wisdom Literature*, 256–59.

192. Richard B. Hays, "Wisdom According to Paul," in *Where Shall Wisdom Be Found?*, ed. S. C. Barton (Edinburgh: T&T Clark, 1999), 116.

poetic parts of each discourse and their relation to the whole. At the microlevel, it will explore the syntax and semantics of clauses, devoting specific attention to word order within specific clauses.[193] This exploration of the syntactical parts will form the basis for the commentary's analysis of macrolevel clause relationships, which will include attention to discourse markers, patterns of constructions, and ellipses, as well as wordplay and sound play.[194] Together, these micro- and macrolevel forms of analysis serve a common goal: to discern *how* the form and architecture of the poetic discourses in Proverbs convey *meaning*.

Brief Outline of Proverbs

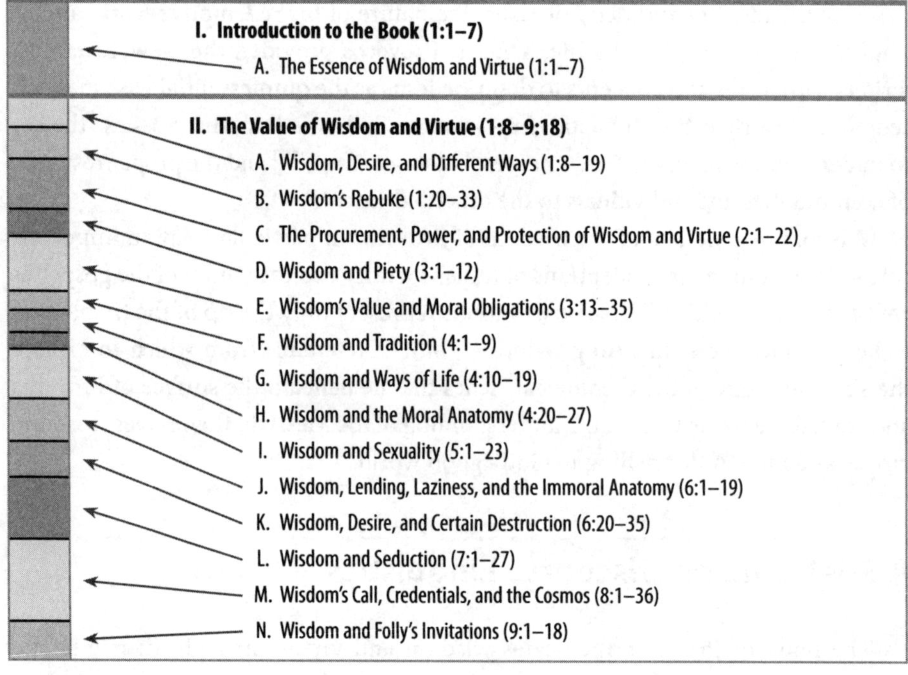

193. Robert D. Holmstedt, "Word Order in the Book of Proverbs," in *Seeking Out the Wisdom of the Ancients: Essays Offered to Honor Michael V. Fox on the Occasion of His Sixty-Fifth Birthday*, ed. R. L. Troxel, K. G. Friebel, and D. R. Magary (Winona Lake, IN: Eisenbrauns, 2005), 135–54.

194. This commentary will utilize terms and concepts from *IBHS*; Joüon; *BHRG*; Thomas P. McCreesh, *Biblical Sound and Sense: Poetic Sound Patterns in Proverbs 10–29*, JSOTSup 128 (Sheffield: Sheffield Academic, 1991); and Cynthia L. Miller, "A Linguistic Approach to Ellipsis in Biblical Poetry," *BBR* 13 (2003): 251–70.

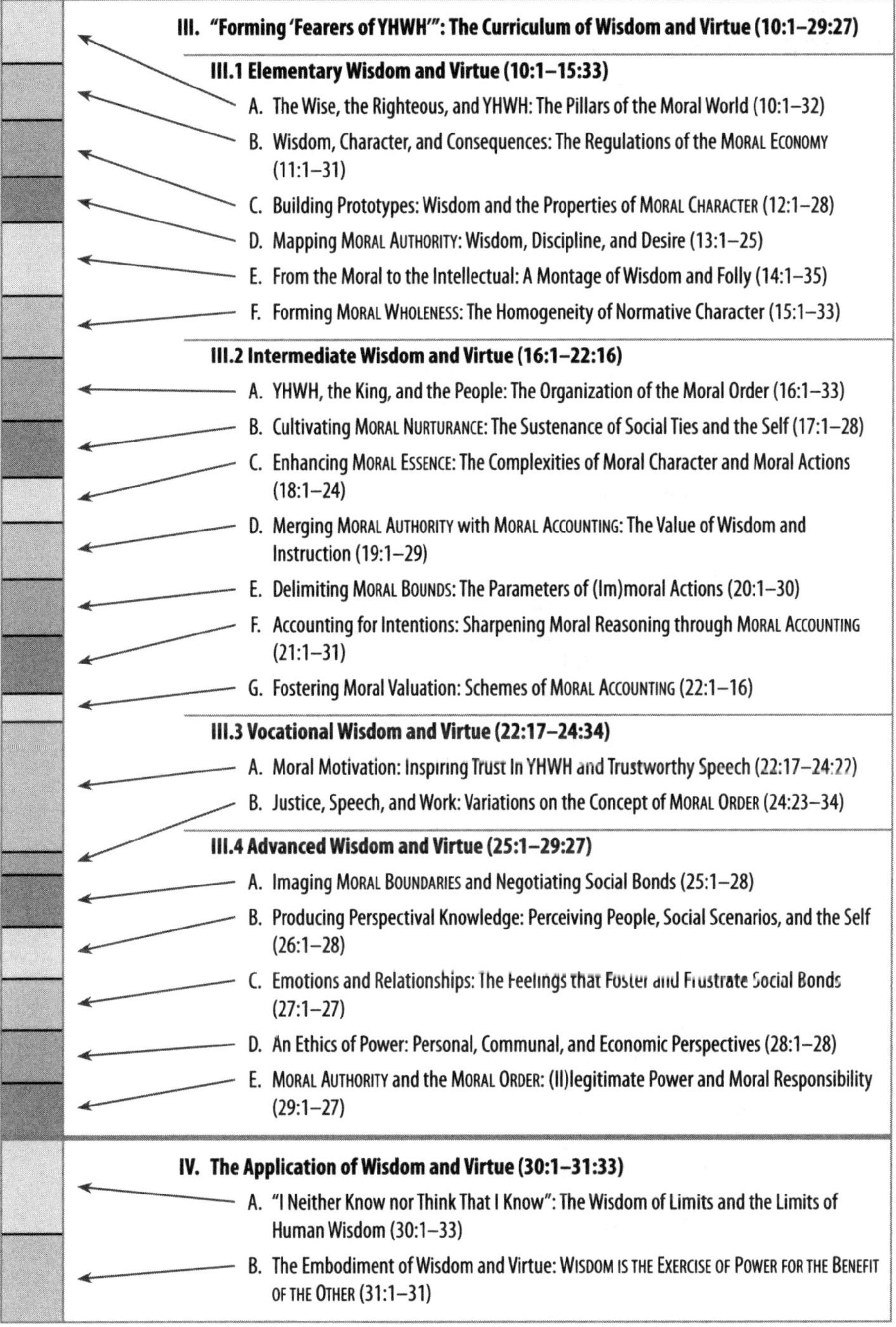
III. "Forming 'Fearers of YHWH'": The Curriculum of Wisdom and Virtue (10:1–29:27)
III.1 Elementary Wisdom and Virtue (10:1–15:33)
A. The Wise, the Righteous, and YHWH: The Pillars of the Moral World (10:1–32)
B. Wisdom, Character, and Consequences: The Regulations of the MORAL ECONOMY (11:1–31)
C. Building Prototypes: Wisdom and the Properties of MORAL CHARACTER (12:1–28)
D. Mapping MORAL AUTHORITY: Wisdom, Discipline, and Desire (13:1–25)
E. From the Moral to the Intellectual: A Montage of Wisdom and Folly (14:1–35)
F. Forming MORAL WHOLENESS: The Homogeneity of Normative Character (15:1–33)
III.2 Intermediate Wisdom and Virtue (16:1–22:16)
A. YHWH, the King, and the People: The Organization of the Moral Order (16:1–33)
B. Cultivating MORAL NURTURANCE: The Sustenance of Social Ties and the Self (17:1–28)
C. Enhancing MORAL ESSENCE: The Complexities of Moral Character and Moral Actions (18:1–24)
D. Merging MORAL AUTHORITY with MORAL ACCOUNTING: The Value of Wisdom and Instruction (19:1–29)
E. Delimiting MORAL BOUNDS: The Parameters of (Im)moral Actions (20:1–30)
F. Accounting for Intentions: Sharpening Moral Reasoning through MORAL ACCOUNTING (21:1–31)
G. Fostering Moral Valuation: Schemes of MORAL ACCOUNTING (22:1–16)
III.3 Vocational Wisdom and Virtue (22:17–24:34)
A. Moral Motivation: Inspiring Trust in YHWH and Trustworthy Speech (22:17–24:22)
B. Justice, Speech, and Work: Variations on the Concept of MORAL ORDER (24:23–34)
III.4 Advanced Wisdom and Virtue (25:1–29:27)
A. Imaging MORAL BOUNDARIES and Negotiating Social Bonds (25:1–28)
B. Producing Perspectival Knowledge: Perceiving People, Social Scenarios, and the Self (26:1–28)
C. Emotions and Relationships: The Feelings that Foster and Frustrate Social Bonds (27:1–27)
D. An Ethics of Power: Personal, Communal, and Economic Perspectives (28:1–28)
E. MORAL AUTHORITY and the MORAL ORDER: (Il)legitimate Power and Moral Responsibility (29:1–27)
IV. The Application of Wisdom and Virtue (30:1–31:33)
A. "I Neither Know nor Think That I Know": The Wisdom of Limits and the Limits of Human Wisdom (30:1–33)
B. The Embodiment of Wisdom and Virtue: WISDOM IS THE EXERCISE OF POWER FOR THE BENEFIT OF THE OTHER (31:1–31)

Outline of Proverbs

I. Introduction to the Book (1:1–7)

A. The Essence of Wisdom and Virtue (1:1–7)
  1. The Title(1:1)
  2. The Goal: The Inculcation of Wisdom and Virtue (1:2–6)
    a. Intellectual Virtue (1:2)
    b. Instrumental and Moral Virtues (1:3)
    c. Instrumental and Intellectual Virtues (1:4–5)
    d. Interpretive Dexterity (1:6)
  3. The Prerequisite for the Inculcation of Wisdom and Virtue (1:7)

II. The Value of Wisdom and Virtue (1:8–9:18)

A. Wisdom, Desire, and Different Ways (1:8–19)
  1. The Introductory Exhortation (1:8–9)
    a. The Admonition (1:8)
    b. The Motivation (1:9)
  2. The Lesson: Sinners, Speech, and Steps (1:10–18)
    a. The General Command: Temptation and the Will (1:10)
    b. The Sinners' Deceptive Speech and Desires (1:11–14)
      (1) The Invitation (1:11–12)
      (2) The Promised Reward (1:13–14)
    c. The Speech Interpreted: Wrong Ways and Misplaced Desire (1:15–18)
      (1) The Command (1:15)
      (2) The Rationale (1:16)
      (3) A Proverb: The Seeing Bird (1:17)
      (4) The Ironic Fate of Blind Sinners (1:18)
  3. The Conclusion (1:19)

B. Wisdom's Rebuke (1:20–33)
  1. The Prelude to Wisdom's Rebuke (1:20–21)
  2. Wisdom's Rebuke (1:22–31)
    a. Wisdom's Direct Rebuke (1:22–27)
      (1) The Addressees (1:22)
      (2) The Rebuke (1:23)
      (3) The Response of the Addressees (1:24–25)
      (4) Wisdom's Response (1:26–27)
    b. Wisdom's Indirect Rebuke (1:28–31)
      (1) Wisdom's Response (1:28)
      (2) The Response of the Addressees (1:29–30)
      (3) The Reward Promised the Addressees (1:31)
  3. Wisdom's Conclusion (1:32–33)
    a. The Fate of the Unreceptive (1:32)
    b. The Fate of the Receptive (1:33)

C. The Procurement, Power, and Protection of Wisdom and Virtue (2:1–22)
  1. The Preconditions for Wisdom's Procurement (2:1–4)
    a. A Receptive Posture (2:1–2)
    b. An Active Pursuit (2:3–4)

2. The Procurement of Wisdom (2:5–8)
   a. The Essence of the Procurement (2:5)
   b. The Reason for the Procurement (2:6–7)
   c. The Purpose of the Procurement (2:8)
3. The Procurement of Virtue (2:9–22)
   a. The Essence of the Procurement (2:9)
   b. The Reason for the Procurement (2:10–11)
   c. The Purpose of the Procurement (2:12–19)
      (1) The Way of the Evildoer (2:12–15)
      (2) The Way of the Strange Woman (2:16–19)
   d. The Result of the Procurement (2:20–22)

D. Wisdom and Piety (3:1–12)
1. The Retention and Internalization of Parental Teaching (3:1–4)
   a. The Retention of Parental Teaching (3:1)
   b. The Motivation for Retention (3:2)
   c. The Internalization of Virtue (3:3)
   d. The Promise of Internalization (3:4)
2. The Contours of the Pious Life (3:5–10)
   a. The Disposition and Practice of Dependence (3:5–6)
   b. The Disposition and Practice of Humility (3:7–8)
   c. The Disposition and Practice of Homage (3:9–10)
3. A Pious Perspective (3:11–12)
   a. A Pious Attitude (3:11)
   b. The Reason for the Attitude (3:12)

E. Wisdom's Value and Moral Obligations (3:13–35)
1. Wisdom and the Good Life (3:13–18)
   a. Wisdom and Happiness (3:13)
   b. The Rationale for Happiness (3:14–18)
2. Wisdom and the Good Creation (3:19–20)
3. Wisdom and the Secure Life (3:21–26)
   a. The Retention of Wisdom (3:21)
   b. The Reward for Retention: Security (3:22–24)
   c. The Reassurance of the Reward (3:25–26)
4. Wisdom and the Good Neighborhood (3:27–35)
   a. The Characteristics of the Good Neighborhood (3:27–30)
   b. Character and the Good Neighborhood (3:31–35)

F. Wisdom and Tradition (4:1–9)
1. The Father's Exhortation (4:1–2)
2. The Grandfather's Exhortation (4:3–9)
   a. The Setting of the Exhortation (4:3–4a)
   b. The Substance of the Exhortation (4:4b–9)
      (1) The Exhortation (4:4b–5)
      (2) The Motivation (4:6)
      (3) The Exhortation (4:7)
      (4) The Motivation (vv. 8–9)

G. Wisdom and Ways of Life (4:10–19)
1. Introductory Exhortation (4:10)
   a. The Admonition (4:10a)
   b. The Motivation (4:10b)

2. The Ways of Life (4:11–17)
   a. The Way of Wisdom (4:11–13)
      (1) The Nature of the Way (4:11–12)
      (2) The Compass for the Way (4:13)
   b. The Way of the Wicked (4:14–17)
      (1) Avoiding the Way (4:14–15)
      (2) The Rationale (4:16–17)
3. Conclusion: Wisdom and Ways (4:18–19)

H. Wisdom and the Moral Anatomy (4:20–27)
1. Introductory Exhortation (4:20–22)
   a. The Admonitions (4:20–21)
   b. The Motivation (4:22)
2. The Headquarters of the Moral Anatomy (4:23)
3. The Movements of the Moral Anatomy (4:24–27)

I. Wisdom and Sexuality (5:1–23)
1. Introductory Exhortation (5:1–2)
   a. The Admonitions (5:1)
   b. The Motivation (5:2)
2. The Price of Sexual Promiscuity (5:3–14)
   a. The Danger: A Portrait of the Strange Woman (5:3–6)
   b. The Renewed Exhortation (5:7–8)
   c. The Price of Promiscuity (5:9–14)
      (1) The Social Price (5:9)
      (2) The Economic Price (5:10)
      (3) The Physical Price (5:11)
      (4) The Emotional Price (5:12–14)
3. The Satisfaction of Marital Sex (5:15–20)
   a. A Wellspring of Satisfaction (5:15–18)
   b. An Enchanting Doe (5:19–20)
4. The Conclusion: Divine Omniscience and the Retribution Principle (5:21–23)
   a. The Rationale: YHWH's Omniscience (5:21)
   b. The Reward (5:22–23)

J. Wisdom, Lending, Laziness, and the Immoral Anatomy (6:1–19)
1. Surety and Strangers (6:1–5)
   a. The Dangerous Situation (6:1–2)
   b. The Self-Deprecating Course of Action (6:3–5)
2. Industry and Indolence (6:6–11)
   a. The Industry of the Ant (6:6–8)
   b. The Indolence of the Sluggard (6:9–11)
3. A Sketch of the Scoundrel (6:12–19)
   a. The Immoral Anatomy of the Scoundrel (6:12–14)
   b. The Sudden Ruin of the Scoundrel (6:15)
   c. A Register of Revulsion (6:16–19)
      (1) The Introduction (6:16)
      (2) Abominable Body Parts (6:17–18)
      (3) Abominable Character Types (6:19)

K. Wisdom, Desire, and Certain Destruction (6:20–35)
1. The Introduction: The Retention of Parental Instruction (6:20–24)
   a. The Internalization and Remembrance of Parental Instruction (6:20–21)

- b. The Guidance and Protection of Wisdom (6:22–24)
  - (1) Wisdom's Guidance (6:22–23)
  - (2) Wisdom's Protection (6:24)
- 2. The Lesson: Misdirected Desire, Adultery, and Destruction (6:25–32)
  - a. Internal Desire and External Capture (6:25–26)
  - b. The Fiery Consequences of Misdirected Desire and Adultery (6:27–29)
  - c. The Senselessness and Self-Destruction of Misplaced Desire and Adultery (6:30–32)
- 3. The Conclusion: The Certain Punishment of Misdirected Desire and Adultery (6:33–35)
  - a. The Inevitable Punishment for Misplaced Desire and Adultery (6:33)
  - b. The Rationale for the Inevitable Punishment (6:34–35)

L. Wisdom and Seduction (7:1–27)
- 1. Introductory Exhortation: The Retention and Protection of Wisdom (7:1–5)
  - a. The Admonitions: The Retention of Wisdom (7:1–4)
  - b. The Purpose: The Protection of Wisdom (6:5)
- 2. The Lesson: A Cautionary Tale (7:6–23)
  - a. The Setting: Seeing the Senseless (7:6–9)
  - b. The Central Subject: Seeing the Woman (7:10–13)
  - c. The Speech: Hearing the Seduction (7:14–20)
    - (1) The Seductive Preparations (7:14–17)
    - (2) The Seductive Proposition (7:18–20)
  - d. The Consequences of Submitting to Seduction (7:21–23)
- 3. The Conclusion: The Woman, Her Ways, and Her House (7:24–27)
  - a. The Admonitions (7:24–25)
  - b. The Motivation (7:26–27)

M. Wisdom's Call, Credentials, and the Cosmos (8:1–36)
- 1. The Introduction to Wisdom's Encomium (8:1–3)
  - a. The Introduction of Wisdom (8:1)
  - b. The Setting of Wisdom's Speech (8:2–3)
- 2. Wisdom's Opening Exhortation (8:4–11)
  - a. Wisdom's Appeal (8:4–6)
  - b. Wisdom's Virtuous Speech (8:7–9)
  - c. Wisdom's Admonition (8:10–11)
- 3. Wisdom's Credentials and Function in the Present World (8:12–21)
  - a. Wisdom's Credentials (8:12–13)
  - b. Wisdom's Function in the Terrestrial Realm (8:14–16)
  - c. Wisdom's Gifts (8:17–21)
- 4. Wisdom's Preeminence and Position in the Primordial World (8:22–31)
  - a. Wisdom's Emergence before Creation (8:22–26)
  - b. Wisdom's Presence at Creation (8:27–29)
  - c. Wisdom's Activity after Creation (8:30–31)
- 5. Wisdom's Climactic Exhortation (8:32–36)
  - a. The Exhortation (8:32–33)
  - b. The Blessing (8:34)
  - c. The Consequences (8:35–36)

N. Wisdom and Folly's Invitations (9:1–18)
- 1. Lady Wisdom's Banquet (9:1–6)
  - a. The Setting of the Banquet (9:1–3)
    - (1) Wisdom's Preparations (9:1–2)
    - (2) Wisdom's Emissaries and the Location of her Call (9:3)

b. The Invitation to Wisdom's Banquet (9:4–6)
   (1) Wisdom's General Summons (9:4)
   (2) Wisdom's Specific Offer (9:5–6)
2. Character, the Conditions, and the Consequences of the Choice (9:7–12)
   a. The Ineducability of the Scoffer/Wicked (9:7–8a)
   b. The Educability of the Wise/Righteous (9:8b–9)
   c. The Key to Educability (9:10)
   d. The Reward of the Educable (9:11)
   e. The Conclusion: Character, Conditions, and Consequences (9:12)
3. Woman Folly's Banquet (9:13–18)
   a. The Setting of the Banquet (9:13–15)
      (1) The Character of the Hostess (9:13)
      (2) Folly's Location and Call (9:14–15)
   b. The Invitation to Folly's Banquet (9:16–17)
      (1) Folly's General Summons (9:16)
      (2) Folly's Specific Offer (9:17)
   c. The Fate of Folly's Guests (9:18)

III. "Forming 'Fearers of YHWH'": The Curriculum of Wisdom and Virtue (10:1–29:27)

III.1 Elementary Wisdom and Virtue (10:1–15:33)

A. The Wise, the Righteous, and YHWH: The Pillars of the Moral World (10:1–32)
   1. Title (10:1a)
   2. The Wise, the Righteous, and YHWH: The Pillars of the Moral World (10:1b–32)

B. Wisdom, Character, and Consequences: The Regulations of the MORAL ECONOMY (11:1–31)

C. Building Prototypes: Wisdom and the Properties of MORAL CHARACTER (12:1–28)

D. Mapping MORAL AUTHORITY: Wisdom, Discipline, and Desire (13:1–25)

E. From the Moral to the Intellectual: A Montage of Wisdom and Folly (14:1–35)

F. Forming MORAL WHOLENESS: The Homogeneity of Normative Character (15:1–33)

III.2 Intermediate Wisdom and Virtue (16:1–22:16)

A. YHWH, the King, and the People: The Organization of the Moral Order (16:1–33)

B. Cultivating MORAL NURTURANCE: The Sustenance of Social Ties and the Self (17:1–28)

C. Enhancing MORAL ESSENCE: The Complexities of Moral Character and Moral Actions (18:1–24)

D. Merging MORAL AUTHORITY with MORAL ACCOUNTING: The Value of Wisdom and Instruction (19:1–29)

E. Delimiting MORAL BOUNDS: The Parameters of (Im)moral Actions (20:1–30)

F. Accounting for Intentions: Sharpening Moral Reasoning through MORAL ACCOUNTING (21:1–31)

G. Fostering Moral Valuation: Schemes of MORAL ACCOUNTING (22:1–16)

III.3 Vocational Wisdom and Virtue (22:17–24:34)

A. Moral Motivation: Inspiring Trust in YHWH and Trustworthy Speech (22:17–24:22)
   1. Formal Introduction: Saying 1 (22:17–21)
      a. Exhortation and Motivation (22:17–18)
      b. The Theological Purpose of the "Words of the Wise" (22:19)
      c. The Formational Purpose and Result of the "Words of the Wise" (22:20–21)
   2. Saying 2 (22:22–23)
   3. Saying 3 (22:24–25)
   4. Saying 4 (22:26–27)

5. Saying 5 (22:28)
6. Saying 6 (22:29)
7. Saying 7 (23:1–3)
8. Saying 8 (23:4–5)
9. Saying 9 (23:6–8)
10. Saying 10 (23:9)
11. Saying 11 (23:10–11)
12. Saying 12 (23:12–14)
13. Saying 13 (23:15–16)
14. Saying 14 (23:17–18)
15. Saying 15 (23:19–21)
16. Saying 16 (23:22–25)
17. Saying 17 (23:26–28)
18. Saying 18 (23:29–35)
19. Saying 19 (24:1–2)
20. Saying 20 (24:3–4)
21. Saying 21 (24:5–6)
22. Saying 22 (24:7)
23. Saying 23 (24:8–9)
24. Saying 24 (24:10)
25. Saying 25 (24:11–12)
26. Saying 26 (24:13–14)
27. Saying 27 (24:15–16)
28. Saying 28 (24:17–18)
29. Saying 29 (24:19–20)
30. Saying 30 (24:21–22)

B. Justice, Speech, and Work: Variations on the Concept of Moral Order (24:23–34)

III.4 Advanced Wisdom and Virtue (25:1–29:27)

A. Imaging Moral Boundaries and Negotiating Social Bonds (25:1–28)
   1. The Title (25:1)
   2. Imaging Moral Boundaries and Negotiating Social Bonds (25:2–28)
      a. Establishing Epistemological Boundaries and Removing Moral Impurity (25:2–5)
      b. Negotiating Social Relations (25:6–15)
      c. Negotiating Social Conflict (25:16–27)
      d. The (In)stability of Moral Bounds (25:28)

B. Producing Perspectival Knowledge: Perceiving People, Social Scenarios, and the Self (26:1–28)

C. Emotions and Relationships: The Feelings that Foster and Frustrate Social Bonds (27:1–27)

D. An Ethics of Power: Personal, Communal, and Economic Perspectives (28:1–28)

E. Moral Authority and the Moral Order: (Il)legitimate Power and Moral Responsibility (29:1–27)

IV. The Application of Wisdom and Virtue (30:1–31:33)

A. "I Neither Know nor Think I Know": The Wisdom of Limits and the Limits of Human Wisdom (30:1–33)
   1. The Title: The Performance Context of the Words of Agur (30:1a–b)
   2. The Burden of Agur (30:1c–9)
      a. Agur's Humble Confession: The Epistemological Limits of Humans (30:1c–4)
      b. Agur's Dependence: The Relational Resolution to the Epistemological Limits of Humans (30:5–6)
      c. Agur's Prayer: The Embodiment of Humble Dependence (30:7–9)

3. Placing the Burden on the Reader (30:10–33)
    a. Defending the Defenseless (30:10)
    b. A Devouring Generation (30:11–14)
    c. A Devouring Animal (30:15a)
    d. Devouring Things that are Never Satisfied (30:15b–16)
    e. Animals Devouring an Immoral Animal (30:17)
    f. The Wonder of Ways (30:18–20)
    g. The "World Upside Down" (30:21–23)
    h. Success through Limits (30:24–28)
    i. Stride and Self-Exaltation (30:29–31)
    j. Silencing the Arrogance of Self-Exaltation (30:32–33)

B. The Embodiment of Wisdom and Virtue: WISDOM IS THE EXERCISE OF POWER FOR THE BENEFIT OF THE OTHER (31:1–31)
1. The Words of Lemuel (31:1–9)
    a. The Title (31:1)
    b. The Clamor for Attention (31:2)
    c. Admonitions regarding the Exercise of Power (31:3–9)
        (1) Self-Interested Satisfaction: Sex (31:3)
        (2) Self-Interested Satisfaction: Drink (31:4–5)
        (3) Alleviating the Other through Drink (31:6–7)
        (4) Exercising Power for the Benefit of Others (31:8–9)
2. The Poem of the Valiant Woman (31:10–31)
    a. The Exercise of Power for the Benefit of the Household (31:10–18)
    b. The Exercise of Power for the Benefit of the Household and the Poor (31:19–20)
    c. The Exercise of Power for the Benefit of the Household and the Community (31:21–29)
    d. True Beauty and its Recognition (31:30–31)

Introduction to the Book

Main Idea of Proverbs 1:1–7

As the introduction to the book of Proverbs, the preamble serves as the course syllabus for the anthology, delineating the learning outcomes, addressees, and prerequisite for its instruction in wisdom and virtue.

Literary Context of Proverbs 1:1–7

When read within the broad literary context of Proverbs, the preamble orients the reader to the design and content of the anthology. The title shares similarities with other titles within the book (1:1; 10:1a; 25:1), establishing a measure of coherence among the collections and initiating an intratextual dialogue about the relationship between the materials in Proverbs and the biography of Solomon. The preamble introduces key terms and concepts that are reiterated, expanded, and nuanced across the book's instruction in wisdom and virtue (1:2–7). Among these term and concepts, the "fear of YHWH" attunes readers not only to the requisite mode of being for the acquisition of wisdom and virtue, but also to the design and content of Proverbs. The "fear of YHWH" is mentioned at critical junctures in the anthology. It's placement at the climax of the preamble (1:7), at the end of the book's introduction (9:10), and at the conclusion of Proverbs (31:30) creates an envelope around the instructional material, indicating that the fear of YHWH is the beginning of wisdom, the ontological ground for growth in wisdom, and an embodied life of wisdom. Moreover, the placement of the fear of YWH near the center of the anthology sensitizes readers to the content of Proverbs. According to Prov 15:33, the fear of YHWH is instruction in wisdom, that is, the content of wisdom's instruction in Proverbs.

➦ **I. Introduction to the Book (1:1–7)**

II. The Value of Wisdom and Virtue (1:8–9:18)

III. "Forming 'Fearers of YHWH'": The Curriculum of Wisdom and Virtue (10:1–29:27)

III.1 Elementary Wisdom and Virtue (10:1–15:33)

III.2 Intermediate Wisdom and Virtue (16:1–22:16)

III.3 Vocational Wisdom and Virtue (22:17–24:34)

III.4 Advanced Wisdom and Virtue (25:1–29:27)

IV. The Application of Wisdom and Virtue (30:1–31:31)

CHAPTER 1

Proverbs 1:1–7

A. The Essence of Wisdom and Virtue

Main Idea of the Passage

The preamble indicates that the book of Proverbs seeks to (trans)form one's character through the inculcation of wisdom and virtue. This goal is a lifelong process of intellectual, moral, and practical formation that emanates from a perspectival posture engendered by the fear of YHWH.

Literary Context of 1:1–7

As the introduction to Proverbs, the preamble captures the essence of the document's purpose and provides a distillation of its agenda. Within the broader literary context of the anthology, it functions in at least five ways. First, the preamble identifies the poetic medium of the book's instruction: proverbs. Second, the preamble describes the book's aim and method of delivery. Similar to the structure of a course syllabus, it defines the document's objectives, explains its agenda, and answers those questions looming in the minds of most students, questions like, "Why does this course matter? How does it contribute to my education?" Third, by addressing these issues, the preamble calibrates the expectations of readers by identifying the document's pedagogical program and intended results (1:5–6). Fourth, the preamble provides a glossary of key terms, concepts, and character types to help the reader navigate the materials, understand their message, and internalize their teaching. And fifth, the preamble delineates the fundamental prerequisite for achieving the document's goal: the fear of YHWH. This requisite posture is a recurrent theme within the book; it is cast at key junctures within the document and forms a literary envelope around the book as a whole (1:7; 9:10; 31:30). Its contribution to the structure and rhetorical strategy of the anthology is apparent through its use at the close of the preamble (1:7), the end of the prologue (9:10), the center of the book (15:33), and the document's conclusion (31:30), where it moves from the abstract to the concrete, from a requisite posture to an embodied way of life.

In light of the various ways in which the preamble functions within the broader literary context of Proverbs, it is difficult to overestimate its significance. As the entryway into the book, this coherent unit serves as the interpretive lens through which to understand the nature, function, and goal of the anthology as a whole.

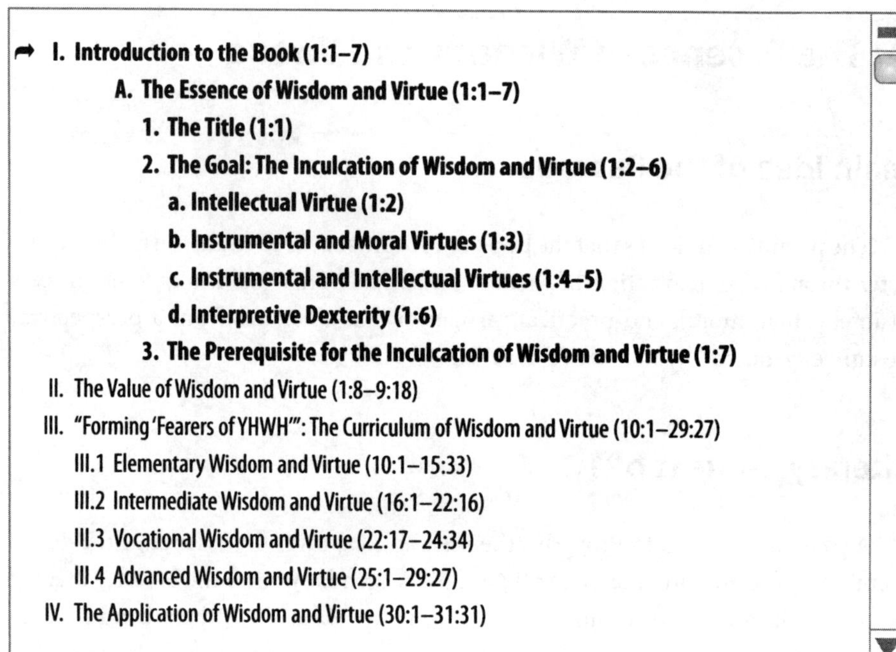

Translation and Exegetical Outline

(See page 107.)

Proverbs 1:1–7

Verse	Hebrew	Translation	Outline
			Macro Unit I: Introduction to the Book (1:1–7)
			A. The Essence of Wisdom and Virtue (1:1–7)
1	מִשְׁלֵי שְׁלֹמֹה בֶן־דָּוִד מֶלֶךְ יִשְׂרָאֵל	The proverbs of Solomon, son of David, king of Israel.	1. The Title (1:1)
			2. The Goal: The Inculcation of Wisdom and Virtue (1:2–6)
2a	לָדַעַת חָכְמָה וּמוּסָר	For learning wisdom and instruction,	a. Intellectual Virtue (1:2)
2b	לְהָבִין אִמְרֵי בִינָה	for understanding insightful words,	
3	לָקַחַת מוּסַר הַשְׂכֵּל צֶדֶק וּמִשְׁפָּט וּמֵישָׁרִים	for acquiring instruction in prudent living: righteousness, justice, and uprightness,	b. Instrumental and Moral Virtues (1:3)
4a	לָתֵת לִפְתָאיִם עָרְמָה	for giving to the uncommitted shrewdness,	c. Instrumental and Intellectual Virtues (1:4–5)
4b	לְנַעַר דַּעַת וּמְזִמָּה	to the young, knowledge and discretion,	
5a	יִשְׁמַע חָכָם וְיוֹסֶף לֶקַח	so the wise may hear and increase instruction,	
5b	וְנָבוֹן תַּחְבֻּלוֹת יִקְנֶה	and one with understanding may acquire guidance,	
6a	לְהָבִין מָשָׁל וּמְלִיצָה	for understanding a proverb and an allusive saying,	d. Interpretive Dexterity (1:6)
6b	דִּבְרֵי חֲכָמִים וְחִידֹתָם	the words of the wise and their riddles.	
7a	יִרְאַת יְהוָה רֵאשִׁית דָּעַת	The fear of YHWH is the beginning of knowledge;	3. The Prerequisite for the Inculcation of Wisdom and Virtue (1:7)
7b	חָכְמָה וּמוּסָר אֱוִילִים בָּזוּ	wisdom and instruction fools despise.	

Structure and Literary Form

Similar to Egyptian instructional texts, the preamble summarizes the aim and agenda of the anthology, namely, the (trans)formation of character through the inculcation of wisdom and virtue.[1] As a self-contained syntactical unit, the title sets the stage for this curricular outline, creating an interpretive frame that associates the diverse materials in the book with the biography of Israel's quintessential wise man: Solomon (v. 1a).[2] Against the backdrop of this interpretive frame, the text shifts to a sequence of purpose clauses, which specify the discrete virtues the document seeks to instill within readers (vv. 2–6). These virtues are not a hodgepodge of terms and concepts within the semantic field of wisdom; rather, they are a carefully constructed sequence of ethical values. When viewed through the general categories of virtue, it appears the values delineated in vv. 2–7 are cast in the form of a chiasm:[3]

A Comprehensive, intellectual values (v. 2a)
  B Literary expressions of wisdom (v. 2b)
    C Instrumental virtue (v. 3a)
      D Moral, communal virtues (v. 3b)
    C′ Instrumental virtues (vv. 4–5)
  B′ Literary expressions of wisdom (v. 6)
A′ Comprehensive, intellectual virtues (v. 7)

These categories illuminate the distinctive types of virtues the document seeks to inculcate in readers. And the placement of specific moral or communal virtues in the nucleus of the prologue's purpose statement identifies their importance in Proverbs's project of education for character formation.

The categories of virtue capture the multifaceted pedagogical agenda of Proverbs and orient one to the potential design of the preamble. The same is true of structural proposals that attend to the literary-aesthetic aspects of the preamble.[4] When the preamble is assessed from a syntactical perspective, however, a different blueprint emerges. As noted above, like the other titles and subtitles in Proverbs

1. "The Instruction of Ptahhotep" (*AEL* 1:61–80); "The Satire of the Trades" (*AEL* 1:184–92); "The Instruction of Amenemope" (*AEL* 2:146–63); Christa Kayatz, *Studien zu Proverbien 1–9* (Neukirchen-Vluyn: Neukirchener Verlag, 1966), 24–25. For discussion of ancient Near Eastern texts that are comparable to Proverbs, see the introduction, Ancient Near Eastern Instructional Literature.

2. Mroczek, *The Literary Imagination in Jewish Antiquity*, 51–85.

3. This structural model is taken from Brown, *Wisdom's Wonder*, 32. Cf. Timothy J. Sandoval, "Revisiting the Prologue of Proverbs," *JBL* 126 (2007): 473.

4. Sandoval, "Revisiting the Prologue of Proverbs," 471–73.

(10:1; 24:23; 25:1; 30:1; 31:1), v. 1 constitutes an independent grammatical unit.[5] The chain of *lamed* + infinitives construct in vv. 2–4 and v. 6, by contrast, are subordinate purposes clauses. These purposes clauses are cast in parallel relationship with one another. And they are dependent upon a main clause. Some identify the imperfects in v. 5 as the main clause.[6] This syntactical construal of the preamble suggests that the "wise" represents the ideal, intended addressee of the book (v. 5), the person who can actualize the anthology's goal (vv. 2–4).[7] What's more, this syntactical construal identifies a rhetorical shift in the preamble: it moves from the pedagogical purpose of the anthology (vv. 2–4) to an invitation for the ideal addressee to engage the book's purposes (vv. 5–6).[8]

The verbs in v. 5 are viable candidates for the main clause in the preamble. But they are not the only candidates. As the climax of the preamble, v. 7 may also serve as the main clause. Two factors seem to legitimize this reading. The first is the repetition of the root ידע ("learning," v. 2a; "knowledge," v. 7a), as well as the nouns "wisdom" (חָכְמָה, vv. 2a, 7b) and "instruction" (מוּסָר, vv. 2a, 7b), which form a literary envelope around the preamble proper. The second concerns the pattern ל + infinitive construct, followed by an imperfect.[9] This pattern occurs elsewhere in Prov 1–9 (2:2, 5; 5:2; cf. 8:21). These occurrences indicate that the imperfect adopts the sense of the preceding ל + infinitive construct. The difference between the forms "is purely formal, as both infinitives and imperfects may head purpose clauses."[10] On this reading, the imperfect verbs in v. 5 continue the string of subordinate purpose clauses, each of which are dependent on v. 7.[11] Far from representing an independent saying situated at the conclusion of the preamble, v. 7 constitutes the main clause, expressing the fundamental prerequisite for achieving Proverbs's pedagogical vision. Put differently, this construal of the syntax indicates that neither "the proverbs of Solomon" (v. 1a) nor the "wise" (v. 5a) serve as the agents for actualizing the goal of the anthology; rather, the goal of the anthology is realized through the agency produced by the "fear of YHWH" (יִרְאַת יְהוָה, v. 7a).

The syntax of the preamble suggests that the discourse unit consists of three

5. John Johnson, "An Analysis of Proverbs 1:1–7," *BSac* 144 (1987): 429; Arthur Jan Keefer, "A Shift in Perspective: The Intended Audience and a Coherent Reading of Proverbs 1:1–7," *JBL* 136 (2017): 105–6.

6. Hans F. Fuhs, *Das Buch der Sprichwörter: Ein Kommentar*, FB 95 (Würzburg: Echter, 2001), 37; Keefer, "A Shift in Perspective," 106–8.

7. Keefer, "A Shift in Perspective," 108–113.

8. Sandoval, "Revisiting the Prologue of Proverbs," 462–71. Cf. James A. Loader, *Proverbs 1-9*, HCOT (Leuven: Peeters, 2014), 51–52; Bernd U. Schipper, *Proverbs 1–15*, Hermeneia (Minneapolis: Fortress, 2019), 67–68.

9. Alex Luc, "The Titles and Structure of Proverbs," *ZAW* 112 (2000): 254; Kyle C. Dunham, "Structure and Theology in Proverbs: Its Function as an Educational Program for Novice Leaders in Ancient Israel," *BBR* 29 (2019): 370–72.

10. Fox, *Proverbs 1–9*, 191.

11. For discussion of the morphology and syntax of jussives and imperfects, see Hélène M. Dallaire, *The Syntax of Volitives in Biblical Hebrew and Amarna Canaanite Prose*, LSAWS 9 (Winona Lake, IN: Eisenbrauns, 2014).

sections: the title (v. 1), a summary of the goal of the anthology (vv. 2–6), and a declaration of the prerequisite for achieving this goal (v. 7). Together with its syntax, the literary coherence of the unit is established through the repetition of constructions as well as terms and expressions. As intimated above, with the exception of the latter half of v. 3, each line within vv. 2–4 begins with a common construction that expresses purpose (*lamed* + infinitive construct; cf. v. 6a). In addition to this construction, the preamble reiterates several key terms and expressions. The term "instruction" (or "discipline," מוּסָר) recurs in vv. 2, 3, and 7. The form and expression "for understanding" (לְהָבִין) is used in vv. 2 and 6, suggesting that the catalogue of difficult literary forms in v. 6 specify the content of "insightful words" within v. 2 (אִמְרֵי בִינָה). And, following the title (v. 1), the entire unit is framed by the expression "wisdom and instruction" (חָכְמָה וּמוּסָר, vv. 2, 7).

These forms of repetition, combined with the intricately woven tapestry of moral values related to wisdom, indicate that the formation of character through the acquisition of wisdom and virtue represents the purpose and driving force of the preamble as well as the book of Proverbs.

Explanation of the Text

As indicated above, the preamble contains three discrete sections (v. 1, vv. 2–6, v. 7). Together, these sections define the nature and purpose of Proverbs and identify the posture or form of being necessary to achieve its objectives.

1. The Title (1:1)

The book of Proverbs opens with a conventional title that is comparable to superscriptions elsewhere in the Old Testament as well as in the ancient Near Eastern instructional tradition (e.g., Isa 1:1; Jer 1:1; Hab 1:1).[12] Similar to these superscriptions, the title defines the nature of the material within the document as well as the identity, genealogy, and status of the one to whom the material is attributed.

The initial word of v. 1 not only serves as the title of the book; it also orients one to the poetic style of the anthology. When read in light of Prov 10:1a and 25:1 as well as the materials that these titles frame, it appears that "proverbs" (מְשָׁלִים, v. 1a) are poetic speech acts that communicate traditional truths. They are popular, memorable expressions that convey cultural values. They are paradigms that project a particular vision of reality and draw listeners into their imaginative world.[13] These general descriptions capture the nature of contemporary proverbs as well as the individual sayings that pervade the central collections of the book of Proverbs. But they do not account for the diverse materials within the anthology as a whole. As a term that orients one to the poetic materials within the book, the designation "proverbs" includes various literary forms, ranging from extended poems

12. Kitchen, "Proverbs and Wisdom Books of the Ancient Near East," 68–114.

13. Timothy Polk, "Paradigms, Parables, and *Měšālîm*: On Reading the *Māšāl* in Scripture," *CBQ* 45 (1983): 569.

and speeches to admonitions and instructions to short, popular sayings. Whether these "proverbs" are cast in the form of an extended speech or a terse saying, they function in a basic way: to inspire the imagination and provoke reflection on one's character, one's conduct, one's situation, and one's view of the world.[14] This is a difficult task, for it demands imagination.[15] It requires readers or hearers to project themselves into situations comparable to those described in these proverbs, to imagine appropriate circumstances within which a proverb may be applied, and to envision an appropriate form of conduct.[16] Without the capacity for "*truthful* imagination,"[17] the wisdom and virtue communicated through these proverbs may be lost and the purpose of the book may not be realized.

In addition to identifying the poetic style of the anthology, the title attributes the materials to a particular person: "Solomon, son of David, king of Israel." While the title ascribes the materials in the book to Solomon, superscriptions elsewhere within the document attribute particular collections to other individuals (i.e., "the words of the wise," 22:17–24:22; "[sayings] of the wise," 24:23–34; "Agur," 30:1; and "King Lemuel," 31:1).[18] In view of these attributions as well as the anonymous nature and communal authority of proverbs, the attribution to Solomon does not mean that the wise king created or wrote all of the materials in the book. Rather, it seems to indicate that the materials in the book are consonant with Solomonic wisdom. The title links the wisdom of Proverbs with the wisdom of Israel's quintessential wise man. In so doing, the title plays an important literary role in the anthology, inviting the reader to consider the materials across the book in light of the biography of Israel's wisest king.

2. The Goal: The Inculcation of Wisdom and Virtue (1:2–6)

Against the backdrop of the title, vv. 2–6 capture the goal and agenda of the book through a sequence of purpose clauses that contain a constellation of virtues. At first glance, the virtues within vv. 2–6 appear to be virtual synonyms for wisdom, a sort of motley collection intended to highlight the comprehensive nature of the book's pedagogical program.[19] Upon closer investigation, however, the terms possess various connotations and distinct shades of meaning. Since the virtues delineated in vv. 2–6 appear throughout the book, particular attention to the meaning of the individual terms or expressions as well as their ethical connotations is in order.

a. Intellectual Virtue (1:2)

The preamble's purpose statement opens with expressions that capture the general intellectual and

14. Herbert, "The Parable [*MĀŠĀL*] in the Old Testament," 180–96. See also Vayntrub, *Beyond Orality*, 70–90; Millar, *Genre and Openness*, 191–221.

15. Schökel, *A Manual of Hebrew Poetics*, 104. For a discussion of imagination in the interpretive process, see Leo G. Perdue, *The Collapse of History: Reconstructing Old Testament Theology* (Minneapolis: Fortress, 1994; repr., Eugene, OR: Wipf and Stock, 2002), 263–98.

16. Davis, *Proverbs*, 19.

17. Davis, *Proverbs*, 19, italics original.

18. The early reception history of Proverbs indicates that those responsible for the translation of the document attempted to clarify the Solomonic nature of the anthology, for the LXX rearranges the collections and conceals certain titles to create one seamless Solomonic composition. For a discussion of the additions and omissions in the LXX and its *Vorlage*, see J. Cook, *The Septuagint of Proverbs: Jewish and/or Hellenistic Colouring of the LXX Proverbs*, VTSup 69 (Leiden: Brill, 1997); Emmanuel Tov, "Recensional Differences between the Masoretic Text and the Septuagint of the Book of Proverbs," in *The Greek and Hebrew Bible: Collected Essays on the Septuagint*, VTSup 72 (Leiden: Brill, 1999), 419–32.

19. Von Rad, *Wisdom in Israel*, 13, 30; Rolf Schäfer, *Die Poesie der Weisen: Dichotomie als Grundstruktur der Lehr-und Weisheitsgedichte in Proverbien 1–9* (Neukirchen-Vluyn: Neukirchener Verlag, 1999), 10.

ethical dimensions of the anthology's agenda (v. 2). The initial purpose clause indicates that Proverbs seeks to enable the reader to learn, internalize, or recognize "wisdom and instruction" (חָכְמָה וּמוּסָר, v. 2a). That is, it attempts to shape one's intellectual faculties through discipline, correction, and guidance so that they may develop the virtuous disposition and cognitive skills necessary to understand the fundamental issues of life. Together with "insightful words" (אִמְרֵי בִינָה, v. 2b), "wisdom and instruction" serve as a cipher for the book's teaching. "Wisdom" refers to the intellectual and moral expertise that the book seeks to inculcate in readers, while "instruction" refers to the various forms of authoritative correction or discipline within the piece, each of which operates under certain verbal or physical conventions to convey ethical teaching that endeavors to shape the character, desires, thinking, and behavior of its readers (1:8; 3:11; 4:1; 6:23; 8:33; 13:1, 24).

b. Instrumental and Moral Virtues (1:3)

In light of this concern with education for character formation, vv. 3–4 clarify the ethical dimensions of the document's pedagogical agenda. Here the practical, moral, and intellectual threads that are woven throughout the anthology's ethical tapestry are given specific attention. The practical and moral aspects of the document's instruction are intimately related to one another in v. 3. The moral virtues "righteousness, justice, and uprightness" (צֶדֶק וּמִשְׁפָּט וּמֵישָׁרִים) are cast in apposition to "instruction in prudent living" (מוּסַר הַשְׂכֵּל, v. 3a); they identify the ethical values that allow one to receive the book's authoritative teaching and to live in accordance with the social and cosmic order. The terms "righteousness" (צֶדֶק) and "justice" (מִשְׁפָּט) frequently occur together in the Old Testament to describe one who lives, judges, and governs rightly (e.g., Gen 18:19; 1 Kgs 10:9; Isa 1:21; Jer 22:3; Ezek 18:5). This general conception of right living is enhanced by the term "uprightness," which denotes behavior that is straight and aligns with the order God has woven into the fabric of the universe. Taken together, these values define the nature of social justice in ancient Israel.[20] They represent the fundamental virtues the book seeks to inculcate in readers, the essential components of a moral compass that leads to practical forms of equitable behavior in a range of social and personal relations.[21]

These practical forms of ethical behavior are captured by the expression "instruction in prudent living." The "instruction" (מוּסָר) mentioned in v. 2 is reiterated and recast in more specific terms in v. 3. Here it is more than a reference to the anthology's authoritative teaching and ethical instruction; it is a particular form of instruction, namely, instruction "in prudent living" or instruction that "effects prudent living."[22] Within the broader context of the document, "prudent living" (הַשְׂכֵּל) encompasses a variety of practical values; it describes concrete actions marked by discretion, persistence, self-control, resourcefulness, and good sense, just to name a few (10:5, 19; 13:15; 14:35; 16:22, 23; 17:2; 23:9). These values are nurtured through instruction, directed by righteousness, justice, and uprightness, and embodied through specific actions in which a person interprets a situation correctly and acts intelligently.[23] In this

20. Moshe Weinfeld, "'Justice and Righteousness'—משפט וצדק—the Expression and Its Meaning," in *Justice and Righteousness: Biblical Themes and Their Influence*, ed. H. G. Reventlow and Y. Hoffman (Sheffield: Sheffield Academic, 1992), 228–46.

21. Fox, *Proverbs 1–9*, 60.

22. For the attributive genitive or genitive of effect, see *IBHS* §9.5.2c, §9.5.3a; Schipper, *Proverbs 1–15*, 65.

23. Fox, *Proverbs 1–9*, 59–60.

respect, "prudent living" is an inclusive, pragmatic virtue that concerns actions and their intended results.[24]

c. Instrumental and Intellectual Virtues (1:4–5)

The same is true of "shrewdness" (עָרְמָה, v. 4a). While the term carries negative connotations related to craftiness and deception (Gen 3:1; Job 5:12), within Proverbs it is used positively to denote the ability to devise clever plans or practices in order to achieve a favorable outcome (8:5, 12; 14:8, 15; 22:3; 27:12). As Wisdom's abode (8:12) and a virtue that the uncommitted lack, prudence is an intellectual value rooted in a commitment to wisdom's way, developed through experience, and manifested through the execution of careful planning.

These intellectual and instrumental dimensions of "shrewdness" correspond with the values delineated in v. 4b: "knowledge and discretion" (דַּעַת וּמְזִמָּה). While "knowledge" is a general term that conveys a basic awareness of an object, "discretion" is much more specific. Similar to "shrewdness," it denotes a person's hidden, private thoughts or schemes, whether positive or negative.[25] When read in conjunction with vv. 2–4a, the comprehensive ethical agenda of the book is clear: the anthology seeks to sharpen the reader's character, cognitive faculties, and practical behavior by cultivating a receptivity to instruction and inculcating an understanding of the fundamental issues of a life.

In addition to describing the book's purpose through an artistically crafted moral tapestry, it is important to note that v. 4 reveals the primary addressee of the material: the uncommitted youth. The terms "uncommitted" (פְּתָאיִם, v. 4a) and "young" (נַעַר, v. 4b) refer to the same type of person, namely, a late adolescent on the brink of adulthood who is committed to neither wisdom nor folly.[26] Among the characters within the book, the uncommitted are situated in a liminal state, that is, a state of limbo, "betwixt and between" the way of life and the way of death.[27] They are inexperienced, prone to folly (1:22; 9:4), and easily seduced.[28] Nonetheless, in contrast to the fool, they are open, malleable, and capable of being shaped by the educational process.[29] This condition explains the rhetorical texture of the discourses and the root metaphors that pervade Prov 1–9, as various voices attempt to win the uncommitted youth's allegiance and convince him to commit to a path, a woman, a house, and a banquet.[30]

While the preamble and poetic interludes within Prov 1–9 identify the uncommitted youth as the principal audience of the anthology (1:20–33; 8:1–36; 9:1–18),[31] the parental lectures introduce

24. Brown, *Character in Crisis*, 25–26.

25. Fox, *Proverbs 1–9*, 34.

26. For the nature of the "young" see 7:7; 20:11; 22:6, 15; 23:13; 29:15. For discussion of the status of the implied addressee, see Ansberry, *Be Wise, My Son*, 64–69.

27. Victor Turner, "Betwixt and Between: The Liminal Period in *Rites de Passage*," in *The Forest of Symbols: Aspects of Nbembu Ritual* (Ithaca, NY: Cornell University Press, 1967), 93–111; Leo G. Perdue, "Liminality as a Social Setting for Wisdom Instruction," *ZAW* 93 (1981): 114–26; Van Leeuwen, "Liminality and Worldview," 111–44.

28. Fox, *Proverbs 1–9*, 42–43; Waltke, *Proverbs: Chapters 1–15*, 111–12.

29. Waltke, *Proverbs: Chapters 1–15*, 111.

30. Aletti, "Seduction et parole en Proverbes I–IX," 129–44; Van Leeuwen, "Liminality and Worldview," 111–44.

31. While the interludes address a variety of individuals, ranging from humanity in general to the scoffer, the fool, and the gullible in particular (1:22; 8:4–5, 9:4, 16), Wisdom's invitation to the scoffer and the fool appears to be rhetorical, for within the book these personages are unable to learn. Since the gullible are malleable and capable of being shaped by the educational process, it seems that they are the principal addressees of the interludes. Michael V. Fox, "Who Can Learn? A Dispute in Ancient Pedagogy," in *Wisdom You Are My Sister: Studies in Honor of Roland E. Murphy, O. Carm., on the Occasion of His Eightieth Birthday*, ed. M. L. Barré, CBQMS 29 (Washington, DC: Catholic Biblical Association of America, 1997), 68.

a second addressee: the son(s) (1:8, 10, 15; 2:1; 3:1, 11, 21; 4:1, 10, 20; 5:1, 7, 20; 6:20; 7:1, 24). Despite the distinctive designations as well as the discrete settings of the parental lectures (i.e., the home) and the poetic interludes (i.e., the public thoroughfares), these addressees are not mutually exclusive. The preamble and interludes present the primary addressee of the book, the gullible or uncommitted youth (1:4), who is represented by the addressee in the parental lectures, "my son(s)" (cf. 7:7).[32] The uncommitted youth identified in the preamble and addressed in the interludes is called to take up the subject position of the son(s) in the lectures in order to receive social and moral training that will enable him to develop into a responsible member of the community.[33] This notion is reinforced by Wisdom's speech, which imitates the rhetoric of the parental lectures and associates the gullible with the sons (8:5, 32). And the same notion is implied by the fact that the father serves as the governing voice across the prologue, the one who speaks for the various characters and to the addressee within the individual discourses in Prov 1–9. These features suggest the uncommitted youth is the primary addressee of the book.[34] Against the backdrop of the virtues delineated in vv. 2–4, it appears that Proverbs seeks to instill these values in the uncommitted, thus transforming the addressee's uncommitted state and inclination to folly by inculcating within him wisdom and virtue.

The uncommitted youth may represent the primary addressee of Proverbs, but this persona is by no means the sole addressee of the document. As noted above, the pair of imperfect verbs in v. 5 adopt the sense of the preceding infinitives construct and open a pair of purpose clauses, each of which express a wish or desire.[35] The wish concerns the formation of the second addressee of the anthology: "the wise" (חָכָם, v. 5a) or "one with understanding" (נָבוֹן, v. 5b). Together with the uncommitted youth, the materials in the document are directed toward those who are teachable and discerning, who accept correction and internalize knowledge (2:1; 9:8; 10:8, 14; 12:5; 13:1; 15:31). That is, the document not only bestows wisdom and virtue on the simple; it also enhances the wisdom and virtue of the mature. The juxtaposition of the uncommitted and the wise (vv. 4–5), combined with the use of the verb "hear" (שׁמע, v. 5a), which punctuates the introduction to the instructions in Prov 1–9 (1:8; 4:1, 10; 5:7; 7:24; 8:6, 32, 33), intimates that both addressees occupy a common subject position. Both the uncommitted youth and the wise are rendered as those in need of instruction as well as those who possess the posture and cognitive capacity to receive and increase in instruction so as to acquire wisdom and virtue.[36]

In addition to its contributions to the construction of the implied addressees of the anthology, v. 5 offers a rough sketch of the document's pedagogical program: "hear" (יִשְׁמַע, v. 5a), "increase instruction" (יוֹסֶף לֶקַח, v. 5a), "acquire guidance" (תַּחְבֻּלוֹת יִקְנֶה, v. 5b). Among the pedagogical techniques within Proverbs, hearing may be the most

32. Fox, *Proverbs 1–9*, 326.

33. Newsom, "Woman and the Discourse of Patriarchal Wisdom," 142–44.

34. Cf. Keefer, "A Shift in Perspective," 103–16.

35. Cf. Sandoval, "Revisiting the Prologue of Proverbs," 455–73.

36. Sandoval, "Revisiting the Prologue of Proverbs," 463–66. Two addressees are also apparent in several ancient Near Eastern instructional texts. The instructions of Ptahhotep and Amenemope, for example, direct their teachings toward a dual audience. The former transmits the "ways of the ancestors" to both his son and those who are willing to hear, while the latter delivers the "teaching for life" to future generations in general and his youngest son in particular. "The Instruction of Ptahhotep" (*AEL* 1:63); "The Instruction of Amenemope" (*AEL* 2:148–49, 162).

significant. It is a defining characteristic of the wise (10:8; 12:15; 13:1; 15:31; 19:20), the primary means of education, and the channel for receiving instruction (cf. 2:2). This listening posture enables the uncommitted as well as the wise to "increase instruction," that is, to grow in their apprehension of the book's teaching of wisdom and virtue (cf. 4:2; 16:21, 23). This growth is not achieved through passive reception of the material; rather, it is attained through an active pursuit in which the reader seeks to obtain "guidance" (תַּחְבֻּלוֹת, v. 5b). This technical term pertaining to nautical expertise captures the educational vision of Proverbs. With a listening posture and through an active pursuit of the book's teaching, the reader is granted an intellectual and moral compass to navigate through life, negotiate various circumstances, formulate effective plans, and proceed down the path of wisdom (11:14; 12:5; 20:18; 24:6).

d. Interpretive Dexterity (1:6)

The sketch of the anthology's educational program sets the stage for the final purpose clause within the preamble, a clause that delineates the document's intended pedagogical outcome (v. 6). This outcome is introduced by the same construction that punctuates vv. vv. 2–4 as well as the same form used in v. 2b. As noted above, the repetition of the form and expression "for understanding" (לְהָבִין) in v. 6 suggests that the catalogue of literary forms in the remainder of the line specify the content of "insightful words" within v. 2. By engaging the anthology's educational program, the audience is granted the ability to grasp its "insightful words" (v. 2b) in general and process or interpret its figures and tropes in particular (v. 6). The cluster of literary expressions listed in v. 6 does not refer to the discrete genres incorporated in the book;[37] rather, the agglomeration of literary forms highlights the multivalent nature of the materials in the book, alerts the audience to the difficult nature of their interpretation, and intimates that diligent study of these complex materials will yield understanding.[38] Put simply, the catalogue of literary forms suggests that the implied addressees will acquire a measure of interpretive dexterity, the ability to read and perceive proverbs, people, and the particulars of life in accord with wisdom and virtue.

3. The Prerequisite for the Inculcation of Wisdom and Virtue (1:7)

This perception and the realization of the book's multifaceted purpose, however, are contingent upon a particular mode of being. This mode of being is articulated in v. 7, which functions as the climactic conclusion to the preamble and the main clause of the string of subordinate purpose clauses in vv. 2–6; it identifies the document's basic prerequisite for the acquisition of wisdom and virtue: "the fear of YHWH" (יִרְאַת יְהוָה, v. 7a). This prerequisite is developed in different ways and from different angles across the anthology. At minimum, these developments indicate that "the fear of YHWH" is a posture or mode of being that is cultivated in relationship with YHWH and through knowledge of his will. To be specific, it is a perspectival posture that shapes, governs, and directs one's emotions, desires, and intellect. This mode of being represents "the beginning" (רֵאשִׁית,

37. While "proverb" (מָשָׁל, v. 6a) and "the words of the wise" (דִּבְרֵי חֲכָמִים, v. 6b) are associated with the sayings in 10:1–22:16 and 22:17–24:34, respectively, "allusive saying" (מְלִיצָה, v. 6a) and "riddles" (חִידֹת, v. 6b) are formally absent from the book. Van Leeuwen, "The Book of Proverbs," 5:33; Murphy, *Proverbs*, 5; Fox, *Proverbs 1–9*, 65–67; Sandoval, "Revisiting the Prologue of Proverbs," 469. See also Schipper, who suggests that the expression "allusive saying" or "allusion" refers to the twice-told proverbs across the anthology (*Proverbs 1–15*, 69, 71).

38. Sandoval, "Revisiting the Prologue of Proverbs," 466–71.

v. 7a), the starting point, or the first principle of knowledge;[39] it is an embodied acknowledgement of humanity's limits, dependence, responsibilities, and place within the cosmos under YHWH's gracious governance (9:10; cf. 30:1–6). That is, it is a recognition of one's contingency and creaturehood, a humble acceptance of one's status in the cosmos in relation to YHWH.[40] The epistemological realization of one's contingency and dependence upon YHWH engenders a particular ontology or mode of being: the fear of YHWH, which may be described as Proverbs's expression for faith.[41] This multifaceted posture not only produces humility, trust, and reverence before God (15:33; 22:4); it also shapes one's worldview and creates a humble, virtuous disposition that serves as the seedbed in which wisdom might germinate and grow.

Far from a strict concern with one's intellect, Proverbs seeks to form the totality of one's character through wisdom and virtue (vv. 2–6). To accomplish this goal, moral or virtuous character is required. As the climactic conclusion of the preamble and the prerequisite for achieving the document's goal, v. 7 indicates that the acquisition of wisdom is dependent upon a virtuous mode of being, and virtuous activity is dependent upon the acquisition of wisdom (vv. 2–6).[42] Wisdom and virtue cannot be separated from one another, for they are inextricably linked in Proverbs's educational agenda and overarching purpose. In this respect, it is not surprising that fools can neither learn nor achieve the goal of the book (v. 7b), for they refuse to adopt the perspectival posture and mode of being necessary to acquire wisdom and virtue.[43]

Canonical and Theological Significance

As the introduction to Proverbs, the preamble summarizes the purpose and agenda of the anthology, namely, the (trans)formation of one's character through the inculcation of wisdom and virtue. In so doing, it provides an interpretive framework within which to understand how the discrete lectures, interludes, and sayings within the book contribute to its overarching purpose. In the context of the anthology as a whole, the preamble combines a variety of intellectual, instrumental, and moral virtues to highlight the holistic nature of the anthology's purpose (vv. 2–6); it specifies the principal audience(s) of the material (v. 4–5); it outlines the document's educational program and its intended result (vv. 5–6); it announces the fundamental prerequisite for achieving the goal of the anthology (v. 7); and it provides the reader with a glossary of key terms, concepts, and character types through which to under-

39. Henri Blocher, "The Fear of the Lord as the 'Principle' of Wisdom," *TynBul* 28 (1977): 3–28.

40. Jindo, "On the Biblical Notion," 433–53.

41. Treier, *Proverbs and Ecclesiastes*, 12. For discussion of the fear of YHWH as a person's conscience, see Fox, *Proverbs 1–9*, 70; Christine Roy Yoder, *Proverbs*, AOTC (Nashville: Abingdon, 2009), 6–7.

42. Ansberry, "What Does Jerusalem Have to Do with Athens?," 161, 171–73.

43. For the moral and intellectual nature of the fool, see Fox, *Proverbs 1–9*, 41–42; Waltke, *Proverbs: Chapters 1–15*, 112–13.

stand the materials in the book. Without the preamble, the purpose, the educational program and expectations, and the prerequisite of the book would be ambiguous at best and lost at worst.

While the preamble is comparable to introductory statements in ancient Near Eastern instructional texts, the objective and worldview of Proverbs is distinct in several respects, two in particular. First, the conflation of intellectual, instrumental, and moral virtues in the preamble's purpose statement indicates that the anthology's *principal* goal is neither the audience's intellectual nor their social development. These forms of development play a formative role in Proverbs's educational program; but they are subservient to its fundamental goal, namely, the formation of character. In contrast to ancient Near Eastern instructional works, whose primary function was to orient readers to the social world through the inculcation of key cultural traditions,[44] the primary function of Proverbs is to shape the dimensions of one's character.[45] Whereas character and virtue appear to be subservient to a utilitarian ethic in ancient Near Eastern instructional literature, practical strategies for coping with life appear to be subservient to the cultivation of character and virtue in Proverbs.[46] Proverbs gives particular attention to the way in which wisdom and moral character yield happiness, success, and social honor. But these rewards and motivations for living in accordance with wisdom are dependent upon virtuous character. Character determines the goal of virtuous activity, while practical wisdom determines the means for achieving that goal in particular situations.[47] The social orientation of ancient Near Eastern instructional literature suggests that practical wisdom is the fundamental goal. The theological orientation of Proverbs, on the other hand, indicates that character and virtue are the fundamental goal, for without a moral disposition wisdom is left without a guide for virtuous activity.

The theological orientation of Proverbs not only provides a rationale for its concern with character and virtue; it also serves as an explanation for the second difference between the anthology and its ancient Near Eastern counterparts: its worldview. The distinctive worldview of Proverbs is defined by the distinctive nature of Israel's God, YHWH. The virtues promoted in the anthology are not based on some principal of primordial order by which the gods and humans were to live (i.e., *mes* in Mesopotamia and Maat in Egypt);[48] rather, they are rooted in the order that YHWH has woven into the fabric of the cosmos. And wisdom is not acquired

44. Assmann, "Kulturelle und literarische Texte," 60–82; Carr, *Writing on the Tablet*, 77.

45. Brown, *Character in Crisis*, 1–21.

46. Lyu, *Righteousness*, 97–114, esp. 114.

47. Aristotle, *Nicomachean Ethics* 6.1142b33; 6.1144a7–9; 6.1144b15–18; Ansberry, "What Does Jerusalem Have to Do with Athens?," 159–60.

48. For a discussion of the *mes* in Mesopotamia, see Thorkild Jacobsen, *The Treasures of Darkness* (New Haven: Yale University Press, 1976), 84–85. For a discussion of Maat in Egypt, see Hornung, *Conceptions of God in Ancient Egypt*, 213–16; Assmann, *Maât*, 127–28; Michael V. Fox, "World Order and Maʿat: A Crooked Parallel," *JANES* 23 (1995): 37–48.

simply through instruction and diligent study; rather, it is acquired through the fear of YHWH (1:7), in relationship with YHWH, and as a gift from YHWH (2:1–6). Whereas the wisdom materials of Egypt and Mesopotamia transmit basic values and advice in order to maintain order in the social realm, Proverbs transmits basic values and advice to maintain relationship with YHWH. While social harmony is the natural implication of applying the principles of wisdom into everyday life, the social function of Israel's wisdom tradition is secondary, whereas relationship with and knowledge of YHWH is primary.

Despite the distinctive nature of Proverbs's purpose and worldview within the ancient Near East, it is important to note that this combination of purpose and worldview is reflected elsewhere in the Old Testament. The anthology's concern with (trans)forming character through wisdom and virtue is reflected in the Torah as well as the Prophets. Just as the preamble indicates that the inculcation of the materials in Proverbs yield wisdom and understanding (1:2), so also Moses indicates that the embodiment of the principles of the covenant yields wisdom and understanding (Deut 4:5–8). The virtues presented in the preamble's purpose statement are by no means unique. These values are cast in distinct forms and communicated in diverse ways within Israel's constitutional literature as well as the oracles of the prophets (e.g., Deut 16:20; 2 Sam 8:15; Jer 17:23; Ezek 18:5–29; Amos 5:24). The pedagogical program of Proverbs is reminiscent of Deuteronomy's philosophy of education.[49] And the attitude that serves as the prerequisite for acquiring wisdom is not limited to Israel's sapiential tradition (Prov 1:7; 8:13; 9:10; 31:30; Job 1:1, 8; 2:3; Eccl 7:18; 12:13; Ps 111:10); the fear of YHWH is also a moral posture that serves as the precondition for covenant obedience in Deuteronomy (Prov 4:10–14; 5:29; 10:12–13; 17:19–20; 28:58; 31:12), an attitude that is encouraged by the Prophets (Isa 50:10; 59:19; Mal 3:5, 16; 4:2 [3:20]), and a disposition that shaped and motivated Paul's cruciform ministry of reconciliation (2 Cor 5:11–21).

The preamble's purpose, pedagogical program, and prerequisite reverberate through the canon. And the theological melodies played by the book's prolegomena resound in the church today. Among the diverse ways in which the prologue speaks to the contemporary church, two deserve specific comment. First, the careful arrangement of intellectual, instrumental, and moral virtues in the preamble's purpose statement indicates that Proverbs is not a self-help book; its intention is not necessarily to provide readers with a how-to guide to parenting, wealth ethics, or social success. Its fundamental intention is education for character formation. The anthology seeks to sharpen the intellect, hone the desires, form the feelings, and construct the worldview of readers in accordance with wisdom and virtue so that

49. Daniel I. Block, "Deuteronomy: The Heart of Theological Education in the First Testament," in *The Triumph of Grace: Literary and Theological Studies in Deuteronomy and Deuteronomic Themes* (Eugene, OR: Cascade, 2017), 1–18.

they might live rightly in relation to God, others, and the created world. In contrast to many inspirational or motivational best sellers, Proverbs does not define wisdom and the good life through personal happiness; rather, it defines wisdom and the good life as virtuous character that is acquired through diligent study in relationship with God.

Second, in light of the preamble's purpose, pedagogical program, and prerequisite, Proverbs provides a vision of true wisdom. Contrary to modern perceptions of wisdom, Proverbs does not define this virtue merely as an intellectual quality, as some value found among those in the ivory towers of the academy or the halls of power who stand aloof from the practical concerns or circumstances of everyday life. For Proverbs, the intellect is a part of wisdom but not the whole of wisdom. Wisdom includes the totality of one's person and character. It is a virtue that is inextricably linked to relationship with God and knowledge of his will. Put differently, it is a way of life that refuses to separate faith from reason, piety from the life of the mind. In fact, according to the preamble's prerequisite (1:7), faith does not hamper reason; rather, it helps reason by situating it in a theological context through which one is able to recognize its limitations and proper place in relation to God. The preamble's concern with character over practical strategies for dealing with life and its theological vision of wisdom provide the church with guideposts on their journey of "faith seeking understanding." These guideposts direct the church away from moralism to theological formation, they prevent the church from compartmentalizing faith and reason, and they guard the church against understanding wisdom as a mere species of knowledge, as a virtue disinterested in everyday affairs and distinct from an embodied way of living.

PART II

Proverbs 1:8–9:18

The Value of Wisdom and Virtue

Main Idea of Proverbs 1:8–9:18

The prologue of Proverbs illuminates the surpassing value of wisdom and virtue through the discourses, dispositions, desires, lifestyles, and worldviews of rival characters in order to persuade the reader to pursue and embrace a life of wisdom and virtue.

Literary Context of Proverbs 1:8–9:18

The prologue of Proverbs serves as an extended introduction that provides an interpretive lens through which to understand the variegated materials in the remainder of anthology.[1] Whereas the preamble offers a distillation of the document's objectives, addressees, key terms, and requisite posture (1:1–7), the prologue delineates the setting of the document's instruction and introduces the characters, virtues, vices, and nuclear symbols that are woven throughout the remaining collections in the anthology. To borrow from one of the document's nuclear symbols, the prologue provides the reader with a roadmap, outlining the terrain, contours, highways, and byways that orient and mark a life of wisdom and virtue. Its literary and hermeneutical significance can hardly be overestimated. Within the context of the anthology, the prologue functions on several levels, two in particular.

1. This conclusion is well attested in the secondary literature. See, for example, Brevard S. Childs, *Introduction to the Old Testament as Scripture* (Philadelphia: Fortress, 1979), 552–53; Otto Plöger, *Sprüche Salomos (Proverbia)*, BKAT 17 (Neukirchen-Vluyn: Neukirchener Verlag, 1984), xxxvi; Steiert, *Die Weisheit Israels*, 217; Fox, *Proverbs 1–9*, 346; Waltke, *Proverbs: Chapters 1–15*, 10–13; Yoder, *Proverbs*, 10.

First, the prologue provides a formal introduction to the central collections within the anthology (10:1–29:27). Similar to several ancient Near Eastern instructional texts,[2] the extended speeches in the prologue establish the discourse setting of the document. That is, they illuminate the world within which the variegated materials in the anthology are to be read and heard; they delineate the speaker in the document, the addressee of the piece, and the setting of the discourse, creating a social and dialogical context through which to view the various components of the anthology as well as the document as a whole (in the introduction see Discourse Setting, pp. 56–58). In addition, the prologue supplies the nuts and bolts, the conventional character types, and the thematic components that are employed, twisted, and turned by various sayings in the central collections to construct a planetarium in which one may see the expanse, dimensions, and paths of the wise and virtuous life. While the prologue introduces the reader to different characters, virtues, vices, desires, and moral worldviews, it does not describe the essence of the wise life in great detail. Instead, the prologue gives particular attention to the value of wisdom and virtue. Against this backdrop, the central collections within the anthology profile the virtues, vices, appetites, and affections embodied in specific character types in order to describe the essence of the wise and virtuous life. The prologue shapes one's approach to the central collections in the anthology; it identifies the discourse setting of the materials, introduces the principal characters and themes that pervade the document, and prepares one to navigate the myriad of sayings in the sentence literature.[3]

Second, the prologue is intimately related to the materials in chs. 30–31. Together, these collections provide a literary envelope around the anthology; they serve as bookends that situate the diverse materials in the document within a formal, literary framework.[4] This framework is formed through certain terms, expressions, concepts, and images characteristic of the prologue as well as the concluding collections.

---

2. See, for example, "The Instruction of Ptahhotep" (*AEL* 1:61–80); "The Instruction Addressed to King Merikare" (*AEL* 1:97–109); "The Instruction of King Amenhemet I for His Son Sesostris I" (*AEL* 1:135–39); "The Instruction of Amenemope" (*AEL* 2:146–63). While the prologue of Proverbs is much longer than the prologues within these ancient Near Eastern instructional texts, it functions in manner comparable to the introductions to these ancient Egyptian instructional texts.

3. Van Leeuwen, "The Book of Proverbs," *NIB* 5:31.

4. Camp, *Wisdom and the Feminine*, 179; Thomas P. McCreesh, "Wisdom as Wife: Proverbs 31:10–31," *RB* 92 (1985): 25–46; repr. in *Learning from the Sages: Selected Studies on the Book of Proverbs*, ed. R. B. Zuck (Grand Rapids: Baker, 1995), 391–410; Arndt Meinhold, *Die Sprüche, Teil 1: Sprüche Kapitel 1–15*, ZBK 16.1 (Zürich: TVZ, 1991), 26; Jutta Hausmann, "Beobachtungen zu Spr 31,10–31," in *Alttestamentlicher Glaube und Biblische Theologie: Festschrift für Horst Dietrich Preuss zum 65. Geburtstag*, ed. J. Hausmann and H.-J. Zobel (Stuttgart: Kohlhammer, 1992), 266; Rick D. Moore, "A Home for the Alien: Worldly Wisdom and Covenantal Confession in Proverbs 30,1–9," *ZAW* 106 (1994): 104; Van Leeuwen, "The Book of Proverbs," *NIB* 5:24; Yoder, *Wisdom as a Woman of Substance*, 2; Brown, "The Pedagogy of Proverbs 10:1–31:9," 153. It is important to note, however, that for some of these scholars Prov 30:1–33 does not play a decisive role in the recontextualization of the sentence literature.

The phrase "knowledge of the Holy One" is found only in 9:10 and 30:3, that is, at the conclusion of the prologue and within Agur's monologue. The maternal voice mentioned in the prologue (1:8; 6:20) is given expression in the instruction of Lemuel's mother (31:1). Just as the book opened in the confines of the home, so also it concludes with a mother instructing her son in the home (31:1–9). And the female figures that dominate the prologue correspond with the female figures that dominate ch. 31. In fact, the poem concerning the "valiant woman" (31:10–31) includes terms and expressions that are used elsewhere only to describe Lady Wisdom. Similar to Lady Wisdom, the valiant woman is difficult to obtain (31:10, cf. 1:28; 8:17), more precious than corals (31:10; cf. 3:15 [Q]; 8:11), the proprietress of a substantial household (31:15, 21, 27; cf. 9:1; 31:15; 9:3), a source of security (31:11; cf. 1:33), and a paragon of the fear of YHWH (31:30; cf. 1:29; 8:13). She is the embodiment of Lady Wisdom's character and the antitype of the strange woman. The female imagery, combined with the use of unique terms and expressions, suggests the discourses within chs. 30–31 coalesce with the prologue to provide a literary framework through which to interpret the materials in the book of Proverbs. The hermeneutical and theological significance of this framework will be the subject of attention in chs. 30–31.

The prologue plays a formative role in the broader context of Proverbs. Its relation to the central collections within the anthology (10:1–29:27) as well as the concluding compositions reveals its hermeneutical significance. The prologue orients and guides the reader of Proverbs; it inculcates receptivity, illuminates the value of wisdom and virtue, and provides the reader with an interpretive framework within which to understand the component parts of the anthology.

Structure and Outline of Proverbs 1:8–9:18

In light of the various ways in which the preamble functions within the broader literary context of Proverbs, it is difficult to overestimate its significance. As the entryway into the book, this coherent unit serves as the interpretive lens through which to understand the nature, function, and goal of the anthology as a whole.

I. Introduction to the Book (1:1–7)

➦ II. The Value of Wisdom and Virtue (1:8–9:18)

- **A. Wisdom, Desire, and Different Ways (1:8–19)**
- **B. Wisdom's Rebuke (1:20–33)**
- **C. The Procurement, Power, and Protection of Wisdom and Virtue (2:1–22)**
- **D. Wisdom and Piety (3:1–12)**
- **E. Wisdom's Value and Moral Obligations (3:13–35)**
- **F. Wisdom and Tradition (4:1–9)**
- **G. Wisdom and Ways of Life (4:10–19)**
- **H. Wisdom and the Moral Anatomy (4:20–27)**
- **I. Wisdom and Sexuality (5:1–23)**
- **J. Wisdom, Lending, Laziness, and the Immoral Anatomy (6:1–19)**
- **K. Wisdom, Desire, and Certain Destruction (6:20–35)**
- **L. Wisdom and Seduction (7:1–27)**
- **M. Wisdom's Call, Credentials, and the Cosmos (8:1–36)**
- **N. Wisdom and Folly's Invitations (9:1–18)**

III. "Forming 'Fearers of YHWH'": The Curriculum of Wisdom and Virtue (10:1–29:27)

- III.1 Elementary Wisdom and Virtue (10:1–15:33)
- III.2 Intermediate Wisdom and Virtue (16:1–22:16)
- III.3 Vocational Wisdom and Virtue (22:17–24:34)
- III.4 Advanced Wisdom and Virtue (25:1–29:27)

IV. The Application of Wisdom and Virtue

CHAPTER 2

Proverbs 1:8–19

A. Wisdom, Desire, and Different Ways

Main Idea of the Passage

The initial lecture seeks to cultivate the virtues of discernment and perception by thrusting the reader into a world of competing worldviews, words, and ways, each of which are shaped by desires that are satisfied through different means by different characters.

Literary Context

In the wake of the preamble's description of the purpose of the anthology and the prerequisite for achieving its goal, the first parental lecture propels the reader into a complex, conflicted world in order to attune one to the fundamental issues within the document and to form in readers the requisite posture for attaining wisdom and virtue.[1] Whether uncommitted or wise (1:4, 5), the reader is invited to assume the subject position or identity of the son and place themselves in the home and under the authority of the parental voice to receive instruction in wisdom and a worldview through which to see and perceive the complexities of life.[2] Far from representing an intrusive discourse that separates the anthology's purpose statement (1:2–6) from the prologue's teaching program (2:1–22), the initial parental lecture provides an invaluable preface to the program proper. As the entryway into the prologue's formal instruction, 1:8–19 functions in at least two ways within the broader context of the book.

1. This is the first of ten parental lectures in the prologue (1:8–19; 2:1–22; 3:1–12, 13–35; 4:1–9, 10–19, 20–27; 5:1–23; 6:30–35; 7:1–27).

2. Newsom, "Woman and the Discourse of Patriarchal Wisdom," 142–44.

First, the lecture actualizes the educational vision of the preamble and situates the document's addressees in a concrete context. The invitation to hear (יִשְׁמַע; 1:5a) and acquire instruction (מוּסָר; 1:2a, 3a) is transformed into a command to hear (שְׁמַע; 1:8a) and obey instruction (מוּסָר; 1:8a). And, as noted above, the addressees identified in the preamble are subsumed in a single figure: a son within the confines of the home who is instructed by his parents. The initial lecture activates the pedagogical program of the preamble and provides the reader with a subject position from which to receive the book's teaching; it cultivates the receptive posture necessary to achieve the document's goal and gives teeth to the authoritative discipline and instruction it bestows on readers.

Second, the initial lecture introduces the fundamental issue that pervades the remainder of the prologue, namely, seductive speech.[3] The discourses within the prologue contain a cast of characters and a cacophony of voices, each of which are vying for the reader's allegiance. This clamor of voices by different characters with different worldviews who offer similar promises raise several questions, questions like: to whom should the reader listen? Or better, whom should the reader trust? The initial lecture provides a partial answer to these questions: the reader should hear, obey, and trust the parents' instruction (see 1:20–33). In addition to identifying a trustworthy voice, 1:8–19 introduces key images and motifs that are reiterated throughout the prologue.[4] The path metaphor that pervades the prologue punctuates the parents' instruction (vv. 15, 19), and the image of the home makes its initial appearance (v. 13; cf. 2:18; 5:8; 7:27; 9:1, 14). While the "sinners" (חַטָּאִים, v. 10) do not appear elsewhere in the prologue (cf. 4:14–17), their attractive promises, projection of an alternative moral worldview, and ultimate fate correspond with the promises, perspectives, and fate of the adulterous woman and Woman Folly (2:16–19; 5:1–14; 7:10–27; 9:13–18). They are members of a larger community, a "community of death."[5] Together with its application of the anthology's educational program and identification of a trustworthy voice, the first parental lecture sketches the contours of this community and its fate, providing the reader with a framework through which to identify its other members.

3. See, for example, Aletti, "Seduction et parole en Proverbes I–IX," 129–44; Fox, *Proverbs 1–9*, 94; Weeks, *Instruction and Imagery*, 79–82.

4. Van Leeuwen, "The Book of Proverbs," *NIB* 5:37.

5. Van Leeuwen, "The Book of Proverbs," *NIB* 5:3.

I. Introduction to the Book (1:1–7)

➦ **II. The Value of Wisdom and Virtue (1:8–9:18)**

- **A. Wisdom, Desire, and Different Ways (1:8–19)**
  - **1. The Introductory Exhortation (1:8–9)**
    - **a. The Admonition (1:8)**
    - **b. The Motivation (1:9)**
  - **2. The Lesson: Sinners, Speech, and Steps (1:10–18)**
    - **a. The General Command: Temptation and the Will (1:10)**
    - **b. The Sinners' Deceptive Speech and Desires (1:11–14)**
      - **(1) The Invitation (1:11–12)**
      - **(2) The Promised Reward (1:13–14)**
    - **c. The Speech Interpreted: Wrong Ways and Misplaced Desire (1:15–18)**
      - **(1) The Command (1:15)**
      - **(2) The Rationale (1:16)**
      - **(3) A Proverb: The Seeing Bird (1:17)**
      - **(4) The Ironic Fate of Blind Sinners (1:18)**
  - **3. The Conclusion (1:19)**
- B. Wisdom's Rebuke (1:20–33)
- C. The Procurement, Power, and Protection of Wisdom and Virtue (2:1–22)
- D. Wisdom and Piety (3:1–12)
- E. Wisdom's Value and Moral Obligations (3:13–35)
- F. Wisdom and Tradition (4:1–9)
- G. Wisdom and Ways of Life (4:10–19)
- H. Wisdom and the Moral Anatomy (4:20–27)
- I. Wisdom and Sexuality (5:1–23)
- J. Wisdom, Lending, Laziness, and the Immoral Anatomy (6:1–19)
- K. Wisdom, Desire, and Certain Destruction (6:20–35)
- L. Wisdom and Seduction (7:1–27)
- M. Wisdom's Call, Credentials, and the Cosmos (8:1–36)
- N. Wisdom and Folly's Invitations (9:1–18)

III. "Forming 'Fearers of YHWH'": The Curriculum of Wisdom and Virtue (10:1–29:27)

IV. The Application of Wisdom and Virtue (30:1–31:31)

Translation and Exegetical Outline

(See pages 128–129.)

Proverbs 1:8–19

	Hebrew	English	Outline
			Macro Unit II: The Value of Wisdom and Virtue (1:8–9:18)
			A. Wisdom, Desire, and Different Ways (1:8–19)
			1. The Introductory Exhortation (1:8–9)
8a	שְׁמַע בְּנִי מוּסַר אָבִיךָ	Hear, my son, your father's instruction,	a. The Admonition (1:8)
8b	וְאַל־תִּטֹּשׁ תּוֹרַת אִמֶּךָ	and do not neglect your mother's teaching,	
9a	כִּי לִוְיַת חֵן הֵם לְרֹאשֶׁךָ	for they are a beautiful garland for your head,	b. The Motivation (1:9)
9b	וַעֲנָקִים לְגַרְגְּרֹתֶךָ	and a necklace for your throat.	
			2. The Lesson: Sinners, Speech, and Steps (1:10–18)
10a	↓ בְּנִי אִם־יְפַתּוּךָ חַטָּאִים	↓ My son, if sinners entice you,	a. The General Command: Temptation and the Will (1:10)
10b	אַל־תֹּבֵא	do not accede.	
			b. The Sinners' Deceptive Speech and Desires (1:11–14)
11a	אִם־יֹאמְרוּ	If they say,	
11b	לְכָה אִתָּנוּ	"Come with us,	(1) The Invitation (1:11–12)
11c	נֶאֶרְבָה לְדָם	let's lurk for blood,	
11d	נִצְפְּנָה לְנָקִי חִנָּם	let's ambush the innocent without cause;	
12a	נִבְלָעֵם כִּשְׁאוֹל חַיִּים	let's swallow them alive like Sheol,	
12b	וּתְמִימִים כְּיוֹרְדֵי בוֹר	the blameless like those who go down into the Pit.	
13a	כָּל־הוֹן יָקָר נִמְצָא	We'll find all sorts of precious wealth;	(2) The Promised Reward (1:13–14)
13b	נְמַלֵּא בָתֵּינוּ שָׁלָל	we'll fill our houses with spoil.	
14a	גּוֹרָלְךָ תַּפִּיל בְּתוֹכֵנוּ	Throw in your lot with us;	
14b	כִּיס אֶחָד יִהְיֶה לְכֻלָּנוּ ↓	↓ we'll all share one purse."	

Verse	Hebrew	English	Outline
			c. The Speech Interpreted: Wrong Ways and Misplaced Desire (1:15–18)
15a	בְּנִי אַל־תֵּלֵךְ בְּדֶרֶךְ אִתָּם	My son, do not go on this way with them;	(1) The Command (1:15)
15b	מְנַע רַגְלְךָ מִנְּתִיבָתָם	hold back your foot from their path,	
16a	כִּי רַגְלֵיהֶם לָרַע יָרוּצוּ	for their feet run to evil,	(2) The Rationale (1:16)
16b	וִימַהֲרוּ לִשְׁפָּךְ־דָּם	and they hurry to shed blood.	
17a	כִּי־חִנָּם מְזֹרָה הָרָשֶׁת	For spreading out the net is useless	(3) A Proverb: The Seeing Bird (1:17)
17b	בְּעֵינֵי כָּל־בַּעַל כָּנָף	in the sight of any bird.	
18a	וְהֵם לְדָמָם יֶאֱרֹבוּ	But they lurk for their own blood;	(4) The Ironic Fate of Blind Sinners (1:18)
18b	יִצְפְּנוּ לְנַפְשֹׁתָם	they ambush their own lives.	
19a	כֵּן אָרְחוֹת כָּל־בֹּצֵעַ בָּצַע	Thus are the ways of all who profit from unjust gain;	3. The Conclusion (1:19)
19b	אֶת־נֶפֶשׁ בְּעָלָיו יִקָּח	it takes away the life of its possessors.	

Structure and Literary Form

The first parental instruction is cast in the form of coherent lecture that seeks to inculcate the virtues of perception and discretion in the reader.[6] The lecture develops its argument through a rhetorical scheme that is emulated by the subsequent instructions. Similar to these parental instructions, the piece opens with an introduction (vv. 8–9), moves to the lesson proper (vv. 10–18), and ends with a formal conclusion (v. 19). The introduction mirrors the exordia within many of the parental lectures in the prologue: it includes an admonition as well as a motivation. The lesson proper contains two conditional clauses (vv. 10, 11–18). And the apodosis of each conditional clause opens with the vocative, "my son" (בְּנִי, vv. 10, 15). These conditional clauses are intimately related to one another. The general situation or condition delineated in the first is given specific attention through the speech of the sinners in the second (vv. 10b, 11b–14d); and the command delivered in the first is reinforced through a vivid description of the way, character, and fate of the sinners in the second (vv. 10b, 16a–18b). Together, they move from the general to the specific, a basic prescription to an extended prohibition. The lesson then gives way to a conclusion, which offers a distillation of the instruction proper (v. 19). The initial colon (v. 19a) summarizes the extended protasis in vv. 11–14, while the second colon captures the fate of the sinners in vv. 15–18 (v. 19b).[7]

In addition to the rhetorical texture and movement of the lecture, the coherence of the discourse is established through a variety of recurring terms that are placed in mouths of different speakers. Just as the sinners open their deceptive invitation with the imperative "come" (לְכָה, v. 11b), so also the parents open their prohibition with the command, "do not go" (אַל־תֵּלֵךְ, v. 15a). Whereas the sinners summon the son to "lurk for blood" (נֶאֶרְבָה לְדָם, v. 11c) and "ambush the innocent" (נִצְפְּנָה לְנָקִי, v. 11d), the parents reveal the ironic consequences of this plot: the sinners "lurk for their own blood" (לְדָמָם יֶאֱרֹבוּ, v. 18a, cf. v. 16b) and "ambush their own lives" (יִצְפְּנוּ לְנַפְשֹׁתָם, v. 18b). The sinners indicate that their violent attack is "without cause" (חִנָּם, v. 11d). In the same way, the parents reveal that setting a trap in the sight of any bird is "useless" (חִנָּם, v. 17a). The repeated terms and play on certain words highlight the coherence of the lecture as well as its rhetorical strategy. The recurring terms create a world of warring words and conflicting moral worldviews. The voices sound the same, but the consequences associated with their directives are different. The parents reiterate and recast the language of the sinners. And in so doing, they attempt to cultivate discretion and persuade the son to choose a particular path.

6. For further discussion of this literary form, in the introduction see Instructions or "Lectures," pp. XX.

7. Loader, *Proverbs 1–9*, 66; Magne Sæbø, *Sprüche*, ATD 16,1 (Göttingen: Vandenhoeck & Ruprecht, 2012), 47.

Explanation of the Text

1. The Introductory Exhortation (1:8–9)

As noted above, the lecture subdivides into three parts. The first seeks to cultivate receptivity and foster appropriate desire (vv. 8–9). The second inculcates discernment and perception through the presentation and interpretation of the sinners' speech, ways, and worldview (vv. 10–18). And the third offers a formal conclusion, summarizing the ironic fate of the sinners' lifestyle (v. 19). The substance of each unit deserves specific comment.

a. The Admonition (1:8)

Similar to the introductory statements of the subsequent parental lectures within the prologue, the instruction opens with a formal admonition. This admonition includes a pair of commands, an identification of the addressee, and a description of the speakers as well as the nature of the lesson that follows.

The commands identify and foster the posture necessary to receive the wisdom articulated in the lecture. The initial command is cast in the positive, while the second is cast in the negative. The positive appeal to "hear" (שְׁמַע, v. 8a) is reminiscent of the educational program delineated in the preamble (v. 5). The verb encompasses listening, understanding, and obedience. This call to hear and obey is strengthened by the negative appeal, "do not neglect" (אַל־תִּטֹּשׁ, v. 8b), which involves ignoring, rejecting, or disregarding the parents' teaching. Together, these verbs recur in the exordia of several instructions within the prologue (4:1, 10; 6:20; cf. 5:7; 7:24; 8:6, 32, 33).[8] The repetition of these verbs, as well as particular direct objects in the introductions to the parental lectures (e.g., instruction, teaching, discipline, commandment, my words), illuminates the function of the admonition in 1:8: it seeks to cultivate the receptivity, discipline, and obedience necessary for acquiring wisdom and virtue.[9]

This receptive, listening posture is reinforced by the addressee and speakers of the material. The admonition, combined with the lesson proper (vv. 10, 15), identifies the addressee as "my son" (בְּנִי, v. 8a). And the introductory exhortation associates the teaching with the son's father and mother. As noted above as well as in the introduction,[10] these designations clarify the discourse setting or dialogical context in which the material is conveyed. They situate the anthology in general and 1:8–19 in particular in the confines of the home, in a stable environment in which the parents seek to shape the character and identity of the son in accordance with wisdom and virtue. This domestic setting provides a window into the relationship between speaker and addressee. As leaders within the home who deserve respect and bear both the authority and the responsibility of teaching, training, and enculturating their children, the parents instruct their silent son, who hears, receives, and obeys their teaching. And through this discursive setting, Proverbs invites the reader to identify with this son, place themselves under the authority of the parents, and receive guidance in wisdom and virtue.

8. For a comparison and discussion of the repetition of 1:8 in 4:1 and 6:20, see Heim, *Poetic Imagination*, 61–70.

9. For further discussion, see Christine Roy Yoder, "Forming 'Fearers of Yahweh': Repetition and Contradiction as Pedagogy in Proverbs" in *Seeking out the Wisdom of the Ancients: Essays Offered to Honor Michael V. Fox on the Occasion of His Sixty-Fifth Birthday*, ed. K. G. Friebel, R. L. Troxel, and D. R. Magary (Winona Lake, IN: Eisenbrauns, 2005), 167–79.

10. For further discussion of the document's discourse setting, see the introduction, Discourse Setting, pp. 56–58.

The wise and virtuous guidance of the parents is described through the terms "instruction" (מוּסַר, v. 8a) and "teaching" (תּוֹרַת, v. 8b). Similar to the verb "hear" (v. 8a), the father's "instruction" links the material to the preamble (vv. 2, 3, 7). The preamble promised instruction; now the father actualizes this goal by delivering the authoritative teaching or discipline described in the document's prolegomenon. The use of the term in the introductory admonition associates the father's teaching with the book's pedagogical agenda and defines the nature of the material that follows in vv. 10–19.

The same is true of the mother's "teaching." While many emphasize the discrete shades of meaning related to this term to differentiate the mother's mild teaching from the father's fierce instruction,[11] it is important to note that both "instruction" and "teaching" describe the nature of the lesson that follows. The terms may have different connotations, but they share the same referent in this context. The mother's teaching is inextricably linked to the father's instruction. And this teaching is described through a familiar term: תּוֹרָה.[12] Though תּוֹרָה is employed throughout the Old Testament to refer to various instructions or commands, in general, it is a designation that encapsulates Israel's constitutional or covenantal tradition. Here it does not appear to carry all of this theological baggage. After all, it is used to describe the practical, familial advice in vv. 10–19. This does not mean, however, that the term is devoid of association with Israel's covenant tradition. In the present context, תּוֹרָה may not refer to this tradition *primarily*. But Israel's covenantal tradition appears to be in the term's semantic periphery, for the instruction that follows addresses matters of violence, economic practice, and communal well-being that are consonant with the regulations and ethical vision of Israel's covenantal tradition (Exod 21:12–14; Lev 19:11; Deut 19:11–13).[13] In this respect, it appears the mother's teaching refracts the ethos of Israel's covenant tradition through prudent, familial advice to inculcate wisdom and covenant loyalty in the son.[14]

b. The Motivation (v. 9)

The introductory admonition gives way to a motivation (v. 9), which is marked off by the causal conjunction "for" (כִּי, v. 9a). This motivation incorporates ornamental imagery to describe the instruction (v. 8a) and teaching (v. 8b) of the parents. While ornamental imagery and language of adornment reappear in many of the lectures (3:3, 22; 4:9; 6:21; 7:3), "a beautiful garland" (לִוְיַת חֵן, v. 9a) and "a necklace" (עֲנָקִים, v. 9b) are reminiscent of the rewards wisdom bestows on the one who seeks her in 4:9. In fact, "a beautiful garland" occurs only in Prov 1:9a and 4:9a within the Old Testament. Just as Prov 4:1a reiterates 1:8a, so also Prov 4:9a reiterates 1:9a to motivate the son to heed the father's "instruction" (מוּסַר, v. 8a; 4:1a) and to describe the benefits wisdom lavishes on her devotees. These benefits are expressed through multivalent metaphors. Together, "a beautiful garland" and "a necklace" may be symbolic apotropaic or mnemonic devices, on the one hand, or designations that capture the favor, honor, and social esteem that accompany receptivity to wisdom and obedience to parental

11. Loader, *Proverbs 1–9*, 71–72.

12. This may be the only place in the Old Testament where a woman teaches torah explicitly. Many thanks to Hélène M. Dallaire, who alerted me to this.

13. William P. Brown, "The Law and the Sages: A Reexamination of in *Tôrâ* in Proverbs," in *Constituting the Community: Studies on the Polity of Ancient Israel in Honor of S. Dean McBride Jr.*, ed. John T. Strong and Steven S. Tuell (Winona Lake, IN: Eisenbrauns, 2005), 251–80.

14. Brown, "The Law and the Sages," 278–80.

instruction, on the other. The pregnant nature of the images allows for both readings. Nonetheless, the latter appears to be primary. The teaching of the parents is attractive and valuable. Its intrinsic value and the social honor associated with obeying parental instruction, however, not only motivate the son to receive and heed instruction; the ornamental imagery also provides the son with an alternative, even appropriate means of satisfying his desire. The sinners will attempt to lure the son into their gang and down their path through the language and desire of wealth (vv. 13–14). In anticipation of this rival motivation, the parents appeal to the son's desires and offer a different motivation: social honor and favor that is bestowed upon the son through obedience to parental advice within the safe, communal confines of the home for his benefit as well as the well-being of the broader community.

2. The Lesson: Sinners, Speech, and Steps (1:10–18)

As the discourse shifts from the introductory exhortation to the lesson proper, the son is transported out of the confines of the home and into a conflicted world, populated by different characters with different moral worldviews that traverse different ways in life. Rather than isolating the son from these rival characters, ways, and worldviews, the parents introduce him to one of the communities of death within the world of the prologue: the community of "sinners" (חַטָּאִים, v. 10a). As noted above, the lesson proper highlights the nature of these characters and their community through two conditional clauses, which are intimately related to one another. The substance and rhetorical texture of each deserves a brief comment.

a. The General Command: Temptation and the Will (1:10)

The first conditional clause moves from a general situation to a clear, straightforward command. Far from peddling a pious platitude, the parents identify the serious and urgent nature of the issue at hand. The placement of the vocative "my son" (v. 10a) before the conditional clause is emphatic, suggesting that the ensuing advice is not to be brushed aside as banal; it requires thoughtful consideration. And this is not surprising, for the issue at hand concerns temptation and its power to sway the will. The temptation the sinners pose is conveyed through the verb "entice" (יְפַתּוּךָ, v. 10b), a verb that is rarely used in a positive sense (16:29; 24:28; Deut 11:16; Judg 14:15; 16:5; Ps 78:36). As a cognate of פֶּתִי (1:4a), it picks up on one of the fundamental characteristics of the "uncommitted" who is interpolated into the prologue through the son: he is inexperienced, prone to folly, and easily enticed. To remedy the matter and form the malleable disposition of the son, the parents pinpoint the root of the matter, namely, the will. The command, "do not accede" (אַל־תֹּבֵא, v. 10b),[15] places the locus of temptation in the subjective consent and approval of the son, which then blossoms in specific actions or forms of behavior.[16] In preparation for the deceptive invitation of the sinners (vv. 11–14), the parents cut off the gang's appeal to the son's will at the rhetorical pass. They attune the son to the issue of temptation and its power to direct the will.

15. While a few manuscripts read תָּבֹא as a jussive from the lexical root בוא ("to go"), the verb appears to be an irregular form derived from the lexical root אבה; it is an apocopated form, which exhibits the normal elision of the consonant *aleph* and a *tsere-aleph* ending that is common in Aramaic. GKC §68h, §75hh; Fox, *Proverbs 1–9*, 85; Loader, *Proverbs 1–9*, 76.

16. E. Gerstenberger, "אבה, *'bh*, to want," *TLOT* 1:17.

b. The Sinners' Deceptive Speech and Desires (1:11–14)

(1) The Invitation (1:11–12)

The first conditional clause and its concern with temptation and the will give way to the second and its concern with the deceptive speech of the sinners (vv. 11–14). The speech of this community is revealing, for it betrays their character, appetites, and distorted moral worldview. While the parents control and convey the sinners' speech, they allow this representative "community of death" to express its appealing invitation and to entice the son. In so doing, the parents attempt to plant the seeds of discernment and perception. They invite the son to hear another discourse, discern the nature of the sinners' character, and perceive the ethos and end of their way.

The parents present the speech of the sinners through an extended protasis. Here the text moves from the first-person parental appeal to the son to a first-person plural invitation from the sinners. This first-person plural address is woven throughout the sinners' speech: "Come with *us* . . . *let's* lurk . . . *let's* ambush . . . *let's* swallow . . . *We'll* find . . . *we'll* fill . . . Throw in your lot with *us* . . . *we'll* all share." And this first-person plural address creates a rhetorical veneer of a unified, egalitarian community that shares a common character, a common goal, and a common worldview. They offer the son camaraderie and provide him with a sense of belonging.

But this is only the tip of the iceberg. The sinners' invitation also reveals the character, desires, and tactics of their fraternity. They depict themselves as mercenaries, even animals on the prowl, poised to pounce on hapless victims ("let's lurk," נֶאֶרְבָה, v. 11c; cf. Judg 16:2; 21:20; Ps 10:9; Lam 3:10–11). Through imagery reminiscent of the Canaanite deity Mot ("let's swallow them," נִבְלָעֵם, v. 12a),[17] they compare their insatiable appetites to the voracious hunger of Sheol and the Pit, which relentlessly consume the living. They direct their attacks "at the innocent" (לְנָקִי, v. 11d) and satisfy their appetites by feeding on "the blameless" (תְמִימִים, v. 12b).[18] Ironically, they acknowledge the virtue and moral rectitude of their victims. Yet they pursue the life of these victims "without cause" (חִנָּם, v. 11d), that is, gratuitously or for no reason.

(2) The Promised Reward (1:13–14)

The character, appetites, tactics, and moral worldview of this community may be despicable and grotesque, but what they offer the son is attractive and desirable. In addition to a unified, egalitarian community ("one purse," כִּיס אֶחָד, v. 14b), the sinners promise the son "all sorts of precious wealth" (כָּל־הוֹן יָקָר, v. 13a) and a house filled with the "spoil" (שָׁלָל, v. 13b) of their violent attacks. These promises mirror the possessions and promises of Wisdom, who enjoys "enduring wealth" (הוֹן עָתֵק; 8:18b) and fills the treasuries of her devotees (8:21). Wealth is desirable and attractive. Here the problem is not the object of desire; rather, it is the means employed to satisfy the desire. The sinners attempt to separate the ends from the means, the acquisition of wealth from the way in which it is accumulated.[19] In light of this promise and the prospect of instant riches, the sinners call the son to throw in his lot with their gang (גּוֹרָלְךָ תַּפִּיל בְּתוֹכֵנוּ,

17. See "The Baʿlu Myth," trans. Dennis Pardee (*COS* 1.86:241–74, esp. 263–66), where Mot (Prince Death) is described as having an enormous mouth and an unquenchable throat that consumes the living. Cf. Isa 5:14; Hab 2:5.

18. While many translations render תְמִימִים as "whole," that is, physically sound, it appears the moral character of the group is in view, for the term is related to the "innocent" in v. 11d. In addition, though תְמִימִים may be translated as "whole," it is never used in this sense to describe humans. Fox, *Proverbs 1–9*, 87.

19. Fox, *Proverbs 1–9*, 94.

v. 14a) and identify with their community. The son is invited to join the sinners; he is challenged to interpret their deceptive rhetoric and identify the consequences associated with their actions. Put differently, he is invited to exercise discernment and perception.

c. The Speech Interpreted: Wrong Ways and Misplaced Desire (1:15–18)

To assist the son in this task, the parents decode the speech of the sinners. Together, vv. 15–18 serve as the apodosis to the extended situation presented in vv. 11–14. While the proverb delineated in v. 17 and the comment presented in v. 18 may stand alone, the causal conjunction "for" (כִּי, v. 17a) and the adversative "but" (וְ, v. 18a) bind the sayings to vv. 15–16 and reinforce the parents' argument.

(1) The Command (1:15)

This argument concerns the path, steps, perception, and fate of the sinners. Similar to the emphatic position of the vocative before the first condition (v. 10a), "my son" precedes the apodosis in the second condition and infuses the parental interpretation with an air of earnestness (v. 15a). Within the apodosis proper, the parents introduce the root metaphor within the prologue to describe the lifestyle represented by the sinners, namely, the "way" (דֶּרֶךְ, v. 15a) or "path" (נְתִיבָה, v. 15b). This metaphor is associated with particular people to describe their orientation to or course of life as well as their character, conduct, and the consequence of their actions.[20] Viewed through the lens of this metaphor, the parents suggest that the sinners' speech is more than mere talk; it is the manifestation of a particular moral worldview, a particular lifestyle, a particular orientation to life. They reiterate and develop the command issued in v. 10b, admonishing the son to decline membership in this community and to reject its accompanying lifestyle.

(2) The Rationale (1:16)

The rationale for this command is introduced by the causal conjunction "for" (כִּי, v. 16a). The parents build on the path imagery delineated in v. 15 and give particular attention to the "feet" (רַגְלֵי, v. 16a) or steps of the sinners. They clarify the nature of their path and indicate that it not only captures the character and lifestyle of the sinners, but it also describes their bodily fixation; it orients, directs, and controls their steps.

(3) A Proverb: The Seeing Bird (1:17)

Against the backdrop of their command and rationale (vv. 15–16), the parents introduce a proverb (v. 17), which provides an additional reason for avoiding the way of sinners. On the surface, the message of the saying is straightforward: it is useless to spread out the net in the sight of any bird, for the creature will avoid the trap. The issue, however, is whom the bird represents. While the bird may represent the son, within the broader context of the lecture, it seems the bird refers to the sinners. And this connection reveals the warped perception of the gang, which is described in v. 18.

(4) The Ironic Fate of Blind Sinners (1:18)

Like the proverbial bird, the sinners should see or perceive the trap set before them. But they do not. They "hurry" (יְמַהֲרוּ, v. 16b) to shed blood in the same way as "a bird rushing to a trap" (מַהֵר צִפּוֹר אֶל־פָּח; 7:23b). In fact, the sinners set their

20. For further discussion of the path metaphor, see Root Metaphor and Its "Satellite Images" in the introduction, pp. 84–87.

own trap. They invite the son to "lurk for blood" (נֶאֶרְבָה לְדָם, v. 11c), unaware that, in so doing, "they lurk for their own blood" (הֵם לְדָמָם יֶאֱרֹבוּ, v. 18a). They call the son to "ambush the innocent" (נִצְפְּנָה לְנָקִי, v. 11d), unaware that, in so doing, "they ambush their own lives" (יִצְפְּנוּ לְנַפְשֹׁתָם, v. 18b). Their desire has blinded their perception and paralyzed their faculties of discernment.[21] And their blindness as well as their fate illuminates the value of discernment and perception, virtues the son must acquire.

d. The Conclusion (1:19)

The path, steps, perception, and fate of the sinners serve as the foundation for the lecture's conclusion (v. 19). Here the way and ironic fate of the sinners are reiterated and generalized through a description of the "ways" (אָרְחוֹת, v. 19a) and ironic fate of "all who profit from unjust gain" (כָּל־בֹּצֵעַ בָּצַע, v. 19a). As noted above, the initial colon of the conclusion provides an apt summary of vv. 11–14 (v. 19a), while the second colon offers a distillation of vv. 15–18 (v. 19b).[22] The "ways" of those who benefit from illicit profit are given particular expression through the speech of the sinners. And the ultimate fate of these character types is described through the parents' interpretation of the speech of the sinners.

The fate assigned to those who profit from unjust gain in general and to sinners in particular suits the crime. But the relationship between the crime and its consequences is ironic (v. 19b; cf. v. 18). The crime is generalized through the phrase "all who profit from unjust gain" (v. 19a). And as the subject of the verb "takes away" (יִקָּח, v. 19b), it is the "unjust gain" (בָּצַע, v. 19a) that brings these racketeers to ruin. This connection between actions and consequences is striking. Whereas Proverbs tends to relate consequences to the character of various personages,[23] the conclusion to the initial lecture relates consequences to specific actions. The means by which this punishment will be executed is ambiguous, and its timing is left open. The parents refuse to get bogged down in the details. Instead, they conclude their lesson with a general rule that reveals an aspect of their worldview: somehow at some time the perpetrators of exploitation and violence will have to pay the piper.

Canonical and Theological Significance

The first parental lecture reflects on the speech, character, ways, and moral worldview of a particular "community of death":[24] the sinners. The parents, however, do not outline the contours and nature of this community simply to warn their son of the dangers that accompany fraternizing with the wrong crowd or falling prey to get-rich-quick schemes. The speech of the sinners, combined with their character, ways, and moral worldview, provides the occasion for teaching a much more fundamental lesson, namely, the value of discernment and perception in the wise and virtuous life. The parents seek to develop these faculties through the rhetorical ploys, destructive

21. Crawford H. Toy, *A Critical and Exegetical Commentary on the Book of Proverbs*, ICC (Edinburgh: T&T Clark, 1899), 17; McKane, *Proverbs*, 271.

22. Loader, *Proverbs 1–9*, 66, 84.

23. Boström, *The God of the Sages*, 90–133; Van Leeuwen, "Wealth and Poverty," 25–36.

24. Van Leeuwen, "The Book of Proverbs," *NIB* 5:3.

actions, and devastating consequences of a community of despicable characters. And the parents illuminate the indispensable value of these virtues through their interpretation of the sinner's speech (vv. 15–18) as well as their diagnosis of the sinners' fate (vv. 18, 19). Discernment and perception pay. Without these virtues, the son is susceptible to the temptations, pseudo-promises, ways, and fate of the sinners as well as other communities of death within the anthology.

This may explain why the lecture is situated at the beginning of the prologue. As noted above, the discourse introduces the fundamental issue that is woven throughout the parental lectures and wisdom interludes: the issue of seductive speech. Through their speech, the sinners offer the son a sense of community, identity, and camaraderie as well as the promise of wealth and desire fulfilled. They are members of the "community of death," a community that also includes the wicked (4:14–17), the adulterous woman (2:16–19; 5:1–14; 7:10–27), and Woman Folly (9:13–18). This community not only shares a common fate; it also shares a common trait: deceptive speech.

In addition to introducing the issue of seductive speech, the initial lecture contains key themes and root metaphors that pervade the anthology in general and the prologue in particular. The path metaphor plays a formative role in the parent's interpretation of the sinners' speech (vv. 15–16) and their description of the fate of all who profit from unjust gain (v. 19). The matter of wealth and the promises as well as the pitfalls of desire are introduced. And the image of the home makes a brief cameo. These images and issues are reiterated and elaborated upon throughout Proverbs. The initial lecture identifies them and lays the groundwork for their development.

The canonical and theological contributions of the lecture, however, are not limited to its introduction of key motifs. Like the broader canonical witness, it acknowledges that the company we keep matters,[25] for bad company corrupts good morals (13:20; 1 Cor 15:33). It suggests that one's words reveal one's character (Ps 37:30; Prov 10:31–32; 15:2; Matt 12:34). And it confirms that a person reaps what they sow (Prov 1:19; Gal 6:7).

Together with these theological principles, the lecture includes words, phrases, and intertextual references that reveal its relationship to and consonance with other voices within the canon. The characterization of the sinners and the rhetorical scenario sketched by the parents may seem extreme and exceptional. But they are all too familiar within the canon. The parental lecture captures particular aspects of the human condition. Both Jeremiah and Ezekiel describe the people and leaders of their day through the same expression that concludes the lecture: they are "those who profit

25. The expression is taken from Wayne Booth's helpful book, *The Company We Keep: An Ethics of Fiction* (Berkeley: University of California Press, 1988).

from unjust gain" (Jer 6:13; 8:10; Ezek 22:13, 27; Prov 1:19). Similar to the sinners, Israel's history is littered with acts of violence in general and the shedding of innocent blood in particular (Judg 9:1–6; 2 Kgs 21:16; 24:4; Jer 2:34; 19:4; 22:17). In fact, with the exception of the term "innocent" (נָקִי; Prov 1:11d), Prov 1:16 and Isa 59:7 are mirror images of one another. Whereas the former describes the way of the sinners, the latter describes the sin of God's people: their feet run to evil and they hurry to shed innocent blood. Violence and bloodshed mark the human condition, so much so that Paul includes this crime in his description of those under sin (Rom 3:15). And the rhetorical scenario presented by the parents is eerily similar to the scenario outlined in Deut 19:11–13.[26] Here Moses offers prescriptions concerning how to treat a perpetrator of intentional murder in order to purge "the blood of the innocent" (דַם־הַנָּקִי; Deut 19:13; cf. Prov 1:11c–d) from Israel. The perpetrator in this scenario "lurks" (אָרַב; Deut 19:11; Prov 1:11, 18) for his neighbor, rises up, and strikes him so that he dies. Upon his arrival to one of the cities of refuge, Moses advises the elders to deliver the perpetrator into the hands of the avenger of blood so that he may die.

The scenario is straightforward, but it raises a question: how do the elders discriminate between intentional murder and accidental death? The answer, it seems, is through the same virtues that the parents employ to diagnose the speech, character, and path of the sinners: discernment and perception. Together with wisdom, these virtues characterize the leaders and judges appointed by the people (Deut 1:13, 15–17); they were bestowed upon Solomon so that he might discriminate between good and evil and reign in accord with justice (1 Kgs 3:9–12). And they are fundamental to the life of faith. They are cultivated and developed by the Spirit so that believers may discern the will of God (Rom 12:2). They are particular gifts granted to people for the benefit of the church (1 Cor 12:10). They are virtues that characterize the mature (Heb 5:14); and they are values that Proverbs in general (Prov 1:2, 6; 2:5, 9) and the first lecture in particular seek to inculcate in readers.

Along with these canonical and theological contributions, the initial lecture gives vivid attention to the process of sin. In fact, it actualizes and illustrates the paradigm delineated in Jas 1:13–15. Just as James traces the trajectory of sin from temptation to an allurement of the will through desire to sin and then to death, so also the first lecture traces the trajectory of sin from temptation (Prov 1:10a) to an allurement of the will through desire (vv. 10b, 13–14) to sin (vv. 11–14) and then to death (vv. 18, 19). James describes this process through the metaphor of birth; Prov 1:8–19 describes it through the parents' warnings and sinners' rhetorical flourish.

In light of the lecture's theological themes and their treatment elsewhere in the canon, much could be said about the way in which this discourse speaks to the

---

26. For the similarities between the scenario in Prov 1:10–19 and Gen 37, see Harris, *Proverbs 1–9*, 45–65.

church. Two matters, however, deserve specific comment. The first concerns the value of discernment and perception in a world filled with rival voices vying for one's allegiance. In the technological age in which we live, there is no shortage of images appealing to our desires, voices contending for our devotion, or moral worldviews requesting our assent. In large measure, one's character and way in life are determined by what one chooses to listen to and whom one chooses to trust.[27] The voices, views, and images that bombard people every day illuminate the indispensable value of discernment and perception. These values must be developed, trained, and sharpened to discern the good from the pseudo-good, the way of life from the way of death, so that one might tread the path of wisdom and virtue.

Second, the parental lecture reflects on the nature of the human condition through the dynamics of human desire. While the language, character, and tactics of the sinners may be deplorable, their offer is attractive. They promise community, camaraderie, identity, belonging, power, and wealth. These desires are not wrong; there is nothing intrinsically evil about them. But the way in which they are attained or fulfilled is wrong. In fact, the way in which the sinners fulfill their desires is abhorrent in God's sight (Prov 6:16–18). The lecture implicitly recognizes the human temptation to separate the ends from the means,[28] desire from the way in which it is satisfied. And in so doing, it challenges the readers to consider what they desire, where that desire may lead, and whom it will affect. This type of reflection, directed by discernment and perception, will help prevent one from falling prey to deceptive voices, rushing headlong to fulfill their desires, and walking into a trap (1:17).

27. Paul E. Koptak, *Proverbs*, NIV Application Commentary (Grand Rapids: Zondervan Academic, 2003), 75.

28. Fox, *Proverbs 1–9*, 94.

CHAPTER 3

Proverbs 1:20–33

A. Wisdom's Rebuke

Main Idea of the Passage

Through the rhetoric of rebuke, Lady Wisdom seeks to cultivate the attitude and the listening posture necessary to acquire wisdom and virtue by highlighting the severe consequences associated with rejecting her reproof.

Literary Context

Lady Wisdom's impassioned rebuke is intimately related to the preamble (1:1–7), the first parental lecture (1:8–19), and the variegated discourses in the remainder of the prologue. The preamble identified the "uncommitted" (פְּתָאיִם, v. 4a) as its principal addressee; now Wisdom inscribes the "uncommitted" into her discourse and directs her rebuke at the inexperienced (vv. 22a; 32a). The preamble promised that the anthology would disseminate knowledge to the young (1:4b); now Wisdom promises that those who hate knowledge will experience a certain fate (v. 29a). The preamble described the listening posture as well as the mode of being necessary to achieve the document's goal (1:5, 7); now Wisdom describes the consequences associated with failing to assume that posture and mode of being (vv. 24–32; esp. 24–25, 29–30). Similar to the first parental instruction, Wisdom incorporates key terms and expressions from the preamble into her warning. In so doing, she actualizes the document's pedagogical program through a specific form of "instruction" (מוּסָר; 1:2, 3, 7, 8): rebuke.

Together with the preamble, Wisdom's warning complements the first parental lecture. The juxtaposition of Wisdom's speech with first parental lecture associates the domestic voice of the parents with the public voice of Wisdom.[1] These figures deliver their discourses in distinct settings; but they share a common perspective, occupy comparable positions of authority, and use common terms. In fact, with the exception of 6:35, the verb אבה ("to accede, accept") occurs only in the first parental lecture and Wisdom's warning within the anthology (1:10b, 25b, 30a). The coordination of the parents' warning and position with Wisdom's warning and position at the beginning of the prologue is significant, for it provides the reader with an indication of the voices they should trust, the authorities they should heed, and the perspectives they should embrace as they prepare to navigate the discourses within the remainder of the prologue.

The discourses within the remainder of the prologue elaborate upon Wisdom's persona and initial speech in diverse ways. Similar to 1:20–33, Wisdom is personified in 8:1–36 and 9:1–6. The former gives particular attention to her character and her activity in terrestrial affairs, as well as her nobility, authority, and rank as one created by YHWH in hoary antiquity; the latter describes her house, her staff, and her banquet. In each discourse, wisdom addresses the "uncommitted" in the public thoroughfares (1:20–22; 8:1–11; 9:3–4). In each discourse, Wisdom "cries out" (תִּקְרָא; 1:21; 8:1; 9:3) and employs different rhetorical strategies to persuade the addressee to embrace her. And in each discourse, Wisdom concludes with a description of the rewards she bestows upon those who listen to or choose her (1:33; 8:34–35; 9:6). Whereas the interludes present Wisdom as a valuable and desirable woman, the parental lectures describe wisdom as a valuable and desirable virtue (2:1–22; 3:13–18; 4:5–9; 7:4–5). The parental discourses move from the metaphorical to the historical in order to elaborate upon Lady Wisdom's speeches and to persuade the addressee to seek her, find her, and acquire her. Lady Wisdom's speeches are intimately related to the parental lectures within the prologue. And Lady Wisdom's persona is integral to the prologue's rhetorical agenda, for she provides an attractive, alternative companion to Woman Folly (9:13–18), on the one hand, and the adulterous woman (2:16–19; 5:1–14; 6:20–35; 7:1–27), on the other.

1. Newsom, "Woman and the Discourse of Patriarchal Wisdom," 145–46; Murphy, *Proverbs*, 11; Van Leeuwen, "Liminality and Worldview," 115.

I. Introduction to the Book (1:1–7)

II. The Value of Wisdom and Virtue (1:8–9:18)

A. Wisdom, Desire, and Different Ways (1:8–19)

B. Wisdom's Rebuke (1:20–33)

1. The Prelude to Wisdom's Rebuke (1:20–21)

2. Wisdom's Rebuke (1:22–31)

a. Wisdom's Direct Rebuke (1:22–27)

(1) The Addressees (1:22)

(2) The Rebuke (1:23)

(3) The Response of the Addressees (1:24–25)

(4) Wisdom's Response (1:26–27)

b. Wisdom's Indirect Rebuke (1:28–31)

(1) Wisdom's Response (1:28)

(2) The Response of the Addressees (1:29–30)

(3) The Reward Promised the Addressees (1:31)

3. Wisdom's Conclusion (1:32–33)

a. The Fate of the Unreceptive (1:32)

b. The Fate of the Receptive (1:33)

C. The Procurement, Power, and Protection of Wisdom and Virtue (2:1–22)

D. Wisdom and Piety (3:1–12)

E. Wisdom's Value and Moral Obligations (3:13–35)

F. Wisdom and Tradition (4:1–9)

G. Wisdom and Ways of Life (4:10–19)

H. Wisdom and the Moral Anatomy (4:20–27)

I. Wisdom and Sexuality (5:1–23)

J. Wisdom, Lending, Laziness, and the Immoral Anatomy (6:1–19)

K. Wisdom, Desire, and Certain Destruction (6:20–35)

L. Wisdom and Seduction (7:1–27)

M. Wisdom's Call, Credentials, and the Cosmos (8:1–36)

N. Wisdom and Folly's Invitations (9:1–18)

III. "Forming 'Fearers of YHWH'": The Curriculum of Wisdom and Virtue (10:1–29:27)

IV. The Application of Wisdom and Virtue (30:1–31:31)

Translation and Exegetical Outline

(See pages 143–144.)

Proverbs 1:20–33

Verse	Hebrew	English	Outline
			B. Wisdom's Rebuke (1:20–33)
20a	חָכְמוֹת בַּחוּץ תָּרֹנָּה	Wisdom shouts in the street,	1. The Prelude to Wisdom's Rebuke (1:20–21)
20b	בָּרְחֹבוֹת תִּתֵּן קוֹלָהּ	in the open plazas she raises her voice;	
21a	בְּרֹאשׁ הֹמִיּוֹת תִּקְרָא	at the busiest intersection she cries out	
21b	בְּפִתְחֵי שְׁעָרִים בָּעִיר אֲמָרֶיהָ תֹאמֵר	at the entrance of the city gates she speaks her words.	
			2. Wisdom's Rebuke (1:22–31)
			a. Wisdom's Direct Rebuke (1:22–27)
22a	עַד־מָתַי פְּתָיִם תְּאֵהֲבוּ פֶתִי	"How long, uncommitted ones, will you love simplicity,	(1) The Addressees (1:22)
22b	וְלֵצִים לָצוֹן חָמְדוּ לָהֶם	and scoffers desire scoffing,	
22c	וּכְסִילִים יִשְׂנְאוּ־דָעַת	and fools hate knowledge?	
23a	תָּשׁוּבוּ לְתוֹכַחְתִּי	Turn to my reproof;	(2) The Rebuke (1:23)
23b	הִנֵּה אַבִּיעָה לָכֶם רוּחִי	look, I want to pour out my spirit on you;	
23c	אוֹדִיעָה דְבָרַי אֶתְכֶם	I want to enlighten you with my words.	
24a	יַעַן קָרָאתִי וַתְּמָאֵנוּ	Because I called and you refused,	(3) The Response of the Addressees (1:24–25)
24b	נָטִיתִי יָדִי וְאֵין מַקְשִׁיב	I extended my hand and no one paid attention;	
25a	וַתִּפְרְעוּ כָל־עֲצָתִי	you ignored all my advice,	
25b	וְתוֹכַחְתִּי לֹא אֲבִיתֶם	and my reproof you did not accept,	
26a	גַּם־אֲנִי בְּאֵידְכֶם אֶשְׂחָק	I, on my part, will laugh in your disaster;	(4) Wisdom's Response (1:26–27)
26b	אֶלְעַג בְּבֹא פַחְדְּכֶם	I will mock when your moment of dread comes,	
27a	בְּבֹא כְשַׁאֲוָה פַּחְדְּכֶם	when your moment of dread comes like a storm,	
27b	וְאֵידְכֶם כְּסוּפָה יֶאֱתֶה	and your disaster comes like a whirlwind,	
27c	בְּבֹא עֲלֵיכֶם צָרָה וְצוּקָה	when distress and anguish come upon you.	

Continued on next page.

Continued from previous page.

Verse	Hebrew	English	Outline
			b. Wisdom's Indirect Rebuke (1:28–31)
28a	אָז יִקְרָאֻנְנִי וְלֹא אֶעֱנֶה	Then they will call for me, but I will not answer;	(1) Wisdom's Response (1:28)
28b	יְשַׁחֲרֻנְנִי וְלֹא יִמְצָאֻנְנִי	they will seek me, but not find me,	
29a	↑ תַּחַת כִּי־שָׂנְאוּ דָעַת	↑ because they hated knowledge,	(2) The Response of the Addressees (1:29–30)
29b	וְיִרְאַת יְהוָה לֹא בָחָרוּ	and the fear of YHWH they did not choose,	
30a	לֹא־אָבוּ לַעֲצָתִי	they did not accept my advice;	
30b	נָאֲצוּ כָּל־תּוֹכַחְתִּי	they spurned all my reproof.	
31a	וְיֹאכְלוּ מִפְּרִי דַרְכָּם	So they will eat the fruit of their way,	(3) The Reward Promised the Addressees (1:31)
31b	וּמִמֹּעֲצֹתֵיהֶם יִשְׂבָּעוּ	and from their counsels they will be satisfied.	
			3. Wisdom's Conclusion (1:32–33)
32a	כִּי מְשׁוּבַת פְּתָיִם תַּהַרְגֵם	Indeed, the turning away of the uncommitted will kill them,	a. The Fate of the Unreceptive (1:32)
32b	וְשַׁלְוַת כְּסִילִים תְּאַבְּדֵם	and the complacency of fools will destroy them.	
33a	וְשֹׁמֵעַ לִי יִשְׁכָּן־בֶּטַח	But the one who listens to me will dwell securely	b. The Fate of the Receptive (1:33)
33b	וְשַׁאֲנַן מִפַּחַד רָעָה	and be at ease from dread of disaster.	

Structure and Literary Form

Lady Wisdom's rebuke is a poetic masterpiece. To borrow a concept from the fine arts, the poem incorporates the technique of *chiaroscuro*; it juxtaposes rhetorical shade with literary light to produce an arresting and evocative rebuke designed to awaken the readers' organs of reception. Similar to da Vinci, Caravaggio, and Rembrandt, the poet places repeated terms and phrases as well as an inverted argument around the center of the poem to create shadows that help illuminate the literary flourish within the nucleus of the piece: a rhetorical avalanche, complete with repeated clauses, alliteration, and assonance (vv. 26–27). The poem is replete with recurring terms and phrases: "uncommitted" (פְּתָיִם, vv. 22a, 32a), "fools" (כְּסִילִים, vv. 22c, 32b), "hate(d) knowledge" (שָׂנֵא דָעַת, vv. 22c, 29a), "my reproof" (תוֹכַחְתִּי, vv. 23a, 25b, 30b), "dread" (פַּחַד, vv. 26b, 27a, 33b), "accept" (אבה, vv. 25b, 30a), and "my advice" (עֲצָתִי, vv. 25a, 30a). The inverted argument delineated in vv. 24–30 provides an envelope around the literary flourish in vv. 26–27. This argument moves from the response of the addressees (vv. 24–25) to Wisdom's response (vv. 26–27), addressing each other in the second person, to Wisdom's response (v. 28) and the response of the addressees (vv. 29–30), addressing each other in the third person. The rhetorical avalanche is placed at the hinge of this argument, at the threshold between Wisdom's direct and indirect rebuke.

A I, on my part, will laugh "in ***your disaster***" (בְּאֵידְכֶם, v. 26a)
  B I will mock **when your moment of dread comes** (v. 26b)
  B′ **when your moment of dread comes** "like a storm" (כְּשַׁאֲוָה, v. 27a)[2]
A′ and ***your disaster***" (וְאֵידְכֶם) comes "like a whirlwind" (כְּסוּפָה, v. 27b)
    C when "distress and anguish" (צָרָה וְצוּקָה, v. 27c) come upon you.

Lady Wisdom's response is cast in a clean, tight chiasm (26–27c), which culminates in a graphic portrayal of distress (v. 27c).[3] Her rebuke snowballs,[4] building intensity before it crashes and settles on a depiction of the addressees' certain anguish. Similar to the use of *chiaroscuro* by da Vinci, Caravaggio, and Rembrandt, the poem deploys this artistic technique to achieve dramatic intensity. And in so doing, it seeks to probe one's attitudes, kindle one's senses, and provoke receptivity.

2. The translation follows *qere* (כְּשַׁאֲוָה) rather than *ketiv* (כְּשׁוֹאָה).

3. In addition to vv. 26–27, many contend that the entire poem is cast in a clean chiasm. This proposal was popularized by Phyllis Trible ("Wisdom Builds a Poem: The Architecture of Proverbs 1:20–33," *JBL* 94 [1975]: 509–18), and it has been adopted or modified by others (e.g., Duane A. Garrett; *Proverbs, Ecclesiastes, Song of Songs*, NAC 14 [Nashville: Broadman & Holman, 1993], 71; Waltke, *Proverbs: Chapters 1–15*, 201). While the rhetorical movement apparent within the poem and its effective use of repetition suggest a variety of interrelationships among its parts, on the whole, it is difficult to see a precise inverted or chiastic structure to the piece. Fox, *Proverbs 1–9*, 104.

4. Fox, *Proverbs 1–9*, 101.

When one steps back from the intricate details of the poem and views it as a literary whole, the piece divides into three parts. The first is a prelude to Wisdom's rebuke (vv. 20–21). Here an omniscient voice introduces the speaker (v. 20a), describes the impassioned nature of Wisdom's address, and identifies the setting of her speech (vv. 20–21). The second section then presents Wisdom's formal rebuke (vv. 22–31). In light of the shift from second person to third person, the rebuke consists of two parts: it moves from a direct rebuke (vv. 22–27) to an indirect rebuke (vv. 28–30) before describing the reward of those who reject Wisdom's reproof (v. 31). The third and final section of the poem concludes the discourse in a manner comparable to the first parental lecture (vv. 32–33); it summarizes and differentiates the fate of those who fail to respond to Wisdom's rebuke with those who receive Wisdom's rebuke. Together, these three sections coalesce to illuminate the rhetorical and pedagogical power of rebuke; they provide an object lesson intended to cultivate the attitude and the listening posture necessary to acquire wisdom and virtue.

Explanation of the Text

Rebuke is a common form of "instruction" or "discipline" (מוּסָר; 1:2, 3, 7, 8) in Proverbs's pedagogical repertoire. As intimated above, Lady Wisdom's rebuke captures the fundamental purpose of this pedagogical technique. Through stinging rhetoric, she seeks to cultivate a listening posture from which the reader may receive instruction in wisdom and virtue and perceive the world rightly. This rhetorical agenda is conveyed through three main sections, each of which deserves specific comment.

1. The Prelude to Wisdom's Rebuke (1:20–21)

Lady Wisdom's warning opens with a prelude. This prelude sets the tone as well as the scene for the formal rebuke, identifying the speaker of the piece, the nature of the discourse, and the setting in which it is delivered. In contrast to the first parental lecture, the introduction is cast in the third person, placed on the lips of an omniscient narrator. While the identity of this narrator is implicit, the immediate context of the poem as well as the broader context of the prologue suggest the parents in general and the father in particular introduce Wisdom's rebuke. Lady Wisdom is depicted as a discrete character with a distinctive voice. Nonetheless, it is important to recognize that, along with the sinners, the adulterous woman, and Woman Folly, the father controls and conveys her speech.

Together with 8:1–36 and 9:1–6 (cf. Sir 24:1–34; Wis 7–9), "Wisdom" (חָכְמוֹת, v. 20a)[5] is personified as a woman. By definition, personification is a figure of speech in which an inanimate object or an

5. While חָכְמוֹת is a plural form, it is linked to a singular verb. Whether the form is a "plural of majesty" or a Phoenicianism, it functions as a singular in reference to Lady Wisdom. For discussion of these options, see Joüon §136d; William F. Albright, "Some Canaanite-Phoenician Sources of Hebrew Wisdom," in *Wisdom in Israel and in the Ancient Near East: Presented to Professor Harold Henry Rowley*, ed. M. Noth and D. Winston Thomas, VTSup 3 (Leiden: Brill, 1955), 8.

abstract concept is endowed with human characteristics. The sages employed this literary device as a pedagogical tool to transform the abstract concept of wisdom into an attractive form. And through this literary device, the sages created a general, conceptual framework within which to understand Lady's Wisdom's multifaceted character.[6] While some argue that Wisdom is presented as a divine mediator, and others contend that she is figured as a prophet, a teacher, a preacher, or a counselor,[7] the fact remains that she is a poetic, personified figure. Personification provides a literary device through which the images of mediator, goddess, lover, prophet, teacher, preacher, and counselor may be subsumed and concertized in a composite figure.[8] Lady Wisdom's attributes and rhetoric in the formal rebuke bear certain similarities to each of these figures and their respective roles. None of these roles, however, can account fully for the agglomeration of images attributed to Wisdom. She is a woman who speaks with authority and delivers an impassioned discourse.

The impassioned nature of Wisdom's speech is expressed through the string of verbs within vv. 20–21. Lady Wisdom "shouts" (תָּרֹנָּה, v. 20a), "raises her voice" (תִּתֵּן קוֹלָהּ, v. 20b), "cries out" (תִקְרָא, v. 21a), and "speaks her words" (אֲמָרֶיהָ תֹאמֵר, v. 21b). Far from merely expressing a desire for a hearing, the heaping up of these verbs for speech and their sequence capture the emphatic nature of Wisdom's discourse. The initial verb conveys something of the passion and volume of her speech (v. 20a; 8:3; 29:6; Isa 54:1); the second tends to be used in contexts of deep distress, communicating the emotional and intense nature of the verbal expression (Prov 1:20b; 8:1; Gen 45:2; Num 14:1). The third verb intensifies the oral character of the call (Prov 1:21a), while the final phrase places the direct object before the verb and reiterates the root אמר. The string of verbs, culminating in the emphatic, final phrase, highlights the impassioned nature of Wisdom's rebuke. What could be conveyed through a single verb is conveyed through four. The piling up of these verbs focuses one's attention on Wisdom, alerts one to the nature of her speech, and intimates that what she has to say is rather important.

Together with the string of verbs that highlight the nature of Wisdom's speech, the string of prepositional phrases highlights the setting of Wisdom's discourse. These prepositional phrases provide the panorama of Lady Wisdom's rebuke; they describe the arena in which Wisdom delivers her speech. And each phrase locates Wisdom's speech in the thick of public life. Lady wisdom expresses her desire for a hearing "in the street" (בַּחוּץ, v. 20a), "in the open plazas" (בָּרְחֹבוֹת, v. 20b), "at the busiest intersection" (בְּרֹאשׁ הֹמִיּוֹת, v. 21a),[9] and "at the entrance of the city gates" (בְּפִתְחֵי שְׁעָרִים בָּעִיר, v. 21b). Taken together, it appears that these phrases do not

6. Camp, *Wisdom and the Feminine*, 215–16; Alice M. Sinnott, *The Personification of Wisdom*, SOTSMS (Burlington, VT: Ashgate, 2005), 18–19.

7. For these characterizations of Wisdom within the prologue in general and 1:20–33 in particular, see the following representative works. For a mediator, see Camp, *Wisdom and the Feminine*, 272–91; Bruce K. Waltke, "Lady Wisdom as Mediatrix: An Exposition of Proverbs 1:20–33," *Presb* 14 (1988): 1–15. For a prophet, see André Robert, "Les Attaches Littéraires Bibliques de Prov I–IX," *RB* 43 (1934): 172–81; Harris, *Proverbs 1-9*, 87–109. For a teacher, see Fox, *Proverbs 1-9*, 340–41. For a blend of prophet, teacher, and preacher, see Berend Gemser, *Sprüche Salomos*, HAT 16 (Tübingen: Mohr, 1963), 16–17; McKane, *Proverbs*, 273–77. And for a counselor, see P. A. H. de Boer, "The Counsellor," in *Wisdom in Israel and in the Ancient Near East: Presented to Professor Harold Henry Rowley*, ed. M. Noth and D. Winston Thomas (VTSup 3; Leiden: Brill, 1955), 52.

8. Camp, *Wisdom and the Feminine*, 216–17; Sinnott, *The Personification of Wisdom*, 19–20.

9. This rendering construes the prepositional phrase as a superlative genitive. *IBHS* 154, 9.5.3j.

attempt to identify one specific locale in which Lady Wisdom delivers her discourse; rather, they identify Wisdom's integral relation to the thresholds of life in general and public affairs in particular.[10] They project Wisdom's association with the hustle and bustle of everyday life as well as her involvement in commercial, judicial, and economic dealings. In contrast to Wisdom's inaccessible and hidden locale in Job 28, the rebuke reveals her communal presence and accessibility. And the public setting of her speech complements the instruction of the parents. While the parents speak about wisdom within the confines of the home, Wisdom speaks about herself in the thoroughfares of public life.

2. Wisdom's Rebuke (1:22–31)

The prelude gives way to Lady Wisdom's formal rebuke. As noted above, this rebuke consists of a direct as well as an indirect rebuke. The direct rebuke is cast in the second person, whereas the indirect rebuke is cast in the third person. The substance and movement of each deserves specific comment.

a. Wisdom's Direct Rebuke (1:22–27)

(1) The Addressees (1:22)

Wisdom opens her direct rebuke in striking fashion. She poses a rhetorical question, which sets the tone for the formal rebuke; and she identifies three groups of people, who represent the rhetorical audience of her speech. The rhetorical question is enlightening in several respects. As an expression common to laments (Jer 4:14, 21; Ps 74:10; 82:2; 94:3), "How long" (עַד־מָתַי, v. 22a) not only captures Wisdom's impatience and displeasure with her addressees; it also passes judgment on their misplaced affections and conveys Wisdom's desire that their affections might be redirected (Exod 10:3; 1 Sam 16:1; Jer 31:22). According to Wisdom, the addressees have fed their distorted desires far too long. The question assumes that Wisdom and the addressees have crossed paths before. To this point, however, they have failed to respond appropriately.

The reason for this failure as well as Wisdom's exasperation is presented through the characterization of the addressees and the objects they either desire or despise. Both the "uncommitted" (פְּתָיִם; Prov 1:22a) and "scoffers" (לֵצִים, v. 22b) adore things that characterize their nature: the former "love simplicity" (תְּאֵהֲבוּ פֶתִי, v. 22a), whereas the latter "desire scoffing" (לָצוֹן חָמְדוּ, v. 22b). The use of the same lexical root to describe these respective characters and their desires indicates that their desires are intimately related to their disposition. They love the very things that mark their character. That is, they love themselves. The same is true of "fools" (כְּסִילִים, v. 22c). Whereas the uncommitted and scoffers are characterized by what they desire, fools are characterized by what they despise. They "hate knowledge" (יִשְׂנְאוּ־דָעַת, v. 22c). That is, they loathe the very wisdom and instruction the anthology seeks to inculcate in readers (1:4, 7). Wisdom's description of these figures highlights the dynamic relationship between character and desire. One's character directs one's desires, and one's desires identify one's character.

The character and desires of these addressees leave little hope for any change. This sentiment is reinforced by the characterization of these figures elsewhere in the anthology. The scoffer is portrayed as the embodiment of hubris (21:24),[11] as a person whose conceited character preempts

10. Bernhard Lang, *Wisdom and the Book of Proverbs: A Hebrew Goddess Redefined* (New York: Pilgrim Press, 1986), 22–29; Van Leeuwen, "The Book of Proverbs," *NIB* 5:89.

11. Fox, *Proverbs 1–9*, 42.

the acceptance of authority (13:1), the reception of instruction (9:7–8; 15:12), and the acquisition of wisdom (14:6). Fools are cut from the same cloth. As the epitome of intellectual vice, they are complacent and indifferent to knowledge (1:22c, 32b). They lack self-control as well as the ability to assess particular situations (10:19; 12:23). The uncommitted, however, are distinct, for they are open, malleable, and capable of receiving instruction (1:4; 19:25; 21:11).[12] In contrast to scoffers and fools, they possess the potential to learn. Nonetheless, they are inexperienced; they lack sense; and their association with scoffers and fools suggests that their wayward tendencies may lead to death (1:22, 32; 7:7; 9:4, 18).

In light of their capacity to receive wisdom, the "uncommitted" may represent the primary addressee of Lady Wisdom's rebuke, while scoffers and fools serve as the rhetorical audience.[13] In this case, despite the fact that scoffers and fools are unable to receive Wisdom's correction, they are included so that they may be held accountable for their response.[14] The uncommitted represent a more ideal or receptive character type. But their propensity for folly and waywardness suggests that they too constitute the rhetorical audience of the rebuke (1:32). Together with scoffers and fools, they offer an invaluable object lesson. Just as the reader was invited to assume the identity or subject position of the uncommitted in the prologue (1:4) and the son in the initial lecture (1:8), so now they are invited to assume the identity or subject position of one of these character types.[15] The reader not only overhears Wisdom's rebuke; the reader is also addressed through Wisdom's use of the second person (vv. 23a, 24–27). The addressees provide the reader with more than a cautionary tale. They invite the reader to inhabit a particular character type and to receive or reject wisdom's speech.

(2) The Rebuke (1:23)

Having identified and described her rhetorical audience, Lady Wisdom unleashes her rebuke (v. 23). This rebuke is the interpretive crux of the speech; it is interpreted in two basic ways. For some, Wisdom issues a call to repentance.[16] For others, she delivers a call to attention.[17] The distinction between these readings hinges on how one renders the phrase in v. 23a. The sense of this phrase is clarified by the preposition *lamed*. While the verb שׁוּב carries the sense "repent" in many texts within the Old Testament (1 Kgs 8:47; Ps 7:12; Jer 5:3),[18] the construction שׁוּב + לְ (v. 23a) conveys something different; it means to turn *to* something (Gen 18:33; 32:10). The use of this construction in v. 23a indicates that Wisdom delivers a call to attention. This call to attention seeks to reorient the posture of the addresses; it attempts to stop them in their tracks, turn their organs of perception toward Wisdom's reprimand and, by implication, away from

12. Fox, *Proverbs 1–9*, 43; Waltke, *Proverbs: Chapters 1–15*, 111; Schipper, *Proverbs 1–15*, 92.

13. Plöger, *Sprüche Salomos*, 18; Harris, *Proverbs 1–9*, 75–76; Waltke, *Proverbs: Chapters 1–15*, 203.

14. Fox, *Proverbs 1–9*, 98.

15. Newsom, "Woman and the Discourse of Patriarchal Wisdom," 146.

16. Waltke, *Proverbs: Chapters 1–15*, 203–4; Koptak, *Proverbs*, 88.

17. McKane, *Proverbs*, 276; Fox, *Proverbs 1–9*, 99; Yoder, *Proverbs*, 18; Loader, *Proverbs 1–9*, 94–95. Still others argue that Wisdom does not invite her audience to attend to her speech; rather, she indicts them for rejecting her reproof (Roland E. Murphy, "Wisdom's Song: Proverbs 1:20–33," *CBQ* 48 [1986]: 458; idem, *Proverbs*, 10).

18. For an extensive discussion of the verb, see William L. Holladay, *The Root* šûbh *in the Old Testament: With Particular Reference to Its Usage in Covenantal Contexts* (Leiden: Brill, 1958).

their distorted desires. Wisdom's summons is not a call to repentance; but some form of repentance may be implicit in her rebuke.[19] By turning toward Wisdom's reproof, the *receptive* addressee turns away from their misdirected affections and toward a verbal form of discipline that possesses the power to transform their posture, their desires, and their character. The turn toward reproof does not represent a definitive turning away from the lifestyles and desires that mark these character types. This turn, however, is a step in the right direction, for it indicates the addressee retains the listening posture necessary to receive Wisdom's reproof (cf. v. 33a).

The designation "reproof" not only serves as the literary backbone of Wisdom's speech (vv. 23a, 25b, 30b); it also captures the nature and function of her discourse. Reproof is a common pedagogical technique in Proverbs. The term encompasses various forms of verbal reproach or chastisement in the document. And in light of the fact that it is juxtaposed to "discipline" or "instruction" (מוּסָר) in the majority of its occurrences,[20] it seems that Wisdom's reproof is much more than a verbal reprimand intended to shock some sense into the addressees; it is a pedagogical tool, a means of discipline, and a literary mechanism for instruction designed to provide the receptive addressee with perspective, a particular moral worldview, and an indication of the consequences associated with their actions.

While the substance of Lady Wisdom's reproof is presented in vv. 24–31 in general and vv. 24–27 in particular, Wisdom's intention in delivering this verbal reprimand is described in the remainder of v. 23. Similar to the formal rebuke (v. 23a), the interjection "look" (הִנֵּה, v. 23b) arrests the audience and calls attention to the speech that follows.[21] Here Wisdom reveals the intention of her rebuke through a pair of volitional verbs. She wishes to "pour out" (אַבִּיעָה, v. 23b) her spirit and "enlighten" (אוֹדִיעָה, v. 23c) her addressees with her words. The parallel expressions "my spirit" (רוּחִי, v. 23b) and "my words" (דְבָרַי, v. 23c) convey the emotional nature of Wisdom's address. They describe her feelings as well as internal thoughts, which come to expression through her speech. As she opens the levee of her lips and unleashes her emotions as well as her words, the addressees can either receive them as a cold wakeup call or reject them and be carried away by their distorted desires.

(3) The Response of the Addressees (1:24–25)

The response delineated in vv. 24–25 indicates that the addressees have chosen the latter of the two options implied by v. 23. Together, vv. 24–25 represent an extended subordinate clause that describes the addressee's past response to Wisdom's reproof. And this response provides a rationale for or justification of Wisdom's response in vv. 26–27.

Wisdom's description of the addressee's response is unsettling, for she does not provide them with an opportunity to reply to her rebuke. Instead, she seems to recall earlier occasions in which she appealed to the addressees, but to no avail. The absence of an explicit rejection of Wisdom's present rebuke may suggest that she has jumped the gun. In view of the addressee's past response, she assumes their present rejection. This explanation may explain the dramatic shift in the discourse, but it overlooks Wisdom's rhetorical strategy. In contrast to the remaining interludes in the prologue (8:1–36; 9:1–6), Wisdom does not offer an explicit or direct invita-

19. Fox, *Proverbs 1–9*, 99.

20. The term "reproof" is used sixteen times in Proverbs and is paired with מוּסָר in nine of these sixteen occurrences (3:11; 5:12; 6:23; 10:17; 12:1; 13:18; 15:5, 10, 32).

21. Waltke, *Proverbs: Chapters 1–15*, 204.

tion to embrace her in the rebuke. That will come later. Her present concern is to shock the reader and inculcate receptivity to her voice by identifying the consequences associated with rejecting her call. She puts the cart before the horse, the indictment before the invitation, in order to sensitize, attune, and (re) orient one's organs of reception.

This pedagogical goal is achieved through a vivid contrast between Wisdom's invitation and the addressee's rejection. Similar to the prelude (v. 21a), Wisdom recounts the way in which she "called" (קָרָאתִי, v. 24a). And she elaborates on this verbal summons through a physical gesture: she "extended" her hand (נָטִיתִי יָדִי, v. 24b). The idiom is used elsewhere in the Old Testament to convey hostility or aggression (e.g., Exod 7:5, 19; 14:16). In the present context, however, it is qualified by neither the preposition עַל (e.g., Exod 9:22; Isa 5:25) nor a weapon that signifies enmity (Exod 8:13; Josh 8:18–19, 26). In view of the idiom's association with Wisdom's positive call as well as her verbal reproof (vv. 23a, 24a), it appears to be a paradoxical image, one that includes both the stern hand of discipline and a gentle gesture of entreaty.[22] Wisdom called (v. 24a), extended her authoritative yet affectionate hand (v. 24b), and offered both counsel (v. 25a) and correction (v. 25b; cf. v. 23a). But in response, the addressees bite the hand that seeks to feed them. Their response builds throughout v. 24 and culminates in v. 25. According to Wisdom, they "refused" (תְּמָאֵנוּ, v. 24a) her call and authority; "no one paid attention" (אֵין מַקְשִׁיב, v. 24b) to her physical gesture; they brushed aside or "ignored" (תִּפְרְעוּ, v. 25a) all her advice; and they "did not accept" (לֹא אֲבִיתֶם, v. 25b) her reproof. That is, they were not willing to receive her correction (cf. 1:10b). As a result, the addressees confirm their characterization, their commitment to unsanctioned desires, and their inability to receive reproof.

(4) Wisdom's Response (1:26–27)

Wisdom responds to the addressee's rejection in turn. The extended subordinate clause ("Because," יַעַן, vv. 24–25) gives way to a main clause, which gives specific attention to Wisdom's sardonic reaction in general (v. 26) and the prospective calamity of the addressees in particular (v. 27). The main clause opens with the emphatic expression "I, on my part" (גַּם־אֲנִי, v. 26a). The adverb combined with the independent personal pronoun focuses attention on the subject of the verb and highlights Wisdom's derisive response.[23] In view of their rejection of her rebuke, Wisdom promises to "laugh" (אֶשְׂחָק, v. 26a) and "mock" (אֶלְעַג, v. 26b) when impending disaster overtakes the addressees. Together, these verbs capture Wisdom's ironic response. Just as despicable characters within the anthology laugh and mock at the circumstances and calamities of others (17:5; 29:9), so now Wisdom laughs and mocks at the calamity of her addressees. And just as YHWH laughs and mocks at his adversaries (Pss 2:4; 37:13; 59:9; cf. Prov 3:34), so also Wisdom laughs and mocks at her adversaries. She does not initiate their impending disaster; rather, she assumes it and responds to it.[24] While their "disaster" (אֵיד, vv. 26a, 27b) is not specified, the term connotes a sudden, unexpected event that causes personal loss and destruction (6:15; 24:22). And the severity of this destruction is sketched by the chiasm within vv. 26–27:

22. Loader, *Proverbs 1–9*, 96.

23. Ronald J. Williams, *Williams' Hebrew Syntax*, 3rd ed. rev. and enl. by John C. Beckman (Toronto: University of Toronto Press) §381.

24. Fox, *Proverbs 1–9*, 101; Waltke, *Proverbs: Chapters 1–15*, 207.

A I, on my part, will laugh "in ***your disaster***" (בְּאֵידְכֶם, v. 26a)
B I will mock **when your moment of dread comes** (v. 26b)
B′ **when your moment of dread comes** "like a storm" (כְשַׁאֲוָה, v. 27a)
A′ "and ***your disaster***" (וְאֵידְכֶם) comes "like a whirlwind" (כְּסוּפָה, v. 27b)
C when "distress and anguish" (צָרָה וְצוּקָה, v. 27c) come upon you.

As noted above, these verses are comparable to an avalanche; they increase in substance before crashing and settling on a description of the addressees' certain anguish (v. 27c). The first two clauses (A, B) identify the general nature of the calamity and establish the terms for its description. The remaining clauses reiterate these terms and specify the nature of the calamity through meteorological images, synonymous terms, alliteration, and assonance. They intensify the impending disaster through the expressions "your moment of dread" (פַּחְדְּכֶם, vv. 26b, 27a) and "distress and anguish" (צָרָה וְצוּקָה, v. 27c), terms that connote emotional panic and physical shaking (Isa 8:22; 30:6; 33:14). And they elaborate on the nature of the calamity through meteorological images. The similes "like a storm" (כְשַׁאֲוָה, v. 27a) and "like a whirlwind" (כְּסוּפָה, v. 27b) envision the imminent, dreadful disaster as a catastrophic gale that batters the addressees. This tempest, combined with Wisdom's derisive laughter and the emotional turmoil of the coming calamity, creates a world of fear and terror. With vivid imagery, repetition, poetic elaboration, and wordplay, Wisdom concludes her direct rebuke with a rhetorical flourish designed to shock the addressees, vivify their organs of reception, and reorient their worldview.

b. Wisdom's Indirect Rebuke (1:28–31)

The same is true of Wisdom's indirect rebuke (vv. 28–31). She shifts from direct address (vv. 22–27) to indirect address (vv. 28–31) and inverts the previous argument in order to cultivate a receptive posture in the addressee. The rhetorical agenda remains the same, but the addressee has changed. Whereas the direct rebuke invited the reader to assume the identity or subject position of one of the addressees mentioned in v. 22, now the reader is invited to step back, to observe, and to overhear Wisdom's rebuke. The move from direct address to indirect address signals a move from the rhetorical audience to the real audience of the discourse. And in this respect, the rhetorical dynamics of Wisdom's speech are comparable to the oracles against the nations within the prophets (e.g., Amos 1–2; Isa 13–23; Jer 46–51; Ezek 25–32). These prophetic oracles describe YHWH's judgment on various nations. The nations addressed in these oracles, however, do not represent the real audience. Rather, they represent the rhetorical audience. The prophets announce judgment on these nations for the benefit of the Israelites or the Judaeans, who constitute the real audience of these oracles. In the same way, Wisdom's shift to indirect address identifies the real audience of her discourse, namely, the reader, who is invited to step back, catch their breath, overhear Wisdom's rebuke, and learn from the mistakes of the uncommitted, scoffers, and fools.

(1) Wisdom's Response (1:28)

Off the back of her direct rebuke, Wisdom opens her indirect rebuke with a reversal of the previous argument.[25] She begins with her response to the addressees (v. 28; cf. vv. 26–27) before describing the rationale for her reply through their twisted disposition and recalcitrance (vv. 29–30; cf. vv. 24–25).

25. Trible, "Wisdom Builds a Poem," 514.

Wisdom's response shares several similarities with the preceding speech. Similar to the prelude and the introduction to the addressee's earlier response (vv. 21a, 24a), Wisdom opens her indirect rebuke with the verb קרא ("call," v. 28a). And similar to her initial reply (v. 26), Wisdom's response resembles the response of YHWH elsewhere in the Old Testament (v. 28).[26] Just as Wisdom refuses to answer the call of those who reject her (v. 28), so also YHWH refuses to answer the call of those who forsake him (Mic 3:4; cf. Isa 65:12; 66:4; Jer 7:13). And just as Wisdom eludes the search of her detractors (v. 28; but cf. 7:15; 8:17), so also YHWH eludes the search of those who reject him (Hos 5:6).

Wisdom's response is comparable to the previous speech in several respects, but it is also distinct. Whereas Wisdom called and the addressees refused (v. 24), now the addressees call and Wisdom refuses to answer (v. 28). And whereas Wisdom extended her hand to the addressees (v. 24b), now the addressees discover that her authoritative yet affectionate hand is nowhere to be found (v. 28). The reversal of Wisdom's argument mirrors the reversal of the situation. The rhetorical audience's rejection of Wisdom gives way to Wisdom's rejection of the rhetorical audience. The poem moves from a description of the rhetorical audience's rejection to the result of their rejection.[27] Their character, desires, and deeds yield consequences (cf. 1:19). And the description of these consequences offers the reader an invaluable object lesson.

(2) The Response of the Addressees (1:29–30)

The object lesson, however, is not complete. Wisdom's description of the consequences associated with the rhetorical audience's rejection gives way to another extended subordinate clause that provides a rationale for Wisdom's response ("because," תַּחַת כִּי, vv. 29–30). This clause recasts the rhetorical audience's earlier rejection, and it recycles several terms and expressions to identify the fundamental reason for their rejection. According to Wisdom, the reason for the rhetorical audience's rejection is twofold: they possess distorted desires and dysfunctional organs of reception. The first is given specific attention in v. 29. Wisdom reiterates her diagnosis of the misdirected affections of fools (vv. 22c, 29a). In the present case, however, she applies this diagnosis to the entire lot: the uncommitted, scoffers, and fools. They hate that which they should love (v. 29a). And their hatred of knowledge reveals their principal problem: their twisted disposition. "They did not choose" (לֹא בָחָרוּ, v. 29b) the fear of YHWH; that is, they refused to assume a humble posture and a receptive attitude cultivated through relationship with YHWH and knowledge of his will. No wonder they reject Wisdom's reproof. The preamble identified the fundamental prerequisite for the acquisition of wisdom and virtue: the fear of YHWH, which is the beginning of "knowledge" (דַּעַת; 1:7a). These despicable characters hate "knowledge" (דַּעַת, v. 29a). Their desires reveal the nature of their character. And their character explains their inability to receive rebuke and acquire wisdom.

This inability to gain wisdom is the logical implication of the rhetorical audience's distorted desires and twisted disposition. And this inability is presented in v. 30. Again, Wisdom recycles several terms and expressions to highlight the rhetorical audience's dysfunctional organs of reception.

26. For discussion of the parallels between Wisdom's response and Jer 7 and 20, see Harris, *Proverbs 1–9*, 93–100. Harris concludes that Wisdom's rebuke represents a recontextualization of Jeremiah's discourses in chs. 7 and 20. While the rebuke shares several features with these texts in Jeremiah, it is important to note that Wisdom's response also shares several features with the response of YHWH elsewhere in the Old Testament as well as the language and rhetoric of the prophets in general.

27. Fox, *Proverbs 1–9*, 101.

"they did not accept" (לֹא־אָבוּ, v. 30a)	"you did not accept" (לֹא אֲבִיתֶם, v. 25b)
"my advice" (לַעֲצָתִי, v. 30a)	"all my advice" (כָל־עֲצָתִי, v. 25a)
"all my reproof" (כָּל־תּוֹכַחְתִּי, v. 30b)	"my reproof" (תוֹכַחְתִּי, v. 25b; cf. 23a)

Wisdom's reiteration of these expressions from v. 25 seals the rhetorical deal. The addressees were unwilling to receive her counsel; "they spurned" (נָאֲצוּ, v. 30b) or trivialized her verbal discipline. In so doing, they demonstrate their inability to hear, to receive, and to respond appropriately to correction. That is, they demonstrate that they do not possess the attitude or the listening posture necessary to acquire wisdom and virtue.

(3) The Reward Promised the Addressees (1:31)

In light of the rhetorical audience's distorted desires, twisted disposition, and dysfunctional organs of reception, Wisdom describes the ironic reward of those who reject her reproof (v. 31). Here it appears that the extended subordinate clause in vv. 29–30 not only provides a rationale for Wisdom's response (v. 28); it also provides a rationale for the rhetorical audience's reward (v. 31). This reward is introduced by the conjunction "So" (וְ, v. 31a), which marks the result of the audience's rejection.[28] And this reward is described through gastronomic metaphors. Wisdom links the distorted desires of the rhetorical audience with their distorted tastes, and she relates their dysfunctional organs of reception with their dysfunctional palate. Similar to the sinners (1:15), the uncommitted, scoffers, and fools embody a particular "way" (דֶּרֶךְ, v. 31a). That is, they epitomize a particular lifestyle, orientation to life, and moral worldview. And this way or lifestyle bears fruit. Wisdom reiterates the principle of retribution expressed by the parents and offers a vivid description of the rhetorical audience's reward (v. 31; cf. 1:19). Instead of chewing on Wisdom's words, they will eat the fruit of their lifestyle. And instead of finding satisfaction in Wisdom's advice, they will find satisfaction in "their counsels" (מִמֹּעֲצֹתֵיהֶם, v. 31b) or schemes. They will eat what their character has cultivated and gratify their tastes by consuming what they desire (cf. v. 22, 29).

3. Wisdom's Conclusion (1:32–33)

Wisdom concludes her rebuke with a description of the fates of the unreceptive and the receptive, respectively.

a. The Fate of the Unreceptive (1:32)

She begins with the unreceptive, where she moves beyond their reward to their ultimate end. This end is introduced by the conjunction "Indeed" (כִּי, v. 32a), which identifies both the certainty of their reward (v. 31) and the certainty of their fate (v. 32).[29] Wisdom's certainty is rooted in the attitude or disposition of the uncommitted as well as fools. She reinscribes these character types into her conclusion (v. 22a, c) and elaborates on their twisted disposition. They not only desire what is bad and hate what is good (vv. 22, 29), but they

28. *IBHS* §31.6.2.

29. For the asseverative function of the conjunction, see Joüon §164b.

also possess a wayward and complacent disposition. Together with scoffers and fools, Wisdom called the uncommitted to "turn" (תָּשׁוּבוּ, v. 23a) to her reproof. Now she employs a derivative of the verb to describe their wayward disposition, their "turning away" (מְשׁוּבַת, v. 32a). This "spiritual-psychological disorder" defines their character,[30] determines their way, and explains their lack of receptivity (Jer 3:6, 8, 12, 22). The same is true of fools. Whereas the uncommitted are led astray by their waywardness, fools are confined by their "complacency" (שַׁלְוַת, v. 32b). They have a false sense of security and are quite satisfied with their condition (Ezek 16:49; Ps 30:7[6]). Together with the disposition of the uncommitted, the attitude of fools defines their character and prevents them from receiving Wisdom's rebuke. These attitudes, however, do more than dull the receptive organs of these characters. According to Wisdom, they destroy the uncommitted and fools.

b. The Fate of the Receptive (1:33)

The attitudes and ultimate fate of the unreceptive stand in sharp contrast to the posture and fate of the receptive. "The one who listens" (שֹׁמֵעַ, v. 33a) to Wisdom adopts the position necessary to achieve the pedagogical program of the anthology (1:5; cf. 1:8). This person listens to counsel, receives instruction, and heeds reproof (Prov 12:15; 13:1; 15:31–32; 19:20). While the wayward and complacent attitudes of the uncommitted and fools lead to destruction, the attentive, the one who accepts Wisdom's rebuke with a receptive posture experiences security. This security is the antithesis of the mirage created by fools. Fools have a false sense of security (v. 32b). The one who listens, on the other hand, "will dwell securely" (יִשְׁכָּן־בֶּטַח, v. 33a). This genuine form of internal confidence and external safety enables the receptive to "be at ease" (שַׁאֲנַן, v. 33b), to find true repose, to live free of fear, without "dread of disaster" (פַּחַד רָעָה, v. 33b). These benefits bring the value of a receptive posture into sharp relief. Whereas the unreceptive will experience "dread" (פַּחַד, vv. 26b, 27a) and disaster (v. 32), the receptive will experience freedom from "dread" (פַּחַד, v. 33b), confidence, and safety. Similar to the first parental lecture, the conclusion summarizes the fate of the unreceptive through the principle of just retribution (v. 32; cf. v. 19). And in so doing, it provides the reader with a cautionary tale, an object lesson designed to awaken their organs of reception. But in contrast to the first parental lecture, the conclusion also offers an alternative through a description of the attitude, posture, and fate of the receptive (v. 33). In fact, the shift in address ("the one who listens *to me*," שֹׁמֵעַ לִי, v. 33a) within the final verse serves as an implicit invitation for reader to discern their receptivity to Wisdom's correction.[31] This receptive posture is key to Proverbs's pedagogy; its importance as well as the rhetorical strategy of Wisdom's rebuke is captured by Prov 19:25:

> Strike a scoffer and the simple becomes
> shrewd,
> but rebuke the discerning, he will gain
> knowledge.

30. Fox, *Proverbs 1–9*, 103.

31. Stewart, *Poetic Ethics*, 90–93.

Canonical and Theological Significance

Rebuke is a common pedagogical technique in Proverbs; it serves as a means of discipline and a literary mechanism for instruction designed to shock the reader and provide the *receptive* addressee with a particular moral worldview. Wisdom's rebuke instructs through the medium of reproof. To borrow a concept from psychotherapy, Wisdom delivers negative reinforcement. She seeks to shape the desires and disposition of the reader by describing the unsavory desires and despicable disposition of various character types. She cultivates normative character through a description of deplorable characters. And she provides the reader with a specific moral worldview through an evaluation of the attitudes, affections, actions, and fate of the uncommitted, scoffers, and fools. These character types are the perfect foil. They illuminate the kind of person one should not be,[32] and they provide the reader with a lens through which to see other people. This pedagogical approach is given particular expression in Christine McKinnon's discussion of character types and ethics:

> Just as it is natural for humans to develop characters, so is it natural for them to judge character-types. Indeed, the practice of judging character-types is one of the means persons employ in making the kinds of informed and objective decisions required to know in what directions to develop their own characters and, when appropriate, to assist others in the development of their characters.[33]

Lady Wisdom judges the character of the uncommitted, scoffers, and fools to assist the reader in the development of their character. She invites the reader to identify with these characters and to receive correction through her direct rebuke (vv. 22–27); then she allows the reader to step back and overhear her judgment of these character types through her indirect rebuke (vv. 28–31). In so doing, Lady Wisdom contributes to Proverbs's project of education for character formation. Her rebuke offers wisdom, correction, and perception. The acquisition of these benefits, however, is contingent upon receptivity. *The one who desires to learn must first learn to listen.* Only those who receive Wisdom's rebuke can benefit from its correction. The uncommitted, the scoffers, and the fools are a case in point. Receptivity to Wisdom is key. Thus, it is not surprising that the fundamental purpose of Wisdom's rebuke is to cultivate a receptive, listening posture, for without it the reader will be unable to acquire wisdom and virtue.

32. This is a significant pedagogical technique, for as Edmund Pincoffs notes, "Learning to become the right sort of person is in large part learning not to become the wrong sort" (Edmund L. Pincoffs, *Quandaries and Virtues: Against Reductivism in Ethics* [Lawrence, KS: University Press of Kansas, 1986], 164).

33. Christine McKinnon, *Character, Virtue Theories, and the Vices* (Orchard Park, NY: Broadview, 1999), 230.

The rebuke's concern with receptivity indicates that it is well placed within the anthology. This listening posture is the hallmark of the wise (12:15; 15:31–32; 25:12). And it is an essential element in the anthology's educational program. Far from merely announcing the necessity of this posture (1:5), the second discourse within the prologue seeks to inculcate this attitude by reflecting on the distorted attitudes, desires, and dispositions of the uncommitted, scoffers, and fools. Wisdom's rebuke attempts to attune the ears and cultivate the disposition necessary to profit from the wisdom delineated in the remainder of the document; it functions as a form of literary shock treatment intended to awaken the reader's organs of reception so that they may receive instruction in wisdom. Receptivity is a matter of first importance. The acquisition of wisdom and the realization of the document's goal depend upon it. The rebuke, however, not only prepares the reader to receive the wisdom that follows; it also complements the first parental lecture. It identifies another authoritative, trustworthy voice that the reader should heed. And it moves beyond the deceptive speech and destructive actions of particular characters (1:8–19) to reflect on the distorted desires, dispositions, tastes, and organs of particular characters. Together with the first parental instruction, Wisdom's rebuke contributes to the (trans)formation of character in general and the cultivation of a moral aesthetic in particular. The first parental lecture gave specific attention to the intellectual dimension of this aesthetic; Wisdom's rebuke attends to the emotional and attitudinal components of this aesthetic.[34]

Receptivity to Wisdom, and by implication to God (cf. vv. 26a–b, 28), plays a formative role in Proverbs's educational vision. The promise of a receptive posture and the problems associated with an unreceptive attitude are given specific attention in Wisdom's rebuke. These topics are prominent themes within ancient Near Eastern instructional texts.[35] And they are concepts that pervade Proverbs as well as the canon of Scripture. Proverbs and the broader canon bear witness to the fact that the receptive receive understanding, Lady Wisdom's blessing, life, and divine favor (8:33–35; 15:31–32; 19:20). The one who listens accepts rebuke and allows it to seep into the inner recesses of their character, where it fertilizes a wise disposition (17:10; cf. Eccl 7:5). And the ideal learner desires a perceptive, discerning disposition that empowers one to live and judge rightly (1 Kgs 3:9). This receptive posture is ideal, and the promises associated with it are attractive; but this disposition is hard to come by. A receptive, obedient disposition is the prerequisite for maintaining covenant fidelity and receiving the blessings of covenant relationship (Deut 28:1–2). Throughout her history, however, Israel is characterized as an unreceptive, disobedient nation

34. For discussion of the components of moral aesthetics and the book of Proverbs, see Fox, "The Epistemology of the Book of Proverbs," 669–84, esp. 681–84.

35. See, for example, "The Instruction of Ptahhotep" (*AEL* 1:73–75), lines 530–98; "The Instruction of Papyrus Insinger" (*AEL* 3.192), lines 9.5–7.

that experiences the covenant curses (Judg 2:16–17; 1 Sam 8:19; 2 Kgs 17:7–23; Neh 9:16–17). The prophets delivered oracles of judgment with the expectation that the people would hear their words and turn from their wicked ways. But these oracles fell on deaf ears. The prophetic corpus is filled with descriptions of the people's failure to listen (Jer 7:25–26; 11:7–8; 17:23; 32:33; Dan 9:6). And many texts associate this failure to listen with the people's twisted disposition and dysfunctional organs of reception (Isa 6:9–10; Ezek 3:7; 12:2). The people may have ears; but they are unable to hear, receive, and heed the prophetic word. Similar to Wisdom's rhetorical audience, these prophetic texts indicate that the people's character has dulled their organs of reception, preventing them from receiving the correction and reproof that would bring healing and hope.

Reproof and its reception or rejection pervades the Old Testament canon. And reproof serves as a significant pedagogical and pastoral approach to various issues in the New Testament. Paul commanded Timothy to rebuke those who persist in sin so that others within the community may learn from their wrongdoing and develop a fear of sinning (1 Tim 5:20). Reproof and the refutation of false teaching are among the fundamental responsibilities of pastor-teachers (2 Tim 4:2; Titus 1:9, 13; 2:15). And similar to the examples noted above, rejection of reproof remains a problem within the New Testament. In fact, the rejection of instruction appears to be a potential problem for the Thessalonians (2 Thess 3:14). The canon bears witness to the pedagogical value of reproof; it serves as an effective instrument of correction and instruction. And through the rhetoric of rebuke, the canon illuminates an aspect of the human condition, namely, the human aversion to rebuke and the human desire for the wrong sorts of things.

These are the primary ways in which Wisdom's rebuke speaks to the church today. Reproof remains an invaluable pedagogical tool. It is not to be delivered causally; rather, it should be administered with an awareness of the recipient and the accompanying circumstances in order to enhance its reception and evoke an appropriate response from the addressee (1 Tim 5:1). Rebuke invites response; it seeks to induce self-reflection and encourage a different way of thinking or acting. Nonetheless, rebuke is difficult to receive, for correction is a hard pill to swallow. It tends to be met with a counterargument, self-justification, and the like. The human aversion to rebuke reveals aspects of the human condition. Similar to Wisdom's diagnosis of the uncommitted and scoffers, reproof may expose one's distorted desires in general and their self-love in particular (Prov 1:22). It may uncover one's true affections, what one desires, and what one despises. And one's response to rebuke will provide an indication of one's attitude and disposition; it will confirm whether one is teachable or self-satisfied, prone to correction or prone to wander, committed to culling Wisdom's fruit or bent on eating the fruit of one's twisted ways. Rebuke serves as a litmus test for one's character. And Wisdom's rebuke serves as an invitation to examine one's character, one's attitudes, one's desires, and one's organs of reception. Whereas the first parental lecture indicated that the company we keep matters, Wisdom's rebuke indicates that our attitudes, desires, and disposition reveal our character and place us in a particular company: the company of the uncommitted, scoffers, and fools, or the company of those who listen to Wisdom.

CHAPTER 4

Proverbs 2:1–22

C. The Procurement, Power, and Protection of Wisdom and Virtue

Main Idea of the Passage

This pedagogical masterpiece describes the preconditions for and the process of wisdom's procurement as well as its transformative power and protection in order to illustrate wisdom's value and persuade the receptive reader to seek it.

Literary Context

The extended description of wisdom's procurement, power, and protection plays a formative role in the literary context of the prologue. This discourse elaborates upon specific matters introduced in the preamble (1:1–7), the parents' initial lecture (1:8–19), and Wisdom's rebuke (1:20–33); and it identifies particular motifs and character types that are developed elsewhere in the prologue. In so doing, it functions as a literary hinge, binding the initial discourses to the materials that follow; and it describes the way in which the acquisition of wisdom and virtue hinge on the reader's active pursuit and God's gracious provision.

The single, conditional sentence within ch. 2 builds on the discrete discourses within ch. 1. While the preamble described the fundamental goal of the document (1:1–7), the discourse in ch. 2 describes the way in which this goal is achieved. The (trans)formation of one's character through the inculcation of wisdom and virtue involves more than a listening posture (1:5a; 2:1–2); it also necessitates an active pursuit (2:3–4). And this pursuit mirrors Lady Wisdom's activity in 1:20–33. Just as Wisdom cried out, raised her voice, and extended her hand to prospective devotees (1:20b, 21b, 24), so also the son must cry out, raise his voice, and stretch out or incline his heart to wisdom (2:2b, 3). The acquisition of wisdom requires an active pursuit of wisdom. And this pursuit is completed by God, who grants the requisite posture to live in accord with wisdom as well as many of the virtues promised in the preamble (1:2, 3, 4b, 7a; 2:2a, 3a, 5a, 6, 9, 11a). The discourse specifies the way in which the goal delineated in the preamble is realized; its description of the search for wisdom is reminiscent of Wisdom's search for receptive followers in 1:20–33. And its portrayal of the protective power of wisdom is comparable to the parents' speech in 1:8–19. Whereas the initial parental lecture highlighted the value of wisdom through the parents' perceptive interpretation of the deceptive rhetoric and alternative moral worldview of the sinners (1:8–19), the second parental lecture highlights the value of wisdom through a description of the way it delivers one from the path, speech, and moral worldview of evildoers and the strange woman (2:12–19).

These motifs and character types are woven throughout the fabric of the remaining discourses in the prologue. The sixth parental instruction as well as several sayings in the central collections of the anthology elaborate upon the way, speech, dispositions, and desires of evildoers (2:12–15; 4:14–17; 12:13). The seductive rhetoric, moral worldview, and way of the "strange woman" (אִשָּׁה זָרָה; 2:16a) or "outsider" (נָכְרִיָּה, v. 16b) are the focus of attention in many of the parental lectures (5:1–23; 6:20–35; 7:1–27; cf. 22:14; 23:27). And the motifs of the way or path (2:8, 9, 12, 13, 15, 18, 19, 20), houses (v. 18a), deceptive speech (vv. 12, 16), and life and death (vv. 18, 19, 21–22) punctuate the collections within the anthology in general and the discourses within the prologue in particular. The second parental lecture not only integrates and develops expressions and concepts from the previous discourses; it also includes expressions, concepts, and symbols that are developed in the discourses that follow.

In light of how succeeding discourses within the prologue develop specific character types, concepts, and themes within ch. 2, some contend that the second parental lecture serves as a formal teaching program for the prologue;[1] it identifies the topics and character types that are unpacked in a progressive fashion within the remainder of Prov 1–9. While the second parental lecture delineates topics and character types that are developed elsewhere in the prologue, the remaining discourses do not address these topics or character types through the scheme presented in ch. 2. The second parental lecture does not provide a formal teaching program for the prologue; rather, it describes the preconditions for and the process of wisdom's procurement. In this respect, it serves as the logical counterpart to Lady Wisdom's rebuke. Through the rhetoric of rebuke, Lady Wisdom attempted to cultivate receptivity in the addressee. This receptive posture is assumed in the preconditions for and the pursuit of wisdom in ch. 2. Whereas Lady Wisdom identified the consequences associated with rejecting her words, the parents identify the rewards associated with receiving their instruction and pursuing wisdom.

1. Meinhold, *Die Sprüche*, 1.43–47.

I. Introduction to the Book (1:1–7)
II. The Value of Wisdom and Virtue (1:8–9:18)
- A. Wisdom, Desire, and Different Ways (1:8–19)
- B. Wisdom's Rebuke (1:20–33)
- ➡ **C. The Procurement, Power, and Protection of Wisdom and Virtue (2:1–22)**
  - **1. The Preconditions for Wisdom's Procurement (2:1–4)**
    - **a. A Receptive Posture (2:1–2)**
    - **b. An Active Pursuit (2:3–4)**
  - **2. The Procurement of Wisdom (2:5–8)**
    - **a. The Essence of the Procurement (2:5)**
    - **b. The Reason for the Procurement (2:6–7)**
    - **c. The Purpose of the Procurement (2:8)**
  - **3. The Procurement of Virtue (2:9–22)**
    - **a. The Essence of the Procurement (2:9)**
    - **b. The Reason for the Procurement (2:10–11)**
    - **c. The Purpose of the Procurement (2:12–19)**
      - **(1) The Way of the Evildoer (2:12–15)**
      - **(2) The Way of the Strange Woman (2:16–19)**
    - **d. The Result of the Procurement (2:20–22)**
- D. Wisdom and Piety (3:1–12)
- E. Wisdom's Value and Moral Obligations (3:13–35)
- F. Wisdom and Tradition (4:1–9)
- G. Wisdom and Ways of Life (4:10–19)
- H. Wisdom and the Moral Anatomy (4:20–27)
- I. Wisdom and Sexuality (5:1–23)
- J. Wisdom, Lending, Laziness, and the Immoral Anatomy (6:1–19)
- K. Wisdom, Desire, and Certain Destruction (6:20–35)
- L. Wisdom and Seduction (7:1–27)
- M. Wisdom's Call, Credentials, and the Cosmos (8:1–36)
- N. Wisdom and Folly's Invitations (9:1–18)

III. "Forming 'Fearers of YHWH'": The Curriculum of Wisdom and Virtue (10:1–29:27)
IV. The Application of Wisdom and Virtue (30:1–31:31)

Translation and Exegetical Outline

(See pages 163–64.)

Proverbs 2:1–22

			C. The Procurement, Power, and Protection of Wisdom and Virtue (2:1–22)
			1. The Preconditions for Wisdom's Procurement (2:1–4)
1a	בְּנִי אִם־תִּקַּח אֲמָרָי	My son, if you receive my words,	a. A Receptive Posture (2:1–2)
1b	וּמִצְוֺתַי תִּצְפֹּן אִתָּךְ	and store up my commands within you,	
2a	לְהַקְשִׁיב לַחָכְמָה אָזְנֶךָ	by making your ear attentive to wisdom,	
2b	תַּטֶּה לִבְּךָ לַתְּבוּנָה	inclining your heart to understanding;	
3a	כִּי אִם לַבִּינָה תִקְרָא	indeed, if you cry out for insight,	b. An Active Pursuit (2:3–4)
3b	לַתְּבוּנָה תִּתֵּן קוֹלֶךָ	raise your voice for understanding;	
4a	אִם־תְּבַקְשֶׁנָּה כַכָּסֶף	if you seek it as silver,	
4b	וְכַמַּטְמוֹנִים תַּחְפְּשֶׂנָּה	and as hidden treasures search for it,	
			2. The Procurement of Wisdom (2:5–8)
5a	אָז תָּבִין יִרְאַת יְהוָה	then you will understand the fear of YHWH,	a. The Essence of the Procurement (2:5)
5b	וְדַעַת אֱלֹהִים תִּמְצָא	and you will find the knowledge of God;	
6a	כִּי־יְהוָה יִתֵּן חָכְמָה	for YHWH grants wisdom;	b. The Reason for the Procurement (2:6–7)
6b	מִפִּיו דַּעַת וּתְבוּנָה	from his mouth comes knowledge and understanding;	
7a	יִצְפֹּן לַיְשָׁרִים תּוּשִׁיָּה	he stores up resourcefulness for the upright;	
7b	מָגֵן לְהֹלְכֵי תֹם	a shield for those who walk with integrity,	
8a	לִנְצֹר אָרְחוֹת מִשְׁפָּט	in order to protect the paths of justice,	c. The Purpose of the Procurement (2:8)
8b	וְדֶרֶךְ חֲסִידָיו יִשְׁמֹר	guard the way of his faithful ones;	
			3. The Procurement of Virtue (2:9–22)
9	אָז תָּבִין צֶדֶק וּמִשְׁפָּט וּמֵישָׁרִים כָּל־מַעְגַּל־טוֹב	then you will understand righteousness, justice, and uprightness—every good path,	a. The Essence of the Procurement (2:9)
10a	כִּי־תָבוֹא חָכְמָה בְלִבֶּךָ	for wisdom will infiltrate your heart,	b. The Reason for the Procurement (2:10–11)
10b	וְדַעַת לְנַפְשְׁךָ יִנְעָם	and knowledge will be pleasant to your soul,	
11a	מְזִמָּה תִּשְׁמֹר עָלֶיךָ	discretion will guard you,	
11b	תְּבוּנָה תִנְצְרֶכָּה	understanding will protect you,	

Continued on next page.

Continued from previous page.

Verse	Hebrew	Translation	Outline
12a	לְהַצִּילְךָ מִדֶּרֶךְ רָע	in order to deliver you from the way of the evildoer,	c. The Purpose of the Procurement (2:12–19) (1) The Way of the Evildoer (2:12–15)
12b	מֵאִישׁ מְדַבֵּר תַּהְפֻּכוֹת	from the person who speaks perversely,	
13a	הַעֹזְבִים אָרְחוֹת יֹשֶׁר	those who forsake the paths of uprightness	
13b	לָלֶכֶת בְּדַרְכֵי־חֹשֶׁךְ	to walk in ways of darkness,	
14a	הַשְּׂמֵחִים לַעֲשׂוֹת רָע	who delight in doing evil,	
14b	יָגִילוּ בְּתַהְפֻּכוֹת רָע	rejoice in the perversity of evil,	
15a	אֲשֶׁר אָרְחֹתֵיהֶם עִקְּשִׁים	whose paths are crooked,	
15b	וּנְלוֹזִים בְּמַעְגְּלוֹתָם	and who are devious in their ways;	
16a	לְהַצִּילְךָ מֵאִשָּׁה זָרָה	in order to deliver you from the strange woman,	(2) The Way of the Strange Woman (2:16–19)
16b	מִנָּכְרִיָּה אֲמָרֶיהָ הֶחֱלִיקָה	from the outsider with her smooth words	
17a	הַעֹזֶבֶת אַלּוּף נְעוּרֶיהָ	who forsakes the companion of her youth,	
17b	וְאֶת־בְּרִית אֱלֹהֶיהָ שָׁכֵחָה	and forgets the covenant of her God,	
18a	כִּי שָׁחָה אֶל־מָוֶת בֵּיתָהּ	for her house sinks down to death,	
18b	וְאֶל־רְפָאִים מַעְגְּלֹתֶיהָ	and her ways to the deceased;	
19a	כָּל־בָּאֶיהָ לֹא יְשׁוּבוּן	all who come to her will never return,	
19b	וְלֹא־יַשִּׂיגוּ אָרְחוֹת חַיִּים	nor will they reach the paths of life;	
20a	לְמַעַן תֵּלֵךְ בְּדֶרֶךְ טוֹבִים	so that you may walk in the way of the good,	d. The Result of the Procurement (2:20–22)
20b	וְאָרְחוֹת צַדִּיקִים תִּשְׁמֹר	and keep the paths of the righteous,	
21a	כִּי־יְשָׁרִים יִשְׁכְּנוּ אָרֶץ	for the upright will dwell in the land,	
21b	וּתְמִימִים יִוָּתְרוּ בָהּ	and the blameless will remain in it;	
22a	וּרְשָׁעִים מֵאֶרֶץ יִכָּרֵתוּ	but the wicked will be cut off from the land,	
22b	וּבוֹגְדִים יִסְּחוּ מִמֶּנָּה	and the treacherous will be uprooted from it.	

Structure and Literary Form

In contrast to the first parental lecture (1:8–19), this speech is not a formal instruction; rather, it is a description of the way in which one may achieve the goal of the anthology (1:1–7), an account of the preconditions for and the process of wisdom's procurement. This does not mean, however, that the discourse is devoid of instruction. It does not instruct through imperatives or formal admonitions; rather, it instructs through description. Or better, it persuades through description. And the persuasion of the speech is integral to Proverbs's pedagogy. As Christine McKinnon notes, character "is not something that comes ready made at birth";[2] rather, character and the virtues that constitute one's character "must be chosen, and they must be chosen for reasons that are related to the agent's conception of a good human life."[3] The parental description of the preconditions for as well as the process of wisdom's procurement addresses these matters. It conceptualizes the "way of the good" (דֶּרֶךְ טוֹבִים; 2:20a) and provides reasons for choosing the good through an exposition of the disposition, understanding, and protection YHWH bestows on those who seek wisdom.

As the main idea and syntactical outline suggest, this description of the preconditions for and the process of wisdom's procurement is a pedagogical masterpiece.[4] The chapter consists of a single, conditional sentence. And this sentence contains three constituent parts. The first identifies the preconditions for wisdom's procurement, namely, receptivity and an active pursuit (vv. 1–4). The second describes the disposition and knowledge God grants to those who seek wisdom (vv. 5–8), while the third delineates the virtues that accompany this disposition and knowledge, virtues that transform one's character, empower one to avoid the wrong people and their respective ways, and lead one down the path of the good (vv. 9–22). While some contend the discourse developed over a period of time under several hands,[5] the syntax suggests it is a coherent piece.[6] The extended protasis gives way to two apodoses, each of which illuminates the process of wisdom's procurement through identical expressions and comparable subordinate clauses. The basic argument of the piece may be illustrated through the following scheme:

2. McKinnon, *Character, Virtue Theories, and the Vices*, 36.

3. McKinnon, *Character, Virtue Theories, and the Vices*, 30.

4. For discussion of the types of parallelism in the unit, see Pardee, *Ugaritic and Hebrew Poetic Parallelism*.

5. For this religious and literary development, see Toy, *Proverbs*, 31–55; R. Norman Whybray, "Some Literary Problems in Proverbs I–IX," *VT* 16 (1966): 482–96; Dieter Michel, "Proverbia 2–ein Dokument der Geschichte der Weisheit," in *Alttestamentlicher Glaube und Biblische Theologie: Festschrift für Horst Dietrich Preuß zum 65. Geburtstag*, ed. J. Hausmann and H.-J. Zobel (Stuttgart: Kohlhammer, 1992), 233–43.

6. Fox, *Proverbs 1–9*, 128; Loader, *Proverbs 1–9*, 106; Schipper, *Proverbs 1–15*, 103–4.

If you receive my words, cry out for insight, and seek understanding (vv. 1–4),
"then you will understand" [אָז תָּבִין] the fear of YHWH and find the knowledge of God (v. 5),
"for" [כִּי, v. 6a] YHWH grants wisdom and stores up resourcefulness (vv. 6–7)
"in order to protect" [לִנְצֹר] the paths of justice (v. 8),
"then you will understand" [אָז תָּבִין] righteousness, justice, and uprightness (v. 9),
"for" [כִּי, v. 10a] wisdom will infiltrate your heart (vv. 10–11)
"in order to deliver you" [לְהַצִּילְךָ, v. 12a] from the way of the evildoer (vv. 12–15)
"in order to deliver you" [לְהַצִּילְךָ, v. 16a] from the strange woman (vv. 16–19)
"so that" [לְמַעַן, v. 20a] you may walk in the way of the good (vv. 20–22)

The syntactical and rhetorical coherence of the unit is reinforced by the recurring words, expressions, and motifs that punctuate the piece. The terms "wisdom" (חָכְמָה, vv. 2a, 6a, 10a), "understanding" (תְּבוּנָה, vv. 2b, 3b, 6b, 11b), "heart" (לֵב, vv. 2b, 10a), "store(s) up" (צָפַן, vv. 1b, 7a), "upright(ness)" (יָשָׁר/ יֹשֶׁר, vv. 7a, 13a, 21a), "guard/keep" (שָׁמַר, vv. 8b, 11a, 20b), "protect" (נצר, vv. 8a, 11b), and "forsake(s)" (עָזַב, vv. 13a, 17a) are reiterated across the discourse. The expressions "then you will understand" (אָז תָּבִין, vv. 5a, 9) and "in order to deliver you from" (לְהַצִּילְךָ מִ-, v. 12a, 16a) open the apodoses and a pair of purpose clauses, respectively. And the image of walking (הלך, vv. 7b, 13b, 20a) as well as the path metaphor pervades the lecture. In fact, the piece includes three of the four distinctive terms used for the nuclear symbol of the "way" or "path" within the anthology (אֳרָחוֹת, vv. 8a, 13a, 15a, 19b, 20b; דֶּרֶךְ, vv. 8b, 12a, 13b, 20a; מַעְגָּל, vv. 9, 15b, 18b). Together with the crisp syntax of the unit, the repetition of these terms, expressions, and motifs illuminates the discourse's rhetorical elocution and contributes to its perlocutionary effect, namely, to persuade the receptive addressee to pursue wisdom and virtue.[7]

7. Some contend that the lecture is cast in the form of an acrostic: it contains twenty-two lines, which mirror the number of consonants in the Hebrew alphabet, and the first half of the poem includes several lines that begin with *'aleph* (vv. 4, 5, 9), while the second half of the poem includes several lines that begin with *lamed* (vv. 12, 16, 20). These consonants divide the lecture into two parts (vv. 1–11, 12–22), each of which contains three sections. While acrostic poems use the Hebrew alphabet in distinctive ways, it is unlikely that Prov 2 was arranged in accordance with this scheme, for the break between vv. 1–11 and vv. 12–22 violates the syntax and logical flow of the discourse. For discussion of the acrostic structure of Prov 2, see Patrick W. Skehan, "The Seven Columns of Wisdom's House in Proverbs 1–9," *CBQ* 9 (1947): 190–98; repr. and rev. in *Studies in Israelite Poetry and Wisdom*, CBQMS 1 (Washington, DC: Catholic Biblical Association of America, 1971), 9–14; Murphy, *Proverbs*, 14; Clifford, *Proverbs*, 45–46.

Explanation of the Text

The preamble (1:1–7), the first parental lecture (1:8–19), and Lady Wisdom's rebuke (1:20–33) share a common concern: receptivity. The preamble announced the necessity of this posture for acquiring wisdom and virtue (1:5). The first parental lecture opened with the call to "hear" (שְׁמַע; 1:8). And Lady Wisdom attempted to cultivate a receptive attitude through a description of the fate of those who reject her reproof as well as the reward bestowed upon "the one who listens" (שֹׁמֵעַ; 1:33). A receptive, listening posture is essential to the acquisition of wisdom and virtue; but this receptive posture is not enough. The acquisition of wisdom and virtue must be accompanied by an active pursuit and received as a divine gift.

1. The Preconditions for Wisdom's Procurement (2:1–4)

The extended protasis that opens the parental lecture indicates that receptivity to instruction and the pursuit of wisdom are inextricably linked in Proverbs's project of education for character formation. Wisdom is acquired neither through osmosis nor through passive acceptance. The acquisition of wisdom requires both a receptive posture as well as an active pursuit, two preconditions that are presented in vv. 1–4.

a. A Receptive Posture (2:1–2)

The receptive posture profiled in the previous discourses is reiterated and unpacked in the initial half of the protasis (vv. 1–2). Similar to the first lecture, the parent opens the discourse by addressing the son (v. 1a; cf. 1:8, 10, 15). This invocation, however, does not include a pair of admonitions; rather, it incorporates a series of conditions, or better, preconditions for the acquisition of wisdom and virtue, each of which are introduced by the particle "if" (אִם; 2:1b, 3a, 4a). The first condition focuses on a familiar topic: the acceptance of parental instruction. This acceptance is expressed through the verbs "receive" (תִּקַּח, v. 1a) and "store up" (תִּצְפֹּן, v. 1b; cf. v. 7a). The former captures the receptive yet passive posture necessary to acquire wisdom and virtue. The latter expresses the internal dimensions of this acceptance through the concept of accumulation; it evokes the image of packing one's internal pantry with parental instruction. The parental instruction is presented through the general phrase "my words" (אֲמָרָי, v. 1a) and developed through the parallel expression "my commands" (מִצְוֹתַי, v. 1b), which constitute authoritative directives delivered by a superior to an inferior (Num 15:39; Deut 4:40; 2 Kgs 18:36; Neh 11:23). And this relational dynamic reveals the nature of the son's acceptance. Acceptance involves more than the reception of commands; it also involves submission to proper authority in a relationship governed by trust.[8]

The acceptance and stockpiling of parental commands, however, is contingent on the orientation and inclination of one's organs of reception. This is the focus of attention in Prov 2:2. The *lamed* + infinitive construct in v. 2a describes the way in which the son is to receive and store up the parental commands (v. 1); the preposition expresses manner ("by," לְ, v. 2a), while the infinitive specifies or explains how the son will receive wisdom and understanding.[9] The function of the infinitive construct

8. Loader, *Proverbs 1–9*, 111.

9. *IBHS* §36.2.3e; Joüon §124o.

is significant, for it influences the rendering of its verbal parallel: "inclining" (תַּטֶּה, v. 2b).[10] Together, these clauses suggest that receptivity to instruction is not innate; rather, it requires one to sensitize their ear and to orient their heart. This move from the external reception of the ear to the internal inclination of the heart mirrors the external-internal dimensions of receptivity sketched in v. 1. And the internal precondition for wisdom's acceptance is given particular attention through the expression "inclining your heart" (תַּטֶּה לִבְּךָ, v. 2b). As the locus of the inner self, the heart encapsulates the mind as well as one's emotions and dispositions (3:1, 5; 11:29; 15:13; 17:22). To incline one's heart, then, is an attitude governed by one's intellectual and emotional faculties and marked by a desire for as well as a commitment to understanding (Judg 9:3; Pss 119:36; 141:4). It involves the preparation of the will and the orientation of one's organs of reception to receive authoritative, parental instruction.

b. An Active Pursuit (2:3–4)

The acceptance of parental instruction and the cultivation of one's organs of reception are fundamental for the acquisition of wisdom and virtue. Nonetheless, they are insufficient for the task; they must be accompanied by the second precondition: an active pursuit (v.v. 3–4). In the event that the son assumed the apodosis would follow the first precondition and explanation (vv. 1–2), the parent introduces the second set of preconditions with the conjunction "indeed" (כִּי, v. 3a), which highlights the certainty of the subsequent conditions.[11] These conditions describe the active search for wisdom. And this search is conceptualized in two ways. The first involves one's mouth (v. 3). Similar to Wisdom's call (1:20, 21, 24), the parent calls the son to "cry out" (תִקְרָא, v. 3a) and "raise your voice" (תִּתֵּן קוֹלֶךָ, v. 3b) for insight and understanding—terms for wisdom that are personified indirectly and envisioned as coveted guests (cf. 1:2). In so doing, the parent indicates that the acquisition of wisdom involves a verbal pursuit, an urgent summons to wisdom. And when this verbal pursuit is read in conjunction with the previous preconditions, it appears that the acquisition of wisdom involves the synchronization of the son's mouth with his ears and his heart.

The same is true of the second way in which the search for wisdom is conceptualized. The final precondition indicates that the son must also launch a diligent search for understanding (v. 4); he must hunt for it, aligning his physical body and desires with his mouth (v. 3), ears (v. 2a), and heart (v. 2b). This hunt for understanding is compared to the pursuit of desirable commodities: "silver" (כָּסֶף, v. 4a) and "hidden treasures" (מַטְמוֹנִים, v. 4b). The move from accessible currency to concealed riches illuminates the effort required to acquire wisdom. Wisdom and understanding must be desired and diligently sought, not just passively received.

2. The Procurement of Wisdom (2:5–8)

The preconditions delineated in the extended protasis suggest that a commitment to and a desire for wisdom precede understanding.[12] They describe the way in which faith seeks understanding.[13] When the preconditions are met, the disposition and cognitive facility for wisdom and

10. While תַּטֶּה is cast in the imperfect, parallelism between infinitives and imperfects elsewhere in Proverbs suggest the latter forms adopt the sense expressed through the former (2:8; 5:2). As Fox suggests, "Such skewed parallelism may be a stylistic fillip to avoid monotony." Fox, *Proverbs 1–9*, 191.

11. *IBHS* §39.3.4e; cf. §40.2.2 a–b; Joüon §164b–c.

12. Newsom, "Woman and the Discourse of Patriarchal Wisdom," 147.

13. Treier, *Proverbs and Ecclesiastes*, 22.

virtue is procured (v. 5). The inclination for and call to understanding precipitates understanding. And the search for wisdom culminates in finding the knowledge of God.

a. The Essence of the Procurement (2:5)

These rewards are presented in the first apodosis, which is introduced by the adverb "then" (אָז, v. 5a). Ironically, the search for wisdom does not result in the acquisition of wisdom per se; rather, it provides the occasion for something much greater: the acquisition of "the fear of YHWH" (יִרְאַת יְהוָה, v. 5a) and intimate relationship with the divine established through "the knowledge of God" (דַעַת אֱלֹהִים; 5b). As noted in the preamble (1:7), the fear of YHWH is the mode of being cultivated in relationship with YHWH that shapes one's intellect, desires, and worldview. It is a posture that that recognizes humanity's responsibilities, contingency, and place within the cosmos under YHWH's gracious governance (Prov 9:10; cf. 30:1–6). And as 2:5 suggests, the fear of YHWH not only represents the beginning of wisdom (1:7); it also serves as the means by which one increases in wisdom (cf. 1:5). As faith and fear seek wisdom and understanding, more mature wisdom and understanding is granted. One's character is sharpened; one's intellect is honed; one's desires are further shaped; and one's worldview is further formed.

As the motto of the anthology, the fear of YHWH is familiar phrase. This is not the case with the expression "the knowledge of God" (דַעַת אֱלֹהִים; 5b). The phrase occurs elsewhere in the Old Testament only in Hos 4:1 and 6:6. These texts, combined with the expression's parallel relationship with the fear of YHWH (cf. 9:10), intimate that "the knowledge of God" is inextricably linked with the anthology's prerequisite. But it is also distinct. It conveys the knowledge that comes from fear and faith seeking understanding. This awareness of God assumes intimacy with God and familiarity with the divine will. And this relational knowledge necessitates commitment and forms of behavior that please the divine partner.[14]

b. The Reason for the Procurement (2:6–7)

The first apodosis presents the procurement of wisdom (v. 5). The son searches for wisdom (vv. 3–4). And in so doing, he searches for God, for when he finds wisdom, he finds God, who hones the requisite disposition and grants knowledge for the cultivation of wisdom and virtue. This is given specific attention in vv. 6–7, which provide the rationale for the acquisition of the fear of YHWH and knowledge of God. The introductory conjunction "for" (כִּי, v. 6a), combined with the emphatic placement of YHWH at the beginning of v. 6, focuses attention on the divine subject in this explanation for the procurement of wisdom. The son pursues wisdom; but it is YHWH who grants wisdom. In fact, YHWH is the source and dispenser of wisdom: it flows from his mouth (v. 6b).[15] And YHWH is the custodian of "resourcefulness" (תּוּשִׁיָּה, v. 7a). Just as the son was called to "store up" (תִּצְפֹּן, v. 1c) parental commands, so YHWH "stores up" (יִצְפֹּן, v. 7a)[16] or conceals ingenuity for the upright. Those who search for wisdom find YHWH's storehouse; they acquire the ingenuity and the mental proficiency

14. Clifford, *Proverbs*, 47; Fox, *Proverbs 1–9*, 111–12; Waltke, *Proverbs: Chapters 1–15*, 223.

15. For discussion of whether the phrase "from his mouth" (מִפִּיו, v. 6b) represents a claim to divine inspiration, see Fox, *Proverbs 1–9*, 113–14; Waltke, *Proverbs: Chapters 1–15*, 224; Longman, *Proverbs*, 120–21; Loader, *Proverbs 1–9*, 117–18. Even if the phrase does not represent a claim to divine inspiration, it identifies YHWH as the source of wisdom. Cf. Schipper, *Proverbs 1–15*, 110, who links the expression with Deut 8:3 and argues that it assumes the late confluence of wisdom and *torah*.

16. This reading follows *qere* rather than *ketiv*.

to navigate the various circumstances of life. This ingenuity serves as a means of protection for those who walk with integrity. While "shield" (מָגֵן, v. 7b) may be read in relation to YHWH, its immediate juxtaposition to resourcefulness suggests the term stands in apposition to the latter.[17] Resourcefulness provides protection. YHWH does not shield the upright directly; rather, YHWH is the one who allows those who search for wisdom to rummage through his storehouse, secure resourcefulness, and apply this mental proficiency to withstand the vicissitudes of life.

c. The Purpose of the Procurement (2:8)

This purpose is expressed in v. 8, which is dependent upon the verb "stores up" (v. 7a); it identifies the reason why YHWH reserves resourcefulness for the upright. This reason is intimately related to the metaphor of a shield. Just as a shield offers protection, so also YHWH empowers the blameless to wield the shield of resourcefulness in order to protect "the paths of justice" (אָרְחוֹת מִשְׁפָּט, v. 8a) and guard "the way of his faithful ones" (דֶּרֶךְ חֲסִידָיו, v. 8b).[18] The initial apodosis culminates in a purpose clause that employs the nuclear symbol of the way. The protection offered by ingenuity allows one to guard not only themselves but also the community in general and the paths of the faithful in particular. It equips one to protect the many manifestations of justice, to preserve forms of righteous behavior that accord with the divine order, and to secure the way of those who are loyal to YHWH.

The first apodosis moves from a declaration of wisdom's procurement (v. 5) to an explanation for this procurement (vv. 6–7) to a description of the purpose of this procurement (v. 8). And this scheme is reproduced in the second apodosis.

3. The Procurement of Virtue (2:9–22)

Whereas the first apodosis focused on the procurement of wisdom (vv. 5–8), the second focuses on the procurement of virtue (vv. 9–22). The disposition and knowledge granted to those who seek and find wisdom does not represent the end of Proverbs's pedagogical process. This disposition and knowledge culminate in the inculcation of genuine virtue, which, like wisdom, protects and preserves the way of the upright.

a. The Essence of the Procurement (2:9)

The intimate relationship between wisdom and virtue is conveyed through the second apodosis, which stands in parallel relationship with the first. Similar to the first, it opens with the expression "then you will understand" (אָז תָּבִין, v. 9). And similar to the preamble (1:3), it describes the essence of virtue through the terms "righteousness, justice, and uprightness" (צֶדֶק וּמִשְׁפָּט וּמֵישָׁרִים, v. 9). In so doing, it captures the spirit of the document's prolegomenon (1:1–7): it links the acquisition of wisdom with the cultivation of virtue in a comprehensive program of education for character formation.

While the repetition in the second apodosis suggests the procurement of virtue is contemporaneous with the procurement of wisdom, the logic of the passage intimates that the fear of YHWH and the knowledge of God provide the soil in which virtue may bloom. YHWH grants wisdom, the requisite posture, and knowledge of his will from which one may live rightly in relation to God and

17. So also, e.g., Longman, *Proverbs*, 121; Loader, *Proverbs 1–9*, 119.

18. This reading follows *qere*. For the rendering of the imperfect form יִשְׁמֹר in accordance with the infinitive construct לִנְצֹר, see p. 281n4 above.

others. That is, wisdom acquired in pursuit of and in relationship with YHWH leads to virtue and proper relations others (v. 9).[19] This description of virtue mirrors not only the language of 1:3 but also its syntax. Like 1:3, "righteousness, justice, and uprightness" are cast in apposition. And like 1:3, they serve as a distillation of the virtues that characterize, guide, and define the wise life. Here, however, they do not explain the type of instruction in prudent living the document seeks to inculcate in readers; rather, they explain "every good path" (כָּל־מַעְגַּל־טוֹב, v. 9), all forms of ethical behavior that accord with the divine order and contribute to human flourishing. The virtues are integrated into the anthology's nuclear symbol. The values that mark instruction in prudent living are actualized through an embodied way of life. And these values overload the poetic line. To be specific, the term "uprightness" tips the poetic scales and disrupts the balance of poetic parallelism within the unit, drawing attention to the procurement of virtue.[20] Just as these values disrupt the syntactical pattern within the preamble, so now they disrupt the poetic pattern of the lecture. They stand out syntactically much in the same way that they stand out practically.

b. The Reason for the Procurement (2:10–11)

Similar to the first apodosis (vv. 5–7), the second moves from a declaration of the procurement of virtue to an explanation for its procurement (vv. 10–11). This explanation is introduced by the conjunction "for" (כִּי, v. 10a) and conceptualized in two ways. The first is the transformative power of wisdom (v. 10). As wisdom seeps into the locus of one's inner self, it (re)orients one's disposition and satisfies one's ethical taste buds.[21] That is, as wisdom penetrates the inner recesses of one's character, it transforms one's desires and cultivates the virtues delineated in v. 9. The second way in which the rationale is conceptualized is comparable to v. 8. Like resourcefulness, discretion and understanding serve as a source of protection (v. 11). And this protection is described through the same verbs that appear in v. 8. Together, the transformative power and protection of wisdom illuminate the internal-external dimensions of virtue. The procurement of virtue is attributed to the internal infiltration of wisdom, which then provides external protection through the powers of discretion and understanding. Wisdom transforms one's inner attitudes and appetites, produces virtue, and offers practical protection.

c. The Purpose of the Procurement (2:12–19)

This practical protection is given specific attention in vv. 12–19. The reason for the procurement of virtue governs the extended description of the purpose of its procurement (vv. 12–19). This extended description elaborates upon the protective power of wisdom mentioned in vv. 8 and 11 through two parallel purposes clauses, each of which is dependent upon the verbs within v. 11. And each of these purposes clauses focuses on the disposition, speech, and way of a particular character type.

(1) The Way of the Evildoer (2:12–15)

The "evildoer" (רָע, v. 12a) represents the first character type from which discretion and understanding offer deliverance. The shift from "guard" (תִּשְׁמֹר, v. 11a) and "protect you" (תִנְצְרֶכָּה, v. 11b)

19. Van Leeuwen, "The Book of Proverbs," *NIB* 5:43.

20. For discussion of the phenomenon of enjambment, see Watson, *Classical Hebrew Poetry*, 332–35.

21. Waltke, *Proverbs: Chapters 1–15*, 228; Yoder, *Proverbs*, 27.

to "deliver you" (הַצִּילְךָ, v. 12a) highlights the development of thought within the unit. Discretion and understanding not only serve as a means of general defense (vv. 8, 11); they also provide a source of active deliverance. They save one from a lifestyle marked by perverse speech, twisted desires, and crooked paths. This lifestyle is sketched throughout vv. 12–15. According to the vignette, the evildoer speaks "perversely" (תַּהְפֻּכוֹת, v. 12b) and rejoices "in the perversity of evil" (בְּתַהְפֻּכוֹת רָע, v. 14b). His speech matches his character and desires. His words and schemes are distorted (v. 12b; 8:13; 10:32); his affections and desires are warped (2:14; 6:14; 16:28, 30). He is the antithesis of the upright. In fact, he is a personage who has forsaken or abandoned the "paths of uprightness" (אָרְחוֹת יֹשֶׁר; 1:13a). He prefers ways of darkness to light, crooked paths to straight. And his crooked paths correspond with his "devious" (נְלוֹזִים, v. 15b) ways. The extended purpose clause employs the nuclear symbol of the way as an organizing principle to describe the dimensions of the evildoers' character: his speech, desires, disposition, actions, and lifestyle. In so doing, the clause concretizes the protective power of wisdom and virtue. Wisdom and virtue save one from the way of the "moral pervert."[22] And they prevent one from forsaking the way of the upright for the way of the crooked.

(2) The Way of the Strange Woman (2:16–19)

The "strange woman" (אִשָּׁה זָרָה, v. 16a) or "outsider" (נָכְרִיָּה, v. 16b) represents the second character type from which discretion and understanding offer deliverance. The designations "strange" and "outsider" carry several distinct connotations. The former is used elsewhere in the Old Testament to designate Israelites who are members of another family or community (Num 18:4, 7; Deut 25:5), as well as to describe ethnic foreignness (Isa 1:7; 61:5; Jer 5:19; 30:8) and apostasy associated with foreign women (Jer 2:25; 3:13).[23] The latter term also conveys these shades of meaning. In the main, however, "outsider" tends to function as a social designation that denotes ethnic or national foreignness (Gen 31:15; Deut 17:15; 1 Kgs 11:1). Taken together, these terms portray the woman as "other," as one outside the boundaries of what is deemed acceptable or appropriate, whether socially, legally, or sexually.[24] And when this ambiguous "other" is considered within the context of the prologue in general (5:1–23; 6:20–35; 7:1–27) and the vivid description within vv. 16–19 in particular, the parent appears to portray her in a specific way: as an adulterous woman.[25] In this respect, she is strange, "other," and off-limits because she is the wife of another as well as one who operates outside the boundaries of the sociomoral order.

Similar to the evildoers, the strange woman embodies a particular lifestyle. And this lifestyle is described through her speech, character, and way. In contrast to the crooked, perverse speech of the evildoers (v. 12), the speech of the strange woman is "smooth" (הֶחֱלִיקָה, v. 16b); it is slippery, seductive, and flattering. Her sweet talk conceals her deceptive character and the bitter consequences associated with indulging in her speech. The rhetoric of the strange woman differs from that of the evildoers; but the actions these character types

22. Fox, *Proverbs 1–9*, 117.

23. 4Q184, lines 9–12; Camp, *Wisdom and the Feminine*, 256–71; Christl Maier, *Die 'Fremde Frau' in Proverbien 1–9: Eine Exegetische und Sozialgeschichtliche Studie*, OBO 144 (Göttingen: Vandenhoeck & Ruprecht, 1995), 92–108; N. Nam Hoon Tan, *The 'Foreignness' of the Foreign Woman in Proverbs 1–9: A Study of the Origin and Development of a Biblical Motif*, BZAW 381 (Berlin: de Gruyter, 2008), 81–105.

24. Yoder, *Proverbs*, 30.

25. So also, among others, Fox, *Proverbs 1–9*, 139–41; Loader, *Proverbs 1–9*, 127.

perform is the same. The evildoers are "those who forsake" (הַעֹזְבִים, v. 13a) the paths of uprightness, while the strange woman is one "who forsakes" (הַעֹזֶבֶת, v. 17a) the companion of her youth. She abandons her husband, her intimate friend. To be specific, she violates her marriage covenant.[26] Her actions and moral worldview mirror the actions and worldview of the evildoers. She abandons a relationship and a lifestyle sanctioned by God and embodies a moral worldview that leads to death.

This telos is presented in vv. 18–19, which explain the protective power and deliverance of wisdom and virtue delineated in v. 16 ("for," כִּי, v. 18a). Again, wisdom and virtue save one from a particular way (cf. vv. 12–15). The way of the strange woman, however, is not simply a path or lifestyle; it is also a portal that leads to a particular place: the place of "the deceased" (רְפָאִים, v. 18b).[27] Her house is a gateway to death; it "sinks down" (שָׁחָה, v. 18a) or descends to the underworld.[28] The parent employs vivid, metaphorical language that blurs the boundaries among the strange woman, her house, and her ways. All lead to the same place. And as the double entendre suggests, whether one "come[s] to her" (בָּאֶיהָ, v. 19a) on foot or through sexual intercourse, the woman, her house, and her way lead to a place from which there is no escape and no return.[29] The strange woman epitomizes a lifestyle that leads to death, a lifestyle and an end from which wisdom and virtue offer protection and deliverance.

d. The Result of the Procurement (2:20–22)

The result of the procurement, protection, and deliverance of wisdom and virtue is delineated in vv. 20–22. This result is introduced by "so that" (לְמַעַן, v. 20a), and the result clause stands in parallel relationship with the purposes clauses introduced in vv. 12 and 16. Similar to these purpose clauses, vv. 20–22 are subordinate to the verbs of protection in v. 11. In view of the procurement of wisdom and virtue (vv. 5, 9), the argument moves from the reasons for their procurement (vv. 6–7, 10–11), to the purpose of their procurement (vv. 8, 12–15, 16–19), to the result of their procurement (vv. 20–22). This result consists of two parts. The first is governed by the path metaphor (v. 20). As noted above, the path metaphor serves as the conceptual backbone of vv. 12–19. The evildoers and the strange woman traverse and embody particular ways. The same is true of the one who procures wisdom and virtue. This person traverses the "way of the good" (דֶּרֶךְ טוֹבִים, v. 20a) and adheres to the "paths of the righteous" (אָרְחוֹת צַדִּיקִים, v. 20b). Wisdom and virtue propel one down a particular path; they associate one with the good and the righteous; and they empower one to live virtuously in accord with God's design.

26. Gordon P. Hugenberger, *Marriage as a Covenant: A Study of Biblical Law and Ethics Governing Marriage Developed from the Perspective of Malachi*, VTSup 52 (Leiden, Brill, 1994), 296–302; Fox, *Proverbs 1–9*, 121; Loader, *Proverbs 1–9*, 128.

27. For discussion of "the deceased," see H. Rouillard, "Rephaim, רפאים," *DDD* 692–700.

28. In light of the fact that the verb "sinks down" (שָׁחָה, v. 18a) is feminine and "house" (בַּיִת, v. 18a) is masculine, many emend "her house" to the feminine noun "her path" (נתיבתה, v. 18a). If, however, v. 19 elaborates upon the imagery in v. 18, the emendation is unnecessary, for the parent moves from a description of the woman's house (v. 18a) to her ways (v. 18b), which highlight the entryway and route to the place of no return (v. 19). The grammatical conflict between "sinks down" and "house," therefore, may be understood through the development of thought between vv. 18–19 and the metaphorical equivalence of the woman, her house, and her ways. Van Leeuwen, "The Book of Proverbs," *NIB* 5:44–45, Loader, *Proverbs 1–9*, 129–31.

29. For the motif of death as a place of no return, see "The Descent of Ishtar to the Underworld," trans. Stephanie Dalley (*COS* 1.108:381–84).

This path or lifestyle is developed in the second part of the lecture's result, which explains the value of the "way of the good" and the "paths of the righteous" through the theme of "land" (אֶרֶץ, vv. 21–22). "The upright" (יְשָׁרִים, v. 21a) and "the blameless" (תְמִימִים, v. 21b) are members of the same class as the good and the righteous (v. 20).[30] They not only walk straight paths (cf. v. 13a), but they also enjoy a secure, long life in the land. The wicked and the treacherous experience the opposite fate: they are "cut off" (יִכָּרֵתוּ, v. 22a) and "uprooted" (יִסְּחוּ, v. 22b) from the land. That is, they experience a brief life, a premature death. The antithesis between these character types and the use of the verbs "remain" and "cut off" with reference to the land is reminiscent of several texts within the Torah and the Prophets, which describe one's relation to the promised land through the dictates of the covenant (Deut 28:63; Zeph 1:3; cf. Deut 5:16, 33; 6:18). While the covenant may serve as the conceptual backdrop of Proverbs, it does not function as the principal framework through which to understand the motif of land in the parental lecture. The land is not necessarily conceptualized through the covenant; rather, the land serves as a metonymy for life and peace on the earth.[31] And this life, combined with a lifestyle and orientation that classifies one among the good and the righteous, constitutes the result of the procurement of wisdom and virtue. The parent concludes the description of the procurement, power, and protection of wisdom and virtue with an attractive portrayal of the good life. In so doing, the parent not only provides reasons for choosing the good but also defines the essence of the good life.[32]

Canonical and Theological Significance

The extended description of the procurement, power, and protection of wisdom and virtue plays a formative role in Proverbs. As intimated above, the parental lecture outlines the preconditions for the acquisition of wisdom and the process by which one may achieve the purpose of the document (1:1–7). It elaborates upon the preamble and the discourses within ch. 1, provides a pedagogical paradigm of faith seeking wisdom and virtue, and introduces concepts that are developed within the remainder of the anthology. The lecture reiterates and develops the educational requirements sounded in the preamble and the discourses in ch. 1. It indicates that the acquisition of wisdom and virtue is dependent upon a receptive posture as well as an active pursuit. Receptivity alone is not enough; rather, one must manifest their commitment to and desire for wisdom and virtue through an active search. This search is governed by faith seeking understanding; it begins with fear and faith (1:7); and it leads to further understanding of God, who grants wisdom, understanding, and virtue as a gracious gift (2:5–6, 9). Humans search for wisdom; and their search leads them to God, who grants wisdom that transforms one's character (v. 10), virtues

30. Loader, *Proverbs 1–9*, 134.

31. Clifford, *Proverbs*, 49; Fox, *Proverbs 1–9*, 123–24; Waltke, *Proverbs: Chapters 1–15*, 234; Yoder, *Proverbs*, 32–33; Loader, *Proverbs 1–9*, 135.

32. McKinnon, *Character, Virtue Theories, and the Vices*, 30.

that protect one from the onslaughts of evildoers and the strange women (vv. 12–19), and the moral capacity to walk in the way of the good (vv. 20–22).

The parental lecture builds on the previous discourses and introduces character types as well as concepts that are woven throughout the materials in the remainder of the document. The character and desires of the evildoers are recast through the disposition and actions of the wicked in 4:14–19 (cf. 6:12–15). The strange woman and her slippery speech are the focus of attention in three of the remaining parental lectures (5:1–23; 6:20–35; 7:1–27). The necessity of pursuing wisdom punctuates many discourses and sayings (3:13; 4:7, 13, 22; 8:9, 35; 15:14; 18:15; 23:23). The protective power of wisdom and virtue recurs within many of the parental lectures (4:6; 6:22–24; 7:5). And the transformative power of wisdom and virtue is developed through the internalization of parental teaching (3:3; 6:21; 7:3) as well as through the patterning of one's character and desires in accordance with the characterization of approved character types.[33]

The motifs that pervade the second parental lecture reverberate across the anthology. And these motifs are the subject of attention elsewhere in the canon. Similar to Prov 2, several Old Testament texts indicate that wisdom is not the product of human striving or ingenuity alone; rather, it is a divine gift bestowed upon humans by the fount of true wisdom (Exod 31:6; 36:1–2; 1 Kgs 3:12; Eccl 2:26). God grants wisdom. Humans nurture and hone this divine gift through skilled practices. The giftedness of wisdom underlies several New Testament texts (2 Cor 4:6; Eph 1:17–19). And it is given clear expression in Jas 1:5: "Now if any of you lacks wisdom, he should ask God, who gives generously to all and without finding fault, and it will be given to him" (author's translation). Humans may search and ask for wisdom, but it is God who gives genuine wisdom.

In addition to wisdom as a divine gift, the intimate relationship between wisdom and virtue within the lecture is reflected in the broader canonical witness. Just as the acquisition of wisdom and the knowledge of God is inseparable from the acquisition of virtue and the embodiment of communal values (Prov 2:5, 9), so also relationship with God through knowledge of the divine will is inseparable from forms of behavior that please the divine partner and nourish the community. The lecture moves from knowledge of and relationship with God (2:5) to virtues that contribute to right relations with others and communal well-being (2:9).[34] This paradigm is reflected in the Decalogue (Exod 20:1–17; Deut 5:6–21), and it is summarized in the greatest commandments: love God and love your neighbor (Mark 12:29–31). Wisdom and virtue are not mutually exclusive. They are inextricably linked in Proverbs's program

33. For discussion of the way in which stories "produce a practical patterning of desire," see Booth, *The Company We Keep*, 201–24.

34. Van Leeuwen, "The Book of Proverbs," *NIB* 5:45.

of education for character formation and in the broader theological witness of the canon. Wisdom is rooted in relationship with God and knowledge of his will. Wisdom yields virtuous conduct. And virtuous conduct manifests one's wisdom.

The link between wisdom and virtue and the recognition that wisdom is acquired through active pursuit and received as a divine gift is relevant to the life and witness of the church today. If genuine wisdom is inseparable from virtue, then forms of behavior oriented toward others that contribute to the health of the community must mark the wise life. Righteousness, justice, and uprightness are not private values; they are virtues that strengthen ethical relations among individuals within a community. And they are ethical diagnostics that help one determine whether they possess wisdom. Wisdom inculcates these moral virtues in the individual, and the individual disperses these virtues through specific forms of behavior within the community.

Together with the link between wisdom and virtue, the recognition that the acquisition of wisdom involves human pursuit and divine generosity calibrates one's expectations and curbs potential arrogance. According to Prov 2, wisdom is not acquired through passive receptivity. It necessitates a commitment; it requires the preparation and orientation of one's ears and heart; and it demands an active search that includes one's mouth and one's body. Wisdom is available and accessible, but it is not a commodity that is simply inherited from others. It requires effort and personal responsibility. Nonetheless, in light of the fact that wisdom is acquired through the combination of human effort and divine generosity, the one who searches for and finds wisdom has no grounds for boasting. Ultimately, wisdom is a gift from God. And the realization that God grants wisdom liberates individuals as they search for this divine gift, curbs potential pride when the gift is bestowed, and provides perspective as the gift is exercised through virtuous conduct for the benefit of others.

CHAPTER 5

Proverbs 3:1–12

D. Wisdom and Piety

Main Idea of the Passage

The third parental lecture indicates that the wise life is a pious life; it identifies how the fear of YHWH and knowledge of God (2:5) should shape one's character and attitudes, producing a lifestyle marked by trust, humility, and homage.

Literary Context

The parental instruction in 3:1–12 offers a healthy corrective to a misreading of the extended description of the procurement of wisdom and virtue within ch. 2. In the event that this description left one with the impression that once wisdom and virtue are acquired the quest is complete, the third parental lecture informs the addressee that the procurement of wisdom and virtue initiates a lifelong journey of piety in which one retains, cultivates, and manifests their wisdom through specific attitudes and concrete actions. And in the event that the parental description in ch. 2 left one with the impression that wisdom automatically produces virtuous behavior, the third parental lecture informs the addressee that virtue and piety must be developed. What was procured must be preserved (2:5, 9; 3:1–4). The active pursuit of wisdom must be accompanied by the active cultivation of character (2:1–4; 3:1, 3, 5–10). And the reception of wisdom and virtue must be demonstrated through pious attitudes and actions that evince genuine wisdom and virtue. That is, an understanding of the "fear of YHWH" (יִרְאַת יְהוָה; 2:5a) and "the knowledge of God" (דַּעַת אֱלֹהִים; 2:5b) must move one to "fear YHWH" (יְרָא אֶת־יְהוָה, 3:7b) and "know him" (דָעֵהוּ, v. 6a) in all their ways. The third parental instruction qualifies the description of wisdom's procurement in the previous lecture by emphasizing the importance of piety in the wise life. To modify an expression from the epistle of James (Jas 2:26), in light of the acquisition of wisdom and virtue in ch. 2, the discourse declares, "Wisdom without piety is dead."

In addition to qualifying the description of wisdom's procurement in ch. 2, the third parental lecture elaborates upon the nature of the good life in general and the "way of the good" (דֶּרֶךְ טוֹבִים; 2:20a) in particular. Whereas ch. 2 identified the "way of the good" (דֶּרֶךְ טוֹבִים, v. 20a) and provided reasons for choosing the good, the third parental lecture defines the essence of this "way" and explains the rewards

I. Introduction to the Book (1:1–7)

II. The Value of Wisdom and Virtue (1:8–9:18)

- A. Wisdom, Desire, and Different Ways (1:8–19)
- B. Wisdom's Rebuke (1:20–33)
- C. The Procurement, Power, and Protection of Wisdom and Virtue (2:1–22)
- **D. Wisdom and Piety (3:1–12)**
    - **1. The Retention and Internalization of Parental Teaching (3:1–4)**
        - **a. The Retention of Parental Teaching (3:1)**
        - **b. The Motivation for Retention (3:2)**
        - **c. The Internalization of Virtue (3:3)**
        - **d. The Promise of Internalization (3:4)**
    - **2. The Contours of the Pious Life (3:5–10)**
        - **a. The Disposition and Practice of Dependence (3:5–6)**
        - **b. The Disposition and Practice of Humility (3:7–8)**
        - **c. The Disposition and Practice of Homage (3:9–10)**
    - **3. A Pious Perspective (3:11–12)**
        - **a. A Pious Attitude (3:11)**
        - **b. The Reason for the Attitude (3:12)**
- E. Wisdom's Value and Moral Obligations (3:13–35)
- F. Wisdom and Tradition (4:1–9)
- G. Wisdom and Ways of Life (4:10–19)
- H. Wisdom and the Moral Anatomy (4:20–27)
- I. Wisdom and Sexuality (5:1–23)
- J. Wisdom, Lending, Laziness, and the Immoral Anatomy (6:1–19)
- K. Wisdom, Desire, and Certain Destruction (6:20–35)
- L. Wisdom and Seduction (7:1–27)
- M. Wisdom's Call, Credentials, and the Cosmos (8:1–36)
- N. Wisdom and Folly's Invitations (9:1–18)

III. "Forming 'Fearers of YHWH'": The Curriculum of Wisdom and Virtue (10:1–29:27)

IV. The Application of Wisdom and Virtue (30:1–31:31)

associated with the attitudes and actions characteristic of this pious lifestyle. Similar to the extended description in ch. 2 (2:5, 9), the parental instruction indicates that wisdom and virtue are inextricably linked; they cannot be separated. In contrast to ch. 2, however, the third parental lecture offers a distinct perspective on this intimate connection. It focuses on the importance of piety. Piety is foregrounded, while wisdom and wisdom terminology are relegated to the background. This emphasis on piety and virtue counterbalances those discourses that give specific attention to wisdom. The lecture reveals that the wise life involves much more than the acquisition of knowledge and the cultivation of appropriate attitudes; it also involves an active piety—specific dispositions and concrete actions that prove one's wisdom.

Translation and Exegetical Outline

(See page 180.)

Structure and Literary Form

Similar to the discourse in 1:8–19, the third parental lecture may be classified as an instruction. In contrast to the extended description in ch. 2, the lecture is dominated by formal admonitions cast in the form of positive and negative injunctions. Even the rewards or promises associated with the attitudes and forms of conduct prescribed by the lecture are expressed through volitional forms (3:4a, 6b, 8a, 10a). These indirect volitives not only illuminate the tone and rhetorical texture of the discourse; they also express certainty or assurance that those who embody the prescribed attitudes and perform the stipulated actions will receive the promised rewards.[1] The prevalent use of direct and indirect volitives within the piece clarifies the discourse's form and function. As a formal instruction, the lecture seeks to persuade the addressee to internalize parental teaching and cultivate internal attitudes and external actions characteristic of pious devotion to YHWH.

Together with the form and function of the discourse, the direct and indirect volitives define the literary architecture of the lecture. At the macrolevel, the piece contains three distinct units. The first focuses on the retention and internalization of parental instruction (vv. 1–4). The second describes the contours of a pious life through internal attitudes and external actions (vv. 5–10), while the third qualifies the grandiose promises delineated in vv. 5–10 with a pious perspective on adversity (vv. 11–12).

1. For discussion of indirect volitives, see GKC §110f–i; Joüon §164f, i.

Proverbs 3:1–12

Verse	Hebrew	English	Outline
			D. Wisdom and Piety (3:1–12)
			1. The Retention and Internalization of Parental Teaching (3:1–4)
1a	בְּנִי תּוֹרָתִי אַל־תִּשְׁכָּח	My son, do not forget my teaching,	a. The Retention of Parental Teaching (3:1)
1b	וּמִצְוֹתַי יִצֹּר לִבֶּךָ	and let your heart keep my commands;	
2a	↑ כִּי אֹרֶךְ יָמִים וּשְׁנוֹת חַיִּים	↑ for length of days and years of life,	b. The Motivation for Retention (3:2)
2b	וְשָׁלוֹם יוֹסִיפוּ לָךְ	and peace will increase for you.	
3a	חֶסֶד וֶאֱמֶת אַל־יַעַזְבֻךָ	Do not let kindness and faithfulness leave you;	c. The Internalization of Virtue (3:3)
3b	קָשְׁרֵם עַל־גַּרְגְּרוֹתֶיךָ	bind them around your neck,	
3c	כָּתְבֵם עַל־לוּחַ לִבֶּךָ	write them on the tablet of your heart,	
4a	וּמְצָא־חֵן וְשֵׂכֶל־טוֹב	then you will find favor and good repute	d. The Promise of Internalization (3:4)
4b	↑ בְּעֵינֵי אֱלֹהִים וְאָדָם	↑ in the sight of God and humans.	
			2. The Contours of the Pious Life (3:5–10)
5a	בְּטַח אֶל־יְהוָה בְּכָל־לִבֶּךָ	Trust in YHWH with all your heart,	a. The Disposition and Practice of Dependence (3:5–6)
5b	וְאֶל־בִּינָתְךָ אַל־תִּשָּׁעֵן	and do not depend on your own understanding.	
6a	בְּכָל־דְּרָכֶיךָ דָעֵהוּ	In all your ways know him,	
6b	וְהוּא יְיַשֵּׁר אֹרְחֹתֶיךָ	then he himself will make your paths smooth.	
7a	אַל־תְּהִי חָכָם בְּעֵינֶיךָ	Do not be wise in your own eyes;	b. The Disposition and Practice of Humility (3:7–8)
7b	יְרָא אֶת־יְהוָה וְסוּר מֵרָע	fear YHWH, and turn away from evil;	
8a	רִפְאוּת תְּהִי לְשָׁרֶּךָ	then it will be healing to your body	
8b	וְשִׁקּוּי לְעַצְמוֹתֶיךָ	and nourishment for your bones.	
9a	כַּבֵּד אֶת־יְהוָה מֵהוֹנֶךָ	Honor YHWH from your wealth	c. The Disposition and Practice of Homage (3:9–10)
9b	וּמֵרֵאשִׁית כָּל־תְּבוּאָתֶךָ	and from the firstfruits of all your produce;	
10a	וְיִמָּלְאוּ אֲסָמֶיךָ שָׂבָע	then your storehouses will overflow with abundance,	
10b	וְתִירוֹשׁ יְקָבֶיךָ יִפְרֹצוּ	and your vats will burst with new wine.	
			3. A Pious Perspective (3:11–12)
11a	מוּסַר יְהוָה בְּנִי אַל־תִּמְאָס	YHWH's discipline, my son, do not reject,	a. A Pious Attitude (3:11)
11b	וְאַל־תָּקֹץ בְּתוֹכַחְתּוֹ	and do not loathe his reproof,	
12a	↑ כִּי אֶת אֲשֶׁר יֶאֱהַב יְהוָה יוֹכִיחַ	↑ for the one whom YHWH loves he will reprove,	b. The Reason for the Attitude (3:12)
12b	↑ וּכְאָב אֶת־בֵּן יִרְצֶה	↑ even as a father the son in whom he delights.	

The unit is framed by the vocative "my son" (בְּנִי, vv. 1a, 11a) as well as a pair of admonitions followed by the conjunction "for" (כִּי, vv. 2a, 12a), which occur only in vv. 1–2 and 11–12.[2] At the microlevel, however, the discourse consists of six couplets. The odd-numbered verses convey the formal admonitions (vv. 1, 3, 5, 7, 9, 11), while the even-numbered verses express the motivations, promises, or reasons associated with the respective commands (vv. 2, 4, 6, 8, 10, 12).[3] Whether the discourse is viewed at the macro- or microlevel, its rhetoric, movement, and frame suggest it is a coherent instruction designed to inculcate piety in the addressee.

Explanation of the Text

1. The Retention and Internalization of Parental Teaching (3:1–4)

Similar to the exordia of the parental lectures elsewhere in the prologue, the discourse opens with a pair of admonitions. These admonitions are concerned with the retention and internalization of parental teaching. The substance of these commands and the motivations or promises associated with each deserves a brief comment.

a. The Retention of Parental Teaching (3:1)

Whereas the previous discourses attempted to cultivate a receptive, listening posture in the addressee, the third parental lecture assumes the son has received the teaching and commands of the parent (1:8; 2:1; 3:1). The issue is not the acceptance of parental instruction; rather, the issue is the retention and cultivation of parental instruction. This concern is expressed through a pair of admonitions, the first negative and the second positive. The negative injunction, "do not forget my teaching" (תּוֹרָתִי אַל־תִּשְׁכָּח, v. 1a), identifies the danger of educational amnesia, the deliberate neglect or abandonment of parental instruction. The positive command, "let your heart keep my commands" (וּמִצְוֹתַי יִצֹּר לִבֶּךָ, v. 1b), reiterates the spirit of the negative injunction, giving particular attention to the intentional protection and cultivation of authoritative parental directives (6:20; cf. Deut 32:10; Isa 42:6). Just as the acquisition of wisdom involved an active, intentional pursuit, so also the life of wisdom involves an active, intentional preservation of the wisdom one has received. This preservation requires remembrance (v. 1b); and it requires one to patrol, guard, and nurture the commands one has stored up within their heart (2:1c; 3:1c). When these commands concerning the retention of parental instruction are read against the backdrop of ch. 2, it appears the third parental lecture develops the process of wisdom's acquisition and application. The lecture moves from storing up commands to retaining commands (2:1; 3:1), and from understanding offering protection (תִּנְצְרֶךָּ; 2:11b) to the son protecting (יִצֹּר; 3:1b) parental teaching.

2. Plöger, *Sprüche Salomos*, 32–35; Arndt Meinhold, "Gott und Mensch in Proverbien III," *VT* 37 (1987): 468; Paul Overland, "Did the Sage Draw from the Shema? A Study of Proverbs 3:1–12," *CBQ* 62 (2000): 427; Loader, *Proverbs 1–9*, 143.

3. Waltke, *Proverbs: Chapters 1–15*, 238–39; Loader, *Proverbs 1–9*, 143.

b. The Motivation for Retention (3:2)

The rationale for this retention of parental teaching is introduced by the conjunction "for" (כִּי, v. 2a), which opens a clause that provides a motivation for adhering to the admonitions delineated in v. 1. Similar to 1:3 and 2:9, the clause disrupts the poetic balance within the unit; it overloads the poetic line with a sequence of phrases that highlight the reward for preserving parental instruction; and the placement of the main verb near the end of the poetic line draws attention to this sequence. The sequenced objects build on one another, developing a portrait of the life enjoyed by one who preserves parental instruction. The initial phrase, "length of days" (אֹרֶךְ יָמִים, v. 2a), captures the extent or quality of this life, while the phrases "years of life" (שְׁנוֹת חַיִּים, v. 2a) and "peace" (שָׁלוֹם, v. 2b) describe the quality of this life. It is a long life of wholeness and wellbeing, a life characterized by inward and outward serenity.[4] This type of life is experienced by those who accept and retain parental instruction (3:2; 4:10); and this type of life is granted to those who embrace Lady Wisdom (9:11; cf. 3:17).[5] The common reward for preserving parental instruction and embracing Lady Wisdom suggests that the instruction of these personae is comparable. The wisdom and life mediated by the parents is the wisdom and life embodied in and offered by Lady Wisdom.[6]

c. The Internalization of Virtue (3:3)

The reward for retaining the parent's instruction mirrors the reward for accepting Lady Wisdom's instruction. And the virtues that characterize the parent's instruction mirror virtues that define aspects of YHWH's character. These virtues are foregrounded in v. 3; they open the second admonition and shape its concern with the internalization of parental instruction. Similar to v. 2, the extended admonition in v. 3 disrupts the balance of poetic parallelism in the unit. The shift from two poetic lines to three lines focuses attention on the importance of the commands and the extent of internalization.[7] The string of commands reiterate in recast form the call to retain parental instruction through terms, images, and expressions that connote active internalization. Whereas the initial pair of admonitions commended the retention of parental teaching (v. 1a, b), the sequence of admonitions in v. 3 commends the retention and assimilation of "kindness" (חֶסֶד, v. 3a) and "faithfulness" (אֱמֶת, v. 3a). These virtues are used elsewhere to describe the covenant commitment, constancy, loyalty, and reliability of both YHWH and humans (Gen 24:27; 47:29; Exod 34:6; Deut 7:9, 12; 2 Sam 2:5–6; Pss 40:11; 89:15[14]).[8] In the present context, however, these virtues appear to be metonymies for the parent's teaching and commands (v. 1a, b).[9] They are closely associated with

4. Oesterley, *The Book of Proverbs*, 19; Loader, *Proverbs 1–9*, 148.

5. For discussion of the nature and significance of the variant repetition among 3:2, 4:10, and 9:11, see Heim, *Poetic Imagination*, 104–9.

6. Van Leeuwen, "The Book of Proverbs," *NIB* 5:48.

7. In light of the fact that tricola are rare in Prov 1–9, many consider either 3:3a or 3:3c as a gloss (e.g., Plöger, *Sprüche Salomos*, 32; Fox, *Proverbs 1–9*, 145; Waltke, *Proverbs: Chapters 1–15*, 236n41, 241–42; Loader, *Proverbs 1–9*, 144–45). The addition of 3:3a is explained with reference to 7:1–3, whereas the addition of 3:3c is explained with reference to its absence in certain Septuagint manuscripts and the influence of 7:3. While 3:3c may have been influenced by the 7:3 (or vice versa), the present form of 3:3 should be accepted. The individual lines in the tricola evince a coherent progression of thought. The combination of the three lines highlights the significance of the commands. And the potential addition of 3:3c is the product of the one(s) responsible for the editing the lecture in conversation with the prologue or the anthology as a whole. For further discussion, see Gerhard Tauberschmidt, *Secondary Parallelism: A Study of the Translation Technique in LXX Proverbs*, AcBib 15 (Leiden: Brill, 2004), 104; Heim, *Poetic Imagination*, 110–15.

8. For discussion, see Katherine Doob Sakenfeld, *The Meaning of Ḥesed in the Hebrew Bible*, HSS 17 (Missoula, MT: Scholars Press, 1978), 233.

9. Toy, *Proverbs*, 57; Waltke, *Proverbs: Chapters 1–15*, 241; Van Leeuwen, "The Book of Proverbs," *NIB* 5:48.

the parent's instruction; they are human virtues that spring from retention of parental instruction; and they are values that are illustrated through the parent's instructions in 3:5–12 as well as 3:21–35. The association of these virtues with parental teaching, combined with their personification, heightens the attractiveness of the instructions and the importance of their retention. The son must court, preserve, and maintain these virtues in the same way that he protects and maintains parental teaching. By retaining parental teaching, the son develops these virtues. And by developing and maintaining these virtues, the son images YHWH.

Imaging YHWH, however, involves more than the retention of the parent's instruction and its accompanying virtues; it also involves internalization, the mnemonic replay of the parent's teaching, and the inscription of kindness and faithfulness onto the core of one's being. This internalization is outlined in the remainder of v. 3 through the metaphorical commands "bind them around your neck" (קָשְׁרֵם עַל־גַּרְגְּרוֹתֶיךָ, v. 3b) and "write them on the tablet of your heart" (כָּתְבֵם עַל־לוּחַ לִבֶּךָ, v. 3c). These metaphors are related to the ornamental imagery within the parental lectures. This imagery is used elsewhere in the lectures to describe the attractiveness (1:8–9), guidance (6:20–23), or protection of the parent's instructions (3:21–23).[10] Here, however, it appears the mnemonic sense of the imagery is primary (3:3; 7:3).[11] The son must wear kindness and faithfulness on his body and brand them onto the core of his character so that they may serve as a permanent, external reminder as well as a fixed, internal register for recollection, retrieval, and action.[12] These virtues must be displayed and remembered; they must become innate, natural values that prompt and prod one's thoughts and actions.[13] The retention of parental teaching and the internalization of these virtues is crucial, for as the following commands suggest, failure to remember these instructions and recall these virtues leads to inflated self-valuation manifested in hubris, self-delusion, and misperception. Memory matters; and the remembrance of these virtues as well as the formation of character depend upon their internalization.

d. The Promise of Internalization (3:4)

The promise or reward for this retention and internalization is presented in v. 4. Similar to v. 2, the promise seeks to motivate the addressee to heed the sequence of commands in v. 3. In contrast to v. 2, however, this promise is conveyed through the imperative (מְצָא, v. 4a); the form and tone of the promise mimics the form and tone of the previous commands. And this form captures the certainty of the promise; it *will* follow from the internalization of kindness and faithfulness.[14] The promise concerns approbation in divine-human as well as interpersonal relations. The expressions "favor" (חֵן, v. 4a) and "good repute" (שֵׂכֶל־טוֹב, v. 4a) describe the way in which others perceive the one who internalizes kindness and faithfulness. As kindness and faithfulness cultivate trustworthy relations with others (14:22; 16:6; 20:28), so others view the one who internalizes and manifests these virtues with respect, honor, and esteem. These favorable relationships create an ideal environment for human flourishing. And these relational dimensions of human existence provide the backdrop for the commands within vv. 5–12 (re: God) and 3:27–35 (re: others).

10. Heim, *Poetic Imagination*, 114.
11. Heim, *Poetic Imagination*, 114–15.
12. Fox, *Proverbs 1–9*, 146–47.
13. Toy, *Proverbs*, 58; Yoder, *Proverbs*, 38.
14. Joüon §164f, §164i.

2. The Contours of the Pious Life (3:5–10)

In light of the retention of parental teaching and the internalization of virtue, the lecture outlines the contours of the pious life through three couplets (vv. 5–6, 7–8, 9–10), each of which moves from prescribed dispositions and practices to a promised reward. These dispositions and practices are viewed in relation to YHWH; and this relationship affects not only one's attitudes and actions but also one's view of oneself.

a. The Disposition and Practice of Dependence (3:5–6)

The first couplet contains three commands pertaining to the disposition and practice of dependence. The initial command is cast in the positive: "Trust in YHWH" (בְּטַח אֶל־יְהוָה, v. 5a). This injunction, combined with the prepositional phrase "with all your heart" (בְּכָל־לִבֶּךָ, v. 5a), captures the essence and extent of pious dependence. It is an exclusive dependence on the object of true faith; it is a complete, confident reliance upon the divine over against wealth (11:28; Ps 52:9[7]), leaders (Ps 146:3), weapons (Isa 31:1) and, most importantly, oneself (Hos 10:13; Ezek 33:13). This sentiment is expressed through the second command, which is cast in the negative (אַל־תִּשָּׁעֵן; Prov 3:5b). If one trusts in YHWH, then, by implication, one should not rely on one's own understanding. To trust in oneself or one's intellectual capacity is the epitome of folly (28:26); it is confidence in the creature rather than the Creator, the limited rather than the eternal.[15] The negative command serves as the counterpart to the positive. It explains the nature of genuine trust and offers an alternative description of the dependent disposition that marks the pious life.

The third and final command in the couplet complements the commands in v. 5 by illustrating how this disposition of dependence informs one's practice. This command is preceded by the prepositional phrase "in all your ways" (בְּכָל־דְּרָכֶיךָ, v. 6a), which focuses attention on one's lifestyle and connects the pious disposition of dependence with the prologue's nuclear symbol. The command proper indicates that trust in YHWH is intimately related to knowledge of YHWH manifested in concrete forms of behavior. Knowledge of and dependence upon YHWH cannot be separated from the expression of this dependence through one's actions. One's ways demonstrate one's dependence. And one's actions prove one's knowledge. The third command brings the injunction in the initial couplet to a climactic conclusion. It reveals that pious dependence involves an internal disposition of trust, faith, and confidence in YHWH exhibited through external actions that corroborate one's trust and evince one's knowledge.[16] This is not a piety divorced from knowledge. It is a piety that proclaims one's knowledge through praxis.

This pious dependence upon YHWH expressed through practical "ways" is rewarded with the promise of a specific way: smooth paths (v. 6b). Together, the personal pronoun combined with the inflected verb highlight YHWH's role in the actualization of the promise. This promise captures the safety and security that accompanies a life of pious dependence demonstrated through praxis. While the verb "make smooth" (ישׁר, v. 6b) carries ethical connotations of straight, upright conduct that aligns with the order of creation (9:15), YHWH's involvement in the leveling or flattening suggests the geographical sense of the verb is envisioned here. YHWH clears the way for those who depend upon him; he removes obstacles, creating a smooth, unencumbered path for the pious.

15. Murphy, *Proverbs*, 21.

16. Fox, *Proverbs 1–9*, 149; Loader, *Proverbs 1–9*, 153–54.

b. The Disposition and Practice of Humility (3:7–8)

The prescriptions concerning the disposition and practice of dependence are intimately related to the prescriptions concerning the disposition and practice of humility (vv. 5, 6a, 7). Similar to the first couplet (vv. 5–6), the second contains three commands, two cast in the positive (v. 7b) and one cast in the negative (v. 7a). And these commands complement one another. The negative command that opens the second couplet develops the negative command in the first (v. 5b). Dependence on one's limited understanding is comparable to the subjective valuation that one is wise (v. 7a). Whereas the former focuses on a disposition of misplaced trust that epitomizes the fool (כְּסִיל; 28:26), the latter focuses on a delusional, prideful disposition that is considered to be worse than the fool (26:12; cf. 26:16; 28:11; Isa 5:21).[17] The lecture moves from the danger of misplaced trust to the danger of misperception, from the condition of the fool to a terminal condition produced by hubris. The command seeks to rein in the son's propensity for arrogance and self-inflation. In so doing, it promotes humility and proper limits, two pillars of the pious life.

Together with the negative admonition, the positive commands in the second couplet complement the positive injunctions in the first (Prov 3:5a, 6a). The disposition of fear commended in v. 7b is rooted in the knowledge of and trust in YHWH delineated in vv. 5a and 6a (cf. 2:5; 9:10). And this disposition of fear is demonstrated by turning away from evil, that is, through concrete forms of behavior that prove one's fear and proclaim one's knowledge of YHWH in their "ways" (3:6a, b; 8:13; 14:16; 16:6; Job 1:1, 8; 28:28). The positive commands seek to inculcate the same virtues as the negative command in Prov 3:7a. These commands intimate that the fear of YHWH and arrogance are like oil and water; they do not mix. An internal disposition of fear cultivates humility and a proper perspective on one's limits. And this internal disposition is expressed through external actions that shun evil. One's pious attitude is reflected in one's pious practices. Like the first couplet, the second refuses to separate one's disposition from praxis. Just as dependence upon YHWH is expressed through knowledge of YHWH in one's ways, so also humility and fear of YHWH are expressed by a lifestyle that turns away from evil.

The reward for cultivating a humble disposition that evinces fear of YHWH through pious practices is health and healing. This promise is expressed through the same verbal form used in v. 7a (תְּהִי, vv. 7a, 8a). And similar to v. 4a, it employs the indirect volitive to convey the certainty of the reward. The health and healing envisioned in the promise is comprehensive. This comprehensive vision is captured by the expressions "your body" (שָׁרֶּךָ, v. 8a) and "your bones" (עַצְמוֹתֶיךָ, v. 8b), which function as a merism. While the former term is used elsewhere to denote one's navel (Song 7:3), here it serves as a synecdoche for the body.[18] This representation of one's external being, combined with one's "bones" or inner being, illuminates the wholeness, health, and wellbeing that accompanies the one who expresses and demonstrates humble dependence upon YHWH. The promise complements and develops the promises delineated in vv. 2 and 6; it moves from a long, peaceful life and smooth, clear paths to a physical condition of vitality and refreshment.

17. Van Leeuwen, *Context and Meaning*, 104–6; Clifford, *Proverbs*, 52; Murphy, *Proverbs*, 21.

18. Waltke, *Proverbs: Chapters 1–15*, 246; Loader, *Proverbs 1–9*, 156–57. In contrast to this reading, some emend the text to read "your flesh" (בשׂרך) rather than "your navel" (שׁרך[ל]), since "flesh" and "bones" is a standard word pair in the Old Testament (e.g., Toy, *Proverbs*, 61; Fox, *Proverbs 1–9*, 151). This emendation is possible but unnecessary if "your navel" is understood as a synecdoche for the body.

c. The Disposition and Practice of Homage (3:9–10)

The third and final couplet in the main body of the lecture commends an attitude and actions that naturally flow from a disposition of dependence upon and humility before YHWH: homage. This attitude is captured by the command "Honor YHWH" (כַּבֵּד אֶת־יְהוָה, v. 9a) and demonstrated through concrete acts of worship. Honor, in this respect, involves both an internal disposition and external expression. It involves a value judgment, the assignment or attribution of esteem, respect, and prominence to another. And it demands the manifestation of this judgment through concrete acts of devotion. In the present text, these concrete acts of devotion pertain to one's wealth in general and the "firstfruits" (רֵאשִׁית, v. 9b) of one's crops in particular.[19] The one deemed the best deserves the best. To modify a New Testament expression, the command challenges one to put their treasure where their heart is (Matt 6:21//Luke 12:34). If one trusts in YHWH (Prov 3:5a) and fears YHWH (v. 7b), then one will honor YHWH and demonstrate this attitude through the allocation of one's wealth in the spirit of worship.

The reward for this internal homage expressed through external worship is substantial. When the son expresses honor and devotion to YHWH by giving the best from his landed property, then his storehouses and wine vats will overflow. Similar to v. 8, "abundance" (שָׂבָע, v. 10a) and "new wine" (תִּירוֹשׁ, v. 10b) function as a merism for the totality of one's produce.[20] The former serves as a metonymy for food or grain, while the latter represents drink. Together, they supplement the previous promises of long life, favor, unobstructed paths, and health with ample produce and provision.

3. A Pious Perspective (3:11–12)

In light of these pious dispositions, virtuous practices, and grandiose promises, the conclusion offers an important qualification. It provides perspective on the dispositions, practices, and promises of the pious life. Piety may pay, but not always. YHWH is not a cosmic vending machine, doling out rewards to all who trust in him, live in humble submission to him, or honor him. The pious life is not that simple. Dependence upon, fear of, and relationship with YHWH involves discipline. And this discipline tempers the promises within the lecture, placing them in proper perspective.[21]

a. A Pious Attitude (3:11)

This perspective is shaped by a receptive posture. Just as the son accepts parental "instruction" (מוּסַר; 1:8), so also he must accept YHWH's "discipline" (מוּסַר; 3:11a). The form of this discipline is ambiguous, but its basic function is clear: it is educative, designed to correct, cultivate character, and inculcate wisdom (13:24; 19:18, 25; 22:15; 23:13–14; 29:15, 17). Accordingly, the parent admonishes the son to welcome this purposeful discipline; and the parent commands the son to train his emotions so that he might receive this discipline rightly. The reception of discipline involves both intellectual ("do not reject," אַל־תִּמְאָס, v. 11a) and emotional ("do not loathe," אַל־תָּקֹץ, v. 11b) acceptance.[22] YHWH's discipline seems inevitable.

19. Cf. Schipper, *Proverbs 1–15*, 133–34.

20. Waltke, *Proverbs: Chapters 1–15*, 248; Loader, *Proverbs 1–9*, 159.

21. Toy, *Proverbs*, 64; Clifford, *Proverbs*, 53; Fox, *Proverbs 1–9*, 152; Loader, *Proverbs 1–9*, 161.

22. While the verb מאס simply denotes the intellectual desire "to want nothing to do with someone or something," קוץ adds the notion of a deep emotional reaction produced by disgust. H. Wildberger, "מאס," *TLOT* 2:653; Gen 27:46; Exod 1:12; Lev 20:23; Num 21:5; 1 Kgs 11:25.

The issue is not whether YHWH will discipline the son; the issue is how the son will receive and perceive this discipline. Thus, the father calls for a pious attitude, for loving acceptance rather than loathsome rejection.

b. The Reason for the Attitude (3:12)

The rationale for this acceptance is conveyed through the causal clause in v. 12, which opens with the conjunction "for" (כִּי, v. 12a; cf. v. 2a). Here the parent depicts YHWH as a parent. This image provides a conceptual framework through which to understand the nature of YHWH's discipline. Like a parent's discipline, YHWH's discipline is dispensed in and directed by love. In fact, this discipline reveals YHWH's commitment to and delight in the son. As Prov 13:24 indicates:

> One who spares the rod hates his son;
> but one who loves him disciplines him
> consistently.

Discipline prompted by love may seem paradoxical. The loving impulse and educative intention of this discipline, however, places it in proper perspective. The parent does not rationalize or theologize correction; rather, the parent views YHWH's discipline as a severe mercy with beneficent intentions. As the only couplet in the lecture without a promise, the final verses offer a qualification that places the promises in vv. 2, 4, 6, 8, and 10 into perspective. Pious dispositions and practices yield particular promises, but these promises do not insulate one from YHWH's discipline.

Canonical and Theological Significance

The third parental lecture gives particular attention to dispositions that represent the pillars of the pious life, namely, dependence, humility, and homage (vv. 5–10). These dispositions are not prescribed in a vacuum; nor are they presented as moral recommendations that enable one to secure the good life. Rather, they are viewed in relation to YHWH and cultivated through the retention and internalization of parental teaching (vv. 1–4), on the one hand, and the acceptance of divine chastisement (vv. 11–12), on the other. The lecture's concern with the dispositions and practices of piety complements and counterbalances the previous discourses. Whereas the previous discourses focused on aspects of wisdom and the wise life, the third lecture focuses on piety and the dimensions of the virtuous life. It moves from the reception of the fear of YHWH and the knowledge of God (2:5) to the actualization of this fear and knowledge through specific attitudes and actions (3:5–8). And it moves from the "instruction" (מוּסָר; 1:8) of the parents and the "reproof" (תּוֹכַחַת; 1:23) of Lady Wisdom to a description of the "discipline" (מוּסָר; 3:11a) and "reproof" (תּוֹכַחַת; 3:11b) of YHWH. The lecture demonstrates that the wise life is a pious life; and it outlines the contours of this life through specific attitudes and actions forged in relationship with YHWH. In so doing, it offers a distillation of what it means to love YHWH and sets the stage for the following description of what it means to love one's neighbor (3:27–35).

As a distillation of the dispositions and practices that characterize pious devotion to YHWH, it is not surprising that the attitudes and actions advocated in the lecture punctuate Proverbs and pervade the canon of Scripture. Trust in YHWH is a valued disposition in Proverbs, the Prophets, and the Psalter. This confident reliance on YHWH occasions blessing, deliverance, and safety (Prov 16:20; 28:25; 29:25; Isa 26:3–4; Jer 17:7; Ps 22:4–5); it allows one to recognize their limitations and place in the divine economy (Prov 26:12; Jas 1:5–8); it cultivates virtue, inculcates fear of YHWH, and motivates forms of behavior that seek the well-being of the community (Isa 50:10; Pss 37:3; 143:8). As an alternative expression for faith, trust in YHWH is a hallmark of both Proverbs's and the canon's conception of genuine piety.

The same is true of fear and homage. These attitudes and their corresponding practices are intimately related to one another, and these attitudes intersect with the disposition of trust in the canon's portrait of piety. This is especially apparent in Deuteronomy. Similar to the third parental lecture, Deuteronomy refuses to separate piety from practice, fear of YHWH from obedience to YHWH. According to Moses's paraenetic speeches, instruction cultivates a disposition of fear that is manifested in external forms of obedience (Deut 6:1–3, 24; 8:6; 10:12–13; 13:4; 17:19; 28:58; cf. 4:10). Whereas Proverbs and several other texts relate this disposition of fear to turning away from evil (Prov 3:7; 16:6; Job 1:1, 8; 2:3; 28:28), Deuteronomy explains this disposition of fear by describing the other side of the coin: turning to YHWH, listening to his voice, and keeping the regulations of the Torah. Fear is demonstrated through concrete acts of obedience. And these acts of obedience involve expressions of homage rooted in dependence on the divine. To be specific, these acts of obedience involve expressions of worship in general and the tithe in particular, each of which evinces one's fear of and trust in YHWH (Deut 6:13–14; 14:22–23). Together with Proverbs, Deuteronomy presents trust, fear, and homage as the fundamental pillars of the pious life. While the third parental lecture outlines these pillars to provide a basic blueprint for personal piety, Deuteronomy offers a more detailed depiction of their contours and application to everyday life in relationship with YHWH.

Relationship with YHWH, however, involves more than pious dispositions and practices; it also entails discipline or correction (3:11–12). This theological perspective on divine discipline recurs elsewhere in the canon. As a father, YHWH loves and reproves Israel in general (Deut 8:5; cf. Deut 10:15; 23:5; 1 Kgs 10:9; Jer 31:3) and the Davidic king in particular (2 Sam 7:14). In contrast to the third parental lecture and the dictates of the Davidic covenant (Prov 3:11–12; 2 Sam 7:11–16), Deuteronomy democratizes this concept of divine discipline. This democratization of divine discipline is reflected in the Septuagint's rendering of Prov 3:12.[23] And the writer to the

23. The Septuagint includes the expression "every son" (πάντα υἱὸν) in Prov 3:12b. Although the expression does not correspond to the Hebrew text, it is a typical addition in Prov 3, for the Greek translator integrates πάς seven times with

Hebrews uses this rendering to provide his audience with a theological perspective on persecution and hardship (Heb 12:5–6; cf. 10:32–39).[24] According to the writer to the Hebrews, membership in God's family does not preclude suffering; rather, sonship entails suffering. In fact, adversity serves as a sign of God's loving correction (Heb 12:5–6). The writer to the Hebrews uses Prov 3:11–12 to provide his audience with a theological lens through which to view their circumstances. The text seeks to encourage persecuted members of the community to persevere. And the quotation sets the stage for Hebrews's discussion of the purpose, nature, and goal of God's discipline in Heb 12:7–11. God's beneficent correction not only produces endurance and demonstrates his familial commitment to the community, but it also cultivates holiness and righteousness in members of the community (Heb 12:10–11).[25] In this respect, the use of Prov 3:11–12 in Heb 12:5–6 is comparable to its function in the third parental lecture. Just as divine discipline provides perspective on the nature and dynamics of the pious life (Prov 3:11–12), so also this perspective produces piety, encouragement, and endurance (Heb 12:5–11).

This theological perspective is invaluable, for the benefits that accompany the pious life in Prov 3:1–10 are not hard-and-fast promises. The lecture does not advocate a retributive dogmatism: insert proper attitudes and actions, pull the lever, and the cosmic genie dispenses the lavish reward. YHWH is not a cosmic vending machine; he is not bound to a strict, mechanical system of retribution and reward. While Proverbs acknowledges that people perform actions in accord with their character and reap appropriate rewards, the document's reflections on human limits as well as divine sovereignty and inscrutability temper the timing and expectations concerning the rewards (16:1–2, 9; 19:21; 20:24; 21:30; 27:1; 30:2–4). This nuanced vision of retribution and reward is woven throughout the witness of Job (Job 11:7–11; 36:26; 42:1–6), and it is expressed in the musings of Qoheleth (Eccl 3:16–17; 6:12; 7:13–14, 23–24; 8:6–8; 9:11–12). Piety may pay in the divine economy (Prov 10:3; 19:23; 29:25; Pss 1:3; 37:3–6; Eccl 2:24–26; 5:18–20). The nature and timing of the payment, however, are ambiguous. The benefits delineated in the third lecture do not represent unqualified promises. They serve as motivations for pious dispositions and practices. They seek to move one to develop these dispositions and model these practices. In this respect, the promises are not the goal; they do not represent the driving force behind the pious attitudes and actions in the third lecture. Rather, they capture the value of piety in relationship with God.

no corresponding "all" (כל) in the Hebrew text (Prov 3:7, 12, 15, 18, 23, 26, 32). This addition in the LXX of 3:12 democratizes the concept of divine discipline. To be specific, it emphasizes that YHWH disciplines all those who live a life of active piety (3:5–10).

24. While the nature of YHWH's discipline is ambiguous in Prov 3:11–12, it appears the LXX and Heb 12:6 envision this discipline as physical, for they replace the simile "as a father" with the verb "he whips/beats" (μαστιγοῖ).

25. Clement of Rome uses Prov 3:11–12 in a similar way (1 Clem. 56.4–16).

From this perspective, the third parental lecture identifies the basis and context of genuine piety. This piety is not a brand of moralism; it is a piety cultivated and actualized in relationship with YHWH. One does not live piously for the reward; rather, one lives piously because one is wise, because fear and knowledge of God produce particular dispositions that are demonstrated through external actions. Just as one demonstrates faith through their deeds (Jas 2:17–18, 26), so one must demonstrate their wisdom through practical piety. This demonstration of practical piety confirms one's wisdom and expresses one's love for and devotion to YHWH. It operates under a proper view of the place and limits of humanity in the divine economy. And it evinces dependence upon the proper object of trust. This vision of piety offers a model for the life of faith. It depicts the life of faith as a life of wisdom and piety. It probes the very basis and motivation of the life of faith. And it challenges one to manifest their wisdom and faith through specific attitudes and actions.

CHAPTER 6

Proverbs 3:13–35

E. Wisdom's Value and Moral Obligations

Main Idea of the Passage

The distinctive parts of this lecture highlight the human, cosmic, personal, and communal value of wisdom to provide a moral worldview, a vision of the good life in a good neighborhood that mirrors the goodness of God's creation.

Literary Context of the Passage

Whereas the previous parental lecture focused on the value of the pious life (3:1–12), the present discourse focuses on the other side of the coin: it gives particular attention to the value of wisdom (3:13–35). The juxtaposition of these discourses indicates that wisdom and virtue are not mutually exclusive in Proverbs's vision of education for character formation (cf. 1:1–7; 2:5–11); rather, they are intimately related to one another. This intimate relationship is evinced through the shared promises that accompany the pious and wise life, namely, "long life" (אֹרֶךְ יָמִים; 3:2, 16), "peace" (שָׁלוֹם; 3:2, 17), and "favor/adornment" (חֵן; 3:4, 22). And this intimate relationship is expressed through shared terms and concepts within the unit and the previous discourses in the prologue. Just as the procurement of wisdom and virtue produced resourcefulness (תּוּשִׁיָּה; 2:7) and discretion (מְזִמָּה; 2:11) to protect one's way (2:11), so now the protection of resourcefulness (תֻּשִׁיָּה; 3:21) and discretion (מְזִמָּה; 3:21) offer one security in the various ways of life (3:21–24). Just as the acquisition of wisdom (חָכְמָה; 2:10), understanding (תְּבוּנָה; 2:11), and discretion (מְזִמָּה; 2:11) safeguarded one from the antisocial way of the evildoer, so now the retention of wisdom (חָכְמָה;

3:19a), understanding (תְּבוּנָה; 3:19b),[1] and discretion (מְזִמָּה; v. 21b) safeguard one from perpetrating evil, from joining this antisocial community, and from poisoning the ethos of society (vv. 27–32). The discrete sections within vv. 13–35 integrate terms and concepts from the previous discourses to emphasize the value of wisdom. This emphasis on the value of wisdom, however, does not attenuate the importance of virtue and piety. If wisdom without piety is dead (vv. 1–12), then piety without wisdom is benighted (vv. 13–35).

In addition to the relationship between vv. 13–35 and the previous discourses, the discrete sections within the piece plant thematic seeds that blossom in subsequent texts. The ethical values promoted in vv. 27–30 and the theological reflections within vv. 31–34 are elaborated upon in the central collections of the anthology.[2] And the beatitudinal reflection on wisdom, YHWH, and the cosmos (3:13–20) is developed in 8:1–36 in general and 8:22–31 in particular. Here Wisdom restates what the father declares about her in 3:13–18: her profit is better than silver and gold (3:14; 8:19); everything desirable cannot compare with her (3:15; 8:11); she possesses riches and honor (3:16; 8:18); and those who find her, keep her ways, and listen to her are blessed (3:13, 18; 8:32, 34). Together with their comparable description of Wisdom, the movement of the poem in 3:13–20 mirrors the movement of Wisdom's aretalogy in 8:1–36: both open with a description of Wisdom's value (3:13–18; 8:6–21); and both justify Wisdom's value by reflecting on her relation to YHWH as well as her role in the creation of the cosmos (3:19–20; 8:22–31).[3] These literary and structural similarities suggest that the beatitudinal poem serves as the metaphorical sermon text for 8:1–36. But it is much more than this. In its present context, the poem functions as a literary hinge, situating the pious and wise life in a cosmic perspective (3:1–12, 21–35).[4] In its broader context, however, the piece elaborates on Wisdom's persona (cf. 1:20–33), offers the addressee with an alternative to the strange woman, prepares the way for Wisdom's aretalogy, and introduces terms and expressions that are used to paint the concluding portrait of the valiant woman (31:10–31).

---

1. While the verb "escape" (יָלֻזוּ; 3:21a) lacks an explicit subject, it appears the previous reference to wisdom and understanding in v. 19 serve as the implied subject of the verb. In this respect, these terms open not only the first two subsections (vv. 13, 19) but also the third (vv. 21–26). For further discussion, see the explanation below.

2. For representative texts in the central collections that reiterate and elaborate upon the virtues and theological perspectives delineated in vv. 27–34, see the explanation of these verses below.

3. Von Rad, *Wisdom in Israel*, 151n4.

4. Meinhold, "Gott und Mensch in Proverbien III," 477; Loader, *Proverbs 1–9*, 164.

I. Introduction to the Book (1:1–7)

II. The Value of Wisdom and Virtue (1:8–9:18)

A. Wisdom, Desire, and Different Ways (1:8–19)

B. Wisdom's Rebuke (1:20–33)

C. The Procurement, Power, and Protection of Wisdom and Virtue (2:1–22)

D. Wisdom and Piety (3:1–12)

➦ **E. Wisdom's Value and Moral Obligations (3:13–35)**

1. Wisdom and the Good Life (3:13–18)

a. Wisdom and Happiness (3:13)

b. The Rationale for Happiness (3:14–18)

2. Wisdom and the Good Creation (3:19–20)

3. Wisdom and the Secure Life (3:21–26)

a. The Retention of Wisdom (3:21)

b. The Reward for Retention: Security (3:22–24)

c. The Reassurance of the Reward (3:25–26)

4. Wisdom and the Good Neighborhood (3:27–35)

a. The Characteristics of the Good Neighborhood (3:27–30)

b. Character and the Good Neighborhood (3:31–35)

F. Wisdom and Tradition (4:1–9)

G. Wisdom and Ways of Life (4:10–19)

H. Wisdom and the Moral Anatomy (4:20–27)

I. Wisdom and Sexuality (5:1–23)

J. Wisdom, Lending, Laziness, and the Immoral Anatomy (6:1–19)

K. Wisdom, Desire, and Certain Destruction (6:20–35)

L. Wisdom and Seduction (7:1–27)

M. Wisdom's Call, Credentials, and the Cosmos (8:1–36)

N. Wisdom and Folly's Invitations (9:1–18)

III. "Forming 'Fearers of YHWH'": The Curriculum of Wisdom and Virtue (10:1–29:27)

IV. The Application of Wisdom and Virtue (30:1–31:31)

Translation and Exegetical Outline

(See pages 194–95.)

Proverbs 3:13–35

			E. Wisdom's Value and Moral Obligations (3:13–35)
			1. Wisdom and the Good Life (3:13–18)
13a	אַשְׁרֵי אָדָם מָצָא חָכְמָה	Blessed is the person who has found wisdom,	a. Wisdom and Happiness (3:13)
13b	וְאָדָם יָפִיק תְּבוּנָה	and the person who gains understanding,	
14a	כִּי טוֹב סַחְרָהּ מִסְּחַר־כָּסֶף	for her profit is better than the profit of silver,	b. The Rationale for Happiness (3:14–18)
14b	וּמֵחָרוּץ תְּבוּאָתָהּ	and her yield is better than gold;	
15a	יְקָרָה הִיא מִפְּנִינִים	she is more precious than corals,	
15b	וְכָל־חֲפָצֶיךָ לֹא יִשְׁווּ־בָהּ	everything desirable cannot compare with her;	
16a	אֹרֶךְ יָמִים בִּימִינָהּ	long life is in her right hand;	
16b	בִּשְׂמֹאולָהּ עֹשֶׁר וְכָבוֹד	in her left, riches and honor;	
17a	דְּרָכֶיהָ דַרְכֵי־נֹעַם	her ways are pleasant ways,	
17b	וְכָל־נְתִיבוֹתֶיהָ שָׁלוֹם	and all her paths are peace;	
18a	עֵץ־חַיִּים הִיא לַמַּחֲזִיקִים בָּהּ	she is a tree of life to those who embrace her,	
18b	וְתֹמְכֶיהָ מְאֻשָּׁר	and those who hold fast to her are blessed.	
19a	יְהוָה בְּחָכְמָה יָסַד־אָרֶץ	YHWH founded the earth by wisdom,	2. Wisdom and the Good Creation (3:19–20)
19b	כּוֹנֵן שָׁמַיִם בִּתְבוּנָה	he established the heavens by understanding;	
20a	בְּדַעְתּוֹ תְּהוֹמוֹת נִבְקָעוּ	by his knowledge the deeps burst open,	
20b	וּשְׁחָקִים יִרְעֲפוּ־טָל	and the clouds drip dew.	
			3. Wisdom and the Secure Life (3:21–26)
21a	בְּנִי אַל־יָלֻזוּ מֵעֵינֶיךָ	My son, do not let these escape from your sight;	a. The Retention of Wisdom (3:21)
21b	נְצֹר תֻּשִׁיָּה וּמְזִמָּה	protect resourcefulness and discretion;	
22a	וְיִהְיוּ חַיִּים לְנַפְשֶׁךָ	then they will be life for your soul,	b. The Reward for Retention: Security (3:22–24)
22b	וְחֵן לְגַרְגְּרֹתֶיךָ	and adornment for your neck;	
23a	אָז תֵּלֵךְ לָבֶטַח דַּרְכֶּךָ	then you will walk on your way securely,	
23b	וְרַגְלְךָ לֹא תִגּוֹף	and your foot will not stumble.	
24a	אִם־תִּשְׁכַּב לֹא־תִפְחָד	When you lie down, you will not be afraid,	
24b	וְשָׁכַבְתָּ וְעָרְבָה שְׁנָתֶךָ	when you lie down, your sleep will be pleasant.	
25a	אַל־תִּירָא מִפַּחַד פִּתְאֹם	Do not fear sudden terror,	c. The Reassurance of the Reward (3:25–26)
25b	וּמִשֹּׁאַת רְשָׁעִים כִּי תָבֹא	or the devastation of the wicked when it comes,	
26a	כִּי־יְהוָה יִהְיֶה בְכִסְלֶךָ	for YHWH will be your confidence,	
26b	וְשָׁמַר רַגְלְךָ מִלָּכֶד	and keep your foot from capture.	

27a	אַל־תִּמְנַע־טוֹב מִבְּעָלָיו	Do not withhold good from those to whom it is due,	4. Wisdom and the Good Neighborhood (3:27–35) a. The Characteristics of the Good Neighborhood (3:27–30)
27b	↑ בִּהְיוֹת לְאֵל יָדְךָ לַעֲשׂוֹת	↑ when you have the power to do it.	
28a	אַל־תֹּאמַר לְרֵעֲךָ	Do not say to your neighbor,	
28b	↑ לֵךְ וָשׁוּב	↑ "Go and return;	
28c	וּמָחָר אֶתֵּן	and I will give it tomorrow,"	
28d	וְיֵשׁ אִתָּךְ	when you have it with you.	
29a	אַל־תַּחֲרֹשׁ עַל־רֵעֲךָ רָעָה	Do not plan evil against your neighbor,	
29b	↑ וְהוּא־יוֹשֵׁב לָבֶטַח אִתָּךְ	↑ while he is living confidently with you.	
30a	אַל־תָּרִיב עִם־אָדָם חִנָּם	Do not accuse a person without cause,	
30b	↑ אִם־לֹא גְמָלְךָ רָעָה	↑ if he has done you no wrong.	
31a	אַל־תְּקַנֵּא בְּאִישׁ חָמָס	Do not envy a violent person,	b. Character and the Good Neighborhood (3:31–35)
31b	וְאַל־תִּבְחַר בְּכָל־דְּרָכָיו	and do not choose any of his ways,	
32a	↑ כִּי תוֹעֲבַת יְהוָה נָלוֹז	↑ for the crooked person is an abomination to YHWH,	
32b	וְאֶת־יְשָׁרִים סוֹדוֹ	but with the upright is his counsel.	
33a	מְאֵרַת יְהוָה בְּבֵית רָשָׁע	The curse of YHWH is on the house of the wicked,	
33b	וּנְוֵה צַדִּיקִים יְבָרֵךְ	but he blesses the dwelling of the righteous.	
34a	אִם־לַלֵּצִים הוּא־יָלִיץ	If it is a matter of mockers, he himself mocks,	
34b	וְלַעֲנָוִים יִתֶּן־חֵן	but if it is a matter of the humble, he bestows favor.	
35a	כָּבוֹד חֲכָמִים יִנְחָלוּ	The wise will inherit honor,	
35b	וּכְסִילִים מֵרִים קָלוֹן	but fools will acquire disgrace.	

Structure and Literary Form

On the surface, Prov 3:13–35 appears to contain distinct poems, proverbs, and instructions that bear little formal or logical resemblance to one another. Irrespective of whether these materials existed independently before they were integrated into their present literary context, they share a common function and several common features, suggesting their substance and arrangement contributes to the developing argument of the prologue in general and Prov 3 in particular. While the boundaries of the units within the discourse are debated, the form and literary features of the materials intimate the piece consists of four parts, each of which deserves specific comment.

The first unit is cast in the form of a macarism (3:13–18)—a poem that celebrates the happiness of a person who possesses certain characteristics or performs certain actions.[5] Far from simply proclaiming the good fortune associated with a virtue or experience, however, the proclamation of happiness possesses a didactic and persuasive force.[6] The beatitudinal poem seeks to motivate readers to find wisdom and embrace her, for she offers the blessing of a good life. This blessing frames the poem. The piece opens with the expression "Blessed is" (אַשְׁרֵי, v. 13a) and concludes with the declaration that those who cling to Wisdom "are blessed" (מְאֻשָּׁר, v. 18b).[7] It pronounces blessing on those who possess wisdom to explain the happiness of her possessor, to describe her value, and to persuade the reader to find her.

The second unit of the discourse builds on the first, intensifying the value of wisdom (vv. 19–20). Similar to the opening lines of the beatitudinal poem (v. 13), the initial lines of the second section include the terms "wisdom" (חָכְמָה, v. 19a) and "understanding" (תְּבוּנָה, v. 19b). The repetition of these terms binds the second section to the first; and their connection with YHWH's creative work strengthens wisdom's value and heightens the happiness of wisdom's possessor.

While the third (vv. 21–26) and fourth (vv. 27–35) units within the discourse appear to be cut from a different literary cloth, they are related to the previous sections. The lack of an explicit subject in v. 21a suggests that "wisdom" and "understanding" in v. 19 serve as the subject of the verb "escape" (יָלֻזוּ, v. 21a). On this account, these terms open the first, second, and third sections of the discourse. Against the backdrop of the first two sections, the third moves from implicit to explicit instruction, from humanity to the son, and from the cosmological realm to the personal realm. The unit is bound together by references to body parts, framed by the synonymous verbs

5. Fox, *Proverbs 1–9*, 156, 161; Loader, *Proverbs 1–9*, 166–67.

6. McKane, *Proverbs*, 294–95; Fox, *Proverbs 1–9*, 161; Loader, *Proverbs 1–9*, 167.

7. For the distinction between אַשְׁרֵי ("blessed") and בָּרוּךְ ("blessed"), see Hélène M. Dallaire, "Blessed (בָּרוּךְ) or Blessed (אַשְׁרֵי) or Both?," in *Devotions on the Hebrew Bible: 54 Reflections to Inspire and Instruct*, ed. Milton Eng and Lee M. Fields (Grand Rapids: Zondervan Academic, 2015), 36–38.

"protect" (נָצַר, v. 21b) and "keep" (שָׁמַר, v. 26b; cf. 2:8), and united by the concept of security.[8] It concretizes the human (vv. 13–18) and cosmological (vv. 19–20) value of wisdom by reflecting on the personal protection it offers the son.

The fourth and final section represents a natural extension of the third, for it offers examples of how wisdom and understanding (v. 21a; cf. 3:19a, b) as well as resourcefulness and discretion (v. 21b) shape one's relation to others (vv. 27–35).[9] The initial half of the unit exhibits a common pattern: a negative construction in the first line, followed by a circumstance that qualifies the command in the second (vv. 27–30). The second half of the section then offers an extended rationale for the ethics prescribed in vv. 27–30 through a series of theological observations. In so doing, it expands the moral vision of 3:1–12; it moves from personal piety and its rewards to personal piety and its communal implications.

On the whole, the seemingly disparate collection of materials in 3:13–35 exhibits a logical progression of thought and a common didactic function. It moves from the human and cosmic value of wisdom (3:13–20) to the individual, ethical, and communal value of wisdom (vv. 21–35). And the collection demonstrates that wisdom involves moral obligations.

Explanation of the Text

1. Wisdom and the Good Life (3:13–18)

In light of the value of personal piety (3:1–12), the parent shifts attention to the value of wisdom (3:13–18). This shift in topic coincides with a shift in perspective. The personal admonitions to the son give way to a beatitudinal poem that reflects on wisdom's value for humanity (v. 13a). The value of wisdom for humankind is expressed through two main parts: an exclamation (v. 13) and a rationale (vv. 14–18).

a. Wisdom and Happiness (3:13)

Similar to other beatitudinal poems (e.g., Pss 1:1–3; 112:1–3; 119:1–3), the adulation of wisdom opens with the exclamation "Blessed is" (אַשְׁרֵי, v. 13a). As noted above, this exclamation celebrates the happiness or good favor of the person who possesses wisdom and understanding. These virtues are the source and reason for the person's happiness. Their possession, however, is neither passive nor static. In accordance with 2:1–4, the verbs "has found" (מָצָא, v. 13a) and "gains" (יָפִיק, v. 13b) indicate that the good favor wisdom lavishes upon its possessor is the result of an active and ongoing search.[10] The first verb is cast in the perfect; it expresses a completed action and explains why the person is blessed: this person *has found* wisdom. In contrast, the second verb is cast in the imperfect; it expresses a continuing or durative action and demonstrates that the search for as well as the application of wisdom remains an

8. Waltke, *Proverbs: Chapters 1–15*, 263.
9. Clifford, *Proverbs*, 57; Longman, *Proverbs*, 140.
10. Oesterley, *The Book of Proverbs*, 23; Fox, *Proverbs 1–9*, 156; Loader, *Proverbs 1–9*, 168.

ongoing process (cf. 1:5). Taken together, the verbs suggest that happiness, good favor, and blessing accompany the person who has acquired wisdom and who continues to utilize and manifest this wisdom in the various circumstances of everyday life.

b. The Rationale for Happiness (3:14–18)

While the exclamation provides the basic reason for the person's happiness, vv. 14–18 offer an extended explanation for this good favor ("for," כִּי, v. 14a). The explanation consists of two strophes (vv. 14–15, 16–17) and a concluding couplet (v. 18), each of which describes different dimensions of wisdom's value. The first strophe casts economic terms in a series of comparative constructions (מִן + טוֹב, vv. 14a, 14b; and מִן + יְקָרָה, v. 15a) to illuminate the surpassing value of wisdom. Here wisdom's value is measured against the financial return of silver (v. 14a) and the intrinsic worth of gold (v. 14b). These comparisons highlight wisdom's superior earnings or profit; what she produces is better than the trade value of silver and the market price of gold. The economic language identifies wisdom's worth and desirability through the benefits she produces.[11] In contrast, the third comparative construction moves beyond the value of wisdom's earnings to the value of wisdom itself (v. 15a): she is more precious than "corals" (מִפְּנִינִים, v. 15a)[12] or jewels. Her quantitative value (v. 14) corresponds to her qualitative value (v. 15a). Together, these comparative constructions set the stage for the final line of the strophe, the unqualified assertion that develops and escalates wisdom's value (v. 15b). Nothing—neither wealth, nor jewels, nor anything else—compares with her. Wisdom is in a class of her own. She is not only incomparable in value, but she is also desirable and the fulfillment of one's desires.[13]

In view of wisdom's quantitative and qualitative value, the second strophe describes the beatific life wisdom offers to those who find her (vv. 16–17). Whereas the previous strophe personified wisdom implicitly, the present strophe personifies her explicitly. Evoking the image of the Egyptian goddess Maat,[14] wisdom is depicted as the proprietress of long life (v. 16a, see 3:2) and "substantive wealth" (v. 16b).[15] She treads pleasant paths, leading those who find her on beneficial ways (v. 17a; cf. 8:20). And she charts a course in life characterized by wholeness, harmony, and well-being (v. 17b, see 3:2). Similar to the previous strophe (v. 15b), the final line intensifies the description of the beatific life offered by wisdom through a comprehensive statement ("all," כָּל, v. 17b). She provides a full life accompanied by prosperity and esteem on peaceable ways.

The final couplet completes the extended description of wisdom's value with a vivid portrayal of the vitality, life, and joy she grants to those who intimately embrace her (v. 18). This vitality is conveyed through the expression "she is a tree of life" (עֵץ־חַיִּים הִיא, v. 18a). The metaphor is used elsewhere in Proverbs to describe the fruit of the righteous (11:30), the nature of a fulfilled desire

11. Sandoval, *The Discourse of Wealth and Poverty*, 80–81.

12. This reading follows *qere* (מִפְּנִינִים) rather than *ketiv* (מִפְּנִיִּים) due to haplography.

13. In light of 8:11 and following *BHS* and LXX, the translation of v. 15b emends "everything you desire" (כָּל־חֲפָצֶיךָ) to "everything desirable" (כל־חפצים), since the introduction of the second-person suffix in a poem that lacks this form of address is unusual.

14. For discussion of this imagery and its relation to Prov 3:16, see Christa Kayatz, *Studien zu Proverbien 1–9*, 105; Fox, *Proverbs 1–9*, 157. Also, for the more general proposal that 3:16 presents wisdom in the guise of a fertility goddess, see Perdue, *Wisdom and Creation*, 80–81; idem, *Wisdom Literature: A Theological History* (Louisville: Westminster John Knox, 2007), 49–51.

15. For this single concept conveyed by the expression "riches and honor" (עֹשֶׁר וְכָבוֹד, v. 16b), see Fox, *Proverbs 1–9*, 157.

(13:12), and the healing power of a gentle tongue (15:4). While the expression "tree of life" evokes an ancient Near Eastern mythological motif in general and the Eden narrative in particular (Gen 2:9; 3:22, 24; cf. Rev 22:2, 14, 19), it is important to note that throughout Proverbs the phrase is indefinite. It is not *the* tree of life; it is *a* tree of life. The expression is a pregnant metaphor for wisdom that recalls the memory of Eden. In view of its use elsewhere in the book, however, it appears the metaphor does not associate wisdom with access to immortality. Rather, the image heightens the desirability of wisdom and captures the good, peaceable life she offers to her devotees.[16] Those who find her, embrace her, and hold fast to her receive the blessing of a full, joyous life (v. 18b).[17]

2. Wisdom and the Good Creation (3:19–20)

The second unit enhances the value of wisdom delineated in the first by identifying wisdom as the instrument through which YHWH ordered the cosmos (vv. 19–20; cf. Pss 104:24; 136:5; Jer 10:12; 51:15). The memory of Eden evoked in v. 18 serves as a transition to the cosmic, creational perspective offered in vv. 19–20.[18] This hymnic colophon is intimately related to the beatitudinal poem; it provides a theological justification for wisdom's value in vv. 13–18 by ascribing the basis of a person's happiness—wisdom and understanding—to YHWH's creative activities (vv. 13, 19). These activities are conveyed through two couplets (vv. 19, 20), each of which move from YHWH's creation of the earth and the deeps below (vv. 19a, 20a) to the heavens and the clouds above (vv. 19b, 20b). This movement, combined with the juxtaposition of terms that are spatial opposites, indicates that each couplet expresses YHWH's creation of the cosmos through a merism. And these merisms highlight YHWH's comprehensive creation and artistic design of the cosmos by means of wisdom.

The first couplet gives particular attention to the way in which YHWH utilized wisdom and understanding to form a strong, stable cosmos (v. 19). As a master builder, YHWH "founded" (יָסַד, v. 19a) the earth and "established" (כּוֹנֵן, v. 19b) the heavens. The former verb envisions YHWH setting the terrestrial realm on a firm foundation (cf. 8:29); the latter depicts YHWH fixing the celestial realm as a secure, permanent dome over the earth. Wisdom and understanding are the tools or powers employed by the divine architect to construct a sure, enduring cosmos. And within this stable, cosmic frame, the second couplet highlights YHWH's providential care for and preservation of the cosmos by means of a synonym for wisdom and understanding: "knowledge" (דַּעַת, v. 20a). The couplet narrows its vision, zooming in on specific moments of creation during which YHWH separated the waters from the dry land and flicked the meteorological switch, allowing the clouds to dispense water to nourish the earth. Together with its parallel terms, wisdom is presented as the instrument of YHWH's cosmic handiwork, as the skill by which creation is fashioned and sustained according to a stable and discernable design.

YHWH's use of wisdom to order his good world reinforces its value. But it does more than this. YHWH's creation of the world by means of wisdom also provides a worldview (vv. 19–20). The poem indicates that the virtues promoted by the father are

16. Van Leeuwen, "The Book of Proverbs," *NIB* 5:53.

17. For the distributive construction, that is, the use of the singular, predicate participle "are blessed" (v. 18b) with the plural subjects "those who embrace her" (v. 18a) and "those who hold fast to her" (v. 18b), see GKC §145l; *IBHS* §15.6c.

18. Plöger, *Sprüche Salomos*, 38.

the very "stuff of reality";[19] they are woven into the fabric of the cosmos; they evince the structure of the world. To find and embrace wisdom, therefore, is valuable, for it empowers one to live a good life in accord with the order and structure of YHWH's good world.

3. Wisdom and the Secure Life (3:21–26)

Having reflected on wisdom's value through poetic accounts of the good life and YHWH's good creation, the third section concretizes its value through the form of an instruction (vv. 21–26). It specifies wisdom's value, narrowing its attention from humanity (vv. 13–18) and the cosmos (vv. 19–20) to the personal security it offers the son (vv. 21–26). Against the backdrop of YHWH's creative activities, the instruction intimates that wisdom is not only the instrument through which YHWH fashioned a secure world; it is also the instrument through which the son may experience a secure life.

a. The Retention of Wisdom (3:21)

This secure life, however, necessitates the retention of wisdom and understanding. As noted above, the verb "escape" (יָלֻזוּ, v. 21a) lacks an explicit subject. Since the verb cannot refer forward to the subjects delineated in v. 21b, it appears to refer back to wisdom and understanding in v. 19.[20] The wisdom and understanding that serve as the basis of the good life (v. 13) and that YHWH employed to order the cosmos (v. 19) are the wisdom and understanding the son must retain to live a secure, harmonious life that is in tune with creation. Through the resumptive use of the vocative, the parent admonishes the son to hold on to wisdom and understanding, keeping them ever in sight, and to guard those virtues that represent the practical application of wisdom, namely, "resourcefulness" (תֻּשִׁיָּה, v. 21b) and "discretion" (מְזִמָּה, v. 21b). These byproducts of wisdom provide one with the ability to think clearly in the exercise of power and the navigation of practical matters as well as to devise clever plans or practices in order to achieve a favorable outcome, respectively (see 1:4; 2:7, 11).[21]

b. The Reward for Retention: Security (3:22–24)

The practical benefits that accompany wisdom are delineated in vv. 22–24; they may be summarized by a single word: security. This security is depicted as both external as well as internal. External or physical security is conveyed through the ornamental imagery and the path metaphor within vv. 22–23, while internal or emotional security is expressed through the absence of fear and the delight of rest in v. 24. The security in view concerns one's body parts, which serve as a synecdoche for the whole person: "throat" or "soul" (נֶפֶשׁ, v. 22a), "neck" (גַּרְגְּרֹת, v. 22b), and "foot" (רֶגֶל, v. 23b). It is comprehensive. The retention and protection of the virtues enables one to navigate through life securely (v. 23a), to avoid the most minor accidents (v. 23b), and to sleep soundly (v. 24). And this security is certain. Similar to 3:4 and 3:8, the parent moves from a pair of commands (v. 21) to a promise cast in the form of an indirect volitive (v. 22a) in order to convey the certainty of the reward. Wisdom and its instrumental byproducts offer vitality and life (v. 22a). They are attractive ornaments that bring protection (v. 22b; cf. 3:3). They empower one to

19. Newsom, "Woman and the Discourse of Patriarchal Wisdom," 151.

20. Waltke, *Proverbs: Chapters 1–15*, 263; Loader, *Proverbs 1–9*, 165–66. Cf. Schipper, *Proverbs 1–15*, 154.

21. Fox, *Proverbs 1–9*, 34, 38.

live a secure, stable life that mirrors the security and stability of the created order (v. 23, vv. 19–20). And they yield peaceful sleep (v. 24b). From walking to lying down, wisdom, resourcefulness, and discretion offer security. And this inclusive security renders the retention and protection of these virtues valuable.

c. The Reassurance of the Reward (3:25–26)

The final verses in the subunit bring the motif of personal security to a climactic conclusion (vv. 25–26). The admonition (v. 25) followed by a causal clause (v. 26) mirrors the syntactical pattern of 3:11–12. Similar to 3:11–12, the couplet concludes the subunit; it reiterates terms and concepts from vv. 23–24 but recasts them in a theological framework. In so doing, it intensifies and develops the previous rewards. The opening admonition of v. 25a reiterates and develops the notion of fear mentioned in v. 24a. This admonition is not a strict command; rather, it serves as a reassurance.[22] The son should not "be afraid" (תִּפְחָד, v. 24a). Put differently, he should not fear "sudden terror" (פַּחַד פִּתְאֹם, v. 25a) or the inevitable catastrophe of the wicked. Here the basis for confidence and security is neither wisdom, nor understanding, nor resourcefulness, nor discretion (vv. 21, 24). It is YHWH (v. 26). The causal clause captures the internal-external dimensions of confidence in the previous verses, repeats the term "foot" (רֶגֶל, vv. 23b, 26b), and recasts v. 23 in a theological framework to provide a definitive assurance of security. Just as wisdom, understanding, resourcefulness, and discretion offer confidence and security, so also YHWH is one's "confidence" (כֶּסֶל, v. 26a) or "at one's side."[23] And just as these virtues keep one's foot from stumbling (v. 23b), so also YHWH keeps one's foot from capture (v. 26b). The couplet offers a fitting conclusion to the third section; it develops the theme of security by attributing one's confidence to YHWH and his activities (cf. vv. 19–20).

4. Wisdom and the Good Neighborhood (3:27–35)

The fourth and final section within 3:13–35 expands the vision of the discourse unit; it moves beyond the human (vv. 13–18), cosmic (vv. 19–20), and personal value of wisdom (vv. 21–26) to reflect on its ethical and communal value (vv. 27–35; cf. 3:1–12). Wisdom affects and involves not only one's personal ethics but also one's relation to others. The ethics of these relations are presented in two parts. The first consists of a series of commands cast in a common pattern: a negative construction in the first line, followed by a circumstance that qualifies the command in the second (vv. 27–30). The second part, vv. 31–35, contains a series of theological observations that bolster the ethical prescriptions in vv. 27–30. Together, these parts offer examples of how wisdom and understanding (v. 21a, cf. v. 19) and resourcefulness and discretion (v. 21b) shape one's communal relationships (vv. 27–35).[24] In so doing, they project a vision of a "good neighborhood." This expression is taken from Patrick Miller;[25] it is a metaphor that captures not only the physical characteristics of a fine neighborhood but also "the character of the persons who live there, how they understand themselves, what they are about in their lives, and how they relate to

22. Loader, *Proverbs 1–9*, 180.

23. The term "confidence" (כֶּסֶל) represents a play on the root for "fool" (כְּסִיל). In contrast to confidence in YHWH, the fool is one characterized by misplaced trust and confidence.

24. Clifford, *Proverbs*, 57; Longman, *Proverbs*, 140.

25. Patrick D. Miller, "The Good Neighborhood: Identity and Community through the Commandments," in *Character and Scripture: Moral Formation, Community, and Biblical Interpretation*, ed. William P. Brown (Grand Rapids: Eerdmans), 55–72.

others in the community."[26] This metaphor serves as an appropriate heuristic guide for understanding the materials in vv. 27–35, for these materials identify ethical principles that create a moral space and ethos that is inviting and good.

a. The Characteristics of the Good Neighborhood (3:27–30)

The prescriptions in vv. 27–30 promote sociomoral principles that confirm one's commitment to wisdom and characterize the good neighborhood. These principles concern three matters: sensitivity to the needs of others (vv. 27–28), the maintenance of communal trust (v. 29), and the preservation of peace (v. 30). The first is expressed through a pair of commands that operate under a basic assumption, namely, the other has a rightful claim on what is good. This assumption and its corresponding practices are cultivated through wisdom and actualized through "resourcefulness" (תֻּשִׁיָּה, v. 21b), that is, the ability to think clearly in *the exercise of power*.[27] The initial couplet assumes one possesses the power to do good (v. 27b); and the expression "from those to whom it is due" (מִבְּעָלָיו, v. 27a) acknowledges that the other has a right to this good. The command calls one to recognize the needs of others and to act in accord with one's power, ability, and means for the benefit of the other (cf. 14:31; 19:17; 2 Cor 8:12). This call is given concrete expression through the second couplet (Prov 3:28; cf. 21:13). Here the parent illustrates the abuse of power delineated in the first through direct discourse. He intensifies the prohibition against withholding in 3:27 by sketching a scenario in which the agent possesses the good but delays or even refuses to dispense it. Whatever is envisioned by this benefit, the point is clear: it belongs to the other, not necessarily by virtue of ownership but by right.[28] Together, the prescriptions commend an ethic of responsibility, a vision of communal relations governed by care and sensitivity rather than the abuse of power for personal privilege. And this ethic fosters an ethos characteristic of the good neighborhood.

The same is true of the admonitions in vv. 29–30, which move from withholding what is deserved to dispensing what is undeserved.[29] The first couplet illustrates the value of "discretion" (מְזִמָּה, v. 21b), that is, the ability to devise clever plans or practices in order to achieve a favorable outcome (v. 29),[30] by describing its opposite: improper thoughts and plans against one's neighbor (cf. 6:14; 12:20; 14:22; 15:26). The couplet addresses the impropriety of exploiting the other's trust in and secure dwelling with the agent. Trust and security are fundamental to any good neighborhood.[31] Malicious scheming, however, poisons this ideal ethos, creating a community characterized by fear and suspicion.[32] The second couplet elaborates on the fear and suspicion peculiar to this alternative neighborhood by reflecting on false accusations against others (v. 30; cf. 22:22–23; 23:10–11; 25:9).[33] The issue is not litigation per se but the gratuitous prosecution of the innocent. Such false accusations not only foster fear and suspicion within the community, but they also disturb the peace. Similar to vv. 27–28, the couplets promote particular ethical principles through negative constructions and specific scenarios. In so doing, they illuminate the impropriety of the prohibited actions, illustrate the value

26. Miller, "The Good Neighborhood," 55.

27. Fox, *Proverbs 1–9*, 34.

28. Fox, *Proverbs 1–9*, 164.

29. Loader, *Proverbs 1–9*, 189–90.

30. Fox, *Proverbs 1–9*, 38.

31. McKane, *Proverbs*, 300.

32. Longman, *Proverbs*, 143.

33. This reading follows the normal spelling represented by *qere* (תָּרִיב), rather than *ketiv* (תָּרוֹב).

of resourcefulness and discretion, and project an ethical vision that creates an ethos characteristic of the good neighborhood.

b. Character and the Good Neighborhood (3:31–35)

The cultivation of a good neighborhood, however, involves more than particular actions. The characteristics of the good neighborhood are dependent upon one's character. This character is profiled within a communal context and in relation to YHWH in vv. 31–35. These verses divide individuals into two groups based on their character: the violent, crooked, wicked, mockers, and fools, on the one hand, and the upright, righteous, humble, and wise, on the other. The specific designations for these character types are distinct but, taken together, they refer two types of people. These people are not distinguished by their actions per se; rather, they are distinguished by their character in general and YHWH's response to their character in particular.

Together, vv. 31–32 introduce the shift from the characteristics of the good neighborhood to the character of those within this neighborhood. While v. 31 continues the sequence of negative constructions from vv. 27–30, unlike the previous couplets, it does not qualify the admonition with a circumstance or scenario in the second line. Instead, it contains two admonitions that concern one's emotions, will, and character. The admonitions assume that the "violent person" (אִישׁ חָמָס, v. 31a), the epitome of antisocial behavior (16:29), is an attractive advertisement for the good life. The apparent success of the violent possesses the power to tempt one to desire their quality of life and to imitate their behavior (cf. Pss 37; 73). To curb this enticement, the parent places the apparent success of the violent in a theological perspective. This perspective is delineated in v. 32, which substantiates the pair of commands in v. 31. Here the violent is characterized as "crooked" (נָלוֹז, v. 32a) and set against the straight or "upright" (יְשָׁרִים, v. 32b). Whereas the former elicits divine disgust and abhorrence (v. 32a; cf. 6:16; 11:1, 20; 12:22; 15:8–9), the latter enjoys intimate fellowship with YHWH and access to his inner circle (v. 32b). The rationale for rejecting the character and way of the violent person does not solve the problem of their apparent success; rather, it places this success in proper perspective. It offers an emotive, theological evaluation of the character of the violent or crooked and illuminates the close communion the upright experience with YHWH.

YHWH's relationship with and response to particular character types is elaborated upon in vv. 33–34. While v. 32 provides the sole syntactical rationale within the final section of the discourse, vv. 33–35 develop this rationale through a sequence of antithetical sayings.[34] With the exception of v. 35, these antithetical sayings follow a conventional pattern: they open with a theological evaluation of a negative character type (vv. 33a, 34a) and then identify the reward YHWH lavishes on the positive counterpart of the negative character type (vv. 33b, 34b). Whereas the curse of or misfortune sent by YHWH rests upon the house of the wicked—its inhabitants, structure, and contents—YHWH blesses the abode of the righteous. With regard to the insolent or the cynical,[35] YHWH operates under the principle of *lex talionis*: he derides or mocks the mockers (v. 34a–b; cf. 1:26–27; Pss 2:4; 37:13).

34. McKane, *Proverbs*, 299; Gemser, *Sprüche Salomos*, 24; Van Leeuwen, "The Book of Proverbs," *NIB* 5:54–55; Waltke, *Proverbs: Chapters 1–15*, 270; Loader, *Proverbs 1–9*, 184–85.

35. The construction ל + אם (vv. 34a, 34b) means "in regard to" or "if it is a matter of" (cf. Job 9:19). Fox, *Proverbs 1–9*, 168; Waltke, *Proverbs: Chapters 1–15*, 254n39.

With the "humble" (עֲנָוִים, v. 34b),[36] however, he grants communal approval and commendation. Again, character counts; it affects one's relation to YHWH, one's household, and one's communal status. Just as the ethics promoted in vv. 27–30 foster an ethos characteristic of a good neighborhood, so also one's character and YHWH's intervention create a peaceful, secure community.

In contrast to the previous antithetical sayings (vv. 33–34), the final proverb reverses the order of character types (positive–negative) and expresses an axiomatic belief indicative of the sages' assumptions or value system (v. 35).[37] It incorporates the sociological concepts of honor and shame to offer an anthropological observation regarding the communal esteem and repute of the wise, on the one hand, and the social ostracism and ignominy of fools, on the other. In so doing, it provides a fitting conclusion to the discourse unit. The one who finds and retains wisdom enjoys a good life (vv. 13–18), for this person possesses the virtues that YHWH utilized to order the cosmos (vv. 19–20), lives securely (vv. 21–26), and cultivates a good neighborhood through their actions (vv. 27–30) and character under YHWH's good governance (vv. 31–34). No wonder this wise individual receives social honor while fools "acquire disgrace" (מֵרִים קָלוֹן, v. 35b).[38]

Canonical and Theological Significance

In light of the value of personal piety (3:1–12), the distinct sections within 3:13–35 highlight the value of wisdom through the human (vv. 13–18), cosmic (vv. 19–20), personal (vv. 21–26), and communal dimensions of existence (vv. 27–35). The juxtaposition of these dimensions and the treatment of wisdom from these vantage points capture wisdom's inclusive, incomparable value. She is the basis of human happiness and the good life (vv. 13–18), the instrument YHWH employed to order the cosmos (vv. 19–20), the principle that offers personal security (vv. 21–26), and the virtue that enables one to foster a good neighborhood (vv. 27–35). Wisdom is valuable; it is fundamental to the good life. And wisdom involves moral obligations; it empowers one to cultivate a good neighborhood within YHWH's good creation.

These facets of wisdom's worth and value are developed elsewhere in Proverbs and the canon of Scripture. To be specific, the poetic portrait of wisdom's benefits (vv. 13–18) and YHWH's use of wisdom (vv. 19–20), as well as the ethical obligations that accompany the acquisition of wisdom (vv. 27–35), are elaborated upon and recontextualized elsewhere in the anthology and the broader canonical witness. As intimated above, the beatitudinal poem (3:13–18) includes terms and expressions that are used to describe both Lady Wisdom (8:4–21) and the valiant woman (31:10–31).

36. This reading follows *qere* (עֲנָוִים, "humble") rather than *ketiv* (עֲנִיִּים, "poor"). Loader, *Proverbs 1–9*, 195–96.

37. Fox, "The Epistemology of the Book of Proverbs," 669–84, esp. 675–84.

38. For רום with the sense of "acquire," see Fox, *Proverbs 1–9*, 169. Also, for the distributive use of the singular predicate (i.e., "acquire," מֵרִים, v. 35b) with a plural subject (i.e., "fools," כְּסִילִים, v. 35b), see *IBHS* §15.6c.

The poem provides the literary and linguistic colors for the subsequent portraits of these female figures. Happiness and the good life are related to finding wisdom (3:13, 18) and manifest in the woman who incarnates wisdom (31:10, 28). The reason for this beatific state is captured by the value of both Wisdom and the valiant woman: they are the source of substantial "profit" (סַחַר; 3:14a; 31:18) and more precious than "corals" (פְּנִיִּים; 3:15a; 8:11; 31:10).[39] Far from serving as a literary figure that merely awakens the son's desire and provides an alternative to the strange woman, Wisdom serves as the metaphorical counterpart to her historical instantiation. Her poetic depiction in 3:13–18 shapes and informs the poetic depiction of the valiant woman in 31:10–31. The concluding discourse in the anthology draws on 3:13–18, transforming the figurative into the physical in order to provide a captivating image of wisdom's inherent value and realization in an exemplary woman (cf. Ruth).

In addition to the poetic portrait of wisdom's benefits (3:13–18), the description of YHWH's use of wisdom plays a formative role in Proverbs as well as the Old Testament (3:19–20). Similar to 3:13–18, the concepts and terms delineated in vv. 19–20 are reiterated and unpacked in 8:1–36 in general and 8:22–31 in particular. And similar to 3:13–18, this poetic description of YHWH's construction of the cosmic house serves as a metaphorical counterpart to humanity's construction of a terrestrial house. Just as YHWH founded the earth "by wisdom" (בְּחָכְמָה; 3:19a), established the heavens "by understanding" (בִּתְבוּנָה; 3:19b), and filled particular realms "by his knowledge" (בְּדַעְתּוֹ; 3:20a), so also a human home is built "by wisdom" (בְּחָכְמָה; 24:3a), established "by understanding" (בִּתְבוּנָה; 24:3b), and filled with precious materials "by knowledge" (בְּדַעַת; 24:4a). The content and sequence of the prepositional phrases in 24:3–4 mirror the content and sequence of phrases in 3:19–20 (cf. Jer 10:12; 51:15), suggesting that the principles of human house building are inextricably linked to YHWH's design and construction of the cosmos.[40] The tools employed by YHWH in the establishment of the cosmos are the tools employed by humans in the establishment of a home. The divine house builder provides a paradigm for human house building.[41]

This conclusion is reinforced by the accounts concerning the construction of the tabernacle and temple. As microcosmic representations of the universe, the tabernacle and temple not only reflect the cosmic creation; they are also constructed in the same manner as the cosmic creation. Similar to Prov 3:19–20 and 24:3–4, Exod 31:3 indicates that YHWH filled the human builder, Bezalel, "with wisdom" (בְּחָכְמָה), "with understanding" (בִּתְבוּנָה), and "with knowledge" (בְּדַעַת) to construct parts of the tabernacle. And 1 Kings 7:14 declares that God filled Hiram "with wisdom"

39. For a catalogue of lexical and thematic similarities between Lady Wisdom and the valiant woman, see Yoder, *Wisdom as a Woman of Substance*, 91–93; Fox, *Proverbs 10–31*, 908–9.

40. Raymond C. Van Leeuwen, "Cosmos, Temple, House: Building and Wisdom in Mesopotamia and Israel," in *Wisdom Literature in Mesopotamia and Israel*, ed. Richard J. Clifford, SymS 36 (Atlanta: SBL Press, 2007), 81.

41. Van Leeuwen, "Cosmos, Temple, House," 81.

(אֶת־הַחָכְמָה), "with understanding" (אֶת־הַתְּבוּנָה), "and with knowledge" (וְאֶת־הַדַּעַת) to construct elements of the temple. While the latter text lacks the preposition *bêt*, the sequence of terms is the same as Prov 3:19–20, 24:3–4, and Exod 31:3 (cf. Exod 35:31; 36:1). Just as human house building mirrors the work of the divine builder, so also the construction of the tabernacle and temple—microcosmic representations of the universe—mirror YHWH's construction of the cosmos. Each builder uses the same tools or instruments; and each text presents these instruments in stereotypical order. The striking similarities among these texts indicate that human wisdom in general and human building in particular are rooted in divine wisdom manifested in the construction, ordering, and filling of the cosmos.[42] One who finds and retains wisdom, then, reflects God's wisdom, imitates his creation order, and manifests his provision for the cosmos through their work, life, and care for others.

From this theological perspective, it is not surprising that the acquisition of wisdom carries certain moral obligations (vv. 27–35). These obligations include, among other things, the responsible exercise of power in interpersonal relations and doing what is good (vv. 27–28). Put differently, they encapsulate those actions that constitute loving one's neighbor (Lev 19:18; Mark 12:31). This vision of love, responsibility, and doing good is commended, commanded, and illustrated elsewhere in the canon (e.g., Lev 19:13–14, 16; Deut 6:18; 12:28; Job 31:16–21; Eccl 3:12). And these ethical actions necessitate moral character, namely, righteousness, uprightness, and humility (Prov 3:31–34). These characteristics of character pervade the beatitudinal declarations in the Sermon on the Mount. Similar to the one who possesses wisdom (vv. 3:13–18, 31–34), the one who embodies these aspects of character is blessed (Matt 5:3, 5, 6, 8, 9). And the disposition of humility observed in 3:34 (cf. 3:7) is quoted and prescribed in both Jas 4:6 and 1 Pet 5:5. One's character and actions reveal one's relation to God; and one's character and actions illuminate one's wisdom and the degree to which one lives in consonance with the created world.

The discourse unit's concern with the good life, the good creation, and the good neighborhood provides a worldview governed by wisdom in general and God's utilization of wisdom in particular. To find, retain, and employ wisdom in the ordering of one's life and one's relation with others is to imitate God's wisdom, created order, and relation to humans. And to find wisdom is to find happiness. As the beatitudinal poem indicates, wisdom is the basis of human happiness. In a world where people are consumed by the pursuit of happiness, this perspective on the good life is significant. According to the poem as well as the subsequent sections of the discourse unit, happiness and the good life are found in neither wealth, nor pleasure,

42. Van Leeuwen, "Cosmos, Temple, House," 89.

nor independence.[43] They are found in the acquisition of wisdom, virtuous character, and dependence on the divine. Wisdom forms one's character, produces personal and communal flourishing, and cultivates *šālôm*—a life of wholeness and rest in relation with God and in accord with the created order. This vision of happiness and human flourishing stands in sharp contrast to many contemporary descriptions of the good life. And this vision of happiness and human flourishing provides the church with a framework within which to understand wisdom's value as well as the good life in a good neighborhood within God's good world.

43. Carol A. Newsom, "Positive Psychology and Ancient Israelite Wisdom," in *The Bible and the Pursuit of Happiness: What the Old and New Testaments Teach Us about the Good Life*, ed. Brent A. Strawn (Oxford: Oxford University Press, 2012), 123.

CHAPTER 7

Proverbs 4:1–9

F. Wisdom and Tradition

Main Idea of the Passage

This unique instruction draws upon and reactualizes the tradition of familial instruction to warm the affections and to persuade one to pursue, acquire, and cherish wisdom at all costs.

Literary Context of the Passage

Among the parental instructions within the prologue, Prov 4:1–9 is distinct. The discourse deviates from the structural scheme characteristic of the parental lectures; and it incorporates an extended quotation or recollection in order to convey its message. Whereas the parental lectures elsewhere in the prologue move from an exordium to a lesson to a conclusion, this lecture lacks a formal conclusion and includes an extended exordium as the lesson proper (vv. 4b–9). And whereas some parental lectures include different voices to illustrate the dispositions, desires, and moral worldviews of despicable character types (1:11–14; 7:14–20; cf. 5:12–14), this lecture includes the voice of familial tradition to cultivate appropriate desires and a proper worldview (4:4b–9). The language of the piece may mirror the rhetoric of several other lectures, but its design and substance differentiate the discourse from the parental instructions within the prologue.

The distinctive characteristics of 4:1–9, however, should not overshadow its relationship to other discourses in Prov 1–9. In addition to its use of language characteristic of the didactic speeches within the prologue, the lecture's attention to the pursuit of wisdom, its erotic overtones, and its inchoate personification of wisdom illuminate its place within and contribution to the prologue as a whole. Just as the father indicated that the acquisition of wisdom requires an active pursuit (2:1–4;

3:13), so now the grandfather indicates that wisdom is acquired through an active pursuit (4:5–7). This pursuit is described through pregnant terms and images with erotic overtones (4:5–9). These terms and images awaken the affections, encourage one to pursue wisdom, and shape the portrayal of wisdom as a valuable and attractive maiden. While the personification of wisdom is underdeveloped in the lecture (4:6, 8–9), the discourse elaborates on the implicit and explicit personifications of her persona within the previous speeches (1:20–33; 3:16–18) and sets the stage for the maturation of her character in the speeches that follow (8:1–36; 9:1–6). These speeches give particular attention to Lady Wisdom's value. The value of wisdom is acknowledged in 4:1–9, but one's desire for wisdom is foregrounded. And this desire is significant. In light of the centrality of desire and the erotic overtones within the

I. Introduction to the Book (1:1–7)
II. The Value of Wisdom and Virtue (1:8–9:18)
  A. Wisdom, Desire, and Different Ways (1:8–19)
  B. Wisdom's Rebuke (1:20–33)
  C. The Procurement, Power, and Protection of Wisdom and Virtue (2:1–22)
  D. Wisdom and Piety (3:1–12)
  E. Wisdom's Value and Moral Obligations (3:13–35)
➡ **F. Wisdom and Tradition (4:1–9)**
    1. The Father's Exhortation (4:1–2)
    2. The Grandfather's Exhortation (4:3–9)
      a. The Setting of the Exhortation (4:3–4a)
      b. The Substance of the Exhortation (4:4b–9)
        (1) The Exhortation (4:4b–5)
        (2) The Motivation (4:6)
        (3) The Exhortation (4:7)
        (4) The Motivation (4:8–9)
  G. Wisdom and Ways of Life (4:10–19)
  H. Wisdom and the Moral Anatomy (4:20–27)
  I. Wisdom and Sexuality (5:1–23)
  J. Wisdom, Lending, Laziness, and the Immoral Anatomy (6:1–19)
  K. Wisdom, Desire, and Certain Destruction (6:20–35)
  L. Wisdom and Seduction (7:1–27)
  M. Wisdom's Call, Credentials, and the Cosmos (8:1–36)
  N. Wisdom and Folly's Invitations (9:1–18)
III. "Forming 'Fearers of YHWH'": The Curriculum of Wisdom and Virtue (10:1–29:27)
IV. The Application of Wisdom and Virtue (30:1–31:31)

discourses that follow (5:1–23; 6:20–35; 7:1–27), the issue of proper desire is of the utmost importance. Unless one desires wisdom and finds satisfaction in the acquisition of wisdom, one may seek fulfillment elsewhere—in unsanctioned relationships in general (4:16–17) and the strange woman in particular (5:1–23; 6:20–35; 7:1–27). To curb this misdirected desire and to preempt one from seeking satisfaction in inappropriate objects of desire, the parent attempts to cultivate affection for the proper object of desire: wisdom.

Translation and Exegetical Outline

(See pages 211.)

Structure and Literary Form

As intimated above, the pedagogical rhetoric and formal admonitions woven through 4:1–9 suggest the discourse may be classified as an instruction. This instruction, however, is unique. It does not contain a formal lesson; rather, its "lesson" is cast in the form of an extended exhortation (vv. 4b–9). And this extended exhortation, complete with motivations, is placed on the lips of the parent's father. The reiteration or creative recollection of the grandfather's speech imbues the instruction with an autobiographical ethos. It situates the instruction in the stream of familial tradition. It blurs the intergenerational divide between father and son, inviting the son(s) to imagine the father in his youth and to overhear the instruction he received from his own father. This appeal to past instruction not only enhances the authority of the discourse, but it also allows the son(s) to see the transformative potential of the material.[1] If the son, like the father, heeds the instruction and acquires wisdom, then he, like the father, may develop into a wise, mature parent. The discourse intermingles memory, autobiography, and instruction in a powerful lecture designed to kindle the son's affections and persuade him to pursue wisdom.

This persuasive call to acquire, love, and embrace wisdom is cast in two parts, each of which is attributed to a different voice. The first consists of an exhortation delivered by the father (vv. 1–2), while the second represents an exhortation delivered by the grandfather (vv. 4b–9). These sections are stitched together by vv. 3–4a, which serve as a transition from the father's speech to the grandfather's speech. Despite the different voices within the discourse, the unit is bound together by several common terms.

1. Newsom, "Woman and the Discourse of Patriarchal Wisdom," 151.

Proverbs 4:1–9

	Hebrew	English	Outline
			F. Wisdom and Tradition (4:1–9)
1a	שִׁמְעוּ בָנִים מוּסַר אָב	Hear, sons, a father's instruction,	1. The Father's Exhortation (4:1–2)
1b	וְהַקְשִׁיבוּ לָדַעַת בִּינָה	pay attention, so that you might know understanding;	
2a	↓ כִּי לֶקַח טוֹב נָתַתִּי לָכֶם	↓ because I give you good instruction,	
2b	תּוֹרָתִי אַל־תַּעֲזֹבוּ	do not forsake my teaching.	
			2. The Grandfather's Exhortation (4:3–9)
3a	כִּי־בֵן הָיִיתִי לְאָבִי	When I was a son to my father,	a. The Setting of the Exhortation (4:3–4a)
3b	↓ רַךְ וְיָחִיד לִפְנֵי אִמִּי	↓ tender and the only one before my mother,	
4a	וַיֹּרֵנִי וַיֹּאמֶר לִי	he taught me and said to me:	
			b. The Substance of the Exhortation (4:4b–9)
4b	יִתְמָךְ־דְּבָרַי לִבֶּךָ	"Let your heart hold on to my words,	(1) The Exhortation (4:4b–5)
4c	שְׁמֹר מִצְוֹתַי וֶחְיֵה	keep my commandments and you will live.	
5a	קְנֵה חָכְמָה קְנֵה בִינָה	Get wisdom! Get understanding!	
5b	אַל־תִּשְׁכַּח וְאַל־תֵּט מֵאִמְרֵי־פִי	Do not forget, and do not turn aside from the words of my mouth.	
6a	אַל־תַּעַזְבֶהָ וְתִשְׁמְרֶךָּ	Do not leave her, and she will keep you;	(2) The Motivation (4:6)
6b	אֱהָבֶהָ וְתִצְּרֶךָּ	love her, and she will protect you.	
7a	רֵאשִׁית חָכְמָה קְנֵה חָכְמָה	The beginning of wisdom: get wisdom!	(3) The Exhortation (4:7)
7b	וּבְכָל־קִנְיָנְךָ קְנֵה בִינָה	With all you possess get understanding!	
8a	סַלְסְלֶהָ וּתְרוֹמְמֶךָּ	Cherish her and she will exalt you;	(4) The Motivation (vv. 8–9)
8b	תְּכַבֵּדְךָ כִּי תְחַבְּקֶנָּה	she will honor you, if you embrace her.	
9a	תִּתֵּן לְרֹאשְׁךָ לִוְיַת־חֵן	She will place a graceful garland on your head;	
9b	עֲטֶרֶת תִּפְאֶרֶת תְּמַגְּנֶךָּ	she will grant you a splendid crown."	

Just as the father gives (נָתַתִּי, v. 2a) good instruction, so also wisdom will give or "place" (תִּתֵּן, v. 9a) a graceful garland on her devotee's head. Whereas the father admonishes the addressees not to "forsake" (תַּעֲזֹבוּ, v. 2b) his teaching, the grandfather commands the addressee not to forsake or "leave" (תַּעַזְבֶהָ, v. 6a) wisdom. If the addressee keeps (שְׁמֹר, v. 4c) the grandfather's commands, then wisdom will "keep" (תִשְׁמְרֶךָּ, v. 6a) him. This protection, however, requires an active pursuit. The addressee must "get wisdom" (קְנֵה חָכְמָה, vv. 5a, 7a) and "get understanding" (קְנֵה בִינָה, vv. 5a, 7b) with all he possesses (בְּכָל־קִנְיָנְךָ, v. 7b). This refrain captures the fundamental purpose and agenda of the lecture. The instruction may contain different voices, but the recurring terms within the discourse suggest that these voices share a common lexicon and pursue a common goal.

Explanation of the Text

1. The Father's Exhortation (4:1–2)

The instruction opens with a conventional exhortation that includes terms indicative of the exordia of the parental lectures elsewhere in the prologue (4:1–2; cf. 1:8; 2:2; 4:10, 20). The repetition of these terms does not indicate that the parent lacks rhetorical creativity. To the contrary, it illuminates the parent's pedagogy. The repetition of key terms from both the preamble (1:2, 3, 4, 5, 6; 4:1a, 1b, 2a) and the exordia of other parental lectures suggest that the parent seeks to cultivate a receptive posture (1:5) and to inculcate specific values in the addressee so that he might embody wisdom and virtue.

While the exhortation mirrors the rhetoric, form, and function of many of the exordia within the prologue, it is distinct in at least two respects. First, the instruction is addressed to "sons" (בָנִים; 4:1a), rather than a singular son. And second, the instruction is presented in generic terms: it is "a father's instruction" (מוּסַר אָב, v. 1a), rather than *your* father's instruction. In light of the previous lectures, the plural address to sons is unique. This plural address, however, recurs in subsequent instructions (5:7; 7:24; cf. 8:32–33), suggesting that the father-son discourse setting is a literary convention with some generic flexibility (cf. Sir 39:13; 41:14).[2] This generic flexibility reveals the rhetorical dynamics of the lecture. The plural addressee (Prov 4:1a), combined with the singular form of address that pervades vv. 4b–9, indicates that the instruction transcends the singular son and speaks to a wider audience. Just as the grandfather speaks across generational boundaries, so also the lecture speaks across generational boundaries. The son may be the primary audience of the discourse, but he is by no means the only audience of the discourse. All those who assume the subject position of the son may join the ranks of the "sons" and receive the lecture's instruction.

The rhetorical function of the plural address provides a backdrop against which to understand the generic nature of the parent's instruction. Just as the lecture moves from a plural addressee (v. 1a) to a singular form of address (vv. 4b–9), so also the

2. Fox, *Proverbs 1–9*, 172; Yoder, *Proverbs*, 51.

lecture moves from general parental instruction (v. 1a) to specific instruction (vv. 2, 4b–9). The progression of the lecture clarifies the nature of this general instruction. "A father's instruction" is co-opted by the parent and described as "my teaching" (תּוֹרָתִי, v. 2b), before it is placed on the lips of the grandfather (vv. 4b–9). This progression suggests that "a father's instruction" is an implicit reference to the grandfather's speech, a discourse that the father has appropriated (v. 2b) and reiterated for the benefit of the son (vv. 4b–9).[3]

To benefit from the instruction, however, the son must receive the speech. In characteristic fashion, the exhortation combines formal admonitions with motivations in order to sensitize the son's organs of reception and highlight the value of the material. The admonitions plot a movement that captures the passive and active dimensions of the learning process. The addressees must "hear" (שִׁמְעוּ, v. 1a) the instruction, "pay attention" (הַקְשִׁיבוּ, v. 1b) or listen attentively to the teaching, and remain vigilant so that they do not "forsake" (תַּעֲזֹבוּ, v. 2b), abandon, or forget the father's instruction. The rationale for receiving and retaining the instruction is delineated in vv. 1b and 2a. The former serves as a result clause ("so that you might know," לָדַעַת, v. 1b) that integrates key terms from 1:2 in order to motivate the addressee to receive and attend to the material. The latter is a causal clause ("because," כִּי; 4:2a) that provides an explanation for heeding the instruction. This explanation concerns the nature of the teaching. It is "good instruction" (לֶקַח טוֹב, v. 2a). In light of the speech that follows, it appears the instruction is good not only because of its content but also because of its transgenerational authority: it shaped the father, and it possesses the power to shape the son.

2. The Grandfather's Exhortation (4:3–9)

a. The Setting of the Exhortation (4:3–4a)

In preparation for the father's reiteration of the grandfather's good teaching, the parent recreates the setting of the speech and defines the nature of the discourse. The conjunction "when" (כִּי, v. 3a) situates the speech in past time. This recollection of the past, combined with the father's identification as a "son" (בֵּן, v. 3a), temporarily eliminates the hierarchical structure of domestic instruction and allows the father to identify with the subject position of his own son. He once assumed the same position. He was once a son to his father. And he was once a delicate, malleable youth, precious and beloved by his mother (v. 3b).[4] The domestic setting, intimate terminology, and autobiographical style of the introduction establish rapport with the addressee and enhance the persuasive force of the speech. The father transports the son back to the home of his youth and invites him to overhear and to receive the authoritative instruction of the previous generation. Just as the grandfather "taught" (ירה, v. 4a) the father, so now the father recalls these words of instruction to teach his son. The verb indicates the discourse is didactic and catechetical. And the attribution of the speech to the grandfather suggests the material has roots, weight, and gravitas; it has endured the test of time, shaped the father's character, and now possesses the potential to form the disposition and hone the affections of the son.

b. The Substance of the Exhortation (4:4b–9)

The citation formula (v. 4a) serves as a formal introduction to the grandfather's speech. As noted above, this speech is an extended exhortation that

3. Fox, *Proverbs 1–9*, 172.

4. Waltke, *Proverbs: Chapters 1–15*, 277–78.

seeks to warm the son's affections and persuade him to pursue, acquire, and cherish wisdom at all costs. This pedagogical goal is achieved through a mixture of exhortations and motivations, each of which deserves a brief comment.

(1) The Exhortation (4:4b–5)

Similar to other lectures within the prologue, the grandfather's speech opens with a formal exhortation (vv. 4b–5). This exhortation consists of a barrage of admonitions that concern the retention of the grandfather's words and the acquisition of wisdom. The first pair of admonitions focus on the preservation of the grandfather's words (vv. 4b–c). Drawing on intimate, erotic language from the beatitudinal poem in ch. 3, the grandfather addresses the center of the intellect and affections ("your heart," לִבֶּךָ, v. 4b), calling the son to "hold on to" (יִתְמָךְ, v. 4b) his words in the same way that the blessed person "holds fast" (תֹמְכֶיהָ; 3:18) to wisdom. The retention, protection, and preservation of the grandfather's commands produce the fruit of wisdom: life (3:2, 16, 18). While both "keep" (שְׁמֹר; 4:4c) and "live" (חְיֵה, v. 4c) are imperatives, the sequence indicates that the latter serves as an assurance or certain result of the action prescribed in the former.[5] By keeping and guarding the grandfather's commandments, then, the addressee will live.

This concern with the retention and preservation of the grandfather's words is reiterated in v. 5, where it is cast in the negative and expressed through intellectual neglect as well as a deliberate abandonment of the teaching. The shift from positive (vv. 4b–c) to negative (v. 5b) admonitions, however, is interrupted by a pair of imperatives concerning the acquisition of wisdom (v. 5a).[6] Here the grandfather introduces a root that recurs throughout the remainder of the lecture: "Get" (קְנֵה, vv. 5a, 7a, 7b). This root possesses different shades of meaning; it refers to the acquisition of various objects through different transactions and carries both economic and erotic connotations. The grandfather plays on these connotations throughout the speech. In the present context, it appears the erotic or marital connotation of the verb is primary. In view of the grasping language in v. 4b (cf. 3:18) and the intimate terminology in 4:6, the grandfather urges the addressee to acquire wisdom as a wife (cf. Ruth 4:10).[7]

(2) The Motivation (4:6)

This acquisition, however, is envisioned as much more than a marriage contract with economic strings attached. It involves commitment and loyalty as well as one's emotions and affections. These dimensions of the relationship are given particular expression in v. 6. Here the grandfather delivers a negative and a positive admonition, each of which is accompanied by a particular motivation that describes wisdom's reciprocal response to the commitment and affection of her devotee. Just as the father commanded the son not to "forsake" (תַּעַזְבוּ,

5. GKC §110f–i. For discussion of the repetition of 4:4c in 7:2, see Heim, *Poetic Imagination*, 137–41.

6. While these imperatives are missing from LXX^{B} and some either omit these admonitions or rearrange the text to create a seamless string of commands concerning the retention of parental teaching, neither the omission of the imperatives nor the rearrangement of the text is necessary. Since wisdom (v. 5a) and understanding (v. 5a) serve as the antecedents to the pronominal suffixes in v. 6, the imperatives should be retained. The sequence of the text may be unusual, but the placement of these imperatives at the beginning of v. 5 and the equation of the grandfather's words with wisdom may contribute to the grandfather's rhetorical strategy. For discussion of these issues, see Fox, *Proverbs 1–9*, 174; idem, *Proverbs: An Eclectic Edition with Introduction and Textual Commentary* (Atlanta: SBL Press, 2015), 108.

7. Meinhold, *Die Sprüche*, 1.91–92; Murphy, *Proverbs*, 27; Waltke, *Proverbs: Chapters 1–15*, 279; Yoder, *Proverbs*, 53; Loader, *Proverbs 1–9*, 204–5.

v. 2b) his teaching, so now the grandfather commands the addressee not to "leave" (תַּעַזְבֶהָ, v. 6a) or forsake wisdom. This form of commitment is reinforced and intensified by the positive command to "love her" (אֱהָבֶהָ, v. 6b), which links the concept of loyalty to one's emotions, affections, and attitudes. The reward for this physical and emotional commitment to wisdom is expressed through the same terms as 2:8 and 2:11. Similar to resourcefulness and discretion (2:8, 11), wisdom will guard or "keep" (שׁמר; 4:6a) the son. She will "protect" (נצר, v. 6b) him in the same way that resourcefulness and understanding "protect" (נצר; 2:8, 11) the one who procures wisdom and virtue. The lecture shifts from keeping the grandfather's commandments (v. 4c) to wisdom keeping the son (v. 6a). This protection serves as the reward or motivation for one's physical and emotional commitment to wisdom. The erotic connotations indicated in vv. 4 and 5 come to clear expression through the admonitions in v. 6. And these admonitions provide the basis for the security that wisdom offers those who love her and remain faithful to her.

(3) The Exhortation (4:7)

In view of the motivations or rewards that accompany the acquisition of wisdom, the grand father resumes and escalates the admonitions delineated in v. 5 through the exhortation in v. 7. Similar to v. 5, the grandfather reiterates the commands "get wisdom" (קְנֵה חָכְמָה, v. 7a) and "get understanding" (קְנֵה בִינָה, v. 7b). But he qualifies these commands with distinct phrases. In a manner reminiscent of 1:7, the grandfather indicates that "the beginning of wisdom" (רֵאשִׁית חָכְמָה, v. 7a) is getting wisdom. This tautology counterbalances and elaborates upon the prerequisite for the acquisition wisdom delineated in 1:7 (cf. 9:10). It suggests that the acquisition of wisdom not only depends upon a posture of fear cultivated in relationship with YHWH and knowledge of his will, but it also requires an active pursuit.[8] This pursuit is conceptualized through the prepositional phrase "with all you possess" (בְּכָל־קִנְיָנְךָ, v. 7b). Here the grandfather employs the nominal form of the root קנה and foregrounds the economic connotation of the term to emphasize wisdom's value and desirability. She is worth all that one possesses; and one must deploy the full range of their economic resources to acquire her. The lecture reaches its crescendo with the grandfather's reiteration of the commands from v. 5 and threefold use of the root קנה. The exhortation merges the erotic sense of "get" with the economic. In so doing, it highlights wisdom's value and identifies the extent to which one must go to acquire her.

(4) The Motivation (4:8–9)

Similar to the movement of vv. 4b–6, admonitions accompanied by motivations follow the formal exhortation in v. 7. And similar to the admonitions in v. 6, these commands contain terms with erotic connotations (v. 8). Here the grandfather develops the emotional and physical dimensions of one's commitment to wisdom. He moves from the command to "love her" (אֱהָבֶהָ, v. 6b) to the command to "cherish her" (סַלְסְלֶהָ, v. 8a),[9] and from the warning "do not leave her" (אַל־תַּעַזְבֶהָ, v. 6a) to the condition "if you embrace her" (כִּי תְחַבְּקֶנָּה, v. 8b). Again, the grandfather refuses to separate one's attitudes or emotions from one's physical orientation toward wisdom. The two

8. Loader, *Proverbs 1–9*, 205–6.

9. The verb סַלְסְלֶהָ is a *hapax legomenon* from the root סלל. In general, the root denotes "to exalt, make high" and connotes "to cherish." For a discussion of the rabbinic use of the verb and its sense "caress, cuddle," see Fox, *Proverbs 1–9*, 175.

are inextricably linked. One's love of wisdom will correspond with one's esteem for wisdom; and this emotional commitment will manifest itself in one's physical, even erotic, embrace of wisdom (cf. 5:20; Song 2:6; 8:3).

Together with these admonitions, the grandfather develops the rewards that accompany emotional and physical commitment to wisdom. He moves beyond the protection she provides (Prov 4:6) to the social honor she bestows (vv. 8–9). If the son cherishes, highly esteems, or exalts wisdom, then she will exalt him (v. 8a). If he embraces her, then she will honor him (v. 8b). These general expressions of social esteem are concretized through ornamental and marital imagery in v. 9. The expression "graceful garland" (לִוְיַת־חֵן, v. 9a) recalls the ornamental imagery of 1:9; it describes the external favor, honor, and beauty that wisdom bestows on her lover. The same is true of the phrase "a splendid crown" (עֲטֶרֶת תִּפְאֶרֶת, v. 9b). The image not only connotes honor and nobility, but it also evokes a marriage ceremony, where the bridegroom donned a crown to enhance his beauty (Song 3:11).[10] Here wisdom grants this beauty, honor, and esteem to those who love, cherish, and embrace her. The climactic motivation and formal conclusion to the lecture envision wisdom as more than an object that one is to attain; she is also a noble woman that one must desire and pursue.

Canonical and Theological Significance

As a document that is concerned with cultivating and shaping the various dimensions of one's character through the inculcation of wisdom and virtue, the diverse materials in Proverbs operate under different rhetorical strategies and focus on different dispositions, attitudes, emotions, and actions. The discourse delivered in 4:1–9 contributes to the fundamental goal of the anthology through a distinct rhetorical strategy and sustained attention to a distinct component of one's character. In contrast to other lectures, the parent does not employ an alternative voice to illustrate the dispositions, desires, and moral worldview of despicable character types. Rather, the parent incorporates an authoritative, trustworthy voice to provide a proper perspective on the pursuit of wisdom. In view of the various voices in the prologue vying for the addressee's allegiance, the parent presents a reliable voice that contributed to the formation of his own character. While some may view the advice of previous generations as old-fashioned and outdated, the parent views his father's advice as a clear expression of wisdom that possesses the power to cultivate the character of his son.

Among the dimensions of character, the grandfather's discourse focuses on a specific component: one's desires or affections. The repeated call to "get wisdom" and "get understanding" (vv. 5, 7), combined with the erotic overtones within the lecture, indicate that one's desires plays a formative role in the construction of character.

10. Waltke, *Proverbs: Chapters 1–15*, 282–83; Yoder, *Proverbs*, 53.

Desires identify who one is by revealing what one wants. Similar to other lectures in the prologue, the discourse suggests that the acquisition of wisdom requires an active pursuit, and it includes motivations that explain why one should pursue wisdom. The grandfather, however, goes a step further. He not only provides a series of reasons or motivations for seeking wisdom; he also explains *how* one should seek wisdom.[11] Herein lies the importance of proper desires. These desires fuel the pursuit of wisdom, and they govern the retention of wisdom. In many respects, the call to love, cherish, and embrace wisdom drives the search for and preservation of wisdom. We seek what we desire; we cling to that which we desire. Desire, character, and action are bound together. In view of the formative role of desire in character formation, the grandfather seeks to warm the affections and direct the desires through commands laden with connotations that awaken one's desires and move one to pursue wisdom.

This attempt to cultivate a proper desire for wisdom is significant, for upcoming lectures reflect on the way in which improper objects of desire lead to destruction (5:1–23; 6:20–35; 7:1–27). Proverbs recognizes that desire itself is neither good nor bad. Rather, the object of desire and the character of the desirer provide a framework within which to determine whether the desire is positive or negative (11:23; 13:2; 21:25). Through the voice of the grandfather, the parent urges the son to desire, pursue, and embrace wisdom. The connection among desire, character, and action is reflected elsewhere in the canon. These components are foregrounded in Gen 3:1–6, explored throughout the Song of Songs, and accentuated in James's description of sin's conception (Jas 1:13–15). And the relationship among these components is reflected in the teaching of Jesus. According to Jesus, one's treasure or desire reveals one's heart (Matt 6:19–21); it illuminates the essence of one's character and explains the nature of one's actions. The interrelationship between desire and action is given particular expression in the parables of the hidden treasure and the costly pearl (Matt 13:44–46). When a person finds a treasure hidden in a field, that person will sell all that they own to purchase that field and possess that treasure. When a merchant seeking fine pearls discovers one of the finest quality and the greatest price, that person will sell all that they own to possess the pearl. In the same way, when one loves and desires wisdom, they will sell all of their possessions to acquire, possess, and embrace her. Following Augustine, James K. A. Smith rightly notes that humans are "essentially and ultimately desiring animals."[12] We are lovers. We are desirers. Desire diagnoses one's character. And desire directs one's actions. While desire is not a bad thing, it must be directed toward the right things. The grandfather identifies one of those approved objects of desire: wisdom. He sketches the contours of the good life offered by wisdom. And he invites the reader to enter into a love affair with wisdom.

11. Stewart, *Poetic Ethics*, 155.

12. James K. A. Smith, *Desiring the Kingdom: Worship, Worldview, and Cultural Formation* (Grand Rapids: Baker Academic, 2009), 50–51 et passim.

CHAPTER 8

Proverbs 4:10–19

G. Wisdom and Ways of Life

Main Idea of the Passage

Through specific attention to the root metaphor of the way, the parent links one's character with one's course, illuminates the life and light of wisdom's way, and admonishes the son to avoid the dark, treacherous path of the wicked.

Literary Context of the Passage

In light of its concern with the nuclear symbol of the way, this instruction provides an appropriate counterpart to 4:1–9. Whereas the previous instruction focused on getting wisdom, this lecture focuses on going along wisdom's way.[1] It moves from acquiring to advancing, from procuring to proceeding. It nurtures a desire for wisdom's way through a vivid description of the distorted desires of the wicked (vv. 16–17). And it shifts from wisdom guarding the addressee (4:6) to the addressee guarding wisdom and instruction (4:13b). The parental lecture complements the previous instruction; it indicates that the getting is for going; and it intimates that the acquisition of wisdom is not a one-time decision but rather a lifelong commitment to a way of life.[2]

Together with its relationship to 4:1–9, the instruction contributes to the prologue's discourse on the root metaphor of the way or path. Similar to other discourses within the prologue, the instruction illuminates the intimate relationship among one's character, one's desires, one's knowledge, and one's way. These elements are inextricably linked to one another in 1:11–19, where the parents equate the twisted character and desires of the sinners with their way, moral worldview, and lack of

1. Loader, *Proverbs 1–9*, 210.

2. Longman, *Proverbs*, 151.

vision. These elements are profiled in 2:12–15, where the despicable disposition and distorted desires of the evildoer corresponds with the darkness that encompasses his way. These elements are outlined in 5:1–14 and 7:13–27, where the way of the strange woman is defined through her character, speech, inappropriate desire, and lack of knowledge. And these elements coalesce in 4:10–19, where the parent describes the way of the wicked through their warped character, perverted desires, and ignorance. The lecture contributes to the prologue's treatment of the way. On the one hand, it reiterates and explores the ways in which character, desire, and knowledge inform the various facets of the prologue's nuclear symbol. On the other hand, it enhances the disposition and desires of the wicked through a vivid description of the appetites that mark their moral worldview and way (4:16–17).

Translation and Exegetical Outline

(See page 221.)

Structure and Literary Form

Similar to the parental discourses elsewhere in the prologue, the lecture is cast in the form of an instruction. This instruction contains three distinct sections. The first is an introductory exhortation that attunes the organs of reception and cultivates the posture necessary to receive the teaching proper (v. 10). The second is a formal lesson devoted to the way of wisdom and the way of the wicked, respectively (vv. 11–17). Here the parent incorporates the root metaphor of the way, verbs of motion, and admonitions to describe the nature and terrain of these respective paths. The third and final section serves as a conclusion, which summarizes and compares the way of wisdom and the way of the wicked (vv. 18–19). This conclusion opens with a disjunctive, captures the essence of the ways mentioned in the lesson, and relates one's way with one's character as well as one's knowledge.

In addition to its logical progression of thought, the discourse is bound together by common constructions and the concept of the way. Just as the first half of the lesson proper opens with a pair of admonitions framed by propositional phrases (v. 11), so also the second half of the lesson opens with a pair of admonitions framed by prepositional phrases (v. 14). And the lesson as well as the conclusion are replete with nouns and verbs from the semantic and conceptual sphere of the instruction's primary theme: the way. This theme is explored through the nouns "way" (דֶּרֶךְ, vv. 11a, 14b, 19a; אֹרַח, v. 14a, 18a), "paths" (מַעְגָּל, v. 11b), and "step" (צַעַד, v. 12a) as well as through the verbs "lead" (דָּרַךְ, v. 11b), "walk" (הָלַךְ, v. 12a), "run" (רוץ, v. 12b), "stumble" (כָּשַׁל, vv. 12b, 16b, 19b), "enter" (בוא, v. 14a), "tread" (אשׁר, v. 14b), "pass through/on" (עבר, vv. 15a, 15b), and "turn away" (שׂטה, v. 15b). The nouns concerning the way, combined with the verbs of movement and the threefold use of the construction לא + כשל (vv. 12b, 16b, cf. 19b), reinforce the coherence of the discourse unit and identify its governing theme.

Proverbs 4:10–19

Verse	Hebrew	English	Outline
			G. Wisdom and Ways of Life (4:10–19)
			1. Introductory Exhortation (4:10)
10a	שְׁמַע בְּנִי וְקַח אֲמָרָי	Hear, my son, and take my words,	a. The Admonition (4:10a)
10b	וְיִרְבּוּ לְךָ שְׁנוֹת חַיִּים	so that years of life may increase for you.	b. The Motivation (4:10b)
			2. The Ways of Life (4:11–17)
			a. The Way of Wisdom (4:11–13)
11a	בְּדֶרֶךְ חָכְמָה הֹרֵתִיךָ	In the way of wisdom, I instruct you,	(1) The Nature of the Way (4:11–12)
11b	הִדְרַכְתִּיךָ בְּמַעְגְּלֵי־יֹשֶׁר	I lead you in upright paths.	
12a	בְּלֶכְתְּךָ לֹא־יֵצַר צַעֲדֶךָ	When you walk, your step will not be hampered;	
12b	וְאִם־תָּרוּץ לֹא תִכָּשֵׁל	and if you run, you will not stumble.	
13a	הַחֲזֵק בַּמּוּסָר אַל־תֶּרֶף	Take hold of instruction, do not let go,	(2) The Compass for the Way (4:13)
13b	נִצְּרֶהָ כִּי־הִיא חַיֶּיךָ	guard it, for it is your life.	
			b. The Way of the Wicked (4:14–17)
14a	בְּאֹרַח רְשָׁעִים אַל־תָּבֹא	On the way of the wicked do not enter,	(1) Avoiding the Way (4:14–15)
14b	וְאַל־תְּאַשֵּׁר בְּדֶרֶךְ רָעִים	and do not tread on the way of evildoers.	
15a	פְּרָעֵהוּ אַל־תַּעֲבָר־בּוֹ	Avoid it; do not pass through it;	
15b	שְׂטֵה מֵעָלָיו וַעֲבוֹר	turn away from it; and pass on,	
16a	↑ כִּי לֹא יִשְׁנוּ אִם־לֹא יָרֵעוּ	↑ for they cannot sleep unless they do harm,	(2) The Rationale (4:16–17)
16b	וְנִגְזְלָה שְׁנָתָם אִם־לֹא יַכְשִׁילוּ	they are robbed of sleep if they cause no stumbling;	
17a	כִּי לָחֲמוּ לֶחֶם רֶשַׁע	for they eat the bread of wickedness,	
17b	וְיֵין חֲמָסִים יִשְׁתּוּ	and drink the wine of violence.	
18a	וְאֹרַח צַדִּיקִים כְּאוֹר נֹגַהּ	Now the way of the righteous is like the shining light,	3. Conclusion: Wisdom and Ways (4:18–19)
18b	הוֹלֵךְ וָאוֹר עַד־נְכוֹן הַיּוֹם	growing brighter until the day is established.	
19a	דֶּרֶךְ רְשָׁעִים כָּאֲפֵלָה	The way of the wicked is like darkness;	
19b	לֹא יָדְעוּ בַּמֶּה יִכָּשֵׁלוּ	they do not know what they stumble over.	

Explanation of the Text

1. Introductory Exhortation (4:10)

The parental instruction opens in typical fashion with an exhortation, complete with admonitions and a motivation (cf. 1:8–9; 4:1–2). Each deserves a brief comment.

a. The Admonition (4:10a)

Together with the address to the son, the introductory exhortation includes a pair of admonitions. The call to "hear" (שְׁמַע, v. 10a) and the invitation to "take my words" (קַח אֲמָרָי, v. 10a) are part and parcel of the pedagogical rhetoric of both the parents and Lady Wisdom (1:8; 2:1; 4:1; 5:7; 7:24; 8:6, 10, 32, 33). In accordance with the educational philosophy of the document (1:5), the parents and Lady Wisdom recognize that a listening posture is fundamental to the acquisition and retention of wisdom and virtue. The parent signals the necessity of this posture through this pair of admonitions. And through the repetition of these common expressions (1:8; 2:1; 4:1; 4:10a–b), the parent seeks to cultivate receptivity to and the retention of his teaching, for the wisdom and instruction delivered through the parent's teaching will provide the addressee with a compass for navigating the way of wisdom (cf. 4:13).

b. The Motivation (4:10b)

To encourage the reception and retention of the instruction, the parent supplements the pair of admonitions with a motivation. This motivation is cast in the form of a result clause.[3] And this clause represents a variant repetition of both 3:2 and 9:11.[4] Similar to 3:2, the reception and retention of parental instruction yields years of life. In light of the fact that Wisdom offers the same reward (9:11), it appears that the parent's words are comparable to Wisdom's words, that the acceptance and retention of one reaps the same rewards as the acceptance and retention of the other. To listen to the parent's words, then, is to hear Wisdom's voice and receive the years of life she offers to her devotees.

2. The Ways of Life (4:11–17)

These words and the nuclear metaphor of the way are delineated in lesson proper (vv. 11–17). Here the parent sketches the nature and moral geography of two distinctive ways: the way of wisdom (vv. 11–13) and the way of the wicked (vv. 14–17).

a. The Way of Wisdom (4:11–13)

(1) The Nature of the Way (4:11–12)

The parent opens the lesson by foregrounding the root metaphor that provides the conceptual framework for the instruction: the way. This metaphor is expressed through two terms (vv. 11a, 11b), which are cast in prepositional phrases that frame the pair of verbs in v. 11. And these verbs correspond with the nuclear symbol of the lecture. The first, "I instruct you" (הֹרֵתִיךָ, v. 11a), is a verb derived from the same root as the noun תּוֹרָה; it not only denotes teaching, but it also connotes guidance and carries the sense of giving directions.[5] The second verb, "I lead you" (הִדְרַכְתִּיךָ, v. 11b), is a form derived from the noun דֶּרֶךְ; it matches its nominal counterpart in v. 11a and complements

3. Following the imperative, the construction *waw* + imperfect marks purpose or result (*IBHS* §34.6a).

4. Heim, *Poetic Imagination*, 104–9.

5. McKane, *Proverbs*, 307–8; Loader, *Proverbs 1–9*, 213.

the previous verb. The parent offers authoritative instruction to direct, guide, and lead the son in a particular way. While the directions are vague and the end or telos of the journey is ambiguous, the nature of the path is clear.

Together, the prepositional phrases in v. 11 highlight the nature and moral geography of the way on which the father instructs the son. It is the "way of wisdom" (דֶּרֶךְ חָכְמָה, v. 11a), a way characterized by delight and peace (3:17). And it is a way distinguished by honesty and moral rectitude. This notion is expressed through the construct phrase "upright paths" (מַעְגְּלֵי־יֹשֶׁר; 4:11b), that is, walkways that are morally straight and marked by movements that accord with the order YHWH has woven into the fabric of the cosmos (2:13). The parent describes this way of life through intellectual and moral terms. In so doing, he intimates that one's way reveals one's character and one's character determines one's way.

The moral geography of the way of wisdom is consonant with its terrain and physical features, which are described in v. 12. The verbs "walk" (הָלַךְ, v. 12a) and "run" (רוּץ, v. 12b) in the temporal and conditional protases form a merism that captures the totality of the movements of life. Whether the circumstances of life demand little effort or considerable exertion,[6] the way of wisdom remains a safe, smooth path. One's "step" (צַעַד, v. 12a) or conduct will be neither impeded nor restricted; and one will "not stumble" (לֹא תִכָּשֵׁל, v. 12b). The way of wisdom is open and clear. Its physical features mirror its moral geography.

(2) The Compass for the Way (4:13)

Although the parent does not provide explicit directions in the way of wisdom, he identifies the compass necessary for the journey, namely, "instruction" (מוּסָר, v. 13a). In a manner reminiscent of the introductory exhortation (v. 10), the parent delivers a series of commands, complete with a motivation. The commands build in intensity, from taking hold of or holding fast to instruction (v. 13a), to clinging to it (v. 13a), to guarding or protecting it (v. 13b). And similar to the introductory exhortation (v. 10), these commands and expressions reverberate throughout the prologue. The call to "take hold of instruction" (הַחֲזֵק בַּמּוּסָר, v. 13a) is redolent of 3:18, where "those who embrace" (מַחֲזִיקִים) Lady Wisdom experience a full, joyous life. And the command to "guard" (נְצָר; 4:13b) recalls previous discourses, where the son is called to "keep" (יָצַר; 3:1) the parent's commandments and "protect" (נָצַר; 3:21) resourcefulness and discretion (cf. 2:11; 4:6). The parent reiterates and recasts traditional pedagogical language elsewhere in the prologue, enjoining the son to lay hold of instruction, on the one hand, and to protect wisdom, on the other. In contrast to the masculine form of the noun "instruction" (v. 13a), the pronominal objects in vv. 13b are feminine, suggesting these feminine suffixes refer back to "wisdom" (חָכְמָה) in v. 11.[7] By looking back to and including "wisdom" in the series of commands, the parent equates "instruction" (מוּסָר, v. 13a) with "wisdom" (חָכְמָה, v. 11a; cf. 1:2). In so doing, he provides the son with a compass. The parent depicts instruction and wisdom as virtual guides that must be seized, clutched, and guarded on the journey along wisdom's way.[8]

The motivation for traversing the way of wisdom in general and following the series of commands in particular is presented in v. 13b. The conjunction "for" (כִּי, v. 13b) opens a causal clause, which

6. For walking and running as expressions of different degrees of effort in life, see Fox, *Proverbs 1–9*, 179; Loader, *Proverbs 1–9*, 214.

7. Toy, *Proverbs*, 92; McKane, *Proverbs*, 307; Fox, *Proverbs 1–9*, 180; Waltke, *Proverbs: Chapters 1–15*, 288; Loader, *Proverbs 1–9*, 216.

8. Habel, "The Symbolism of Wisdom in Proverbs 1–9," 138.

provides a motivation or rationale for grasping instruction and guarding wisdom. This motivation is comparable to v. 10b. Just as the motivation for receiving and retaining the parent's words was "years of life" (שְׁנוֹת חַיִּים, v. 10b), so also the motivation for holding fast to instruction and protecting wisdom is "life" (חַיֶּי, v. 13b). Wisdom and the parent's words are one in the same. Both bring life (cf. 3:18). This life is not the end of wisdom's way; rather, it *is* wisdom's way, a path of life and human flourishing.[9]

b. The Way of the Wicked (4:14–17)

Having described the moral geography of the way of wisdom and the requisite compass for navigating this way, the parent shifts to a different way, the way of the wicked (vv. 14–17). As the second half of the lesson proper, the discourse on the way of the wicked is divided into two parts: admonitions urging the son to avoid the way of the wicked (vv. 14–15) and a rationale focusing on the character and twisted desires of the wicked (vv. 16–17).

(1) Avoiding the Way (4:14–15)

In contrast to the way of wisdom (vv. 11–13), the parent does not describe the nature or moral geography of the way of the wicked. The *way* of the wicked is not necessarily the focus of attention; rather, the *character* of the wicked and the evildoer are the center of gravity. The character of these personages defines their way. And this way is to be avoided at all costs. While one would expect "the way of folly" as the appropriate counterpart to the way of wisdom, the parent reflects of the way of the wicked and evildoers. Similar to the opening verse of the initial half of the lesson (v. 11), the opening verse of the second half includes two prepositional phrases concerning the way that frame a pair of commands (v. 14). And similar to the opening verse of the initial half of the lesson (v. 11), the verbs within these commands correspond to the nuclear symbol of the lecture. The first, "do not enter" (אַל־תָּבֹא, v. 14a), forbids the addressee from setting foot on the way of the wicked. The second, "do not tread" (אַל־תְּאַשֵּׁר, v. 14b), intensifies and develops the first, prohibiting the son from venturing along or marching down "the way of evildoers" (דֶּרֶךְ רָעִים, v. 14b). Whereas the parent commended a way marked by wisdom and moral rectitude in the initial half of the lesson, he prohibits the son from entering and traversing a way marked by moral perversion and evil in the second.

This prohibition is amplified in v. 15. Here the parent delivers four categorical commands, urging the son to steer clear of the way of the wicked. These commands are expressed through verbs within the semantic range of the path metaphor. And these commands recast and develop the pair of prohibitions in v. 14. They assume the son will stumble upon the way of the wicked; and they outline the course of action that the son must take when he arrives at the threshold of this way: he must "avoid it" (פְּרָעֵהוּ, v. 15a), "not pass through it" (אַל־תַּעֲבָר־בּוֹ, v. 15a), "turn away from it" (שְׂטֵה מֵעָלָיו, v. 15b), and "pass on" (עֲבוֹר, v. 15b). The language and imagery of these commands is reminiscent of the language and imagery that punctuates the discourses devoted to the strange woman and Woman Folly (5:8; 7:8, 25; 9:15–16). Like these women and their ways, the son must shun the way of the wicked. The parent moves beyond prohibitions concerning entering and traversing the way of the wicked to commands that indicate entrance to this path should not be entertained. When the way of wisdom intersects with the way of the wicked, the son should change his course and proceed along the right way, persevering in upright paths.

9. Loader, *Proverbs 1–9*, 216.

(2) The Rationale (4:16–17)

These unqualified commands concerning avoidance of the way of the wicked are substantiated by a series of causal clauses governed by the conjunction "for" (כִּי, vv. 16a, 17a). As noted above, the rationale does not focus on the way of the wicked or evildoers per se; rather, it focuses on the character of these figures. The shift from the second-person singular to the third-person plural shifts the focus of attention away from the son and onto the disposition of the wicked and evildoers. This shift mirrors the rhetorical pattern within the initial half of the lesson (vv. 11–13). Just as the final verse in the first half of the lesson referred back to wisdom in the initial verse (vv. 11, 13), so now the final verses in the second half of the lesson refer back to personages mentioned in the initial verse (vv. 14, 16–17). They form an *inclusio*, framing the latter half of the lesson with a description of the disposition of the wicked and evildoers.

The disposition of these character types is profiled through their perverted appetites and desires. The portrait is vivid. And it appears that this portrait is intended to evoke disgust and, in so doing, to motivate the son to avoid the way traversed by these distorted character types.[10] The appetites and desires of the wicked and evildoers are described through the basic activities of life: sleep, food, and drink. These personages are unable to sleep "unless they do harm" (אִם־לֹא יָרֵעוּ, v. 16a), engineer evil, and "cause stumbling" (יַכְשִׁילוּ, v. 16b).[11] The latter verb recontextualizes the root used in v. 12b. Whereas the way of wisdom is a clear, open path on which one "will not stumble" (לֹא תִכָּשֵׁל, v. 12b), the wicked and evildoers epitomize a way in which physical and psychological rest is achieved only through actions that cause others to stumble (cf. Mic 2:1; Ps 36:2–5[1–4]). To modify Augustine's well-known statement, the hearts of the wicked and evildoers are restless until they find rest in the propagation of evil and the downfall of others.[12] Their repose is found in the ruination of others. Their inner impulses and appetites are satiated only through the dissemination of destruction.

The distorted desires of the wicked and evildoers are extended in v. 17. These personages not only require a sordid sedative in order to sleep; they also survive on a depraved diet: they "eat the bread of wickedness" (לָחֲמוּ לֶחֶם רֶשַׁע, v. 17a) and "drink the wine of violence" (יֵין חֲמָסִים יִשְׁתּוּ, v. 17b). These construct phrases illuminate the perverted appetites of the wicked and evildoers. Literally, they are what they eat. They are "wicked" (רְשָׁעִים, v. 14a), so they feed on the food of wickedness (v. 17a).[13] They desire harm and violence (v. 16a; 13:2), so they quench their thirst with "violent acts" (חֲמָסִים, v. 17b). While some argue that these construct phrases refer to food and drink gained by acts of violence, and others interpret them as expressions that capture the metaphorical nourishment of the wicked, the two options are not mutually exclusive.[14] The wicked and evildoers not only find rest through real acts of evil and unjust violence (v. 16), but they also survive on and satisfy their gastronomic appetite through evil and unjust violence. Their palate reveals their desires. Their desires identify their character. And their character defines their way.

10. Lyu, *Righteousness*, 64.

11. The translation follows *qere*, for the causative form matches v. 16a and captures the actions of the wicked on others.

12. Augustine, *Confessions*, 1.1.1.

13. The expression "they eat the bread of wickedness" is a *figura etymologica* or cognate accusative, a construction in which the verb and its nominal object derive from the same root.

14. Loader, *Proverbs 1–9*, 219.

3. Conclusion: Wisdom and Ways (4:18–19)

The character types and ways delineated in the lesson proper are summarized and developed in the lecture's conclusion (vv. 18–19). This conclusion opens with a disjunctive *waw* ("now"), which signals the close of the lecture and introduces a contrast between the way of the wicked (vv. 14–17, 19) and the way of the righteous (v. 18).[15] The nuclear symbol of the way remains the focus of attention. The conclusion, however, enhances this root metaphor in two respects. First, it includes a character type that is missing from the formal lesson: the "righteous" (צַדִּיקִים, v. 18a). In so doing, it associates the way of wisdom with the way of the righteous, morally straight paths (v. 11d) with a virtuous way of life (v. 18a). Second, the conclusion incorporates the images of light and darkness. These images illuminate and explore another dimension of the lecture's nuclear symbol: they link one's character and one's way with the concept of knowledge. Just as one's character defines and determines one's way, so also one's way reveals one's knowledge, sight, and perception. The metaphor of sight or knowledge expands the root metaphor of the way by including an intellectual dimension that supplements the lesson's concern with the moral geography, dispositions, and desires that mark the way of wisdom and the way of the wicked.

Together, light and darkness, sight and purblindness, knowledge and ignorance govern the ways described in the conclusion. The way of the righteous is compared to a gleaming light that grows in intensity, ever illuminating and clarifying the contours and terrain of the path (v. 18). Whether the comparison refers to the gradual emergence of the sun at dawn or to its intensification from sunrise to midday, the general thrust is that the righteous walk in a light that progressively grows in brightness. This brightness allows the righteous to see the path, determine their step (v. 12a), perceive obstacles (v. 12b), avoid the way of the wicked, and walk in accord with the order God has established in the cosmos. Light provides sight; sight generates perception; and perception breeds the knowledge necessary to increase in wisdom and walk in the way of the righteous.

This is not the case with the way of the wicked. The final verse of the lecture clarifies the conceptual dimensions of the light/darkness metaphor through a description of the nature of the way of the wicked. The way of the wicked is compared to "darkness" (אֲפֵלָה, v. 19a), a negative term that connotes gloom, calamity, and lack of perception (Exod 10:22; Deut 28:29; Isa 8:22). The intellectual and physical nuances of the image are foregrounded in Prov 4:19b. The wicked "do not know what they stumble over" (לֹא יָדְעוּ בַּמֶּה יִכָּשֵׁלוּ, v. 19b). They lack sight, perception, and knowledge. They survive on causing others to stumble (v. 16), and yet they are ignorant of the timing and cause of their own stumbling. Similar to the adulterous woman and Woman Folly (Prov 5:6; 9:13), the wicked suffer from a lack of knowledge and perception. As the culmination of the lecture, this description of the way of the wicked is the icing on the pedagogical cake. This is why one must avoid the way of the wicked. Their character is warped; their desires are depraved; their appetite is perverted; their way is dark; their vision is clouded; and their knowledge is deficient.

15. In view of the disjunctive *waw*, it is unnecessary to follow Toy, *Proverbs*, 93, and the proposal of *BHS* and invert the final verses.

Canonical and Theological Significance

The nuclear metaphor of the way governs the content, movement, pedagogy, and worldview of this parental lecture; it is a pregnant symbol that integrates one's character, one's desires, and one's knowledge with one's course of life. And, as noted in the introduction, it is a symbol that orients one to the larger metaphoric system and pedagogical discourse of Proverbs. All characters traverse paths that lead to one of two destinations: life or death. The physical and moral geography of these paths foreshadow their telos. The way of life is a clear, open, straight, secure pathway marked by wisdom, instruction, understanding, justice, and uprightness (3:6, 23; 4:11, 18; 6:23; 8:20; 9:6; 11:5; 12:28). The way of death, by contrast, is a dark, crooked, impeded pathway marked by wickedness, ignorance, arrogance, perverted speech, and distorted desires (2:12–15; 4:16–17, 19; 8:13; 21:8). The sharp distinction between the terrain and telos of these paths mirrors the distinctions between the character types that traverse them. Whereas the wise and righteous tread the way of life, the fool, wicked, and lazy walk the way of death. The polarity between the two paths matches the polarity between the character types profiled in the antithetical sayings of Prov 10–29. And the polarity between these paths parallels the polarity between the women and houses within the prologue. The path metaphor provides a powerful, multidimensional symbol for mapping character, attitudes, actions, and ends in Proverbs's pedagogical program of education for character formation. Proverbs 4:10–19 focuses on this symbol and several of its facets, illuminating the interrelationship among one's way, disposition, desires, and intellect as well as the pivotal role of wisdom and instruction in the determination of one's steps, conduct, and course of life.

The metaphor of the way and its accompanying dimensions play an important role in the worldview and pedagogy of Proverbs. This metaphor, however, is the sole property of neither Proverbs nor the wisdom literature. It appears throughout the canon of Scripture. The image pervades the hortatory discourses of Deuteronomy, where walking in the way is equated with covenant obedience, which yields life (Deut 5:33; 8:6; 9:12, 16; 11:22, 28; 13:5; 26:17; 30:16). The metaphor recurs throughout the Deuteronomistic History, where it describes the character, lifestyle, and orientation of the people as well as particular individuals in relation to the standards of covenant relationship (Josh 22:5; Judg 2:17; 1 Kgs 2:3–4; 3:14; 8:36; 15:26; 22:52; 2 Kgs 22:2). The symbol punctuates the oracles of the prophets and the poems within the Psalter, where it refers to a life of righteousness or wickedness (Isa 64:4[5]; Jer 3:21; 6:16; 18:15; 26:3; Ezek 3:18–19; Hos 14:9[10]; Zech 1:4; Pss 1:1, 6; 35:6; 36:5[4]; 37:14; 107:17). The image is used in the New Testament to describe alternative pathways in life (Matt 7:13–14), the identity of Jesus (John 14:6), and the Christian community

(Acts 9:2). And the motif of walking as well as the images of light and darkness are employed to portray one's course of life, commitments, and knowledge (John 8:12; 12:35; Gal 5:16; Eph 4:1; 5:8; 1 John 1:6–7). Similar to Prov 4:10–19, the canon of Scripture bears witness to the multifaceted dimensions of the metaphor of the way; it is a path oriented toward a particular telos with a distinctive physical and moral geography that is associated with one's character, commitments, attitudes, actions, and knowledge.

As Prov 4:10–19 indicates, the way of wisdom and the way of the wicked are open to prospective travelers. One must choose a path. And, according to 4:13, this choice and the subsequent journey are governed by one's possession of instruction and wisdom. The way of wisdom is navigated with a moral compass. This compass guides one along upright paths trodden by others, and it advises one to turn away from the path of the wicked. The parent does not advise the son to blaze a new path with whatever skills he may be able to muster. He identifies the paths and provides the resources necessary to choose the right way. Just as the son was called to pursue and acquire wisdom (4:5, 7), so also he must retain instruction, protect wisdom, and choose the right path. The lecture places the reader at the crossroads of the way of wisdom and the way of the wicked. Just as Jesus commanded his disciples to enter the narrow way that leads to life (Matt 7:13–14), so also the parent commands the son to enter the way of wisdom, which is the son's life. The lecture demands that the reader choose a path. The choice will determine one's steps. The choice will illuminate one's character, conduct, and movements. The choice will identify one's destination. And the choice will reveal whether one has acquired, retained, and protected wisdom and instruction.

CHAPTER 9

Proverbs 4:20–27

H. Wisdom and the Moral Anatomy

Main Idea of the Passage

This parental lecture demonstrates that wisdom's way is an embodied way of life, a journey in which the headquarters of the heart direct and govern one's posture, orientation, and body parts.

Literary Context of the Passage

The nuclear metaphor of the way, which predominated the former lecture, plays a significant role in the present instruction. This metaphor, however, is subordinate to terms and images pertaining to the members and movements of the body. Whereas the previous lecture described the moral geography of the way of wisdom (4:11–13), this instruction describes the moral anatomy of the way of wisdom. And whereas the previous lecture admonished the addressee to avoid the way of the wicked (4:14–15), this instruction urges the addressee to walk straight on the straight path (4:24–27). Both lectures acknowledge the dangers associated with traversing the wrong way (4:14–15, 26–27). And both lectures encourage walking along the right way through distinct pedagogical strategies. In view of their common features and discrete emphases, it appears that these lectures complement one another. What the previous lecture lacked in concrete directions, the present lecture provides;[1] it offers a paradigmatic portrait of the moral anatomy of wisdom's way. Put differently, the lecture presents an impressionistic sketch of the corporeal orientation and kinesthetic movements of the right way. In so doing, it demonstrates that one's character, desire, and knowledge not only reveal one's way (4:10–19), but one's body also reveals one's path.

1. Loader, *Proverbs 1–9*, 222.

In addition to its relationship with the previous lecture, the instruction serves as a positive counterpart to the discourse in 6:12–15 (cf. 6:16–19). The portraits painted in these pieces are mirror images of one another. While the parent exhorts the son to distance himself from a "crooked mouth" (עִקְּשׁוּת פֶּה; 4:24a), the scoundrel is described as one who goes about with a "crooked mouth" (עִקְּשׁוּת פֶּה; 6:12). While the parent urges the son to fix his eyes straight ahead and to watch the path of his feet (4:25–26), the scoundrel is depicted as one who winks his eyes and shuffles his feet (6:13; cf. 6:17–18). While the parent calls the son to guard his heart from evil thoughts and schemes (v. 23), the scoundrel is characterized as one with perversions in his heart who constantly plans evil (6:14; cf. 6:18). And while the reception and retention of the parent's words produces "healing" (מַרְפֵּא; 4:22b), the scoundrel is portrayed as one who will be broken, without "remedy" (מַרְפֵּא; 6:15). Just as the right way is marked by movements in which one's members reveal one's character, so also the wrong way is marked by movements in which one's members reveal one's character. Far from viewing wisdom merely as an intellectual enterprise, the lecture identifies how the body illuminates one's wisdom, character, and way.

Translation and Exegetical Outline

(See page 232.)

Structure and Literary Form

Similar to the parental discourses elsewhere in the prologue, this lecture is cast in the form of an instruction; its introductory address, admonitions, and motivations illuminate its literary form and didactic function. Although the instruction lacks a formal conclusion, the piece may be divided into three sections. The first is a conventional introduction, complete with admonitions and a motivation (4:20–22). The second section functions as a literary hinge (v. 23).[2] On the one hand, it looks back to vv. 20–22, reiterating and recasting specific terms from the introductory exhortation. On the other hand, it looks forward to the third section of the lecture (vv. 24–27), which describes the "outcomes" or "sources of life" (תּוֹצְאוֹת חַיִּים, v. 23b) that flow from the heart. The heart is the focus of attention in v. 23. From an anthropological perspective, the heart is the very center of the human being in Israelite thought. And from a literary perspective, the heart is situated at the very center of the instruction.[3]

The design and unity of the lecture is reinforced by repeated terms as well as references to the human body in general and its parts in particular. As for repeated terms, "life" (חַיִּים) is reiterated in vv. 22a and 23b. The verbal form of the root שׁמר is used in v. 21b ("keep," שָׁמְרֵ-), while the nominal form of the root is employed in v. 23a ("protected," מִשְׁמָר). The verb נטה recurs in vv. 20b ("incline," הַט) and 27a ("turn aside," תֵּט), creating a formal frame around the lecture. And the imperatival form of סור opens v. 24 and closes v. 27 ("keep . . . away," הָסֵר), forming an *inclusio* around the third section of the instruction. Together with these repeated terms, references to the body and its parts pervade the lecture. Along with "one's body" (בְּשָׂרוֹ, v. 22b), the instruction refers to the "ear" (אׇזֶן, v. 20b), "eyes" (עֵינֶיךָ, vv. 21a, 25a), "heart" (לְבָב, v. 21b; לֵב, v. 23a), "mouth" (פֶּה, v. 24a), "lips" (שְׂפָתַיִם, v. 24b), "pupils" (עַפְעַפַּיִם, v. 25b), "feet" (רַגְלַיִם, v. 26a), and "foot" (רֶגֶל, v. 27b). These repeated terms and references to the human body unify the lecture and illuminate its purpose.

2. So also Waltke, *Proverbs: Chapters 1–15*, 295–96; Loader, *Proverbs 1–9*, 223–24.

3. So also Waltke, *Proverbs: Chapters 1–15*, 296; Loader, *Proverbs 1–9*, 222.

Proverbs 4:20–27

			H. Wisdom and the Moral Anatomy (4:20–27)
			1. Introductory Exhortation (4:20–22)
20a	בְּנִי לִדְבָרַי הַקְשִׁיבָה	My son, listen attentively to my words,	a. The Admonitions (4:20–21)
20b	לַאֲמָרַי הַט־אָזְנֶךָ	incline your ear to my sayings;	
21a	אַל־יַלִּיזוּ מֵעֵינֶיךָ	they must not escape from your eyes,	
21b	שָׁמְרֵם בְּתוֹךְ לְבָבֶךָ	keep them within your heart;	
22a	כִּי־חַיִּים הֵם לְמֹצְאֵיהֶם	for they are life to those who find them,	b. The Motivation (4:22)
22b	וּלְכָל־בְּשָׂרוֹ מַרְפֵּא	and healing to the whole of one's body.	
23a	מִכָּל־מִשְׁמָר נְצֹר לִבֶּךָ	More than anything to be protected, guard your heart,	2. The Headquarters of the Moral Anatomy (4:23)
23b	כִּי־מִמֶּנּוּ תּוֹצְאוֹת חַיִּים	for from it flow the sources of life.	
24a	הָסֵר מִמְּךָ עִקְּשׁוּת פֶּה	Keep a crooked mouth away from yourself,	3. The Movements of the Moral Anatomy (4:24–27)
24b	וּלְזוּת שְׂפָתַיִם הַרְחֵק מִמֶּךָּ	and remove devious lips far from you.	
25a	עֵינֶיךָ לְנֹכַח יַבִּיטוּ	Let your eyes look straight ahead,	
25b	וְעַפְעַפֶּיךָ יַיְשִׁרוּ נֶגְדֶּךָ	and let your pupils look straight in front of you.	
26a	פַּלֵּס מַעְגַּל רַגְלֶךָ	Watch the path of your feet,	
26b	וְכָל־דְּרָכֶיךָ יִכֹּנוּ	so that all your ways may be sure.	
27a	אַל־תֵּט־יָמִין וּשְׂמֹאול	Do not turn aside to the right or to the left;	
27b	הָסֵר רַגְלְךָ מֵרָע	keep your foot away from evil.	

They indicate that wisdom's way is an embodied way of life, a liturgy in which one's body synchronizes with one's character, orientation, movements, way, and telos.

Explanation of the Text

1. Introductory Exhortation (4:20–22)

In conventional fashion, the lecture opens with a formal exhortation, which includes both admonitions and a motivation. The structure and rhetoric of the exhortation illuminates the parent's pedagogical penchant for repetition, as the introduction follows the design and reiterates key terms of other instructions.

a. The Admonitions (4:20–21)

The introductory exhortation commences with admonitions that seek to awaken the son's organs of reception, adjust his posture, and encourage the retention of the parent's words. This is a familiar approach. The call to receive and retain instruction is a hallmark of the exordia within the parental lectures. And the terms employed in this call are reminiscent of introductory exhortations elsewhere in Prov 1–9. The invitation to "listen attentively" (הַקְשִׁיבָה, v. 20a) recurs in 2:2; 4:1; 5:1; and 7:24; and similar to 5:1 (cf. 2:2), this invitation is cast in parallel relationship with the expression "incline your ear" (הַט־אָזְנֶךָ, v. 20b). The command "they must not escape from your eyes" (אַל־יַלִּיזוּ מֵעֵינֶיךָ, v. 21a)[4] reiterates 3:21. The call to "keep" (שְׁמֹר־, v. 21b) the parent's words or commandments is repeated in 4:4; 7:1; and 7:2. And the description of the heart as the storehouse of wisdom and parental instruction is reflected in 2:10; 3:1; 4:4; and 4:21b. The admonitions within the introductory exhortation recycle terms, expressions, and concepts from exordia elsewhere in the prologue. This pattern of repetition suggests that the principle serves as an important pedagogical technique within the lectures.[5] Repetition shapes receptivity to the instruction and creates a pedagogical experience of reliability.

In addition to the use of repetition for the sake of cultivating receptivity, the admonitions seek to form the addressee's posture or orientation. Anticipating the commands within the lesson proper (vv. 24–27), the admonitions focus on particular body parts. They move from ears attentive to the parent's sayings, to vigilant eyes, to a heart that preserves their counsel. The admonitions develop from attending to the parent's words to internalizing them. In so doing, these admonitions seek to do much more than encourage the reception and retention of the parent's instruction. In view of their attention to particular body parts, they also attempt to shape the posture and orientation of the addressee. That is, they attempt to synchronize the son's anatomy with his attitude.

b. The Motivation (4:22)

The motivation for assuming the attitude and posture delineated in the admonitions is presented in v. 22. This motivation is introduced by the conjunction "for" (כִּי, v. 22a), which opens a causal

4. In contrast to Fox (*Proverbs: An Eclectic Edition*, 111), it is unnecessary to emend the *hiphil* יליזו to the *qal* ילוזו, for the form appears to be an internal *hiphil* of לוז. GKC §72ee; *IBHS* §27.2f; Waltke, *Proverbs: Chapters 1–15*, 293n2; Loader, *Proverbs 1–9*, 225n2.

5. Yoder, "Forming 'Fearers of Yahweh,'" 172–79.

clause that provides the rationale for heeding the admonitions within vv. 20–21. The reception and retention of the parent's words is attractive, for these words are a source of life as well as an agent of health and healing to one's body. Whereas elsewhere in the prologue "life" (חַיִּים) is the reward of those who find Wisdom (8:35; cf. 3:18, 22; 4:13), here the parent's words provide life to those who find them (v. 22a). Again, the parent associates his words with Wisdom; the reward for finding and retaining the parent's words is the same as the reward for finding Wisdom: life. This life is elaborated upon in v. 22b. Here the parent's words are portrayed as an instrument of healing. They preserve the health and restore the body of anyone who finds them. When one orients the body to the parent's words and stores them in the middle of one's heart, these words sustain one's health and cure one's body. Similar to the introductory admonitions and the lesson that follows, the motivation relates the parent's teaching with the body. The two cannot be separated. The teaching received by the ear, monitored by the eyes, and stored in the heart affects one's body and health.

2. The Headquarters of the Moral Anatomy (4:23)

The health of one's external, physical frame, however, is dependent upon the protection of one's inner being. Storing the words of the parent in the heart is not enough. The heart must also be "protected" (מִשְׁמָר, v. 23a) from internal and external threats; that is, it must be controlled and restrained from evil attitudes, schemes, and actions.[6] The importance of this surveillance is signaled by the comparative construction "more than anything" (מִכָּל, v. 23a), which opens the verse. The heart takes priority over any other object of protection. This is not surprising, for the heart is the center of the human being in Israelite thought. It is situated at the center of the parent's lecture. And from a syntactical perspective, the command to guard the heart is the center of v. 23; it is framed by the comparative construction, on the one hand (v. 23a), and a rationale or motivation, on the other (v. 23b). Whereas the former is cast at the beginning of the verse to highlight the significance of the command, the latter is situated at the end of the verse to substantiate the command.

As the literary hinge of the lecture, v. 23 looks back to the introductory exhortation (vv. 20–22) as well as forward to the lesson proper (vv. 24–27). It reiterates and recasts specific roots and terms from vv. 20–22. Just as the son was commanded to "keep" (-שָׁמְר, v. 21b) the parent's words in his "heart" (לֵבָב, v. 21b) because they are a source of "life" (חַיִּים, v. 22a), so now he is commanded to guard his "heart" (לֵב, v. 23a) above anything that is to be "protected" (מִשְׁמָר, v. 23a) because from it flows the sources of "life" (חַיִּים, v. 23b). The command moves from storing the parent's words in the heart to protecting the heart, and from a description of the life associated with the parent's words to the sources of life that flow from the heart. These "sources of life" (תוֹצְאוֹת חַיִּים, v. 23b) spill out in vv. 24–27 through specific parts and movements of the body. These movements illustrate the way in which the heart controls and directs the members of the body, manifesting life along the way of wisdom. The heart gives what it receives. When it accepts and protects the parent's teaching, life flows through one's members and manifests itself in one's movements.

6. Fox, *Proverbs 1–9*, 185; Waltke, *Proverbs: Chapters 1–15*, 297–98.

3. The Movements of the Moral Anatomy (4:24–27)

The members of the body and the life manifested through their movements are the focus of attention throughout vv. 24–27. This final section of the lecture is framed by the imperative "keep . . . away" (הָסֵר, vv. 24a, 27b); it is united by a concern with specific body parts; and the orientation of these body parts are described through terms and images pertaining to the root metaphor of the way. The dyad of posture and way encouraged by the parent is straight. This dyad straight of posture and path is sketched through three particular body parts: the lips, the eyes, and the feet, each of which deserve specific comment.

The parent opens this paradigmatic portrait of the moral anatomy with a pair of commands concerning one's "mouth" (פֶּה, v. 24a) and "lips" (שְׂפָתַיִם, v. 24b). These organs function as a synecdoche for speech. The parent combines them with directional terms and spatial images redolent of the path metaphor in order illuminate the relationship among one's body, one's speech, and one's way. A "crooked mouth" (עִקְּשׁוּת פֶּה, v. 24a) and "devious lips" (לְזוּת שְׂפָתַיִם, v. 24b)[7] are forms of speech that deviate from the way of wisdom and life (8:8). They mirror the character, speech, and way of the scoundrel (6:12). They distort wisdom and depart from what is right. And they represent the alternative to the straight talk and straight ways of the upright (3:6; 4:11; 11:5; 15:21). Just as the way of wisdom is straight, so also one's mouth, lips, and speech must be straight. To cultivate this posture and mode of discourse the parent intensifies the commands; he moves from staying away from these perverse forms of speech to removing them from oneself. And he strengthens the commands with a spatial expression. These deviant types of speech are not to be kept at arm's length; they are to be removed "far away from you" (הַרְחֵק מִמֶּךָּ, v. 24b). The parent delivers a polished pair of commands; he combines body parts with spatial images and terms associated with the way in order to form a posture and mode of speech that is straight and in accord with the way of wisdom and life.

The same is true in the second pair of commands, which focus on the eyes (v. 25). Straight talk along the straight way corresponds with a straight gaze. Again, the parent seeks to synchronize the body with one's direction and path. The expressions "your eyes" (עֵינֶיךָ, v. 25a) and "your pupils" (עַפְעַפֶּיךָ, v. 25b)[8] open each line. They are foregrounded to highlight the organs of sight. And each line includes a term or phrase for straightness that captures the line of sight. While the initial line expresses straightness through the adverbial qualifier "straight ahead" (לְנֹכַח, v. 25a), the second line employs the verb "look straight" (יַיְשִׁרוּ, v. 25b). Similar to straight speech, a straight gaze reflects one's posture, orientation, and way.

The final verses of the lecture focus on the orientation and movements of the third body part: the feet (vv. 26–27). Whereas the path metaphor was implicit in the previous commands, it is explicit in v. 26. Similar to YHWH (5:21) and in contrast to the adulterous woman (5:6), the son must "watch" (פַּלֵּס, v. 26a) or observe the way on which his feet

7. The noun "devious" (לְזוּת, v. 24b) is a *hapax legomenon*. Whether the noun is a derivative of לזה or a by-form of לוז, context in general and the parallel noun "crooked" (עִקְּשׁוּת, v. 24a) in particular suggest that the term refers to duplicitous or deceitful speech. For discussion of the root, see Fox, *Proverbs 1–9*, 187; Loader *Proverbs 1–9*, 228.

8. While the LXX and the Syria Peshitta read "your eyelids," evidence from Ugarit and Qumran suggest the expression refers to "your eyeballs" or "your pupils." Irrespective of the precise nuance of the expression, the sense of the line remains clear. For discussion, see Fox, *Proverbs 1–9*, 187; Loader *Proverbs 1–9*, 228.

trod. The command serves as a logical counterpart to v. 25. As one fixes one's gaze straight ahead toward a particular telos, one must watch the way one travels. The result of straight sight and vigilant attention to one's path is ways that are "sure" (יִכֹּנוּ, v. 26b) or established (cf. 21:29). While the verb in 4:26b may be read as an imperfect, in light of the use of volitionals in vv. 24–27, it appears to be a jussive. And since the jussive follows the imperative in v. 26a, it expresses the assurance or certain result of careful observance of one's path.[9] Sure ways are the reward of those who synchronize their sight and feet with the straight path.

This concern with aligning the feet with the straight path is reinforced by v. 27. The parent encourages movement along the right way through a negative admonition and a positive command. The negative admonition reiterates the verbal root from v. 20b. The parent combines this root with the merism "to the right or to the left" (יָמִין וּשְׂמֹאול, v. 27a), urging the son to remain on the straight path. This prescription is elaborated upon in the positive command, which complements and clarifies the negative admonition. Here the parent reiterates the imperative from v. 24a. In addition to a crooked mouth, the son is to keep his foot away from evil. To swerve to the right or the left is to deviate from the right way. The avoidance of evil is contingent on feet that are fixed on the straight way. And the proper orientation of one's foot is contingent on a protected heart. When viewed against the backdrop of the whole, the lecture ends where it began: with a verbal root that focuses on the proper posture and orientation of a body part (vv. 20b, 27a). And the lesson ends where it began: with an imperative urging the son to keep his members away from movements that stray from the straight path (vv. 24a, 27b).

Canonical and Theological Significance

The body is integral to a life lived in accord with the way of wisdom. Wisdom is, after all, not only an intellectual quality; it is also an embodied way of life. This embodied way of life is the focus of attention in Prov 4:20–27. The body receives parental wisdom through the organs of reception; it stores and protects this wisdom in the headquarters of the heart; and the heart releases this wisdom and displays the manifestations of life as it directs the external members and movements of the body along the straight path. The lecture's attention to the moral anatomy indicates that Proverbs is interested in much more than the formation of one's character, desires, worldview, and way; it is also interested in the formation of one's being.

This interest in the body, however, is not novel. Body parts play a formative role in the educational program of many ancient Near Eastern instructional texts. The demotic instructions of Ankhsheshonq, for example, observe that a person's character is "on his face" as well as "one of his limbs."[10] The body reveals one's disposition; it is a walking advertisement of one's way. In the same way, the mouth reveals one's inner attitude, the core of one's character. Together with the preponderance of commands

9. GKC §110f.

10. "The Instruction of Ankhsheshonq" (*AEL* 3:168).

pertaining to controlling one's mouth and guarding one's speech in ancient Near Eastern instructional tradition,[11] many texts link the heart or belly with the mouth. According to Ptahhotep, the heart of the wise and great match their tongue.[12] In the initial chapter of his work, Amenemope encourages the addressee to bolt the words of his instruction to the heart so that they might serve as a mooring post for the tongue.[13] And in the final chapter of his work, he urges the addressee to put the words of the instruction in his heart.[14] In light of this relationship between the heart and the mouth, it is not surprising that, in the manner of Prov 4:23, Ahiqar commands his nephew to guard his mouth more than anything else.[15] Just as the body reveals one's character, so also the mouth reveals the heart. They are inextricably linked. While actions may speak louder than words, words illuminate the nature and state of one's internal transmitter, the heart.

Interest in the body in general and the relationship between the heart and the mouth in particular is reflected throughout ancient Near Eastern instructional tradition. And interest in the body as well as the relationship between the heart and the mouth is reflected throughout Proverbs. Many sayings within the central collections of Proverbs focus on the members and movements of the moral anatomy. Similar to Prov 4:23–24, several sayings indicate that the heart instructs and directs the mouth (15:28; 16:23). Just as the son is called to guard his heart, so also particular proverbs call the reader to guard their mouth (13:3; 21:23), for just as the sources of life flow from the heart (4:23), so also life springs from the lips and tongue (10:11; 14:3; 15:4; 18:21). The crooked speech prohibited by the parent is profiled through the perverse speech of the wicked and the fool in chs. 10–29 (10:32; 18:6–7; 19:28). And the movements of the feet commended by the parent are illustrated through the depiction of the wise within the central collections (14:16; 16:17; cf. 13:19). Whereas the materials in these central collections focus on the way in which one's body parts reveal one's character, the instructions in Prov 4:23–27 focus on the way in which one's body parts reveal one's path. The materials in chs. 10–29 complement the parental lecture, illuminating the interplay among one's posture, orientation, movements, path, and character.

Together with Proverbs, the members and movements of the moral anatomy are explored elsewhere in the canon. Job diagnoses his character and way through explicit attention to the internal and external members of his body—his heart, foot, hands, and mouth (Job 31:1–40). Jesus declares that the mouth serves as the megaphone for the heart; it reveals the essence of one's character (Matt 12:34; 15:8; Luke 6:45). And from a more general perspective, Paul indicates that Christ's life is manifested

11. See, for example, "The Counsels of Wisdom" (*BWL* 101, 105); "The Instruction of Ptahhotep" (*AEL* 1:65, 75); "The Instruction of Papyrus Insinger" (*AEL* 3:202).

12. "The Instruction of Ptahhotep" (*AEL* 1:73).

13. "The Instruction of Amenemope" (*AEL* 2:149).

14. "The Instruction of Amenemope" (*AEL* 2:162).

15. "Ahiqar" (*OTP* 2:500).

through the Christian's body (2 Cor 4:10–11). That is, the body displays the redemptive life accomplished through Christ; and its members function as instruments of righteousness that project God's glory (Rom 6:13; 1 Cor 6:20). The body and its parts are not trappings that play a trivial role in the wise life; they are a fundamental part of the wise life. They serve as a window into one's character and a mirror that reveals one's orientation and way.

Wisdom is an embodied way of life. And this way of life is written on the body and reflected through the movements of its members. The parent's attention to moral anatomy in Prov 4:20–27 highlights the importance of the body in the wise life. In the same way, the lecture provides a healthy corrective to disembodied conceptions of the way of wisdom and the Christian life. For some, the way of wisdom is an intellectual quest, and the Christian life is a doctrinal checklist. The mind, of course, is important; and Christian doctrine is indispensable. But wisdom and the Christian life are more than this. They are more than the life of the mind. And they are more than intellectual assent to particular doctrines and confessions. Both are embodied. Both are written on one's body. Both are manifested through one's members. According to Prov 4:23–27, the body reveals one's heart; the parts of the body reveal one's path. The way of wisdom and the Christian life are not disembodied; they are embodied. They are not theoretical; they are actual. The body wears one's character, and its members as well as its movements illustrate its master as well as its way.

CHAPTER 10

Proverbs 5:1–23

I. Wisdom and Sexuality

Main Idea of the Passage

Through provocative images and polysemic language, the parent taps into primal desires, passions, and fears to warn the son of the dangers of adultery and to persuade him to find satisfaction in his wife as well as the way of wisdom.

Literary Context of the Passage

Women play a significant role in Prov 1–9. As one of the prominent symbols within the prologue, they serve as an effective pedagogical device, a means to explore the interrelationship among one's desires, character, commitments, and way. This is the case in Prov 5:1–23. The didactic poem contributes to the worldview and pedagogical agenda of the prologue through a graphic description of the strange woman as well as one's wife. It enhances the vignette sketched in 2:16–18, painting an impressionistic portrait of the speech, taste, touch, way, and house of the strange woman. It integrates erotic language from the previous discourses in order to relate one's commitment to and embrace of Lady Wisdom with one's commitment to and embrace of the strange woman (5:20; 4:8). It builds on 4:20–27 by attending to the movements and moral anatomy of the adulterous (5:3–6). And it sets the stage for 6:20–35 and 7:1–27, each of which elaborates upon the character, seductive rhetoric, and way of this femme fatale. The lecture devotes considerable attention to one of the dominant symbols within the prologue. It develops the description of the strange woman in 2:16–18 and foreshadows her depiction in both 6:20–35 and 7:1–27.

The interrelationship among these texts, however, should not overshadow the unique contribution of 5:1–23 within Proverbs. In contrast to 2:16–18, 6:20–35,

I. Introduction to the Book (1:1–7)
II. The Value of Wisdom and Virtue (1:8–9:18)
- A. Wisdom, Desire, and Different Ways (1:8–19)
- B. Wisdom's Rebuke (1:20–33)
- C. The Procurement, Power, and Protection of Wisdom and Virtue (2:1–22)
- D. Wisdom and Piety (3:1–12)
- E. Wisdom's Value and Moral Obligations (3:13–35)
- F. Wisdom and Tradition (4:1–9)
- G. Wisdom and Ways of Life (4:10–19)
- H. Wisdom and the Moral Anatomy (4:20–27)
- ➦ **I. Wisdom and Sexuality (5:1–23)**
  - **1. Introductory Exhortation (5:1–2)**
    - **a. The Admonitions (5:1)**
    - **b. The Motivation (5:2)**
  - **2. The Price of Sexual Promiscuity (5:3–14)**
    - **a. The Danger: A Portrait of the Strange Woman (5:3–6)**
    - **b. The Renewed Exhortation (5:7–8)**
    - **c. The Price of Promiscuity (5:9–14)**
      - **(1) The Social Price (5:9)**
      - **(2) The Economic Price (5:10)**
      - **(3) The Physical Price (5:11)**
      - **(4) The Emotional Price (5:12–14)**
  - **3. The Satisfaction of Marital Sex (5:15–20)**
    - **a. A Wellspring of Satisfaction (5:15–18)**
    - **b. An Enchanting Doe (5:19–20)**
  - **4. The Conclusion: Divine Omniscience and the Retribution Principle (5:21–23)**
    - **a. The Rationale: YHWH's Omniscience (5:21)**
    - **b. The Reward (5:22–23)**
- J. Wisdom, Lending, Laziness, and the Immoral Anatomy (6:1–19)
- K. Wisdom, Desire, and Certain Destruction (6:20–35)
- L. Wisdom and Seduction (7:1–27)
- M. Wisdom's Call, Credentials, and the Cosmos (8:1–36)
- N. Wisdom and Folly's Invitations (9:1–18)

III. "Forming 'Fearers of YHWH'": The Curriculum of Wisdom and Virtue (10:1–29:27)
IV. The Application of Wisdom and Virtue (30:1–31:31)

and 7:1–27, the lecture counterbalances the dangers of illicit sexual activity with the delights of marital sex. While each of the texts devoted to the strange woman admonish the addressee to avoid the adulterous, only 5:15–19 describe the alternative: the satisfaction of sexual desire within the confines of marriage. This alternative sets commitment to and intercourse with the strange woman against commitment to and intercourse with one's wife. And the antithesis between the strange woman and one's wife is reflected in the antithesis between Lady Wisdom and Woman Folly (9:1–6; 13–18). While these antitheses operate at different levels within the discourse, it appears that they are organically related. One's commitment to one's wife reflects one's commitment to Lady Wisdom and her way, whereas one's commitment to the strange woman reflects one's commitment to Woman Folly and her way. By offering an alternative to illicit sexual relations with the strange woman, 5:1–23 establish a female antithesis that is reflected at another level of the discourse. And by focusing on the appropriate context for sexual expression, the lecture contributes to Proverbs's vision of marriage. While many texts within the anthology describe the qualities and value of a good wife (11:16, 22; 12:4; 14:1; 18:22; 19:14; 31:10–31), only 5:1–23 describes the place of erotic love in the marital relationship. In so doing, the lecture addresses a significant aspect of the wise life and contributes to the document's discourse on marriage.

Translation and Exegetical Outline

(See pages 242–43.)

Structure and Literary Form

As a didactic poem, Prov 5:1–23 is comparable to the parental lectures elsewhere in the prologue; its introductory addresses (vv. 1a, 7a; cf. v. 20a), commands, motivations, and rationales suggest it is a form of instructional literature. The language and imagery of the poem, however, indicate that it also includes features reminiscent of another genre, namely, love poetry. In fact, the poem contains many images and expressions that are used in the Song of Songs (see the Explanation of the Text below). The correspondence between the poem and the Song illuminates the rhetorical and pedagogical agenda of the piece. While it incorporates elements characteristic of the instructional form, it is much more than an instructional text. The poem integrates and invokes the sensual imagery and erotic language of love poetry in order to capture the nature and consequences of appropriate and inappropriate objects of desire. The parent, so it seems, recognizes that proper desire cannot be directed by imperatives alone.

Proverbs 5:1–23

			I. Wisdom and Sexuality (5:1–23)
			1. Introductory Exhortation (5:1–2)
1a	בְּנִי לְחָכְמָתִי הַקְשִׁיבָה	My son, listen attentively to my wisdom;	a. The Admonitions (5:1)
1b	לִתְבוּנָתִי הַט־אָזְנֶךָ	incline your ear to my understanding,	
2a	לִשְׁמֹר מְזִמּוֹת ↑	↑ so that you may keep discretion,	b. The Motivation (5:2)
2b	וְדַעַת שְׂפָתֶיךָ יִנְצֹרוּ	and your lips may guard knowledge.	
			2. The Price of Sexual Promiscuity (5:3–14)
3a	כִּי נֹפֶת תִּטֹּפְנָה שִׂפְתֵי זָרָה	For the lips of the strange woman drip honey,	a. The Danger: A Portrait of the Strange Woman (5:3–6)
3b	וְחָלָק מִשֶּׁמֶן חִכָּהּ	and her palate is smoother than oil.	
4a	וְאַחֲרִיתָהּ מָרָה כַלַּעֲנָה	But her aftertaste is bitter as wormwood,	
4b	חַדָּה כְּחֶרֶב פִּיּוֹת	sharp as a two-edged sword.	
5a	רַגְלֶיהָ יֹרְדוֹת מָוֶת	Her feet descend to death,	
5b	שְׁאוֹל צְעָדֶיהָ יִתְמֹכוּ	her steps cling to Sheol;	
6a	אֹרַח חַיִּים פֶּן־תְּפַלֵּס	so that she does not watch the path of life,	
6b	נָעוּ מַעְגְּלֹתֶיהָ	her ways wander;	
6c	לֹא תֵדָע ↓	↓ she does not know.	
7a	וְעַתָּה בָנִים שִׁמְעוּ־לִי	So now, sons, listen to me,	b. The Renewed Exhortation (5:7–8)
7b	וְאַל־תָּסוּרוּ מֵאִמְרֵי־פִי	and do not depart from the words of my mouth.	
8a	הַרְחֵק מֵעָלֶיהָ דַרְכֶּךָ	Keep your way far from her,	
8b	וְאַל־תִּקְרַב אֶל־פֶּתַח בֵּיתָהּ	and do not come near to the door of her house,	
			c. The Price of Promiscuity (5:9–14)
9a	פֶּן־תִּתֵּן לַאֲחֵרִים הוֹדֶךָ	lest you give your splendor to others	(1) The Social Price (5:9)
9b	וּשְׁנֹתֶיךָ לְאַכְזָרִי	and your honor to the ruthless;	
10a	פֶּן־יִשְׂבְּעוּ זָרִים כֹּחֶךָ	lest strangers be filled with your strength	(2) The Economic Price (5:10)
10b	וַעֲצָבֶיךָ בְּבֵית נָכְרִי	and your toil end up in the house of an alien;	
11a	וְנָהַמְתָּ בְאַחֲרִיתֶךָ	and at your end you groan,	(3) The Physical Price (5:11)
11b	בִּכְלוֹת בְּשָׂרְךָ וּשְׁאֵרֶךָ ↑	↑ when your body and flesh languish	
12a	וְאָמַרְתָּ	and you say,	(4) The Emotional Price (5:12–14)
12b	אֵיךְ שָׂנֵאתִי מוּסָר	"How I hated discipline,	
12c	וְתוֹכַחַת נָאַץ לִבִּי	and my heart despised reproof.	
13a	וְלֹא־שָׁמַעְתִּי בְּקוֹל מוֹרָי	I did not listen to the voice of my teachers;	
13b	וְלִמְלַמְּדַי לֹא־הִטִּיתִי אָזְנִי	nor incline my ear to my instructors.	

14a	כִּמְעַט הָיִיתִי בְכָל־רָע	I have come to the brink of sheer calamity	
14b	↑ בְּתוֹךְ קָהָל וְעֵדָה	↑ in the assembly and congregation."	
			3. The Satisfaction of Marital Sex (5:15–20)
15a	שְׁתֵה־מַיִם מִבּוֹרֶךָ	Drink water from your own cistern,	a. A Wellspring of Satisfaction (5:15–18)
15b	וְנֹזְלִים מִתּוֹךְ בְּאֵרֶךָ	and running water from your well.	
16a	יָפוּצוּ מַעְיְנֹתֶיךָ חוּצָה	Should your springs flow about,	
16b	בָּרְחֹבוֹת פַּלְגֵי־מָיִם	water channels in the squares?	
17a	יִהְיוּ־לְךָ לְבַדֶּךָ	Let them be yours alone,	
17b	וְאֵין לְזָרִים אִתָּךְ	and not for strangers with you.	
18a	יְהִי־מְקוֹרְךָ בָרוּךְ	Let your fountain be blessed,	
18b	וּשְׂמַח מֵאֵשֶׁת נְעוּרֶךָ	and take pleasure from the wife of your youth,	
19a	↑ אַיֶּלֶת אֲהָבִים וְיַעֲלַת־חֵן	↑ a lovely hind, a graceful doe;	b. An Enchanting Doe (5:19–20)
19b	דַּדֶּיהָ יְרַוֻּךָ בְכָל־עֵת	her breasts should always satisfy you;	
19c	בְּאַהֲבָתָהּ תִּשְׁגֶּה תָמִיד	may you be intoxicated always by her love.	
20a	וְלָמָּה תִשְׁגֶּה בְנִי בְזָרָה	Why should you be intoxicated, my son, by a strange woman	
20b	וּתְחַבֵּק חֵק נָכְרִיָּה	or embrace the bosom of an adulteress?	
			4. The Conclusion: Divine Omniscience and the Retribution Principle (5:21–23)
21a	כִּי נֹכַח עֵינֵי יְהוָה דַּרְכֵי־אִישׁ	For a man's ways are before the eyes of YHWH,	a. The Rationale: YHWH's Omniscience (5:21)
21b	↓ וְכָל־מַעְגְּלֹתָיו מְפַלֵּס	↓ and he observes all his paths.	
22a	עֲוֺנוֹתָיו יִלְכְּדֻנוֹ	His iniquities will ensnare him,	b. The Reward (5:22–23)
22b	אֶת־הָרָשָׁע וּבְחַבְלֵי חַטָּאתוֹ יִתָּמֵךְ	and in the chords of his sin he will be caught.	
23a	הוּא יָמוּת בְּאֵין מוּסָר	He will die for lack of discipline,	
23b	וּבְרֹב אִוַּלְתּוֹ יִשְׁגֶּה	and in the abundance of his folly he will stray.	

So, he includes language and imagery redolent of love poetry so that the son may taste, see, and experience the bitter consequences of adultery, on the one hand, and the satisfaction of sex in the confines of marriage, on the other. The mixture of forms in the poem reveals its pedagogical agenda. It is neither an instructional text nor love poetry in the strict sense of the term. Rather, it is a combination of the two, a hybrid that blends elements of instruction with elements of love poetry to achieve a particular pedagogical result.

Together with the genre of the poem, its structure contributes to its pedagogical agenda. The piece may be divided into three basic sections. The first is a traditional introduction (vv. 1–2), which includes admonitions as well as motivations. The second provides the lesson proper (vv. 3–20).[1] This lesson consists of two distinct subunits. The initial subunit offers an extended description of the strange woman and the multifaceted consequences that follow from falling prey to her speech (vv. 3–14). The second subunit then incorporates vivid imagery and language to describe the delights of sexual activity with one's wife (vv. 15–20). Against the backdrop of these descriptions, the third and final section of the poem serves as a formal conclusion (vv. 21–23), which situates the teaching in a theological framework governed by YHWH's omniscience and the principle of retribution. Viewed as a whole, the introductory exhortation (vv. 1–2) and final warning (vv. 21–23) frame an extended discourse devoted to the dangers and delights of sexual desire. They invite one to experience via the discourse the fear and pain of unsanctioned desire as well as the joy and satisfaction of sanctioned desire.

The pedagogy and unity of the poem is also exhibited through the repetition of particular terms, wordplays, and references to the human body. In addition to the recurrent call to the son(s) (vv. 1a, 7a, 20a), the parent reiterates and recasts particular terms: "to incline the ear" (נטה אזן, vv. 1b, 13b), "lips" (שְׂפָתֵי, vv. 2b, 3a), "strange woman" (זָרָה, vv. 3a, 20a), "strangers" (זָרִים, vv. 10a, 17b), "aftertaste/end" (אַחֲרִית, v. 4a, 11a), "cling/be caught" (תמך, vv. 5b, 22b), "watch/observes" (פלס, vv. 6a, 21b), "listen" (שׁמע, vv. 7a, 13a), "way(s)" (דֶּרֶךְ, vv. 8a, 21a), "house" (בַּיִת, vv. 8b, 10b), "discipline" (מוּסָר; 12b, 23a), and "be intoxicated/stray" (שׁגה, vv. 19c, 20a, 23b). Together with the pervasive use of double entendre, the parent employs a wordplay on the "palate" (חֵךְ, v. 3b) and "bosom" (חֵק, v. 20b) of the strange woman. And the introduction as well as the lesson opens with various references to the human body (vv. 1–6). The recasting of repeated terms and references to body parts reveal the unity and pedagogy of the poem. They indicate that the parent's wisdom and the virtue of discretion are pivotal in the interpretation of the strange woman's speech, perception of her end, and protection against the ironic recitation of the parent's words in the context of public demise (vv. 12–14).

1. Meinhold, *Die Sprüche*, 1.100–101; Fox, *Proverbs 1–9*, 205; Loader, *Proverbs 1–9*, 233. While some read vv. 3–6 as an extended rationale within the introduction of the poem, it appears this rationale opens the lesson proper. In fact, it seems this rationale is frontloaded for rhetorical and pedagogical purposes. For discussion of the matter, see the explanation below.

Explanation of the Text

1. Introductory Exhortation (5:1–2)

Similar to the parental discourses elsewhere in the prologue, the poem opens with an introductory exhortation. And this exhortation includes admonitions and motivations that reiterate terms and expressions from other exordia in Prov 1–9. Far from modeling a brand of monotonous, even boring instruction, the standard introduction contributes to the parent's pedagogical agenda; it creates a pedagogical experience of familiarity and reliability; and it illuminates the parent's suasive intent, repetitive rhetoric, and commitment to inscribing the teaching on the memory of the addressee.[2]

a. The Admonitions (5:1)

Together with the introductory address to the son, the exhortation includes a pair of admonitions. These admonitions are both familiar and unusual. They are familiar in that the verbs and their corresponding objects occur elsewhere in the exordia of the parental discourses within the prologue. In fact, the invitation to "listen attentively" (הַקְשִׁיבָה, v. 1a) and "incline your ear" (הַט־אָזְנֶךָ, v. 1b) reiterates the introductory admonition of the previous lecture (4:20; cf. 2:2). And the objects of the verbs—"wisdom" (חָכְמָה, v. 1a) and "understanding" (תְּבוּנָה, v. 1b)—constitute a traditional word pair in Prov 1–9 (2:2, 6; 3:13, 19; 8:1). The admonitions are familiar. But they are also unusual in that that the objects include the first-person pronominal suffix "my." This does not occur elsewhere in Proverbs. In contrast to other exordia in the prologue, where the parent commands the addressee to listen to his "words," "sayings," "instructions," or "commands," here the father introduces his teaching with a distinct pair of terms. In so doing, he not only characterizes the teaching in the piece as a manifestation of wisdom and understanding, but he also indicates that this teaching has universal applicability (cf. 3:13, 19; 8:1).[3] It is neither limited to a particular time period nor restricted to a particular group. Similar to the exordia of the other parental discourses, the admonitions seek to inculcate receptivity in the addressee and form the posture necessary to receive the teaching. The inclusion of distinct objects to describe the teaching, however, produces a jarring effect. They intimate that the teaching is not trivial. It is significant.

b. The Motivation (5:2)

The significance of the teaching is reinforced by a pair of motivations, which are cast in the form of a result clause. As the head of the clause, the *lamed* + infinitive construct ("so that you may keep," לִשְׁמֹר, v. 2a) introduces the result of heeding the parent's wisdom and influences the rendering of the parallel imperfect verb "may guard" (יִנְצֹרוּ, v. 2b).[4] Reception of the parent's wisdom yields a twofold reward. The first is the retention of prudence or "discretion" (מְזִמּוֹת, v. 2a). In the context

2. For discussion of these didactic techniques in Deuteronomy, see Brent A. Strawn, "Keep/Observe/Do—Carefully—Today! The Rhetoric of Repetition in Deuteronomy," in *A God So Near: Essays on Old Testament Theology in Honor of Patrick D. Miller*, ed. B. A. Strawn and N. R. Bowen (Winona Lake, IN: Eisenbrauns, 2003), 215–40.

3. Fox, *Proverbs 1–9*, 190; Loader, *Proverbs 1–9*, 234.

4. For discussion of this phenomenon, see Fox, *Proverbs 1–9*, 191, as well as the explanation of 2:2.

of the poem, this virtue is invaluable, for it provides the addressee with the perception necessary to interpret the speech of others, to discern the consequences associated with one's actions, and to act accordingly. The second reward intensifies the first, as it moves from the internal preservation of discretion to the external protection of knowledge. While "lips" (שְׂפָתֶיךָ, v. 2b) may function as a metonymy for speech, suggesting that reception of the parent's wisdom will enable the addressee to speak appropriately, this reading does not exhaust the sense of the verset. Similar to the description of the moral anatomy in the previous lecture, the lips are the focus of attention. In fact, the lips are depicted as border agents.[5] They not only guard one's inner thoughts, preventing the inappropriate disclosure of knowledge, but they also protect one from the pseudo-wisdom of others. They are the gatekeepers that allow one to both keep discretion and guard knowledge.

2. The Price of Sexual Promiscuity (5:3–14)

The introductory exhortation and its concern with the ear and lips of the addressee sets the stage for the lesson proper and its initial concern with lips, palate, feet, and steps of the strange woman. As noted above, the lesson consists of two distinct subunits (vv. 3–14, 15–20). The first includes an impressionistic portrait of the strange woman (vv. 3–6), a renewed exhortation (vv. 7–8), and an extended account of the price of sexual promiscuity (vv. 9–14). The substance of each deserves specific comment.

a. The Danger: A Portrait of the Strange Woman (5:3–6)

Just as the lecture opened with unusual terms for the parent's teaching (v. 1), so also the lesson opens in an unusual way. In view of the rhetorical pattern of previous lectures, one would expect a sequence of parental commands pertaining to a particular issue or series of issues regarding wisdom and the wise life to follow the introductory exhortation. But this is not the case.[6] Instead, v. 3 begins with the conjunction "for" (כִּי, v. 3a), which governs an extended causal clause (vv. 3–6). This subordinate clause requires a main clause.[7] And the design of the poem identifies two possible candidates. On the one hand, the extended causal clause may be dependent upon the imperatives in v. 1. In this case, vv. 3–6 would complement the motivations in v. 2, offering a rationale for heeding the parent's wisdom within the introduction of the poem.[8] On the other hand, the extended causal clause may be dependent upon the parallel commands in v. 7.[9] In this case, the clause would foreground the rationale for heeding the parent's words in vv. 8–14. While both options are possible, the latter is preferred for two reasons. First, this pattern mirrors the syntac-

5. Van Leeuwen, "The Book of Proverbs," *NIB* 5:66.

6. It appears the LXX expected this pattern, for it inserts the clause "Do not pay attention to the base woman" (μὴ πρόσεχε φαύλῃ γυναικί) in v. 3a to govern the rationale introduced by "for" in v. 3b (γὰρ). In a similar fashion, Goldingay contends that the question posed in 5:20 originally stood between vv. 2–3, providing a transition to the topic of the strange woman and a clause to govern the subsequent rationale in v. 3 (John Goldingay, "Proverbs V and IX," *RB* 84 [1977]: 80–93). And in light of other passages devoted to the strange woman (2:16–18; 6:23–24; 7:4–5), each of which includes a promise of protection after the parent's introductory exhortation, Fox proposes a conjectural addition on literary grounds "to fill the logical gap between vv. 2 and 3" (*Proverbs: An Eclectic Edition*, 114–15). Among these proposals, the latter is especially appealing. But the addition of a statement between vv. 2 and 3 to solve an apparent logical issue fails to account for the rhetorical and pedagogical strategy of the parent (see below).

7. Alternatively, the conjunction may function as an asseverative (i.e., "indeed, surely, truly") and render the search for a main clause unnecessary. On contextual and logical grounds, however, the causal use of כִּי appears to make best sense.

8. Waltke, *Proverbs: Chapters 1–15*, 305, 307.

9. Loader, *Proverbs 1–9*, 233.

tical design of the poem's conclusion (vv. 21–23), which opens with a causal clause (v. 21) and then moves to a series of main clauses (cf. 1:2–7). And second, this proposal illuminates the rhetorical and pedagogical approach of the parent. By front-loading the rationale for heeding the instruction, the parent signposts its significance, answers the fundamental question "why does this matter?," and provides an incentive for accepting the material.[10] The introduction to the lesson proper is unusual. And it appears that this is precisely the point. It deviates from the traditional pattern, catches the listener or reader off guard, and highlights the importance of the teaching.

The teaching within this extended causal clause concerns the speech, orientation, and path of the strange woman.[11] This woman is dangerous. And her danger is profiled in two basic ways. The first is through her speech, taste, and touch (vv. 3–4). Similar to v. 2b, the "lips" (שִׂפְתֵי, v. 3a) of the strange woman serve as a metonymy for speech. The parent describes her speech through erotic imagery reminiscent of the Song of Songs. Just as the lips of the young woman "drip honey" (נֹפֶת תִּטֹּפְנָה; Song 4:11a), so also the lips of the strange woman "drip honey" (נֹפֶת תִּטֹּפְנָה; Prov 5:3a). Her lips and speech are sweet and appetizing. But they are also sticky; they neither satisfy one's hunger nor quench one's thirst.[12] The imagery and assonance of the expression suggest that the strange woman's lips are polysemous. They are sweet, sticky, and sexually appealing. Among these shades of meaning, the sexual appeal of the strange woman's mouth is accentuated in v. 3b. Whereas lips serve as a metonymy for speech, this is not the case with "palate" (חֵךְ, v. 3b), which refers to the inside of the mouth.[13] The term clarifies the erotic overtones in v. 3a, emphasizing the notion of taste. And when the smooth, oily palate of the strange woman is read alongside descriptions of the sweetness of the palate and its comparison to fluids flowing down the throats of lovers in the Song (5:16; 7:10[9]), it appears the eroticism of kissing is in view.[14] The parent paints a vivid, inviting portrait of the strange woman's mouth. Her lips, speech, and palate are smooth and appetizing. And her organs of love are attractive.

But appearances can be deceiving, and "liquids of delight" may prove to be dangerous.[15] Despite her promise and appeal, the parent indicates that the "aftertaste" (אַחֲרִית; Prov 5:4a) of the strange woman is bitter and sharp. Through the use of the *waw* adversative ("But"), the parent draws a sharp contrast between the flavor of the strange woman's mouth and the aftereffect of tasting her organs of love. While her lips appear to be sweet, she is "bitter as wormwood" (מָרָה כַלַּעֲנָה, v. 4a). In light of the fact that wormwood is often cast in parallel relationship with something poisonous elsewhere in the canon (Deut 29:17[18]; Jer 9:14[15]; Amos 6:12; Lam 3:19), it seems the term connotes the dangerous effects of the strange woman. She is toxic. And according to Prov 5:4b, she is sharp. While her palate appears to be smoother than oil, its aftertaste is sharp as a double-mouthed or "two-edged sword" (חֶרֶב פִּיּוֹת, v. 4b). What seemed smooth to the touch turns out to be a harsh, devouring bite. This vivid description of the aftertaste of the strange woman complements other texts that describe the seductive and destructive nature

10. Loader, *Proverbs 1–9*, 235.

11. For discussion of the strange woman, see 2:16–19.

12. Yoder, *Proverbs*, 62.

13. Meinhold, *Die Sprüche*, 1.102; Sæbø, *Sprüche*, 86; Loader, *Proverbs 1–9*, 235.

14. Loader, *Proverbs 1–9*, 235.

15. Yoder, *Proverbs*, 62.

of her discourse (2:16; 6:24; 7:5, 14–21). And this description illuminates the importance of heeding the parent's wisdom (5:1–2), for reception of this wisdom allows the addressee to exercise the powers of discretion, to perceive the nature of the strange woman's speech, and to arm his lips so that he may avoid her sweet lips and slippery palate.

In addition to the speech, taste, and touch of the strange woman, the parent describes her orientation and paths (vv. 5–6). This is the second way in which the parent profiles the danger of the strange woman. Similar to the description of her house in 2:18 (cf. 7:27), the strange woman's feet are oriented toward death. Her feet descend to death in the same way that her house sinks down to death (5:5a; 2:18). In fact, her steps "cling" (יִתְמֹכוּ; 5:5b) to Sheol; they lay hold of and march resolutely toward the underworld (cf. Ps 17:5).[16] To borrow a title track from AC/DC, the strange woman is depicted as one on a highway to hell. Her direction is dangerous. And the implicit implication is that those who embrace her will follow in her footsteps.

The orientation and footsteps of the strange woman correspond with her paths. These paths are outlined in 5:6. While the conjunction פֶּן is placed after the object (v. 6a), it opens a negative result clause, which qualifies v. 5b. The steps of the strange woman cling to Sheol (v. 5b). As a result, she does not "watch" (תְּפַלֵּס, v. 6a) the path of life. Whereas the parent urged the son to "watch" (פַּלֵּס; 4:26a) the path of his feet in the previous discourse, now he indicates that the strange woman does not "watch" the path he commended. She is headed in a different direction. Though the verb "watch" may be read as second-person imperfect, describing the son's failure to observe the path of life as a result of clinging to the strange woman, the shift to the second person within an extended third-person description of the strange woman would be intrusive. The third person makes good sense. The same is true of the expression "she does not know" (לֹא תֵדָע, v. 6c). Again, though the verb may be read as a second-person imperfect, identifying the son's failure to recognize the path on which he is traveling, the negative construction appears to describe the strange woman's lack of knowledge. Similar to the wicked in 4:19, this woman "does not know." She embodies and moves along a way marked by ignorance. And this ignorance is expressed through fact that her ways "wander" (נָעוּ, v. 6b). She meanders about, twisting and turning, charting a crooked course that ultimately ends in Sheol. With this description of the orientation and paths of the strange woman, the parent does not warn the son through an explicit explanation of the fate that will befall him should he embrace this femme fatale. Rather, in a manner similar to vv. 3–4, the parent offers an implicit warning through his ethical evaluation of this woman's orientation and path. She is a dangerous woman who walks a dangerous path that leads to a destructive end. The natural implication is that, should the son entertain this woman, he will be in grave danger.

b. The Renewed Exhortation (5:7–8)

In the event the addressee failed to catch this implicit warning, the parent delivers a pair of admonitions that clarify how the son(s) should respond to the threat of the strange woman. These admonitions follow a renewed exhortation and call to listen (v. 7). Against the backdrop of the extended description of the dangers of the strange woman (vv. 3–6), the parent reins in the imaginative digression and resumes direct discourse with the addressee. This resumption is introduced by the expression "So now" (וְעַתָּה, v. 7a; cf. 7:24; 8:32).

16. Fox, *Proverbs 1–9*, 192.

The expression establishes logical continuity with the introductory exhortation (5:1–2) and signals a shift in the rhetorical agenda of the lesson.[17] This continuity is expressed through the renewed call to listen, which recapitulates the admonitions in v. 1 and reorients the addressee's attention away from the mouth of the strange woman to the parent's "mouth" (פֶּה, v. 7b). And the vocative "sons" (בָנִים, v. 7a) reinforces the general applicability of the teaching announced in v. 1. The parent's wisdom is directed specifically to the son, but it remains applicable to all.

In addition to establishing logical continuity with the introductory exhortation, the expression "so now" also marks a shift in the rhetorical agenda of the lesson. This shift is apparent in v. 8. Here the parent moves from a description and ethical evaluation of the strange woman (vv. 3–6) to explicit advice concerning how one should respond to her. The woman is not named; rather, her description in vv. 3–6 is assumed through the use of pronominal suffixes. With the command not to depart from the parent's words still ringing in the addressees' ears (v. 7b), the father urges each son to depart from the strange woman (v. 8a). That is, in a manner reminiscent of 4:24, he commands the son to keep his way far from her (הַרְחֵק מֵעָלֶיהָ, v. 8a). Distance is key. And this distance is specified in v. 8b: the son should not go near "the door of her house" (פֶּתַח בֵּיתָהּ, v. 8b). Along with women, houses are among the "satellite images" within Prov 1–9; they are the symbols that orbit and inform the root metaphor of the way.[18] In view of the orientation and way of the strange woman (5:5–6) as well as the description of her house in 2:18 (cf. 7:8, 11, 27; 9:14), the rationale for the parent's injunction is clear: the door of this woman's home is the portal to death. And if, similar to 2:18, the parent employs a double entendre, then the warning includes more than the opening of her home; it also concerns the opening of her body, namely, her vagina.[19] Both are off-limits.

c. The Price of Promiscuity (5:9–14)

The rationale for these general admonitions is implicit in the description of the strange woman in vv. 3–6. Now the parent makes the rationale for keeping this woman at arm's length explicit. Through the powers of discretion and perception, he explains the devastating effects and personal consequences associated with sexual activity with the strange woman. The consequences are terrifying. And the price of promiscuity is high; it affects the social (v. 9), economic (v. 10), physical (v. 11), and emotional dimensions of one's life (vv. 12–14).

(1) The Social Price (5:9)

The social price of sexual promiscuity is presented in v. 9, which is cast in the form of a negative purpose clause ("lest," פֶּן, v. 9a). This negative purpose clause seeks to prevent the son from drawing near to the strange woman and the door of her house (v. 8). And it attempts to curb this behavior by describing the loss of social esteem that accompanies such promiscuous activity. This social esteem is expressed through the terms "splendor" (הוֹד, v. 9a) and "honor" (שְׁנֹתֶיךָ, v. 9b).[20] The former refers to one's majesty or dignity,[21] whereas the latter captures one's distinction. The terms overlap in

17. *IBHS* §39.3.4f.

18. Habel, "The Symbolism of Wisdom in Proverbs 1–9," 133–34, and the section entitled Root Metaphor in the introduction.

19. Alter, *The Art of Biblical Poetry*, 182.

20. Following Waltke and Loader, this rendering takes the noun as a derivative of III שׁנה, meaning "to be elevated, exalted." Waltke, *Proverbs: Chapters 1–15*, 312; Loader, *Proverbs 1–9*, 240.

21. For a clear explanation of why הוֹד does not refer to sexual vigor, see Loader, *Proverbs 1–9*, 240.

some respects, reflecting different aspects of one's social admiration and power. A rendezvous with the strange woman, however, will force the son to hand over these aspects of social admiration and power to others. To be specific, it will require the son to surrender these social powers "to the ruthless" (לְאַכְזָרִי, v. 9b), that is, to cruel individuals outside the family unit. The promise of sexual satisfaction will end with the relinquishment of social esteem.

(2) The Economic Price (5:10)

The surrender of social esteem is intimately related to the loss of one's assets (v. 10). The conceptual relationship between these losses is reflected in the syntactical structure of vv. 9 and 10. Similar to v. 9, v. 10 is cast in the form of a negative purpose clause; it opens with the conjunction "lest" (פֶּן, v. 10a) and includes parallel expressions for those outside of the domestic unit that will benefit from the son's base behavior. The benefits enjoyed by these outsiders are economic. They will be filled with the son's "strength" (כֹּחַ, v. 10a). The nature of this strength is clarified in v. 10b; it concerns the son's "toil" (עֲצָבֶי, v. 10b), his hard-earned produce and fortune (14:23). The energy exerted to achieve this fortune will be for naught, for this produce will end up in the hands of "strangers" (זָרִים, v. 10a) and "the house of an alien" (בֵית נָכְרִי, v. 10b). Entrance into the strange woman's house will require the son to fill the house of male strangers with the profit of his labor. Similar to v. 9, the expressions for these strangers are masculine. Their precise identity is ambiguous. And the details concerning the transfer of assets are obscure. But the personal, familial, and economic consequences of sexual indiscretion are crystal clear.

(3) The Physical Price (5:11)

Together with the loss of social esteem and economic assets, promiscuity takes a physical toll on one's body. This toll is due not only to the forfeiture of honor and the transfer of one's economic resources to strangers but also to the taste of the strange woman's mouth. The son's "end" (אַחֲרִית, v. 11a) represents a play on the "aftertaste" (אַחֲרִית, v. 4a) of the strange woman. This end does not refer to the imminent death of the son; rather, it concerns the outcome of his affair with the strange woman. When her sweet lips turn to wormwood and her oily palate devours his honor and assets, the son will "groan" (נָהַמְתָּ, v. 11a). The physical and painful nature of this groaning is captured by the temporal clause in v. 11b; the moaning will arise out of physical exhaustion, as the body languishes, perhaps by disease (cf. Job 33:21). Both body and flesh will pine away in pain. Far from simply affecting one's social status and economic resources, promiscuity has a physical price.

(4) The Emotional Price (5:12–14)

And this physical toll infiltrates and influences one's emotional condition (vv. 12–14). The psychological price of sexual promiscuity is dramatized through quoted speech in vv. 12–14. The parent puts words in the son's mouth. These words do not represent a confession of sexual indiscretion with the strange woman per se. The confession addresses a much more fundamental matter: remorse and regret for failing to seek wisdom. This concern with wisdom is reflected in the terminology of the confession, which recalls the exhortations within the poem as well as the exordia of the parental lectures elsewhere in the prologue (1:8, 23; 2:2; 4:1, 20; 5:1, 7; cf. 3:11). Rather than listening to the parent's discipline, inclining his ear to the father's teaching, and turning to Wisdom's reproof, the son will confess that he "hated discipline" (שָׂנֵאתִי מוּסָר; 5:12b), despised "reproof" (תוֹכַחַת, v. 12c), "did not listen" (לֹא־שָׁמַעְתִּי, v. 13a) to his teachers or incline his ear to his instructors (הִטִּיתִי אָזְנִי,

v. 13b).[22] The organs of reception are recast as the organs of rejection. And the responsive disposition and appropriate desires fostered by the parent are described through their antitheses: a hatred of instruction, a foolish disposition, and distorted desires (1:22; 15:5).

The avalanche of first-person indictments concerning the son's failure to seek wisdom culminate in 5:14, where he describes the ruin experienced at the end of his encounter with the strange woman. He will find himself on the brink of sheer calamity, in a dismal swamp of misery (v. 14a). This state will not be a private matter but rather a public affair, endured in the midst of the "assembly and congregation" (קָהָל וְעֵדָה, v. 14b). Private promiscuity climaxes in open shame. And this personal confession of open shame summarizes the consequences delineated in vv. 9–14: the loss of social honor (v. 9), the forfeiture of one's assets to those outside the family unit (v. 10), physical disintegration (v. 11), and psychological trauma (vv. 12–14).

3. The Satisfaction of Marital Sex (5:15–20)

In view of the danger of the strange woman and the price of sexual promiscuity, the parent shifts the discussion to the satisfaction that is found in this woman's positive counterpart: the son's wife. The satiation and delight of marital sex stand in sharp contrast to the deprivation and disaster caused by sexual engagement with the strange woman. This satisfaction is described through two basic metaphors: a wellspring and a doe. Each image recalls the love poetry of the Song of Songs. And each deserves specific comment.

a. A Wellspring of Satisfaction (5:15–18)

Just as the parent incorporated images from the Song to describe the attractive yet deceitful nature of the strange woman, so also he includes expressions and images from the Song to describe the satisfaction of sexual intercourse in the context of marriage. He counterbalances the danger of promiscuous sexual expression with the delights of marital sex. This delight is conceptualized in vv. 15–18 through images of water from distinctive sources, each of which represents the wife. This water both satisfies and stimulates one's thirst. In light of these powers, the parent invites the son to drink water "from your own cistern" (מִבּוֹרֶךָ, v. 15a) and running water "from your own well" (מִתּוֹךְ בְּאֵרֶךָ, v. 15b). Whereas the former is a basin in which rainwater is collected and preserved, the latter is a shaft through which underground water may be drawn. Both offer refreshment. The same is true of one's wife. She is a personal source of fulfillment. Similar to the lover in the Song, the wife is depicted as a well of fresh or living water (Song 4:15). And similar to the Song, drinking from her brings satisfaction and sexual enjoyment (Song 8:2).[23]

This notion is developed in v. 16 through additional images from the sphere of water: "springs" (מַעְיְנֹת, v. 16a) and "water channels" (פַּלְגֵי־מָיִם, v. 16b). Nonetheless, the precise nature of the development is unclear, for the verb "flow about"

22. The mention of "my teachers" (מוֹרָי, v. 13a) and "my instructors" (מְלַמְּדַי, v. 13b) may suggest the existence of formal educational institutions within ancient Israel in general and a school setting for the discourse in particular. In view of the semantic range of these terms, however, it is doubtful that they should be understood in a technical sense (i.e., school teachers) and to the exclusion of the parents and others within the community. Crenshaw, *Education in Ancient Israel*, 208; Fox, *Proverbs 1–9*, 198.

23. Michael V. Fox, *The Song of Songs and the Ancient Egyptian Love Songs* (Madison: University of Wisconsin Press, 1985), 138–39.

(יָפוּצוּ, v. 16a) may be understood in several different ways. Among other readings, it may be taken as a command (i.e., "let your springs flow about") or as a promise ("your springs will flow about"). But these readings are unlikely, since they assume that the water imagery related the wife in v. 15 now shifts to the man, describing his semen or its generative power to produce offspring. If the water imagery in vv. 16–17 is consistent with the imagery in v. 15, then it appears the wife is in view. In view of this referent, v. 16 may be read as an unmarked interrogative, raising a rhetorical question.[24] For some, this question assumes that sexual neglect of one's wife, that is, failure to drink from her well, will compel her to look elsewhere for satisfaction.[25] For others, it functions as a threat: if the son goes to the strange woman for satisfaction, then his unfaithfulness will be met with his wife's sexual exploitation by others.[26] This sort of tit-for-tat understanding of the question is consistent with Proverbs's view of retribution. But it may assume too much. The question is rhetorical. And if it is understood rhetorically, then it may be read in a way that does not presume the wife will allow her water channels to overflow in the public thoroughfares for consumption by others (cf. Song 4:12). It appears that the question turns the rhetorical tables on the son. Does he want his private water supply, his personal source of refreshment, to become a public watering hole? The obvious answer is, "Of course not." And the implication is that, just as he does not want his wife's springs refreshing strangers in the public square, so also he should not search for refreshment in the squares and seek satisfaction through the strange woman.

This idea is reinforced in v. 17, where the verb "let them be" (יִהְיוּ, v. 17a) takes the plural expressions "springs" and "water channels" as its antecedent. The wife's refreshing sources of water are the son's alone; they are not for others. Just as the wife's water supply is off-limits to "strangers" (זָרִים, v. 17a), so also the "strange woman" (זָרָה, v. 3a, 20a) is off-limits to the son. The jussive form of the verb conveys the parent's wish or desire. This desire for exclusive sexual satisfaction with one's wife may focus on the erotic needs of the husband at the expense of the wife. But it also expresses the desire for exclusive commitment and loyalty to one's wife. Finding satisfaction in one's wife alone is intimately related to one's absolute allegiance and fidelity to one's wife.

In view of this satisfaction within the confines of exclusive allegiance, the parent concludes his use of the water imagery with a blessing and a command (v. 18). The blessing concerns the wife, who is depicted as a "fountain" (מְקוֹר, v. 18a). Her blessing, however, is also the son's. Whereas v. 17 focused on the sexual satisfaction of the son at the expense of the wife, v. 18 focuses on both parties. Both will experience the blessing of sexual pleasure and gratification. The erotic nature of this blessing is clarified in v. 18b, which offers the denouement to the allegory in vv. 15–18. The source of water and refreshment is explicitly identified as "the wife of your youth" (אֵשֶׁת נְעוּרֶךָ, v. 18b). And the sexual gratification of the blessing is expressed through

24. Alternatively, following the LXX, the text may be emended to include a negative particle (Fox, *Proverbs 1–9*, 200; idem, *Proverbs: An Eclectic Edition*, 119–20). This particle would open a negative purpose clause ("lest your springs flow about"), which seeks to warn the son of the dangers involved in neglecting sex with his wife: if he fails to drink from her well, then she will search for satisfaction in the public thoroughfares.

25. Murphy, *Proverbs*, 32; Yoder, *Proverbs*, 66; Loader, *Proverbs 1–9*, 244.

26. Fox, *Proverbs 1–9*, 200–201; Van Leeuwen, "The Book of Proverbs," *NIB* 5:69.

the imperative "take pleasure" (שְׂמַח, v. 18b; cf. Song 1:4) as well as the preposition "from." The command urges the son to find joy and erotic pleasure in his wife, to draw "from" her water sources and receive satisfaction. If the son drinks from his own wife (Prov 5:15a), recognizing that she is for him alone (v. 17), then both he and his wife will be blessed with the delights of sexual enjoyment (v. 18).

Taken as a whole, the parent's use of water imagery to describe the satisfaction of sexual desire in the context of marriage creates a world of pleasure, fulfillment, refreshment, joy, and exclusive allegiance. In contrast to the honeyed lips and oily palate of the strange woman (v. 3), which neither quench one's thirst nor satisfy one's appetite, the son's wife is a depicted as a sustained source of satisfaction and pleasure.

b. An Enchanting Doe (5:19–20)

This satisfaction is amplified in v. 19. Similar to the preceding verses, the parent includes erotic imagery reminiscent of the Song and terms with connotations in the metaphorical domain of water. But the image of water no longer governs the discourse; rather, the parent shifts to an animal metaphor to further describe the wife. This shift in metaphor is accompanied by a shift in the poetic structure of the discourse. In contrast to the preceding and following lines of the poem, all of which are cast in the form of a distich, v. 19 is cast in the form of a tristich. The parent disrupts the balance of poetic parallelism. And this disruption illuminates the significance of the verse's content; it provides a condensed yet vivid description of the wife's beauty as well as the pleasure she brings to her husband.

This alternative description of the wife is cast in apposition to "the wife of your youth" (v. 18b). That is, it refers to and offers a more elaborate portrayal of the wife. This portrayal involves erotic animal images reminiscent of the Song. As a "lovely hind" (אַיֶּלֶת אֲהָבִים, v. 19a) and a "graceful doe" (יַעֲלַת־חֵן, v. 19a), the wife is considered beautiful, tender, and desirable (cf. Song 4:5). But she is much more than an object of desire; she is also able to quench and stimulate the son's desires. This is clarified in the remainder of the verse. Returning to the metaphorical domain of water, the parent invites the son to drink deeply from his wife's "breasts" (דַּדֶּי; Prov 5:19b)[27] and "love" (אַהֲבָת, v. 19c). Her nipples should serve as a frequent source of satisfaction and saturation (v. 19b). And her love should be imbibed to the extent that the son becomes "intoxicated" (תִּשְׁגֶּה, v. 19c). While the verb is used elsewhere in a negative sense, connoting a swerving or straying from proper boundaries, here it is viewed positively.[28] The parent invites the son to stray, overindulge, and lose himself in the luxury of lovemaking with his wife (cf. Song 5:1). As both an object of desire and one who is able to fulfill the son's desire, the wife is depicted as the source of sexual satisfaction and ecstasy.

In view of this reality, the parent poses the question in Prov 5:20: why would the son seek sexual satisfaction in the strange woman? The rhetorical question serves as a fitting conclusion to the lesson proper. The mention of the "strange woman" (זָרָה, v. 20a) creates an *inclusio* around the lesson; it ends where it began (v. 3a). The question reiterates the verb from v. 19c, pitting intoxication by one's wife against intoxication by the strange woman. And it offers an implicit comparison between the erotic

27. While "her breasts" may be revocalized as "her lovemaking," thus matching the construction in 7:18, the change is unnecessary in a text steeped in erotic language and sexual imagery. Loader, *Proverbs 1–9*, 247.

28. Fox, *Proverbs 1–9*, 203.

pleasure of the adulteress's "bosom" (חֵק, v. 20b) and the satisfaction found in the wife's breasts (v. 19b). While the question is rhetorical, its placement at the end of the lesson and its reiteration of particular terms and images indicates that it passes judgment on the strange woman. Against the backdrop of the parent's description of the wife, it appears that any thought of entertaining or engaging the strange woman is sheer lunacy.

4. The Conclusion: Divine Omniscience and the Retribution Principle (5:21–23)

The parent's extended assault on the son's senses and sexual desires culminates in a formal conclusion where the parent reflects more calmly on the implications of the teaching. This conclusion situates the discussion of wisdom and sexuality in a theological framework, governed by YHWH's omniscience and justice (vv. 21–23).

a. The Rationale: YHWH's Omniscience (5:21)

Similar to the lesson proper, the conclusion opens with the conjunction "for" (כִּי, v. 21a). This conjunction introduces a causal clause that provides a rationale for both the preceding lesson (vv. 3–20) as well as the following theological judgments (vv. 22–23). The rationale concerns YHWH's omniscience. And this omniscience is described through terms used elsewhere in the poem. The parent reinforces his earlier command to keep one's "way" (v. 8a) far from the strange woman with the theological assertion that all of one's "ways" (דַּרְכֵי, v. 21a) are before the eyes of YHWH. And he observes that while the strange woman does not "watch" (תְּפַלֵּס, v. 6a) the path of life, YHWH "observes" (מְפַלֵּס, v. 21b) and assesses every path. He sees and evaluates everything. Neither clandestine encounters with the adulteress nor sexual activities with one's wife are hidden from his sight. All is laid bare before his eyes. This reality places the content of the lesson into theological perspective. To be specific, it situates unsanctioned sexual intercourse with the strange woman as well as sanctioned sexual intercourse with one's wife under the purview of YHWH's gaze, concern, and maintenance of the cosmos.

b. The Reward (5:22–23)

In addition to providing a theological lens through which to understand the lesson proper, the causal clause serves as the basis for understanding the reward delineated in vv. 22–23. This reward focuses on the punishment experienced by the one who commits iniquity, despises discipline, and engages in illicit sex with the strange woman.[29] Similar to v. 21, it describes this punishment through terms used elsewhere in the poem. Just as the strange woman's steps "cling" (יִתְמֹכוּ, v. 5b) to Sheol, so also the one who entertains her will be ensnared by his iniquities and "caught" (יִתָּמֵךְ, v. 22b) in the chords of his sin. In accord with his hatred of "discipline" (מוּסָר, v. 12b), he will die for lack of "discipline" (מוּסָר, v. 23a). And by becoming "intoxicated" (תִּשְׁגֶּה, v. 20a) by the strange woman, rather than his wife (v. 20c), he will "stray" (יִשְׁגֶּה, v. 23b) in the abundance of his folly. The repetition of these terms links promiscuous sexual expression with one's punishment. More specifically, it defines illicit sex as sin and relates the punishment to the lack of discipline. Sex is the issue. But this issue is inextricably linked to wisdom and discipline.

29. While the MT includes the expression "the wicked" (אֶת־הָרָשָׁע, v. 22a) to clarify the third person masculine singular suffix "his" in v. 22a, in light of its absence in the LXX, it appears the expression is a gloss. This gloss was included to specify the person who will experience this punishment and distinguish this person from the one who finds sexual satisfaction in his wife (vv. 15–20). Fox, *Proverbs 1–9*, 204–5; Waltke, *Proverbs: Chapters 1–15*, 305n46.

Without them, one is in danger of transgressing appropriate boundaries and losing oneself in one's libido.

Like the conclusion to other parental lectures in the prologue, vv. 21–23 operate under a doctrine of retribution (cf. 1:17–19, 31–32). Under the observant eyes and evaluation of YHWH, he oversees the punishment of one's sin.[30] But in contrast to the conclusions of other parental lectures, the didactic poem does not counterbalance this negative punishment with a description of the positive reward. This, it seems, is unnecessary, for the reward is outlined throughout vv. 15–19. And the conclusion's exclusive attention to the consequences associated with despising discipline and engaging the strange woman serves as an effective pedagogical device. It leaves the son with a warning and a theological perspective that discourages illicit sexual expression.

Canonical and Theological Significance

Sex is an innate, carnal desire. This desire is acknowledged and directed in Prov 5 through an antithesis between the strange woman and one's wife. The strange woman is depicted as dangerous, off-limits, the instantiation of adultery, whereas the wife is portrayed as the object of commitment and the sanctioned means of sexual satisfaction. As noted above, the antithesis between the strange woman and one's wife mirrors the antithesis between Woman Folly and Lady Wisdom. One's desire for and commitment to Wisdom corresponds with one's desire for and commitment to one's wife. Wisdom and the boundaries of sexual expression are closely related. While sexual activity outside of these boundaries brings about social, economic, physical, and psychological ruin (vv. 9–14), sexual activity within these boundaries produces joy, delight, and satiation (vv. 15–20).

The didactic poem focuses on the proper object of sexual desire as well as the proper context for sexual expression. This concern with sex and the marital relationship is by no means unique. The issue of inappropriate or unsanctioned sexual activity will occupy the discourses in Prov 6:20–35 and 7:1–27. And the matter of marriage is developed throughout the subsequent collections in Proverbs. These collections include many sayings that complement 5:1–23. Whereas the parental discourse describes the place of erotic love in the marital relationship, materials elsewhere in the anthology describe the qualities and value of a good wife.

Among these materials, the qualities of a good wife are profiled in 11:16, 22; 12:4; and 14:1. Together, these aphorisms focus on the moral and intellectual virtues of an ideal wife. And these virtues are comparable to the moral and intellectual qualities of Lady Wisdom. Similar to Lady Wisdom, a noble wife possesses a gracious disposition that produces social honor and communal admiration (11:16; cf. 3:16; 8:18). She enhances the status of her husband (12:4; cf. 4:9; 31:23). She employs wisdom in the

30. Boström, *The God of the Sages*, 99.

management of her household (14:1; cf. 9:1; 24:3–4; 31:10–31). And she possesses a genuine, lasting form of beauty: inner rectitude (31:30; cf. 11:22).[31] No wonder she is considered a divine gift and a source of divine favor (18:22; 19:14; cf. 8:35).[32] These aphorisms build upon Prov 5:1–23, providing the addressee with an ethical framework for marriage preparation.[33] While the didactic poem focuses on the joy and satisfaction of marital sex (5:15–20), these sayings describe the qualities and value of a good wife.

The value of a good wife is enhanced by other sayings that reflect on the vexation caused by an ignoble wife. This type of wife is the subject of several aphorisms (19:13; 21:9, 19; 25:24; 27:15), each of which incorporates the term "quarrels" (מִדְיָן) with vivid images that illuminate the domestic environment produced by this woman.[34] The domicile of the disputatious wife is portrayed as a chaotic domain of constant assault (19:13; 27:15), a place of perpetual dissention and dissonance. In view of this tumultuous environment, the corner of a roof and the arid desert offer more peace and security than the home (21:9, 19; 25:24). These striking images provide an impressionistic portrait of a domestic environment that stands in contradistinction to the irenic home of a noble wife. Whereas a virtuous wife procures social honor, enhances the status of her husband, and forms the foundation of a stable home (11:16; 12:4a; 14:1a), a contentious wife produces personal torment and domestic conflict. These sayings contribute to the discourse on marriage preparation within Proverbs. They focus on the character and domestic environment fostered by an ignoble wife in order to place the qualities and value of a good wife into sharp relief.

The sayings within the central collections of the book do not represent the final word on the matter of marriage, however. The anthology's discourse on marriage preparation as well as its description of a good wife culminates in the climactic acrostic poem (31:10–31). This poem depicts a woman who stands in sharp contrast to the strange woman and embodies the characteristics of Lady Wisdom. It elaborates on earlier aphorisms concerning marriage preparation (11:16; 12:4; 14:1; 18:22; 19:14) to provide a veritable mosaic that delineates the fundamental features of a virtuous woman. This woman is the feminine embodiment of wisdom, the incarnation of moral nobility, and the paragon of the fear of YHWH. She is a rare find (31:10). But she remains the ideal wife described in Prov 5:15–20.

In addition to marriage, Prov 5:1–23 is concerned with sexual desire and sexual activity within appropriate boundaries. These matters are addressed elsewhere in

31. Knut M. Heim, "A Closer Look at the Pig in Proverbs xi 22," *VT* 58 (2008): 13–27, esp. 24–25; Fox, *Proverbs 10–31*, 541.

32. For an analysis of the comparable elements in Prov 18:22 and 8:35, see Daniel C. Snell, *Twice-Told Proverbs and the Composition of the Book of Proverbs* (Winona Lake, IN: Eisenbrauns, 1993), 39.

33. Heim, "A Closer Look at the Pig," 26.

34. For an analysis of the comparable elements in Prov 21:9, 19; 25:24, see Snell, *Twice-Told Proverbs*, 41, 58.

Proverbs as well as the canon of Scripture. The potent powers of sexual desire are explored throughout the Song of Songs. Similar to Prov 5:15–20, the Song creates a world of erotic passion and ecstatic pleasure in which exclusive commitment to one's covenant partner produces delight and satisfaction. Sex within these boundaries is portrayed as beautiful, wonder-full, and even mysterious (Prov 30:18–19). In contrast, sex outside of these boundaries is portrayed as dangerous (5:9–14), an overstepping of appropriate boundaries and a blatant violation of divine design (23:27–28; 30:20). Both Proverbs and the Song assume the boundary established in the decalogic command concerning adultery (Exod 20:14; Deut 5:18; cf. Gen 1:17–28; 2:21–24). Both elaborate on this command by describing the joy and fulfillment of sexual activity within the confines of marriage. And Prov 5 develops the severe consequences of transgressing the divine boundary, of failing to live in accord with the way of wisdom, and of violating the moral order YHWH has woven into the fabric of the cosmos (8:36).[35]

Illicit sexual activity mars the marital relationship, destroys the fabric of the household, and dissolves the foundations of the community (Mal 2:14). In accordance with Prov 5 and the witness of the canon, sexual desire is to be satisfied in a specific relationship and within a particular context. And sexual desire must be directed and disciplined by wisdom. This is a difficult task, for contemporary culture is inundated with sexual images and innuendos that constantly bombard Christians, calling them to break free from the boundaries of divine design. It is a culture in which autonomy and self-centered sexual desire are elevated above submission to and self-sacrifice for the benefit of one's partner. It is a culture in which lust trumps love, where compatibility, or the lack thereof, replaces commitment, and where one's personal, sexual proclivities determine the length of the relationship or the amount of sexual partners. The outward forms of temptation may be different in modern culture, but the danger remains the same. According to Prov 5, the consequences of unsanctioned desire and illicit sexual activity are devastating. The satisfaction of sexual desire in the confines of marriage, by contrast, is the epitome of delight.

35. Mark E. Biddle, *Missing the Mark: Sin and Its Consequences in Biblical Theology* (Nashville: Abingdon, 2005), 57.

CHAPTER

11

Proverbs 6:1–19

J. Wisdom, Lending, Laziness, and the Immoral Anatomy

Main Idea of the Passage

The parent evaluates the dangers associated with surety and indolence as well as the immoral anatomy of the scoundrel in order to inculcate perception, form the feelings of the addressee, and shape his character in accord with wisdom and virtue.

Literary Context of the Passage

In light of the parent's concern with sex and the strange woman in both the previous (5:1–23) and the subsequent discourses (6:20–35; 7:1–27), the placement of these epigrams pertaining to lending, laziness, and the scoundrel within the literary context of the prologue is rather puzzling. While these pithy poems include certain terms and themes deployed by the parent in the preceding discourse,[1] they do not provide a logical progression of thought within their immediate context. Moreover, they depart from the style and structure of the parental discourses elsewhere in the prologue.[2] On logical and formal grounds, it appears that they are out of place, poetic victims of a sloppy scribe who slipped them into an inappropriate literary locale.

From a logical and formal perspective, the placement of these epigrams in the literary context of the prologue is unclear. From a rhetorical and pedagogical perspective, however, their placement is rather apropos. Together, these epigrams interrupt the discourses concerning the strange woman (5:1–23; 6:20–35; 7:1–27). In so doing, they serve as a literary interlude and a pedagogical intermission on the

1. Plöger, *Sprüche Salomos*, 67; Meinhold, *Die Sprüche*, 1.108–9.

2. McKane, *Proverbs*, 320.

topic of sex.[3] They provide the addressee with a measure of pedagogical relief. They prevent the addressee from drifting off or blurring together the parent's distinctive discourses on sex. And they indicate that the wise life involves much more than avoiding sinners, evil people, and the strange woman. It also concerns economic

- I. Introduction to the Book (1:1–7)
- **II. The Value of Wisdom and Virtue (1:8–9:18)**
  - A. Wisdom, Desire, and Different Ways (1:8–19)
  - B. Wisdom's Rebuke (1:20–33)
  - C. The Procurement, Power, and Protection of Wisdom and Virtue (2:1–22)
  - D. Wisdom and Piety (3:1–12)
  - E. Wisdom's Value and Moral Obligations (3:13–35)
  - F. Wisdom and Tradition (4:1–9)
  - G. Wisdom and Ways of Life (4:10–19)
  - H. Wisdom and the Moral Anatomy (4:20–27)
  - I. Wisdom and Sexuality (5:1–23)
  - ➦ **J. Wisdom, Lending, Laziness, and the Immoral Anatomy (6:1–19)**
    - **1. Surety and Strangers (6:1–5)**
      - **a. The Dangerous Situation (6:1–2)**
      - **b. The Self-Deprecating Course of Action (6:3–5)**
    - **2. Industry and Indolence (6:6–11)**
      - **a. The Industry of the Ant (6:6–8)**
      - **b. The Indolence of the Sluggard (6:9–11)**
    - **3. A Sketch of the Scoundrel (6:12–19)**
      - **a. The Immoral Anatomy of the Scoundrel (6:12–14)**
      - **b. The Sudden Ruin of the Scoundrel (6:15)**
      - **c. A Register of Revulsion (6:16–19)**
        - **(1) The Introduction (6:16)**
        - **(2) Abominable Body Parts (6:17–18)**
        - **(3) Abominable Character Types (6:19)**
  - K. Wisdom, Desire, and Certain Destruction (6:20–35)
  - L. Wisdom and Seduction (7:1–27)
  - M. Wisdom's Call, Credentials, and the Cosmos (8:1–36)
  - N. Wisdom and Folly's Invitations (9:1–18)
- III. "Forming 'Fearers of YHWH'": The Curriculum of Wisdom and Virtue (10:1–29:27)
- IV. The Application of Wisdom and Virtue (30:1–31:31)

3. Loader, *Proverbs 1–9*, 251.

matters (6:1–5), neighborly relations (6:1–5), the avoidance of indolence (6:6–11), the recognition of the scoundrel (6:12–15), and an understanding of those attitudes, actions, and personas that evoke divine disgust (6:16–19).

In addition to the rhetorical and pedagogical role of these epigrams in their immediate literary context, each poem addresses issues developed elsewhere in Proverbs. The epigram pertaining to the immoral anatomy of the scoundrel (6:12–15), for example, functions as the negative counterpart to the moral anatomy sketched in 4:23–27. And the poems devoted to surety (6:1–5) and indolence (6:6–11) introduce matters concerning the wise life that are unpacked and elaborated upon in the central collections within the anthology. Within the broader context of Proverbs, these epigrams resume its discussion of particular character types (1:8–19; 2:12–15; 4:14–19, 23–27) and introduce topics pertaining to the wise life that will be developed in the subsequent collections.

Translation and Exegetical Outline

(See pages 261–62.)

Structure and Literary Form

As intimated above, this pedagogical intermission includes four distinct units, each of which is cast in the form of an epigram. While epigrams may be cast in any mode, they tend to be "terse, pointed, and witty."[4] And they tend to function in a particular way: they are designed to evoke a sense of shock or surprise, which is then satisfied in an unexpected way.[5] The same may be said of the poetic units in Prov 6:1–19. In different ways, these epigrams create a sense of astonishment and then satisfy that incredulity with a particular resolution.

Though these epigrams may stand alone, in view of their shared terminology and imagery, it appears that they have been deliberately arranged in diametrically opposed conceptual pairs. The first pair is linked by the use of the vocative ("my son," בְּנִי, vv. 1a, 3a; "you sluggard," עָצֵל, vv. 6a, 9a), the command "go" (לֵךְ, vv. 3c, 6a), the terms "sleep" (שֵׁנָה, vv. 4a, 10a) and "slumber" (תְּנוּמָה, vv. 4b, 10a), the reference to the hand(s) (יָד, כַּף, vv. 1b, 3b, 5a, 5b, 10b), the concern with staying awake (vv. 4, 9), and animal imagery (vv. 5, 6–8; cf. v. 2). The second pair is bound together by its attention to body parts as well as its use of common verbs and expressions. In many respects, the final two epigrams are mirror images of one another (see chart on p. 263).

4. M. H. Abrams, *A Glossary of Literary Terms*, 11th ed. (Boston: Wadsworth; Cengage Learning, 2014), 84.

5. Abrams, *A Glossary of Literary Terms*, 339.

Proverbs 6:1–19

			J. Wisdom, Lending, Laziness, and the Immoral Anatomy (6:1–19)
			1. Surety and Strangers (6:1–5)
1a	בְּנִי אִם־עָרַבְתָּ לְרֵעֶךָ	My son, if you have given surety to your neighbor,	a. The Dangerous Situation (6:1–2)
1b	תָּקַעְתָּ לַזָּר כַּפֶּיךָ	shaken hands for a stranger,	
2a	נוֹקַשְׁתָּ בְאִמְרֵי־פִיךָ	ensnared yourself by the words of your mouth,	
2b	נִלְכַּדְתָּ בְּאִמְרֵי־פִיךָ ↓	↓ trapped yourself by the words of your mouth,	
3a	עֲשֵׂה זֹאת אֵפוֹא בְּנִי וְהִנָּצֵל	do this then, my son, in order to save yourself,	b. The Self-Deprecating Course of Action (6:3–5)
3b	↑ כִּי בָאתָ בְכַף־רֵעֶךָ	↑ for you have come into your neighbor's power:	
3c	לֵךְ הִתְרַפֵּס וּרְהַב רֵעֶיךָ	Go, humble yourself, and hassle your neighbor;	
4a	אַל־תִּתֵּן שֵׁנָה לְעֵינֶיךָ	do not give sleep to your eyes,	
4b	וּתְנוּמָה לְעַפְעַפֶּיךָ	nor slumber to your eyelids;	
5a	הִנָּצֵל כִּצְבִי מִיָּד	save yourself like a gazelle from someone's hand,	
5b	וּכְצִפּוֹר מִיַּד יָקוּשׁ	and like a bird from the fowler's hand.	
			2. Industry and Indolence (6:6–11)
6a	לֵךְ־אֶל־נְמָלָה עָצֵל	Go to the ant, you sluggard,	a. The Industry of the Ant (6:6–8)
6b	רְאֵה דְרָכֶיהָ וַחֲכָם	observe its ways, and become wise.	
7	↓ אֲשֶׁר אֵין־לָהּ קָצִין שֹׁטֵר וּמֹשֵׁל	↓ Although it has no leader, overseer or ruler	
8a	תָּכִין בַּקַּיִץ לַחְמָהּ	it prepares its food in summer,	
8b	אָגְרָה בַקָּצִיר מַאֲכָלָהּ	it gathers its fare during the harvest.	
9a	עַד־מָתַי עָצֵל תִּשְׁכָּב	How long, you sluggard, will you lie down?	b. The Indolence of the Sluggard (6:9–11)
9b	מָתַי תָּקוּם מִשְּׁנָתֶךָ	When will you rise from your sleep?	
10a	מְעַט שֵׁנוֹת מְעַט תְּנוּמוֹת	A little sleep, a little slumber,	
10b	מְעַט חִבֻּק יָדַיִם לִשְׁכָּב	a little folding of the hands to rest,	
11a	וּבָא־כִמְהַלֵּךְ רֵאשֶׁךָ	and poverty will come upon you like a vagabond,	
11b	וּמַחְסֹרְךָ כְּאִישׁ מָגֵן	and need like an armed warrior.	

Continued on next page.

Continued from previous page.

Verse	Hebrew	Translation	Outline
			3. A Sketch of the Scoundrel (6:12–19)
12a	אָדָם בְּלִיַּעַל אִישׁ אָוֶן	A scoundrel is a vile person,	a. The Immoral Anatomy of the Scoundrel (6:12–14)
12b	הוֹלֵךְ עִקְּשׁוּת פֶּה	who goes around with a crooked mouth,	
13a	קֹרֵץ בְּעֵינָו מֹלֵל בְּרַגְלָו	who winks with his eyes, who shuffles with his feet,	
13b	מֹרֶה בְּאֶצְבְּעֹתָיו	who signals with his fingers,	
14a	תַּהְפֻּכוֹת בְּלִבּוֹ	perversions are in his heart,	
14b	חֹרֵשׁ רָע בְּכָל־עֵת	he constantly plans evil,	
14c	מִדְיָנִים יְשַׁלֵּחַ	he stirs up strife.	
15a	עַל־כֵּן פִּתְאֹם יָבוֹא אֵידוֹ	Therefore his ruin will come suddenly;	b. The Sudden Ruin of the Scoundrel (6:15)
15b	פֶּתַע יִשָּׁבֵר וְאֵין מַרְפֵּא	he will be broken unexpectedly and without a remedy.	
			c. A Register of Revulsion (6:16–19)
16a	שֶׁשׁ־הֵנָּה שָׂנֵא יְהוָה	There are six things that YHWH hates,	(1) The Introduction (6:16)
16b	וְשֶׁבַע תּוֹעֲבַת נַפְשׁוֹ	even seven that are an abomination to him:	
17a	עֵינַיִם רָמוֹת לְשׁוֹן שָׁקֶר	haughty eyes, a lying tongue,	(2) Abominable Body Parts (6:17–18)
17b	וְיָדַיִם שֹׁפְכוֹת דָּם־נָקִי	and hands that shed innocent blood,	
18a	לֵב חֹרֵשׁ מַחְשְׁבוֹת אָוֶן	a heart that plans vile schemes,	
18b	רַגְלַיִם מְמַהֲרוֹת לָרוּץ לָרָעָה	feet that hasten to run to evil,	
19a	יָפִיחַ כְּזָבִים עֵד שָׁקֶר	a lying witness who blows out deceits,	(3) Abominable Character Types (6:19)
19b	וּמְשַׁלֵּחַ מְדָנִים בֵּין אַחִים	and one who stirs up strife between brothers.	

The Immoral Anatomy of the Scoundrel (vv. 12–15)	A Register of Revulsion (vv. 16–19)
"a crooked mouth" (עִקְּשׁוּת פֶּה, v. 12b)	"a lying tongue" (לְשׁוֹן שָׁקֶר, v. 17a)
"who winks with his eyes" (קֹרֵץ בְּעֵינָו, v. 13a)	"haughty eyes" (עֵינַיִם רָמוֹת, v. 17a)
"with his feet" (בְּרַגְלָו, v. 13a)	"feet" (רַגְלַיִם, v. 18b)
"with his fingers" (בְּאֶצְבְּעֹתָיו, v. 13b)	"hands" (יָדַיִם, v. 17b)
"in his heart" (בְּלִבּוֹ, v. 14a)	"a heart" (לֵב, v. 18a)
"he ... plans evil" (חֹרֵשׁ רָע, v. 14b)	"plans vile schemes" (חֹרֵשׁ מַחְשְׁבוֹת אָוֶן, v. 18a)
"he stirs up strife" (מְדָנִים יְשַׁלֵּחַ, v. 14c)	"one who stirs up strife" (מְשַׁלֵּחַ מְדָנִים, v. 19b)

These similarities suggest that, while each epigram conveys a distinct message, each piece may be read in relation to its counterpart. When they are read as two corresponding pairs, it seems that the first reflects on forms of behavior that threaten personal and social well-being;[6] the second indicates that the actions and attitudes of the scoundrel (vv. 12–14) epitomize that which YHWH despises (vv. 16–19).[7] Far from exhibiting haphazard arrangement, the sequence and shared terminology between the epigrams betray signs of deliberate design. The specific design of each epigram will be discussed under the section headings below.

Explanation of the Text

1. Surety and Strangers (6:1–5)

The initial poem is cast in the form of an extended condition; it consists of two parts: the protasis presents the dangers of going surety through a description of specific circumstances (vv. 1–2),[8] while the apodosis offers a solution to the dangerous situation through a sequence of admonitions (vv. 3–5). These parts are bound together syntactically. They are linked by the terms "hand(s)/power" (כַּף, vv. 1b, 3b; יָד, vv. 5a, 5b) and "neighbor" (רֵעַ, vv. 1a, 3c) as well as hunting imagery (vv. 2, 5). And the apodosis is framed by the verb "save yourself" (הִנָּצֵל, vv. 3a, 5a). These recurring terms and images highlight the dangers of going surety, heighten the emotional intensity of the poem, and contribute to its concern with perception in economic matters.

a. The Dangerous Situation (6:1–2)

As noted above, the poem opens with a protasis that describes the dangers of going surety through a specific situation. In contrast to parental lectures elsewhere in the prologue, the introductory address to the son is not accompanied by an invitation

6. Waltke, *Proverbs: Chapters 1–15*, 329; Yoder, *Proverbs*, 70.

7. Van Leeuwen, "The Book of Proverbs," *NIB* 5:75–76; Waltke, *Proverbs: Chapters 1–15*, 341; Yoder, *Proverbs*, 70; Loader, *Proverbs 1–9*, 253.

8. While certain versions begin the apodosis in v. 1b (LXX, Peshitta), the introductory particle "if" (אִם, v. 1a) can govern subsequent clauses. This possibility, combined with the renewed address to the son and the use of the conjunction "then" in v. 3, suggests that v. 3 opens the apodosis of the extended conditional construction.

to receive the father's words or wisdom. Instead, the parent plunges into an imagined economic scenario, writing the son into a precarious script. This scenario concerns taking responsibility for a loan. The matter is sketched through the verb "have given surety" (עָרַבְתָּ, v. 1a) and the idiom "shaken hands" (תָּקַעְתָּ כַפֶּיךָ, v. 1b). The former refers to a commitment or guarantee, according to which one assumed responsibility for another's debt (11:15; 17:18; 20:16; 22:26; 27:13; cf. Gen 43:9; 44:32). And the latter identifies the physical gesture that ratified the pledge (Prov 11:15; 17:18; 22:26). Together, they describe the nature and establishment of the same financial agreement. The essence of the agreement is clear. But the parities involved in the pledge are debated.

The fundamental issue concerns the identity of the creditor and the debtor. For some, the "neighbor" (רֵעַ, v. 1a) and "stranger" (זָר, v. 1a) are coreferential; that is, they refer to the same person.[9] In this case, the son has assumed responsibility for the debt of one who lives within his geographical locale (i.e., a neighbor) but remains outside of his familial and social unit (i.e., a stranger). Here the debtor is the focus of attention. The creditor is not mentioned. For others, the neighbor and the stranger are different individuals; one represents the creditor, while the other functions as the debtor.[10] Opinions differ on the dynamics of this financial agreement. Two factors, however, seem to clarify the envisioned situation.

The first is the unusual construction in v. 1a. Whereas the verb "go surety" (עָרַבְתָּ, v. 1a) is followed by the accusative elsewhere in the Old Testament (Gen 44:32; 43:9; Ps 119:122), in Prov 6:1a it governs a distinct construction: the preposition *lamed* + "your neighbor" (רֵעֶךָ). Whether or not the construction was incorporated to correspond with the same construction in v. 1b, it is unusual, for it does not identify the beneficiary of the surety. That is, it does not refer to the addressee going surety "for" his neighbor; rather, it indicates that the addressee has given surety "to" his neighbor.[11] When this rendering of the construction is read alongside v. 1b, it appears the addressee has given surety "to" his neighbor "for" a stranger. He has vouched for a stranger and assumed responsibility for the debt "to" his neighbor. In view of the unusual construction, it seems the neighbor and the stranger are different individuals. The neighbor represents the creditor, while the stranger functions as the debtor.[12]

This reading is reinforced by the second consideration, namely, the use of the expression "your neighbor" in v. 3b, c. This expression mirrors v. 1a; and it portrays the neighbor as the one under whose power the addressee has fallen. While the addressee is dependent upon the debtor to repay the loan, ultimately he has come under the power and authority of the creditor. This contextual observation, combined with the syntactical construction in v. 1a, intimates that the parent paints a precarious financial scenario. The addressee finds himself in a situation where his economic and per-

9. Toy, *Proverbs*, 120, Gemser, *Sprüche Salomos*, 28; Murphy, *Proverbs*, 37; Waltke, *Proverbs: Chapters 1–15*, 331.

10. For a reading that classifies the stranger as the creditor and the neighbor as the debtor, see Meinhold, *Die Sprüche*, 1.109–10. For a reading of the stranger as the debtor and the neighbor as the creditor, see McKane, *Proverbs*, 321–22; Plöger, *Sprüche Salomos*, 111; Fox, *Proverbs 1–9*, 212; Loader, *Proverbs 1–9*, 255–57.

11. For an alternative reading of the construction, see Waltke, who argues that, in light of Aramaic and Talmudic Hebrew, the construction *lamed* + "your neighbor" is equivalent to accusative construction (*Proverbs: Chapters 1–15*, 325n1).

12. For those who follow this reading, see n10 above.

sonal well-being hang in the balance; he has shaken hands for the debt of a stranger and fallen into the hand of his neighbor.

In a word, the addressee is trapped. This notion is captured by the language and imagery in v. 2. Here the parent elaborates on the establishment of the contractual agreement. The addressee assumed the responsibility of guarantor orally (v. 2) before ratifying the deal with a handshake (v. 1b). The repetition of the phrase "by the words of your mouth" (בְּאִמְרֵי־פִיךָ, v. 2) not only highlights the oral nature of the contract, but it also emphasizes that the addressee's precarious situation is self-inflicted.[13] In the same way that a hunter captures or traps prey, the addressee has "ensnared" (נוֹקַשְׁתָּ, v. 2a) and "trapped" (נִלְכַּדְתָּ, v. 2b) himself. He is vulnerable and helpless. Irrespective of the potential motives for the financial agreement, the parent projects a dangerous scenario. He writes the son into the script, where he serves as a guarantor whose lack of wisdom and perception has jeopardized his economic and personal well-being.

b. The Self-Deprecating Course of Action (5:3–5)

In light of the dangerous situation sketched in the protasis, the apodosis offers a solution through a sequence of admonitions. For the parent, it appears that desperate times call for desperate measures. These measures are introduced in a general yet emphatic way in the initial half of v. 3. The command "do this then" (עֲשֵׂה זֹאת אֵפוֹא, v. 3a), combined with the renewed address to the son, accentuates the urgency and intensity of the prescribed form of action. Before disclosing the details of this course of action, however, the parent identifies the purpose and rationale for the self-deprecating measures that follow. The *waw* + imperative in v. 3a is linked to the command "do this" (עֲשֵׂה זֹאת, v. 3a); it expresses the intended purpose or result of the prescribed form of action, namely, "in order to save yourself" (וְהִנָּצֵל, v. 3a).[14] This deliverance is necessary, for the addressee is in a vulnerable situation. This situation is described in the rationale, which is introduced by the conjunction "for" (כִּי, v. 3b). The addressee has come "into the power" (בְכַף, v. 3b) of his neighbor. As the guarantor, he has entered a state of utter helplessness, a condition in which his property or financial resources serve as collateral for the loan and, for all intents and purposes, are under the power of his neighbor.

In view of the purpose and rationale for the prescribed form of action, the parent specifies what the son should "do" in order to deliver himself from the predicament (v. 3c). The plan consists of a sequence of five imperatives. Among these imperatives, the first three capture the self-deprecating course of action: "go" (לֵךְ, v. 3c), "humble yourself" (הִתְרַפֵּס, v. 3c), and "hassle" (רְהַב, v. 3c) your neighbor. In the context of an honor-shame culture, this form of action is striking. The reflexive and intensive form of the *hithpael* imperative captures the disposition and demeanor of the addressee's approach. He must "totally trample himself down,"[15] that is, humble himself or "grovel."[16] And from this humble disposition and posture he must "hassle" (רְהַב, v. 3c) or "badger"[17] his neighbor (cf. Isa 3:5; Ps 138:3). Put simply, the guarantor must humbly and unrelent-

13. While the LXX and the Peshitta avoid the repetition of the phrase by reading "lips" rather than "words" in v. 2a, this emendation is unnecessary, for the repetition of the phrase highlights the guarantor's personal culpability in the envisioned predicament. Loader, *Proverbs 1–9*, 259.

14. GKC §110f; Loader, *Proverbs 1–9*, 259.

15. Ezekiel 34:18 and Loader, *Proverbs 1–9*, 260.

16. Fox, *Proverbs 1–9*, 213.

17. Fox, *Proverbs 1–9*, 213; Waltke, *Proverbs: Chapters 1–15*, 333–34.

ingly beseech his neighbor, appealing to his mercy and testing his patience, in order to receive release from his economic and legal obligation.

This self-deprecating form of action should be executed immediately. The urgency of the command (v. 3) corresponds with the urgency of the prescribed approach (v. 4). The parent indicates that there is no time for either "sleep" (שֵׁנָה, v. 4a) or "slumber" (תְּנוּמָה, v. 4b). That is, there is neither time for an extended rest nor opportunity for a brief snooze (cf. Ps 121:4). The latter term escalates the first,[18] emphasizing the immediacy of the prescribed form of action. The precarious nature of the situation demands that the addressee act instantly and directly.

The final verse of the unit delivers a command and a comparison that summarize the purpose of the parent's prescribed plan of action. Just as the protasis opened with trapping imagery (Prov 6:2), so the apodosis closes with trapping imagery (v. 5). And just as the parent framed the plan as an attempt to save the guarantor (הִנָּצֵל, v. 3a), so he closes the sequence of admonitions with the command "save yourself" (הִנָּצֵל, v. 5a). This command forms an *inclusio* around the apodosis. Deliverance from the financial and legal predicament is the goal of the addressee's humble harassment of his neighbor. And this deliverance is expressed through trapping imagery. It is comparable to the escape of a gazelle (v. 5a) and the flight of a bird from the fowler's hand (v. 5b). According to the parent, the one who ratified the pledge with an indiscriminate handshake (v. 1b) must seek release from the creditor's hand (v. 5). The one who became trapped by the words of his mouth (v. 2) must seek deliverance through persistent pestering. And the situation born of indiscretion must be solved through shameless audacity.

2. Industry and Indolence (6:6–11)

Against the backdrop of the first epigram (vv. 1–5), the second focuses on additional forms of behavior that threaten personal and social well-being.[19] While the piece is concerned with matters of industry and indolence, it shares several similarities with the previous poem. As noted above, these epigrams are linked by the use of the vocative (vv. 1a, 3a, 6a, 9a), the command "go" (vv. 3c, 6a), the terms "sleep" (vv. 4a, 10a) and "slumber" (vv. 4b, 10a), the reference to the hand(s) (vv. 1b, 3b, 5a, 5b, 10b), the concern with staying awake (vv. 4, 9), and animal imagery (vv. 5, 6–8; cf. v. 2). In addition, they offer variations on the theme of perception or foresight. Whereas the guarantor and the sluggard lack these virtues, they are embodied by the ways and wisdom of a wee creature: the ant.

Despite the poem's relationship with the previous epigram, it may stand alone. Similar to the previous piece, it consists of two sections. The first focuses on the industry of the ant (vv. 6–8), while the second profiles the indolence of the sluggard (vv. 9–11). The subject matter of these sections, the renewed address to the sluggard (vv. 6a, 9a), and the shift from observation (vv. 6–8) to accusation (vv. 9–11) provides a rationale for this division. The substance of each section deserves specific comment.

a. The Industry of the Ant (6:6–8)

In contrast to the previous poem and the parental lectures elsewhere in the prologue, the epigram does not open with an address to the son(s). Rather, it is directed to the "sluggard" (עָצֵל, v. 6a). The sluggard serves as the rhetorical addressee of the epigram, but the son remains the real ad-

18. Fox, *Proverbs 1–9*, 213–14; Waltke, *Proverbs: Chapters 1–15*, 334; Loader, *Proverbs 1–9*, 260.

19. Waltke, *Proverbs: Chapters 1–15*, 329; Yoder, *Proverbs*, 70.

dressee of the piece. He is invited to overhear the discourse, observe the ways of the ant, perceive the disposition of the sluggard, and receive the parental evaluation of this character type. Similar to Lady Wisdom's rebuke (1:20–33), the parent teaches the son what type of person he should be by reflecting on the sort of person he should not be.[20] The parent's evaluation of the sluggard's character and (in)activity provides the addressee with a lens through which to evaluate his own character, to assess the character of others, and to discover the value of industriousness.[21]

Industriousness defines the "ways" (דְּרָכֶי-, v. 6b) of the ant. According to the parent, these ways are worthy of observation, for they exemplify aspects of the way of wisdom and possess the capacity to make one wise (v. 6b). Among the aspects of wisdom's way exemplified by the ant, the parent focuses on three matters. The first is the initiative of the ant. This value is expressed through a concessive clause, "although," introduced by the relative pronoun אֲשֶׁר (v. 7). In spite of the fact that the ant does not operate within a defined social hierarchy, it exhibits self-motivation and resourcefulness, harvesting food in the appropriate seasons. It requires neither command nor coercion, for it possesses initiative. Second, the ant is a model of industry and foresight. In anticipation of the cold season, it diligently "prepares" (תָּכִין, v. 8a) its food and "gathers" (אָגְרָה, v. 8b) its fare throughout the harvest season (cf. 10:4). And third, the ant acts in accord with the rhythm of creation. Similar to the wise, the ant recognizes the patterns woven into the fabric of the cosmos and aligns its activities in accordance with the seasons. The "ways" of the ant mirror aspects of wisdom's way. The implication is that, if this wee creature can exercise diligence and foresight, act in harmony with the created order, and operate without a social hierarchy, how much more should humans exercise diligence and foresight in accord with the created order within a social hierarchy?[22]

b. The Indolence of the Sluggard (6:9–11)

In view of the wise ways of the ant, the parent resumes the address to the sluggard. This address includes an accusation and a warning, each of which focuses on the indolence of the sluggard. The accusation is delivered through a pair of rhetorical questions. The first opens with the expression "How long?" (עַד־מָתַי, v. 9a). This expression not only betrays the parent's impatience and displeasure with the sluggard, but it also passes judgment on his inaction. In a word, it functions as a rebuke (see 1:22). This rebuke is developed in the second rhetorical question (6:9b). Whereas the first passed judgment on the sluggard's inaction, the second focuses on the particular time when this inaction will turn into action. It functions as an exhortation, urging the sluggard to awake and arise (v. 9b).

This rebuke and exhortation provide the basis for the warning in vv. 10–11. In contrast to the industry and foresight of the ant, the sluggard is marked by indolence and folly. He is unable to perceive the consequences of his inaction. These consequences are outlined in vv. 10–11, first through an astute observation of the sluggard's twisted thinking (v. 10) and then through a declaration of the sluggard's fate (v. 11).[23] The sluggard's twisted thinking is delineated in the development or inten-

20. Pincoffs, *Quandaries and Virtues*, 164.

21. McKinnon, *Character, Virtue Theories, and the Vices*, 230.

22. As a complement to the ant, the LXX includes an extended description of the industry of bees following v. 8. While this description represents a later addition, the vignette reinforces the way in which weak creatures reflect wisdom through their diligent work.

23. Following Waltke, it appears that vv. 10–11 are comparable to 6:1–2: v. 10 is cast in the form of an implied protasis, while v. 11 serves as the apodosis (*Proverbs: Chapters 1–15*,

sification of thought in v. 10: a little sleep, a little snoozing, a little lying around with hands folded to rest (cf. 6:4). Obsessed with sleep, the sluggard transgresses appropriate limits for rest and refuses to exercise diligence.[24] As a result, poverty and destitution will strike the sluggard unexpectedly. This sudden onslaught is compared to the unpredictable visit of a disreputable "vagabond" (מְהַלֵּךְ, v. 11a)[25] as well as to the hostile approach of an "armed warrior" (אִישׁ מָגֵן, v. 11b).[26] Together, these comparisons capture the swift and forceful way in which deprivation will overtake the sluggard. His desire for a little more sleep dulls his senses, warps his character, and ends with the possession of little to no resources.

3. A Sketch of the Scoundrel (6:12–19)

Whereas the first pair of epigrams attended to forms of behavior that threaten personal and social well-being,[27] the second pair reflects on the actions and attitudes of the scoundrel (vv. 12–14), which epitomize the actions and attitudes that YHWH despises (vv. 16–19).[28] As illustrated in the table above (p. 263), the epigrams in the second pair focus on the immoral movements of body parts as well as despicable attitudes and actions. These body parts, attitudes, and actions, however, are evaluated from different vantage points. The initial epigram offers a character sketch of the scoundrel (vv. 12–15); it catalogs the movements, attitudes, and actions characteristic of this sort of person, culminating in the inevitable fate of this character type. The second epigram, on the other hand, outlines movements, attitudes, and actions that YHWH abhors. It counterbalances the first, providing a theological valuation of the anthropological portrait painted in vv. 12–15. While the epigrams are cast in different modes and assume distinctive vantage points, they coalesce to offer an anthropological and theological assessment of the scoundrel.

These sketches of the scoundrel may be divided into three main sections. As intimated above, the first catalogs the immoral movements, attitudes, and actions of the scoundrel (vv. 12–14). The second describes the fate or end of the scoundrel (v. 15). And the third reframes these immoral movements, attitudes, and actions, evaluating them from a divine perspective and through the form of a numerical saying (vv. 16–19).

a. The Immoral Anatomy of the Scoundrel (6:12–14)

In contrast to the previous epigrams, the portrait of the scoundrel is cast in the form of a description. This third-person account is not directed toward an explicit addressee, nor does it include any normative advice. Its addressee and advice are implicit yet intelligible. In light of the context of the epigram, it appears the son remains the addressee. And similar to the previous epigram, he is invited to observe the parent's sketch of the scoundrel. This sketch is not intended to dissuade the addressee

339). Although some suggest v. 10 may represent the response of the sluggard (Toy, *Proverbs*, 124; Murphy, *Proverbs*, 38), in light of the fact that vv. 10–11 recur in 24:33–34, where they are not in the form of a dialogue, it seems best to take vv. 10–11 as the observations of the parent. Loader, *Proverbs 1–9*, 264. For discussion of the relationship between 6:10–11 and 24:33–34 as well as the difficulties in determining the direction of dependence, see Heim, *Poetic Imagination*, 161–66.

24. Van Leeuwen, "The Book of Proverbs," *NIB* 5:75.

25. The form מְהַלֵּךְ in the *piel* expresses the speed by which one walks. The form is found elsewhere only in Eccl 4:15. For discussion of the form, see Fox, *Proverbs 1–9*, 217.

26. For discussion of various explanations of the unique expression אִישׁ מָגֵן, see Fox, *Proverbs 1–9*, 217–18; Schipper, *Proverbs 1–15*, 228–30.

27. Waltke, *Proverbs: Chapters 1–15*, 329; Yoder, *Proverbs*, 70.

28. Van Leeuwen, "The Book of Proverbs," *NIB* 5:75–76; Yoder, *Proverbs*, 70; Loader, *Proverbs 1–9*, 253.

from developing the vices characteristic of this sort of person; rather, it provides the addressee with a profile so that he might diagnose this character type and avoid him.[29]

As a character sketch, the epigram opens with pair of expressions that offer a general description of the central subject. This subject is classified as a "scoundrel" (אָדָם בְּלִיַּעַל, v. 12a) and a "vile person" (אִישׁ אָוֶן, v. 12a). The former is used elsewhere in the Old Testament to describe idolaters (Deut 13:14[13]), rapists (Judg 19:22), murderers (Judg 20:13), and slanderers (1 Kgs 21:10), as well as those who abuse their power and distort justice (2 Sam 2:12–17, 22–25). In view of its use as well as the description in vv. 12–14, it appears the expression refers to a general type of person: a "good-for-nothing"[30] or scoundrel. This characterization is reinforced by the expression's counterpart. This individual is a vile person, one marked by injustice and wickedness. Taken together, the expressions capture the general nature of the poem's central subject: a person devoid of moral character and prone to all forms of depravity.

With this general sketch, vv. 12b–14 infuse the portrait with depth and color by depicting the immoral movements (vv. 12b–13), attitudes (vv. 14a–b), and actions (v. 14c) of the scoundrel. In contrast to the movements of the moral anatomy (4:23–27), the scoundrel is marked by a misuse of body parts and the transmission of "sinister sign language."[31] He walks about with a "crooked mouth" (עִקְּשׁוּת פֶּה, v. 12b), distorting the truth and twisting his lips in order to send devious signals to comrades. He "winks with his eyes" (קֹרֵץ בְּעֵינָו, v. 13a),[32] confirming malicious forms of behavior or conveying envy and disdain (cf. 10:10; 16:30). He "shuffles with his feet" (מֹלֵל בְּרַגְלָו, v. 13a),[33] shifting or sliding to communicate subtle schemes. And he "signals with his fingers" (מֹרֶה בְּאֶצְבְּעֹתָיו, v. 13b), perhaps accusing others or directing some along a particular path. Whatever the precise nuances of these underhanded gestures, they illustrate the deplorable character and devious ways of the scoundrel.[34] The sequence of participles and body parts depict the scoundrel as dishonest, conniving, shifty, and malicious (vv. 12b–13).

The misuse of body parts and the external movements of the scoundrel's immoral anatomy correspond with the internal attitudes of this character type. Just as the heart represented the headquarters of the moral anatomy (4:23), so also it functions as the headquarters of the immoral anatomy. The scoundrel's heart is the residence of various "perversions" (תַּהְפֻּכוֹת, 6:14a). These perversions distort his disposition and explain his distorted movements. In light of this disposition, it is not surprising that the scoundrel constantly "plans" (חֹרֵשׁ, v. 14b), designs, or cultivates evil.[35] Like a craftsman or a farmer, the headquarters of his anatomy is hard at work, devising and nurturing discord (cf. 3:29; 11:12; 14:22). And this constant planning comes to fruition through the spreading

29. Fox, *Proverbs 1–9*, 222; Waltke, *Proverbs: Chapters 1–15*, 342.

30. Fox, *Proverbs 1–9*, 219; Yoder, *Proverbs*, 75.

31. McKane, *Proverbs*, 325.

32. This reading follows *qere* rather *ketiv*, which includes the singular "eye."

33. This reading follows *qere* rather than *ketiv*, which includes the singular "foot."

34. While Fox argues that the movements in v. 13 are not signals but rather "symptoms of a personality disorder," his reading is unconvincing (*Proverbs 1–9*, 220–21). Among the scoundrel's movements, the expression "signals with his fingers" (v. 13b) refers to a gesture, not a personality disorder. And the absence of an explicit recipient of these signals does not mean they do not transmit a message. See also Waltke, *Proverbs: Chapters 1–15*, 344n90; Loader, *Proverbs 1–9*, 266–67.

35. Following the Masoretic punctuation, the adverbial phrase "constantly" (בְּכָל־עֵת, v. 14b) modifies the participle "he plans" (חֹרֵשׁ) rather than the verb "he stirs up" (יְשַׁלֵּחַ).

of poisonous fruit. The scoundrel's immoral movements and internal attitudes are expressed through actions that sow, spread, or stir up strife and discord (6:14c; cf. 16:28). The immoral movements of the scoundrel match his immoral disposition and actions. This disposition and actions bring the character sketch of the scoundrel to climactic conclusion. The final tristich indicates that the "sinister sign language" of the scoundrel is a symptom of his perverse disposition and plans, which sow conflict within the community (v. 14).

b. The Sudden Ruin of the Scoundrel (6:15)

The extended description of the scoundrel's character, movements, attitudes, and actions explain his sudden ruin (v. 15). The expression "therefore" (עַל־כֵּן, v. 15a) introduces the formal conclusion to the epigram and identifies the causal relationship between its parts. The scoundrel will experience sudden ruin (v. 15) because of his despicable character, movements, attitudes, and actions (vv. 12–14). While the nature of this ruin is ambiguous, its timing and scope is clear: it will come abruptly, and it will be absolute. The former is expressed through the adverbs "suddenly" (פִּתְאֹם, v. 15a) and "unexpectedly" (פֶּתַע, v. 15b), each of which is situated at the beginning of the parallel clauses. And the latter is conveyed through the irremediable nature of the scoundrel's punishment (vv. 15b; cf. 29:1). The sudden ruin of the scoundrel assumes that one's character and accompanying actions produce certain consequences. The poetic sketch of the character and consequences of the scoundrel seeks not only to reinforce this truth but also to prevent the addressee from associating with this type of person.

c. A Register of Revulsion (6:16–19)

Whereas the previous section assessed the character, movements, attitudes, and actions of the scoundrel from an anthropological perspective, the final unit evaluates comparable movements, attitudes, and actions from a theological perspective. This theological evaluation complements the anthropological. It reframes the movements, attitudes, and actions of the scoundrel, characterizing them as representative of that which elicits divine disgust.

The catalogue or register of things that YHWH abhors is cast in the form of a numerical saying. As noted in the introduction, numerical sayings open with a conventional formula (X + 1) and systematize various phenomena that share a common denominator to achieve a particular purpose.[36] This is the case in 6:16–19. The unit opens with a conventional introduction, identifying six phenomena (v. 16a), along with a seventh (v. 16b), that share a common theme. These common phenomena are then cataloged in the main body of the unit, which may be divided into two sections. The first focuses on misused or dysfunctional body parts (vv. 17–18), while the second identifies despicable character types (v. 19). Each deserves a brief comment.

(1) The Introduction (6:16)

The introduction to the numerical saying not only presents the number of phenomena under discussion, but it also explains what these phenomena share in common. They are things that YHWH detests. Just as the number of phenomena develops from six to seven, so also the sense of disgust develops from "hates" (שָׂנֵא, v. 16a) to "an abomination

36. Roth, "The Numerical Sequence x/x + 1 in the Old Testament," 300–11; idem, *Numerical Sayings in the Old Testament*, 5–9 et passim; Forti, *Animal Imagery in the Book of Proverbs*, 120.

to him" (תּוֹעֲבַת נַפְשׁוֹ, v. 16b).[37] The latter expression intensifies the first, portraying this hatred in terms of moral revulsion, loathing, and contempt. This revulsion characterizes YHWH's emotive response to the body parts and character types that follow, for these body parts and character types are out of step with divine design and incompatible with YHWH's character (cf. 3:32; 11:1, 20; 12:22; 15:8, 9, 26; 16:5; 17:15; 20:10, 23).[38] And this revulsion leads to judgment on these dysfunctional movements and character types.

(2) Abominable Body Parts (6:17–18)

Against the backdrop of the number of items and their common denominator, the formal list opens with a sequence of abominable body parts, which moves from the top of the human person to the bottom.[39] Each body part functions as a synecdoche; its aberrant orientation or action represents the character and behavior of a person who transgresses the divine order. "Haughty eyes" (עֵינַיִם רָמוֹת, v. 17a) refer to a proud, arrogant disposition that fails to recognize one's proper place in relation to both YHWH and others (cf. 30:13; Isa 10:12; 37:23). "A lying tongue" (לְשׁוֹן שָׁקֶר, Prov 6:17a) distorts reality and destroys others (cf. 10:18; 26:28). "Hands that shed innocent blood" (יָדַיִם שֹׁפְכוֹת דָּם־נָקִי, v. 17b) describes one who subverts the created order by intentionally killing another (cf. 1:11–14). "A heart that plans vile schemes" (לֵב חֹרֵשׁ מַחְשְׁבוֹת אָוֶן, v. 18a) cultivates and calculates iniquitous plans (cf. 6:14). And the expression "feet that hasten to run to evil" (רַגְלַיִם מְמַהֲרוֹת לָרוּץ לָרָעָה, v. 18b) captures the fervor and enthusiasm with which one pursues harm (cf. 1:16). These dysfunctional body parts are representative of dispositions and behaviors that misrepresent YHWH's character and operate outside of YHWH's design. They project an abominable body out of sync with the created order and in opposition to both YHWH and the human community.

(3) Abominable Character Types (6:19)

This opposition to both YHWH and the human community is exemplified in the final two items, which focus on specific character types. These abominable character types are described in different ways, but they share a common interest: communal conflict. This conflict is actualized through specific forms of speech (v. 19a) and general antisocial activities (v. 19b). The former is expressed through the designation "a lying witness" (עֵד שָׁקֶר, v. 19a), which is set in apposition to "who blows out deceits" (יָפִיחַ כְּזָבִים, v. 19a). Whether in the confines of the court or among members of the community, this individual utters falsehoods and traffics in deception. On this account, a lying witness is a specific instantiation of "one who stirs up strife between brothers" (מְשַׁלֵּחַ מְדָנִים בֵּין אַחִים, v. 19b), sowing discord in the family as well as the broader community. Character types that cultivate communal conflict conclude the numerical saying (cf. v. 14c). Just as the abominable body parts illustrated dispositions and behaviors that conflict with YHWH's character and design, so also these character types exemplify individuals who create and thrive on conflict. While these individuals occupy the final and climactic position within the numerical saying, they do not embody or exhaust all that YHWH abhors. Rather, like the body parts, they illustrate the conflict, disorder, and hostility that YHWH detests.

37. While it makes little difference to the sense of the line, this translation follows *qere* rather than the plural *ketiv*, "abominations."

38. Loader, *Proverbs 1–9*, 269.

39. Meinhold, *Die Sprüche*, 1.115; Fox, *Proverbs 1–9*, 223.

Canonical and Theological Significance

To some extent, judgments involve emotions. Emotions are not necessarily at odds with one's cognitive faculties; rather, they influence and inform one's intellectual and social life.[40] The intimate relationship between emotions and the intellect is conveyed through the constituent epigrams in 6:1–19. As noted above, these epigrams create a sense of astonishment and then satisfy that incredulity in a particular way. They traffic in terror and shame (vv. 1–5), sarcasm and utter destitution (vv. 9–11), moral revulsion and divine loathing (vv. 12–19). These shocking accounts and their resolution link one's feelings with one's perception of specific social and moral affairs. They envision scenarios or sketch character types to cultivate emotions that align with judgments that are perceptive and wise.

These perceptive judgments concern matters that are significant for the wise and virtuous life. The significance of these matters is evinced by their treatment elsewhere in Proverbs. The warning against standing surety for a stranger reverberates throughout the individual collections in the document. Sayings concerned with the practice reinforce and develop aspects addressed in 6:1–5, highlighting the risks involved in the agreement (11:15; 22:26–27), the indiscretion of guarantor (17:18), the payment required at the time of the transaction (20:16; 27:13), and the social exploitation that accompanies the financial arrangement (22:7). While Proverbs commends social concern and generosity toward the needy (11:24–26; 14:21, 31; 19:17; 21:13; 27:10), it appears that the personal and social risks of standing surety for a stranger outweigh the rewards.[41] Similar to 6:1–5, sayings within the remainder of the work reinforce and elaborate on the dangers of the practice through pithy observations, pointed admonitions, and palpable images.

The same is true of industry and indolence. Diligence is commended throughout the anthology, for it yields food, profit, and satisfaction (12:11, 24, 27; 14:23; 28:19). This form of diligence is not haphazard; rather, it is performed in the right way and at the right time. The ant is a model of this industry, wisdom, and sensitivity to the rhythm of creation (6:7–8; 30:25). A prudent son is depicted as the human instantiation of hard work performed in accord with the created order (10:5). The sluggard, on the other hand, is portrayed as the embodiment of indolence and folly. This comical character type neither works nor observes the seasons within the cre-

40. Martha C. Nussbaum, *Upheavals of Thought: The Intelligence of Emotions* (Cambridge: Cambridge University Press, 2001), 60 et passim.

41. Ben Sirach identifies both the social benefits and the risks of standing surety (Sir 29:14–20). It is important to note, however, that Sirach discusses the social benefits of the practice in the context of standing surety for a neighbor, not a stranger. The same is true in 4QInstruction (4Q416 2 II, 4–17), where the gravitas and relational implications of making a pledge for one's neighbor is emphasized.

ated order (20:4; 21:25). Instead, the sluggard invests in farcical speech and ludicrous actions; he traverses a painful path and possesses a deluded sense of self (15:19; 19:24; 22:13; 26:13–16). The sketch of the sluggard's character and fate in 6:9–11 is enhanced through satirical vignettes in the remainder of the anthology. And the assessment of the sluggard in 6:10–11 is reiterated and recast as the conclusion to the autobiographical reflection in 24:30–34. Industry and indolence play a significant role in the moral vision of Proverbs. And the degree to which the collections within the book develop these concepts through common terms, expressions, and proverbs reveals the coherence of its moral vision.

Together with surety, industry, and indolence, the immoral anatomy of the scoundrel (6:12–15) and the items delineated in the register of divine revulsion (6:16–19) recur elsewhere in the anthology. The immoral movements of the scoundrel (vv. 12–15) find a positive counterpart in 4:23–27. And the despicable gestures, dispositions, and actions profiled in 6:12–19 find lexical and thematic parallels in the central collections of the book. These collections affirm that YHWH abhors many of the items catalogued in 6:16–19, such as a perverted heart (6:18; 11:20), a lying tongue or lips (6:17; 12:22), evil schemes (6:18; 15:26), and an arrogant disposition (6:17; 16:5).[42] Several proverbs reinforce the character, speech, and fate of a lying witness (6:19; 12:17; 14:5; 19:5, 9; 25:18). The sudden ruin (6:15a) and irremediable punishment of the scoundrel (6:15b) is applied to rebellious officials (24:22) and the obstinate (29:1), respectively. And certain sayings offer variations on the immoral anatomy, attitudes, and actions presented in 6:12–19. Among these sayings, Prov 16:27–30 share several lexical and conceptual similarities with 6:12–19:[43]

Proverbs 16:27–30	**Proverbs 6:12–19**
27 "A scoundrel" (אִישׁ בְּלִיַּעַל) digs up evil, and on his lips it is like a scorching fire.	12a "A scoundrel" (אָדָם בְּלִיַּעַל)
28 "A perverse person stirs up strife" (אִישׁ תַּהְפֻּכוֹת יְשַׁלַּח מָדוֹן), and a slanderer separates friends.	14a "perversions" (תַּהְפֻּכוֹת) are in his heart 14c "he stirs up strife" (מְדָנִים יְשַׁלֵּחַ) 19b one who stirs up strife between brothers
29 A violent person entices his neighbor, and leads him on a way not good.	
30 He squints "his eyes" (עֵינָיו) "to plan perversities" (לַחְשֹׁב תַּהְפֻּכוֹת), "pinching" (קֹרֵץ) his lips, he accomplishes "evil" (רָעָה).	13a who winks "with his eyes" (בְּעֵינָו) 14a "perversions" (תַּהְפֻּכוֹת) are in his heart 14b he constantly "plans evil" (חֹרֵשׁ רָע) 13a "who winks" (קֹרֵץ) with his eyes

42. Plöger, *Sprüche Salomos*, 65; Waltke, *Proverbs: Chapters 1–15*, 345–46.

43. This comparison is adapted from Fox, *Proverbs 1–9*, 224–25.

These similarities suggest that the character types delineated in Prov 16:27–30—the scoundrel, the perverse, and the violent—are species of the good-for-nothing (6:12). They are not mutually exclusive; rather, they are designations that describe the disposition and behavior of the same type of person. Like the epigrams devoted to surety as well as industry and indolence, the sketch of the scoundrel (6:12–15) and the items catalogued in the register of divine revulsion (6:16–19) include character types, expressions, and proverbs that recur elsewhere in the distinct collections within the anthology. Their recurrence illuminates the importance of these matters within Proverbs's vision of the wise and virtuous life as well as the intratextual relationship among the various collections.

While the issues addressed in 6:1–19 reverberate throughout the central collections of Proverbs, they receive little direct attention elsewhere in the canon. The mechanics of guaranteeing a loan are described in a few constitutional texts (Exod 22:24–26[25–27]; Deut 24:6, 10–13). And the dire consequences of borrowing are portrayed in Neh 5:3–5. At best, however, these texts offer an implicit warning of the dangers involved in going surety. In the same way, indolence is viewed with ignominy and industry is commended in several texts (Eccl 3:13; 4:5; Col 3:23; 2 Thess 3:10). But the value of the latter is qualified by Qoheleth, who observes its risks as well as its limited rewards (Eccl 2:10–11, 18–22). The silhouette of the scoundrel is profiled in Deuteronomy and the Deuteronomistic History, confirming the aberrant nature and despicable actions of this character type (Deut 13:14[13]; Judg 19:22; 20:13; 1 Sam 2:12; 10:27; 25:17, 25; 2 Sam 20:1; 1 Kgs 21:10–13). And the attitudes and actions that elicit divine disgust are reinforced and developed in various passages (Isa 14:4–20; Rom 3:15; Gal 5:20).

The canonical witness affirms and, in some cases, elaborates upon the personal, economic, social, and moral issues discussed in Prov 6:1–19. The relative lack of attention to these matters, however, may leave one with the impression that they are insignificant. Nothing could be further from the truth. When matters of money, indolence, and industry as well as immoral attitudes and actions are viewed from a theological perspective, they not only outline the terrain of the way of wisdom, on the one hand, and the way of folly, on the other; they also illuminate the many facets of sin. The epigrams in Prov 6:1–19 construe sin as both overstepping appropriate boundaries (6:1–5, 12–19) as well as underachieving human potential (6:6–11). Sin affects not only oneself but also others. It can threaten the social and economic welfare of the family (6:1–5) as well as the stability of the community (6:14, 18–19). As a power, sin warps one's character, motivates malicious movements (6:12–14, 17–18), and sows conflict in the broader community (6:14, 19). And as an embodied phenomenon, sin elicits divine loathing and judgment (6:11, 15, 16). The epigrams focus on the dangers of standing surety, the dangers of indolence, and the detestable anatomy of the scoundrel, as well as abominable body parts and actions. They traffic in fear, shame, anger, disgust, and revulsion. They evoke these emotions to hone one's perception. Put differently, they link emotions with socioeconomic affairs as well as the evaluation of particular characters and actions so that these emotions and their accompanying judgments might become ingrained in one's intelligence, moral discretion, and practical judgments.

This attention to emotions, the intellect, and moral judgments is valuable pedagogically. But more than this, the interrelationship among emotions, the intellect, moral judgments, and embodied portrayals of sin is instructive for the church. Too often, sin is viewed as entity that only affects the sinner; it is considered as a phenomenon that can be contained. Additionally, sin tends to be perceived as missing the mark or transgressing appropriate boundaries but not as underachieving or failing to operate within appropriate boundaries. The dangers sketched in the individual epigrams of Prov 6:1–19 depict embodied forms of sin and its effects. These effects are not limited to the individual; rather, they infect and implicate others. They produce social shame, economic instability, communal conflict, and divine disgust. Sin contaminates the heart, circulates through one's bodily members and actions, infiltrates society, and poisons interpersonal, divine-human as well as communal relationships. According to the epigrams in 6:1–19, the manifestation of sin through foolish economic agreements, sloth, and immoral attitudes and actions is both disastrous and disgusting. Standing surety for a stranger is not a bad business decision; it is a sin that jeopardizes the stability and security of the household. Indolence is not a leisure activity; it is a lifestyle that fails to actualize human potential in the *imago Dei*. The "sinister sign language" of the scoundrel is not characterized as harmless but as morally repulsive. And the attitudes and actions catalogued in the register of revulsion are not regarded as tolerable but as abominable. This disgust captures YHWH's emotive response to sin. And this disgust should characterize the Christian's response to sin. The epigrams in Prov 6:1–19 seek to sensitize one's emotions and train one's perception and judgment so that that they mirror God's response to and perception of sin in general and its manifestation in standing surety, indolence, and immoral attitudes and actions in particular.

CHAPTER 12

Proverbs 6:20–35

K. Wisdom, Desire, and Certain Destruction

Main Idea of the Passage

This parental lecture seeks to train one's desires by describing the complete and inevitable destruction of the adulterer, a destruction designed to evoke terror and scare the hell out of the addressee.[1]

Literary Context of the Passage

As a discourse concerned with the protective power of wisdom (6:20–24), the dangers of erotic desire (6:25–32), and the slippery speech of the strange woman (6:24), this parental lecture reinforces and develops the prologue's discussion of sex and the strange woman in particular ways (2:16–19; 5:1–23; cf. 7:1–27). Similar to other lectures, the discourse affirms that wisdom and parental instruction offer protection and guidance (2:11, 16; 4:6; 6:22, 24; 7:5). In fact, the piece blurs the boundaries between parental instruction and wisdom, intermingling references to parental teaching with inchoate personifications of wisdom in order to highlight their preventive and didactic power (6:20–23). The lecture reiterates admonitions and images from earlier discourses (3:3; 4:18; 6:21, 23; cf. 7:3). And its depiction of the character and seductive speech of the strange woman as well as the severe consequences that accompany those who "enter" (בוא; 2:19; 6:29) her correspond with 2:16–19 and 5:1–23 (cf. 7:1–27).

1. Limitations of space preclude an extensive treatment of Prov 6:20–35. This chapter does not include an Explanation of the Text. For discussion of Prov 6:20–35 in conversation with the pedagogies of Prov 5 and Prov 7, see the Canonical and Theological Significance section following the treatment of Prov 7:1–27.

The parental lecture includes terms, concepts, and characterizations reminiscent of other discourses within the prologue. But the piece does not simply repeat previous instruction; it also develops this instruction. Whereas Prov 2:16–17 describe the strange woman as one who forsakes the companion of her youth and forgets the covenant of her God, 6:24–35 describe her as the wife of another man who hunts for precious life.

I. Introduction to the Book (1:1–7)
II. The Value of Wisdom and Virtue (1:8–9:18)
- A. Wisdom, Desire, and Different Ways (1:8–19)
- B. Wisdom's Rebuke (1:20–33)
- C. The Procurement, Power, and Protection of Wisdom and Virtue (2:1–22)
- D. Wisdom and Piety (3:1–12)
- E. Wisdom's Value and Moral Obligations (3:13–35)
- F. Wisdom and Tradition (4:1–9)
- G. Wisdom and Ways of Life (4:10–19)
- H. Wisdom and the Moral Anatomy (4:20–27)
- I. Wisdom and Sexuality (5:1–23)
- J. Wisdom, Lending, Laziness, and the Immoral Anatomy (6:1–19)
- ➡ **K. Wisdom, Desire, and Certain Destruction (6:20–35)**
  - **1. The Introduction: The Retention of Parental Instruction (6:20–24)**
    - **a. The Internalization and Remembrance of Parental Instruction (6:20–21)**
    - **b. The Guidance and Protection of Wisdom (6:22–24)**
      - **(1) Wisdom's Guidance (6:22–23)**
      - **(2) Wisdom's Protection (6:24)**
  - **2. The Lesson: Misdirected Desire, Adultery, and Destruction (6:25–32)**
    - **a. Internal Desire and External Capture (6:25–26)**
    - **b. The Fiery Consequences of Misdirected Desire and Adultery (6:27–29)**
    - **c. The Senselessness and Self-Destruction of Misplaced Desire and Adultery (6:30–32)**
  - **3. The Conclusion: The Certain Punishment of Misdirected Desire and Adultery (6:33–35)**
    - **a. The Inevitable Punishment for Misplaced Desire and Adultery (6:33)**
    - **b. The Rationale for the Inevitable Punishment (6:34–35)**
- L. Wisdom and Seduction (7:1–27)
- M. Wisdom's Call, Credentials, and the Cosmos (8:1–36)
- N. Wisdom and Folly's Invitations (9:1–18)

III. "Forming 'Fearers of YHWH'": The Curriculum of Wisdom and Virtue (10:1–29:27)
IV. The Application of Wisdom and Virtue (30:1–31:31)

She is not divorced but married. And her marital status plays a significant role in the inevitable punishment recounted in the lecture. In contrast to 2:16–19 and 5:1–23, which indicate that death, the loss of honor, the forfeiture of economic resources, and psychological anguish accompany engagement with the strange woman, 6:20–35 indicate that when one plays with the fire of a married woman, one will be burned with physical affliction, lasting public shame, self-destruction, and the vengeance of an enraged and uncompassionate husband. The consequences of adultery delineated in the lecture are vivid, pointed, and terrifying. Unlike 5:1–23, the parent does not mention the sexual satisfaction that may be found in one's wife. Exclusive attention is devoted to the severe and inevitable punishment of the adulterer.[2] And the description of this punishment shares much in common with the epigrams in 6:1–19. Just as these epigrams evoke particular emotions in order to cultivate perception and train one's moral judgment, so also the parental lecture evokes fear at the prospect of sexual engagement with the strange woman in order to train one's desires. Its sharp rhetorical questions, frightening scenarios, and graphic descriptions of physical pain, social humiliation, and an infuriated husband awaken unsettling emotions and arouse sheer terror. The lecture integrates elements from earlier discourses in order to train one's desires, form one's feelings, and shape one's character in accord with wisdom and virtue.

Translation and Exegetical Outline

(See pages 279–80.)

Structure and Literary Form

Similar to parental lectures elsewhere in the prologue, the discourse is cast in the form of an instruction. It opens with a conventional introduction, delivers a formal lesson, and concludes with a word of inevitable punishment. In light of its form and syntax, the piece may be divided into three basic parts.[3] The first is an exordium (vv. 20–24), complete with admonitions (vv. 20–22), a causal clause (v. 23), and a purpose clause (v. 24). The admonitions encourage the retention of parental instruction and highlight the protective power of wisdom through the reiteration of verbs, expressions, and half-lines from other parental lectures (1:8b; 3:3; 7:3; cf. Deut 6:7–8; 11:19–20).

2. Fox, *Proverbs 1–9*, 237; Weeks, *Instruction and Imagery*, 86; Loader, *Proverbs 1–9*, 272.

3. While the majority of commentators recognize that the discourse consists of three parts, there is little unanimity regarding the boundaries of these parts. To be specific, there is disagreement regarding the place of v. 24 and the boundaries of the conclusion within the lecture's literary design. In view of the syntax of the discourse, it seems the piece may be divided as follows: (1) vv. 20–24; (2) vv. 25–32; (3) vv. 33–35. Loader, *Proverbs 1–9*, 273–74. Cf. Plöger, *Sprüche Salomos*, 69; Meinhold, *Die Sprüche*, 1.117; Fox, *Proverbs 1–9*, 236–37; Waltke, *Proverbs: Chapters 1–15*, 350; Yoder, *Proverbs*, 70.

Proverbs 6:20–35

			K. Wisdom, Desire, and Certain Destruction (6:20–35)
			1. The Introduction: The Retention of Parental Instruction (6:20–24)
20a	נְצֹר בְּנִי מִצְוַת אָבִיךָ	Keep, my son, your father's commandment,	a. The Internalization and Remembrance of Parental Instruction (6:20–21)
20b	וְאַל־תִּטֹּשׁ תּוֹרַת אִמֶּךָ	and do not neglect your mother's teaching.	
21a	קָשְׁרֵם עַל־לִבְּךָ תָמִיד	Bind them upon your heart always,	
21b	עָנְדֵם עַל־גַּרְגְּרֹתֶךָ	tie them around your neck.	
			b. The Guidance and Protection of Wisdom (6:22–24)
22a	בְּהִתְהַלֶּכְךָ תַּנְחֶה אֹתָךְ	When you walk about, she will lead you;	(1) Wisdom's Guidance (6:22–23)
22b	בְּשָׁכְבְּךָ תִּשְׁמֹר עָלֶיךָ	when you lie down, she will watch over you;	
22c	וַהֲקִיצוֹתָ הִיא תְשִׂיחֶךָ	and when you awake, she will teach you.	
23a	כִּי נֵר מִצְוָה וְתוֹרָה אוֹר	For the commandment is a lamp and the teaching a light,	
23b	וְדֶרֶךְ חַיִּים תּוֹכְחוֹת מוּסָר	and corrective reproofs are the way of life	
24a	לִשְׁמָרְךָ מֵאֵשֶׁת רָע	to guard you from the wife of another,	(2) Wisdom's Protection (6:24)
24b	מֵחֶלְקַת לָשׁוֹן נָכְרִיָּה	from the smooth tongue of the strange woman.	
			2. The Lesson: Misdirected Desire, Adultery, and Destruction (6:25–32)
25a	אַל־תַּחְמֹד יָפְיָהּ בִּלְבָבֶךָ	Do not desire her beauty in your heart,	a. Internal Desire and External Capture (6:25–26)
25b	וְאַל־תִּקָּחֲךָ בְּעַפְעַפֶּיהָ	and do not let her capture you with her eyelashes,	
26a	כִּי בְעַד־אִשָּׁה זוֹנָה עַד־כִּכַּר לָחֶם	for a prostitute's fee is just a loaf of bread,	
26b	וְאֵשֶׁת אִישׁ נֶפֶשׁ יְקָרָה תָצוּד	but the wife of another man hunts for precious life.	
27a	הֲיַחְתֶּה אִישׁ אֵשׁ בְּחֵיקוֹ	Can a man carry fire in his bosom,	b. The Fiery Consequences of Misdirected Desire and Adultery (6:27–29)
27b	וּבְגָדָיו לֹא תִשָּׂרַפְנָה	without his clothes being burnt?	
28a	אִם־יְהַלֵּךְ אִישׁ עַל־הַגֶּחָלִים	Can a person walk on burning embers,	
28b	וְרַגְלָיו לֹא תִכָּוֶינָה	without his feet being scorched?	
29a	כֵּן הַבָּא אֶל־אֵשֶׁת רֵעֵהוּ	So is he who enters his neighbor's wife,	
29b	לֹא יִנָּקֶה כָּל־הַנֹּגֵעַ בָּהּ	none who touches her remains unpunished.	

Continued on next page.

Continued from previous page.

	Hebrew	Translation	Outline
30a	לֹא־יָבוּזוּ לַגַּנָּב כִּי יִגְנוֹב	People do not despise a thief if he steals	c. The Senselessness and Self-Destruction of Misplaced Desire and Adultery (6:30–32)
30b	↑ לְמַלֵּא נַפְשׁוֹ כִּי יִרְעָב	↑ to satisfy his desire when hungry.	
31a	וְנִמְצָא יְשַׁלֵּם שִׁבְעָתָיִם	But if caught, he must repay sevenfold,	
31b	אֶת־כָּל־הוֹן בֵּיתוֹ יִתֵּן	all the wealth of his house he must give.	
32a	נֹאֵף אִשָּׁה חֲסַר־לֵב	One who commits adultery with a woman lacks sense;	
32b	מַשְׁחִית נַפְשׁוֹ הוּא יַעֲשֶׂנָּה	one who destroys his own life, he is the one who does this.	
			3. The Conclusion: The Certain Punishment of Misdirected Desire and Adultery (6:33–35)
33a	נֶגַע־וְקָלוֹן יִמְצָא	He will find affliction and shame,	a. The Inevitable Punishment for Misplaced Desire and Adultery (6:33)
33b	וְחֶרְפָּתוֹ לֹא תִמָּחֶה	and his reproach will not be removed.	
34a	↑ כִּי־קִנְאָה חֲמַת־גָּבֶר	↑ For jealousy is a man's wrath,	b. The Rationale for the Inevitable Punishment (6:34–35)
34b	וְלֹא־יַחְמוֹל בְּיוֹם נָקָם	and he will not show compassion on the day of vengeance.	
35a	לֹא־יִשָּׂא פְּנֵי כָל־כֹּפֶר	He shall not accept any ransom,	
35b	וְלֹא־יֹאבֶה כִּי תַרְבֶּה־שֹׁחַד	nor be satisfied though you increase the bribe.	

The causal clause (v. 23) provides a rationale for the guidance of wisdom and parental instruction presented in v. 22a. And the purpose clause (v. 24) clarifies the goal of wisdom's protection delineated in v. 22b–c. In so doing, it not only marks the conclusion of the exordium, but it also identifies the subject of the lesson proper, serving as a hinge between the introduction and the main body of the discourse. Against the backdrop of the exordium, the second section conveys the formal lesson, which consists of admonitions, rhetorical questions, and a scenario concerned with the dangers of misdirected desire as well as the terrifying consequences of adultery (vv. 25–32). These consequences are brought into sharp relief in the third and final section of the lecture, where the inevitable punishment for adultery (v. 33) is substantiated by a specific rationale: the inextinguishable wrath of the woman's husband (vv. 34–35).

In contrast to the conclusions to other lectures in the prologue, the discourse ends with neither a crisp summary of the lesson nor a moral or theological rationale for the inevitable judgment of the adulterer. While it mirrors the general architecture of other lectures in the prologue, it remains distinct. The same is true of its coherence. Whereas other lectures in the prologue are bound together by recurring terms, expressions, or images, the discourse is bound together by a coherent argument, a common emotion, and attention to a particular theme.[4] In view of the guidance and protection of wisdom (vv. 20–24), the lesson prosecutes a particular argument: if one desires and is captured by a married woman, severe punishment is unavoidable. Adultery with the strange woman is the focus of attention. And fear is the emotion that pervades the discourse's comparisons, analogies, rhetorical questions, and evaluations.

4. This does not mean that repeated terms and images are absent from the lecture; the root "to watch, guard" (שׁמר) occurs twice (vv. 22b, 24a), the verbal and nominal form of the root נגע is used in vv. 29b and 33a, and conflagration imagery appears in vv. 27–28.

CHAPTER 13

Proverbs 7:1–27

L. Wisdom and Seduction

Main Idea of the Passage

The parent invites the addressee to see, hear, touch, taste, and smell the strange woman so that he might experience the power of seduction, perceive the dark side of the woman's smooth speech, and recognize the protection of another woman: Wisdom.

Literary Context of the Passage

As the final parental discourse in the prologue, this imaginative piece plays a significant role within the literary context of Prov 1–9; it fits within and contributes to the prologue in at least three ways. First, the discourse includes language and imagery redolent of the first lecture to create a literary envelope around the parental speeches (1:8–19; 7:1–27).[1] The actions and speech of the strange woman mimic the actions and speech of the sinners (7:12, 15, 15, 18; cf. 1:11, 13, 18); and the subhuman description of the sinners' fate is reflected in the subhuman description of the fate that befalls the lad lacking sense (7:23; cf. 1:17). Second, the discourse sets the stage for the interludes that follow (8:1–36; 9:1–18). The speech, character, way, and house of the strange woman serve as a counterpart to and a foil for the speech, character, ways, and houses of the women who occupy the symbolic register in the remainder of the prologue. Third, the discourse reinforces and develops previous texts devoted to the strange woman (2:16–19; 5:1–23; 6:20–33). Similar to these texts, the piece attends to the seductive rhetoric of the strange woman (2:16; 5:3; 6:24; 7:5, 14–20, 21), the dangers of unsanctioned desire (5:9–14; 6:27–35; 7:22–23), and the disastrous

1. Gale Yee, "'I Have Perfumed My Bed with Myrrh': The Foreign Woman (ʾiššâ) in Proverbs 1–9," *JSOT* 43 (1989): 56; Clifford, *Proverbs*, 84; Van Leeuwen, "The Book of Proverbs," *NIB* 5:83–84.

consequences that accompany passage along her way and entrance into her house (2:18–19; 5:5–6, 8, 22–23; 7:25–27). These similarities, however, should not overshadow the distinctive contributions of Prov 7:1–27 to the prologue's discussion of the strange woman. Whereas the previous instructions talk about her smooth speech, Prov 7 allows this composite figure to speak. In addition, like 5:1–23 and 6:20–33, the discourse delivers its teaching through a distinctive pedagogical approach.

- I. Introduction to the Book (1:1–7)
- **II. The Value of Wisdom and Virtue (1:8–9:18)**
  - A. Wisdom, Desire, and Different Ways (1:8–19)
  - B. Wisdom's Rebuke (1:20–33)
  - C. The Procurement, Power, and Protection of Wisdom and Virtue (2:1–22)
  - D. Wisdom and Piety (3:1–12)
  - E. Wisdom's Value and Moral Obligations (3:13–35)
  - F. Wisdom and Tradition (4:1–9)
  - G. Wisdom and Ways of Life (4:10–19)
  - H. Wisdom and the Moral Anatomy (4:20–27)
  - I. Wisdom and Sexuality (5:1–23)
  - J. Wisdom, Lending, Laziness, and the Immoral Anatomy (6:1–19)
  - K. Wisdom, Desire, and Certain Destruction (6:20–35)
  - ➡ **L. Wisdom and Seduction (7:1–27)**
    - **1. Introductory Exhortation: The Retention and Protection of Wisdom (7:1–5)**
      - **a. The Admonitions: The Retention of Wisdom (7:1–4)**
      - **b. The Purpose: The Protection of Wisdom (7:5)**
    - **2. The Lesson: A Cautionary Tale (7:6–23)**
      - **a. The Setting: Seeing the Senseless (7:6–9)**
      - **b. The Central Subject: Seeing the Woman (7:10–13)**
      - **c. The Speech: Hearing the Seduction (7:14–20)**
        - **(1) The Seductive Preparations (7:14–17)**
        - **(2) The Seductive Proposition (7:18–20)**
      - **d. The Consequences of Submitting to Seduction (7:21–23)**
    - **3. The Conclusion: The Woman, Her Ways, and Her House (7:24–27)**
      - **a. The Admonitions (7:24–25)**
      - **b. The Motivation (7:26–27)**
  - M. Wisdom's Call, Credentials, and the Cosmos (8:1–36)
  - N. Wisdom and Folly's Invitations (9:1–18)
- III. "Forming 'Fearers of YHWH'": The Curriculum of Wisdom and Virtue (10:1–29:27)
- IV. The Application of Wisdom and Virtue (30:1–31:31)

Whereas 5:1–23 counterbalances the multifaceted consequences of illicit sexual activity with the delights of marital sex and 6:20–35 traffics in terror to scare the pants on the prospective adulterer, 7:1–27 deals in indeterminacy, the powers of seduction, and the paradoxical pain and pleasure of desire.[2] The discourse may treat a common theme, but it explores this theme through a distinctive pedagogical approach. And this approach illuminates the unit's place within and contribution to the prologue's discussion of sexual desire, speech, and the strange woman.

Beyond the boundaries of the prologue, Prov 7:1–27 serves as the seedbed out of which the sayings concerning illicit sexual activity in the remainder of the book sprout (22:14; 23:27; 29:3; 30:20; 31:3). And together with 5:1–23 and 6:20–35, the discourse provides a foil for the impressionistic portrait of the valiant woman in 31:10–31. This woman is the antithesis of the strange woman. She labors during the night (31:15, 18) rather than prowling the public spaces for prospective sexual partners (7:9). She possesses a permanent form of "beauty" (31:30) rather than a deceptive façade (6:25). And she drapes her bed with "coverings" (31:22) in order to enhance her household rather than to entice the senseless to partake in illicit sexual acts (7:16). The discourse includes distinctive terms and images that are redeployed in the anthology's climactic poem to portray the positive counterpart to the strange woman.

Translation and Exegetical Outline

(See pages 285–85.)

Structure and Literary Form

The distinctive pedagogical strategy of the discourse unit coincides with the distinctive literary form of the piece. While the poem is framed by admonitions characteristic of the parental lectures elsewhere in the prologue (7:1–5, 24–27), the center of the piece is quite different (7:6–23). The lesson proper is a fictional story cast in a conventional type scene that draws on elements of erotic poetry and deals in indeterminate language to stimulate the imagination, arouse the senses, and inculcate discretion.[3] Whether the lesson is classified as an example story, an autobiographical narrative, or a cautionary tale, it is the product of fictional imagination.[4]

2. Scott C. Jones, "Wisdom's Pedagogy: A Comparison of Proverbs VII and 4Q184," *VT* 53 (2003): 65–80; Stewart, *Poetic Ethics*, 158-61.

3. Alter, *The Art of Biblical Poetry*, 64–73; Jones, "Wisdom's Pedagogy," 65–80; Estes, "Fiction and Truth," 387–99; Stewart, *Poetic Ethics*, 158–61.

4. Alter, *The Art of Biblical Poetry*, 73.

Proverbs 7:1–27

Verse	Hebrew	English	Outline
			L. Wisdom and Seduction (7:1–27)
			1. Introductory Exhortation: The Retention and Protection of Wisdom (7:1–5)
1a	בְּנִי שְׁמֹר אֲמָרָי	My son, keep my words,	a. The Admonitions: The Retention of Wisdom (7:1–4)
1b	וּמִצְוֺתַי תִּצְפֹּן אִתָּךְ	and store my commandments within you;	
2a	שְׁמֹר מִצְוֺתַי וֶחְיֵה	keep my commandments so that you may live	
2b	וְתוֹרָתִי כְּאִישׁוֹן עֵינֶיךָ	and my teaching as the pupil of your eye;	
3a	קָשְׁרֵם עַל־אֶצְבְּעֹתֶיךָ	bind them on your fingers,	
3b	כָּתְבֵם עַל־לוּחַ לִבֶּךָ	write them on the tablet of your heart.	
4a	אֱמֹר לַחָכְמָה אֲחֹתִי אָתְּ	Say to Wisdom, "You are my sister,"	
4b	וּמֹדָע לַבִּינָה תִקְרָא	and call Understanding, "companion,"	
5a	לִשְׁמָרְךָ מֵאִשָּׁה זָרָה	so that they may keep you from a strange woman,	b. The Purpose: The Protection of Wisdom (6:5)
5b	מִנָּכְרִיָּה אֲמָרֶיהָ הֶחֱלִיקָה	an outsider who makes her words smooth.	
			2. The Lesson: A Cautionary Tale (7:6–23)
6a	כִּי בְּחַלּוֹן בֵּיתִי	When, at the window of my house,	a. The Setting: Seeing the Senseless (7:6–9)
6b	בְּעַד אֶשְׁנַבִּי נִשְׁקָפְתִּי	I looked down through my lattice,	
7a	וָאֵרֶא בַפְּתָאיִם	then I saw among the uncommitted,	
7b	אָבִינָה בַבָּנִים נַעַר חֲסַר־לֵב	perceived among the youths, a lad lacking sense,	
8a	עֹבֵר בַּשּׁוּק אֵצֶל פִּנָּהּ	passing through the street by her corner,	
8b	וְדֶרֶךְ בֵּיתָהּ יִצְעָד	striding along the way of her house	
9a	בְּנֶשֶׁף־בְּעֶרֶב יוֹם	at dusk, in the evening,	
9b	בְּאִישׁוֹן לַיְלָה וַאֲפֵלָה	in the black of night and darkness	
10a	וְהִנֵּה אִשָּׁה לִקְרָאתוֹ	And look – a woman meets him,	b. The Central Subject: Seeing the Woman (7:10–13)
10b	שִׁית זוֹנָה וּנְצֻרַת לֵב	in a harlot's garment, with hidden intent.	
11a	הֹמִיָּה הִיא וְסֹרָרֶת	She is turbulent and defiant,	
11b	בְּבֵיתָהּ לֹא־יִשְׁכְּנוּ רַגְלֶיהָ	her feet do not stay in her house;	
12a	פַּעַם בַּחוּץ פַּעַם בָּרְחֹבוֹת	a foot in the street, a foot in the squares,	
12b	וְאֵצֶל כָּל־פִּנָּה תֶאֱרֹב	and beside every corner she lurks.	
13a	וְהֶחֱזִיקָה בּוֹ וְנָשְׁקָה־לּוֹ	Then she seized him and kissed him,	
13b	הֵעֵזָה פָנֶיהָ וַתֹּאמַר לוֹ	with a brazen face she said to him:	

Continued on next page.

Continued from previous page.

14a	זִבְחֵי שְׁלָמִים עָלָי	"I had to make peace offerings.	c. The Speech: Hearing the Seduction (7:14–20)
14b	הַיּוֹם שִׁלַּמְתִּי נְדָרָי	Today I paid my vows!	(1) The Seductive Preparations (7:14–17)
15a	עַל־כֵּן יָצָאתִי לִקְרָאתֶךָ	Therefore, I came out to meet you,	
15b	לְשַׁחֵר פָּנֶיךָ וָאֶמְצָאֶךָּ	to seek your face, and I found you!	
16a	מַרְבַדִּים רָבַדְתִּי עַרְשִׂי	I've prepared my couch with coverings,	
16b	↑ חֲטֻבוֹת אֵטוּן מִצְרָיִם	↑ embroidered cloth, Egyptian linen.	
17a	נַפְתִּי מִשְׁכָּבִי	I've perfumed my bed –	
17b	↑ מֹר אֲהָלִים וְקִנָּמוֹן	↑ myrrh, aloes, and cinnamon.	
18a	לְכָה נִרְוֶה דֹדִים עַד־הַבֹּקֶר	Come, let's drink lovemaking until morning,	(2) The Seductive Proposition (7:18–20)
18b	נִתְעַלְּסָה בָּאֳהָבִים	let's indulge ourselves in love;	
19a	↑ כִּי אֵין הָאִישׁ בְּבֵיתוֹ	↑ for the man is not at home,	
19b	הָלַךְ בְּדֶרֶךְ מֵרָחוֹק	he's gone on a far journey.	
20a	צְרוֹר־הַכֶּסֶף לָקַח בְּיָדוֹ	He took a bag of money in his hand,	
20b	לְיוֹם הַכֵּסֶא יָבֹא בֵיתוֹ	he will return to his house at the full moon."	
21a	הִטַּתּוּ בְּרֹב לִקְחָהּ	She seduces him with her powerful instruction,	d. The Consequences of Submitting to Seduction (7:21–23)
21b	בְּחֵלֶק שְׂפָתֶיהָ תַּדִּיחֶנּוּ	with her smooth lips she tempts him.	
22a	הוֹלֵךְ אַחֲרֶיהָ פִּתְאֹם	He follows her at once,	
22b	↑ כְּשׁוֹר אֶל־טָבַח יָבוֹא	↑ like an ox goes to slaughter,	
22c	וּכְעֶכֶס אֶל־מוּסַר אֱוִיל	and like a stag skipping into a trap,	
23a	עַד יְפַלַּח חֵץ כְּבֵדוֹ	until an arrow pierces his liver,	
23b	כְּמַהֵר צִפּוֹר אֶל־פָּח	as a bird rushing to a trap,	
23c	וְלֹא־יָדַע כִּי־בְנַפְשׁוֹ הוּא	so he does not know that his life is the cost.	
			3. The Conclusion: The Woman, Her Ways, and Her House (7:24–27)
24a	וְעַתָּה בָנִים שִׁמְעוּ־לִי	So now, sons, listen to me,	a. The Admonitions (7:24–25)
24b	וְהַקְשִׁיבוּ לְאִמְרֵי־פִי	and pay attention to the words of my mouth.	
25a	אַל־יֵשְׂטְ אֶל־דְּרָכֶיהָ לִבֶּךָ	Do not let your heart turn aside to her ways,	
25b	אַל־תֵּתַע בִּנְתִיבוֹתֶיהָ	do not wander into her paths.	
26a	↑ כִּי־רַבִּים חֲלָלִים הִפִּילָה	↑ for many are the slain she has toppled,	b. The Motivation (7:26–27)
26b	וַעֲצֻמִים כָּל־הֲרֻגֶיהָ	and numerous all those killed by her.	
27a	דַּרְכֵי שְׁאוֹל בֵּיתָהּ	The ways of Sheol [run through] her house,	
27b	יֹרְדוֹת אֶל־חַדְרֵי־מָוֶת	descending to the chambers of death.	

When this imaginative account is read in concert with the frame of the discourse unit, it appears that the piece is not a pure form; it defies strict classification. At best, it is a didactic poem that intermingles elements common to instructional texts, love poetry, and imaginative literature in order to awaken one's moral imagination, hone the faculties of discernment, and illuminate the value of wisdom through one's active participation in the world of the discourse.

The formal diversity of the poem clarifies its pedagogical agenda and literary design. The discourse consists of three main sections. The first is a conventional introduction (7:1–5) complete with admonitions and a purpose clause, which serves as a transition to the lesson proper. The second section delivers the formal lesson (7:6–23). This lesson contains several subunits, each of which appeal to the senses. The third and final section of the poem returns to the admonitory style of the introduction (7:24–27), providing a climactic warning that includes the root metaphor of the way and the satellite images of women and houses.

The design of the poem contributes to its suasive intent. And the recurring terms and expressions within the piece strengthen its coherence.[5] In addition to repeating language from discourses elsewhere in the prologue, the poem reiterates many words and phrases: the verb "keep" (שׁמר, vv. 1a, 2a, 5a); the expression "my commandments" (מִצְוֹתַי, vv. 1b, 2a); the nouns for "pupil, black" (אִישׁוֹן, vv. 2b, 9b), "corner" (פִּנָּה, vv. 8a, 12b), "house" (בַּיִת, vv. 6a, 8b, 11b, 19a, 20b, 27a), and "way" (דֶּרֶךְ, vv. 8b, 19b, 25a, 27a); the infinitive construct "to meet" (קְרָאת-, vv. 10a, 15a); the root "smooth" (חלק, vv. 5b, 21b); and the verb "go, walk" (הלך, vv. 18a, 19b, 22a). These recurring terms and expressions highlight the poem's rhetorical texture and complement its pedagogical agenda.

Explanation of the Text

1. *Introductory Exhortation: The Retention and Protection of Wisdom (7:1–5)*

a. The Admonitions: The Retention of Wisdom (7:1–4)

The poem opens in conventional fashion with a sequence of admonitions. Similar to the introductory exhortations to the parental lectures elsewhere in the prologue, these admonitions recycle terms and lines from other exordia. The recurrence of these terms and lines illuminates the significance of repetition in the prologue's pedagogical approach. In several parental lectures, repetition cultivates receptivity. Here repetition inspires retention. Retention is the focus of attention in vv. 1–3. And this retention is conveyed through the verbs "keep"

5. R. N. Whybray reflects on the compositional history of the unit, arguing that the poem originated as a brief instruction (vv. 1–3, 5, 25–27) into which a moral tale was inserted (*Proverbs*, NCB [Grand Rapids: Eerdmans, 1994], 110–11). While this proposal recognizes the instructional frame of the unit, the recurring terms within the frame and the moral tale as well as the tale's place within the conventional tripartite structure of the parental lectures render Whybray's reconstruction unconvincing.

(שְׁמֹר, vv. 1a, 2a), "store" (תִּצְפֹּן, v. 1b), "bind" (-קָשְׁר, v. 3a), and "write" (-כָּתְב, v. 3b). These verbs capture the internal and external dimensions of retention. The parental commands are to be preserved (v. 1a) and packed into one's internal pantry (v. 1b; cf. 2:1). This vision of retention is intensified in v. 2, which repeats the verb from v. 1a and the object from v. 1b. According to the parent, the preservation of his commandments yields life (v. 2a; cf. 4:4);[6] that is, retention of his teaching preserves one's life. Accordingly, it is to be guarded as the "pupil" (אִישׁוֹן, v. 2b) of one's eye and positioned at the very center of one's attention. What's more, parental teaching is to be fixed on one's being and inscribed on one's heart (v. 3; cf. 3:3; 6:21; Deut 6:8–9; 11:18–21), where it may serve as an external reminder and an internal guide that prompts wise conduct. The admonitions in vv. 1–3 emphasize the internal and external retention, preservation, and instillation of the parent's commandments. These commandments are valuable, so valuable that they are to be protected like the very locus of one's vision (v. 2b).

To the retention of parental teaching, v. 4 adds another instrument of defense: relationship. This relationship is expressed through an inchoate personification of Wisdom and Understanding. The son is urged to call these ladies "my sister" (אֲחֹתִי, v. 4a) and "companion" (מֹדָע, v. 4b), respectively. The former is a term of intimacy and endearment common to the Song of Songs (Song 4:9, 10, 12; 5:1, 2),[7] while the latter is a designation that connotes relational knowledge and kinship solidarity (Ruth 2:1; 3:2).[8] Together with parental teaching (Prov 7:1–3) and similar to one's wife (5:15–19), it appears that relationship with Lady Wisdom will protect one from the wrong type of woman.[9]

b. The Purpose: The Protection of Wisdom (7:5)

This protection is specified through a purpose clause in v. 5. Keeping parental instruction and intimate relationship with Wisdom will keep one from the wiles of the strange woman. These wiles are linked to her words, which she "makes smooth" (הֶחֱלִיקָה, v. 5b). The strange woman's smooth speech is the hallmark of her literary characterization (2:16; 5:3; 6:24; 7:21). And her smooth speech is the focus of attention in the lesson proper (vv. 14–20). The purpose clause marks the conclusion to the introductory exhortation and provides a smooth transition to the formal lesson.[10] It reiterates the verb "keep" from v. 1, forming an *inclusio* around the exordium;[11] and it introduces the central subject as well as the type of speech that will occupy the following lesson.

2. The Lesson: A Cautionary Tale (7:6–23)

As noted above, the formal lesson differs from the lessons within the parental lectures elsewhere in the prologue. The parent does not seek to persuade through admonitions (5:7–8; 6:25–26), allegory (5:15–19), or analogies (6:27–32); rather, he attempts to train one's desires and cultivate one's moral discernment through the powers of imaginative literature. This imaginative lesson functions as

6. Following the imperative "keep" (שְׁמֹר, v. 2a), the *waw* + imperative "and live" (וֶחְיֵה, v. 2a) opens a result clause that conveys "the certain consequence of the previous action" (GKC §110f).

7. Fox, *The Song of Songs and the Ancient Egyptian Love Songs*, 136.

8. McKane, *Proverbs*, 334.

9. Clifford, *Proverbs*, 84.

10. The use of the *lamed* + infinitive construct to introduce a purpose clause that serves as the conclusion to the exordium and a transition to the formal lesson also occurs in 2:12, 5:2, and 6:24.

11. Waltke, *Proverbs: Chapters 1–15*, 370.

a cautionary tale; it tantalizes one's senses, allowing one to experience both the excitement and pleasure of misplaced desire before delivering a cold shower of catastrophic consequences. In view of the syntax of and voices within the lesson, the tale may be divided into four subunits: the setting of the story (7:6–9), a description of the central subject (vv. 10–13), the seductive speech of the woman (vv. 14–20), and the consequences of succumbing to seduction (vv. 21–23).

a. The Setting: Seeing the Senseless (7:6–9)

The cautionary tale opens with a temporal clause that sketches the setting and vantage point of the parent's observation (כִּי; "when," v. 6). Shifting to the first person, the father invites the addressee to approach his window and look down through the lattice.[12] From this bird's-eye perspective, the parent spots a group of uncommitted youths; and among them he perceives a "lad lacking sense" (נַעַר חֲסַר־לֵב, v. 7b). Against the backdrop of the subordinate temporal clause (v. 6), the main clause employs language from the semantic domain of sight and perception to focus attention on a particular type of individual (v. 7). This individual is easy prey. He is among the "uncommitted" (פְתָאיִם, v. 7a), that is, those prone to folly and easily seduced (cf. 1:22; 9:4).[13] As a "youth" (בָנִים, v.7b), he is inexperienced. And as one "lacking sense" (חֲסַר־לֵב, v. 7b), he does not possess the cognitive capacity for wisdom (cf. 6:32; 11:12; 12:11; 15:21; 17:18; 24:30). The characterization of this youth indicates that he is a sitting duck. Or better, he is a roaming duck.

Together, vv. 8–9 modify the main clause of v. 7, describing the direction and the timing of the lad's movements. With the declaration of wisdom's ability to protect one from the strange woman still ringing in the addressee's ear (v. 5), the parent notices this lad passing through the public thoroughfares "by her corner" (אֵצֶל פִּנָּהּ, v. 8a), "striding along" (יִצְעָד, v. 8b) or marching resolutely along the way of her house. The woman needs no introduction. The father is aware of her base of operations. But it appears that the lad is not. He does not search for this woman; rather, he meanders in her direction at the most dangerous time of the day. This dangerous setting is accentuated through the sequence of terms pertaining to darkness in v. 9, culminating in the "pupil" or "black of night" (אִישׁוֹן לַיְלָה, v. 9b) and darkness. With this description, the scene is set: the parent peers into the darkness to perceive an ignorant youth, marching along the way of "her" house in the black of night.

It is important to note that the setting of the story not only provides the backdrop for the events that follow, but it also interpolates the son (and, by implication, the reader) into the tale. The father

12. The lesson is cast in a conventional "type scene" where one looks out the window. This type scene is reflected in several biblical texts and illustrated on ivory plaques from Samaria, Assyria, Cyprus, and Syria (Josh 2:13–21; Judg 5:26–30; 1 Sam 19:11–12; 2 Sam 6:16; 2 Kgs 9:30, 33; Philip J. King and Lawrence E. Stager, *Life in Biblical Israel*, LAI [Louisville: Westminster John Knox, 2001], 30–31). In light of the prominence of women looking through the window in this type scene, the LXX changes the masculine pronoun and the verb to feminine forms, making the strange woman the subject. But it is difficult to see such a sudden shift to a female voice, especially in a lecture delivered by the father where the woman is in the streets, not in the window. And, despite the prominence of women looking through the window in this type-scene, the literary motif is not restricted to a feminine posture (Gen 26:8). The father, then, remains the observer. For a discussion of the issues, see Robert H. O'Connell, "Proverbs VII 16–17: A Case of Fatal Deception in a 'Women and the Window' Type-Scene," *VT* 41 (1991): 235–41; Fokkelien van Dijk-Hemmes, "The I Persona in Proverbs 7," in *On Gendering Texts: Female and Male Voices in the Hebrew Bible*, ed. A. Brenner and F. van Dijk-Hemmes, BibInt 1 (Leiden: Brill, 1993), 57–62; Loader, *Proverbs 1–9*, 300–301.

13. Fox, *Proverbs 1–9*, 42–43; Waltke, *Proverbs: Chapters 1–15*, 111–12.

invites the son to peer through his window and perceive the disposition of the lad lacking sense. Then he shifts the son's subject position, moving him from observant onlooker to a senseless street roamer. From this position, the son will both see what the father sees and experience the sensory seduction of the lad lacking sense.[14]

b. The Central Subject: Seeing the Woman (7:10–13)

The father's discriminating evaluation of the lad lacking sense corresponds with his evaluation of the central subject of the lesson: the woman. The particle "look" (הִנֵּה, v. 10a) focuses attention on the woman and ushers her to the center of the stage, a place she will occupy through v. 21. Similar to the lad lacking sense (vv. 7–9), the father profiles this woman's character and movements (vv. 10b–12). This profile is parenthetical to the actions the father witnessed (vv. 7, 10a, 13a). The parenthesis, however, reveals the father's moral discretion as well as the woman's immoral disposition. On the surface, the father recognizes that the woman is dressed as a harlot (v.10b; cf. Gen 38:14); her identity is hidden from view. But he sees behind the veil and diagnoses her character. She is a woman "with hidden intent" (נְצֻרַת לֵב, v. 10b), cunning and crafty.[15] She is "turbulent" (הֹמִיָּה, v. 11a; cf. 9:13) and "defiant" (סֹרָרֶת, v. 11a), that is, boisterous and resistant to authority (cf. Deut 21:18). And "her feet are all over town,"[16] in the street and squares, but not at home (Prov 7:11b–12a).[17] She not only occupies a corner (v. 8a); she also "lurks" (תֶאֱרֹב, v. 12b) at every corner. Like the sinners in 1:11 (cf. 1:18), the father paints this woman as a devious hunter on the prowl, who lies behind dark corners prepared to ambush her prey.

Having evaluated the inward disposition and outward movements of the woman, the father resumes the main line of action, recounting what he saw (7:13a). After meeting the lad (v. 10a), the woman performs a contemptuous public act: she seizes him and kisses him (v. 13a; cf. Song 8:1). And with "a brazen face" (הֵעֵזָה פָנֶיהָ, Prov 7:13b) she unleashes her seductive discourse. The expression "brazen face" provides a fitting introduction to the speech of the woman; it captures her impudence through a facial expression that indicates what follows is a straight-faced lie.[18]

c. The Speech: Hearing the Seduction (7:14–20)

This lie is dressed in indeterminate language and imagery throughout vv. 14–20, where the parent moves from the sight of the woman to her deceptive speech. This extended speech is dependent on the introductory expression "[and] she said" (וַתֹּאמַר) in v. 13b. And this speech consists of two sections: the seductive preparations of the woman (vv. 14–17) and the seductive proposition of the woman (vv. 18–20).

14. For discussion of the pedagogical contribution of these shifting subject positions, see Stewart, *Poetic Ethics*, 158–60.

15. G. R. Driver, "Hebrew Notes," *VT* 1 (1950): 250.

16. Fox, *Proverbs 1–9*, 245.

17. While פַּעַם may denote some aspect of time, it also carries the sense of "foot" or "step." Many translations and commentators opt for the former ("now in the street, now in the squares"). In light of the description of the woman's feet in v. 11b, however, it appears the latter sense is in view. So also, Longman, *Proverbs*, 184; Stewart, *Poetic Ethics*, 156. In addition to describing the physical movements of the woman, the language of feet may also depict her sexual movements. Since foot/feet may serve as a euphemism for genitalia, Longman suggests that the description serves as a double entendre: this woman has taken her sexual desire and activity from marriage and the home to the public thoroughfares (Longman, *Proverbs*, 189). If this is the case, the double entendre contributes to the indeterminacy that pervades the lesson.

18. Duane A. Garrett, "Votive Prostitution Again: A Comparison of Proverbs 7:13–14 and 21:28–29," *JBL* 109 (1990): 681–82; idem, *Proverbs*, 104.

(1) The Seductive Preparations (7:14–17)

The preparations open with a pair of pregnant declarations that are designed to project the woman's religious commitment and to present the lad with an implicit invitation. These declarations concern cultic matters: "peace offerings" (זִבְחֵי שְׁלָמִים, v. 14a) and "vows" (נְדָרָי, v. 14b). The former refers to a particular type of celebrative sacrifice, according to which the deity consumed the fat and certain organs, a cultic official received a portion of the offering, and the worshipper retained the rest for a joyous feast (Lev 3:15–17; 7:15–16, 29–38).[19] The latter is a more general designation for votive offerings, which may be paid through peace offerings (Lev 7:16). With these expressions, the woman professes her dedication to cultic obligations,[20] her religious devotion, and her ritual purity.[21] And the mention of peace offerings intimates that she has fresh meat at home for a celebratory meal (Lev 7:15–16). On the surface, she is a devout worshipper prodding the lad to participate in a sumptuous meal. Beneath the surface, however, her smooth, polysemic words betray her hidden intent (Prov 7:10b). Her "brazen face" (v. 13b) indicates these declarations are a sham; she feins cultic devotion in order to soothe the religious sensibilities of the lad.[22] And her claim "I paid my vows" (שִׁלַּמְתִּי נְדָרָי, v. 14b) is ambiguous. The perfective verb suggests that she has fulfilled her vows and meat is available for a joyous banquet. But the verb may also denote an incomplete action, one that will be performed in the near future.[23] In this case, her vows are not quite fulfilled, for the sacrifice and its fresh meat are before her.[24] While the lad appears to understand the declaration in the former sense, it appears the woman intends it in the latter sense: he is the sacrificial ox she is leading to slaughter (v. 22b).[25] The ambiguity of her declarations reveals the nature of her discourse. Her speech is smooth. And her language is indeterminate.

The rhetoric of religion coincides with the rhetoric of relationship (v. 15). Against the backdrop of her religious commitment, the woman expresses her relational desire. The lad is the prize whom she has urgently and specifically sought. She has come to "seek" (שַׁחֵר, v. 15b) and "find" (אֶמְצָא, v. 15b) him.[26] He is the object of her desire. And he is the one for whom the woman has made lavish preparations: a bed spread with "coverings" (מַרְבַדִּים, v. 16a; cf. 31:22), "embroidered cloth" (חֲטֻבוֹת, 7:16b), and "Egyptian linen" (אֵטוּן מִצְרָיִם, v. 16b)[27] perfumed with "myrrh, aloes, and cinnamon" (מֹר אֲהָלִים וְקִנָּמוֹן, v. 17b). Similar to her opening declarations, these preparations are ambiguous. On the one

19. For further discussion of the ritual, see Gary A. Anderson, "Sacrifice and Sacrificial Offerings (OT)," *ABD* 5:878–79.

20. The preposition עַל in v. 14a marks an obligation or duty. *IBHS* §11.2.13c.

21. Fox, *Proverbs 1–9*, 246.

22. Garrett, "Votive Prostitution Again," 682.

23. According to Joüon §112g, this future use of the *qatal* refers to "an action which in fact belongs to the (usually near) future, but which is represented as being performed at the very moment of utterance." See also Karel van der Toorn, "Female Prostitution in Payment of Vows in Ancient Israel," *JBL* 108 (1989): 198.

24. Reading the *qatal* in the future sense does not entail that one must follow Boström and others in concluding the woman is a devotee of Aphrodite who has taken a vow to engage in sexual activity with a stranger during a cultic festival (Gustav Boström, *Proverbiastudien: Die Weisheit und das fremde Weib in Sprüche 1–9*, LUÅ 3 [Lund: Gleerup, 1935], 106). A plain reading of the *qatal* suggests that she has completed her offering and fulfilled her vows. The statement is a clever ruse to lure the lad into her home. But the seductive and polyphonic nature of her speech suggests that, from her perspective, the lad is the offering. Garrett, "Votive Prostitution Again," 682; Clifford, *Proverbs*, 88.

25. Clifford, *Proverbs*, 88.

26. The seek-and-find motif punctuates the discourses within Prov 1–9. Whereas elsewhere the addressee is exhorted to seek and find Wisdom (1:28; 3:13; 8:17, 35), here the strange woman seeks and finds him. Yoder, *Proverbs*, 87.

27. For discussion of these imported fabrics, see Douglas R. Edwards, "Dress and Ornamentation," *ABD* 2:235.

hand, the couch and spices are symbols evocative of opulence and sexual satisfaction (Song 1:16; 4:6, 14, 15; 5:5). On the other hand, linen, myrrh and aloes are associated with burial rites.[28] Again, the woman's language is indeterminate. She massages the lad's ego and tantalizes his senses, leading him to believe she has searched for him alone to enjoy an evening of gastronomic and erotic pleasure. But more is at stake; her slippery words suggest "her couch is his coffin"[29] and her chamber is prepared for his burial.

(2) The Seductive Proposition (7:18–20)

The extravagant preparations of the woman and her appeal to the lad's religious sensibilities, taste, self-image, touch, and smell culminate in an enticing proposition (vv. 18–20). This proposition opens with the long imperative "Come" (לְכָה, v. 18a), which functions as an interjection.[30] And this proposition holds out the promise of sexual satiation without fear of consequences. The woman's sexual interests are no longer implicit. Using language characteristic of the Song of Songs, she invites the lad to an evening of erotic excess in which the partners overindulge their sexual taste buds (v. 18). To be specific, she invites the lad to drink lovemaking with her rather than with his spouse (5:19). The language of drinking and "lovemaking" (דֹּדִים, 7:18a) punctuate the Song of Songs (Song 1:2, 4; 4:10; 5:1; 7:13). This language, however, is recast within a different relationship. The language of love, mutuality, and exclusive commitment within the Song is twisted and deployed to serve the interests of lust and infidelity.[31] Legitimate delights are situated in an illegitimate context.[32]

In view of the risks that accompany this illegitimate expression of sexual satisfaction, the woman attempts to assuage the lad's fears with a pair of statements (Prov 7:19–20). These statements provide a motivation and rationale for her seductive proposition (כִּי, v. 19a) and focus on the whereabouts and itinerary of the man. According to the woman, the man is not in his house but away on a far journey (v. 19). The bag of money he took suggests he will be traveling for some time. And the calendar indicates he is not scheduled to return until the full moon. This description of the man's whereabouts quells the fear of the lad and counters the parent's warning concerning the wrath the adulterer will experience at the hands of a jealous husband (6:34–35). What's more, the woman uses this description to distance herself from her husband. He is "the man" (הָאִישׁ, v. 19a); and he is not, formally, "at his house" (בְּבֵיתוֹ, v. 19a).[33] Fear of consequences should not deter the lad from enjoying sexual satiation.

d. The Consequences of Succumbing to Seduction (7:21–23)

For the parent, however, consequences are inevitable. The voice of the woman gives way to the voice of the father, who describes the power of the woman's speech and the severe consequences that follow from succumbing to her seductive proposition. The father observes that the woman's speech achieved its intended effect, seducing and tempting

28. O'Connell, "Proverbs VII 16–17," 237–38; Clifford, *Proverbs*, 88–89; Dell, *The Book of Proverbs*, 46–47. While the Old Testament in silent on the role of these commodities in burial customs, several New Testament texts bear witness to their use in funeral rites (Matt 27:59; Mark 15:46; Luke 23:53; John 19:39–40). If, as O'Connell suggests, burial customs tend to be conservative in cultures, then these commodities may serve as ambivalent symbols.

29. Jones, "Wisdom's Pedagogy," 70.

30. When a woman attempts to seduce a man to sleep with her, the long imperative tends to be used (e.g., Gen 39:7, 12). Many thanks to Hélène M. Dallaire, who alerted me to this.

31. Daniel Grossberg, "Two Kinds of Sexual Relationships in the Hebrew Bible," *HS* 35 (1994): 7–25; Clifford, *Proverbs*, 86–87.

32. Van Leeuwen, "The Book of Proverbs," *NIB* 5:85.

the lad (v. 21). This speech is presented in striking terms. Together with the conventional description of the woman's speech and lips as "smooth" (חֵלֶק, v. 21b; cf. 2:16; 5:3; 6:24; 7:5), the father characterizes her discourse as "powerful instruction" (בְּרֹב לִקְחָהּ, v. 21a). Elsewhere in the preamble and prologue, instruction refers to the teaching that the anthology in general and the parents in particular seek to inculcate within the youth (1:5; 4:2; cf. 9:9). But this is not the only instruction available. The woman's speech represents an alternative form of instruction that operates under a different moral worldview and leads to a different end.

This end is sketched through vivid language and imagery in 7:22–23. For the first time since v. 8, the passive lad performs an action: he follows her suddenly (v. 22a).[34] And this journey is depicted in subhuman terms throughout the remainder of vv. 22–23.[35] The lad is compared to an ignorant ox entering the slaughterhouse (v. 22b), to a stag mindlessly skipping into a trap where he will be shot (v. 22c–23a),[36] and to a senseless bird rushing into a snare (v. 23b). The ignorance of these creatures in their journey toward death is specified in the conclusion to the formal lesson. Just at these animals do not know their life is at stake, so also the lad lacking sense does not know that the price of his journey is his life (v. 23c). The pair of tristichs in vv. 22–23 disrupt the flow of poetic parallelism in the piece and highlight the severe consequences that accompany submission to the woman's seductive speech. The parent concludes the lesson in the same way that he began, peering behind the veil to illustrate the power of perception and the value of moral discretion.

3. The Conclusion: The Woman, Her Ways, and Her House (7:24–27)

These virtues are also applied in the conclusion of the discourse (vv. 24–27), which resumes the instructional style of the introduction and summarizes the essence of the lesson with a pair of admonitions and motivations.

a. The Admonitions (7:24–25)

The conclusion opens with a renewed call to attention (v. 24). Similar to 5:7 (cf. 8:32), the expression "so now" (וְעַתָּה, 7:24a) establishes logical continuity with the preceding lesson and signals a shift in the rhetorical agenda of the piece.[37] And the use of the plural "sons" (בָנִים, v. 24a) highlights the general applicability of the instruction. The parent alters the subject position of the addressee once

33. These expressions may be conventional idioms for "husband" and "house," respectively (Waltke, *Proverbs: Chapters 1–15*, 381). But the use of the definite article and the third-person pronominal suffix in the context of the woman's seductive speech suggests the expressions convey a measure of alienation from the man. Fox, *Proverbs 1–9*, 248; Loader, *Proverbs 1–9*, 311.

34. In contrast to the MT (פִּתְאֹם; "suddenly, at once"), the LXX reads κεπφωθείς (פתאים; "simple"). Rather than representing a vocalization error, the Septuagint translation appears to be an interpretation of פתאם (McKane, *Proverbs*, 340; *BHQ*; Loader, *Proverbs 1–9*, 313n60). While the MT is preferred, it is important to note that פתאם may be a play on פתאים (7:7), capturing both the immediacy of the lad's response as well as his folly (Stewart, *Poetic Ethics*, 157n86).

35. Several commentators modify the order of lines in v. 23 on logical grounds. For example, Toy and Fox argue that v. 23a interrupts the sequence of similes and should be placed at the conclusion of v. 23 (Toy, *Proverbs*, 156–57; Fox, *Proverbs 1–9*, 250). But this reading is unconvincing, since the sequence of lines makes good sense. Verse 23a describes the way in which the ensnared stag is killed (v. 22c). This slaughter may be performed through an arrow; it is not limited to a knife.

36. The MT of v. 22c reads "and like the fetters/ankle chain of a disciplined fool." This reading seems unlikely, since it breaks the sequence of animal comparisons. With many commentators, it seems best to follow the LXX and read "like a stag skipping into a trap." For further discussion of the emendation, see Fox, *Proverbs 1–9*, 249–50; Waltke, *Proverbs: Chapters 1–15*, 365n33; Loader, *Proverbs 1–9*, 313–14.

37. *IBHS* §39.3.4f.

more, moving him from a senseless street roamer to an attentive student focused on his "words" (אִמְרֵי, v. 24b) rather than the woman's words (v. 5b). From this receptive posture, the parent admonishes the son to attend to the headquarters of his moral anatomy and the seat of his desires. His heart must not desire or turn to her ways (v. 25a; cf. 4:15) and, by implication, meander about in her paths (v. 25b).[38] That is, he must train his desires and anatomy so that they do not stray into the lifestyle and adopt the orientation of the woman.

b. The Motivation (7:26–27)

The rationale or motivation for this warning is delineated in vv. 26–27. Here the parent returns to the military and hunting imagery employed earlier in the discourse (vv. 12b, 23a; cf. 6:26b), noting that the seductress has claimed many "slain" or "pierced ones" (חֲלָלִים, 7:26a). This is not surprising, for the woman's house is depicted as the gateway to Sheol. Similar to 2:18, the parent blurs the boundaries among the woman, her ways, and her house.[39] All forms of behavior oriented toward Sheol pass through her home, leading one to the inner chambers of the vast subterranean mausoleum where the most vile individuals reside (cf. Ezek 32:17–32). The cosmological imagery provides a backdrop for the parent's climactic use of the nuclear symbol of the way and the satellite images of a woman and a house. This conclusion captures the thrust of the cautionary tale and indicates that the lesson outlines the pattern by which many are destroyed.[40] The way and house of this woman lead to death. No wonder the discourse leads one to that fearful place, ending with the word "death" (מָוֶת, v. 27b).[41]

Canonical and Theological Significance

Research from the fields of cognitive science, pain studies, and linguistics provide a rationale for a particular rhetorical technique deployed across Prov 5:1–23, 6:20–35, and 7:1–27. According to the findings of these fields, pain is pedagogically productive. Pain is an inescapable sensation. Every person experiences pain. And every person responds to the sensation, sight, or description of pain in different ways, ranging from empathy and vicarious experience to aversion and anticipation.[42] When philosophical and linguistic analyses of pain are read in relation to Prov 5:1–23, 6:20–35, and 7:1–27, it appears that the parent's rhetoric of pain is deployed to direct one in a life of wisdom and virtue. More specifically, this rhetoric is designed to inspire an avoidance of immoral behaviors.[43] Just as pain serves as God's "megaphone

38. Fox, *Proverbs 1–9*, 250–51.

39. This blurring of boundaries is also apparent in the use of the term "chambers" (חַדְרֵי, v. 27b), which may refer to both the compartments within Sheol as well as the woman's genitalia. Newsom, "Woman and the Discourse of Patriarchal Wisdom," 155–56; Jones, "Wisdom's Pedagogy," 70; Waltke, *Proverbs: Chapters 1–15*, 384–86.

40. Estes, "Fiction and Truth," 395.

41. Stewart, *Poetic Ethics*, 158n90.

42. Ryan P. O'Dowd, "Pain and Danger: Unpleasant Sayings and the Structure of Proverbs," *CBQ* 80 (2019): 619.

43. O'Dowd, "Pain and Danger," 624.

to rouse a deaf world,"[44] so pain serves as the parent's rhetorical megaphone to rouse the moral self.

This rhetorical megaphone resounds across Prov 5:1–23, 6:20–35, and 7:1–27 to engender an aversion to illicit sexual activity. The parent depicts the strange woman as a sharp, two-edged sword (5:4). A neighbor's wife is a fire and embers, which burn one's bosom and scorch one's feet (6:27–28). Those who fall prey to the smooth speech of the strange woman experience groaning and physical disintegration (5:11). An arrow pierces their liver, and they are ensnared by a trap (7:23). These descriptions of cutting, burning, deterioration, wounding, and trapping elicit terror. This perlocutionary effect may explain the pedagogical approach of these discourses, especially the approaches of Prov 6:20–35 and 7:1–27. On the surface, the pedagogical approaches of these discourses may feel counterintuitive. Should one seek to induce terror in another to teach a lesson? And should one allow a vulnerable person to hear, touch, taste, and smell sexual seduction? These are difficult questions. The rhetoric of Prov 6:20–35 and 7:1–27, however, suggests that these pedagogical techniques are appropriate. They are appropriate because humans are embodied, fearful, pain-averse creatures.

Together with pain, the parent arouses terror by focusing on the social and physical consequences of illicit sexual activity. This form of activity occasions public shame, the forfeiture of economic resources, psychological anguish, the vengeance of an immovable husband, and, ultimately, death. The parent puts words of guilt and remorse in the addressee's mouth (5:12–14). The parent writes the son into the adulterous script, promising that the offended husband will not accept his bribe (6:35). And the parent concludes each discourse pertaining to the strange or adulterous woman with a frightening word: capture under the ever-watchful gaze of YHWH (5:21–23), lifelong disgrace at the hands of an enraged husband (6:33–35), and death (7:25–27).

In different ways, the discourses concerning the strange or adulterous woman explore and contextualize the decalogic command prohibiting adultery (Exod 20:14; Deut 5:18). But they do more than this. On another level, they also explore and contextualize idolatry. Many construe the strange or adulterous woman as an instantiation of idolatrous worship.[45] She is a symbol of apostasy. The language and imagery of adultery is deployed elsewhere in Scripture to describe the nature of idolatry and apostasy (Hos 4:13–14; Jer 3:6–10; 5:7–8; Ezek 23:36–45). This is not surprising, since all forms of idolatry parody something good and true in the divine economy. In this instance, idolatry parodies marriage as well as covenant relationship with

44. C. S. Lewis, *The Problem of Pain* (New York: Macmillan, 1962), 91.

45. Maier, *Die 'Fremde Frau' in Proverbien 1–9*; Nam Hoon Tan, *The 'Foreignness' of the Foreign Woman in Proverbs 1–9*.

God; it places a genuine relationship into a framework of falsehood. This recasting of genuine relationship is captured by Mike Ovey, who contends,

> The concept of idolatry helps us to see the spiritually counterfeit, for it exposes a parody of true spiritual relationship. Idolatrous practice parodies the relation of creation by reversing it, with humans making the god of their choice; it parodies true worship in true relationship by offering a lying fiction; it parodies the relation of holy marriage by offering unholy harlotry; and parodies the victory of Christ by understating it. Tertullian memorably envisaged idolatry as fraud. It is doubly so, defrauding God of his glory, and humanity of true relationship. It cruelly counterfeits real spiritual currency: spiritually, it is "funny money."[46]

As "funny money," adultery and idolatry trade on true spiritual realities. This explains why they are attractive. Among other things, they promise satisfaction without commitment. They offer control and affirm self-sufficiency. In light of the stakes in this spiritual economy, how does one discern the true from the counterfeit? The discourses pertaining to the strange or adulterous woman seek to cultivate discernment and perception through various techniques: admonitions (Prov 5:7–8; 6:25–26), love poetry (5:15–19), analogies (6:27–32), and imaginative literature (7:6–23). These techniques feed and fund one's moral imagination. That is, they direct one's seeing of and being in the world. In implicit and explicit ways, the discourses concerning the strange woman appeal to male fantasies, causing the reader to participate in and feel the force of seduction.[47] The same is true of contemporary advertising and media. They appeal to one's fantasies. They arouse the powers of one's imagination. A heathy, moral imagination is necessary to perceive the persuasive powers of the counterfeit and its vision of life. The discourses across Prov 5:1–23, 6:20–35, and 7:1–27 seek to nurture a moral imagination that sees through the parody of true spiritual reality and loves that which is good. These discourses unmask the fraudulent and stock one's moral imagination. These pedagogical dynamics also define the book of Revelation, which attempts to unmask idolatry and counter its appeal by nurturing one's moral imagination. As Richard Bauckham writes,

> One of the functions of Revelation was to purge and to refurbish the Christian imagination. It tackles people's imaginative response to the world, which is at least as deep and influential as their intellectual convictions. It recognizes the way a dominant culture, with its images and ideals, constructs the world for us, so that we perceive and

46. Mike Ovey, "Idolatry and Spiritual Parody: Counterfeit Faiths," in *The Goldilocks Zone: Collected Writings of Michael J. Ovey*, ed. Chris Green (London: IVP, 2018), 145.

47. Estes, "Fiction and Truth," 396.

> respond to the world in its terms. Moreover, it unmasks this dominant construction of the world as an ideology of the powerful which serves to maintain their power. In its place, Revelation offers a different way of perceiving the world which leads people to resist and to challenge the effects of the dominant ideology. Moreover, since this different way of perceiving the world is fundamentally to open it to transcendence it resists any absolutizing of power or structures or ideals within this world. This is the most fundamental way in which the church is called always to be counter-cultural.[48]

Like Revelation, the discourses pertaining to the strange or adulterous woman offer a different way of perceiving the world. This perception of the world is governed by wisdom and virtue, which form and fund one's moral imagination. It is a healthy moral imagination that enables one to resist and to challenge the lure of illicit sexual activity and adultery.

48. Richard Bauckham, *The Theology of the Book of Revelation* (Cambridge: Cambridge University Press, 1993), 159–60.

CHAPTER 14

Proverbs 8:1–36

M. Wisdom's Call, Credentials, and the Cosmos

Main Idea of the Passage

Wisdom praises her character, credentials, cosmic preeminence, and intimate relationship with YHWH to woo her audience, direct their moral consciousness, and encourage them to listen to and embrace her.[1]

Literary Context of the Passage

Wisdom's discourse in ch. 8 plays a formative role in the literary context of the anthology in general and the prologue in particular.[2] The piece contributes to the broad literary context of the prologue in several ways, three in particular. First, the poem complements and counterbalances Wisdom's discourse in 1:20–33. Whereas Wisdom's initial discourse is cast in the form of a rebuke, this speech is cast in the form of self-praise. And whereas Wisdom's initial discourse offered a moral evaluation of prospective devotees, this speech offers a moral evaluation of Wisdom's character. Second, the piece weaves the document's principal virtues through Wisdom's persona. Wisdom's speech and disposition are marked by those virtues that pervade the preamble and define the anthology's agenda (1:1–7): "integrity/uprightness" (מֵישָׁרִים, 8:6b; 1:3), "righteousness" (צֶדֶק, 8:8a; 1:3), "knowledge" (דַעַת, 8:10b; 1:4), "wisdom" (חָכְמָה, 8:11a; 1:2), "shrewdness" (עָרְמָה; 8:12a; 1:4), "discretion" (מְזִמָּה, 8:12b; 1:4), "the fear of YHWH" (יִרְאַת יְהוָה, 8:13a; 1:7), and "understanding" (בִינָה,

1. William P. Brown, *The Ethos of the Cosmos: The Genesis of Moral Imagination in the Bible* (Grand Rapids: Eerdmans, 1999), 272; idem, *Wisdom's Wonder*, 50.

2. For the potential hermeneutical and theological significance of the discourse within the document, see Schwáb, *Toward an Interpretation*, 175–189. Here Schwáb sketches a reading strategy that views the book of Proverbs through the theological vision of ch. 8.

8:14b; 1:2). The intimate relationship between these virtues and Wisdom's character indicates that wisdom and virtue are inextricably linked in Proverbs's moral vision. Put differently, Lady Wisdom is the incarnation of the book's fundamental virtues. Third, Wisdom's discourse elaborates upon many of the inchoate personifications of wisdom in the parental lectures (Prov 3:13–18; 4:5–9; 7:4–5); it elevates one's search and desire for wisdom from the literal level to the metaphorical, and from the historical to the cosmological. This is especially clear in the way in which Wisdom's discourse reiterates and recasts aspects of 3:13–18:

Proverbs 3:13–18	Proverbs 8:1–36
13 Blessed is the person who has found wisdom (אַשְׁרֵי אָדָם מָצָא חָכְמָה), and the person who gains understanding (וְאָדָם יָפִיק תְּבוּנָה),	1 Is not Wisdom (חָכְמָה) calling, and Understanding (תְבוּנָה) raising her voice? 32b for blessed (אַשְׁרֵי) are those who keep my ways 34a Blessed is the person (אַשְׁרֵי אָדָם) who listens to me 35 for the one who finds me finds (מצא) life and gains (וַיָּפֶק) favor from YHWH
14 for her profit is better (טוֹב) than the profit of silver (כָּסֶף), and her yield (תְּבוּאָתָהּ) is better than gold (חָרוּץ);	19 My fruit is better (טוֹב) than gold (מֵחָרוּץ), even fine gold, and my produce (תְבוּאָתִי) than choice silver (מִכֶּסֶף).
15 she is more precious than corals (מִפְּנִינִים), everything desirable cannot compare with her (וְכָל־חֲפָצֶיךָ לֹא יִשְׁווּ־בָהּ);	11 for wisdom is better than corals (פְּנִינִים), and nothing delightful can compare with it (וְכָל־חֲפָצִים לֹא יִשְׁווּ־בָהּ).
16 long life is in her right hand, in her left, riches and honor (עֹשֶׁר וְכָבוֹד);	18 Riches and honor (עֹשֶׁר־וְכָבוֹד) are with me, enduring wealth and righteousness.
17 her ways are pleasant ways, and all her paths are peace;	
18 she is a tree of life (עֵץ־חַיִּים) to those who embrace her, and those who hold fast to her are blessed.	35 for the one who finds me finds life (חַיִּים) and gains favor from YHWH

The shared terms, expressions, and forms in 3:13–18 and 8:1–36 suggest that these texts are intimately related to one another. Similar to the inchoate personification of wisdom elsewhere in the parental lectures, Prov 3:13–18 serves as a well from which Prov 8 draws to develop Wisdom's nature and value.[3]

Together with its contribution to the broad literary context of the prologue, Wisdom's discourse fits within the immediate literary context of Prov 1–9. As noted in

3. Cf. Schipper, *Proverbs 1–15*, 288–90, for discussion of the relationship between Prov 8:22–31 and Gen 1:1–2:4a.

I. Introduction to the Book (1:1–7)

II. The Value of Wisdom and Virtue (1:8–9:18)

- A. Wisdom, Desire, and Different Ways (1:8–19)
- B. Wisdom's Rebuke (1:20–33)
- C. The Procurement, Power, and Protection of Wisdom and Virtue (2:1–22)
- D. Wisdom and Piety (3:1–12)
- E. Wisdom's Value and Moral Obligations (3:13–35)
- F. Wisdom and Tradition (4:1–9)
- G. Wisdom and Ways of Life (4:10–19)
- H. Wisdom and the Moral Anatomy (4:20–27)
- I. Wisdom and Sexuality (5:1–23)
- J. Wisdom, Lending, Laziness, and the Immoral Anatomy (6:1–19)
- K. Wisdom, Desire, and Certain Destruction (6:20–35)
- L. Wisdom and Seduction (7:1–27)
- **M. Wisdom's Call, Credentials, and the Cosmos (8:1–36)**
  - **1. The Introduction to Wisdom's Encomium (8:1–3)**
    - **a. The Introduction of Wisdom (8:1)**
    - **b. The Setting of Wisdom's Speech (8:2–3)**
  - **2. Wisdom's Opening Exhortation (8:4–11)**
    - **a. Wisdom's Appeal (8:4–6)**
    - **b. Wisdom's Virtuous Speech (8:7–9)**
    - **c. Wisdom's Admonition (8:10–11)**
  - **3. Wisdom's Credentials and Function in the Present World (8:12–21)**
    - **a. Wisdom's Credentials (8:12–13)**
    - **b. Wisdom's Function in the Terrestrial Realm (8:14–16)**
    - **c. Wisdom's Gifts (8:17–21)**
  - **4. Wisdom's Preeminence and Position in the Primordial World (8:22–31)**
    - **a. Wisdom's Emergence before Creation (8:22–26)**
    - **b. Wisdom's Presence at Creation (8:27–29)**
    - **c. Wisdom's Activity after Creation (8:30–31)**
  - **5. Wisdom's Climactic Exhortation (8:32–36)**
    - **a. The Exhortation (8:32–33)**
    - **b. The Blessing (8:34)**
    - **c. The Consequences (8:35–36)**
- N. Wisdom and Folly's Invitations (9:1–18)

III. "Forming 'Fearers of YHWH'": The Curriculum of Wisdom and Virtue (10:1–29:27)

IV. The Application of Wisdom and Virtue (30:1–31:31)

the discussion of ch. 7, Wisdom's speech, character, and way provide an alternative to the speech, character, and way of the strange woman. And the telos that awaits those who linger at Wisdom's door serves as a counterpart to the telos reserved for those who enter the strange woman's house (7:26–27; 8:34–36). While Wisdom's speech shifts to the metaphorical register, it presents a woman who represents an attractive alternative to the strange woman.[4] This female antithesis is significant, for it mirrors the antithesis in ch. 9. In this respect, Wisdom's discourse functions as a literary hinge: it provides a foil for the discourse of the strange woman, on the one hand, and foreshadows the antithetical women, houses, and invitations in 9:1–18, on the other.

Translation and Exegetical Outline

(See pages 302–04.)

Structure and Literary Form

In contrast to Wisdom's rebuke in 1:20–33, her discourse in ch. 8 is cast in the form of an encomium. Similar to royal inscriptions and divine aretalogies throughout the ancient Near East, self-praise pervades the piece;[5] and this praise concerns Wisdom's virtuous character, associates, and desires as well as her gifts, antiquity, unique relationship with YHWH, and knowledge of the fundamental patterns woven into the fabric of reality. Self-praise defines the nature and ethos of Wisdom's discourse. This self-praise, however, is situated within a didactic frame that is comparable to the exordia within the parental lectures elsewhere in the prologue (8:10–11, 32–36; cf. 1:8–9; 3:1–2; 4:20–22; 5:7–8; 6:20–24; 7:24–27). The intermingling of these literary forms suggests that the discourse seeks to cultivate one's desires and persuade one to pursue Wisdom, for she embodies and possesses all that is desirable.[6]

The literary forms within the discourse of Prov 8 contribute to its perlocutionary force. And these forms clarify the movement and architecture of the unit. The piece consists of five main sections: (1) a third-person introduction of Wisdom and the setting of her discourse (vv. 1–3); (2) Wisdom's opening exhortation, complete with a profile of her virtuous speech (vv. 4–11); (3) Wisdom's credentials and function within the present world (vv. 12–21); (4) Wisdom's preeminence and position in the

4. In addition to Lady Wisdom, one's wife (5:15–19) and the "valiant woman" (31:10–31) also provide a positive counterpart to the strange woman.

5. For discussion of these ancient Near Eastern texts, see Kayatz, *Studien*, 76–93; Lang, *Wisdom and the Book of Proverbs*, 57–62; Fox, "World Order and Maʿat," 44–47.

6. Stewart, *Poetic Ethics*, 166.

Proverbs 8:1–36

Verse	Hebrew	English	Outline
			M. Wisdom's Call, Credentials, and the Cosmos 8:1–36)
			1. The Introduction to Wisdom's Encomium (8:1–3)
1a	הֲלֹא־חָכְמָה תִקְרָא	Is not Wisdom calling,	a. The Introduction of Wisdom (8:1)
1b	וּתְבוּנָה תִּתֵּן קוֹלָהּ	and Understanding raising her voice?	
2a	↓ בְּרֹאשׁ־מְרוֹמִים עֲלֵי־דָרֶךְ	↓ On top of the heights, beside the way,	b. The Setting of Wisdom's Speech (8:2–3)
2b	בֵּית נְתִיבוֹת נִצָּבָה	at the crossroads she takes her stand;	
3a	↓ לְיַד־שְׁעָרִים לְפִי־קָרֶת	↓ beside the gates at the city entrance,	
3b	מְבוֹא פְתָחִים תָּרֹנָּה	at the entry of the portal she cries aloud:	
			2. Wisdom's Opening Exhortation (8:4–11)
4a	אֲלֵיכֶם אִישִׁים אֶקְרָא	"To you, men, I call out,	a. Wisdom's Appeal (8:4–6)
4b	וְקוֹלִי אֶל־בְּנֵי אָדָם	my voice goes out to humankind.	
5a	הָבִינוּ פְתָאיִם עָרְמָה	Learn shrewdness, you uncommitted!	
5b	וּכְסִילִים הָבִינוּ לֵב	Learn sense, you fools!	
6a	שִׁמְעוּ כִּי־נְגִידִים אֲדַבֵּר	Listen, for I speak straightforward things,	
6b	וּמִפְתַּח שְׂפָתַי מֵישָׁרִים	and the opening of my lips contains integrity.	
7a	כִּי־אֱמֶת יֶהְגֶּה חִכִּי	Indeed, my palate utters truth,	b. Wisdom's Virtuous Speech (8:7–9)
7b	וְתוֹעֲבַת שְׂפָתַי רֶשַׁע	and wickedness is an abomination to my lips.	
8a	בְּצֶדֶק כָּל־אִמְרֵי־פִי	All the words of my mouth are in accord with righteousness;	
8b	אֵין בָּהֶם נִפְתָּל וְעִקֵּשׁ	nothing in them is twisted or perverse.	
9a	כֻּלָּם נְכֹחִים לַמֵּבִין	All of them are straight to the one who understands	
9b	וִישָׁרִים לְמֹצְאֵי דָעַת	and right to those who find knowledge.	
10a	קְחוּ־מוּסָרִי וְאַל־כָּסֶף	Take my instruction instead of silver,	c. Wisdom's Admonition (8:10–11)
10b	וְדַעַת מֵחָרוּץ נִבְחָר	and knowledge rather than choice gold;	
11a	↑ כִּי־טוֹבָה חָכְמָה מִפְּנִינִים	↑ for wisdom is better than corals,	
11b	וְכָל־חֲפָצִים לֹא יִשְׁווּ־בָהּ	and nothing delightful can compare with it.	
			3. Wisdom's Credentials and Function in the Present World (8:12–21)
12a	אֲנִי־חָכְמָה שָׁכַנְתִּי עָרְמָה	I, Wisdom, inhabit shrewdness,	a. Wisdom's Credentials (8:12–13)
12b	וְדַעַת מְזִמּוֹת אֶמְצָא	and knowledge of discretion I find.	
13a	יִרְאַת יְהוָה שְׂנֹאת רָע	The fear of YHWH is hating evil.	
13b	גֵּאָה וְגָאוֹן וְדֶרֶךְ רָע	Pride and arrogance and the way of evil	
13c	וּפִי תַהְפֻּכוֹת שָׂנֵאתִי	and perverse speech I hate.	

Verse	Hebrew	English	Outline
14a	לִי־עֵצָה וְתוּשִׁיָּה	Mine are counsel and resourcefulness;	b. Wisdom's Function in the Terrestrial Realm (8:14–16)
14b	אֲנִי בִינָה לִי גְבוּרָה	I am Understanding; strength is mine.	
15a	בִּי מְלָכִים יִמְלֹכוּ	By me kings reign,	
15b	וְרוֹזְנִים יְחֹקְקוּ צֶדֶק	and rulers decree justice.	
16a	בִּי שָׂרִים יָשֹׂרוּ	By me princes rule,	
16b	וּנְדִיבִים כָּל־שֹׁפְטֵי צֶדֶק	and nobles, all judges of justice.	
17a	אֲנִי אֹהֲבַי אֵהָב	I love those who love me,	c. Wisdom's Gifts (8:17–21)
17b	וּמְשַׁחֲרַי יִמְצָאֻנְנִי	and those who seek me find me.	
18a	עֹשֶׁר־וְכָבוֹד אִתִּי	Riches and honor are with me,	
18b	הוֹן עָתֵק וּצְדָקָה	enduring wealth and righteousness.	
19a	טוֹב פִּרְיִי מֵחָרוּץ וּמִפָּז	My fruit is better than gold, even fine gold,	
19b	וּתְבוּאָתִי מִכֶּסֶף נִבְחָר	and my produce than choice silver.	
20a	בְּאֹרַח־צְדָקָה אֲהַלֵּךְ	I walk on the way of righteousness,	
20b	↑ בְּתוֹךְ נְתִיבוֹת מִשְׁפָּט	↑ in the midst of the paths of justice,	
21a	לְהַנְחִיל אֹהֲבַי יֵשׁ	to cause those who love me to inherit wealth,	
21b	וְאֹצְרֹתֵיהֶם אֲמַלֵּא	and I will fill their treasuries.	
			4. Wisdom's Preeminence and Position in the Primordial World (8:22–31)
22a	יְהוָה קָנָנִי רֵאשִׁית דַּרְכּוֹ	YHWH begat me at the beginning of his way,	a. Wisdom's Emergence before Creation (8:22–26)
22b	↑ קֶדֶם מִפְעָלָיו מֵאָז	↑ the earliest of his works from that time.	
23a	מֵעוֹלָם נִסַּכְתִּי	In the distant past I was formed,	
23b	↑ מֵרֹאשׁ מִקַּדְמֵי־אָרֶץ	↑ at the beginning, at the earliest times of the earth.	
24a	↓ בְּאֵין־תְּהֹמוֹת	↓ When there were no deeps,	
24b	חוֹלָלְתִּי	I was brought forth,	
24c	↑ בְּאֵין מַעְיָנוֹת נִכְבַּדֵּי־מָיִם	↑ when there were no springs abounding with water.	
25a	בְּטֶרֶם הָרִים הָטְבָּעוּ	Before the mountains were founded,	
25b	↓ לִפְנֵי גְבָעוֹת	↓ before the hills,	
25c	חוֹלָלְתִּי	I was brought forth,	
26a	↑ עַד־לֹא עָשָׂה אֶרֶץ וְחוּצוֹת	↑ before he made the earth and the open fields,	
26b	וְרֹאשׁ עַפְרוֹת תֵּבֵל	or the world's first lumps of soil.	

Continued on next page.

Continued from previous page.

27a	↓ בַּהֲכִינוֹ שָׁמַיִם	↓ When he established the heavens,	b. Wisdom's Presence at Creation (8:27–29)
27b	שָׁם אָנִי	I was there —	
27c	↑ בְּחוּקוֹ חוּג עַל־פְּנֵי תְהוֹם	↑ when he inscribed a circle on the face of the deep,	
28a	בְּאַמְּצוֹ שְׁחָקִים מִמָּעַל	when he made firm the clouds above,	
28b	בַּעֲזוֹז עִינוֹת תְּהוֹם	when he fixed the fountains of the deep,	
29a	בְּשׂוּמוֹ לַיָּם חֻקּוֹ	when he set for the sea its limit,	
29b	↑ וּמַיִם לֹא יַעַבְרוּ־פִיו	↑ so that the waters do not transgress his command,	
29c	בְּחוּקוֹ מוֹסְדֵי אָרֶץ	when he marked out the foundations of the earth.	
30a	וָאֶהְיֶה אֶצְלוֹ אָמוֹן	And I have been beside him faithfully,	c. Wisdom's Activity after Creation (8:30–31)
30b	וָאֶהְיֶה שַׁעֲשֻׁעִים יוֹם יוֹם	and I have been delighting before him day after day,	
30c	↑ מְשַׂחֶקֶת לְפָנָיו בְּכָל־עֵת	↑ rejoicing before him always,	
31a	מְשַׂחֶקֶת בְּתֵבֵל אַרְצוֹ	rejoicing in his inhabitable world,	
31b	וְשַׁעֲשֻׁעַי אֶת־בְּנֵי אָדָם	and delighting in humankind.	
			5. Wisdom's Climactic Exhortation (8:32–36)
32a	וְעַתָּה בָנִים שִׁמְעוּ־לִי	So now, sons, listen to me,	a. The Exhortation (8:32–33)
32b	↑ וְאַשְׁרֵי דְּרָכַי יִשְׁמֹרוּ	↑ for blessed are those who keep my ways.	
33a	שִׁמְעוּ מוּסָר וַחֲכָמוּ	Listen to discipline so that you become wise,	
33b	וְאַל־תִּפְרָעוּ	and do not neglect it.	
34a	אַשְׁרֵי אָדָם שֹׁמֵעַ לִי	Blessed is the person who listens to me,	b. The Blessing (8:34)
34b	↑ לִשְׁקֹד עַל־דַּלְתֹתַי יוֹם יוֹם	↑ by keeping vigil at my doors day after day,	
34c	לִשְׁמֹר מְזוּזֹת פְּתָחָי	by watching the posts of my doorways;	
35a	כִּי מֹצְאִי מָצָא חַיִּים	for the one who finds me finds life	c. The Consequences (8:35–36)
35b	וַיָּפֶק רָצוֹן מֵיְהוָה	and gains favor from YHWH;	
36a	וְחֹטְאִי חֹמֵס נַפְשׁוֹ	but the one who offends me harms himself;	
36b	כָּל־מְשַׂנְאַי אָהֲבוּ מָוֶת	all who hate me love death."	

primordial world (vv. 22–31); and (5) Wisdom's climactic exhortation (vv. 32–36).[7] These sections are distinguished by their tone, focus (i.e., "you" [vv. 4–11], "I" [vv. 12–21], "YHWH" [vv. 22–31]), vantage point, and thematic emphases. And they are linked by recurring terms and expressions, such as "humankind" (בְּנֵי אָדָם, vv. 4, 31), "shrewdness" (עָרְמָה, vv. 5, 12), "knowledge" (דַעַת, vv. 9, 10, 12), "instruction" (מוּסָר, vv. 10, 33), and "decree/inscribed/marked out" (חקק, vv. 15, 27, 29). The architecture of the piece and the relationship among its parts evinces deliberate design. Wisdom's introductory exhortation corresponds with her concluding exhortation (vv. 4–11, 32–36). These exhortations frame the central section of the piece, which focuses on Wisdom's prominence in the present world and the primordial world (vv. 12–21, 22–31). And this prominence provides the basis and motivation for Wisdom's exhortations.

Explanation of the Text

1. The Introduction to Wisdom's Encomium (8:1–3)

Similar to Wisdom's initial discourse (1:20–33), the encomium opens with a formal introduction, which introduces both the speaker and the setting of the piece.

a. The Introduction of Wisdom (8:1)

The introduction of Wisdom shares several similarities with 1:20–21: it is cast in the third person, delivered by the parent, and characterized by the expressions "calling" (תִקְרָא, 8:1a; 1:21) as well as "raising her voice" (תִתֵּן קוֹלָהּ, 8:1b; 1:20; cf. 8:3b; 1:20). But the introduction is also distinct; it differs from the prelude to Wisdom's initial speech on two counts. The first concerns the form of the introduction. Whereas Wisdom's introduction in 1:20 is expressed through a pair of indicative statements, the introduction to her encomium is expressed through a rhetorical question (v. 1). The negative form of the question demands a positive answer. More than this, the rhetorical question attunes the audience to Wisdom's voice. The world projected in Prov 1–9 consists of various characters with discrete voices.[8] If the one to whom one listens influences what one thinks and how one lives,[9] then identifying Wisdom's voice is of primary importance. The rhetorical question invites the addressee to hear Wisdom's call, recognize her voice and, by implication, distinguish her voice from that of others.

7. McKane, *Proverbs*, 344–58; Meinhold, *Die Sprüche*, 1.136–48; Murphy, *Proverbs*, 48; Fox, *Proverbs 1–9*, 291–92; Sæbø, *Sprüche*, 120; Loader, *Proverbs 1–9*, 320–21. While there is general agreement regarding the basic contours of the discourse's structure, some include vv. 1–3 in the initial section of the speech (e.g., Van Leeuwen, "The Book of Proverbs," *NIB* 5:88; Clifford, *Proverbs*, 93; Waltke, *Proverbs: Chapters 1–15*, 392–93). In light of the fact that these introductory verses are cast in the third person, it appears that they may be distinguished from the first-person discourse in vv. 4–11. Together with the initial section of the unit, it is important to note that since some take v. 11 as a late addition, this verse is not included in their structural proposals. For a discussion of v. 11, see the explanation below.

8. Aletti, "Seduction et parole en Proverbes I–IX," 129–44.

9. Dru Johnson, *Biblical Knowing: A Scriptural Epistemology of Error* (Eugene, OR: Cascade, 2013).

Second, in contrast to 1:20–33, the introduction associates Wisdom (8:1a) with Understanding (v. 1b). The relationship between the poetic lines intimates that both are personified. And in light of the prevalence of this word pair in the parental lectures of the prologue (Prov 2:2, 6; 3:13, 19; 5:1), it appears that Understanding is an alternative designation for Wisdom. The wisdom and understanding of which the parent has spoken about now speaks for herself. The designations link the voice of the discourse with the wisdom proffered by the parent and correlate the object of the addressee's search in the lectures with a particular persona.

b. The Setting of Wisdom's Speech (8:2–3)

This persona does not deliver her discourse within the confines of the home; rather, she broadcasts her speech in an urban locale. Similar to 1:20–21, Wisdom's speech is set in the city amid the clamor and congestion of everyday life (8:2–3). This setting is expressed through a string of adverbial phrases, each of which is foregrounded in the individual poetic lines to emphasize Wisdom's presence and involvement in the hustle and bustle of commercial, judicial, and economic dealings. Wisdom stations herself in the middle of the community, among the centers of power, on an elevated part of the city, and beside the gate.[10] The conflation of these urban locales illuminates Wisdom's accessibility, association with ordinary affairs, and position among the thresholds of human life.[11] Whether these locales refer to a single place or to different areas within the city,[12] they situate Wisdom at an ideal site or sites from which to address her audience. And they indicate that Wisdom is neither detached from nor disinterested in the practicalities of life; rather, she resides among and relates to those negotiating the hullabaloo of being-in-the-world.

2. Wisdom's Opening Exhortation (8:4–11)

Against the backdrop of the introduction, Wisdom opens her formal discourse with an exhortation, which consists of an appeal (vv. 4–6), an account of her virtuous speech (vv. 7–9), and an admonition, complete with a motivation (vv. 10–11).

a. Wisdom's Appeal (8:4–6)

Wisdom introduces her exhortation with an appeal that is forceful and emphatic. The placement of the expression "To you" (אֲלֵיכֶם, v. 4a) at the beginning of v. 4, combined with the sequence of imperatives in vv. 5–6, catch the audience's attention, crystallize the pitch of Wisdom's voice (vv. 1b, 4b), and capture the intention of her call. Wisdom's call corresponds with the setting of her speech. She addresses everyone (v. 4). All may hear and heed her voice. But among the masses, two species of humankind are singled out as the rhetorical audience of Wisdom's speech: the "uncommitted" (פְּתָאיִם, v. 5a) and "fools" (כְּסִילִים, v. 5b). As noted in 1:4, the uncommitted are "betwixt and between" the way of life and the way of death.[13] This character type is inexperienced, prone to folly (1:22; 9:4), and easily seduced,[14] but remains malleable and possesses the capacity to acquire wisdom.[15] Fools, by contrast, are characterized as complacent and indifferent

10. Yoder, *Proverbs*, 90.

11. Fox, *Proverbs 1–9*, 267; Van Leeuwen, "The Book of Proverbs," *NIB* 5:89.

12. For discussion of these locales and the setting of Wisdom's speech, see Fox, *Proverbs 1–9*, 265–67; Loader, *Proverbs 1–9*, 325–27.

13. Turner, "Betwixt and Between," 93–111; Perdue, "Liminality as a Social Setting for Wisdom Instruction," 114–26; Van Leeuwen, "Liminality and Worldview," 111–44.

14. Fox, *Proverbs 1–9*, 42–43; Waltke, *Proverbs: Chapters 1–15*, 111–12.

15. Waltke, *Proverbs: Chapters 1–15*, 111.

to knowledge (1:22, 32). They neither assume the listening posture nor possess the moral character necessary for the acquisition of wisdom and virtue. The disposition of these character types explains Wisdom's appeal to each. The uncommitted must learn "shrewdness" (עָרְמָה, 8:5a), while fools must learn "sense" (לֵב, v. 5b). That is, the uncommitted must acquire good judgment in order to decipher and deflect deceptive speech (see 1:4),[16] while fools must acquire the heart and mind to snap out of their obstinate state and receive wisdom.[17] Although Proverbs holds out little hope for the education and transformation of fools, this character type is invited to learn and, by implication, to assume responsibility for their response.[18]

In addition to learning, Wisdom enjoins her audience to "listen" (שִׁמְעוּ, 8:6). The command to listen followed by the causal conjunction "for" (כִּי, v. 6a) mirrors the rhetoric of the exordia within the parental lectures of the prologue (cf. 1:8–9; 4:1–2).[19] This construction serves as the conclusion to Wisdom's appeal. The rationale for listening to Wisdom is the nature of her speech. Wisdom utters "straightforward things" (נְגִידִים, 8:6a);[20] and "integrity" (מֵישָׁרִים, v. 6b; cf. 1:3) resides on her lips, directing the words of her mouth. Together, these terms indicate that Wisdom's speech is forthright, trustworthy, and morally upright.[21] If one's speech reflects one's character, then Wisdom is presented as the embodiment of virtue. And if the one to whom one listens shapes how one lives, then Wisdom is depicted as a reliable guide, one whose straight talk corresponds with the straight paths within the created order.

b. Wisdom's Virtuous Speech (8:7–9)

In light of the importance of speech and its relationship to the character, moral worldview, and promises of various voices in Prov 1–9, it is not surprising that Wisdom elaborates on the nature of her speech in 8:7–9. While the subordinate causal clause in v. 6 (כִּי; "for") described the trustworthy nature of Wisdom's speech in order to substantiate her call to listen, the asseverative use of the conjunction in v. 7 (כִּי; "Indeed") introduces a main clause and a distinct subsection within Wisdom's opening exhortation in order to provide an extended rationale for why her words should be heard and heeded.[22] This rationale is preoccupied with the moral quality of Wisdom's speech.[23] And the moral quality of her speech reveals Wisdom's association with YHWH as well as the way in which she serves as a positive foil for the strange woman.

The terms used to describe Wisdom's speech correspond with various characterizations of YHWH's character and speech. Just as Wisdom utters "truth" (אֱמֶת, v. 7a), so also YHWH and his words are true (Exod 34:6; 2 Sam 7:28). Wickedness is an abomination to Wisdom's lips (Prob 8:7b) in the same way that lying lips are an abomination to

16. Loader, *Proverbs 1–9*, 328; Fox, *Proverbs 1–9*, 268.

17. Yoder, *Proverbs*, 90.

18. Fox, *Proverbs 1–9*, 98.

19. Loader, *Proverbs 1–9*, 328.

20. Some commentators read נְגִידִים as a derivative of נגיד and render the term "princely things" or "noble things" (e.g., Meinhold, *Die Sprüche*, 1.138; Longman, *Proverbs*, 194). While this reading retains the text's concern with the quality of Wisdom's speech, it appears that נְגִידִים is a plural form of the preposition נֶגֶד ("in front of, opposite") (R. P. L. Grollenberg, "A propos de Prov. VIII,6 et XVII,27," *RB* 59 [1952], 41; *HALOT* 2:666, s.v. נֶגֶד). Accordingly, the term expresses the straightforward and truthful nature of Wisdom's speech and provides a more suitable parallel to "integrity" in v. 6b. For this reading and discussion of the issues, see Fox, *Proverbs 1–9*, 269; Waltke, *Proverbs: Chapters 1–15*, 387n14; Loader, *Proverbs 1–9*, 328–29. Cf. H. H. Hardy II, *The Development of Biblical Hebrew Prepositions*, ANEM 28 (Atlanta: SBL Press, 2022), 94–97.

21. Fox, *Proverbs 1–9*, 269; Waltke, *Proverbs: Chapters 1–15*, 397.

22. Loader, *Proverbs 1–9*, 329.

23. Van Leeuwen, "The Book of Proverbs," *NIB* 5:90.

YHWH (12:22). Both Wisdom and YHWH speak "in accord with righteousness" (בְּצֶדֶק, 8:8a; Ps 65:6[5]; cf. 11:7; 19:10[9]; 33:5; Isa 45:19); and their words are "right" (יְשָׁרִים, Prov 8:9b; Pss 19:9[8]; 33:4; 119:137; Isa 45:19; Neh 9:13). The nature of Wisdom's speech reflects YHWH's character and speech.[24] The correlation between their words betrays the correlation of their character; and the similarity of their speech indicates that Wisdom speaks with an authority comparable to YHWH.[25]

In addition to the correspondence between Wisdom's words and YHWH's speech, Wisdom's discourse stands in sharp contrast to the discourse of the strange woman. Wisdom's palate is neither smooth nor slippery (Prov 5:3); rather, it is straightforward, marked by truth (8:7a). And Wisdom's speech is clear and comprehensible (v. 9),[26] not polysemous and deceptive (5:3; 7:21). It is important to note, however, that the intelligibility of Wisdom's words requires a particular moral posture. Only "one who understands" (מֵבִין, 8:9a) and "those who find knowledge" (מֹצְאֵי דָעַת, v. 9b) can comprehend her words and recognize their virtuous nature.[27] Listening is not enough (v. 6); it must be accompanied by a discerning disposition and an active search for knowledge. From this moral posture, Wisdom's speech is perceived as clear, attractive, and virtuous, worthy of one's attention and reception.

c. Wisdom's Admonition (8:10–11)

The virtuous nature of Wisdom's speech provides the rhetorical foundation for her admonition and motivation (vv. 10–11), which form the conclusion to her opening exhortation. Both employ economic language to draw a comparison. And each comparison highlights Wisdom's surpassing value. If Wisdom's words are virtuous (vv. 7–9), then one should not only listen to her straightforward speech (v. 6), but also take action. To be specific, one should "take" (קְחוּ, v. 10a) or "choose" her instruction and knowledge (v. 10; cf. 1:3; 2:1; 4:10)[28] above "silver" (כָּסֶף, 8:10a)[29] and "choice gold" (חָרוּץ נִבְחָר, v. 10b). These precious commodities are desirable and valuable. While Wisdom possesses these commodities and dispenses wealth to her devotees (8:18–21), she remains more desirable and valuable than material riches. The admonition recasts the language of 3:14 in order to highlight the qualitative value of Wisdom's instruction. Her moral instruction exceeds the quality of silver and fine gold (8:10) in the same way that she exceeds the quantitative market price of silver and gold (3:14).

Wisdom's qualitative value is reinforced in 8:11, which offers a motivation and rationale for the closing admonition. Whereas v. 10 recasts the language of 3:14, 8:11 recasts 3:15. The subordinate

24. Maurice Gilbert, "Le discours de la sagesse en Proverbes 8," in *La Sagesse De l'Ancien Testament*, ed. M. Gilbert (Leuven: Leuven University, 1979), 205; Gerlinde Baumann, *Die Weisheitsgestalt in Proverbien 1–9*, FAT 16 (Tübingen: Mohr Siebeck, 1996), 78–79; Schwáb, *Toward an Interpretation*, 179.

25. Loader, *Proverbs 1–9*, 329–30.

26. Loader, *Proverbs 1–9*, 330.

27. Fox, *Proverbs 1–9*, 270; Loader, *Proverbs 1–9*, 330.

28. For "choose" as the sense of imperative קְחוּ, see Fox, *Proverbs 1–9*, 270; Waltke, *Proverbs: Chapters 1–15*, 399. With regard to the text-critical issue in v. 10a, some follow the LXX and read "instruction" (מוּסָר) rather than "my instruction" (מוּסָרִי). While the inclusion of the pronominal suffix in the MT may be due to dittography and the reading "instruction" may provide a better parallel to "knowledge" (דַעַת, v. 10b), the emendation seems unnecessary. The pronominal suffix in v. 10a may be implied in v. 10b (Waltke, *Proverbs: Chapters 1–15*, 388n20). And the emendation ignores the potential variation or development between the lines (Loader, *Proverbs 1–9*, 331–32).

29. Similar to the comparative use of the inseparable preposition מִן in v. 10b, the construction וְאַל in v. 10a functions as a comparative. Franz Delitzsch, "The Book of Proverbs," in *Commentary on the Old Testament*, trans. M. G. Easton, 5th ed. (1874; repr., Peabody, MA: Hendrickson, 1996), 6:177 (1:265; this latter citation is for those who use an edition bound in more than the ten volumes of *Commentary on the Old Testament*).

causal clause (כִּי, 8:11a) introduces a comparison, first through a better-than saying (v. 11a; cf. 3:14) and then through an unqualified assertion of wisdom's inestimable value (8:11b). Similar to 3:15, wisdom is compared to jewels: its quality is better than that of "corals" (פְּנִינִים, 8:11a). And similar to 3:15, the final line of the strophe offers an unequivocal declaration of wisdom's worth: its quality and desirability are without equal (8:11b). In light of the comparable logic and language between 3:14–15 and 8:10–11, some conclude that 8:11 is an interpolation.[30] Among other reasons, the third-person cast of the verse seems intrusive, especially in a first-person discourse delivered by Wisdom. The fact that Wisdom evaluates the quality of wisdom in the third person, however, is quite appropriate.[31] The personified figure speaks of the non-personified value that is intrinsic to her worth and inseparable from both her character and the nature of her discourse.[32] In so doing, Wisdom relates the quality of her teaching (v. 10) with the quality of wisdom (v. 11) and substantiates the value of the former by highlighting the incomparable worth of the latter. Wisdom's instruction and wisdom are in a class of their own. The comparisons provide a fitting conclusion to Wisdom's opening exhortation. Together, the admonition and motivation strengthen the call to "listen" (v. 6a) to and "choose" (v. 10a) Wisdom's instruction by emphasizing the inestimable quality of Wisdom's teaching as well as wisdom itself.

3. Wisdom's Credentials and Function in the Present World (8:12–21)

Wisdom's value, however, is not limited to the nature of her speech (vv. 7–9) and the quality of her instruction (vv. 10–11); it is also exhibited through her credentials (vv. 12–13), manifested in the present world through her role in the social order (vv. 14–16), and demonstrated through the gifts that she bestows on her devotees (vv. 17–21).

a. Wisdom's Credentials (8:12–13)

Wisdom develops her value and preeminence by describing her credentials in vv. 12–13. She introduces these credentials with a self-identification formula that resembles many royal inscriptions and divine aretalogies throughout the ancient world.[33] Similar to its use in the ancient world and the Old Testament, this formula is foregrounded to link Wisdom's identity with particular descriptions of her character (Gen 15:7; 17:1; 41:44; Isa 41:4; 45:19; Jer 17:10).[34] These self-descriptions of Wisdom's character are familiar, for they mirror the fundamental values that Proverbs seeks to inculcate in readers (cf. Prov 1:1–7).

Wisdom's relationship with and possession of these values is presented through a description of her residence and the object of her pursuit. Wisdom resides in a virtuous environment. She "inhabits shrewdness" (שָׁכַנְתִּי עָרְמָה, 8:12a); that is, she abides in and is intimately associated with the prudence

30. See, for example, Patrick W. Skehan, "Structures in Poems on Wisdom: Proverbs 8 and Sirach 24," *CBQ* 41 (1979): 368; Meinhold, *Die Sprüche*, 1.137; Van Leeuwen, "The Book of Proverbs," *NIB* 5:88.

31. Fox, *Proverbs 1–9*, 271; Loader, *Proverbs 1–9*, 333.

32. Loader, *Proverbs 1–9*, 333.

33. For discussion of these texts, see n5 above as well as Van Leeuwen, "The Book of Proverbs," *NIB* 5:90. These texts include the characteristic expression "I am (personal name)." While the expression אֲנִי־חָכְמָה in v. 12a could be rendered "I am Wisdom," the use of the *maqqep* to link the independent personal pronoun with Wisdom suggests the terms are set in apposition and treated as a compound construction, "I, Wisdom." *IBHS* §64, 4.2.1a; Loader, *Proverbs 1–9*, 333–34.

34. Yoder, *Proverbs*, 92.

that the uncommitted must learn (1:4; 8:5a). If one finds and embraces Wisdom, then it appears that one acquires the insight and good judgment that Proverbs proffers in its prolegomenon (1:4).[35] The same is true of "knowledge of discretion" (דַּעַת מְזִמּוֹת, 8:12b). Proverbs promises knowledge and discretion to those uncommitted characters that participate in its pedagogical program (1:4). But these virtues are not acquired by rote reception of instruction alone. They are also obtained through relationship with Wisdom. Wisdom pursues and finds what those who rightly perceive her words find (8:9b, 12b). And she secures knowledge of careful planning and prudent ways of conduct that the uncommitted lack (1:4; 8:12b). Her credentials match the virtues that mark the prolegomenon of Proverbs (1:1–7); and her character mirrors the type of character the book seeks to form in readers.

In light of the correspondence between wisdom's credentials and the vision of character formation projected in the preamble (1:1–7), it is not surprising that Wisdom also embodies the form of being required to achieve the anthology's goal (8:13; 1:7). This form of being is defined in terms of Wisdom's moral tastes; and these moral tastes are developed through a tricolon. The tricolon evinces a logical progression of thought and provides a conclusion to Wisdom's catalogue of credentials.[36] The initial line describes the fear of YHWH as hating evil (v. 13a). The final two lines then profile particular manifestations of evil. The evil in view has to do with certain attitudes, dispositions, and actions that are contrary to the fear of YHWH and repulsive to Wisdom's moral tastes. Pride (גֵּאָה, v. 13b) and arrogance (גָּאוֹן, v. 13b) are attitudes incompatible with the humble, lowly disposition produced by the fear of YHWH and characteristic of the wise (11:2; 15:33; 16:19). The twisted terrain and telos of "the way of evil" (דֶּרֶךְ רָע, 8:13b) stands in opposition to the smooth, straight paths of the way of wisdom and life (3:23; 4:11–12, 18; 11:5). And the perverse speech that defines those who traverse the way of evil (8:13c; 2:12–15) is the antithesis of the straightforward speech that marks both Lady Wisdom and the wise (8:6–9). No wonder Wisdom finds these attitudes, dispositions, and actions abhorrent. Her moral tastes match her moral character, and both are trained by the fear of YHWH.

b. Wisdom's Function in the Terrestrial Realm (8:14–16)

Wisdom elaborates upon her character and qualifications in vv. 14–16 by identifying her possession and implementation of particular skills in the terrestrial realm. These skills include "counsel" (עֵצָה, v. 14a), "resourcefulness" (תוּשִׁיָּה, v. 14a), and "strength" (גְּבוּרָה, v. 14b). Wisdom is an accomplished consultant, one who possesses the capacity both to conceive a plan and to communicate it to others.[37] Her counsel is informed by

35. Loader, *Proverbs 1–9*, 334.

36. While some consider the whole of v. 13 as a late gloss (Toy, *Proverbs*, 164; Meinhold, *Die Sprüche*, 1.140) and others restrict the editorial addition to v. 13a–b (Clifford, *Proverbs*, 92nb; Fox, *Proverbs 1–9*, 261, 272; Sæbø, *Sprüche*, 117), the arguments for these excisions remain unconvincing. In view of the similarities between the preamble (1:4) and 8:12, the mention of "the fear of YHWH" (יִרְאַת יְהוָה, v.13a) and its exposition in v. 13a makes good sense in context (pace Clifford). And the positive sense of both "shrewdness" (עָרְמָה, v.12a) and "discretion" (מְזִמּוֹת, v. 12b) in the context of the prologue in general and the encomium (v. 5a) in particular raises questions over whether it was necessary to insert v. 13a in order to counteract the possible amoral connotations of these terms (McKane, *Proverbs*, 348; Fox, *Proverbs 1–9*, 272). Verse 13 is retained in all the ancient versions. And it provides a fitting climax to the brief catalogue of credentials that define Wisdom's character. Loader, *Proverbs 1–9*, 335–36.

37. For examples of counsel given and taken, see 2 Sam 15:31, 34; 16:20, 23; 17:7, 14, 23; 1 Kgs 1:12; Jer 19:7; Prov 20:18; Ezra 10:8; 2 Chr 22:5.

resourcefulness, that is, by the mental proficiency required to perceive and to navigate the various circumstances of life (cf. 2:7). And her plans are actualized by means of strength. These terms from the semantic field of governance indicate that Wisdom possesses those skills that contribute to the order and maintenance of a just society. They are the same skills that mark the ideal king (Isa 11:2) and define YHWH's governance of the cosmos (Job 12:13–16). And they are skills that are related to and directed by Wisdom's character. Between the repeated declaration of Wisdom's possession of these skills ("mine," לִי, Prov 8:14a, 14b), she offers a self-characterization: "I am Understanding" (אֲנִי בִינָה, v. 14b; cf. 4:5, 7; 7:4). This self-characterization is inextricably linked to Wisdom's possession and implementation of the "faculties of statecraft."[38] Understanding both nurtures counsel, resourcefulness, and strength and directs the intelligent implementation of these political skills.

The way in which Wisdom employs these skills in the terrestrial realm is delineated in 8:15–16. She acts through agents: kings, rulers, princes, nobles, and all judges. These are not the only agents through whom Wisdom manifests her sociopolitical skills. As those in positions of power, however, they are the agents through whom these skills are manifested most clearly. The repetition of the construction "By me" (בִּי, vv. 15a, 16a) at the beginning of vv. 15–16 identifies and emphasizes Wisdom's instrumental role in the establishment of an ordered society. And the recurrence of the noun "justice" (צֶדֶק, vv. 15b, 16b)[39] at the end of vv. 15 and 16 indicates that the order established through Wisdom's agents is right and good. Wisdom does not withhold her skills from humans; rather, she bestows them on those in positions of power, grants them to those who embrace her, and manifests them through the operation of a just society.

c. Wisdom's Gifts (8:17–21)

The social value of Wisdom coincides with the emotional and material gifts that she bestows on individuals (vv. 17–21). These emotional and material gifts are related to one another. The expression "those who love me" (אֹהֲבַי, vv. 17a, 21a)[40] frames the subunit, binding the erotic and emotional longing for Wisdom (v. 17) with the material benefits that she lavishes on her devotees (v. 21). Wisdom expresses her mutual love through an emphatic construction. The repetition of the root for "love" (אהב, v. 17a), combined with the placement of the personal pronoun "I" (אֲנִי, v. 17a) in the first position and the object "those who love me" (אֹהֲבַי, v. 17a) before the verb, highlights Wisdom's sure commitment to those who love her. This mutual love is reinforced in v. 17b. With language very reminiscent of the Song of Songs, Wisdom promises that those who seek her will find her (v. 17b; cf. Song 3:1–4; 5:6). The motif of seeking and finding develops the thought of Prov 8:17a, as it moves from the feeling of love to the active pursuit of the

38. Fox, *Proverbs 1–9*, 273.

39. In contrast to many MT manuscripts, the LXX and other texts read "earth" (ארץ) rather than "justice" (צדק) in v. 16b. In light of the universal description of Wisdom's involvement in the terrestrial realm and the fact that the phrase "judges of the earth" occurs elsewhere in the Old Testament (Isa 40:23; Pss 2:10; 148:11), the alternative reading makes good sense (e.g., Fox, *Proverbs 1–9*, 274; idem, *Proverbs: An Eclectic Edition*, 154–55). From a literary perspective, however, the reading "justice" is preferable. When read together, Prov 8:15 and 16 both begin with the expression "By me" (בִּי, vv. 15a, 16a); both include a subject and a verb formed from the same root (i.e., מְלָכִים יִמְלֹכוּ, v. 15a; שָׂרִים יָשֹׂרוּ, v. 16a); and it seems that both end with the expression "justice." The repetition of the term enhances the design and artistry of the text, without negating Wisdom's universal involvement in terrestrial rule. Loader, *Proverbs 1–9*, 338.

40. The reading of v. 17a follows *qere* (אֹהֲבַי, "those who love me") rather than *ketiv* (אֹהֲבֶיהָ, "those who love her").

one who is loved.[41] Wisdom assures her lovers that she will not stand them up; she will love them in return and allow them to find her.

In addition to relational commitment and emotional satisfaction, Wisdom promises to grant material gifts to her lovers. Together, vv. 18–20 catalogue Wisdom's economic and ethical worth; they move from the type of wealth Wisdom possesses (v. 18), to the material benefits she produces (v. 19), to her virtuous lifestyle and character (v. 20). The language of the catalogue and its characterization of Wisdom's worth are comparable to the beatitudinal poem in 3:13–20 (esp. vv. 14–17). What the father said about wisdom's nature and value Wisdom now says herself. Similar to 3:16, Wisdom possesses "wealth and honor" or "honorable wealth";[42] her riches bring repute, and these riches are acquired through honorable practices. This ethical valuation of Wisdom's economic worth is reinforced in 8:18b–20. In contrast to the "precious wealth" offered by the sinners (1:13), Wisdom possesses lasting or "enduring wealth" (הוֹן עָתֵק, 8:18b), which is stable, reliable, and attained in accord with righteousness.[43] Her profits or benefits are in a class of their own; they exceed both the intrinsic worth and the financial return of fine gold and choice silver (8:19; cf. v. 10; 3:14).[44] And Wisdom's character corresponds with the dignity and desirability of her wealth and ethical practices, for her orientation, lifestyle, and conduct manifest the moral contours and movements characteristic of righteousness and justice (8:20). The conflation of economic and ethical concepts in this catalogue of Wisdom's materials gifts indicates that the two are inseparable. Wisdom's wealth must be understood through her moral character, and her moral character manifests its worth through her enduring wealth. The fusion of economic and ethical concepts specifies the nature of Wisdom's worth, enhancing her value and desirability.[45]

Her value and desirability, however, are found not only in who she is and what she possesses but also in the gifts she bestows on those who love her (v. 21). These gifts are the focus of attention in v. 21. The repetition of the expression "those who love me" (אֹהֲבַי, vv. 17a, 21a), combined with the introductory *lamed* + infinitive construct (v. 21a), suggests that v. 21 marks the conclusion of the subunit (vv. 17–21). This conclusion identifies the purpose or entailments of Wisdom's economic and ethical worth.[46] Those who love Wisdom receive more than reciprocal love (v. 17a); they also inherit "wealth" (יֵשׁ, v. 21a)[47] and the promise of treasuries filled with abundance. A desire for and an intimate relationship with Wisdom bring benefits: mutual love, sure commitment, stability, legitimate wealth, abundance, and satisfaction. These benefits highlight Wisdom's value, and they capture the beatific life that Wisdom bestows on her devotees.

41. Loader, *Proverbs 1–9*, 339.

42. For this single concept conveyed by the expression "riches and honor" (עֹשֶׁר־וְכָבוֹד, v. 18a), see Fox, *Proverbs 1–9*, 277.

43. Sandoval, *The Discourse of Wealth and Poverty*, 95–97; Lyu, *Righteousness*, 79–80.

44. For the comparative construction in v. 19, see 3:14.

45. Sandoval, *The Discourse of Wealth and Poverty*, 93, 101; Stewart, *Poetic Ethics*, 165–67.

46. It is difficult to determine the function of the *lamed* + infinitive construct in v. 21a. If the construction introduces a clause that is subordinate to v. 20 alone, then Loader's suggestion that it marks attendant circumstances or the entailments of Wisdom's moral lifestyle is convincing: Wisdom's moral orientation (v. 20) entails that she grants wealth (Loader, *Proverbs 1–9*, 343; cf. GKC §114o). If, however, the construction is subordinate to the extended catalogue in vv. 18–20, then it may identify the purpose of Wisdom's economic and ethical worth. This does not mean that Wisdom's "sole purpose" is to bestow wealth on her lovers, but it does mean that one of Wisdom's purposes is to confer these possessions on her devotees.

47. While the term יֵשׁ tends to function as a substantive that identifies the existence of someone or something, here as well as in Sir 42:3 it functions as a noun, meaning "property, wealth" (*HALOT* 2:443, s.v. יֵשׁ).

4. Wisdom's Preeminence and Position in the Primordial World (8:22–31)

Wisdom has built a convincing case: in light of her virtuous speech (vv. 7–9), her credentials (vv. 12–13), her function in the terrestrial realm (vv. 14–16), and the gifts she bestows on those who love her (vv. 17–21), Wisdom is valuable, honorable, and the epitome of all this is desirable. But a question remains: Is this merely propagandistic self-praise? Is there any basis or justification for Wisdom's fantastic claims? There is, and this justification is delineated in vv. 22–31.[48] As noted above, this section legitimizes Wisdom's character, credentials, and function in the present world (vv. 12–21) through an account of her preeminence and position in the primordial world (vv. 22–31). The account is divided into three constituent parts, each of which assumes a distinctive vantage point: Wisdom's emergence before creation (vv. 22–26), Wisdom's presence at creation (vv. 27–29), and Wisdom's activity after creation (vv. 30–31).[49]

a. Wisdom's Emergence before Creation (8:22–26)

Wisdom's portrait of her preeminence and place within YHWH's creation of the cosmos marks a shift in the broader discourse (vv. 22–31). The poetic subunit moves from first-person self-praise (vv. 12–21) to a third-person account of YHWH's creative ways (vv. 22–31), from Wisdom's function in the terrestrial realm (vv. 14–16) to her generation in the primordial realm (vv. 22–26), and from Wisdom's portrayal as a patroness and lover (vv. 14–21) to her depiction as the delighted daughter of YHWH (vv. 22–31). Temporal expressions dominate the discourse, orienting one to Wisdom's whereabouts within YHWH's wonderous arrangement of the cosmos. And distinctive metaphors govern the individual subsections, providing a conceptual framework through which to perceive Wisdom's character and the nature of her relationships. The temporal expressions and images of birth within vv. 22–26 distinguish the strophe from the poetic units that follow. They situate Wisdom's emergence in hoary antiquity and illuminate her temporal and qualitative preeminence in relation to the rest of creation.[50]

Wisdom's preeminence is conveyed through a preponderance of temporal expressions within vv. 22–26. These expressions place Wisdom's emergence in the realm of nonexistence, prior to creation. The repetition of "earliest" (קֶדֶם, vv. 22b, 23b) and "when there were no" (בְּאֵין; 24a, 24c), combined with synonymous terms for "beginning" (רֵאשִׁית, v. 22a; רֹאשׁ; 23b) and "before" (בְּטֶרֶם, v. 25a; לִפְנֵי, v. 25b; עַד־לֹא, v. 26a), situate Wisdom's preexistence relative to God's creative activities. She preceded creation. In fact, she was the first of God's works (v. 22a; cf. Job 15:7–9).[51] The avalanche of temporal expressions illuminates Wisdom's antiquity, chronological priority, and temporal preeminence in creation. And the geographical movement sketched in vv. 24–26

48. Gale A. Yee, "The Theology of Creation in Proverbs 8:22–31," in *Creation in Biblical Traditions*, ed. R. J. Clifford and J. J. Collins, CBQMS 24 (Washington, DC: Catholic Biblical Association of America, 1992), 87; Stuart Weeks, "The Context and Meaning of Proverbs 8:30a," *JBL* 125 (2006): 436; Loader, *Proverbs 1–9*, 344.

49. Weeks, "The Context and Meaning," 437–38; cf. Victor A. Hurowitz, "Nursling, Advisor, Architect? אמן and the Role of Wisdom in Proverbs 8.22–31," *Bib* 80 (1999): 392–94.

50. Yee, "The Theology of Creation in Proverbs 8:22–31," 90–91; Waltke, *Proverbs: Chapters 1–15*, 408.

51. While the phrase "at the beginning of his way" (רֵאשִׁית דַּרְכּוֹ) may mark a second object or serve as an appositional phrase to the pronominal suffix "me," it appears to function as an adverbial qualifier that positions Wisdom chronologically as the first of God's creative ways. GKC §118i; Fox, *Proverbs 1–9*, 280; Loader, *Proverbs 1–9*, 348–50.

highlights Wisdom's preeminent position. The text moves the reader's vantage point from the depths below to the earth above: from the primeval deeps and subterranean springs (v. 24), to the foundation of the mountains (v. 25a), to the emergence of the hills from the subsiding waters (v. 25b), to the land, the open fields, and the first lumps of soil (v. 26).[52] Wisdom emerged before the cosmic waters (v. 24a; cf. Gen 1:2), the establishment of the earth's pillars, and the creation of the land. She existed in the nothingness from which YHWH created the cosmos before the creation of time itself.

While the subordinate temporal expressions in Prov 8:22–26 capture Wisdom's temporal preeminence, the main clauses emphasize Wisdom's qualitative preeminence. These main clauses are governed by three verbs, each of which is related to the metaphor of birth.[53] And these verbs appear to chart a chronological sequence from Wisdom's conception (v. 22) to her gestation (v. 23) to her delivery (vv. 24–26). Wisdom's conception is expressed through a pregnant verb. Among its shades of meaning, קנה carries the sense "to acquire" (Prov 1:5; 4:5, 7; 15:32; 16:16; 17:16),[54] "to create" (Gen 4:1; 14:19, 22; Deut 32:6; Ps 139:13),[55] and "to beget" or "bring forth."[56] Though the verb means "to acquire" elsewhere in Proverbs, when read in conjunction with the verbs that follow (Prov 8:23a, 24a, 25b), it seems to signify Wisdom's conception or creation.[57] The precise nature of Wisdom's creation, however, remains unclear; and YHWH's creation of Wisdom may also involve his acquisition of her.[58] The semantic potential of the verb allows for different senses, but the verbs that follow and the overarching metaphor of birth in vv. 22–26 intimate that creation, conception, or, theologically speaking, generation, is the primary nuance of קנה in v. 22.[59]

If קנה expresses Wisdom's creation or generation, then the pair of passive verbs that follow describe her (eternal) gestation and delivery, respectively. Wisdom's conception naturally leads to a description of her prenatal development. She was "formed" (נִסַּכְתִּי, v. 23a) like a child in the womb, where organs, bone, sinew, and flesh were woven and knit together (cf. Ps 139:13; Job 10:11).[60] And when the time arrived, she "was brought forth" (חוֹלָלְתִּי, vv. 24b, 25c; cf. Deut 32:18; Job 39:1; Pss 29:9; 90:2). The repetition of the verb in Prov 8:24b and 25c introduces the final two main clauses in the subsection (vv. 22–26). Together, these main clauses reinforce Wisdom's temporal and qualitative

52. Gilbert, "Le discours de la sagesse," 211; Meinhold, *Die Sprüche*, 1.144–45; cf. Loader, *Proverbs 1–9*, 352.

53. These verbs stand at the center of early Christian Christological debates. For an excellent discussion of the hermeneutical and theological issues within these debates, see Hans Boersma, "The Sacramental Reading of Nicene Theology: Athanasius and Gregory of Nyssa on Proverbs 8," *JTI* 10 (2016): 1–30.

54. See the Vulgate and Bruce Vawter, "Prov 8:22: Wisdom and Creation," *JBL* 99 (1980): 205–16.

55. For the use in Prov 8:22, see LXX, Toy, *Proverbs*, 173; McKane, *Proverbs*, 352–54; Meinhold, *Die Sprüche*, 1.133, 144; Fox, *Proverbs 1–9*, 279–80; Loader, *Proverbs 1–9*, 345–48.

56. William A. Irwin, "Where Shall Wisdom Be Found," *JBL* 80 (1961): 133–42; Murphy, *Proverbs*, 47; Clifford, *Proverbs*, 96; Waltke, *Proverbs: Chapters 1–15*, 408–9; Longman, *Proverbs*, 204; Sæbø, *Sprüche*, 117.

57. When קנה means "acquire" or "buy" elsewhere in Proverbs, it takes as its object guidance, wisdom, understanding, knowledge, or the like (Prov 1:5; 4:5, 7; 15:32; 16:16; 17:16; 18:15; 19:8). In v. 22, however, YHWH is the subject and Wisdom is the object.

58. Fox, *Proverbs 1–9*, 279. Though one can acquire something by means of creation, it appears that acquisition would be a derivative of creation and thus creation would remain primary. Waltke, *Proverbs: Chapters 1–15*, 409; Loader, *Proverbs 1–9*, 346.

59. C. F. Burney, "Christ as the APXH of Creation," *JTS* 27 (1926): 160–77.

60. While the vocalization of the MT indicates that the verb derives from the root נסך ("to pour out"), *BHS* revocalizes the form to סכך ("to form, weave, shape"). In light of the use of both קנה and סכך in Ps 139:13 and the birth metaphor that frames vv. 22–26, the latter appears to be the best reading.

preeminence: she was delivered in the nothingness before YHWH created the cosmos as his personal procreation. She was conceived in YHWH's uterus, formed in his womb, and delivered as his daughter. Analogically, she was created in the same way as humans. And like a human child, she shares a unique relationship with the one who bore her.

b. Wisdom's Presence at Creation (8:27–29)

Whereas vv. 22–26 describe Wisdom's temporal and qualitative preeminence through the metaphor of birth, vv. 27–29 present her preeminent position through the metaphor of construction. Similar to the preceding verses, temporal clauses dominate the subsection. The temporal frame of reference shifts, however, from Wisdom's emergence before creation to her presence during YHWH's creation of the cosmos ("when," vv. 27–29). This eyewitness account of creation develops 3:19–20; and its cosmic geography represents a mirror image of 8:24–26. Against the backdrop of the movement from the realm below to the realm above (vv. 24–26), the subunit portrays YHWH's construction of the cosmos from the realm above to the realm below.[61] To be specific, it recounts the way in which YHWH "established" (-הֵכִין, v. 27a) the heavens, carved or "inscribed" (חוק, v. 27c) the horizon (cf. Gen 1:2), "made firm" (-אַמְּצ, v. 28a) the clouds, "fixed" (עזז, v. 28b)[62] the foundations of the deep, circumscribed the sea (v. 29a), and "marked out" (חוק, v. 29c)[63] the foundations of the earth. The repetition of the verb "inscribed/marked out" (חוק, vv. 27c, 29c) not only frames the subunit, but it also accentuates YHWH's architectural prowess and relates YHWH's construction of the cosmos with Wisdom's role in the construction of a stable society (vv. 15b, 27c, 29c). Wisdom's ability to empower rulers with the skills necessary for the establishment of social order is inextricably linked to her observance of YHWH's establishment of the cosmic order.

This observance of YHWH's creative handiwork is expressed through the lone main clause in vv. 27–29: "I was there" (שָׁם אָנִי, v. 27b). This clause governs all the contemporaneous temporal clauses in vv. 27–29. Similar to the syntactical pattern evinced in vv. 22–26 (esp. vv. 24–26), according to which main clauses govern temporal subordinate expressions that both precede and follow them, the declaration "I was there" governs the subordinate temporal clause that precedes it (v. 27a) as well as the series of temporal clauses that follow (vv. 27c–29). This clause specifies Wisdom's location during YHWH's construction of the cosmos. And when read together with 3:19–20, it provides an alternative perspective on YHWH's creative work. Whereas 3:19–20 focus on YHWH's use of wisdom in his creation and filling of the cosmos, 8:27–29 focus on Wisdom's observance of YHWH's establishment and ordering of the universe. Her eyewitness account of YHWH's construction of the cosmos enhances her authority and preeminence. Wisdom's preeminent place during creation and her observance of YHWH's design of the universe entails that she understands the patterns and bound-

61. Gilbert, "Le discours de la sagesse," 211; Meinhold, *Die Sprüche*, 1.144–45; Fox, *Proverbs 1–9*, 281–82; Waltke, *Proverbs: Chapters 1–15*, 414; cf. Loader, *Proverbs 1–9*, 352.

62. With the LXX and *BHS*, this reading assumes that the final *waw* and *zayin* (MT) are the result of metathesis. When the consonants are reversed, the infinitive construct receives a subject and matches the sequence of infinitives construct with pronominal suffixes in vv. 27, 28, and 29.

63. With the LXX, some read "when he marked out" (בְּחוּקוֹ) as "when he made strong" (בחזקו). The difference between the forms appears to be due to a confusion of the second consonant: the former has a *waw*, while the latter has a *zayin*. While the alternative reading explains the way in which foundations are laid (Fox, *Proverbs: An Eclectic Edition*, 159–60), in light of the architectural metaphor within vv. 27–29, "when he marked out" makes very good sense. It envisions YHWH marking the parameters of the earth's foundations in accord with the divine blueprint so that they may be laid. Loader, *Proverbs 1–9*, 356.

aries YHWH ingrained in the created world.[64] Accordingly, she can guide her devotees in accord with these patterns and within these boundaries.

c. Wisdom's Activity after Creation (8:30–31)

In light of the governing metaphors within vv. 22–29, the text moves from Wisdom's birth before creation (vv. 22–26) to her observance of YHWH's construction of the cosmos during creation (vv. 27–29). Disagreement persists, however, regarding the place of vv. 30–31 in this temporal scheme. Many contend that vv. 30–31 continue the description of Wisdom's presence during creation.[65] Others maintain that vv. 30–31 mark a temporal shift from Wisdom's presence during creation to her activity after creation.[66] Both proposals are possible. The syntactical design of vv. 27–29 and the repetition of terms in vv. 30–31, however, suggest that these verses move from Wisdom's observance of YHWH's creative works *during* creation to a period *after* creation.[67]

As noted above, similar to the syntax of vv. 22–26, the main clause in v. 27b ("I was there") governs the temporal clause that precedes it as well as the temporal clauses that follow. It completes the portrait of Wisdom's presence during YHWH's creation of the cosmos.[68] The main clause introduced in v. 30a, then, is not required to complete the contemporaneous temporal clauses in vv. 28–29. Rather than providing the apodosis for the string of temporal clauses in vv. 28–29, v. 30a breaks the temporal scheme envisioned in vv. 27–29 and marks a shift in the poem's plot progression.

This temporal shift is marked by the repetition of "And I have been" (וָאֶהְיֶה, vv. 30a, 30b) and reinforced by the prepositional phrases within vv. 30–31. Wisdom has remained at YHWH's side since the creation of the cosmos. Her presence at YHWH's side is not restricted to the period of YHWH's construction of the world; rather, it extends beyond that time to the period after creation. The same is true of Wisdom's "delighting" (שַׁעֲשֻׁעִים, vv. 30b, 31b) and "rejoicing" (מְשַׂחֶקֶת, vv. 30c, 31a). The repetition of these terms link vv. 30–31; and the temporal phrases that accompany them suggest that Wisdom's delighting and rejoicing continues beyond YHWH's formation of the universe. This development is implicit in v. 31. Wisdom's rejoicing in the goodness of YHWH's creation and particular delight in humankind not only demands that they exist, but also suggests that this rejoicing and delighting is not confined to YHWH's stabilization of the inhabitable world and creation of humankind.[69] To assume that vv. 30–31 only describe Wisdom's presence at and role during creation obscures her activity and delight after creation. And to break the temporal scheme at v. 30b only recognizes the repetition and continuity between vv. 30b–31 at the expense of the repetition and continuity between vv. 30a and 30b. The repetition of terms links v. 30 more closely with v. 31 than with the preceding verses; and the prepositional phrases highlight Wisdom's constant presence with YHWH and continuing delight in YHWH's world from creation to the present.[70] Whereas vv. 27–29 are linked by a string of infinitives that highlight Wisdom's ob-

64. Van Leeuwen, "The Book of Proverbs," *NIB* 5:93–94.

65. Toy, *Proverbs*, 177; Fox, *Proverbs 1–9*, 285; Van Leeuwen, "The Book of Proverbs," *NIB* 5:93–94; Waltke, *Proverbs: Chapters 1–15*, 406; Longman, *Proverbs*, 203; Loader, *Proverbs 1–9*, 321.

66. Weeks, "The Context and Meaning," 437–38; Treier, *Proverbs and Ecclesiastes*, 48.

67. Weeks, "The Context and Meaning," 437–38. The following adheres to the logic and conclusions of Weeks's argument.

68. Weeks, "The Context and Meaning," 437.

69. Weeks, "The Context and Meaning," 437.

70. Weeks, "The Context and Meaning," 438.

servation of YHWH's creative acts, vv. 30–31 are connected by a series of catchwords that emphasize Wisdom's delight in YHWH's created order.[71] The poem envisages a progression from Wisdom's birth and presence at the construction of the cosmos to her delight in the created order and humankind after creation.[72]

If vv. 30–31 envision a period after the creation of the cosmos, then the meaning of the infamous crux in v. 30a becomes clearer. Reading אמון as "craftsman" does not make much sense,[73] for creation is complete and the preceding verses portray Wisdom as a passive observer of YHWH's creative acts rather than an active participant in creation (vv. 27–29). The same may be said of the reading "child" or "nursling."[74] While this reading aligns with Wisdom's birth (vv. 22–26) and accounts for her "cultic play"[75] and rapturous celebration (vv. 30b–31), it contributes little to her portrait of preeminence. Context raises questions concerning each reading. And both readings operate under an important assumption, namely, that אמון specifies, or at least explains, Wisdom's role. If the term describes Wisdom's role, then "child" or "nursling" is the best reading. But if the term clarifies Wisdom's relation to YHWH, then "faithfully" or "constantly" provides the best contextual reading of אמון.[76] From creation or eternal generation to the present, Wisdom has faithfully resided at YHWH's side. This notion is developed by the adverbial temporal expressions in vv. 30b and 30c, which indicate that Wisdom's delighting and rejoicing in YHWH's presence is constant: "day after day" (יוֹם יוֹם, v. 30b) and "always" (בְּכָל־עֵת, v. 30c). These expressions not only specify the nature and extent of Wisdom's playful activity, but they also situate her play in intimate

71. Weeks, "The Context and Meaning," 437–38.

72. Weeks, "The Context and Meaning," 437–38.

73. For this reading, see the LXX, Vulgate, Delitzsch, "Proverbs of Solomon," 6:137–40 (1:188–91); Oesterley, *The Book of Proverbs*, 64–65; Murphy, *Proverbs*, 47; Van Leeuwen, "The Book of Proverbs," *NIB* 5:94–95; Longman, *Proverbs*, 207. Clifford offers a variant proposal, reading אמון as "scribe" or "sage" (*Proverbs*, 100–101). And others argue that אמון is cast in apposition to "his side" (אֶצְלוֹ, v. 30a), thus referring to YHWH's activity as an "artisan" or "craftsman" (P. E. Bonnard, "De la Sagesse personnifieé dans l'Ancien Testament à la Sagesse en personne dans le Nouveau," in *La Sagesse de l'Ancien Testament*, ed. M. Gilbert [Louven: Peeters, 1979], 121–22; Cleon L. Rogers III, "The Meaning and Significance of the Hebrew Word אמון in Proverbs 8,30," *ZAW* 109 [1997]: 208–21). These proposals are promising, for they recognize that Wisdom does not play an active role in creation. Nonetheless, they remain problematic. Similar to the reading "craftsman," Clifford's proposal relates אמון to the Akkadian cognate *ummānu*. But if this were the case, the Hebrew form would be אמן (Song 7:2), not אמון (Fox, *Proverbs 1–9*, 286). As for אמון as appositional to "his side," one would expect the definite article on אמון. The absence of the article may signal an exception to the general rule. This exception, however, has little support elsewhere in the Old Testament. Loader, *Proverbs 1–9*, 357.

74. For this reading, see Toy, *Proverbs*, 177–78; Meinhold, *Die Sprüche*, 1.146; Baumann, *Die Weisheitsgestalt in Proverbien 1–9*, 131–40; Leo G. Perdue, *Proverbs*, IBC [Louisville: John Knox Press, 2000), 145; Loader, *Proverbs 1–9*, 358–60. Fox offers a variation of this reading, taking אמון as an infinitive absolute that serves as an adverbial complement meaning "growing up" (Michael V. Fox, "ʾAmon Again," *JBL* 125 [1996]: 699–702; idem, *Proverbs 1–9*, 266–87). Together with those who take אמון as an infinitive absolute and read "nursling," this reading is attractive, for it requires no emendation of the Hebrew and explains why אמון is neither feminine nor passive. For the argument that the reading "nursling, child" and "growing up" obscures the technical sense of אמן in the context of child rearing, see Weeks, "The Context and Meaning," 434–35.

75. Brown, *The Ethos of the Cosmos*, 278. The expression "rejoicing before him" (מְשַׂחֶקֶת לְפָנָיו, v. 30c) is comparable to 2 Sam 6:5, where David and all the house of Israel are "dancing before YHWH" (מְשַׂחֲקִים לִפְנֵי יְהוָה; cf. 2 Sam 6:21). For the possible military and cultic connotations of this form of celebration, see C. L. Seow, *Myth, Drama, and The Politics of David's Dance*, HSM 44 (Atlanta: Scholars Press, 1989), 93–97.

76. In this case, following Weeks, אמון is taken as a noun or an adjective that derives from אמן I and functions adverbially, for it does not agree with the gender of the subject. This reading mirrors the parallel expression "day after day" in v. 30b, which consists of the juxtaposition of two nouns that function adverbially. And it accounts for the use of אמון as a personal name in the Old Testament, meaning "faithful" (*HALOT* 1:62, s.v. אמון). Weeks, "The Context and Meaning," 439–40; Symmachus and Theodotian.

relationship with YHWH. Whether this relationship is understood as familial ("child, nursling") or simply faithful, Wisdom's relation to YHWH, rather than her role in relation to the creation of the cosmos, is the climax of the account. And this climax accentuates Wisdom's preeminence.

Wisdom's preeminence is given particular expression in the repetition of the terms "delighting" (שַׁעֲשֻׁעִים, vv. 30b, 31b) and "rejoicing" (מְשַׂחֶקֶת, vv. 30c, 31a). Wisdom delights and rejoices before YHWH.[77] And she rejoices and delights in God's good creation as well as in humankind. Play and delight characterize Wisdom's relationship with YHWH, creation, and humanity. They serve as a bridge between YHWH, creation, and humanity. And they function as the climax of Wisdom's case. In view of her credentials (vv. 12–13), function in the present world (vv. 14–16), gifts (vv. 17–21), emergence in primordial time (vv. 22–26), presence at creation (vv. 27–29), and position at YHWH's side (v. 30), Wisdom epitomizes all that is desirable: virtue, the principles of statecraft, reciprocal love, wealth, intimate relationship with YHWH, knowledge of the fundamental structures of the world, faithfulness, and perpetual access to the divine. Despite her status, possessions, and preeminent position, humans are the object of her affections, her prized preoccupation within the cosmic playhouse constructed by YHWH. No wonder Wisdom frames her formal encomium with a reference to "humankind" (בְּנֵי אָדָם, vv. 4, 31). Her play in the presence of YHWH and her delight in the moral and aesthetic beauty of the cosmos coincide with her play in the inhabitable world and her delight in humankind. She communes with Creator and creatures, expressing a joy that traverses the transcendent and imminent realms and incorporates Creator and creature in a harmonious celebration of creation's goodness.[78]

5. Wisdom's Climactic Exhortation (8:32–36)[79]

In view of the content of Wisdom's extended justification of her value, desirability, and preeminence (vv. 12–31), it is not surprising that those who listen to her are blessed. This blessing naturally flows from Wisdom's own joy and mirth. And this state is the focus of attention in Wisdom's climactic exhortation (vv. 32–36). The expression "So now" (וְעַתָּה, v. 32a), combined with the address to "sons" (בָנִים, v. 32a) and the repetition of the imperative "listen" (שִׁמְעוּ, vv. 32a, 33a), mimics the rhetoric of the parental lectures elsewhere in the prologue and distinguishes vv. 32–36 from the cosmic portrait painted in vv. 22–31 (5:7; 7:24).[80] Wisdom resumes the role of a teacher, urging her audience to listen to her and to take up residence at her doorstep so that they might live and receive divine favor (8:35; cf. 3:2, 22; 4:22).[81] Similar to the style and structure of the exhortations within the parental lectures, the conclusion to Wisdom's discourse consists of three basic parts: the exhortation (8:32–33), the blessing (v. 34), and the consequences (vv. 35–36).

77. In contrast to the MT's "I was delights" (וָאֶהְיֶה שַׁעֲשֻׁעִים, v. 30b), the LXX reads "I was his delight" (ἐγὼ ἤμην ᾗ προσέχαιρεν, v. 30b). The LXX includes the implied 3ms suffix from v. 30a. The translation above assumes that the expression "before him" (לְפָנָיו) in v. 30c is implied in v. 30b. For discussion of this reading, see Waltke, *Proverbs: Chapters 1–15*, 420–21.

78. Brown, *The Ethos of the Cosmos*, 278.

79. While the LXX rearranges certain verses within Wisdom's climactic exhortation and omits v. 33, it is not necessary to emend the MT. The LXX may provide a well-ordered text with respect to parallelism and logic, but the design and flow of the MT makes very good sense. Fox, *Proverbs 1–9*, 289.

80. Waltke, *Proverbs: Chapters 1–15*, 423. In addition to the way in which Wisdom's call (v. 32a) reiterates the parent's call in 7:24, Waltke also observes that the discourses in chs. 7 and 8 end with the same word: death (7:27; 8:36).

81. Fox, *Proverbs 1–9*, 289.

a. The Exhortation (8:32–33)

The concluding exhortation mirrors Wisdom's opening exhortation (vv. 4–11); it resumes the mode of direct address and reinforces the universal relevance of Wisdom's self-portrait. This resumption is introduced by the expression "So now" (וְעַתָּה, v. 32a; cf. 5:7; 7:24), which establishes logical continuity with the preceding sections (8:12–31) and signals a shift in the rhetorical agenda of the encomium.[82] In light of her character, credentials, and cosmic preeminence (vv. 12–21, 22–31), Wisdom recapitulates her introductory call to listen (v. 32a; cf. v. 6a) and reveals the real audience of her discourse: "sons" (בָנִים, v. 32a). Whereas the opening exhortation identified "humankind" (בְּנֵי אָדָם, v. 4b) in general and the "uncommitted" (פְּתָאיִם, v. 5a) and "fools" (כְּסִילִים, v. 5b) in particular as the rhetorical audience of the encomium, the concluding exhortation identifies "sons" as the real audience of Wisdom's discourse. The audience remains general, and the relevance of Wisdom's encomium remains universal. But the familial language of the concluding exhortation reorients the subject position of the addressees and aligns this audience with the audience of the parental lectures. As the daughter of YHWH, Wisdom addresses sons, urging them to heed her voice, keep her way, and enjoy the blessed state and filial relationship that she enjoys with God.

In many respects, Wisdom's introductory appeal serves as a distillation of the admonition and blessing that follow. It consists of two basic parts: an exhortation and a rationale. The exhortation is simple: "listen to me" (שִׁמְעוּ־לִי, v, 32a). The rationale for observing this admonition is expressed through a paratactic construction that implies a causal relationship between vv. 32a and 32b.[83] One should attend to Wisdom's directives because the one who follows her ways is blessed (v. 32b). As the first of YHWH's creative ways (v. 22a) and as one who walks on the paths of justice and righteousness (v. 20), Wisdom's way brings blessing. The one who listens to her is socialized in a moral worldview and oriented toward a way of life characterized by happiness, good favor, and wholeness.

These aspects of Wisdom's appeal are developed in vv. 33–34. The repetition of the imperative "Listen" (שִׁמְעוּ, vv. 32a, 33a) in v. 33 links the admonition to Wisdom's opening exhortation. And the object of the imperative supplements Wisdom's opening call; it indicates that listening to Wisdom means listening to "discipline" (מוּסָר, v. 33a), that is, to verbal forms of authoritative reproof that possess the power to shape one's worldview, desires and, ultimately, one's character. This form of listening requires a receptive posture, it demands attention and response to the right voice without neglect, and it produces the pedagogical goal of Proverbs. This goal is expressed through the imperative "become wise" (חֲכָמוּ, v. 33a). This second imperative complements the first, "listen" (שִׁמְעוּ, v. 33a), and marks the purpose or result of listening to discipline.[84] The reception of authoritative correction makes one wise, forming one into the virtuous person profiled and projected throughout the diverse materials in Proverbs.

b. The Blessing (8:34)

If v. 33 develops v. 32a, then v. 34 develops v. 32b. The repetition of the macaristic expression "Blessed is" (אַשְׁרֵי, v. 34a) as well as the term "listens" (שֹׁמֵעַ, v. 34a) binds the blessing to Wisdom's

82. *IBHS* §39.3.4f.
83. *IBHS* §39.2.1c.
84. GKC §110f; Loader, *Proverbs 1–9*, 365.

opening appeal. This blessing provides a vivid exposition of what it means to keep Wisdom's ways (v. 32b).[85] The exposition employs architectural imagery, which positions the addressee at a particular locale. The locale is familiar. As one of the nuclear symbols within the prologue, houses are part and parcel of a larger metaphoric system that includes the concepts of wisdom and folly, life and death.[86] Wisdom draws on language and imagery reminiscent of the parental lectures concerning the strange woman to describe the alternative fate that awaits those who listen to her. Whereas the "door" (פֶּתַח; 5:8) of the strange woman's house is the portal to death (5:8), the "doorways" (פְּתָח, 8:34c) of Wisdom's house offer entry into the beatific life. This blessed state is achieved by listening to Wisdom in a particular way. The infinitives construct "by keeping vigil" (לִשְׁקֹד, v. 34b) and "by watching" (לִשְׁמֹר, v. 34c) function adverbially, describing the manner in which one listens to Wisdom. The form of listening delineated in v. 34 moves beyond reception of Wisdom's words to include a position and posture that one must assume. One listens to Wisdom by attentively and persistently watching her doors and by orienting one's gaze at her doorways. Put differently, one demonstrates one's desire and love for Wisdom by aligning one's body and geographical position with their inward disposition. This physical posture and geographical position complement the receptive disposition required to listen to and receive Wisdom. And similar to v. 32, this posture, position, and disposition toward Wisdom bring blessing, happiness, and wholeness.

c. The Consequences (8:35–36)

This reward for listening to and receiving Wisdom is substantiated by the concluding verses of the discourse (vv. 35–36). The conjunction "for" (כִּי, v. 35a) introduces a causal clause, which provides a rationale for the blessing announced in v. 34. While v. 34 employed architectural imagery to describe the physical posture and geographical position of the blessed person, v. 35 includes the search and find motif to legitimize the blessed state of the one who listens to Wisdom (cf. 3:13). With language very reminiscent of 3:18 (cf. 4:13; cf. 18:22), Wisdom indicates that she is the source of life. If one finds her, then one finds life as well as divine favor. That is, one experiences happiness through the horizontal blessing of life and the vertical blessing of divine favor.

The opposite is true for those who hate Wisdom (8:36). The antithetical conjunction "but" (וְ, v. 36a) introduces another type of person. This person "offends" (-חֹטְא, v. 36a)[87] Wisdom, harming oneself in the process. And this person possesses perverted emotions and misdirected desires: rather than hating evil (v. 13), they hate Wisdom (v. 36b); and rather than loving Wisdom (v. 17; 4:6), they love death (8:36b). The declaration is clear and crisp. While the consequence of death is implied, the self-harm inflicted by the one who offends Wisdom is explicit. The conclusion to Wisdom's discourse legitimizes the blessing announced in vv. 32–34 (cf. 3:13–20) and confirms the conclusion announced in Wisdom's initial speech: listening to Wisdom brings security; complacency brings destruction (1:32–33).

85. Loader, *Proverbs 1–9*, 366.

86. Van Leeuwen, "Liminality and Worldview," 111.

87. Since חטא is cast in the *qal* stem and moral sin does not appear to be in view, the sense "offends me" provides an appropriate, emotional parallel to "hate me" (v. 36b) and captures the nature of the affront committed by the person in view.

Canonical and Theological Significance

Wisdom's evocative encomium is masterful; its "'I'-witness"[88] account connects the communal sphere with the home (vv. 2–3, 34), the primordial world with the present (vv. 12–21, 22–29), the transcendent realm with the imminent (vv. 22–30, 31), and Wisdom's character with the moral vision of Proverbs (vv. 8–9, 12–13; cf. 1:2–7). Wisdom raises her voice amid the clamor of competing characters and moral worldviews, wooing prospective devotees through a captivating portrait of her character, social value, personal benefits, and cosmic preeminence. This portrait limns a vision of life suffused with the ethos of truth, trust, justice, righteousness, stability, safety, wonder, joy, and delight. Its rhetorical richness awakens one's desires and enchants one's moral imagination. And its thematic pigments point one to other texts in Proverbs, the Old Testament, and the New that were created with the same colors that produced Prov 8.

When viewed within the book of Proverbs, Wisdom's encomium exhibits lexical and thematic shades used elsewhere in the document. As noted above, Wisdom's self-presentation provides a positive, metaphorical counterpart to the seductive speech of the strange woman: Wisdom's speech is straightforward (vv. 7, 9), not slippery (5:3; 7:21); she walks on the way of righteousness and justice (8:20); her paths do not meander about (5:6); and the door of her house is the threshold of the beatific life (8:34) rather than the entry to death (5:8; cf. 9:14). Wisdom is portrayed as a mirror image of the strange woman, as a legitimate object of desire and as the fulfillment of one's desires. This female antithesis anticipates the comparable, yet conflicting women, houses, and invitations of ch. 9. And Wisdom's metaphorical portrait provides the lexical palette for the historical portrait painted in 31:10–31.[89] The lexical and thematic shades within Wisdom's encomium provide a contrast to ch. 7, an orientation to ch. 9, and the color for 31:10–31. The discourse functions as a literary hinge within the prologue, and its links with the concluding poem in the anthology create a literary framework around the central collections.

In addition to its structural significance, Wisdom's rich encomium filters the document's fundamental virtues through Wisdom's literary persona. She embodies that which Proverbs seeks to inculcate in readers: "integrity/uprightness" (מֵישָׁרִים, 8:6b; 1:3), "righteousness" (צֶדֶק, 8:8a, 18b, 20a; 1:3), "justice" (מִשְׁפָּט, 8:20b; 1:3), "knowledge" (דַּעַת, 8:10b; 1:4), "wisdom" (חָכְמָה, 8:11a; 1:2), "shrewdness" (עָרְמָה; 8:12a; 1:4), "discretion" (מְזִמָּה, 8:12b; 1:4), "the fear of YHWH" (יִרְאַת יְהוָה, 8:13a;

88. Brown, *Wisdom's Wonder*, 50.

89. McCreesh, "Wisdom as Wife," 391–410; Camp, *Wisdom and the Feminine*, 186–208; R. Norman Whybray, *The Composition of the Book of Proverbs*, JSOTSup 168 (Sheffield Academic, 1994), 153–62; Yoder, *Wisdom as a Woman of Substance*, 91–93.

1:7), and "understanding" (בִּינָה, 8:14b; 1:2). By embodying the fundamental virtues proffered in the anthology, Wisdom is presented as the epitome of what is desirable and a legitimate object of love.

The colors that characterize Wisdom's self-portrait correspond with the moral vision of Proverbs, capture her antithetical relationship with the strange woman as well as Woman Folly, and evince her consonance with the valiant woman. More than this, Wisdom's self-portrait illuminates her intimate and enigmatic relation to YHWH, for it portrays Wisdom in a manner comparable to YHWH's depiction elsewhere in the Old Testament. Similar to YHWH, Wisdom's words are true (v. 7a; Exod 34:6; 2 Sam 7:28) and right (Prov 8:9b; Pss 19:9[8]; 33:4; 119:137; Isa 45:19; Neh 9:13); she speaks "in accord with righteousness" (בְּצֶדֶק, Prov 8:8a; Pss 65:6[5]; cf. 11:7; 19:9[10]; 33:5; Isa 45:19); and wickedness is an abomination to her lips (Prov 8:7b; 12:22).[90] Similar to YHWH, Wisdom possesses and implements those skills that contribute to the establishment of an ordered society: counsel, resourcefulness, and strength (v. 14; Job 12:13, 16; cf. Isa. 11:2). Similar to YHWH, relationship with Wisdom brings life (Prov 8:35–36; Jer 21:8; Prov 14:27).[91] And similar to YHWH, Wisdom transcends creation (vv. 22–31; Gen 1:1–2:4; Ps 104). Whereas Prov 3:19–20 describe Wisdom's relation to creation in instrumental terms, 8:22–31 express this relationship through presence, observation, delight, and dance. Wisdom is among the tools or powers employed by the divine architect to construct a sure, enduring cosmos (3:19) as well as an independent, exuberant eyewitness within YHWH's stable world (8:22–31).

These distinctive accounts of W/wisdom's relation to creation, combined with her intimate association with YHWH and YHWH's prerogatives, raise questions concerning her nature and function within ch. 8, each of which has theological, and especially Christological implications. Many seek to address these questions, with or without regard to their theological consequences, by exploring the origin(s) or sociohistorical context of Wisdom's literary creation. While these investigations are not unimportant, they contribute little to an understanding of Wisdom's literary and theological portrayal. As a personified figure, Wisdom does not appear to have a single referent.[92] This is not surprising, since personification is a rhetorical convention that provides a general, conceptual framework within which multiple images and

90. Gilbert, "Le discours de la sagesse," 205; Baumann, *Die Weisheitsgestalt in Proverbien 1–9*, 78–79; Schwáb, *Toward an Interpretation*, 179.

91. Baumann, *Die Weisheitsgestalt in Proverbien 1–9*, 156–57; Schwáb, *Toward an Interpretation*, 178.

92. Van Leeuwen, "The Book of Proverbs," *NIB* 5:96. In addition, it is important to note that the personification of Wisdom has no precedent in texts from the ancient world. While many have appealed to a personified Wisdom in the Aramaic Ahiqar, this personification is due to a questionable arrangement of the text. In view of Porten and Yardeni's new arrangement of Ahiqar, which organizes the fragmentary text according to the commercial document underlying the papyri rather than according to content, Seth Bledsoe has demonstrated convincingly that Ahiqar does not present a personified wisdom figure and, therefore, cannot be used as evidence for such a figure independent of the biblical tradition. Seth A. Bledsoe, "Can *Ahiqar* Tell Us Anything about Personified Wisdom?," *JBL* 132 (2013): 119–37.

roles may be subsumed and concretized in a composite figure.[93] Wisdom's literary persona may integrate and gesture to images and concepts reminiscent of goddesses, lovers, mothers, counselors, teachers, prophets, and real women,[94] but her multifaceted description refuses classification into one category alone. Wisdom wears many hats, none of which lay claim to the fullness of her literary identity.

If one looks beyond Wisdom's wardrobe and focuses on her literary and theological function, then her characterization and contribution to the prologue becomes clearer. As a personified figure, Wisdom absorbs and embodies the various aspects of wisdom presented in the parental lectures.[95] She is a divine gift who grants gifts in filial relationship with YHWH and within creation (2:6; 3:19–20; 8:17–21, 22–31). She is the emanation of YHWH's mouth and the frolicking daughter brought forth from his womb (2:6; 8:22–31). She is the substance of parental instruction and the constant companion of YHWH (2:2, 10; 4:5, 7; 5:1; 7:4; 8:30). She directs one on the path of the righteous and walks along the way of righteousness (2:20; 8:20). She is the authorized object of love and the one who loves her devotees (4:6; 8:17). Wisdom is inextricably linked with the wisdom of the parental lectures. And she is inextricably linked to YHWH.

The nature of this link, however, is unclear. Despite the insightful observations of many proposals for Wisdom's identity, it appears that she is neither a personified divine attribute nor a mediator, at least in the conventional sense of the term.[96] If anything, Lady Wisdom is a divine hypostasis. She is depicted as a distinct, personal agent. She speaks for herself. She shares the prerogatives of YHWH. She presents herself as one who subsists through time both beside YHWH and before YHWH.[97] And her intermediate position between YHWH and humanity provides one with access to the wisdom, will, and presence of God.[98] Similar to the personification of other divine attributes, Wisdom is portrayed as a distinct, personal being. When her poetic portrayal is viewed within the conceptual world of the Old Testament, it appears that Lady Wisdom participates in the unique being and identity of the one God of Israel, who creates through wisdom, speaks through his word, enlivens through his Spirit,

93. Camp, *Wisdom and the Feminine*, 215–17; Sinnott, *The Personification of Wisdom*, 18–20.

94. For a summary and discussion of these proposals along with others, see Baumann, *Die Weisheitsgestalt in Proverbien 1–9*, 4–25; Fox, *Proverbs 1–9*, 333–45; Sinnott, *The Personification of Wisdom*, 34–51.

95. Gerlinde Baumann, "A Figure of Many Facets: The Literary and Theological Functions of Personified Wisdom in Proverbs 1–9," in *Wisdom and Psalms: A Feminist Companion to the Bible*, ed. A. Brenner and C. R. Fontaine (Sheffield: Sheffield Academic, 1998), 52–56.

96. As Fox rightly notes, Wisdom "exists on an intermediate plane" between God and the world. "But she does not *mediate.* God never speaks to her, and she does not quote him, even indirectly, or transmit his word to mankind" (*Proverbs 1–9*, 334, italics original).

97. Donald Collett, "A Place to Stand: Proverbs 8 and the Construction of Ecclesial Space," *SJT* 70 (2017): 176–81.

98. Schwáb, *Toward an Interpretation*, 184–85. Along these lines, Van Leeuwen rightly notes that, similar to the "the angel of the Lord," "the word of the Lord," "the Name (of the Lord)," and "the Presence," Wisdom expresses "the working or presence of YHWH in the world and cannot be separated from God's being." At the same time, however, Wisdom and these entities "are not identical with it." Van Leeuwen, "The Book of Proverbs," *NIB* 5:96.

and reveals himself through intimate, covenant relationship with his people.[99] The Old Testament reveals a unique God who is not Unitarian but who exists "in a class of his own," who remains distinct from "all other reality" yet graciously relates to his creatures in such a way that allows for "distinction within the unique identity of the one God."[100] Wisdom's testimony across Prov 8 bears witness to this distinction within the unique identity of the one God of Israel. And Wisdom's poetic portrait focuses attention on the wonder, supremacy, delight, and goodness of God's wisdom.

While the precise nature of Wisdom's relationship with YHWH and creation evades simple classification, her polysemous portrayal may be more of an asset than a liability. The semantic potential of the terms used to paint her portrait and the poetic cast of her presentation create space within which to understand and appreciate the diverse ways in which Wisdom has been received and appropriated, from the Second Temple period into the New Testament and beyond. According to Ben Sirach, Wisdom was created before all things (Sir 1:4; 24:9; cf. Prov 8:22–26). As the emanation of YHWH's mouth (Sir 24:3; cf. Prov 2:6), she traverses the heavens above and the abyss below (Sir 24:5). And as one who holds sway over all the nations (Sir 24:6; cf. Prov 8:14–16), she is manifest in, even equivalent to, the Torah (Sir 24:23; cf. Bar 4:1). For Wisdom of Solomon, Wisdom was present at YHWH's construction of the cosmos (Wis 9:9; cf. Prov 8:27–29). Far from merely observing YHWH's creative work, however, Wisdom participated in the process as "the fashioner of all things" (Wis 7:22) and as the one by whom God "formed humankind" (Wis 9:2). She is "a breath of the power of God and a pure emanation of the glory of the Almighty" (Wis 7:25; cf. Prov 2:6), one who encompasses the earth, penetrating the hearts of people to make them friends with God (Wis 7:27; 8:1). This narrow account of Wisdom's reception indicates that both Ben Sirach and Wisdom of Solomon develop aspects of Wisdom latent in Prov 8. The former equates Wisdom with Torah and identifies her dwelling in Jerusalem to describe the way in which God directs and cares for his people (Sir 24:8–12, 23). The latter grants Wisdom an active role in creation, elevating her to the position of "God's chief agent."[101] The Wisdom of Ben Sirach and Wisdom of Solomon resembles the Wisdom of Prov 8. Certain contours remain, but the portrait has changed: differing landscapes and particular pigments have altered the depiction of Wisdom's place, function, and persona within the divine economy.

These alterations provide a necessary backdrop for exploring Wisdom within the New Testament. In light of the rough reception history sketched above, it appears that, while certain New Testament texts portray Jesus and the gospel message through

99. Christopher Seitz, "The Trinity in the Old Testament," in *The Oxford Handbook of the Trinity*, ed. Gilles Emery and Matthew Levering (Oxford: Oxford University Press, 2011), 30.

100. Richard Bauckham, *God Crucified: Monotheism and Christology in the New Testament* (Carlisle: Paternoster, 1998), 22.

101. Larry W. Hurtado, *One God, One Lord: Early Christian Devotion and Ancient Jewish Monotheism*, 3rd ed. (Bloomsbury T&T Clark, 2015), 44.

terms and concepts redolent of Wisdom's encomium, the pigments of these texts are closer to Ben Sirach and Wisdom of Solomon than to Prov 8. Or, to change the metaphor, Prov 8 is the flower from which Ben Sirach and Wisdom of Solomon trim and plant a cutting, each of which germinates and blossoms into an independent flower. And Ben Sirach and Wisdom of Solomon are the flowers from which several New Testament authors trim and plant a cutting, each of which germinates and blossoms into Christological flora. These flowers are organically related; but their genealogy and development indicate that certain New Testament texts are more closely related to Ben Sira and Wisdom of Solomon than to Prov 8. This does not deny the resonance between Prov 8 and certain New Testament texts; rather, it reframes the relationship among these texts. The prologue of John's Gospel depicts the *logos* through terms and concepts reminiscent of Prov 8 but, despite their lexical and conceptual correspondence in general and the way in which the *logos* assumed the pedigree and powers of Wisdom in Hellenistic thought in particular, it is important to note that the *logos* of the Johannine prologue possesses characteristics and functions that go well beyond the characteristics and functions of Wisdom in Prov 8. With the exception of Wisdom's primordial presence with God "in the beginning" and her association with life (Prov 8:23, 27, 35), Prov 8 contributes little to John's depiction of the *logos*. The paucity of parallels, combined with Wisdom's passive observance of creation in Prov 8, suggests that Gen 1, Ben Sirach, Wisdom of Solomon, and Philo's readings of Genesis provide better intertextual and conceptual parallels to the Johannine prologue than Wisdom's encomium.[102] The same is true of the early Christological hymn in Col 1:15–20 (cf. Heb 1:2–4). Similar to John 1, the Colossian hymn praises Christ's preeminence through expressions and concepts redolent of Prov 8. Again, however, Wisdom's primordial birth and passive observance of creation within the encomium intimate that the hymn's Christological portrait shares much more in common with expressions and concepts that pervade Wisdom of Solomon and Philo than with Prov 8.[103] And so the argument could continue with reference to particular portrayals of Jesus in the Synoptics.[104] The point is that Prov 8 does not serve as a direct

102. For a detailed catalogue of the parallels between John 1:1–18 and Gen 1–2, Exod 33–34, Jewish wisdom traditions, and Philo, see Craig A. Evans, *Word and Glory: On the Exegetical and Theological Background of John's Prologue*, JSNTSup 89 (Sheffield: Sheffield Academic, 1993), 78–94, 101–3.

103. For a catalogue of the striking verbal and conceptual parallels between Col 1:15–20 and Wisdom of Solomon, see Witherington, *Jesus the Sage*, 267. Also, see Christopher A. Beetham, *Echoes of Scripture in the Letter of Paul to the Colossians*, BibInt 96 (Atlanta: SBL Press, 2008), 111–41, esp. 135–36. In essence, Beetham argues that Paul does not draw on Prov 8 directly to formulate the hymn; rather, Paul draws on the interpretive development of Prov 8 in early and late Judaism, especially Wisdom of Solomon and Philo.

104. Witherington, *Jesus the Sage*, 155–83, 336–68; Barton, "Gospel Wisdom," 93–110. Paul's discussion of wisdom in 1 Corinthians may seem like a missing piece in the canonical puzzle, but Prov 8 does not contribute to the apostle's argument. While Paul's description of Jesus as "the wisdom of God" (1 Cor 1:24; cf. 1:30) bears witness to the apostle's use of wisdom as a theological category, it is important to note that, in the context of 1 Cor 1:18–3:23, this "wisdom" is thoroughly subversive. As Richard Hays rightly notes, throughout this text Paul counters the Corinthians' boasting in their distinguished knowledge and powerful eloquence "by performing an ironic counter-reading of wisdom in light of the cross." The death of the crucified Messiah "confounds all human wisdom and redefines wisdom in a new and paradoxical way." In light of Paul's argument, it appears

intertext with New Testament texts that contribute to Christology; rather, Prov 8, as developed and refracted through particular texts in early and late Judaism, serves as the well from which New Testament authors draw to express their Christological convictions. This account of Prov 8 removes the text, at least directly, as an intertext with certain New Testament passages and their contribution to Christology. This does not mean, however, that Prov 8 contributes nothing to the witness of the New Testament. On the contrary, the terms and concepts employed in Wisdom's evocative and enigmatic portrait are redeployed by several New Testament texts to demonstrate that the ultimate embodiment and expression of God's preeminent wisdom is found in the person of Jesus Christ. The conceptual resonances of Wisdom's primordial existence, presence at creation, and intermediary position between YHWH and humans do not indicate that Wisdom and Jesus are one and the same. Rather, following Raymond Van Leeuwen, these resonances suggest that "Christ is the hidden reality underlying and fulfilling the cosmic and personal imagery of Wisdom in Proverbs 8."[105] Put differently, Christ is the referent, reality, or *res* of Lady Wisdom's poetic portrait in Prov 8. If this is the case, then early, pro-Nicene readers were not fanciful interpreters; rather, they were wise, theological interpreters who pierced through the literal surface of the text to discover the reality of Christ projected through the shadowy images of Wisdom's encomium.[106]

The fact that Prov 8 offers a faint witness to New Testament conceptions of Jesus and expressions of Christology does not mean that is has nothing to say to the church. It has several things to say, four in particular. First, when read against the backdrop of ch. 7, Wisdom's self-portrait revisits the matter of human desire. Wisdom epitomizes all that is desirable: virtuous character, straightforward speech, the responsible exercise of power, reciprocal love, material benefits, intimate relationship with YHWH, and a beatific life. Her portrait of praise awakens and directs one's desires. Her concluding admonition questions what one loves or desires. And her resume defines what it means to fear YHWH in terms of desire; it is to hate pride, arrogance, the way of evil, and perverse speech (8:13). In many ways, Prov 8 probes one's desires, challenging one to diagnose and determine what is most desirable.

Second, Wisdom's self-portrait demonstrates that wisdom and virtue are inseparable. Wisdom defines her character through both intellectual and moral qualities. And the moral qualities that characterize Wisdom's character are indistinguishable from the attributes that define YHWH's character. Wisdom's words and ways image God's words and ways. In the same way, one who is wise images both YHWH's and

that Prov 8 does not contribute to the discussion; rather, Greco-Roman conceptions of wisdom and Paul's theological interpretation of the Christ event drive the argument. Hays, "Wisdom According to Paul," 111–23, esp. 112–13.

105. Van Leeuwen, "The Book of Proverbs," *NIB* 5:99.

106. Boersma, "The Sacramental Reading of Nicene Theology," 1–30.

Wisdom's words and ways. Contrary to modern conceptions, Proverbs refuses to define wisdom in terms of the intellectual possession of knowledge alone. Wisdom is much more than this. It is a power that forms, cultivates, and expresses itself though one's character.[107] Just as faith without works is dead, so also wisdom without works is dead. Or, to borrow Jesus's proverbial declaration, wisdom is proved right—not by intellectual prowess or sophisticated argumentation but *by her actions* (Matt 11:19).

The worldview that governs and informs these actions constitutes the third contribution of Prov 8. Wisdom's self-portrait links the primordial world with the present, the transcendent with the imminent, the order of the cosmos with the order of human life, and Wisdom's delight before YHWH with her delight in humankind. This wonderous vision enlivens and enchants one's worldview; it indicates that freedom, joy, and mirth are found in intimate relationship with YHWH and Wisdom within the boundaries of God's good creation.[108] Wisdom's exuberant rejoicing awakens the pathos appropriate to the ethos of God's wonderful order. Here joy and life are found within God's good boundaries rather than without. And here the order and stability of creation is deemed as the arena of delight rather than the domain of drudgery.

Fourth and finally, the encomium expresses the reality that wisdom is available and accessible. In contrast to Job 28, Wisdom's whereabouts are neither hidden nor unknown. She cries out to all from the centers of social life, summoning devotees to listen to her and to darken her door. The one who seeks her will find her (Prov 8:17). The one who cries aloud for her will receive her (2:1–6). And whoever lacks her may ask God, who promises to grant wisdom to those who trust in him (Jas 1:5).

107. Fox, *Proverbs 1–9*, 183, where Fox defines wisdom as "*moral character*," italics original.

108. Van Leeuwen, "The Book of Proverbs," *NIB* 5:97–98.

CHAPTER 15

Proverbs 9:1–18

N. Wisdom and Folly's Invitations

Main Idea of the Passage

The dramatic climax of Prov 1:8–9:18 weaves the prologue's nuclear symbol and satellite images through rival invitations to force the reader to make a choice, one that hinges on one's character and leads to different destinations.

Literary Context of the Passage

As a door turns on its hinges, so the prologue and the central collections within the anthology turn on Prov 9:1–18. The discourse marks the threshold between Prov 1:8–9:18 and 10:1–22:16; and it swings the door that faces the prologue, on the one hand, and the central collections, on the other.[1] The literary craftsmanship of this door and the way in which its sides resemble features characteristic of the prologue and the central collections deserves a brief comment.

When viewed as the climax of the prologue, the discourse throws key images, motifs, and expressions into sharp relief. The nuclear symbol and satellite images woven throughout the prologue are engraved on its epilogue: ways, women, and houses as well as wisdom and folly, life and death mark the exit of the anthology's introduction.[2] The antithesis between the strange woman and Lady Wisdom in chs. 7–8 is heightened by the antithetical invitations of Lady Wisdom and Woman Folly in ch. 9. And Wisdom's blessing upon those who keep vigil at her doors and watch the posts of her doorways (8:34) provides an appropriate precursor to Wisdom's

1. The recognition that Prov 9:1–18 looks back on the prologue as well as forward to the central collections is noted by many. Among others, see Clifford, *Proverbs*, 102; Yoder, *Proverbs*, 103–4; Loader, *Proverbs 1–9*, 377.

2. Habel, "The Symbolism of Wisdom in Proverbs 1–9," 133–34; Van Leeuwen, "Liminality and Worldview," 111; Fox, *Proverbs 1–9*, 128–29.

invitation into her home.[3] If the governing metaphor of the way and the accompanying concepts of women and houses, wisdom and folly, life and death represent the nuclear symbol and satellite images within the prologue, then this symbol and its corresponding images converge and culminate in the epilogue.[4]

The epilogue includes additional terms, motifs, and expressions reminiscent of the discourses elsewhere in the prologue. Three are of particular importance. First, Wisdom's invitation resembles her previous discourses. The unusual use of the plural "Wisdom" (חָכְמוֹת, v. 1a) corresponds with the introduction to Wisdom's initial speech (1:20). The urban locale and general site of her call reflects the locale and setting of her previous calls (9:3; 1:20–21; 8:1–3; cf. 9:14) and, similar to the preamble and her previous speeches, Wisdom's invitation targets the "uncommitted" (v. 4a; 1:22, 32; 8:5; cf. 9:16a). Second, Woman Folly is a mirror image of the strange woman. Both address the uncommitted in general and one lacking sense in particular (v. 16; 7:7). Both are characterized as "turbulent" (הֹמִיָּה, 9:13a; 7:11) and as those who "know nothing" (בַל־יָדְעָה מָּה, 9:13b; 5:6; cf. 4:19; 9:18). And the house of both women is depicted as the entrance to Sheol (v. 18b; 5:5; 7:27; cf. 1:12), the portal to fellowship with the community of the dead (9:18a; 2:18). Third, and finally, the collection of aphorisms in 9:7–12 link the epilogue with other portions of the prologue. The repeated mention of the "scoffer" (vv. 7a, 8a) recalls Wisdom's initial speech and the conclusion to the fourth parental discourse (1:22; 3:34). Wisdom's promise of years of life reiterates the promises presented in 3:2 and 4:10 (9:11). The teaching program described in the preamble is reiterated and recast in 9:9 (1:5). And the fundamental prerequisite for the acquisition of wisdom is delineated at both the climax of the preamble (1:7) and the climax of the prologue (9:10a), forming a literary envelop around the introduction to the anthology.[5] Together with the logical and conceptual parallels among chs. 7–9, the epilogue combines the prologue's nuclear symbol and satellite images with key terms and expressions from the preamble (1:1–7) and Wisdom's previous discourses (1:20–33; 8:1–36) to provide a fitting conclusion to the anthology's introduction.

The epilogue serves as the climax of Prov 1–9. But, as noted above, it also functions as the entrance into the central collections. When viewed from this vantage point, the epilogue prepares one to navigate the subsequent materials in at least four ways. First, the collection of aphorisms in 9:7–12 introduce one to distinctive forms that pervade 10:1–29:27. They represent an amuse-bouche, whetting the appetite for a feast on Wisdom's fare. Second, this collection of aphorisms orients one to the nature and interrelationship among certain character types in the central collections.

3. Among others, see Van Leeuwen, "The Book of Proverbs," *NIB* 5:95; Fox, *Proverbs 1–9*, 296; Yoder, *Proverbs*, 99; Loader, *Proverbs 1–9*, 366.

4. Van Leeuwen, "The Book of Proverbs," *NIB* 5:100–101.

5. Van Leeuwen, "The Book of Proverbs," *NIB* 5:100.

Just as these aphorisms relate the scoffer with the wicked and the wise with the righteous (9:7, 9), so also the central collections assume the coreferential relationship among particular character types. Third, the contrasts between Lady Wisdom and Woman Folly, the scoffer and the wise, the righteous and the wicked anticipate the contrasting characters portrayed throughout the central collections.[6] Fourth, similar to its relationship with the prologue, the epilogue includes themes and expressions that bind the discourse with the subsequent collections. The nexus of wisdom, folly, women, and housebuilding recurs at certain junctures within the central collections (14:1; 24:3, 27; cf. 31:10–31). In addition to forming an *inclusio* around the introduction (1:7; 9:10), "the fear of YHWH" is reiterated in 31:30, creating a literary framework around the anthology as a whole. And the expression "knowledge of the Holy One" (דַּעַת קְדֹשִׁים, 9:10b) occurs elsewhere only in 30:3, linking the prologue with Agur's discourse. As a literary hinge within the anthology, Prov 9:1–18 prepares one for the subsequent collections. It includes forms, character types, and expressions that connect the epilogue to the central collections in general and the concluding compositions within the anthology in particular (30:3; 31:30).

6. Loader, *Proverbs 1–9*, 377.

(2) Wisdom's Emissaries and the Location of her Call (9:3)
b. The Invitation to Wisdom's Banquet (9:4–6)
(1) Wisdom's General Summons (9:4)
(2) Wisdom's Specific Offer (9:5–6)
2. Character, the Conditions, and the Consequences of the Choice (9:7–12)
a. The Ineducability of the Scoffer/Wicked (9:7–8a)
b. The Educability of the Wise/Righteous (9:8b–9)
c. The Key to Educability (9:10)
d. The Reward of the Educable (9:11)
e. The Conclusion: Character, Conditions, and Consequences (9:12)
3. Woman Folly's Banquet (9:13–18)
a. The Setting of the Banquet (9:13–15)
(1) The Character of the Hostess (9:13)
(2) Folly's Location and Call (9:14–15)
b. The Invitation to Folly's Banquet (9:16–17)
(1) Folly's General Summons (9:16)
(2) Folly's Specific Offer (9:17)
c. The Fate of Folly's Guests (9:18)
III. "Forming 'Fearers of YHWH'": The Curriculum of Wisdom and Virtue (10:1–29:27)
IV. The Application of Wisdom and Virtue (30:1–31:31)

Translation and Exegetical Outline

(See pages 332–33.)

Structure and Literary Form

As noted above, Prov 9 may be described as the hinge upon which the prologue and the central collections within the anthology turn. This image conceptualizes the epilogue's place and function within the book; and it corresponds with the epilogue's design. Following Luis Alonso Schökel, the contrasting portraits and rival invitations in ch. 9 form a diptych (vv. 1–6, 13–18).[7] Each panel moves from a description of the scene (vv. 1–3, 13–15), to a formal invitation (vv. 4–6, 16–17), to a declaration of the fate that awaits those who attend the different banquets (vv. 6, 18).

7. Schökel, *A Manual of Hebrew Poetics*, 198.

Proverbs 9:1–18

Verse	Hebrew	English	Outline
			N. Wisdom and Folly's Invitations (9:1–18)[1]
			1. Lady Wisdom's Banquet (9:1–6)
			a. The Setting of the Banquet (9:1–3)
1a	חָכְמוֹת בָּנְתָה בֵיתָהּ	Wisdom – having built her house,	(1) Wisdom's Preparations (9:1–2)
1b	חָצְבָה עַמּוּדֶיהָ שִׁבְעָה	set up her seven pillars,	
2a	טָבְחָה טִבְחָהּ מָסְכָה יֵינָהּ	prepared her meat, mixed her wine,	
2b	אַף עָרְכָה שֻׁלְחָנָהּ	then arranged her table,	
3a	שָׁלְחָה נַעֲרֹתֶיהָ תִקְרָא	having sent out her maidservants – calls out	(2) Wisdom's Emissaries and the Location of her Call (9:3)
3b	עַל־גַּפֵּי מְרֹמֵי קָרֶת	at the tops of the city's heights:	
			b. The Invitation to Wisdom's Banquet (9:4–6)
4a	מִי־פֶתִי יָסֻר הֵנָּה	"Whoever is uncommitted, let him turn aside here!"	(1) Wisdom's General Summons (9:4)
4b	חֲסַר־לֵב	"Whoever lacks sense" –	
4c	אָמְרָה לּוֹ	she says to him:	
5a	לְכוּ לַחֲמוּ בְלַחֲמִי	"Come, eat of my food,	(2) Wisdom's Specific Offer (9:5–6)
5b	וּשְׁתוּ בְּיַיִן מָסָכְתִּי	and drink of the wine I have mixed.	
6a	עִזְבוּ פְתָאִים וִחְיוּ	Abandon agnosticism, so that you may live;	
6b	וְאִשְׁרוּ בְּדֶרֶךְ בִּינָה	and tread on the way of understanding!"	
			2. Character, the Conditions, and the Consequences of the Choice (9:7–12)
7a	יֹסֵר לֵץ לֹקֵחַ לוֹ קָלוֹן	Whoever disciplines a scoffer receives an insult,	a. The Ineducability of the Scoffer/Wicked (9:7–8a)
7b	וּמוֹכִיחַ לְרָשָׁע מוּמוֹ	and whoever reproves a wicked person receives a blemish.	
8a	אַל־תּוֹכַח לֵץ פֶּן־יִשְׂנָאֶךָּ	Do not reprove a scoffer lest he hate you;	
8b	הוֹכַח לְחָכָם וְיֶאֱהָבֶךָּ	reprove a wise person and he will love you.	b. The Educability of the Wise/Righteous (9:8b–9)
9a	תֵּן לְחָכָם וְיֶחְכַּם־עוֹד	Give [reproof] to the wise person, and he will become even wiser;	
9b	הוֹדַע לְצַדִּיק וְיוֹסֶף לֶקַח	instruct the righteous person and he will maximize learning.	
10a	תְּחִלַּת חָכְמָה יִרְאַת יְהוָה	The beginning of wisdom is the fear of YHWH,	c. The Key to Educability (9:10)
10b	וְדַעַת קְדֹשִׁים בִּינָה	and knowledge of the Holy One is understanding.	
11a	כִּי־בִי יִרְבּוּ יָמֶיךָ	"Surely through me your days will be many,	d. The Reward of the Educable (9:11)
11b	וְיוֹסִיפוּ לְּךָ שְׁנוֹת חַיִּים	and years of life will be added to you."	
12a	אִם־חָכַמְתָּ חָכַמְתָּ לָּךְ	If you are wise, you are wise for yourself;	e. The Conclusion: Character, Conditions, and Consequences (9:12)
12b	וְלַצְתָּ לְבַדְּךָ תִשָּׂא	but if you scoff, you will bear it alone.	

			3. Woman Folly's Banquet (9:13–18)
			a. The Setting of the Banquet (9:13–15)
13a	אֵשֶׁת כְּסִילוּת הֹמִיָּה	Woman Folly is turbulent –	(1) The Character of the Hostess (9:13)
13b	פְּתַיּוּת וּבַל־יָדְעָה מָּה	imprudence itself – and she knows nothing.	
14a	וְיָשְׁבָה לְפֶתַח בֵּיתָהּ	And she sits at the door of her house,	(2) Folly's Location and Call (9:14–15)
14b	עַל־כִּסֵּא מְרֹמֵי קָרֶת	on a throne at the city's heights	
15a	לִקְרֹא לְעֹבְרֵי־דָרֶךְ	calling out to those passing by,	
15b	הַמְיַשְּׁרִים אֹרְחוֹתָם ↑	those going straight on their way, ↑	
			b. The Invitation to Folly's Banquet (9:16–17)
16a	מִי־פֶתִי יָסֻר הֵנָּה	"Whoever is uncommitted, let me turn aside here!	(1) Folly's General Summons (9:16)
16b	וַחֲסַר־לֵב	And whoever lacks sense,"	
16c	וְאָמְרָה לּוֹ	she says to him:	
17a	מַיִם־גְּנוּבִים יִמְתָּקוּ ↑	↑ "Stolen water is sweet,	(2) Folly's Specific Offer (9:17)
17b	וְלֶחֶם סְתָרִים יִנְעָם	and food taken secretly is a delight!"	
18a	וְלֹא־יָדַע כִּי־רְפָאִים שָׁם	But he does not know that the dead are there,	c. The Fate of Folly's Guests (9:18)
18b	בְּעִמְקֵי שְׁאוֹל קְרֻאֶיהָ	in the depths of Sheol are her guests.	

1. This English outline is adapted from Fox, *Proverbs 1–9*, 303.

While vv. 7–12 do not appear to play a role in the formation of this bi-coda, they make a valuable contribution. If the invitations of Lady Wisdom and Woman Folly form a diptych, then the collection of aphorisms in vv. 7–12 serve as the hinge that holds the panels together.[8] These aphorisms connect the panels, on the one hand, and determine the way one will turn, on the other.[9] In view of this design, the discourse divides into three equal parts, each of which are illustrated below:

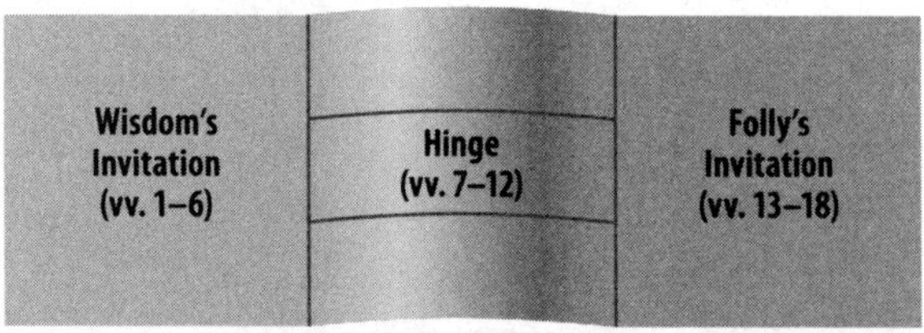

This threefold design is also reflected in the literary texture of the discourse. The two main panels are cast in the form of an invitation (vv. 1–6, 13–18), which, from an illocutionary perspective, seeks to instruct and persuade through description, directives, and promises. The hinge or spine of the unit includes a sequence of aphorisms, ranging from declarative sayings (vv. 7, 10, 12) to admonitions (vv. 8, 9).[10] Together, these distinctive forms contribute to the didactic intention of the unit. And this intention is augmented by one of the hallmarks of Proverbs's pedagogy: repetition. The discourse contains a variety of repeated terms and expressions. The invitations of Lady Wisdom and Woman Folly are linked by the repetition of "city's heights" (מְרֹמֵי קָרֶת, vv. 3b, 14b) and the near verbatim reiteration of the initial half of each summons (vv. 4, 16),[11] while the collection of aphorisms in vv. 7–12 are framed by the root "scoff" (ליץ, vv. 7a, 12b) and bound together by the repetition of "scoffer" (לֵץ, vv. 7a, 8a), "reprove" (יכח, vv. 7b, 8a, 8b), and "wise person" (חָכָם, vv. 8b, 9a). These repeated terms illuminate the relationship between Wisdom and Folly's invitations in general and the prologue's concern with deceptive or seductive speech in particular. They clarify the logical and conceptual relationship among the aphorisms in vv. 7–12. And they capture the coherence and deliberate design of the discourse.

8. Rick W. Byargeon, "The Structure and Significance of Prov 9:7–12," *JETS* 40 (1997): 375.

9. In light of the formal and thematic differences between these aphorisms (vv. 7–12) and the invitations (vv. 1–6, 13–18), many conclude that they represent a later insertion. This appears to be the case, but their inclusion is neither haphazard nor unintelligent (Toy, *Proverbs*, 183; Oesterley, *The Book of Proverbs*, 66–67). In addition to linking the epilogue with the preamble (1:1–7), with discourses elsewhere in the prologue, and with the collections that follow (10:1–22:16), these aphorisms distill and recast the contrast between wisdom and folly through different character types and identify the conditions that determine which invitation one will entertain (Byargeon, "The Structure and Significance of Prov 9:7–12," 373–74; Loader, *Proverbs 1–9*, 378). On formal grounds, they appear out of place. But their vision of pedagogy and concern with the educability of antithetical character types indicate that they offer a conceptual parallel to the rival invitations and provide an appropriate interlude to these invitations. For discussion, see Fox, "Who Can Learn?," 62–69; Byargeon, "The Structure and Significance of Prov 9:7–12," 367–75, and the explanation below.

10. Loader, *Proverbs 1–9*, 380.

11. With the exception of two *waw* conjunctions in v. 16b–c, the initial half of Wisdom and Folly's summons is the same.

Explanation of the Text

1. Lady Wisdom's Banquet (9:1–6)

a. The Setting of the Banquet (9:1–3)

Wisdom's final discourse opens in conventional fashion. Similar to her previous speeches, the parent sets the scene, introducing the speaker and the setting of Wisdom's call (1:20–21; 8:1–3). This scene is constructed through a series of perfect verbs, which provide background information for Wisdom's formal invitation.[12] They create the context for Wisdom's call, envisioning her preparations as well as the location from which her call is delivered.

(1) Wisdom's Preparations (9:1–2)

Wisdom's preparations project a palatial environment: she has built a stable, spacious home, prepared sumptuous fare, and arranged her table. The smell of mouthwatering meat fills her home. The sight of spiced wine fosters a celebratory mood. And her table creates an atmosphere of warmth, relationship, and intimacy. If nothing else, Wisdom's preparations reveal her generosity, her hospitality, and her desire for relationship. Not content with devotees keeping vigil at her doors, she appears to be intent on expressing her delight with humankind by welcoming them into her home (8:31, 34).

Despite the general impression conveyed through Wisdom's preparations, the opening scene raises questions concerning the nature of Wisdom's house in general and her seven pillars in particular.[13] Is Wisdom's house a symbol of the cosmos, a cipher for the temple, or merely a home? And what, if anything, do the seven pillars represent? As for Wisdom's house, in light of the building-banquet paradigm common in the ancient world and Wisdom's presence at YHWH's formation of the universe (8:22–30; cf. 3:19–20), her home may represent the cosmos.[14] But if, as we have argued, Wisdom plays a passive role in the formation of the universe and appears to occupy a home within YHWH's created order (8:22–29, 34), then the equation of Wisdom's house with the cosmos creates more questions than answers. The same is true of the temple. While YHWH's construction of the cosmic house (3:19–20) serves as a counterpart to the construction of the tabernacle/temple (Exod 31:3; 1 Kgs 7:14; cf. Prov 24:3–4),[15] in contrast to the intertextual connections among texts that deal with these building projects, the relationship between Wisdom's house and the temple is implicit and indefinite in Prov 9.[16] The intimate relationship between the concepts of wisdom,

12. Alviero Niccacci, *The Syntax of the Verb in Classical Hebrew Prose*, trans. W. G. E. Watson, JSOTSup 86 (Sheffield: JSOT Press, 1990), §15–16; Fox, *Proverbs 1–9*, 296–97.

13. In addition to these matters, disagreement over whether Wisdom "has hewn out" (חצבה, v. 1b) or "has set up" (הצבה, v. 1b) her seven pillars persists. The former reading follows the MT, while the latter emends the text, understanding the verb as a *hiphil* perfect of נצב with defective spelling and confusion between ח and ה in the first consonant. While the LXX's rendering could be used to support either reading, both the Syriac Peshitta and the Targum appear to support the emendation, which makes more logical sense than the MT (built—set up vs. built—hewn). Loader, *Proverbs 1–9*, 381–82; Fox, *Proverbs: An Eclectic Edition*, 162.

14. For this reading, see Van Leeuwen, "The Book of Proverbs," *NIB* 5:100–102. Also, for the intersection of wisdom and building-filling in ancient Near Eastern and Old Testament accounts pertaining to the cosmos, a temple, or a house, see Van Leeuwen, "Cosmos, Temple, House," 67–90.

15. Van Leeuwen, "Cosmos, Temple, House," 77–89.

16. Even Schwáb, who offers a nuanced reading of Wisdom's house as the (Solomonic) temple, admits that the temple interpretation is not explicit (*Toward an Interpretation*, 202). For his canonical, "temple-building" reading of Prov 8–9 in conversation with Camp and Van Leeuwen, see *Toward an Interpretation*, 190–209, esp. 198–209.

building, and filling in relation to the cosmos and the tabernacle/temple is well attested in ancient Near Eastern as well as Old Testament literature. Proverbs 9 inhabits this thought world; but it does not bear enough conceptual or intertextual marks to warrant a connection between Wisdom's house and the cosmos or the temple. This does not mean that the conceptual world of the text contributes nothing to a reading of Prov 9:1. It does. The cosmic housebuilder provides the paradigm for terrestrial house building.[17] Just as the wise among women builds a home (Prov 14:1; 24:3–4), so also Lady Wisdom builds a home (9:1). As one who manifests God's presence, Wisdom's home is among the dwelling places of God. The divine presence is not restricted to the temple. It infiltrates the everyday, the place of common communion and intimacy, the holy place of the home.[18]

On this account, the seven pillars of Wisdom's home are neither "the pillars of the earth"[19] nor the pillars of the temple. Rather, in the first instance, they represent a spacious, complete home. When these pillars are viewed within the literary architecture of the anthology, however, they may also represent the discrete collections within the book.[20] If the preamble (1:1–7) is regarded as a part of the prologue (1:8–9:18), then the anthology contains seven collections, each of which is marked off by a title or subtitle (1:1–9:18; 10:1–22:16; 22:17–24:22; 24:23–34; 25:1–29:27; 30:1–33; 31:1–31). From this literary vantage point, Wisdom's seven-pillared house is more than a luxurious residence that manifests God's presence; it is also the book of Proverbs, the place where Wisdom dwells and where one learns to image God's wisdom and presence within the world.[21]

(2) Wisdom's Emissaries and the Location of Her Call (9:3)

With the preparations complete in her spacious home of sapiential nourishment, the parent completes the scene: the maidservants are sent out (v. 3a). The perfect verb provides the final panel of the backdrop. This panel sets the tableau for the shift to the imperfect ("calls out," תִּקְרָא, v. 3a) and the delivery of Wisdom's invitation, and it enhances both Wisdom's desirability and the attractiveness of her call. Wisdom's retinue of attendants is sent out to issue an invitation to her luxurious home and opulent banquet. The fact that Wisdom has maidservants indicates that she is no ordinary woman; she is a woman of substance.[22] And yet, Wisdom does not limit her invitation to a privileged few. Her call is delivered from the city's heights (v. 3b). All may hear; but Wisdom has a particular audience in mind.

b. The Invitation to Wisdom's Banquet (9:4–6)

This audience is specified in Wisdom's invitation. The invitation moves from a general summons to a specific offer, each of which deserves a brief comment.

(1) Wisdom's General Summons (9:4)

Wisdom's general summons is familiar. Similar to her previous speeches, she addresses the "un-

17. Van Leeuwen, "Cosmos, Temple, House," 81.

18. Cf. Schipper, *Proverbs 1–15*, 323–25, who entertains the idea that the Greek symposium may serve as the backdrop of the dual invitations in Prov 9.

19. Van Leeuwen, "The Book of Proverbs," *NIB* 5:102.

20. Raymond J. Tournay, "Review of Gerhard von Rad, *Weisheit in Israel*," *RB* 80 (1973): 130; Baumann, *Die Weisheitsgestalt in Proverbien 1–9*, 206–9; Murphy, *Proverbs*, 58–59; Loader, *Proverbs 1–9*, 383–84; cf. Waltke, *Proverbs: Chapters 1–15*, 431.

21. Loader, *Proverbs 1–9*, 384.

22. Carolyn S. Leeb, *Away from the Father's House: The Social Location of* Na'ar *and* Na'arah *in Ancient Israel*, JSOTSup 301 (Sheffield: Sheffield Academic, 2000), 43.

committed" (פֶּתִי, v. 4a; cf. 1:4, 22, 32; 8:5), that is, those "betwixt and between" the way of wisdom and folly, life and death.[23] Drawing from the conceptual sphere of repentance, Wisdom challenges this character type to snap out of their uncommitted state, to "turn aside" (יָסֻר, 9:4a) to her dwelling.[24] The uncommitted youth can remain agnostic no longer. A fate awaits. To brace the addressee for this decision, the parent chimes in, introducing a second addressee as well as Wisdom's specific offer (v. 4b–c). In contrast to the naïve yet malleable character of the "uncommitted," this addressee is characterized as one who "lacks sense" (חֲסַר־לֵב, v. 4b).[25] Whereas the "uncommitted" are depicted as those who can make a choice, those lacking sense are portrayed as imprudent and thoughtless.[26] Wisdom delivers her offer to these character types. And this offer elaborates on her general summons, identifying the food, way, and fate prepared for her devotees.

(2) Wisdom's Specific Offer (9:5–6)

Wisdom's specific offer traffics in relational imagery; it consists of a coming to and a departing from, or better, a commitment to and an abandonment of a particular way, woman, and house. To the nuclear metaphor of the way and the satellite images of women and houses, Wisdom includes a new symbolic ingredient: food.[27] Similar to 4:17, one's character, way, desires, and appetite intersect in Wisdom's formal invitation (cf. 7:14; 24:13–14). Reiterating the language of 9:2, she invites the uncommitted to find satisfaction in her food and drink (v. 5). This satisfaction, however, comes at a cost; it requires the uncommitted to abandon their "agnosticism" (פְּתָאיִם, v. 6a).[28] Put differently, it demands those lacking sense to leave their senselessness. The uncommitted must change. And this change, however hard it may be, will yield a particular result. The imperative "abandon" (עִזְבוּ, v. 6a) followed by the *waw* + imperative indicates that the outcome of abandoning agnosticism is life (וִחְיוּ, v. 6a).[29] Wisdom offers much more than food; she reorients one's telos and redirects one's movements along a particular way, a way characterized by understanding (v. 6b). Her invitation is clear; and, unlike Woman Folly's invitation, the consequences associated with accepting her offer are unambiguous.

---

23. Turner, "Betwixt and Between," 93–111; Perdue, "Liminality as a Social Setting for Wisdom Instruction," 114–26; Van Leeuwen, "Liminality and Worldview," 111–44. Here the interrogative functions as an indefinite pronoun, meaning "whoever" (GKC §137c).

24. The language of turning aside is comparable to the prophetic concept of turning or returning, that is, to repentance. Since the uncommitted, however, have committed to neither wisdom nor folly, a return to wisdom is unnecessary. Rather, a commitment to Wisdom is in order. Loader, *Proverbs 1–9*, 388.

25. Many assume that the "uncommitted" and those who "lack sense" refer to the same type of person (e.g., Fox, *Proverbs 1–9*, 298; Waltke, *Proverbs: Chapters 1–15*, 437; Longman, *Proverbs*, 217; Loader, *Proverbs 1–9*, 388). While these character types may be "nearly identical" (Fox, *Proverbs 1–9*, 40), it appears they are distinct. The summons evinces a development from the "uncommitted" to "whoever lacks sense." The former is able to make a choice, whereas the latter is an instantiation of one who makes the wrong choice (cf. vv. 15–16). Heim, *Poetic Imagination*, 203–4.

26. Fox, *Proverbs 1–9*, 39–40, 42–43.

27. Fox, *Proverbs 1–9*, 305.

28. While some take פְּתָאיִם as the object of the imperative (i.e., "Abandon [the class of] the gullible," Delitzsch, "Proverbs of Solomon," 6:146 [1:200]; Meinhold, *Die Sprüche*, 1.155; cf. Weeks, *Instruction and Imagery*, 192, 222) and others treat it as a vocative by supplying an elided object (e.g., "Leave your ways, you gullible ones," Waltke, *Proverbs: Chapters 1–15*, 427n11), the term may be understood as an abstract plural ("Abandon agnosticism/simpleness/callowness," LXX; Fox, *Proverbs: An Eclectic Edition*, 163–64; Loader, *Proverbs 1–9*, 389–90). Similar to 9:13, the feminine form would clarify the abstract sense of the term. The plural, however, is used with numerous words to convey an abstract sense, suggesting it carries a "conventional idiomatic use" (Loader, *Proverbs 1–9*, 390n55; GKC §124d). And the distinctive form of the abstract פְּתָאיִם may be used to differentiate the agnosticism of the addressee (v. 6) from the impudence of Woman Folly (v. 13).

29. GKC §110f.

2. Character, the Conditions and the Consequences of the Choice (9:7–12)

Why would one refuse Lady Wisdom's generous offer? In anticipation of Woman Folly's alternative invitation, the collection of seemingly random aphorisms in vv. 7–12 provide an answer. Together, these sayings sketch conflicting character types to describe the way in which one's character determines the path, woman, house, food, and fate one will choose. If the son, who occupies the subject position of the uncommitted youth,[30] is the primary addressee of Prov 9, then these aphorisms, in the first instance, do not provide teachers with an explanation of why certain people cannot learn.[31] Rather, the aphorisms and admonitions provide a mirror in which one may see who they are and perceive why one will choose a particular path, woman, house, banquet, and fate. The decision depends on one's character, and one's character creates the (in)educable conditions that determine one's choice and one's fate.

a. The Ineducability of the Scoffer/Wicked (9:7–8a)

This connection between character and educability is illustrated through two classes of character: the scoffer/wicked and the wise/righteous. The former is the focus of attention in vv. 7–8a, which are framed by the mention of "a scoffer" (לֵץ, vv. 7a, 8a). Returning to the character type introduced in Wisdom's first speech (1:22), these lines associate the "scoffer" (לֵץ, vv. 7a, 8a) with the "wicked" (רָשָׁע, v. 7b) and sharpen the silhouette of this coreferential personage. As the embodiment of hubris, conceit, and moral corruption (13:1; 21:24),[32] the scoffer/wicked refuses to accept authority and receive correction. This person responds to disciplinary reproof with verbal and physical abuse (9:7).[33] And these outward forms of abuse mirror the scoffer's inward disposition of hatred toward the one who offers correction (v. 8a). These responses to discipline characterize the scoffer/wicked as uneducable. This person will not acknowledge their limits and accept correction. The statement in v. 7 suggests that the risks of instructing the scoffer/wicked far outweigh the rewards; one is better off, therefore, saving one's breath (v. 8a).

b. The Educability of the Wise/Righteous (9:8b–9)

This is not the case in vv. 8b–9. The repetition of the root "reprove" (יכח, vv. 8b; 7b; 8a; cf. 9a) opens a positive admonition that serves as a transition to a different class of character: the wise/righteous. Similar to the contrast between Lady Wisdom and Woman Folly, the wise/righteous are a mirror image of the scoffer/wicked. They respond to reproof with love, not hate (v. 8b; cf. v. 8a). They receive correction. In fact, the wise/righteous reflect the pedagogical vision of Proverbs: by accepting instruction, they "maximize learning" (יוֹסֵף לֶקַח, v. 9b; 1:5), growing in wisdom and maturity. The sequence of commands in vv. 8b–9 illuminate the receptivity and response of a different type of character. This character is intellectually and morally distinct from the scoffer/wicked. This character possesses a distinct posture and disposition. And these factors indicate that, in contrast to the scoffer/fool, the wise/righteous are educable.

30. Newsom, "Woman and the Discourse of Patriarchal Wisdom," 142–44.

31. Fox, *Proverbs 1–9*, 306–17; Longman, *Proverbs*, 216–18; Loader, *Proverbs 1–9*, 392.

32. Fox, *Proverbs 1–9*, 42.

33. While מום may denote a moral or physical blemish, the latter is foregrounded in v. 7b. The pronominal suffix parallels לוֹ in v. 7a and serves as the subject, indicating that one who reproves the wicked receives a physical injury rather than a moral blemish. Fox, *Proverbs 1–9*, 307.

c. The Key to Educability (9:10)

The educable disposition of the wise/righteous is clarified in v. 10, which situates love for and growth in wisdom within a theological framework. Just as the statement in v. 7 provides a logical rationale for the admonition in v. 8a, so also the statement in v. 10 provides a logical rationale for the commands in vv. 8b–9.[34] The statement is familiar, for it is a development of the motto of the anthology. The initial half of the line resembles 1:7a, but it is distinct in several respects. In addition to word order (predicate-subject vis-à-vis subject-predicate), the line replaces "beginning/first principle" (רֵאשִׁית; 1:7a) with "beginning" (תְּחִלַּת, 9:10a) and "knowledge" (דַּעַת; 1:7a) with "wisdom" (חָכְמָה, 9:10a). The latter pair evinces a movement from the general ("knowledge") to the specific ("wisdom"), while the former contributes to the anthology's construal of the "fear of YHWH" and the acquisition of wisdom. The contours of this construal may be sketched by placing 1:7, 2:5, and 9:10 in conversation with one another.[35] According to 1:7, the fear of YHWH is the "beginning," "starting point," or "first principle" of knowledge.[36] It is important to note that the term רֵאשִׁית is polysemous;[37] whether a chronological ("beginning") or logical ("first principle") connotation is foregrounded, 1:7a seems to suggest that the fear of YHWH is a disposition or mode of being, according to which one recognizes one's need for knowledge. This need is assumed in 2:5 (cf. 4:7), where one's reception and active pursuit of wisdom culminates in understanding the fear of YHWH. When read within the broader context of the anthology, however, this understanding remains incomplete. Growth in wisdom and maturity is assumed, especially in 9:9 (cf. 1:5). And this growth is affirmed in 9:10a: the fear of YHWH is the "beginning of wisdom" (תְּחִלַּת חָכְמָה), that is, the fear of YHWH is a relational mode of being from which one not only begins but also progresses in the acquisition of wisdom.[38]

This progression is elaborated upon in 9:10b, where "knowledge of the Holy One" (דַּעַת קְדֹשִׁים, v. 10b; cf. 30:3) develops a dimension of the fear of YHWH. If nothing else, the epithet gives particular attention to divine transcendence and, by implication, human creaturehood. The fear of YHWH, then, entails cognitive and relational knowledge of God and God's transcendence, on the one hand, and humanity's limits and place in the divine economy, on the other.[39] This knowledge explains, in part, what the fear of YHWH means; and it cultivates the mode of being from which one might grow in wisdom and understanding.

d. The Reward of the Educable (9:11)

In accord with Proverbs's pedagogy, this educable mode of being is not without a reward. In striking fashion, a first-person voice interrupts the discourse, offering a familiar promise of life (v. 11; cf. 3:2; 4:10). This shift, along with the conventional structure of most discourses within the prologue, has led many to conclude that 9:11 is misplaced. It should be located at the conclusion of Wisdom's formal invitation (i.e., v. 6).[40] This conclusion

34. Fox, *Proverbs 1–9*, 308.

35. This conversation follows the texts and hermeneutical scheme presented by Fox, *Proverbs 1–9*, 308, and Heim, *Poetic Imagination*, 59–61.

36. Blocher, "The Fear of the Lord as the 'Principle' of Wisdom," 14–16.

37. In addition to "beginning," "starting point," or "first principle," it may denote "the first and best" or "first-fruit, choicest portion" (*HALOT* 3:1169–1170, s.v. רֵאשִׁית).

38. For תְּחִלַּת as the start or beginning of a process, see 2 Kgs 17:25; Hos 1:2; and Weeks, *Instruction and Imagery*, 118. Also see Fox, *Proverbs 1–9*, 68–69; Heim, *Poetic Imagination*, 59–60.

39. Waltke, *Proverbs: Chapters 1–15*, 441–42.

40. Goldingay, "Proverbs V and IX," 87–93, Clifford, *Proverbs*, 101–2; Fox, *Proverbs 1–9*, 299–300.

is reasonable. But in light of the second-person address that punctuates vv. 5–9 (vv. 5, 6, 8, 9; cf. vv. 11–12) as well as the repetition of "understanding" (בִּינָה) at the end of both Wisdom's speech and the previous statement (vv. 6b, 10b), the editor(s) may have included this first-person motivation at this juncture to indicate that the sequence of aphorisms should be understood as an extension of Wisdom's speech.[41] The reward of long life is delayed, for it applies to those who listen to Wisdom's voice—to those who fear YHWH and join the class of the wise/righteous. For this type of person, Lady Wisdom serves as the instrument through which one enjoys the good life.

e. The Conclusion: Character, Conditions and Consequences (9:12)

The enjoyment of this life, however, is not passed on as an inheritance. As Wisdom's invitation indicates, it requires a choice. And personal choices reap personal consequences. These personal consequences are the focus of attention in v. 12, which returns to the roots "wise" (חכם, v. 12a; cf. 8b, 9a) and "scoff" (ליץ, v. 12b; cf. vv. 7a, 8a), forming a literary envelope around vv. 7–12.[42] The pair of conditional sentences brings the aphoristic discussion of character, conditions, and consequences to a formal conclusion. The wise enjoy the benefits of wisdom personally, though not necessarily exclusively. Scoffers, by contrast, bear the consequences of their character and behavior alone. They may inflict others (v. 7), but in the end, they will be the sole recipients of their own contempt.

3. Woman Folly's Banquet (9:13–18)

The antithesis between the scoffer/wicked and the wise/righteous provides the backdrop for Lady Wisdom's antithesis: Woman Folly.[43] As noted above, this personified figure resembles her human counterpart: the strange woman. And her invitation mimics Lady Wisdom's invitation, bringing the prologue's concern with seductive or deceptive speech to a dramatic climax. Like Wisdom's banquet, the depiction of Folly's feast moves from a description of its setting to a formal invitation to an interpretation of the consequences associated with dining at her home.

a. The Setting of the Banquet (9:13–15)

The setting of Woman Folly's banquet is comparable to the scene of Wisdom's invitation. Again, the parent introduces the speaker, the site, and the target of the Woman's summons. The contextual components of the two calls are commensurate, and their differences are conspicuous.

(1) The Character of the Hostess (9:13)

Whereas Lady Wisdom is depicted as a generous hostess who reorients the character and way of the uncommitted, "Woman Folly" (אֵשֶׁת כְּסִילוּת, v. 13a) is characterized as the embodiment of those things the uncommitted must abandon.[44] Like the strange

41. Delitzsch, "Proverbs of Solomon," 6:146 (1:200); McKane, *Proverbs*, 360; Meinhold, *Die Sprüche*, 1.155–57; Garrett, *Proverbs*, 114–15; Heim, *Poetic Imagination*, 58; Loader, *Proverbs 1–9*, 395. This reading follows the MT rather than emending the first common singular pronominal suffix to a third feminine singular suffix (LXX; Waltke, *Proverbs: Chapters 1–15*, 428n21).

42. While Fox contends that v. 12 is a separate addition inserted after the inclusion of vv. 7–10, its semantic links with vv. 7–9 suggest that it fits within and contributes to the content and literary design of the unit. Fox, *Proverbs 1–9*, 317.

43. Byargeon, "The Structure and Significance of Prov 9:7–12," 373–74; Loader, *Proverbs 1–9*, 378.

44. While *BHS* suggests that אֵשֶׁת may be a case of dittography, it is unnecessary to delete the word. The chiastic arrangement of the consonants תשא (the last word in v. 12b) and אשת (the first word in v. 13a) may be a deliberate poetic device, linking the aphorisms in vv. 7–12 with Folly's invitation

woman, she is "turbulent" (הֹמִיָּה, v. 13a; 7:11) and unruly. She incarnates "imprudence" (פְּתַיּוּת, v. 13b) or simplemindedness.[45] And her moral knowledge is reminiscent of the wicked and the strange woman: "she knows nothing" (בַּל־יָדְעָה מָּה, v. 13b; 4:19; 5:6; 7:23). She is the antithesis of Lady Wisdom, a woman whose profile reflects the silhouette of moral outsiders elsewhere within the prologue.

(2) Folly's Location and Call (9:14–15)

This antithesis is enhanced in vv. 14–15. Similar to Wisdom, Folly delivers her invitation "at the city's heights" (מְרֹמֵי קָרֶת, v. 14b). And she has a home. But her passivity pales in comparison with Wisdom's preparations and pursuit. Whereas Wisdom builds, prepares, mixes, and arranges (vv. 1–2), Folly sits (v. 14a). Whereas Wisdom sends out a retinue of maidservants to deliver her invitation (v. 3a), Folly positions herself at an opportune locale to entice prospective guests (vv. 14b–15). She sits on a "throne" (כִּסֵּא, v. 14b), a seat of honor. And she addresses passersby, those attempting to walk the "straight and narrow" (v. 15b; cf. 3:6; 4:11, 25–26).[46] Her seat and location are attractive, but looks can be deceiving. Folly occupies a public place, the same playing field as Wisdom. And she focuses on those negotiating and navigating the moral thresholds of life. Wisdom calls one to abandon a self-destructive way of life. Folly, by contrast, seeks to derail those walking the virtuous highways and byways of the moral life.

b. The Invitation to Folly's Banquet (9:16–17)

This deceptive scheme is laid bare in Folly's formal invitation, which, like Wisdom's, includes a general summons and a specific offer.

(1) Folly's General Summons (9:16)

With the exception of two *waw* conjunctions in v. 16b–c, Folly's general summons repeats Wisdom's general summons (v. 4). Similar to v. 4a, Folly invites the uncommitted to "turn aside" (יָסֻר, v. 16a) to her dwelling. And similar to v. 4c, the parent chimes in, introducing a second addressee as well as Folly's specific offer.[47] In light of their position and speech, Wisdom and Folly are difficult to distinguish. They occupy the same place. They appeal to the same clientele. And they sound the same.

(2) Folly's Specific Offer (9:17)

This is not the case, however, with the specific offer. Here Woman Folly departs from Wisdom's invitation. She appeals to baser human instincts and desires.[48] She does not demand a turning away from the agnosticism that besets the uncommitted; rather, she invites one to turn inward on oneself, to satisfy one's illicit desires, and to bask in the adrenaline rush of secret sin.[49] Folly accomplishes this in a distinctive way. In contrast to Wisdom's offer, her invitation is cast in the form of a statement (v. 17) rather than a sequence of commands (vv. 5–6). The form of the locution differs from that of Wisdom's

(Byargeon, "The Structure and Significance of Prov 9:7–12," 371). Together, אֵשֶׁת כְּסִילוּת functions as an attributive genitive (*IBHS* §9.5.3b); and on contextual grounds, this foolish woman should be understood as a personification of Folly (e.g., Murphy, *Proverbs*, 57; Fox, *Proverbs 1–9*, 300; Loader, *Proverbs 1–9*, 397).

45. Just as the participle "turbulent" (הֹמִיָּה, v. 13a) functions as a predicate of "Woman Folly," so also the abstract noun "imprudence" (פְּתַיּוּת, v. 13b) functions as a predicate of "Woman Folly." While the abstract noun "imprudence" occurs only here, it identifies an innate attribute of Folly. For discussion, see Fox, *Proverbs 1–9*, 301; Loader, *Proverbs 1–9*, 397–98.

46. Yoder, *Proverbs*, 108.

47. While the LXX and Syriac Peshitta read ואמרה as a first-person singular ("and I will say"), its third-person feminine singular vocalization in the MT is preferred, for it mirrors v. 4c and represents the more difficult reading.

48. Longman, *Proverbs*, 221.

49. Treier, *Proverbs and Ecclesiastes*, 59.

offer. And the distinctive locutions perform different illocutionary acts. Whereas Wisdom seeks to persuade one by means of directives or commands, Folly entices one by means of an assertion.[50] She asserts something that is true. Her words match a reality: clandestine enjoyment of illicit things is attractive and satisfying.

This reality is expressed through polysemous and cunning language. Like Wisdom, Woman Folly incorporates the image of food into the symbolic matrix of ways, women, and houses. The meal she describes may seem meager in comparison with Wisdom's opulent banquet, but her declaration is no less attractive. Far from merely referring to basic staples, the terms "water" (מַיִם, v. 17a) and "food/bread" (לֶחֶם, v. 17b) may serve as a merism for an entire feast.[51] What's more, if these terms are used metaphorically as elsewhere in the anthology (5:15–17; 30:20; cf. Song 4:12, 15; 5:1; 7:9), then they capture the gratification of illicit sexual indulgence. And this gastronomic/sexual satisfaction is heightened by the fact that these elements are "stolen" (גְּנוּבִים, v. 17a) and "taken secretly" (סְתָרִים, v. 17b). Folly tantalizes one's gastronomic, sexual, and psychological desires by describing something that is true. The consequences associated with this truth, however, are as concealed as the consumption of the elements. The degree to which one is able to discern these consequences will determine whether Woman Folly's assertion is received as a warning or accepted as a motivation for indulging in illicit pleasures.[52]

c. The Fate of Folly's Guests (9:18)

Since the uncommitted lack the discernment necessary to perceive the consequences of seeking satisfaction in these illicit pleasures, the parent provides a clear explanation of the fate of Folly's guests. This explanation is familiar. Just as the strange woman and her house are depicted as the gateway to Sheol and the place of the deceased (2:18; 5:5; 7:27), so also Woman Folly's house is portrayed as the entrance to Sheol and the residence of the dead (v. 18). Her guests enter a home from which there is no departure. And the one who crosses Folly's threshold demonstrates that s/he has become like this Woman, not knowing or possessing moral knowledge (v. 18a).

Canonical and Theological Significance

"You are what you eat." This popular expression captures the way in which food affects one's physical health and state of mind. When applied to Prov 9, however, it diagnoses one's moral health and forecasts one's end. The fare on offer at Wisdom and Folly's feasts brings the prologue's extended discourse on desire and deception to a climax, and the inclusion of food with the nuclear symbol of the way and the satellite images of women and houses introduces the appetite and human omnivorousness

50. To distinguish between assertives and directives/commands, Searle appeals to the concept of "*differences in the direction of fit between words and the world*." In light of this concept, assertives perform the illocutionary action of matching words to the world (i.e., representing a state of affairs), while directives perform the inverse action, seeking to match the world to the words (i.e., moving one to act in accord with the words). John R. Searle, *Expression and Meaning: Studies in the Theory of Speech Acts* (Cambridge: Cambridge University Press, 1979), 3–4, italics original.

51. Waltke, *Proverbs: Chapters 1–15*, 446.

52. Fox, *Proverbs 1–9*, 302.

into the prologue's projection of human life. Character types and conditions, paths and destinations, intimacy and relationships, hospitality and community, hunger and food coalesce in Prov 9 to form a choice. This persistent choice reveals who one is, where one is going, what one loves, where one is nurtured, and what one considers good. It is dictated, in part, by one's (in)educability and (im)moral tastes. And it is contingent on one's (in)discretion.

The prologue concludes at the crossroads, where the dominant metaphor, images, themes, and expressions of Prov 1–9 converge in rival invitations, forcing one to make a choice.[53] This choice bears particular consequences. Those who enter Folly's home descend into the netherworld to dwell among the community of the deceased. Those who enter Wisdom's house, by contrast, enjoy a feast, life, and entrance into the way of understanding (9:5–6). This feast and way are spread out in the central collections. As intimated in the discussion of literary context, Prov 9 serves as the entryway into the remainder of the anthology. It orients one to the materials in the central collections. The antithetical characters throughout the discourse (i.e., Wisdom and Folly, scoffer and wise, righteous and wicked) prepare one for the terrain of antithetical characters and their coreferential counterparts in Prov 10–29.[54] The expressions "knowledge of the Holy One" (דַּעַת קְדֹשִׁים, 9:10b) and "the fear of YHWH" (יִרְאַת יְהוָה, v. 10a) link the prologue's dramatic conclusion with chs. 30 and 31, respectively (30:3; 31:30; cf. 1:7; 15:33), signposting the destinations on the horizon. And the interrelationship between wisdom, folly, women, and housebuilding within the invitations provides a paradigm that is utilized and applied by several sayings in the central collections (14:1; 24:3, cf. 24:27; 31:10–31).[55] Proverbs 9 serves as a hinge within the anthology. From a literary and structural perspective, it is the binding on which the prologue and the remaining collections turn and to which they relate. From a thematic perspective, it introduces a critical choice. How one decides determines whether one passes through its threshold into the central collections.

Choice constitutes the crux of Prov 9. This choice is, to some degree, a matter of (moral) taste. The food offered by Wisdom and Folly appeals to the needs of whole, formed, desiring beings: hunger's satisfaction, human community, and the nourishment that both promise. Whereas Folly's food satisfies the desire to turn inward on oneself and to find enjoyment in the transgression of appropriate boundaries, Wisdom's food forces one to look outside of oneself and to receive satisfaction in and sustenance for a life within proper boundaries. Food provides a hearty metaphor; it connects human need with human desire and human omnivorousness with human choice.[56]

53. Yoder, *Proverbs*, 109.

54. Loader, *Proverbs 1–9*, 377.

55. For discussion of the variant repetitions in and relationship among these texts, see Heim, *Poetic Imagination*, 192–201.

56. Leon R. Kass, *The Hungry Soul: Eating and the Perfecting of Our Nature* (Chicago: University of Chicago Press, 1999), 208.

This metaphor and its conceptual ingredients create a meal of choice. This meal, however, is not unique; it is prepared and served elsewhere in the canon of Scripture. In fact, it is reminiscent of the dish served in Gen 3. Similar to the rival women and invitations in Prov 9, Gen 3 turns on rival voices and guides: God and the serpent (3:1–3). These rival voices focus on food: the tree in the middle of the garden (3:1–3). The rival perspectives on food form a meal of choice. This choice is directed by desire (3:6). And it carries particular consequences: life and death (3:3–5). Just as Prov 9 creates a meal of choice with rival voices and food, so also Gen 3 creates a meal of choice with rival voices and perspectives on food. Both link human omnivorousness with choice. And both envision this choice as a matter of life and death.

While food and choice represent the main course in Prov 9, it is important to note that this entrée is served within the context of a banquet. The banquet motif carries the symbolic resonances of celebration, nourishment, community, and belonging. And these resonances resound throughout the Old Testament and the New. They appear, for example, in Isa 55:1–3 (cf. Isa 65:11–14), where the prophet bids the exiles to come and dine at the lavish banquet prepared by the divine host.[57] Like Wisdom's banquet, this feast is open, free, and opulent. And like Wisdom's banquet, it offers more than physical nourishment; it also provides life, relationship, and community (Isa 55:3). As hostess, Wisdom's generous provision, hospitality, and desire for relationship correspond with the divine host. Whether the table is spread in the wilderness (Pss 78:19–29; 105:40–41; Exod 16:1–17:7) or envisioned as a land flowing with milk and honey in which one will lack nothing (Deut 6:3; 8:7–9), the divine host spares no expense, lavishing abundance, satisfaction, and joy on his people. This composite portrait of divine hospitality resembles Wisdom's hospitality. And the hospitality of both Wisdom and YHWH is reflected in Jesus's person and teaching within the Gospels. Jesus is the bread of life, the one who offers definitive satisfaction and eternal life (John 6:35–59). Jesus provides water that quenches one's thirst and bestows everlasting life (John 4:13–14; 7:37–39). He is both the host and the meal, the one whose body and life provide forgiveness, create relationship, form community, and evoke celebration. Like Wisdom's meal, however, the enjoyment of this meal and its benefits is contingent on a choice, on a response to an invitation. This invitation is given particular expression in the parable of the great banquet (Matt 22:1–14; Luke 14:15–24). Here the kingdom of heaven is compared to a banquet. The meal is prepared. The invitations are delivered; but many on the guest list decline. Similar to those who reject Wisdom's offer, they refuse to lose their own life in order to find it (14:25–27). They turn inward on themselves. They embrace folly.

The banquet motif and its resonances are as rich as Wisdom's fare. The same is true of the image of a house. The prologue of Proverbs ends at the crossroads and in

57. Baumann, *Die Weisheitsgestalt in Proverbien 1–9*, 214–20.

the same fashion as the Sermon on the Mount: with different houses, constructed by different people, who epitomize different fates (Matt 7:24–27; Luke 6:46–49).[58] The image of the house differs in these accounts, but it functions in a comparable way. Those who hear Jesus's sermon and embody its vision of righteousness and kingdom life are like the wise who build their house on a sure, stable foundation (Matt 7:24–25; cf. 5:20). They will weather the tempests and live. Those who fail to practice Jesus's vision of kingdom life, by contrast, are described as fools who build their house on sand (7:26–27). The storm will erode the foundation and topple the home, bringing destruction. Just as Jesus concludes the Sermon on the Mount with a depiction of two houses, two ways, two responses to his words, so also Prov 1–9 concludes with two houses, two ways, two responses to the prologue's instruction. Both demand a decision.

The end of Proverbs's prologue may be the end for some, but it is the beginning for others. In Wisdom's house, one finds food, community, and nourishment for passage along the way of understanding. The same is true of the church, the house built by the Father, governed by the Son, and filled with the Spirit (Heb 3:1–6; 1 Pet 2:5). As both members of the household and living stones of the building (Eph 2:19–22), the Christian sees the church as the place in which one receives food, community, and nourishment for passage along the narrow way. Enjoyment of this food and fellowship is, of course, dependent on a response to an invitation. This invitation is not contingent on one's social or economic status. Similar to Prov 9, it is contingent on a turn toward a person, a house, and a way. And it is governed by what one loves or desires. Proverbs 9 reframes and elaborates upon the Augustinian aphorism "you are what you love" as you are what you eat and you become like where you eat.[59] If you fancy Wisdom's house, fare, and path, the book of Proverbs invites you to cross her threshold, take a seat at her table, and prepare for a feast on the way wisdom sees, hears, feels, tastes and smells the world, its inhabitants, and its activities. This multisensory experience is presented in the central collections. And it is to this experience that we now turn.

58. Witherington, *Jesus the Sage*, 224–25; Robert C. Stallman, "Divine Hospitality and Wisdom's Banquet in Proverbs 9:1–6," in *The Way of Wisdom: Essays in Honor of Bruce K. Waltke*, ed. J. I. Packer and Sven K. Soderlund (Grand Rapids: Zondervan Academic, 2000), 117–133, esp. 128.

59. For an exposition of this Augustinian aphorism, see James K. A. Smith, *You are What You Love: The Spiritual Power of Habit* (Grand Rapids: Brazos, 2016).

PART III

Proverbs 10:1–29:27

"Forming 'Fearers of YHWH'": *The Curriculum of Wisdom and Virtue*

Main Idea of Proverbs 10–29

As a curriculum of wisdom and virtue, the aphorisms within the central collections form the fearer of YHWH by providing patterns on and through which the self, the senses, and the imagination are shaped in accord with wisdom and virtue.[1]

Literary Context Proverbs 10–29

While many, in principle, would be happy with the hermeneutical proverb "a text without a context becomes a pretext for a prooftext,"[2] some contend that this aphorism does not apply to the materials in the central collections of Proverbs. William McKane, for example, concludes that "there is, for the most part, no context in the sentence literature" (i.e., Prov 10:1–29:27).[3] The individual sayings represent independent entities that stand on their own and convey a discrete message(s). No literary context is required. They are, one might say, autonomous items within a catalogue or inventory. Or, to borrow from Wolfgang Mieder's well-worn expression, the proverbs within the central collections are "dead";[4] by virtue of their dislocation from oral use and their resettlement within an anthology, the collections may be viewed as cemeteries, filled with separate graves, arranged in orderly rows with headstones

1. For this concept of formation on a pattern, see Athanasius's theological approach to the Psalter: Athanasius, *The Life of Antony and the Letter to Marcellinus*, 108.

2. D. A. Carson, *Exegetical Fallacies*, 2nd ed. (Grand Rapids: Baker Academic, 1996), 115. While the "proverb" is taken from Carson's work, it appears that its origin is debated.

3. McKane, *Proverbs*, 10.

4. Mieder, "The Essence of Literary Proverb Study," 892.

that bear some resemblance to one another. Hope remains, however, for these dead aphorisms. They may be revived. But their resurrection requires a dislocation from the anthology and a recontextualization within an imagined scenario or some form of discourse, which bestows tendons, flesh, and the life breath upon these dead sayings once confined to the boneyard.

Revitalization through recontextualization represents one approach to treating the individual sayings in the central collections. But not all would agree with McKane's vision of contextual independence or Mieder's obituary. For others, the hermeneutical proverb noted above appertains to reading the materials within Prov 10–29. Irrespective of whether the proverbs in these collections evince signs of deliberate arrangement into "pairs," "clusters," "poems," or "sequences of value-statements,"[5] the sayings and collections are situated within a formal literary framework, a context within which they may be read and through which they may be understood.

This framework is formed through the prologue (chs. 1–9) and the concluding discourses (chs. 30–31).[6] The common terms, expressions, images, and setting within these collections create a literary envelope around Prov 10–29.[7] If nothing else, this envelope situates the diverse sayings in the central collections within a particular performance context, namely, the context of domestic instruction (e.g., 1:8; 31:1). Here the youth, and one might add, the implied reader, is formed.[8] Or better, here the youth is fed. The prologue culminates in Wisdom's invitation to her banquet (9:1–6). The youth is invited to leave the parental home and enter Wisdom's home. Her food is prepared. Her table is set. And the one who enters Wisdom's home may feast on her sumptuous fare. The domestic context of the anthology's literary framework corresponds with the domestic context of Wisdom's invitation. The banquet scene within ch. 9 creates a metaphorical setting through which to read the aphorisms in the central collections.[9] These aphorisms are Wisdom's fare, "a multi-course meal" designed to stimulate the moral taste buds, nourish the moral life, and sustain one

5. For a discussion and defense of coherent "pairs," "clusters" and "poems" in the sentence literature and their significance for interpretation, see Hildebrandt, "Proverbial Pairs," 207–24; Van Leeuwen, *Context and Meaning*, 3; McCreesh, *Biblical Sound and Sense*; Meinhold, *Die Sprüche*, 1:25–26; Ruth Scoralick, *Einzelspruch und Sammlung*, BZAW 232 (Berlin: de Gruyter, 1995); Garrett, *Proverbs*, 46–48; Heim, *Like Grapes of Gold*; Waltke, *Proverbs: Chapters 1–15*, 17–21. For discussion of the arrangement of the aphorisms according to "*sequences of value-statements*," see T. A. Perry, *Wisdom Literature and the Structure of Proverbs* (University Park: Pennsylvania State University Press, 1993), 72–75. For discussion of the lack of coherence among the materials in the sentence literature and/or the interpretive insignificance of these purported units, see Weeks, *Early Israelite Wisdom*, 20–40; Longman, *Proverbs*, 38–42. For a *via media* approach, see Fox, *Proverbs 10–31*, 477–83.

6. For further discussion, see the sections entitled Discourse Setting and The Central Collections (10:1–29:27): Chaos or Coherence? in the introduction to the volume.

7. Among others, see Camp, *Wisdom and the Feminine*, 186–208, who discusses not only the themes, language, and imagery reiterated in the anthology's frame but also instances in which these themes, terms, and images are deployed in particular aphorisms within the central collections to unify the diverse materials in a compositional whole.

8. As noted in our discussion of the parental lectures, and following Carol Newsom, the son or youth provides the subject position one is to assume and with which one is to identify. Newsom, "Woman and the Discourse of Patriarchal Wisdom," 142–44.

9. William P. Brown, "The Didactic Power of Metaphor in the Aphoristic Sayings of Proverbs," *JSOT* 29 (2004): 137–38.

on the journey of "fear seeking understanding."[10] When the aphorisms in Prov 10–29 are read within the literary framework of the anthology and against the backdrop of both the preamble (1:2–7) and Wisdom's climactic invitation (9:1–6), they may be viewed as much more than a random assemblage of sayings grafted into discrete collections. They are sayings cast in the context of domestic instruction that contribute to Proverbs's project of education for character formation. As the guidance of the parents and Lady Wisdom fade into the background, the reader is invited to discern the wisdom of these proverbs and to develop the perception necessary to hear, taste, see, smell, and feel their way through the world in accord with wisdom and virtue.

Structure and Outline of Proverbs 10–29

Within the general literary and performance context created by the prologue (Prov 1–9) and concluding discourses in the anthology (30:1–33; 31:1–31), the variegated sayings in Prov 10–29 are arranged in four collections, each of which opens with a formal heading (10:1; 22:17; 24:23; 25:1). These collections share much in common. The aphorisms are cast in conventional poetic forms. The collections address comparable themes; and they include variant repetitions, that is, sayings or parts of sayings found in other collections within the anthology.[11] This intimates that, to some degree, the collections exhibit a uniform perspective.

The formal and thematic correspondence among the collections, however, should not overshadow their distinctive characteristics. As many have noted, the predominance of antithetical sayings in 10:1–15:33 distinguishes the material from the variety of poetic forms that pervade 16:1–22:16, suggesting that the first Solomonic collection should be subdivided into two units: 10:1–15:33 and 16:1–22:16.[12] The same is true of the second Solomonic collection (25:1–29:27). Whereas vivid imagery, rich poetic analogies, and larger, coherent units characterize Prov 25–27, the materials in chs. 28–29 return to the terse, antithetical style of Prov 10–15, indicating that the collection contains two sections.[13] The poetic texture of the aphorisms in

10. Brown, "The Didactic Power of Metaphor," 138; idem, *Wisdom's Wonder*, 24.

11. Snell, *Twice-Told Proverbs*; Heim, *Poetic Imagination*.

12. Oesterley, *The Book of Proverbs*, xiv; Plöger, *Sprüche Salomos*; Meinhold, *Die Sprüche*, 1:26; Whybray, *The Composition of the Book of Proverbs*, 89, 131; Van Leeuwen, "The Book of Proverbs," *NIB* 5:105; Clifford, *Proverbs*, 108; Leo G. Perdue, *Wisdom Literature*, 58; Fox, *Proverbs 10–31*, xviii–xix, 509; Sæbø, *Sprüche*, 160. Others follow a similar structural model but mark the division of the collection at different places. Waltke, for example, argues that 15:30–33 functions as an introduction to the second subcollection, while Weeks observes that the lower frequency of antithetical sayings in ch. 15 suggests it constitutes "a grey area" between the two subcollections. Waltke, *Proverbs: Chapters 1–15*, 16; idem, *Proverbs: Chapters 15–31*, 5–8; Weeks, *Early Israelite Wisdom*, 26–27.

13. Toy, *Proverbs*, 457; Oesterley, *The Book of Proverbs*, xix; Van Leeuwen, "The Book of Proverbs," *NIB* 5:215; Perdue, *Proverbs*, 223; Waltke, *Proverbs: Chapters 1–15*, 25; Yoder, *Proverbs*, 245. Again, others agree that the collection should be divided into two subunits, but they mark the division at different places. Fox, for example, argues that 27:1 serves as the boundary between the subcollections (25:1–26:28; 27:1–29:27). Fox, *Proverbs 10–31*, 775–76.

Prov 10:1–22:16 and 25:1–29:27 intimate that the collections may be split in two. And the division of these collections into two units appears to correspond with the thematic emphases of each subsection. Following William Brown, the subcollections in Prov 10–29 focus on particular motifs and offer a nuanced development of certain themes to form the character and shape the moral vision of the reader in a progressive fashion.[14] The arrangement of these subcollections is comparable to modern educational curricula;[15] they move from elementary wisdom (10:1–15:33), to intermediate wisdom (16:1–22:16), to vocational wisdom (22:17–24:34), to advanced wisdom (25:1–29:27).[16] That is, the subcollections exhibit a "didactic movement."[17] This movement mirrors the progressive (trans)formation of the reader and contributes to the fundamental agenda of Proverbs, namely, the cultivation of character through the inculcation of wisdom and virtue.

It is important to note that this developmental scheme does not imply that the aphorisms in the central collections move from a simplistic to a more complex vision of the world. The development among the central collections is not one of moral worldview.[18] The development is, as Brown's expression suggests, didactic.[19] The pedagogical stability and dependency created by the pastiche of antithetical sayings in Prov 10–15 is interrupted by an avalanche of diverse poetic and rhetorical forms in the subsequent collections, which heighten the "discursive elocution" of the material and hone the moral reasoning of the reader.[20] The development of particular themes across the subcollections, combined with the introduction of motifs not mentioned in previous subunits, enhance the reader's "moral purview" and illuminate the elusiveness of the world.[21] The many sayings that acknowledge the limits of human wisdom, the ambiguities of life, and the inevitable contingencies that accompany the inscrutability of the divine indicate that the pedagogy and moral worldview of the central collections is neither naïve nor simplistic, neither dogmatic nor disconnected from reality (11:4; 16:1–2, 9).[22] The central collections exhibit a pedagogical or didactic development, not a development of moral worldview per se.

The commentary below will operate under this developmental model. Unfortunately, limitations of space preclude an extensive treatment of each aphorism in

14. Brown, "The Pedagogy of Proverbs 10:1–31:9," 181–82.

15. Brown, "The Pedagogy of Proverbs 10:1–31:9," 158.

16. Ansberry, *Be Wise, My Son*, 71–161.

17. Brown, "The Pedagogy of Proverbs 10:1–31:9," 164–65 et passim.

18. For an excellent discussion and critique of this (implicit) assumption, see Stewart, *Poetic Ethics*, 71–79.

19. Brown, "The Pedagogy of Proverbs 10:1–31:9," 153–54, 164–65. Cf. Schipper, *Proverbs 1–15*, 32–36. According to Schipper, the sayings in Proverbs 10:1–29:27 stage a "critical dialogue" through the juxtaposition of aphorisms that reflect "different levels of sapiential thought." These levels or modes of thought include (1) mundane observations (useful//harmful); (2) sapiential evaluations (wise//foolish); and (3) theological reflections (righteous//wicked). The confluence of these levels of thought across Prov 10:1–29:27 not only creates the conditions for the production of a "discursive" or "critical wisdom"; it also redefines "the basis of sapiential thought," affirming that "insight into human nature before God" is of primary importance, not "practical knowledge based on experience."

20. Brown, "The Pedagogy of Proverbs 10:1–31:9," 174–75.

21. Brown, "The Pedagogy of Proverbs 10:1–31:9," 164–65.

22. Stewart, *Poetic Ethics*, 77–78.

Prov 10–29. Certain chapters will receive full consideration; the discussion of others will be restricted to matters of literary context as well as structure and literary form. The acceptance of the medieval chapter divisions as a means by which to explore the sayings in the central collections is due more to the commentary genre than to the assumption that these divisions mark the boundaries of coherent proverbial units. In the event that a coherent unit of sayings transgresses the chapter division, it will be discussed under the sections devoted to Structure and Literary Form.

This sort of discussion is contingent on the presence of coherent groupings in the sentence literature. While the aphorisms in the central collections evince signs of deliberate arrangement into "proverbial pairs" and, to a lesser degree, into coherent strings or clusters of sayings (e.g., 16:1–9, 10–15; 26:1–12), on the whole, it appears that they are neither arranged into larger units nor organized according to a consistent design. Each saying is a unique, innovative creation that conveys a clear and often pregnant message. The commentary below, therefore, will explore each saying individually and consider its relationship with neighboring proverbs, its position within a group, and the interpretive implications of this contextual relationship where applicable. The hope is that the more detailed exploration of sayings in certain chapters will provide the reader with some assistance in their analysis of other aphorisms. In anticipation of the nuance and development evinced in the successive subcollections of Prov 10–29, we will begin with the basics, the ABC's:[23] elementary wisdom and virtue (10:1–15:33).

23. Van Leeuwen, "The Book of Proverbs," *NIB* 5:105.

III.1 Proverbs 10:1–15:33

Elementary Wisdom and Virtue

The world is both ordered and elusive; and human beings as well as human interactions are both predictable and complex. The central collections of Proverbs acknowledge these realities. The individual aphorisms probe the revealed and the concealed, the transparent and the hidden. They capture stable patterns and principles of life; and they contemplate the multiplex, mysterious, almost inarticulable nature of being-in-the-world. Each aphorism is fraught with meaning. And each traffics in terse expressions and pregnant turns of phrase that nurture the imagination, stimulate moral reasoning, and form character. As the opening course, Prov 10–15 provides an appropriate starter. The preponderance of antithetical sayings that focus on the fortunes of conflicting characters ease the reader into Lady Wisdom's curricular meal. They create a pedagogical experience of dependability and familiarity; and they awaken the palate to both recognizable tastes as well as surprises and rich subtleties that characterize life in the world. Whether the sayings are consumed or ingested, they offer nourishment and growth in a life of wisdom and virtue.[1] Let's taste and see what they have to offer.

1. This distinction between consumption and ingestion is inspired by George Steiner, *Real Presences* (Chicago: University of Chicago Press, 1989), 10; consumption is mere accumulation of data while ingestion is the comprehension and application of that data into one's life.

III. "Forming 'Fearers of YHWH'": The Curriculum of Wisdom and Virtue (10:1–29:27)

III.1 Elementary Wisdom and Virtue (10:1–15:33)

- **A. The Wise, the Righteous, and YHWH: The Pillars of the Moral World (10:1–32)**
- **B. Wisdom, Character, and Consequences: The Regulations of the MORAL ECONOMY (11:1–31)**
- **C. Building Prototypes: Wisdom and the Properties of MORAL CHARACTER (12:1–28)**
- **D. Mapping MORAL AUTHORITY: Wisdom, Discipline, and Desire (13:1–25)**
- **E. From the Moral to the Intellectual: A Montage of Wisdom and Folly (14:1–35)**
- **F. Forming MORAL WHOLENESS: The Homogeneity of Normative Character (15:1–33)**

III.2 Intermediate Wisdom and Virtue (16:1–22:16)

III.3 Vocational Wisdom and Virtue (22:17–24:34)

III.4 Advanced Wisdom and Virtue (25:1–29:27)

Proverbs 10:1–32

CHAPTER 16

A. The Wise, the Righteous, and YHWH:
The Pillars of the Moral World

Main Idea of the Passage

These sayings sketch the basic pillars of the moral order by profiling certain facets of the primary prototypes in the anthology, each of whom model and motivate the moral life through their divergent dispositions, body parts, and fates.

Literary Context

Wisdom's home may be spacious and her food may be sumptuous (9:1–6), but settling into a seat at her table can be unnerving. The formal shift from the extended discourses in the prologue to the pithy sayings in the central collections corresponds with a shift in the reader's subject position and responsibilities.[1] Wisdom's "curricular cuisine" is served,[2] but it is tasted and ingested without the help of authorized guides. Responsibility for discerning the wisdom of these sayings now lies with the reader. And digesting the spate of aphorisms and the variety of topics is contingent on the dexterity of one's moral imagination. There is no more handholding, no more spoon-feeding. One must participate in the process of moral reasoning and maturation independent of the parents and Wisdom.

The transition from the prologue to the central collections may be disorienting, but this transition is alleviated to some extent by the interrelationship between the prologue and the introductory verses of ch. 10. These verses link the prologue with the central collections in at least four ways. First, the title that opens the extended collection of aphorisms reiterates the expression that opens the anthology: "The proverbs of Solomon" (מִשְׁלֵי שְׁלֹמֹה; 1:1; 10:1a). Second, the mention of father, mother,

1. Yoder, *Proverbs*, 110, 114.

2. Brown, "The Didactic Power of Metaphor," 138.

and son in the initial saying recalls the pedagogical setting of the parental lectures (10:1bc; 1:8; 6:20).[3] Third, the contrast between the wise and foolish son mirrors the contrast between Lady Wisdom and Woman Folly in ch. 9 (10:1b–c; 9:1–6, 13–18). And fourth, the antithesis between the righteous and the wicked resumes the characterization of these personages in the hinge of the previous chapter (10:3; 9:7, 9; cf. 3:33). On formal and pedagogical grounds, ch. 10 marks a significant shift in the anthology. The language of its opening aphorisms, however, links the collection with the prologue in general and the material in ch. 9 in particular.

The opening aphorisms look back to the prologue, but they also look forward to the materials that follow. Their concern with the wise and the fool (10:1b–c), the righteous and the wicked (10:3) as well as YHWH (10:3a) foreground the categories of character along with the intellectual, moral, and theological dimensions of life that dominate the landscape of the central collections. And when taken as a whole, the sayings in ch. 10 focus on *the* prototypical character within the anthology and introduce a formative technique in its pedagogical repertoire, namely, motivation.

While the wise, the fool, and their coreferential counterparts play a prominent role throughout the central collections,[4] the righteous and the wicked receive considerable attention in ch. 10. In fact, the righteous is mentioned more frequently in ch. 10 than in the other chapters within the initial subcollection (chs. 11–14) and the entirety of the second subcollection (16:1–22:16).[5] This is not surprising, for the righteous is *the* prototypical character within Proverbs, the personage that Sun Myung Lyu designates as "the sages' chosen exemplar of the ethical and pious life" who induces desire "*by showing what is desirable*."[6] The frequency with which this paradigmatic personage appears in ch. 10 is instrumental in the pedagogical agenda of the central collections. The righteous is featured in the opening chapter of the central collections as the one who embodies and reflects all that is desirable.[7] And the sayings throughout ch. 10 reinforce this pedagogical program of seduction through motivation. As Anne Stewart has demonstrated, the sayings appeal to various motives, ranging from parental favor (10:1), wealth (10:2, 4), satiety (v. 3), and renown (10:5, 7) to blessing (10:6), safety (10:9), life (10:11, 16, 17, 25, 27), security (10:15, 29, 30) and joy (10:23, 28, 32).[8] These motivations are not delivered through formal motive clauses; rather, they are latent in the antithetical sayings.[9] Chapter 10, *in nuce*,

3. John Goldingay, "The Arrangement of Sayings in Proverbs 10–15," *JSOT* 61 (1994): 81; Waltke, *Proverbs: Chapters 1–15*, 14.

4. For discussion of these characters and their coreferential counterparts, see Heim, *Like Grapes of Gold*, 77–103.

5. The righteous appears 13x in ch. 10 (vv. 3, 6, 7, 11, 16, 20, 21, 24, 25, 28, 30, 31, 32), 8x both in chs. 11 and 12 (11:8, 9, 10, 21, 23, 28, 30, 31; 12:3, 5, 7, 10, 12, 13, 21, 26), 5x in ch. 13 (vv. 5, 9, 21, 22, 25), 2x in ch. 14 (vv. 19, 32) and 3x in ch. 15 (vv. 6, 28, 29). On the whole, the righteous is mentioned only 10x in 16:1–22:16 (17:15, 26; 18:5, 10, 17; 20:7; 21:12, 15, 18, 26).

6. Lyu, *Righteousness*, 62 (italics original).

7. Lyu, *Righteousness*, 62–63.

8. Stewart, *Poetic Ethics*, 118.

9. Ted Hildebrandt, "Motivation and Antithetic Parallelism in Proverbs 10–15," *JETS* 35 (1992): 433–44. Rather than exploring motivation through grammatical or syntactical constructions, Hildebrandt investigates the semantic motiva-

acclimates the reader to the materials that follow by introducing the character types and dimensions of life that populate the central collections, by promoting the righteous as the prototype of the wise and virtuous life, and by revealing the instrumental role of motivation in the anthology's pedagogy.

In light of these observations, Katharine Dell's and Anne Stewart's observations concerning the literary and contextual significance of ch. 10 capture its contribution to the central collections. The initial verses of the chapter "provide a kind of programme for what follows."[10] On the whole, ch. 10 offers "a hermeneutical orientation toward the proverbial collections that follow," especially with regard to its use of motivation;[11] it serves as a primer, identifying the prototypical character within the anthology as well as the interconnection of character, consequence, and motive in its pedagogy.[12]

III: "Forming 'Fearers of YHWH'": The Curriculum of Wisdom and Virtue (10:1–29:27)

III.1 Elementary Wisdom and Virtue (10:1–15:33)

➡ **A. The Wise, the Righteous, and YHWH: The Pillars of the Moral World (10:1–32)**

1. Title (10:1a)

2. The Wise, the Righteous, and YHWH: The Pillars of the Moral World (10:1b–32)

B. Wisdom, Character, and Consequences: The Regulations of the MORAL ECONOMY (11:1–31)

C. Building Prototypes: Wisdom and the Properties of MORAL CHARACTER (12:1–28)

D. Mapping MORAL AUTHORITY: Wisdom, Discipline, and Desire (13:1–25)

E. From the Moral to the Intellectual: A Montage of Wisdom and Folly (14:1–35)

F. Forming MORAL WHOLENESS: The Homogeneity of Normative Character (15:1–33)

III.2 Intermediate Wisdom and Virtue (16:1–22:16)

III.3 Vocational Wisdom and Virtue (22:17–24:34)

III.4 Advanced Wisdom and Virtue (25:1–29:27)

Translation and Exegetical Outline

(See pages 358–60.)

tional structures inherent in the aphorisms within the sentence literature through "approach/avoidance" motivational theory, which opens the "deep structure" of proverbial motivations by means of psycholinguistic analysis.

10. Dell, *The Book of Proverbs*, 61.

11. Stewart, *Poetic Ethics*, 118.

12. Stewart, *Poetic Ethics*, 119. In view of the concentration of sayings regarding the righteous in the opening chapters of Prov 10–15, Goldingay contends that these aphorisms establish "an ethical context for the material on human behaviour in 10:1–22:16 as a whole" (Goldingay, "The Arrangement of Sayings in Proverbs 10–15," 76).

Proverbs 10:1–32

III.1 Elementary Wisdom and Virtue (10:1–15:33)

A. The Wise, the Righteous, and YHWH: The Pillars of the Moral World (10:1–32)

1. Title (10:1a)
2. The Wise, the Righteous, and YHWH: The Pillars of the Moral World (10:1b–32)

1a	מִשְׁלֵי שְׁלֹמֹה	The Proverbs of Solomon
1b	בֵּן חָכָם יְשַׂמַּח־אָב	A wise son gladdens the father;
1c	וּבֵן כְּסִיל תּוּגַת אִמּוֹ	but a foolish son, the grief of his mother.
2a	לֹא־יוֹעִילוּ אוֹצְרוֹת רֶשַׁע	Treasures of wickedness will not profit;
2b	וּצְדָקָה תַּצִּיל מִמָּוֶת	but righteousness delivers from death.
3a	לֹא־יַרְעִיב יְהוָה נֶפֶשׁ צַדִּיק	YHWH will not let the righteous person starve;
3b	וְהַוַּת רְשָׁעִים יֶהְדֹּף	but he will push away the desire of the wicked.
4a	רָאשׁ עֹשֶׂה כַף־רְמִיָּה	A slack palm produces poverty;
4b	וְיַד חָרוּצִים תַּעֲשִׁיר	but the hand of the diligent brings riches.
5a	אֹגֵר בַּקַּיִץ בֵּן מַשְׂכִּיל	One who gathers in the summer, a perceptive son;
5b	נִרְדָּם בַּקָּצִיר בֵּן מֵבִישׁ	one who sleeps in the harvest, a disgraceful son.
6a	בְּרָכוֹת לְרֹאשׁ צַדִּיק	Blessings for the head of the righteous;
6b	וּפִי רְשָׁעִים יְכַסֶּה חָמָס	but the mouth of the wicked conceals violence.
7a	זֵכֶר צַדִּיק לִבְרָכָה	The memory of the righteous, for a blessing;
7b	וְשֵׁם רְשָׁעִים יִרְקָב	but the name of the wicked rots.
8a	חֲכַם־לֵב יִקַּח מִצְוֹת	The wise of heart receives commands,
8b	וֶאֱוִיל שְׂפָתַיִם יִלָּבֵט	but one with foolish lips will be ruined.
9a	הוֹלֵךְ בַּתֹּם יֵלֶךְ בֶּטַח	One who walks uprightly walks securely;
9b	וּמְעַקֵּשׁ דְּרָכָיו יִוָּדֵעַ	but one who twists his ways will be discovered.
10a	קֹרֵץ עַיִן יִתֵּן עַצָּבֶת	One who winks the eye brings grief,
10b	וֶאֱוִיל שְׂפָתַיִם יִלָּבֵט	and one with foolish lips will be ruined.
11a	מְקוֹר חַיִּים פִּי צַדִּיק	A fount of life – the mouth of the righteous;
11b	וּפִי רְשָׁעִים יְכַסֶּה חָמָס	but the mouth of the wicked conceals violence.
12a	שִׂנְאָה תְּעוֹרֵר מְדָנִים	Hate awakens conflict;
12b	וְעַל כָּל־פְּשָׁעִים תְּכַסֶּה אַהֲבָה	but love covers all offenses.
13a	בְּשִׂפְתֵי נָבוֹן תִּמָּצֵא חָכְמָה	On the lips of the discerning wisdom is found;
13b	וְשֵׁבֶט לְגֵו חֲסַר־לֵב	and a rod for the back of the senseless.

14a	חֲכָמִים יִצְפְּנוּ־דָעַת	The wise store knowledge;
14b	וּפִי־אֱוִיל מְחִתָּה קְרֹבָה	but the mouth of the fool, impending ruin.
15a	הוֹן עָשִׁיר קִרְיַת עֻזּוֹ	The wealth of the rich, his fortified city;
15b	מְחִתַּת דַּלִּים רֵישָׁם	the ruin of the poor, their poverty.
16a	פְּעֻלַּת צַדִּיק לְחַיִּים	The wages of the righteous, for life;
16b	תְּבוּאַת רָשָׁע לְחַטָּאת	the produce of the wicked, for sin.
17a	אֹרַח לְחַיִּים שׁוֹמֵר מוּסָר	One who observes instruction, a path to life;
17b	וְעוֹזֵב תּוֹכַחַת מַתְעֶה	but one who rejects reproof leads astray.
18a	מְכַסֶּה שִׂנְאָה שִׂפְתֵי־שָׁקֶר	One who conceals hatred, lying lips;
18b	וּמוֹצִא דִבָּה הוּא כְסִיל	and one who spreads slander is a fool.
19a	בְּרֹב דְּבָרִים לֹא יֶחְדַּל־פָּשַׁע	In a multitude of words, offense will not cease;
19b	וְחֹשֵׂךְ שְׂפָתָיו מַשְׂכִּיל	but one who restrains his lips is prudent.
20a	כֶּסֶף נִבְחָר לְשׁוֹן צַדִּיק	The tongue of the righteous, choice silver;
20b	לֵב רְשָׁעִים כִּמְעָט	the heart of the wicked, of little value.
21a	שִׂפְתֵי צַדִּיק יִרְעוּ רַבִּים	The lips of the righteous nourish many;
21b	וֶאֱוִילִים בַּחֲסַר־לֵב יָמוּתוּ	but fools die through senselessness.
22a	בִּרְכַּת יְהוָה הִיא תַעֲשִׁיר	The blessing of YHWH, it brings riches;
22b	וְלֹא־יוֹסִף עֶצֶב עִמָּהּ	and strenuous work adds nothing to it.
23a	כִּשְׂחוֹק לִכְסִיל עֲשׂוֹת זִמָּה	Lewd behavior is like pleasure for a fool;
23b	וְחָכְמָה לְאִישׁ תְּבוּנָה	but wisdom for a person of understanding.
24a	מְגוֹרַת רָשָׁע הִיא תְבוֹאֶנּוּ	What the wicked fears, it will come upon him;
24b	וְתַאֲוַת צַדִּיקִים יִתֵּן	but what the righteous desire he will grant.
25a	כַּעֲבוֹר סוּפָה וְאֵין רָשָׁע	When the whirlwind passes, the wicked is no more;
25b	וְצַדִּיק יְסוֹד עוֹלָם	but the righteous, an enduring foundation.
26a	כַּחֹמֶץ לַשִּׁנַּיִם וְכֶעָשָׁן לָעֵינָיִם	Like vinegar to the teeth and smoke to the eyes,
26b	כֵּן הֶעָצֵל לְשֹׁלְחָיו	so the sluggard to those who send him.
27a	יִרְאַת יְהוָה תּוֹסִיף יָמִים	The fear of YHWH increases days;
27b	וּשְׁנוֹת רְשָׁעִים תִּקְצֹרְנָה	but the years of the wicked are shortened.

Continued on next page.

Continued from previous page.

28a	תּוֹחֶלֶת צַדִּיקִים שִׂמְחָה	The expectation of the righteous, joy;
28b	וְתִקְוַת רְשָׁעִים תֹּאבֵד	but the hope of the wicked perishes.
29a	מָעוֹז לַתֹּם דֶּרֶךְ יְהוָה	A stronghold for the upright, the way of YHWH;
29b	וּמְחִתָּה לְפֹעֲלֵי אָוֶן	but ruin for those who commit iniquity.
30a	צַדִּיק לְעוֹלָם בַּל־יִמּוֹט	The righteous will never be shaken;
30b	וּרְשָׁעִים לֹא יִשְׁכְּנוּ־אָרֶץ	and the wicked will not dwell in the land.
31a	פִּי־צַדִּיק יָנוּב חָכְמָה	The mouth of the righteous produces wisdom;
31b	וּלְשׁוֹן תַּהְפֻּכוֹת תִּכָּרֵת	but the tongue of the perverse is cut off.
32a	שִׂפְתֵי צַדִּיק יֵדְעוּן רָצוֹן	The lips of the righteous know what is pleasing;
32b	וּפִי רְשָׁעִים תַּהְפֻּכוֹת	but the mouth of the wicked, perversity.

Structure and Literary Form

The structure of Prov 10 is, to some extent, in the interpretive eye of the beholder. Some see general contours: the repetition of the terms "son" (בֵּן, vv. 1b, 1c, 5) and "blessing(s)" (בְּרָכוֹת, v. 6a; בִּרְכַּת, v. 22a), for example, may illuminate the boundaries or introductions to discrete units, each of which focuses on particular themes (vv. 1b–5, vv. 6–21, vv. 22–32).[13] Others recognize these contours but perceive a sharper blueprint, where catchwords and the recurrence of prototypical characters clarify subtler aspects of the chapter's architecture (vv. 6–7, 11–12, 14–15, 16–17, 20–21, 24–25, 27–28, 31–32).[14] And still others discern a meticulous design in which verbal and syntactical repetition, paronomasia, and subject matter form proverbial pairs and delineate units that constitute well-defined rooms in the chapter's configuration (vv. 1b–5, 6–11, 12–18, 19–22, 23–30, 31–32).[15] Each structural proposal isolates and elucidates semantic, syntactical, and thematic elements that place particular sayings in dialogical relationship with others. These elements are not insignificant. But the interpretive fruit of these proposals is disputed. The proof of the structural pudding, to modify a modern proverb, will have to be in the eating.

Before we taste the individual sayings from these potential units, a word on the recurring terms and motifs within the chapter is in order. As many have noted, the sayings devote considerable attention to the prototypical character within the anthology, viz., the righteous (צַדִּיק, vv. 3a, 6a, 7a, 11a, 16a, 20a, 21a, 24b, 25b, 28a, 30a, 31a, 32a), and this exemplar's antithetical counterpart, the wicked (רָשָׁע, vv. 3b, 6b, 7b, 11b, 16b, 20b, 24a, 25a, 27b, 28b, 30b, 32b). Many aphorisms recycle terms that link adjacent proverbs, such as "blessing(s)" (בְּרָכוֹת, v. 6a; בְּרָכָה, v. 7a; cf. בִּרְכַּת, v. 22a), "conceals/covers" (יְכַסֶּה, v. 11b; תְּכַסֶּה; 12b; cf. מְכַסֶּה, v. 18a), "ruin" (מְחִתָּה, v. 14b; מְחִתַּת, v. 15b; cf. v. 29), "for/to life" (לְחַיִּים, vv. 16a, 17a), and "perverse/perversity" (תַּהְפֻּכוֹת, v. 31b, 32b).[16] Two lines are reiterated within the chapter (v. 6b//11b, v. 8b//10b); and, in addition to the fate of the righteous and wicked, speech and body parts predominate in the aphorisms. The recurrence of these terms, lines, themes,

13. For this general design, see Koptak, *Proverbs*, 283. It is important to note that Koptak identifies particular pairs within these units in the commentary proper.

14. Van Leeuwen, "The Book of Proverbs," *NIB* 5:106, 110–13; Yoder, *Proverbs*, 118. Whereas Yoder considers vv. 1b–5 as a unit and restricts catchwords to more conspicuous terms, Van Leeuwen regards vv. 1b–8 as a unit and allows the antithesis between the righteous and the wicked to serve as a link between sayings (e.g., vv. 24–25, 27–28).

15. For a defense of these units and comparable groups with slight variations, see Meinhold, *Die Sprüche*, 1:163; Garrett, *Proverbs*, 117–22; Heim, *Like Grapes of Gold*, 111–134; cf. Whybray, *The Composition of the Book of Proverbs*, 94–96; Waltke, *Proverbs: Chapters 1–15*, 450, 465, 468; Schipper, *Proverbs 1–15*, 362–64.

16. In addition to these catchwords, the terms "son" (בֵּן, vv. 1b, 1c, 5), "hate/hatred" (שִׂנְאָה, vv. 12a, 18a), "perceptive/prudent" (מַשְׂכִּיל, vv. 5a, 19b) and "brings riches" (תַּעֲשִׁיר, vv. 4b, 22a) are repeated in the chapter.

and images suggests that the sayings are not a hodgepodge of random aphorisms. At minimum, it indicates they were composed or organized through a process of "associative thinking" to guide the reader in their ingestion of the material.[17]

Using the concept of "associative thinking" as a heuristic guide, the commentary below will analyze the individual sayings in their present sequence, identifying links between aphorisms and the interpretive horizons that their association may open. The individual sayings will represent the focus of attention. In light of the structural proposals noted above, however, the discussion will also consider the presence and the interpretive payoff of larger units or groups.

Explanation of the Text

1. Title (10:1a)

The second collection opens with a title. On formal grounds, this title initiates a transition from the discourses of the prologue to a collection of short, pithy sayings. On compositional grounds, it relates the collection of proverbs with the title that opens the anthology (מִשְׁלֵי שְׁלֹמֹה; 10:1a; 1:1). And on numerical grounds, it identifies the number of sayings in Prov 10:1–22:16.[18] The title serves as a bridge between the collections; it establishes continuity with the attribution and agenda of the anthology (1:1–7), on the one hand, and introduces the extent of the curricular course that awaits the reader, on the other.

2. The Wise, the Righteous, and YHWH: The Pillars of the Moral World (10:1b–32)

This bridge between the collections is reinforced by the first aphorism (**v. 1b, c**). As noted above, the mention of son, father, and mother recalls the exordium of the initial parental lecture (1:8–9). The sequence of terms is the same. The domestic setting is the same. But, as Christine Roy Yoder notes, "the reader's location with respect to it is different."[19] Direct address disappears (cf. 19:27), and the guidance of both parents and Wisdom recedes from the material. At Wisdom's table, one must learn to fend for oneself, discerning the wisdom of the sayings, developing moral reasoning, and refining moral

17. Fox, *Proverbs 10–31*, 480.

18. The numerical value of the consonants in the name Solomon is 375, which matches the number of sayings in the collection. Patrick W. Skehan, "A Single Editor for the Whole Book of Proverbs," *CBQ* 10 (1948): 115–30; repr. and rev. in *Studies in Israelite Poetry and Wisdom*, 15–26; idem, "Wisdom's House," *CBQ* 29 (1967): 162–80; repr. and rev. in *Studies in Israelite Poetry and Wisdom*, 27–45. Skehan argues that the book of Proverbs was organized according to an intricate design. The compositional layout of this design forms the blueprint of "Wisdom's house," and the numerical value of particular terms within the titles of the collections confirms this design. While Skehan's rearrangement of particular texts to form the "columns" of Wisdom's house may be a case of hermeneutical opportunism, and his use of gematria may be characterized as both questionable and anachronistic, the fact remains that the numerical value of the consonants in Solomon corresponds with the number of sayings in the second collection.

19. Yoder, *Proverbs*, 118.

tastes with a view toward the maturation of one's character.

The first aphorism provides an appropriate point of entry into the central collections. Against the backdrop of Wisdom and Folly's invitations, the reader encounters a wise and a foolish son. The saying focuses on an intimate interpersonal relationship within the most fundamental social unit in the moral order. The parent-child relationship and the household create the conditions for exploring the way in which one's character is intertwined with the emotional state of one's parents (cf. 15:20; 17:21, 25; 19:13). On one level, the antithetical saying affirms that a wise son "gladdens" (יְשַׂמַּח, v. 1b) the father, while a foolish son arouses maternal heartache, anxiety, and shame. At a deeper level, however, the aphorism promotes the wise life, motivating the reader to create a domestic environment of delight by fulfilling a fundamental human desire: the desire to please and honor one's parents.[20] Parental emotions and their implications on the emotional fabric of the home offer a powerful motivation for wise character.

The same is true of wealth, which serves as the motivational bait of **v. 2**. The meaning of the opening expression, "Treasures of wickedness" (אוֹצְרוֹת רֶשַׁע, v. 2a), is unclear; it could refer to either treasures procured by wicked practices or treasures possessed by the wicked. What is clear is that, despite wickedness, wealth is acquired. But paradoxically, this wealth is of little value, for it neither profits nor protects. The phrase "will not profit" (לֹא־יוֹעִילוּ, v. 2a) is used elsewhere in reference to useless things (1 Sam 12:21; Isa 30:5), such as idols (Isa 57:12–13; Jer 2:11) and false prophets (Jer 23:32). Like these things, treasures of wickedness are worthless. This is not the case with righteousness. This quality of character is more valuable and more powerful than the wealth of wickedness, for it secures the sure, stable dividend of deliverance. The antithetical saying elevates righteousness over illicit wealth and long-term, personal security over the short-term gain of fleeting wealth and wickedness, which cannot deliver from death.

This striking assertion of the personal value and protection of righteousness is substantiated by the theological conviction conveyed in **v. 3**. Similar to v. 2, the aphorism opens with the construction לֹא + imperfect (vv. 2a, 3a). And similar to the other YHWH sayings within the central collections, it situates v. 2 in a broader theological perspective.[21] Treasures of wickedness are worthless and righteousness provides protection (v. 2) because YHWH is the sovereign accountant, defender, and provider of the moral order (v. 3). The proverb reflects on a fundamental human desire: satiation. And it captures YHWH's provision for human life. As the divine host, YHWH ensures the appetite of the righteous is satisfied. He appeases their hunger with his rich bounty. But he pushes away that which the wicked desire, moving out of reach the plate they crave. Sustenance, satisfaction, and longing (un)fulfilled are not generated by human effort alone; they are also granted by YHWH and contingent on one's character.

This theological perspective informs the reading of **v. 4**, which returns to the motivational lure of wealth. Whereas v. 3 emphasizes divine provision, v. 4 stresses the place of human effort in the acquisition of riches. The proverb expresses a general principle that is reiterated and qualified elsewhere

20. Hildebrandt, "Motivation and Antithetic Parallelism in Proverbs 10–15," 437.

21. R. Norman Whybray, "Yahweh-Sayings and their Contexts in Proverbs, 10,1–22,16," in *La Sagesse de l'Ancien Testament*, 2nd ed., ed. M. Gilbert, BETL 51 (Leuven: Peeters, 1990), 153–65.

in the anthology, viz., laziness causes poverty, while diligence produces wealth (e.g., Prov 12:11, 24; 13:4; 24:30–34). Like many other aphorisms in the chapter, this principle is communicated through synecdoche. The "palm" (כַּף, v. 4a) and "hand" (יָד, v. 4b) represent the whole body of the individual. They identify the power of these particular body parts for inducing poverty and producing wealth. Perhaps more importantly, however, they indicate that laziness and diligence are embodied qualities, not merely intellectual concepts. Riches are desirable; but their acquisition, to a certain extent, lies in one's hands.[22]

This vision of work is recast in intellectual and emotional terms in **v. 5**. These terms modify the "son" in each line. Similar to v. 1b–c, the mention of the son situates the saying in the context of the home. Using alliteration, assonance, and language reminiscent of the ant (cf. 6:6–8), the first line depicts a perceptive son as one who gathers at the appropriate time. He is discerning and astute, sensitive to the seasons and the rhythm of creation. The disgraceful son, by contrast, is dazed and confused, insensible to the seasons and indifferent to the needs of the household.[23] He is a son who, like the foolish child in v. 1c, strains the emotional fabric of the home, heaping shame and disgrace on the household. When the aphorism is read in conjunction with v. 1, it illustrates the emotional effects of wise and foolish children on the home through a particular activity. And when read in conjunction with v. 4, it clarifies Proverbs's vision of diligence, which involves not only hard work but also hard work performed at the right time.

Just as vv. 3–5 may be read in relation to one another, so also **vv. 1–5** may be read as a unit. Many contend that the repetition of "son" in vv. 1 and 5 forms an *inclusio*, framing a sequence of aphorisms cast in a chiasm.[24] This frame creates a context within which to read the individual proverbs; and the chiasm places particular sayings in dialogue with one another. This dialogue does not mitigate the basic message of the aphorisms. If anything, it opens a fruitful conversation among the sayings that identifies *some of the ways* in which they might be construed.[25] When the sayings are read within this context and in accord with the chiasm, the son is the focus of attention. The wise son honors his parents, acts justly, and works hard while acknowledging his dependence on God, who is the source of provision and the sovereign overseer of the wise life.[26] The foolish son, by contrast, is lazy and disgraceful (vv. 4a, 5b). He craves wickedness, acquires wealth by illicit practices (vv. 3b, 2a), and experiences insecurity, hunger, and deprivation, which explains his mother's misery (v. 1c).[27] The interplay among the sayings suggests that they form a montage of the wise and foolish son.[28]

22. Van Leeuwen, "The Book of Proverbs," *NIB* 5:107; Yoder, *Proverbs*, 120.

23. The root רדם ("to sleep deeply") denotes inopportune sleep or a daze (Judg 4:21; Jonah 1:5–6; Ps 76:7[6]).

24. Plöger, *Sprüche Salomos*, 124; Meinhold, *Die Sprüche*, 1:164–69; Garrett, *Proverbs*, 117; Whybray, *The Composition of the Book of Proverbs*, 94; Murphy, *Proverbs*, 72; Heim, *Like Grapes of Gold*, 111–12; Waltke, *Proverbs: Chapters 1–15*, 450–52; Koptak, *Proverbs*, 287–90; Yoder, *Proverbs*, 118–19; Sæbø, *Sprüche*, 168. Cf. Fox, *Proverbs 10–31*, 514–15, who considers 10:1–6 as a cluster, and Van Leeuwen, "The Book of Proverbs," *NIB* 5:106–8, who deems 10:1–8 as a unit.

25. For a discussion and illustration of this sort of dialogue, see Zoltán Schwáb, "The Sayings Clusters in Proverbs: Towards an Associative Reading Strategy," *JSOT* 38 (2013): 59–79.

26. Yoder, *Proverbs*, 119; Koptak, *Proverbs*, 289–90.

27. Heim, *Poetic Imagination*, 211–12. In accord with this reading, Heim contends that vv. 1b–5 describe the foolish son's behavior and the consequences of his actions, which provide a more detailed rationale for the mother's grief (v. 1c).

28. Fox, *Proverbs 10–31*, 515.

The montage produces a general impression of the character and presumed consequences that accompany each figure. The individual sayings, however, provide detailed stills that enhance this montage and generate other imaginative scenarios in which they may be placed or applied.

While the links among vv. 1–5 are varied, the relationship between **vv. 6 and 7** is fixed and clear. Both move from a description of the righteous to a description of the wicked. And both include the noun "blessing(s)" (בְּרָכוֹת, v. 6a, בְּרָכָה, v. 7a) in the first line. The noun evokes a tangible state of peace, prosperity, favor, and harmonious relationships. This state is explored from different angles in the adjacent aphorisms. The first conceptualizes blessings as a garland or crown (v. 6a; cf. 1:9). Whether they are bestowed by God or granted by members of the community, they adorn the head of the righteous, revealing this prototypical character's favor, desirability, and moral worth. The wicked, by contrast, may be difficult to spot, for they prefer concealing to revealing (10:6b). Whereas the head of the righteous showcases blessings, the mouth of the wicked covers up violence and veils wrongdoing (v. 6b).[29] What the body reveals about the righteous, it conceals about the character and inclinations of the wicked. The second aphorism conceptualizes blessing in terms of renown (v. 7). Both "memory" (זֵכֶר, v. 7a) and "name" (שֵׁם, v. 7b) refer to one's reputation in life and even after death. The memory of the righteous endures, entering the collective speech and memory of the community. But the name of the wicked rots; its stench triggers moral nausea, its substance decays, and its remembrance fades. Crown and renown, revealing and concealing, endurance and evanescence structure this proverbial pair, which links one's character with communal consequences in both the present and the future.

With language and imagery reminiscent of the prologue, **vv. 8–10** sketch the posture, movements, and orientation of distinctive characters. Again, body parts feature prominently in the sayings. And v. 8b is reiterated verbatim in v. 10b. Returning to the contrast between the wise and the fool (vv. 1b–c), **v. 8** focuses on one's attitude toward speech. The wise of heart receive the speech of the other (v. 8a). They possess that which the exordia within the parental lectures attempted to inculcate in readers: a receptive posture (2:1; 3:1; 4:10). One with foolish lips, however, is more interested in speaking than listening. The constant movement of their lips prevents their hearts from hearing and heeding commands. As an example of "asymmetrical antithetical parallelism," the second line implies that one with foolish lips does not receive commands.[30] It is not surprising, then, that one with foolish lips "will be ruined" (יִלָּבֵט, v. 8b) or destroyed.[31] Nor is it a stretch to assume that, in light of the asymmetrical parallelism, the wise of heart "will be delivered."[32] The parallelism is imprecise; but the components provide a guide for the imagination to fill in the gaps.

29. In contrast to this reading, some take "violence" as the subject of v. 6b (i.e., "but violence overwhelms/conceals the mouth of the wicked"); so Delitzsch, "Proverbs of Solomon," 6:154 (1:212–13), and Waltke, *Proverbs: Chapters 1–15*, 449n29. This reading creates a clearer antithesis with v. 6a. The repetition of v. 6b in v. 11b, however, suggests that "mouth" is the subject, not "violence." Garrett, *Proverbs*, 118n199; Fox, *Proverbs 10–31*, 514. Cf. Heim, *Poetic Imagination*, 218.

30. William E. Mouser Jr., *Walking in Wisdom: Studying the Proverbs of Solomon* (Downers Grove, IL: InterVarsity Press, 1983), 35–52, reprinted as "Filling in the Blank: Asymmetrical Antithetic Parallelisms," in *Learning from the Sages: Selected Studies on the Book of Proverbs*, ed. R. B. Zuck (Grand Rapids: Baker, 1995), 137–50, and Heim, *Poetic Imagination*, 225–26.

31. With the exception of Prov 10:8b and 10:10b, the verb לבט occurs elsewhere only in Hos 4:14, where it depicts the destruction or ruination of a people without understanding. For discussion of the verbs use in Rabbinic Hebrew, see Fox, *Proverbs 10–31*, 516.

32. Heim, *Poetic Imagination*, 225.

Just as one's attitude toward speech reveals one's disposition and destiny (v. 8), so also one's gait reveals one's character and its consequences (v. 9). The nuclear symbol of the prologue recurs in **v. 9**, merging moral movements with the terrain of a path. And the prospect of personal security provides the motivational substructure of the saying. Similar to the parents' projection of (im)moral movements, one's walk is indicative of one's character (cf. 4:20–27; 6:12–15). Those who walk "uprightly" (בַּתֹּם, 10:9a) embody an honest way of life that is safe and secure, while those who twist their ways embody perversity and deceit (v. 9b; cf. 2:15). Far from covering their winding way of life, the twisted will be discovered, caught unawares in their wrongdoing. The agent and timing of the discovery is undetermined, but the consequence is certain.

This antithetical account of (im)moral movements is developed in **v. 10**, which offers a pair of negative statements concerning the anatomy and speech of nefarious figures. Similar to 6:13, the first line describes the effects of "sinister sign language."[33] One "who winks the eye" (קֹרֵץ עַיִן, v. 10a) conveys malicious schemes and inflicts pain on others (cf. 16:30). One with foolish lips, however, inflicts self-destruction (v. 10b). As noted above, the second line repeats v. 8b. This repetition, combined with the disruption of antithetical sayings, has prompted some to conclude that the verset is a scribal error.[34] In view of the prevalence of repetitions and variant repetitions within Proverbs, however, the recurrence of the line may be intentional.[35] The parallel lines associate the malicious gesture of winking the eye with foolish lips. The former action may inflict pain on others, but the association suggests that this pain will return upon the one with these dysfunctional facial organs, bringing ruin.[36] These images and concepts resemble the sketch of the scoundrel in 6:12–15. Both consider the immoral mouth and winking eyes. And both culminate in destruction. Whether or not the repeated line contributes to the structure of the aphorisms in the chapter, it signals the importance of repetition in Proverbs's pedagogical program and illustrates the way in which repeated lines open new horizons of meaning. Whereas the asymmetrical parallelism in 10:8 suggested that one with foolish lips does not receive commands, the association of foolish lips with one who winks the eye intimates that, like the scoundrel, those characterized by these facial movements will experience the pain and destruction they sought to sow among others.

The repetition in v. 10 reverberates through **v. 11**, where the second line is a verbatim reiteration of 10:6b.[37] Against the backdrop of the babbling fool (v. 10b), the aphorism explores the "mouth"

33. McKane, *Proverbs*, 325.

34. Murphy, *Proverbs*, 71; Clifford, *Proverbs*, 111; Fox, *Proverbs 10–31*, 517. The LXX offers a clear antithesis to the components in v. 10a; it reads "but one who reproves openly makes peace."

35. Heim, *Poetic Imagination*, 224–27 et passim. Heim also notes Snell's discussion of repeated verses in the Septuagint. In conversation with Jack Berezov's unpublished essay, Snell concludes with Berezov that the Septuagint's tendency to avoid repeating words or verses in the MT may be due to the translators' "esthetic judgment that repetition was inelegant" (Snell, *Twice-Told Proverbs*, 23–33, esp. 23).

36. Heim, *Poetic Imagination*, 226–27.

37. As noted above, some construe vv. 6–11 as a coherent group of sayings that evince deliberate editorial arrangement. Heim, for example, argues that the repetition of two lines in close proximity betrays intentional design (vv. 6b//11b; vv. 8b//10b). Taken together, these repeated lines create "an imprecise chiastic sequence (A–B–C–D–C′–A′)," a sequence that situates "verse 9 (=D) at the center" (Heim, *Poetic Imagination*, 221). When read as a unit and through the nucleus of v. 9, the sayings identify the interconnection between character, speech, and particular consequences. Heim, *Like Grapes of Gold*, 117–19.

(פִּי, v. 11a, b) of the righteous and the wicked. The mouth of the former is portrayed as "a fount of life" (מְקוֹר חַיִּים, v. 11a)—as a spring from which listeners may draw and drink cool, refreshing words that sustain life (cf. 13:14; 14:27; 16:22). For the thirsty, it is open and free, a reservoir of satiety. The mouth of the wicked, by contrast, is closed and concealed; it harbors violence and masks evil intent, veiling wrongdoing with words.

Concealment may carry negative connotations (10:6b, 11b, 18a), but it is important to note that it has its benefits. One benefit is delineated in **v. 12**, which is linked to the previous aphorism through the catchword "conceals/covers" (יְכַסֶּה, v. 11b, תְּכַסֶּה, v. 12b). Hate is a powerful emotion that possesses the power to awaken conflict. But love is more powerful; it dispels and quells conflict in forbearance. In the spirit of 1 Cor 13, love endures all offenses and overlooks all wrongs against oneself. It is like a bandage that covers a wound, promoting healing and harmony (cf. 1 Pet 4:8; Jas 5:20).[38]

Love may cover wounds, but wounds serve as a means of discipline and correction. This aspect of instruction is expressed in **v. 13b** (cf. 19:29; 26:3). But its relationship to **v. 13a** is unclear. The initial line identifies wisdom's locale. Wisdom resides "on the lips" (בְּשִׂפְתֵי, v. 13a) of the discerning. They are the throne on which she dwells and the place from which she manifests her presence. The "senseless" (חֲסַר־לֵב, v. 13b), by contrast, relate to wisdom through a material object and a different part of the body. Whether the "rod" (שֵׁבֶט, v. 13b) refers to a stick or serves as a metaphor for verbal reprimand, this disciplinary instrument is "for the back" (לְגֵו, v. 13b) of the senseless. If the body and the concept of place govern the relationship between the parallel statements, then the lines identify the locale of particular things: wisdom is found on the lips of the discerning, whereas a physical rod or verbal chastisement is found on the back of the senseless.[39] If, however, the saying is another example of "asymmetrical parallelism,"[40] then it forces the reader to fill in the gaps and form two antithetical sayings. Following Knut Heim, these antithetical sayings may be formulated as follows:[41]

a On the lips of the discerning wisdom
is found,
a′ on the lips of the fool folly is found.
b There is no rod for the back of the
discerning,
b′ but a rod for the back of the senseless.

Irrespective of one's reading of v. 13, the first line explores the issue of wisdom and speech (v. 13a), two issues that are also considered in **v. 14**. The initial line profiles the wise through commercial imagery. As custodians of wisdom, they "store knowledge" (יִצְפְּנוּ־דָעַת, v. 14a), collecting it, curating it, and protecting it for personal and communal benefit. The mouth of the wicked, however, stores something else: impending ruin (v. 14b). It is a container of corruption. The verb is implied in the second line. And this entails that the consequence presented in the second may be recast to complete the thought of the first: the wise store knowledge for preservation.

The concept of storage or accumulation is reformulated in **v. 15**. The noun "ruin" (מְחִתָּה, v. 14b; מְחִתַּת, v. 15b) links the aphorism to the preceding

38. Koptak, *Proverbs*, 293.

39. Fox, *Proverbs 10–31*, 518.

40. Mouser, "Filling in the Blank," 137–50; Heim, *Poetic Imagination*, 232.

41. This is an adaptation of Heim's reconstruction in *Poetic Imagination*, 232.

saying. This ruin and the object of accumulation, however, pertain to wealth and poverty. Rather than storing knowledge (v. 14a), the rich store wealth, which offers safety and protection (v. 15a). Wealth forms the walls of a fortified city, but ruin represents the rubble on which the poor reside. Poverty leaves one vulnerable and defenseless, exposed to attacks and open to danger. These parallel statements concerning the value of wealth and the dangers of poverty are clear. It is important to note, however, that they constitute only a piece of a broader discourse within the anthology, which counterbalances the advantages of wealth and the dangers of poverty by addressing matters of wisdom, virtue, and responsibility to the other (Prov 11:4; 18:10–11; 19:1, 17, 22; 23:4–5; 28:6).

Similar to v. 15, economics is the focus of attention in **v. 16**. The contrast between the righteous and the wicked, however, indicates that money is now considered in moral rather than social terms. And the parallel prepositional phrases signal that the way in which the righteous and the wicked use their economic resources is the crux of the contrast. The "wages" (פְּעֻלַּת, v. 16a) of the righteous are "for life" (לְחַיִּים, v. 16a). They bankroll human flourishing and well-being. The "produce" (תְּבוּאַת, v. 16b) of the wicked, by contrast, is "for sin" (לְחַטָּאת, v. 16b); it contributes to the economy of evil and death (cf. Rom 6:23). The relationship between "life" and "sin" may be imprecise. But, like several sayings above, this asymmetry invites a fuller reading of the aphorism: The wages of the righteous, for virtue and life//the produce of the wicked, for sin and death.

While the prepositional phrase "to/for life" (לְחַיִּים, vv. 16a, 17a) links vv. 16 and **17**, the latter saying moves from matters of money to one's receptivity to instruction (cf. v. 8). The aphorism returns to the nuclear metaphor of the path, but it uses this metaphor in a distinctive way. Elsewhere the path is a way of life associated with one's character, orientation, and telos. Here the one who heeds instruction *is* "a path to life" (אֹרַח לְחַיִּים, v. 17a). This individual *is* the way, one who embodies and paves the way to life.[42] The one who rejects or abandons reproof serves as an alternative role model, misguiding others and leading them astray. The aphorism conflates receptivity with an embodied way of life and describes a person as a particular path.

With this holistic vision of the self, **vv. 18–21** narrow their focus to the mouth and matters of speech. The repetition of the noun "lips" (שָׂפָה, vv. 18a, 19b) connects **vv. 18 and 19**. The former reflects on two types of illegitimate speech, one hidden and the other dispersed. The initial line returns to the concept of concealment (v. 18a; cf. vv. 6b, 11b, 12b).[43] Rather than arousing conflict (v. 12a), hatred may be concealed. One who conceals enmity, however, does not cover offenses. He possesses lying lips, for he veils his inward hatred through deceitful speech. This veil is lifted in the second line, which considers one who spreads slander (v. 18b). The manner of speech may differ from the first line, but the purpose is the same. Disseminating malicious words denigrates others, distorts reality, and demonstrates the verbal incompetence of the fool.[44] Verbal (in)competence is explored

42. Murphy, *Proverbs*, 74; Clifford, *Proverbs*, 115; Fox, *Proverbs 10–31*, 520.

43. In view of catchwords as well as the repetition of "hate/hatred" (שִׂנְאָה, vv. 12a, 18a) and "covers/conceals" (תְּכַסֶּה, v. 12b, מְכַסֶּה, v.18a), some read vv. 12–18 as a coherent unit. In general, this unit profiles certain coreferential characters and culminates with a definitive judgment on the wicked/fool (v. 18), who represents one of the principal subjects of vv. 12–17. Meinhold, *Die Sprüche*, 1:173–77; Heim, *Like Grapes of Gold*, 123.

44. Fox, *Proverbs 1–9*, 41.

from a different angle in **v. 19**, which concerns the matter of many words. Excessive speech creates conditions ripe for the activation and perpetuation of personal offences (v. 19a). One who restrains his lips, therefore, is prudent, manifesting the intellectual insight that accompanies verbal caution and reticence.

It is important to note that speech involves more than the lips; ultimately, it flows from the heart. The interconnection between the heart and speech is profiled in **vv. 20–21**. Precious commodities and economic value furnish the motivation in **v. 20**. Here the tongue of the righteous is "choice silver" (כֶּסֶף נִבְחָר, v. 20a); it is pure, unadulterated, and desirable (cf. 8:19). The wellspring of the wicked person's words, however, is shallow and insubstantial. Their heart or mind is trivial and of little value (10:20b). This concern with the value of virtuous speech is developed in **v. 21**. The saying shifts the motivational metaphor from economic worth to physical sustenance and satisfaction. This shift is marked by the verb "nourish" (יִרְעוּ, v. 21a). The root conveys the activities of a shepherd and envisions the "lips" (שִׂפְתֵי, v. 21a) or speech of the righteous as that which feeds, sustains, and even guides a multitude.[45] Those who long for this sort of speech will receive nourishment. Fools who refuse to feed on this speech will wither away. Deprived of this food, they will shrivel in their "senselessness" (חֲסַר־לֵב, v. 21b) and die.

The sequence of aphorisms concerning speech is interrupted by a saying devoted to the blessing of YHWH in **v. 22**. This blessing has to do with wealth. And the saying's theological account of the acquisition of wealth places it in conversation with v. 4. Whereas v. 4b affirmed that diligence "brings riches" (תַּעֲשִׁיר, v. 4b), v. 22a contends that the blessing of YHWH "brings riches" (תַּעֲשִׁיר, v. 22a). Both are true and both must be considered together. Like 10:3, the aphorism conveys a theological conviction that places wealth and work in proper perspective. Work performed and wealth pursued through human striving and self-sufficiency is limited, frustrating, and fleeting (cf. 21:5; 28:20; Eccl 4:7–8; 5:13–16), for it overestimates the power of human planning and activity. The YHWH saying reins in this human centered perspective on work and wealth. It does not question the value of hard work in the pursuit of profit; rather, it broadens one's vision of work and recalibrates one's expectations concerning the acquisition of wealth. YHWH plays a formative role in this process. He lavishes rich benefits on individuals (Prov 10:22a), and his blessing brings such peace and contentment that no amount of human work can add to it (v. 22b).[46]

The motives of wealth (vv. 20, 22) and satisfaction (v. 21) provide an appropriate backdrop for **v. 23** and its consideration of one's affections and desires. What one desires reveals one's character. The aphorism profiles this connection through the moral tastes of the fool and the person of understanding. For the fool, "lewd behavior" (עֲשׂוֹת זִמָּה, v. 23a; cf. Judg 20:6; Ezek 16:27, 43, 58) or shameful activity is a source of joy. Like a favorite sport, it generates laughter and satisfaction. But for the person of understanding, wisdom and the virtuous forms of conduct that flow from it are the objects of delight. They align with and satisfy the moral

45. Brown, "The Didactic Power of Metaphor," 142; Fox, *Proverbs 10–31*, 522.

46. The subject of the second line is unclear. Some take YHWH as the subject and render עֶצֶב as "sorrow" or "trouble" to read, "and he adds no trouble with it" (Toy, *Proverbs*, 212–13; McKane, *Proverbs*, 422; Waltke, *Proverbs: Chapters 1–15*, 473; Longman, *Proverbs*, 239–40). According to this reading, God grants wealth, and this wealth comes without the sorrow or trouble of human labor.

taste buds. The saying profiles the interrelationship between one's character and one's desires. And in so doing, it offers the reader a taste test, a means to check one's moral tastes and character.

Desire and aversion also inform the contrast between the wicked and the righteous in **v. 24** of Prov 10. But the aphorism reorients these matters from present pleasures to future fates. Through language reminiscent of Wisdom's opening speech (1:26), the first line traffics in terror. Far from merely haunting them, what the wicked fears will come upon them (10:24a). The punishment is just and the recompense is certain. This certainty also applies to the fate of the righteous, who receive what they desire (v. 24b). And the certainty of these fates is affirmed by divine agency. The string of passive constructions within the chapter is broken in the second line, where the verb "he will grant" (יִתֵּן, v. 24b) implicitly refers to YHWH (cf. v. 22a).[47] He oversees and guarantees retribution and reward, overcoming the wicked with what they fear and granting the righteous what they desire.

The fate of the wicked and the righteous is accentuated in **v. 25**. Again, in a manner reminiscent of Wisdom's opening rebuke (1:27), the fate of the wicked is described in vivid terms. The image of a whirlwind captures the force and feeling of a devastating storm. This gale sweeps across the land, striking everyone. When the dust settles, the wicked are no more (10:25a). Like chaff, they are blown away. The righteous, by contrast, remain, for they are an "enduring foundation" (יְסוֹד עוֹלָם, v. 25b). Their moral character offers stability and safety in the storms of life. And their moral infrastructure allows them to weather the whirlwind.

The sequence of antithetical sayings devoted to the righteous and the wicked is disrupted in **v. 26**, which reflects on the pain caused by the sluggard. This pain is conveyed through a threefold comparison. The first two analogies involve irritants to the body: the sharp burn of an acidic drink on decaying teeth and the sting of smoke in the eyes (v. 26a). The third concerns the social and personal pain the sluggard wreaks on those who send him (v. 26b). The aphorism seems to assume the sluggard serves as a messenger, one who represents the words, wishes, and character of the one who sent him. As an unreliable emissary, the sluggard inflicts social and personal agony on a patron. Shame, economic losses, broken relationships, and botched business deals are among some of the scenarios envisioned by the saying, which offers an implicit warning to both messengers and the masters who send them.[48]

The fate of the wicked reemerges in **v. 27**. Rather than considering this fate through the concept of safety or stability (v. 25), the saying explores one's future through the motive of longevity and life. The initial line links the promises of the prologue with the fear of YHWH. According to the discourses within the prologue, the fear of YHWH is the beginning of wisdom (1:7; 9:10); and Wisdom grants her devotee's years of life (9:11). It is not surprising, then, that the saying depicts the fear of YHWH as a disposition, relationship, and state of being that increases days. This coveted blessing, however, is not experienced by the wicked. They suffer the curse of premature death (10:27b). The sharp antithesis appeals to the natural desire for a full, long life and accentuates the surpassing value of the fear of YHWH.

47. While some revocalize the verb as a passive form and eliminate divine agency from the line, the change is unnecessary.

48. For discussion of messengers in the ancient world, see A. D. Crown, "Messengers and Scribes: The ספר and מלאך in the Old Testament," *VT* 24 (1974): 366–70; Samuel A. Meier, *The Messenger in the Ancient Semitic World*, HSM 45 (Atlanta: Scholars Press, 1988), 21–22, 158–59.

In light of the fates of the fearer of YHWH and the wicked, **v. 28** explores the way in which the aspirations of the righteous and the wicked relate to their end. The saying serves as an appropriate counterpart to v. 24. By virtue of their character, the righteous possess a sure hope, an expectation that is a lifelong source of joy (vv. 24b; 28a).[49] The hope of the wicked, on the other hand, is dashed. The wicked not only experience hope unfulfilled, but they receive that which they feared (vv. 24a, 28b). This prospect of joy and hope fulfilled provides a powerful motivation for righteousness.

To the previous reflections on the blessing of YHWH (v. 22a) and the fear of YHWH (v. 27a), **v. 29** offers a word on "the way of YHWH" (דֶּרֶךְ יְהוָה, v. 29a). While the expression does not occur elsewhere in Proverbs, it corresponds with the Deuteronomic phrase "his [YHWH's] ways" (e.g., Deut 8:6; 10:12; 11:22; 28:9; cf. 2 Sam 22:22; Hos 14:9; Jer 5:4–5).[50] This entails that, like the way of wisdom, the way of YHWH is the prescribed pattern for human conduct, a way of life that mirrors God's character. For the innocent or "upright" (תֹּם, Prov 10:29a; cf. v. 9a), this way is a stronghold. Similar to the wealth of the rich (v. 15a), it offers safety and security. But those who commit iniquity experience ruin (v. 29b; cf. vv. 14b, 15b). The way of YHWH could be the instrument of this ruin; but in light of the variant repetition of the line in 21:15, it seems that the iniquity committed by evildoers is their ruin.[51] The stronghold in 10:29a, in this respect, is for the upright; but rubble and ruin are for those who commit iniquity.[52]

This vision of safety and security is reinforced in **v. 30**. In fact, the saying provides the natural implication of v. 29.[53] If the way of YHWH is a stronghold, then the righteous will never be shaken (v. 30a). Their enduring foundation remains (v. 25b; cf. 12:3; Ps 112:6). As residents of ruin, by contrast, the wicked will not dwell in the land. The term "land" (אֶרֶץ, Prov 10:30b) is polysemous; it could refer to the promised land or to the entire earth. Irrespective of the precise geographical locale, the second line strikes a chord of horror. The wicked will be severed from a community, whether the community of Israel or the community of the living, and exiled to live in an isolated place.

The final two aphorisms within the chapter form a proverbial pair (**vv. 31–32**). This pair is linked by the theme of speech, the terms "mouth" (פִּי, vv. 31a, 32b), "righteous" (צַדִּיק, vv. 31a, 32a), and "perverse/perversity" (תַּהְפֻּכוֹת, vv. 31b, 32b), as well as an identical syntactical structure. To varying degrees, both sayings draw from the metaphorical domain of food. The first aphorism envisions the mouth of the righteous as a healthy tree that produces sweet fruit (v. 31a; cf. 12:14; 13:2; 18:20). The verb "produces" (יָנוּב, 10:31a) conveys the sense of thriving, prospering, and sprouting. As a thriving tree, the mouth of the righteous yields the mouthwatering fruit of wisdom (v. 31a), which nourishes the speaker and satisfies those who consume it. As a diseased tree, the tongue of the wicked is ripe for destruction (v. 31b). The asymmetrical or imprecise parallelism between the lines generates food for further thought. The image of a tree is foregrounded in the second line. But the accompanying concept of fruit is supplied by

49. Yoder, *Proverbs*, 128.

50. Since the expression "the way of YHWH" does not occur elsewhere in the anthology and the phrase "upright of way" appears in 13:6, some read the first line as: "A stronghold for the upright of way is YHWH" (Toy, *Proverbs*, 217; McKane, *Proverbs*, 427). This reading revocalizes לַתֹּם as לְתָם, following 13:6. While this reading is possible, as Delitzsch notes, we would expect the construction מָעוֹז יְהוָה לְתַם דֶּרֶךְ, not מָעוֹז לַתֹּם דֶּרֶךְ יְהוָה (Delitzsch, "Proverbs of Solomon," 6:154 [1:227]).

51. Heim, *Poetic Imagination*, 247–48.

52. Heim, *Poetic Imagination*, 248–49.

53. Heim, *Like Grapes of Gold*, 132; Fox, *Proverbs 10–31*, 528.

the first. When read together, it appears the mouth of the righteous produces wisdom and flourishes, while the tongue of the perverse produces folly and is chopped down. It is a diseased tree that yields unsavory fruit and is destined for the fire.

The lexical and syntactical links between vv. 31–32 intimate that the metaphor of food seasons **v. 32**. Whereas v. 31 focused on the health and produce of speech, v. 32 emphasizes its taste. According to the first line, the lips of the righteous "know what is pleasing" (יֵדְעוּן רָצוֹן, v. 32a).[54] As a synecdoche for the whole person, these lips possess the moral capacity and the situational perception to taste or discern what is fitting and favorable. The mouth of the wicked, however, has different tastes; it knows or discerns perversity (v. 32b). In a chapter filled with aphorisms devoted to speech (vv. 6, 8, 10, 11, 13, 14, 18, 19, 20, 21, 31, 32), the final two sayings provide an appropriate conclusion. They underscore the value of virtuous speech through rich metaphors and savory images that allow the reader to taste and to see its goodness.

54. In light of the fact that knowing is attributed to "lips," which is rather odd, some understand the verb to denote "flow" or "pour forth" (LXX; Mitchell Dahood, *Proverbs and Northwest Semitic Philology* [Rome: Pontifical Biblical Institute, 1963], 20–21), while others emend the verb to read "pour out, express" (יבעון; Toy, *Proverbs*, 219; Fox, *Proverbs 10–31*, 529–30). If "lips" serve as a synecdoche, however, the attribution of knowledge to the whole person makes good sense.

CHAPTER 17

Proverbs 11:1–31

B. Wisdom, Character, and Consequences: *The Regulations of the Moral Economy*

Main Idea of the Passage

These sayings map the interconnection between character, actions, and consequences through the metaphorical concepts of MORAL ACCOUNTING and MORAL STRENGTH in order to structure one's moral reasoning and motivate the virtuous life.[1]

Literary Context[2]

The formation of one's character, worldview, and moral reasoning through the promotion of moral prototypes and the presentation of various actions defines, in large part, the vision and agenda of Prov 10–29. Proverbs 10 set the tone for this program. The aphorisms in Prov 11 further this pedagogical plan. Similar to ch. 10, antithetical sayings predominate, and the righteous and the wicked figure prominently in the chapter's gradual construction of normative character. The pronounced concern with the fates of these characters, however, extends the purview of the collection's vision of the moral order. The attention to the communal implications of one's character and actions situates the consequences of personal behavior in a broader network of relationships (11:9–14). And the conspicuous use of the MORAL ACCOUNTING and

1. For these metaphorical concepts and their contribution to moral reasoning, see Mark Johnson, *Moral Imagination: Implications of Cognitive Science for Ethics* (Chicago: University of Chicago Press, 1993), 40–52; George Lakoff and Mark Johnson, *Philosophy in the Flesh: The Embodied Mind and Its Challenge to Western Thought* (New York: Basic Books, 1999), 292–301. For the application of these concepts to Proverbs, see Anne W. Stewart, "Wisdom's Imagination," 363–68; idem, *Poetic Ethics*, 181–87.

2. This chapter does not include the Explanation of the Text or the Canonical and Theological Significance sections. See pp. xv and 276n1 for justification. Also, see pp. 424–28 for the Canonical and Theological Significance of Prov 10–15.

MORAL STRENGTH metaphors to conceptualize the fates of character types contributes to the pedagogical and motivational repertoire of the central collections. Whereas the aphorisms in ch. 10 operated under a variety of metaphorical concepts to motivate the moral life, the majority of sayings in ch. 11 are governed by the conceptual system of a regulated moral market in which virtue endows one with the power to both survive and thrive. The MORAL ACCOUNTING and MORAL STRENGTH metaphors that structure many of the sayings in ch. 11 orient one to the moral economy of the cosmos and motivate the moral life by conceptualizing the consequences of one's character in terms of financial exchange and physical strength.[3]

The use of these metaphors to organize the relationship between character, actions and consequences clarifies the chapter's contribution to the anthology's developing curriculum and explains many of its features. The opening aphorism, for example, acknowledges YHWH's concern with "fair trade" (v. 1).[4] This theological valuation of economic practices creates a conceptual framework for many of the sayings in the chapter, which redeploy the idea of "fair trade" in the moral economy and in accord with the MORAL ACCOUNTING metaphor (e.g., vv. 4, 17, 18, 19, 21, 24, 25, 26, 27, 28, 29, 31). Moral character and moral acts are construed as transactions in which one receives what one is due.[5]

The MORAL STRENGTH metaphor complements this construal of moral interactions. Together with the righteous, several sayings devoted to the "upright" (יְשָׁרִים) punctuate ch. 11. This designation captures not only one's moral posture but also one's moral strength.[6] The virtue of the upright is portrayed as a power that guides, supports, and delivers the individual, on the one hand, and fortifies the community, on the other (vv. 3, 6, 11; cf. v. 5). The vice of various characters, by contrast, is figured as a power that brings destruction (vv. 3, 5, 6, 9, 11, 17, 27). The destructive force of vice returns on the individual to square moral accounts and confirm the cosmic order. The MORAL ACCOUNTING and MORAL STRENGTH metaphors inform the majority of the sayings in ch. 11. Whereas the aphorisms in ch. 10 focused on the character of the righteous and the wicked through body parts and the theme of speech, the sayings in ch. 11 focus on the effects and fates of the righteous and the wicked through particular metaphorical concepts and expressions from the semantic fields of life, death, and business (vv. 1, 3–11, 15–16, 18–19, 21, 24, 27–28, 31).[7] These concepts and expressions create a prototypical vision of the moral order that forms one's worldview and structures one's moral understanding.

3. Stewart, "Wisdom's Imagination," 363–68.

4. Heim, *Like Grapes of Gold*, 138.

5. Johnson, *Moral Imagination*, 46–47.

6. Stewart, "Wisdom's Imagination," 367. Also see Lakoff and Johnson, *Metaphors We Live By*, 14–21.

7. For these semantic fields and the expressions in chapter 11 that fall under these semantic categories, see Heim, *Like Grapes of Gold*, 136–37, 140.

III. "Forming 'Fearers of YHWH'": The Curriculum of Wisdom and Virtue (10:1–29:27)

III.1 Elementary Wisdom and Virtue (10:1–15:33)

A. The Wise, the Righteous, and YHWH: The Pillars of the Moral World (10:1–32)

➡ **B. Wisdom, Character, and Consequences: The Regulations of the MORAL ECONOMY (11:1–31)**

C. Building Prototypes: Wisdom and the Properties of MORAL CHARACTER (12:1–28)

D. Mapping MORAL AUTHORITY: Wisdom, Discipline, and Desire (13:1–25)

E. From the Moral to the Intellectual: A Montage of Wisdom and Folly (14:1–35)

F. Forming MORAL WHOLENESS: The Homogeneity of Normative Character (15:1–33)

III.2 Intermediate Wisdom and Virtue (16:1–22:16)

III.3 Vocational Wisdom and Virtue (22:17–24:34)

III.4 Advanced Wisdom and Virtue (25:1–29:27)

Translation and Exegetical Outline

(See pages 376–77.)

Structure and Literary Form

As noted above, with the exception of a few aphorisms (vv. 7, 22, 25, 29, 30), antithetical sayings dominate the literary landscape of ch. 11. While the MORAL ACCOUNTING and MORAL STRENGTH metaphors provide a conceptual framework through which to understand the placement of the aphorisms in the chapter, many have detected signs of arrangement that suggest certain sayings may be divided into coherent units. On the microlevel, catchwords, comparable syntax, and common themes appear to unite contiguous sayings. In addition to the familiar contrast between the righteous and the wicked, the repetition of the root ישר ("upright," vv. 3a, 6a; "makes straight," v. 5a), the verbs "delivers" (נצל, vv. 4b, 6a) and "delivered" (חלץ, vv. 8a, 9b) as well as the terms "only" (אַךְ, vv. 23–24) and "blesses/blessing" (בְּרָכָה, vv. 25a, 26b) create proverbial pairs. With the exception of v. 12b, each line in vv. 9–12 opens with the consonant ב, forming a string of aphorisms concerned with the communal implications of one's character. And the themes of generosity and selfishness appear to link vv. 24–26.

On the macrolevel, these smaller units may be viewed as parts within an extensive design. This design may be rather simple. The תּוֹעֵבָה ("abomination") sayings in vv. 1 and 20, for example, may form an envelope around the first unit within the chapter

Proverbs 11:1–31

B. Wisdom, Character, and Consequences: The Regulations of the Moral Economy (11:1–31)

1a	מֹאזְנֵי מִרְמָה תּוֹעֲבַת יְהוָה	Fraudulent scales, an abomination to YHWH;
1b	וְאֶבֶן שְׁלֵמָה רְצוֹנוֹ	but an accurate weight, his delight.
2a	בָּא־זָדוֹן וַיָּבֹא קָלוֹן	Arrogance comes, then shame comes;
2b	וְאֶת־צְנוּעִים חָכְמָה	but with the humble, wisdom.
3a	תֻּמַּת יְשָׁרִים תַּנְחֵם	The integrity of the upright guides them;
3b	וְסֶלֶף בּוֹגְדִים יְשָׁדֵּם	but the perversity of the treacherous destroys them.
4a	לֹא־יוֹעִיל הוֹן בְּיוֹם עֶבְרָה	Wealth is no benefit on the day of wrath;
4b	וּצְדָקָה תַּצִּיל מִמָּוֶת	but righteousness delivers from death.
5a	צִדְקַת תָּמִים תְּיַשֵּׁר דַּרְכּוֹ	The righteousness of the blameless makes his way straight;
5b	וּבְרִשְׁעָתוֹ יִפֹּל רָשָׁע	but the wicked falls through his wickedness.
6a	צִדְקַת יְשָׁרִים תַּצִּילֵם	The righteousness of the upright delivers them;
6b	וּבְהַוַּת בֹּגְדִים יִלָּכֵדוּ	but the treacherous are caught by desire.
7a	בְּמוֹת אָדָם רָשָׁע תֹּאבַד תִּקְוָה	When a wicked person dies, hope perishes;
7b	וְתוֹחֶלֶת אוֹנִים אָבָדָה	and the expectation of power perishes.
8a	צַדִּיק מִצָּרָה נֶחֱלָץ	The righteous is delivered from trouble;
8b	וַיָּבֹא רָשָׁע תַּחְתָּיו	and the wicked takes his place.
9a	בְּפֶה חָנֵף יַשְׁחִת רֵעֵהוּ	With the mouth the impious destroys his neighbor;
9b	וּבְדַעַת צַדִּיקִים יֵחָלֵצוּ	but through knowledge the righteous are delivered.
10a	בְּטוּב צַדִּיקִים תַּעֲלֹץ קִרְיָה	When the righteous prosper, a city rejoices;
10b	וּבַאֲבֹד רְשָׁעִים רִנָּה	and when the wicked perish, jubilation.
11a	בְּבִרְכַּת יְשָׁרִים תָּרוּם קָרֶת	By the blessing of the upright a city is exalted;
11b	וּבְפִי רְשָׁעִים תֵּהָרֵס	but by the mouth of the wicked it is ruined.
12a	בָּז־לְרֵעֵהוּ חֲסַר־לֵב	The senseless despises his neighbor;
12b	וְאִישׁ תְּבוּנוֹת יַחֲרִישׁ	but a discerning person keeps silent.
13a	הוֹלֵךְ רָכִיל מְגַלֶּה־סּוֹד	A slanderer reveals secrets;
13b	וְנֶאֱמַן־רוּחַ מְכַסֶּה דָבָר	but a reliable spirit covers a matter.
14a	בְּאֵין תַּחְבֻּלוֹת יִפָּל־עָם	Without guidance, a people fall;
14b	וּתְשׁוּעָה בְּרֹב יוֹעֵץ	but in a multitude of counselors, victory.
15a	רַע־יֵרוֹעַ כִּי־עָרַב זָר	One will be harmed severely when one goes surety for a stranger;
15b	וְשֹׂנֵא תֹקְעִים בּוֹטֵחַ	but one who hates agreements is secure.
16a	אֵשֶׁת־חֵן תִּתְמֹךְ כָּבוֹד	A gracious woman grasps honor;
16b	וְעָרִיצִים יִתְמְכוּ־עֹשֶׁר	but violent men grasp wealth.

17a	גֹּמֵל נַפְשׁוֹ אִישׁ חָסֶד	A merciful person benefits himself;
17b	וְעֹכֵר שְׁאֵרוֹ אַכְזָרִי	but the cruel harms himself.
18a	רָשָׁע עֹשֶׂה פְעֻלַּת־שָׁקֶר	The wicked makes a deceitful wage;
18b	וְזֹרֵעַ צְדָקָה שֶׂכֶר אֱמֶת	but one who sows righteousness, a true reward.
19a	כֵּן־צְדָקָה לְחַיִּים	So righteousness [heads] to life;
19b	וּמְרַדֵּף רָעָה לְמוֹתוֹ	and one who pursues evil, to death.
20a	תּוֹעֲבַת יְהוָה עִקְּשֵׁי־לֵב	An abomination to YHWH, those crooked of heart;
20b	וּרְצוֹנוֹ תְּמִימֵי דָרֶךְ	but his delight, those whose way is blameless.
21a	יָד לְיָד לֹא־יִנָּקֶה רָּע	Be assured, the evil will not go unpunished;
21b	וְזֶרַע צַדִּיקִים נִמְלָט	but the descendants of the righteous will escape.
22a	נֶזֶם זָהָב בְּאַף חֲזִיר	A gold ring in a pig's snout—
22b	אִשָּׁה יָפָה וְסָרַת טָעַם	a beautiful woman who lacks discretion.
23a	תַּאֲוַת צַדִּיקִים אַךְ־טוֹב	The desire of the righteous, only good;
23b	תִּקְוַת רְשָׁעִים עֶבְרָה	the hope of the wicked, wrath.
24a	יֵשׁ מְפַזֵּר וְנוֹסָף עוֹד	There is this: one who gives freely and gets more;
24b	וְחוֹשֵׂךְ מִיֹּשֶׁר אַךְ־לְמַחְסוֹר	and one who withholds what is right, only to lack.
25a	נֶפֶשׁ־בְּרָכָה תְדֻשָּׁן	One who blesses will be satisfied;
25b	וּמַרְוֶה גַּם־הוּא יוֹרֶא	and one who refreshes will himself be refreshed.
26a	מֹנֵעַ בָּר יִקְּבֻהוּ לְאוֹם	One who withholds grain—people will curse him;
26b	וּבְרָכָה לְרֹאשׁ מַשְׁבִּיר	but blessing for the head of one who sells it.
27a	שֹׁחֵר טוֹב יְבַקֵּשׁ רָצוֹן	One who diligently seeks good seeks favor;
27b	וְדֹרֵשׁ רָעָה תְבוֹאֶנּוּ	but one who seeks evil, it will come upon him.
28a	בּוֹטֵחַ בְּעָשְׁרוֹ הוּא יִפֹּל	One who trusts in his wealth—he will fall;
28b	וְכֶעָלֶה צַדִּיקִים יִפְרָחוּ	but the righteous will sprout like foliage.
29a	עוֹכֵר בֵּיתוֹ יִנְחַל־רוּחַ	One who troubles his house will inherit wind;
29b	וְעֶבֶד אֱוִיל לַחֲכַם־לֵב	and a fool will be a servant to the wise of heart.
30a	פְּרִי־צַדִּיק עֵץ חַיִּים	The fruit of the righteous, a tree of life;
30b	וְלֹקֵחַ נְפָשׁוֹת חָכָם	and one who takes lives is wise.
31a	הֵן צַדִּיק בָּאָרֶץ יְשֻׁלָּם	If the righteous is repaid on the earth,
31b	אַף כִּי־רָשָׁע וְחוֹטֵא	how much more the wicked and the sinner!

or mark the introduction to two general sections within the collection of aphorisms.[8] Alternatively, the design may be more intricate. The attention to the personal and communal consequences of one's character, matters of speech, wealth, women, and the paradoxical conditions of life among particular sayings may suggest that the aphorisms are organized into several larger units.[9] Whether or not the aphorisms evince deliberate arrangement into these larger units, these structural proposals provide fertile plots in which to till, harvest, taste, and see the meaning, depth, and versatility of the individual sayings within the chapter.

8. Garrett, *Proverbs*, 124; Koptak, *Proverbs*, 316.

9. In light of these thematic features and other formal considerations, some divide the aphorisms into larger units. Heim, for example, argues that the sayings are arranged into three larger sections (vv. 1 + 2–14, vv. 15–21, vv. 22–31), whereas Waltke perceives five units, with v. 9 serving as a janus between the first two sections (vv. 1–8, v. 9, vv. 10–15, vv. 16–22, vv. 23–27, vv. 28–31). Heim, *Like Grapes of Gold*, 135–46; Waltke, *Proverbs: Chapters 1–15*, 481, 489–91, 499, 505, 511; cf. Meinhold, *Die Sprüche*, 1:185–202; Whybray, *The Composition of the Book of Proverbs*, 96–97.

Proverbs 12:1–28

CHAPTER 18

C. Building Prototypes: *Wisdom and the Properties of Moral Character*

Main Idea of the Passage

These sayings privilege the concept of MORAL ESSENCE to illuminate the quintessential features of prototypical characters and, in so doing, to help one see the world, think about the world, and be-in-the-world in accord with wisdom and virtue.

Literary Context[1]

Characters are critical to the pedagogy of the central collections. The individual aphorisms contain conventional characters. These characters exhibit particular (im)moral properties. These properties clarify the general contours and essential traits of moral prototypes. And these moral prototypes structure the way in which one sees the world, thinks about the world, and lives within the world.[2] Like the sayings that populate the central collections of Proverbs, the aphorisms in ch. 12 contribute to the anthology's construction of moral categories and configuration of moral prototypes. But they contribute to this project in a particular way. The sayings privilege the concept of MORAL ESSENCE, orienting one to the inherent properties and central traits of particular prototypes.[3] Whereas the aphorisms in ch. 10 seduced the reader through their preoccupation with the anthology's moral exemplar and the sayings in ch. 11 conceptualized the fates of certain figures through the MORAL ACCOUNTING and MORAL STRENGTH metaphors, the materials in ch. 12 construe

1. This chapter does not include the Canonical and Theological Significance section. See pp. xv and 276n1 for justification. Also, see pp. 424–28 for the Canonical and Theological Significance of Prov 10–15.

2. Josef Stern, *Metaphor in Context* (Cambridge: MIT Press, 2000), 281–82.

3. For discussion of the MORAL ESSENCE metaphor, see Lakoff and Johnson, *Philosophy in the Flesh*, 306–7.

characters as containers with moral properties that define their essence. This concern with the essence of moral prototypes complements the interests and emphases of chs. 10–11. And the concern with moral essence plays a formative role in the developing curriculum of the central collections. Many of the sayings in ch. 12 identify the core characteristics of moral prototypes (12:1, 5, 8, 10, 11, 12, 14, 15, 16, 17, 18, 20, 21, 23). In so doing, they stabilize the inherent traits of these prototypical figures, providing the reader with a conceptual framework within which to recognize family resemblances among character types and to understand the "fuzzy boundaries" of moral categories that emerge in the subsequent collections.[4]

While the concept of moral essence informs many of the aphorisms in ch. 12, it is important to note that these sayings bear a close resemblance with the materials in the previous chapters as well as the subsequent collections. Similar to chs. 10 and 11, antithetical sayings saturate the literary landscape. The righteous and the wicked represent the most prominent moral prototypes. Many sayings construe character through the metaphors of MORAL ACCOUNTING (12:2, 11a, 14, 21a, 22, 24, 28; cf. 10:2, 16; 11:18, 19, 31) and MORAL STRENGTH (12:3, 6, 7, 13, 19; cf. 10:25, 30; 11:6, 9). Familiar themes mark the chapter's evaluation of character, such as words, work, and ways. And the aphorisms traffic in the motivational drives of well-being, honor, safety, and satiety. In addition to these similarities with chs. 10 and 11, a number of sayings in ch. 12 are reiterated and recast as variant repetitions elsewhere in the central collections.[5] These variant repetitions illuminate the organic unity among the materials in Prov 10–29; and the prevalence of variants in ch. 12 is indicative of

4. Lakoff and Johnson, *Metaphors We Live By*, 71–72, 122–25; Stewart, "Wisdom's Imagination," 359–63.

5. These variant repetitions include **12:11**//28:19; **12:13**//29:6; **12:14a**//13:2a//18:20a; **12:15a**//16:2//21:2//14:12//16:25; **12:16b**//12:23a; **12:23**//13:16//15:2//15:14. For a discussion of each variant, see Heim, *Poetic Imagination*, 288–328.

the didactic development within the central collections. These variant repetitions profile different aspects of moral prototypes, each of which are repeated, modified, and extended in relation to different phenomena within different cola in different contexts within the unfolding curriculum of the central collections.

Translation and Exegetical Outline

(See pages XX.)

Structure and Literary Form

The didactic rhythm and pedagogical stability created by the profusion of antithetical sayings in Prov 10–11 continues in ch. 12. But antithesis does not mark all of the aphorisms; there are a few poetic scratches on the rhetorical record (12:9, 14, 28). For some commentators, these scratches signal the general structure of the unit. The placement of nonantithetical sayings in vv. 14 and 28, for example, may indicate that the chapter consists of two equal subunits (vv. 1–14; 15–28).[6] Each unit opens with an "educational aphorism" (12:1, 15; cf. 10:1; 13:1); each closes with a nonantithetical saying (vv. 14, 28); and each contains several smaller units.[7] The nature and boundaries of these smaller units, however, are unclear. The sequence of certain sayings may evince a progression of thought (vv. 1–3, vv. 5–7).[8] Others may be linked by common imagery (vv. 9–11) or a particular theme (vv. 8–13; 13–23).[9] And still others may be distinguished by catchwords or repeated expressions (vv. 2–3, 9–11, 15–16, 18–19, 20–21).[10] While some have detected complex structural units among the aphorisms,[11] at minimum the chapter consists of several proverbial pairs (vv. 15–16, 18–19, 20–21); it includes a series of sayings pertaining to speech (vv. 13–20, 22–23); and it evinces a particular interest in the righteous, the wicked, and their co-referential counterparts.

6. For this proposal, see Waltke, *Proverbs: Chapters 1–15*, 518–19. Cf. Whybray, *The Composition of the Book of Proverbs*, 98; Koptak, *Proverbs*, 336–37n1.

7. Waltke, *Proverbs: Chapters 1–15*, 518–19. Waltke also observes that the second subunit is framed by the term "way" (דֶּרֶךְ, vv. 15a, 28b), which serves as a formal *inclusio* (*Proverbs: Chapters 1–15*, 532).

8. Meinhold, *Die Sprüche*, 1:203–5; Whybray, *The Composition of the Book of Proverbs*, 98; Heim, *Like Grapes of Gold*, 147; Waltke, *Proverbs: Chapters 1–15*, 519, 521; Yoder, *Proverbs*, 141.

9. Meinhold, *Die Sprüche*, 1:209; Whybray, *The Composition of the Book of Proverbs*, 98; Murphy, *Proverbs*, 88; Van Leeuwen, "The Book of Proverbs," *NIB* 5:125; Heim, *Like Grapes of Gold*, 150, 153, 158; Waltke, *Proverbs: Chapters 1–15*, 519, 532; Yoder, *Proverbs*, 141; Koptak, *Proverbs*, 337; Fox, *Proverbs 10–31*, 555; Sæbø, *Sprüche*, 191.

10. Whybray, *The Composition of the Book of Proverbs*, 98; Murphy, *Proverbs*, 89.

11. Garrett, *Proverbs*, 128–33; Heim, *Like Grapes of Gold*, 153–57.

Proverbs 12:1–28

1a	אֹהֵב מוּסָר אֹהֵב דָּעַת	One who loves discipline loves knowledge;	C. Building Prototypes: Wisdom and the Properties of Moral Character (12:1–28)
1b	וְשֹׂנֵא תוֹכַחַת בָּעַר	but one who hates reproof is a brute.	
2a	טוֹב יָפִיק רָצוֹן מֵיְהוָה	A good man receives favor from YHWH;	
2b	וְאִישׁ מְזִמּוֹת יַרְשִׁיעַ	but the schemer he condemns.	
3a	לֹא־יִכּוֹן אָדָם בְּרֶשַׁע	No one is established through wickedness;	
3b	וְשֹׁרֶשׁ צַדִּיקִים בַּל־יִמּוֹט	but the root of the righteous will never totter.	
4a	אֵשֶׁת־חַיִל עֲטֶרֶת בַּעְלָהּ	A virtuous woman, the crown of her husband;	
4b	וּכְרָקָב בְּעַצְמוֹתָיו מְבִישָׁה	but a disgraceful one, like rot in his bones.	
5a	מַחְשְׁבוֹת צַדִּיקִים מִשְׁפָּט	The plans of the righteous, just;	
5b	תַּחְבֻּלוֹת רְשָׁעִים מִרְמָה	the guidance of the wicked, deceptive.	
6a	דִּבְרֵי רְשָׁעִים אֱרָב־דָּם	The words of the wicked, a murderous ambush;	
6b	וּפִי יְשָׁרִים יַצִּילֵם	but the mouth of the upright delivers them.	
7a	הָפוֹךְ רְשָׁעִים וְאֵינָם	Overturn the wicked and they are no more;	
7b	וּבֵית צַדִּיקִים יַעֲמֹד	but the house of the righteous stands.	
8a	לְפִי־שִׂכְלוֹ יְהֻלַּל־אִישׁ	A person is praised according to his intelligence;	
8b	וְנַעֲוֵה־לֵב יִהְיֶה לָבוּז	but the perverse of heart will be despised.	
9a	טוֹב נִקְלֶה וְעֶבֶד לוֹ	Better the lightly regarded who has a servant,	
9b	מִמְּתַכַּבֵּד וַחֲסַר־לָחֶם	than one who honors himself and lacks food.	
10a	יוֹדֵעַ צַדִּיק נֶפֶשׁ בְּהֶמְתּוֹ	The righteous knows the desire of his livestock;	
10b	וְרַחֲמֵי רְשָׁעִים אַכְזָרִי	but the compassion of the wicked is cruel.	
11a	עֹבֵד אַדְמָתוֹ יִשְׂבַּע־לָחֶם	One who works his land will be satisfied with food;	
11b	וּמְרַדֵּף רֵיקִים חֲסַר־לֵב	but one who pursues worthless things lacks sense.	
12a	חָמַד רָשָׁע מְצוֹד רָעִים	The wicked desires a snare for evil things;	
12b	וְשֹׁרֶשׁ צַדִּיקִים יִתֵּן	but the root of the righteous gives forth.	
13a	בְּפֶשַׁע שְׂפָתַיִם מוֹקֵשׁ רָע	In the transgression of lips, an evil snare;	
13b	וַיֵּצֵא מִצָּרָה צַדִּיק	but the righteous escapes from trouble.	
14a	מִפְּרִי פִי־אִישׁ יִשְׂבַּע־טוֹב	From the fruit of his mouth, one is satisfied with good things,	
14b	וּגְמוּל יְדֵי־אָדָם יָשִׁיב לוֹ	and the work of one's hands returns to him.	

15a	דֶּרֶךְ אֱוִיל יָשָׁר בְּעֵינָיו	A fool's way, upright in his eyes;
15b	וְשֹׁמֵעַ לְעֵצָה חָכָם	but one who listens to counsel is wise.
16a	אֱוִיל בַּיּוֹם יִוָּדַע כַּעְסוֹ	A fool makes known his anger at once;
16b	וְכֹסֶה קָלוֹן עָרוּם	but the shrewd conceals an insult.
17a	יָפִיחַ אֱמוּנָה יַגִּיד צֶדֶק	A faithful witness declares what is right;
17b	וְעֵד שְׁקָרִים מִרְמָה	but a lying witness, deceit.
18a	יֵשׁ בּוֹטֶה כְּמַדְקְרוֹת חָרֶב	There is this: one who chatters like a sword's stabs;
18b	וּלְשׁוֹן חֲכָמִים מַרְפֵּא	but the tongue of the wise, healing.
19a	שְׂפַת־אֱמֶת תִּכּוֹן לָעַד	Truthful lips endure forever;
19b	וְעַד־אַרְגִּיעָה לְשׁוֹן שָׁקֶר	but a lying tongue is only for a moment.
20a	מִרְמָה בְּלֶב־חֹרְשֵׁי רָע	Deceit is in the heart of those who devise evil;
20b	וּלְיֹעֲצֵי שָׁלוֹם שִׂמְחָה	but those who advise peace have joy.
21a	לֹא־יְאֻנֶּה לַצַּדִּיק כָּל־אָוֶן	No calamity will befall the righteous;
21b	וּרְשָׁעִים מָלְאוּ רָע	but the wicked are filled with evil.
22a	תּוֹעֲבַת יְהוָה שִׂפְתֵי־שָׁקֶר	An abomination to YHWH, lying lips;
22b	וְעֹשֵׂי אֱמוּנָה רְצוֹנוֹ	but one who acts honestly, his delight.
23a	אָדָם עָרוּם כֹּסֶה דָּעַת	A shrewd person covers knowledge;
23b	וְלֵב כְּסִילִים יִקְרָא אִוֶּלֶת	but the heart of fools proclaims folly.
24a	יַד־חָרוּצִים תִּמְשׁוֹל	The hand of the diligent rules;
24b	וּרְמִיָּה תִּהְיֶה לָמַס	but the slack will be put to forced labor.
25a	דְּאָגָה בְלֶב־אִישׁ יַשְׁחֶנָּה	Anxiety in a person's heart weighs it down;
25b	וְדָבָר טוֹב יְשַׂמְּחֶנָּה	but a good word makes it merry.
26a	יָתֵר מֵרֵעֵהוּ צַדִּיק	The righteous shows the way to his companion;
26b	וְדֶרֶךְ רְשָׁעִים תַּתְעֵם	but the way of the wicked leads them astray.
27a	לֹא־יַחֲרֹךְ רְמִיָּה צֵידוֹ	A slacker will not roast his game;
27b	וְהוֹן־אָדָם יָקָר חָרוּץ	but the precious wealth of a person, diligence.
28a	בְּאֹרַח־צְדָקָה חַיִּים	In the path of righteousness, life;
28b	וְדֶרֶךְ נְתִיבָה אַל־מָוֶת	and along that way, no death.

To these general reflections on the varied design of the chapter, recurring themes and repeated expressions deserve specific comment. As intimated above, the aphorisms focus on several themes, three in particular: words (vv. 6, 13–20, 22–23, 25), work (vv. 11, 14, 24, 27), and ways (vv. 15, 26, 28).[12] Terms related to truth and falsehood (אֱמֶת; אֱמוּנָה; שֶׁקֶר, vv. 17, 19, 22) as well as diligence and negligence (חָרוּץ; וּרְמִיָּה, vv. 24, 27) appear in a few sayings. The expressions YHWH's "favor/delight" (רָצוֹן, vv. 2a, 22b) and "the root of the righteous" (שֹׁרֶשׁ צַדִּיקִים, vv. 3b, 12b) are reiterated; and v. 23a constitutes a variant repetition of v. 16b. The poetic forms within the chapter may be familiar, and the precise structure of the whole may be unclear. But recurring themes and repeated expressions orient one to the types of properties privileged by the aphorisms and the way in which these properties contribute to the chapter's construction of moral prototypes.

Explanation of the Text

The metaphor of MORAL ESSENCE plays a significant role in the conceptualization of character. According to the metaphor, people are containers with (im)moral properties. These properties are developed over time through instruction and habituation. They are manifested through a person's actions. And those actions are indicative of a person's character or moral essence.[13] The metaphor of moral essence structures many of the sayings in Proverbs. In fact, the aphorisms in the central collections depict *developed* characters with essential moral properties. These characters reveal their moral essence through their actions; and their actions betray their moral essence. But actions and appearances can be deceiving. Moral prototypes, like the ideal reader of Proverbs, are malleable.[14] And characters are fluid, possessing both moral and immoral properties. These characters, however, retain a moral essence; that is, they have essential properties that orient one to the core characteristics of the moral prototype. Many of the aphorisms in Prov 12 explore and uncover these inherent traits of moral character, including the first.

The initial saying describes two innate dispositions in order to demonstrate that the object of one's inner affections reveals the essence of one's character (**v. 1**). Whereas the lectures and interludes in Prov 1–9 attempted to inculcate a love for and a receptivity to "discipline" (מוּסָר, 1:8, 22; 6:23; 9:8), 12:1 observes that what one loves determines one's being. The relationship between "loves knowledge" (אֹהֵב דָּעַת, v. 1a) and "is a brute" (בָּעַר, v. 1b) is imprecise. But the components of the parallel lines help one to fill in the gaps. One who loves discipline not only possesses a humble posture that receives correction; this person is also fully human. The one who hates reproof, by contrast, is subhuman, even animal-like, for this person hates both reproof and knowledge.[15] The aphorism is as illogical from a natural perspective as it is consistent

12. Heim, *Like Grapes of Gold*, 150–59; Waltke, *Proverbs: Chapters 1–15*, 518.

13. For discussion of the metaphor, see Lakoff and Johnson, *Philosophy in the Flesh*, 306–7.

14. Lakoff and Johnson, *Metaphors We Live By*, 122–24; Johnson, *Moral Imagination*, 191; Stewart, "Wisdom's Imagination," 362–63. Also see the discussion of the "uncommitted" (פתי) in Characters and Characterization in the introduction, pp. XX.

15. Yoder, *Proverbs*, 141–42.

with the pedagogical vision of the anthology. One must love in order to know;[16] and one must love correction to love knowledge. The objects of one's desires disclose the inherent properties of one's character and the health of one's being.

In addition to internal affections, external evaluation of others contributes to the diagnosis of one's character. Character is clarified and constituted before the face of the other, especially the divine Other. This is the focus of **v. 2**, which describes YHWH's evaluation of the good man and the schemer through the MORAL ACCOUNTING metaphor. While the designation "good man" (טוֹב, v. 2a) is rather vague, in light this figure's association with the righteous (2:20; 14:19), it is not surprising that he receives a fundamental human desire: divine favor, acceptance, and approval (cf. 11:1; 12:22). The "schemer" (אִישׁ מְזִמּוֹת, v. 2b), however, receives divine disapproval; his hidden thoughts incur the public pronouncement of guilt. It is important to note that hidden thoughts or schemes are not inherently evil. In fact, the term used to characterize the schemer is among the virtues that Proverbs seeks to instill in readers (מְזִמָּה; "discretion," 1:4; 3:21; 8:12). When directed by wisdom, schemes are virtuous and valuable. But when they are condemned by YHWH, these hidden thoughts are exposed for what they are: malicious and destructive.

The divine evaluation of the good and the schemer in 12:2 places **v. 3** in a broader theological context.[17] Whereas v. 2 evaluated character through the MORAL ACCOUNTING metaphor, v. 3 assesses character through the MORAL STRENGTH metaphor. The concepts of (im)permanence and (in)stability inform the aphorism. But the images in the respective lines differ. The first employs an architectural image that depicts a life built on wickedness as unstable, insecure, constructed on an uneven, shifting foundation (v. 3a). The second utilizes a common agricultural image that presents the righteous as an unshakeable root, firmly anchored in and nourished by the fertile foundation of the created order (v. 3b; cf. Pss 1:3; 92:13–15[12–14]; 112:6; Prov 10:30; 11:28, 30). Despite the distinctive images, the concept of moral strength unifies the saying, captures the stability of moral character, and motivates the moral life through the expectation of safety.

While **vv. 1–3** may be read in a progressive fashion,[18] each aphorism operates under a different metaphorical concept. The same is true of **v. 4**, which integrates the metaphors of MORAL BEAUTY and MORAL ESSENCE. With language and imagery redolent of the prologue and the concluding acrostic poem (1:9; 4:9; 31:10; cf. Ruth 3:11), the first line describes the glamour, worth, and influence of a "virtuous woman" (אֵשֶׁת־חַיִל, Prov 12:4a). Her moral beauty enhances the public appearance of her husband, bringing favor, stature, and repute to the household. A "disgraceful" wife (מְבִישָׁה, v. 4b), by contrast, erodes a man's internal bodily frame. Far from bestowing public acclamation, she inflicts personal disintegration, infecting her husband with the impurity symptomatic of her moral essence. Like several other sayings, the aphorism indicates that external beauty is deceitful (11:22; 31:30); but the moral beauty of a wife offers domestic health and public honor. The saying may sound strange to our modern ears. But its elevation of character and underlying motivation contribute to the book's discourse on marriage preparation.[19]

16. Esther Lightcap Meek, *Loving to Know: Introducing Covenant Epistemology* (Eugene, OR: Cascade, 2011).

17. Whybray, "Yahweh-Sayings and their Contexts," 153–65.

18. See Heim, *Like Grapes of Gold*, 147–48, who argues that the sayings indicate that the good man (v. 2a) receives discipline (v. 1a) and is righteous (v. 3b).

19. Knut M. Heim, "A Closer Look at the Pig," 26–27; Ansberry, *Be Wise, My Son*, 93–95.

Just as the metaphor of MORAL ESSENCE structured the construal of the disgraceful wife (12:4b), so also it organizes the evaluation of the righteous and the wicked in **v. 5**. Using terms from the semantic field of thoughts and intentions, the saying observes how one's character directs deliberations to certain ends. By virtue of their character, the thoughts or "plans" (מַחְשְׁבוֹת, v. 5a) of the righteous are just. Their moral essence informs their planning, which aligns with the moral order of the cosmos. In the same way, the guidance of the wicked conforms to their character; it is deceptive and misleading. Deceit is among the inherent properties of this moral prototype (v. 5b; cf. vv. 17, 20). And the deception of the wicked is reflected through the use of the term "guidance" (תַּחְבֻּלוֹת, v. 5b). Elsewhere in the book, the term is used in a positive sense (1:5; 11:14; 20:18; 24:6). This is the only instance in which it is used negatively. Guidance may seem good, but its directives and ends are contingent on the essence of one's character.

Together, **vv. 6–7** may develop the thought of v. 5, extending the intentions of the righteous and the wicked through a description of their acts (v. 6) and ultimate fates (v. 7). The acts and fates of these character types, however, are conceptualized through a different metaphor: MORAL STRENGTH. This metaphor is foregrounded in **v. 6**. The words of the wicked are depicted as a powerful force; they are a "murderous ambush" (אֱרָב־דָּם, v. 6a), a deadly trap sprung on unsuspecting victims (cf. 1:8–19). The strong moral posture of the "upright" (יְשָׁרִים, 12:6b), however, evades this verbal assault.[20] Their mouth or words exact their deliverance (v. 6b; cf. 10:2; 11:6, 8, 9). The MORAL STRENGTH metaphor illuminates the posture and power of virtuous character, and it motivates the moral life through the prospect of safety and security. This motivation is reiterated in **12:7**, which reflects on the fate of the righteous and the wicked. The latter are capsized in judgment, powerless to reestablish their fortunes and restore their existence. The "house of the righteous" (בֵּית צַדִּיקִים, v. 7b), however, endures, for its moral structure and firm foundation protect its members and material property from the storms of life (cf. 10:25, 30; 12:3).

Moral character requires strength to survive and thrive within the world in accord with wisdom and virtue. And moral character requires the other to see and to know itself rightly. This is given particular expression in **vv. 8–9**. Whereas v. 2 evaluated particular characters before the face of YHWH, **v. 8** assesses character in relation to the community. This assessment includes both intellectual and moral qualities.[21] "Intelligence" or good sense elicits communal praise and honor (לְפִי־שִׂכְלוֹ, v. 8a). The "perverse of heart" (נַעֲוֵה־לֵב, v. 8b), by contrast, receive social scorn. The piercing eye of the community diagnoses their twisted mind and punishes their perverted character with public shame. The aphorism acknowledges that the essence of one's character is constituted and confirmed in relation to one's community. And moral character is motivated by means of social honor and shame.

Public perception may serve as a useful gauge of one's character, but according to **v. 9**, social honor is not the goal.[22] Like the other better-than sayings in the central collections, the aphorism relativizes the worth of something through a valuational scheme that elevates something far more desirable, even if it is accompanied by something of little value.[23] Fame and subsistence are the focus

20. See Stewart, "Wisdom's Imagination," 366–67, who discusses the relationship between the MORAL STRENGTH metaphor and the metaphor BEING MORAL IS BEING UPRIGHT.

21. Fox, *Proverbs 10–31*, 550.

22. Yoder, *Proverbs*, 143.

23. For discussion of the structure and logic of better-than sayings, see Perry, *Wisdom Literature and the Structure of Proverbs*, 40–44; Fox, *Proverbs 10–31*, 597–98.

of the comparison. While communal praise is good (v. 8a), it remains a relative good. Modesty and low social esteem, when combined with even the most meager resources that sustain life, are far better than self-glorification without sustenance. One may manufacture an honorable self-image, but this reputation is of little value when one lacks the most basic victuals of life. Whether the end of the initial line reads "who has a servant" (עֶבֶד לוֹ, v. 9a), "who works for himself" (עֹבֵד לוֹ), or "who has produce" (עֲבֻר לוֹ), the point is clear.[24] Self-awareness and lowliness with subsistence are better than the façade of self-importance without food.

The repetition of both "food" and "lack(s)" in vv. 9 and 11 (לָחֶם, vv. 9b, 11a; חֲסַר, vv. 9b, 11b), combined with the agricultural backdrop of **vv. 10–11**, may suggest that these sayings form a coherent unit.[25] The concept of MORAL ESSENCE in general and MORAL EMPATHY in particular informs **v. 10**.[26] More than empathizing with and nurturing other people (21:26; 29:7), the righteous is sensitive to the needs and well-being of his livestock. His character is so in touch with the grain of creation that he understands the particularity and needs of his animals.[27] This form of care stands in sharp contrast to the "compassion" (רַחֲמֵי, v. 10b) of the wicked, for the mercy of this character type is considered "cruel" (אַכְזָרִי, v. 10b). The characterization may be an oxymoron,[28] but it captures an essential trait of the wicked: even their empathy is inhumane.

The agrarian setting of v. 10 lingers in **v. 11**, which reflects on the satisfaction and stability afforded by one's field. Both lines depict diligent characters. But their diligence is directed toward different things. One cultivates his land and is satisfied by its bounty; the other chases empty things and remains empty. In light of the fact that the latter "lacks sense" (חֲסַר־לֵב, v. 11b), it is not surprising that he pursues things that lack substance.[29] The objects of his desire and the nature of his pursuit match his moral essence. The imprecise relationship between "will be satisfied with food" (יִשְׂבַּע־לָחֶם, v. 11a) and "lacks sense" (חֲסַר־לֵב, v. 11b) indicates that the lines are unbalanced; and the imprecision invites the reader to complete the parallelism: one who works his land *has good sense and* will be satisfied with food; but one who pursues worthless things lacks sense *and will starve* (cf. 28:19).[30]

Just as the one who lacks sense pursues things that match his moral essence (12:11), so also the character of the wicked matches the object of their desires in **v. 12**. The rendering of the end of the first line is debated. The object of the wicked person's desire may be "the catch of evil people," that is, the prey entangled in the net of the evil.[31] The object could be rendered "a snare for the wicked," that is, something that, in reality and unbeknown to the wicked, is a snare.[32] Or it could be construed as "a snare for evil things"—a trap that captures all they desire. The latter translation makes good sense and provides a suitable parallel to the second line without requiring its emendation. When read together, the aphorism observes that the wicked desire a snare for things that nourish their charac-

24. For these readings, see Waltke, *Proverbs: Chapters 1–15*, 515–16n11 (following the MT); Heim, *Like Grapes of Gold*, 150 (LXX); and Fox, *Proverbs 10–31*, 550–51, respectively.

25. Van Leeuwen, "The Book of Proverbs," *NIB* 5:125; Yoder, *Proverbs* 1:41; cf. Heim, *Like Grapes of Gold*, 150–51.

26. For the MORAL EMPATHY metaphor, see Lakoff and Johnson, *Philosophy in the Flesh*, 309–10.

27. Van Leeuwen, "The Book of Proverbs," *NIB* 5:126.

28. Van Leeuwen, "The Book of Proverbs," *NIB* 5:126; Fox, *Proverbs 10–31*, 552.

29. Longman, *Proverbs*, 274.

30. Fox, *Proverbs 10–31*, 552.

31. Clifford, *Proverbs*, 131.

32. Fox, *Proverbs 10–31*, 553.

ter and satisfy their longings, while the "root of the righteous" (שֹׁרֶשׁ צַדִּיקִים, v. 12b; cf. v. 3) gives forth, nourishing others and satisfying their longings.[33]

The language of trapping, the adjective "evil" (רָעִים, v. 12a; רָע, v. 13a), and the concept of moral essence link **vv. 12 and 13**. But the latter moves from the essence of desire to the essence of discourse and from moral nurturance to moral strength. Character types recede from view in the first line, and the character of speech takes center stage (v. 13a). One's lips are conceptualized as both a conduit and a container. When they transmit verbal transgressions, they set an evil snare. The openness of the line creates space for the snare to trap the speaker, others, or both. Its relationship with the second line, however, indicates that the righteous elude this verbal trap. Their moral strength enables them to escape from trouble and avoid the evil force of verbal offences.

The concern with speech in v. 13 is shared by many of the following sayings. In fact, with the exception of v. 21, **vv. 13–23** deal with the declaration, suppression, and reception of words.[34] Words and work are the focus of attention in **v. 14**. The nonantithetical saying associates one's mouth with one's hands; and it highlights the satisfaction that one receives from both in order to motivate fruitful speech and diligent work (cf. 13:2; 18:20).

Together, **vv. 15 and 16** in ch. 12 consider the moral essence of the "fool" (אֱוִיל, vv. 15a, 16a) by attending to matters of verbal reception and suppression, respectively. With a negative expression used elsewhere in the anthology, v. 15a exposes the deluded self-perception of the fool (cf. 3:7; 16:2; 21:2; 26:5, 12, 16; 28:11; 30:12). His distorted character distorts his vision, for he considers his way of life morally upright. And as the second line suggests, he refuses to see himself and his ways before the face of and through the advice of the other. The "one who listens to counsel" (שֹׁמֵעַ לְעֵצָה, 12:15b), by contrast, is receptive to the words of others. And this receptivity marks the moral posture and essential properties of the wise. The reception of words is a hallmark of the wise. But their reception may also entail their concealment. This motif is explored in **v. 16**. Whereas the fool reveals his moral essence through the "reflex action" of anger,[35] the shrewd covers up an affront, perhaps in the interest of nurturing interpersonal relationships (cf. 11:13; 12:23; 17:9). Whether received or concealed (12:15b, 16b), rejected or released through exasperation (vv. 15a, 16a), one's use of and response to words reveals one's moral essence.

The concept of MORAL ESSENCE and the theme of words continue in **vv. 17–19**, which explore the moral, medicinal, and temporal qualities of speech. According to **v. 17**, the moral quality of one's character determines the moral quality of one's words: "one who breathes out truth" (formal translation) is a faithful witness (יָפִיחַ אֱמוּנָה, v. 17a), while one who traffics in deceit is a fraud (cf. 6:19; 14:5, 25; 19:5, 9). Words convey moral qualities, and moral qualities are presented as words.[36] In addition to

33. The second line reads "but the root of the righteous gives forth." The lack of an explicit object makes the sense of the line unclear. Some argue that the verb may be elliptical for the idiom "to produce fruit" (Clifford, *Proverbs*, 131; cf. Lev 24:6, 20; Ps 1:3). Others emend the verb to איתן and read "but the root of the righteous is secure" (Toy, *Proverbs*, 249–50; Fox, *Proverbs: An Eclectic Edition*, 200). The lack of an object may render the line unclear; but this lack of clarity is an asset, not a liability. It engages the imagination and contributes to Proverbs's pedagogical program.

34. Meinhold, *Die Sprüche*, 1:209; Whybray, *The Composition of the Book of Proverbs*, 98; Murphy, *Proverbs*, 88; Heim, *Like Grapes of Gold*, 153; Waltke, *Proverbs: Chapters 1–15*, 532–33; Yoder, *Proverbs*, 141; Koptak, *Proverbs*, 340; Fox, *Proverbs 10–31*, 555; Sæbø, *Sprüche*, 191.

35. McKane, *Proverbs*, 442.

36. For the metaphorical concept MORAL QUALITIES ARE WORDS, see Nicole L. Tilford, *Sensing World, Sensing Wisdom: The Cognitive Foundation of Biblical Metaphors*, AIL 31 (Atlanta: SBL Press, 2017), 88–89.

their moral quality, **12:18** indicates that words possess a medicinal quality. Their power can be wielded to harm or to heal.[37] And reiterating the term "tongue" (לָשׁוֹן, vv. 18b, 19b), **v. 19** combines the concepts of MORAL ESSENCE and MORAL STRENGTH to illuminate the temporal quality of words. Truthful speech endures because it is strong and stable. A lying tongue, however, is momentary, fleeting, and ephemeral.

While the motif of speech is implicit in **v. 20**, the metaphor of MORAL ESSENCE is explicit. The saying returns to the matter of "deceit" (מִרְמָה, vv. 20a, 5b, 17b). Similar to v. 5, it uses terms from the semantic field of intentions and plans. But rather than describing how one's character directs one's deliberations (v. 5), it explores the way in which these plans reveal the essence and emotional state of one's character. Deceit makes its home in the heart of those who plan evil; it is an essential trait of those who provoke strife (cf. 6:14). Those who advise peace and cultivate communal well-being, by contrast, experience joy. Like 12:1 and 11, the relationship between "deceit" (מִרְמָה, v. 20a) and "joy" (שִׂמְחָה, v. 20b) is imprecise. And like vv. 1 and 11, the asymmetrical parallelism invites the reader to exercise their moral reasoning by filling out the saying: those who harbor deceit and devise evil are *unhappy*, whereas those who are *honest* advise peace and are filled with joy.[38]

On thematic grounds, **v. 21** interrupts the sequences of sayings devoted to speech in order to consider the nature and (in)stability of the righteous and the wicked. But the adjective "evil" (רָע, vv. 20a, 21b) and concept of MORAL ESSENCE link v. 20 to v. 21. By virtue of their moral strength and position in the moral economy, the righteous will not capitulate to trouble or calamity. Their moral character offers safety and well-being. The wicked, by contrast, are not offered such immunity, for their character carries a disease. They are "filled with evil" (מָלְאוּ רָע, v. 21b), contaminated containers brimming with an inherent trait that defines their moral essence.

Similar to v. 2, **v. 22** offers a theological evaluation of character through the emotive language of YHWH's "favor" or "delight" (רָצוֹן, vv. 2a, 22b). And similar to vv. 13–19, it evaluates character with reference to the theme of speech. Lying lips are not only deceitful and momentary (vv. 17b, 19b); they also evoke divine disgust. But one who deals honestly in word and deed enjoys YHWH's acceptance and pleasure.

The sequence of sayings concerned with words concludes in **v. 23**. While the initial line is a variant repetition of v. 16b, its distinctive elements and relationship with the adjacent line provide a fresh angle on the concealment of speech. The shrewd do more than swallow their pride by concealing an insult (v. 16b);[39] in modesty and humility, they cover knowledge so as to not trumpet their wisdom (v. 23a); and with perception, they discern the appropriate time and context within which to reveal their knowledge (v. 23a; cf. 13:16; 14:8, 15).[40] The fool, however, does not possess such modesty or discretion. Rather, his unrestrained heart advertises the essence of his character (v. 23b; cf. 13:16; 15:2, 14).

Whereas the dimensions and entailments of

37. For the use of the יֵשׁ of reflection to introduce the opposing pair, see Agustinus Gianto, "On יֵשׁ of Reflection in the Book of Proverbs," in *"When the Morning Stars Sang": Essays in Honor of Choon Leong Seow on the Occasion of his Sixty-Fifth Birthday*, ed. Scott C. Jones and Christine Roy Yoder, BZAW 500 (Berlin: de Gruyter, 2018), 159.

38. Fox, *Proverbs 10–31*, 556–57.

39. Fox, *Proverbs 10–31*, 555.

40. Waltke, *Proverbs: Chapters 1–15*, 539; Yoder, *Proverbs*, 147.

speech dominate **12:13–23**, work (vv. 24, 27) and ways (vv. 26, 28) are the focus of attention in **vv. 24–28**. Similar to 10:4, **v. 24** explores industry and indolence through the character of the "diligent" (חָרוּצִים, v. 24a) and the "slack" (רְמִיָּה, v. 24b). And similar to 10:4, the saying employs a synecdoche to depict diligence as an embodied quality (i.e., יַד; "hand," 12:24a). But in contrast to 10:4, 12:24 traffics in politics rather than economics. The opposite poles of political power reinforce and motivate a characteristic principle of Proverbs's moral vision: hard work. More than generating wealth (10:4), the hand of the diligent "rules" (תִּמְשׁוֹל, 12:24a), enjoying authority, influence, and a measure of independence.[41] And more than suffering poverty, the slack are subjected to "forced labor" (מַס, v. 24b). They are rendered powerless and assigned the burdensome tasks associated with corvée, a form of labor that was often imposed upon ethnic outsiders and those of the lowest social status (Josh 16:10; 2 Sam 20:24; 1 Kgs 9:15–23; cf. Exod 1:11; 1 Kgs 5:13–14). Like wealth and poverty, political authority and social degradation serve as a powerful motivation for diligence in the moral economy of Proverbs.

The physical weight projected by forced labor provides an appropriate backdrop to **12:25**, which reflects on the emotional weight of worry. The aphorism recognizes that anxiety possesses a thing-like quality; it is a load that burdens the heart and overwhelms the mind. This load may be lifted, however, through the power of a good word. And the goodness of this word is enhanced by an elegant sound play between the verbs in the constituent lines: "weighs it down" (יַשְׁחֶנָּה, v. 25a) and "makes it merry" (יְשַׂמְּחֶנָּה, v. 25b).[42]

The health and happiness produced by a good word guide one to an obscure sequence of words in **v. 26**, which appear to address the conventional relationship between one's character and one's way. While the second line is clear, the first is uncertain. The uncertainty may be resolved if the verb in the second line is permitted to shed light on the sense of the first. Whereas the way of the wicked transgresses moral boundaries and leads both themselves and others astray, the righteous person walks in accord with the grain of creation and "shows" (יָתֵר, v. 26a) or directs "his companion" (מֵרֵעֵהוּ, v. 26a) in a fitting way of life.[43] The aphorism reinforces a traditional motif within Proverbs. But rather than simply reflecting on the consequences associated with one's character and one's way, it gives particular attention to the implications of the embodied and verbal direction offered by one's way for others.

Similar to v. 26, uncertainty overshadows the particulars of **v. 27**. On the surface, the aphorism utilizes the metaphor of MORAL ESSENCE to identify an innate trait of the indolent and industrious by

41. Yoder, *Proverbs*, 148.

42. The use of assonance may explain the grammatical inconsistences within the verse, viz., the masculine singular verb "weighs it down" (יַשְׁחֶנָּה, v. 25a) does not correspond with the feminine subject "anxiety" (דְּאָגָה, v. 25a); and the feminine singular pronominal suffixes on the verbs do not agree with their masculine singular antecedent, "a person's heart" (לֶב־אִישׁ, v. 25a). For discussion of these difficulties, see Waltke, *Proverbs: Chapters 1–15*, 518n33. For an emendation of the MT, see Fox, *Proverbs 10–31*, 558.

43. These renderings interpret יָתֵר as the *hiphil* of תור ("to make explore, to show the way") and מֵרֵעֵהוּ as the noun מרע with a pronominal suffix ("his companion," cf. Gen 26:26; Judg 14:20; 15:6; Prov 19:7). While others read the former as either the *hophal* of נתר ("delivered") or a noun from the root יתר ("have an advantage") and the latter as either the construction מן + רעה ("from harm, misfortune, evil") or מן + רע ("over his neighbor"), the present interpretation makes good sense and does not require an emendation of the MT. For discussion of these readings, see J. A. Emerton, "A Note on Proverbs 12:26," *ZAW* 76 (1964): 191–93; Meinhold, *Die Sprüche*, 1:213; Murphy, *Proverbs*, 88; Fox, *Proverbs 10–31*, 559. Cf. Clifford, *Proverbs*, 133.

means of a contrast (cf. 10:4; 12:24). But the precise nature of this contrast is unclear. The word order of the second line is difficult. And the verb in the first line is a *hapax legomenon*. But in light of post-biblical Hebrew, the verb in the initial line may be rendered as "roast" (יַחֲרֹךְ, v. 27a).[44] The slack, then, is depicted as one who cannot enjoy the benefits of a basic staple. His character prevents him from completing a simple task and receiving the nourishment necessary for life (cf. Prov 19:24; 26:15). Another type of person, by contrast, enjoys the benefits of virtue for virtue's sake. While the syntax of the second line is awkward, following Kimchi and Delitzsch, it may be read in accord with the sequence of the MT.[45] In this case, the aphorism does not compare the slack and the diligent per se. Rather, it compares the enjoyment or lack thereof experienced by two different characters. One does not experience enjoyment or satisfaction by virtue of his character (v. 27a). The other finds enjoyment in virtue on account of his character (v. 27b). For this person, diligence is a precious commodity; industry itself is the reward.

The final saying combines with vv. 26–27 to form a trinity of uncertain aphorisms. Similar to v. 26, **v. 28** focuses on one's character and one's way. And similar to v. 26, one of the lines is obscure. The initial line is both conventional and clear: life itself is the ethos and air that inhabits the path of righteousness (cf. 10:16; 11:19). It is a way characterized by wholeness and happiness.[46] The life-nurturing and sustaining nature of this way stands in contrast to the mention of death in the second line. The expression "no(t) death" (אַל־מָוֶת, v. 28b), however, is odd, even unprecedented in the Old Testament.[47] And the opening phrase "the way of a path" (דֶרֶךְ נְתִיבָה, v. 28b) is awkward. In light of the parallel between life and death in the respective lines, many assume that the aphorism is an antithetical saying and emend elements in the second line to create a clear contrast with the first.[48] But if, like v. 14, the aphorism represents a nonantithetical saying, then the two words for "way" and the unusual expression "no(t) death" in the second line may extend the thought of the first. From this perspective, life resides in the path of righteousness (v. 28a); and it is along that way that there is no death (v. 28b). While some balk at a nonantithetical reading because it seems to imply the concept of immortality (cf. Dan 12:1–3), this concept is far from clear in the saying. The aphorism, like many of the sayings in the central collections of Proverbs, is pregnant, polysemous, and open.[49] It may create space for the concept of immortality, but principally it seems to project a temporal life and lifestyle that is full and fruitful.

44. Waltke, *Proverbs: Chapters 1–15*, 542–43n120.

45. For the reading of v. 27b reflected in the translation above, see Delitzsch, "Proverbs of Solomon," 6:193–94 (1:267–68). For representative readings of v. 27b that either transpose certain words or render יָקָר ("precious") and חָרוּץ ("diligence") in particular ways, see McKane, *Proverbs*, 444–45; Murphy, *Proverbs*, 88; Heim, *Like Grapes of Gold*, 157–58; Waltke, *Proverbs: Chapters 1–15*, 542–43; Fox, *Proverbs 10–31*, 559.

46. Lyu, *Righteousness*, 56–59.

47. The particle אַל is used to negate volitional forms, not nouns.

48. These elements include a replacement of "path" (נְתִיבָה, v. 28b) for a word that provides an antithesis to "righteousness" (צְדָקָה, v. 28a) and the repointing of "no(t)" (אַל, v. 28b) to "to" (אֶל, v. 28b; cf. Prov 2:18). For possible proposals, see McKane, *Proverbs*, 450–52; Murphy, *Proverbs*, 88; Fox, *Proverbs 10–31*, 560.

49. For discussion of the literary and linguistic openness of many sayings in Prov 10:1–22:16, see Millar, *Genre and Openness*.

CHAPTER 19

Proverbs 13:1–25

D. Mapping MORAL AUTHORITY: *Wisdom, Discipline, and Desire*

Main Idea of the Passage

Utilizing the metaphorical concept of MORAL AUTHORITY, these sayings focus on the dynamics of discipline and the way in which they intersect with emotions and economics in order to sharpen one's moral reasoning and direct one's moral desires.[1]

Literary Context[2]

The opening aphorism of ch. 13 is familiar. It envisions a relationship and assumes a setting that pervades the prologue (e.g., 1:8; 2:1; 3:1; 4:1, 10, 20; 5:1). The expression "a wise son" (בֵּן חָכָם, 13:1a) echoes the entryway into the central collections (10:1b); and the mention of "discipline" (מוּסָר, 13:1a) recalls the initial saying of ch. 12 (12:1a). The aphorism reiterates a familiar theme through a familiar relationship and context. But more than this, the introductory aphorism revives a motif and a metaphorical concept that animates many of the sayings within ch. 13. Similar to v. 1, many of the sayings in the chapter focus on the dynamics of discipline (vv. 1, 10, 13, 14, 18, 20, 24). They attend to the value of receptivity (vv. 1, 10, 13, 18), the parents' obligation to discipline their child (v. 24), the role of one's community in the formation of one's character (v. 20), and the well-being that accompanies those who

1. See also Koptak, *Proverbs*, 354; Yoder, *Proverbs*, 149–50; and Ryan P. O'Dowd, *Proverbs*, The Story of God Biblical Commentary (Grand Rapids: Zondervan Academic, 2017), 216, each of whom note the emphasis on and interrelationship between discipline and desire in ch. 13.

2. This chapter does not include the Explanation of the Text or the Canonical and Theological Significance sections. See pp. xv and 276n1 for justification. Also, see pp. 424–28 for the Canonical and Theological Significance of Proverbs 10–15.

drink from the teaching of the wise (v. 14). Moreover, similar to v. 1, these sayings operate under the metaphorical concept of MORAL AUTHORITY, according to which parents and legitimate authorities have the responsibility of protecting, nurturing, and educating children, while children bear the responsibility of responding to these authorized authorities with respect and obedience.[3] The MORAL AUTHORITY metaphor informs many of the aphorisms in ch. 13. And the metaphor's vision of domestic order aligns with Proverbs's conception of the moral order enshrined in the natural world (30:21–23).[4] The exercise and reception of authentic moral authority, then, not only structures the majority of sayings in the chapter but also mirrors the moral order of creation and "the pedagogical logic of Proverbs."[5]

This concern with moral authority and the dynamics of discipline is not novel (cf. 10:1, 8, 17; 12:1, 15). But the attention devoted to the motif of discipline, its relationship to other prominent themes in the unit, and the moral reasoning required by many of the aphorisms reveal the chapter's contributions to the pedagogical program of the central collections. In addition to discipline, emotions and appetites as well as wealth and poverty occupy many of the sayings in Prov 13 (vv. 2, 4, 5, 7, 8, 9, 11, 13, 18, 19, 22, 23, 24, 25). These themes are not mutually exclusive; rather, they are intimately related to the matter of discipline. As Christine Roy Yoder notes, the chapter expresses the need for discipline through "the language of desire, emotions, and physical appetites."[6] This language permeates the chapter, identifying the dispositions and desires that define one's posture toward moral authority and instruction (vv. 10, 13, 24).[7] If the emotive language of many aphorisms identifies the need for discipline, then the language of wealth and poverty in certain sayings motivates receptivity to discipline. While some sayings reflect on wealth and poverty through the concepts of diligence and retribution (vv. 11, 22), others relate one's economic status to one's

3. For a discussion of the MORAL AUTHORITY metaphor, see Lakoff and Johnson, *Philosophy in the Flesh*, 301–3. For the use of the concept in Proverbs, see Stewart, "Wisdom's Imagination," 369–70. As Lakoff and Johnson note, the metaphor is rooted in the reality of the parents' physical dominance over the child. This logic of physical dominance is also reflected in the social order of ancient Israel and the ancient Near East, where the hierarchy of the household shaped the concept of authority and the structure of other spheres in society. Max Weber, *Economy and Society: An Outline of Interpretive Sociology*, trans. E. Fischoff, ed. G. Roth and C. Wittich, 3 vols. (New York: Bedminster, 1968), 2:1007; J. David Schloen, *The House of the Father as Fact and Symbol: Patrimonialism in Ugarit and the Ancient Near East*, Studies in the Archaeology and History of the Levant 2 (Winona Lake, IN: Eisenbrauns, 2001), 135–83, 359–60; and Daniel M. Master, "State Formation Theory and the Kingdom of Ancient Israel," *JNES* 60 (2001): 128–29.

4. For the MORAL ORDER metaphor and its relationship to the MORAL AUTHORITY metaphor, see Lakoff and Johnson, *Philosophy in the Flesh*, 303–4; Stewart, "Wisdom's Imagination," 369–70.

5. Stewart, "Wisdom's Imagination," 369.

6. Yoder, *Proverbs*, 150.

7. Together with these sayings regarding discipline, the emotions and appetites mentioned throughout the chapter include the terms "eat(s)" (יֹאכַל, v. 2a, אֹכֵל, v. 25a), "throat" (נֶפֶשׁ, v. 2b), "craves" (מִתְאַוָּה, v. 4a), "appetite" (נֶפֶשׁ, vv. 4a, 4b, 25a), "hates" (יִשְׂנָא, v. 5a, שׂוֹנֵא, v. 24a), "rejoices" (יִשְׂמָח, v. 9a), "despises" (בָּז, v. 13a), "fears" (יָרֵא, v. 13b), "sweet" (תֶּעֱרַב, v. 19a), "abomination" (תוֹעֲבַת, v. 19b), "food" (אֹכֶל, v. 23a), "loves" (אֹהֲבוֹ, v. 24b).

reception of discipline and reproof (vv. 8, 18). Economics and emotions intersect with the chapter's construal of moral authority, creating a network of aphorisms that associate receptivity to discipline with desire, wealth, and well-being.

Wealth and poverty contribute to the chapter's discourse on discipline. And they inhabit a pair of paradoxical sayings that discipline one's moral reasoning and enhance the pedagogical repertoire of the central collections. Like 11:24 and 12:18, 13:7 and 23 include the particle יֵשׁ. Whereas elsewhere it functions as a common noun ("wealth," Prov 8:21) or as a particle of existence ("there is/are," Prov 3:28; 19:18; 23:18; 24:14), here it serves as a particle that introduces "a reflection on some opposing situation or paradox" ("There is this," 13:7a; "the reality is this," v. 23b; cf. Prov 11:24; 12:18; 14:12; 16:25; 18:24; 20:15).[8] It invites meditation on enigmatic affairs and encourages the exercise of one's moral imagination. The particle is included in sayings that force one to reflect on the reality that things may not be what they seem (13:7); and the fortune of the poor is not invulnerable (v. 23). Together with the indefinite subjects that mark many of the aphorisms (e.g., vv. 2a, 7, 8a, 10, 13a, 19a),[9] these sayings play a formative role in the chapter's cultivation of discipline. They complement the motif's explicit treatment in several sayings through poetic forms and particular constructions that discipline one's moral imagination and direct one's moral reasoning.

The thematic emphases and poetic forms of the chapter converge with the MORAL AUTHORITY metaphor to discipline one's character, desires, and thinking. But it is important to note that the collection of aphorisms in ch. 13 share several similarities with the surrounding materials. While the righteous and the wicked are less prominent in the chapter's construal of character, conventional prototypes occupy the aphorisms, such as "the treacherous" (בֹּגְדִים, v. 2b, 15b; 11:3, 6; 21:18; 22:12), "the diligent" (חָרֻצִים, v. 4b; 10:4; 12:24, 27; 21:5), and the "shrewd" (עָרוּם, v. 16a; 12:16, 23; 14:8, 15, 18; 22:3). The themes of discipline (13:1; cf. 9:7–8; 15:12; 21:24; 22:10), speech (13:2–3; cf. 10:14, 19; 11:13; 12:23; 15:2), and wealth (13:8, 11; cf. 10:15; 11:16, 28; 14:24; 18:11) treated elsewhere are reinforced and extended by several aphorisms. Similar to the previous chapters, the MORAL ACCOUNTING and MORAL ESSENCE metaphors structure many of the sayings (e.g., 13:2, 4, 5, 9, 16). Various aphorisms appeal to the conventional motivational drives of satisfaction, safety, and well-being (e.g., 13:2, 3, 4, 6, 9, 11, 25). Variant repetitions associate certain apho-

8. These observations and translations follow Gianto, "On יֵשׁ of Reflection in the Book of Proverbs," 158–62, esp. 158. Cf. Hans-Jürgen Hermisson, *Studien zur israelitischen Spruchweisheit*, WMANT 28 (Neukirchen-Vluyn: Neukirchener Verlag, 1968), 148.

9. In light of the fact that these indefinite subjects do not correspond explicitly with the moral prototypes projected within the anthology, they require the reader to pause and reflect on their family resemblance to particular character types. In so doing, they hone the reader's moral reasoning. For a discussion of the indefinite subject, see GKC §144d–i; *IBHS* §4.4.2.

risms with other sayings in the chapter (13:1b//8b), with proverbs in the adjacent chapters (**13:2a**//12:14a//18:20a; **13:14**//14:27), and with materials elsewhere in the central collections (**13:3**//21:23//16:17b//19:16a; **13:9b**//24:20b).[10]

III. "Forming 'Fearers of YHWH'": The Curriculum of Wisdom and Virtue (10:1–29:27)

III.1 Elementary Wisdom and Virtue (10:1–15:33)

A. The Wise, the Righteous, and YHWH: The Pillars of the Moral World (10:1–32)

B. Wisdom, Character, and Consequences: The Regulations of the Moral Economy (11:1–31)

C. Building Prototypes: Wisdom and the Properties of Moral Character (12:1–28)

➡ **D. Mapping Moral Authority: Wisdom, Discipline, and Desire (13:1–25)**

E. From the Moral to the Intellectual: A Montage of Wisdom and Folly (14:1–35)

F. Forming Moral Wholeness: The Homogeneity of Normative Character (15:1–33)

III.2 Intermediate Wisdom and Virtue (16:1–22:16)

III.3 Vocational Wisdom and Virtue (22:17–24:34)

III.4 Advanced Wisdom and Virtue (25:1–29:27)

Translation and Exegetical Outline

(See pages 396–97.)

Structure and Literary Form

Taken as a whole, the central collections may be compared to a pointillist painting. Each aphorism is a work of art, a dot of pure color and genuine wisdom. These dots correspond to and complement those in close proximity, and they throw into sharp relief those distinctive colors dotted at a distance. The individual aphorisms collected in Prov 13 contribute to the central collection's pointillist portrait of wisdom and virtue. Like chs. 10–12, antithetical sayings cover this portion of the canvas. But a nonantithetical saying (13:14) as well as a pair of paradoxical reflections (vv. 7, 23) introduce different colored dots. The former disrupts the general pattern of sayings in chs. 10–15.

10. For discussion of these variant repetitions, see Heim, *Poetic Imagination*, 329–58.

Proverbs 13:1–25

D. Mapping Moral Authority: Wisdom, Discipline, and Desire (13:1–25)

1a	בֵּן חָכָם מוּסַר אָב	A wise son—a father's discipline;
1b	וְלֵץ לֹא־שָׁמַע גְּעָרָה	but a scoffer does not listen to reproof.
2a	מִפְּרִי פִי־אִישׁ יֹאכַל טוֹב	From the fruit of his mouth, one eats good things;
2b	וְנֶפֶשׁ בֹּגְדִים חָמָס	but the throat of the treacherous, violence.
3a	נֹצֵר פִּיו שֹׁמֵר נַפְשׁוֹ	One who guards his mouth protects his life;
3b	פֹּשֵׂק שְׂפָתָיו מְחִתָּה־לוֹ	one who opens wide his lips—ruin is his.
4a	מִתְאַוָּה וָאַיִן נַפְשׁוֹ עָצֵל	It craves but has nothing: the appetite of the sluggard;
4b	וְנֶפֶשׁ חָרֻצִים תְּדֻשָּׁן	but the appetite of the diligent is satisfied.
5a	דְּבַר־שֶׁקֶר יִשְׂנָא צַדִּיק	The righteous hates a false word;
5b	וְרָשָׁע יַבְאִישׁ וְיַחְפִּיר	but the wicked bring shame and disgrace.
6a	צְדָקָה תִּצֹּר תָּם־דָּרֶךְ	Righteousness guards the way of the upright;
6b	וְרִשְׁעָה תְּסַלֵּף חַטָּאת	but wickedness ruins the sinner.
7a	יֵשׁ מִתְעַשֵּׁר וְאֵין כֹּל	There is this: one who pretends to be rich and has nothing;
7b	מִתְרוֹשֵׁשׁ וְהוֹן רָב	one who pretends to be poor and has great wealth.
8a	כֹּפֶר נֶפֶשׁ־אִישׁ עָשְׁרוֹ	The ransom of a person's life, his wealth;
8b	וְרָשׁ לֹא־שָׁמַע גְּעָרָה	but the poor does not listen to reproof.
9a	אוֹר־צַדִּיקִים יִשְׂמָח	The light of the righteous rejoices;
9b	וְנֵר רְשָׁעִים יִדְעָךְ	but the lamp of the wicked is extinguished.
10a	רַק־בְּזָדוֹן יִתֵּן מַצָּה	Indeed, arrogance produces strife;
10b	וְאֶת־נוֹעָצִים חָכְמָה	but those who accept advice, wisdom.
11a	הוֹן מֵהֶבֶל יִמְעָט	Wealth in haste dwindles;
11b	וְקֹבֵץ עַל־יָד יַרְבֶּה	but one who gathers by hand increases.
12a	תּוֹחֶלֶת מְמֻשָּׁכָה מַחֲלָה־לֵב	A drawn-out hope makes the heart sick;
12b	וְעֵץ חַיִּים תַּאֲוָה בָאָה	but a tree of life is a desire fulfilled.
13a	בָּז לְדָבָר יֵחָבֶל לוֹ	One who despises a word, it will go badly for him;
13b	וִירֵא מִצְוָה הוּא יְשֻׁלָּם	but one who fears a commandment, he will be rewarded.

14a	תּוֹרַת חָכָם מְקוֹר חַיִּים	The teaching of the wise, a fount of life
14b	לָסוּר מִמֹּקְשֵׁי מָוֶת	for avoiding the snares of death.
15a	שֵׂכֶל־טוֹב יִתֶּן־חֵן	Good sense produces favor;
15b	וְדֶרֶךְ בֹּגְדִים אֵיתָן	but the way of the treacherous is their ruin.
16a	כָּל־עָרוּם יַעֲשֶׂה בְדָעַת	Every shrewd person acts with knowledge;
16b	וּכְסִיל יִפְרֹשׂ אִוֶּלֶת	but a fool spreads folly.
17a	מַלְאָךְ רָשָׁע יִפֹּל בְּרָע	A wicked messenger falls into evil;
17b	וְצִיר אֱמוּנִים מַרְפֵּא	but a faithful envoy brings healing.
18a	רֵישׁ וְקָלוֹן פּוֹרֵעַ מוּסָר	Poverty and shame: one who neglects discipline;
18b	וְשׁוֹמֵר תּוֹכַחַת יְכֻבָּד	but one who listens to reproof will be honored.
19a	תַּאֲוָה נִהְיָה תֶּעֱרַב לְנָפֶשׁ	A desire realized is sweet to a person;
19b	וְתוֹעֲבַת כְּסִילִים סוּר מֵרָע	and an abomination of fools: turning away from evil.
20a	הוֹלֵךְ אֶת־חֲכָמִים יֶחְכָּם	One who walks with the wise becomes wise;
20b	וְרֹעֶה כְסִילִים יֵרוֹעַ	but the companion of fools suffers harm.
21a	חַטָּאִים תְּרַדֵּף רָעָה	Evil pursues sinners;
21b	וְאֶת־צַדִּיקִים יְשַׁלֶּם־טוֹב	but the righteous will be rewarded with good.
22a	טוֹב יַנְחִיל בְּנֵי־בָנִים	A good person leaves an inheritance to grandchildren;
22b	וְצָפוּן לַצַּדִּיק חֵיל חוֹטֵא	but stored up for the righteous: the wealth of the sinner.
23a	רָב־אֹכֶל נִיר רָאשִׁים	An abundance of food—the fallow ground of the poor;
23b	וְיֵשׁ נִסְפֶּה בְּלֹא מִשְׁפָּט	but the reality is this: it is swept away without justice.
24a	חוֹשֵׂךְ שִׁבְטוֹ שׂוֹנֵא בְנוֹ	One who spares the rod hates his son;
24b	וְאֹהֲבוֹ שִׁחֲרוֹ מוּסָר	but one who loves him disciplines him consistently.
25a	צַדִּיק אֹכֵל לְשֹׂבַע נַפְשׁוֹ	The righteous eats to satisfy his appetite;
25b	וּבֶטֶן רְשָׁעִים תֶּחְסָר	but the stomach of the wicked is empty.

The latter signals the mystery and indeterminacy that infiltrates the order and harmony of life in the world. While neither the nonantithetical saying nor the pair of paradoxes contribute to the apparent structure of the chapter, they indicate that wisdom for life is not necessarily black and white.

The affairs of reality may not always be clear. But, for many, the general structure of ch. 13 is transparent. The introductory and concluding aphorisms appear to form a formal framework. The repetition of the terms "discipline(s)" (מוּסָר, vv. 1a, 24b) and "throat/appetite" (נֶפֶשׁ, vv. 2b, 25a) as well as the root אכל ("eats," vv. 2a, 25a) may create an *inclusio*, providing an envelope around the diverse aphorisms in the chapter.[11] Within this framework, many have detected four basic units (vv. 1–6, 7–11, 12–19, 20–25).[12] These units are delineated by different phenomena, ranging from catchwords and *inclusios* to chiasms and common themes.[13] At minimum, it appears that several adjacent aphorisms are linked by conventional terms or distinct expressions, such as נֶפֶשׁ ("throat," v. 2b; "life," v. 3a; "appetite," vv. 4a, 4b), פֶּה ("mouth," vv. 2a, 3a), צְדָקָה ("righteous[ness]") and רִשְׁעָה ("wicked[ness]") (vv. 5–6), רוּשׁ ("pretends to be poor," v. 7b; "poor," v. 8b), כְּסִילִים ("fools," vv. 19b, 20b), and חוֹטֶא, חַטָּאִים ("sinner(s)," vv. 21a, 22b), טוֹב ("good," vv. 21b, 22a), and צַדִּיק ("righteous," vv. 21b, 22b). And in addition to the chapter's concern with discipline and pervasive use of emotive language, the aphorisms recycle several words or roots.[14] Together, these recurring terms and motifs intimate that, like the sayings elsewhere in Prov 10–15, the aphorisms in ch. 13 contribute to a unified view of wisdom and virtue that remains open to literary variation and thematic disruption.

11. Whybray, *The Composition of the Book of Proverbs*, 99; Waltke, *Proverbs: Chapters 1–15*, 550; Koptak, *Proverbs*, 355. Together with its contribution to the literary framework of ch. 13, v. 1 may play a formative role in the design of Prov 10–15. In light of the shared terms and constructions in 10:1b–c, 13:1, and 15:20, 13:1 may have been situated in its present location to mark the middle of the first subcollection. For a discussion of these "wise son" sayings and their potential contributions to the composition and redaction of Prov 10–15, see Mathias Winkler, "Die drei Sprüche „weisen Sohn" Zur Diskussion um Komposition und Redaktion in Spr 10–15," *BZ* 62 (2018): 81–99.

12. Meinhold, *Die Sprüche*, 1:217–26; Heim, *Like Grapes of Gold*, 160–69; Waltke, *Proverbs: Chapters 1–15*, 550–51; O'Dowd, *Proverbs*, 216; Koptak, *Proverbs*, 355. For slight variations to the boundaries of these units, see Garrett, *Proverbs*, 134–40. Cf. Delitzsch, "Proverbs of Solomon," 6:193–207 (1:270–86), who perceives several smaller collections of sayings (vv. 1–4, 5–6, 7–8, 9–11, 12–14, 15–18, 19–20, 20–21, 23–25).

13. For example, the repetition of "wealth" (הוֹן, vv. 7b, 11a) may indicate that vv. 7–11 represent a coherent unit. In addition to those mentioned in the previous note, others argue that vv. 12–19 constitute a discrete section: it is framed by aphorisms that employ the term "desire" (תַּאֲוָה, vv. 12b, 19a) and organized as a chiasm. Van Leeuwen, "The Book of Proverbs," *NIB* 5:132–33; Yoder, *Proverbs*, 150.

14. For these recurring words and roots, see Waltke, *Proverbs: Chapters 1–15*, 551.

CHAPTER 20

Proverbs 14:1–35

E. From the Moral to the Intellectual: *A Montage of Wisdom and Folly*

Main Idea of the Passage

With language reminiscent of Prov 1–9, these aphorisms reinstate the MORAL ESSENCE metaphor and profile character through intellectual categories in order to sketch the prototypical features of the wise and hone the moral reasoning of the reader.

Literary Context[1]

The aphorisms assembled in ch. 14 introduce a new scene within the opening act of the central collections. In contrast to the previous chapters, which privilege the antithesis between the righteous and the wicked and profile the central features of Proverbs's moral prototype, ch. 14 privileges the wise and the fool along with their coreferential counterparts in order to profile the central features of Proverbs's intellectual prototype. This is not to say that the righteous and the wicked disappear backstage. They continue to play a role, but their role is minimal. They fade into the background, allowing the wise and the fool to step into the spotlight and display their contributions to Proverbs's conception of virtue and the moral life.[2]

The characters and categories that predominate in ch. 14 signal the shift to a new scene that features a different character type. The script of this new scene, however, is familiar. In fact, it appears that this script was composed from the language and

1. This chapter does not include the Canonical and Theological Significance section. See pp. xv and 276n1 for justification. Also, see pp. 424–28 for the Canonical and Theological Significance of Proverbs 10–15.

2. This shift from a particular concentration on the righteous and the wicked in chs. 10–13 to the relative scarcity of these character types in chs. 14–20 is noted by Goldingay, "The Arrangement of Sayings in Proverbs 10–15," 76.

imagery of the preamble and prologue (1:1–7, 1:8–9:18). Characters, terms, and concepts introduced in the preamble and prologue occupy the individual aphorisms (with the exception of a few sayings [14:20, 28]). Some of the links are rather unremarkable, such as the mention of the wise and the fool (חָכָם, vv. 1a, 3b, 16a, 24a; אֱוִיל, vv. 3a, 9a; כְּסִיל, vv. 7a, 8b, 16b, 24b, 33b), wisdom and folly (חָכְמָה, vv. 6a, 8a, 33a; אִוֶּלֶת, vv. 1b, 8b, 17a, 18a, 24b [2x], 29b), and the image of the way (דֶּרֶךְ, vv. 2b, 8a, 12a, 14a, cf. v. 15b). Others are more evocative of the preamble and prologue. The terms "scoffer" (לֵץ, v. 6a; cf. 1:22, 9:7–8, 12; 13:1), "discerning" (נָבוֹן, 14:6b, 33a; cf. 1:5; 10:13), and "schemer/discretion" (אִישׁ מְזִמּוֹת, 14:17b; cf. 1:4; 2:11; 3:21; 5:2; 8:12; 12:2), along with the expressions "turns away from evil" (סָר מֵרָע, 14:16a; cf. 3:7; 4:27; 13:19), "devisers of evil" (חֹרְשֵׁי רָע, 14:22a; cf. 3:29; 6:14; 12:20), and "the fear of YHWH" (יִרְאַת יְהוָה, 14:26a, 27a; cf. 1:7, 29; 2:5; 8:13; 9:10; 10:27) recall the introduction to the anthology. And still other intertextual links with the preamble and prologue are quite striking. Seven deserve specific comment:

A. The language of wisdom, folly, women, houses, and building is reminiscent of Prov 9:1–18 (14:1; cf. 24:3).
B. Among the character types profiled in Prov 10–15, the "simple" (פֶּתִי, 14:15a, 18a) has been conspicuously absent. The character introduced as one of the anthology's primary addressees and identified as the principal audience of the wisdom interludes now returns to the stage, making a cameo in two aphorisms (vv. 15a, 18a; cf. 1:4, 22, 32; 8:5; 9:4, 6, 16).
C. The expression "house of the wicked" (בֵּית רְשָׁעִים, 14:11a) resembles 3:33 (cf. 21:12).
D. The noun "end" (אַחֲרִית), which links 14:12–13, recalls the distinctive ends associated with entertaining the strange woman (5:4, 11; cf. 16:25; 19:20; 20:21).
E. The macaristic exclamation, "blessed is he" (אַשְׁרָיו, 14:21b), echoes the beatific state that accompanies those who embrace wisdom (3:13; 8:32, 34; cf. 16:20; 20:7; 28:14).
F. The collocation "loyalty and faithfulness" (חֶסֶד וֶאֱמֶת, 14:22b) evokes the admonition in 3:3 (cf. 16:6; 20:28).
G. And 14:5b constitutes a variant repetition of 6:19a.[3]

Taken together, the range of links between the aphorisms in ch. 14 and the discourses of the prologue intimate that the script of this new scene was composed from the lexicon of Prov 1–9 or provided the vocabulary for the composition of Prov 1–9.

3. In addition to this variant repetition, ch. 14 includes four others: **14:1a**//9:1a//24:3a (noted above); **14:12**//16:25//12:15a //16:2//21:2; **14:27**//13:14; and **14:17a**//14:29. For discussion of these repetitions, see Heim, *Poetic Imagination*, 181–85, 192–201, 303–15, 353–62.

Whereas the previous chapters focused on the moral prototype of Proverbs, ch. 14 employs the language of the prologue and the metaphor of MORAL ESSENCE to develop the intellectual prototype of the anthology. The wise, the fool, and folly figure prominently among the aphorisms.[4] And the recurrence of the "fear of YHWH" (יִרְאַת יְהוָה, vv. 26a, 27a; cf. vv. 2a, 16a) as well as the incorporation of sayings that illuminate human limits (vv. 10, 12, 13) correspond to and enhance the chapter's intellectual orientation. The attention devoted to these categories and motifs suggests that this collection of sayings seeks to clarify the moral essence of the prototype that embodies the anthology's prerequisite (1:7), to create an aversion to folly, and to cultivate a desire for wisdom. Certain aphorisms look back to the previous collections. The all but forgotten figure of the "simple" (פֶּתִי, 14:15a, 18a), for example, reemerges in a pair of sayings that shed light on the "fuzzy border" this character occupies between the wise and the fool (cf. 19:25; 21:11; 22:3; 27:12).[5] And other aphorisms look forward to the subsequent collections, like those concerned with the king (14:28, 35; cf. 16:10–15). In so doing, they reinforce and expand the sociomoral purview of the central collections and, by implication, sharpen the character, moral reasoning, and worldview of the reader.

4. Murphy, *Proverbs*, 108; Yoder, *Proverbs*, 157; Sæbø, *Sprüche*, 201–2; O'Dowd, *Proverbs*, 226.

5. The concept of "fuzzy borders" stems from Lotfi Zadeh's mathematical "fuzzy set" theory, according to which certain items are not entirely members of a set, on the one hand, and yet not completely a nonmember of the set, on the other (Lofti A. Zadeh, "Fuzzy Sets," *Information and Control* 8 [1965]: 338–53). This theory has been applied to semantics as well as prototype theory. George Lakoff, *Women, Fire, and Dangerous Things: What Categories Reveal about the Mind* (Chicago: University of Chicago Press, 1987); Johnson, *Moral Imagination*, 8–9, 189–92; Stewart, *Poetic Ethics*, 170–200; Millar, *Genre and Openness*, 92–110.

Translation and Exegetical Outline

(See pages 403–5.)

Structure and Literary Form

While terms from the semantic fields of wisdom and folly orient one to the conceptual and thematic concerns of the aphorisms arranged in ch. 14, these concerns do not necessarily translate into an intelligible structural blueprint. Like the previous chapters, antithetical sayings predominate; but a handful of nonantithetical aphorisms add an alternative texture that pairs well with the distinctive intellectual concepts that prevail in the unit (vv. 7, 10, 13, 14, 17, 19, 26, 27).[6] If one tastes the sayings sequentially, common flavors emerge. Several verses are linked by catchwords, forming proverbial pairs (vv. 12–13, 17–18, 20–21, 26–27). In addition to these smaller bites, the consumption of a series of sayings may create the impression of a coherent dish. Repeated terms or roots may create a framework, delineating the literary boundaries of a unit and the context within which the individual sayings should be read.[7] And the concentration of particular themes or the recurrent use of language from general semantic spheres may suggest that the chapter consists of several sections.[8] The aphorisms collected in ch. 14 form a pie that may be cut in more than one way. The precise structure of the chapter is unclear. But the preponderance of terms pertaining to wisdom in general and folly in particular offer a measure of coherence amid the structural ambiguity of the aphorisms.

6. Among the nonantithetical sayings in the chapter, 14:12 is comparable to 11:24, 12:18, and 13:7 (cf. 13:23; 16:25; 18:24; 20:15). Following Gianto, it is introduced by a יֵשׁ of reflection; and when this יֵשׁ of reflection opens the aphorism, the adjacent saying continues the contrast presented by the aphorism (14:13). Gianto, "On יֵשׁ of Reflection in the Book of Proverbs," 158–62, esp. 160.

7. The repetition of terms for wisdom and folly, for example, may demarcate vv. 1–3 or 1–7; and the recurrence of מֶלֶךְ and לְאֹם (vv. 28, 34, 35) as well as the wordplay between רָזוֹן ("ruler's," v. 28b) and רְצוֹן ("favors," v. 35a) may form an *inclusio*, marking the parameters of a unit concerned with the communal orientation of the monarchy. For discussion of these cases as well as other potential examples of *inclusio* in ch. 14, see Meinhold, *Die Sprüche*, 1:229, 242–46; Garrett, *Proverbs*, 140, 144–47; Heim, *Like Grapes of Gold*, 177–88; Waltke, *Proverbs: Chapters 1–15*, 583–84, 588; O'Dowd, *Proverbs*, 230–31.

8. For subunits formed through thematic and semantic connections, see Delitzsch, "The Book of Proverbs," 6:209–27 (1:293–313); Toy, *Proverbs*, 298–301; Murphy, *Proverbs*, 105–106; Yoder, *Proverbs*, 157.

Proverbs 14:1–35

E. From the Moral to the Intellectual: A Montage of Wisdom and Folly (14:1–35)

1a	חַכְמוֹת נָשִׁים בָּנְתָה בֵיתָהּ	The wisdom of women builds her house;
1b	וְאִוֶּלֶת בְּיָדֶיהָ תֶהֶרְסֶנּוּ	but folly tears hers down with her own hands.
2a	הוֹלֵךְ בְּיָשְׁרוֹ יְרֵא יְהוָה	One who walks uprightly fears YHWH;
2b	וּנְלוֹז דְּרָכָיו בּוֹזֵהוּ	but one whose ways are twisted despises him.
3a	בְּפִי־אֱוִיל חֹטֶר גַּאֲוָה	In the mouth of the fool, a sprig of pride;
3b	וְשִׂפְתֵי חֲכָמִים תִּשְׁמוּרֵם	but the lips of the wise guard them.
4a	בְּאֵין אֲלָפִים אֵבוּס בָּר	Without oxen, the manger has grain;
4b	וְרָב־תְּבוּאוֹת בְּכֹחַ שׁוֹר	but abundant produce, by the bull's strength.
5a	עֵד אֱמוּנִים לֹא יְכַזֵּב	A trustworthy witness does not deceive;
5b	וְיָפִיחַ כְּזָבִים עֵד שָׁקֶר	but a false witness breathes lies.
6a	בִּקֶּשׁ־לֵץ חָכְמָה וָאָיִן	The scoffer seeks wisdom, but nothing;
6b	וְדַעַת לְנָבוֹן נָקָל	while knowledge comes easy for the discerning.
7a	לֵךְ מִנֶּגֶד לְאִישׁ כְּסִיל	Go before a fool,
7b	וּבַל־יָדַעְתָּ שִׂפְתֵי־דָעַת	and you will not know knowledgeable lips.
8a	חָכְמַת עָרוּם הָבִין דַּרְכּוֹ	The wisdom of the shrewd: understanding his way;
8b	וְאִוֶּלֶת כְּסִילִים מִרְמָה	but the folly of fools, deceit.
9a	אֱוִלִים יָלִיץ אָשָׁם	Fools mock at guilt;
9b	וּבֵין יְשָׁרִים רָצוֹן	but among the upright, favor.
10a	לֵב יוֹדֵעַ מָרַּת נַפְשׁוֹ	The heart knows its own bitterness;
10b	וּבְשִׂמְחָתוֹ לֹא־יִתְעָרַב זָר	and a stranger cannot share in its joy.
11a	בֵּית רְשָׁעִים יִשָּׁמֵד	The house of the wicked will be destroyed;
11b	וְאֹהֶל יְשָׁרִים יַפְרִיחַ	but the tent of the upright will blossom.
12a	יֵשׁ דֶּרֶךְ יָשָׁר לִפְנֵי־אִישׁ	There is this: a way that is straight before a person;
12b	וְאַחֲרִיתָהּ דַּרְכֵי־מָוֶת	but its end, ways to death.
13a	גַּם־בִּשְׂחוֹק יִכְאַב־לֵב	Even in laughter the heart may hurt;
13b	וְאַחֲרִיתָהּ שִׂמְחָה תוּגָה	and the end of joy, grief.

Continued on next page.

Continued from previous page.

14a	מִדְּרָכָיו יִשְׂבַּע סוּג לֵב	The wayward of heart will be satisfied from his ways;
14b	וּמֵעָלָיו אִישׁ טוֹב	and a good person, from his.
15a	פֶּתִי יַאֲמִין לְכָל־דָּבָר	The simple believes anything;
15b	וְעָרוּם יָבִין לַאֲשֻׁרוֹ	but the shrewd considers his step.
16a	חָכָם יָרֵא וְסָר מֵרָע	The wise fears and turns away from evil;
16b	וּכְסִיל מִתְעַבֵּר וּבוֹטֵחַ	but the fool, quick-tempered and overconfident.
17a	קְצַר־אַפַּיִם יַעֲשֶׂה אִוֶּלֶת	A short-tempered person commits folly;
17b	וְאִישׁ מְזִמּוֹת יִשָּׂנֵא	and a schemer is hated.
18a	נָחֲלוּ פְתָאיִם אִוֶּלֶת	The simple inherit folly;
18b	וַעֲרוּמִים יַכְתִּרוּ דָעַת	but the shrewd are crowned with knowledge.
19a	שַׁחוּ רָעִים לִפְנֵי טוֹבִים	The evil bow before the good;
19b	וּרְשָׁעִים עַל־שַׁעֲרֵי צַדִּיק	and the wicked at the gates of the righteous.
20a	גַּם־לְרֵעֵהוּ יִשָּׂנֵא רָשׁ	Even by his neighbor the poor is hated;
20b	וְאֹהֲבֵי עָשִׁיר רַבִּים	but those who love the rich, many.
21a	בָּז־לְרֵעֵהוּ חוֹטֵא	One who despises his neighbor, a sinner;
21b	וּמְחוֹנֵן עֲנָיִים אַשְׁרָיו	but one who is gracious to the poor, blessed is he.
22a	הֲלוֹא־יִתְעוּ חֹרְשֵׁי רָע	Do not devisers of evil go astray,
22b	וְחֶסֶד וֶאֱמֶת חֹרְשֵׁי טוֹב	while devisers of good, loyalty and faithfulness?
23a	בְּכָל־עֶצֶב יִהְיֶה מוֹתָר	In all hard work there is profit;
23b	וּדְבַר־שְׂפָתַיִם אַךְ־לְמַחְסוֹר	but mere talk, only to deprivation.
24a	עֲטֶרֶת חֲכָמִים עָשְׁרָם	The crown of the wise, their wealth;
24b	אִוֶּלֶת כְּסִילִים אִוֶּלֶת	the folly of fools, folly.
25a	מַצִּיל נְפָשׁוֹת עֵד אֱמֶת	A reliable witness saves lives;
25b	וְיָפִחַ כְּזָבִים מִרְמָה	but a deceiver breathes lies.
26a	בְּיִרְאַת יְהוָה מִבְטַח־עֹז	In the fear of YHWH, strong confidence;
26b	וּלְבָנָיו יִהְיֶה מַחְסֶה	and for his children it will be a refuge.

27a	יִרְאַת יְהוָה מְקוֹר חַיִּים	The fear of YHWH, a fountain of life
27b	לָסוּר מִמֹּקְשֵׁי מָוֶת	for avoiding the snares of death.
28a	בְּרָב־עָם הַדְרַת־מֶלֶךְ	In a multitude of people, a king's splendor;
28b	וּבְאֶפֶס לְאֹם מְחִתַּת רָזוֹן	but in a lack of a nation, a ruler's ruin.
29a	אֶרֶךְ אַפַּיִם רַב־תְּבוּנָה	Slow to anger, great understanding;
29b	וּקְצַר־רוּחַ מֵרִים אִוֶּלֶת	but the short-tempered exalts folly.
30a	חַיֵּי בְשָׂרִים לֵב מַרְפֵּא	The life of the body, a gentle heart;
30b	וּרְקַב עֲצָמוֹת קִנְאָה	but rot in the bones, jealousy.
31a	עֹשֵׁק דָּל חֵרֵף עֹשֵׂהוּ	One who oppresses the poor insults his maker,
31b	וּמְכַבְּדוֹ חֹנֵן אֶבְיוֹן	but one who is kind to the needy honors him.
32a	בְּרָעָתוֹ יִדָּחֶה רָשָׁע	The wicked is thrust down by his evil;
32b	וְחֹסֶה בְמוֹתוֹ צַדִּיק	but the righteous finds refuge in his death.
33a	בְּלֵב נָבוֹן תָּנוּחַ חָכְמָה	Wisdom rests in the heart of the discerning;
33b	וּבְקֶרֶב כְּסִילִים תִּוָּדֵעַ	and in the midst of fools she makes herself known.
34a	צְדָקָה תְרוֹמֵם־גּוֹי	Righteousness exalts a nation;
34b	וְחֶסֶד לְאֻמִּים חַטָּאת	but the disgrace of peoples, sin.
35a	רְצוֹן־מֶלֶךְ לְעֶבֶד מַשְׂכִּיל	The king favors a competent servant;
35b	וְעֶבְרָתוֹ תִּהְיֶה מֵבִישׁ	but his wrath is for a disgraceful one.

Explanation of the Text

The intellectual cast of the aphorisms in the chapter is introduced by the initial saying, which traffics in a distinctive intertextual topos (**v. 1**). The association between wisdom and house building recalls YHWH's construction of the cosmic house (3:19–20) and Lady Wisdom's establishment of her domicile (9:1; cf. Exod 31:3; 1 Kgs 7:14). And the antithesis between wisdom's house and folly's house evokes the invitations delivered in Prov 9. The present aphorism, however, transforms the cosmological and metaphorical into the historical. The skill of the divine architect and the work of Lady Wisdom is manifest in the construction of human homes.[9] Just as Lady Wisdom "builds her house" (חָכְמוֹת בָּנְתָה בֵיתָהּ; 9:1), so also "the wisdom of women builds her house" (חַכְמוֹת נָשִׁים בָּנְתָה בֵיתָהּ, v. 1a; cf. 24:3–4; 31:10–31). With the exception of "women" (נָשִׁים, v. 1a), the initial line is a mirror image of Prov 9:1. Whether or not "women" is an editorial addition or a corruption that should be omitted,[10] "wisdom" identifies a class of women, each of whom instantiate the skill of YHWH and Lady Wisdom.[11] These wise women build their homes; that is, they establish and cultivate an orderly environment directed by and oriented to shalom. Those within the class of folly, by contrast, destroy the structures, people, possessions, and posterity that make up the home. The home that folly tears down by the work of her hands may be the house that the wise among women build, or it could refer to her own home. Irrespective of the precise referent, the aphorism captures the antithetical ways in which wisdom and folly relate to the most fundamental social structure within society. By virtue of their MORAL ESSENCE, wise women imitate the divine builder, creating a household characterized by the moral order and ethos of wisdom. In the same way, by virtue of their MORAL ESSENCE, foolish women unleash chaos in the domestic sphere, destroying the foundational building block of society. On one level, the aphorism contributes to Proverbs's discourse on marriage preparation through its attention to the value of a wise woman. On another level, the proverb expresses the stability and moral symmetry of a home founded on and organized according to (divine) wisdom.

Whereas the character of wise and foolish women explains their actions and identifies their MORAL ESSENCE, the actions of "one who walks uprightly" (הוֹלֵךְ בְּיָשְׁרוֹ, v. 2a) and "one whose ways are twisted" (נְלוֹז דְּרָכָיו, v. 2b) explain their character and reveal their MORAL ESSENCE (**v. 2**). The first line combines the metaphor of MORAL ESSENCE with the concept of MORAL STRENGTH. One who walks "uprightly" (בְּיָשְׁרוֹ, v. 1b) manifests a strong, physically straight posture that epitomizes his moral fortitude.[12] This physical posture corresponds with the inward, moral posture of the individual: he fears YHWH. Recognizing his creatureliness and contingency, one who walks uprightly displays his moral ontology or mode of being through a manner of life that is vertically

9. Van Leeuwen, "Cosmos, Temple, House," 67–90.

10. For discussion of the different proposals, see Van Leeuwen, "The Book of Proverbs," *NIB* 5:138; Waltke, *Proverbs: Chapters 1–15*, 576; Fox, *Proverbs 10–31*, 572.

11. For the genitive of relation, see *IBHS* §9.5.1i. For the use of the abstract plural חָכְמוֹת with the singular verb בָּנְתָה, see GKC §145k.

12. For the metaphor of MORAL STRENGTH and its related concept BEING MORAL IS BEING UPRIGHT, see Lakoff and Johnson, *Philosophy in the Flesh*, 299.

straight and an inner attitude that is attuned to vertical relationship with YHWH.[13] One whose ways are twisted, however, displays a perverse form of life. This twisted form of life aligns with the individual's twisted disposition: he despises YHWH. One's way, actions, moral essence, and attitudes are combined through different metaphorical concepts in each line, but the interrelationship among these elements may be construed differently. The noun phrases in each line may serve as either the subject or the predicate. Put differently, either one who walks uprightly fears YHWH or the one who fears YHWH walks uprightly, and either one whose ways are twisted despises him or one who despises him is perverse in his ways. Whether one's actions reveal one's MORAL ESSENCE or one's MORAL ESSENCE is reflected though one's actions, the aphorism illuminates the intimate relationship between character and behavior; and the flexibility of the subject and predicate in each line hones the readers' moral reasoning as they consider the dynamics of this relationship.

Similar to v. 2, the MORAL ESSENCE and MORAL STRENGTH metaphors structure the respective lines in **v. 3**. While some emend the end of the first line to create a precise parallel with its counterpart in the second, in view of the phenomenon of imprecise parallelism in Proverbs, the change is unnecessary.[14] The fool's discourse is depicted through an inchoate pair of metaphors that sprout in the reader's imagination. These metaphors include PEOPLE ARE TREES and ARROGANCE IS HIGH. The fool is portrayed as a tree, and his mouth is projected as the top of the trunk from which a "sprig" (חֹטֶר, v. 3a) springs. The "sprig" may be a small and delicate shoot (cf. Isa 11:1),[15] but its characterization as proud suggests otherwise. This characterization engenders an orientational metaphor frequently associated with arboreal images elsewhere in the Old Testament, namely, ARROGANCE IS HIGH.[16] The fool "sp(r)outs" arrogant speech;[17] but, ironically, his high, haughty words are nothing more than a small stem springing from his mouth. This sprig of arrogant speech may assault others, but it is unable to overcome the verbal prowess of the wise (Prov 14:3b).

If v. 3 trains one's moral reasoning through an unusual image, **v. 4** hones the reader's hermeneutical skills through semantic fecundity. The noun בָּר at the end of the first line may be rendered as either "clean" or "grain." Without oxen, the manger is clean, that is, free of dung and empty of fodder. Alternatively, without oxen, the manger has grain since there are no draught animals to consume it. Whether or not the moral sense of בָּר ("pure") can include the physical sense of cleanness, when the initial line is read together with its counterpart, it describes an alternative household economy. And the reversal of this economy in the second line is signaled by a reversal of consonants.[18] The initial line ends with בָּר ("grain," "clean," v. 4a); the second line begins with רֹב ("abundant," v. 4b). In the

13. For the fear of YHWH as a mode of being, see Jindo, "On the Biblical Notion,'" 433–53.

14. See *BHS*; McKane, *Proverbs*, 463; Garrett, *Proverbs*, 140, who emend גַּאֲוָה ("pride") to גוו ("his back") to form a clear antithesis between the self-destructive speech of the fool and the protective speech of the wise.

15. In light of the ancient versions and its rendering in Aramaic, חֹטֶר may be translated as "rod." Since the term is used elsewhere only in Isa 11:1 and the arboreal connotation makes good sense in the line, it is retained. Walter Bühlmann, *Vom Rechten Reden und Schweigen: Studien zu Proverbien 10–31*, OBO 12 (Göttingen, Vandenhoeck & Ruprecht, 1976), 127–29.

16. William R. Osborne, *Trees and Kings: A Comparative Analysis of Tree Imagery in Israel's Prophetic Tradition and the Ancient Near East*, BBRSup 18 (University Park: Eisenbrauns, 2018), 116–33.

17. Yoder, *Proverbs*, 158.

18. Clifford, *Proverbs*, 143.

absence of oxen, the manger may be clean, but it is also empty of produce necessary to nourish the household. In the same way, without oxen the manger may have grain, but not for long since the harvest is dependent on draught animals. More than advocating animal husbandry, the aphorism links the productivity and health of the household with the creatures, and it sharpens the moral reasoning of the reader through semantic ambiguity.

This ambiguity recedes in **v. 5**, which returns to the metaphor of MORAL ESSENCE. A trustworthy witness acts in accord with his character, refusing to deceive and impede the establishment of truth and justice (v. 5a). In the same way, a false witness speaks in accord with his moral essence. This individual "breathes lies" (יָפִיחַ כְּזָבִים, v. 5b; cf. 6:19a; 14:25). Deceit is the air that fills his lungs; and lies are the natural breath exhaled from his mouth. The aphorism deploys the metaphor of MORAL ESSENCE to organize a familiar topos within the anthology, namely, one's moral ontology corresponds with one's speech.

Just as one's moral ontology aligns with one's speech (v. 5), so also one's moral ontology determines one's ability to acquire and to convey wisdom (vv. 6–7). The noun דַּעַת ("knowledge," v. 6b; "knowledgeable," v. 7b) links **vv. 6 and 7**, forming a proverbial pair concerned with the acquisition and communication of wisdom, respectively. According to **v. 6**, the acquisition of wisdom is dependent on one's mode of being. The scoffer may seek wisdom; but by virtue of his disdain for reproof and refusal to receive correction (Prov 9:7–8; 15:12), he does not possess the moral ontology necessary to receive and acquire it. For the discerning, however, knowledge "comes easy" (נָקָל, v. 6b) because they possess a mode of being that is receptive to the instruction of others. One's moral ontology determines one's ability to acquire wisdom.

The same is true of one's ability of convey wisdom (v. 7). In contrast to many of the sayings in Prov 10–15, **v. 7** is cast in the form of an admonition.[19] The instruction offered does not direct one to a source of wisdom (cf. 6:6); rather, it identifies where wisdom may not be found. On account of their moral ontology, fools neither possess nor dispense wisdom (Prov 1:22; 12:23; 15:7, 14; 17:16). Their being is incompatible with and unable to produce knowledgeable speech. The imperative and prepositional phrase that open v. 7 do not represent a call to stay away from a fool; rather, the construction indicates that if one faces a fool, then one will be confronted by their mode of being through their foolish speech.[20]

The discourse on one's moral essence is extended in **v. 8**, which considers the character of the shrewd and the fool. Perception and discretion are among the ways in which the shrewd exercise wisdom. This persona perceives the nature of his actions, understands their potential consequences, and discerns the appropriate path (v. 8a). The fool, by contrast, does not possess the perception, discretion, and self-awareness of the shrewd. Whereas wisdom defines the moral essence of the shrewd, folly defines the moral essence of the fools (v. 8b). And this folly manifests itself through deceit. Whether this natural by-product of fools includes both self-deceit and the deception of others, its relationship with the predicate in the initial line is imprecise. The asymmetry invites the reader to expand the individual cola: the wisdom of the shrewd is avoiding deceit and understanding his way, but

19. McKane, *Proverbs*, 464.

20. While many read לֵךְ מִנֶּגֶד לְאִישׁ כְּסִיל as a command to stay away from the presence of a fool (Murphy, *Proverbs*, 100; Clifford, *Proverbs*, 144; Longman, *Proverbs*, 294), the construction מִנֶּגֶד לְ means "before," "opposite," or "facing," not "away from." See Judg 20:34; Fox, *Proverbs 10–31*, 574–75.

the folly of fools is deceit and inattentiveness to their ways.[21]

The extent of this "folly" (אִוֶּלֶת, v. 8b) is developed in **v. 9**. More than manifesting (self-)deceit and inattentiveness to their ways, "fools" (אֱוִלִים, v. 9a) mock at guilt.[22] While אָשָׁם may refer to a guilt or reparation offering (Lev 4:13, 22; 5:2–6), it appears that a general state of guilt in is view (Jer 50:7; 51:5; Hab 1:11).[23] Fools, on account of their moral ontology, scorn their guilty state, refusing to accept responsibility for their actions and make appropriate reparations. The upright, on the other hand, fund a socioreligious economy of favor (Prov 14:9b). By virtue of their moral posture and fortitude, they avoid the charge of guilt, accept responsibility for their actions, and cultivate a community of benevolence "among the upright" (בֵּין יְשָׁרִים, v. 9b). One's moral ontology and actions carry communal consequences. By denying any culpability, fools find no communal favor. By funding an economy of favor, the upright cultivate a community of goodwill.

But a benevolent community can neither comprehend nor experience the profundity of personal sorrow and joy (v. 10). The parallel expressions "its own bitterness" (מָרַּת נַפְשׁוֹ, v. 10a) and "its joy" (שִׂמְחָתוֹ, v. 10b) in **v. 10** constitute a merism that captures the full range of human emotions.[24] From an internal perspective, these emotions are known and existentially experienced only in the core of one's being (לֵב, v. 10a). And from an external perspective, even a stranger cannot interfere with or share in one's emotional experiences, whether positive or negative. The complexity and depth of human emotions and experiences engender a recognition of the limits of human knowledge.[25] While human hearts are open to YHWH (15:11), the emotions and experiences of the heart remain too profound to be fully understood by the self and too intense to be grasped by others.

Against the backdrop of the personal and interpersonal limits of one's emotions and experiences in 14:10, **v. 11** expresses the certain fate of the wicked and the upright. The antithetical saying intermingles the MORAL ACCOUNTING metaphor with the concept of MORAL STRENGTH. The former informs the initial line. Despite the stability of its physical structure, "the house of the wicked will be destroyed" (בֵּית רְשָׁעִים יִשָּׁמֵד, v. 11a);[26] that is, the residents, property, and posterity will pay the price for its moral makeup. The posture and moral strength of the upright, on the other hand, ensure that their "tent" (אֹהֶל, v. 11b) endures. The character of the tent's inhabitants renders it more stable than the house of the wicked. And the moral virtue of its members provides a rationale for its prosperity. Like a healthy tree, the tent of the upright will blossom, producing fruit for its inhabitants as well as for the community (cf. 11:28, 30; Ps 1).

Returning to the matter of human limits (14:10), **vv. 12–13** offer a pair of reflections pertaining to appearances and unanticipated ends. The aphorisms are linked by the expression "its end" (אַחֲרִיתָהּ, vv. 12b, 13b), but the end in view within each saying is distinct. The first opens with a יֵשׁ of reflection that, following Agustinus

21. Waltke, *Proverbs: Chapters 1–15*, 589.

22. While some take "guilt" (אָשָׁם, v. 9a) as the subject in the initial line (e.g., Meinhold, *Die Sprüche*, 1:233), it makes better sense as the object, since the personification of guilt scorning fools would be quite unusual.

23. Heim, *Like Grapes of Gold*, 177.

24. Van Leeuwen, "The Book of Proverbs," *NIB* 5:140.

25. Murphy, *Proverbs*, 104.

26. For the assonance and alliteration generated by the combination of רְשָׁעִים יִשָּׁמֵד (v. 11a) and יְשָׁרִים יַפְרִיחַ (v. 11b), see Clifford, *Proverbs*, 144–45.

Gianto, introduces "a contrast between appearance and reality" (**v. 12**).[27] And this contrast is conveyed through the pedagogical technique of the "false lead."[28] The initial line foregrounds an apparent reality for reflection: "a way that is straight before a person" (דֶּרֶךְ יָשָׁר לִפְנֵי־אִישׁ, v. 12a). Elsewhere in the anthology, straight ways are established by YHWH (3:6), paved by righteousness (11:5), and embodied by a person of understanding (15:21). A way that is straight, then, is a good way, a path that stands in opposition to the crooked paths of the wicked. The second line, however, bursts the bubble of this reading, for the end of this straight way is "ways to death" (דַּרְכֵי־מָוֶת, 14:12b). This end alerts the reader to the "false lead" of the initial line and demands a rereading.[29] The straight way *before* a person is not so straight after all; rather, it is a way that *seems* straight to a person. The prepositional phrase לִפְנֵי ("before") appears to function in a manner comparable to בְּעֵינֵי ("in the sight of"; cf. Prov 12:15; 16:25; 21:2; Neh 2:5–6).[30] The straight way, in the end, is not a morally approved way.[31] The יֵשׁ of reflection and the pedagogical technique of the "false lead" not only train the reader's moral reasoning but also reinforce the limits of creaturehood by guiding one through a process in which one recognizes that appearances do not always match reality. The same truth is reiterated in Prov 14 at **v. 13** through an emotional framework. Laughter may disguise heartache (v. 13a), but, in the end, the reality of melancholy will emerge from the masquerade of merriment (v. 13b). Appearances are deceiving and reality is opaque because humans are limited.

In spite of human limits and the ambiguity of reality, **v. 14** expresses the sages' confidence in the character-consequence connection. This connection is described through the concept of satiation. Both the "wayward of heart" (סוּג לֵב, v. 14a) and the "good person" (אִישׁ טוֹב, v. 14b) will be sated. The former will be filled by the fruit of his devious ways, while the latter will be satisfied by his virtuous deeds.[32] The aphorism awakens the reader's moral taste, appealing to the types of satiation engendered by one's character.

This concern with character is extended in **vv. 15–16**. These sayings profile various character types through the MORAL ESSENCE metaphor. According to the metaphor, one's character determines one's actions and one's actions determine one's character.[33] This reciprocal relationship structures the characterization of the intellectual prototypes in vv. 15–16. The "simple" (פֶּתִי, v. 15a) may be open to instruction (8:5; 9:4, 6; 19:25); but the malleability of this persona carries a moral liability. On account of his lack of discretion, the simple "believes anything" (יַאֲמִין לְכָל־דָּבָר, 14:15a); he does not possess the prudence to filter the words or deeds of others through the worldview of wisdom. The "shrewd" (עָרוּם, v. 15b), by contrast, embodies and exercises moral intelligence by considering and observing every step. The same is true of the "wise" (חָכָם, v. 16a). The substantival participle that modifies the subject indicates that

27. Gianto, "On יֵשׁ of Reflection in the Book of Proverbs," 160.

28. Suzanna R. Millar, "When a Straight Road Becomes a Garden Path: The 'False Lead' as a Pedagogical Strategy in the Book of Proverbs," *JSOT* 43 (2018): 67–82.

29. Millar, "When a Straight Road Becomes a Garden Path," 80.

30. Waltke, *Proverbs: Chapters 1–15*, 591; Millar, "When a Straight Road Becomes a Garden Path," 80.

31. Millar, "When a Straight Road Becomes a Garden Path," 80.

32. When read in conjunction with "from his ways" (מִדְּרָכָיו, v. 14a), the prepositional phrase "from upon him" (מֵעָלָיו, v. 14b) in the MT appears to be a case of haplography. Assuming that the consonants *mem* and *lamed* have dropped out, the expression should be rendered "from his deeds" (וממעלליו). For discussion, see Waltke, *Proverbs: Chapters 1–15*, 579.

33. Lakoff and Johnson, *Philosophy in the Flesh*, 306.

the wise are marked by a particular mode of being. This persona "fears" (יָרֵא, v. 16a); and if the term is elliptical, then the wise is one who fears YHWH.[34] Similar to 3:7, this moral ontology is manifested in "turning away from evil" (סָר מֵרָע, 14:16a; cf. 8:13; 16:6). The wise person's mode of being is expressed through a form of being in the world. In the same way, the fool's immoral mode of being is evinced through his behavior. As one who refuses to acknowledge the limits of creaturehood and his dependence on the divine, the fool oversteps moral boundaries. He is impulsive, indiscriminate in his expression of anger, and has an inflated view of self (14:16b).[35] Together, vv. 15–16 explore the moral essence of various character types. In so doing, these proverbs provide patterns through which to perceive people and on which one may recognize the value of discretion, prudence, and fear.

The characterization of the fool sets the stage for a pair of descriptions concerning folly (vv. 17–18). The noun אִוֶּלֶת ("folly," vv. 17a, 18a) links **vv. 17–18**, which integrate the MORAL ESSENCE and MORAL ACCOUNTING metaphors to cultivate moral aversions and values. Moral aversion captures the perlocutionary force of **v. 17**. In a rare departure from the antithetical cast of the sayings in Prov 10–15, the aphorism evaluates the external action of the short-tempered and the internal action of the schemer. As the antithesis to the patient or one "long of nose" (אֶרֶךְ אַפַּיִם, 14:29), the "short-tempered" is "short of nose" (קְצַר־אַפַּיִם, v. 17a); his impulsive, uncontrolled outbursts are the epitome of folly. This evaluation is escalated in the second line. The schemer may conceal his emotions, but his secret plans arouse communal hatred and shame. The distinctive evaluations of the short-tempered and the schemer may serve as an invitation to read these assessments together. On this account, the character and actions of the short-tempered as well as the schemer exemplify folly and generate communal loathing.

If v. 17 cultivates moral aversion, **v. 18** fosters the value of shrewdness. Whereas the character and actions of the short-tempered and schemer exemplified "folly" (אִוֶּלֶת, v. 17a), the simple are depicted as natural heirs of "folly" (אִוֶּלֶת, v. 18a). By virtue of their vulnerability to moral corruption, they possess the potential to inherit or gain possession of folly. The shrewd, on the other hand, receive a different gift. They are "crowned with knowledge" (יַכְתִּרוּ דָעַת, v. 18b); that is, they are adorned with external symbols that are indicative of their internal disposition. The dignity of their moral essence is reflected in the magnificence of their outward appearance.

The royal imagery of v. 18 provides the backdrop for the royal homage projected in **v. 19**. The aphorism operates under the MORAL STRENGTH metaphor, depicting the "good" (טוֹבִים, v. 19a) and the "righteous" (צַדִּיק, v. 19b) as those who rule over and judge the wicked. Moving from a physical and reverential posture of servitude before the good to a position of homage "at the gates of the righteous" (עַל־שַׁעֲרֵי צַדִּיק, v. 19b), the saying captures the power of moral character. And this power may be construed in judicial and material terms. Whether the mention of "gates" places the righteous as head of the judiciary or as the owner of a substantial

34. Van Leeuwen, "The Book of Proverbs," *NIB* 5:141; Waltke, *Proverbs: Chapters 1–15*, 595.

35. While מִתְעַבֵּר means "to show oneself angry" (*HALOT* 2:781, s.v. II עבר) and makes good sense in v. 16b, in an attempt to create a more precise parallel with "turns away from evil" (v. 16a), some read "interferes" (מתערב; LXX; Fox, *Proverbs: An Eclectic Edition*, 221). The verbs look similar and may have been confused. In any case, as Fox notes, these verbs focus attention on two aspects of the same act: the cause ("to be angry") and the effect ("interferes"). Fox, *Proverbs 10–31*, 579.

estate,[36] the term concretizes the moral strength of the righteous. More than the exemplar of the moral life, this figure is portrayed as a powerful agent of communal rule.[37]

While v. 19 explores the ethics of power in moral and judicial terms, **vv. 20–21** describe the ethics of power in socioeconomic terms. The proverbial pair is bound together by the mention of "his neighbor" (רֵעֵהוּ, vv. 20a, 21a) as well as a concern for the "poor" (רָשׁ, v. 20a; עֲנָיִים, v. 21b).[38] And the juxtaposition as well as the syntactical structure of the sayings critique and redefine the categories and character of these social relationships. The introductory גַּם ("even," v. 20a) functions in an emphatic fashion,[39] foregrounding the unfortunate certainty of the observation in **v. 20.** The fact of the matter is that the poor is hated by his neighbor, but the rich court a multitude of lovers (v. 20). The syntactical design of the individual lines indicates that the emotions of hate and love separate and secure social relationships, respectively.[40] The verb "is hated" (יִשָּׂנֵא, v. 20a) stands between "by his neighbor" (לְרֵעֵהוּ, v. 20a) and "the poor" (רָשׁ, v. 20a). And the substantival participle "those who love" (אֹהֲבֵי, v. 20b) connects the multitude of admirers with the rich. This social observation is realistic, but according to **v. 21**, it is not right. The initial line reiterates the expression "his neighbor" (לְרֵעֵהוּ, v. 21a). By associating one's response to a neighbor with one's response to the poor (v. 21b), however, the aphorism redefines the terms in v. 20.[41] The poor *is* one's neighbor, not a social outcast who should be shunned. One who despises his neighbor or hates the poor (vv. 20a, 21a), therefore, is a sinner (v. 21a), the one who deserves social shame.[42] But one who is gracious to the poor and, by implication, to one's neighbor, is blessed (v. 21b). This beatific state accompanies the one who recognizes that socioeconomic boundaries do not offer an answer to the question, "Who is my neighbor?" (Luke 10:29). Rather, the common dignity of all humans by virtue of their creation in the image of God determines one's neighbor and informs one's gracious, loving response to the other (Prov 14:31; 17:5; 22:2; 29:13).

This response corresponds with the experience of the "devisers of good" (חֹרְשֵׁי טוֹב, 14:22b) in **v. 22.** Cast in the form of a rhetorical question (הֲלוֹא; "do not," v. 22a), the aphorism considers the consequences that accompany different devisors, inviting the reader to affirm their respective fates. Whereas devisors of evil craft plans that ensure moral meandering, devisors of good experience "loyalty and faithfulness" (חֶסֶד וֶאֱמֶת, v. 22b). As virtues that convey the covenant commitment, constancy, loyalty, and reliability of both YHWH and humans (Exod 34:6; Deut 7:9, 12; 2 Sam 2:5–6; Ps 40:11),[43] these qualities outline the personal and relational worth of those who plan good. The precise relationship between these qualities and devisors of good, however, is unclear. The absence of a verb in the second line creates a lacuna that provokes the reader's moral imagination and solicits interpretive suggestions. Whether devisors of good "are" loyalty and faithfulness, "do" loyalty and faithfulness, or "experience" loyalty and faithful-

36. Murphy, *Proverbs*, 105; Waltke, *Proverbs: Chapters 1–15*, 598.

37. Lyu, *Righteousness*, 47–48.

38. While it makes little difference to the sense of the line, this reading follows *ketiv* (עֲנָיִים; "poor") rather than *qere* (עֲנָוִים; "oppressed") to retain the contrast between "rich" and "poor" in vv. 20–21.

39. *IBHS* §39.3.4d.

40. Yoder, *Proverbs*, 162–63.

41. Yoder, *Proverbs*, 163.

42. Yoder, *Proverbs*, 163.

43. Sakenfeld, *The Meaning of Ḥesed in the Hebrew Bible*, 233.

ness, these virtues are inextricably linked to their character and plans.[44]

The interrelationship between character and consequence in Prov 14 is extended in **vv. 23–24** through terms taken from the semantic field of wealth.[45] Similar to other aphorisms regarding diligence (10:4; 12:24, 27), v. 23 observes that all work yields some profit, while "a word of the lips" or "mere talk" (דְּבַר־שְׂפָתַיִם, v. 23b) without action brings only scarcity. The economic transaction between one's deeds and their consequences is reframed in v. 24, which describes the transaction generated by one's character. Just as the shrewd wear external symbols that reflect their moral essence (v. 18b), so also the wise wear wealth as an external indication of their character and connection to Lady Wisdom (4:9; 8:18). The worth of their moral essence is manifested in the dignity and splendor of their appearance. The "folly of fools" (אִוֶּלֶת כְּסִילִים, v. 24b), on the other hand, produces the immoral dividend of "folly" (אִוֶּלֶת, v. 24b). On account of their immoral essence, fools can only produce folly; and folly can only beget folly.[46]

Just as the metaphor of MORAL ESSENCE structures v. 24, so also the metaphor organizes **v. 25.** When the individual lines are read together, each highlights aspects of character or consequences that fill particular gaps in the other. A reliable witness saves lives, presumably because he breathes out truth (v. 25a). A deceiver, by contrast, breathes lies and, by implication, destroys lives (v. 25b).[47] Both act in accord with their character. Their character or moral essence determines their behavior and explains the consequences of their actions. The character and actions of a reliable witness testify to the liberating power and desirability of truthful speech; the air the deceiver breathes and the destructive power of his words bear witness to the repulsive nature of this character type.

The concern with one's moral essence continues in **vv. 26–27**. These aphorisms are linked by the expression "fear of YHWH" (יִרְאַת יְהוָה, vv. 26–27), which, as Job Jindo notes, is the "norm that constitutes the normative mode of human existence."[48] This normative moral ontology defines one's being as fully human. It creates a particular form of life; and vv. 26–27 explore the nature of this life through the metaphor of MORAL STRENGTH. Modified by the *bet* of the norm (בְּ, v. 26a), v. 26 identifies the fear of YHWH as a state or condition.[49] Far from inspiring angst or anxiety, this form of fear engenders "strong confidence" (מִבְטַח־עֹז, v. 26a) and provides a refuge for the God-fearer's offspring. That is, one in the state of the fear of YHWH experiences emotional stability and creates an environment of safety and security (cf. Pss 34:9[8]; 52:9[7]). The strength that accompanies the fear of YHWH is expanded and intensified in Prov 14:27. The juxtaposition of "the fear of YHWH" (יִרְאַת יְהוָה, v. 27a) with "a fountain of life" (מְקוֹר חַיִּים, v. 27a) projects the God-fearer as a source of vitality and refreshment. By virtue of his moral ontology, the God-fearer is a fount who sustains the life and quenches the thirst of the community (cf. 13:14). This life-sustaining

44. Yoder, *Proverbs*, 163; Fox, *Proverbs 10–31*, 581.

45. Heim, *Like Grapes of Gold*, 184.

46. Some emend "folly" (אִוֶּלֶת, v. 24b) to "garland" (לוית), since it provides a suitable parallel to "crown" and eliminates the tautology in the second line (e.g., Toy, *Proverbs*, 296–97; Fox, *Proverbs 10–31*, 582). But in light of the metaphor of MORAL ESSENCE and the fact that garlands or crowns are not associated with vices elsewhere in the book, the MT's reading should be retained. Waltke, *Proverbs: Chapters 1–15*, 581.

47. While יָפִחַ may be construed as a noun ("witness," v. 25b), it appears to function as a verb ("breathes") that supplies an appropriate counterpart to the verb in the initial line (cf. Prov 14:5). Fox, *Proverbs 10–31*, 592.

48. Jindo, "On the Biblical Notion," 449.

49. Williams, *Williams' Hebrew Syntax*, §252.

power is unpacked in 14:27b through the use of the epexegetical ל + infinitive construct (לָסוּר; "for avoiding," v. 27b).[50] As a fountain of life, the fear of YHWH empowers one to walk along the way of wisdom and avoid the snares of death. When taken together, vv. 26–27 portray the power of the fear of YHWH; it is a state of being that satisfies the human desire for assurance, stability, safety, satisfaction, and life.

The implicit communal orientation of v. 27 is explicit in **v. 28**. The king appears for the first time in the central collections (cf. Prov 1:1; 8:15); and his status is inextricably bound up with his people. A large population reflects a king's "splendor" (הַדְרַת, v. 28a)—a term used elsewhere only for the way in which one should worship YHWH (Pss 29:2; 96:9; 1 Chr 16:29; 2 Chr 20:21). That is, a king's glory resides in his just, competent rule, which produces communal prosperity and strengthens popular allegiance. If an abundant population serves as an indication of the character of a king's rule, then "a lack of a nation" (אֶפֶס לְאֹם, Prov 14:28b)[51] signifies its weakness, feeble kinship bonds, and inept governance, which portends a ruler's ruin.

Together, **vv. 29–30** move from the reciprocal relationship between the ruler and the ruled to the reciprocal relationship between one's emotions and their effects. This relationship is evaluated from an external as well as internal perspective. From an external perspective, one's emotions reveal one's MORAL ESSENCE. Just as patience exhibits one's great understanding and imitation of God (v. 29a; cf. Exod 34:6), so also unrestrained anger displays one's embodiment and advertisement of folly. From an internal perspective, one's emotions reveal one's MORAL HEALTH. While a "gentle heart" or a calm mind (לֵב מַרְפֵּא, Prov 14:30a) enlivens and sustains the self, jealousy eats away at one's insides, splintering the bones. Emotions have public and private faces, and these faces disclose the condition as well as the (un)desirability of one's moral essence and moral health.

To these emotional and moral diagnostics, **v. 31** offers a theological evaluation of social relationships. Returning to the theme of treatment of the poor (vv. 20–21), the aphorism highlights the theological basis for social ethics. This basis is founded on the fundamental conviction that all people are created in the *imago Dei* (Gen 1:26). All human beings, irrespective of their socioeconomic standing, have a common dignity that derives from their common Creator (cf. Prov 17:5; 22:2; 29:13). One who oppresses or exploits the poor, therefore, denigrates God's workmanship, while the one who is gracious to the poor honors both the Maker and the one whom he has made.

This theological evaluation in 14:31 serves as a backdrop for **v. 32**, which explores the intimate relationship between character and consequences through the metaphor of MORAL STRENGTH. By virtue of his moral instability, the wicked "is thrust down" (יִדָּחֶה, v. 32a), shattered by means of his own evil (cf. Pss 35:5; 36:13[12]; 62:5[4]).[52] The moral strength of the righteous, by contrast, is manifest in the protection and security this exemplar finds throughout the course of life. Character serves as a stronghold, and if YHWH is the unstated object of "finds refuge" (חֹסֶה, Prov 14:32b), then this shelter is sought in the divine.[53] These sources of safety provide a hedge for the righteous "in his death" (בְמוֹתוֹ, v. 32b).[54] While the expression may

50. *IBHS* §36.2.3e; Heim, *Like Grapes of Gold*, 186.

51. For the privative use of אֶפֶס, see Williams, *Williams' Hebrew Syntax*, §426.

52. For the בְּ of agency, see *IBHS* §23.2.2f.

53. Meinhold, *Die Sprüche*, 1:245; Heim, *Like Grapes of Gold*, 190; Waltke, *Proverbs: Chapters 1–15*, 582.

54. The LXX and Syriac versions read בתמו ("in his integrity") rather than בְמוֹתוֹ ("in his death"), based on a metathesis

gesture to a vague conception of the afterlife, the active nature of the verb suggests that the righteous receives protection throughout the course of life.[55] Character and YHWH accompany the righteous on their lifelong journey, satisfying the basic human longing for safety and protection.

Strength of character offers protection; and according to **v. 33**, the essence of one's character determines one's receptivity to wisdom. Similar to the inchoate personification of Wisdom in certain parental lectures within Prov 1–9, the aphorism employs vivid imagery to identify the place where Wisdom rests. Wisdom not only invites others to enter her home (9:1–6); she also "rests" (תָּנוּחַ, 14:33a) or makes her home in the heart of the discerning. The *waw* conjunctive that opens the second line may introduce coordination ("and") or an antithesis ("but"). Whether it marks coordination or an antithesis, the line intimates that wisdom reveals herself in distinctive ways to both parties: she dwells in the heart of the discerning but manifests herself in the middle of fools. The way in which Wisdom manifests herself in the midst of fools is open and ambiguous.[56] What is clear, however, is that one's moral essence determines one's relation to Wisdom. The character of the discerning creates a home for Wisdom to rest. The moral ontology of fools, by contrast, ensures that Wisdom remains one who may enter their midst but not their heart.

Wisdom's distinctive relationship with the discerning and fools corresponds with the distinctive relationship between virtue/vice and a nation in **v. 34**. Righteousness exalts a nation through its cultivation of an environment of mutual flourishing (v. 34a). At first glance, the opening phrase of the second line appears to unpack aspects of this moral environment, for, with the exception of one other instance (Lev 20:17), the term חֶסֶד means "kindness" or "covenant commitment."[57] When one reaches the evaluation "sin" (חַטָּאת, Prov 14:34b) at the end of the line, however, one recognizes the "false lead."[58] The covenant commitment or loyalty of peoples is not sin; rather, sin is the "disgrace of peoples." The evaluation hones the reader's moral reasoning, forcing one to double back and reinterpret the rare homonym. This reinterpretation yields a clear antithesis that locates a nation's status in the (im)moral character of its constituents.

The final saying elaborates on the communal orientation of v. 34 by giving particular attention to the king's response to discrete servants (**v. 35**). Just as the status of the nation is dependent on the moral character of its members, so also the king is dependent on capable servants. The prudence and aptitude of a competent courtier elicits the king's pleasure, while his wrath is manifested in and experienced by an inept, disgraceful servant. On one level, this straightforward statement may serve as an admonition to the king, encouraging him to cultivate capable administrators by rewarding the

---

of מ and ת as well as the insertion of ו in the MT. Many follow this reading, arguing, among other things, that the MT seems to affirm a belief in the afterlife that is anachronistic (e.g., McKane, *Proverbs*, 475; Fox, *Proverbs 10–31*, 585–86). Whether one follows the MT or the LXX, the sense that character and YHWH offer protection throughout one's temporal life remains (cf. Prov 10:2; 11:4).

55. Waltke, *Proverbs: Chapters 1–15*, 582–83.

56. In light of the fact that Proverbs suggests fools are unable to learn, many render the second line in two different ways. First, following the LXX and Syriac versions, some insert the particle לא to read "among fools Wisdom is unknown" (Gemser, *Sprüche Salomos*, 67; Garrett, *Proverbs*, 147; Van Leeuwen, "The Book of Proverbs," *NIB* 5:145). Second, despite the absence of an appropriate marker, others read the second line as a rhetorical question, with the sense "will Wisdom come to be known?" (Meinhold, *Die Sprüche*, 1:242; Murphy, *Proverbs*, 102n33a). Both proposals provide possible readings, but the MT remains the more difficult and the most probable reading.

57. Fox, *Proverbs 10–31*, 587; Yoder, *Proverbs*, 166.

58. Millar, "When a Straight Road Becomes a Garden Path," 67–82, esp. 72–73.

competent and reproving the corrupt.[59] On another level, however, the saying calls royal servants to demonstrate prudence and competence in their work in order to secure the favor of the king and avert his fury.

In light of the shared language between v. 28 and vv. 34–35, some contend that these sayings frame a coherent unit that explores the social conditions of a just reign. The frame is formed through the repetition of the terms מֶלֶךְ (vv. 28a, 35a) and לְאֹם (vv. 28b, 34b), on the one hand, and the wordplay between רְזוֹן and רְצוֹן (vv. 28b, 35a), on the other.[60] This frame recontextualizes the individual aphorisms in vv. 29–33. When read through this communal and monarchical framework, the individual aphorisms sketch the reciprocal relationship between the ruler and the ruled.[61] Patience and quietude are presented as virtues that reinforce the king's ability to execute justice and increase the welfare of the community (vv. 29–30). By embodying righteousness and exercising kindness to the needy (vv. 31b, 32b), the king and the individual find refuge in YHWH while the wicked are consumed by their evil. And as one with a discerning disposition, wisdom resides within the king and provides him with an indispensable resource for dealing with fools (v. 33). On this account, the royal establishment requires prudent advisors to secure communal welfare (v. 35), while the king is responsible to maintain justice by acting on behalf of the people (v. 28), protecting the rights of the disenfranchised (vv. 31–32), and inspiring righteousness through his character and leadership (vv. 29–30, 33, 34–35). The sayings within vv. 28 and 34–35 may outline the communal orientation and responsibilities of the king. But this represents only one way of construing these aphorisms.[62] The sayings allow for other readings, which form emotions, cultivate social relations, and nourish moral virtues and dispositions characteristic of the wise life.

59. Waltke, *Proverbs: Chapters 1–15*, 612.

60. Plöger, *Sprüche Salomos*, 174–76; Meinhold, *Die Sprüche*, 1:242–46; idem, "Das Wortspiel רזון-רצון in Prov 14,28–35," *ZAW* 110 (1998): 615–16; Garrett, *Proverbs*, 145–47; Heim, *Like Grapes of Gold*, 187–89.

61. For a reading of the sayings within this framework, see Meinhold, *Die Sprüche*, 1:242–46; Garrett, *Proverbs*, 145–47; Heim, *Like Grapes of Gold*, 188–91.

62. Schwáb, "The Sayings Clusters in Proverbs," 59–79.

CHAPTER 21

Proverbs 15:1–33

F. Forming Moral Wholeness: *The Homogeneity of Normative Character*

Main Idea of the Passage

These aphorisms devote considerable attention to the physical, emotional, attitudinal, and divine-human dimensions of selfhood, producing a homogeneous portrait of moral wholeness that attunes one to the unity and stability of normative character.

Literary Context[1]

Similar to the metaphor of MORAL BOUNDARIES,[2] the metaphor of MORAL WHOLENESS provides a way to conceptualize uniform standards of behavior and the symmetry of normative character.[3] Among other things, the metaphor entails an overall unity of form that makes an entity strong and capable of functioning in its natural capacity.[4] On this account, the concept is related to the metaphor of MORAL ESSENCE. But these metaphors remain distinct. Whereas the MORAL ESSENCE metaphor considers the reciprocal relationship between character and actions, the MORAL WHOLENESS metaphor explores the homogeneity of the moral self; it integrates one's physical, emotional, attitudinal, and moral qualities into the whole of normative character. These discrete qualities pervade the individual aphorisms gathered in Prov 15. When read together, the sayings outline the facets of moral wholeness and the homogeneous nature of normative character. Their attention to the body, emotions, attitudes, actions, and divine-human relations illuminates the wholeness, unity, and stability of the moral life.

1. This chapter does not include the Explanation of the Text section. See pp. xv and 276n1 for justification.

2. For discussion of the metaphor, see Lakoff and Johnson, *Philosophy in the Flesh*, 304–6.

3. George Lakoff, *Moral Politics: How Liberals and Conservatives Think*, 3rd ed. (Chicago: University of Chicago Press, 2016), 90.

4. Lakoff, *Moral Politics*, 90–92.

The consideration of these motifs may not be new, but their conspicuous coverage and combination within the chapter attunes one to the harmonious interrelationship among these components of moral wholeness. The relationship between physical and moral wholeness is engendered by the juxtaposition of body parts, character types, and images of human flourishing. One's moral wholeness is commensurate with the physical wholeness of one's tongue (לָשׁוֹן, v. 2a), mouth (פֶּה, vv. 2b, 14b [Q], 23a, 28b), lips (שָׂפָה, v. 7a), ear (אֹזֶן, v. 31a), and, most importantly, one's "heart/mind" (לֵב, vv. 7b, 14a, 28a, 32b). Heart/mind is mentioned more frequently here than in any other chapter in Proverbs (vv. 7b, 11b, 13a, 13b, 14a, 15b, 28a, 30a, 32b). Its use not only reinforces the intimate link between one's character and actions, but it also accentuates the psychosomatic unity of the self. The emotional state of the heart brightens or breaks one's countenance (v. 13; cf. v. 4), nourishes one's condition, irrespective of circumstances (v. 15b), and manifests itself through one's beaming appearance (v. 30a). Body parts feature prominently in the sayings within Prov 15. And body parts inform the chapter's construal of divine-human relations. Wholeness includes more than one's physical and moral homogeneity; it also includes one's relationship with YHWH, who sees everything, even the condition of human hearts (vv. 3, 11).

The attention to body parts and physical-moral wholeness coincides with the chapter's concern with the emotional and attitudinal dimensions of moral wholeness. These emotions and attitudes range from wrath (vv. 1a, 18a), anger (v. 1b), disdain (vv. 5a, 20b, 32a), and hatred (vv. 10b, 17b, 27b) to love (vv. 9b, 12a, 17a), joy (vv. 13a, 20a, 21a, 23a, 30a), and delight (v. 8b). They define one's character (v. 21a, 23), response to discipline (vv. 5a, 10b, 12a, 20b, 32a), and the ethos of one's community (v. 17, 20), as well as the personal and social implications of one's actions (vv. 1, 18, 27). Furthermore, similar to the relationship between physical and moral wholeness, these attitudes and emotions inform the chapter's consideration of divine-human relations. Loathing and love, abhorrence and delight characterize YHWH's response to certain characters, cultic activities, ways, and actions (vv. 8, 9, 26; cf. v. 29). What's more, the fear of YHWH determines one's moral ontology, producing a mode of being marked by humility (v. 33) and a perspectival frame of reference that allows one to experience peace with "a little" (מְעַט, v. 16a). Attitudes and emotions are key components of the moral self. Together with its concern with physical and moral wholeness, Prov 15 gives particular attention to the emotional and attitudinal dimensions of moral wholeness through personal, interpersonal, and divine-human relations. The homogeneity of one's body, emotions, and attitudes manifest the unity of normative character and the stability of the moral life.

While the configuration of sayings pertaining to the physical, emotional, and attitudinal dimensions of the moral life provides a fresh angle on the homogeneity of normative character, these facets of the wise and virtuous life are addressed in both the preceding and subsequent chapters. In addition to the many thematic resemblances that Prov 15 shares with other materials in the anthology, the chapter contains a variety of variant repetitions, which provide clear intertextual links with sayings across the sentence literature.[5] More striking than these variant repetitions is the intimate relationship between the materials in Prov 15 and the sayings situated at the seams of the preceding and subsequent collections. The final aphorism (15:33a) mirrors the conclusion of the preamble (1:7a) and the hinge that closes the prologue (9:10a). And, as Raymond Van Leeuwen has noted, many of the sayings in Prov 15 resemble materials from Prov 10.[6] The opening aphorism of the Solomonic collection is reiterated and recast in 15:20 (10:1b–c; cf. 15:5).[7] The impotence of the wealth of the wicked (15:6) and YHWH's relation to satiation (15:16–17) recall 10:2–3. The aphorisms devoted to observing or rejecting discipline and reproof (15:5; 10, 12, 31–32) allude to 10:17, 12:1, and 13:1. And the expression "fear of YHWH" (יִרְאַת יְהוָה; 15:16a, 33a) echoes 10:27 (cf. 14:26–27). The unusual intertextual connections between Prov 15 and the compositional seams of the preamble (1:7; 15:33), prologue (9:10; 15:33), and first Solomonic collection (10:1b–c; 15:20), combined with the thematic parallels between its aphorisms and ch. 10, intimate that the chapter forms "a verbal and thematic envelope to mark off the first Solomonic subcollection."[8] If, as many assume, Prov 10:1–15:33 represents the first of two subcollections within Prov 10:1–22:16,[9] the variant repetitions within and the subject matter of ch. 15 suggest that it serves as an appropriate conclusion.

These observations, however, represent only half of the contextual story. Similar to 9:7–12, Prov 15 also provides an appropriate introduction to the materials in ch. 16. Both 15:16 and 15:33b are cast in lexical and syntactical templates that resemble 16:8 and 16:18a, respectively. The dense concentration of YHWH sayings in ch. 15 sets the stage for the sequence of YHWH sayings that open the second half of the Solomonic collection (15:3, 8, 9, 11, 16, 25, 26, 29, 33; 16:1–9). And, when read in relation to the subsequent materials, 15:33 appears to identify the mode of being necessary for ingesting the aphorisms that follow. On contextual grounds, ch. 15 functions as a hinge within Prov 10:1–22:16. It concludes the first Solomonic subcollection, on the one hand, and eases the reader into the second Solomonic subcollection, on the other.

5. These variant repetitions include **15:33a**//1:7a//9:10a; **15:20**//10:1b–c; **15:22**//11:14; **15:2**//15:14//12:23//13:16; **15:8a**//21:27a; **15:13**//17:22; **15:14a**//18:15a; **15:16**//16:8; **15:18a**//29:22a; **15:22b**//24:6b; **15:33b**//18:12//16:18a. For discussion of these variant repetitions, see Heim, *Poetic Imagination*, 51–61, 208–13, 267–73, 320–28, 363–98.

6. Van Leeuwen, "The Book of Proverbs," *NIB* 5:148.

7. Winkler, "Die drei Sprüche „weisen Sohn," 81–99. Winkler argues that the variant repetition concerning the "wise son" was placed at the beginning (10:1b–c), middle (13:1), and end (15:20) of Prov 10–15 to create compositional coherence across a distance.

8. Van Leeuwen, "The Book of Proverbs," *NIB* 5:148.

9. Meinhold, *Die Sprüche*, 1:26; Van Leeuwen, "The Book of Proverbs," *NIB* 5:105; Clifford, *Proverbs*, 108; Yoder, *Proverbs*, 167; Fox, *Proverbs 10–31*, xviii–xix, 509; Sæbø, *Sprüche*, 160. Others follow a similar structural model but mark the division of the collection at different places. Waltke, *Proverbs: Chapters 1–15*, 16; idem, *Proverbs: Chapters 15–31*, 5–8; Weeks, *Early Israelite Wisdom*, 26–27.

Translation and Exegetical Outline

(See pages 421–23.)

Structure and Literary Form

Just as the YHWH sayings within Prov 15 ease the reader into the second Solomonic subcollection, so also the poetic texture of the aphorisms prepares one for the materials that follow. While different types of sayings punctuate Prov 10:1–14:35, on the whole, antithetical sayings pervade the literary landscape. These sayings maintain a presence in ch. 15, but they are far less pronounced. "Better-than" proverbs (vv. 16–17), תּוֹעֵבָה ("abomination") templates (vv. 8–9, 26), and other poetic forms occupy the terrain.[10] And several sayings exhibit asymmetrical parallelism, inviting the reader to exercise their moral reasoning by filling in particular gaps (vv. 5, 6, 16, 20).[11] The poetic texture of Prov 15 is similar to and different from the preceding and subsequent materials. In light of the formal diversity of the sayings, it appears that ch. 15 represents a "grey area" between the Solomonic subcollections.[12] Or, to borrow an expression from Roland Murphy, it "is a mixture of *nova et vetera*, the new and the old."[13]

10. For a discussion of the better-than proverb and תּוֹעֵבָה template, see Fox, *Proverbs 10–31*, 491, 597–98.

11. For discussion of these asymmetrical or disjointed proverbs, see Fox, "The Rhetoric of Disjointed Proverbs," 169–71; idem, *Proverbs 10–31*, 600.

12. Weeks, *Early Israelite Wisdom*, 26.

13. Murphy, *Proverbs*, 115.

Proverbs 15:1–33

1a	מַעֲנֶה־רַּךְ יָשִׁיב חֵמָה	A soft answer turns away wrath;	F. Forming Moral Wholeness: The Homogeneity of Normative Character (15:1–33)
1b	וּדְבַר־עֶצֶב יַעֲלֶה־אָף	but a harsh word provokes anger.	
2a	לְשׁוֹן חֲכָמִים תֵּיטִיב דָּעַת	The tongue of the wise adorns knowledge;	
2b	וּפִי כְסִילִים יַבִּיעַ אִוֶּלֶת	but the mouth of fools pours out folly.	
3a	בְּכָל־מָקוֹם עֵינֵי יְהוָה	In every place, the eyes of YHWH,	
3b	צֹפוֹת רָעִים וטוֹבִים	observing the evil and the good.	
4a	מַרְפֵּא לָשׁוֹן עֵץ חַיִּים	A soothing tongue, a tree of life;	
4b	וְסֶלֶף בָּהּ שֶׁבֶר בְּרוּחַ	but perversion in it breaks the spirit.	
5a	אֱוִיל יִנְאַץ מוּסַר אָבִיו	A fool despises his father's discipline;	
5b	וְשֹׁמֵר תּוֹכַחַת יַעְרִם	but one who observes reproof is shrewd.	
6a	בֵּית צַדִּיק חֹסֶן רָב	The house of the righteous, much wealth;	
6b	וּבִתְבוּאַת רָשָׁע נֶעְכָּרֶת	but in the produce of the wicked, ruin.	
7a	שִׂפְתֵי חֲכָמִים יְזָרוּ דָעַת	The lips of the wise disperse knowledge;	
7b	וְלֵב כְּסִילִים לֹא־כֵן	but the heart of fools, not so.	
8a	זֶבַח רְשָׁעִים תּוֹעֲבַת יְהוָה	The sacrifice of the wicked, an abomination to YHWH;	
8b	וּתְפִלַּת יְשָׁרִים רְצוֹנוֹ	but the prayer of the upright, his delight.	
9a	תּוֹעֲבַת יְהוָה דֶּרֶךְ רָשָׁע	An abomination to YHWH, the way of the wicked;	
9b	וּמְרַדֵּף צְדָקָה יֶאֱהָב	but one who pursues righteousness he loves.	
10a	מוּסָר רָע לְעֹזֵב אֹרַח	Severe discipline for one who abandons the way;	
10b	שׂוֹנֵא תוֹכַחַת יָמוּת	one who hates reproof will die.	
11a	שְׁאוֹל וַאֲבַדּוֹן נֶגֶד יְהוָה	Sheol and Abaddon are before YHWH—	
11b	אַף כִּי־לִבּוֹת בְּנֵי־אָדָם	how much more human hearts!	
12a	לֹא יֶאֱהַב־לֵץ הוֹכֵחַ לוֹ	A scoffer does not love being reproved;	
12b	אֶל־חֲכָמִים לֹא יֵלֵךְ	to the wise he will not go.	
13a	לֵב שָׂמֵחַ יֵיטִב פָּנִים	A joyful heart brightens the face;	
13b	וּבְעַצְּבַת־לֵב רוּחַ נְכֵאָה	but in a troubled heart, a broken spirit.	

Continued on next page.

Continued from previous page.

14a	לֵב נָבוֹן יְבַקֶּשׁ־דָּעַת	The heart of the discerning seeks knowledge;
14b	וּפִי כְסִילִים יִרְעֶה אִוֶּלֶת	but the mouth of fools feeds on folly.
15a	כָּל־יְמֵי עָנִי רָעִים	All the days of the poor, bad;
15b	וְטוֹב־לֵב מִשְׁתֶּה תָמִיד	but a cheerful heart, a continual feast.
16a	טוֹב־מְעַט בְּיִרְאַת יְהוָה	Better a little with the fear of YHWH,
16b	מֵאוֹצָר רָב וּמְהוּמָה בוֹ	than great treasure and turmoil with it.
17a	טוֹב אֲרֻחַת יָרָק וְאַהֲבָה־שָׁם	Better a portion of greens with love,
17b	מִשּׁוֹר אָבוּס וְשִׂנְאָה־בוֹ	than a fattened ox with hatred.
18a	אִישׁ חֵמָה יְגָרֶה מָדוֹן	A hothead provokes strife;
18b	וְאֶרֶךְ אַפַּיִם יַשְׁקִיט רִיב	but the patient quiets disputes.
19a	דֶּרֶךְ עָצֵל כִּמְשֻׂכַת חָדֶק	The way of the sluggard, like a hedge of thorns;
19b	וְאֹרַח יְשָׁרִים סְלֻלָה	but the path of the upright, a highway.
20a	בֵּן חָכָם יְשַׂמַּח־אָב	A wise son brings joy to a father;
20b	וּכְסִיל אָדָם בּוֹזֶה אִמּוֹ	but a foolish person despises his mother.
21a	אִוֶּלֶת שִׂמְחָה לַחֲסַר־לֵב	Folly, joy to the senseless;
21b	וְאִישׁ תְּבוּנָה יְיַשֶּׁר־לָכֶת	but a person of understanding walks straight.
22a	הָפֵר מַחֲשָׁבוֹת בְּאֵין סוֹד	Plans are thwarted without counsel;
22b	וּבְרֹב יוֹעֲצִים תָּקוּם	but with many counselors they succeed.
23a	שִׂמְחָה לָאִישׁ בְּמַעֲנֵה־פִיו	A person takes delight in the answer of his mouth;
23b	וְדָבָר בְּעִתּוֹ מַה־טּוֹב	and a word in its time, how good!
24a	אֹרַח חַיִּים לְמַעְלָה לְמַשְׂכִּיל	The way of life, upward for the prudent,
24b	לְמַעַן סוּר מִשְּׁאוֹל מָטָּה	that he might turn aside from Sheol below.
25a	בֵּית גֵּאִים יִסַּח יְהוָה	YHWH tears down the house of the proud;
25b	וְיַצֵּב גְּבוּל אַלְמָנָה	and he establishes the boundary of the widow.

26a	תּוֹעֲבַת יְהוָה מַחְשְׁבוֹת רָע	An abomination to YHWH, plans of the evil;
26b	וּטְהֹרִים אִמְרֵי־נֹעַם	but pleasant words are pure.
27a	עֹכֵר בֵּיתוֹ בּוֹצֵעַ בָּצַע	One who troubles his house: one who profits from unjust gain;
27b	וְשׂוֹנֵא מַתָּנֹת יִחְיֶה	but one who hates bribes will live.
28a	לֵב צַדִּיק יֶהְגֶּה לַעֲנוֹת	The heart of the righteous reflects before answering;
28b	וּפִי רְשָׁעִים יַבִּיעַ רָעוֹת	but the mouth of the wicked pours out evil things.
29a	רָחוֹק יְהוָה מֵרְשָׁעִים	YHWH is far from the wicked;
29b	וּתְפִלַּת צַדִּיקִים יִשְׁמָע	but the prayer of the righteous he hears.
30a	מְאוֹר־עֵינַיִם יְשַׂמַּח־לֵב	The light of the eyes brings joy to the heart;
30b	שְׁמוּעָה טוֹבָה תְּדַשֶּׁן־עָצֶם	a good report fattens the bones.
31a	אֹזֶן שֹׁמַעַת תּוֹכַחַת חַיִּים	The ear that listens to the reproof of life
31b	בְּקֶרֶב חֲכָמִים תָּלִין	dwells among the wise.
32a	פּוֹרֵעַ מוּסָר מוֹאֵס נַפְשׁוֹ	One who neglects discipline despises his life;
32b	וְשׁוֹמֵעַ תּוֹכַחַת קוֹנֶה לֵּב	but one who listens to reproof acquires sense.
33a	יִרְאַת יְהוָה מוּסַר חָכְמָה	The fear of YHWH, instruction in wisdom;
33b	וְלִפְנֵי כָבוֹד עֲנָוָה	and before honor, humility.

The literary texture of the aphorisms in Prov 15 may indicate that it constitutes a generic grey area between the Solomonic subcollections; but lexical, thematic, and conceptual affinities among the sayings suggest that certain aphorisms are organized into intentional units. These units vary among interpreters who see coherence in the central collections. For most, catchwords and common motifs between juxtaposed sayings reveal several proverbial pairs (vv. 1–2, 8–9, 13–14, 16–17, 20–21, 25–26, 28–29, 32–33).[14] For some, shared vocabulary and themes within a sequence of sayings signal that these proverbial pairs are parts within larger clusters (vv. 1–4, 5–12, 13–19, 20–24, 25–33).[15] And for a few, the materials in ch. 15 form part of an extended diptych: the content of vv. 1–17 matches the content of Prov 15:18–16:8.[16] Irrespective of the way in which one cuts this structural pie, the micro- and macro-grouping of the aphorisms accentuate the recurrent mention of body parts, emotions, and attitudes as well as matters of speech, instruction, and YHWH. In so doing, they offer different vantage points on the design of the whole and its integration of the parts that comprise moral wholeness.

Canonical and Theological Significance

According to Charles Taylor, "Moral philosophy has tended to focus on what it is right to do rather than on what it is good to be, on defining the content of obligation rather than the nature of the good life."[17] If Taylor's assessment is right, then Proverbs bucks this tendency, for it focuses on the nature of the good life through the nature of its moral exemplar: the righteous. Among the character types profiled in Prov 10:1–15:33, the righteous is foregrounded and rendered in such a way as to show one "what it is good to be." The righteous is *the* prototypical character within Proverbs, the anthology's "ideal virtuous agent."[18] Put differently, "any and every positive characteristic in the book is embodied in the righteous."[19] Far from representing a bald assertion concerning the moral centrality of this character type, it is important to note that the righteous remains distinct from his/her intellectual counterpart, the wise. Whereas the wise as well as the righteous possess the moral ontology and epistemological capacity to increase in wisdom or learning (9:9), it is striking that the righteous is unable to increase in righteousness. The state of the righteous is

14. Among others, see Toy, *Proverbs*, 305–17; Sæbø, *Sprüche*, 219.

15. While the boundaries of these units vary among interpreters, the general contours are comparable. Meinhold, *Die Sprüche*, 1:227; Heim, *Like Grapes of Gold*, 191–205; Waltke, *Proverbs: Chapters 1–15*, 609–31; idem, *Proverbs: Chapters 15–31*, 5; Schipper, *Proverbs 1–15*, 490–91.

16. Garrett, *Proverbs*, 149–50.

17. Charles Taylor, *Sources of the Self: The Making of Modern Identity* (Cambridge: Harvard University Press, 1989), 3.

18. Rosalind Hursthouse, *On Virtue Ethics* (Oxford: Oxford University Press, 1999), 148.

19. Millar, *Genre and Openness*, 107.

fixed.[20] Or, to borrow a category from Aquinas, it appears that the righteousness of the righteous is an infused virtue.[21] The righteous constitutes the embodiment of moral virtue and human flourishing in Proverbs.

From a moral perspective, the righteous epitomizes virtue across Prov 10:1–15:33, and from a pedagogical perspective, the righteous induces desire for virtuous character "*by showing what is desirable*."[22] The poetic snapshots of the righteous trace the contours and illuminate the substance of the good life. But the literary presentation of the righteous is not all about show; it is equally about admiration. Here Linda Trinkaus Zagzebski's work is especially helpful. In accord with her exemplarist moral theory, Zagzebski maintains that moral exemplars engender "moral admiration" for a particular sort of person.[23] By definition, admiration trades on attraction. This is the case with the righteous. The poetic renderings of the righteous are attractive advertisements, pedagogical marketing ploys that evoke admiration and compel one to emulate the good life. Like modern marketing firms, Proverbs banks its advertising on a fundamental anthropological assumption: human beings are lovers or desirers. If one is or becomes what one admires or loves, then Proverbs impels one to admire and love the righteous.

Desire, admiration, and attraction animate modern advertising. Gatorade, for example, invited people to "Be like Mike" (i.e., Michael Jordan).[24] Proverbs, in comparable fashion, invites one to be like the righteous.

This example may be trite. But it captures the dynamics of desire, admiration, attraction, and emulation. Zagzebski is right: concrete moral exemplars are primary; they precede the virtues we associate with them. Michael Jordan precedes the characterization many associate with him: the GOAT in basketball. The same is true of the righteous. That one is the GOAT in the moral life. And the poetic presentation of the righteous invites one to apply the characterization to concrete exemplars in one's own life: to parents, friends, and teachers.

The sayings across Prov 10:1–15:33 move one to admire the righteous and to emulate their form of life by appealing to basic human loves or desires. A few deserve specific comment. Many sayings traffic in the desire for safety or security. The righteous and the virtue of righteousness are depicted as powers that bring about deliverance and ensure stability (10:2, 25, 30; 11:4, 6, 8, 9; 12:3, 13, 21; 13:6). Other sayings gesture to the desire for satisfaction. YHWH will never allow the righteous to starve (10:3). In fact, YHWH will satisfy the righteous, granting them their desire

20. Lyu, *Righteousness*, 61.

21. Thomas Aquinas, *Summa Theologiae*, 5 vols., ed. Thomas Gilby (Cambridge: Cambridge University Press, 2006), I–II, q. 65, art 2.

22. Lyu, *Righteousness*, 62 (italics original).

23. Linda Trinkaus Zagzebski, *Exemplarist Moral Theory* (Oxford: Oxford University Press, 2017), 30–59.

24. Bernie Pitzel, "Be Like Mike," music by Ira Antelis and Steve Shafer (1991).

(10:24). And the righteous, in turn, will satisfy others through their speech (10:21). Still other sayings entice readers through the prospect of honor (10:6; 14:19), moral worth (10:20), good (13:21), and wealth (13:22; 15:6). When taken together, it is not surprising that the righteous enjoy that which all humans long to possess: a full, flourishing life (11:10, 19, 28, 30; 12:12, 28).

The righteous represent Proverbs's prime pedagogical stimulus for a life of wisdom and virtue. This prototype models and motivates the moral life. As a moral prototype, the righteous are idealized, just as people and products are idealized in modern advertising. The righteous, like airbrushed figures in advertising campaigns, resemble people in the real world; but they are not designed to mirror people in the real world. They are designed to show what is desirable and to direct one's desires to a form of life that is good by evoking "emotions, moods, erotic desire, empathy, and a host of typical affective states that motivate" one's embodied actions in the world.[25] In so doing, the righteous shape "the reader's desires and satisfactions," coaxing one to become this "*kind of desirer*," this type of person.[26]

The righteous is a particular type of person in Proverbs. By virtue of their characterization, "righteous" awakens a host of ideas and canonical connotations. To the Protestant ear, the Reformation's construal of the "righteous" or "righteousness" as an imputed forensic status immediately springs to mind. From a canonical perspective, this understanding may be a latent theological judgment within Proverbs's use of the concepts of the "righteous" and "righteousness."[27] But it is not the primary sense of these terms. Like the characterization of other characters in Proverbs, the "righteous" and "righteousness" are best interpreted as ethical designations. They denote being and behavior in accord with some standard.[28] And yet, like their use elsewhere in the canon, this standard is implicit in Proverbs. Gerhard von Rad captures this sentiment: righteousness operates under a norm, but "no matter how urgently it was sought, no satisfactory answer to this question of an absolute norm could be found in the Old Testament."[29] Despite the absence of an explicit norm, scholars have proposed an implicit standard for the "righteous" and "righteousness" in Proverbs. While some identify this norm for being and behavior as "world order" or "created order,"[30] it appears that the norm for righteousness is "God himself—his Being and doing."[31] The righteous are not righteous by virtue of their conformity to a "world order"; rather, the righteous are righteous because they conform to God's righteous-

25. Johnson, *Moral Imagination*, 191.

26. Booth, *The Company We Keep*, 204.

27. For this distinction between judgments and concepts, see David Yeago, "The New Testament and Nicene Dogma," *ProEccl* 3 (1993): 152–64.

28. Reimer, "צדק," *NIDOTTE* 3.750.

29. Gerhard von Rad, *Old Testament Theology, Volume 1: The Theology of Israel's Historical Traditions*, trans. D. M. G. Stalker, OTL (Louisville: Westminster John Knox, 2001), 371.

30. Schmid, *Gerechtigkeit als Weltordnung*, 66–67.

31. Jeffrey J. Niehaus, "Righteousness and the Created Order: Appreciation and Critique of a Novel Idea," *JETS* 63 (2020): 235.

ness and, by implication, live in accord with the created order.[32] In this respect, the righteous one images God. That is, the righteous one participates in and imitates God's righteousness for the sake of shalom.

Proverbs's moral and pedagogical use of the "righteous" and "righteousness" may not fund a dogmatic account of justification; but its use of the "righteous" and "righteousness" contributes to accounts of ethics and sanctification. In fact, the didactic function of the righteous in Proverbs counters the charge that imputed righteousness and justification by faith alone inevitably lead to antinomianism or libertinism. Like the righteous and righteousness in the Sermon on the Mount, Proverbs depicts the righteous as the "whole person" (τέλειος, Matt 5:48) who embodies and enacts righteousness "through behavior that accords with God's nature" and will.[33] This embodiment and enaction of righteousness corresponds with Oliver O'Donovan's definition of sanctification:

> Sanctification is the gracious work of God in our human living that leads out the gift of righteous agency in Christ into reconciled participation in the world, shaping within us the multifaceted virtue of love.[34]

According to Proverbs, the righteous manifest their character and evince virtue through embodied human living. This embodied human living is fueled and funded by covenant relationship with God in general and the mode of being engendered by the fear of YHWH in particular. On this account, the righteous model a form of life in union with the God of Israel and through the gift of his transformative agency so as to participate in the reconciliation of community and cosmos, which cultivates and rightly orders the theological virtue of love.

The participation of the righteous in the reconciliation of community and cosmos is the hallmark of their characterization across Prov 10:1–15:33. The righteous are the object of communal blessing (10:6), their life sustains communal memory (10:7), their speech slakes the thirst and nourishes the body of the community (10:11, 21, 31), their prosperity engenders communal jubilation (11:10), their life allures and wins others over (11:30),[35] their being is attuned to the desire of creatures (12:10), and their moral orientation guides others (12:26). If nothing else, the righteous embody righteousness in relation. This moral prototype models a form of life in union with

32. Niehaus, "Righteousness and the Created Order," 253.

33. Jonathan T. Pennington, *The Sermon on the Mount and Human Flourishing: A Theological Commentary* (Grand Rapids: Baker Academic, 2017), 69–91, esp. 91.

34. Oliver O'Donovan, "Sanctification and Ethics," in *Sanctification: Explorations in Theology and Practice*, ed. Kelly M. Kapic (Downers Grove: IVP Academic, 2014), 156.

35. In light of the fact that the phrase "takes lives" (לֹקֵחַ נְפָשׁוֹת) is characterized as "wise" (11:30b), it appears that the idiom is used contrary to its conventional sense (i.e., killing). The phrase should be understood as "one who wins lives." Meinhold, *Die Sprüche*, 1:201; Fox, *Proverbs 10–31*, 45.

YHWH (10:24; 15:9, 29). This form of life provides the form on which one might form oneself. And this form of life reflects the character of God, which is embodied most clearly in the person of God the Son: Jesus Christ the righteous (1 John 2:1). By imaging the righteous in Proverbs, one images the Image of God (2 Cor 4:4) and is conformed to the image of God the Son (Rom 8:29).

III.2 Proverbs 16:1–22:16

Intermediate Wisdom and Virtue

If Prov 10:1–15:33 functions as the pedagogical starter in Wisdom's "curricular cuisine,"[1] the second subcollection offers a more variegated didactic dish (16:1–22:16). This dish pairs well with the first; it includes characters and motifs redolent of chs. 10–15. The wise and the fool, domestic matters, attentiveness to discipline, speech ethics, and the connection between one's character and consequences, among others, remain familiar smells and spices. But certain flavors and forms are more pronounced in Prov 16:1–22:16, and additional themes introduce fresh ingredients that contribute to the maturation of the reader's moral palate. The formal shift initiated by the sayings in ch. 15 prepares the reader for the new norm in chs. 16:1–22:16. Antithetical sayings recede and various poetic forms emerge as the instruments of moral formation. The pedagogical experience of dependability and familiarity engendered by the preponderance of antithetical sayings gives way to a pedagogical encounter with diverse aphorisms. This formal and pedagogical shift coincides with the second subcollection's shifting attention to particular character types. Whereas the righteous and the wicked featured prominently in chs. 10–15, these characters appear less frequently in chs. 16:1–22:16.[2] They move from the center to the periphery, creating space for the subcollection's attention to other characters, communal figures, and social relationships. And this attention to other characters, communal figures, and social relationships occasions the treatment of fresh themes. As both William Brown and Christine Roy Yoder observe, the second subcollection addresses topics that either do not find precedent in the first or receive only a cursory treatment in Prov 10–15, such as friendship, justice, and elocution.[3] Moreover, the subcollection's exploration of wealth and poverty, the monarchy, interpersonal disputes, human limits, and the role of YHWH in the socioreligious world nuance and extend their

1. Brown, "The Didactic Power of Metaphor," 138.

2. While the righteous//wicked (צַדִּיק // רָשָׁע) appear in antithetical parallelism thirty times in Prov 10–15 (10:3, 6, 7, 11, 24, 25, 28; 11:8, 10, 23; 12:3, 5, 7; 13:5, 9, 25; 14:19; 15:28, 29), the pair occurs only four times in chs. 16:1–22:16 (17:15; 18:5; 21:12, 18). When the adjectives צַדִּיק and רָשָׁע are employed independently of one another in the latter half of the collection, צַדִּיק appears six times (17:26; 18:10, 17; 20:7; 21:15, 26) and רָשָׁע occurs eleven times (16:4, 12; 17:23; 18:3; 19:28; 20:26; 21:4, 7, 10, 27, 29).

3. Brown, "The Pedagogy of Proverbs 10:1–31:9," 158–62; Yoder, *Proverbs*, 176–78.

depiction in chs. 10–15.[4] When taken together, these formal and thematic features suggest that Prov 16:1–22:16 serves the reader a discrete entrée. This entrée contains familiar flavors, privileges particular spices, and introduces additional ingredients to nourish growth in a life of wisdom and virtue—growth from elementary wisdom and virtue (10:1–15:33) to intermediate wisdom and virtue (16:1–22:16).

4. Brown, "The Pedagogy of Proverbs 10:1–31:9," 162–65; Yoder, *Proverbs*, 176–79.

CHAPTER 22

Proverbs 16:1–33

A. YHWH, the King, and the People: *The Organization of the Moral Order*

Main Idea of the Passage

These sayings sketch the hierarchy of the cosmos through the MORAL ORDER and MORAL BOUNDS metaphors to form one's worldview, disposition, and moral responsibilities in accord with the organization of and interrelationship between divine and human realms.

Literary Context[1]

Just as the first Solomonic subcollection opened with a series of sayings that profiled the prototypes and pillars of the moral order (Prov 10:1–32), so also the second subcollection opens with a series of sayings that profile the organization of and limits within the cosmic order. This order is constructed through the chapter's sequential and extended attention to YHWH, the king, and particular people (16:1–9, 10–15, 16–33);[2] its contours are outlined by aphorisms that explore the intellectual, attitudinal, and behavioral dimensions of human limits; and its ethos is shaped by the MORAL ORDER and MORAL BOUNDS metaphors. The former maps the hierarchy of the cosmic order onto the moral order to promote a vision of legitimate power relations and the moral responsibilities that superintend those relations.[3] The latter

1. This chapter does not include the Canonical and Theological Significance section. See pp. xv and 276n1 for justification. Also, see pp. 510–14 for the Canonical and Theological Significance of Proverbs 16:1–22:16.

2. This movement is noted by Fox, *Proverbs 10–31*, 605; O'Dowd, *Proverbs*, 246.

3. Lakoff and Johnson, *Philosophy in the Flesh*, 303–4. Lakoff and Johnson find the consequences of the MORAL ORDER metaphor "morally repugnant," since the concept "legitimizes a certain class of existing power relations as being natural and therefore moral," making "certain social movements, such as feminism, appear to be unnatural and therefore counter to the moral order."

metaphorical concept complements this vision of order through its conceptualization of attitudes and actions that either conform to or transgress the moral boundaries of the social order.[4] While the MORAL ORDER and MORAL BOUNDS metaphors do not inform every aphorism within ch. 16, they structure the majority of the sayings and reflect their arrangement. They serve as concepts that orient one to the order, boundaries, and moral worldview of Proverbs.

This moral worldview shares much in common with the preceding materials. Several aphorisms employ terms and ideas reminiscent of the prologue (1:8–9:18). The species of scoundrel sketched in 16:27–30, for example, recalls the portrait of the scoundrel in 6:12–19.[5] The expressions "acquiring wisdom" (קְנֹה־חָכְמָה, 16:16a) and "acquiring understanding" (קְנוֹת בִּינָה, v. 16b) reiterate the instruction of the grandfather in 4:5 and 7. The comparison of this process of acquisition with gold and silver in 16:16 echoes 3:14, 8:10, and 8:19. The expressions "turning aside from evil" (סוּר מֵרָע, 16:17a), watching one's way, and guarding one's life (v. 17b) allude to key concepts in Prov 1–9 (3:7; 4:10–27). The striking similarities between 16:16–17 and the materials in the prologue may be the product of deliberate design. These aphorisms not only sit within the middle of ch. 16 but, according to the Masoretes, v. 17 is also the center of the book. The midpoint of Proverbs seems to evoke the prologue, reminding one of its hermeneutical guidance and its recurring call to get wisdom.[6]

Together with its relationship to the prologue, Prov 16 bears various similarities with the first Solomonic subcollection as well as the materials that follow. Variant repetitions punctuate the chapter, indicating that its aphorisms exist in a dynamic intertextual relationship with sayings across the central collections.[7] These intertextual links suggest that the sayings in ch. 16 share some unity of perspective with the sentence literature. This homogeneity is reinforced by the chapter's treatment of common themes. Sayings devoted to YHWH, the king, and speech, for example, recur throughout chs. 10–29. But when these themes are read against the backdrop of chs. 10–15, it appears that they undergo development in ch. 16. The sequence of YHWH sayings accentuates the transcendence, justice, and wisdom of the divine (vv. 1–9, 11, 33; cf. 17:3, 15; 20:27; 21:3, 30–31).[8] The cluster of aphorisms pertaining to the king elaborates on the royal sayings in chs. 10–15 (14:28, 35), outlining the monarch's socioeconomic authority, moral character, and sovereign power (16:10–15; cf. 19:12;

4. Lakoff and Johnson, *Philosophy in the Flesh*, 304–6.

5. Meinhold, *Die Sprüche*, 1:113; Whybray, *The Composition of the Book of Proverbs*, 109–10; Achim Müller, *Proverbien 1–9: Der Weisheit neue Kleider*, BZAW 291 (Berlin: de Gruyter, 2000), 42–43; Fox, *Proverbs 1–9*, 224–25, idem, *Proverbs 10–31*, 621.

6. Van Leeuwen, "The Book of Proverbs," *NIB* 5:162; Yoder, *Proverbs*, 180–81.

7. These variant repetitions include **16:6b**//3:7b; **16:28a**//6:14; 16:5//11:20a//11:21a; **16:2**//16:25//12:15a//21:2//14:12; **16:17b**//13:3//21:23//19:16a; **16:8**//15:16; **16:18a**//15:33b//18:12b//18:12a; **16:12b**//20:28b//25:5b//29:14b. For discussion of these variant repetitions, see Heim, *Poetic Imagination*, 116–20, 167–74, 283–87, 303–15, 334–47, 376–83, 392–98, 399–411.

8. Brown, "The Pedagogy of Proverbs 10:1–31:9," 164; Ansberry, *Be Wise, My Son*, 114–17.

20:2, 8, 28, 29; 29:12).[9] And several sayings concerning speech give particular attention to an aspect of communication mentioned only briefly in the first subcollection (15:2), namely, eloquence (16:21, 23, 24).[10] While variant repetitions and common themes intimate that the aphorisms in ch. 16 are comparable to the materials in chs. 10–15, these aphorisms do not simply reiterate previous motifs. They also reinforce and extend these motifs in fresh ways. In so doing, they signal a development in the material and alert one to the pedagogical progression within the subcollection.

This development mirrors the development of the reader. The progressive formation of the reader, however, is contingent on a particular mode of being. And this mode of being is mentioned in 15:33. Before receiving the second course of Wisdom's "curricular cuisine," one is reminded that the fear of YHWH is necessary for growth in wisdom and virtue. The recognition of one's limits and dependence on the divine create a state of mind that is prepared for instruction in wisdom and a mode of being marked by humility (15:33).[11] As the final verse within the first Solomonic subcollection, 15:33 plays a pivotal role.[12] It identifies the mode of existence that is required to progress in the acquisition of wisdom and virtue; and it serves as an appropriate introduction to the group of YHWH sayings (16:1–9), which focus on divine transcendence, the mystery of God's immanent actions in the world, and the severe limits of humans.

9. Ansberry, *Be Wise, My Son*, 104–7.

10. Brown, "The Pedagogy of Proverbs 10:1–31:9," 161–62; Ansberry, *Be Wise, My Son*, 108–10.

11. Jindo, "On the Biblical Notion,'" 433–53.

12. Whybray, *The Composition of the Book of Proverbs*, 89; Fox, *Proverbs 10–31*, 605.

Translation and Exegetical Outline

(See pages 435–37.)

Structure and Literary Form

As noted above, the arrangement of the aphorisms in Prov 16 reflects the hierarchical organization of the cosmic order. The movement from YHWH and divine-human relations to the king, to the people captures the mystery and symmetry of both the vertical and horizontal, the perpendicular and parallel structures of the moral order. This order may be projected through several orderly clusters, but these clusters consist of a variety of poetic forms. The compilation of sayings completes what ch. 15 began: a move away from antithetical sayings to a pastiche of parallel relations. These relations range from better-than sayings (16:8, 19, 32) and reflective sayings (v. 25) to admonitions (v. 3) and diverse types of intralinear parallelism (vv. 16, 20, 22, 24, 26, 31). Far from exhibiting a lack of order, the variety of forms attests to the manifest diversity of the cosmic order as well as to the didactic development of the material in the second Solomonic subcollection.

While the organization or structural arrangement of the materials in the central collections varies among interpreters, broad consensus exists concerning the design of Prov 16.[13] With a few exceptions, most see three coherent units (vv. 1–9, 10–15, 27–30) as well as a literary frame around the chapter formed through aphorisms concerned with YHWH's sovereign intervention (vv. 1, 9, 33).[14] To this, others perceive loose units in vv. 16–19 and 20–24, organized according to common language and themes.[15] And still others discern a final cluster extending into ch. 17 (16:31–17:6), established through the repetition of "crown" (עֲטֶרֶת; 16:31a; 17:6a) and "splendid/splendor" (תִּפְאֶרֶת; 16:31a; 17:6b).[16] The coherence engendered by the organization of the aphorisms is also felt in the shared language among the sayings. The repetition of the terms "wicked" (רָשָׁע, 16:4b; רֶשַׁע, v. 12a), "abomination" (תּוֹעֲבַת, vv. 5a, 12a), and "favor/delight" (רְצוֹת, v. 7a; רְצוֹן; 13a, 15b) as well as the verb "atone/appease" (כפר, vv. 6a, 14b) place the sayings on YHWH and the king in an intertextual and dialogical relationship.[17]

13. For discussion of the potential structural contribution of ch. 16 within the second Solomonic subcollection, see Sæbø, *Sprüche*, 268–69. Building on his structural observations of chs. 10–15, Sæbø contends that ch. 16 and chs. 20–21 provide a theological lens through which to read chs. 17–19.

14. McKane, *Proverbs*, 487; Whybray, *The Composition of the Book of Proverbs*, 106–10; Murphy, *Proverbs*, 118–22; Clifford, *Proverbs*, 157–61.

15. Toy, *Proverbs*, 327–28; Meinhold, *Die Sprüche*, 2:263–79; Van Leeuwen, "The Book of Proverbs," *NIB* 5:161–62; Heim, *Like Grapes of Gold*, 207–23; Yoder, *Proverbs*, 180–81; Fox, *Proverbs 10–31*, 605.

16. Waltke, *Proverbs: Chapters 15–31*, 35–36. Cf. Delitzsch, "Proverbs of Solomon," 6:252 (1:350).

17. Meinhold, *Die Sprüche*, 2:263–64, Waltke, *Proverbs: Chapters 15–31*, 8–9, Sæbø, *Sprüche*, 224.

Proverbs 16:1–33

Verse	Hebrew	Translation
1a	לְאָדָם מַעַרְכֵי־לֵב	The reflections of the heart belong to humans;
1b	וּמֵיְהוָה מַעֲנֵה לָשׁוֹן	but the answer of the tongue, from YHWH.
2a	כָּל־דַּרְכֵי־אִישׁ זַךְ בְּעֵינָיו	All the ways of a person, pure in his eyes;
2b	וְתֹכֵן רוּחוֹת יְהוָה	but YHWH weighs motives.
3a	גֹּל אֶל־יְהוָה מַעֲשֶׂיךָ	Commit your works to YHWH,
3b	וְיִכֹּנוּ מַחְשְׁבֹתֶיךָ	and your plans will succeed.
4a	כֹּל פָּעַל יְהוָה לַמַּעֲנֵהוּ	YHWH made everything for its purpose—
4b	וְגַם־רָשָׁע לְיוֹם רָעָה	even the wicked for an evil day.
5a	תּוֹעֲבַת יְהוָה כָּל־גְּבַהּ־לֵב	An abomination to YHWH, every proud heart;
5b	יָד לְיָד לֹא יִנָּקֶה	be assured: it will not go unpunished.
6a	בְּחֶסֶד וֶאֱמֶת יְכֻפַּר עָוֹן	By loyalty and faithfulness iniquity is atoned for;
6b	וּבְיִרְאַת יְהוָה סוּר מֵרָע	and by the fear of YHWH, a turning away from evil.
7a	בִּרְצוֹת יְהוָה דַּרְכֵי־אִישׁ	When YHWH favors a person's ways,
7b	גַּם־אוֹיְבָיו יַשְׁלִם אִתּוֹ	he makes even his enemies at peace with him.
8a	טוֹב־מְעַט בִּצְדָקָה	Better a little with righteousness,
8b	מֵרֹב תְּבוּאוֹת בְּלֹא מִשְׁפָּט	than abundant produce without justice.
9a	לֵב אָדָם יְחַשֵּׁב דַּרְכּוֹ	A person's heart plans his way,
9b	וַיהוָה יָכִין צַעֲדוֹ	but YHWH directs his step.
10a	קֶסֶם עַל־שִׂפְתֵי־מֶלֶךְ	An oracle on the king's lips:
10b	בְּמִשְׁפָּט לֹא יִמְעַל־פִּיו	in judgment his mouth is not unfaithful.
11a	פֶּלֶס וּמֹאזְנֵי מִשְׁפָּט לַיהוָה	A just balance and scales belong to YHWH;
11b	מַעֲשֵׂהוּ כָּל־אַבְנֵי־כִיס	his work, all the weights of the bag.
12a	תּוֹעֲבַת מְלָכִים עֲשׂוֹת רֶשַׁע	An abomination to kings, doing wicked deeds,
12b	כִּי בִצְדָקָה יִכּוֹן כִּסֵּא	for a throne is established by righteousness.
13a	רְצוֹן מְלָכִים שִׂפְתֵי־צֶדֶק	Righteous lips, the delight of kings,
13b	וְדֹבֵר יְשָׁרִים יֶאֱהָב	and one who speaks uprightly he loves.

III.2 Intermediate Wisdom and Virtue (16:1–22:16)

A. YHWH, the King, and the People: The Organization of the Moral Order (16:1–33)

Continued on next page.

Continued from previous page.

14a	חֲמַת־מֶלֶךְ מַלְאֲכֵי־מָוֶת	The king's wrath, a messenger of death,
14b	וְאִישׁ חָכָם יְכַפְּרֶנָּה	but a wise person appeases it.
15a	בְּאוֹר־פְּנֵי־מֶלֶךְ חַיִּים	In the light of the king's face, life,
15b	וּרְצוֹנוֹ כְּעָב מַלְקוֹשׁ	and his favor, like a cloud of spring rain.
16a	קְנֹה־חָכְמָה מַה־טּוֹב מֵחָרוּץ	Acquiring wisdom—how much better than gold!
16b	וּקְנוֹת בִּינָה נִבְחָר מִכָּסֶף	And acquiring understanding, preferable to silver.
17a	מְסִלַּת יְשָׁרִים סוּר מֵרָע	The highway of the upright, turning aside from evil;
17b	שֹׁמֵר נַפְשׁוֹ נֹצֵר דַּרְכּוֹ	one who watches his way guards his life.
18a	לִפְנֵי־שֶׁבֶר גָּאוֹן	Before destruction, pride;
18b	וְלִפְנֵי כִשָּׁלוֹן גֹּבַהּ רוּחַ	and before stumbling, a haughty spirit.
19a	טוֹב שְׁפַל־רוּחַ אֶת־עֲנָוִים	Better a humble spirit with the oppressed
19b	מֵחַלֵּק שָׁלָל אֶת־גֵּאִים	than to divide spoil with the proud.
20a	מַשְׂכִּיל עַל־דָּבָר יִמְצָא־טוֹב	One prudent in a matter finds good,
20b	וּבוֹטֵחַ בַּיהוָה אַשְׁרָיו	and one who trusts in YHWH, blessed is he.
21a	לַחֲכַם־לֵב יִקָּרֵא נָבוֹן	The wise of heart is called discerning,
21b	וּמֶתֶק שְׂפָתַיִם יֹסִיף לֶקַח	and sweetness of lips increases learning.
22a	מְקוֹר חַיִּים שֵׂכֶל בְּעָלָיו	Insight, a fountain of life for its possessor,
22b	וּמוּסַר אֱוִלִים אִוֶּלֶת	but the instruction of fools, folly.
23a	לֵב חָכָם יַשְׂכִּיל פִּיהוּ	The heart of the wise makes his mouth insightful,
23b	וְעַל־שְׂפָתָיו יֹסִיף לֶקַח	and enhances instruction on his lips.
24a	צוּף־דְּבַשׁ אִמְרֵי־נֹעַם	Pleasant words, a honeycomb—
24b	מָתוֹק לַנֶּפֶשׁ וּמַרְפֵּא לָעָצֶם	sweet to the throat and healing to the bones.
25a	יֵשׁ דֶּרֶךְ יָשָׁר לִפְנֵי־אִישׁ	There is this: a way that is straight before a person;
25b	וְאַחֲרִיתָהּ דַּרְכֵי־מָוֶת	but its end, ways to death.

26a	נֶפֶשׁ עָמֵל עָמְלָה לּוֹ	The appetite of the worker works for him,
26b	כִּי־אָכַף עָלָיו פִּיהוּ	because his mouth compels him.
27a	אִישׁ בְּלִיַּעַל כֹּרֶה רָעָה	A scoundrel, one who mines evil,
27b	וְעַל־שְׂפָתָיו כְּאֵשׁ צָרָבֶת	and on his lips, like a scorching fire.
28a	אִישׁ תַּהְפֻּכוֹת יְשַׁלַּח מָדוֹן	A perverse person spreads strife,
28b	וְנִרְגָּן מַפְרִיד אַלּוּף	and a slanderer separates friends.
29a	אִישׁ חָמָס יְפַתֶּה רֵעֵהוּ	A violent person entices his neighbor
29b	וְהוֹלִיכוֹ בְּדֶרֶךְ לֹא־טוֹב	and leads him on a way not good.
30a	עֹצֶה עֵינָיו לַחְשֹׁב תַּהְפֻּכוֹת	One who winks his eyes, to plan perversities;
30b	קֹרֵץ שְׂפָתָיו כִּלָּה רָעָה	one who pinches his lips has accomplished evil.
31a	עֲטֶרֶת תִּפְאֶרֶת שֵׂיבָה	A splendid crown, grey hair;
31b	בְּדֶרֶךְ צְדָקָה תִּמָּצֵא	it is found on the way of the righteous.
32a	טוֹב אֶרֶךְ אַפַּיִם מִגִּבּוֹר	Better the patient than the mighty,
32b	וּמֹשֵׁל בְּרוּחוֹ מִלֹּכֵד עִיר	and one who controls his spirit than one who captures a city.
33a	בַּחֵיק יוּטַל אֶת־הַגּוֹרָל	The lot is cast in the bosom,
33b	וּמֵיְהוָה כָּל־מִשְׁפָּטוֹ	but from YHWH, its every judgment.

And the recurrence of body parts across the sayings illuminates their common concern with the embodiment of particular virtues and vices (vv. 1, 2a, 5a, 9, 10, 13a, 15a, 21, 23, 24b, 26, 27b, 30, 31a, 32b, 33a). On semantic and thematic grounds, the aphorisms in ch. 16 evince signs of deliberate design. This design not only produces a sense of coherence; it also complements the chapter's consideration of the organization of the moral order.

Explanation of the Text

With the mode of being engendered by the fear of YHWH and the epistemic awareness of humanity's limits and place within the cosmos (15:33),[18] one is primed to ingest Wisdom's second course (16:1–22:16). This course begins with a substantial helping of YHWH sayings (vv. 1–7, 9), which explore the transcendence, omniscience, and omnipotence of the divine. The thematic cluster is framed by aphorisms that traffic in shared terminology and explore the mystery of YHWH's immanent intervention in human affairs (לֵב, vv. 1a, 9a; אָדָם, vv. 1a, 9a). The combination of these sayings and their concern with the dimensions of divine-human relations not only legitimize YHWH's place at the top of the cosmic hierarchy; they also scrutinize human limits and one's moral responsibilities in relationship with YHWH. Whether the aphorisms are read individually or as component parts of a coherent unit, they confirm von Rad's insightful reflection on the dialectic between divine freedom and activity, on the one hand, and human action and responsibility, on the other: "Man must always keep himself open to the activity of God, an activity which completely escapes all calculation, for between the putting into practice of the most reliable wisdom and that which then actually takes place, there always lies a great unknown."[19]

This "great unknown" manifests itself in a multitude of human affairs. Among them is speech (**v. 1**). The opening aphorism moves from internal thoughts to external utterance. The connection between the "reflections of the heart" (מַעַרְכֵי־לֵב, v. 1a) and the utterance of the tongue may appear straightforward, even one firmly under the control of human agents. But when one accounts for divine intervention, a "great unknown" lies between the plans of the heart and the answer of the tongue. While one may organize his reflections and craft his thoughts, the verbal locution may yield unintended illocutionary and perlocutionary effects. Successful speech is dependent on divine mediation.[20] Far from minimizing the importance of organizing one's reflections before bringing them to speech, the aphorism emphasizes the limitations of human control over the connection between internal thoughts, their external utterance, and their intended effects. YHWH is involved in this process of successful speech, mediating the "great unknown" and actualizing the answer of the tongue.

The limits of human control are extended in **v. 2** to include the limits of human self-understanding

18. Jindo, "On the Biblical Notion," 433–53.

19. Von Rad, *Wisdom in Israel*, 101.

20. Whether the *waw* that links the lines is considered conjunctive ("and") or disjunctive ("but"), YHWH's intervention in successful speech remains.

(cf. Prov 21:2; 24:12). Whereas v. 1 explored the disconnect between the thoughts of the heart and the answer of the tongue, this saying examines the disconnect between one's eyes and one's "spirits" or "motives" (רוּחוֹת, 16:2b). The eyes are depicted as potential sources of self-deceit. One's manner of life and particular actions may be pure or undefiled "in his eyes" (בְּעֵינָיו, v. 2a; cf. 3:7), but YHWH operates under a different moral metric: he weighs the inner life or motives of a person. The aphorism compares the superficial evaluation of human self-perception with the depth dimension of YHWH's moral measurements, impressing on reader's the severe limitations of human understanding before the scales of the divine.

In light of the limits of human control and self-understanding, **v. 3** offers a remedy: dependence on YHWH. Shifting to direct address, the aphorism deploys the idiomatic expression "roll to YHWH" (גֹּל אֶל־יְהוָה, v. 3a; cf. Pss 22:9[8]; 37:5), admonishing one to "commit" or "turn over" his plans to the divine. The admonition is comparable to Prov 3:5–6. But the sequence of "your works" (מַעֲשֶׂיךָ, 16:3a) to "your plans" (מַחְשְׁבֹתֶיךָ, v. 3b) is unusual; one would expect the reverse.[21] While one's external works and internal thoughts or plans are not mutually exclusive, the sequence inspires confidence in the efficacy of divine activity. YHWH receives the works entrusted to him and brings the intentions of those works to fulfillment.[22] Whether present or future works are in view, their fruition is rooted in dependence on YHWH and realized through divine implementation.

More than materializing one's plans, **v. 4** indicates that YHWH made everything "for its purpose" (לַמַּעֲנֵהוּ, v. 4a).[23] But the object of the verb and the antecedent of the pronominal suffix in the initial line is unclear. If YHWH is the antecedent of the suffix, the line may read as, "YHWH made everyone/everything for his purpose." If, on the other hand, "everyone/everything" is the antecedent of the suffix, then the initial line may be rendered as, "YHWH made everyone/everything for its purpose." Irrespective of whether YHWH or everyone/everything is the antecedent of the pronominal suffix, the line gives particular attention to the proper place and purpose of every entity in the economy of creation. As creator of all, YHWH made everything to function in accord with its purpose or end. The second line conveys the certainty of this moral order by foregrounding the emphatic use of "even" (גַּם, v. 4b). Among other things, the purpose of the wicked is singled out. Even this type of character serves a particular role in the divine economy: a destiny with "an evil day" (לְיוֹם רָעָה, v. 4b). The saying captures the order of the moral world; and it construes the function of its members in terms of YHWH's dominion and design.

Whereas v. 4 expressed certainty over YHWH's purpose for and judgment of the wicked, **v. 5** expresses certainty over YHWH's judgment on a specific form of wickedness. This form of wickedness is cast in a תּוֹעֵבָה template ("abomination to"), a conventional syntactical pattern that serves as a mold for exploring those things that evoke divine disgust.[24] Divine disgust is directed toward a particular disposition: "every proud heart" (כָּל־גְּבַהּ־לֵב, v. 5a). The expression employs the orientational

21. Van Leeuwen, "The Book of Proverbs," *NIB* 5:158; Murphy, *Proverbs*, 120.

22. Boström, *The God of the Sages*, 121–22.

23. The form of the prepositional phrase is unusual; it contains both a definite article and a pronominal suffix, and it appears to be an anomalous form of מַעֲנֶה ("answer"), which makes little sense in the saying. If the expression is revocalized to לְמַעֲנֵהוּ, however, it may be read as a form related to לְמַעַן and rendered "for its purpose." GKC §127i; Joüon §140c; *IBHS* §13.6b; Fox, *Proverbs 10–31*, 611.

24. Fox, *Proverbs 10–31*, 488, 491.

metaphor ARROGANCE IS HIGH to conceptualize a mode of being that overestimates humanity's place in the moral order.[25] This inflated mode of being transgresses the boundaries appropriate to creaturehood, engendering divine disgust and certain judgment. The certainty of this judgment is conveyed through the expression "hand to hand," that is, "be assured" (יָד לְיָד, v. 5b; cf. 11:21), as well as the idiom "will not go unpunished" (לֹא יִנָּקֶה, v. 5b; cf. 6:29; 11:21; 17:5; 19:5, 9; 28:20). The high heart may be a hidden disposition, but YHWH sees and will bring each one under judgment.

Judgment may be certain (16:5b), but as **v. 6** intimates, atonement for sin is available.[26] This atonement is qualified by the prepositional phrase "by loyalty and faithfulness" (בְּחֶסֶד וֶאֱמֶת, v. 6a), which identifies the means by which iniquity is covered.[27] These qualities are attributed to both God and humans (Exod 34:6–7; Prov 3:3; 14:22; 20:28), raising questions concerning the agent of atonement in view. While humans may imitate God's loyal faithfulness and cover offences (Prov 3:3; 10:12; 14:22; 17:9), only YHWH can atone for "iniquity" (עָוֹן, 16:6a) by means of his loyalty and faithfulness (Exod 34:6–7).[28] These divine attributes are manifested in YHWH's actions. The same is true of humans. The second line expands on the first, mirroring its syntax but developing an account of the interrelationship between one's moral ontology and moral actions.[29] By means of the fear of YHWH, one possesses a mode of being that manifests itself in "turning away from evil" (סוּר מֵרָע, Prov 16:6b; cf. v. 17). Just as YHWH's being is displayed through his actions, so also one who fears YHWH reveals his ontology through his actions.

This interest in moral action continues in **v. 7**. The saying opens with בְּ + infinitive construct, establishing a particular circumstance and a contemporaneous time frame through which to understand the main clause in the second line.[30] This circumstance concerns YHWH's evaluation of one's moral orientation and manner. When YHWH is pleased with one's ways, he offers protection and interpersonal favor, bringing peace. And the extent of this peace is foregrounded through the emphatic use of גַּם ("even," v. 7b) at the beginning of the second line; it includes even one's enemies.

YHWH's evaluation of one's ways serves as a backdrop for the valuation of certain virtues and vices in **v. 8**. Echoing 15:16, the better-than saying integrates economic language with (im)moral qualities in order to minimize the value of material resources and elevate the worth of normative character.[31] When read as an independent saying, it offers an axiomatic belief, funded by the fundamental assumptions of the sages and designed to shape the moral worldview of the reader. But when read in conversation with the surrounding aphorisms, it seems to qualify the nature and timing of YHWH's retribution and rewards (16:3–7), on the one hand, and anticipate the discussion of righteousness and justice in the royal sayings (vv. 10–13), on the other.[32]

The valuation of character and wealth gives way to a declaration of human limits in **v. 9**. The repetition of "heart" (לֵב, vv. 1a, 9a) and "person" (אָדָם, vv. 1a, 9a), combined with the aphorism's attention

25. Tilford, *Sensing World, Sensing Wisdom*, 162–64.

26. Whybray, *Proverbs*, 241.

27. For the instrumental בְּ, see Joüon §132e.

28. Van Leeuwen, "The Book of Proverbs," *NIB* 5:158–59; Fox, *Proverbs 10–31*, 612.

29. Fox, *Proverbs 10–31*, 612.

30. *IBHS* §11.2.5c.

31. For the logical structure of the saying, see Sandoval, *The Discourse of Wealth and Poverty*, 131.

32. Meinhold, *Die Sprüche*, 2:268; Van Leeuwen, "The Book of Proverbs," *NIB* 5:159; Waltke, *Proverbs: Chapters 15–31*, 15.

to the limits of human planning, associates the saying with v. 1, forming a literary envelope around the thematic cluster of YHWH sayings (vv. 1–9). Whereas v. 1 explored the "great unknown"[33] between the heart and the tongue, this saying probes the "great unknown" between the one's heart and one's step. Humans bear the responsibility for planning their way. In fact, planning is considered necessary, valuable, and effective (11:14; 15:22; 20:18; 24:6). Nonetheless, to adapt von Rad's observation noted above, between this planning and that which then actually takes place lies YHWH's activity. YHWH secures or "directs one's steps" (יָכִין, 16:9b) in accord with his purposes, ensuring success.[34] Human and divine agency coalesce in this aphoristic account of the limits of human planning and the efficacy of YHWH's sovereign and immanent action.

Taken together, **vv. 1–9** paint a portrait of YHWH's transcendence and immanence in human affairs, which throws the limits that attend creaturehood into sharp relief. The thematic cluster legitimizes YHWH's place at the top of the cosmic hierarchy; and it gestures to one's moral responsibilities in relationship with and dependence upon the divine. The sayings not only occupy the center of the first Solomonic collection (10:1–22:16) and play an important role as the introduction to the second Solomonic subcollection (16:1–22:16);[35] they also inform the construal of the figure who occupies the second tier within the moral and cosmic order: the king.[36] The juxtaposition of the royal sayings (16:10–15) with the YHWH sayings (vv. 1–9) supports the common ancient Near Eastern perception that the king served as the representative of the gods. This representation is reflected in the shared language between the two clusters. And their arrangement intimates that, while the king enjoys a privileged position in the moral order, he too is a mortal and subject to YHWH.[37]

The cluster of royal sayings consists of three proverbial pairs, each of which is linked by common terms and concepts. The first sketches the socioeconomic authority and responsibilities of the king (vv. 10–11). The repetition of מִשְׁפָּט ("judgment," v. 10b; "just," v. 11a) forms **vv. 10–11** into a unit and clarifies their complementary depiction of certain dimensions of royal justice. In accord with ancient Near Eastern royal ideology, **v. 10** portrays the king as an agent who delivers infallible judicial decisions. The source of these oral decisions, however, is unusual. Elsewhere in the Old Testament, "oracle" (קֶסֶם, v. 10a) is a pejorative term, designating illegitimate forms of divination (Deut 18:10; 1 Sam 15:23; Jer 14:14; Ezek 13:6). Whether or not it refers to an authorized means of divination,[38] the parallel relationship between "oracle" and "judgment" (מִשְׁפָּט, Prov 16:10b) indicates that the former possesses a positive connotation in the present context. The king's judgments are oracular

33. Von Rad, *Wisdom in Israel*, 101.

34. Fox, *Proverbs 10–31*, 613.

35. In addition to the contextual and structural comments above, it is important to note that Whybray describes 15:33–16:9 as "the theological kernel" of Prov 10:1–22:16. Whybray, "Yahweh-Sayings and their Contexts," 159.

36. For discussion, see Schmid, *Gerechtigkeit als Weltordnung*, 83–89; Schmid, *Altorientalische Welt in der alttestamentliche Theologie* (Zürich: TVZ, 1974), 100–101.

37. Whybray, *The Composition of the Book of Proverbs*, 88–89.

38. Eryl W. Davies, "The Meaning of *qesem* in Prv 16,10," *Bib* 61 (1980): 554–56. Davies reads Prov 16:10 in light of Ezek 21:23–28 and argues that קֶסֶם refers to a process of lot casting based on its use with "to shake/cast arrows" (קִלְקַל בַּחִצִּים). This proposal is possible but unconvincing, since Ezekiel classifies casting arrows, consulting idols, and examining the liver as forms of קֶסֶם. In light of the fact that consulting idols and examining the liver are prohibited in the Old Testament, it follows that casting arrows are also proscribed. Daniel I. Block, *The Book of Ezekiel: Chapters 1–24*, NICOT (Grand Rapids: Eerdmans, 1997), 686–87; Waltke, *Proverbs: Chapters 15–31*, 17n61.

and inerrant. The saying may be idealistic; but in light of that fact that the king serves as the official representative of the divine and the answer of the tongue belongs to YHWH (v. 1b), the monarch's judicial infallibility may be the product of divine wisdom (Prov 8:14–16; 2 Sam 14:17, 20; 16:23; 1 Kgs 3:16–28; Isa 11:1–5)[39] rather than the result of some divinatory procedure.

Beyond the judicial sphere, **v. 11** intimates that the king also mediated YHWH's justice in the economic sphere. While the aphorism does not mention the king, the repetition of מִשְׁפָּט (vv. 10b, 11a) and the juxtaposition of the sayings associates the king's judicial activity and divine guidance with his maintenance of economic affairs. If just economic practices are the creation and concern of YHWH, then economic equity and the standardization of weights are the concern of his earthly representative.[40] Scales and weights are mentioned elsewhere in the central collections (11:1; 20:10, 23). But in contrast to these sayings, 16:11 describes the economic practice in a positive manner. It does not offer YHWH's value judgment on commercial practices (תּוֹעֲבַת יְהוָה; "abomination to YHWH"); rather, it emphasizes his role in the institution of economic justice and places the maintenance of commercial ethics under the authority of the king.

Against the backdrop of the king's socioeconomic prerogatives and responsibilities, **vv. 12–13** profile the monarch's moral character. The expression "kings" (מְלָכִים, vv. 12a, 13a) and the conventional word pair תּוֹעֲבַת . . . רְצוֹן ("abomination . . . delight," vv. 12a, 13a; cf. 11:1, 20; 12:22; 15:8) link the aphorisms, foregrounding their attention to the monarch's emotional and moral tastes.[41] These tastes match those of YHWH and Lady Wisdom. Just as the way of the wicked is an abomination to YHWH (15:9), so also wicked deeds are an abomination to kings (**16:12**).[42] While "abomination" (תּוֹעֲבַת, v. 12a) typically occurs with YHWH, here it refers to the king's moral sensibilities. The ideal king must embody both YHWH's (6:16; 15:8, 9; 17:5) and Lady Wisdom's (8:7) moral tastes and detest the wicked actions of his people in general and his officials in particular (20:8, 26; 29:12). This moral and emotional obligation is grounded in a particular rationale, introduced by the particle "for" (כִּי, 16:12b): the king's righteousness serves as the means by which his throne is established. His moral tastes determine the order and stability of the kingdom (v. 12b; cf. 20:28).[43] And his moral tastes determine the nature of his relationship with his subjects (**v. 13**). Those with righteous, upright speech not only emulate Lady Wisdom's vernacular (8:8–9), but they also elicit the king's love, for he favors honest discourse (16:13). When read together,

39. Meinhold, *Die Sprüche*, 2:269; Clifford, *Proverbs*, 159; Waltke, *Proverbs: Chapters 15–31*, 17.

40. Fox, *Proverbs 10–31*, 615.

41. Plöger, *Sprüche Salomos*, 192; Hildebrandt, "Proverbial Pairs," 209n7; Meinhold, *Die Sprüche*, 2:270–71; Heim, *Like Grapes of Gold*, 212.

42. The construct phrase תּוֹעֲבַת מְלָכִים ("abomination to kings," v. 12a) introduces a subjective genitive rather than an objective genitive, making others the agents of עֲשׂוֹת רֶשַׁע ("doing wicked deeds," v. 12a) rather than the king (cf. LXX, Targ., Vulg.). For an extended discussion of the issue, see Heim, *Like Grapes of Gold*, 213–14. Cf. Fox, *Proverbs 10–31*, 615.

43. Following Hellmut Brunner, some argue that the concept of righteousness as the foundation of the royal throne (Prov 16:12; 20:28; 25:5) is comparable with Egyptian royal ideology. This proposal is based on the fact that the hieroglyph for both the royal pedestal and *ma'at* are identical. The imagery in Prov 16:12 and the significance of the throne in Israelite royal thought reflect the concepts associated with *ma'at* and the pharaonic throne; but these similarities do not necessarily lead to the conclusion that Egyptian thought influenced the description in 16:12, for this imagery is found elsewhere in the Old Testament (cf. Pss 89:15; 97:2). For a discussion of these issues, see Hellmut Brunner, "Gerechtigkeit als Fundament des Thrones," *VT* 8 (1958): 426–28; McKane, *Proverbs*, 492–93.

vv. 12–13 move from deeds to words, describing the moral tastes and the emotional disposition the king *should* embody.[44] Similar to vv. 10–11, this profile of the king's moral character may not be realistic, but it remains the ideal.

If vv. 12–13 describe the moral tastes and obligations that ought to epitomize the king, then **vv. 14–15** identify the powers intrinsic to the royal institution. The repetition of "king" (מֶלֶךְ, vv. 14a, 15a) and the antonyms "death" (מָוֶת, v. 14a) and "life" (חַיִּים, v. 15a) call attention to these powers. In fact, when read together, life and death serve as a merism for the king's absolute power.[45] This power is portrayed through graphic imagery. The king's wrath is presented as "messenger of death" (formally for מַלְאֲכֵי־מָוֶת, v. 14a), envoys of execution that can only be assuaged and withdrawn by the tactics of the wise. And the king's friendship and favor are depicted through images of light, life, and natural renewal (v. 15). These images are used in reference to YHWH elsewhere in the Old Testament (Num 6:25; Deut 11:14; 33:28; Pss 4:7[6]; 31:17[16]; Hos 6:3; Hag 1:10; Zech 10:1). The verb "appeases" (יְכַפְּרֶ, Prov 16:14b) recalls the use of the root in v 6; it associates the wise person's appeasement of the king's wrath with YHWH's atonement for sin. These graphic and verbal parallels strengthen the interrelationship between YHWH and the king. They place the prerogatives of the human king in relationship with the prerogatives of the divine king, thus mapping the hierarchical organization of the cosmic order and the powers that maintain the moral order.

On the whole, the cluster of royal sayings, **vv. 10–15**, intermingle idealistic aphorisms concerning the king's socioeconomic responsibilities and moral character with realistic sayings pertaining to his power. Some provide the king with a model on which to form his reign (vv. 11, 12, 13); others may offer advice to those who serve the king (vv. 12, 13, 14, 15). But all contribute to the formation of the reader's worldview and the anthology's developing account of the monarchy. This cluster of aphorisms elaborates on the royal sayings in Prov 10–15 (14:28, 35), complementing the king's communal orientation with depictions of his judicial and economic responsibilities, moral character, and power. These sayings anticipate aphoristic accounts of the king in subsequent collections, which reinforce and qualify the ideal portrait presented in vv. 10–15. As the earthly representative of YHWH and the leader of the nation, the king plays a significant role in Proverbs's projection of the cosmic and moral order. This order and the king's splendor, however, include a multitude of people (14:28). These people occupy the third tier within the cosmic hierarchy as well as many of the remaining sayings within the chapter.

In preparation for the profile of these variegated people within the moral order, **16:16** delivers an evaluative exclamation of the anthology's educational program.[46] With language redolent of the instructions and interludes within the prologue (3:14; 4:5, 7; 8:10, 19), the saying elevates the acquisition of wisdom over the value of gold and silver. And the form of the exclamation accentuates an inchoate aspect of Proverbs's conception of the educational enterprise. The infinitives construct

44. Fox, *Proverbs 10–31*, 615–16.

45. Waltke, *Proverbs: Chapters 15–31*, 20.

46. The interrogative particle מַה ("how," v. 16a) is included in the MT but omitted by the ancient versions. Since it follows חָכְמָה ("wisdom," v. 16a), its inclusion may be the product of dittography, and its omission may be due to haplography. On syntactical grounds, the inclusion of the particle creates a complex exclamation, suggesting it should be retained. For discussion, see Meinhold, *Die Sprüche*, 2:272; Heim, *Like Grapes of Gold*, 216.

"acquiring" (קְנֹה, 16:16a; קְנוֹת, v. 16b) are gerunds.[47] They do not express the value of wisdom's *possession* (i.e., "to acquire wisdom"); rather, they convey the surpassing worth of the *process* of wisdom's acquisition, the value of the investigating and learning of wisdom (cf. 2:1–4).[48] On the cusp of the document's central saying, v. 16 reiterates language reminiscent of the prologue, reminding one of the pedagogical agenda of the anthology. The form of the exclamation, however, prepares one for the materials that follow, proclaiming that the entire process of wisdom's acquisition is worth far more than precious metals.

As the central verse within the anthology, **16:17** assesses character through the central or root metaphor of the book. The path metaphor creates a framework through which to explore the interrelationship between moral character, moral actions, and moral bounds. The initial line describes the avoidance of evil as a bounded movement that manifests a permissible path.[49] This path is a "highway" (מְסִלַּת, v. 17a), a main road that is even and free of obstacles (1 Sam 6:12; Isa 11:16; 40:3). The elevated nature of this road matches the moral and physical posture of the "upright" (יְשָׁרִים, 16:17a; cf. Isa 49:11). And its smooth terrain reflects the safety and security that accompanies turning away from evil (Isa 40:3). This safety serves as the underlying motivation of the second line. Just as one who watches his mouth protects his life (Prov 13:3), so also one who attends to his manner of life protects himself (16:17b). Movement along particular paths and within moral boundaries brings security and well-being.

Insecurity, by contrast, informs the construal of dispositions that transgress moral boundaries in **v. 18**. The saying privileges the metaphorical concept PRIDE IS HIGH; and it includes certain consequences that exploit the orientational source domain of the metaphor.[50] A "break" or "destruction" (שֶׁבֶר; 18a) and "stumbling" (כִּשָּׁלוֹן, v. 18b) are presented as the natural corollaries of a disposition that fails to acknowledge the limits of creaturehood. This disposition is described in orientational terms: "height" or "pride" (גָּאוֹן, v. 18a) as well as a "high" or "haughty spirit" (גֹּבַהּ רוּחַ, v. 18b). Both are attitudes that reach beyond appropriate moral boundaries. They are precursors of a calamity that makes that which is high low. Insecurity and the threat of disastrous reversal animate the individual lines, creating an aversion to inflated dispositions and motivating a life of humility (cf. v. 5; 18:12).

The virtue of humility and the vice of pride are recast in a better-than saying in **v. 19**. This saying extends the orientational frame of reference in v. 18, associating that which is low with "a humble spirit" (שְׁפַל־רוּחַ, v. 19a), and it evaluates humility and pride in socioeconomic terms.[51] According to the saying's socioeconomic metric, low in spirit with the "oppressed" (עֲנָוִים, v. 19a)[52] is superior to dividing spoil with the proud. The poor are considered a healthier community than the arrogant; and lowliness with these marginalized members of society is preferred to apportioning booty with those who refuse to acknowledge and live within appropriate sociomoral boundaries. Like the other better-than sayings in the anthology, the aphorism

47. The form of the infinitive construct in v. 16a differs from the form of the infinitive in v. 16b. The former follows the pattern of the strong verb, while the latter follows the expected pattern of III-ה verbs. For discussion, see Delitzsch, "Proverbs of Solomon," 6:248 (1:345); Joüon §79p.

48. Delitzsch, "Proverbs of Solomon," 6:248 (1:345); Fox, *Proverbs 10–31*, 618.

49. Lakoff and Johnson, *Philosophy in the Flesh*, 304.

50. Clifford, *Proverbs*, 160.

51. Yoder, *Proverbs*, 186.

52. This reading follows *qere* (עֲנָוִים; "oppressed") rathe than *ketiv* (עֲנִיִּים; "poor") to enhance the contrast with th "arrogant."

offers a value judgment that appears counterintuitive: it promotes a humble disposition and solidarity with the oppressed over wealth and power with the proud.

The language of the "good" is redeployed in **v. 20** to provide a complementary evaluation of one's intellectual and moral ontology. But this evaluation remains open. The general sense of "good" (טוֹב, v. 20a) creates interpretive space to contemplate the social, economic, or personal benefits gained;[53] and the phrase that introduces the initial line invites different renderings. This phrase may be construed in several ways, two in particular: as "one prudent in a matter" or as "one who pays attention to a word" (מַשְׂכִּיל עַל־דָּבָר, v. 20a). Both the participle and the term "matter/word" (דָּבָר, v. 20a) are open to different meanings. And these meanings generate different readings. If prudence in a matter is in view, then "good" is the general benefit gained from one's application of insight in a particular situation.[54] But if attentiveness to a word is in view, then "good" accompanies one who heeds either a wise word or a divine word.[55] The opening line is spacious; it welcomes different readings, cultivating the reader's moral imagination. And these readings promote particular construals of the second line. The first suggests that the second line escalates or intensifies the thought of the opening line; it moves from the intellectual value of prudence to the moral value of dependence on YHWH and from the "good" gained in a particular matter to a beatific state that encompasses the whole of life.[56] The second reading, by contrast, indicates that the lines are synonymous. One who pays attention to a (divine) word exhibits a receptivity rooted in trust in YHWH; and the "good" this person finds is indicative of a life of blessing and human flourishing. Whichever reading is preferred, the aphorism evaluates the value of certain intellectual and moral forms of being, each of which constitutes normative character in Proverbs's moral vision.

Intellectual valuation continues in **vv. 21–24**. These aphorisms exhibit a shared concern with eloquent speech and instruction;[57] and they traffic in the concept of taste in general and the metaphor WORDS ARE FOOD in particular. As Greg Schmidt Goering rightly argues, taste tends to mark "the consumption and production of wisdom" and folly in Proverbs.[58] This is the case in **v. 21**. The "wise of heart" is one who possesses a mode of being that is receptive to instruction. By virtue of this disposition, it is not surprising that this person is dubbed "discerning" (נָבוֹן, v. 21a) by the community. The reason for this communal characterization is delineated in the second line, which appears to extend the thought of the first. The wise of heart is one with "sweetness of lips" (מֶתֶק שְׂפָתַיִם, v. 21b), with eloquent speech that satisfies the taste buds of the community and contributes to the anthology's goal of increasing learning (cf. 1:5). The disposition of the wise of heart allows him to ingest instruction and produce sweet, effective speech that nourishes the community and wins from them the title discerning.

Satiation also serves as the underlying motivation of **v. 22**. Returning to the root שׂכל (מַשְׂכִּיל; "one

53. Sandoval, *The Discourse of Wealth and Poverty*, 178–80.

54. Longman, *Proverbs*, 335; Fox, *Proverbs 10–31*, 619.

55. Delitzsch, "Proverbs of Solomon," 6:264 (1:346); McKane, *Proverbs*, 498; Meinhold, *Die Sprüche*, 2:275; Van Leeuwen, "The Book of Proverbs," *NIB* 5:162; Yoder, *Proverbs*, 186–87.

56. Fox, *Proverbs 10–31*, 619.

57. Murphy, *Proverbs*, 122; Van Leeuwen, "The Book of Proverbs," *NIB* 5:161; Heim, *Like Grapes of Gold*, 218–20; Waltke, *Proverbs: Chapters 15–31*, 28; Yoder, *Proverbs*, 186–87; Fox, *Proverbs 10–31*, 619.

58. Greg Schmidt Goering, "Honey and Wormwood: Taste and the Embodiment of Wisdom in the Book of Proverbs," *HBAI* 5 (2016): 27.

prudent," v. 20a; שֵׂכֶל; "insight," v. 22a), the aphorism describes that which flows from the intellectual essence of different character types. One who possesses insight is "a fountain of life" (מְקוֹר חַיִּים, v. 22a), a reciprocal source of vitality that slakes the thirst of the individual and the community. Fools, by contrast, offer something quite different. They provide instruction, but this instruction flows from and corresponds to their state of being. Like fools, their instruction is folly. They perpetuate their state of being, while one who possesses insight provides satisfaction and life.

The concern with instruction, the reiteration of the root שׂכל (מַשְׂכִּיל; "one prudent," v. 20a; שֵׂכֶל; "insight," v. 22a; יַשְׂכִּיל; "makes insightful," v. 23a), and the concept of MORAL ESSENCE link **v. 23** to the previous sayings. Whereas the instruction of fools is folly (v. 22b), the moral essence of the wise produces effective speech and instruction. His "mind" or "heart" (לֵב, v. 23a) not only instructs his mouth; it also enhances the persuasiveness of his speech (cf. v. 21; 1:5). Just as the "wise of heart" produce sweet, efficacious speech that increases instruction (16:21), so also "the heart of the wise" informs his mouth and provides eloquent, compelling speech that increases instruction. This instruction is effectual and attractive, and according to **v. 24**, its efficacy is the product of its sweet, medicinal qualities. The metaphor WORDS ARE FOOD structures the saying. Pleasant and eloquent words are conceptualized as a honeycomb; they are a nourishing substance that satisfies the "appetite" or "throat" (נֶפֶשׁ, v. 24b) and restores the body of those who ingest them.[59] Building on the concepts of MORAL ESSENCE, taste, and satisfaction in the previous sayings, the aphorism captures the aesthetic appeal and moral nourishment of eloquent speech.

Eloquent speech may be tasty, therapeutic, and effective, but it is constrained by the conditions of human limits. These limits are described in **v. 25**. The saying is governed by the יֵשׁ of reflection ("there is this," v. 25a), which introduces a "paradoxical state of affairs."[60] And these paradoxical affairs are a mirror image of 14:12. Similar to 14:12, the verbatim repetition in 16:25 presents a contrast between human perception and reality through the pedagogical technique of the "false lead."[61] The initial line leads one astray with the expression "a way that is straight" (דֶּרֶךְ יָשָׁר, v. 25a). Straight ways may be good ways elsewhere in the anthology; but as the second line demonstrates, the telos of this way is ways to death. The saying reinforces the chapter's discourse on the conditions of creaturehood (vv. 1–9, 33), accentuating the severe limits of human perception. The straight way is not so straight after all; it just seems straight from one's limited vantage point. This paradoxical state of affairs also informs the striking description of the worker in **v. 26**. The worker does not work for a human master. In truth, he toils for his appetite; his longings drive his labors. Far from possessing mastery over his appetites, the worker is mastered by them, compelled to satisfy their unrelenting demands (cf. Eccl 6:7).

The harsh lot of the laborer gives way to a catalogue of despicable character types in **vv. 27–30**. These aphorisms are intimately related to 6:12–19;[62] they offer a complementary montage of aberrant individuals, each of whom transgress moral boundaries and threaten social well-being through their immoral speech and actions. The montage is

59. Tova Forti, "Bee's Honey—From Realia to Metaphor in Biblical Wisdom Literature," *VT* 56 (2006): 333–36.

60. Gianto, "On יֵשׁ of Reflection in the Book of Proverbs," 159.

61. Suzanna R. Millar, "When a Straight Road Becomes a Garden Path," 67–82.

62. Fox, *Proverbs 1–9*, 224–25.

formed according to a particular pattern: the first three aphorisms open with the noun "person" (אִישׁ, 16:27a, 28a, 29a), followed by a negative qualifier, and the final saying offers an appropriate conclusion, highlighting the base body language that marks this class of characters (v. 30). On one level, the group of sayings may furnish the reader with a moral diagnostic, informing one of the characteristics of these immoral characters and warning one to avoid them.[63] On another level, the graphic vignettes may seek to engender moral revulsion, training one to detest the characters and actions that YHWH deems abhorrent (cf. 6:16–19).

Similar to 6:12–19, the catalogue in 16:27–30 opens with a sketch of the "scoundrel" (אִישׁ בְּלִיַּעַל, v. 27a). This "good-for-nothing"[64] is characterized by his searching and his speech. He "mines evil" (כֹּרֶה רָעָה, v. 27a),[65] digging around in his inner recesses for a word or scheme that traps others. When he finds it, he unleashes it through his lips, searing others with his scorching speech.[66] While the scoundrel singes others with speech, the perverse person and the slanderer destroy social relationships (v. 28). The former is depicted as a messenger of discord, as one who spreads communal strife (v. 28a) The latter operates in more intimate relationships, separating friends through gossip and false accusations (v. 28b). The violent person, by contrast, takes a different approach (v. 29). He, too, moves in intimate relationships, enticing his neighbor. Yet, despite his characterization as violent, his tactics are subtle. Like the sinners in 1:10–19, he tempts and guides, leading one along a mode of life that transgresses moral boundaries. These species of the good-for-nothing—the perverse, the slanderer, and the violent—may employ speech or subtle tactics to sow social discord. But according to 16:30, these tactics may manifest themselves in visible, bodily forms. The aphorism reiterates and extends the "sinister sign language" of the scoundrel in 6:12–14,[67] highlighting the interconnection between one's physical gestures and moral character. Winking or squinting eyes are symptomatic of a particular purpose, namely, plotting perversities (cf. 6:13; 10:10).[68] And the fulfillment of these perverse schemes is publicized through pinched lips. The saying focuses on different forms of body language and moves from the development of malicious schemes to their completion; it complements the portraits sketched in 16:27–29, identifying physical features that accompany the verbal tactics and immoral character of the scoundrel.

More than revealing deplorable characters and actions, **v. 31** indicates that physical features also reveal the righteous. As a metonymy for old age, "grey hair" (שֵׂיבָה, v. 31a; cf. Lev 19:32) bears the marks of a long, abundant life; and this form of life is imbued with honor and dignity though the image of "a splendid crown" (עֲטֶרֶת תִּפְאֶרֶת, Prov 16:31a). This crown, along with years of life, is not only the gift of wisdom (3:2, 4:9, 10); it is also an emblem of one's virtue, righteous character, and endurance on an authorized way. The aphorism focuses on a specific aspect of old age and employs vivid, ornamental imagery to motivate perseverance on a path that brings honor.

63. Whybray, *Proverbs*, 250; Waltke, *Proverbs: Chapters 15–31*, 32.

64. Fox, *Proverbs 1–9*, 219; Yoder, *Proverbs*, 75.

65. While some read כור רעה ("a furnace of evil"), rather than כרה רעה ("mines evil"), to conform the imagery in the first line with the second, the change is unnecessary (cf. LXX). Gemser, *Sprüche Salomos*, 73; Murphy, *Proverbs*, 118.

66. McKane, *Proverbs*, 494; Fox, *Proverbs 10–31*, 622.

67. McKane, *Proverbs*, 325.

68. The reading construes the infinitive construct לַחְשֹׁב ("to plan") as expressing purpose.

Shifting to military imagery, **16:32** assesses the value of self-mastery to inculcate the virtues of patience and restraint. The better-than saying compares internal powers with physical powers. These comparisons, however, are partial and elliptical. The elements in the initial line appear to be asymmetrical, for the expected counterpart of "patient" (אֶרֶךְ אַפַּיִם, v. 32a) is "short-tempered" (קְצַר־רוּחַ; 14:29) or "hothead" (אִישׁ חֵמָה; 15:18), and the presumed parallel to "mighty" (גִּבּוֹר, 16:32a) would be "weak." The disjointed parallelism awakens the moral reasoning of the reader, inviting one to supply the concealed elements to complete the comparison. Following Fox, the complete comparison would read: "Better (A) a weak man who is (B) patient than (A′) a mighty man who is (B′) impatient."[69] The full comparison elevates physical weakness with an internal disposition of patience over physical strength with an internal disposition of impatience. Moral virtue and internal self-mastery are more valuable than physical power. This valuation is reiterated in elliptical fashion within the second line. The adjective "better" (טוֹב, v. 32a) is elided but assumed; and, again, military language is deployed to promote "one who rules over" (formally for מֹשֵׁל, v. 32b) his passions over one who captures a city. The virtues of patience, restraint, and self-mastery outweigh physical power, for they govern a more turbulent realm than the external world.

The final saying in the chapter returns to a theme that occupied vv. 1–9, namely, YHWH's omnipotence and mysterious intervention in human affairs. This sovereign intervention is conveyed through the divinatory technique of lot casting. The procedure involved the throwing of stones to obtain a decision or judgment (18:18; cf. Josh 7:14–18; Judg 20:9; 1 Sam 10:20–21; Esth 3:7), and it represented a permissible divinatory practice, most likely because it lacked hermeneutical ambiguity (Deut 18:9–13). The lot may be cast "in the bosom" (בַּחֵיק, v. 33a), that is, in the fold of the garment, where it remained concealed.[70] Yet, even here, YHWH intervenes, for he delivers the lot's "every judgment" (כָּל־מִשְׁפָּט, v. 33b). From the answer of the tongue (v. 1) to the decision of the lot (v. 33), YHWH manifests his mysterious sovereignty in the "great unknown" that exists between human planning or action and that which actually takes place.[71]

69. Fox, *Proverbs 10–31*, 598.

70. *HALOT* 1:312, s.v. חֵיק.

71. Von Rad, *Wisdom in Israel*, 101.

Proverbs 17:1–28

CHAPTER 23

B. Cultivating Moral Nurturance: *The Sustenance of Social Ties and the Self*

Main Idea of the Passage

These sayings devote considerable attention to various social relations and explore these relations through the metaphor of MORAL NURTURANCE to form moral actions and attitudes that nurture social bonds and the self for the sake of others.

Literary Context[1]

In light of the hierarchy of the moral order and the moral responsibilities that attend its arrangement (16:1–33), one might conclude that Proverbs privileges a moral world governed by authority and power. The aphorisms in ch. 17 indicate otherwise. These sayings give particular attention to various social relations that comprise the moral order. They are populated by grandparents, fathers and mothers, children and grandchildren, friends and neighbors, nobles and the poor. They explore these relations through domestic, interpersonal, judicial, and economic ties. And they structure these relations through the metaphor of MORAL NURTURANCE.[2] This metaphorical concept maps the dynamics of family nurturance onto society. On this account, society is conceptualized as a family, with moral agents who nurture those in need of care by means of moral acts. Nurturance is engendered by a moral obligation to care for others. As Lakoff and Johnson note, this ethics of care operates

1. This chapter does not include the Explanation of the Text or the Canonical and Theological Significance sections. See pp. xv and 276n1 for justification. Also, see pp. 510–14 for the Canonical and Theological Significance of Prov 16:1–22:16.

2. For the metaphor, see Lakoff, *Moral Politics*, 108–42, Lakoff and Johnson, *Philosophy in the Flesh*, 310–11.

on two levels. One level concerns the nurturance of social relations, the cultivation of "*social ties* that bind people together in communities";[3] the other concerns self-nurturance, the responsibility to care for oneself so that one can, in turn, care for others.[4] Both forms of nurturance inform the chapter's construal of social ties, capture the illocutionary force of its relational sayings, and infuse the moral world of Proverbs with an ethic of care and responsibility.

The nurturance of social relations occupies the vast majority of aphorisms. These relations range from domestic and interpersonal ties to economic and judicial bonds. The initial aphorism elevates the value of domestic tranquility, even with meager fare, over a sumptuous feast accompanied by strife (v. 1). Other sayings develop this domestic environment of security, motivating children to honor their familial responsibilities (v. 2) and embody wisdom for the emotional well-being of the household (vv. 21, 25) so as to preserve and strengthen generational bonds (v. 6, cf. v. 13). These intimate relational bonds extend beyond the household to include friendship. Forgiveness and loyalty, even at personal cost, are commended as moral actions that foster friendship (v. 9); and a friend, like a brother, is portrayed as one who should love his companion, irrespective of circumstances (v. 17). Deciphering a true "friend" or "neighbor" (רֵעַ, vv. 17a, 18b), however, is necessary, especially in economic affairs. The desire to offer financial help may contribute to the nurturance of social ties, but going surety for one's neighbor may overextend one's resources and inhibit one from self-nurturance (v. 18). Moral actions nurture the self and various social ties. The same is true of moral attitudes. The poor are identified as those who need care and empathy, and these forms of nurturance are cultivated through recognizing their Creator and envisioning their plight (v. 5). What's more, justice provides a moral foundation for society. Its nurturance, however, requires more than just judges; it necessitates moral judgments and moral attitudes that nurture the sentiment that injustice is more than "not good" (לֹא־טוֹב, v. 26a); it is a sentiment that is also abhorrent (v. 15; cf. v. 23).

The attention to domestic, interpersonal, economic, and judicial ties illuminates the chapter's concern with social relations. While most of the aphorisms that consider these relations evaluate them in negative terms, their illocutionary force indicates that they function to motivate and cultivate various forms of care and communal nurturance. Nurturance of the other, however, is not considered in isolation from nurturance of the self. Self-nurturance occupies many of the remaining aphorisms. The recognition that YHWH tests hearts motivates moral purity and self-care before the face of YHWH (v. 3). The description of the evildoer and the liar challenges one to consider to whom they listen and whom they heed (v. 4). Receptivity to rebuke

3. Lakoff and Johnson, *Philosophy in the Flesh*, 311, italics original.

4. Johnson, *Philosophy in the Flesh*, 311.

diagnoses the health of one's disposition and one's openness to growth (v. 10). The shocking depiction of the danger of a fool in his folly motivates one to steer clear of the fool and the subtle ways in which foolishness may malnourish the self (v. 12). And the avoidance of strife or the abandonment of a conflict in the interest of peace protects and preserves the self (v. 14). These forms of self-nurturance complement the chapter's exploration of various forms of social nurturance. And the juxtaposition of chs. 16 and 17 place the concept of MORAL ORDER in conversation with the concept of MORAL NURTURANCE. Within the hierarchical and moral order of Proverbs (16:1–33), it appears that authority and power do not reign supreme. Just as moral responsibilities inform one's position and authority in the moral order, so also moral and self-nurturance informs one's care for both others and the self within the various social relations that comprise the moral order.

In addition to the metaphorical concept that structures many of the sayings in ch. 17 and the way in which this concept supplements the metaphor of MORAL ORDER in ch. 16, it is important to note that the aphorisms reinforce and develop motifs within the prologue (1:8–9:18) and the first Solomonic subcollection (10:1–15:33). The risk of granting surety is reiterated (17:18; cf. 6:1–5; 11:15; 20:16); and the language of acquiring wisdom is redeployed to satirize the fool's defective disposition and inability to buy wisdom (v. 16; cf. 4:5–7). Silence is promoted yet complicated in connection with a fool (vv. 27–28; cf. 10:19; 11:12; 13:3; 21:23); and a cohesive household is prized (vv. 1, 6, 21, 25; cf. 10:1, 5; 13:1; 15:20; 19:13).

To these familiar themes, several aphorisms introduce or elaborate on motifs that receive little or no attention in the previous collections. Bribery, for example, is explored from different perspectives (vv. 8, 23; cf. 21:14), expanding the moral purview of the central collections and their treatment of justice. And friendship emerges as an invaluable relationship beyond the domestic unit (vv. 9, 17; cf. 16:28; 18:24; 19:6, 7).[5] While ch. 17 includes only a few variant repetitions that create intertextual links with both previous and subsequent materials,[6] its aphorisms reinforce common topics and introduce fresh themes, which contribute to the pedagogical development of the central collections.

Translation and Exegetical Outline

(See pages 453–54.)

Structure and Literary Form

Whereas order characterizes the content and arrangement of the materials in ch. 16, "hodgepodge" is a representative description of the aphorisms in ch. 17.[7] A better-than saying (v. 1) and a proverb cast in the form of a rhetorical question (v. 16) accompany aphorisms that exhibit various types of intralinear parallelism. Certain sayings traffic in hyperbole, eliciting an emotional response from the reader (vv. 10, 12, 16). But, in comparison with previous chapters, proverbial pairs are scarce (vv. 1–2, 17–18, 21–22, 27–28). The aphorisms evince neither lexical nor thematic relationships with their neighbors. In light of these features, it is not surprising that most claim that the materials show no sign of deliberate design.[8] The chapter represents the first with little discernable arrangement.

This is not to say that the materials bear no signs of coherence. Fools feature prominently in the chapter (נָבָל, vv. 7a, 21b; כְּסִיל, vv. 10b, 12b, 16a, 21a, 24b, 25a; אֱוִיל, v. 28a). As noted above, the metaphor of MORAL NURTURANCE and the attention to various social relations infuse the aphorisms with a measure of conceptual coherence. And common themes as well as catchwords across a contextual distance may suggest that ch. 17 operates under a method of design that "differs from previous sections in Prov 10:1–22:16."[9] The method may differ, but the design of the chapter is far from clear.

5. Brown, "The Pedagogy of Proverbs 10:1–31:9," 158–59.

6. These variant repetitions include **17:22**//15:13; **17:3a**//27:21a; **17:15a**//24:24a; **17:15b**//20:10b. For discussion of these repetitions, see Heim, *Poetic Imagination*, 368–73, 411–27.

7. Murphy, *Proverbs*, 127.

8. Whybray, *The Composition of the Book of Proverbs*, 110.

9. Heim, *Like Grapes of Gold*, 226.

Proverbs 17:1–28

1a	טוֹב פַּת חֲרֵבָה וְשַׁלְוָה־בָהּ	Better a dry crust and tranquility with it,	B. Cultivating Moral Nurturance: The Sustenance of Social Ties and the Self (17:1–28)
1b	מִבַּיִת מָלֵא זִבְחֵי־רִיב	than a house full of contentious feasting.	
2a	עֶבֶד־מַשְׂכִּיל יִמְשֹׁל בְּבֵן מֵבִישׁ	A competent servant will rule over a disgraceful son,	
2b	וּבְתוֹךְ אַחִים יַחֲלֹק נַחֲלָה	and divide an inheritance among brothers.	
3a	מַצְרֵף לַכֶּסֶף וְכוּר לַזָּהָב	A crucible for silver and a furnace for gold,	
3b	וּבֹחֵן לִבּוֹת יְהוָה	but the one who tests hearts, YHWH.	
4a	מֵרַע מַקְשִׁיב עַל־שְׂפַת־אָוֶן	An evildoer, one who listens to iniquitous lips;	
4b	שֶׁקֶר מֵזִין עַל־לְשׁוֹן הַוֹּת	a liar, one who heeds a destructive tongue.	
5a	לֹעֵג לָרָשׁ חֵרֵף עֹשֵׂהוּ	One who mocks the poor insults his maker,	
5b	שָׂמֵחַ לְאֵיד לֹא יִנָּקֶה	and one who rejoices at disaster will not go unpunished.	
6a	עֲטֶרֶת זְקֵנִים בְּנֵי בָנִים	The crown of the aged, grandchildren,	
6b	וְתִפְאֶרֶת בָּנִים אֲבוֹתָם	and the splendor of children, their fathers.	
7a	לֹא־נָאוָה לְנָבָל שְׂפַת־יֶתֶר	An excessive lip, not fitting for a fool;	
7b	אַף כִּי־לְנָדִיב שְׂפַת־שָׁקֶר	how much more a lying lip for a noble.	
8a	אֶבֶן־חֵן הַשֹּׁחַד בְּעֵינֵי בְעָלָיו	A bribe, a beautiful charm in the eyes of its possessor;	
8b	אֶל־כָּל־אֲשֶׁר יִפְנֶה יַשְׂכִּיל	wherever he turns he succeeds.	
9a	מְכַסֶּה־פֶּשַׁע מְבַקֵּשׁ אַהֲבָה	One who seeks love covers an offense,	
9b	וְשֹׁנֶה בְדָבָר מַפְרִיד אַלּוּף	but one who repeats a matter separates friends.	
10a	תֵּחַת גְּעָרָה בְמֵבִין	A rebuke goes deeper into the discerning	
10b	מֵהַכּוֹת כְּסִיל מֵאָה	than a hundred blows on a fool.	
11a	אַךְ־מְרִי יְבַקֶּשׁ־רָע	The evil seek only rebellion,	
11b	וּמַלְאָךְ אַכְזָרִי יְשֻׁלַּח־בּוֹ	and a cruel messenger will be sent against him.	
12a	פָּגוֹשׁ דֹּב שַׁכּוּל בְּאִישׁ	Encounter a bear bereft of her young by a man,	
12b	וְאַל־כְּסִיל בְּאִוַּלְתּוֹ	but not a fool in his folly.	
13a	מֵשִׁיב רָעָה תַּחַת טוֹבָה	One who returns evil for good—	
13b	לֹא־תָמוּשׁ רָעָה מִבֵּיתוֹ	evil will never depart from his house.	
14a	פּוֹטֵר מַיִם רֵאשִׁית מָדוֹן	Releasing water, the beginning of strife,	
14b	וְלִפְנֵי הִתְגַּלַּע הָרִיב נְטוֹשׁ	so before the conflict breaks out, leave!	
15a	מַצְדִּיק רָשָׁע וּמַרְשִׁיעַ צַדִּיק	One who acquits the wicked and condemns the righteous—	
15b	תּוֹעֲבַת יְהוָה גַּם־שְׁנֵיהֶם	an abomination to YHWH, both of them.	

Continued on next page.

Continued from previous page.

16a	לָמָּה־זֶּה מְחִיר בְּיַד־כְּסִיל	Why is it that a payment is in the fool's hand
16b	לִקְנוֹת חָכְמָה וְלֶב־אָיִן	to buy wisdom, when there is no brain?
17a	בְּכָל־עֵת אֹהֵב הָרֵעַ	A friend loves at all times,
17b	וְאָח לְצָרָה יִוָּלֵד	and a brother is born for adversity.
18a	אָדָם חֲסַר־לֵב תּוֹקֵעַ כָּף	A senseless person shakes hands,
18b	עֹרֵב עֲרֻבָּה לִפְנֵי רֵעֵהוּ	going surety for his neighbor.
19a	אֹהֵב פֶּשַׁע אֹהֵב מַצָּה	One who loves an offense loves strife,
19b	מַגְבִּיהַּ פִּתְחוֹ מְבַקֶּשׁ־שָׁבֶר	and one who makes his door high seeks destruction.
20a	עִקֶּשׁ־לֵב לֹא יִמְצָא־טוֹב	One with a perverted heart never finds good,
20b	וְנֶהְפָּךְ בִּלְשׁוֹנוֹ יִפּוֹל בְּרָעָה	and one with a twisted tongue falls into evil.
21a	יֹלֵד כְּסִיל לְתוּגָה לוֹ	One who begets a fool has grief,
21b	וְלֹא־יִשְׂמַח אֲבִי נָבָל	and the father of a fool never rejoices.
22a	לֵב שָׂמֵחַ יֵיטִב גֵּהָה	A joyful heart enhances healing,
22b	וְרוּחַ נְכֵאָה תְּיַבֶּשׁ־גָּרֶם	but a broken spirit dries up the bones.
23a	שֹׁחַד מֵחֵיק רָשָׁע יִקָּח	The wicked takes a bribe from the bosom
23b	לְהַטּוֹת אָרְחוֹת מִשְׁפָּט	to divert the paths of justice.
24a	אֶת־פְּנֵי מֵבִין חָכְמָה	Before the face of the discerning, wisdom;
24b	וְעֵינֵי כְסִיל בִּקְצֵה־אָרֶץ	but the eyes of the fool, on the ends of the earth.
25a	כַּעַס לְאָבִיו בֵּן כְּסִיל	A foolish son, a vexation to his father
25b	וּמֶמֶר לְיוֹלַדְתּוֹ	and bitterness to the one who bore him.
26a	גַּם עֲנוֹשׁ לַצַּדִּיק לֹא־טוֹב	Surely, punishing the righteous, not good—
26b	לְהַכּוֹת נְדִיבִים עַל־יֹשֶׁר	striking noble people for uprightness.
27a	חוֹשֵׂךְ אֲמָרָיו יוֹדֵעַ דָּעַת	One who restrains words, a knowledgeable person,
27b	וְקַר־רוּחַ אִישׁ תְּבוּנָה	and the calm, a person of understanding.
28a	גַּם אֱוִיל מַחֲרִישׁ חָכָם יֵחָשֵׁב	Even a fool who keeps silent is regarded wise;
28b	אֹטֵם שְׂפָתָיו נָבוֹן	one who closes his lips, discerning.

Among the potential units, some agreement exists concerning the coherence of 16:31–17:6 or 17:1–6,[10] and several scholars read vv. 21–28 as either a cluster or a combination of two smaller units (vv. 21–25, 26–28).[11] These units create fruitful contexts within which to read the individual aphorisms. The moral and intellectual nourishment provided by the aphorisms, however, is not contingent on these contexts; they simply offer an alternative way to taste and see their wisdom.

10. Delitzsch, "Proverbs of Solomon," 6:252 (1:350); Meinhold, *Die Sprüche*, 2:282; Waltke, *Proverbs: Chapters 15–31*, 35–36. Cf. Heim, *Like Grapes of Gold*, 228–30.

11. Whybray, *The Composition of the Book of Proverbs*, 111; Meinhold, *Die Sprüche*, 2:293; Heim, *Like Grapes of Gold*, 237–39; Waltke, *Proverbs: Chapters 15–31*, 59–60; Koptak, *Proverbs*, 433.

CHAPTER 24

Proverbs 18:1–24

C. Enhancing MORAL ESSENCE: *The Complexities of Moral Character and MORAL ACTIONS*

Main Idea of the Passage

Negotiating the interrelationship between moral character and moral actions, these aphorisms privilege the concept of MORAL ESSENCE and nuance various themes to enhance the complexities of being-in-the-world and sharpen one's moral reasoning.

Literary Context[1]

Moral character and moral action—the stuff that constitutes MORAL ESSENCE—are complex. Among other reasons, this complexity is due to the fact that one does not have direct or immediate access to oneself, to others, or to the variegated situations of life. This access is always partial and mediated. Proverbs recognizes these complexities of the moral life, and many of the sayings in ch. 18 accentuate these complexities through their depiction of moral character and moral actions.

Similar to many of the sayings in ch. 12 and elsewhere in the central collections, the metaphor of MORAL ESSENCE and the intricate relationship between moral character and moral action are explored by various aphorisms in ch. 18. This exploration, however, differs from the previous materials. The themes are familiar; but they are developed and nuanced in particular ways. The sayings reveal the desire of fools (v. 2; cf. 3:15; 8:11), not simply this figure's loquaciousness (12:23; 13:16). In striking

1. This chapter does not include the Canonical and Theological Significance section. See pp. xv and 276n1 for justification. Also, see pp. 510–14 for the Canonical and Theological Significance of Proverbs 16:1–22:16.

fashion, they affirm the value of loquaciousness, so long as it springs from a fountain of wisdom (18:4b; cf. 10:8, 18, 19; 11:12, 13; 12:23; 17:27, 28).[2] They acknowledge, in contrast to previous sayings, the sweet taste of slander (18:8; cf. Prov 16:28; 26:20, 22). They raise questions about the security of wealth (18:11; cf. 10:15). They reinforce the value of listening, not only to counsel (12:15), or rebuke (13:1), or reproof (15:31) but also to others generally (18:13, 17). They question one's psychosomatic ability to cope with a crushed spirit (18:14; cf. 15:13; 17:22). They introduce the efficacy of gift giving, promoting a dialogue between the wisdom of the practice and the matter of bribery (18:16; cf. 15:27; 17:8, 23; 19:6; 21:14; 25:6–7).[3] They extend the power of lots (18:18; cf. 16:33) as well as the power of a brother (18:19; cf. 17:17). They entertain the idea that the fruit of one's mouth may not be good (18:20; cf. 12:14; 13:2; 18:21). They provide a theological evaluation of a wife (18:22; cf. 12:4; 19:13, 14). They ask the reader whether the rich person's harsh response to the poor is problematic or merely a prevalent social reality (18:23; cf. 14:20). Finally, they identify gradations of friendship (18:24; cf. 17:17; 19:4, 6). The sayings consider familiar aspects of moral character and common moral actions. But these repeated themes are cast in discrete scenarios and developed in distinctive ways to highlight the complexities of moral character and moral actions.

The nuanced development of familiar themes and the complexities of the moral life are funded, in part, by the variant repetitions within ch. 18. These repetitions create intertextual links with previous and subsequent materials, intimating the collections share comparable concerns and a homogenous moral vision. More than this, these repetitions generate a dialogue among sayings, where subtleties, tensions, and the depth dimension of topics are expressed and explored. Divine favor, for example, accompanies not only one who finds Lady Wisdom (8:35) and the good person (12:2a) but also one who finds a wife (18:22). The wealth of the rich may be a fortified city (10:15a), but, ultimately, this source of security is illusive (18:11). The fruit of one's mouth may yield good things and bring satisfaction (12:14; 13:2), but equally it may simply fill the speaker as well as others with death (18:20; cf. v. 21). Other variant repetitions extend the moral ontology of the wise (18:15; cf. Prov 15:14), consider the consequences of humility and pride (18:12; cf. 15:33b; 16:18a), illuminate different aspects of the metaphor "deep waters" (18:18; cf. 20:5), reinforce the tasty words of the slanderer (18:8; cf. 26:22), and develop the family tree of the destroyer (18:9; cf. 28:24).[4] Whereas variant repetitions were scarce in ch. 17, they are more prevalent in ch. 18. They complement the chapter's nuanced construal of common themes and contribute to the didactic development of the central collections.

2. Hatton, *Contradiction in the Book of Proverbs*, 150–54.

3. Hatton, *Contradiction in the Book of Proverbs*, 137–48.

4. For discussion of the variant repetitions in chapter 18, see Heim, *Poetic Imagination*, 186–92, 235–40, 295–303, 373–76, 392–98, 427–37.

Translation and Exegetical Outline

(See pages 459–60.)

Structure and Literary Form

The complexities of moral character and moral actions explored by many of the aphorisms in ch. 18 coincide with its complex poetic forms and opaque design. While most of the sayings exhibit some form of intralinear parallelism, syntactic or semantic correspondence between elements in juxtaposed lines does not characterize others. Similar to a handful of aphorisms (11:24, 12:18, 13:7, 23; 14:12; 16:25; 20:15), 18:24 is cast in the form of a reflection.[5] The second line of several sayings expand aspects of the first rather than providing an equivalent element (vv. 1, 8, 9, 13).[6] At least one aphorism integrates asymmetrical parallelism with "semantic extension" (v. 11);[7] and another uses metaphoric parallelism to plumb the semantic depths of partial equivalents (v. 4).[8]

5. Gianto, "On יֵשׁ of Reflection in the Book of Proverbs," 158–62, esp. 160–61.

6. McKane, *Proverbs*, 512–13; Heim, *Poetic Imagination*, 434.

7. Adele Berlin, *The Dynamics of Biblical Parallelism*, rev. and enl. ed. (Grand Rapids: Eerdmans, 2008), 95.

8. Berlin, *The Dynamics of Biblical Parallelism*, 99–102.

Proverbs 18:1–24

C. Enhancing Moral Essence: The Complexities of Moral Character and Moral Actions (18:1–24)

1a	לְתַאֲוָה יְבַקֵּשׁ נִפְרָד	A loner seeks his own desire;
1b	בְּכָל־תּוּשִׁיָּה יִתְגַּלָּע	he breaks out against all sound wisdom.
2a	לֹא־יַחְפֹּץ כְּסִיל בִּתְבוּנָה	A fool does not delight in understanding,
2b	כִּי אִם־בְּהִתְגַּלּוֹת לִבּוֹ	but only in disclosing his heart.
3a	בְּבוֹא־רָשָׁע בָּא גַם־בּוּז	When the wicked enters, contempt enters too,
3b	וְעִם־קָלוֹן חֶרְפָּה	and with shame, reproach.
4a	מַיִם עֲמֻקִּים דִּבְרֵי פִי־אִישׁ	The words of a person's mouth, deep waters,
4b	נַחַל נֹבֵעַ מְקוֹר חָכְמָה	a flowing stream, a fountain of wisdom.
5a	שְׂאֵת פְּנֵי־רָשָׁע לֹא־טוֹב	Showing the wicked favor, not good,
5b	לְהַטּוֹת צַדִּיק בַּמִּשְׁפָּט	thrusting aside the righteous in judgment.
6a	שִׂפְתֵי כְסִיל יָבֹאוּ בְרִיב	A fool's lips bring strife,
6b	וּפִיו לְמַהֲלֻמוֹת יִקְרָא	and his mouth calls for blows.
7a	פִּי־כְסִיל מְחִתָּה־לוֹ	A fool's mouth, his ruin,
7b	וּשְׂפָתָיו מוֹקֵשׁ נַפְשׁוֹ	and his lips, a snare for his life.
8a	דִּבְרֵי נִרְגָּן כְּמִתְלַהֲמִים	The words of a slanderer, like delicacies,
8b	וְהֵם יָרְדוּ חַדְרֵי־בָטֶן	and they descend into one's innermost being.
9a	גַּם מִתְרַפֶּה בִמְלַאכְתּוֹ	Even one slack in his work—
9b	אָח הוּא לְבַעַל מַשְׁחִית	he is a brother to a destroyer.
10a	מִגְדַּל־עֹז שֵׁם יְהוָה	The name of YHWH, a strong tower;
10b	בּוֹ־יָרוּץ צַדִּיק וְנִשְׂגָּב	into it the righteous runs and is secure.
11a	הוֹן עָשִׁיר קִרְיַת עֻזּוֹ	The wealth of the rich, his fortified city;
11b	וּכְחוֹמָה נִשְׂגָּבָה בְּמַשְׂכִּיתוֹ	and like a high wall, in his imagination.
12a	לִפְנֵי־שֶׁבֶר יִגְבַּהּ לֶב־אִישׁ	Before destruction one's heart is haughty,
12b	וְלִפְנֵי כָבוֹד עֲנָוָה	but before honor, humility.
13a	מֵשִׁיב דָּבָר בְּטֶרֶם יִשְׁמָע	One who replies before listening—
13b	אִוֶּלֶת הִיא־לוֹ וּכְלִמָּה	it is folly to him, and shame.

Continued on next page.

Continued from previous page.

14a	רוּחַ־אִישׁ יְכַלְכֵּל מַחֲלֵהוּ	A person's spirit can endure his sickness,
14b	וְרוּחַ נְכֵאָה מִי יִשָּׂאֶנָּה	but a broken spirit—who can bear it?
15a	לֵב נָבוֹן יִקְנֶה־דָּעַת	The heart of the discerning acquires knowledge,
15b	וְאֹזֶן חֲכָמִים תְּבַקֶּשׁ־דָּעַת	and the ear of the wise seeks knowledge.
16a	מַתָּן אָדָם יַרְחִיב לוֹ	A person's gift makes room for him,
16b	וְלִפְנֵי גְדֹלִים יַנְחֶנּוּ	and leads him before the great.
17a	צַדִּיק הָרִאשׁוֹן בְּרִיבוֹ	The first in his case, right,
17b	יָבֹא־רֵעֵהוּ וַחֲקָרוֹ	until his neighbor comes and examines him.
18a	מִדְיָנִים יַשְׁבִּית הַגּוֹרָל	The lot stops quarrels,
18b	וּבֵין עֲצוּמִים יַפְרִיד	and separates the powerful.
19a	אָח נִפְשָׁע מִקִּרְיַת־עֹז	An offended brother, like a strong city,
19b	וּמִדְיָנִים כִּבְרִיחַ אַרְמוֹן	and quarrels, like the bar of a palace.
20a	מִפְּרִי פִי־אִישׁ תִּשְׂבַּע בִּטְנוֹ	From the fruit of his mouth one's belly is satisfied;
20b	תְּבוּאַת שְׂפָתָיו יִשְׂבָּע	he is satisfied by the produce of his lips.
21a	מָוֶת וְחַיִּים בְּיַד־לָשׁוֹן	Death and life, in the power of the tongue;
21b	וְאֹהֲבֶיהָ יֹאכַל פִּרְיָהּ	those who love it eat its fruit.
22a	מָצָא אִשָּׁה מָצָא טוֹב	One who has found a wife has found good,
22b	וַיָּפֶק רָצוֹן מֵיְהוָה	and receives favor from YHWH.
23a	תַּחֲנוּנִים יְדַבֶּר־רָשׁ	The poor speak entreaties;
23b	וְעָשִׁיר יַעֲנֶה עַזּוֹת	but the rich answer harshly.
24a	אִישׁ רֵעִים לְהִתְרֹעֵעַ	There are friends to associate with,
24b	וְיֵשׁ אֹהֵב דָּבֵק מֵאָח	but the reality is this: a true friend sticks closer than a brother.

The rich variety of poetic forms bears witness to the pedagogical development in the central collections. These forms invite the reader to contemplate the relationship between the parts of a saying. This contemplation cultivates one's moral reasoning, and it shapes one's moral worldview.

In addition to a variety of poetic forms, one encounters an opaque design within ch. 18. Like ch. 17, many claim the material "lacks apparent structure"[9] and "contains no extended groups" of sayings.[10] Others, by contrast, perceive signs of structural arrangement at the macro- and microlevels. At the macrolevel, the repetition of "brother" (אָח, 18:9b, 19a, 24b) may serve as a lexical marker, dividing the aphorisms into three constituent groups (vv. 1–9, 10–19, 20–24).[11] Alternatively, thematic concerns may reveal two larger subunits, each of which is concerned with different forms of speech (vv. 1–11, 12–21).[12] At the microlevel, wordplay as well as thematic and verbal links may disclose the presence of clusters or the formation of proverbial pairs (e.g., vv. 1–2; 6–8, 10–12, 16–19, 20–24).[13] Whether or not these macro and micro signs of arrangement illuminate the design of the chapter, most agree that the sayings exhibit a particular concern with speech, listening, and disputes.[14] The aphorisms may not evince clear signs of structural arrangement, but they intimate a measure of thematic coherence. This coherence, however, does not conceal the formal, structural, or moral complexity of the aphorisms; rather, it creates a sense of unity amid disparity.

Explanation of the Text

The metaphor of MORAL ESSENCE entails that one's moral actions reveal one's moral character and that one's moral character is revealed through one's moral actions.[15] The interrelationship between character and actions, however, is not always clear. As Prov 17:28 notes, even a fool may be considered wise when he exercises verbal restraint. Individual actions do not always provide an accurate diagnosis of one's character. But, in most cases, they do. The stability of this interrelationship is reestablished in

18:1. The misfit or "loner" (נִפְרָד, v. 1a) emerges for the first and only time within Proverbs. His character is inchoate, but his social isolation and verbal actions clarify the contours of his moral essence. Whether the recluse's estrangement from the community is due to his individualism or antisocial behavior, his isolation creates the ideal environment to seek "his own desire" (לְתַאֲוָה, v. 1a).[16] Pursuing the satisfaction of his own urges, he nourishes self-separation; and by breaking out

9. Yoder, *Proverbs*, 196.

10. Whybray, *The Composition of the Book of Proverbs*, 112. Also see Murphy, *Proverbs*, 134.

11. Meinhold, *Die Sprüche*, 2:296. Cf. Delitzsch, "Proverbs of Solomon," 6:276 (2:14).

12. Waltke, *Proverbs: Chapters 15–31*, 68.

13. Toy, *Proverbs*, 358–65; Heim, *Like Grapes of Gold*, 241–50; Fox, *Proverbs 10–31*, 638, 640, 642.

14. McKane, *Proverbs*, 513; Murphy, *Proverbs*, 134; Yoder, *Proverbs*, 196; Fox, *Proverbs 10–31*, 640; Sæbø, *Sprüche*, 237; O'Dowd, *Proverbs*, 266.

15. Lakoff and Johnson, *Philosophy in the Flesh*, 306–7.

16. Following the LXX, many emend לְתַאֲוָה ("desire") to לתאנה ("pretexts"), since the suffix "his" is absent from the MT and "pretexts" provides an appropriate backdrop for the association between breaking out and quarreling in the second

against all sound wisdom, he seeks to sow separation within the community. Far from concealing his character through verbal restraint (Prov 17:28), the loner's quarreling and attack on social competence discloses his anticommunitarian ethos. His moral actions mirror his moral character.

The same is true of the fool, who is profiled in **18:2.**[17] This figure's heart may be concealed from sight, but it delights in disclosing its immoral ontology. Similar to other sayings in the central collections, the aphorism utilizes the metaphor of MORAL ESSENCE to describe the fool's propensity for self-disclosure (12:23; 13:16). In contrast to these sayings, however, 18:2 casts this self-disclosure in terms of desire. The aphorism develops the moral ontology of the fool. This personage not only has a habit of revealing his heart; he reveals his moral essence because he delights in self-disclosure, having no inclination for understanding.

Whereas the fool reveals his moral essence through self-disclosure, the wicked reveals his moral essence through his traveling companions (**v. 3**).[18] The initial בְּ + infinitive construct introduces contemporaneous time, casting the action in the main clause as simultaneous with the entrance of the wicked (v. 3a). The wicked travels with contempt. When one enters, the other enters (v. 3a; cf. 11:2). Both share a disdain for creatures and created goods (14:21).[19] And, as the second line suggests, both keep company with shame and reproach.[20] The entourage of the wicked is united by an internal disposition of contempt and the communal reputation of disgrace. The aphorism indicates that the company one keeps complements moral actions and moral character, revealing one's moral essence.

Drawing from the source domain of water, **18:4** explores the depths of one's moral essence through words (cf. 20:5).[21] The words of one's mouth is the topic of the saying (18:4a). The expressions pertaining to water extend and interpret the quantity, consistency, and quality of these words through metaphorical parallelism.[22] As the opening of a well, the mouth contains words that are "deep waters" (מַיִם עֲמֻקִּים, v. 4a), cool, revitalizing, and plentiful. These words, however, are not confined to the well, for they are also "a flowing stream" (נַחַל נֹבֵעַ, v. 4b), a river of refreshment that is continually fed by its moral source. And these words possess a particular character: they are "a fountain of wisdom" (מְקוֹר חָכְמָה, v. 4b). This final expression clarifies the previous two, identifying wisdom as the source of these waters and words. Words contain and convey the depth and refreshment of wisdom. In contrast to aphorisms that associate wisdom with verbal reticence and folly with verbosity (10:8, 18, 19; 11:12, 13; 12:23; 17:27, 28), this saying suggests that wisdom may flow through a perpetual "outpouring of words."[23] Loquaciousness, when springing from the moral essence of the wise, provides wisdom and

line (17:14; 20:3; *BHS*; Fox, *Proverbs 10–31*, 638). While emendation involves only a consonantal change from *waw* to *nun*, it is unnecessary, for the MT makes good sense. Delitzsch, "Proverbs of Solomon," 6:268 (2:1); McKane, *Proverbs*, 519; Heim, *Like Grapes of Gold*, 240.

17. The saying may be linked to v. 1 by means of the wordplay between יִתְגַּלָּע (v. 1b; "breaks out") and בְּהִתְגַּלּוֹת (v. 2b; "disclosing). Clifford, *Proverbs*, 170.

18. Yoder, *Proverbs*, 197. Also see Delitzsch, "Proverbs of Solomon," 6:269 (2:3).

19. Van Leeuwen, "The Book of Proverbs," *NIB* 5:172.

20. Delitzsch, "Proverbs of Solomon," 6:269 (2:3).

21. While 18:4a is a variant repetition of 20:5a, these sayings use the metaphor "deep waters" (מַיִם עֲמֻקִּים) in distinctive ways. As Knut Heim rightly notes, the former captures the quantity and clarity of one's words, whereas the latter considers the "concealment and discovery" of one's words (Heim, *Poetic Imagination*, 429).

22. Berlin, *The Dynamics of Biblical Parallelism*, 99–102; Heim, *Poetic Imagination*, 428.

23. Hatton, *Contradiction in the Book of Proverbs*, 150–54, esp. 153.

refreshment for all who will come to the waters and drink (cf. Isa 55:1).

Moving away from the matter of words (Prov 17:27–18:4), **18:5** considers justice and judicial partiality. The ironic, understated evaluation "not good" (לֹא־טוֹב, v. 5a) places the aphorism in conversation with others that employ the rhetorical technique of litotes (16:29; 17:26; 19:2; 20:23). Among these sayings, 18:5 bears a close resemblance to 17:26. Just as punishing the righteous or striking the noble for uprightness is "not good" (17:26), so also showing partiality to the guilty is "not good" (18:5a). While the judicial context of 17:26 is implicit, it is explicit in the second half of 18:5. The initial infinitive construct functions epexegetically,[24] explaining the circumstances that attend showing favoritism toward the wicked or guilty: it thrusts aside the righteous or innocent in judgment. From both an ethical and pragmatic perspective, this inversion of justice is "not good."[25] The saying contributes to the second subcollection's particular concern with justice, evaluating the virtue in relation to the righteous and the wicked (cf. 17:15, 23, 26).[26]

Whether or not 18:5 implies a "verbal crime,"[27] **vv. 6–8** return to the topic of speech and the metaphor of MORAL ESSENCE. This metaphorical concept structures the interrelationship between moral character and moral actions within these aphorisms; and it creates a framework for their use of the complex metaphorical concepts WORDS ARE A FORCE and WORDS ARE FOOD.[28] The former is employed in **v. 6**. The fool's speech possesses a particular power. His lips incite strife; and his mouth either summons listeners to physical punishment or invites others to punish him (v. 6b). The ambiguity regarding the object of punishment is alleviated by the portrait of the fool's speech in **v. 7**. The fool's mouth remains powerful. His speech, however, ruins him and ensnares his life (cf. 10:14; 13:3). Destructive speech is the product of the fool's immoral ontology (18:6–7); it is a power that sows social strife and engenders self-ruin. The speech of the slanderer, by contrast, operates under a different power, namely, the potency of taste (**v. 8**). The complex metaphor WORDS ARE FOOD fills out different dimensions of the metaphor of MORAL ESSENCE. By virtue of his character, the slanderer produces malicious speech. Despite the nature of this speech, it tastes savory, "like delicacies" (כְּמִתְלַהֲמִים, v. 8a).[29] This irresistible dish is quickly consumed by others. And once consumed, it descends into the innermost parts of the listener's being, where it shapes their perception and nourishes their (im)moral essence.[30] Whereas the speech of the slanderer separates friends and increases strife elsewhere in the central collections (16:28; 26:20), its tantalizing taste and (mal)nourishing qualities are the focus of attention in 18:8 (cf. 26:22). The effects of malicious speech may be disastrous; but to the ear, gossip is delicious.

The discourse on speech gives way to an aphorism on work in **18:9**. The introductory particle "even" (גַּם, v. 9a) is emphatic, expressing the certainty of the saying in general and its expanded evaluation in the second line in particular.[31]

24. Waltke, *Proverbs: Chapters 15–31*, 66; Fox, *Proverbs 10–31*, 639; *IBHS* §36.2.3e.

25. Fox, *Proverbs 10–31*, 639.

26. Brown, "The Pedagogy of Proverbs 10:1–31:9," 160.

27. Fox, *Proverbs 10–31*, 640.

28. Tilford, *Sensing World, Sensing Wisdom*, 184–91.

29. While the precise sense of the term "delicacies" (כְּמִתְלַהֲמִים) is unclear, its root appears to be related to the Arabic *lahima*, meaning "to devour greedily" (*HALOT* 2:521, s.v. להם). Accordingly, the *hithpael* participle conveys the image "of someone wolfing down gossip like food" (Fox, *Proverbs 10–31*, 641).

30. Tilford, *Sensing World, Sensing Wisdom*, 187.

31. Williams, *Williams' Hebrew Syntax*, §379. Cf. Waltke, *Proverbs: Chapters 15–31*, 74, who contends that the particle marks the climax or conclusion to vv. 1–9. Also see, *IBHS* §36.3.4d.

This evaluation integrates the slacker into the family tree of a destroyer. They share a striking resemblance. Like a destroyer, the negligent devastate themselves as well as kith and kin (cf. 28:24). More than inflicting physical pain (cf. 10:27), one slack in his work reveals his moral relations and, by implication, his moral essence.

The theme of security, shared imagery, and the catchwords "strong/fortified" (עֹז, 18:10a, 11a) and "secure/high" (שׂגב, vv. 10b, 11b) create an intimate relationship between **vv. 10–11**. These aphorisms observe that the righteous and the rich trust in different sources of safety. With language reminiscent of certain psalms, v. 10 construes the name of YHWH as an impregnable tower (v. 10a; cf. Ps 20:2[1]; 61:4[3]). YHWH's name signifies his person and character, which provides a high, safe place for the righteous to run and find security. Security, however, may be sought in other places. The wealth of the rich is comparable to the name of YHWH; it constitutes a "fortified city" (קִרְיַת עֻזּוֹ, 18:11a) and "a high wall" (חוֹמָה נִשְׂגָּבָה, v. 11b). Similar to 10:15a, 18:11 acknowledges that wealth offers safety. But the aphorism's juxtaposition to v. 10 and its inclusion of the final phrase "in his imagination" (בְּמַשְׂכִּיתוֹ, v. 11b) relativize wealth as a sure source of security.[32] Compared to YHWH's person and character, wealth is a vulnerable and illusory safety net. The righteous recognize this and run to YHWH. The rich, by contrast, seek security behind a wall that cannot offer the protection one imagines.

Just as v. 11a repeats 10:15a, so also the individual lines in **18:12** repeat 16:18a and 15:33b, respectively. The saying recasts these variant repetitions into a contrast. In so doing, it rehearses Proverbs's concern with pride and humility to form a moral ontology appropriate to creaturehood through the power of motivation. Similar to its use elsewhere in the Old Testament (Isa 3:16; Jer 49:16; Ezek 17:24), the verb "high" or "haughty" (יִגְבַּהּ, Prov 18:12a) describes the vice of pride in orientational terms; it is a disposition that transgresses moral boundaries, engendering destruction and insecurity. Humility, by contrast, is depicted as a lowly disposition that serves as a precondition for exaltation. Insecurity and renown animate the individual lines, creating an aversion to pride and an inclination for humility.

Motivation continues to play a formative role in **v. 13** and its evaluation of the social dishonor that accompanies one's failure to listen. Listening is a defining feature of the wise (1:5; 12:15; 13:1; 15:31, 32). This characteristic posture is illustrated through the teachability of the wise in general and their receptivity to counsel (12:15), rebuke (13:1), and reproof in particular (15:31, 32). Listening, however, is not limited to receiving instruction. According to 18:13, it involves a more general openness to the words of others. The saying expands Proverbs's description of the virtue of listening; it cultivates mutual communication by associating the refusal to listen to another with social disgrace and the immoral actions of a babbling, resistant fool (cf. v. 2).

Whereas v. 13 expands the virtue of listening, **v. 14** develops Proverbs's discussion of a "broken spirit" (רוּחַ נְכֵאָה, v. 14b). This psychosomatic condition is related to a troubled heart and a withering body elsewhere in the central collections (Prov 15:13; 17:22); it connotes an internal state of distress that determines the condition of the body. This intimate interrelationship between body and spirit is explored in the individual lines of 18:14. The first indicates that a healthy, internal spirit

32. Although the specific meaning of "in his imagination" (בְּמַשְׂכִּיתוֹ) is uncertain, in light of the use of the noun in Ps 73:7, it appears to convey the sense of "delusions." Fox, *Proverbs 10–31*, 642.

enables one to endure bodily sickness (v. 14a). The second, however, contends that a sick spirit is unable to withstand the weight of physical affliction, for it possesses no other source of support (v. 14b). By casting the unbearable nature of a broken spirit in the form of a rhetorical question, the second line extends Proverbs's discourse on this psychosomatic condition. A broken spirit may be comparable to a troubled heart that infiltrates the bones and infects the body (Prov 15:13; 17:22). More than representing a physical and psychological state of being, however, this condition may be emotionally intolerable (18:14b).

The interrelationship between one's inner being and body is explored further in **v. 15**. The aphorism moves from the heart to the ear, describing the moral essence and actions of the wise. Far from representing passive body parts, the heart and ear are portrayed as active organs through which wisdom is obtained (cf. 2:2). The heart of the discerning continually engages in the process of acquiring knowledge (18:15a; cf. 16:16); and the ear of the wise constantly searches for wisdom (18:15b).[33] The inclinations of these organs reinforce and expand the moral essence of the wise. By reiterating and extending 15:14a, the aphorism develops the moral ontology of the discerning through the interrelationship between this personage's internal and external organs.

The moral ontology of the discerning serves as an appropriate backdrop for **18:16** and its consideration of the wisdom of gift giving.[34] While the practice was common in the ancient world, it receives little attention in Proverbs (v. 16; cf. 19:6; 21:14). This is the first mention of the custom within the anthology. On the surface, it is considered efficacious, as a means of opening doors so that one may climb the social ladder and associate with the great. But when the saying is read together with 17:8 and 23 in general and 21:14 in particular, it raises questions concerning the distinction between gift giving and bribery. Since "gift" (מַתָּן, 18:16a) is a more neutral term than "bribe" (שֹׁחַד; 17:8, 23; 21:14),[35] the difference between these practices may reside in the intention of the giver.[36] If self-interest at the expense of the social good is intended, then the practice may be regarded as both unscrupulous and potentially damaging, for standing in the place of the great may provide the occasion for personal humiliation (Prov 25:6–7).[37] If, on the other hand, the saying simply observes a social reality, then it may encourage gift giving in order to secure some form of advancement.[38] Gift giving may be effective, but circumstances may indicate that the practice is not wise. The openness of the aphorism shapes one's moral reasoning, calling one to discern the wisdom of the practice in light of one's intentions, the social situation, and potential consequences.

The same is true of **18:17**, which seeks to cultivate the virtue of discernment. Developing the value of listening from v. 13, the aphorism envisions a scenario in which the first to make his case seems right until another scrutinizes the person, exposing him and his one-sided case. Whether or not the saying developed in the context of the legal court,

33. Fox, *Proverbs 10–31*, 643.

34. While vv. 16–19 may constitute a coherent unit of sayings that share a judicial setting, these aphorisms are by no means limited to this purported context. Murphy, *Proverbs*, 137.

35. Hatton, *Contradiction in the Book of Proverbs*, 146.

36. Fox, *Proverbs 10–31*, 643.

37. For the dialogue between Prov 18:16 and 25:6–7 as well as 19:6, see Hatton, *Contradiction in the Book of Proverbs*, 146–47. Many view the practice of gift giving in 18:16 negatively, construing it as a form of bribery by virtue of the saying's juxtaposition to v. 17. Van Leeuwen, "The Book of Proverbs," *NIB* 5:174; Heim, *Like Grapes of Gold*, 248; Waltke, *Proverbs: Chapters 15–31*, 81–82.

38. Toy, *Proverbs*, 362–63; McKane, *Proverbs*, 517; Meinhold, *Die Sprüche*, 2:304–5.

it promotes listening to all sides of a dispute. The warning inculcates the virtue of discernment by acknowledging that the truth of a matter is sought out and sifted through multiple perspectives.

Examining both sides of a case, however, may not resolve a dispute. In the event of such a stalemate, **v. 18** commends the power of the lot. Elsewhere in the Old Testament, lots were used to identify perpetrators and to allocate one's territorial inheritance (Num 34:13; 36:2; Josh 7:14–18; 14:2; Jonah 1:7). The present saying expands its function, promoting its use in interpersonal conflicts. The lot possesses the power to end conflict; its decision separates powerful disputants from one another. When viewed in light of Israelite thought and read together with Prov 16:33, it appears that the power of the lot is funded by a particular conception of YHWH's immanent intervention in human affairs. The divine sovereign reveals his verdict through a few stones, which separate litigants.

Nonetheless, certain disputes cannot be settled by the lot. The catchword "quarrels" (מִדְיָנִים, 18:18a, 19b)[39] links **v. 19** with the previous saying. And the terms and expressions employed by the aphorism develop particular topics within the central collections. Reiterating language and imagery from v. 11, the initial line likens an "offended brother" (אָח נִפְשָׁע, v. 19a) to a "strong city" (מִקִּרְיַת־עֹז, v. 19a).[40] Whereas 17:17 portrayed a brother as an indispensable source of support in adversity, 18:19a depicts an irreconcilable brother as unconquerable fortress. And whereas the metaphor "strong city" is used positively in several sayings (10:15; 18:10, 11), v. 19a construes it negatively.[41] The elliptical line creates interpretive space for different renderings of this negative image. An offended brother may be "like" a fortified city or "more unconquerable than" a fortified city. In both cases, the brother is irreconcilable. The second line appears to extend the sense of the first, indicating that the condition of the offended brother is engendered by quarrels and comparable to "the bar of a palace" (בְּרִיחַ אַרְמוֹן, v. 19b; cf. Judg 16:3; Neh 3:3). Quarrels transform an intimate, loyal companion into a fortified city that is impregnable from the outside and bolted from the inside.

The fortress imagery gives way to a pair of sayings pertaining to fruit (Prov 18:20–21). The initial line of **v. 20** is a variant repetition of 12:14a and 13:2a. Similar to these aphorisms, 18:20 explores one's moral essence through the conceptual metaphors PEOPLE ARE TREES and WORDS ARE FOOD. These fertile metaphors not only structure the saying. Following Tilford, they also encapsulate a compressed sequence.[42] The branches of the mouth produce fruit through speech. This fruit satisfies or fills others. Others then produce discursive fruit. And this fruit satisfies or fills the speaker. The aphorism compresses this act-consequence connection into a single event: the mouth that produces the fruit of edible speech is the mouth that consumes the fruit.[43] Whereas this condensed event "increases the immediacy of the speaker's reward and emphasizes the inherent benefit of speaking wisely" in 12:14a and 13:2a,[44] this does not appear to be the case in 18:20. In contrast to

39. While the sense of v. 18b remains the same, this reading follows *qere* ("quarrels") rather than *ketiv* ("contentions").

40. The syntax of the initial line is difficult. The LXX reads "a brother helped by a brother is a like a strong and lofty city," which, as Fox notes, amounts to a guess (*Proverbs: An Eclectic Edition*, 268). To clarify the simile, the inseparable preposition מן may be corrected to כ. Alternatively, מן may function as a comparative with an elided but implied word. For discussion of the textual difficulties see, Delitzsch, "Proverbs of Solomon," 6:275–76 (2:13–14); Toy, *Proverbs*, 363–64; McKane, *Proverbs*, 520; Fox, *Proverbs 10–31*, 644–45.

41. Hatton, *Contradiction in the Book of Proverbs*, 95–96.

42. Tilford, *Sensing World, Sensing Wisdom*, 190.

43. Tilford, *Sensing World, Sensing Wisdom*, 190.

44. Tilford, *Sensing World, Sensing Wisdom*, 190.

12:14a and 13:2a, 18:20a does not associate the fruit of one's mouth with "good things" (טוב, 12:14a; 13:2a). The quality of the fruit is unclear. The neutral nature of this fruit suggests that the verbs in each line may be rendered as either "satisfied" or simply "filled."[45] The fruit of one's mouth is the product of one's character. But the quality of one's words must be discerned by one's moral palate. The aphorism cultivates one's moral reasoning, inviting one to determine whether words bring satisfaction or merely a full stomach.

The effects of speech are escalated in **18:21**. More than producing satisfied stomachs or full bellies, words wield the power of life and death. The open, neutral description of speech in v. 20 is conceptualized in terms of life and death in v. 21. The tongue holds and controls life and death, and the tongue or form of speech that each person loves determines one's fate.[46] When the sayings are read together, it appears that those who love wise and honest speech will consume this edible fruit, receive satisfaction, and enjoy the gift of life. Those who do not produce, consume, or love wise and honest speech, by contrast, may be filled by words; but their dish will demonstrate that they dine on death. Words are powerful and, as noted above, their effects are determined by one's loves and moral tastes.

The feminine gender of "tongue" and its association with death and life recall the antithesis between Wisdom and Folly within Prov 9:1–18 (18:21).[47] In light of these resonances as well as its striking similarities with 8:35, it is not surprising that **18:22** considers finding a wife. The aphorism evaluates the value of a wife, celebrating the goodness of the marital relationship within God's good creation without entertaining exceptions. Whereas other aphorisms devoted to a wife evaluate her in moral terms, this saying evaluates her in theological terms. Just as one who finds Lady Wisdom receives "favor from YHWH" (רָצוֹן מֵיְהוָה, 8:35; cf. 12:2a), so also one who finds a wife receives "favor from YHWH" (רָצוֹן מֵיְהוָה, 18:22b). The saying offers both a theological evaluation and an androcentric perspective on finding a wife. This perspective, however, may be recontextualized to affirm the divine favor that accompanies finding a spouse.

Explicit evaluation recedes from view in **v. 23**, leading many to conclude that the aphorism offers "a general rule" concerning "the way the world is."[48] When the saying is read as a "'neutral' comment on a reality of social life,"[49] it observes that the poor, by virtue of their socioeconomic vulnerability, "speak entreaties" (תַּחֲנוּנִים יְדַבֶּר, v. 23a), while the rich, on account of their socioeconomic power, "answer harshly" (יַעֲנֶה עַזּוֹת, v. 23b). Power literally governs the rhetoric and relationship between poor and rich.[50] As a social observation, the aphorism may simply bear witness to "the manners of the time."[51] But when the saying is placed in conversation with other aphorisms within the anthology, this social observation invites ethical evaluation. Far from representing a neutral comment, it calls for critique. And when the saying is read closely,

45. Murphy, *Proverbs*, 137; Heim, *Poetic Imagination*, 300.

46. For the distributive sense of the singular predicate with a plural subject, see GKC §145l. While "death" (מָוֶת, v. 21a) or "life" (חַיִּים, v. 21a) may serve as the antecedent of the feminine singular pronominal suffixes in v. 21b, it is unlikely that both are in view, especially since neither noun agrees grammatically with the pronominal suffixes. On syntactical grounds, "tongue" (לָשׁוֹן, v. 21a) is the antecedent of the pronouns in the second line. For discussion of these options as well as the proposal that "wisdom" is the implied antecedent of the pronouns, see Delitzsch, "Proverbs of Solomon," 6:276 (2:15); Clifford, *Proverbs*, 173; Fox, *Proverbs 10–31*, 645.

47. Van Leeuwen, "The Book of Proverbs," *NIB* 5:174–75.

48. Toy, *Proverbs*, 366; McKane, *Proverbs*, 518; Clifford, *Proverbs*, 174; Meinhold, *Die Sprüche*, 2:308–9.

49. Whybray, *Proverbs*, 274.

50. Sandoval, *The Discourse of Wealth and Poverty*, 192.

51. Toy, *Proverbs*, 366.

it criticizes the callousness of the rich. The noun "supplications" or "entreaties" derives from the root חנן, which is used elsewhere in Proverbs to describe one who is gracious to the poor and honors YHWH (14:21, 31; 19:17; 28:8). The noun "entreaties" also punctuates the Psalter, where it is placed on the lips of one in need, petitioning the divine (Pss 28:2, 6; 31:23[22]; 86:6; 116:1; 130:2; 140:7[6]; 143:1). Like the psalmists, the poor entreat the rich for help. The rich, however, refuse the claim of the poor and reject their obligation to meet the needs of the vulnerable.[52] That is, they refuse to be constituted before the face of and through the voice of the poor, speaking strong things in response to the supplications of the marginalized. The saying may be read as a neutral social observation. Read ethically and in dialogue with other sayings, however, it houses perlocutionary disgust toward those who fail to use their resources in acknowledgment that YHWH is the maker of and the one who cares for both the rich and the poor (Prov 22:2).

The relational dynamics between poor and rich set the stage for the relational dynamics between different types of friends in **18:24**. The aphorism's concern with friendship develops previous sayings pertaining to this amicable relationship (Prov 14:20; 17:17). Similar to 13:23, 18:24 employs the יֵשׁ of reflection to introduce the second colon.[53] The initial line lures the reader into the topic of sociable relationships. Certain people make for mixing (v. 24a).[54] The introductory יֵשׁ of the second line, however, reveals the reality: a true friend sticks closer than a brother (v. 24b). This reality nuances other sayings by identifying gradations of friendship. One may share company with plenty of people, but true friendship is manifested through loyal commitment.

52. Sandoval, *The Discourse of Wealth and Poverty*, 192.

53. Gianto, "On יֵשׁ of Reflection in the Book of Proverbs," 160.

54. The initial line may be rendered in several different ways. Following the Masoretic note, the Greek versions, the Peshitta, and the Targum, the opening אִישׁ ("a man") in the MT may be read as a particle of existence יֵשׁ ("there are"). Whether or not the emendation is accepted, the sense of the opening phrase remains the same. This is not the case, however, with the infinitive construct "to associate with" (לְהִתְרֹעֵעַ, v. 24a). The form may derive from the roots רעע I ("to be bad, displeasing"), רעע II ("to smash, be broken"), or רעה ("to befriend, be involved with"), among others. In light of v. 24b, it appears to be a *hithpolel* infinitive construct from רעע, which is a by-form of רעה, meaning "to befriend" or "to associate with" (Fox, *Proverbs 10–31*, 647). For other proposals, see Delitzsch, "Proverbs of Solomon," 6:277–78 (2:17–18); McKane, *Proverbs*, 518–19; Whybray, *Proverbs*, 274; Waltke, *Proverbs: Chapters 15–31*, 87.

CHAPTER 25

Proverbs 19:1–29

D. Merging MORAL AUTHORITY with MORAL ACCOUNTING: *The Value of Wisdom and Instruction*

Main Idea of the Passage

Many of these sayings consider the value of wisdom and instruction through the metaphors of MORAL AUTHORITY and MORAL ACCOUNTING in order to cultivate receptivity to discipline and to motivate a moral life marked by well-being.

Literary Context[1]

Wisdom and instruction animate Proverbs's program of education for character formation. They discipline, shape, and motivate the moral self through various techniques and through an account of reality designed to form one's "moral equipment" and inform one's being-in-the-world.[2] Many of the aphorisms in ch. 19 reflect on the value of wisdom and instruction.[3] Some utilize the metaphor of MORAL AUTHORITY and traffic in parental emotions, the promise of life, and success to encourage instruction and engender receptivity to discipline (vv. 13, 18, 20, 25, 26, 27).[4] Others operate under the metaphor of MORAL ACCOUNTING, linking characters and actions to rewards and punishments in order to motivate a life of wisdom and well-being

1. This chapter does not include the Explanation of the Text or the Canonical and Theological Significance sections. See pp. xv and 276n1 for justification. Also, see pp. 510–14 for the Canonical and Theological Significance of Proverbs 16:1–22:16.

2. For the expression "moral equipment" and its relation to the concept of "'virtuous' moral selfhood," see Jacqueline E. Lapsley, *Can These Bones Live? The Problem of the Moral Self in the Book of Ezekiel*, BZAW 301 (Berlin: De Gruyter, 2000), 8–10.

3. McKane, *Proverbs*, 523; Meinhold, *Die Sprüche*, 2:310–11; Whybray, *Proverbs*, 275; Heim, *Like Grapes of Gold*, 262; Waltke, *Proverbs: Chapters 15–31*, 117; Yoder, *Proverbs*, 202.

4. For the metaphor, see Lakoff and Johnson, *Philosophy in the Flesh*, 301–3. Also see the discussion in ch. 13 of this volume.

(vv. 2, 5, 8, 9, 15, 16, 17, 19, 23, 29).[5] These familiar metaphorical concepts and motivations structure and underlie many of the aphorisms in ch. 19. They illuminate their attention to the significance of wisdom and instruction and these thematic emphases clarify the chapter's unusual use of admonitions (vv. 18, 19, 20, 27). While these metaphorical concepts, motivations, and motifs do not encapsulate all of the aphorisms in ch. 19, they account for its prominent concerns and play a formative role in the didactic development of the central collections.

This development is evinced through the chapter's treatment of common themes and variant repetitions, each of which place the aphorisms in conversation with previous and subsequent materials. The initial saying contributes to the anthology's complex discussion of wealth and poverty (v. 1). In contrast to previous sayings, which reflect on the vulnerability of the poor or the moral culpability of poverty (10:4, 15; 13:18, 23; 14:20; 18:23), 19:1 associates the poor with virtue. Companionship with the poor may be preferable to camaraderie with the proud (16:19); and it may be better to be poor than a liar (19:22b). But according to v. 1, the poor are more than a lowly socioeconomic class. The poor may live a virtuous life. Their poverty may have nothing to do with vice. The opening better-than saying problematizes perspectives that attribute poverty only to vice; it sharpens one's moral worldview. Moreover, as a variant repetition of 28:6, the saying also trains one's moral reasoning. Whereas 28:6 follows the structure and logic of better-than sayings, 19:1b disrupts the logic of this evaluative scheme. Neither perverted lips nor foolishness are desirable (v. 1b). This explains why some emend "a fool" (כְּסִיל, v. 1b) to "rich" (עָשִׁיר), which aligns the saying with 28:6b.[6] When 19:1 is read as another example of asymmetrical parallelism, however, the aphorism invites the reader to extend the saying, not to emend it. In this case, the poor who walks in his integrity is wise and better than one with perverted lips, who is both rich and a fool.[7] The aphorism contributes to Proverbs's discourse on wealth and poverty, shaping one's moral worldview and moral reasoning.

In addition to wealth and poverty, several sayings contribute to the development of other strands of Proverbs's moral vision. Friendship, for example, may be valuable (17:9, 17), but according to 19:4 and 7, friendships are also varied. These aphorisms expand the reality of gradations of friendship in 18:24 by introducing wealth and one's socioeconomic status as the tie that (un)binds friendships. The quantity and quality of friendships are evaluated: some are fraudulent and the refusal to participate in others is morally misanthropic. Money and friendship are associated with the practice of gift giving in 19:6, placing the custom in dialogue with 18:16. Gifts may open doors to the great (18:16), but they may also attract a multitude of pseudo-

5. For the metaphor, see Lakoff and Johnson, *Philosophy in the Flesh*, 292–98. Also see the discussion in ch. 11 of this volume.

6. Toy, *Proverbs*, 368; *BHS*; Fox, *Proverbs 10–31*, 447–48.

7. Waltke, *Proverbs: Chapters 15–31*, 98; Heim, *Poetic Imagination*, 440.

friends (19:6b). Perjury occupies the variant repetitions in vv. 5 and 9. These sayings move beyond previous aphorisms and their attention to the moral essence of a false witness to consider the moral bill this person must pay. A false witness will not only face certain punishment (v. 5); he will receive the death penalty (v. 9b; cf. 21:28).[8] To these developments, others could be mentioned, such as the initial mention of the "quarrelsome wife" (מִדְיְנֵי אִשָּׁה, 19:13b; cf. 21:9, 19; 25:24; 27:15–16), the specification that a "prudent wife" is a divine gift (19:14b; cf. 18:22), and the unique construal of one's treatment of the poor in terms of moral accounting (19:17; cf. 14:21, 31; 21:10; 28:8), where the poor serve as "some sort of ancient automatic teller machine through which one could make a deposit directly to one's heavenly account."[9] The characters, actions, and relationships enshrined in these aphorisms are well known within the context of the anthology. Their distinctive features, however, reveal their particular contributions to the pedagogical development within the central collections.

More than developing previous themes, it is important to note that the sayings in ch. 19 also reinforce common motifs. The foolish son's emotional and social toll on parents and the fabric of the household reappears (vv. 13a, 26; cf. 10:1b–c; 17:21, 25). Rich imagery accompanies the wrath and favor of the king (19:12; cf. 16:14–15). The sluggard is subjected to satire (19:24; cf. 10:26; 13:4; 15:19; 26:13–16).

III. "Forming 'Fearers of YHWH'": The Curriculum of Wisdom and Virtue (10:1–29:27)

- III.1 Elementary Wisdom and Virtue (10:1–15:33)
- **III.2 Intermediate Wisdom and Virtue (16:1–22:16)**
  - A. YHWH, the King, and the People: The Organization of the Moral Order (16:1–33)
  - B. Cultivating MORAL NURTURANCE: The Sustenance of Social Ties and the Self (17:1–28)
  - C. Enhancing MORAL ESSENCE: The Complexities of Moral Character and Moral Actions (18:1–24)
  - ➡ **D. Merging MORAL AUTHORITY with MORAL ACCOUNTING: The Value of Wisdom and Instruction (19:1–29)**
  - E. Delimiting MORAL BOUNDS: The Parameters of (Im)moral Actions (20:1–30)
  - F. Accounting for Intentions: Sharpening Moral Reasoning through MORAL ACCOUNTING (21:1–31)
  - G. Fostering Moral Valuation: Schemes of MORAL ACCOUNTING (22:1–16)
- III.3 Vocational Wisdom and Virtue (22:17–24:34)
- III.4 Advanced Wisdom and Virtue (25:1–29:27)

8. Heim, *Poetic Imagination*, 445.

9. Gary A. Anderson, *Sin: A History* (New Haven: Yale University Press, 2009), 140.

Human limits and divine sovereignty are reiterated (19:21; cf. 16:1, 9). And the importance of discipline and receptivity to instruction is rehearsed (19:18, 20, 25, 27; cf. 1:8; 9:7–9; 13:24; 22:15; 23:13–14; 29:15, 17). The treatment of these themes complements their construal in previous materials and anticipates their exploration in subsequent collections. The "high concentration of variant repetitions" in ch. 19 also creates intertextual connections between its aphorisms and those that follow.[10] When taken together, these features indicate that Prov 19 contributes to the "didactic movement" of the central collections;[11] it strengthens and develops previous themes, on the one hand, and signposts the treatment of these motifs in subsequent collections, on the other.

Translation and Exegetical Outline

(See pages 473–74.)

Structure and Literary Form

On formal and structural grounds, the aphorisms in Prov 19 have not fared well with commentators. In accordance with the literary pattern manifest in chs. 17 and 18, William McKane goes so far as to claim that the sayings in ch. 19 evince "disintegration of form."[12] This decay may be substantiated by the variegated sayings in the chapter. Antithetical parallelism is present but minimal (vv. 4, 12, 14, 16, 21, 25). If one retains the MT, then v. 1 deviates from the logic of better-than sayings.[13] Some aphorisms are cast in the form of continuous sentences rather than parallel lines (vv. 17, 24, 26). Others represent a fortiori arguments (vv. 7, 10). And still others are admonitions more at home in the prologue or Prov 22:17–24:34 than in the first Solomonic collection (19:18, 19, 20, 27). While conventional forms of intralinear parallelism are woven throughout the fabric of ch. 19, the presence of a fortiori arguments and admonitions, the direct address "my son" (בְּנִי, v. 27a), and an unusual tricolon (v. 7) create a peculiar literary texture.

10. Heim, *Poetic Imagination*, 438. Heim explores several variant repetitions in Prov 19 (**19:29b**//10:13b//26:3b; **19:16a**//13:3//16:17b//21:23; **19:1**//28:6; **19:5**//19:9; **19:9**//21:28a; **19:12a**//20:2a; **19:13b**//27:15–16; **19:24**//26:15; **19:25**//21:11) and considers whether Prov **19:11**//20:3 is "a case of conceptual repetition." Heim, *Poetic Imagination*, 228–35, 334–47, 438–76.

11. Brown, "The Pedagogy of Proverbs 10:1–31:9," 164–65 et passim.

12. McKane, *Proverbs*, 522.

13. For this better-than saying and its proposed emendation, see the discussion under Literary Context above.

Proverbs 19:1–29

1a	טוֹב־רָשׁ הוֹלֵךְ בְּתֻמּוֹ	Better the poor who walks in his integrity	D. Merging Moral Authority with Moral Accounting: The Value
1b	מֵעִקֵּשׁ שְׂפָתָיו וְהוּא כְסִיל	than one with perverted lips who is a fool.	of Wisdom and Instruction (19:1–29)
2a	גַּם בְּלֹא־דַעַת נֶפֶשׁ לֹא־טוֹב	Indeed, without knowledge, desire, not good,	
2b	וְאָץ בְּרַגְלַיִם חוֹטֵא	and one who hurries with his feet sins.	
3a	אִוֶּלֶת אָדָם תְּסַלֵּף דַּרְכּוֹ	A person's folly leads him astray,	
3b	וְעַל־יְהוָה יִזְעַף לִבּוֹ	but his heart rages against YHWH.	
4a	הוֹן יֹסִיף רֵעִים רַבִּים	Wealth adds many friends,	
4b	וְדָל מֵרֵעֵהוּ יִפָּרֵד	but the poor is separated from his friend.	
5a	עֵד שְׁקָרִים לֹא יִנָּקֶה	A false witness will not go unpunished,	
5b	וְיָפִיחַ כְּזָבִים לֹא יִמָּלֵט	and one who tells lies will not escape.	
6a	רַבִּים יְחַלּוּ פְנֵי־נָדִיב	Many seek the favor of the noble,	
6b	וְכָל־הָרֵעַ לְאִישׁ מַתָּן	and everyone is a friend to the gift giver.	
7a	כָּל אֲחֵי־רָשׁ שְׂנֵאֻהוּ	All the poor person's brothers hate him.	
7b	אַף כִּי מְרֵעֵהוּ רָחֲקוּ מִמֶּנּוּ	How much more do his friends avoid him!	
7c	מְרַדֵּף אֲמָרִים לֹא־הֵמָּה	Pursuing words—they are not there.	
8a	קֹנֶה־לֵּב אֹהֵב נַפְשׁוֹ	One who acquires a heart loves himself,	
8b	שֹׁמֵר תְּבוּנָה לִמְצֹא־טוֹב	one who guards understanding, to find good.	
9a	עֵד שְׁקָרִים לֹא יִנָּקֶה	A false witness will not go unpunished,	
9b	וְיָפִיחַ כְּזָבִים יֹאבֵד	and one who tells lies will perish.	
10a	לֹא־נָאוֶה לִכְסִיל תַּעֲנוּג	Not fitting for a fool, luxury.	
10b	אַף כִּי־לְעֶבֶד מְשֹׁל בְּשָׂרִים	How much more for a servant to rule over princes!	
11a	שֵׂכֶל אָדָם הֶאֱרִיךְ אַפּוֹ	A person's insight makes him patient,	
11b	וְתִפְאַרְתּוֹ עֲבֹר עַל־פָּשַׁע	and his splendor, overlooking an offense.	
12a	נַהַם כַּכְּפִיר זַעַף מֶלֶךְ	Like a lion's growl, a king's wrath,	
12b	וּכְטַל עַל־עֵשֶׂב רְצוֹנוֹ	but his favor like dew on the grass.	
13a	הַוֹּת לְאָבִיו בֵּן כְּסִיל	A disaster to his father, a foolish son,	
13b	וְדֶלֶף טֹרֵד מִדְיְנֵי אִשָּׁה	and a constant dripping, a quarrelsome wife.	
14a	בַּיִת וָהוֹן נַחֲלַת אָבוֹת	House and wealth, an inheritance from fathers,	
14b	וּמֵיְהוָה אִשָּׁה מַשְׂכָּלֶת	but a prudent wife, from YHWH.	

Continued on next page.

Continued from previous page.

15a	עַצְלָה תַּפִּיל תַּרְדֵּמָה	Laziness induces a deep sleep,
15b	וְנֶפֶשׁ רְמִיָּה תִרְעָב	and the slacker goes hungry.
16a	שֹׁמֵר מִצְוָה שֹׁמֵר נַפְשׁוֹ	One who keeps a commandment keeps his life,
16b	בּוֹזֵה דְרָכָיו יָמוּת	but one who despises his ways will die.
17a	מַלְוֵה יְהוָה חוֹנֵן דָּל	One who is gracious to the poor lends to YHWH,
17b	וּגְמֻלוֹ יְשַׁלֶּם־לוֹ	and he will repay him for his deed.
18a	יַסֵּר בִּנְךָ כִּי־יֵשׁ תִּקְוָה	Discipline your son, for there is hope,
18b	וְאֶל־הֲמִיתוֹ אַל־תִּשָּׂא נַפְשֶׁךָ	and do not direct your desire to his death.
19a	גְּדָל־חֵמָה נֹשֵׂא עֹנֶשׁ	The hothead bears a penalty,
19b	כִּי אִם־תַּצִּיל וְעוֹד תּוֹסִף	for if you deliver him, you must do so again.
20a	שְׁמַע עֵצָה וְקַבֵּל מוּסָר	Listen to counsel and receive discipline,
20b	לְמַעַן תֶּחְכַּם בְּאַחֲרִיתֶךָ	that you may be wise in the future.
21a	רַבּוֹת מַחֲשָׁבוֹת בְּלֶב־אִישׁ	Many plans are in a person's heart,
21b	וַעֲצַת יְהוָה הִיא תָקוּם	but the counsel of YHWH, it stands.
22a	תַּאֲוַת אָדָם חַסְדּוֹ	A person's desire, his kindness,
22b	וְטוֹב־רָשׁ מֵאִישׁ כָּזָב	so better a poor person than a liar.
23a	יִרְאַת יְהוָה לְחַיִּים	The fear of YHWH, for life,
23b	וְשָׂבֵעַ יָלִין בַּל־יִפָּקֶד רָע	that one spends the night content, undisturbed by evil.
24a	טָמַן עָצֵל יָדוֹ בַּצַּלָּחַת	The sluggard has buried his hand in the bowl;
24b	גַּם־אֶל־פִּיהוּ לֹא יְשִׁיבֶנָּה	he will not even bring it back to his mouth.
25a	לֵץ תַּכֶּה וּפֶתִי יַעְרִם	Strike a scoffer and the simple become shrewd,
25b	וְהוֹכִיחַ לְנָבוֹן יָבִין דָּעַת	but rebuke the discerning, he will gain knowledge.
26a	מְשַׁדֶּד־אָב יַבְרִיחַ אֵם	One who mistreats a father and drives away a mother,
26b	בֵּן מֵבִישׁ וּמַחְפִּיר	a shameful and disgraceful son.
27a	חֲדַל־בְּנִי לִשְׁמֹעַ מוּסָר	Cease, my son, to listen to instruction,
27b	לִשְׁגוֹת מֵאִמְרֵי־דָעַת	to stray from words of knowledge!
28a	עֵד בְּלִיַּעַל יָלִיץ מִשְׁפָּט	A worthless witness mocks justice,
28b	וּפִי רְשָׁעִים יְבַלַּע־אָוֶן	and the mouth of the wicked swallows iniquity.
29a	נָכוֹנוּ לַלֵּצִים שְׁפָטִים	Judgments are prepared for scoffers,
29b	וּמַהֲלֻמוֹת לְגֵו כְּסִילִים	and blows for the back of fools.

These features may bear witness to a "disintegration of form." Alternatively, they may serve as poetic threads stitched into the chapter to stretch the moral dexterity and reasoning of the reader. If this is the case, then the didactic function of these variegated forms seems to align with the chapter's content. Many sayings emphasize the value of wisdom and instruction (vv. 2, 8, 13, 16, 18, 19, 20, 23, 25, 26, 27, 29). And the ambiguity of others instructs the moral reasoning of the reader. The final line of the unusual tricolon (v. 7c), for example, is nonsensical, leading Michael Fox to conclude that it is "a meaningless group of four words."[14] The MT's reading of v. 16b raises questions concerning whether "his ways" (דְּרָכָיו) refers to God's ways or the sage's teaching.[15] The use of the homonym חֶסֶד in v. 22a creates space to render the line as either "A person's desire, his kindness" (חֶסֶד I) or "A person's desire/greed/lust, his shame" (חֶסֶד II).[16] And the admonition in v. 27a is strange, for it runs counter to the fundamental teaching of Proverbs. Perhaps a scribe misread the infinitive construct "to listen" (לִשְׁמֹעַ).[17] Perhaps the admonition is ironic.[18] Perhaps it is a pedagogical wake-up call. Whatever it is, the command, combined with the ambiguity of certain sayings, appears to contribute to the pedagogical movement of the central collections. Both the forms within and the subject matter of ch. 19 contribute to the maturation of one's moral reasoning.

The evaluation of the formal texture of ch. 19 is comparable to the assessment of its structure. Similar to chs. 17 and 18, it appears the sayings exhibit "no obvious structure."[19] Signs of structural design may be perceived, however, within the chapter and across its boundaries. Common themes may mark the boundaries of larger units (18:22–19:14; 19:15–20:4).[20] Coreferential terms, comparable proverbs, and repeated expressions, on the other hand, indicate that extended clusters may be drawn along different lines (Prov 18:22–19:7; 19:8–15; 19:16–23; 19:24–20:1).[21] And other criteria for coherence suggest that ch. 19 consists of several smaller units.[22] These distinctive

14. Fox, *Proverbs 10–31*, 651. The final line of v. 7 has baffled interpreters, not only because it represents the only tricolon in Prov 10:1–22:16, but also because it appears to make no sense. Some have attempted to recover another line, presumably missing in the MT, by consulting the additional four lines in the LXX (Delitzsch, "Proverbs of Solomon," 6:282–83 [2:24–25]; Gemser, *Sprüche Salomos*, 77). But this pursuit has not yielded a satisfactory reading; and in light of the fact that the LXX Proverbs "is not a formal correspondence translation," the use of the Greek version here to correct or reconstruct the text is questionable (*BHQ*). As a result, many conclude that v. 7c is the initial line of a lost aphorism. Toy, *Proverbs*, 370; Fox, *Proverbs 10–31*, 651. For an attempt to account for v. 7c within the context of the surrounding sayings, see Meinhold, *Die Sprüche*, 2:313–15; Heim, *Poetic Imagination*, 446–47.

15. For the former reading, see John A. Emerton, "Notes on Some Passages in the Book of Proverbs," *JTS* 20 (1969): 208; for the latter, see Murphy, *Proverbs*, 144. For the emendation of "his ways" (דרכיו) to "a word" (דבר), see, among others, Toy, *Proverbs*, 375; *BHS*, Fox, *Proverbs 10–31*, 655–56.

16. For discussion of these readings as well as the emendation of "desire" (תַּאֲוַת) to "fruit" (תבואת; cf. LXX), see Murphy, *Proverbs*, 141n22.a.; Fox, *Proverbs 10–31*, 659.

17. For the variants "to hate" (לשׂנא) or "to spurn" (לפרע) for "to listen" (לשמע), see Toy, *Proverbs*, 381; Fox, *Proverbs 10–31*, 661, 1022–23.

18. McKane, *Proverbs*, 525; Clifford, *Proverbs*, 179; Murphy, *Proverbs*, 146.

19. Murphy, *Proverbs*, 142.

20. Garrett, *Proverbs*, 169.

21. Waltke, *Proverbs: Chapters 15–31*, 93, 120. Cf. Meinhold, *Die Sprüche*, 2:310; Heim, *Like Grapes of Gold*, 254–68.

22. Toy, *Proverbs*, 368–82, Van Leeuwen, "The Book of Proverbs," *NIB* 5:178–82; Sæbø, *Sprüche*, 243.

proposals recognize different forms of coherence and design across a contextual distance. Whether one privileges a particular proposal or sees the structure of the chapter as more porous, catchwords and the juxtaposition of common forms imply that certain sayings should be read together (19:1–2, 6–7, 13–14, 18–20, 20–21, 28–29). The design of the chapter may not be obvious, but its attention to particular themes imbues the material with a measure of unity.

CHAPTER 26

Proverbs 20:1–30

E. Delimiting Moral Bounds: *The Parameters of (Im)moral Actions*

Main Idea of the Passage

Taken together, these sayings explore (im)moral actions through the MORAL BOUNDS metaphor. They devote particular attention to human limits and the maintenance of moral boundaries to cultivate conduct in accord with the contours of creation.

Literary Context[1]

More than serving as a token of one's character, moral actions reveal the space within which one lives and moves. More specifically, they indicate whether or not one lives within the moral bounds of the community and moves within authorized areas of the moral order. Moral actions, on this account, are conceptualized through the metaphor of MORAL BOUNDS, a concept that is related to the prologue's root metaphor, LIFE IS A PATH.[2] The MORAL BOUNDS metaphor informs many of the sayings within Prov 20. These sayings are not concerned with the topography of one's path or the orientation of one's character (2:12–13; 4:18; 11:5; 12:28; 16:17); rather, they focus on particular moral actions and delimit specific moral boundaries. These boundaries range from the consumption of alcohol (20:1) and economic affairs (vv. 10, 14, 21, 23) to work (v. 4), sleep (v. 13), disputes (v. 3), retributive justice (v. 22), vows (v. 25), and social protocol before the king (v. 2). While other sayings within the chapter operate under different metaphorical concepts, many consider various limits or

1. This chapter does not include the Canonical and Theological Significance section. See pp. xv and 276n1 for justification. Also, see pp. 510–14 for the Canonical and Theological Significance of Proverbs 16:1–22:16.

2. For discussion of the MORAL BOUNDS metaphor, see Lakoff and Johnson, *Philosophy in the Flesh*, 304–5.

boundaries. Several admonitions, for example, prescribe particular moral actions (vv. 13, 16, 18, 19, 22), mapping areas within which one should or should not move. Certain aphorisms attend to the role of YHWH and the king in the establishment and maintenance of boundaries in the moral order (vv. 8, 22, 26, 28). And a number of sayings reflect on the limits of human perception (vv. 5, 6, 9, 11, 24). The construal of moral actions through the metaphor of MORAL BOUNDS and the attention to limits within the majority of sayings in ch. 20 intimate that these materials seek to cultivate moral movements that abide within and strengthen the moral order.

Among the distinctive emphases within ch. 20, many have noted the unusual attention to YHWH and the king (vv. 2, 8, 10, 12, 22, 23, 24, 26, 27, 28). The arrangement of these YHWH and royal sayings may suggest that they mimic the pattern of Prov 16, exploring the relationships between YHWH and people, YHWH and the king, and the king and the people.[3] Whether or not this is the case, the placement of the YHWH and royal sayings among others concerned with moral boundaries intimate that they function in a different framework than ch. 16. Whereas the content and arrangement of the materials in ch. 16 foreground the metaphor of MORAL ORDER, the content and arrangement of the materials in ch. 20 foreground the metaphor of MORAL BOUNDS. These metaphors are related to one another, but each offers a discrete view of the moral world. The former promotes a vision of legitimate power relations and the moral responsibilities that superintend those relations;[4] the latter focuses on moral actions that either conform to or transgress the moral boundaries of the social order.[5] The sayings within ch. 20 privilege particular moral actions and the bounded areas of the moral life.

The moral actions profiled in Prov 20 reinforce and develop materials in the previous subcollections, and these moral actions are reiterated and nuanced in subsequent collections. Many could be mentioned. Particular attention to the thirteen variant repetitions within the chapter, however, may serve as a window into the variety of contextual and intertextual links between Prov 20 and other collections.[6] Some of the variant repetitions recast lines through alternative terms or with different forms of parallelism to accentuate particular motifs, such as YHWH's abhorrence of false weights (20:10, 23; 11:1; cf. 17:15), the nature of the slanderer (20:19; 11:13), the foundation of the king's throne (20:28b; 16:12b; 25:5b; 29:14b), the ways in which the king discerns evil (20:8, 26a), and the practice of providing surety (20:16; 27:13). Other variant repetitions extend common themes through their juxtaposition with different lines. These themes include the value of old age (20:29; 16:31a), the instrument necessary to draw up deep waters (20:5; 18:4), the nature of the king's

3. Meinhold, *Die Sprüche*, 2:329; Whybray, *Proverbs*, 288, 299; Heim, *Like Grapes of Gold*, 282; Waltke, *Proverbs: Chapters 15–31*, 134, 148, 165; Sæbø, *Sprüche*, 256.

4. Lakoff and Johnson, *Philosophy in the Flesh*, 303–4.

5. Lakoff and Johnson, *Philosophy in the Flesh*, 304–6.

6. For detailed discussion of these variant repetitions, see Heim, *Poetic Imagination*, 252–54, 263–67, 399–411, 415–30, 455–60, 477–503.

anger (20:2; 19:12), the conduct of the pure (20:11b; 21:8b), the results of military planning (20:18b; 24:6a; cf. 11:14; 15:22), and the expansion of those who curse father and mother (20:20a; 30:11). Far from merely recycling lines or partial lines, the variant repetitions in ch. 20 reinforce and reconfigure particular motifs to shape the character, actions, and moral reasoning of the reader.

Translation and Exegetical Outline

(See pages 480–81.)

Structure and Literary Form

If beauty lies in the eye of the beholder, then the forms within Prov 20 may be evaluated in different ways. The manifest diversity of forms and the lack of parallelism within many sayings may evince the "formlessness" of the materials.[7] The diverse forms and variegated types of parallelism, on the other hand, may evince the unique design of each saying. The design of each requires careful attention; and the investigation of each shapes one's moral reasoning in discrete ways.

7. McKane, *Proverbs*, 535.

Proverbs 20:1–30

E. Delimiting Moral Bounds: The Parameters of (Im)moral Actions (20:1–30)

1a	לֵץ הַיַּיִן הֹמֶה שֵׁכָר	Wine, a mocker; beer, a brawler,
1b	וְכָל־שֹׁגֶה בּוֹ לֹא יֶחְכָּם	and whoever is intoxicated by them will never be wise.
2a	נַהַם כַּכְּפִיר אֵימַת מֶלֶךְ	Like a lion's growl, the dread of a king;
2b	מִתְעַבְּרוֹ חוֹטֵא נַפְשׁוֹ	one who provokes his anger forfeits his life.
3a	כָּבוֹד לָאִישׁ שֶׁבֶת מֵרִיב	Abstaining from strife, to a person's honor,
3b	וְכָל־אֱוִיל יִתְגַּלָּע	but every fool quarrels.
4a	מֵחֹרֶף עָצֵל לֹא־יַחֲרֹשׁ	From the winter, the sluggard does not plow.
4b	וְשָׁאַל בַּקָּצִיר וָאָיִן	At the harvest, he inquires, but nothing!
5a	מַיִם עֲמֻקִּים עֵצָה בְלֶב־אִישׁ	The counsel in a person's heart, deep waters,
5b	וְאִישׁ תְּבוּנָה יִדְלֶנָּה	but an understanding person draws it up.
6a	רָב־אָדָם יִקְרָא אִישׁ חַסְדּוֹ	Many people – each one proclaims his own loyalty,
6b	וְאִישׁ אֱמוּנִים מִי יִמְצָא	but a trustworthy person, who can find?
7a	מִתְהַלֵּךְ בְּתֻמּוֹ צַדִּיק	One who goes about in his integrity: the righteous.
7b	אַשְׁרֵי בָנָיו אַחֲרָיו	Blessed are his children after him!
8a	מֶלֶךְ יוֹשֵׁב עַל־כִּסֵּא־דִין	A king sits on the throne of judgment
8b	מְזָרֶה בְעֵינָיו כָּל־רָע	scattering all evil with his eyes.
9a	מִי־יֹאמַר זִכִּיתִי לִבִּי	Who can say, "I have made my heart pure,
9b	טָהַרְתִּי מֵחַטָּאתִי	I am cleansed from my sin?"
10a	אֶבֶן וָאֶבֶן אֵיפָה וְאֵיפָה	Variant weights, variant measures:
10b	תּוֹעֲבַת יְהוָה גַּם־שְׁנֵיהֶם	an abomination to YHWH, both of them.
11a	גַּם בְּמַעֲלָלָיו יִתְנַכֶּר־נָעַר	Even by his actions a youth makes himself known,
11b	אִם־זַךְ וְאִם־יָשָׁר פָּעֳלוֹ	whether his conduct is pure and upright.
12a	אֹזֶן שֹׁמַעַת וְעַיִן רֹאָה	A hearing ear and a seeing eye:
12b	יְהוָה עָשָׂה גַם־שְׁנֵיהֶם	YHWH has made both of them.
13a	אַל־תֶּאֱהַב שֵׁנָה פֶּן־תִּוָּרֵשׁ	Do not love sleep lest you become impoverished.
13b	פְּקַח עֵינֶיךָ שְׂבַע־לָחֶם	Open your eyes; be satisfied with food!
14a	רַע רַע יֹאמַר הַקּוֹנֶה	"Bad, bad," says the buyer,
14b	וְאֹזֵל לוֹ אָז יִתְהַלָּל	but when he goes away, he boasts.
15a	יֵשׁ זָהָב וְרָב־פְּנִינִים	There is this: gold and an abundance of corals,
15b	וּכְלִי יְקָר שִׂפְתֵי־דָעַת	but a precious ornament, knowledgeable lips.

16a	לְקַח־בִּגְדוֹ כִּי־עָרַב זָר	Take his garment, for he has gone surety for a stranger!
16b	וּבְעַד נָכְרִים חַבְלֵהוּ	And for outsiders, impound it.
17a	עָרֵב לָאִישׁ לֶחֶם שָׁקֶר	Sweet to a person, the bread of deceit,
17b	וְאַחַר יִמָּלֵא־פִיהוּ חָצָץ	but afterward his mouth is filled with gravel.
18a	מַחֲשָׁבוֹת בְּעֵצָה תִכּוֹן	Plans are established by counsel,
18b	וּבְתַחְבֻּלוֹת עֲשֵׂה מִלְחָמָה	so wage war with guidance.
19a	גּוֹלֶה־סּוֹד הוֹלֵךְ רָכִיל	A slanderer reveals secrets,
19b	וּלְפֹתֶה שְׂפָתָיו לֹא תִתְעָרָב	so do not mix with a big-mouth.
20a	מְקַלֵּל אָבִיו וְאִמּוֹ	One who curses his father or his mother,
20b	יִדְעַךְ נֵרוֹ בְּאִישׁוֹן חֹשֶׁךְ	his lamp will be extinguished in deep darkness.
21a	נַחֲלָה מְבֹהֶלֶת בָּרִאשֹׁנָה	An inheritance quickly gained at first,
21b	וְאַחֲרִיתָהּ לֹא תְבֹרָךְ	in the end will not be blessed.
22a	אַל־תֹּאמַר אֲשַׁלְּמָה־רָע	Do not say, "I will repay evil."
22b	קַוֵּה לַיהוָה וְיֹשַׁע לָךְ	Wait for YHWH, and he will save you.
23a	תּוֹעֲבַת יְהוָה אֶבֶן וָאָבֶן	An abomination to YHWH, variant weights,
23b	וּמֹאזְנֵי מִרְמָה לֹא־טוֹב	and fraudulent scales are not good.
24a	מֵיְהוָה מִצְעֲדֵי־גָבֶר	One's steps, from YHWH,
24b	וְאָדָם מַה־יָּבִין דַּרְכּוֹ	and a person—how can he understand his way?
25a	מוֹקֵשׁ אָדָם יָלַע קֹדֶשׁ	A trap for a person to say rashly, "Holy,"
25b	וְאַחַר נְדָרִים לְבַקֵּר	and after vows to appraise.
26a	מְזָרֶה רְשָׁעִים מֶלֶךְ חָכָם	A wise king scatters the wicked,
26b	וַיָּשֶׁב עֲלֵיהֶם אוֹפָן	and rolls the wheel over them.
27a	נֵר יְהוָה נִשְׁמַת אָדָם	The human life-breath, the lamp of YHWH,
27b	חֹפֵשׂ כָּל־חַדְרֵי־בָטֶן	searching all the innermost parts.
28a	חֶסֶד וֶאֱמֶת יִצְּרוּ־מֶלֶךְ	Kindness and faithfulness protect the king,
28b	וְסָעַד בַּחֶסֶד כִּסְאוֹ	and he supports his throne by kindness.
29a	תִּפְאֶרֶת בַּחוּרִים כֹּחָם	The splendor of the young, their strength,
29b	וַהֲדַר זְקֵנִים שֵׂיבָה	and the adornment of the aged, grey hair.
30a	חַבֻּרוֹת פֶּצַע תַּמְרִיק בְּרָע	Bruised wounds clean away evil,
30b	וּמַכּוֹת חַדְרֵי־בָטֶן	and blows, the innermost parts.

The variety of forms may contribute to the pedagogical development of the central collections and their progressive formation of the reader. If this is the case, the reader is formed through many forms within ch. 20. Some antithetical sayings are clear (vv. 3, 5, 6); the construal of the *waw* conjunctive in others is not (v. 29b). Semilinear parallelism characterizes certain lines (vv. 1a, 10a, 12a, 23a), while consequential parallelism distinguishes other aphorisms (vv. 4, 7, 17, 19, 21). The second line of certain sayings elaborates on the first (vv. 28b, 30b); in others, it extends only one element from the first (v. 11b).[8] And the "parallelism" of several sayings is marked by general correspondences between phrases or metaphors in juxtaposed lines rather than precise correlations (vv. 2, 8, 26, 27). In addition to these various forms of parallelism, some sayings are admonitions (vv. 13, 16, 18, 19, 22b). Others include rhetorical questions (vv. 6b, 9, 24b) or direct speech (vv. 14a, 22a, 25a). And similar to previous sayings, v. 15 is cast in the form of a reflection.[9] The forms, types of parallelism, and literary devices in Prov 20 vary. This variety, however, may bear witness to the varied ways in which its materials seek to form readers.

The same may be true of the structure of Prov 20. Despite the metaphor of MORAL BOUNDS and the concern with limits in many sayings, the boundaries or limits of discrete units within ch. 20 are unclear. But certain units may be discerned by means of themes, vocabulary, and similar or repeated terms; and each proposed unit creates a distinct context within which to read and contextualize the individual proverbs. At the microlevel, catchwords or comparable themes may link juxtaposed sayings or mark off certain units (אִישׁ, vv. 5, 6a; זַךְ ,זִכִּיתִי, vv. 9a, 11b; גַּם־שְׁנֵיהֶם, vv. 10b, 12b; עַיִן, vv. 12a, 13b; the root ערב, vv. 16a, 17a, 19b; יְהוָה, vv. 22b, 23a, 24a).[10] At the macrolevel, a variety of larger blocks have been proposed, with little agreement concerning their precise boundaries. Among these blocks, several commentators agree that vv. 5–12(13) and Prov 20:20–21:4 constitute coherent units. The former is united by its concern with discerning the secrets of human character; the latter is framed by the word "lamp" (נֵר, vv. 20b; 21:4b) and characterized by its consideration of YHWH and the king's relation to one another as well as the people.[11]

While the forms within and the structural proposals for Prov 20 vary, the repetitions within the chapter supply a sense of unity to the material.[12] Two sets of variant repetitions explore the winnowing of the king (vv. 8, 26) and YHWH's evaluation of false weights (vv. 10, 23). Two sayings consider laziness and food (vv. 4, 13). And two sayings probe the value of "loyalty/kindness" (חֶסֶד, v. 6a; 28a, 28b) and

8. Heim, *Poetic Imagination*, 488.

9. Gianto, "On יֵשׁ of Reflection in the Book of Proverbs," 158–62, esp. 160.

10. Yoder, *Proverbs*, 208.

11. Garrett, *Proverbs*, 175, 178; Whybray, *Proverbs*, 291, 298–99; Heim, *Like Grapes of Gold*, 273, 282–84. Cf. Meinhold, *Die Sprüche*, 2:329; Waltke, *Proverbs: Chapters 15–31*, 93, 120–21, 127, 148–50.

12. Koptak, *Proverbs*, 491–92.

trustworthiness/faithfulness (אֱמוּן, v. 6b; אֱמֶת, v. 28a) from different angles. These repetitions, combined with the use of the MORAL BOUNDS metaphor and the attention to limits within certain aphorisms, provide a measure of unity in the rich diversity of Prov 20.

Explanation of the Text

According to the MORAL BOUNDS metaphor, moral actions performed within authorized boundaries fund human flourishing, whereas immoral actions performed outside prescribed boundaries threaten the parameters of the moral order. It is important to note, however, that some moral boundaries are porous and open to transgression, like the intoxication of love with one's spouse (Prov 5:19). Others, by contrast, are fixed. This is the case in **v. 1**. The initial line personifies wine and beer in order to epitomize the way in which these strong drinks transform the overindulgent. Recasting the root לִיץ from Prov 19:28–29, wine turns one into a "mocker" (לֵץ, 20:1a) and, reiterating the description of the strange woman and Woman Folly (Prov 7:11; 9:13), beer makes one loud and turbulent (הֹמֶה, 20:1a). When enjoyed within proper limits, these strong drinks are a source of delight (Prov 3:10; 9:2, 5). But those who lose themselves in these beverages nourish a moral ontology that can never be wise. They transgress the moral bounds of drinking to the extent that they cannot determine the limits of appropriate conduct.[13]

This arresting vignette of transgressing moral bounds serves as an appropriate backdrop to **v. 2**, which explores the consequences of impermissible social protocol before the king. Similar to other sayings, the aphorism considers the wrath of the king (14:35; 16:14; cf. 24:21–22; 28:15). Similar to 19:12a, the dread of the king is depicted as a lion's growl. The sound inspires fear. The snarl reveals the frightening fangs of the king. And his presence anticipates the imminent unsheathing of his claws. More than engendering fright, however, the presence of the king identifies the rules of social engagement. Those who acknowledge these rules and act within the boundaries set are safe. Those who fail to acknowledge the king's fearsome powers and provoke his anger violate appropriate boundaries and forfeit their life.

Moral actions within moral or social bounds carry consequences. This truth is expressed from a different angle in **v. 3**. The aphorism depicts strife as a moral, bounded space. The person who abstains or stays away from strife receives public acclamation. This person refuses to enter a conflict in order to gain honor. This is not the case with the fool, whose character compels participation in the realm of quarreling. Whether or not the fool believes that quarreling serves as the appropriate occasion for gaining social honor, the second line fails to provide a complete antithesis to the first. The aphorism is unbalanced, and this imbalance awakens the reader's moral reasoning, inviting one to complete the saying. When the lines are read together, the generic "person" in the first line appears to be the wise, the intellectual counterpart to the fool. And in contrast to the honor attributed to the one who abstains from strife, it seems that every fool has no honor.

13. Van Leeuwen, "The Book of Proverbs," *NIB* 5:185.

Whereas vv. 1–3 consider the bounded areas of drinking, social protocol, and strife, **v. 4** aligns human behavior with the rhythm and calendrical pattern of the created order. The temporal expressions "from the winter" (מֵחֹרֶף, v. 4a) and "at the harvest" (בַקָּצִיר, v. 4b) designate bounded seasons, each of which required particular actions.[14] The wet winter season called for ploughing and planting, while the harvest demanded reaping. The fittingness of these forms of activity are reflected in the assonance in the initial line: "winter" (חֹרֶף, v. 4a) is congruous with "plow" (יַחֲרֹשׁ, v. 4a). The sluggard, however, neither lives in accord with the rhythm of creation nor acts in accord with its bounded seasons. And ironically, he has the chutzpah to inquire after the yield of his crop, only to discover nothing. More than satirizing the sluggard, the aphorism associates moral actions with the bounded seasons of creation, demonstrating that the one who does not sow does not reap.

In light of the agricultural seasons in v. 4, **v. 5** projects the agricultural image of a well through the metaphor "deep waters" (מַיִם עֲמֻקִּים, v. 5a). The metaphor, combined with the noun "person" (אִישׁ, v. 5a), indicates that the initial line represents a variant repetition of 18:4. The "deep waters" in these twice-told proverbs, however, function in distinctive ways. As Knut Heim rightly notes, 18:4 captures the quantity and clarity of one's words, whereas 20:5 considers the "concealment and discovery" of one's words.[15] Like Prov 18:4a, the counsel in a person's heart is plentiful. But in contrast to Prov 18:4b, this counsel is not depicted as a perpetual fountain of wisdom; rather, it is portrayed as a resource that the competent person draws from the well of another's heart. Whether these deep waters are brought to the surface for the refreshment of the understanding person, the community, or both, the task is not characterized as difficult. The competent discover and receive the counsel of others in the same way that one draws up deep waters from a well for refreshment.[16]

Deep waters of counsel may be plentiful; but according to **v. 6**, a trustworthy person is hard to find. The characterization of the trustworthy and the illocutionary force of the rhetorical question in the second line of the saying are clear. The syntax of the initial line, by contrast, is obscure. While various renderings and emendations are possible, the MT is by no means ambiguous.[17] The opening phrase in the initial line functions as a nominative absolute; it emphatically foregrounds the subject "many people" (רָב־אָדָם, v. 6a).[18] The clause that follows then distributes the evaluation of the many to each member of the group: "each one proclaims his own loyalty" or kindness (יִקְרָא אִישׁ חַסְדּוֹ, v. 6a).[19] On this reading, the aphorism does not pit the loyal person against the trustworthy; rather, it sets the self-declaration of the many against the concrete and reliable action of a rare individual: the trustworthy. In so doing, the saying reinforces the anthology's discourse concerning the dangers of self-evaluation (26:5, 12, 16; 27:2) and contributes to its conception of the gradations of friendship (17:9, 17; 18:24; 19:4, 6, 7).

Just as v. 6 opened with a nominative absolute, so also **v. 7** opens with the emphatic construction. More than focusing attention on the subject, the initial line gives particular attention to the state or condition of the subject. The subject "one who

14. For the temporal function of מִן and בְּ, see *IBHS* §11.2.11c; §11.2.5c.

15. Heim, *Poetic Imagination*, 429.

16. Fox, *Proverbs 10–31*, 664–65.

17. For alternative renderings and possible emendations, see Delitzsch, "Proverbs of Solomon," 6:295 (2:42); Clifford, *Proverbs*, 180; Fox, *Proverbs: An Eclectic Edition*, 282.

18. *IBHS* §4.7; Waltke, *Proverbs: Chapters 15–31*, 132.

19. Murphy, *Proverbs*, 149n6a.

goes" or "walks about" (מִתְהַלֵּךְ, v. 7a) introduces the concept of moral action as a bounded movement.[20] The physical space of movement, however, is not mentioned. Instead, the condition or state of moral movement is emphasized. This condition is expressed through the prepositional phrase "in his integrity" (בְּתֻמּוֹ, v. 7a) as well as the accusative "the righteous" (צַדִּיק, v. 7a).[21] Integrity identifies the manner or state in which the righteous walk about. The initial line gestures to the metaphor of MORAL BOUNDS but structures its description of the subject through the metaphor of MORAL ESSENCE. And in an unexpected turn, the second line is cast in the form of a beatitudinal expression, creating consequential parallelism. A form of life conditioned by integrity and righteousness results in transgenerational blessing.

This blessing stands in sharp contrast to the judgment of a king, which is the focus on attention in **v. 8** (cf. v. 26). The aphorism attends to a king's powers of perception and ability to adjudicate a matter. Taken together, the lines do not fit into any particular category of parallelism. This does not mean, however, that each line is an independent entity. The relationship between the component parts of the parallel lines reflects general metaphorical correspondences, not precise logical or grammatical relations.[22] The initial line delineates the place and posture of the king, clarifying the judicial setting of the saying. The second line specifies the way in which the king adjudicates evil through a pregnant metaphorical expression. The phrase "scattering . . . with his eyes" (מְזָרֶה בְעֵינָיו, v. 8b) depicts the forensic discernment of the king through the process of winnowing grain.[23] Like the winnowing fork, the eyes of the king serve as the instrument by which the chaff of evil is separated from the grain of the good and scattered by the wind.[24] Whether the saying is idealistic or aspirational, the incisiveness of the king's discernment and the nature of his judgment in the second line clarify the nature of his character in the first. This king is a wise or righteous king (cf. v. 26) who establishes moral order and moral bounds by eradicating evil (cf. 16:12; 25:5; 29:14; Ezek 5:10–12).

The ideal king may eradicate all evil, but no one, not even the king, can eradicate the evil of human sin. This is the essence of **20:9**. The aphorism is cast in the form of a rhetorical question, which demands a negative answer. It operates under the metaphorical concept of MORAL PURITY, according to which "Morality Is Cleanliness,"[25] and it elicits a response through the repetition of the first-person pronominal suffix "I . . . my . . . I . . . my . . ." The reiteration of the first-person pronominal suffix indicates that only a self-righteous person could answer this question in the affirmative, declaring "me . . . me . . . me!"[26] Those who acknowledge the limits of human perception and the inevitable transgression of moral bounds confess that the appropriate answer to the question is "No one."[27] The saying captures the nature of humanity internally as well as externally: the human heart is impure and human nature is defiled by sin.

A particular sin that evokes divine loathing is explored in **v. 10**, namely, unjust weights and

20. Lakoff and Johnson, *Philosophy in the Flesh*, 303–4.

21. For the בְּ of manner, marking a state or a condition, see Joüon §133c. For the accusative of state, see *IBHS* §10.2.2d.

22. Heim, *Poetic Imagination*, 478.

23. For the instrumental function of the preposition בְּ that opens the prepositional phrase "with his eyes" (בְּעֵינָיו, v. 8b), see *IBHS* §11.2.5d.

24. Heim, *Poetic Imagination*, 478.

25. Lakoff and Johnson, *Philosophy in the Flesh*, 307.

26. McCreesh, *Biblical Sound and Sense*, 74; Stewart, *Poetic Ethics*, 46.

27. Murphy, *Proverbs*, 151.

measures. This practice is mentioned elsewhere in the central collections (11:1; 20:23; cf. 16:11; Deut 25:13–16; Mic 6:11). Whereas other sayings distribute fraudulent weights and measures across parallel lines, Prov 20:10a juxtaposes them in a single line. This juxtaposition creates semilinear parallelism.[28] The poetic balance of the line, however, stands in sharp contrast to the economic imbalance reflected in the practice.[29] Disparate stones and variant dry measures transgress the moral bounds of economic transactions. And they engender divine disgust. This response not only offers a theological evaluation of unjust economic practices; it also forms the reader's emotional and moral stance toward financial fraudulence.

For some, the financial fraud addressed in v. 10 serves as an appropriate backdrop to **v. 11** and its apparent treatment of fraudulent behavior.[30] But the behavior sketched in the aphorism is by no means clear. The initial line opens with the adverb "even" (גַּם, v. 11a). If the aphorism is considered as the conclusion to a larger cluster (i.e., vv. 9–11), then the adverb may introduce an a fortiori argument.[31] But if the saying is considered as a coherent proverb that has its own integrity, then the adverb functions emphatically, signaling an exaggerated case.[32] The exaggerated case is expressed through the instrumental, prepositional phrase "by his actions" (בְּמַעֲלָלָיו, v. 11a). While the noun "actions" (מַעֲלָל) refers to evil deeds in most cases, it can also refer to good deeds. And while the verb יִתְנַכֶּר may be rendered as "to disguise oneself," it may also be construed as "to make oneself recognizable." Taken as a whole, the initial line of the aphorism is ambiguous: the nature of the youth's actions is undecidable and the verb is polysemous. Many resolve the ambiguity by identifying particular relationships between elements in the second line with those in the first. This approach, however, overlooks the fact that the elements in the second line do not exist in close relationship with those in the first. The lines do not exhibit conventional parallelism; rather, they are fashioned in such a way that the second line is parallel only to "his actions" in the first.[33] On this account, the saying is structured in accord with the metaphor of MORAL ESSENCE. One's actions, even if childish, identify whether one's conduct is "pure and upright" (אִם־זַךְ וְאִם־יָשָׁר, v. 11b).[34] This truth may strike one as banal. But the hermeneutical exertion required to acquire this truth may indicate that the process of discovery, rather than the end, is the pedagogical point.

This process of discovery is followed by a YHWH saying in **v. 12**, which offers a theological perspective on the organs of perception. These organs are cast in semilinear parallelism within the initial line. They are foregrounded as focal points through the nominative absolute construction. And their sequence reveals the process of human perception: hearing directs and informs seeing.[35] By listening to the instruction of authorized guides, one is invited to see the world in a particular way (chs. 1–9).[36] Wisdom is not simply read from creation; it comes by hearing, which trains one's sight. As the creation of YHWH, the hearing ear and the seeing eye are divine gifts bestowed on humans to

28. Heim, *Poetic Imagination*, 482–83.

29. Yoder, *Proverbs*, 210.

30. Clifford, *Proverbs*, 183–84; Waltke, *Proverbs: Chapters 15–31*, 137–38; Longman, *Proverbs*, 379–80.

31. Waltke, *Proverbs: Chapters 15–31*, 137.

32. Takamitsu Muraoka, *Emphatic Words and Structures in Biblical Hebrew* (Leiden: Brill, 1985), 143–44.

33. Heim, *Poetic Imagination*, 488–89.

34. Fox, *Proverbs 10–31*, 668.

35. Murphy, *Proverbs*, 151.

36. Johnson, *Biblical Knowing*.

perceive the richness of created reality. Perception, like wisdom, is gifted. The implication is that humans are responsible for the use of these organs in their pursuit of wisdom or folly (15:31; 17:24).[37]

This implication is developed in **20:13**, which offers a variation on the theme of sight. The saying consists of two admonitions, the first a prohibition, the second an exhortation. The prohibition addresses an improper desire: the love of sleep. More than preventing one from using the eyes to pursue and perceive wisdom (v. 12), this improper desire funds underachievement, a falling short of moral boundaries. And it engenders a state of poverty, which is conveyed through a negative purpose clause (פֶּן, "lest," v. 13a). The remedy for the improper love of sleep and moral inaction is expressed through an exhortation in the second line. The pair of positive commands seek to awaken attentiveness and direct desire away from sleep to food. Among the aphorisms pertaining to laziness, this saying is comparable to the exhortation in 6:6–11; rather than painting a satirical portrait of the sluggard (10:26; 13:4; 15:19; 19:15, 24; 22:13; 26:13–16), the proverb admonishes the lazy to redirect their desires by dangling the carrot of satiety.

While 20:13 reflects on a case of falling short of moral bounds, **v. 14** narrates the transgression of moral bounds. The initial line sets the scene, depicting a buyer haggling with a seller over the price of goods. The declaration "bad, bad" (רַע רַע, v. 14a) captures the buyer's assessment of these goods as inferior. The second line, however, tells a different story. It opens with a circumstantial clause (v. 14b), describing the aftermath of the negotiation. And it ends with the buyer boasting over the acquisition of the goods, presumably at a lower cost. The condensed narrative projects dissembling speech and behavior. The buyer oversteps moral bounds through deceptive actions, and the buyer breaches moral bounds by boasting in a form of life that subverts the moral order. More than serving as a cautionary tale regarding transactions in the marketplace, the aphorism attunes one to the reality of hypocrisy in social relations and the "fuzzy boundaries" of character, speech, and behavior.[38]

In contrast to the narrative description of v. 14, **v. 15** is cast in the form of a paradoxical reflection. Similar to several other sayings in the central collections (Prov 11:24; 12:8; 13:7, 23; 14:12; 16:25; 18:24), this reflection is marked by the particle "there is this" (יֵשׁ, 20:15a), which modifies the entire statement.[39] The paradox is engendered by the antithetical evaluation. The initial line foregrounds the qualitative value of gold and the quantitative value of many rubies or corals. These costly materials, however, are incomparable to a singular, precious ornament: "knowledgeable lips" (שִׂפְתֵי־דָעַת, v. 15b). The comparison elevates knowledgeable speech over lavish commodities, recalibrating one's evaluative framework and aesthetic taste. And the comparison invites one to imagine how knowledgeable speech is more precious than gold and abundance of corals. The paradoxical reflection traffics in the concept of MORAL BEAUTY; it ignites the imagination and awakens desire for a form of speech that exceeds the value of choice materials.

The surpassing value of knowledgeable speech serves as appropriate backdrop to **v. 16** and its consideration of presumptuous speech. The aphorism includes a pair of admonitions. And both pertain to the practice of surety. Like other sayings that deal with the practice (6:1–5; 11:15;

37. Boström, *The God of the Sages*, 64–65.

38. Lakoff and Johnson, *Metaphors We Live By*, 71–72, 122–25; Stewart, "Wisdom's Imagination," 359–63.

39. Gianto, "On יֵשׁ of Reflection in the Book of Proverbs," 158–62.

17:18; 22:26; 27:13), the admonitions trade in terror, highlighting the severe consequences associated with standing surety. They contribute to the anthology's economic discourse by focusing on a particular consequence: the confiscation of the guarantor's garment. The parallel admonitions conflate the economic agreement.[40] They assume that the debtor—a "stranger" (זָר, 20:16a) and "outsiders" (נָכְרִים, v. 16b)[41]—has defaulted on the loan. The guarantor is responsible to the creditor for the financial malfeasance of the debtor, who is described as one outside of the immediate family unit or community. The imperatives "take" (לְקַח, v. 16a) and "impound" (-חֲבְלֵ, v. 16b), combined with the conflation of the economic agreement, emphasize the immediacy of the consequence. The guarantor's garment, that is, his personal source of warmth and protection from the elements, is stripped from his body. This penalty is striking. In contrast to the covenant regulations (Exod 22:25–26; Deut 24:12–13), which require the creditor to return the debtor's garment every evening, the admonitions implicate the guarantor.[42] His garment is impounded. This state of affairs heightens the danger of standing surety. The admonitions serve as a form of rhetorical shock treatment, warning readers against serving as a guarantor in financial agreements.

The shock generated by 20:16 thrusts the reader into **v. 17**, which destabilizes the connection between taste and satisfaction.[43] This destabilization is achieved though the imagery and syntax of the individual lines as well as their consequential relationship. The initial line foregrounds the phrase "sweet to a person" (עָרֵב לָאִישׁ, v. 17a). In light of other aphorisms, one might expect "honey" (דְּבַשׁ; 24:13; 25:16) or "the fruit of one's mouth" (פְּרִי פִי־אִישׁ; 12:14; 13:2; 18:20) to follow.[44] Bread emerges as a suitable counterpart, but the final element in the line characterizes this bread as deceitful. While this characterization may be unsettling, it is not surprising, for Woman Folly banks on the momentary gratification and adrenaline rush of sweet, stolen food (9:17). The initial line follows the same logic, but the second line indicates that the sweetness of "bread gained by deceit" turns out to be "bread that deceives."[45] When placed in the mouth, it turns into gravel, scraping one's taste buds and cracking one's teeth. The unpleasing nature of the bread and the painful consequences of gravel in one's mouth train one's discernment through the concept of moral taste.[46]

Discernment, however, is more than an individual affair. According to **20:18**, it is also a collective achievement. The saying is comparable to other aphorisms that commend the value of many counselors for the welfare of the community (11:14), the establishment of plans (15:22), and victory in warfare (24:6). While the general message of the saying in 20:18 corresponds to these aphorisms, it differs from them in at least two respects. First, it focuses on the instrumental power of counsel to establish plans rather than a multitude of counselors. And second, the saying moves from a statement (v. 18a) to an admonition (v. 18b), encouraging the reader the pursue this particular form of action.[47]

40. The second line of the saying is elliptical. That is, while the causal clause "for he has gone surety" (כִּי־עָרַב, v. 16a) is absent from the second line, it is assumed.

41. This reading follows *ketiv* (נָכְרִים, v. 16b), rather than *qere* (נָכְרִיָּה, v. 16b), in light of the parallel "stranger" and the unlikelihood that a strange woman would seek surety for a loan (cf. 27:13). Fox, *Proverbs 10–31*, 670.

42. Fox, *Proverbs 10–31*, 670.

43. Stewart, *Poetic Ethics*, 148–49.

44. Brown, "The Didactic Power of Metaphor," 144.

45. Fox, *Proverbs 10–31*, 671.

46. Goering, "Honey and Wormwood," 23–41.

47. In light of the unusual switch to the second-person imperative "wage war" (עֲשֵׂה מִלְחָמָה, v. 18b), some follow certain

The reader is addressed directly. Hermeneutical exertion is unnecessary.

The same is true in **v. 19**, which mirrors the design of v. 18. The initial line sketches the moral essence of the slanderer, depicting this character type as one who moves about divulging secrets. But in contrast to its variant counterpart (11:13), the second line does not paint a portrait of the slanderer's antitype; rather, like 20:18, it expresses the logical consequence in the form of an admonition. Since the slanderer is a "big-mouth" (לְפֹתֶה שְׂפָתָיו, v. 19b), one should not associate with him, lest his open lips consume one's reputation. The admonition placed at the end of the second line breaks the grammatical and phonic pattern of the saying, differentiating it from the other phrases that constitute the aphorism;[48] it is set apart in the same way that one is to remain separate from the slanderer.

The speech of the slanderer serves as an appropriate entrée into **v. 20** and its attention to maledictory discourse. As a form of speech, cursing is not inappropriate (Deut 27:9–26; Judg 9:27); it is the object of the curse that determines whether it is appropriate. In this respect, cursing one's father or mother is detestable, for it degrades a relationship governed by self-sacrificial love, transgresses moral bounds, and upends the moral order (20:20a; cf. 30:11, 17; Exod 20:12; 21:17; Lev 20:9). Similar to the structure of the previous sayings, the second line presents the consequence of cursing one's parents. Under the metaphorical concept of MORAL ACCOUNTING, the degradation of parents engenders the extinction of life. The curse blows out the lamp of one's existence. And if "lamp" includes one's posterity (1 Kgs 11:36; 15:4; 2 Kgs 8:19), then the one who curses his parents is not only snuffed out but also this person, ironically, ensures that he will never be a parent.[49]

Just as the concept of cursing and consequential parallelism structure Prov 20:20, so also they structure **v. 21**. The aphorism extends the theme of domestic offences to include familial property. The offense against family patrimony, however, is unclear. Following *ketiv* (מְבֻחֶלֶת; "greedily guarded," v. 21a), the saying suggests that, if an inheritance is received in an avaricious fashion, then, in the end, it will not be blessed.[50] By contrast, following *qere* (מְבֹהֶלֶת; "quickly gained," v. 21a), the saying indicates that, if an inheritance is pursued in a premature fashion, then, in the end, it will not be blessed. In light of Proverbs's attention to the dangers of haste (19:2; 21:5; 28:20), the latter reading is preferable.[51] Together with cursing one's parents, any attempt to grasp the patrimonial gift in a rash or hasty manner is accursed. "At first" (בָּרִאשֹׁנָה, 20:21a), it may appear to be good; but "in the end" (אַחֲרִית, v. 21b), the lack of discretion and the disregard for moral bounds will demonstrate that it "will not be blessed" (לֹא תְבֹרָךְ, v. 21b).

The direct and indirect formulations for cursing in vv. 20 and 21 grease the conceptual wheel for the matter of vengeance in **v. 22**. Like vv. 9 and 14, the initial line includes direct speech. And with 3:28 and 24:29, the aphorism is among the three "do not say" (אַל־תֹּאמַר, 20:22a) sayings in the anthology.[52] The proscribed form of speech concerns the promise of personal vengeance (v. 22a). This

versions and emend the verb to the passive "is made" (תֵּעָשֶׂה). The use of the second person in both v. 19b and the aphorism's variant counterpart (Prov 24:6a) suggest that the emendation is unnecessary.

48. McCreesh, *Biblical Sound and Sense*, 93.

49. Fox, *Proverbs 10–31*, 672; Yoder, *Proverbs*, 213.

50. Clifford, *Proverbs*, 181–82, 185.

51. So also, e.g., Toy, *Proverbs*, 391; McKane, *Proverbs*, 539; Waltke, *Proverbs: Chapters 15–31*, 148; Fox, *Proverbs: An Eclectic Edition*, 286.

52. Yoder, *Proverbs*, 214.

proscription seems to be grounded in the conviction that vengeance is not the business of human beings (Deut 32:35). Rather than taking vengeance into one's own hands, the second line offers an alternative response to repaying evil; it opens with a command and closes with a promise. The command to "wait for YHWH" (קַוֵּה לַיהוָה, Prov 20:22b) elevates divine agency, divine timing, and the divine means of recompense over human agency, expectations, and adjudication.[53] And when read in conjunction with the initial line, the promise "he will save you" (וְיֹשַׁע לָךְ, v. 22b) telescopes divine vengeance with the deliverance of the individual. Taken together, the prohibition (v. 22a), prescription (v. 22b), and promise (v. 22b) affirm that vengeance belongs to YHWH (Deut 32:35). Accordingly, to take vengeance into one's own hands is to perform a moral action that transgresses moral bounds.

The metaphor of MORAL BOUNDS also structures **Prov 20:23**. As a variant repetition, the aphorism recycles and rearranges terms and expressions from 11:1 and 20:10 to reinforce YHWH's abhorrence of deceptive economic practices.[54] But this conventional evaluation is constructed in a distinctive way. The initial line is cast in the form of a תּוֹעֵבָה ("abomination") template, expressing divine revulsion over variant weights.[55] The second line reformulates this revulsion in ironic terms. The understated evaluation "not good" (לֹא־טוֹב, 20:23b) drips with sarcasm and places the aphorism in conversation with others that employ the rhetorical technique of litotes (16:29; 17:26; 18:5; 19:2). While the saying reiterates divine disgust over deceptive economic practices, it conveys this disgust through different modes to shape one's emotions and attune one to the moral bounds of economic practices.

Together with 20:22 and 23, YHWH and the concept of MORAL BOUNDS hem the reader in within **v. 24**. This sense of constraint is conveyed not only through the content of the saying but also through its syntax. The initial line opens with the prepositional phrase "from YHWH" (מֵיְהוָה, v. 24a); he is the source of one's steps, the one who funds human agency. The second line, by contrast, opens with the nominative absolute "and a person" (וְאָדָם, v, 24b), focusing attention on human agency. And the rhetorical question highlights the severe limits of human understanding. Humans may plan, perform, and perceive various activities in life, but they lack the capacity to see and understand the entire sweep of their life, for they are limited creatures sustained and directed by YHWH. The saying reinforces the limits of creaturehood in light of divine sovereignty (cf. 16:1–9). Far from breeding despair, it seeks to engender trust in and absolute dependence on YHWH by mapping the bounded space of human perception.

The limits of human perception provide an appropriate backdrop to **20:25**, for the saying considers the pronouncement of a solemn promise without due attention to its future implications. The precariousness of impetuous promises is signaled in the initial line, which foregrounds the predicate nominative "a trap for a person" (מוֹקֵשׁ אָדָם, v. 25a). Similar to vv. 6, 9, and 22, this trap is expressed through direct speech. And the form of speech is regarded as rash. By declaring "Holy" (קֹדֶשׁ, v. 25a), one consecrates an item to God, transferring one's personal property to the divine. The practice is not

53. It is important to note, however, that divine and human agency in retribution are "complementary rather than mutually exclusive" (Boström, *The God of the Sages*, 105).

54. For discussion of these variant repetitions, see Heim, *Poetic Imagination*, 252–54; 482–87.

55. For the concept of "proverb templates," see Fox, *Proverbs 10–31*, 489–91.

the problem; rather, the lack of contemplation is the problem. This is clarified in the second line, which opens with the adverb "after" (אַחַר, v. 25b). After consecrating an item to God, the one who vowed "appraises" (לְבַקֵּר, v. 25b) whether the promise can be kept and how it could be fulfilled. The sequence sketched between the lines reverses logical expectations, explaining why the vow is reckless. In so doing, it sharpens the reader's moral reasoning by depicting an inverted process of unreason.

Inversion also serves as the organizing principle of **v. 26**. The saying develops v. 8, intensifying the nature of the king's judgment through vivid agricultural imagery. Similar to v. 8b, the initial line conceptualizes the judgment of the king through the process of winnowing grain. The king "scatters" (מְזָרֶה, v. 26a) the wicked as chaff to be driven away by the wind. The metaphor assumes that the kernels of grain have been separated from the chaff. The second line, however, describes this initial stage of the threshing process, according to which heavy wheels were rolled over the grain to split the husk (cf. Isa 28:27–28). This process captures the powers of the king's discernment; his piercing perception creates the pressure necessary to crack individuals, sifting the righteous from the wicked. While the second line inverts the traditional process, it also escalates the judicial prowess of the wise king. More than inspiring awe, this idealistic portrait paints the king as the one who establishes moral order and moral bounds by eradicating the wicked (cf. Prov 16:12; 20:8; 25:5; 29:14).

The piercing perception of the king, however, pales in comparison with YHWH's penetrating gaze, which is the focus of attention in **v. 27**. The noun phrases in the initial line project the nature of YHWH's vision through rich imagery. The juxtaposition of "human life-breath" (נִשְׁמַת אָדָם, v. 27a; cf. Gen 2:7) and "the lamp of YHWH" (נֵר יְהוָה, Prov 20:27a) places air and the instrument of being in intimate relationship with the illuminating light of YHWH. This light is not the conscience; rather, it refers to the clarity of divine sight.[56] The second line expands on this sight, highlighting the extent of YHWH's vision: it penetrates the depths of the self. Just as the human life-breath flows through the hidden, innermost parts of one's being, so also YHWH sees and knows the hidden thoughts and desires of one's being. The life-breath is the divine lamp, illuminating the recesses of the self to the one who is the source of life. For some, this expression of divine omniscience may inspire fear. For others, the extent to which one is known by YHWH brings comfort.

In light of concern with the king and YHWH in vv. 26 and 27, it is not surprising that these two figures converge in **v. 28**. "Kindness" (חֶסֶד, v. 28a) and "faithfulness" (אֱמֶת, v. 28a) are personified as royal guards, keeping watch over the king. While these virtues may be qualities that mark the character of the king, elsewhere they are divine gifts, bestowed on the king for protection (Pss 40:11[10]; 57:4[3]; 61:8[7]; 89:34[33]). If the initial line describes kindness and faithfulness as agents of protection, then the second line delineates the agency of the king in maintaining his throne. This throne is supported by "kindness" (בַּחֶסֶד, 20:28b). Whether or not "faithfulness" (אֱמֶת) is assumed in the second line, the prepositional phrase may be construed in two ways: the king's throne is supported either *on* the pedestal of kindness or *by means of* kindness. Both are possible, leaving the matter undecidable. What is clear, however, is that the second line appears to move beyond divine agency to the king's responsibility. The aphorism, like the other royal sayings in the chapter (vv. 2, 8, 26, 28), depicts the

56. Fox, *Proverbs 10–31*, 677.

royal ideal, providing a model on which the king and other leaders may form themselves.

The security endowed on the king provides an appropriate backdrop to **v. 29** and its attention to the endowments of the young and the aged. These endowments are clear: physical strength beautifies the young, whereas grey hair adorns the aged. But when read together, the evaluation of these endowments is unclear. If the *waw* conjunction that opens the second line is rendered as "and," then the aphorism delineates the splendor that characterizes particular seasons of life and describes the "grey hair" (שֵׂיבָה, v. 29b) of the aged as a power comparable to the strength of the young. If, on the other hand, the *waw* conjunction functions as an adversative ("but"), then old age—the mark of a wise life—is deemed more majestic and powerful that the vigor of the young. Both readings are possible. When the saying is read in conjunction with its variant counterpart, however, it appears to elevate old age over physical strength, for "grey hair" is the emblem of righteous character and endurance on an authorized path (16:31). Whether or not 16:31 clarifies the relationship between the lines in 20:29, the ambiguity of the *waw* conjunction and the dynamics of innertextual reading within the central collections hone the reader's moral reasoning and, in so doing, contribute to the anthology's project of character formation.

Together with the ambiguity of certain sayings, corporal punishment is an invaluable pedagogical technique in the sages' vision of character formation (13:24; 19:25, 29; 22:15; 23:13–14; 29:15). The value of this technique is sketched in **v. 30**, which traffics in pain.[57] The construct phrase "bruised wounds" (חַבֻּרוֹת פֶּצַע, v. 30a) captures the severity of physical discipline. And the verb "clean away" (תַּמְרִיק, v. 30a) or "rub" describes the way in which corporal punishment brings about moral cleansing.[58] While the verb is absent from the second line, it is implied. The terseness of this line contributes to the intensification of the saying. More than rubbing out moral evil, corporal discipline rubs out one's "innermost parts" (חַדְרֵי־בָטֶן, v. 30b; cf. v. 27b). It is a comprehensive pedagogical technique, designed to purify the whole of the human person.

57. For the role of pain in Proverbs's pedagogy, see O'Dowd, "Pain and Danger," 619–35.

58. This reading follows *ketiv* (תַּמְרִיק; "clean, rub, scour") rather than *qere* (תַּמְרוּק; "cosmetic, ointment"), for the latter makes little sense.

Proverbs 21:1–31

CHAPTER 27

F. Accounting for Intentions: *Sharpening Moral Reasoning through Moral Accounting*

Main Idea of the Passage

These sayings focus on embodied actions as well as internal desires or intentions to extend the anthology's conception of moral character and sharpen the reader's understanding of the interconnection among character, intention, action, and consequence.

Literary Context[1]

From a literary, pedagogical, and rhetorical perspective, the aphorisms in ch. 21 stretch one's intellectual and perceptual acuity. To this point in the central collections, the reader's moral reasoning has been trained through various techniques to perceive the contours of moral prototypes, imagine moral actions, anticipate particular consequences, taste specific rewards, and desire that which is good. These learning outcomes are extended in a particular way in ch. 21. Antithetical sayings punctuate the chapter, providing one with a helpful pedagogical guide to certain characters, moral actions, and their consequences. And many of the aphorisms operate under the metaphorical concepts of MORAL ACCOUNTING or MORAL ESSENCE—the common conceptual stock of proverbial lore.[2] They reinforce one's understanding of the act-, or better, character-consequence nexus. But they do so in an unusual way. Most of

1. This chapter does not include the Explanation of the Text or the Canonical and Theological Significance sections. See pp. xv and 276n1 for justification. Also, see pp. 510–14 for the Canonical and Theological Significance of Prov 16:1–22:16.

2. For these metaphorical concepts, see Lakoff and Johnson, *Philosophy in the Flesh*, 292–98, 306–7.

the sayings in the chapter are cast in the form of sentences that defy the traditional logic and categorization of parallelism. What's more, many of the antithetical sayings are imprecise. The poetic form of the sayings forms one's moral reasoning in discrete ways. To modify the exhortation of Immanuel Kant, these forms train one to "have the courage to use your own [moral] reason[ing]."[3] They refuse to follow the logic of straightforward antithesis or synonymity. In so doing, they extend one's conception of moral character, moral actions, and consequences by elaborating on particular topics introduced in the initial lines of the sayings.

Moral reasoning is honed through the form of the materials, and moral perception is directed through particular metaphorical concepts. As noted above, among these concepts, the majority of the sayings privilege the metaphors of MORAL ACCOUNTING and MORAL ESSENCE. The former structures the connection between (im)moral acts and consequences (vv. 5, 6, 7a, 12, 13, 16, 17, 18, 21, 25, 28), while the latter is employed to diagnose the qualities and actions characteristic of certain characters (vv. 4, 8, 11b, 24, 26, 29). Far from serving as discrete modes of moral motivation and perception, these metaphorical concepts converge in many sayings that attend to intentions (vv. 1a, 2b, 5a) and desires (vv. 1b, 10a, 15, 17, 20, 21a, 25a, 26a, 27b). This attention to intentions and desires links one's embodied actions and their consequences with one's inner life, illuminating the depth dimension of (im)moral character. Character, intention/desire, action, and consequence coalesce to motivate the moral life and sharpen one's moral reasoning.

In addition to a conspicuous concern with the extent of (im)moral character, the sayings in ch. 21 reinforce and extend familiar themes. Similar to the juxtaposition of YHWH sayings and royal sayings in Prov 16:1–9 and 10–15, respectively, the opening pair of sayings in ch. 21 temper the power of the king (vv. 1–2).[4] Against the backdrop of ch. 20, these sayings place the wrath and just judgment of the king (21:2, 8, 26, 28) under YHWH's sovereign and mysterious designs. The same is true of the concluding verses of the chapter (vv. 30–31). Whereas several sayings commend the value of counsel and careful planning (11:14; 15:22; 20:18; 24:6), 21:30–31 highlight the severe limits of human wisdom, planning, and power before YHWH's sovereign purposes. Humans may plan and perceive their way, but YHWH perceives one's subconscious intentions and the end of one's way (v. 2; 16:2).

The paradoxical relationship between human responsibility and YHWH's mysterious sovereignty frames other sayings that extend common motifs and develop fresh perspectives. In contrast to the broader witness of the Old Testament, 21:14 unashamedly presents the efficacy of bribery (cf. 6:34–35; 15:27; 17:8, 23; 18:16; 19:7).[5]

3. Immanuel Kant, "An Answer to the Question: 'What is Enlightenment?,'" in *Kant: Political Writings*, ed. Hans Reiss; trans. H. B. Nisbet; 2nd enl. ed. (Cambridge: Cambridge University Press, 1991), 54.

4. Meinhold, *Die Sprüche*, 2:347; Whybray, *Proverbs*, 305; Van Leeuwen, "The Book of Proverbs," *NIB* 5:192; Heim, *Like Grapes of Gold*, 282; Sæbø, *Sprüche*, 259–60.

5. Hatton, *Contradiction in the Book of Proverbs*, 137–48.

And contrary to the broader witness of Proverbs, 21:12 indicates that the righteous person "is a capable and powerful agent of justice" who executes judgment on the wicked.[6] While previous sayings identified a wife as a divine gift (5:15–20; 12:4; 18:22; and after this text, 31:10–31), 21:9 and 19 depict the tortuous environment engendered by a contentious wife (cf. 19:13; 25:24; 27:15–16). The circumstances and educational means noted in 21:11 extend those mentioned in 19:25. The protective power of circumspect speech expressed in 21:23 expands its variant counterpart in 13:3. And the fate of the false witness in 21:28 recasts 19:9, situating the punishment in an elliptical judicial scenario.[7] Taken together, the reiteration of common motifs and the development of alternative perspectives in ch. 21 broaden one's moral worldview and sharpen one's moral reasoning.

III. "Forming 'Fearers of YHWH'": The Curriculum of Wisdom and Virtue (10:1–29:27)
- III.1 Elementary Wisdom and Virtue (10:1–15:33)
- **III.2 Intermediate Wisdom and Virtue (16:1–22:16)**
  - A. YHWH, the King, and the People: The Organization of the Moral Order (16:1–33)
  - B. Cultivating MORAL NURTURANCE: The Sustenance of Social Ties and the Self (17:1–28)
  - C. Enhancing MORAL ESSENCE: The Complexities of Moral Character and Moral Actions (18:1–24)
  - D. Merging MORAL AUTHORITY with MORAL ACCOUNTING: The Value of Wisdom and Instruction (19:1–29)
  - E. Delimiting MORAL BOUNDS: The Parameters of (Im)moral Actions (20:1–30)
  - ➦ **F. Accounting for Intentions: Sharpening Moral Reasoning through MORAL ACCOUNTING (21:1–31)**
  - G. Fostering Moral Valuation: Schemes of MORAL ACCOUNTING (22:1–16)
- III.3 Vocational Wisdom and Virtue (22:17–24:34)
- III.4 Advanced Wisdom and Virtue (25:1–29:27)

Translation and Exegetical Outline

(See pages 496–97.)

6. Lyu, *Righteousness*, 48. Since "the righteous" (צַדִּיק) do not serve as agents of judgment elsewhere in the anthology, many commentators construe צַדִּיק as a divine epithet, "The Righteous One" (cf. Isa 24:16; McKane, *Proverbs*, 561; Murphy, *Proverbs*, 160; Clifford, *Proverbs*, 191; Waltke, *Proverbs: Chapters 15–31*, 177–78). This reading is possible. In light of the fact that the term lacks the definite article and that "righteous" always refers to a human being elsewhere in the book, human agency appears to be in view.

7. Heim, *Poetic Imagination*, 447–50.

Proverbs 21:1–31

1a	פַּלְגֵי־מַיִם לֶב־מֶלֶךְ בְּיַד־יְהוָה	Water channels, the heart of the king in YHWH's hand;
1b	עַל־כָּל־אֲשֶׁר יַחְפֹּץ יַטֶּנּוּ	he guides it wherever he desires.
2a	כָּל־דֶּרֶךְ־אִישׁ יָשָׁר בְּעֵינָיו	A person's every way, upright in his eyes,
2b	וְתֹכֵן לִבּוֹת יְהוָה	but the one who examines hearts, YHWH.
3a	עֲשֹׂה צְדָקָה וּמִשְׁפָּט	Doing righteousness and justice,
3b	נִבְחָר לַיהוָה מִזָּבַח	more preferable to YHWH than sacrifice.
4a	רוּם־עֵינַיִם וּרְחַב־לֵב	Haughty eyes and an arrogant heart—
4b	נִר רְשָׁעִים חַטָּאת	the lamp of the wicked, sin.
5a	מַחְשְׁבוֹת חָרוּץ אַךְ־לְמוֹתָר	The plans of the diligent, only for profit,
5b	וְכָל־אָץ אַךְ־לְמַחְסוֹר	but all haste, only to poverty.
6a	פֹּעַל אוֹצָרוֹת בִּלְשׁוֹן שָׁקֶר	Acquiring treasures by a deceitful tongue—
6b	הֶבֶל נִדָּף מְבַקְשֵׁי־מָוֶת	the fleeting vapor of those pursuing death.
7a	שֹׁד־רְשָׁעִים יְגוֹרֵם	The violence of the wicked drags them away,
7b	↑ כִּי מֵאֲנוּ לַעֲשׂוֹת מִשְׁפָּט	↑ for they refuse to do justice.
8a	הֲפַכְפַּךְ דֶּרֶךְ אִישׁ וָזָר	The way of the guilty person, crooked,
8b	וְזַךְ יָשָׁר פָּעֳלוֹ	but the pure, his conduct is straight.
9a	טוֹב לָשֶׁבֶת עַל־פִּנַּת־גָּג	Better to dwell on the corner of a roof
9b	מֵאֵשֶׁת מִדְיָנִים וּבֵית חָבֶר	than a shared house with a quarrelsome woman.
10a	נֶפֶשׁ רָשָׁע אִוְּתָה־רָע	The soul of the wicked desires evil;
10b	לֹא־יֻחַן בְּעֵינָיו רֵעֵהוּ	his neighbor finds no favor in his eyes.
11a	בַּעְנָשׁ־לֵץ יֶחְכַּם־פֶּתִי	When a scoffer is punished, the simple become wise;
11b	וּבְהַשְׂכִּיל לְחָכָם יִקַּח־דָּעַת	and when the wise is instructed, he receives knowledge.
12a	מַשְׂכִּיל צַדִּיק לְבֵית רָשָׁע	The righteous attends to the house of the wicked,
12b	מְסַלֵּף רְשָׁעִים לָרָע	turning the wicked to ruin.
13a	אֹטֵם אָזְנוֹ מִזַּעֲקַת־דָּל	One who shuts his ear from the outcry of the poor—
13b	גַּם־הוּא יִקְרָא וְלֹא יֵעָנֶה	he too will cry out and not be answered.
14a	מַתָּן בַּסֵּתֶר יִכְפֶּה־אָף	A gift in secret averts anger,
14b	וְשֹׁחַד בַּחֵק חֵמָה עַזָּה	and a bribe in the bosom, fierce wrath.
15a	שִׂמְחָה לַצַּדִּיק עֲשׂוֹת מִשְׁפָּט	Doing justice, joy for the righteous,
15b	וּמְחִתָּה לְפֹעֲלֵי אָוֶן	but ruin for evildoers.
16a	אָדָם תּוֹעֶה מִדֶּרֶךְ הַשְׂכֵּל	A person who wanders from the way of insight
16b	בִּקְהַל רְפָאִים יָנוּחַ	will rest in the community of the dead.

F. Accounting for Intentions: Sharpening Moral Reasoning through Moral Accounting (21:1–31)

17a	אִישׁ מַחְסוֹר אֹהֵב שִׂמְחָה	One who loves pleasure, a needy person;
17b	אֹהֵב יַיִן־וָשֶׁמֶן לֹא יַעֲשִׁיר	one who loves wine and oil will never grow rich.
18a	כֹּפֶר לַצַּדִּיק רָשָׁע	A ransom for the righteous, the wicked,
18b	וְתַחַת יְשָׁרִים בּוֹגֵד	and the treacherous in the place of the upright.
19a	טוֹב שֶׁבֶת בְּאֶרֶץ־מִדְבָּר	Better to dwell in a desert land
19b	מֵאֵשֶׁת מִדְיָנִים וָכָעַס	than with a contentious and vexing wife.
20a	אוֹצָר נֶחְמָד וָשֶׁמֶן בִּנְוֵה חָכָם	Desirable treasure and oil in the dwelling of the wise,
20b	וּכְסִיל אָדָם יְבַלְּעֶנּוּ	but a foolish person swallows it up.
21a	רֹדֵף צְדָקָה וָחָסֶד	One who pursues righteousness and kindness
21b	יִמְצָא חַיִּים צְדָקָה וְכָבוֹד	finds life, righteousness, and honor.
22a	עִיר גִּבֹּרִים עָלָה חָכָם	A wise person went up against a city of the mighty
22b	וַיֹּרֶד עֹז מִבְטֶחָה	and brought down the stronghold of its reliance.
23a	שֹׁמֵר פִּיו וּלְשׁוֹנוֹ	One who guards his mouth and his tongue
23b	שֹׁמֵר מִצָּרוֹת נַפְשׁוֹ	guards himself from troubles.
24a	זֵד יָהִיר לֵץ שְׁמוֹ	Proud, arrogant—scoffer is his name;
24b	עוֹשֶׂה בְּעֶבְרַת זָדוֹן	who acts in the rage of insolence.
25a	תַּאֲוַת עָצֵל תְּמִיתֶנּוּ	The sluggard's desire kills him,
25b	↑ כִּי־מֵאֲנוּ יָדָיו לַעֲשׂוֹת	↑ for his hands refuse to work.
26a	כָּל־הַיּוֹם הִתְאַוָּה תַאֲוָה	All day he longs longings,
26b	וְצַדִּיק יִתֵּן וְלֹא יַחְשֹׂךְ	but the righteous gives without restraint.
27a	זֶבַח רְשָׁעִים תּוֹעֵבָה	The sacrifice of the wicked, an abomination;
27b	אַף כִּי־בְזִמָּה יְבִיאֶנּוּ	how much more when he brings it with evil intent.
28a	עֵד־כְּזָבִים יֹאבֵד	A false witness will perish,
28b	וְאִישׁ שׁוֹמֵעַ לָנֶצַח יְדַבֵּר	but the person who listens will speak successfully.
29a	הֵעֵז אִישׁ רָשָׁע בְּפָנָיו	The wicked person puts on a strong face,
29b	וְיָשָׁר הוּא יָבִין דַּרְכּוֹ	but the upright, he discerns his way.
30a	אֵין חָכְמָה וְאֵין תְּבוּנָה	There is no wisdom, and no understanding,
30b	וְאֵין עֵצָה לְנֶגֶד יְהוָה	and no counsel before YHWH.
31a	סוּס מוּכָן לְיוֹם מִלְחָמָה	The horse is prepared for the day of battle,
31b	וְלַיהוָה הַתְּשׁוּעָה	but victory belongs to YHWH.

Structure and Literary Form

As noted above, the diverse forms in Prov 21 form the reader in discrete ways. Variant repetitions cast in the form of better-than sayings punctuate the chapter (vv. 9, 19). These better-than sayings not only shape one's valuation of a contentious wife, they also awaken one's moral imagination, for they omit elements of comparison, inviting the reader to complete the conventional construction (i.e., "B with Y is better than A with X").[8] The a fortiori argument in v. 27b attunes one's religious sensibilities and prods the reader to consider the evil intent of the wicked as well as whether their sacrifice is an abomination "to YHWH" (v. 27a; cf. 15:8a). Antithetical sayings reemerge as a prominent poetic form in the chapter. Their presence has led some to conclude that, in contrast to "the disintegration of form" in the previous chapters,[9] a measure of poetic stability returns in ch. 21. This assessment, however, overlooks the fact that, with the exception of vv. 2, 5 and 11, these antithetical sayings are either unbalanced (vv. 20, 28) or imprecise (vv. 8, 15, 26, 29). Their asymmetry suggests that they are not simplistic comparisons; rather, they are designed to sharpen the moral reasoning of the reader.

The same is true of the other sayings in chapter, most of which are continuous sentences. These sentences take different forms. Some move from the subject in the initial line to the predicate in the second line (vv. 3, 21, 23, 24). Causal clauses modify the initial line of vv. 7 and 25, providing a rationale. A condensed narrative appears in v. 22 (cf. Eccl 9:13–16). Most of the sentences in Prov 21 contain a consequence in the second line, which intensifies or elaborates on a particular topic in the first (vv. 1, 4, 6, 10, 12, 13, 16, 30). These types of sentences elude the traditional categories of parallelism. This does not mean that the sayings lack parallelism; it suggests they are a form of "creative poetry."[10] These forms of "creative poetry" form the reader in particular ways. To be specific, they form one's moral reasoning and perception, challenging one to think differently about the interconnection among character, intention, action, and consequence.

The diverse forms in Prov 21 serve as a window into its design. These forms and the variety of themes that they address are cast within a clear framework. The YHWH sayings at the boundaries of the chapter enclose the materials in vv. 4–29 (vv. 1–3, 30–31). The interpretive implications of this theological framework, however, are unclear. For some, the frame infuses the material with a theological bent.[11] For others, it situates the material in the context of YHWH's sovereignty, "exercised

8. For discussion of the form of better-than sayings, see Fox, *Proverbs 10–31*, 597–98; Lyu, *Righteousness*, 83–88.

9. McKane, *Proverbs*, 522, 535; cf. 501, 512.

10. Heim, *Poetic Imagination*, 249.

11. Meinhold, *Die Sprüche*, 2:329, 361; Sæbø, *Sprüche*, 258.

through his king."[12] For still others, the frame forms an a fortiori argument: "if even kings are subject to YHWH's control, this is even more true of ordinary people,"[13] who populate the remaining materials in the chapter. While the frame of the chapter is rich with hermeneutical potential, at minimum, it creates a degree of structural coherence. But beyond this frame, it is difficult to detect an intelligible design within vv. 4–29. Catchwords across juxtaposed sayings form proverbial pairs (שׂכל, vv. 11b, 12a; תַּאֲוָה, vv. 25a, 26a; cf. לֵב, vv. 1a, 2b, vv. 30–31); and variant repetitions (vv. 9, 19) as well as the motif of "doing justice" (vv. 3a, 7b, 15a) signal common concerns. These common concerns may constitute structural pillars within the chapter. That is, they may orient one to distinctive units and the general themes that bind together the sayings within certain clusters. The boundaries of these potential clusters vary among commentators. But most discern thematic clusters in vv. 4–8, 10–18, 20–29.[14] Whether or not they define the design of the chapter, these clusters engender a dialogue among the sayings that allows for differing yet fruitful fusions of horizons between the sayings and the reader.[15]

12. Waltke, *Proverbs: Chapters 15–31*, 165.

13. Whybray, *The Composition of the Book of Proverbs*, 117.

14. Heim, *Like Grapes of Gold*, 287–303; Waltke, *Proverbs: Chapters 15–31*, 165–83; cf. Delitzsch, "Proverbs of Solomon," 6:308, 312, 316 (2:63, 68, 75); Garrett, *Proverbs*, 179–85; Meinhold, *Die Sprüche*, 2:347–61.

15. Hans-Georg Gadamer, *Truth and Method*, trans. Joel Weinsheimer and Donald G. Marshall; 2nd rev. ed. (London: Continuum, 2004), 299–306, esp. 305.

CHAPTER 28

Proverbs 22:1–16

G. Fostering Moral Valuation: *Schemes of MORAL ACCOUNTING*

Main Idea of the Passage

These sayings explore the social capital of normative character as well as moral interactions between rich and poor through schemes of the MORAL ACCOUNTING metaphor to motivate a life of virtue and to foster one's moral valuation.

Literary Context

Among the moral "metaphors we live by," MORAL ACCOUNTING may be the most prominent.[1] This is not surprising, for the dynamics of this capacious metaphorical concept are rooted in the embodied social interactions that define everyday life.[2] The concept governs the way in which one understands various moral interactions. These interactions are conceptualized through several moral schemes, each of which represents a facet of the MORAL ACCOUNTING metaphor. These schemes include reciprocation, retribution, revenge, restitution, and altruism, just to name a few.[3] Many of the aphorisms in the book of Proverbs evaluate moral actions through these schemes. In fact, most of the sayings in ch. 21 privileged the MORAL ACCOUNTING metaphor, devoting particular attention to the interconnection among character, intention/desire, action, and consequence. The sayings in Prov 22:1–16 also privilege this metaphorical concept. This concept's schemes serve as a lens through which to

1. Lakoff and Johnson, *Metaphors We Live By*. For discussion of the metaphor, see Lakoff and Johnson, *Philosophy in the Flesh*, 292–98.

2. Lakoff and Johnson, *Philosophy in the Flesh*, 290.

3. Lakoff and Johnson, *Philosophy in the Flesh*, 293–98.

understand the value of moral character as well as the interactions among YHWH, the generous, the rich, and the poor.

As the final installment within the first Solomonic collection (Prov 10:1–22:16),[4] the sayings in this brief unit reinforce and develop common themes in the preceding materials. The mention of "strange women" (זָרוֹת, 22:14) and the educational effectiveness of discipline (v. 15) at the end of the collection recall the prologue (1:8–9:18), suggesting a measure of homogeneity across the compendia.[5] Familiar motifs and pedagogical techniques populate the sayings. Moral virtue is elevated over material prosperity (22:1; 15:17; 16:19; 17:1). Social observations cast in the indicative probe one's moral valuation (22:2, 7, 16; 10:15; 18:11, 23).[6] Paradoxes illuminate the mysteries of being-in-the-world and stimulate one's moral reasoning (22:16; cf. 11:24; 13:7, 23; 14:12; 16:25; 18:24). Generosity to the poor is commended (22:2, 9; 14:31; 17:5; 19:7; 21:12; 28:27). And the fear of YHWH is linked to the virtue of humility (22:4; 15:33).

In addition to these familiar motifs and techniques, the sayings in 22:1–16 develop previous materials and anticipate aphorisms in subsequent collections.

III. "Forming 'Fearers of YHWH'": The Curriculum of Wisdom and Virtue (10:1–29:27)
- III.1 Elementary Wisdom and Virtue (10:1–15:33)
- **III.2 Intermediate Wisdom and Virtue (16:1–22:16)**
  - A. YHWH, the King, and the People: The Organization of the Moral Order (16:1–33)
  - B. Cultivating Moral Nurturance: The Sustenance of Social Ties and the Self (17:1–28)
  - C. Enhancing Moral Essence: The Complexities of Moral Character and Moral Actions (18:1–24)
  - D. Merging Moral Authority with Moral Accounting: The Value of Wisdom and Instruction (19:1–29)
  - E. Delimiting Moral Bounds: The Parameters of (Im)moral Actions (20:1–30)
  - F. Accounting for Intentions: Sharpening Moral Reasoning through Moral Accounting (21:1–31)
  - ➦ **G. Fostering Moral Valuation: Schemes of Moral Accounting (22:1–16)**
- III.3 Vocational Wisdom and Virtue (22:17–24:34)
- III.4 Advanced Wisdom and Virtue (25:1–29:27)

4. For an analysis of the sections of the central section, see Structure and Outline of Proverbs 10–29, pp. 349–51 above.

5. Whybray, *Proverbs*, 321–22; Waltke, *Proverbs: Chapters 15–31*, 210–11, 214.

6. For further discussion, see Sandoval, *The Discourse of Wealth and Poverty*, 189–93.

The complexities of the simple person's character are developed in v. 3 (cf. Prov 14:15, 18; 19:25; 21:11; 27:12). Whereas preceding aphorisms described the value of parental discipline (Prov 10:1, 5; 13:1, 24; 14:26; 15:20; cf. 19:18), 22:6 and 15 prescribe the practice.[7] In the same way, while previous materials observed the character of the scoffer (Prov 13:1; 14:6; 15:12; 19:29; 21:24; 24:9), 22:10 advises one to take a particular form of action in the company of this character type (cf. 19:25). And in contrast to previous sayings that sketched the nature of the sluggard (6:6–11; 10:26; 13:4; 15:19; 19:24; 20:4; 21:25), 22:13 introduces the reader to this figure's speech and logic (cf. 26:13). Several sayings develop earlier materials in the first Solomonic collection. The variant repetitions in 22:1–16, on the other hand, foreshadow twice-told proverbs in the subsequent collections (**22:2**//29:13; **22:3**//27:12; **22:13**//26:13; **22:14**//23:27a).[8] The sayings reinforce particular themes, develop certain motifs, and anticipate the materials that follow.

Translation and Exegetical Outline

(See pages 503–4.)

Structure and Literary Form

If "perception takes place precisely in and with the poetic composition,"[9] then the poetic form of the materials in Prov 22:1–16 directs the perception and forms the moral reasoning of the reader in various ways. A better-than saying sharpens one's valuation of virtue (v. 1), and admonitions direct particular actions (vv. 6, 10). The majority of the sayings, however, exhibit "a paucity of precise parallelism."[10] They are cast in sentences, where the second line develops a topic introduced within the first (vv. 2, 4, 5, 8, 9, 11, 13, 14, 15). Correspondences between poetic lines are either imprecise (v. 3) or governed by conceptual relations rather than balanced associations between specific words or phrases. Far from exhibiting poor poetry, the diversity of poetic forms fund Proverbs's pedagogical program. They force the reader to determine the relationship between the poetic lines. And differing determinations produce different readings, which reveal the depth of the saying's meaning potential.

The richness of meaning within the sayings coincides with the design of the unit. The root עשׁר ("rich") and terms from the semantic fields of wealth and poverty frame the material (vv. 1, 2, 16). Words from these semantic fields also populate vv. 4, 7, and 9.

7. Yoder, *Proverbs*, 222.

8. For discussion of these variant repetitions, see Heim, *Poetic Imagination*, 508–27.

9. Von Rad, *Wisdom in Israel*, 24. Also see, Stewart, *Poetic Ethics*, 29–69.

10. McKane, *Proverbs*, 562.

Proverbs 22:1–16

1a	נִבְחָר שֵׁם מֵעֹשֶׁר רָב	A name is preferable to great wealth,	G. Fostering Moral Valuation: Schemes of Moral Accounting (22:1–16)
1b	מִכֶּסֶף וּמִזָּהָב חֵן טוֹב	and graciousness is better than silver and gold.	
2a	עָשִׁיר וָרָשׁ נִפְגָּשׁוּ	The rich and the poor meet together;	
2b	עֹשֵׂה כֻלָּם יְהוָה	YHWH is the maker of both.	
3a	עָרוּם רָאָה רָעָה וְיִסָּתֵר	The shrewd sees evil and hides,	
3b	וּפְתָיִים עָבְרוּ וְנֶעֱנָשׁוּ	but the simple pass on and are punished.	
4a	עֵקֶב עֲנָוָה יִרְאַת יְהוָה	The reward of humility, the fear of YHWH,	
4b	עֹשֶׁר וְכָבוֹד וְחַיִּים	wealth and honor and life.	
5a	צִנִּים פַּחִים בְּדֶרֶךְ עִקֵּשׁ	Thorns, snares, in the way of the perverse,	
5b	שׁוֹמֵר נַפְשׁוֹ יִרְחַק מֵהֶם	one who guards his life stays far from them.	
6a	חֲנֹךְ לַנַּעַר עַל־פִּי דַרְכּוֹ	Train a youth according to his way,	
6b	גַּם כִּי־יַזְקִין לֹא־יָסוּר מִמֶּנָּה	even when he becomes old he will not depart from it.	
7a	עָשִׁיר בְּרָשִׁים יִמְשׁוֹל	The rich rules over the poor,	
7b	וְעֶבֶד לֹוֶה לְאִישׁ מַלְוֶה	and the borrower, a slave to the lender.	
8a	זוֹרֵעַ עַוְלָה יִקְצָר־אָוֶן	One who sows iniquity reaps disaster,	
8b	וְשֵׁבֶט עֶבְרָתוֹ יִכְלֶה	and the rod of his wrath will fail.	
9a	טוֹב־עַיִן הוּא יְבֹרָךְ	The generous person, he will be blessed,	
9b	כִּי־נָתַן מִלַּחְמוֹ לַדָּל	for he shares his food with the poor.	

Continued on next page.

Continued from previous page.

10a	גָּרֵשׁ לֵץ וְיֵצֵא מָדוֹן	Drive out the scoffer and strife departs,
10b	וְיִשְׁבֹּת דִּין וְקָלוֹן	even quarreling and shame cease.
11a	אֹהֵב טְהָר־לֵב	One who loves purity of heart—
11b	חֵן שְׂפָתָיו רֵעֵהוּ מֶלֶךְ	his lips are gracious; the king is his friend.
12a	עֵינֵי יְהוָה נָצְרוּ דָעַת	The eyes of YHWH guard knowledge,
12b	וַיְסַלֵּף דִּבְרֵי בֹגֵד	but he subverts the words of the treacherous.
13a	אָמַר עָצֵל אֲרִי בַחוּץ	The sluggard says, "A lion outside,
13b	בְּתוֹךְ רְחֹבוֹת אֵרָצֵחַ	in the squares I'll be killed!"
14a	שׁוּחָה עֲמֻקָּה פִּי זָרוֹת	A deep pit, the mouth of strange women;
14b	זְעוּם יְהוָה יִפָּל־שָׁם	one cursed by YHWH falls into it.
15a	אִוֶּלֶת קְשׁוּרָה בְלֶב־נָעַר	Folly is bound in a youth's heart;
15b	שֵׁבֶט מוּסָר יַרְחִיקֶנָּה מִמֶּנּוּ	the rod of discipline drives it far from him.
16a	עֹשֵׁק דָּל לְהַרְבּוֹת לוֹ	One who oppresses the poor, to enrich him;
16b	נֹתֵן לְעָשִׁיר אַךְ־לְמַחְסוֹר	one who gives to the rich, only to lack.

Their use, combined with the reiteration of the verb "shares/gives" (נתן, vv. 9b, 16b) and the construction "far from them/him" (רחק + מִן + pronominal suffix, vv. 5b, 15b), has served as the basis for differing macrostructural proposals. Some identify vv. 1–9 and 10–16 as the basic parts of the unit;[11] others discern vv. 1–5 and 6–16 as the macrostructural parts.[12] Both are possible. And both bound particular contexts within which individual sayings may be read.

Explanation of the Text

The MORAL ACCOUNTING metaphor plays a formative role in the motivational pedagogy of Proverbs.[13] The embodiment of normative character and the pursuit of wisdom are fueled by the promise of wealth and well-being. According to **22:1**, however, material wealth cannot hold a candle to virtuous character. This valuation is not described; rather, it is declared through two parallel better-than sayings. The first is formed through the adjectival participle נִבְחָר + מִן ("preferable to," v. 1a), while the second follows the conventional construction טוֹב + מִן ("better than," v. 1b). Taken together, they heighten the value of one's reputation and graciousness. These virtues exceed the value of material wealth. Unlike material wealth, they are forms of social capital that endure within the life and memory of the community. The juxtaposition of these unqualified comparative clauses conditions one's system of valuation. That is, they urge one not to "consider the 'better' to be what everyone else considers to be the better"; instead, they invite the reader to decide after one has "reflected on whether it is truly the better!"[14]

The moral valuation of v. 1 serves as an appropriate backdrop to the theological valuation in **v. 2.** Again, economics figures prominently in the saying, distinguishing two classes of people: the rich and the poor. Members from these classes "meet together" (נִפְגָּשׁוּ, v. 2a); but the context and the occasion of their meeting is open and ambiguous, inviting the reader to exercise their moral imagination. Whether the rich and poor rub shoulders in the everyday affairs of public life or meet in the context of conflict, when viewed in relation to their maker (עֹשֵׂה, v. 2b; cf. 14:31; 17:5), they are mere creatures. Their common creaturehood defines the essence of their being, which relativizes the socioeconomic constructs of society. On the surface, the saying appears to be a neutral observation. No observation, however, is neutral. At this point within the anthology, the observation calls for evaluation (cf. 29:13). As many suggest, it seems to function as an implicit admonition, encouraging the rich to alleviate economic inequality in society through responsible care for the poor.[15] The saying's theological valuation summons the reader's moral valuation and, in so doing, nurtures altruism.

The powers of perception summoned by 22:2

11. Waltke, *Proverbs: Chapters 15–31*, 197. Cf. Delitzsch, "Proverbs of Solomon," 6:320–25 (2:82–88), who connects 21:30–31 to 22:1–2 and views three parts as 21:20–22:2; 22:3–7; and 22:8–9.

12. Heim, *Like Grapes of Gold*, 305–9. Cf. Garrett, *Proverbs*, 186–87; Meinhold, *Die Sprüche*, 2:363–73.

13. Stewart, "Wisdom's Imagination," 365.

14. Westermann, *Roots of Wisdom*, 71.

15. Boström, *The God of the Sages*, 66; Murphy, *Proverbs*, 84; Fox, *Proverbs 10–31*, 695.

are foregrounded in **v. 3**. The aphorism reflects on the protection and security of discernment. And it hones the reader's discernment through its form. From a syntactical perspective, the parallel lines mirror one another.[16] But from a conceptual perspective, they are imprecise. With the exception of the antithetical correspondence between "the shrewd" (עָרוּם, v. 3a) and "the simple" (פְתָיִים, v. 3b), the parallel elements between the lines are asymmetrical.[17] This asymmetry invites the reader to complete the saying. In light of the second line, it appears that the shrewd not only sees evil and hides; by virtue of their perception, the shrewd also "escapes."[18] The simple, by contrast, do not "see evil" (רָאָה רָעָה, v. 3a). This expression is missing from the second line; its absence indicates that the simple do not possesses discernment.[19] This figure does not perceive imminent danger. As a result, instead of hiding, the simple pass on and rather than escaping, the simple are fined or "punished" (נֶעֱנָשׁוּ, v. 3b). This punishment is economic. Virtuous character is more valuable than great wealth (v. 1). A lack of discernment, however, is costly.

The economics of the moral order also inform **v. 4**. The saying is cast in the form of a single sentence that considers "the normative mode of human existence" through the metaphorical concept WELL-BEING IS WEALTH.[20] The initial line identifies the subject through an appositional construction.[21] In accord with this construction, the "fear of YHWH" is not "the first reward of humility";[22] rather, humility is defined as the fear of the YHWH (cf. 15:33). This is not surprising, for humility is a posture that is inextricably linked to a perspectival recognition of one's place in the cosmos and relationship with YHWH.[23] The reward for this lowly state of being is described in terms of the rewards that Lady Wisdom bestows on those who love her, namely, wealth, honor, and life (v. 4b; 8:18, 35). Paradoxically, humility engenders the optimal form of human existence.

The life of the perverse, by contrast, is far from optimal. Similar to 22:4a, **v. 5** opens with an appositional construction: "Thorns, snares" (צִנִּים פַּחִים, v. 5a). While the former term is uncertain, its juxtaposition with "snares" indicates that some sort of trap is in view. The crooked lifestyle of the perverse is littered with these traps. They spell impending death. One who guards his life, on the other hand, preserves his soul. This persona perceives the snares of the perverse person's way and steers clear of them, traversing a path of life.

The term "way" (דֶּרֶךְ, vv. 5a, 6a) is reiterated in **v. 6**, which is cast in the form of an admonition. But the pedagogical "way" prescribed is unclear. The initial line may be read in several ways, three in particular. First, it may be construed as an ironic warning against teaching a child in accord with their juvenile taste: "Train a youth in the way that he wants."[24] Second, the line may be rendered as a

16. Whether one follows *ketiv* (וְיִסָּתֵר, v. 3a) or *qere* (וְנִסְתָּר), the meaning of the saying remains the same. The *qere* may be an attempt to harmonize the form of the verb in the initial line with its counterpart in the second.

17. Waltke, *Proverbs: Chapters 15–31*, 201–2; Heim, *Poetic Imagination*, 514.

18. Heim, *Poetic Imagination*, 514.

19. Heim, *Poetic Imagination*, 515.

20. Jindo, "On the Biblical Notion," 449. For the metaphor WELL-BEING IS WEALTH, see Lakoff and Johnson, *Philosophy in the Flesh*, 292–93.

21. Waltke, *Proverbs: Chapters 15–31*, 193n6; *IBHS* §12.2c.

22. Fox, *Proverbs 10–31*, 697.

23. Jindo, "On the Biblical Notion," 449.

24. Clifford, *Proverbs*, 197. The verb חנך means "to dedicate, consecrate" elsewhere in the Old Testament (Deut 20:5; 1 Kgs 8:63; 2 Chr 7:5). Here it carries the sense "train." For discussion of the verb, see S. C. Reif, "Dedicated to חנך," *VT* 22 (1972): 495–501; Fox, *Proverbs 10–31*, 698.

directive to teach a child in a manner appropriate to their aptitude or age, that is, "Train a youth in a way that is suitable for him."[25] Alternatively, third, the line may be read as a command to instruct a child in a moral way of life, that is, "Train a youth in the right way—the way he ought to go."[26] The terse line is patient with each of these renderings. In light of the effectiveness of this training in the second line as well as Proverbs's broader vision of pedagogy (cf. v. 15; 23:13), the third reading may be the best. Whether or not one reads the admonition in this way, the openness of the saying contributes to Proverbs's pedagogy; it nurtures the imagination and necessitates the exercise of discernment.[27]

The same is true of **v. 7**. Similar to v. 2, the saying appears to be a neutral observation regarding "the way the world wags." The poor will always persist in society (Deut 15:11); and business requires borrowing. But the saying's construal of the socioeconomic power of the rich and the lender calls for evaluation: is this the way things ought to be?[28] The terms used to define the economic relationships with the poor and the borrower are questionable. Both "rules" (יִמְשׁוֹל, v. 7a) and "slave" (עֶבֶד, v. 7a) render these relationships in terms of subjugation, with the latter term unearthing the memory of Israel's status in Egypt.[29] "Rich" (עָשִׁיר, v. 7a) and "poor" (רָשִׁים, v. 7b) may be linked by alliteration in the first line, and "borrower" and "lender" share the same root in the second.[30] The nature of the relationship between these parties, however, awakens one's moral valuation and, in the process, cultivates the virtue of discernment.

Discernment is also demanded in **v. 8**. When read together, the individual lines exhibit semantic parallelism, but the conceptual relationship between these lines is unclear. The initial line traffics in the retributive scheme of moral accounting: one reaps what one sows (11:18; Job 4:8; Gal 6:7). The second line appears to extend this scheme. The way in which it elaborates on the nature of retribution is contingent on one's construal of the construct phrase "rod of his wrath" (שֵׁבֶט עֶבְרָתוֹ, v. 8b). This rod may represent a scepter of authority in general or a weapon in particular (2 Sam 23:21; Isa 14:5–6), which will prove ineffective in the face of disaster.[31] If the second line develops the agricultural imagery in the first, however, the phrase refers to a threshing rod (Isa 28:27).[32] This image intensifies the retributive scheme sketched in the first line. The iniquity sown will produce a harvest of disaster; and the flail, that is, the sower's wrath, will prove futile in threshing the crop of calamity.[33] The ambiguous imagery in the second line stimulates one's moral reasoning, inviting one to amplify the nature of retribution outlined in the first.

In contrast to the retributive scheme of moral accounting delineated in Prov 22:8, **v. 9** describes the "moral credit" accumulated through altruism.[34] This altruism is embodied and exercised by "the generous person," one "good of eye" (טוֹב־עַיִן, v. 9a). Whether the generous is blessed by God, the poor, or both, they experience well-being, for they see and meet the needs of the poor. Similar to several other sayings in the central collections (Prov 14:31; 17:5; 19:7; 28:27), the aphorism inculcates care for

25. Delitzsch, "The Book of Proverbs," 6:324 (2:86–87); Toy, *Proverbs*, 415–16.

26. McKane, *Proverbs*, 564; Murphy, *Proverbs*, 165; Waltke, *Proverbs: Chapters 15–31*, 205; Yoder, *Proverbs*, 224; Fox, *Proverbs 10–31*, 698.

27. Stewart, *Poetic Ethics*, 50.

28. Sandoval, *The Discourse of Wealth and Poverty*, 190.

29. Sandoval, *The Discourse of Wealth and Poverty*, 193.

30. McCreesh, *Biblical Sound and Sense*, 66–67.

31. Yoder, *Proverbs*, 225.

32. Clifford, *Proverbs*, 197.

33. Fox, *Proverbs 10–31*, 699.

34. Lakoff and Johnson, *Philosophy in the Flesh*, 295.

the marginalized through the motivation of social honor.[35]

While the generous is welcomed by the community in Prov 22:9, **v. 10** admonishes the reader to banish the scoffer from social gatherings. This familiar figure is associated with "strife" (מָדוֹן, v. 10a), which is personified as the scoffer's partner in crime. When one expels the scoffer, strife also departs. The imperative followed by the *waw* + jussive marks result (v. 10a). And the second line expounds on the contentious qualities that are quelled with the departure of the scoffer. The aphorism develops other sayings devoted to the scoffer (13:1; 14:6; 15:12; 19:29; 21:24; 24:9); it moves beyond a description of this figure's character to prescribe a particular form of action (cf. 19:25).

The admonition in 22:10 is straightforward. If Norman Whybray is right, the extended description in **v. 11**, by contrast, "hardly makes sense in the Hebrew."[36] The individual phrases are clear, but their relationship is ambiguous. This ambiguity has engendered various emendations. Following the LXX, some include YHWH as the subject of the first line.[37] Others transpose the term "king" from the end of the second line to the subject of the first.[38] Both emendations, however, are conjectural and unnecessary. The aphorism includes three asyndetic phrases. The absence of particles to clarify the syntactical relationship between the individual phrases rouses the moral reasoning of the reader, inviting one to plug these syntactical holes in order to understand the saying. These holes may be filled in two ways. First, in light of the nominative absolute "one who loves purity of heart" (אֹהֵב טְהוֹר־לֵב, v. 11a), the second phrase may be construed as an unmarked relative clause (חֵן שְׂפָתָיו, "whose lips are gracious"), followed by the predicate.[39] Second, off the back of the nominative absolute in the first line, the phrases in the second line may be read as the predicate.[40] Whichever reading is preferred, the saying moves from the internal desires of normative character to its external expression in speech and the companionship it cultivates with the king. The way in which they relate to one another requires moral reasoning and discernment.

Similar to v. 11, **v. 12** focuses on speech. This motif is implicit in the first line but explicit in the second. According to the initial line, the eyes of YHWH "guard knowledge" (נָצְרוּ דָעַת, v. 12a). The object "knowledge" may be construed as an abstract for a concrete. That is, following Roland Murphy, "'knowledge' stands for 'the one who knows.'"[41] In light of the parallel expression in the second line, however, it appears that the term "is a metonymy for '*words* of knowledge' (cf. Prov 22:17)."[42] On this account, the eyes of YHWH survey speech; he protects words of knowledge, ensuring their efficacy, whereas he undermines the words of the treacherous, guaranteeing their failure. The aphorism reinforces the retributive scheme of the MORAL ACCOUNTING metaphor, associating the inefficacious speech of the treacherous with YHWH's legitimate authority.

The inefficacy of the speech of the treacherous serves as an appropriate entrée into **v. 13** and its presentation of the speech of the sluggard. In contrast to previous descriptions of the sluggard

35. Sandoval, *The Discourse of Wealth and Poverty*, 181–82.
36. Whybray, *Proverbs*, 321.
37. Whybray, *Proverbs*, 321.
38. Toy, *Proverbs*, 417–18; G. R. Driver, "Problems in the Hebrew Text of Proverbs," *Bib* 32 (1951): 186–87; McKane, *Proverbs*, 568; Clifford, *Proverbs*, 195.
39. Waltke, *Proverbs: Chapters 15–31*, 195–96nn22–24; Fox, *Proverbs 10–31*, 700–701.
40. Murphy, *Proverbs*, 164n11.a.
41. Murphy, *Proverbs*, 166.
42. Fox, *Proverbs 10–31*, 701, italics original.

(6:6–11; 10:26; 13:4; 15:19; 19:24; 20:4; 21:25), the saying allows this personage to speak (cf. 26:13). This speech is introduced by the expression "the sluggard says" (אָמַר עָצֵל, 22:13a), which has no counterpart in the second line. The absence of a parallel element creates space to develop the sluggard's logic and the lengths to which he will go to avoid any form of physical exertion.[43] This development is exhibited through the parallel prepositional phrases "outside" (בַחוּץ, v. 13a) and "in the squares" (בְּתוֹךְ רְחֹבוֹת, v. 13b). Here the sluggard clarifies his location. He does not live in a rural area, where lions might roam. He lives in a settlement, complete with open squares surrounded by buildings.[44] Lions do not tend to wander into these populated areas. The threat is not only unlikely; the sluggard's logic is also ludicrous. His speech and logic are presented to expose his underachievement, his failure to live within appropriate boundaries.

Together with vv. 11–13, speech seems to be in view within **v. 14** (cf. 23:27a). The saying reintroduces a familiar figure (2:16–19; 5:1–23; 6:20–35; 7:1–27), who is represented through the plural "strange women" (זָרוֹת, v. 14a). In light of the description of the strange woman's seductive speech across Prov 1–9 (2:16; 5:3–4; 6:24; 7:5, 14–21), "deep pit" (שׁוּחָה עֲמֻקָּה, 22:14a) appears to depict her mouth as a deadly snare. The sound and sense of her words may promise cool, refreshing water; but her mouth proves to be a trap, devoid of satisfaction. The second line delineates the consequence of lingering around this deep pit. When read in relation to the initial line, the saying defies the traditional categories of parallelism. Conceptual relations, rather than syntactical or semantic similarities, generate meaning between the lines.[45] One who drinks from the pit of strange women will be cursed by YHWH and fall into it. Similar to v. 12, the saying traffics in retribution, connecting the judgment for adultery with YHWH's agency and legitimate authority.

Retribution under YHWH's legitimate authority informs **v. 15** and its description of discipline under the educator's legitimate MORAL AUTHORITY.[46] This discipline is conceptualized through a form of corporal punishment. The gravest species of "folly" (אִוֶּלֶת, v. 15a) is depicted as bound in a youth's heart. Elsewhere, this term for folly designates a personage who is unable to learn (12:15, 16; 15:5; 27:22).[47] Here, by contrast, hope remains, and this hope is linked to physical punishment, which serves as the means by which folly is expelled from the youth's heart. Far from the intellectual apprehension of information, learning includes tactility and the sensation of pain, which shapes one's character by releasing one from certain forms of behavior (cf. 13:24; 19:25, 29; 23:13–14; 29:15).[48]

The final saying returns to the root עשׁר ("rich," 22:16b) and terms from the semantic fields of wealth and poverty that opened the unit (vv. 1, 2, 16). Just as vv. 1 and 2 summoned and shaped one's moral valuation, so also **v. 16** challenges one to exercise their moral valuation. This challenge is solicited by the ambiguities and gaps that mark the individual lines. From a syntactical perspective, the lines mirror one another. But their relationship is unclear, for the noun clause that opens the second line is asyndetic. And the subject at the

43. Heim, *Poetic Imagination*, 519.

44. Heim, *Poetic Imagination*, 519–20.

45. Heim, *Poetic Imagination*, 524.

46. For discussion of the metaphorical concept, see Lakoff and Johnson, *Philosophy in the Flesh*, 301–3.

47. Fox, *Proverbs 1–9*, 40; idem, *Proverbs 10–31*, 703.

48. Tilford, *Sensing World, Sensing Wisdom*, 110.

end of each line is equivocal. These difficulties prompted Norman Whybray to conclude that the lines were "originally unconnected fragments which have been erroneously set side by side because of their formal parallelism."[49] And they moved Richard Clifford to construe the saying "as a typical dispassionate observation on the rich and the poor."[50] The saying is far from disinterested. It awakens one's moral valuation and calls for the exercise of one's moral reasoning. As many have noted, it presents a pair of paradoxes. In fact, from a syntactical and conceptual perspective, the saying mirrors 11:24 (cf. 13:7, 23). Like 11:24, 22:16 ends with the expression "only to lack" (אַךְ־לְמַחְסוֹר, v. 16b). And like 11:24, 22:16 juxtaposes paradoxes. But these paradoxes are marked by the יֵשׁ of reflection in 11:24. If v. 16 is governed by an asyndetic יֵשׁ of reflection, which observes "some opposing situation or paradox," then it may be rendered as follows:[51]

There is this: one who oppresses the poor
so as to enrich him
(i.e., the poor);
one who gives to the rich
only to lack (i.e., the rich).

These unmarked paradoxes invite meditation on enigmatic affairs and encourage the exercise of one's moral valuation. They serve as an appropriate conclusion to the first Solomonic collection. The second half of the collection opened with a sequence of sayings that explored the mystery of YHWH's intervention in human affairs (16:1–9). The final saying in the subcollection reinforces the paradoxical realities of being-in-the-world.

Canonical and Theological Significance

Creation serves as one of the primary means by which Proverbs participates in and contributes to biblical-theological and dogmatic reflection.[52] Aspects of the doctrine of creation preoccupy certain collections within Proverbs. In the most general terms, the instructional materials in chs. 1–9 give particular attention to YHWH's creation of the cosmos (3:19–20; 8:22–30), while the aphoristic sayings in chs. 10–29 focus on YHWH as the creator of human beings (14:31; 20:12; 22:2; 29:13). From a tradition-historical perspective, these aspects of the doctrine of creation serve as a window into the date, audience, and oral-written setting of Prov 1–9 and 10–29.[53] But from a canonical and theological perspective, the movement from YHWH's creation of the cosmos to YHWH's creation of human beings and involvement in ordinary life reflects the logic of the doctrine of creation, which moves from YHWH's creation of all things to YHWH's providential preservation and ordering of all things.

49. Whybray, *Proverbs*, 323.

50. Clifford, *Proverbs*, 199.

51. Gianto, "On יֵשׁ of Reflection in the Book of Proverbs," 158–62, esp. 158. Cf. Fox, *Proverbs 10–31*, 704.

52. Perdue, *Wisdom and Creation*.

53. Westermann, *Roots of Wisdom*, 123–24; Peter Doll, *Menschenschöpfung und Weltschöpfung in der alttestamentlichen Weisheit*, SBS 117 (Stuttgart: Katholisches Bibelwerk, 1985).

YHWH's providential activity underlies many of the sayings across Prov 16:1–22:16. These sayings contribute to the doctrine of providence. They serve as the dichroscope through which the facets of the doctrine are examined and illuminated. These aphorisms do not traffic in the technical, dogmatic term "providence." No biblical text does. Instead, they focus on YHWH, who is mentioned more frequently in 16:1–22:16 than in any other subcollection in the anthology.[54] And they juxtapose divine agency with human agency. The confluence of divine agency and human agency is real. What's more, the confluence of these forms of agency is mysterious. This mystery is "dimensional in character," that is, it is due to "an unimaginable depth or density that transcends our rational capacities and all of our other capacities as well."[55] Many sayings in 16:1–22:16 plumb the depths of this mystery by considering divine and human involvement in ordinary affairs. In so doing, they fund two aspects of the doctrine of providence: government and concurrence.[56]

If "providence concerns God's continuing relation to the world he has created,"[57] specifically to "that act of God by which from moment to moment he preserves and governs all things,"[58] then government refers to God's active and sovereign rule over all created things. This aspect of the doctrine of providence is the focus of attention in many sayings across Prov 16:1–22:16. YHWH directs each creature to its established end, even the wicked and the arrogant to judgment (16:4, 5; cf. 17:5). In contrast to human self-valuation, YHWH operates under a different moral metric: he weighs motives, tests hearts, and searches the innermost recesses of one's being (16:2; 17:3; 20:27; 21:2). YHWH establishes and oversees economic and judicial affairs (16:11; 17:15; 20:10, 23). He orders and reveals judgments (16:33). He executes vengeance and enacts salvation (20:22). He guides the hearts of all (21:1). He is the maker of all (22:2). And he guards all speech acts, orchestrating their intended end (22:12).

This sketch of divine governance may strike a note of determinism. But this is not the case, for divine government is inextricably bound up with concurrence in Proverbs's conception of providence. According to John Webster, concurrence specifies God's preserving activity "by speaking of how God's providential work is not simply a force brought to bear upon creation from outside, but is integral or interior to creation: providence works through creaturely working."[59] That is, "God's

54. Boström, *The God of the Sages*, 33.

55. Steven D. Boyer and Christopher A. Hall, *The Mystery of God: Theology for Knowing the Unknowable* (Grand Rapids: Baker Academic, 2012), 13. Also see Paul S. Fiddes, *Seeing the World and Knowing God: Hebrew Wisdom and Christian Doctrine in a Late-Modern Context* (Oxford: Oxford University Press, 2013), 108.

56. In addition to government and concurrence, the doctrine of providence includes a third aspect that is implicitly assumed rather than explicitly addressed in Prov 16:1–22:16: preservation. For discussion of these aspects, see Herman Bavinck, *Reformed Dogmatics*, ed. John Bolt; trans. John Vriend, 4 vols. (Grand Rapids: Baker Academic, 2004), 2:604–19.

57. John Webster, "Providence," in *Mapping Modern Theology: A Thematic and Historical Introduction*, ed. Kelly M. Kapic and Bruce L. McCormack (Grand Rapids: Baker Academic, 2012), 203.

58. Bavinck, *Reformed Dogmatics*, 2:596.

59. Webster, "Providence," 207.

acts concur with creaturely acts."[60] This construal of providence necessitates an account of primary and secondary causality, according to which the former does not eliminate the latter. Both primary, divine causality and secondary, human causality are genuine. Divine causality enables creaturely causality. This concurrent, noncontrastive rendering of providence is foregrounded by many sayings in 16:1–22:16 that juxtapose human agency with divine agency.

The concurrence of human and divine agency emerges in several sayings pertaining to speech, planning, and interpersonal relationships throughout Prov 16:1–22:16. The interrelationship between one's internal thoughts and their external expression is characterized by concurrence: humans arrange their thoughts and bring these cognitive arrangements to verbal expression, while YHWH directs these cognitive arrangements and their verbal expression to their intended communicative ends (16:1; cf. 19:21). Humans plan, while YHWH directs their steps (16:9; 20:24). Humans commit their works to YHWH, and YHWH ensures their success (16:3). Humans prepare for battle, while YHWH brings about victory (21:30–31). One who finds a wife receives divine favor (18:22), and a prudent wife is a divine gift (19:14). YHWH's favor engenders peace with one's enemies (16:7). YHWH repays the one who is gracious to the poor (19:17). And relational dependence upon YHWH brings blessing (16:20), security (18:10), and safety (19:23). The concurrence of divine and human agency across the aphorisms in Prov 16:1–22:16 not only testifies to the reality of YHWH's providential activity in and through human activity; it also probes the mysterious confluence of divine freedom and human freedom.

Many of the aphorisms in Prov 16:1–22:16 lay bare the depth and density of certain aspects of providence. While 16:1–22:16 foregrounds government and concurrence as essential aspects of providence, these aspects of the doctrine are not dependent on the witness of Proverbs alone. They reverberate across the canon of Scripture. Government, for example, is evinced through theological interpretations of history. Across Deut 2, Israel is prohibited from provoking certain people groups to war because YHWH has allotted to each of these groups their land (Deut 2:5, 9, 19). According to Amos 9:7, just as YHWH brought the Israelites out of Egypt, so also he brought the Philistines out of Caphtor and the Arameans out from Kir. The oracles against the nations in the Prophets bear witness to YHWH's just and sovereign judgment of all peoples (Isa 13–23; Jer 46–51; Ezek 25–32; Amos 1:3–2:16). The respective exiles of Israel and Judah are attributed to YHWH's covenant faithfulness and governance of geopolitical events (2 Kgs 17:7–23; 21:10–15). And Jesus's rule over nature, sickness, and death attests to the reality that all authority in heaven and on earth has been entrusted to him (Matt 28:18).

Together with governance, concurrence pervades the biblical witness. In many

60. Webster, "Providence," 220.

cases, the juxtaposition of divine and human agency is explicit. Joseph, for example, interprets his brothers' treacherous actions in terms of YHWH sending him to Egypt to preserve life (Gen 45:5–8). Joseph's brothers intended to harm him, but God intended it for good (Gen 50:20). The seamless narrative of Ezra–Nehemiah attributes the waves of Judean exiles returning to the land (Ezra 1:5; 7:1–10; 8:31; Neh 2:1–9), the restoration of the community (Ezra 7:27–28; Neh 2:11–17; 6:15–19), and the preservation of the Levitical priesthood to both human agency and "the good hand of YHWH" (Ezra 8:15–18). And Peter construes the crucifixion of Jesus of Nazareth as the product of God's deliberate plan and foreknowledge, on the one hand, and the work of wicked people, on the other (Acts 2:23). In other cases, the concurrence of divine and human agency is implicit. Having returned to Bethlehem with her mother-in-law, Ruth "chanced upon" (וַיִּקֶר מִקְרֶהָ) the portion of the field belonging to Boaz (Ruth 2:3). This apparent coincidence mirrors the remarkable sequence of coincidences that unfold across the narrative of Esther: Xerxes's selection of Esther as queen, Mordecai's discovery of a plot to assassinate the king, Xerxes's insomnia on the evening that Haman planned to speak to the king about impaling Mordecai, and the portion of the royal chronicles read to the king, as well as Esther's precarious identification with the people of God and their preservation within the empire. YHWH's activity is not specified in Ruth 2:3 or the narrative of Esther, but it is assumed. YHWH's activity concurs with human activity, guiding human actions to their intended telos (cf. Rom 8:28).

Whether implicitly or explicitly, aspects of the doctrine of providence are woven throughout the canonical tapestry. And many aphorisms in Prov 16:1–22:16 represent significant threads in this tapestry. These threads are easily overlooked or unnoticed, like God's providential activity. But they are not insignificant. Neither is the doctrine of providence. Far from representing an abstraction, the doctrine of providence is practical;[61] it provides "orientation and consolation to believers by instructing them in how to read the world as an ordered, not random, reality—ordered by divine love and directed by divine power for God's glory and the creature's good."[62] As Webster notes, the doctrine of providence offers one a lens through which "to read the world." In so doing, it engenders hope, solace, and courage. The same is true of the YHWH sayings in Prov 16:1–22:16. This sentiment is captured by Gerhard von Rad, who observed:

> When did Israel ever complain of this mysterious presence of God in every human activity? This divine presence, on the one hand limiting human planning, on the

61. Bruce Riley Ashford and Craig G. Bartholomew, *The Doctrine of Creation: A Constructive Kuyperian Approach* (Downers Grove, IL: IVP Academic, 2020), 296–98.

62. Webster, "Providence," 207.

> other carrying men beyond the goal which they had envisaged—to experience human limitations in this way was, in the last resort, a comforting doctrine.[63]

The doctrine of providence is comforting. And the YHWH sayings in Prov 16:1–22:16 offer comfort by providing one with a liberating vision of being in a world that is preserved by YHWH and governed by YHWH in such a way that divine and human agency do not conflict but concur in a beautiful yet mysterious harmony that reflects the beautiful yet mysterious harmony of the created world.

63. Von Rad, *Wisdom in Israel*, 105–6.

III.3 Proverbs 22:17–24:34

Vocational Wisdom and Virtue

The materials in the book of Proverbs evince an understanding of how humans tick. Among other things, they bank on human self-interest to motivate the moral life. While this form of motivation is implicit in many of the sayings within 10:1–22:16,[1] it is explicit in the short collections attributed to the "wise" (22:17–24:22; 24:23–34). Emerging from the rugged literary terrain of indicative sayings that sharpened one's moral imagination and perception (16:1–22:16), the reader encounters an avalanche of admonitions, most of which are modified by a clause that appeals to self-preservation, honor/shame, or parental approval to motivate a particular form of action.

This shift in form coincides with a shift in the reader's subject position. Like the lectures and interludes in chs. 1–9, the reader is placed under the teaching of an authorized guide and called to assume "the subject position of son in relation to an authoritative father" (23:15–16, 22–28; 24:13–14, 21).[2] But in contrast to chs. 1–9, the reader does not remain in the comfortable confines of the home. The admonitions and sayings place the reader *in* varying social roles: a messenger (22:21), a citizen (22:24, 28, 10–11, 23:20–21; 24:10–12, 15), a dinner guest (23:1–3, 6–8), a parent (23:13–14), a drunkard (23:33–34), and a military leader (24:6).[3] More than shaping the character and social relations of the reader, the movement between these subject positions contributes to the goal of the "words of the wise": to inculcate trust in YHWH and to form one into a reliable communicator who may flourish in the dynamic vocations of life (22:19, 21).

1. Hildebrandt, "Motivation and Antithetic Parallelism in Proverbs 10–15," 427–44; Stewart, *Poetic Ethics*, 102–29; Schwáb, *Toward an Interpretation*, 100–27.

2. Newsom, "Woman and the Discourse of Patriarchal Wisdom," 143.

3. Brown, "The Pedagogy of Proverbs 10:1–31:9," 169; Yoder, *Proverbs*, 229.

III. "Forming 'Fearers of YHWH'": The Curriculum of Wisdom and Virtue (10:1–29:27)

- III.1 Elementary Wisdom and Virtue (10:1–15:33)
- III.2 Intermediate Wisdom and Virtue (16:1–22:16)
- ➡ **III.3 Vocational Wisdom and Virtue (22:17–24:34)**
  - **A. Moral Motivation: Inspiring Trust in YHWH and Trustworthy Speech (22:17–24:22)**
  - **B. Justice, Speech, and Work: Variations on the Concept of MORAL ORDER (24:23–34)**
- III.4 Advanced Wisdom and Virtue (25:1–29:27)

CHAPTER 29

Proverbs 22:17–24:22

A. Moral Motivation: *Inspiring Trust in YHWH and Trustworthy Speech*

Main Idea of the Passage

In accord with the formal introduction to the collection (22:17–21), the "words of the wise" seek to inculcate trust in YHWH and to cultivate trustworthy speakers by providing concrete counsel on how to interpret or deal with diverse people in particular situations.

Literary Context[1]

Direct address is rare in the rhetoric of Prov 10:1–22:16 (14:7; 19:18–20, 27; 20:13, 16, 19, 22; 22:10). This is not the case in the "words of the wise" (22:17–24:22). These "words" mimic the language, rhetoric, and pedagogical techniques of the discourses in chs. 1–9 (cf. 31:1–9). Similar to the discourses in chs. 1–9, the "words of the wise" traffic in admonitions and exhortations, complete with subordinate clauses designed to shape one's desires, reasoning, and behavior in accord with wisdom and virtue. And similar to chs. 1–9 (1:8; 6:20), the parents emerge as authorized, authoritative guides, while the reader resumes the receptive posture of "son" (23:15, 19, 22, 25, 26; 24:13, 21). The "words of the wise" place the reader in familiar pedagogical territory. This territory serves as the setting within which common themes and fresh motifs converge to extend the purpose of the book of Proverbs.

The convergence and development of these common themes and fresh motifs

1. This chapter does not include the Canonical and Theological Significance section. See pp. xv and 276n1 for justification. Also, see pp. 543–47 for the Canonical and Theological Significance of Proverbs 22:17–24:34.

may be illustrated through the variant repetitions within the collection.[2] The tools employed by YHWH (3:19–20), Lady Wisdom (9:1), and women (14:1) to construct and fill cosmic and terrestrial homes are redeployed to describe the formation and provisioning of domestic spheres (24:3–4).[3] With language reminiscent of 3:31, the appeal not to envy immoral characters serves as a refrain in the collection (23:17a; 24:1a, 19a), indicating that the prosperity of the wicked and the absence of retribution produced an appealing advertisement for a lifestyle that threatened the perseverance of the wise. Twice-told proverbs pertaining to the displacement of landmarks (22:28a; 23:10a), the delicacies of a host (23:3a; 6b), and the certain hope of the wise punctuate the collection (23:18; 24:14b, 20). And YHWH's personal involvement in the circumstances of life (22:23; 23:11; 24:12, 18, 21–22) overshadows his enigmatic involvement in human affairs (16:1–9).[4] The collection's reiteration of common themes and its attention to dinner etiquette (23:1–3, 6–8), the dangers of unrestrained eating, drinking, and work (23:4–5, 20–21, 29–35), as well as the company that one keeps (22:24–25, 26–27; 23:20–21) contribute to a thread of Proverbs's pedagogical goal. The embedded title of the collection—the "words of the wise"—recalls 1:6 and the description of the anthology's purpose. And the stated purpose of the "words of the wise" complements of the goal delineated in the preamble.[5] Just as the book seeks to (trans)form the character of those who fear YHWH through the inculcation of wisdom and virtue (1: 2–7), the "words of the wise" seek to inculcate trust in YHWH and form one into a trustworthy speaker through the promotion of practical virtues (22:19a, 21b).

III. "Forming 'Fearers of YHWH'": The Curriculum of Wisdom and Virtue (10:1–29:27)
- III.1 Elementary Wisdom and Virtue (10:1–15:33)
- III.2 Intermediate Wisdom and Virtue (16:1–22:16)
- **III.3 Vocational Wisdom and Virtue (22:17–24:34)**
  - ➡ **A. Moral Motivation: Inspiring Trust in YHWH and Trustworthy Speech (22:17–24:22)**
    - **1. Formal Introduction: Saying 1 (22:17–21)**
      - **a. Exhortation and Motivation (22:17–18)**
      - **b. The Theological Purpose of the "Words of the Wise" (22:19)**
      - **c. The Formational Purpose and Result of the "Words of the Wise" (22:20–21)**

2. For a detailed analysis of these as well as other variant repetitions in the collection, see Heim, *Poetic Imagination*.

3. Van Leeuwen, "Cosmos, Temple, House," 67–90.

4. Brown, "The Pedagogy of Proverbs 10:1–31:9," 166–67; Yoder, *Proverbs*, 230.

5. Meinhold, *Die Sprüche*, 2:374. Cf. Keefer, *Proverbs 1–9 as an Introduction*, 161–67.

Translation and Exegetical Outline

(See pages 520–524.)

Proverbs 22:17–24:22

Verse	Hebrew	Translation	Outline
			III.3 Vocational Wisdom and Virtue (22:17–24:34) A. Moral Motivation: Inspiring Trust in YHWH and Trustworthy Speech (22:17–24:22) 1. Formal Introduction: Saying 1 (22:17–21)
17a	הַט אָזְנְךָ וּשְׁמַע דִּבְרֵי חֲכָמִים	Incline your ear and hear the words of the wise,	a. Exhortation and Motivation (22:17–18)
17b	וְלִבְּךָ תָּשִׁית לְדַעְתִּי	and direct your heart to my knowledge;	
18a	↑ כִּי־נָעִים כִּי־תִשְׁמְרֵם בְּבִטְנֶךָ	↑ for it will be pleasant if you keep them in your belly,	
18b	יִכֹּנוּ יַחְדָּו עַל־שְׂפָתֶיךָ	if all of them are secured on your lips.	
19a	↓ לִהְיוֹת בַּיהוָה מִבְטַחֶךָ	↓ In order that your trust may be in YHWH,	b. The Theological Purpose of the "Words of the Wise" (22:19)
19b	הוֹדַעְתִּיךָ הַיּוֹם אַף־אָתָּה	I teach you today—even you.	
20a	הֲלֹא כָתַבְתִּי לְךָ שְׁלֹשִׁים	Have I not written for you thirty sayings	c. The Formational Purpose and Result of the "Words of the Wise" (22:20–21)
20b	↑ בְּמוֹעֵצֹת וָדָעַת	↑ as counsel and knowledge	
21a	לְהוֹדִיעֲךָ קֹשְׁטְ אִמְרֵי אֱמֶת	to teach you truth, words of truth,	
21b	↑ לְהָשִׁיב אֲמָרִים אֱמֶת לְשֹׁלְחֶיךָ	↑ so as to bring back true reports to those who send you?	
22a	אַל־תִּגְזָל־דָּל כִּי דַל־הוּא	Do not rob the poor because they are poor,	2. Saying 2 (22:22–23)
22b	וְאַל־תְּדַכֵּא עָנִי בַשָּׁעַר	and do not crush the needy at the gate;	
23a	↑ כִּי־יְהוָה יָרִיב רִיבָם	↑ for YHWH will contest their case	
23b	וְקָבַע אֶת־קֹבְעֵיהֶם נָפֶשׁ	and will snatch the life of those who snatch from them.	
24a	אַל־תִּתְרַע אֶת־בַּעַל אָף	Do not befriend an angry person,	3. Saying 3 (22:24–25)
24b	וְאֶת־אִישׁ חֵמוֹת לֹא תָבוֹא	and with a hothead do not go;	
25a	↑ פֶּן־תֶּאֱלַף אֹרְחֹתָו	↑ lest you learn his ways,	
25b	וְלָקַחְתָּ מוֹקֵשׁ לְנַפְשֶׁךָ	and get yourself ensnared.	
26a	אַל־תְּהִי בְתֹקְעֵי־כָף	Do not be among those who seal a deal,	4. Saying 4 (22:26–27)
26b	בַּעֹרְבִים מַשָּׁאוֹת	among those who guarantee a loan,	
27a	↓ אִם־אֵין־לְךָ לְשַׁלֵּם	↓ if you do not have the means to pay,	
27b	לָמָּה יִקַּח מִשְׁכָּבְךָ מִתַּחְתֶּיךָ	why should he take your bed from beneath you?	
28a	אַל־תַּסֵּג גְּבוּל עוֹלָם	Do not displace an ancient boundary	5. Saying 5 (22:28)
28b	↑ אֲשֶׁר עָשׂוּ אֲבוֹתֶיךָ	↑ which your ancestors made.	
29a	חָזִיתָ אִישׁ מָהִיר בִּמְלַאכְתּוֹ	Have you seen a person skilled in his work?	6. Saying 6 (22:29)
29b	לִפְנֵי־מְלָכִים יִתְיַצָּב	He will stand before kings.	
29c	בַּל־יִתְיַצֵּב לִפְנֵי חֲשֻׁכִּים	He will not stand before the obscure.	

Verse	Hebrew	English	Saying
23:1a	↓ כִּי־תֵשֵׁב לִלְחוֹם אֶת־מוֹשֵׁל	↓ When you sit to dine with a ruler,	7. Saying 7 (23:1–3)
23:1b	בִּין תָּבִין אֶת־אֲשֶׁר לְפָנֶיךָ	look carefully at what is before you,	
2a	וְשַׂמְתָּ שַׂכִּין בְּלֹעֶךָ	and put a knife to your throat,	
2b	↑ אִם־בַּעַל נֶפֶשׁ אָתָּה	↑ if you are an insatiable person.	
3a	אַל־תִּתְאָו לְמַטְעַמּוֹתָיו	Do not desire his delicacies,	
3b	↑ וְהוּא לֶחֶם כְּזָבִים	↑ for they are deceptive food.	
4a	אַל־תִּיגַע לְהַעֲשִׁיר	Do not struggle to get rich.	8. Saying 8 (23:4–5)
4b	מִבִּינָתְךָ חֲדָל	Desist from your own understanding!	
5a	הֲתָעִיף עֵינֶיךָ בּוֹ וְאֵינֶנּוּ	Will you let your eyes fly to it? It is no more!	
5b	↑ כִּי עָשֹׂה יַעֲשֶׂה־לּוֹ כְנָפַיִם	↑ for it will surely grow wings for itself,	
5c	כְּנֶשֶׁר יָעוּף הַשָּׁמָיִם	and fly to the sky like an eagle.	
6a	אַל־תִּלְחַם אֶת־לֶחֶם רַע עָיִן	Do not eat the food of a stingy person,	9. Saying 9 (23:6–8)
6b	וְאַל־תִּתְאָיו לְמַטְעַמֹּתָיו	nor desire his delicacies.	
7a	↓ כִּי כְּמוֹ־שָׁעַר בְּנַפְשׁוֹ כֶּן־הוּא	↓ For like one who calculates within himself, thus is he:	
7b	אֱכֹל וּשְׁתֵה יֹאמַר לָךְ	"Eat and drink," he says to you,	
7c	וְלִבּוֹ בַּל־עִמָּךְ	but his heart is not with you.	
8a	פִּתְּךָ־אָכַלְתָּ תְקִיאֶנָּה	You eat your morsel, you will vomit it up,	
8b	וְשִׁחַתָּ דְּבָרֶיךָ הַנְּעִימִים	and you will waste your pleasant words.	
9a	בְּאָזְנֵי כְסִיל אַל־תְּדַבֵּר	Do not speak in the ears of a fool,	10. Saying 10 (23:9)
9b	↑ כִּי־יָבוּז לְשֵׂכֶל מִלֶּיךָ	↑ for he will despise the insight of your words.	
10a	אַל־תַּסֵּג גְּבוּל עוֹלָם	Do not displace an ancient boundary,	11. Saying 11 (23:10–11)
10b	וּבִשְׂדֵי יְתוֹמִים אַל־תָּבֹא	nor encroach on the fields of orphans,	
11a	↑ כִּי־גֹאֲלָם חָזָק	↑ for their redeemer is strong;	
11b	הוּא־יָרִיב אֶת־רִיבָם אִתָּךְ	he will contest their case with you.	
12a	הָבִיאָה לַמּוּסָר לִבֶּךָ	Apply your heart to discipline,	12. Saying 12 (23:12–14)
12b	וְאָזְנֶךָ לְאִמְרֵי־דָעַת	and your ear to words of knowledge.	
13a	אַל־תִּמְנַע מִנַּעַר מוּסָר	Do not withhold discipline from a youth,	
13b	כִּי־תַכֶּנּוּ בַשֵּׁבֶט לֹא יָמוּת	if you strike him with a rod, he shall not die.	
14a	אַתָּה בַּשֵּׁבֶט תַּכֶּנּוּ	Strike him with a rod,	
14b	וְנַפְשׁוֹ מִשְּׁאוֹל תַּצִּיל	and you will deliver his life from Sheol.	

Continued on next page.

Continued from previous page.

15a	↓ בְּנִי אִם־חָכַם לִבֶּךָ	↓ My son, if your heart becomes wise,	13. Saying 13 (23:15–16)
15b	יִשְׂמַח לִבִּי גַם־אָנִי	my heart, too, will rejoice,	
16a	וְתַעְלֹזְנָה כִלְיוֹתָי	and my kidneys will exalt,	
16b	↑ בְּדַבֵּר שְׂפָתֶיךָ מֵישָׁרִים	↑ when your lips speak what is upright.	
17a	אַל־יְקַנֵּא לִבְּךָ בַּחַטָּאִים	Let not your heart envy sinners,	14. Saying 14 (23:17–18)
17b	כִּי אִם־בְּיִרְאַת־יְהוָה כָּל־הַיּוֹם	but rather those who fear YHWH every day.	
18a	כִּי אִם־יֵשׁ אַחֲרִית	Surely, there is a future,	
18b	וְתִקְוָתְךָ לֹא תִכָּרֵת	and your hope shall not be cut off.	
19a	שְׁמַע־אַתָּה בְנִי וַחֲכָם	You yourself listen, my son, and become wise,	15. Saying 15 (23:19–21)
19b	וְאַשֵּׁר בַּדֶּרֶךְ לִבֶּךָ	and stride in the way of your heart.	
20a	אַל־תְּהִי בְסֹבְאֵי־יָיִן	Do not be among winebibbers,	
20b	בְּזֹלֲלֵי בָשָׂר לָמוֹ	among those who overindulge on meat,	
21a	↑ כִּי־סֹבֵא וְזוֹלֵל יִוָּרֵשׁ	↑ for the inebriated and the glutton will be impoverished,	
21b	וּקְרָעִים תַּלְבִּישׁ נוּמָה	and stupor will clothe them in rags.	
22a	שְׁמַע לְאָבִיךָ זֶה יְלָדֶךָ	Listen to your father, who begot you,	16. Saying 16 (23:22–25)
22b	וְאַל־תָּבוּז כִּי־זָקְנָה אִמֶּךָ	and do not despise your mother when she grows old.	
23a	אֱמֶת קְנֵה וְאַל־תִּמְכֹּר	Buy truth, and do not sell it;	
23b	חָכְמָה וּמוּסָר וּבִינָה	wisdom and discipline and understanding.	
24a	גִּיל יָגִיל אֲבִי צַדִּיק	The father of a righteous son will greatly exult;	
24b	וְיוֹלֵד חָכָם יִשְׂמַח־בּוֹ	one who begets a wise son will rejoice in him.	
25a	יִשְׂמַח־אָבִיךָ וְאִמֶּךָ	Your father and your mother will rejoice,	
25b	וְתָגֵל יוֹלַדְתֶּךָ	and she who bore you will exult.	
26a	תְּנָה־בְנִי לִבְּךָ לִי	Give me, my son, your heart,	17. Saying 17 (23:26–28)
26b	וְעֵינֶיךָ דְּרָכַי תִּצֹּרְנָה	and let your eyes observe my ways,	
27a	↑ כִּי־שׁוּחָה עֲמֻקָּה זוֹנָה	↑ for a deep pit, a harlot,	
27b	↓ וּבְאֵר צָרָה נָכְרִיָּה	↓ and a narrow well, a strange woman.	
28a	אַף־הִיא כְּחֶתֶף תֶּאֱרֹב	Surely, she lies in wait like a bandit,	
28b	וּבוֹגְדִים בְּאָדָם תּוֹסִף	and increases traitors among men.	
29a	לְמִי אוֹי לְמִי אֲבוֹי	Who cries "Alas"? Who cries "Woe"?	18. Saying 18 (23:29–35)
29b	לְמִי מִדְיָנִים לְמִי שִׂיחַ	Who has strife? Who has complaints?	
29c	לְמִי פְּצָעִים חִנָּם	Who has wounds for no reason?	
29d	לְמִי חַכְלִלוּת עֵינָיִם	Who has bloodshot eyes?	

30a	לַמְאַחֲרִים עַל־הַיָּיִן	Those who linger over wine,	
30b	לַבָּאִים לַחְקֹר מִמְסָךְ	those who come to taste mixed wine.	
31a	אַל־תֵּרֶא יַיִן כִּי יִתְאַדָּם	Do not look at wine when it sparkles red,	
31b	↑ כִּי־יִתֵּן בַּכּוֹס עֵינוֹ	↑ when it shines in the cup,	
31c	יִתְהַלֵּךְ בְּמֵישָׁרִים	going down smoothly.	
32a	אַחֲרִיתוֹ כְּנָחָשׁ יִשָּׁךְ	In the end, it bites like a serpent,	
32b	וּכְצִפְעֹנִי יַפְרִשׁ	and it stings like an adder.	
33a	עֵינֶיךָ יִרְאוּ זָרוֹת	Your eyes will see strange things,	
33b	וְלִבְּךָ יְדַבֵּר תַּהְפֻּכוֹת	and your heart will utter perverse things.	
34a	וְהָיִיתָ כְּשֹׁכֵב בְּלֶב־יָם	And you will be like one who lies down in the heart of the sea,	
34b	↑ וּכְשֹׁכֵב בְּרֹאשׁ חִבֵּל	↑ even like one who lies at the top of a mast.	
35a	הִכּוּנִי בַל־חָלִיתִי	"They struck me – I feel no pain,	
35b	הֲלָמוּנִי בַּל־יָדָעְתִּי	they beat me – I did not know it.	
35c	מָתַי אָקִיץ	When shall I awake?	
35d	אוֹסִיף אֲבַקְשֶׁנּוּ עוֹד	I'll continue seeking it."	
24:1a	אַל־תְּקַנֵּא בְּאַנְשֵׁי רָעָה	Do not envy evil people,	19. Saying 19 (24:1–2)
24:1b	וְאַל־תִּתְאָיו לִהְיוֹת אִתָּם	nor desire to be with them,	
2a	↑ כִּי־שֹׁד יֶהְגֶּה לִבָּם	↑ for their heart ponders destruction,	
2b	וְעָמָל שִׂפְתֵיהֶם תְּדַבֵּרְנָה	and their lips speak mischief.	
3a	בְּחָכְמָה יִבָּנֶה בָּיִת	By wisdom a house is built,	20. Saying 20 (24:3–4)
3b	וּבִתְבוּנָה יִתְכּוֹנָן	and by understanding it is established;	
4a	וּבְדַעַת חֲדָרִים יִמָּלְאוּ	and by knowledge rooms are filled	
4b	↑ כָּל־הוֹן יָקָר וְנָעִים	↑ with all wealth, precious and pleasant.	
5a	גֶּבֶר־חָכָם בַּעוֹז	A wise man – strength,	21. Saying 21 (24:5–6)
5b	וְאִישׁ־דַּעַת מְאַמֶּץ־כֹּחַ	and a person of knowledge grows in power.	
6a	כִּי בְתַחְבֻּלוֹת תַּעֲשֶׂה־לְּךָ מִלְחָמָה	For by guidance you should wage war,	
6b	וּתְשׁוּעָה בְּרֹב יוֹעֵץ	and with many counselors, victory.	
7a	רָאמוֹת לֶאֱוִיל חָכְמוֹת	Wisdom, too high for a fool;	22. Saying 22 (24:7)
7b	בַּשַּׁעַר לֹא יִפְתַּח־פִּיהוּ	at the gate he cannot open his mouth.	
8a	מְחַשֵּׁב לְהָרֵעַ לוֹ	The one who plans to do evil—	23. Saying 23 (24:8–9)
8b	בַּעַל־מְזִמּוֹת יִקְרָאוּ	he will be called a master of schemes.	

Continued on next page.

Continued from previous page.

9a	זִמַּת אִוֶּלֶת חַטָּאת	Foolish scheming, sin;	23. Saying 23 (24:8–9) *cont.*
9b	וְתוֹעֲבַת לְאָדָם לֵץ	and an abomination to a person, a scoffer.	
10a	↓ הִתְרַפִּיתָ בְּיוֹם צָרָה	↓ If you show yourself lax in the day of distress,	24. Saying 24 (24:10)
10b	צַר כֹּחֶכָה	your strength, meager.	
11a	הַצֵּל לְקֻחִים לַמָּוֶת	Deliver those who are being taken away to death,	25. Saying 25 (24:11–12)
11b	וּמָטִים לַהֶרֶג אִם־תַּחְשׂוֹךְ	and those stumbling to slaughter do not refrain from sparing.	
12a	↓ כִּי־תֹאמַר הֵן לֹא־יָדַעְנוּ זֶה	↓ If you say, "We did not know about this,"	
12b	הֲלֹא־תֹכֵן לִבּוֹת הוּא־יָבִין	does not he who weighs hearts perceive it?	
12c	וְנֹצֵר נַפְשְׁךָ הוּא יֵדָע	Does not he who guards your life know?	
12d	וְהֵשִׁיב לְאָדָם כְּפָעֳלוֹ	And will he not repay a person according to his deed?	
13a	אֱכָל־בְּנִי דְבַשׁ כִּי־טוֹב	Eat honey, my son, because it is good,	26. Saying 26 (24:13–14)
13b	וְנֹפֶת מָתוֹק עַל־חִכֶּךָ	and honeycomb, sweet upon your palate.	
14a	כֵּן דְּעֶה חָכְמָה לְנַפְשֶׁךָ	So know wisdom is such for your life.	
14b	אִם־מָצָאתָ וְיֵשׁ אַחֲרִית	If you find it, there is a future,	
14c	וְתִקְוָתְךָ לֹא תִכָּרֵת	and your hope shall not be cut off.	
15a	אַל־תֶּאֱרֹב רָשָׁע לִנְוֵה צַדִּיק	Do not lie in wait as a wicked person against the dwelling of the righteous;	27. Saying 27 (24:15–16)
15b	אַל־תְּשַׁדֵּד רִבְצוֹ	do not destroy his resting place;	
16a	כִּי שֶׁבַע יִפּוֹל צַדִּיק וָקָם	though the righteous may fall seven times, he will rise;	
16b	וּרְשָׁעִים יִכָּשְׁלוּ בְרָעָה	while the wicked will stumble in evil.	
17a	בִּנְפֹל אוֹיִבְךָ אַל־תִּשְׂמָח	When your enemy falls, do not rejoice,	28. Saying 28 (24:17–18)
17b	וּבִכָּשְׁלוֹ אַל־יָגֵל לִבֶּךָ	and when he stumbles, do not let your heart exult;	
18a	↑ פֶּן־יִרְאֶה יְהוָה וְרַע בְּעֵינָיו	↑ lest YHWH see and it will be evil in his sight,	
18b	וְהֵשִׁיב מֵעָלָיו אַפּוֹ	and turn his anger away from him.	
19a	אַל־תִּתְחַר בַּמְּרֵעִים	Do not fret at evildoers,	29. Saying 29 (24:19–20)
19b	אַל־תְּקַנֵּא בָּרְשָׁעִים	nor envy the wicked,	
20a	↑ כִּי לֹא־תִהְיֶה אַחֲרִית לָרָע	↑ for there is no future for the evil,	
20b	נֵר רְשָׁעִים יִדְעָךְ	the lamp of the wicked will be extinguished.	
21a	יְרָא־אֶת־יְהוָה בְּנִי וָמֶלֶךְ	Fear YHWH, my son, and the king.	30. Saying 30 (24:21–22)
21b	עִם־שׁוֹנִים אַל־תִּתְעָרָב	Do not disobey either of them.	
22a	↑ כִּי־פִתְאֹם יָקוּם אֵידָם	↑ For their ruin will arise suddenly,	
22b	וּפִיד שְׁנֵיהֶם מִי יוֹדֵעַ	and the destruction of them both – who knows?	

Structure and Literary Form

The form of the materials in the "words of the wise" confirm its pedagogical agenda and bear witness to its concern with moral motivation. Admonitions cast in the form of אַל + jussive predominate, proscribing certain forms of behavior (22:22, 24, 26, 28; 23:3a, 4a, 6, 9a, 10, 13a, 17a, 20, 31; 24:1, 15, 17, 19, 21b). And imperatives introduce exhortations as well as renewed calls to attention, which cultivate a posture of receptivity (22:17a; 23:12, 19, 22a, 26a). Whether cast in the form of an admonition or exhortation, the vast majority of sayings are modified by a clause that motivates the moral life. These subordinate clauses take different forms, ranging from causal and conditional clauses to interrogatives (22:23, 27; 23:3b, 5b–c, 7a, 9b, 11, 13b, 21, 27; 24:2, 6, 12a, 13a, 14b, 20, 22). The variety of motivational techniques, combined with the use of direct address, rhetorical questions (22:29; 23:5a, 29; 24:12b–d, 22b), and aphoristic sayings (24:3–4, 7–10), illuminates the ethos of the collection. The materials inspire trust in YHWH and trustworthy speech through the rhetoric of prohibition and prescription.

The general homogeneity of form coincides with general agreement regarding the structure of the "words of the wise." In light of the similarities between Prov 22:17–23:11 and the Instruction of Amenemope, most interpreters emend the MT's unusual "previously" (שִׁלְשׁוֹם; *ketiv*) or "noble things" (שָׁלִישִׁים; *qere*) in Prov 22:20 to "thirty [sayings]" (שְׁלֹשִׁים), a number that mirrors the thirty chapters of the Egyptian instructional text.[6] While there remains no consensus regarding the precise numbering of these thirty sayings, it is striking that, even before E. A. W. Budge's publication of the Instruction of Amenemope as well as Erman's and Gressmann's rendering of Prov 22:20 as "thirty,"[7] some commentators divided the text into approximately thirty sayings.[8] The emendation, combined with the syntactical design of the collection's exordium (22:17–21), provide a window into its nature and structure. The collection consists of the "words of the wise" (דִּבְרֵי חֲכָמִים; 22:17a), which were adapted by an author/editor ("my knowledge," דַּעְתִּי; 22:17b) and cast in the form of "thirty sayings"

6. Cf. the LXX's rendering "three times" (τρισσῶς). As Emerton notes, the emendation is minor; it replaces consonants that were indistinguishable in certain manuscripts, viz., the *waw* of the *ketiv* with a *yod*. John A. Emerton, "The Teaching of Amenemope and Proverbs XXII 17–XXIV 22: Reflections on a Long-Standing Problem," *VT* 51 (2001): 431–65, esp. 452.

7. E. A. W. Budge, *Facsimiles of Egyptian Hieratic Papyri in the British Museum, Second Series* (London: British Museum, 1923); Adolf Erman, "Eine ägyptische Quelle der 'Spruch Salomos,' SPAW 15 (1924): 86–93; Hugo Gressmann, "Die neugefundene Lehre des Amen-em-ope und die vorexilische Spruchdichtung Israels," *ZAW* 42 (1924): 272–94. With few exceptions, the majority of scholars have followed Erman's and Gressmann's rendering. Cf. Thierry Maire, "Proverbes XXII 17ss: Enseignement à Shalishom?," *VT* 45 (1995): 227–38, who, following the conventional pattern of introductions to instructional texts, reads שָׁלִישׁוֹם as the name of the addressee.

8. Delitzsch, for example, commented on the text in thirty-two groups, including the introduction (22:17–21); and Toy discussed the sayings in the collection under thirty-one headings, including the introduction. See Delitzsch, "Proverbs of Solomon," 6:330–59 (2:95–140); Toy, *Proverbs*, 422–51.

(שְׁלִשִׁים; 22:20a) in order to inspire trust in YHWH and to teach words of truth (22:19a, 21a) so as to form the reader into a reliable speaker (22:23b).

From a macrostructural perspective, the "words of the wise" include thirty sayings. These sayings are marked off by the subtitles "words of the wise" (דִּבְרֵי חֲכָמִים; 22:17a) and "These also are of/to the wise" (גַּם־אֵלֶּה לַחֲכָמִים; 24:23), and they are framed by the expressions "in order that your trust may be in YHWH" (לִהְיוֹת בַּיהוָה מִבְטַחֶךָ; 22:19a) and "fear YHWH" (יְרָא־אֶת־יְהוָה; 24:21a).[9] Within this frame, most divide the "words of the wise" into two subcollections: Prov 22:17–23:11 and 23:12–24:22. As noted above, the former exhibits a close relationship with the Instruction of Amenemope. The latter, by contrast, evinces a more general relationship with ancient Near Eastern instructional texts.[10] In addition to comparative evidence, formal and thematic features support the boundaries and illuminate the structural contours of these subcollections. The repetition of "he will contest their case" (יָרִיב רִיבָם; 22:23a; 23:11b) reinforces the conclusion that 22:17–23:11 constitutes the initial subcollection within the "sayings of the wise." The second subcollection opens with a renewed call to attention that recycles key terms from the collection's introduction (23:12; 22:17). Despite the repeated calls to attention within the subcollection (23:19, 22, 26), many divide it into two parts. The first is defined by its persistent concern with discipline and forms of debauchery (23:12–23:35), whereas the second may represent a non-alphabetic acrostic, focusing on the fate of the wicked (24:1–22).[11]

Explanation of the Text

1. Formal Introduction: Saying 1 (22:17–21)[12]

The collection opens with a formal introduction reminiscent of the exordia that initiate the parental lectures in Prov 1:8–9:18. This introduction consists of three parts: (1) an exhortation, complete with a motivation (vv. 17–18); (2) a declaration of the purpose of the "words of the wise" (v. 19); and (3) a rhetorical question modified by a description of an additional purpose of the materials and their intended result (vv. 20–21).

9. Waltke, *Proverbs: Chapters 1–15*, 22.

10. Harold C. Washington, *Wealth and Poverty in the Instruction of Amenemope and the Hebrew Proverbs*, SBLDS 142 (Atlanta: Scholars Press, 1994), 135–45; Nili Shupak, "The Instruction of Amenemope and Proverbs 22:17–24:22 from the Perspective of Contemporary Research," in *Seeking Out the Wisdom of the Ancients: Essays Offered to Honor Michael V. Fox on the Occasion of his Sixty-Fifth Birthday*, ed. R. L. Troxel, K. G. Friebel, and D. R. Magary (Winona Lake, IN: Eisenbrauns, 2005), 203–20.

11. Meinhold, *Die Sprüche*, 2:374; Clifford, *Proverbs*, 199; Fox, *Proverbs 10–31*, 735, 743; Sæbø, *Sprüche*, 277. For comparable structural proposals, see Diethard Römheld, *Wege der Weisheit: Die Lehren Amenemopes und Proverbien 22,17–24,22*, BZAW 184 (Berlin: de Gruyter, 1989); Waltke, *Proverbs: Chapters 15–31*, 246, 249, 270, 280.

12. While some do not include the formal introduction in their enumeration of the thirty sayings (e.g., McKane, *Proverbs*, 372), the similarities between the introduction and the first chapter of Amenemope suggest that it represents the first saying. "The Instruction of Amenemope" (*AEL* 2:149); Glendon E. Bryce, *A Legacy of Wisdom: The Egyptian Contribution to the Wisdom of Israel* (Lewisburg: Bucknell University Press, 1979), 101–2; Waltke, *Proverbs: Chapters 1–15*, 22–23; Fox, *Proverbs 10–31*, 711.

a. Exhortation and Motivation (22:17–18)

Against the expansive backdrop of individual aphorisms (10:1–22:16), 22:17–18 marks a formal, pedagogical, and compositional shift in the anthology. Direct address replaces indicative sayings. The reader moves from the position of observer and interpreter to that of a receptive student. And having digested "the proverbs of Solomon" (10:1a), the reader is served a new compositional dish: "the words of the wise" (22:17a).

With language redolent of the exordia to the instructions in 1:8–9:18, 22:17 awakens the attention of the reader. The call to "incline your ear" (הַט אָזְנְךָ, v. 17a) and "direct your heart" (לִבְּךָ תָּשִׁית, v. 17b) seeks to cultivate a receptive posture, according to which one's external and internal faculties are open and attuned to the materials that follow (cf. 4:20, 21; 5:1, 13; 6:21; 7:3). These materials are characterized as "the words of the wise" (דִּבְרֵי חֲכָמִים, v. 17a).[13] They are teachings drawn from ancient Near Eastern and Israelite wisdom that the speaker has adapted to suit the purposes of the collection (לְדַעְתִּי, "my knowledge," v. 17b). The nature of this adaptation is apparent in v. 18, which offers a rationale and motivation for receiving the words of the wise (כִּי, "for," v. 18a). Modifying the conventional Egyptian metaphor "casket of the belly,"[14] the speaker appeals to the aesthetic benefits associated with storing these words "in your belly" (בְּבִטְנֶךָ, v. 18a) and securing them "on your lips" (עַל־שְׂפָתֶיךָ, v. 18b): delight. The internal and external conditions of this delight mirror the internal and external requirements of the exhortation. One with a receptive ear and an attentive heart that stores the words of the wise in the belly of their being and readies them for redeployment on their lips will embody and reflect the beauty of a wise life.

b. The Theological Purpose of the "Words of the Wise" (22:19)

The beauty and delight that accompanies the assimilation of the words of the wise accords with the theological purpose of the collection. This purpose is expressed in v. 19 through emphatic word order. The subordinate purpose clause is foregrounded, indicating that the collection seeks to inspire trust in YHWH (v. 19a). This attitudinal and relational goal is infused with immediacy in the main clause. The use of the performative perfect signals that the speaker executes the act of teaching through the reading of the text (v. 19b). The temporal modifier "today" (הַיּוֹם, v. 19b) marks the "emphatic contemporaneity" of this teaching;[15] it is delivered here and now. And the reference to "you," followed by the emphatic phrase "even you" (אַף־אָתָּה, v. 19b), places the reader in the position of addressee. The theological purpose of the collection's teaching transcends the circumstances of its original composition. The act of cultivating a disposition of trust in YHWH is performed whenever one reads or hears this teaching and assumes the mantle of "you."

c. The Formational Purpose and Result of the "Words of the Wise" (22:20–21)

In addition to the theological purpose of the collection, vv. 20–21 describe the formational

13. In light of Prov 24:23a and in accord with the LXX, many emend the MT and read "words of the wise" as a formal title to the collection that is syntactically independent from 22:17. The emendation is possible but unnecessary for two reasons. First, the MT makes sense as it stands. Second, the subtitle in Prov 24:23a does not require a syntactically independent subtitle in 22:17a. The latter may refer to the embedded expression in 22:17a, which clearly introduces a new unit. Luc, "The Titles and Structure of Proverbs," 252–53; Waltke, *Proverbs: Chapters 15–31*, 217–18n106.

14. Whereas the heart serves as the essence of one's innermost being within Hebrew thought, the belly represents one's innermost being in Egyptian thought. For discussion, see Shupak, *Where Can Wisdom Be Found?*, 293–97.

15. The expression "emphatic contemporaneity" is taken from von Rad, *The Problem of the Hexateuch*, 29.

purpose and the intended result of the words of the wise. This purpose and result are governed by a rhetorical question in v. 20. The question expresses certainty. More specifically, it gives the assurance that the author/speaker has composed a document, consisting of "thirty sayings" (שְׁלִשִׁים, v. 20a)[16] to serve "as counsel and knowledge" (בְּמוֹעֵצֹת וָדָעַת, v. 20b).[17] This assurance is qualified by the initial line of v. 21, which expresses the purpose of the composition in emphatic fashion. Reiterating the root from the main clause of v. 19, the sayings were composed "to teach you truth" (לְהוֹדִיעֲךָ קֹשְׁטְ-, v. 21a). The addition of the genitive "words of truth" (אִמְרֵי אֱמֶת, v. 21a) suggests that the clause functions as a quasi-superlative. The sayings were designed to teach "the most honest words of truth."[18] And the intended result of this teaching is articulated in v. 21b: "so as to bring back true reports to those who send you" (לְהָשִׁיב אֲמָרִים אֱמֶת לְשֹׁלְחֶיךָ, v. 21b). While the identity of "those who send you" is ambiguous, it appears that these true words are designed to produce trustworthy speakers. When this purpose and intended result are read together with the theological goal of the collection (v. 19), the words of the wise seek to inculcate trust in YHWH and to teach the most truthful words so as to produce trustworthy speakers. Trust and truth—the brick and mortar of the wise life—are the materials employed to construct reliable representatives.

2. Saying 2 (22:22–23)

Whereas the formal introduction resembles the first chapter of Amenemope, the second saying resembles the subject matter of the second chapter of the Egyptian instruction, namely, oppression of the vulnerable.[19] Similar to many of the sayings within the words of the wise, the maxim moves from an admonition to a motivation. The admonition is expressed through a pair of אַל + jussives (v. 22). Together, they prohibit particular forms of oppression through intensification. Stealing the property of the poor because of their socioeconomic vulnerability is specified and intensified in the second line as crushing the needy in the communal court of law. These prohibitions are qualified by a causal clause (כִּי, "for," v. 23a), which supplies a self-interested theological motivation. YHWH is depicted as the personal advocate of the vulnerable. As the advocate of the poor and needy, YHWH "will contest their case" (יָרִיב רִיבָם, v. 23a) and "snatch the life of those who snatch from them" (קָבַע אֶת־קֹבְעֵיהֶם נָפֶשׁ, v. 23b). The repetition of lexical roots in the individual lines of v. 23 creates the impression of even-handed, retributive justice. The punishment, however, exceeds the crime. Those who exploit the vulnerable will face their divine advocate, who will steal or despoil the lives of oppressors (cf. 14:31; 17:5). The causal clause describes YHWH's personal involvement on behalf of the needy and severe punishment of the powerful in order to rein in the potential exploitation of power through an appeal to one's desire for self-preservation.

3. Saying 3 (22:24–25)

Self-preservation and safety also serve as the motivational bait of the third saying. Like the previous saying, the maxim moves from an admonition to a

16. For discussion of the reading, see Structure and Literary Form above. Also see, Waltke, *Proverbs: Chapters 15–31*, 219–20n113; Fox, *Proverbs 10–31*, 710–12.

17. For the בְּ of identity or *essentiæ*, see *IBHS* §11.2.5e.

18. Fox, *Proverbs 10–31*, 712.

19. "The Instruction of Amenemope" (*AEL* 2:150).

motivation. The admonition prohibits consorting with those characterized by anger;[20] it assumes that one's character is shaped by the company one keeps (cf. 13:20; 16:29).[21] This assumption is confirmed in v. 25, which is cast in the form of a negative purpose clause (פֶּן, "lest," v. 25a). One who hangs around with a hothead will become influenced by his example, trained by his ways, and entangled in his fate (v. 25). The negative purpose clause appeals to one's desire for safety by sketching the consequences of associating with a hothead.

4. Saying 4 (22:26–27)

Safety and security also animate the advice of the fourth saying, which contributes to Proverbs's discourse on the dangers involved in standing surety (cf. 6:1–5; 11:15; 17:18; 20:16). Similar to the previous saying, the maxim opens with an admonition pertaining to the company one keeps; it prohibits consorting with "those who seal a deal" (בְתֹקְעֵי־כָף, v. 26a) or, more specifically, with "those who guarantee a loan" (בַּעֹרְבִים מַשָּׁאוֹת, v. 26b). Following the pattern of the previous sayings, v. 27 supplies the motivation. The syntax of the motivation, however, differs from the previous sayings. The initial line is cast in the form of a conditional protasis (אִם, "if," v. 27a) describing the economic state of the reader who has been written into the saying. In light of the fact that "you" do not have the financial resources to serve as the guarantor of the loan (v. 27a), "your bed" (מִשְׁכָּבְךָ, v. 27b) is at risk of confiscation as collateral (v. 27b). While the apodosis is a question, the interrogative pronoun functions in a manner comparable to the particle that marks a negative purpose clause (i.e., פֶּן, "lest").[22] In contrast to covenant regulations that protected the garments of debtors (Exod 22:25–26), guarantors are not offered comparable protections. The motivation arouses one's desire for security and comfort by threatening the ground in exchange for a bed.

5. Saying 5 (22:28)

Just as the risks involved in serving as a guarantor gestured to covenant regulations pertaining to loans, so the concern with boundary markers in the fifth saying recalls covenant regulations prohibiting their displacement (Deut 19:14; 27:17; cf. Prov 23:10).[23] While the saying does not include a marked motive clause, the rationale for the admonition is latent in the language of the maxim. The admonition describes the boundary of one's ancestral allotment as "ancient" (עוֹלָם, 22:28a), and the relative clause qualifies this ancient boundary as one established by "your ancestors" (אֲבוֹתֶיךָ, v. 28b). The appeal to ancestral precedent links the boundary of one's property to the past. To displace this boundary is more than an abuse of power; it constitutes a shameful break with the parameters, history, and tradition of a family's very basis of security.

6. Saying 6 (22:29)

Whereas the fifth saying traffics in shame, the sixth traffics in the prospect of honor and success. The maxim breaks the sequence of admonitions

20. The "heated man" figures prominently in Amenemope. "The Instruction of Amenemope" (*AEL* 2:153–55).

21. Yoder, *Proverbs*, 232; Fox, *Proverbs 10–31*, 717.

22. Fox, *Proverbs 10–31*, 718.

23. Also see "The Instruction of Amenemope" (*AEL* 2:151).

through an unmarked interrogative "have you seen?" (חָזִיתָ, 22:29a; cf. 26:12; 29:20). The question compels the reader to identify a paradigmatic person skilled in his/her work and to measure oneself against that person. But before the reader can respond, the speaker describes the social position and success of such a proficient person through a pair of main clauses, the first positive and the second negative. The placement of the prepositional phrase "before kings" (לִפְנֵי־מְלָכִים, v. 29b) in the initial position of v. 29b highlights the honorable place of the proficient. This person will serve or stand before kings (v. 29b), not before the "obscure" (חֲשֻׁכִּים, v. 29c). The saying presents the employment path of the proficient and, in so doing, motivates the reader to emulate and pursue such skill through the expectation of social honor and success.

7. Saying 7 (23:1–3)

Matters of honor, shame, and one's social position are explored further in the seventh saying, which deals with dining etiquette.[24] The initial line of the maxim sets the scene through a subordinate temporal clause (כִּי, "when," v. 1a). The reader is positioned at the table of a "ruler" (מוֹשֵׁל, v. 1a), one who occupies an ambiguous administrative post. This occasion calls for discretion and restraint. Both are prescribed through the main clauses in vv. 1b and 2a. The former is conveyed through the injunction to "look carefully" (בִּין תָּבִין, v. 1b) at what one is served, while the latter is expressed through the metaphor "put a knife to your throat" (שַׂמְתָּ שַׂכִּין בְּלֹעֶךָ, v. 2a). This striking metaphor for self-restraint is directed specifically to one with an insatiable appetite (v. 2b). Rather than succumbing to overindulgence, this person is to curb their voracious desire by slitting their throat. Whether or not one is prone to intemperance, the admonition and rationale delivered in v. 3 capture the speaker's counsel regarding dining etiquette. And this counsel concerns desire. When discretion restrains desire, the ruler's delicacies may be perceived for what they are: "deceptive food" (לֶחֶם כְּזָבִים, v. 3b), that is, food that reveals the nature of one's desires and the essence of one's character. Far from merely offering advice concerning table etiquette, the saying nurtures discretion and restraint by appealing to the prospect of social shame, on the one hand, and advancement, on the other.

8. Saying 8 (23:4–5)

The themes of restraint and appropriate limits are redeployed in the eighth saying and applied to work and wealth. The saying opens with a pair of admonitions. The first constrains the exertion of physical effort in order to attain riches (v. 4a), whereas the second appears to rein in the belief that one can secure wealth by means of their intellectual prowess alone (v. 4b). These physical and intellectual forms of overreaching for wealth are relativized through the question, answer, and rationale of v. 5, which emphasizes the ephemeral nature of riches. Similar to v. 29a, the reader is positioned in the question: Will *you* let *your* eyes fly to riches (v. 5a)? The one-word answer in Hebrew—"It is no more" (וְאֵינֶנּוּ, v. 5a)—is sharp. And the graphic rationale for the evanescence of riches extends and fills the semantic space opened by the verb "fly" (תָּעִיף, v. 5a). Riches will sprout

24. This etiquette is comparable to the advice offered in several ancient Near Eastern instructional texts. "The Instruction Addressed to Kagemni" (*AEL* 1:59–60); "The Instruction of Ptahhotep" (*AEL* 1:65); "The Instruction of Amenemope" (*AEL* 2:160).

wings, dart away, and disappear into the horizon because overhastiness has failed to provide a secure anchor for their possession.[25] When the saying is read together with aphorisms that commend diligence (10:4; 12:24, 27; 14:23), it appears to place the virtue of industriousness between the extremes of laziness and overwork. In so doing, it maps the appropriate limits of work and the pursuit of wealth by appealing to self-preservation.

9. Saying 9 (23:6–8)[26]

The ninth saying reiterates the virtues of discretion and restraint at the table, recontextualizing the advice delineated in the seventh saying (23:1–3). Again, the reader is prohibited from desiring delicacies (v. 6b; cf. v. 3a); but these delicacies are the fare of the "stingy person" (רַע עָיִן, v. 6a).[27] The character of the host explains the pair of admonitions in v. 6, and the causal clause in v. 7 provides the rationale for these admonitions (כִּי, "for," v. 7a). The rationale is rooted in the hypocritical character of the host. The stingy is characterized as one who "calculates within himself" (שָׁעַר בְּנַפְשׁוֹ, v. 7a),[28] producing a financial record of the delicacies ingested. In accord with social protocol, he invites the reader to "eat and drink" (אֱכֹל וּשְׁתֵה, v. 7b). His internal disposition, however, is repulsed by the companionship and consumption of his guest (v. 7c). This disgust extends beyond the disposition of the host; it also captures the sentiment of the reader seated at the table of the stingy. If one ignores the admonition "do not eat" (אַל־תִּלְחַם, v. 6a) and accepts the stingy one's invitation to "eat" (אֱכֹל, v. 7b; אָכַלְתָּ, v. 8a), then even pleasant words will be wasted around the table, for one will be unable to keep down their disgust. The delicacies and dialogue will perpetuate a feeling of nausea shared by both the host and the guest. This unpleasant feeling, combined with the desire for self-preservation, serves as a powerful motivation to refrain from dining with a miser.

10. Saying 10 (23:9)

Just as words are wasted at the table of the stingy (v. 8b), so also the tenth saying assumes that words are wasted on the fool (v. 9a). Similar to many of the previous sayings, the maxim moves from an admonition to a rationale. The admonition sits in tension with 26:4, for it proscribes speaking urgently and directly to a fool (23:9a). This is not a universal rule for the wise. When read in conversation with other aphorisms pertaining to speech, the admonition requires one to interpret specific situations so as to determine whether to speak, how to speak, and with whom to speak. And when the admonition is read in light of the causal clause in v. 9b, it appears that speaking to a fool is not the point of the saying. The point is to shape the

25. For a comparable image of the ephemerality of wealth, see "The Instruction of Amenemope" (*AEL* 2:152–53).

26. The theme of dining with nefarious characters as well as the language of the saying are reflected in several ancient Near Eastern instructional texts. "The Instruction Addressed to Kagemni" (*AEL* 1:60); "The Instruction of Any" (*AEL* 2:142); "The Instruction of Amenemope" (*AEL* 2:154–55).

27. The expression "evil of eye" (רַע עָיִן, v. 6a) denotes a stingy person, just as the expression "good of eye" (טוֹב־עַיִן; 22:9a) denotes a generous person.

28. Rather than rendering שָׁעַר בְּנַפְשׁוֹ as "he calculated in himself" or repointing the verb to read "one who calculates within himself," many render בְּנַפְשׁוֹ as "his throat" and, following the LXX, read the *hapax legomenon* שׁער as "hair." This produces the sense "for it is like a hair in his throat." This reading may explain why the miser's food engenders vomiting in v. 8a. But it fails to account for the fact that the pronominal suffix "his" in v. 7a refers to the stingy, not the reader. Since the reading does not explain the reader's vomiting in v. 8a, it is better to understand this vomiting as a metaphor of disgust and to retain the translation above. Fox, *Proverbs 10–31*, 726–27.

expectations of the reader by describing the typical response of the fool. Since fools do not possess a receptive posture, it is not surprising that they will "despise" (יָבוּז, v. 9b; cf. 1:7) even insightful words. The rationale sketches the disposition and desire of fools. In so doing, it identifies the expected perlocutionary effect of one's words and provides another perspective from which to determine whether one should speak to a fool.

11. Saying 11 (23:10–11)

The eleventh saying recycles lines and expressions from previous materials in the collection to develop the displacement of boundary markers (**23:10a**//22:28) and YHWH's personal involvement on behalf of the vulnerable (**23:11b**//22:23). Following the pattern of previous sayings, it consists of an admonition as well as motivation. The first admonition (23:10a) reiterates 22:28a. The second extends this admonition; it moves away from history and tradition (22:28b) to encroachment on the fields of orphans (23:10b). This class of marginalized people was particularly vulnerable. In the absence of a human protector, they were a target of exploitation (Deut 24:17; Jer 7:6; Ezek 22:7). Taken together, the admonitions in Prov 23:10 create the social context for the rationale and motivation in v. 11 (כִּי, "for," v. 11a). In light of the fact that the orphan lacks a human protector, YHWH assumes the familial role of "redeemer" (גֹּאֲלָם, v. 11a). In accord with the responsibilities of the redeemer (Lev 25:25), he acts to recover the extent of the patrimonial land. And he accomplishes this through judicial prowess, demonstrating his strength by contesting "their case with you" (אֶת־רִיבָם אִתָּךְ, Prov 23:11b; cf. 22:23a). Similar to many of the sayings, the reader is written into the maxim (23:11b). Those who wish to wield their power by encroaching on the land of the marginalized must contest with YHWH. The motivation not only highlights YHWH's familial relationship with and personal involvement on behalf of the weak; it also reins in the potential exploitation of power by appealing to one's desire for safety and security.

12. Saying 12 (23:12–14)

In light of the renewed call to attention in v. 12 and the fact that the remaining materials within the "words of the wise" do not exhibit a close relationship with the Instruction of Amenemope, it appears that the twelfth saying opens a new subcollection. The renewed call to attention may be treated as a discrete saying.[29] The concern with education and the repetition of the term "discipline" (מוּסָר, vv. 12a, 13a), however, suggest that vv. 12–14 should be read together. When taken together, the exhortations and admonition situate the reader in different subject positions.

The introductory exhortation reiterates the expressions "your heart" (לִבֶּךָ, v. 12a) and "your ear" (אָזְנֶךָ, v. 12b) from 22:17, renewing within the reader a posture of receptivity to discipline and knowledgeable words. The admonition that follows shifts the reader's subject position from that of receptive student to disciplinarian (23: 13a). The one who received discipline is admonished to dispense it. The rationale for dispensing discipline is cast in the form of a conditional clause (כִּי, "if," v. 13b). Discipline is conceptualized as a physical, tactile act that produces pain and drives out folly from

29. McKane, *Proverbs*, 385; Waltke, *Proverbs: Chapters 15–31*, 251.

the youth.[30] On an initial reading, the apodosis appears to motivate corporal punishment with the promise that the rod will not harm the youth. The exhortation in v. 14, however, reconfigures death in terms of deeds that lead to death.[31] Moving from a condition (כִּי־תַכֶּנּוּ בַשֵּׁבֶט, "if you strike him with a rod," v. 13b) to an obligation, the speaker exhorts the reader to "strike him with a rod" (אַתָּה בַּשֵּׁבֶט תַּכֶּנּוּ, v. 14a) so as to save the youth's life. The promise of life motivates the practice and situates the pain of discipline in proper perspective.[32]

13. Saying 13 (23:15–16)

The pain of discipline is transformed into a parent's joy over a wise son in the thirteenth saying. Parental pleasure animates the maxim, and the emotional bond between parent and son is established through the body parts of each. The saying is framed by subordinate clauses, which describe the desired condition of the son's character. The first condition is a heart that becomes wise (v. 15a); the second are lips that speak what is upright (v. 16b). The condition of these body parts triggers a chain reaction in the parent's body. This reaction is expressed through a pair of main clauses in the middle of the saying (vv. 15b, 16a). If the son's heart becomes wise, then the parent's heart will rejoice (v. 15b). And when the son's lips speak what is upright, the inner life or "kidneys" (כִלְיוֹתָי, v. 16a) of the parent will exalt. The saying links the character of the son with the emotional well-being of the parent, motivating the wise life through the natural desire to please one's father.

14. Saying 14 (23:17–18)

Proper desire is the focus of attention in the admonitions that open the fourteenth saying. These admonitions seek to direct one's desire away from sinners to those who fear YHWH. The first admonition assumes that the prosperity of sinners is a powerful advertisement for an alternative form of life. The prohibition focuses on the heart, censuring a desire for the lifestyle and rewards of sinners. While the second admonition does not include a verb, "envy" (יְקַנֵּא, v. 17a) from the first seems to be implied. When read with the expression "those who fear YHWH every day" (בְּיִרְאַת־יְהוָה כָּל־הַיּוֹם, v. 17b),[33] the verb takes the positive sense of zeal.[34] Rather than envying sinners, the reader is exhorted to be zealous for Godfearers. The rationale for this zeal is introduced by the asseverative "surely" (כִּי אִם, v. 18a),[35] which expresses the certain future and hope that accompanies those who fear YHWH. The confident future of God fearers places the presumed prosperity of sinners into perspective and motivates proper zeal through the promise of life.

15. Saying 15 (23:19–21)

Coveting the prosperity of sinners serves as an appropriate backdrop to the fifteenth saying and its consideration of consorting with the self-indulgent. The saying opens with the emphatic, renewed call to attention: "you yourself listen, my son" (שְׁמַע־אַתָּה בְנִי, v. 19a). This exhortation returns the reader to the subject position of a receptive student, who is commanded to become

30. Tilford, *Sensing World, Sensing Wisdom*, 110.
31. McKane, *Proverbs*, 386; Fox, *Proverbs 10–31*, 733–34.
32. "Ahiqar" (*OTP* 2:498).
33. This construction is construed as an abstract for a concrete. Driver, "Problems in the Hebrew Text of Proverbs," 196.
34. Waltke, *Proverbs: Chapters 15–31*, 254–55.
35. Joüon §164c; *IBHS* §40.2.2b.

wise by striding "in the way of your heart" (בְּדֶרֶךְ לִבֶּךָ, v. 19b). This "way" is not whatever the heart desires; rather, it is a way directed by one who has become wise (v. 19a). And it is a way that is illustrated through the admonition and motivation in vv. 20–21. Returning to the theme of the company one keeps (22:24, 26), the admonition prohibits associating with the overindulgent. This prohibition is modified by a causal clause (כִּי, "for," v. 21a), which provides a rationale and motivation for the admonition. The inebriation of winebibbers and the gluttony of the overindulgent will engender poverty and insensibility. The rationale appeals to self-preservation and security in order to curb the desire to consort with the dissolute.

16. Saying 16 (23:22–25)

The momentary joy of the dissolute and the dangers of keeping company with them stand in sharp contrast with the lasting joy and intimacy shared by the parents of a wise son. This joy and intimacy pervade the sixteenth saying; it is framed by the verb ילד ("begot," v. 22a; "bore," v. 25b) and bound together by the repetition of father and mother (vv. 22, 24a, 25a) as well as "exult" (גיל, vv. 24a, 25b) and "rejoice" (יִשְׂמַח, vv. 24b, 25a). The renewed call to attention reinforces a posture of receptivity (v. 22); and the prohibition not to despise one's mother "when she grows old" (כִּי־זָקְנָה, v. 22b) requires this posture across the lifetime of one's parents. The parents' exhortation is familiar. Echoing the grandfather's lecture in 4:4–9, they urge the reader to acquire truth at all costs. The nature of this commodity is elaborated upon in 23:23b, where the objects stand in apposition to "truth" (אֱמֶת, v. 23a), namely, wisdom, discipline, and understanding. In light of the syntax of previous sayings, one might expect a subordinate clause to motivate the acquisition of truth. Instead, the reader encounters a pair of sayings that describe the parents' joy over a righteous, wise son. The first expresses this joy indirectly (v. 24). The second conveys this joy directly; it is the rejoicing of "your father and your mother" (אָבִיךָ וְאִמֶּךָ, v. 25a). Again, the desire to please one's parents provides a powerful motivation for the acquisition of truth and the embodiment of righteousness and wisdom (cf. Prov 10:1b–c; 23:15–16).

17. Saying 17 (23:26–28)

Parental joy turns to parental sternness in the seventeenth saying, which revisits a familiar figure: the "strange woman" (נָכְרִיָּה, v. 27b). The introductory exhortation captures the reader's attention, seizing the possession and direction of one's body parts (v. 26). Rather than giving one's heart to the strange woman, the father exhorts the son to place his heart in the parent's possession (v. 26a); and with this mental and emotional assent, the father expresses the desire that the son would emulate his ways (v. 26b). The reason for this form of attention is expressed in v. 27 (כִּי, "for," v. 27a), which modifies vv. 26 and 28. The parent redeploys familiar imagery to conceptualize the dangers of the strange woman. She is depicted as a deep, barren pit (שׁוּחָה עֲמֻקָּה, v. 27a; cf. 22:14) and as a "narrow well" (בְּאֵר צָרָה, 23:27b; cf. 5:15)—a double entendre that characterizes the woman or her vulva as a meagre source of refreshment. The final lines of the saying fuse the metaphorical domain of holes with the metaphorical domain of hunting. Far from representing a passive threat, the strange woman poses an active danger.[36]

36. Waltke, *Proverbs: Chapters 15–31*, 261; Fox, *Proverbs 10–31*, 739.

The adverb "surely" (אַף, 23:28a), combined with the independent personal pronoun "she" (הִיא, v. 28a), focuses attention on what follows.[37] The woman is portrayed as a "bandit" (חֶתֶף, v. 28a; cf. Job 9:12), prepared to ambush the son and add to the number of traitors that betray their marriage covenant. The portrait inspires fear, and it provides an emotional stimulus to steer clear of the strange woman.

18. Saying 18 (23:29–35)

The dangers of inappropriate sexual desire are comparable to the dangers of drunkenness sketched in the eighteenth saying (cf. 21:17; 23:20–21).[38] This extended epigram renders the drunkard with creativity, imagination, and "condescending irony."[39] It opens with a series of scathing questions (v. 29). The speaker then articulates the answer (v. 30) before drawing the reader into the epigram through an admonition (v. 31), an extended rationale (vv. 32–34), and direct speech (v. 35).

The barrage of questions that initiate the epigram establish the tone of the piece. Taken together, they sketch the emotional (v. 29a), relational (v. 29b), and physical possessions of a particular person (v. 29c–d). They invite the reader to identify this figure, one characterized by emotional exclamations, broken relationships, and a bruised body. The veil is lifted in v. 30 with a pair of clauses: "those who linger over wine" (לַמְאַחֲרִים עַל־הַיָּיִן, v. 30a) and "those who come to taste mixed wine" (לַבָּאִים לַחְקֹר מִמְסָךְ, v. 30b). The former depicts drunkards as those who tarry long into the night; the latter elaborates on this description, portraying drunkards as those who come to inspect or taste the substance that consumes their lives. With the subject of the epigram in view, the speaker delivers an exaggerated admonition: "do not [even] look at wine" (אַל־תֵּרֶא יַיִן, v. 31a). The subordinate clauses that modify the prohibition evoke the attractiveness of the drink: its hypnotizing sparkle (v. 31a), its shining eye (v. 31b), and its smooth taste (v. 31c).[40] The immediate rationale for the prohibition, by contrast, expresses the pain of lingering long over wine (v. 32); and this pain is captured through onomatopoeia, as the similes vocalize the sound of hissing snakes.[41]

The logical rationale for abstaining from excessive drinking continues in vv. 33–35. But the rhetoric of the rationale shifts from the reception of direct address to personal involvement. The reader is written into the script, positioned in a drunken state. According to vv. 33–34, "your eyes" (עֵינֶיךָ, v. 33a) will see deranged things, "your heart" (לִבְּךָ, v. 33b) will speak perversities, and "you" will feel as one strapped to the top of a mast, tossed by waves in the middle of the sea (v. 34). This poetic participation in nausea gives way to direct speech (v. 35). Whether the words are placed in the reader's mouth or heard by one's ear is contingent on one's subject position. Just as the epigram opened with direct speech (v. 29a), so also it closes with direct discourse. The disorientation and irrationality of the drunkard is delineated in four crisp, poetic lines. The first pair describe the drunkard's physical pain and intellectual ignorance (v. 35a–b). The second pair recreates a vicious circle: a reawakening of sorts to repeat the process (v. 35c–d). The irony and mockery of the epigram is thick. This derision serves as a form of literary shock treatment to dissuade the reader from overindulging in drink.

37. Muraoka, *Emphatic Words*, 141–43.

38. For similar advice, see "The Instruction of Any" (*AEL* 2:137); Washington, *Wealth and Poverty*, 142–43.

39. Schökel, *A Manual of Hebrew Poetics*, 16–17.

40. McKane, *Proverbs*, 394.

41. Watson, *Classical Hebrew Poetry*, 27.

19. Saying 19 (24:1–2)

The parent turns from dissuading one from drunkenness to discouraging one from desiring the company of the evil in the nineteenth saying. Similar to 23:17, the admonitions assume the prosperity of the evil (24:1); and they presume that this prosperity poses a threat to the perseverance of the wise. To curb one's desire to consort with the evil, the parent offers a motivation cast in the form of a causal clause (כִּי, "for," v. 2a). The motivation profiles the destructive character of the evil; it is designed to engender moral disgust. The heart and lips of the evil breed destruction; and it seems that this destruction will typify the company of the evil as well as their fate.

20. Saying 20 (24:3–4)

The string of admonitions and motivations is broken by the twentieth saying, which introduces a series of sentences (vv. 3–10). Reiterating expressions redolent of YHWH's construction of the cosmos, the saying accentuates the value of wisdom for constructing and filling human homes. The sequence of prepositional phrases "by wisdom . . . by understanding . . . and by knowledge" (בְּחָכְמָה . . . בִּתְבוּנָה . . . וּבְדַעַת, vv. 3a, 3b, 4a) mirrors 3:19–20. The tools employed by the divine architect to found and fill the cosmos are also the tools granted to humans to found and fill domestic and social spheres (cf. Exod 31:3; 35:31). The formation and filling of the cosmos, by implication, is paradigmatic for the formation and filling of the sociomoral order. In view of its intertextual links, the saying indicates that humans imitate the divine architect's ordering of the cosmos through their ordering of society.[42] The aesthetic beauty of this imitation, combined with the expectation of wealth (v. 4b), produces a compelling account of human flourishing in accord with the order of creation.

21. Saying 21 (24:5–6)

The aesthetic beauty and sociomoral significance of wisdom serve as an appropriate entrée into the twenty-first saying and its description of wisdom's power. The nature of this description is unclear, for the initial line lacks a verb. Some follow the LXX and construe the line as a comparative saying (i.e., "Stronger a wise man than a mighty one").[43] Others argue that the preposition בְּ implies an elided verb, like "prevail" or "endure."[44] Whichever reading is preferred, the statement highlights the power of the wise, a power that is escalated in v. 5b. And this power is illustrated in v. 6 through the theme of guidance and many counselors for waging war (cf. 11:14b; 15:22b; 20:18b).[45] The saying defines the wise as powerful individuals, who grow in strength, establish stability, and achieve success.

22. Saying 22 (24:7)

Wisdom's power, by contrast, is beyond fools. The twenty-second saying expresses this conviction through spatial and judicial imagery. According to the initial line, wisdom is too lofty for a fool; it escapes his reach (v. 7a). This inaccessibility is demonstrated in the second line, where the fool's speech is situated in the judicial and communal center of life (v. 7b). The notion that the fool "cannot open his mouth" (לֹא יִפְתַּח־פִּיהוּ, v. 7b)

42. Van Leeuwen, "Cosmos, Temple, House," 77–87.

43. McKane, *Proverbs*, 397; Fox, *Proverbs: An Eclectic Edition*, 320–21.

44. Waltke, *Proverbs: Chapters 15–31*, 269n2.

45. On logical grounds, v. 6 does not appear to introduce a causal clause providing a rationale for v. 5. Rather the כִּי seems to function as an "evidential" particle, substantiating the truth of v. 5. Fox, *Proverbs 1–9*, 103; idem, *Proverbs 10–31*, 744.

may be construed in at least two ways. First, the verb may be rendered as a modal, indicating that the fool "must not open his mouth" at the gate.[46] On this reading, the line demands that the reader silence the fool. Second, in light of the fact that the fool is not known for verbal restraint (10:10, 14; 18:6; 20:3), the line may offer an evaluation of his speech. In this case, a fool may speak at the gate. But his speech will prove to be ineffective;[47] it will fail to sway public opinion and judicial decisions.

23. Saying 23 (24:8–9)

Social evaluation continues in the twenty-third saying, which is bound together by the root זמם (מְזִמּוֹת, "schemes," v. 8b; זִמַּת, "scheming," v. 9a). The saying traffics in social shame. Those who plot evil are named "master of schemes" (בַּעַל־מְזִמּוֹת, v. 8b) by the public. While schemes directed by wisdom may achieve a desired effect, foolish scheming is considered as sin itself (v. 9a). And these internal schemes engender an internal, emotional response to the scoffer, who is loathsome to people (v. 9b). The public shaming of the schemer and the scoffer hone the moral valuation of the reader and nurture moral disgust for these character types.

24. Saying 24 (24:10)

The twenty-fourth saying returns to the second-person singular form of address and places the reader within its evaluation of strength in distress. In light of its thematic resemblance to what follows, many take vv. 10–12 as a coherent saying.[48] The verse should be treated independently, however, since the strength required in vv. 11–12 is considered meagre or constrained in v. 10. What's more, "the day of distress" (יוֹם צָרָה, v. 10a) is a day of personal reckoning elsewhere (Gen 35:3; 2 Kgs 19:3; Jer 16:19), not merely a day of danger for others (Prov 24:11–12).[49] When read as a discrete saying, the maxim turns on the paronomasia of "distress" (צָרָה, v. 10a) and "meager" (צַר, v. 10b), which conclude and open the respective parallel lines. If one follows the MT, the saying moves from a verbal to a verbless clause, equating one's lack of courage in distress with meager strength. But if one reads the saying as an unmarked conditional clause, then it warns one that lack of courage in distress will reduce one's capacity to respond with fortitude in future situations.[50] Personal danger will test one's courage and determine their moral strength.

25. Saying 25 (24:11–12)

Moral strength remains in view in the twenty-fifth saying, though the circumstances for exercising it differ from the previous maxim. The opening exhortations sketch the contours of the situation requiring moral strength through the expressions "those who are being taken away to death" (לְקֻחִים לַמָּוֶת, v. 11a) and "those stumbling to slaughter" (מָטִים לַהֶרֶג, v. 11b). While the details remain ambiguous, the call to deliver these individuals indicates that those escorted to their execution are in danger of being killed, not necessarily those who have been unjustly accused.[51] This situation calls for immediate moral action, but it is met with inaction in v. 12, which delineates the condition and consequences of feigning ignorance. This feigned ignorance is cast in a conditional protasis and expressed through direct speech (v. 12a). The direct

46. Waltke, *Proverbs: Chapters 15–31*, 269n7.

47. Fox, *Proverbs 10–31*, 744.

48. Whybray, *Proverbs*, 346–47; Murphy, *Proverbs*, 181; Waltke, *Proverbs: Chapters 15–31*, 274–75.

49. Fox, *Proverbs 10–31*, 746.

50. McKane, *Proverbs*, 400; Waltke, *Proverbs: Chapters 15–31*, 275; Fox, *Proverbs 10–31*, 745–76.

51. Whybray, *Proverbs*, 346–47.

speech moves from the second-person singular (v. 11) to the first-person plural (v. 12a), distributing the claim of ignorance to a larger group. But the rhetorical questions that constitute the apodosis refuse to acquit the individuals within the group. These questions place the excuse of ignorance under divine scrutiny. The one who weighs the motives of the heart and "guards your life" (נֹצֵר נַפְשְׁךָ, v. 12c) sees through the sham and will inflict retribution on those who refuse to rescue others. The rhetorical questions appeal to one's desire for safety and security. They seek to nurture courage and compassion before the face of the one who guards every life.

26. Saying 26 (24:13–14)

The protection of life serves as the backdrop for wisdom's nourishment of life in the twenty-sixth saying. This nourishment is expressed through an analogy. The opening exhortation calls the son to eat honey (v. 13a); and the causal clauses within each line provide a rationale for its consumption.[52] This rationale awakens one to the pleasant, therapeutic, and satisfying qualities of honey, each of which are comparable to wisdom. The formal comparison is marked by the particle "so" (כֵּן, v. 14a), which opens v. 14. Like honey, wisdom sustains and animates one's life with its sweetness and healing powers. And as the conditional clause that concludes v. 14 indicates (v. 14b–c), those who pursue and find wisdom will enjoy a full, abundant life. Life and delight motivate this pursuit, and satisfaction marks the ingestion of wisdom.

27. Saying 27 (24:15–16)

Among the character types mentioned in the "words of the wise," the wicked have been conspicuously absent. This figure makes their first appearance in the twenty-seventh saying. The saying is cast in the form of a warning (v. 15), followed by a concessive clause that functions as a motivation (v. 16). The warning prohibits one from destroying or plundering the property of the righteous (v. 15). While many omit the term רָשָׁע or render it as a vocative (i.e., "O wicked"),[53] it seems to represent an accusative of state, describing the nature of the one who lies in wait "as a wicked person."[54] This person may plunder the property of the righteous, but the plundering will engender an unexpected outcome. This outcome is delineated through the concessive clause (כִּי, "though," v. 16a). Irrespective of the number of times that the righteous fall into hardship, they will rise. The wicked, by contrast, will stumble in evil and not receive restoration. The concessive clause focuses on the security of the righteous and the instability of the wicked. And it nuances Proverbs's conception of retribution. The righteous may experience misfortune and failure. But misfortune and failure will not overcome them; it will strengthen their resilience.[55]

28. Saying 28 (24:17–18)

The concept of stability and the roots "fall" (נפל, vv. 16a, 17a) and "stumble" (כשל, vv. 16b, 17b) are reiterated in the twenty-eighth saying. Together, they shape the temporal context for the admoni-

52. The causal clause is unmarked in the v. 13b. But in light of its relationship with v. 13a, it is assumed.

53. See, for example, Toy, *Proverbs*, 447–48; Murphy, *Proverbs*, 179; and Fox, *Proverbs 10–31*, 749, who omit the term, and Delitzsch, "Proverbs of Solomon," 6:356 (2:135); and Longman, *Proverbs*, 439, who render it as a vocative.

54. Waltke, *Proverbs: Chapters 15–31*, 278n38; *IBHS* §10.2.2d.

55. William P. Brown, "When Wisdom Fails," in *"When the Morning Stars Sang": Essays in Honor of Choon Leong Seow on the Occasion of his Sixty-Fifth Birthday*, ed. Scott C. Jones and Christine Roy Yoder; BZAW 500 (Berlin: de Gruyter, 2018), 209–23.

tions pertaining to *Schadenfreude*. The prohibition against external rejoicing and internal exultation at the downfall of one's enemy is striking, for the practice is commended elsewhere in the Old Testament (11:10; Pss 52:7–9 [5–7]; 58:11–12 [10–11]; cf. Prov 25:21–22; Job 31:29). The rationale for its prohibition is intimated in the negative purpose clause (פֶּן, "lest," Prov 24:18a), which offers a theological evaluation of such rejoicing. YHWH will consider this rejoicing as evil (v. 18a); and in a shocking turn of events, YHWH will turn his anger away from one's enemy (v. 18b). Whether or not YHWH turns his anger toward the one who exulted over an enemy's punishment is unclear. As many have noted, the underlying rationale for YHWH's response may be one's delight in vengeance and lack of compassion.[56] The expression of delight in vengeance seems to represent the primary reason for YHWH's response.[57] Vengeance belongs to YHWH (Deut 32:35); it is not the business of humans. And to involve oneself in this business is to cross the line of creaturehood. This recognition cultivates compassion, even for one's enemies.

29. Saying 29 (24:19–20)

Returning to the theme of envy, the twenty-ninth saying recycles previous maxims to inspire perseverance in the wise life (**24:19b**//23:17a; 24:1a; **24:20b**//13:9b). Similar to 23:17 and 24:1, the saying assumes that the prosperity of the wicked may entice the wise to embrace their way of life. To rein in this temptation, the causal clause places the admonitions in broader perspective (כִּי, "for," v. 20a); it expresses the certain extinction of the wicked. In so doing, it motivates perseverance through the promise of life and security.

30. Saying 30 (24:21–22)

Security and well-being also serve as the motivational bait of the final saying within the "words of the wise." Similar to many of the sayings in the collection, the maxim moves from a pair of admonitions to a motivation. The initial admonition exhorts one to respect both YHWH and the king as legitimate authorities in positions of power. The second is cast in the negative, and the crux of the admonition is the expression שׁוֹנִים (v. 21b). Some read the intransitive term ("to change") with a transitive sense (i.e., "to be different") and construe it as "detractors" or "rebels."[58] Others read the participle in light of Arabic cognates to argue that it conveys the sense "those of high rank."[59] And still others follow the LXX and propose a slight emendation to produce a clearer reading: "do not disobey either of them" (עִם־שְׁנֵיהֶם אַל־תִּתְעַבָּר, v. 21b).[60] Whether the admonition prohibits provoking YHWH and the king or associating with underhanded officials, the motivation provides a clear rationale (כִּי, "for," v. 22a). The causal clause reiterates 6:15a to forecast the certain and sudden destruction of those who cross YHWH and the king; it engenders appropriate fear, appealing to one's desire for self-preservation, security, and life.

56. McKane, *Proverbs*, 404; Whybray, *Proverbs*, 350–51.

57. Van Leeuwen, "The Book of Proverbs," *NIB* 5:212.

58. Delitzsch, "Proverbs of Solomon," 6:357–58 (2:137–38); Meinhold, *Die Sprüche*, 2:408; Longman, *Proverbs*, 435.

59. David W. Thomas, "The Root *snh* = *sny* in Hebrew, II," *ZAW* 55 (1937): 174–76; McKane, *Proverbs*, 249; Waltke, *Proverbs: Chapters 15–31*, 279–80n45.

60. Garrett, *Proverbs*, 200n445; Fox, *Proverbs 10–31*, 752.

CHAPTER 30

Proverbs 24:23–34

B. Justice, Speech, and Work: *Variations on the Concept of* MORAL ORDER

Main Idea of the Passage

This brief collection supplements "the words of the wise" (22:17–24:22), focusing on the themes of justice, speech, and work through the metaphorical concept of MORAL ORDER to attune one to the natural, social, and moral patterns of the world.

Literary Context[1]

While a rationale for the separation of twelve sayings attributed to the wise is unclear and the compositional history of the collection is unknown, the maxims exhibit two particular affinities with materials elsewhere in the book. The first is the title: "these also are of the wise" (גַּם־אֵלֶּה לַחֲכָמִים, v. 23a).[2] The use of the adverb "also" (גַּם) suggests that that those responsible for the inclusion of Prov 24:23–34 in the anthology associated the compendium with the existing collection attributed to the wise.[3] Second, the short collection includes several variant repetitions that establish intertextual links across various compendia in the book. The single-line evaluation of partiality (v. 23b), for example, is developed across two parallel lines in 28:21. The expression of divine retribution in 24:12d is recast in the context of personal vengeance in v. 29b. And, as the only example of a variant repetition across

1. This chapter does not include the Explanation of the Text section. See pp. xv and 276n1 for justification.

2. While many construe the preposition as a לְ of authorship (i.e., "of the wise"), in light of the fact that the syntax of 24:23a differs from 1:1a and 10:1a, others render the preposition as a לְ of advantage (i.e., "for the wise"; cf. LXX). This reading indicates that Prov 24:23a is not a title to a formal collection (Luc, "The Titles and Structure of Proverbs," 252–55); rather, it introduces a distinct section designed for one of Proverbs's addressees, viz., the wise (1:5; Schipper, *Proverbs 1–15*, 6–7).

3. In contrast to the arrangement of the MT, the LXX places Prov 30:1–14 between 24:22 and 24:23–34.

two couplets,[4] vv. 33–34 replay the consequences of laziness through an anecdote of personal discovery (6:10–11).[5] These variant repetitions place the short collection in conversation with materials from other collections within the anthology. They reinforce familiar motifs and encourage reflection on matters of justice, speech, and work, each of which strengthens aspects of the moral order or undermines the moral responsibilities that underpin that order.

III. "Forming 'Fearers of YHWH'": The Curriculum of Wisdom and Virtue (10:1–29:27)
- III.1 Elementary Wisdom and Virtue (10:1–15:33)
- III.2 Intermediate Wisdom and Virtue (16:1–22:16)
- **III.3 Vocational Wisdom and Virtue (22:17–24:34)**
  - A. Moral Motivation: Inspiring Trust in YHWH and Trustworthy Speech (22:17–24:22)
  - ➡ **B. Justice, Speech, and Work: Variations on the Concept of Moral Order (24:23–34)**
- III.4 Advanced Wisdom and Virtue (25:1–29:27)

Translation and Exegetical Outline

(See page 542.)

Structure and Literary Form

In contrast to the formal consistency of the maxims in the "words of the wise," its supplement consists of a variety of different forms. It opens with a monostich, which is unusual within the central collections (24:23a; cf. 27:5). The antithesis across 24:24–25 operates under interlinear parallelism rather than intralinear parallelism. The aesthetic satisfaction of honest speech is expressed through a sentence in which the predicate precedes the subject (v. 26). What is more, the epigram that concludes the collection is more at home in chs. 1–9 than the central collections. The diversity of forms, however, does not entail that the sayings are discrete, disconnected entities. They may not be bound together syntactically, but they exhibit thematic coherence.

4. David M. Carr, *The Formation of the Hebrew Bible: A New Reconstruction* (New York: Oxford University Press, 2011), 27.

5. Following Michael Fox, Prov 24:30–34 does not sketch a process of epistemic discovery initiated by empirical observation. Put differently, the anecdote does not describe a normative epistemological process, according to which an individual empirically reads truth from creation. Instead, the anecdote reports "an experience that reinforces a known principle. The observation serves as an occasion for reflection, not inference, and the anecdote is testimonial to an axiomatic belief" (Fox, *Proverbs 10–31*, 966).

Proverbs 24:23–34

Verse	Hebrew	English	Outline
23a	גַּם־אֵלֶּה לַחֲכָמִים	These also are of the wise.	B. Justice, Speech, and Work: Variations on the Concept of MORAL ORDER (24:23–34)
23b	הַכֵּר־פָּנִים בְּמִשְׁפָּט בַּל־טוֹב	Showing partiality in judgment, not good.	
24a	אֹמֵר לְרָשָׁע צַדִּיק אָתָּה	The one who says to the guilty, "You are innocent" –	
24b	יִקְּבֻהוּ עַמִּים יִזְעָמוּהוּ לְאֻמִּים	peoples will curse him, nations will condemn him.	
25a	וְלַמּוֹכִיחִים יִנְעָם	But for those who rebuke, it will be pleasant,	
25b	וַעֲלֵיהֶם תָּבוֹא בִרְכַּת־טוֹב	on them shall come a blessing of good.	
26a	שְׂפָתַיִם יִשָּׁק	He kisses lips –	
26b	מֵשִׁיב דְּבָרִים נְכֹחִים	the one who returns honest words.	
27a	הָכֵן בַּחוּץ מְלַאכְתֶּךָ	Prepare your outside work,	
27b	וְעַתְּדָהּ בַּשָּׂדֶה לָךְ	and ready it in the field for yourself.	
27c	אַחַר וּבָנִיתָ בֵיתֶךָ	Afterwards build your house.	
28a	אַל־תְּהִי עֵד־חִנָּם בְּרֵעֶךָ	Do not be a witness against your neighbor without cause,	
28b	וַהֲפִתִּיתָ בִּשְׂפָתֶיךָ	or would you deceive with your lips?	
29a	אַל־תֹּאמַר כַּאֲשֶׁר עָשָׂה־לִי כֵּן אֶעֱשֶׂה־לּוֹ	Do not say, "Just as he did to me, so I will do to him;	
29b	אָשִׁיב לָאִישׁ כְּפָעֳלוֹ	I will repay the man according to his deed."	
30a	עַל־שְׂדֵה אִישׁ־עָצֵל עָבַרְתִּי	I passed by the field of a sluggard,	
30b	וְעַל־כֶּרֶם אָדָם חֲסַר־לֵב	by the vineyard of a man lacking sense.	
31a	וְהִנֵּה עָלָה כֻלּוֹ קִמְּשֹׂנִים	And look – all of it was overgrown with thorns,	
31b	כָּסּוּ פָנָיו חֲרֻלִּים	the ground was covered with nettles,	
31c	וְגֶדֶר אֲבָנָיו נֶהֱרָסָה	and its stone wall was broken down.	
32a	וָאֶחֱזֶה אָנֹכִי אָשִׁית לִבִּי	And I looked; I took it to heart;	
32b	רָאִיתִי לָקַחְתִּי מוּסָר	I saw; I received instruction:	
33a	מְעַט שֵׁנוֹת מְעַט תְּנוּמוֹת	A little sleep, a little slumber,	
33b	מְעַט חִבֻּק יָדַיִם לִשְׁכָּב	a little folding of the hands to rest,	
34a	וּבָא־מִתְהַלֵּךְ רֵישֶׁךָ	and poverty will come upon you like a vagabond,	
34b	וּמַחְסֹרֶיךָ כְּאִישׁ מָגֵן	and need like an armed warrior.	

And the thematic coherence of the materials is strengthened by the metaphorical concept of MORAL ORDER as well as the moral obligations that underwrite this order. To show partiality as a judge by inverting the standard of justice shared by the "nations" is to fail to fulfill one's moral responsibilities in a position of power (24:24). Those who fulfill their moral responsibilities through rebuke, by contrast, will receive a blessing (v. 25). In fact, honest or straightforward words are an expression of moral affection (v. 26). Prioritizing one's moral responsibilities includes work (v. 27). One's place in the moral order justifies the prohibition against vengeance (v. 29). And one's dereliction of duty to nature and failure to live in accord with the rhythm of the seasons reflects one's moral negligence and economic deprivation (vv. 30–34). Despite the various forms, the concept of MORAL ORDER in general and one's moral responsibilities in particular inform the thematic coherence of the materials in the short collection.

The thematic coherence of the materials has contributed to the formulation of a coherent structural design. The vast majority of commentators follow Arndt Meinhold and argue that the collection is arranged into two parallel groups, each of which consists of three blocks of material that fall under the respective headings "behavior in the law court" (vv. 23b–25//v. 28), "speaking and thinking" (vv. 26//v. 29), and "behavior in work" (v. 27//vv. 30–34).[6] This structural proposal captures the primary themes within the collection, but the headings mischaracterize and mis-divide certain maxims.[7] The prohibition against vengeance (v. 29), for example, is designated as a "false answer" under the heading "speaking and thinking." And this prohibition is separated from v. 28, which supplies the antecedent to the subject "he" in v. 29a. In light of the thematic coherence of materials, it appears that the collection contains several groups: vv. 23b–25, vv. 28–29, vv. 30–34. These groups, however, do not form a threefold symmetrical structure.

Canonical and Theological Significance

Taken together, the collections attributed to the wise (Prov 22:17–24:22; 24:23–34) make explicit that which is implicit in the aphorisms across the central collections: motivation.[8] The implicit motivations that underwrite the pedagogy of chs. 10:1–22:16 are made explicit through the syntax of the admonitions that pervade Prov 22:16–24:34. Moral motivation is a common pedagogical technique across the Old Testament,[9] and moral motivation is a fundamental component in Proverbs's

6. Meinhold, *Die Sprüche*, 2:410.

7. Fox, *Proverbs 10–31*, 770.

8. Hildebrandt, "Motivation and Antithetic Parallelism in Proverbs 10–15," 433–44.

9. Rifat Sonsino, *Motive Clauses in Hebrew Law: Biblical Forms and Near Eastern Parallels*, SBLDS 45 (Chico, CA: Scholars Press, 1980).

pedagogy.[10] But the motivational carrots attached to Proverbs's pedagogical stick raise questions. To be specific, they raise questions concerning the place, nature, and viability of human self-interest. From a pedagogical perspective, Proverbs banks on human self-interest. But does self-interest have a legitimate place in the Christian life in general and in Christian discipleship in particular?

These are contested questions. And they are especially contested among scholars of Augustine.[11] In the shadow of Luther's extension of the inchoate, Augustinian concept of *homo incurvatus in se* (i.e., humanity curved inward on themselves), it appears that love of anyone or anything other than God has no place in the Christian vision of the good life.[12] Here we find the tension with Proverbs's pedagogy and, by implication, its theological anthropology. According to both Proverbs and Augustine, humans are desirers. They are lovers. Pedagogical carrots, therefore, are quite appropriate: they orient and direct desire to proper things and proper ends in the economy of salvation. For Luther, by contrast, humans are intrinsically and inescapably egocentric. Human self-interest is a fundamental problem. This problem runs so deep that humans are prone to pervert material and spiritual gifts from God, making them idolatrous ends in themselves, divorced from proper relationship with the giver of every good and perfect gift (Jas 1:17).[13] In contrast to Augustine, Luther contends that human loves in general and proper self-love in particular cannot be ordered rightly. Human self-love is always contaminated by egoism. On this account, human egocentrism moves creatures to love created things rather than the creator. And self-interest moves humans to use God for their own sake, that is, to use God for his gifts, which are enjoyed for their own sake.

The debate over the nature and legitimacy of human self-interest as well as the distinction between "using" (*usus*) and "enjoying" (*fruitio*) is not an antiquated dispute that has little bearing on instruction in the good life.[14] These matters are foregrounded in both Job and Ecclesiastes. The book of Job asks whether disinterested piety is possible (Job 1:9); and it affirms that one can serve God simply for who God is. Job's losses are incalculable. The absence of God's gifts tests the very basis and motivation of Job's piety. Throughout this test, Job maintains his integrity (27:2–6). He never asks God to restore the gifts that he has taken away. He simply pursues God. And their restored relationship is enough; it brings comfort (42:6). While the book of Job explores the possibility of disinterested piety, the observa-

10. Stewart, *Poetic Ethics*, 102–29.

11. Anders Nygren, *Agape and Eros*, trans. Philip S. Watson (New York: Harper & Row, 1969), 449–562; Oliver O'Donovan, *The Problem of Self-Love in St. Augustine* (New Haven: Yale University Press, 1980).

12. Matt Jenson, *The Gravity of Sin: Augustine, Luther, and Barth on* Homo Incurvatus in Se (London: T&T Clark, 2006), 6–97.

13. Jenson, *The Gravity of Sin*, 79–97.

14. For the distinction between "using" and "enjoying," see Augustine, *On Christian Teaching* 1 (trans. R. P. H. Green [Oxford: Oxford University Press, 2008], 8-29) Oliver O'Donovan, "*Usus* and *Fruitio* in Augustine, *De Doctrina Christiana I*," *JTS* 33 (1982): 361–97.

tions of Qoheleth probe the relationship between using and enjoying. When human pursuits and achievements are considered as ends in themselves or as the means to achieve "profit" (יִתְרוֹן), frustration and pain are the inevitable result. But when human pursuits and achievements are perceived as divine gifts, bestowed on finite creatures for enjoyment, then humans learn to accept their "portion" (חֵלֶק) and use these gifts to enjoy God and his good creation. Self-interest as well as using and enjoying animates Job and Ecclesiastes. Each offers a discrete perspective on these matters. The same is true of the "words of the wise" (Prov 22:17–24:22; 24:23–34). These words not only acknowledge the power and productivity of self-interested motivation for the formation of character;[15] they also situate this motivation in a context that refuses to divorce individual self-interest from the human community and relationship with God.[16]

The introduction to the "words of the wise" establishes the purpose and relational context through which to interpret the self-interested moral motivations within the subcollections (22:17–21). This purpose and relational context consist of three dimensions. The first concerns the self. By orienting one's internal and external organs of reception to the "words of the wise" and by securing them in one's belly and on one's lips, one will reflect the beauty of the wise life (22:17–18). The aesthetic benefits of the words of the wise motivate one to receive their teaching. The second dimension places this self-interested motivation in a broader context, specifically in relationship with YHWH. The emphatic word order of 22:19 focuses attention on the attitudinal and relational goal of the subcollections' teachings: they are designed to cultivate trust in YHWH. The beauty and delight of the wise life is not an end in itself; it is inextricably linked to relationship with and trust in YHWH. More than this, the beauty and delight of the wise life is bound up with a third dimension: relationship with others. The result clause that closes the introduction to the "words of the wise" indicates that the sayings seek to form one into a trustworthy speaker who represents others truthfully and returns true reports to the one who sent him (22:21). The causal, purpose, and result clauses that punctuate the introduction to the "words of the wise" motivate the reception of the subcollections' teaching. These motivations focus on the self, relationship with YHWH, and relationship with the human community. In so doing, they acknowledge the place of self-interest in moral formation, but they place this self-interest in intimate relationship with YHWH and others.

When read within this multidimensional relational context, the nature and legitimacy of human self-interest becomes clear. This multidimensional relational context clarifies *how* one is self-interested, not *how much* one is self-interested.[17] The vast

15. Stewart, *Poetic Ethics*, 126.

16. Schwáb, *Toward an Interpretation*, 99. Schwáb derives this relational network from his reading of Thomas Aquinas.

17. Schwáb, *Toward an Interpretation*, 99.

majority of the "words of the wise" appeal to self-interest. More specifically, they appeal to self-preservation. Some focus on the preservation of the self through promises of security, satisfaction, life, and a future (23:17–18, 20–21, 29–35; 24:13–14). Others threaten one's self-preservation by placing certain (in)actions before the judgment of YHWH (22:22–23; 23:10–11; 24:10–12, 17–18, 21–22). Still others place one's self-preservation in relation with members of the community (22:24–25, 26–27, 29; 23:1–3, 13–14, 15–16, 24–25, 26–28; 24:5–6, 15–16, 26, 28–29). Self-preservation dominates the moral motivations within the "words of the wise." This preservation concerns the self. But it is not exclusive to the self, for the self is always and ever situated in relation to YHWH and the community. On this account, self-preservation is rendered as the preservation of one's relationship with YHWH and the preservation of one's relationship with others in the community.

Put in terms of the purpose of the "words of the wise" (22:17–21), self-preservation is secured through trust and truth in relationship with YHWH and members of the community. Trust and truth are the brick and mortar of these relationships. They ensure that the self is never isolated but always in relation. And they create the conditions for appropriate self-interest. Appropriate self-interest has no place in Luther's program; self-love is the problem that finds its remedy outside the self, in divine intervention. Appropriate self-interest does have a home in Augustine's vision of the good life; it is maintained through the proper ordering of love, as one directs their desire to God and all things in relation to God. Appropriate self-interest is woven into Thomas's moral vision, where self-preservation and a hierarchy of ends contextualize and countenance its legitimacy. Appropriate self-interest is assumed across 22:17–24:34. This construal of self-interest is appropriate by virtue of its interrelationship with YHWH and the community as well as its consideration of trust and truth. These ingredients are key to the moral motivation of the "words of the wise." And these ingredients are key to the use of self-interest in the Christian life in general and in Christian discipleship in particular. Each is captured through the greatest commandment: Love the Lord your God with all your heart and with all your soul and with all your mind and with all your strength; and love your neighbor *as yourself* (Mark 12:30–31; cf. Deut 6:5; Lev 19:18). Christians are called to love their neighbor and this love of the other is conditioned by self-interest: Christians love their neighbor just as they love themselves.

If self-interest or self-love is hardwired into human beings, then trust and truth as well as relationship with God and others are necessary for its appropriate use in education for character formation. That's the perspective of the "words of the wise." Whereas Luther identified humanity's depravity and *incurvatus in se* as factors that mitigate the legitimacy of self-interest, mistrust in people and communal institutions may represent the factors that mitigate the power of appropriate self-interest for character formation today. In the 1960s, 77 percent of American's agreed that "most people can be trusted"; according to a recent Gallop poll, that number now stands at 55 percent.[18] For some, the results of national elections cannot be trusted. Trust in the federal government to manage international and national affairs is low.[19] In addition to weaponizing the remarks of others, social media has contributed to the "continual chipping-away of trust" in social life.[20] These observations illustrate a simple point: Americans have lost trust in both one another and the institutions that govern their manner of life. Trust is the issue. The "words of the wise" alert one to the necessary conditions for appropriate self-interest. In the absence of these conditions, Luther is right: self-interest does not have a place in the Christian life or Christian discipleship. Its place, if it there is one, is found in the "words of the wise": in trust and truth, in relationship with God and others.

18. Robert D. Putnam, *Bowling Alone: The Collapse and Revival of American Community* (New York: Simon & Schuster, 2000), 17; Justin McCarthy, "In U.S., Trust in Politicians, Voters Continues to Ebb," Gallup, October 7, 2021, news.gallup.com /poll/355430/trust-politicians-voters-continues-ebb.aspx.

19. Megan Brenan, "Americans' Trust in Government Remains Low," Gallup, September 30, 2021, news.gallup.com/poll /355124/americans-trust-government-remains-low.aspx.

20. Jonathan Haidt, "After Babel: How Social Media Dissolved the Mortar of Society and Made America Stupid," *The Atlantic*, May 2022, 54–66, esp. 58.

III.4 Proverbs 25:1–29:27

Advanced Wisdom and Virtue

If the central collections within Proverbs are conceptualized as the fare at Lady Wisdom's table (9:1–6), then the reader is served a hearty dish of Wisdom's "curricular cuisine" in the second Solomonic collection (25:1–29:27).[1] This dish is for the advanced. While its ingredients consist of familiar topics and themes, they deliver subtle nuances, contain sharp flavors, and require refined moral taste buds to appreciate their pedagogical depth. Having digested the admonitions, exhortations, and motivations of the "words of the wise" (22:17–24:34), the reader is dished out rich analogies, thematic clusters, and a healthy portion of antithetical sayings in the second Solomonic collection. The analogies and thematic clusters mark chs. 25–27, which most consider the initial subunit. These analogies and clusters traffic in vivid images and the majority of the analogies are either asyndetic or turn on a *waw* conjunctive, requiring the reader to chew on them a bit longer before swallowing their advice. Antithetical sayings, by contrast, characterize chs. 28–29, which most regard as the second subunit within the collection. These antithetical sayings return the reader to the pedagogical stability of Prov 10:1–15:33. But this stability is disrupted by the power struggles between the righteous and the wicked and the subcollection's striking attention to the king's nefarious, totalitarian regime. Far from the context of the home, the reader finds themselves in a world of friends and enemies, neighbors and superiors, the righteous and the wicked. The collection projects a world that is conflicted,[2] a world that refuses to legitimize the idea of "safetyism."[3] Pull up a seat, acclimate to the moral cutlery, and prepare for Proverbs's dish of advanced wisdom and virtue.

1. Brown, "The Didactic Power of Metaphor," 138.
2. Brown, "The Pedagogy of Proverbs 10:1–31:9," 174–75.
3. Greg Lukianoff and Jonathan Haidt, *The Coddling of the American Mind: How Good Intentions and Bad Ideas Are Setting Up a Generation for Failure* (New York: Penguin, 2019).

CHAPTER 31

Proverbs 25:1–28

A. Imaging Moral Boundaries and Negotiating Social Bonds

Main Idea of the Passage

The vivid analogies, admonitions, and sentences prescribe sociomoral boundaries and negotiate social bonds through the metaphorical concepts of MORAL BEAUTY, MORAL NURTURANCE, MORAL STRENGTH, and MORAL PURITY to inculcate a sense of place, personhood, and interpersonal relations within a hierarchical world.

Literary Context[1]

Just as the appendix to the "words of the wise" (24:23) evinced a compositional awareness of the "words of the wise" (22:17), so also the materials transcribed by the men of Hezekiah evince a compositional awareness of the "proverbs of Solomon" (10:1a). Similar to the "words of the wise," this awareness is signaled by the adverb "also" (גַּם, v. 1a) as well as the reiteration of the construct phrase "proverbs of Solomon" (מִשְׁלֵי שְׁלֹמֹה; 10:1a; 25:1a). More than acknowledging the previous collection attributed to Solomon, the title creates a sense of literary and compositional continuity in the anthology.

The same is true of the subject matter of Prov 25. While the motifs are reminiscent of topics addressed in Prov 10:1–22:16,[2] they are conveyed through rich imagery and sophisticated forms that cast new light on these familiar themes. The security of the

1. This chapter does not include the Canonical and Theological Significance section. See pp. xv and 276n1 for justification. Also, see pp. 604–7 for the Canonical and Theological Significance of Proverbs 25:1–29:27.

2. Whybray, *Proverbs*, 359; Dell, *The Book of Proverbs*, 79.

royal throne, for example, is established not only through moral revulsion (16:12) but also through metallurgical moral action (v. 5; cf. 20:28; 29:14). The king's powers of perception are depicted as enigmatic and comparable to God's unsearchable wisdom (vv. 2–3; 16:10; 20:8). A timely word is both delightful (15:23) and beautiful (v. 11). In addition to diffusing wrath (15:1), a soft word possesses the power to break a bone (v. 15). A faithful envoy brings both healing (13:17; 15:30) and refreshment (vv. 13, 25). And the unrestrained may exalt folly (14:29), but they remain vulnerable to attack (v. 28). The motifs explored in Prov 25 are addressed across Prov 10:1–22:16. But their convergence in ch. 25 creates a complex sociomoral arena populated by kings, nobles, neighbors, masters, messengers, and enemies.[3] And the vivid analogies in which these motifs are cast engender fresh perspectives that fund the pedagogical development within the central collections.

3. Yoder, *Proverbs*, 246–47.

Translation and Exegetical Outline

(See pages 554–55.)

Structure and Literary Form

If perception is formed through the poetic form of the materials in Proverbs,[4] then the poetic cast of the sayings in Prov 25 shapes the perception of readers in dynamic ways. Admonitions, complete with motivations, direct moral action by appealing to the prospect of honor and shame (vv. 6–7, 8, 9–10, 16–17, 21–22). A better-than saying hones one's moral valuation (v. 24; cf. 21:9, 19). And the preponderance of poetic analogies sharpens one's moral reasoning as well as one's moral imagination. The form of these analogies demands a hermeneutical deftness rarely required elsewhere in the book. The vast majority of the poetic analogies operate under intralinear parallelism. One is conveyed through interlinear parallelism (vv. 4–5). In each case, the opening line(s) or the initial saying supplies the metaphor or simile (vv. 3a, 4, 11a, 12a, 13a, 14a, 18a, 19a, 20a–b, 23a, 25a, 26a, 28a). The subsequent line(s) or saying provides the referent. But the introduction of this referent is startling. Most of the lines that furnish the referent are asyndetic (vv. 11b, 12b, 13b, 14b, 18b, 19b, 26b, 28b); others are marked by a *waw* conjunction (vv. 3b, 20c, 23b, 25b). The unusual syntax of these lines forces the reader to double back to make sense out of the sayings, for their analogies are not formed through formal syntactical constructions; rather, they are formed through parallelism. The parallel lines or sayings are "grammatically equivalent but semantically unequivalent."[5] This semantic asymmetry forms an analogy through parallelism.[6] The structure of the analogies forms the perception and reasoning of the reader. And the relative scarcity of these analogies elsewhere in book evinces the didactic movement across the central collections.[7]

The sophisticated analogies that pervade Prov 25 may correspond to the intricate structure of the chapter. Following Glendon Bryce and Raymond Van Leeuwen, some perceive a coherent "wisdom 'book'" or "proverb poem" in vv. 2–27.[8] According to Bryce, this wisdom "book" is constructed around the repetition of key terms.

4. Von Rad, *Wisdom in Israel*, 24. Also see, Stewart, *Poetic Ethics*, 29–69.

5. Berlin, *The Dynamics of Biblical Parallelism*, 100.

6. For discussion of the phenomenon of metaphorical parallelism, see Berlin, *The Dynamics of Biblical Parallelism*, 99–101.

7. Brown, "The Pedagogy of Proverbs 10:1–31:9," 171, 174. Also see Fox, *Proverbs 10–31*, 775, who notes that the form of the poetic analogies in Prov 25:1–29:27 occur elsewhere only in 10:23, 26; and 11:22.

8. Glendon E. Bryce, "Another Wisdom-'Book' in Proverbs," *JBL* 91 (1972): 145–57; Van Leeuwen, *Context and Meaning*, 57–86.

Proverbs 25:1–28

			III.4 Advanced Wisdom and Virtue (25:1–29:27)
			A. Imaging MORAL BOUNDARIES and Negotiating Social Bonds 25:1–28)
1a	גַּם־אֵלֶּה מִשְׁלֵי שְׁלֹמֹה	These also are proverbs of Solomon,	1. The Title (25:1)
1b	↑ אֲשֶׁר הֶעְתִּיקוּ אַנְשֵׁי חִזְקִיָּה מֶלֶךְ־יְהוּדָה	↑ which the men of Hezekiah, king of Judah, transcribed.	
			2. Imaging MORAL BOUNDARIES and Negotiating Social Bonds (25:2–28)
2a	כְּבֹד אֱלֹהִים הַסְתֵּר דָּבָר	The glory of God, to conceal a matter,	a. Establishing Epistemological Boundaries and Removing Moral Impurity (25:2–5)
2b	וּכְבֹד מְלָכִים חֲקֹר דָּבָר	and the glory of kings, to examine a matter.	
3a	שָׁמַיִם לָרוּם וָאָרֶץ לָעֹמֶק	The heavens for height and the earth for depth,	
3b	וְלֵב מְלָכִים אֵין חֵקֶר	and the heart of kings, unsearchable.	
4a	הָגוֹ סִיגִים מִכָּסֶף	Remove dross from silver,	
4b	וַיֵּצֵא לַצֹּרֵף כֶּלִי	and a vessel comes forth for the refiner.	
5a	הָגוֹ רָשָׁע לִפְנֵי־מֶלֶךְ	Remove the wicked from before a king,	
5b	↑ וְיִכּוֹן בַּצֶּדֶק כִּסְאוֹ	↑ so that his throne will be established by righteousness.	
6a	אַל־תִּתְהַדַּר לִפְנֵי־מֶלֶךְ	Do not honor yourself before a king,	b. Negotiating Social Relations (25:6–15)
6b	וּבִמְקוֹם גְּדֹלִים אַל־תַּעֲמֹד	and do not stand in the place of the great,	
7a	↑ כִּי טוֹב אֲמָר־לְךָ עֲלֵה הֵנָּה	↑ for better that one say to you, "Come up here,"	
7b	מֵהַשְׁפִּילְךָ לִפְנֵי נָדִיב	than one humiliate you before a nobleman.	
7c	↓ אֲשֶׁר רָאוּ עֵינֶיךָ	↓ What your eyes have seen,	
8a	אַל־תֵּצֵא לָרִב מַהֵר	do not bring hastily to argue,	
8b	↑ פֶּן מַה־תַּעֲשֶׂה בְּאַחֲרִיתָהּ	↑ lest – what will you do afterwards,	
8c	↑ בְּהַכְלִים אֹתְךָ רֵעֶךָ	↑ when your neighbor puts you to shame?	
9a	רִיבְךָ רִיב אֶת־רֵעֶךָ	Contest your case with your neighbor,	
9b	וְסוֹד אַחֵר אַל־תְּגָל	but do not reveal the secret of another,	
10a	↑ פֶּן־יְחַסֶּדְךָ שֹׁמֵעַ	↑ lest one who hears revile you,	
10b	וְדִבָּתְךָ לֹא תָשׁוּב	and the slander against you never ceases.	
11a	תַּפּוּחֵי זָהָב בְּמַשְׂכִּיּוֹת כָּסֶף	Apples of gold in settings of silver:	
11b	דָּבָר דָּבֻר עַל־אָפְנָיו	a word spoken in a fitting fashion.	
12a	נֶזֶם זָהָב וַחֲלִי־כָתֶם	A ring of gold and an ornament of fine gold:	
12b	מוֹכִיחַ חָכָם עַל־אֹזֶן שֹׁמָעַת	a wise person rebuking a listening ear.	
13a	כְּצִנַּת־שֶׁלֶג בְּיוֹם קָצִיר	Like the cold of snow on a day of harvest,	

13b	צִיר נֶאֱמָן לְשֹׁלְחָיו	a trustworthy envoy to those who send them;	
13c	וְנֶפֶשׁ אֲדֹנָיו יָשִׁיב	they refresh the life of their masters.	
14a	נְשִׂיאִים וְרוּחַ וְגֶשֶׁם אָיִן	Clouds and wind but no rain,	
14b	אִישׁ מִתְהַלֵּל בְּמַתַּת־שָׁקֶר	a man who boasts of a deceitful gift.	
15a	בְּאֹרֶךְ אַפַּיִם יְפֻתֶּה קָצִין	By patience a ruler can be persuaded,	
15b	וְלָשׁוֹן רַכָּה תִּשְׁבָּר־גָּרֶם	and a soft tongue breaks a bone.	
16a	דְּבַשׁ מָצָאתָ אֱכֹל דַּיֶּךָּ	If you find honey, eat what you require,	c. Negotiating Social Conflict (25:16–27)
16b	↑ פֶּן־תִּשְׂבָּעֶנּוּ וַהֲקֵאתוֹ	↑ lest you become sated and vomit it up.	
17a	הֹקַר רַגְלְךָ מִבֵּית רֵעֶךָ	Rarely visit your neighbor's house,	
17b	↑ פֶּן־יִשְׂבָּעֲךָ וּשְׂנֵאֶךָ	↑ lest he become sated with you and hate you.	
18a	מֵפִיץ וְחֶרֶב וְחֵץ שָׁנוּן	A club and a sword and a sharpened arrow,	
18b	אִישׁ עֹנֶה בְרֵעֵהוּ עֵד שָׁקֶר	a person who testifies against his neighbor as a false witness.	
19a	שֵׁן רֹעָה וְרֶגֶל מוּעָדֶת	A broken tooth and a shaky foot,	
19b	מִבְטָח בּוֹגֵד בְּיוֹם צָרָה	trusting a treacherous person in a day of trouble.	
20a	מַעֲדֶה בֶּגֶד בְּיוֹם קָרָה	One who removes a garment on a cold day,	
20b	מֶץ עַל־נָתֶר	vinegar on a wound,	
20c	וְשָׁר בַּשִּׁרִים עַל לֶב־רָע	and one who sings songs to a troubled heart.	
21a	אִם־רָעֵב שֹׂנַאֲךָ הַאֲכִלֵהוּ לָחֶם	If your enemy is hungry, feed him food;	
21b	וְאִם־צָמֵא הַשְׁקֵהוּ מָיִם	and if he is thirsty, give him water to drink.	
22a	↑ כִּי גֶחָלִים אַתָּה חֹתֶה עַל־רֹאשׁוֹ	↑ For you will heap burning coals on his head,	
22b	│ וַיהוָה יְשַׁלֶּם־לָךְ	│ and YHWH will reward you.	
23a	רוּחַ צָפוֹן תְּחוֹלֵל גָּשֶׁם	The north wind brings rain,	
23b	וּפָנִים נִזְעָמִים לְשׁוֹן סָתֶר	and a secretive tongue, angry faces.	
24a	טוֹב שֶׁבֶת עַל־פִּנַּת־גָּג	Better to dwell on the corner of a roof,	
24b	מֵאֵשֶׁת מִדְיָנִים וּבֵית חָבֶר	than a shared house with a quarrelsome woman.	
25a	מַיִם קָרִים עַל־נֶפֶשׁ עֲיֵפָה	Cold water for a thirsty throat,	
25b	וּשְׁמוּעָה טוֹבָה מֵאֶרֶץ מֶרְחָק	and a good report from a distant land.	
26a	מַעְיָן נִרְפָּשׂ וּמָקוֹר מָשְׁחָת	A muddied spring and a polluted fountain,	
26b	צַדִּיק מָט לִפְנֵי־רָשָׁע	a righteous person tottering before the wicked.	
27a	אָכֹל דְּבַשׁ הַרְבּוֹת לֹא־טוֹב	Eating much honey, not good,	
27b	וְחֵקֶר כְּבֹדָם כָּבוֹד	and searching out difficult things is without glory.	
28a	עִיר פְּרוּצָה אֵין חוֹמָה	A breached city without a wall:	d. The (In)stability of Moral Bounds (25:28)
28b	אִישׁ אֲשֶׁר אֵין מַעְצָר לְרוּחוֹ	a person whose spirit is unrestrained.	

These terms serve as "structural rubrics" that mark the beginning, middle, and end of the "book," forming the following chiasm:[9]

Glory (כָּבֹד, v. 2)
  Honey (דְּבַשׁ, v. 16a)
  Honey (דְּבַשׁ, v. 27a)
Glory (כָּבוֹד, v. 27b)

Van Leeuwen nuances this macrostructural design, detecting a double chiastic *inclusio*:[10]

A Examine . . . Glory (כָּבֹד . . . חֲקֹר, v. 2)
  B Wicked . . . By Righteousness (רָשָׁע . . . בַּצֶּדֶק, v. 5)
  B′ Righteous . . . Wicked (צַדִּיק . . . רָשָׁע, v. 26b)
A′ Searching . . . Glory (חֵקֶר . . . כָּבוֹד, v. 27b)

According to Van Leeuwen, these chiastic *inclusio*s outline the macrostructure of the "proverb poem." The first furnishes a formal framework around the unit (vv. 2, 27b); the second reinforces the poetic parameters of the piece (vv. 5, 26b). When Bryce's and Van Leeuwen's proposals are taken together, vv. 2–27 may be divided into three units, each of which offer variations on two prominent themes. The first serves as a formal introduction, delineating the themes of God-king-subjects and the conflict between good and evil that drive the unit (vv. 2–3, 4–5).[11] The second (vv. 6–15) and third (vv. 16–27) develop these motifs by attending to various issues pertaining to social hierarchy, the moral order, and social conflict and its resolution. Whether or not Bryce and Van Leeuwen's structural proposals ring true with one's experience of reading,[12] they identify the repetition of key terms, sketch the general contours of the unit, and orient one to prominent themes within the chapter.

9. Bryce, "Another Wisdom-'Book,'" 151–53.

10. Van Leeuwen, *Context and Meaning*, 70–71.

11. Bryce, "Another Wisdom- 'Book,'" 151; Van Leeuwen, *Context and Meaning*, 63.

12. Fox, *Proverbs 10–31*, 776. Also see Whybray, *Proverbs*, 358, who expresses appreciation for Bryce's and Van Leeuwen's structural observations but finds their contention that the proverb poem was composed for a courtly audience unconvincing.

Explanation of the Text

1. Title (25:1)

Similar to the first Solomonic collection (10:1a), the second opens with a title. On formal grounds, this title initiates a transition from the admonitions and exhortations of the "words of the wise" (22:17a; 24:23a) to a collection of rich analogies and politicized antithetical sayings. On compositional grounds, the adverb "also" (גַּם, v. 1a), combined with the expression "proverbs of Solomon" (מִשְׁלֵי שְׁלֹמֹה, v. 1a), relates the materials to the titles of previous collections (1:1a; 10:1a). But in contrast to previous titles, v. 1b introduces a relative clause, which sketches the compositional history of the collection. This history remains a sketch, for the social status of Hezekiah's men and the nature of their literary activities are unclear.[13] If nothing else, the relative clause situates the production of the collection in the late eighth century under the patronage of Hezekiah; it bears witness to the close connection between writing and the royal court as well as Hezekiah's attempt to usher in a new golden age by recovering the literature of a past golden age.[14] Hezekiah entrusted a group of literate individuals with proverbs attributed to Solomon. And this group moved these Solomonic proverbs from one place to another; that is, they "transcribed" them (הֶעְתִּיקוּ, v. 1b).[15]

2. Imaging Moral Boundaries and Negotiating Social Bonds (25:2–28)

a. Establishing Epistemological Boundaries and Removing Moral Impurity (25:2–5)

In light of the royal context of the collection's transcription, it is not surprising that it opens with a series of sayings pertaining to kings and members of the court (vv. 2–7b). The first couplet is bound together by the catchwords "kings" (מְלָכִים, vv. 2b, 3b) and "examine/unsearchable" (חקר, vv. 2b, 3b). The proverbial pair addresses the hierarchical structure of the moral order through the concept of boundaries. These boundaries are epistemological. They concern the prerogatives, knowledge, and glory appropriate to God, kings, and subjects. God obtains glory by concealing his complex, mysterious activities within the cosmos (v. 2a). Kings, by contrast, obtain glory by executing their royal prerogatives, investigating human motives and actions in matters concerning the state or judicial affairs (v. 2b). Just as kings cannot grasp the depths of God's equivocal acts in the cosmos, so also the king's subjects cannot penetrate the profundity of his unfathomable heart (v. 3). Whereas v. 2 distinguishes the epistemological boundaries appropriate to God and kings, the imagery and language of v. 3 blur these boundaries. The cosmic merism

13. For an excellent discussion of the status of scribes and the nature of scribal education in ancient Israel, see Christopher A. Rollston, *Writing and Literacy in the World of Ancient Israel: Epigraphic Evidence from the Iron Age*, ABS 11 (Atlanta: SBL Press, 2010), 85–126.

14. Schniedewind, *How the Bible Became a Book*, 64–90, esp. 76. Also see Eva Mroczek, "Hezekiah the Censor and Ancient Theories of Canon Formation," *JBL* 140 (2021): 481–502.

15. The verb conveys the notion of moving something from one place to another. The LXX, Syriac, and Targum render the verb "to copy, write down," while the Vulgate reads "to transfer." In each case, the compositional activities of Hezekiah's men are vague.

"heavens and earth" and the expression "unsearchable" (אֵין חֵקֶר, v. 3b) are employed elsewhere in the Old Testament with reference to God (Job 5:9; 9:10; 26:14; Pss 115:15–16; 145:3).[16] By applying these images and expressions to kings, Prov 25:3 places the monarch's wisdom and glory in intimate relationship with the divine. The couplet maps the hierarchy of the moral order. But it does not focus on one's moral responsibilities within this order; rather, it foregrounds the epistemological boundaries of kings and subjects under God's governance, identifying the epistemological space one is to inhabit.

The second couplet extends the royal prerogatives mentioned in the first, focusing attention on the elimination of wicked officials in cooperation with righteous courtiers (vv. 4–5). The anaphoric infinitive absolute "remove" (הָגוֹ, vv. 4a, 5a) links the aphorisms. And metallurgical imagery shapes the analogy across the adjacent poetic lines. This analogy operates under the metaphorical concept of MORAL PURITY.[17] The severe process of purification, however, is terse and elliptical. The initial saying telescopes the production of a vessel: it moves from the metallurgist's extraction of dross from silver to the immediate appearance of a durable vessel (v. 4). The immediacy of the process may express the expectation of immediate security when the wicked are removed from the presence of the king.[18] The yawning gap in this process, on the other hand, may create space to imagine the manner by which the king's throne is established in righteousness. The purification process delineated in v. 4 depicts the work of an artisan. This artisan may serve as a model for the king or for righteous courtiers. If the former, then the analogy urges the king to secure righteous rule by removing moral scum from the court.[19] If the latter, then the analogy invites one into a world of political intrigue and calls righteous courtiers to participate in a partisan agenda that ousts the wicked so as to secure the royal throne.[20] The openness of the analogy intimates that both options are possible; it invites both kings and righteous courtiers to establish just rule by cleansing the court from moral impurity.

b. Negotiating Social Relations (25:6–15)

The open and implicit role of members of the court in the establishment of righteous rule provides a fitting entrée into vv. 6–15, which situate the reader in various social situations in order to cultivate virtues that contribute to personal and communal flourishing. Similar to the previous proverbial pairs, vv. 6–7b consider one's place "before a king" (לִפְנֵי־מֶלֶךְ, vv. 5a, 6a) within a defined social hierarchy (vv. 2–3). The word order of the admonitions places the reader on the periphery, outside the king's presence and the place of the great.[21] The verbs proscribe an attitude of self-aggrandizement as well as a self-selected presence among nobles. Within this liminal social space, humility and prudence nurture a self-awareness that may engender social mobility. These virtues are advocated through a causal clause (כִּי, "for," v. 7a), which motivates modesty in the form of a better-than saying (v. 7a–b). The reader is written into the saying and invited to hear the invitation to social promotion (v. 7a), on the one hand, and to experience the shame of social degradation (v. 7b), on the other. Perceiving one's place among the po-

16. Van Leeuwen, *Context and Meaning*, 75–76.

17. For discussion of this metaphorical concept, see Lakoff and Johnson, *Philosophy in the Flesh*, 307–8.

18. Fox, *Proverbs 10–31*, 779.

19. Van Leeuwen, *Context and Meaning*, 79–80; Fox, *Proverbs 10–31*, 779.

20. Heim, *Poetic Imagination*, 403.

21. Yoder, *Proverbs*, 249.

litically powerful evinces prudence. And a posture of humility moves one from the social periphery to a position of influence.

Just as the prospect of social shame motivates a particular posture among the powerful (vv. 6–7b), so also the prospect of social shame directs personal relations with one's neighbor. While vv. 7c–8 and 9–10 may be read as independent admonitions, complete with motivations, their catchwords (רִיב, "argue/case," vv. 8a, 9a; רֵעֶךָ, "your neighbor," vv. 8c, 9a) and concern with social humiliation indicate that they may be read together. Taken together, they promote particular virtues associated with quarreling from two distinct angles. The first employs optical imagery to cultivate discernment and foresight (v. 7c–8).[22] Since appearances can be deceiving, one should avoid impetuous litigation against one's neighbor. The motive for exercising caution in this situation is expressed through an anacoluthon.[23] The conjunction "lest" opens a negative purpose clause (v. 8b); but the clause is immediately broken by the introduction of a rhetorical question. The question writes the reader into the saying, asking one to consider the social dishonor one will suffer for their haste.

The second proverbial pair employs aural imagery to encourage confidentiality (vv. 9–10). The exhortation permits dispute with one's neighbor (v. 9a); but the admonition prohibits betraying his confidence (v. 9b). The motivation for the prohibition is supplied by a negative purpose clause (פֶּן; "lest," v. 10a). Again, the reader is written into the clause and invited to envision the experience of reproach and unending slander (v. 10). Social shame and defamation of character fund vv. 7c–10, providing powerful motivations for the development of foresight, discernment, and confidentiality in personal relationships.

Admonitions pertaining to interpersonal disputes give way to a pair of sayings that compare eloquent speech with elegant jewelry (vv. 11–12). These sayings are intimately related to one another. They are linked by the catchword "gold" (זָהָב, vv. 11a, 12a). Each saying opens with a pair of metaphors. The referent of these metaphors is delivered through an unmarked, asyndetic clause (vv. 11b; 12b). And the analogies drawn in each saying operate under the metaphor of MORAL BEAUTY. The beauty of fine speech is explored from two different angles. The first considers the beauty of a word spoken "in a fitting fashion" (עַל־אָפְנָיו, v. 11b), that is, in the right manner and circumstances.[24] This word is comparable to the allurement of an intricately crafted ornament.[25] The second saying describes the beauty of a listening ear that receives rebuke (v. 12). Far from representing a mismatch, they form the perfect pedagogical pair. Each enhances the elegance of the other, just as golden

22. The Masoretes connected the relative clause אֲשֶׁר רָאוּ עֵינֶיךָ ("whom your eyes have seen") in 25:7c to נָדִיב ("nobleman") in v. 7a–b. This reading is possible, but it seems the relative clause is linked to v. 8a: the former introduces the object, while the latter supplies the subject and predicate (*IBHS* §19.3c). This reading eliminates the ambiguity in both vv. 7 and 8 by identifying what one is not to bring hastily. LXX, Syriac, Symmachus, Meinhold, *Die Sprüche*, 2:417.

23. Delitzsch, "Book of Proverbs," 6:368 (2:154).

24. The meaning of the phrase עַל־אָפְנָיו is obscure. In general, scholars render the *hapax legomenon* אָפְנָיו as a dual form from אוֹפַן ("wheel") or as a plural form that may be countable ("circumstances, moment") or abstract ("time"). The latter proposal is supported by the cognate Arabic term *iffan* ("time") and the use of בְּעִתּוֹ in Prov 15:23. But as a dual form, the idiom may be construed as a word spoken "in its ways," that is, in a fitting manner. For discussion, see Whybray, *Proverbs*, 364; Fox, *Proverbs 10–31*, 783.

25. While the sense of the imagery in Prov 25:11a is clear, the meaning of תַּפּוּחֵי ("apples") and מַשְׂכִּיּוֹת ("settings") is unclear. The former occurs five times in the Old Testament (Joel 1:12; Prov 25:11; Song 2:3, 5; 7:9; 8:5), where it denotes some sort of fruit. The latter carries several different nuances, ranging from carved, idolatrous images (Lev 26:1; Num 33:52; Ezek 8:12) to an image produced by the mind (Ps 73:7; Prov 18:11). For discussion of the terms, see Whybray, *Proverbs*, 364.

rings and ornaments enhance the appearance of the one who wears them. When the different angles of these sayings converge, they offer an aesthetics of speech, delivered in the right way (v. 11b) and by the right person to one who possesses the right posture (v. 12b).

Against the backdrop of this aesthetics of speech, v. 13 depicts the refreshment that faithful speakers bring to their superiors. In contrast to the previous analogies, it opens with a marked simile (v. 13a). Like the previous analogies, however, the referent of the simile is expressed through an unmarked, asyndetic clause (v. 13b). The saying considers the relationship between messengers and their masters through the metaphor of MORAL NURTURANCE. And this nurturance is conveyed through imagery of relief. As those who assume the responsibility of faithfully representing their masters, a trustworthy envoy revives their senders. More specifically, a trustworthy envoy refreshes the "throat" or "life" (נֶפֶשׁ, v. 13c) of their masters, just as the cold of snow refreshes the life of the landowner during the heat of harvest. The imagery captures the way in which faithful messengers care for and sustain their masters, and it explores how messengers nurture social bonds.

If v. 13 reflects on the way in which messengers nurture social bonds, v. 14 explores the way in which a poseur cuts social ties. Similar to many of the analogies in the chapter, the saying opens with a metaphor (v. 14a) and the second line introduces the referent through an asyndetic clause (v. 14b). On an initial reading, the meteorological metaphor offers the promise of refreshment: "clouds and wind and rain" (נְשִׂיאִים וְרוּחַ וְגֶשֶׁם, v. 14a). It is only when one arrives at the final word of the initial line that the promise dissipates: "there is not" (אָיִן, v. 14a). Despite the promising conditions, the hope of refreshment remains unfulfilled. The same is true of the windbag. This person boasts of a gift but fails to deliver. In so doing, the poseur is portrayed as one whose fraud fractures social relations.

In addition to fracturing relationships, words possess the paradoxical power to break people. This oxymoron is the focus of attention in v. 15. The initial line describes the persuasive power of patience. This virtuous disposition serves as the quiet means by which a social superior is "persuaded," even "gulled" (יְפֻתֶּה, v. 15a).[26] The second line intensifies the thought of the first, moving from the power of a patient disposition to the force of tender speech. The imagery is shocking. A soft tongue is rendered as weapon capable of shattering one of the hardest tissues in the human body. More than persuading people or dispelling wrath (v. 15a; 15:1), gentle speech can overcome recalcitrance.

c. Negotiating Social Conflict (25:16–27)

Similar to the second subunit within the chapter (vv. 6–15), the third explores interpersonal relationships in general and social conflict in particular. The subunit is framed by the terms "eat" (אכל, vv. 16a, 27a) and "honey" (דְּבַשׁ, vv. 16a, 27a);[27] and it devotes specific attention to the virtues of moderation and self-control. These virtues are foregrounded in vv. 16–17, which outline the dangers of transgressing authorized boundaries. These boundaries are both personal and interpersonal. An unmarked conditional clause creates the conditions for the establishment of proper personal limits (v. 16a). Honey may be pleasant, therapeutic, and satisfying (cf. 24:13), but overindulgence

26. McKane, *Proverbs*, 584.

27. Bryce, "Another Wisdom-'Book,'" 153; Van Leeuwen, *Context and Meaning*, 70–71.

induces vomiting. This warning against personal excess is applied to interpersonal relationships in 25:17. The repetition of the verb "sated" (שׂבע, vv. 16b, 17b) within a parallel negative purpose clause ("lest," פֶּן, vv. 16b, 17b) maps the dangers of excessive eating onto the dangers of excessive time in a neighbor's house. Just as inordinate eating engenders vomiting, so also inordinate visits to one's neighbor engenders conflict. The exhortations and motivations highlight the value of moderation by sketching the consequences of violating moral boundaries.

The motif of social conflict in interpersonal relations is developed in vv. 18–20. These sayings follow the same syntax; each opens with a metaphor that guides the evaluation of an aberrant character type, and these aberrant character types are cast in either an asyndetic clause (vv. 18b, 19b) or a clause marked by *waw* (v. 20c). The cache of deadly weapons introduced in v. 18a captures the nature of one who testifies against his neighbor as a false witness (v. 18b; cf. Exod 20:16). The perjurer is a force of evil within the community, one whose words wound and kill. Similar to the perjurer, the treacherous one fails to nurture social bonds (Prov 25:19). Like a decaying tooth and a dilapidated foot, this untrustworthy personage disappoints and inflicts pain during a time of need. This experience of interpersonal pain is elaborated upon in v. 20, which compares the insensitivity of one who sings songs to a troubled heart with the bite of exposure to the cold and the sting of vinegar on a wound.[28] Far from nurturing social ties, this trinity of aberrant characters tear the relational fabric of the community. The vivid metaphors associated with each indicate that they not only instigate conflict; they also inflict pain.

The pain inflicted on the community by aberrant characters furnishes the occasion for providing an ethical paradigm for resolving social conflict in vv. 21–22.[29] The pair of conditional protases project the circumstances of potential conflict, while the apodoses prescribe a particular form of action (v. 21). In the face of a vulnerable enemy, one is to provide for their needs rather than seize the opportunity to exact vengeance. The rationale and motivation for this expression of charity is presented through a causal clause ("for," כִּי, v. 22a). While the meaning of the expression "you will heap burning coals on his head" (גֶּחָלִים אַתָּה חֹתֶה עַל־רֹאשׁוֹ, v. 22a) is uncertain, in the present context it appears that the metaphor describes the contrition of the enemy and the reconciliation of the hostile parties, as YHWH's reward extends beyond the compassionate to restore the relationship between the antagonists.[30] Charity serves as the means by which relational enmity is pacified.

In spite of the proposed paradigm for conflict resolution in vv. 21–22, social conflict continues in vv. 23–24. The former is cast in the form of an analogy that reiterates the relationship between wind and words to portray the odious effects of secret slander (v. 23; cf. v. 14). But the metaphor that governs the analogy is puzzling, since rain is produced by the west wind in Israel. Whether the image of the "north wind" (רוּחַ צָפוֹן, v. 23a) is a generalization that does not require meteorological precision within a proverb or a wordplay on "hidden wind" (רוּחַ צָפוֹן, with the homonym צָפוֹן), the comparison is clear: just as the (hidden) north

28. For the reading "wound" rather than "natron," see G. R. Driver, "Problems and Solutions," *VT* 4 (1954): 240–42; Waltke, *Proverbs: Chapters 15–31*, 306n42. Cf. Fox, *Proverbs 10–31*, 786.

29. Van Leeuwen, *Context and Meaning*, 85.

30. Whybray, *Proverbs*, 368; Murphy, *Proverbs*, 193, 195; Waltke, *Proverbs: Chapters 15–31*, 331–32. Cf. Boström, *The God of the Sages*, 110; Fox, *Proverbs 10–31*, 787.

wind produces rain, so also one who whispers (hidden) gossip produces communal anger.[31] Though cloaked in secrecy, slander unleashes social strife.

The communal conflict engendered by secret gossip is comparable to the contentious domestic environment produced by a quarrelsome woman (v. 23; cf. 21:9, 19). Against the backdrop of the meteorological imagery in 25:23, the "corner of a roof" (עַל־פִּנַּת־גָּג, v. 24a) may connote exposure to the natural elements, which is considered better than a shared house with a tumultuous woman.[32] The corner of a roof, on the other hand, may refer to a roof chamber (cf. 2 Kgs 4:10)—the ancient equivalent to a single, dormitory room. In this case, the better-than saying commends living in the relative inconvenience of such a place over marrying and establishing a household with a quarrelsome woman.[33] Whichever reading is preferred, conflict and contention animate the sayings, identifying their presence within the community (Prov 25:23) as well as the household (v. 24).

Relief from both communal and domestic conflict is provided by v. 25, which returns to the promise of refreshment and the metaphor of MORAL NURTURANCE. The saying recasts the simile in v. 13, focusing attention on the restorative power of a good report from afar. Waiting for news from a distant land can make one weary (עֲיֵפָה, v. 25a). But the arrival of good news revives the soul and satisfies desire, just as cold water quenches a "thirsty throat" (נֶפֶשׁ עֲיֵפָה, v. 25a). The news nourishes one's life and nurtures social relations.

This is not the case in v. 26, which muddies the water imagery in v. 25. The analogy reflects on the downfall of the righteous before the wicked through the metaphorical concept of MORAL PURITY. Nuancing aphorisms that indicate the righteous will never "totter" (יִמּוֹט, 10:30a; 12:3b), the saying bears witness to the reality of the righteous "tottering" (מָט, 25:26b) before the wicked. This oppression at the hands of the wicked is catastrophic for the community; it contaminates the waters of justice and pollutes the resources necessary for communal well-being. The analogy qualifies the litany of sayings concerning the stability of the righteous and develops that notion that the righteous may fall (24:16a).

The final aphorism in the subunit returns to the topic of eating honey and the metaphorical concept of boundaries (25:27; cf. v. 2b, 16a). Similar to other sayings within the central collections, the initial line employs the rhetorical technique of litotes to express the dangers of excessive indulgence (v. 27a; cf. 16:29; 17:26; 18:5; 19:2; 20:23). But excessive eating is not the issue. Just as the matter of excess in 25:16 was applied in v. 17, so also the matter of excess in the initial line is applied in the second line. But the nature of the analogy is unclear. The second line of the MT reads "and the search of their glory is glory" (וְחֵקֶר כְּבֹדָם כָּבוֹד, v. 27b). The sense of the line is puzzling, and the pronominal suffix lacks a clear antecedent. Various emendations have been proposed to resolve the ambiguity. Among them, it seems best to read the line as "and searching out difficult things is without glory."[34] In view of this reading, the aphorism compares the consumption

31. Whybray, *Proverbs*, 368–69; Fox, *Proverbs 10–31*, 789.

32. Van Leeuwen, *Context and Meaning*, 85.

33. Heim, *Poetic Imagination*, 507–8n11.

34. This rendering repoints כְּבֹדָם as a plural adjective used substantively (כְּבֵדִים; "heavy, difficult things") and reads כָּבוֹד as מִכָּבוֹד ("apart from/without glory"), understanding the *min* as a case of haplography. See Delitzsch, "Book of Proverbs," 6:379 (2:171–72); Bryce, "Another Wisdom-'Book,'" 150; Raymond C. Van Leeuwen, "Proverbs XXV 27 Once Again," *VT* 36 (1986): 105–14, esp. 110–11; Waltke, *Proverbs: Chapters 15–31*, 307–8n53. Cf. Fox, *Proverbs 10–31*, 790.

of excessive honey with the investigation of difficult things. Just as the ingestion of excess sweets is not good, so also the intellectual exploration of matters that lie beyond one's epistemological capacity is not honorable. Both lines capture the importance of living within proper boundaries. This motif as well as the terms "searching" (חֵקֶר, vv. 27b, 2b) and "glory" (כָּבוֹד, vv. 27b, 2b) recall the opening sayings of the chapter (vv. 2–3). They establish the literary boundaries of the broader discourse unit and reinforce one of the prominent themes within the piece.

d. The (In)Stability of Moral Bounds (25:28)

The concern with moderation and proper boundaries in the previous sayings intersects in v. 28. The analogy compares one who is unable to limit or curb his spirit with a city vulnerable and defenseless from external attacks. The imagery within the initial line appears to telescope an assault, moving from a breach to the dissolution of a city wall. One who cannot restrain his spirit not only lacks moral strength (cf. 16:32), but this person also transgresses proper limits and leaves themselves without the protection of boundaries.

CHAPTER 32

Proverbs 26:1–28

B. Producing Perspectival Knowledge: *Perceiving People, Social Situations, and the Self*

Main Idea of the Passage

The materials attend to the actions and interrelations of particular immoral prototypes in order to produce a form of perspectival knowledge that enables one to perceive people, social situations, and the self through the prism of wisdom and virtue.

Literary Context[1]

When read against the backdrop of ch. 25, the initial saying in ch. 26 elaborates upon the proper parameters of glory (v. 1; cf. v. 8). Just as the exploration of matters that lie beyond one's epistemological capacity is without "glory" (כָּבוֹד; 25:27b; cf. 25:2), so also the bestowal of "honor" (כָּבוֹד, 26:1b) on a fool is not fitting, for it transgresses normative policies regarding the distribution of social capital.[2] But when ch. 26 is read within the broader context of the central collections, one encounters familiar characters, and the variant repetitions within the chapter indicate that the portraits of these characters are painted with common hues.[3] Familiarity with these characters and colors should not breed contempt, for their portraits contain subtleties and surprises that not only sharpen one's perception of the central features

1. This chapter does not include the Explanation of the Text or the Canonical and Theological Significance sections. See pp. xv and 276n1 for justification. Also, see pp. 604–7 for the Canonical and Theological Significance of Prov 25:1–29:27.

2. For discussion of the "world upside down" topos underlying v. 1, see Raymond C. Van Leeuwen, "Proverbs 30:21–23 and the Biblical World Upside Down," *JBL* 105 (1986): 599–610.

3. The variant repetitions include **26:12**//10:13b//19:29b//23:3b; 22:29a//29:20a; **26:13**//22:13; **26:15**//19:24; **26:22**//18:8; **26:1b**//26:8b; **26:4a**//26:5a; **26:7b**//26:9b. For discussion of each variant set, see Heim, *Poetic Imagination*.

of these prototypes but also sketch their fuzzy boundaries.[4] Take, for example, the fool (vv. 1–12). He is rendered as one who knows and deploys proverbs (vv. 7, 9), finds prestigious employment (vv. 6, 10), and receives social honor (vv. 1, 8; cf. 17:7; 19:10)—all to the detriment of the community. Nonetheless, the fool is considered better than "a person wise in his own eyes" (אִישׁ חָכָם בְּעֵינָיו, 26:12). This is not the case with the sluggard, who, in contrast to previous materials (6:6–11; 24:30–34), embodies a fatal moral vision rather than the prospect of poverty.[5] Despite his ironic excuses (26:13; cf. 22:13), habitual turning over in bed (26:14), and eating habits (v. 15; cf. 19:24), he considers himself wiser than those who answer with discernment (26:16). This striking failure of self-perception serves as the backdrop against which many of the malevolent characters manifest a measure of social discretion. They know what people like to eat (26:22; cf. 18:8); and in light of their understanding of social and relational norms, they put on a façade and play their relational part, all the while concealing inner evil and deceit (26:23, 24–25, 26a).

The subtle portraits of the fool (vv. 1–12), the sluggard (vv. 13–16), and the malevolent (vv. 17–28) demonstrate that the problem with these aberrant character types is not their ignorance or lack of propositional knowledge. That is, the problem is not their lack of a descriptive knowledge—a "knowing that" or "knowing about" things. Whether the fool delivers a harmless or a perilous proverb (vv. 7, 9), he knows and performs popular sayings. The sluggard possesses a particular self-perception (v. 16); and the malevolent navigate relationships with an understanding of sociomoral norms (vv. 22, 23, 24, 26). The problem with these aberrant character types is their lack of perspectival knowledge, a knowledge that would allow them to see themselves and the world through a particular mode of cognition.[6] This mode of cognition is shaped by an understanding of the conditions of creaturehood and the limits of wisdom in relationship with YHWH. And the failure to perceive oneself and the world from this perspectival perspective is seen most clearly through the unique expression that punctuates the chapter: "one who is wise in his own eyes" (חָכָם בְּעֵינָיו, vv. 5b, 12a, 16a; cf. 3:7; 16:2; 28:26). As Raymond Van Leeuwen rightly notes, this type of individual engages "in a fatal act of self-perception" that is rooted in a "failure of self-knowledge."[7] This failure of self-knowledge evinces a lack of perspectival knowledge. Without perspectival knowledge, aberrant characters know neither their place in the cosmos nor themselves.

More than revealing the nuanced nature of these aberrant characters and their fuzzy boundaries, the materials in ch. 26 produce perspectival knowledge.[8] To be

4. Johnson, *Moral Imagination*, 8–9, 189–92; Stewart, *Poetic Ethics*, 170–200; Millar, *Genre and Openness*, 89–110.

5. Brown, "The Pedagogy of Proverbs 10:1–31:9," 174.

6. Jindo, "On the Biblical Notion," 433–53.

7. Van Leeuwen, *Context and Meaning*, 105.

8. This is comparable to Van Leeuwen's contention that vv. 1–12 are a "'treatise' on the 'hermeneutics' of wisdom." Van Leeuwen, *Context and Meaning*, 99. The hermeneutical concerns of vv. 1–12 are extended by Heim to include "the hermeneutics of proverb reception" and "proverb performance

specific, they provide a perspectival evaluation of certain people, social relations, and actions. They force the reader to perceive themselves before the face of certain people in certain situations (vv. 4–5, 12a; cf. 22:29a; 29:20a). And they nurture the discernment necessary to interpret and answer people in the right way and in accord with the right strategy (26:4–5, 24–25).[9] In so doing, the materials offer a perspectival lens through which to view people, social situations, and the self. This perspectival lens cultivates perception—a faculty of discrimination that recognizes concrete particulars in specific circumstances.[10] The focused and extended attention to the fool, the sluggard, and the malevolent as well as the perspective through which they are construed contributes to the pedagogical movement within the central collections of Proverbs. Familiar characters are painted with common colors, but the vivid texture of their portraits and the interrelationship among their sayings broaden the construal of particular people, actions, and relations in the social world so as to (re)calibrate one's perspectival knowledge.

III. "Forming 'Fearers of YHWH'": The Curriculum of Wisdom and Virtue (10:1–29:27)
- III.1 Elementary Wisdom and Virtue (10:1–15:33)
- III.2 Intermediate Wisdom and Virtue (16:1–22:16)
- III.3 Vocational Wisdom and Virtue (22:17–24:34)
- **III.4 Advanced Wisdom and Virtue (25:1–29:27)**
  - A. Imaging MORAL BOUNDARIES and Negotiating Social Bonds (25:1–28)
  - ➡ **B. Producing Perspectival Knowledge: Perceiving People, Social Scenarios, and the Self (26:1–28)**
  - C. Emotions and Relationships: The Feelings that Foster and Frustrate Social Bonds (27:1–27)
  - D. An Ethics of Power: Personal, Communal, and Economic Perspectives (28:1–28)
  - E. MORAL AUTHORITY and the MORAL ORDER: (Il)legitimate Power and Moral Responsibility (29:1–27)

Translation and Exegetical Outline

(See pages 567–68.)

response." Knut M. Heim, "Prov 26:1–12: A Crash Course on the Hermeneutics of Proverb Reception and a Case Study in Proverbs Performance Response," *WO* 40 (2010): 34–53.

9. Heim, "Prov 26:1–12," 48–51; Fox, *Proverbs 10–31*, 793–94.

10. Martha C. Nussbaum, *The Fragility of Goodness: Luck and Ethics in Greek Tragedy and Philosophy* (Cambridge: Cambridge University Press, 1986), 300–301.

Proverbs 26:1–28

1a	כַּשֶּׁלֶג בַּקַּיִץ וְכַמָּטָר בַּקָּצִיר	Like snow in summer and like rain at harvest,	B. Producing Perspectival Knowledge: Perceiving People, Social Scenarios, and the Self (26:1–28)
1b	כֵּן לֹא־נָאוֶה לִכְסִיל כָּבוֹד	so honor is not fitting for a fool.	
2a	כַּצִּפּוֹר לָנוּד כַּדְּרוֹר לָעוּף	As a bird for wandering, as a swallow for flying,	
2b	כֵּן קִלְלַת חִנָּם לֹא תָבֹא	so a curse without cause never arrives.	
3a	שׁוֹט לַסּוּס מֶתֶג לַחֲמוֹר	A whip for the horse, a bridle for the donkey,	
3b	וְשֵׁבֶט לְגֵו כְּסִילִים	and a rod for the back of fools.	
4a	אַל־תַּעַן כְּסִיל כְּאִוַּלְתּוֹ	Do not answer a fool according to his folly,	
4b	↑ פֶּן־תִּשְׁוֶה־לּוֹ גַם־אָתָּה	↑ lest you become like him, even you!	
5a	עֲנֵה כְסִיל כְּאִוַּלְתּוֹ	Answer a fool according to his folly	
5b	↑ פֶּן־יִהְיֶה חָכָם בְּעֵינָיו	↑ lest he be wise in his own eyes.	
6a	מְקַצֶּה רַגְלַיִם חָמָס שֹׁתֶה	Cutting off one's feet, drinking violence:	
6b	שֹׁלֵחַ דְּבָרִים בְּיַד־כְּסִיל	one who sends word by the hand of a fool.	
7a	דַּלְיוּ שֹׁקַיִם מִפִּסֵּחַ	Legs dangle from the lame,	
7b	וּמָשָׁל בְּפִי כְסִילִים	and a proverb in the mouth of fools.	
8a	כִּצְרוֹר אֶבֶן בְּמַרְגֵּמָה	Like one who binds a stone in a sling,	
8b	כֵּן־נוֹתֵן לִכְסִיל כָּבוֹד	so is one who gives honor to a fool.	
9a	חוֹחַ עָלָה בְיַד־שִׁכּוֹר	A thornbush coming into the hand of a drunk,	
9b	וּמָשָׁל בְּפִי כְסִילִים	and a proverb in the mouth of a fool.	
10a	רַב מְחוֹלֶל־כֹּל	An archer who pierces everyone,	
10b	וְשֹׂכֵר כְּסִיל וְשֹׂכֵר עֹבְרִים	and one who hires a fool and one who hires a passerby.	
11a	כְּכֶלֶב שָׁב עַל־קֵאוֹ	Like a dog returning to its vomit,	
11b	כְּסִיל שׁוֹנֶה בְאִוַּלְתּוֹ	a fool repeating his folly.	
12a	רָאִיתָ אִישׁ חָכָם בְּעֵינָיו	Have you seen a person wise in his own eyes?	
12b	תִּקְוָה לִכְסִיל מִמֶּנּוּ	There is more hope for a fool than for him.	
13a	אָמַר עָצֵל שַׁחַל בַּדָּרֶךְ	The sluggard says, "A lion in the street!	
13b	אֲרִי בֵּין הָרְחֹבוֹת	A lion in the squares!"	
14a	הַדֶּלֶת תִּסּוֹב עַל־צִירָהּ	The door turns on its hinge,	
14b	וְעָצֵל עַל־מִטָּתוֹ	and the sluggard on his bed.	
15a	טָמַן עָצֵל יָדוֹ בַּצַּלָּחַת	The sluggard buries his hand in the bowl,	
15b	נִלְאָה לַהֲשִׁיבָהּ אֶל־פִּיו	he is too weary to bring it back to his mouth.	

Continued on next page.

Continued from previous page.

16a	חָכָם עָצֵל בְּעֵינָיו	The sluggard is wiser in his own eyes
16b	מִשִּׁבְעָה מְשִׁיבֵי טָעַם	than seven who answer with discernment.
17a	מַחֲזִיק בְּאָזְנֵי־כָלֶב עֹבֵר	One who seizes the ears of a passing dog,
17b	מִתְעַבֵּר עַל־רִיב לֹּא־לוֹ	one who meddles in a dispute not his own.
18a	כְּמִתְלַהְלֵהַּ הַיֹּרֶה	Like a madman shooting
18b	זִקִּים חִצִּים וָמָוֶת	firebrands, arrows, and death
19a	כֵּן־אִישׁ רִמָּה אֶת־רֵעֵהוּ	so is a person who deceives his neighbor
19b	וְאָמַר הֲלֹא־מְשַׂחֵק אָנִי	and says, "Was I not joking?"
20a	בְּאֶפֶס עֵצִים תִּכְבֶּה־אֵשׁ	Without wood, a fire dies out,
20b	וּבְאֵין נִרְגָּן יִשְׁתֹּק מָדוֹן	and when there is no slanderer, strife calms down.
21a	פֶּחָם לְגֶחָלִים וְעֵצִים לְאֵשׁ	Charcoal for burning embers and wood for fire
21b	וְאִישׁ מִדְיָנִים לְחַרְחַר־רִיב	and a contentious man for kindling strife.
22a	דִּבְרֵי נִרְגָּן כְּמִתְלַהֲמִים	The words of a slanderer, like delicacies,
22b	וְהֵם יָרְדוּ חַדְרֵי־בָטֶן	and they descend into the chambers of the belly.
23a	כֶּסֶף סִיגִים מְצֻפֶּה עַל־חָרֶשׂ	Silver gloss glazed upon earthenware:
23b	שְׂפָתַיִם דֹּלְקִים וְלֶב־רָע	burning lips and an evil heart.
24a	בִּשְׂפָתָיו יִנָּכֵר שׂוֹנֵא	An enemy disguises himself in his speech,
24b	וּבְקִרְבּוֹ יָשִׁית מִרְמָה	while he harbors deceit within.
25a	כִּי־יְחַנֵּן קוֹלוֹ אַל־תַּאֲמֶן־בּוֹ	Though he makes his voice gracious, do not trust him,
25b	↑ כִּי שֶׁבַע תּוֹעֵבוֹת בְּלִבּוֹ	↑ for seven abominations are in his heart.
26a	תִּכַּסֶּה שִׂנְאָה בְּמַשָּׁאוֹן	Hatred is covered by deceit,
26b	תִּגָּלֶה רָעָתוֹ בְקָהָל	his evil will be exposed in the assembly.
27a	כֹּרֶה־שַּׁחַת בָּהּ יִפֹּל	One who digs a pit will fall into it,
27b	וְגֹלֵל אֶבֶן אֵלָיו תָּשׁוּב	and one who rolls a stone – it will come back on him.
28a	לְשׁוֹן־שֶׁקֶר יִשְׂנָא דַכָּיו	A lying tongue hates those it afflicts,
28b	וּפֶה חָלָק יַעֲשֶׂה מִדְחֶה	and a smooth mouth works ruin.

Structure and Literary Form

Just as the evaluations offered by the individual sayings and the dialogical relationship among the maxims nurture perception, so also the form of the materials nurture perception. The juxtaposition of the twice-told admonition and exhortation in vv. 4–5 creates interlinear parallelism, forcing the reader to consider the sayings together rather than as separate aphorisms pertaining to discrete circumstances.[11] And the juxtaposition of vivid images within the initial line of several sayings creates semilinear parallelism (vv. 1a, 2, 3a, 6a, 21a), which ignites the imagination of the reader. While some sayings exhibit general correspondences between poetic lines rather than parallelism in the strict sense of the term (vv. 12, 22), like ch. 25, the majority of the materials are cast in the form of poetic analogies. Most of these analogies move from a metaphor(s) in the opening line to the referent in the subsequent line (vv. 3, 6, 7, 9, 10, 14, 20, 21, 23). Other analogies are cast in the form of a comparative clause.[12] The syntactical variety of the analogies, combined with the vivid imagery of the comparisons, contributes to Proverbs's pedagogical program. They shape the perception, sharpen the moral reasoning, and stimulate the imagination of readers.

The same is true of the structure of the materials in the chapter. In light of the repetition of key terms for particular character types, widespread agreement exists concerning the macrostructure of the chapter, consisting of three subunits: vv. 1–12 profile the "fool" (כְּסִיל, vv. 1, 3–12) "*in his various relations*,"[13] vv. 13–16 sketch the character of the "sluggard" (עָצֵל),[14] while vv. 17–28 explore various characters that instigate social conflict, especially through their speech.[15] The attention to these character types within extended thematic units engenders a dialogue among the sayings. This dialogue is facilitated through the repetition of key terms and catchwords, such as "fool" (כְּסִיל), "sluggard" (עָצֵל), "fire" (אֵשׁ, vv. 20a, 21a), "lips/speech" (שָׂפָה, vv. 23b, 24a), and the root "to hate" (שׂנא, vv. 24a, 26a, 28a). It is fueled by variant repetitions within the chapter (vv. 1b//8b, 4a//5a, 5b//12a//16a, 7b//9b) and across the central collections. This same dialogue is supported by recurrent themes and conceptual metaphors. The theme of (un)fittingness is woven throughout vv. 1–12;[16]

11. Schökel, *A Manual of Hebrew Poetics*, 60; Heim, *Poetic Imagination*, 583–84. Taken together, v. 4 admonishes one to respond to a fool, just not according to the manner of a fool, and v. 5 exhorts one to expose the folly of the fool. Waltke, *Proverbs: Chapters 15–31*, 349; Fox, *Proverbs 10–31*, 793–94. Cf. Kenneth G. Hoglund, "The Fool and the Wise in Dialogue," in *The Listening Heart: Essays in Wisdom and the Psalms in Honor of Roland E. Murphy, O. Carm.*, ed. E. F. Huwiler et al. (Sheffield: Sheffield Academic, 1987), 161–80.

12. Joüon §174c, h.

13. Van Leeuwen, *Context and Meaning*, 90, italics original.

14. The subunits devoted to the fool (vv. 1–12) and the sluggard (vv. 13–16) both conclude with the expression "wise in his own eyes" (חָכָם בְּעֵינָיו, vv. 12a, 16a).

15. At the microstructural level of the discourse, many commentators divide vv. 17–28 into different parts, ranging from vv. 17–19 and 20–28 to vv. 17, 18–19, 20–22, 23–28 (Delitzsch, "Book of Proverbs," 6:391–92 (2:190, 192); Waltke, *Proverbs: Chapters 15–31*, 343–44).

16. Van Leeuwen, *Context and Meaning*, 90–106.

and many of the aphorisms traffic in the conceptual metaphor EVIL IS A FORCE (vv. 6, 9, 10, 17, 18–19, 21, 28). While the subunits do not evince a logical progression of thought, the third subunit concludes on a fitting note. The malevolent characters in vv. 18–25 harm members of the community, but they suffer no consequences. This retributive gap is closed in the final sayings, which intimate that these characters will be exposed publicly (v. 26), receive their just deserts (v. 27), and experience ruin (v. 28).[17]

17. Whybray, *The Composition of the Book of Proverbs*, 124–25.

CHAPTER 33

Proverbs 27:1–27

C. Emotions and Relationships: *The Feelings that Foster and Frustrate Social Bonds*

Main Idea of the Passage

The aphorisms explore the interrelationship between emotions and various social bonds to cultivate self-knowledge and to attune one to the feelings that strengthen as well as erode interpersonal relations.

Literary Context[1]

Whereas the thematic subunits in ch. 26 attempted to engender perception and perspectival knowledge through their extended evaluation of particular immoral prototypes, the materials in ch. 27 invite one to feel the pain and promise of various social relations. Emotions overwhelm the aphorisms in the chapter. They include the weight of a fool's vexation (v. 3), the force of jealousy (v. 4), the wounds of a friend (v. 5, 6a), the kisses of an enemy (v. 6b), the power of the appetite (v. 7, 20), the vulnerability of the placeless (v. 8), the sweetness of a friend (v. 9; cf. v. 10), the joy of a parent (v. 11), the annoyance of a chipper neighbor (v. 14), the irritation of a contentious woman (v. 15), the violent pounding of an attacking neighbor (v. 17), and an empathy for the individuality and particularity of one's livestock (v. 23). These varied emotions not only attune one to an interconnected community populated by parents and wives, friends and neighbors, masters and strangers, households and animals, fools and enemies. These emotions and relations also provide a mirror

1. This chapter does not include the Canonical and Theological Significance section. See pp. xv and 276n1 for justification. Also, see pp. 604–7 for the Canonical and Theological Significance of Proverbs 25:1–29:27.

for the self. They reveal that knowledge of oneself is not self-generated; rather, it is discovered before the face of another (vv. 2, 19, 21).

The attention to emotions and social relations across the sayings in ch. 27 serve as a window into their contributions to the pedagogical development within the central collections. When read in light of ch. 26, the personal danger of presumptuousness as well as a particular species of fool are thrown into sharp relief. Several sayings offer a remedy for becoming "wise in one's own eyes" (חָכָם בְּעֵינָיו; 26:5b, 12a, 16a). More than casting aspersions on one's self-valuation, these sayings identify the evaluation of others as a reliable touchstone of one's character (27:2, 19, 21; cf. 12:8; 17:13). The one "wise in his own eyes" may be worse than a "fool" (כְּסִיל; 26:12), but this figure shares much in common with a particular species of "fool" (אֱוִיל, 27:22a) that is unresponsive to even the most severe forms of corporal punishment. Certain sayings in ch. 27 nuance and extend motifs in ch. 26.

The same is true when these sayings are placed in the broader dialogical context of the central collections. The efficacy of planning, for example, is attenuated by the limitations of human wisdom and power (v. 1; cf. 11:14; 15:22; 16:1, 9; 20:18; 21:5; 24:6, 27). In addition to the desire for economic return (6:1–5; 11:15; 17:18; 20:16; 22:26–27), the physical attractiveness of a debtor short circuits one's due diligence and heightens the risk of financial investment (27:13b).[2] A contentious woman is not only irritating but also irrepressible (vv. 15–16; cf. 19:13; 21:9, 19; 25:24). Nonetheless, the irritation engendered by her continual dripping only occurs "on a rainy day" (בְּיוֹם סַגְרִיר, 27:15a). And this is due, at least in part, to the husband's failure

2. Heim, *Poetic Imagination*, 493–94.

to patch the proverbial roof.[3] The implicit virtues that foster a healthy relationship with one's wife are explicit in several sayings devoted to friendship. These sayings elaborate on previous aphorisms pertaining to the nature of genuine friendship as well as gradations of friendship (17:17; 18:24; 19:4, 6). They traffic in pain, taste, smell, sight, safety, and shame to depict true and false friends in paradoxical and powerful ways (27:5, 6, 9, 10, 17). In so doing, they develop the dynamics of a close, interpersonal relationship that lies outside of the domestic sphere.

Translation and Exegetical Outline

(See pages 574–75.)

Structure and Literary Form

As Roland Murphy notes, the literary "'atmosphere'" of Prov 27 is more variable than previous chapters.[4] This does not mean that the form of the materials differs substantially from chs. 25 and 26. Similar to these chapters, admonitions and exhortations punctuate the discourse unit (27:1, 2, 10a–b, 11, 13, 23–27). And several sayings are cast in the form of analogies. Some of these analogies are marked comparative clauses (vv. 8, 19), while others are conveyed through metaphorical parallelism (vv. 3, 4, 15, 16, 17, 18, 20, 21).[5] But to these familiar forms, the chapter adds materials reminiscent of previous collections, such as a monostich (v. 5, cf. v. 10c; 24:23b), sentences (vv. 14, 22), antithetical sayings (vv. 6, 7), and "disjointed proverbs" (vv. 6, 12). The literary variety in the chapter not only sharpens the reader's moral and hermeneutical agility; it also suggests that the discourse unit functions in a manner comparable to Prov 15. Just as the literary variety of ch. 15 intimated that it served as a "grey area" between subcollections (i.e., 10:1–15:33; 16:1–22:16),[6] so also the literary variety in ch. 27 may indicate that it constitutes a "grey area" between subcollections (i.e., 25:1–27:27; 28:1–29:27).

The formal diversity of the sayings distinguishes Prov 27 from the previous chapters and the various forms clarify the macrostructural contours of the chapter. In accord with many commentators, the sayings may be divided into three sections (vv. 1–10, 11–22, 23–27).[7] Each opens with direct address (vv. 1, 11, 23).

3. Heim, *Poetic Imagination*, 464–66.
4. Murphy, *Proverbs*, 206.
5. Berlin, *The Dynamics of Biblical Parallelism*, 99–102.
6. Weeks, *Early Israelite Wisdom*, 26–27.
7. Meinhold, *Die Sprüche*, 2:449; Whybray, *Proverbs*, 382; Van Leeuwen, "The Book of Proverbs," *NIB* 5:231; Clifford, *Proverbs*, 238; Waltke, *Proverbs: Chapters 15–31*, 371, 390; Sæbø, *Sprüche*, 330–31.

Proverbs 27:1–27

C. Emotions and Relationships: The Feelings that Foster and Frustrate Social Bonds (27:1–27)

1a	אַל־תִּתְהַלֵּל בְּיוֹם מָחָר	Do not boast about tomorrow,
1b	↑ כִּי לֹא־תֵדַע מַה־יֵּלֶד יוֹם	↑ for you do not know what a day may bear.
2a	יְהַלֶּלְךָ זָר וְלֹא־פִיךָ	Let a stranger praise you, and not your own mouth,
2b	נָכְרִי וְאַל־שְׂפָתֶיךָ	an outsider, and not your own lips.
3a	כֹּבֶד־אֶבֶן וְנֵטֶל הַחוֹל	The weight of stone and the burden of sand,
3b	וְכַעַס אֱוִיל כָּבֵד מִשְּׁנֵיהֶם	but the vexation of a fool is heavier than both.
4a	אַכְזְרִיּוּת חֵמָה וְשֶׁטֶף אָף	The cruelty of wrath and a flood of anger,
4b	וּמִי יַעֲמֹד לִפְנֵי קִנְאָה	but who can stand before jealousy?
5	טוֹבָה תּוֹכַחַת מְגֻלָּה מֵאַהֲבָה מְסֻתָּרֶת	Better open rebuke than hidden love.
6a	נֶאֱמָנִים פִּצְעֵי אוֹהֵב	Faithful, the wounds of a friend,
6b	וְנַעְתָּרוֹת נְשִׁיקוֹת שׂוֹנֵא	but profuse, the kisses of an enemy.
7a	נֶפֶשׁ שְׂבֵעָה תָּבוּס נֹפֶת	A sated appetite tramples on honey,
7b	וְנֶפֶשׁ רְעֵבָה כָּל־מַר מָתוֹק	but a hungry appetite, everything bitter is sweet.
8a	כְּצִפּוֹר נוֹדֶדֶת מִן־קִנָּהּ	Like a bird wandering from its nest,
8b	כֵּן־אִישׁ נוֹדֵד מִמְּקוֹמוֹ	so is a person who wanders from his place.
9a	שֶׁמֶן וּקְטֹרֶת יְשַׂמַּח־לֵב	Oil and incense make the heart glad,
9b	וּמֶתֶק רֵעֵהוּ מֵעֲצַת־נָפֶשׁ	and the sweetness of one's friend more than his own counsel.
10a	רֵעֲךָ וְרֵעַ אָבִיךָ אַל־תַּעֲזֹב	Do not forsake your friend or your father's friend,
10b	וּבֵית אָחִיךָ אַל־תָּבוֹא בְּיוֹם אֵידֶךָ	and do not enter your brother's house on the day of your calamity.
10c	טוֹב שָׁכֵן קָרוֹב מֵאָח רָחוֹק	Better a close neighbor than a distant brother.
11a	חֲכַם בְּנִי וְשַׂמַּח לִבִּי	Be wise, my son, and make my heart glad,
11b	↑ וְאָשִׁיבָה חֹרְפִי דָבָר	↑ so that I may answer the one who reproaches me.
12a	עָרוּם רָאָה רָעָה נִסְתָּר	The shrewd perceives danger—he hides;
12b	פְּתָאיִם עָבְרוּ נֶעֱנָשׁוּ	the immature pass on—they pay for it.
13a	קַח־בִּגְדוֹ כִּי־עָרַב זָר	Take his garment, for he has gone surety for a stranger;
13b	וּבְעַד נָכְרִיָּה חַבְלֵהוּ	and for a foreign woman, impound it!
14a	מְבָרֵךְ רֵעֵהוּ בְּקוֹל גָּדוֹל בַּבֹּקֶר	One who blesses his neighbor with a loud voice early in the morning—
14b	הַשְׁכֵּים קְלָלָה תֵּחָשֶׁב לוֹ	it will be reckoned to him as a curse.

15a	דֶּלֶף טוֹרֵד בְּיוֹם סַגְרִיר	A continual dripping on a rainy day
15b	וְאֵשֶׁת מִדְיָנִים נִשְׁתָּוָה	and a contentious woman are alike.
16a	צֹפְנֶיהָ צָפַן־רוּחַ	Whoever hides her, hides wind,
16b	וְשֶׁמֶן יְמִינוֹ יִקְרָא	and oil meets his right hand.
17a	בַּרְזֶל בְּבַרְזֶל יָחַד	Iron sharpens iron,
17b	וְאִישׁ יַחַד פְּנֵי־רֵעֵהוּ	and a person sharpens the face of his neighbor.
18a	נֹצֵר תְּאֵנָה יֹאכַל פִּרְיָהּ	One who tends a fig tree will eat its fruit,
18b	וְשֹׁמֵר אֲדֹנָיו יְכֻבָּד	and one who keeps his master will be honored.
19a	כַּמַּיִם הַפָּנִים לַפָּנִים	As water, a face to a face,
19b	כֵּן לֵב־הָאָדָם לָאָדָם	so a heart of a person to a person.
20a	שְׁאוֹל וַאֲבַדּוֹ לֹא תִשְׂבַּעְנָה	Sheol and Abaddon are never satisfied,
20b	וְעֵינֵי הָאָדָם לֹא תִשְׂבַּעְנָה	and the eyes of humans are never satisfied.
21a	מַצְרֵף לַכֶּסֶף וְכוּר לַזָּהָב	A crucible for silver and a furnace for gold,
21b	וְאִישׁ לְפִי מַהֲלָלוֹ	and a person by the mouth of one who praises him.
22a	אִם תִּכְתּוֹשׁ־אֶת־הָאֱוִיל בַּמַּכְתֵּשׁ ↓	↓ Though you crush the fool in a mortar,
22b	↑ בְּתוֹךְ הָרִיפוֹת בַּעֱלִי ↓	↓ ↑ with a pestle among the grains,
22c	לֹא־תָסוּר מֵעָלָיו אִוַּלְתּוֹ	his folly will not depart from him.
23a	יָדֹעַ תֵּדַע פְּנֵי צֹאנֶךָ	Know well the face of your flock,
23b	שִׁית לִבְּךָ לַעֲדָרִים	pay attention to your herds.
24a	↑ כִּי לֹא לְעוֹלָם חֹסֶן	↑ For wealth is not forever,
24b	וְאִם־נֵזֶר לְדוֹר וָדוֹר	and surely not a crown from generation to generation.
25a	גָּלָה חָצִיר וְנִרְאָה־דֶשֶׁא ↓	↓ When the grass disappears and new growth appears,
25b	וְנֶאֶסְפוּ עִשְּׂבוֹת הָרִים ↓	↓ and the vegetation of the mountains is gathered,
26a	כְּבָשִׂים לִלְבוּשֶׁךָ	lambs will provide for your clothing,
26b	וּמְחִיר שָׂדֶה עַתּוּדִים	and goats, the price of a field;
27a	וְדֵי חֲלֵב עִזִּים לְלַחְמְךָ	and enough goat's milk for your food,
27b	↑ לְלֶחֶם בֵּיתֶךָ	↑ for the food of your house,
27c	וְחַיִּים לְנַעֲרוֹתֶיךָ	and sustenance for your maidservants.

Each concludes with a tricolon (vv. 10, 22, 27). And similar to the poems in Prov 24:30–34 and 31:10–31, the poem in vv. 23–27 marks the conclusion to both the chapter as well as the subcollection (i.e., 25:1–27:27).[8] Within these structural contours, repeated terms and motifs infuse the discourse unit with a measure of unity. Catchwords and comparable syntax link adjacent sayings (27:1–2, 3–4, 5–6, 9–10, 15–16, 19–20). Certain expressions are reiterated across non-contiguous aphorisms (הלל, "boast/praise," vv. 1a, 2a, 21b; זָר, "stranger," vv. 2a, 13a; יְשַׂמַּח־לֵב, "make the/my heart glad," vv. 9a, 11a); and the attention to interpersonal relationships in general as well as feelings and friendship in particular are prominent motifs. The collection of sayings may not resemble the thematic and structural consistency of Prov 26; however, its forms and motifs exhibit aspects of unity in diversity.

Explanation of the Text

"Only he is really wise who does not consider himself wise."[9] Following von Rad, this posture is not the product of false humility; rather, it is a posture engendered by a recognition of the limits that accompany human finitude. These limits are sketched in **vv. 1–2**, which are linked by the root הלל ("boast/praise," vv. 1a, 2a). The opening admonition and motivation carve out the limits of human knowledge, power, and planning. In light of the fact that humans do not possess the power to determine even the imminent future (בְּיוֹם מָחָר, "tomorrow," v. 1a), boasting about what lies ahead breaches the epistemological boundaries of creaturehood. These boundaries are foregrounded in the causal clause (כִּי, "for," v. 1b), which furnishes the motivation. The day will give birth to certain events, but these events elude human knowledge and manipulation. Whereas v. 1 focuses on the limits of human knowledge, v. 2 attends to the limits of self-knowledge. The exhortation assumes that self-valuation is deceiving; and it acknowledges that one knows oneself only as one is known by another. This other is characterized as a "stranger" (זָר, v. 2a) and an "outsider" (נָכְרִי, v. 2b), figures that are construed in a negative fashion elsewhere in the book (v. 13; 2:16; 5:10; 6:24; 7:5; 20:16; 23:27). Here, however, these individuals outside of the domestic unit provide a litmus test of one's character. When read together, vv. 1–2 capture particular aspects of human finitude that cultivate humility, gratitude for the giftedness of each day, and self-awareness before the face of another.

In view of human limits, **vv. 3–4** explore the weight and force of particular feelings. The sayings traffic in the same syntax, moving from a pair of images cast in semilinear parallelism (vv. 3a, 4a) to the referent of these images (vv. 3b, 4b). They follow the same logical scheme, and they focus on specific emotions. The anger or "vexation" (כַּעַס, v. 3b) of a fool serves as the standard of comparison

8. See Van Leeuwen, *Context and Meaning*, 140–42, who argues that, in light of the shared terminology between Prov 24:30–34, 27:23–27, and 31:10–31, vv. 23–27 serve as an intentional, editorial boundary.

9. Von Rad, *Wisdom in Israel*, 101.

in v. 3. The emotional weight of this anger exceeds the physical burden of a back-breaking load. But this weight pales in comparison to the force of jealousy (v. 4). Wrath may bring physical or mental harm; and anger may sweep over one as a flood (v. 4a). But harms heal and floods abate. Jealousy, by contrast, is a force that overwhelms oneself as well as another. The power of its zeal is conveyed through the rhetorical question in v. 4b, which demands a negative response. Taken together, the analogies draw on the physical and emotional power of feelings in interpersonal relationships, creating a holistic view of the self in relation.

Feelings also fund **vv. 5–6**, which are linked by the root אהב ("love," v. 5; "friend," v. 6a). The sayings attend to love; and they portray it as a complex, even paradoxical emotion. The paradoxical nature of genuine love is assessed though a terse better-than saying in v. 5. The monostich does not pit verbal reproof against love; rather, it privileges disciplinary expressions of open love over hidden love, for the former reveal one's faults and enable one to grow in wisdom and self-knowledge. This paradoxical expression of love is generalized through a pair of oxymorons in v. 6. The painful wounds of a friend are deemed faithful, whereas the tender kisses of a feigned friend are considered profuse. The asymmetry between "faithful" (נֶאֱמָ־נִים, v. 6a) and "profuse" (נַעְתָּרוֹת, v. 6b) invites one to exercise their moral reasoning by developing the thought of each line.[10] If the kisses of an enemy are profuse, then the wounds of a friend are faithful *but few*.[11] And if the wounds of a friend are faithful, then the profuse kisses of an enemy are *perfidious*. These oxymoronic expressions of love capture the painful yet positive nature of loyalty in close interpersonal relationships.

Whereas vv. 5–6 explore the pains that sustain interpersonal relations, **vv. 7–8** focus on the self. This concern with the self is signaled by the repetition of the term "appetite" (נֶפֶשׁ) in v. 7, which refers to the seat of one's desire. Desire is not only powerful. According to v. 7, it is also paradoxical. A sated appetite despises that which is good and sweet. The initial line assumes that the regular consumption of good things warps one's moral taste buds and dulls one's perception. The same is true of the hungry. Their lack of fulfillment twists their moral palate and perception to the extent that everything bitter tastes sweet. The saying sketches the extremes of desire, taste, and perception. In so doing, it gestures to the middle way of moderation as the means to satisfy desire, hone one's moral taste buds, and nurture one's perception.

The dangers of the (un)fulfilled self provides an entrée into v. 8 and its depiction of the placeless self. The analogy compares the forced displacement of a bird from its nest with the forced displacement of a person from their place (cf. Isa 10:31; 16:2; Jer 4:25; 9:10); it presumes that everyone has a natural environment that offers security, identity, and a sense of belonging. And it invites one to consider the vulnerability and loneliness of forced migration. The self flourishes in a particular communal place. The displaced self, by contrast, withers in an unnatural environment.

Returning to the theme of close interpersonal relationships, **vv. 9–10** attend to the smell and security of a genuine "friend" (רֵעַ, vv. 9b; 10a). Smell and taste direct the comparison in v. 9. Just as the

10. The root עתר means "to plead, supplicate" elsewhere in the Old Testament, which makes little sense in the saying. While various emendations have been proposed, it seems best to understand נַעְתָּרוֹת as an Aramaism, meaning "profuse" (Waltke, *Proverbs: Chapters 15–31*, 367n6; Fox, *Proverbs 10–31*, 805–6).

11. Fox, *Proverbs 10–31*, 805.

smell of scented oil and incense gladden the heart, so also the sweet counsel of a friend gladdens the heart more than one's own counsel.[12] The saying moves from the aesthetic delight of certain scents to the aesthetic delight of a friend's advice. Both bring refreshment and both are beneficial. The benefits of genuine friendship are developed in v. 10. The tripartite saying opens with a pair of admonitions that envision different relationships and circumstances. The first commends the faithful cultivation of relationships with one's friend in general and a family friend in particular (v. 10a). The second, by contrast, appears to prohibit reliance on a brother in a day of trouble (v. 10b). On the surface, this prohibition is strange, for a brother is a certain source of help—one "born for adversity" (לְצָרָה יִוָּלֵד; 17:17b). But when it is read in conjunction with the better-than saying in v. 10c, the rationale for the prohibition is clear. A brother may be born for adversity. A distant brother, however, is little help compared to a close neighbor and a family friend. The second prohibition does not disparage brotherhood; it uses brotherhood as a point of comparison in order to highlight the benefits of neighbors and family friends. Like a brother, these relations serve as a source of support and security, especially on a day of trouble.

Just as friends provide a source of support and security, so also one may serve as a source of support and security to one's parents. Familial solidarity, honor, and protection motivate the exhortation in **v. 11**. The interjection places one in the subject position of a receptive son. And the *waw* + cohortative in the second line introduces the certain consequence that accompanies one who becomes wise.[13] More than engendering parental joy, a wise son becomes a defense against public reproach. The saying assumes that the son's character reflects the father's character. And it inspires the pursuit of wisdom and perseverance in the wise life by appealing to a basic human desire, namely, the desire to please one's parents and to protect the family's honor.

The security afforded by wisdom is developed along different lines in **v. 12**. With the exception of the *waw* conjunctions, the saying reiterates 22:3. Like its variant counterpart, the aphorism not only delineates the security of discernment, but it also shapes the reader's discernment through imprecise parallelism. The imprecision invites the reader to discern the gaps between the parallel lines and to complete the saying.[14] According to the initial line, the shrewd perceives danger. By virtue of their perception, they not only hide, they also escape. The immature, by contrast, do not perceive danger. As a result, they pass on and pay for it. Perception pays: it provides one with the power to see the world and to act in a way that secures safety.

A failure to perceive the world and to act in a way that effects security is specified through the practice of going surety in **v. 13**. The saying represents a variant repetition of 20:16. In addition to the alternative spelling of the imperative "take," the aphorism mentions "a foreign woman" (נָכְרִיָּה, v. 13b) rather than "foreigners" (נָכְרִים). The alteration may be slight, but it appears to introduce a

12. The comparison expressed in the second line is unclear. "Sweetness" (מֶתֶק) is compared with "counsel" (עֲצַת), and the third-person singular pronominal suffix lacks an antecedent. While several proposals produce a clear reading of the line (Delitzsch, "Book of Proverbs," 6:401–2 [2:204–7]; McKane, *Proverbs*, 613), they depart from the syntax and sense of the MT. If the second line is elliptical, then it seems to compare the sweetness of a friend's counsel with one's own counsel. And the third person singular pronominal suffix may refer to the "heart" in the initial line, which serves as a synecdoche for one's being. Waltke, *Proverbs: Chapters 15–31*, 378; Fox, *Proverbs 10–31*, 807.

13. *IBHS* §34.5.2.

14. Heim, *Poetic Imagination*, 514–15.

particular risk that may influence the decision to serve as a financial guarantor. The foreign woman is a pregnant figure elsewhere in the book. She is the epitome of seduction and one who embodies an alternative way of life (2:16; 5:20; 6:24; 7:5). If the mention of a foreign woman includes these connotations, then the saying suggests that physical attraction may influence the provision of a loan, heightening the financial risk of the transaction.[15] The saying traffics in terror and extends the dangers involved in going surety elsewhere in the book by accounting for the way in which sexual desire may short circuit sound financial decisions.

The value of perception is recast in interpersonal terms in **27:14**. The saying depicts "a failure of fittingness," that is, a failure to perceive and to act within appropriate social boundaries.[16] The transgression of these boundaries is expressed through the pair of prepositional phrases in the initial line: "with a loud voice" (בְּקוֹל גָּדוֹל, v. 14a) and "early in the morning" (בַּבֹּקֶר הַשְׁכֵּים, v. 14b). One who greets his neighbor in this manner at this time fails to act within the bounds of social propriety. The inappropriate tone and timing of the greeting explain why the blessing is reckoned as a curse. The saying places one before the face of a neighbor, and it foregrounds the neighbor's evaluation in order to highlight the relational value of perception and propriety.

Against the backdrop of the neighborhood, **vv. 15–16** zoom in on the household and portray a domestic environment occupied by a contentious wife. The initial saying is cast in the form of a comparison, which extends its variant counterpart in 19:13b. Like 19:13b, a contentious wife is compared to a "continual dripping" (דֶּלֶף טוֹרֵד, 27:15a). The addition of the prepositional phrase "on a rainy day" (בְּיוֹם סַגְרִיר, v. 15a), however, nuances the characterization of this woman elsewhere in the anthology. It suggests that a contentious wife is contentious only on a rainy day.[17] And just as rainy days were relatively rare in Israel, so also the contentions of a quarrelsome wife are relatively rare.[18] More than describing the annoyance of a contentious wife, the unnecessary prepositional phrase invites the husband to exercise relational responsibility. One cannot control the rain. In the same way, one can neither determine nor control the arrival of a crisis—the conceptual equivalent to a rainy day.[19] But one can exercise relational care with one's spouse so as to minimize the outburst of contention on the proverbial rainy day. The saying introduces a sporadic meteorological phenomenon that lies outside of one's control to elicit relational responsibility that lies within one's control.[20] This call for relational responsibility is amplified in v. 16. The third-person feminine singular pronominal suffix, combined with the meteorological imagery in v. 16a, elaborates on the uncontrollable nature of a contentious wife. She is compared to the wind and to oil, both of which cannot be restrained.[21] When read together, vv. 15–16 describe a hostile domestic environment with an irrepressible wife. They not only provide a warning against marrying a contentious woman, they also encourage one to cultivate a domestic environment marked by care.

15. Heim, *Poetic Imagination*, 493–94.

16. Van Leeuwen, "The Book of Proverbs," *NIB* 5:231.

17. Heim, *Poetic Imagination*, 464.

18. Heim, *Poetic Imagination*, 464.

19. Heim, *Poetic Imagination*, 465.

20. Heim, *Poetic Imagination*, 465–67.

21. The clause "and oil meets his right hand" (וְשֶׁמֶן יְמִינוֹ יִקְרָא, v. 16b) is unclear. Following the ancient versions, some read קרא I ("call") rather than קרא II ("meet") and emend שֶׁמֶן ("oil") to "his name." This reading appears to produce an ironic comment on the wife, but it remains obscure. It seems best to retain the MT and to understand the clause as an elliptical description of the way in which oil slips through one's fingers. For discussion, see Meinhold, *Die Sprüche*, 2:457–58; Fox, *Proverbs 10–31*, 810–11.

The hostile environment created by a contentious wife corresponds to the hostile encounter with one's neighbor depicted in **v. 17**. While the image in v. 17a and the referent in v. 17b tend to be construed as positive expressions pertaining to the way in which one sharpens the character or wits of another, the process of ironsmithing and expressions for parts of the face that are sharp elsewhere in the Old Testament suggest that the saying describes a contentious encounter with one's neighbor. The terse image in the opening line telescopes the art of ironsmithing in ancient Israel, according to which a hammer was used to pound a soft, heated piece of iron into a weapon or vessel.[22] The forceful nature of this process is reinforced by the verb "sharpens" (יָחַד, vv. 17a, 17b), its synonym "sharp" (שׁנן; 25:18), and the LXX's use of the verb ὀξύνει ("sharpens"), each of which are used to describe acts of violence elsewhere (Ezek 21:19–21[14–16]; Hab 1:8).[23] This violent act of smithing is applied to interpersonal relations in the second line through the expression "sharpens the face" (יַחַד פְּנֵי, Prov 27:17b). Although the expression is not found elsewhere in the Old Testament, it is comparable to descriptions of sharp eyes, a sharp lip, or a sharp tongue—parts of the face that attack others (Pss 52:4[2]; 57:5[4]; Job 16:9).[24] When the smithing process in the initial line is applied to interpersonal relations in the second, it appears that just as a smith pounds soft iron into a sharp instrument, prepared for battle, so also a person may pound one's neighbor, causing him to attack.[25] The analogy attunes one to the nature of animosity in neighborly relations. In so doing, it seeks to cultivate amity and harmony in communal relationships.

The hostile relationship between neighbors in Prov 27:17 gives ways to the loyal servant's reception of honor in **v. 18**. The saying is cast in the form of metaphorical parallelism, mirroring the syntax of the previous aphorism. Both the metaphor and its referent link moral strength and fidelity to a satisfying reward. One who "tends" (נֹצֵר, v. 18a) a fig tree protects its developing fruit and responds to its needs. The tree, in turn, provides its servant with satisfying fruit. This agricultural expectation is mapped onto the hierarchical relationship between masters and servants in the second line: a servant who guards his master's interests and reputation "will be honored" (יְכֻבָּד; 18b). The passive form of the servant's reception of social capital suggests that the reward extends beyond advancement in the household; it also includes increased status within the community. The comparison assumes a moral order that dictates one's moral responsibilities within that order, and it encourages loyalty through the desire for satisfaction and honor.

Whereas v. 18 assumes knowledge of one's place in the hierarchy of the moral order, **v. 19** explores the nature of self-knowledge. This motif is expressed through a marked comparative construction (כֵּן . . . -כְּ, "as . . . so"). Its form is clear, but its sense is ambiguous. The opening line depicts water as a mirror that allows one to perceive their external appearance (v. 19a). The second line moves from the external appearance of one's face to the internal condition of one's heart (v. 19b).

22. Ronald L. Giese Jr., "'Iron Sharpens Iron' as a Negative Image: Challenging the Common Interpretation of Proverbs 27:17," *JBL* 135 (2016): 70–71.

23. Giese, "'Iron Sharpens Iron,'" 65–68. In contrast to the ancient versions, Fox construes the verb as a *qal* perfect from the root יחד ("to join") rather than a *hiphil* imperfect from the root חדד ("to sharpen). This reading is possible, but it is unattested among the ancient versions, and, as Fox notes, the attendant syntactical circumstances of the verb's use indicate that "No entirely viable emendation presents itself." For discussion, see Giese, "'Iron Sharpens Iron,'" 69–70; Fox, *Proverbs: An Eclectic Edition*, 355–56.

24. Giese, "'Iron Sharpens Iron,'" 65–67.

25. Giese, "'Iron Sharpens Iron,'" 76.

This move raises a pair of questions: does one's heart, like water, serve as introspective mirror that generates self-knowledge? Or does the heart of another serve as an interpersonal mirror that enables self-knowledge? The saying is patient with both readings. Self-introspection may produce self-knowledge. But in light of the distorted nature of self-valuation (vv. 2, 21), it appears that one comes to a knowledge of oneself before another. The analogy highlights the value of close interpersonal relationships; it indicates that one knows oneself as one is known by others.[26]

Just as the other serves as a mirror in which to perceive oneself (v. 19b), so also **v. 20** serves as a mirror in which to perceive the power of human desire. The aphorism compares the insatiable appetite of Death with the insatiable appetite of human eyes. The eyes function as a metonymy for human desire.[27] Like Sheol and Abaddon, the eyes are personified to portray their voracious nature. Drawing on imagery from Canaanite mythology, the initial line gestures to the gaping mouth of deified Death, which is never sated by the influx of the deceased (30:15–16; cf. Isa 5:14). The comparison of Death with human eyes indicates that the power and peril of unquenchable desire resides within humans. The eyes seduce the self (cf. Gen 3:6). Similar to the mouth or stomach of Sheol, they are never satisfied. The saying employs vivid imagery to attune one to the nature of human desire; it encourages restraint by locating the insatiable appetite of Death in the self.

The theme of self-knowledge is extended in Prov **27:21**, which returns to the matter of praise and the interpersonal instrument of character evaluation (v. 2). Reiterating 17:3a, the initial line frames the matter of evaluation through a pair of metallurgical images. The crucible and the furnace test precious metals, separating silver and gold from dross. In the same way, the mouth of one who praises functions as a furnace, evaluating the mettle of the one praised. In contrast to its variant counterpart (17:3b), public praise, rather than YHWH, reveals one's character. While these forms of valuation are not mutually exclusive, 27:21 foregrounds the place of the community in the appraisal of one's character. The self is known in relation. But it is important to note that the saying does not go so far as to maintain that the communal assessment of character is always right. Instead, it places the self in the crucible of public praise and evaluates the self in relation to the character and content of the one who praises him.

Imagery associated with sifting seeps into **v. 22** and its characterization of the fool's unmalleable nature. Whereas discipline is deemed an effective pedagogical technique elsewhere in Proverbs (13:24; 19:18; 22:15; 23:13–14), even the most severe form of education is unable to penetrate the obstinate. The tristich explores this reality through a concessive clause (אִם, "though," v. 22a). The saying opens with a pair of subordinate clauses that compare the educational process with the crushing of grains by a pestle in a mortar (vv. 22a–b). This technical process was designed to separate the grain from its husk; it includes a range of firm pedagogical practices intended to chip away at one's intractability and to cultivate receptivity to wisdom. This process may be efficacious for many of the grains in a mortar, but it proves to be ineffective on the "fool" (אֱוִיל, v. 22a). This unexpected result is delineated through the main clause (v. 22c), which describes the hardened nature of the fool. His husk cannot be cracked; educational means cannot engender a change in his character. The saying highlights the moral essence of a particular species of fool.

26. Van Leeuwen, "The Book of Proverbs," *NIB* 5:232.

27. Clifford, *Proverbs*, 240.

In so doing, it nuances other educational sayings, indicating that the conventional means of character formation are ineffectual with this moral prototype (cf. Prov 17:10; 29:1).[28]

The final verses of the chapter constitute a coherent poem (**27:23–27**). On the surface, the piece sketches the advantages of the agrarian economy over the acquisition of ephemeral forms of wealth and social capital. The opening exhortation is emphatic, expressing the intensity of the action in view.[29] The reader is placed in a position of personal responsibility for the welfare of their livestock. This responsibility is governed by an empathy and a care for the individuality and particularity of one's flocks and herds. The rationale for this responsibility is expressed through a causal clause (כִּי, "for," v. 24a), which privileges the art of animal husbandry over the transitory commodities of wealth and prestige. These commodities do not endure. In fact, they pale in comparison to the socioeconomic advantages of the agrarian economy delineated in vv. 25–27. An unmarked temporal clause sets the scene (v. 25), foregrounding renewable resources that fund the farm and the farmer. The seasonal rhythms of creation produce grass, new growth, and vegetation that provide food for lambs and goats. And these animals, in turn, support the domestic economy, providing clothing (v. 26a), finances to purchase land (v. 26b), and food to sustain members of the household (v. 27). The poem paints an idyllic portrait of a renewable economy maintained by interdependence and mutual care, which stands in sharp contrast to the autonomous pursuit of transient forms of wealth for personal benefit.

The dynamics of this economy, combined with the imagery and terminology of the poem, intimate that it may also be read on another level. The ethic of responsibility and care delineated in the poem, its implicit use of shepherd imagery, and its explicit use of the term "crown" (נֵזֶר, v. 24b) suggest that it may point beyond its ostensive reference to describe the manner in which the wise shepherd-king cares for his subjects.[30] Following Raymond Van Leeuwen, this parabolic reading of the poem is signaled by the use of the term "crown" (נֵזֶר, v. 24b)—a symbol that is used elsewhere only for royalty.[31] This symbol pushes the reader to reconsider the exhortation in v. 23. Care for one's flock is more than good husbandry advice; it may also be construed against the backdrop of "the shepherd-sheep metaphor for king and his people" that pervades the Old Testament.[32] When read through this metaphorical frame of reference, the poem admonishes members of the royal institution to care for their subjects, who provide material resources and sustenance for the "house." Whether or not this royal reading "hangs too much on too little,"[33] it aligns with the plain sense of the discourse. The piece emphasizes the importance of responsibility and care, and it exhorts one to act in the interests of those entrusted to their care rather than exercising their authority in self-interest.

28. Stewart, *Poetic Ethics*, 179.

29. Joüon §123j.

30. Van Leeuwen, *Context and Meaning*, 131–43. Also see, Bruce V. Malchow, "A Manual for Future Monarchs: Proverbs 27:23–29:27," *CBQ* 47 (1985): 243–45; Waltke, *Proverbs: Chapters 15–31*, 390–94.

31. Some emend נֵזֶר ("crown") to אוֹצָר ("treasures") or עֹשֶׁר ("wealth"), since these readings form a stronger parallel with חֹסֶן ("wealth") in 27:24a (McKane, *Proverbs*, 618; Plöger, *Sprüche Salomos*, 327; Clifford, *Proverbs*, 236–37). These emendations offer a possible solution to the obscure reference to royalty in the present context. Nonetheless, they are unnecessary, for they operate under a view of parallelism that demands semantic correspondence between elements, and they propose readings that share only a single consonant with the MT. Van Leeuwen, *Context and Meaning*, 136–37; Waltke, *Proverbs: Chapters 15–31*, 389n78.

32. Van Leeuwen, *Context and Meaning*, 138.

33. Fox, *Proverbs 10–31*, 815.

CHAPTER 34

Proverbs 28:1–28

D. An Ethics of Power: *Personal, Communal, and Economic Perspectives*

Main Idea of the Passage

The aphorisms devote considerable attention to the (mis)use of power from personal, communal, and economic perspectives, creating a vision of the character, constituents, and interpersonal responsibilities that mark a "good neighborhood."[1]

Literary Context[2]

Whether the poem in Prov 27:23–27 is read as an exhortation to exercise responsible care over renewable resources or the people placed under one's charge, its ethics of power serve as an appropriate entrée into the aphorisms within Prov 28.[3] Many of these aphorisms depict the dynamics of power from discrete angles. Some render power from a personal perspective, describing the emotional stability (v. 1b), sure standing (vv. 6, 10c, 14a, 19, 20), perception (v. 11), and preservation of virtuous character (vv. 13, 18, 26). Others probe the interpersonal and communal (mis)use of power through the nature of those in authority (vv. 2, 15, 16a), forms of oppression and violence (v. 3, 17), (in)justice (vv. 5, 16b, 21), the character of constituencies (v. 4, 12, 28), and the subversion of the household hierarchy (v. 24; cf. v. 7). And still others construe power in socioeconomic terms (vv. 3, 6, 8, 11, 19, 22, 25, 27). The concepts of character, conflict, and control pervade the materials. These concepts structure

1. For the metaphor of the "good neighborhood," see Miller, "The Good Neighborhood," 55–72.

2. This chapter does not include the Explanation of the Text or the Canonical and Theological Significance sections. See pp. xv and 276n1 for justification. Also, see pp. 604–7 for the Canonical and Theological Significance of Proverbs 25:1–29:27.

3. Malchow, "A Manual for Future Monarchs," 243–45; Van Leeuwen, "The Book of Proverbs," *NIB* 5:234.

familiar themes, reinforce subtle nuances, and introduce fresh motifs within the central collections to engender a nuanced vision of being in a broken world.

Among the themes within the chapter, the conflict between the righteous and the wicked, the interrelationship between character and prayer (v. 9; 15:8, 29), and the characterization of one "wise in his own eyes" (28:11a; 26:5, 12; cf. 28:26a), as well as hastening after wealth (28:20, 22; 13:11; 20:21), partiality in justice (28:21; 16:29; 17:26; 18:5; 19:2; 24:23b), reproof (28:23; 19:25; 25:12; 27:5), and generosity toward the poor recall earlier materials (28:27; 11:24; 14:31; 17:5; 21:13; 22:9). These familiar themes, however, are not simply recapitulated. Many are recast to suit the distinctive concerns of the chapter. Reiterating Prov 19:1 and 12:11, respectively, 28:6 and 19 replace moral valuations ("who is a fool," 19:1b; "lacks sense," 12:11b) with economic valuations ("who is rich," 28:6b; "will be filled with poverty," v. 19b) to foreground the chapter's appraisal of wealth and poverty. In the same way, v. 24b serves as a variant repetition of 18:9b. Whereas 18:9b applies the harsh evaluation of a "destroyer" (מַשְׁחִית, 28:24b) to "one slack in his work" (מִתְרַפֶּה בִמְלַאכְתּוֹ; 18:9a), 28:24a associates it with one who abuses their power by subverting the moral authority and order of the household. Power—whether personal, interpersonal, or economic—informs and extends the chapter's treatment of common themes; and these developments serve to sharpen one's moral worldview.

The same is true with several other sayings in the chapter that reinforce subtle nuances or introduce fresh motifs within the central collections. These nuances and fresh motifs offer a shocking portrait of reality. The poor, for example, are not only exploited by the powerful (13:23; 18:23; 22:7, 16), they are also oppressed by the poor (28:3a). Far from being wicked, foolish, or lazy, the poor may be virtuous. Their economic status does not necessarily reflect the nature of their character and the power of their perception (vv. 6, 11b; cf. 19:1, 22). Wealth, on this account, is not a reliable sign of wisdom. In addition to these matters pertaining to wealth and poverty, other sayings traffic in unexpected assertions. The upright may be misled (28:10a). The wicked arise to rule (vv. 12b, 28a). One may conceal the offense of another (10:12; 11:13; 17:9) but must not conceal their own transgressions (28:13). And kings and rulers, who embody the ideals of justice and righteousness elsewhere in the central collections (14:35; 16:10–15; 20:2, 8, 26, 28), are painted in harsh hues (28:2, 15, 16). The most striking portrait is enshrined in v. 15. The saying redeploys the image of a growling lion from 19:12 but transforms it to portray the ruler's abuse of power rather than his legitimate use of authority. Taken together, these sayings project a chaotic, conflicted world, and into this world several sayings introduce "instruction" (תּוֹרָה, vv. 4, 7a, 9a) as the "weapon against the wicked" (v. 4),[4] the foundation of domestic order (v. 7), and the crux of relationship with YHWH (v. 9). Elsewhere within the

4. Brown, "The Pedagogy of Proverbs 10:1–31:9," 175.

anthology, the term denotes parental instruction or the teaching of the sages (1:8; 3:1; 6:20; 13:14). Here, however, the absolute form of the term and its use among sayings that assume regulations from Israel's covenantal tradition suggest that it refers to some form of divine instruction.[5] This instruction is the guide amid communal conflict, political power struggles, and socioeconomic injustice. In a world where YHWH is separated from kings and rulers, divine instruction serves as the blueprint and bastion of wisdom and well-being in the battle against illegitimate power and social injustice.

III. "Forming 'Fearers of YHWH'": The Curriculum of Wisdom and Virtue (10:1–29:27)
- III.1 Elementary Wisdom and Virtue (10:1–15:33)
- III.2 Intermediate Wisdom and Virtue (16:1–22:16)
- III.3 Vocational Wisdom and Virtue (22:17–24:34)
- **III.4 Advanced Wisdom and Virtue (25:1–29:27)**
  - A. Imaging Moral Boundaries and Negotiating Social Bonds (25:1–28)
  - B. Producing Perspectival Knowledge: Perceiving People, Social Scenarios, and the Self (26:1–28)
  - C. Emotions and Relationships: The Feelings that Foster and Frustrate Social Bonds (27:1–27)
  - ➡ **D. An Ethics of Power: Personal, Communal, and Economic Perspectives (28:1–28)**
  - E. Moral Authority and the Moral Order: (Il)legitimate Power and Moral Responsibility (29:1–27)

Translation and Exegetical Outline

(See pages 586–87.)

Structure and Literary Form

The content of the sayings in ch. 28 mark a shift to a conflicted, chaotic world, and this thematic shift coincides with a shift in form. As many have noted, the poetic texture of the aphorisms stands in sharp contrast to the materials in chs. 25–27.

5. Among the sayings, v. 7b recalls Deut 21:18–21, while Prov 28:8a evokes Exod 22:24; Lev 25:36; and Deut 23:20. For תּוֹרָה as a reference to some form of Israel's covenantal tradition, see McKane, *Proverbs*, 623; Van Leeuwen, "The Book of Proverbs," *NIB* 5:234; Murphy, *Proverbs*, 214.

Proverbs 28:1–28

D. An Ethics of Power: Personal, Communal, and Economic Perspectives (28:1–28)

1a	נָסוּ וְאֵין־רֹדֵף רָשָׁע	The wicked flee, though no one pursues,
1b	וְצַדִּיקִים כִּכְפִיר יִבְטָח	while the righteous are as confident as a lion.
2a	בְּפֶשַׁע אֶרֶץ רַבִּים שָׂרֶיהָ	Because of the transgression of a land – many are its princes,
2b	וּבְאָדָם מֵבִין יֹדֵעַ כֵּן יַאֲרִיךְ	but because of an intelligent person, one who knows, right endures.
3a	גֶּבֶר רָשׁ וְעֹשֵׁק דַּלִּים	A person who is poor and oppresses the lowly:
3b	מָטָר סֹחֵף וְאֵין לָחֶם	a rain that washes away and leaves no food.
4a	עֹזְבֵי תוֹרָה יְהַלְלוּ רָשָׁע	Those who forsake instruction praise the wicked,
4b	וְשֹׁמְרֵי תוֹרָה יִתְגָּרוּ בָם	but those who observe instruction strive against them.
5a	אַנְשֵׁי־רָע לֹא־יָבִינוּ מִשְׁפָּט	Evil people do not understand justice,
5b	וּמְבַקְשֵׁי יְהוָה יָבִינוּ כֹל	but those who seek YHWH understand everything.
6a	טוֹב־רָשׁ הוֹלֵךְ בְּתֻמּוֹ	Better a poor person who walks in his integrity
6b	מֵעִקֵּשׁ דְּרָכַיִם וְהוּא עָשִׁיר	than one of twisted ways who is rich.
7a	נוֹצֵר תּוֹרָה בֵּן מֵבִין	A discerning son keeps instruction,
7b	וְרֹעֶה זוֹלְלִים יַכְלִים אָבִיו	while one who associates with gluttons shames his father.
8a	מַרְבֶּה הוֹנוֹ בְּנֶשֶׁךְ וְתַרְבִּית	One who increases his wealth by interest and usury –
8b	לְחוֹנֵן דַּלִּים יִקְבְּצֶנּוּ	gathers it for one who is kind to the poor.
9a	מֵסִיר אָזְנוֹ מִשְּׁמֹעַ תּוֹרָה	One who turns aside his ear from listening to instruction –
9b	גַּם־תְּפִלָּתוֹ תּוֹעֵבָה	even his prayer is an abomination.
10a	מַשְׁגֶּה יְשָׁרִים בְּדֶרֶךְ רָע	One who misleads the upright into an evil path –
10b	בִּשְׁחוּתוֹ הוּא־יִפּוֹל	he will fall into his own pit,
10c	וּתְמִימִים יִנְחֲלוּ־טוֹב	but the blameless will inherit good.
11a	חָכָם בְּעֵינָיו אִישׁ עָשִׁיר	A rich person, wise in his own eyes,
11b	וְדַל מֵבִין יַחְקְרֶנּוּ	but a discerning poor person sees through him.
12a	בַּעֲלֹץ צַדִּיקִים רַבָּה תִפְאָרֶת	When the righteous rejoice, great glory,
12b	וּבְקוּם רְשָׁעִים יְחֻפַּשׂ אָדָם	but when the wicked arise, people hide.
13a	מְכַסֶּה פְשָׁעָיו לֹא יַצְלִיחַ	One who conceals his transgressions shall not prosper,
13b	וּמוֹדֶה וְעֹזֵב יְרֻחָם	while one who confesses and abandons them will receive mercy.
14a	אַשְׁרֵי אָדָם מְפַחֵד תָּמִיד	Blessed is the person who fears continually,
14b	וּמַקְשֶׁה לִבּוֹ יִפּוֹל בְּרָעָה	while the one who hardens his heart will fall into trouble.

15a	אֲרִי־נֹהֵם וְדֹב שׁוֹקֵק	A growling lion and a charging bear:
15b	מֹשֵׁל רָשָׁע עַל עַם־דָּל	a wicked ruler over a poor people.
16a	נָגִיד חֲסַר תְּבוּנוֹת וְרַב מַעֲשַׁקּוֹת	A prince lacking understanding and abundant in oppressions –
16b	שֹׂנְאֵי בֶצַע יַאֲרִיךְ יָמִים	one who hates unjust gain will prolong days.
17a	אָדָם עָשֻׁק בְּדַם־נָפֶשׁ	A person who oppresses by bloodshed
17b	עַד־בּוֹר יָנוּס אַל־יִתְמְכוּ־בוֹ	will flee to a pit – let no one lay hold of him.
18a	הוֹלֵךְ תָּמִים יִוָּשֵׁעַ	One who walks blamelessly will be saved,
18b	וְנֶעְקַשׁ דְּרָכַיִם יִפּוֹל בְּאֶחָת	while one of twisted ways will fall into one.
19a	עֹבֵד אַדְמָתוֹ יִשְׂבַּע־לָחֶם	One who works his land will be satisfied with food,
19b	וּמְרַדֵּף רֵקִים יִשְׂבַּע־רִישׁ	while one who pursues worthless things will be filled with poverty.
20a	אִישׁ אֱמוּנוֹת רַב־בְּרָכוֹת	A faithful person, many blessings,
20b	וְאָץ לְהַעֲשִׁיר לֹא יִנָּקֶה	but one who hastens to get rich shall not go unpunished.
21a	הַכֵּר־פָּנִים לֹא־טוֹב	Showing partiality, not good;
21b	וְעַל־פַּת־לֶחֶם יִפְשַׁע־גָּבֶר	and even for a piece of bread a person may transgress.
22a	נִבְהָל לַהוֹן אִישׁ רַע עָיִן	A greedy person hastens after wealth,
22b	וְלֹא־יֵדַע כִּי־חֶסֶר יְבֹאֶנּוּ	but he is unaware that loss will come upon him.
23a	מוֹכִיחַ אָדָם אַחֲרַי חֵן יִמְצָא	One who reproves a person finds favor afterward
23b	מִמַּחֲלִיק לָשׁוֹן	more than one who is smooth-tongued.
24a	גּוֹזֵל אָבִיו וְאִמּוֹ וְאֹמֵר	One who robs his father and mother and says,
24b	אֵין־פָּשַׁע	"There is no crime,"
24c	חָבֵר הוּא לְאִישׁ מַשְׁחִית	he is a companion to a destroyer.
25a	רְחַב־נֶפֶשׁ יְגָרֶה מָדוֹן	The greedy stir up strife,
25b	וּבוֹטֵחַ עַל־יְהוָה יְדֻשָּׁן	but the one who trusts in YHWH will be refreshed.
26a	בּוֹטֵחַ בְּלִבּוֹ הוּא כְסִיל	The one who trusts in his own heart – he is a fool;
26b	וְהוֹלֵךְ בְּחָכְמָה הוּא יִמָּלֵט	but the one who walks in wisdom – he will be delivered.
27a	נוֹתֵן לָרָשׁ אֵין מַחְסוֹר	One who gives to the poor lacks nothing,
27b	וּמַעְלִים עֵינָיו רַב־מְאֵרוֹת	while the one who closes his eyes, abundant curses.
28a	בְּקוּם רְשָׁעִים יִסָּתֵר אָדָם	When the wicked rise, people hide,
28b	וּבְאָבְדָם יִרְבּוּ צַדִּיקִים	and when they perish, the righteous increase.

Vivid images and analogies (such as 28:1b, 3, 15) fade. Several sayings are continuous sentences (vv. 8, 9, 10a–b, 17, 22, 24). Most of the aphorisms are cast in the form of antithetical couplets. The antithetical style of the sayings, combined with the renewed attention to the opposition between the righteous and the wicked (vv. 1, 4, 12, 15, 28), intimates that the chapter returns to the poetic design of Prov 10:1–15:33, bringing the central collections full circle.[6] To some extent, this is true. On the surface, antitheses dominate the literary landscape of ch. 28. When one attends to the semantic and syntactical design of these antitheses, however, one discovers that they do not represent a formal return to the antithetical consistency of 10:1–15:33. With the exception of a few antithetical sayings (28:1, 5, 14, 19, 28), the majority of the antitheses in the chapter are disjointed. Their parallel lines engender a conceptual antithesis, but corresponding elements between the lines are semantically imprecise.[7] These imprecisions force the reader to associate asymmetrical elements (cf. vv. 11, 13, 16, 18, 20, 25, 27), such as "many are its princes" (רַבִּים שָׂרֶיהָ, v. 2a) and "right endures" (כֵּן יַאֲרִיךְ, v. 2b),[8] praising the wicked and striving against them (v. 4), keeping instruction and shaming one's father (v. 7), falling into a pit and inheriting good (v. 10b–c), and "great glory" (רַבָּה תִפְאָרֶת, v. 12a) and "people hide" (יְחֻפַּשׂ אָדָם, v. 12b), and "he is a fool" (הוּא כְסִיל, v. 26a) and "he will be delivered" (הוּא יִמָּלֵט, v. 26b). The semantic asymmetry between corresponding elements creates gaps that awaken the reader's moral imagination, shape their moral reasoning, and stretch their powers of perception. While the antithetical style of many of the aphorisms creates the impression of literary and moral symmetry, the semantic imbalance between the lines reveals a deeper structure that trains and forms readers.

The deep structure of most of the antithetical couplets may signal that the sayings within Prov 28 are arranged within a sophisticated structural design. When read in conjunction with ch. 29, some maintain that the righteous-wicked sayings function as formal markers that orient one to the macrostructure of the subcollection (28:1,

6. Murphy, *Proverbs*, 213; Van Leeuwen, "The Book of Proverbs," *NIB* 5:234; Yoder, *Proverbs*, 263.

7. Many of these disjointed proverbs are noted by Waltke and Fox. Waltke, *Proverbs: Chapters 15–31*, 415–28; Fox, *Proverbs 10–31*, 823, 831.

8. The imprecise parallelism, combined with the obscure sense of כֵּן, has given rise to several emendations of 28:2 (Driver, "Problems in the Hebrew Text of Proverbs," 191–92; *BHS*). The LXX reads δι᾽ ἁμαρτίας ἀσεβῶν κρίσεις ἐγείρονται, ἀνὴρ δὲ πανοῦργος κατασβέσει αὐτάς ("through the sins of the wicked disputes break out, but an intelligent person will extinguish them"). This rendering does not provide a firm basis for textual emendations, for it appears to represent a different *Vorlage* (Murphy, *Proverbs*, 213). While the second colon of the MT is difficult, the sense of the initial verset is rather clear: sociomoral anarchy produces revolts that either necessitate a large bureaucracy or ensure a succession of leaders in volatile times. Within the second colon, it seems that מֵבִין יֹדֵעַ serves as an asyndeton ("an intelligent person who knows") and כֵּן functions as an adjective indicating the affirmative ("right, order"; cf. 11:19; 15:7 [see LXX]). In this case, the second colon of 28:2 may be rendered "but because of an intelligent person, one who knows, right endures." The polyvalent nature of the verset suggests that the enduring "right" refers to both the land and the perceptive leader. Although this interpretation does not form a precise parallel with the initial verset, it implies that a discerning person has an advantage over many princes in securing order within society. For a discussion of the textual issues, see Murphy, *Proverbs*, 213; Waltke, *Proverbs: Chapters 15–31*, 408; Fox, *Proverbs 10–31*, 819–20.

12, 28; 29:2, 16, 27). The subcollection is framed by these antithetical character types (28:1; 29:27); and the literary and thematic links between the righteous-wicked sayings across chs. 28–29 may indicate that they serve as structural beams, outlining the major divisions within the material (i.e., 28:2–11, 13–27; 29:3–15, 17–26).[9] On this account, the placement of the righteous-wicked sayings not only reveals the structural contours of the subcollection and its concern with the themes of one's relationship to Torah, YHWH, education, and rulership;[10] it also suggests that chs. 28–29 "are an intricately arranged collection serving as a manual for future monarchs."[11]

The literary and thematic links between the righteous-wicked sayings in Prov 28–29 are striking, but the diverse subject matter of the aphorisms within the purported subdivisions calls into question their thematic and compositional unity. And the relevance of the materials to kings, courtiers, and the common folk undermines the contention that the subcollection was composed exclusively for future rulers. This is not to say that the aphorisms in ch. 28 are a haphazard collage of maxims irrelevant to those in positions of power. The repetition of the term "instruction" (תּוֹרָה, vv. 4, 7a, 9a) and the root בין (vv. 2b, 5, 7a, 11b), combined with the attention to the righteous and the wicked (vv. 1, 4a, 12, 15b, 28), wealth and poverty (vv. 3, 6, 8, 11, 15, 19, 20, 22, 27), and the (mis)use of power, indicates that the aphorisms share common concerns. Even if particular sayings or the subcollection as a whole were composed for future rulers, the materials have been democratized so that all might consider the nature and exercise of power.[12] The aphorisms in ch. 29 may not exhibit a clear, coherent structure. Their shared forms and motifs, however, suggest that they constitute a loose instruction on the dynamics of power.[13]

9. Malchow, "A Manual for Future Monarchs," 238–41; Meinhold, *Die Sprüche*, 2:464. Cf. Daniel P. Bricker, "Proverbs 28.1–11: A Small Poem?," *JSOT* 34 (2010): 315–30.

10. Meinhold, *Die Sprüche*, 2:464–65.

11. Malchow, "A Manual for Future Monarchs," 243.

12. Waltke, *Proverbs: Chapters 15–31*, 405–6; Ricardo Tavares, *Eine königliche Weisheitslehre? Exegetische Analyse von Sprüche 28–29 und Vergleich mit den ägyptischen Lehren Merikaras und Amenemhats*, OBO 234 (Göttingen: Vandenhoeck & Ruprecht, 2007); Fox, *Proverbs 10–31*, 817–18.

13. Whybray, *The Composition of the Book of Proverbs*, 126.

CHAPTER 35

Proverbs 29:1–27

E. MORAL AUTHORITY and the MORAL ORDER: *(Il)legitimate Power and Moral Responsibility*

Main Idea of the Passage

Assuming the close relationship between the concepts of MORAL AUTHORITY and MORAL ORDER, the majority of sayings consider the exercise of power and its implications for the stability of the community and the household to cultivate an ethos of moral responsibility within these spheres of society.

Literary Context

Similar to the sayings within ch. 28, power relations permeate the aphorisms in Prov 29. These relations operate under a hierarchy of authority, which acquires legitimation through the exercise of moral responsibility toward those placed under one's charge.[1] Many of the aphorisms probe the nature of these power relations and the legitimacy of authoritative figures in the household as well as the community by exploring the way in which they exercise power. The well-being of the household, for example, is contingent on the moral action of the parents. Several sayings link the emotional health of parents, the honor of the family, and the stability of the domestic unit to the exercise of parental discipline (vv. 3, 15, 17, 19, 21). This responsible use of power legitimizes the parents' authority; and following Lakoff and Johnson, it "creates the moral imperative for children to obey their parents" as well as for servants to obey their masters.[2] The same dynamic structures the nature of communal rule. The legitimacy of kings, rulers, and constituencies is determined by their character, concern for the administration of justice, and commitment to the flourishing of

1. Lakoff and Johnson, *Philosophy in the Flesh*, 301–3.

2. Lakoff and Johnson, *Philosophy in the Flesh*, 301.

all members of society (vv. 2, 4, 7, 8, 10, 12, 16, 18, 26). Whether the communal or domestic sphere is in view, the concepts of MORAL AUTHORITY and MORAL ORDER shape many of the sayings in ch. 29 and their particular interest in power relations.

When read within the broader context of the book of Proverbs, these metaphorical concepts and thematic concerns are nothing new. Parental discipline and the prospect of familial honor or shame populate the instructions in chs. 1–9 as well as individual sayings in the central collections (29:3, 15, 17, 19, 21; cf. 10:1; 13:24; 15:20; 19:18; 22:15; 23:24–25; 27:11). Righteous rule and the maintenance of justice recall earlier aphorisms that consider the body politic (29:4, 7, 12, 14; cf. 16:10–13; 20:28; 25:5). The sharp contrast between the righteous and the wicked is reminiscent of previous materials in general and the concentrated attention to these character types in the opening chapters of the central collections in particular (i.e., 10:1–11:13).[3]

The recurrence of these familiar themes, combined with the variant repetitions within ch. 29,[4] has contributed to the impression that the chapter serves as a "summary" of the central collections.[5] To the extent that the sayings reiterate key motifs, repeat parts of earlier aphorisms, and revisit conventional character types, they provide "a sort of summary" to the dynamic dialogue among the materials in chs. 10–29.[6] This summary, however, does not bring the thematic dialogue among the sayings to a close.[7] To the contrary, many sayings extend the thematic dialogue in

3. Keefer, *Proverbs 1–9 as an Introduction*, 51.

4. These variant repetitions include **29:1b**//6:15b; **29:6**//12:13; **29:14b**//16:12b//20:28b//25:5b; **29:20a**//11:14a//29:18a; 22:29a//26:12; **29:22a**//15:18a; **29:2, 16**//cf. 28:12//28:28. For discussion of these variant repetitions, see Heim, *Poetic Imagination*.

5. Whybray, *Proverbs*, 398; Hatton, *Contradiction in the Book of Proverbs*, 61, 67; Dell, *The Book of Proverbs*, 81.

6. Hatton, *Contradiction in the Book of Proverbs*, 61.

7. Hatton, *Contradiction in the Book of Proverbs*, 61, 68.

distinctive ways. Similar to the aphorisms in ch. 28, in Prov 29 the righteous and the wicked are construed as political constituencies (vv. 2, 7, 16, 27; cf. 28:4, 5, 12, 28).[8] Far from their idealized characterization elsewhere in the anthology, kings and rulers are subjected to harsh criticism (vv. 4, 12, 14, 26; cf. 16:10–15; 19:12; 21:1; 24:21–22). Counter to expectations, reproof may prove ineffective (v. 1; cf. 1:20–33; 6:23; 13:18; 15:5; 15:31–32). In addition to children, servants require discipline within the household (vv. 19, 21). And together with the wisdom of the sages, prophetic revelation and divine instruction are identified as authoritative means of communal guidance (v. 18). The sayings collected in ch. 29 reinforce and develop familiar themes. In so doing, they bolster and sharpen the reader's moral vision.

Translation and Exegetical Outline

(See pages 593–94.)

Structure and Literary Form

The poetic texture of the materials in Prov 29 mirrors the literary forms sewn into the fabric of ch. 28. Colorful images and imaginative comparisons are scarce (v. 5). A number of sayings defy the conventional categories of parallelism, taking the form of continuous sentences or a rhetorical question, followed by a response (vv. 1, 5, 9, 12, 13, 14, 19, 20, 21). Antithetical couplets dominate the formal make-up of the materials (e.g., vv. 2, 8, 11, 27). In light of its poetic texture, Roland Murphy's characterization of the chapter is not surprising: it lacks "the color" of previous materials, conveying its advice through "humble literary dress."[9] The prominence of antithetical couplets may give the impression that the aphorisms are clothed in "humble literary dress." But when one examines the semantic fabric and poetic stitching of these antithetical couplets, their sophisticated design becomes apparent. Similar to the majority of antithetical couplets in ch. 28, most of the antithetical couplets in ch. 29 are disjointed (vv. 3, 4, 6, 7, 15, 16, 18, 23, 25, 26). Corresponding elements between parallel lines are imprecise; and some elements are elided.[10] While the poetic lines of these couplets create a conceptual antithesis, an analysis of their semantics and syntax reveals their asymmetry.

8. Brown, "The Pedagogy of Proverbs 10:1–31:9," 172, where Brown contends that "the theme of mortal conflict between the righteous and the wicked is more pronounced in this collection than in any other. . . . The issue of conflict is set no longer in the abstract but on the concrete level of social struggle over authority within and outside the royal court (see 29:12)."

9. Murphy, *Proverbs*, 220, 224.

10. Many of these disjointed proverbs are noted by Waltke and Heim. Waltke, *Proverbs: Chapters 15–31*, 432–53; Heim, *Poetic Imagination*, 274–76, 292–93, 385. Also see Fox, *Proverbs 10–31*, 834.

Proverbs 29:1–27

Verse	Hebrew	English	Outline
1a	אִישׁ תּוֹכָחוֹת מַקְשֶׁה־עֹרֶף	A person reproved who stiffens his neck	E. Moral Authority and the Moral Order: (Il)legitimate Power and Moral Responsibility (29:1–27)
1b	פֶּתַע יִשָּׁבֵר וְאֵין מַרְפֵּא	will suddenly be broken and without remedy.	
2a	בִּרְבוֹת צַדִּיקִים יִשְׂמַח הָעָם	When the righteous increase, the people rejoice,	
2b	וּבִמְשֹׁל רָשָׁע יֵאָנַח עָם	but when the wicked rule, people groan.	
3a	אִישׁ־אֹהֵב חָכְמָה יְשַׂמַּח אָבִיו	A person who loves wisdom makes his father glad,	
3b	וְרֹעֶה זוֹנוֹת יְאַבֶּד־הוֹן	but one who associates with prostitutes destroys wealth.	
4a	מֶלֶךְ בְּמִשְׁפָּט יַעֲמִיד אָרֶץ	By justice a king brings stability to a land,	
4b	וְאִישׁ תְּרוּמוֹת יֶהֶרְסֶנָּה	but a person who exacts contributions tears it down.	
5a	גֶּבֶר מַחֲלִיק עַל־רֵעֵהוּ	A person who flatters his neighbor,	
5b	רֶשֶׁת פּוֹרֵשׂ עַל־פְּעָמָיו	spreading a net for his feet.	
6a	בְּפֶשַׁע אִישׁ רָע מוֹקֵשׁ	In the transgression of an evil person, a snare,	
6b	וְצַדִּיק יָרוּן וְשָׂמֵחַ	but the righteous will sing and rejoice.	
7a	יֹדֵעַ צַדִּיק דִּין דַּלִּים	The righteous know the rights of the poor,	
7b	רָשָׁע לֹא־יָבִין דָּעַת	but the wicked do not understand knowledge.	
8a	אַנְשֵׁי לָצוֹן יָפִיחוּ קִרְיָה	Scoffers inflame a city,	
8b	וַחֲכָמִים יָשִׁיבוּ אָף	while the wise turn away anger.	
9a	אִישׁ־חָכָם נִשְׁפָּט אֶת־אִישׁ אֱוִיל	A wise person disputes with a foolish person,	
9b	וְרָגַז וְשָׂחַק וְאֵין נָחַת	and he rages and laughs, but there is no rest.	
10a	אַנְשֵׁי דָמִים יִשְׂנְאוּ־תָם	Men of blood hate the blameless,	
10b	וִישָׁרִים יְבַקְשׁוּ נַפְשׁוֹ	but the upright seeks his life.	
11a	כָּל־רוּחוֹ יוֹצִיא כְסִיל	A fool lets out all of his spirit,	
11b	וְחָכָם בְּאָחוֹר יְשַׁבְּחֶנָּה	while the wise quiet it down.	
12a	מֹשֵׁל מַקְשִׁיב עַל־דְּבַר־שָׁקֶר	A ruler who listens to a deceptive word –	
12b	כָּל־מְשָׁרְתָיו רְשָׁעִים	all his officials, wicked.	
13a	רָשׁ וְאִישׁ תְּכָכִים נִפְגָּשׁוּ	A poor man and an oppressor meet:	
13b	מֵאִיר־עֵינֵי שְׁנֵיהֶם יְהוָה	YHWH is the one who gives light to the eyes of both.	
14a	מֶלֶךְ שׁוֹפֵט בֶּאֱמֶת דַּלִּים	A king who judges the poor in truth,	
14b	כִּסְאוֹ לָעַד יִכּוֹן	his throne will be established forever.	

Continued on next page.

Continued from previous page.

15a	שֵׁבֶט וְתוֹכַחַת יִתֵּן חָכְמָה	The rod and reproof give wisdom,
15b	וְנַעַר מְשֻׁלָּח מֵבִישׁ אִמּוֹ	while a youth set loose shames his mother.
16a	בִּרְבוֹת רְשָׁעִים יִרְבֶּה־פָּשַׁע	When the wicked increase, transgression increases,
16b	וְצַדִּיקִים בְּמַפַּלְתָּם יִרְאוּ׃	but the righteous will see their downfall.
17a	יַסֵּר בִּנְךָ וִינִיחֶךָ	Discipline your son so that he may bring you comfort,
17b	וְיִתֵּן מַעֲדַנִּים לְנַפְשֶׁךָ	and give delight to your life.
18a	בְּאֵין חָזוֹן יִפָּרַע עָם	When there is no vision, a people cast off restraint,
18b	וְשֹׁמֵר תּוֹרָה אַשְׁרֵהוּ׃	but the one who keeps instruction, blessed is he!
19a	בִּדְבָרִים לֹא־יִוָּסֶר עָבֶד	A servant is not disciplined by words;
19b	כִּי־יָבִין וְאֵין מַעֲנֶה	though he understands, there is no response.
20a	חָזִיתָ אִישׁ אָץ בִּדְבָרָיו	Have you seen a man hasty with his words?
20b	תִּקְוָה לִכְסִיל מִמֶּנּוּ׃	There is more hope for a fool than for him.
21a	מְפַנֵּק מִנֹּעַר עַבְדּוֹ	One who pampers his servant from youth –
21b	וְאַחֲרִיתוֹ יִהְיֶה מָנוֹן	afterward he will be insolent.
22a	אִישׁ־אַף יְגָרֶה מָדוֹן	An angry man provokes strife,
22b	וּבַעַל חֵמָה רַב־פָּשַׁע	and a hothead, abundant transgression.
23a	גַּאֲוַת אָדָם תַּשְׁפִּילֶנּוּ	A person's pride will bring him low,
23b	וּשְׁפַל־רוּחַ יִתְמֹךְ כָּבוֹד	but a lowly spirit will hold honor.
24a	חוֹלֵק עִם־גַּנָּב שׂוֹנֵא נַפְשׁוֹ	One who partners with a thief hates his life.
24b	אָלָה יִשְׁמַע וְלֹא יַגִּיד	He hears a curse, but he will not testify.
25a	חֶרְדַּת אָדָם יִתֵּן מוֹקֵשׁ	Fear of people lays a snare,
25b	וּבוֹטֵחַ בַּיהוָה יְשֻׂגָּב	but one who trusts in YHWH will be protected.
26a	רַבִּים מְבַקְשִׁים פְּנֵי־מוֹשֵׁל	Many are those who seek the face of a ruler,
26b	וּמֵיְהוָה מִשְׁפַּט־אִישׁ	but from YHWH: a person's judgment.
27a	תּוֹעֲבַת צַדִּיקִים אִישׁ עָוֶל	An unjust person is an abomination to the righteous,
27b	וְתוֹעֲבַת רָשָׁע יְשַׁר־דָּרֶךְ	while one whose way is upright is an abomination to the wicked.

This asymmetry funds the pedagogical goals of Proverbs; it sharpens one's perception, nurtures the powers of discernment, and awakens one's imagination so as to understand "insightful words" (1:2) and to process difficult sayings (1:6).

Some commentators have exercised these interpretive virtues to elucidate the macro and microstructural contours the materials in Prov 29. Many of their observations concerning the macrostructural design of the chapter merit attention. Together with ch. 28, the righteous and wicked sayings may serve as structural beams, marking off larger units (28:12, 28; 29:2, 16, 27; cf. 29:7).[11] The mention of both YHWH and the ruler (מוֹשֵׁל) at the end of Prov 29 is reminiscent of the opening verses of the Hezekian collection (25:2–3; 29:25, 26), forming an envelope around the compendium.[12] And the double use of the consonant ת—the final letter in the Hebrew alphabet, which opens and closes the initial word in the individual lines of 29:27 (תּוֹעֲבַת, "abomination")—may signal the formal end of the collection.[13] These observations orient one to the general, structural contours of the chapter within the broader context of the Hezekian collection. When the sayings are viewed from a microstructural perspective, however, recourse to the concepts of leapfrogging between sayings, chiastic *inclusios*, paronomasia, and thematic groupings fail to form a satisfying fusion between content and structure.[14] This dissatisfaction does not mean that "uniform" structural proposals that discern the strategic placement of sayings should be dismissed out of hand.[15] To extend the metaphor from Prov 9, this dissatisfaction reveals the nature of one's interpretive palate more than the depth of potential flavor in the interpretive dish. Yet, irrespective of one's palate, certain thematic tastes bring together many sayings in ch. 29. The righteous and the wicked (vv. 2, 7, 16, 27), the administration of justice (vv. 2, 4, 7, 9, 12, 13, 14, 16, 26), discipline (vv. 1, 15, 17, 19, 21), and the use of the term "person" (אִישׁ, vv. 1a, 3a, 4b, 6a, 9a, 10a, 13a, 20a, 22a, 26b, 27a) infuse the diverse materials with a measure of coherence, focusing attention on particular themes that have been placed in this final chapter of the central collections.

11. Malchow, "A Manual for Future Monarchs," 239–43; Meinhold, *Die Sprüche*, 2:464; Waltke, *Proverbs: Chapters 15–31*, 403–6.

12. Whybray, *Proverbs*, 405.

13. Delitzsch, "Book of Proverbs," 6:437 (2:259); Skehan, "A Single Editor for the Whole Book of Proverbs," 23; Clifford, *Proverbs*, 256; Waltke, *Proverbs: Chapters 15–31*, 403.

14. For these concepts, see Meinhold, *Die Sprüche*, 2:481, 488; Garrett, *Proverbs*, 227–33; Van Leeuwen, "The Book of Proverbs," *NIB* 5:243–44; Waltke, *Proverbs: Chapters 15–31*, 429–30; Sæbø, *Sprüche*, 346.

15. Malchow, "A Manual for Future Monarchs," 239; Meinhold, *Die Sprüche*, 2:464.

Explanation of the Text

Among the educational techniques within Proverbs, rebuke plays a formative role. Rebuke is designed to disrupt the recipient and to direct their character by orienting them toward dispositions and practices authorized by the community.[16] The efficacy of rebuke, however, is dependent on the character of the recipient (e.g., 10:17; 12:1; 13:18; 15:31–32; 17:10).[17] This dependence is reinforced by the opening saying of Prov 29 (**v. 1**). But in contrast to previous aphorisms devoted to the topic, the saying offers a "much bleaker judgment."[18] It traffics in terror and focuses on the hard, unmalleable nature of the defiant across two lines, refusing to balance its depiction of the incorrigible with the receptivity of a moral exemplar.[19] This lack of balance is also reflected in the form of the saying. The individual lines exhibit semilinear parallelism.[20] When read together, they form a single sentence that defies the traditional categories of parallelism. This sentence moves from a description of the incorrigible to his demise. The description focuses on "a man of rebukes" (אִישׁ תּוֹכָחוֹת, v. 1a),[21] that is, a person often reproved. In response to relentless reproof, this man "stiffens his neck" (מַקְשֶׁה־עֹרֶף, v. 1a), physically modeling his internal disposition of obstinacy to correction (cf. Deut 10:16; 2 Kgs 17:4; Jer 7:26). His demise is sudden and conveyed with the same words employed to describe the fate of the scoundrel (Prov 29:1b; 6:15b). This terse account of irremediable brokenness serves as a striking warning, alerting both the incorrigible and the receptive to the dangers of spurning reproof.

The nexus of character and consequence is widened in **v. 2**, which portrays the community's response to the character of political constituencies. The conventional contrast between the righteous and the wicked is reiterated. Similar to sayings in ch. 28, however, this conventional contrast concretizes these characters, rendering them as powerful, political parties (28:12, 28; cf. 29:16). Each line opens with a temporal clause that delineates the circumstances under which the community offers differing responses. While the asymmetry between the infinitives construct "increase" (רְבוֹת, v. 2a) and "rule" (מְשֹׁל, v. 2b) has compelled some to emend the initial line in order to improve the parallelism,[22] emendation is unnecessary. The imprecision ignites the reader's moral reasoning, inviting them to place the denotation of "rule" in conversation with the semantic connotations of "increase."[23] When the population and power of the righteous increase, merriment fills the mouths of the people. When the wicked rule, by contrast, inarticulate expressions of despair fill the communal air. The saying politicizes conventional characters; and it bears witness to the interrelationship among (im)moral authority, moral responsibility, and the welfare of those placed under one's care.

Against this communal backdrop, **v. 3** considers the emotional health of the household. Love of wis-

16. Stewart, *Poetic Ethics*, 83–84.

17. Stewart, *Poetic Ethics*, 85.

18. Hatton, *Contradiction in the Book of Proverbs*, 61.

19. Hatton, *Contradiction in the Book of Proverbs*, 61.

20. Heim, *Poetic Imagination*, 177–78.

21. Together with many other interpreters, אִישׁ תּוֹכָחוֹת is construed as an abstract subjective genitive, according to which אִישׁ ("person") serves as the object of the implicit verbal action performed by תּוֹכָחוֹת ("reproved"). *IBHS* §9.5.1e; Waltke, *Proverbs: Chapters 15–31*, 398n30; Fox, *Proverbs 10–31*, 833–34.

22. Toy, *Proverbs*, 507; *BHS*.

23. Yoder, *Proverbs*, 272; Fox, *Proverbs 10–31*, 834; Heim, *Poetic Imagination*, 592–608.

dom, parental joy, and the stability of the domestic unit are familiar topics and motivations within Proverbs (cf. 10:1; 15:20; 17:21). But these familiar topics and motivations are expressed in an unusual way. The saying is cast in the form of a disjointed proverb. The corresponding elements between the parallel lines are semantically imprecise, and this imprecision forces the reader to fill in particular gaps. The opening line focuses on appropriate desire and the emotions: one who loves wisdom engenders parental delight. The second line, by contrast, attends to the financial loss that accompanies the sexually immoral. Each line is funded by a different frame of reference, and each line welcomes the other to complement its comment. If one were to complete the individual lines, the saying may be construed as follows: A sexually moral person loves wisdom and makes his father glad, but one who associates with prostitutes makes his father grieve and destroys wealth.[24] The natural desire to please one's parents and contribute to the emotional and financial stability of the household motivates the saying, cultivating appropriate desires and inspiring implicit obedience to moral authority.

The concepts of moral authority, moral responsibility, and the stability of the community structure **v. 4** (cf. 16:10–13; 20:2). But the ambiguous subject in the second line and the semantic imprecision between elements in the parallel lines challenge the reader to resolve the intralinear logic of the saying. While the semantics and syntax of the predicates in each line form a clear contrast, the elision of a prepositional phrase in the second and the nature of its subject stimulate the reader's moral reasoning. Just as justice serves as the instrument through which a king brings stability to a community (v. 4a), so injustice is the implicit means by which a community crumbles (v. 4b). The implicit injustice in the second line is made explicit through the subject "a person who exacts contributions" (אִישׁ תְּרוּמוֹת, v. 4b). This expression is unusual, for the noun "contributions" (תְּרוּמָה) refers to voluntary cultic donations sanctioned by YHWH elsewhere in the Old Testament (Deut 12:6, 11). These donations are not deemed unjust. The expression creates an asymmetrical relationship with the first line, engendering a fresh dialogue between the subjects. Whether "a person who exacts contributions" refers to a ruler or someone other than the king, the second line may develop the king's responsibility to exercise justice through appropriate oversight of government funds.[25] If, on the other hand, bribes and taxation lie outside of the semantic range of "contributions," the phrase may be considered as a scribal corruption of "a deceitful person" (תַּרְמִית אִישׁ), which would supply a more precise parallel to the concept of justice mentioned in the opening line.[26] The saying is open to both readings, each of which offers a different angle on the intersection of moral authority, moral responsibility, and the stability of a land.

The stability of a land gives way to the interpersonal dangers of slippery speech in **v. 5**. Terms for speech, however, are not mentioned.[27] They slip through the saying's terse sentence, which conceptualizes the smooth interaction with a neighbor through the spreading of a net. In fact, when read together, the participles "who flatters" (מַחֲלִיק, v. 5a) and "spreading" (פּוֹרֵשׂ, v. 5b) may represent a play on words, where smooth speech is equated

24. Waltke, *Proverbs: Chapters 15–31*, 432; Fox, "The Rhetoric of Disjointed Proverbs," 171–72.

25. Meinhold, *Die Sprüche*, 2:483; Van Leeuwen, "The Book of Proverbs," *NIB* 5:242; Waltke, *Proverbs: Chapters 15–31*, 432–33.

26. Fox, *Proverbs 10–31*, 834–35.

27. The participle "who flatters" or "who makes smooth" (מַחֲלִיק) is not accompanied by terms for speech, such as words, mouth, or tongue.

with smoothing out a hidden trap.[28] The goal of the flatterer's seduction is unknown. The same is true of the antecedent of the third-person masculine singular suffix (v. 5b). The smooth words may be designed to trap the neighbor, but the flatterer may be ensnared by the net. The saying rehearses the dangers of slippery speech (2:16; 5:3; 28:23), warning one of the power of words to seduce and entrap.

A trap also appears in **v. 6**, which represents a variant repetition of 12:13. The initial line depicts a snare as a device inherent within the transgression of the evil person. Similar to v. 5b, it remains unclear whether this snare entangles the evil or another. The second line does not clarify the matter, for it reveals that the saying is a disjointed proverb; its elements do not correspond semantically with those in the opening line.[29] Instead, they identify gaps that extend the sense of the saying. One gap may be filled by the aphorism's variant counterpart. Whereas a snare lies in the transgression of the evil, the righteous escapes from trouble (12:13b). Another gap is opened by the emotional exuberance of the righteous (29:6b). The rejoicing of this moral exemplar extends the sense of the saying, focusing attention on the expression of delight that finds no counterpart in the initial line.[30] This attention to the emotions of the righteous produces an attractive model for emulation; it moves beyond the desire for safety to include one's desire for satisfaction.

The exemplary character of the righteous is developed in **v. 7**. The saying links character with knowledge, that is, one's (im)moral ontology with epistemology. By virtue of their moral ontology, it is not surprising that the righteous know the legal rights of the poor (v. 7a). In light of the portrait of the righteous within Proverbs, it appears that this is not knowledge for knowledge's sake; it is the active pursuit of knowledge, borne of empathy, that seeks the welfare of the marginalized. The wicked, by contrast, embody an immoral ontology that is reflected in their epistemology, for they do not understand knowledge in general or the legal rights of the poor in particular (v. 7b; cf. 28:5). Ontology, epistemology, moral responsibility, and moral nurturance converge in this saying to identify another attractive attribute of the righteous: their understanding of and empathy for the condition of others.

And yet, the ability to understand the feelings of others can be used for destructive ends. This is the reality observed in **v. 8**. Alert to communal passions, scoffers possess an uncanny capacity to inflame a city (v. 8a; cf. Isa 28:14). They are depicted as blowtorches, breathing out strife that ignites and consumes the community. The wise, by contrast, mollify the flames of anger (Prov 29:8b); but the manner by which the wise assuage anger is open and ambiguous (cf. Prov 13:14; 15:2, 7; 16:21, 23). The second line focuses on the moral essence and moral action of the wise rather than their means of mollification. In so doing, it reinforces the moral character of the wise as those committed to the peace and stability of society.

Whereas the wise produce communal peace in 29:8, brokering peace in interpersonal relationships or judicial disputes may fail. This is the scenario staged in **v. 9**. The saying is cast in the form of a single sentence, which moves from a debate between the wise and the fool to a description of the derisive demeanor of the latter. Arguing with a foolish person is a dangerous business (cf. 18:2; 20:3; 23:9; 27:3). The prospect of rage and ridicule does not excuse the wise from disputing with or correcting fools (cf. 26:4–5), but it does provide

28. Fox, *Proverbs 10–31*, 835.

29. Heim, *Poetic Imagination*, 291–93.

30. Heim, *Poetic Imagination*, 292–93.

the wise with a warning that shapes expectations concerning the nature and outcome of the debate. The dispute may never reach a resolution. In fact, it may provide the fool with an occasion to rant and rave, and rest may prove to be elusive.

The search for resolution continues in **v. 10**, which poses a semantic problem that requires the powers of discernment. The opening line is clear: it associates the character of the murderous with a distorted desire (v. 10a). When one moves to the second line, the initial expression creates the impression that the saying will conclude with a description of a sanctioned desire that characterizes the upright. But the use of the idiom "seeks his life" (יְבַקְשׁוּ נַפְשׁוֹ, v. 10b) forces the reader to double back and reconsider the relationship between the upright and the idiom, for the phrase is a negative expression that refers to killing elsewhere in the Old Testament (e.g., Exod 4:19; Jer 19:7; Ps 35:4). The notion of the upright seeking the life of the blameless is inconceivable within the moral vision of Proverbs. The incongruity demands reexamination. While many resolve the issue through emendation,[31] if the line traffics in the technique of the "false lead,"[32] then semantic and syntactical considerations provide alternative readings that reconceive the difficulties of the line. From a semantic perspective, "seeks his life" could be construed as an anomaly and rendered as the upright's active preservation of the life of the blameless.[33] Alternatively, the syntax of the elements in the line could be reclassified. To be specific, the upright could be taken as a nominative absolute rather than as the subject of the idiom "seeks his life." On this reading, the "men of blood" would serve as the subject of both lines, and the pronominal suffix "his" would refer back to the "upright." This alternative syntactical account produces an intelligible reading: "Men of blood hate the blameless; as for the upright, they [men of blood] seek his [the upright's] life."[34] The second line intensifies the thought of the first, moving from hatred to murder.[35] And the saying nurtures the moral reasoning of the reader and awakens the powers of discernment through a semantic problem that finds its resolution in a syntactical adjustment.

The interrelationship between one's character and one's emotions overflows into **v. 11**. While many restrict the emotional antithesis between the fool and the wise to their expression or restraint of anger,[36] the semantics of the saying suggests that one's "spirit" (רוח, v. 11a) eclipses this emotional comparison.[37] A fool expels all of his emotions; he is unable to contain the emotional wind that blows within his being. The wise, on the other hand, possess the powers of self-restraint. They exercise moral strength by stilling and subduing their emotions. This snapshot of self-control serves as an attractive portrait that inspires imitation of the wise.

This is not the case in **v. 12**, which engenders moral disgust. In contrast to sayings that describe the king's administration of justice and establishment of communal stability (v. 4; cf. 14:28, 35; 16:10–15; 25:5), this sentence portrays an immoral authority who shirks his moral responsibilities and

31. *BHS*; Driver, "Problems in the Hebrew Text of Proverbs," 194; Toy, *Proverbs*, 509–10.

32. Millar, "When a Straight Road becomes a Garden Path," 67–82, esp. 75–77.

33. Clifford, *Proverbs*, 252; Fox, *Proverbs 10–31*, 837.

34. For this reading, see Delitzsch, "Book of Proverbs," 6:428–29 (2:246–47); Waltke, *Proverbs: Chapters 15–31*, 400n51–53, 438; Millar, "When a Straight Road becomes a Garden Path," 75–77.

35. Millar, "When a Straight Road becomes a Garden Path," 77.

36. Van Leeuwen, "The Book of Proverbs," *NIB* 5:243; Waltke, *Proverbs: Chapters 15–31*, 439; Fox, *Proverbs 10–31*, 837–38.

37. Keefer, *Proverbs 1–9 as an Introduction*, 87–90.

cultivates transcommunal corruption. The ruler stands at the top of the human hierarchy of moral authority. When a ruler evinces an attentiveness to deceptive speech, he cultivates and motivates institutional perfidy, and this perfidy destabilizes the foundations of the sociomoral order. As many note, from an illocutionary perspective, the sentence functions as a warning. From a perlocutionary perspective, however, it arouses moral revulsion.

The immoral authority and sociomoral corruption of 29:12 bump into the ultimate authority and his power in **v. 13**. Similar to 22:2, the sentence in 29:12 projects a meeting. This meeting is between the two very different parties, divided according to power: the poor and the oppressor. More than capturing the power differential between these parties, the character designations concretize the interpersonal dynamics of abuse. Irrespective of the social nature of the meeting between the poor and the oppressor, when both are placed before YHWH, socioeconomic classifications fade, for YHWH "gives light to the eyes of both" (מֵאִיר־עֵינֵי שְׁנֵיהֶם, v. 13b). Both are utterly dependent on YHWH for their life, breath, and existence. This realization of absolute dependence is designed not only to censure abuse and to nurture empathy but also to identify the source of all existence, who does not discriminate according to socioeconomic class.[38]

Like vv. 12 and 13, **v. 14** addresses the intersection of power and moral responsibility but, in contrast to the previous sayings, it renders this relationship in a positive fashion. The initial line presents the royal ideal: a king who exercises his moral responsibility by protecting and securing the rights of the poor. While the second line represents a variant repetition of 16:12b, 28:28b, and 25:5b, it extends these partial aphorisms in a distinctive way. Cast in the form of a promise, it adds a temporal dimension to the establishment of the king's throne (לָעַד, "forever," 29:14b). And it associates the establishment of the royal throne with the king's maintenance of justice for the poor.[39] Among several sayings that are critical of an authority's failure to exercise their moral responsibilities, this aphorism reclaims the moral ideal. Those in positions of moral authority are responsible to exercise their power in order to protect the vulnerable.

The responsibilities that accompany moral authority in the community mirror the responsibilities that accompany moral authority in the household. The importance of parental discipline is foregrounded in **v. 15**. And this familiar theme is motivated by a basic desire. The initial line highlights the pedagogical value of different forms of discipline. Both physical (שֵׁבֶט, "rod," v. 15a) and verbal (תוֹכַחַת, "reproof," v. 15a) correction are instrumental to the cultivation of wisdom. But when parents fail to use these instruments, a youth breaks loose like an untamed animal, bringing social shame on the household (v. 15b). Taken on their own, each line traffics in a well-known principle (cf. 10:1; 13:24; 19:18, 26; 22:15; 23:13–24). When read together, the lines exhibit asymmetrical parallelism.[40] They stimulate one's moral imagination and invite one to exercise their moral reasoning. Their juxtaposition suggests that the rod and reproof not only give wisdom; they also engender parental honor. On the other hand, the lack of parental discipline not only sets a youth loose; it also brings parental shame. Parental authority entails parental responsibility, and the abdication of responsibility betrays a lack of proper authority.

The wild child's humiliation of the household serves as an appropriate entrée into **v. 16** and its

38. Boström, *The God of the Sages*, 67.

39. Heim, *Poetic Imagination*, 405–7.

40. Waltke, *Proverbs: Chapters 15–31*, 442–43.

consideration of the communal havoc wreaked by the wicked. The conditions of the community are delineated through the temporal clause that opens the initial line (v. 16a). The repetition of the root רבה in both the temporal clause and the main clause link the extent of the wicked with the ethos of the community. An increase in the population of the wicked engenders an increase in communal crime and unrest. In light of the similarities between the opening line and previous sayings (28:12, 28; 29:2), one expects the second line to describe the communal flourishing associated with the increase of the righteous. Instead, the second line presents an axiomatic belief, promising that the righteous will see the downfall of the wicked. The main clause in the first line does not have a parallel counterpart in the second. That is, "transgression increases" (יִרְבֶּה־פָּשַׁע, v. 16a) does not have an appropriate parallel in the second line. This line requires elaboration, inviting the reader to supply concepts of communal stability or peace to complete the saying. As another example of imprecise parallelism, the aphorism nurtures the reader's moral reasoning, encouraging one to consider the social implications of the righteous overseeing the downfall of the wicked.

In an astonishing shift, **v. 17** breaks the sequence of aphorisms and directly addresses the reader through an admonition. The admonition places the reader in the subject position of a parent who is exhorted to discipline their son. Off the back of the opening imperative, the *waw* + jussives "may bring you comfort" (וִינִיחֶךָ, v. 17a) and "give" (וְיִתֵּן, v. 17b) mark parallel result clauses, each of which traffics in powerful motivations.[41] Whereas a lack of parental discipline brings shame on the household (v. 15b), the exercise of discipline ensures parental comfort and delight, captured through the image of ingesting delicacies (מַעֲדַנִּים לְנַפְשֶׁךָ, "delight to your life" or "delicacies for your throat," v. 17b). Parental discipline may prove hard and painful; but the rewards of rest, pleasure, and satisfaction serve as powerful motivations for exercising one's moral authority and moral responsibilities in the household.

The alternation between household and community continues in **v. 18** (cf. vv. 15–16, 17), which moves from general social conditions to individual responsibility. The opening line is reminiscent of 11:14a. Whereas the latter links the downfall of the community to a lack of guidance, 29:18a associates communal anarchy with a lack of "vision" (חָזוֹן, v. 18a). This term occurs only here in the book of Proverbs. Although it designates the vision of a prophet elsewhere in the Old Testament (1 Sam 3:1; Isa 1:1; Obad 1), many assume that prophetic guidance is incongruous with wisdom literature and construe the term as communal guidance in general or "the sage's inspired revelation of wisdom" in particular.[42] The juxtaposition of "vision" and "instruction" (תוֹרָה, v. 18b), however, intimate that these terms refer to discrete yet comparable forms of divine guidance (cf. Lam 2:9; Ezek 7:26).[43] And the assumption that the sages were a distinct group of literati who produced texts in isolation from the broader literary, social, and religious traditions of ancient Israel is questionable.[44] Whether the initial construction opens a causal ("because there is no") or a temporal clause ("when there is no"), v. 18a observes that the absence of prophetic guidance engenders communal chaos. Rather than offering an alternative account of communal conditions, the second line focuses on the individual,

41. *IBHS* §34.6a.

42. Waltke, *Proverbs: Chapters 15–31*, 446. Also see Toy, *Proverbs*, 512; Longman, *Proverbs*, 507.

43. Van Leeuwen, "The Book of Proverbs," *NIB* 5:244; Murphy, *Proverbs*, 222–23; Clifford, *Proverbs*, 253–54. Cf. Fox, *Proverbs 10–31*, 840–42.

44. Sneed, "Is the 'Wisdom Tradition' a Tradition?," 50–71; Kynes, *An Obituary*.

Torah-obedience, and personal blessing (v. 18b). Thesc elements do not provide precise antitheses to the expressions in the initial line.[45] They create gaps that require the exercise of moral imagination to complete the saying. To be specific, they require one to include misery with communal anarchy in the first line and the absence of prophetic guidance with one who keeps instruction in the second.[46] The saying highlights the indispensable value of divine guidance for both the community and the individual. Happiness and stability depend on these forms of guidance and their embodiment by the community and the individual.

Just as divine guidance orders the life of the community in v. 18, so also discipline serves as a means of ordering and sustaining the hierarchy of the household in **v. 19**. The concepts of moral authority and moral responsibility structure the opening line. The observation assumes that an authority in the household dispenses verbal discipline for the benefit of a servant. But words are not enough; corporal discipline is also necessary. The value of corporal discipline is disclosed in the second line. Whether כִּי marks a conditional ("if") or a concessive clause ("though"), the main clause identifies the obstinance of the servant. He understands the verbal reprimand, but contrary to expectations, he refuses to respond. The saying directs the moral authority in the household to fulfill their moral responsibilities by administering verbal and physical forms of discipline so as to maintain the order and well-being of the domestic unit.

Words remain the focus of attention in **v. 20**, which moves from the insufficiency of verbal reprimand for disciplining a servant to the sufficiency of speech for revealing one's moral essence. Channeling the rhetoric of 22:29 and 26:12, the opening line addresses the reader through an unmarked rhetorical question. The question invites the reader to call to mind an undisciplined person who is hasty with his words. Haste in any form within Proverbs tends to betray a lack of discretion (19:2; 21:5; 28:20); and hasty speech reveals the impetuous nature of one's character. Little hope remains for this character type. As a repetition of Prov 26:12b, 29:20b associates the outlook of one hasty in speech with the outlook of one wise in his own eyes. This evaluation may represent a "deliberate exaggeration."[47] Whether or not this is the case, it alerts one to the severity of hasty speech and the way in which it deforms one's character.

Returning to the theme of disciplining one's servant (v. 19), **v. 21** profiles a moral authority's failure to execute their moral responsibilities in the household. This profile is painted with a pair of *hapax legomena*. The first—"One who pampers" (מְפַנֵּק, v. 21a)—depicts the householder as one who spoils a servant from youth, bestowing upon him tokens of luxury that are unbefitting to his position in the household. The second—"Insolent" (מָנוֹן, v. 21b)—captures the consequence of this form of rearing. Having grown accustomed to ease, the servant will transgress the boundaries appropriate to their position and incite domestic misery.[48] Moral authority carries moral responsibilities, and the failure to fulfill these responsibilities endangers the stability of the household.

The potential effects of a servant's arrogance in the household give way to the potential effects of anger in **v. 22**. The initial line represents a variant repetition of 15:18a, depicting anger as the heat that kindles the flames of strife. But the forest in

45. Waltke, *Proverbs: Chapters 15–31*, 445–46.
46. Heim, *Poetic Imagination*, 274–76.
47. Murphy, *Proverbs*, 223.
48. For an excellent discussion of the potential renderings of מָנוֹן, see Fox, *Proverbs 10–31*, 844–45.

which these flames burn is unclear. That is, the context of strife is ambiguous; it may be interpersonal, communal, or both. This openness fuels the ambiguity of the second line, which elaborates on the thought of the first through an imprecise parallel element. The hothead serves as an appropriate counterpart to the angry person. But "abundant transgression" (רַב־פָּשַׁע, v. 22b) does not provide a semantic counterpart to "strife" (מָדוֹן, v. 22a),[49] and the verb is elided in the second line. Whether the hothead is the source of transgression or the match that inflames transgression,[50] when read together, the saying scorches the reader, providing them with a literary lesson: if you play with a heated person, you'll get burned.

If v. 22 plays with fire, **v. 23** plays with the concepts of high and low.[51] These concepts structure the characterization of certain dispositions as well as their paradoxical outcomes. The initial line operates under the orientational metaphor ARROGANCE IS HIGH. Pride transgresses the boundaries appropriate to creaturehood, exalting one beyond proper limits. This inflated sense of self-importance will bring one low. The lowly, by contrast, will hold the social capital of honor. While the subjects within each line form a clear antithesis, the predicates are imprecise.[52] And this imprecision introduces gaps within each line that welcome corresponding elements. On this account, a person's pride will bring that person low and breed dishonor; but a lowly spirit will be exalted and hold honor.

The self-destructive nature of pride coincides with the self-destructive scenarios sketched in **v. 24**. The opening line describes one who shares the spoil with a thief as one who despises their life. The partnership evinces a self-hatred, that is, a fundamental lack of concern over the dire consequences of the deed. Among the potential consequences, the second line specifies a perilous situation. This situation is reminiscent of the scenario delineated in Lev 5:1: if a person hears the public declaration of the curse and can testify as one who has seen or known about the crime but fails to do so, this person will bear his guilt. When read against the backdrop of this judicial scenario, the second line depicts the partner of a thief as one who hears the public adjuration of the curse and knows about the crime but refuses to testify. The one who hates his life seeks to preserve his life. This partner may evade the judgment of the community. But if the final clause of Lev 5:1 applies to the present proverb, then this partner will not evade the judgment of God, for God executes judgment on the one who "bears his guilt" (וְנָשָׂא עֲוֹנוֹ; Lev 5:1). Interpersonal, situational, and theological factors converge in the scenarios across the saying to form a cautionary tale that traffics in fear.

The implicit fear that motivates the warning in Prov 29:24 is foregrounded in **v. 25**. But the fear in view is not a fear of judicial or divine judgment; it is a "fear of people" (חֶרְדַּת אָדָם, v. 25a).[53] This paralyzing brand of fear overestimates the nature and power of humans; it stands in sharp contrast to one who trusts in YHWH, for this person perceives the utter dependence and absolute powerlessness of all humans before the divine. The relational bond of trust forms a fortress, engendering emotional and physical safety (v. 25b). This safety, however, eludes the one who fears people, for they are terrorized by the emotional and physical snares set by others.

The contrast between human and divine power is extended in **v. 26**, which considers the matter of

49. Heim, *Poetic Imagination*, 385.

50. Fox, *Proverbs 10–31*, 845.

51. Yoder, *Proverbs*, 277.

52. Waltke, *Proverbs: Chapters 15–31*, 450.

53. While חֶרְדַּת אָדָם may be construed as a subjective genitive (i.e., "a person's own fear"), in light of its relationship with "one who trusts in YHWH" (וּבוֹטֵחַ בַּיהוָה) in the second line, it should be read as an objective genitive (i.e., "fear of people").

judgment. From an anthropocentric perspective, a ruler possesses the moral authority and moral responsibility to dispense just judgment. In view of this authority, it is not surprising that many "seek the face" (מְבַקְשִׁים פְּנֵי, v. 26a) or favor of a ruler. When viewed from a theological perspective, however, YHWH is the ultimate source of a person's judgment. While this judgment may be mediated through a ruler (16:10; 21:1), the saying suggests that seeking the face of a ruler should never replace seeking the face of YHWH (Hos 5:15; Pss 24:6; 27:8; 105:4). Many may place their trust in the former, but in the end each person will face the judgment of the latter.

The final saying within the central collections in general and the Hezekian collection in particular opens with the final consonant in the Hebrew alphabet (Prov **29:27**). And it compares familiar moral prototypes: the righteous and the wicked. This comparison, however, does not focus on the (im)moral actions of these antithetical figures; rather, it attends to the distinctive tastes and values that are indicative of their moral essence.[54] These tastes and values are conveyed through the repetition of the term "abomination" (תּוֹעֲבַת, vv. 27a, 27b). The righteous loathe those who are characterized by injustice, whereas the wicked loathe the moral posture and way of the upright. The attention to moral taste recalls the metaphorical scene set at the entryway to the central collections (9:1–6). Those who have entered Lady Wisdom's house and taken a seat at her table have been served various courses of her "curricular cuisine."[55] The final bite confirms the nature of their moral palate: it either loathes that which YHWH and Wisdom loathe (3:32; 11:20; 15:9, 26; 16:5), or it loathes that which the wicked loathe. It is an appropriate end to an exquisite pedagogical meal.

Canonical and Theological Significance

One of the most striking features of the book of Proverbs is its optimism regarding the human agent's ability to acquire wisdom. Wisdom is accessible and available for the taking. The acquisition of wisdom, however, is contingent on certain conditions. One's moral ontology, for example, determines one's perspectival knowledge and receptivity to wisdom. That is, the recognition of one's creaturehood and contingency create the epistemological and ontological mode of being necessary for the acquisition of wisdom (Prov 1:7; 9:10; 15:33).[56] More than this, the recognition of one's creaturehood and contingency illuminate the necessity of the Other for the acquisition of wisdom. According to Proverbs, wisdom is not innate within the human self (22:15). In fact, Rene Descartes's autonomous *cognito* serves as the foil for coming to know in the anthology (12:15; 14:12; 16:2, 25; 21:2). The autonomous self cannot learn. One only comes to learn wisdom through interpersonal relationship with YHWH and others (25:12; 26:12, 16; 28:5, 9, 26). Wisdom comes from outside of the self; it is the gift of another.

54. Lyu, *Righteousness*, 70.

55. Brown, "The Didactic Power of Metaphor," 138.

56. Jindo, "On the Biblical Notion," 433–53.

Interpersonal relations frame and fund the process of coming to know and acquire wisdom in Proverbs.[57] In light of this epistemological reality, it is not surprising that Proverbs attends to the value of relationships in general and friendship in particular. Anticipating Aristotle's reflections on the subject, Proverbs intimates that friendship is indispensable for the good life. As ancient and modern commentators attest, the reasons for its value are manifold. Friends are "the flora and fauna in a life that hasn't much diversity"; they are unique relationships that remain available as one ages, filling roles once occupied by those with whom one coexisted: mothers and fathers, sisters and brothers, grandparents, aunts and uncles.[58] More than making life appealing, friends constitute the form of life that makes the good and moral life possible.[59] They are "most necessary for living."[60] This necessity is engendered by the acceptance of one's finitude, which provides an impetus to enjoy life the fullest. "Friends can be a sensible way of doing just this," and friends can serve as "the helpful mirror, the other self, and a great benefactor."[61] If one only ever knows themselves before the face of the other, then the other is indispensable for the good life. And a friend is an indispensable other. Put simply, friendship is among "the greatest of external goods."[62]

Proverbs acknowledges that friendship is invaluable for a good, moral, and flourishing life. And Proverbs has its own reasons for this. Friends offer forgiveness (17:9). They love at all times (17:9). They exhibit loyal commitment (18:24). They dispense correction and counsel (27:5, 6, 9). And they provide support (27:10). A genuine friend is comparable to a family member. In fact, a genuine friend serves as a surrogate for the paradigmatic intimate: a brother (17:17; 18:24; 19:7; 27:10).[63] Yet unlike a brother, a friend willingly enters into relationship with the other. Blood may be thicker than water, but faithful friends are an essential relationship in Proverbs's moral vision.

While Proverbs does not provide a detailed description of the duties of a genuine friend,[64] its aphorisms sketch the nature of true friendship. True friendship is sustained by the virtues, specifically the virtues of love, loyalty, and perseverance (17:9, 17; 18:24; 27:5, 6, 9, 10). These virtues establish and nourish friendship. And these virtues are illustrated and embodied in friendships across the canon. They are

57. Meek, *Loving to Know*; Johnson, *Biblical Knowing*.

58. Jennifer Senior, "It's Your Friends who Break Your Heart," *The Atlantic*, March 2022, 35, 39.

59. Paul J. Wadell, "Friendship, Friendship Ethics," in *Dictionary of Scripture and Ethics*, ed. Joel B. Green et al. (Grand Rapids: Baker Academic, 2011), 316.

60. Aristotle, *The Nicomachean Ethics*, trans. J. A. K. Thomson, rev. ed. (New York: Penguin, 2004), 8.1155a.

61. Lorraine Smith Pangle, *Aristotle and the Philosophy of Friendship* (Cambridge: Cambridge University Press, 2003), 191.

62. Aristotle, *Nicomachean Ethics* 9.1169b.

63. Saul M. Olyan, *Friendship in the Hebrew Bible*, ABRL (New Haven: Yale University Press, 2017), 27.

64. Graham Davies, "The Ethics of Friendship in Wisdom Literature," in *Ethical and Unethical in the Old Testament: God and Humans in Dialogue*, ed. Katharine Dell, LHBOTS 528 (London: T&T Clark, 2010), 140–41.

exhibited in Ruth's relationship with her mother-in-law, Naomi. More specifically, they are captured by Ruth's solemn declaration,

> Do not pressure me to leave you, to turn from following you. Indeed, where you go, I will go, and where you lodge, I will lodge. Your people are my people, and your God is my God. Where you die, I will die, and there I will be buried. Thus may YHWH do to me and thus may he add. . . . Indeed, only death will separate me and you! (Ruth 1:16–17)

Just as a true friend "clings" (דָּבֵק; Prov 18:24) closer than a brother, so Ruth "clung" (דָּבְקָה; Ruth 1:14) to her mother-in-law. She demonstrated love, loyalty, and perseverance, even at great personal cost. As the narrative portrait of Ruth indicates, these virtues are evinced through embodied actions, not through mere emotions. Both the emotional and behavioral aspects of these virtues are displayed across David and Jonathan's friendship (1 Sam 18:1–4; 19:1–7; 20:1–42; 23:15–18). They are absent in Job's relationship with his "friends" (Job 19:2–22, 28–29) as well as the psalmist's relationship with enemies (Pss 35; 38; 109).[65] And they are epitomized in Jesus's relationship with his disciples. Jesus loved his own to the end (John 13:1). He endured the cross and opposition from sinners to redeem those given to him by the Father. In light of his love, loyalty, and perseverance for his own, it's not surprising that Jesus calls his disciples "friends" (φίλοι; John 15:14–15).

True friendship is sketched by the aphorisms in Proverbs and exemplified through specific relationships in the canon. True friendship is the ideal, but friendships vary. Proverbs attests to this reality; it describes different types of friendships. And these types of friendships bear striking similarities to Aristotle's threefold classification of friendships.[66] According to Aristotle, different types of friendship are distinguished by different motivations for love. Some love "on the ground of utility": they "do not love each other from their personal qualities, but only in so far as they derive some benefit from each other."[67] Others love "on the ground of pleasure."[68] And still others love on the ground of what is good. This is the perfect form of friendship. "It is those who desire the good of their friends for the friends' sake that are most truly friends, because each loves the other for what he is, and not for any incidental quality."[69] This ideal form of friendship is explored by several aphorisms in Proverbs (17:9, 17; 18:24; 27:5–6, 9–10). The same is true of the other types of friendships. Wealth creates the utilitarian basis of certain friendships (14:20; 19:4). The gift giver engenders

65. For discussion of friendship in Job, see Patricia Vesely, *Friendship and Virtue Ethics in the Book of Job* (Cambridge: Cambridge University Press, 2019).

66. Olyan, *Friendship in the Hebrew Bible*, 36, 107.

67. Aristotle, *Nicomachean Ethics* 8.1156a.

68. Aristotle, *Nicomachean Ethics* 8.1156a.

69. Aristotle, *Nicomachean Ethics* 8.1156b.

friendships grounded on both utility and pleasure (19:6). The poor, by contrast, have no social or economic capital to offer. They are hated by their own brothers and separated from their friends (Prov 19:7). This unfortunate fact invites moral reflection. When considered in conversation with Aristotle, this is the way things ought to be, for social and economic equality form the foundation of friendship. But when read in conversation with the canonical witness, this is not the way things ought to be, for friendship is not founded on social or economic equality. Friendship is founded on a common covenantal relationship with God (Acts 2:44–46; 4:32).[70]

As creatures, humans are dependent. They are dependent on God, and they are dependent on others. Friends are indispensable others who create the conditions for a good, moral, and flourishing life. Neither Proverbs nor Aristotle prescribe an appropriate number of friends. Social media and technology have allowed people to connect with others more easily. They have created tools to enable people to cultivate friendships. But they have also produced unintended results. They have engendered a sense of loneliness.[71] According to the Survey Center on American Life, "the percentage of Americans who say they don't have a single close friend has quadrupled since 1990."[72] Social media and technology have contributed to poor mental health.[73] The decrease in in-person social interaction has produced inferior social skills.[74] And the decline in in-person social interaction has "created a world in which forgiveness has become almost impossible."[75] Whether online or offline, friendship is indispensable for a life of wisdom and virtue. And whether online or offline, friendship is constituted and sustained by the virtues of love, loyalty, and perseverance.

70. Wadell, "Friendship, Friendship Ethics," 317.

71. Jean M. Twenge, *iGen: Why Today's Super-Connected Kids Are Growing Up Less Rebellious, More Tolerant, Less Happy—and Completely Unprepared for Adulthood—and What That Means for the Rest of Us* (New York: Atria, 2017), 79–91 et passim.

72. Senior, "It's Your Friends who Break Your Heart," 35.

73. Twenge, *iGen*, 93–118.

74. Twenge, *iGen*, 90.

75. Douglas Murray, *The Madness of Crowds: Gender, Race and Identity* (London: Bloomsbury Continuum, 2019), 182.

PART IV

Proverbs 30:1–31:31

The Application of Wisdom and Virtue

Main Idea of Proverbs 30–31

Taken together, the words of Agur and the words of Lemuel sketch two aspects of the application of wisdom and virtue. Agur impresses on readers the meta-skill of the wise person: humility. Lemuel defines wisdom as an embodied skill, where WISDOM IS THE EXERCISE OF POWER FOR THE BENEFIT OF THE OTHER.

Literary Context Proverbs 30–31

The words of Agur and the words of Lemuel are intimately related to both the preamble (1:1–7) and the prologue (1:8–9:18). Agur's discourse reiterates key terms from Proverbs's learning outcomes (30:2–3; 1:2) and a unique expression from the conclusion of the prologue (30:3; 9:10) to cast the acquisition of wisdom within a theological frame of reference (30:5–6). Lemuel's discourse mirrors and develops the discourses in the prologue. Situated in a domestic setting, Lemuel's discourse conveys the mother's voice (1:8; 6:20; 31:1–9) and urges the silent, passive son of the prologue to speak (31:8–9). And the portrait of the valient woman includes terms and expressions used elsewhere only for Lady Wisdom (31:10–31). These distinctive links suggest that the words of Agur and the words of Lemuel coalesce with the preamble and the prologue to form an interpretive framework through which to understand the nature and function of the central collections (10:1–29:27).

Structure and Outline of Proverbs 30–31

CHAPTER 36

Proverbs 30:1–33

A. "I Neither Know nor Think That I Know":[1] *The Wisdom of Limits and the Limits of Human Wisdom*

Main Idea of the Passage

As the gadfly of Proverbs, Agur emphasizes the severe limits of human wisdom and explores the boundaries of the sociomoral order to engender humility and absolute dependence on YHWH through his revealed word and within the authorized boundaries of his wondrous world.

Literary Context

When the "words of Agur" are heard against the presumed optimism regarding the acquisition of wisdom in the preceding collections (Prov 2:1–5; 4:5, 7; 14:6, 33; 23:23; 24:13–14),[2] their testimony is both shocking and profound. The placement of these words by a foreign sage, in the twilight of his life, at the end of the anthology, qualify the quest for wisdom in radical fashion. In the event that one has accepted Lady Wisdom's invitation (9:4–6), pulled up a seat at her table, ingested the varied courses of her "curricular cuisine" (10:1–29:27),[3] and emerged from her pedagogical meal with the sense that one is full of wisdom, Agur serves a bitter dessert. Put simply, the foreign sage alerts one to the reality that one never arrives in the life of wisdom.[4] This is the reality of creaturehood, for absolute, even certain, knowledge is

1. Plato, *Apol.*, 21d, in *The Dialogues of Plato: Translated into English with Analyses and Introductions*, trans. Benjamin Jowett, 5 vols., 3rd ed. (Oxford: Clarendon, 1892), 2:113–14.

2. The construct expression "words of" (דִּבְרֵי) mirrors the titles in 22:17 and 31:1 (cf. 1:6).

3. Brown, "The Didactic Power of Metaphor," 138.

4. Davis, *Proverbs*, 138.

above the paygrade of finite creatures. The way in which Agur articulates this reality appears to be at odds with the very purpose of Proverbs (1:1–7). And the semantics of his lament seem to confirm this. From both a pedagogical and theological perspective, however, these words affirm that Agur embodies the goal of the anthology. That is, he embodies the epistemological and ontological mode of being that defines the fearer of YHWH.[5] The foreign sage expresses what every teacher yearns to hear: it is the confession of Socrates, whom the Oracle at Delphi declared was the wisest of all men: "I neither know nor think that I know."[6] If one is to know one thing, this is it, for this is what it means to be a contingent creature. Agur leaves the reader with the ontological, ethical, and hermeneutical meta-skill of the wise: humility.

This meta-skill is by no means novel; it is mentioned elsewhere in the book (11:2; 15:33; 22:4; cf. 16:1–9). But Agur seeks to inculcate the virtue of humility in a distinctive way, namely, through sustained attention to the severe limits of creaturehood. Agur opens his discourse with the conceptual metaphor MAN IS AN ANIMAL (30:2a)[7] and in light of this subhuman state, he intimates that the wisdom the anthology aspires to cultivate within readers has eluded his grasp (v. 3a). The shared language and dialogical relationship between Agur's confession (vv. 2b–3), the preamble (1:2), and the process of wisdom's acquisition (2:1–7) may be construed in different ways.[8] When Agur's confession is heard within the anthology, however, it appears that he puts the finishing touch on this intratextual dialogue. The foreign sage draws together the concepts of wisdom as a divine gift (2:6), humility (15:33; 22:4), and the fear of YHWH (1:7; 15:33) through his own idiom. He indicates that, like an animal, humans receive wisdom as a divine gift, through humility, from the mode of being formed through the fear of YHWH.[9]

In addition to the intratextual dialogue engendered by Agur's confession, the materials attributed to the foreign sage reinforce and develop motifs from previous collections. Analogies and observations concerning the relational ruin precipitated by slander are recast as an admonition and contextualized in master-servant relations (v. 10; cf. 16:28; 25:23; 26:20, 28). Rhetorical questions magnify the yawning gulf between divine transcendence and human finitude (v. 4a–e; cf. 16:1–9). Numerical sayings shape one's perception of domestic anarchy (v. 11–14; cf. v. 17; 20:20), distorted

5. Christine Roy Yoder, "On the Threshold of Kingship: A Study of Agur (Proverbs 30)," *Int* 63 (2009): 254–63; Jindo, "On the Biblical Notion," 433–53.

6. Plato, *Apol.*, 21d (Jowett, Oxford), 2:113–14.

7. Alexander T. Kirk, "Moral Animals: The Literary Nexus of Metaphor, Virtue Ethics, and Animal Imagery in Proverbs 30" (paper presented at the annual meeting of the Evangelical Theological Society, Denver, CO, 14 November 2018), 5–16. For discussion of "The Great Chain of Being"—the cultural model that serves as the wide-angle lens for the conceptual metaphor MAN IS AN ANIMAL—see George Lakoff and Mark Turner, *More than Cool Reason: A Field Guide to Poetic Metaphor* (Chicago: University of Chicago Press, 1989), 166–213.

8. Bernd U. Schipper, "When Wisdom Is Not Enough! The Discourse on Wisdom and Torah and the Composition of the Book of Proverbs," in *Wisdom and Torah: The Reception of "Torah" in the Wisdom Literature of the Second Temple Period*, ed. B. U. Schipper and D. A. Teeter, JSJSup 163 (Leiden: Brill, 2013), 55–79; Keefer, *Proverbs 1–9 as an Introduction*, 121–26.

9. Kirk, "Moral Animals," 22.

self-valuation (v. 12; cf. 16:2; 20:9; 26:12), a topsy-turvy social world (vv. 21–23; cf. 19:10; 26:1), arrogance (vv. 13, 32; cf. 6:17; 16:5; 21:4), and greed (vv. 15a, 15b–16; cf. 23:4–5). These are familiar themes within the anthology, but they are rendered in striking ways, evincing a degree of intensification. This intensification is exhibited through the pervasive use of animals and animal imagery. Animals are depicted as people (vv. 15a, 25a, 26a). And people are depicted as animals (vv. 2a, 14a–b; cf. v. 17c–d).[10] While Proverbs makes extensive use of animals and animal imagery to explore human nature and activity (5:19; 6:5; 7:22–23; 11:22; 19:12; 23:32; 27:8), the concentrated attention to animals and animal imagery within the chapter blurs the boundaries between these species,[11] framing human activity as animal activity.[12]

IV. The Application of Wisdom and Virtue (30:1–31:31)

- **A. "I Neither Know nor Think That I Know": The Wisdom of Limits and the Limits of Human Wisdom (30:1–33)**
  - **1. The Title: The Performance Context of the Words of Agur (30:1a–b)**
  - **2. The Burden of Agur (30:1c–9)**
    - **a. Agur's Humble Confession: The Epistemological Limits of Humans (30:1c–4)**
    - **b. Agur's Dependence: The Relational Resolution to the Epistemological Limits of Humans (30:5–6)**
    - **c. Agur's Prayer: The Embodiment of Humble Dependence (30:7–9)**
  - **3. Placing the Burden on the Reader (30:10–33)**
    - **a. Defending the Defenseless (30:10)**
    - **b. A Devouring Generation (30:11–14)**
    - **c. A Devouring Animal (30:15a)**
    - **d. Devouring Things that are Never Satisfied (30:15b–16)**
    - **e. Animals Devouring an Immoral Animal (30:17)**
    - **f. The Wonder of Ways (30:18–20)**
    - **g. The "World Upside Down" (30:21–23)**
    - **h. Success through Limits (30:24–28)**
    - **i. Stride and Self-Exaltation (30:29–31)**
    - **j. Silencing the Arrogance of Self-Exaltation (30:32–33)**
- B. The Embodiment of Wisdom and Virtue: WISDOM IS THE EXERCISE OF POWER FOR THE BENEFIT OF THE OTHER (31:1–31)

10. Kirk, "Moral Animals," 8–14.
11. Yoder, "On the Threshold of Kingship," 261.
12. Kirk, "Moral Animals," 17–22.

In light of the fact that Agur assumes the position of an animal (v. 2a), it is not surprising that he conceptualizes humans as animals. Both contribute to his attempt to emphasize and extend a pair of themes woven throughout the fabric of the anthology: the severe limits of finite creatures and the necessity of humility.[13]

Translation and Exegetical Outline

(See pages 615–17.)

Structure and Literary Form

Whether viewed from a structural or a literary perspective, the materials arranged in Prov 30 defy modern standards of coherence. This sentiment is evinced through various structural and formal proposals. These proposals identify and explain the signs of incoherence in differing ways, but they share common structural conclusions and a comparable conception of genre. From a macrostructural perspective, ch. 30 may be divided into two parts. In light of the fact that the LXX places vv. 1–14 after Prov 24:22, some follow this compositional clue and distinguish vv. 1–14 from vv. 15–33.[14] Others, by contrast, identify v. 10 as the structural boundary in the chapter. On this account, vv. 1–9 represent a coherent, logical monologue,[15] whereas vv. 10–33 constitute a collection of aphorisms and numerical sayings.[16] This proposal captures the shift in address and mode of instruction within the chapter. And it perceives three signs of deliberate design: (1) the syntactical similarities between vv. 6, 9, and 10 suggest that v. 10 serves as a structural hinge in the chapter;[17]

13. Yoder, "On the Threshold of Kingship," 262–63; William P. Brown, "Rebuke, Complaint, Lament, and Praise: Reading Proverbs and Psalms Together," in *Reading Proverbs Intertextually*, ed. Katharine Dell and Will Kynes, LHBOTS 629 (London: T&T Clark, 2019), 73–74.

14. Plöger, *Sprüche Salomos*, 356; Meinhold, *Die Sprüche*, 2:496, 505; Murphy, *Proverbs*, 227; Longman, *Proverbs*, 517–18, 527–28; Schipper, "When Wisdom Is Not Enough!," 70. Meinhold and Schipper also note the ways in which vv. 1–14 allude to the Deuteronomic Decalogue and mirror its movement from divine-human relations to interpersonal relations. With regard to the LXX, it is important to note that it represents a secondary arrangement of Proverbs and does not demonstrate that ch. 30 consists of two independent parts (Tov, "Recensional Differences," 419–31).

15. Despite the syntax and logical coherence of Agur's discourse in vv. 1–9, others hear two voices in vv. 1c–4 and vv. 5–6 (or vv. 5–14): the voice of Agur, the skeptic (vv. 1c–4), and the voice of an orthodox Yahwist who places Agur's confession in proper perspective (Toy, *Proverbs*, 517–23; Crenshaw, "Clanging Symbols," in *Justice and the Holy*, ed. D. A Knight and P. J. Paris [Philadelphia: Fortress, 1989], 51–64).

16. Van Leeuwen, "The Book of Proverbs," *NIB* 5:250, 253; Yoder, *Proverbs*, 278; Sæbø, *Sprüche*, 358; Waltke, *Proverbs: Chapters 15–31*, 464, 481–82, Fox, *Proverbs 10–31*, 849–51.

17. Clifford, *Proverbs*, 257.

Proverbs 30:1–33

			IV. The Application of Wisdom and Virtue (30:1–31:33)
			A. "I Neither Know nor Think That I Know": The Wisdom of Limits and the Limits of Human Wisdom (30:1–33)
1a	דִּבְרֵי אָגוּר בִּן־יָקֶה	The words of Agur, son of Yaqeh,	1. The Title: The Performance Context of the Words of Agur (30:1a–b)
1b	הַמַּשָּׂא נְאֻם הַגֶּבֶר	the burden, the oracle of the man:	
			2. The Burden of Agur (30:1c–9)
1c	לאיתי אל לאיתי אל ואכל	"I am weary, God, I am weary, God, but I will overcome.	a. Agur's Humble Confession: The Epistemological Limits of Humans (30:1c–4)
2a	כִּי בַעַר אָנֹכִי מֵאִישׁ	Indeed, I am more beast than human,	
2b	וְלֹא־בִינַת אָדָם לִי	that is, I do not have human understanding.	
3a	וְלֹא־לָמַדְתִּי חָכְמָה	I have not learned wisdom,	
3b	וְדַעַת קְדֹשִׁים אֵדָע	but knowledge of the Holy One I will know.	
4a	מִי עָלָה־שָׁמַיִם וַיֵּרַד	Who has gone up to heaven and come down?	
4b	מִי אָסַף־רוּחַ בְּחָפְנָיו	Who has gathered the wind in the hollow of his hands?	
4c	מִי צָרַר־מַיִם בַּשִּׂמְלָה	Who has wrapped the waters in a garment?	
4d	מִי הֵקִים כָּל־אַפְסֵי־אָרֶץ	Who has established all the ends of the earth?	
4e	מַה־שְּׁמוֹ וּמַה־שֶּׁם־בְּנוֹ	What is his name? And what is the name of his son?	
4f	כִּי תֵדָע	Surely, you know!	
5a	כָּל־אִמְרַת אֱלוֹהַּ צְרוּפָה	Every word of God, refined;	b. Agur's Dependence: The Relational Resolution to the Epistemological Limits of Humans (30:5–6)
5b	מָגֵן הוּא לַחֹסִים בּוֹ	he is a shield to those who take refuge in him.	
6a	אַל־תּוֹסְףְּ עַל־דְּבָרָיו	Do not add to his words,	
6b	↑ פֶּן־יוֹכִיחַ בְּךָ וְנִכְזָבְתָּ	↑ lest he reprove you and you be proved a liar.	
7a	שְׁתַּיִם שָׁאַלְתִּי מֵאִתָּךְ	Two things I have asked from you;	c. Agur's Prayer: The Embodiment of Humble Dependence (30:7–9)
7b	אַל־תִּמְנַע מִמֶּנִּי בְּטֶרֶם אָמוּת	do not withhold them from me before I die:	
8a	שָׁוְא וּדְבַר־כָּזָב הַרְחֵק מִמֶּנִּי	Falsehood and deceit keep far from me.	
8b	רֵאשׁ וָעֹשֶׁר אַל־תִּתֶּן־לִי	Poverty or wealth do not give to me;	
8c	הַטְרִיפֵנִי לֶחֶם חֻקִּי	provide me my apportioned food,	
9a	↑ פֶּן אֶשְׂבַּע וְכִחַשְׁתִּי	↑ lest I become sated and disavow,	
9b	וְאָמַרְתִּי מִי יְהוָה	and say, 'Who is YHWH?'	
9c	וּפֶן־אִוָּרֵשׁ וְגָנַבְתִּי	and lest I become impoverished and steal,	
9d	וְתָפַשְׂתִּי שֵׁם אֱלֹהָי	and desecrate the name of my God."	

Continued on next page.

Continued from previous page.

Verse	Hebrew	English	Outline
10a	אַל־תַּלְשֵׁן עֶבֶד אֶל־ אֲדֹנָיו	Do not slander a servant to his master,	3. Placing the Burden on the Reader (30:10–33) a. Defending the Defenseless (30:10)
10b	↑ פֶּן־יְקַלֶּלְךָ וְאָשָׁמְתָּ	↑ lest he curse you and you be held guilty.	
11a	דּוֹר אָבִיו יְקַלֵּל	A generation – it curses its father,	b. A Devouring Generation (30:11–14)
11b	וְאֶת־אִמּוֹ לֹא יְבָרֵךְ	and does not bless its mother.	
12a	דּוֹר טָהוֹר בְּעֵינָיו	A generation – pure in its own eyes,	
12b	וּמִצֹּאָתוֹ לֹא רֻחָץ	and not cleansed of its filth.	
13a	דּוֹר מָה־רָמוּ עֵינָיו	A generation – how lofty are its eyes	
13b	וְעַפְעַפָּיו יִנָּשֵׂאוּ	and haughty are its eyelids.	
14a	דּוֹר חֲרָבוֹת שִׁנָּיו	A generation – its teeth are swords,	
14b	וּמַאֲכָלוֹת מְתַלְּעֹתָיו	and its fangs are knives	
14c	↑ לֶאֱכֹל עֲנִיִּים מֵאֶרֶץ	↑ to devour the poor from the earth	
14d	| וְאֶבְיוֹנִים מֵאָדָם	| and the destitute from humankind.	
15a	לַעֲלוּקָה שְׁתֵּי בָנוֹת הַב הַב	The leech has two daughters: "Give," "Give."	c. A Devouring Animal (30:15a)
15b	שָׁלוֹשׁ הֵנָּה לֹא תִשְׂבַּעְנָה	Three things are never satisfied,	d. Devouring Things that are Never Satisfied (30:15b–16)
15c	אַרְבַּע לֹא־אָמְרוּ הוֹן	four never say, "Enough":	
16a	↑ שְׁאוֹל וְעֹצֶר רָחַם	↑ Sheol, a barren womb,	
16b	| אֶרֶץ לֹא־שָׂבְעָה מַּיִם	| the earth not quenched with water,	
16c	| וְאֵשׁ לֹא־אָמְרָה הוֹן	| and fire, never saying, "Enough!"	
17a	עַיִן תִּלְעַג לְאָב	An eye that mocks a father,	e. Animals Devouring an Immoral Animal (30:17)
17b	וְתָבוּז לִיקְּהַת־אֵם	and despises obedience to a mother –	
17c	יִקְּרוּהָ עֹרְבֵי־נַחַל	the ravens of the valley will pluck it out,	
17d	וְיֹאכְלוּהָ בְנֵי־נָשֶׁר	and the brood of eagles will devour it.	
18a	שְׁלֹשָׁה הֵמָּה נִפְלְאוּ מִמֶּנִּי	Three things are too wonderful for me,	f. The Wonder of Ways (30:18–20)
18b	וְאַרְבָּעָה לֹא יְדַעְתִּים	and four I do not understand:	
19a	↑ דֶּרֶךְ הַנֶּשֶׁר בַּשָּׁמַיִם	↑ the way of the eagle in the sky,	
19b	| דֶּרֶךְ נָחָשׁ עֲלֵי צוּר	| the way of a serpent on a rock,	
19c	| דֶּרֶךְ־אֳנִיָּה בְלֶב־יָם	| the way of a ship in the heart of the sea,	
19d	| וְדֶרֶךְ גֶּבֶר בְּעַלְמָה	| and the way of a man with a maiden.	
20a	כֵּן דֶּרֶךְ אִשָּׁה מְנָאָפֶת	This is the way of an adulterous woman:	
20b	אָכְלָה וּמָחֲתָה פִיהָ	she eats and wipes her mouth,	
20c	וְאָמְרָה לֹא־פָעַלְתִּי אָוֶן	and says: "I have not done wrong."	

Verse	Hebrew	Translation	Outline
21a	תַּחַת שָׁלוֹשׁ רָגְזָה אֶרֶץ	Under three things the earth quakes,	g. The "World Upside Down" (30:21–23)
21b	וְתַחַת אַרְבַּע לֹא־תוּכַל שְׂאֵת	and under four it cannot endure:	
22a	תַּחַת־עֶבֶד כִּי יִמְלוֹךְ	↑ under a servant, when he becomes king,	
22b	וְנָבָל כִּי יִשְׂבַּע־לָחֶם	and a fool, when sated with food;	
23a	תַּחַת שְׂנוּאָה כִּי תִבָּעֵל	under a scorned woman, when she is married,	
23b	וְשִׁפְחָה כִּי־תִירַשׁ גְּבִרְתָּהּ	and a maidservant, when she displaces her mistress.	
24a	אַרְבָּעָה הֵם קְטַנֵּי־אָרֶץ	Four things – they are smallest on earth,	h. Success through Limits (30:24–28)
24b	וְהֵמָּה חֲכָמִים מְחֻכָּמִים	yet they are inherently wise:	
25a	הַנְּמָלִים עַם לֹא־עָז	↑ Ants, a people not strong,	
25b	וַיָּכִינוּ בַקַּיִץ לַחְמָם	but they prepare their food in the summer.	
26a	שְׁפַנִּים עַם לֹא־עָצוּם	Badgers, a people not powerful,	
26b	וַיָּשִׂימוּ בַסֶּלַע בֵּיתָם	but they set their homes in the rock.	
27a	מֶלֶךְ אֵין לָאַרְבֶּה	Locusts have no king,	
27b	וַיֵּצֵא חֹצֵץ כֻּלּוֹ	but they all go forth in ranks.	
28a	שְׂמָמִית בְּיָדַיִם תְּתַפֵּשׂ	Lizards – you can seize them by the hand,	
28b	וְהִיא בְּהֵיכְלֵי מֶלֶךְ	yet they are in the palaces of kings.	
29a	שְׁלֹשָׁה הֵמָּה מֵיטִיבֵי צָעַד	Three things are stately of stride,	i. Stride and Self-Exaltation (30:29–31)
29b	וְאַרְבָּעָה מֵיטְבֵי לָכֶת	and four are stately of gait:	
30a	לַיִשׁ גִּבּוֹר בַּבְּהֵמָה	↑ A lion, mighty among the beasts,	
30b	וְלֹא־יָשׁוּב מִפְּנֵי־כֹל	and never retreats before anything.	
31a	זַרְזִיר מָתְנַיִם אוֹ־תָיִשׁ	A strutting rooster or a he-goat,	
31b	וּמֶלֶךְ אַל קוּם עִמּוֹ	and a king no one can resist.	
32a	אִם־נָבַלְתָּ בְהִתְנַשֵּׂא	If you have acted foolishly by exalting yourself,	j. Silencing the Arrogance of Self-Exaltation (30:32–33)
32b	וְאִם־זַמּוֹתָ	↓ or if you have schemed,	
32c	יָד לְפֶה	hand over your mouth!	
33a	כִּי מִיץ חָלָב יוֹצִיא חֶמְאָה	↑ for pressing milk produces curds,	
33b	וּמִיץ־אַף יוֹצִיא דָם	and pressing the nose produces blood,	
33c	וּמִיץ אַפַּיִם יוֹצִיא רִיב	and pressing anger produces strife.	

(2) both v. 10 and v. 32 are cast in the form of an admonition, forming an *inclusio* around the second part of the chapter;[18] and (3) despite the oscillatory mode of address, the chapter is framed by direct address (vv. 1c–9, 32–33), inviting one to read the piece as the words of Agur.[19] When vv. 1–9 and 10–33 are read together, it appears that the foreign sage moves from a personal expression of human limits, humility, and dependence on the divine to materials that seek to inculcate a sense of limits, wonder, and humility within readers.

While these macrostructural features may not meet modern standards of coherence, they imbue the collection with a measure of cohesion. The same is true of the literary texture of the collection. Agur's opening words mirror the pattern of many laments, which move from a confession to an affirmation of trust (vv. 1c–4, 5–6).[20] This trust is embodied and expressed in vv. 7–9, which represent the only prayer within Proverbs. Against the backdrop of Agur's prayer, the reader encounters admonitions (vv. 10, 32; cf. v. 6), an aphorism (v. 17), and numerical sayings. The numerical sayings are cast in either graded (X, X + 1, vv. 15b–16, 18–20, 21–23, 29–31) or simple form (vv. 24–28). Others are fashioned by means of anaphora (vv. 11–14, 33). These sayings bear some resemblance to ancient Near Eastern onomastica, but they do not function as scientific or naturalistic observations designed to "broaden one's knowledge of the world."[21] They systematize various phenomena so as to shape one's perception of human behavior and social organization.[22] The final or climactic element within each list serves as the hermeneutical key, integrating the disparate phenomena around a specific focus.[23] As a form of poetic art, these sayings help one to see the world and oneself anew. In the words of Iris Murdoch, they show "us the world, our world and not another one, with a clarity which startles and delights us simply because we are not used to looking at the real world at all."[24]

Despite the diversity of forms within the collection, it is important to note that they are set within a frame that delineates the performance situation of the whole: "the burden, the oracle of the man" (הַמַּשָּׂא נְאֻם הַגֶּבֶר, v. 1b).[25] But the way in which this frame organizes the disparate materials into a meaningful whole has proven to be a riddle, for these materials bear no formal resemblance to prophetic oracles designated as מַשָּׂא elsewhere in the Old Testament (Isa 13:1; Nah 1:1; Hab 1:1;

18. Waltke, *Proverbs: Chapters 15–31*, 464.

19. Georg Sauer, *Die Sprüche Agurs: Untersuchungen zur Herkunft, Verbreitung und Bedeutung einer biblischen Stilform under besonderer Berücksichtigung von Proverbia c. 30*, BWA(N)T 84 (Stuttgart: Kohlhammer, 1963), 112; Yoder, *Proverbs*, 278; Waltke, *Proverbs: Chapters 1–15*, 26–27; Sæbø, *Sprüche*, 358.

20. Yoder, *Proverbs*, 279; Brown, "Rebuke, Complaint, Lament," 72.

21. Toy, *Proverbs*, 529. For this sentiment, see also Roth, *Numerical Sayings in the Old Testament*, 21.

22. Meinhold, *Die Sprüche*, 2:506; Forti, *Animal Imagery in the Book of Proverbs*, 120, 131.

23. Haran, "The Graded Numerical Sequence," 261–67.

24. Iris Murdoch, *The Sovereignty of the Good* (London: Routledge, 1971), 63.

25. Vayntrub, *Beyond Orality*, 199–204.

Zech 9:1; 12:1; Mal 1:1).[26] Alexander Kirk has identified two problems that have contributed to the production of this riddle: (1) lexicographical methods rooted in etymological assumptions that seal off the different senses of מַשָּׂא ("burden, load," "oracle, pronouncement," "Massa"); and (2) conceptions of genre wedded to generic realism, which perceive literary forms as pure, fixed, ontological categories.[27] If the semantic boundaries established by a lexicon and the generic fences erected by form criticism are torn down so as to allow words and literary forms to roam in textual spaces, then the way in which Prov 30:1b organizes the whole of Agur's discourse comes into focus.

Agur's מַשָּׂא may be construed "as a figurative extension of the concrete meaning of *burden*," that is, as a "weighty message."[28] And in accord with generic nominalism, this weighty message need not conform to a pure form of prophecy. This blurring of formal boundaries is supported by the appositional expression "the oracle of the man" (נְאֻם הַגֶּבֶר, v. 1b). In light of the fact that this expression occurs elsewhere only in Num 24:3, 15, and 2 Sam 23:1, Agur's weighty oracle may elude the category of prophecy altogether. Balaam's oracles are instructive here. Although the performance frame of these oracles indicate that Balaam is speaking for YHWH (Num 24:3–4, 15–16), the content of the speeches reveals that the words are the product of the prophet's own perception.[29] Like the oracles of Balaam, the oracle of Agur may represent a form of instruction.[30] This instruction concerns the severe limits of creaturehood. Agur confesses the weight of these limits and identifies the way in which the burden is removed, namely, through a humble embrace of these limits as well as a relationship with God through his revealed word (vv. 1–9). The foreign sage, then, places this burden on the reader in order to inspire humility in light of the wonder and boundaries of God's good creation (vv. 10–33).

26. For discussion of this type of prophetic discourse under the form-critical commitment to generic realism, see Richard Weis, "Oracle," *ABD* 5:28–29; Michael H. Floyd, "The (maśśāʾ) as a Type of Prophetic Book," *JBL* 121 (2002): 401–22. Cf. Mark J. Boda, "Freeing the Burden of Prophecy: Maśśāʾ and the Legitimacy of Prophecy in Zech 9–14," *Bib* 87 (2006): 338–57.

27. Alexander T. Kirk, "The Burden of the Sages: Tracing the Semantic Typography of משא with Proverbs 30:1 as a Test Case" (paper presented at the annual meeting of the Society of Biblical Literature, Boston, MA, 7 December 2020), 1–28. See also Mark R. Sneed, "Inspired Sages: *Massa'* and the Confluence of Wisdom and Prophecy," in *Scribes as Sages and Prophets: Scribal Traditions in Biblical Wisdom Literature and in the Book of the Twelve*, ed. Jutta Krispenz, BZAW 496 (Berlin: de Gruyter, 2021), 15–32. Sneed righty contends that faulty assumptions concerning prophecy and wisdom as distinct, hermetically sealed traditions explain why many have explained away the presence of "burden, oracle" in 30:1 and 31:1.

28. Kirk, "The Burden of the Sages," 1 et passim. Also see, Henry S. Gehman, "The 'Burden' of the Prophets," *JQR* 31 (1940): 107–21; J. A. Naudé, "Maśśāʾ in the Old Testament with Special Reference to the Prophets," *OTWSA* 12 (1969): 91–100.

29. Vayntrub, *Beyond Orality*, 125–34.

30. Vayntrub, *Beyond Orality*, 134.

Explanation of the Text

The words of Agur may be divided into two parts (vv. 1–9, 10–33). The first opens with a formal title (vv. 1a–b), which frames Agur's confession of epistemological limits (vv. 1c–4), his relational resolution to these limits (vv. 5–6), and his prayer (vv. 7–9). Each deserves specific comment.

1. The Title: The Performance Context of the Words of Agur (30:1a–b)

The words of Agur open with a formal title that functions as the performance frame of the discourse. The expression "words of" (דִּבְרֵי, v. 1a) recalls the title that opens the collection attributed to the wise (22:17); but the performance situation sketched in v. 1a–b is much more specific than the performance frames of the previous collections within Proverbs. Whether the materials in these collections are ascribed to Solomon or the wise, the titles do not stage these materials as the oral performance of these figures (1:1; 10:1; 24:23; 25:1).[31] And while the lectures and interludes in Prov 1:8–9:18 as well as the "words of the wise" (22:17) are cast as oral performances, these speeches are placed in the mouths of stereotypical figures.[32] Agur son of Yaqeh remains an unknown figure, but in contrast to the other titles and speeches within Proverbs, he is named *and* he speaks.[33]

The nature of Agur's speech is conveyed through the term "the burden" (מַשָּׂא, v. 1b),[34] which is cast in apposition to the phrase "the oracle of the man" (נְאֻם הַגֶּבֶר, v. 1b). As noted above, the former designates a "weighty message."[35] In light of the intertextual links between the latter and Balaam's speeches (Num 24:3–4, 15–16; cf. 2 Sam 23:1), "the oracle of the man" specifies this weighty message as a form of instruction.[36] This weighty instruction forms the performance framework for Agur's discourse; and the weight of this instruction is expressed through a personal confession in vv. 1c–9.

2. The Burden of Agur (30:1c–9)

Agur's confession focuses on the epistemological limits of human beings and their absolute dependence on the divine. It develops in logical fashion, moving from the limits of human wisdom (vv. 1c–4), to a resolution to these limits (vv. 5–6), to a prayer (vv. 7–9).

a. Agur's Humble Confession: The Epistemological Limits of Humans (30:1c–4)

While the logic of Agur's confession is relatively clear, his opening words are fraught with ambiguity. The MT appears to identify the addressees of Agur's burden, reading "to Ithiel, to Ithiel and Ucal" (לְאִיתִיאֵל לְאִיתִיאֵל וְאֻכָל, v. 1c). The mention of

31. Vayntrub, *Beyond Orality*, 195–205.

32. Vayntrub, *Beyond Orality*, 202–3.

33. Vayntrub, *Beyond Orality*, 203–4.

34. Many scholars emend the noun to include a gentilic ending (המשי, "the Massaite") or a preposition (ממשא, "from Massa") in order to establish the ethnic or locative origin of Agur (Sauer, *Die Sprüche Agurs*, 97; McKane, *Proverbs*, 644; Meinhold, *Die Sprüche*, 2:494; Murphy, *Proverbs*, 227; Clifford, *Proverbs*, 260). But these emendations are unnecessary, for Agur's name and lineage betray his foreign identity. The emendations do not seek to clarify an obscure term; rather, they appear to be driven by the clearer use of Massa in 31:1 as well as the assumption that a מַשָּׂא is out of place in "wisdom literature."

35. Kirk, "The Burden of the Sages," 1 et passim.

36. Vayntrub, *Beyond Orality*, 134.

addressees in the prologue of instructional texts is not uncommon.[37] And the personal name “Ithiel” appears in Neh 11:7. But the repetition of Ithiel is unusual. Ucal is unattested as a personal name, and in contrast to instructional texts that name an addressee, the relationship between Agur and these figures is unknown (“his sons,” “his nephews,” “his apprentices”?).[38] These ambiguities have engendered a variety of alternative readings, most of which divide the consonantal text along different lines and repoint the words. Following this pattern, Agur’s opening words may be construed as a personal plea directed to God that intermingles expressions of exhaustion with a declaration of confidence: “I am weary, God, I am weary, God, but I will overcome” (לאיתי אל לאיתי אל ואכל).[39]

Although the main lines of this construal are followed by many, it remains a conjectural reading. This conjectural reading resonates with other features within Agur’s monologue. The expressions of exhaustion, for example, correspond to the frame of Agur’s prayer, where the foreign sage indicates that he is in the twilight of his life, near death (v. 7b).[40] And the confluence of weariness and confidence captures the movement from human limits to relationship with God through his revealed will across Agur’s burden (vv. 2–6).[41] These points of contact may confirm the proposed reading of Agur’s opening words. But it is important to note that they are funded by a circular argument.

The conjectural main clause in v. 1c serves as the entryway into Agur’s shocking yet humble confession in vv. 2–4. This confession develops the severe limits of human wisdom in two parts. The first is cast in the form of a lament (vv. 2–3).[42] This lament opens with the conjunction כִּי, which, in light of its relation to v. 1c, may be interpreted in several different ways. Among the ways in which the conjunction may function, its use as an asseverative (“indeed,” v. 2a) avoids several potential pitfalls and calls attention to the certainty of the main clauses that follow (vv. 2–3).[43]

If Agur is certain of anything, it is his limits (vv. 2–3). These limits are ontological and epistemological. The foreign sage assumes the metaphorical concept MAN IS AN ANIMAL (v. 2a).[44] That is, he adopts a subhuman ontological status, claiming “I am more beast than human” (בַעַר אָנֹכִי מֵאִישׁ,

37. “The Instruction of Prince Hardjedef” (*AEL* 1:58); “The Instruction Addressed to Kagemni” (*AEL* 1:60); “The Instruction of Ptahhotep” (*AEL* 1:63, 76); “The Satire of the Trades” (*AEL* 1:185); “Ahiqar” (*OTP* 2:479–508).

38. Fox, *Proverbs 10–31*, 853–54.

39. This proposal divides לְאִיתִיאֵל (2x) into לאיתי אל (“I am weary, O God”) and construes וְאֻכָל as a defective form from the root יכל (“to be able, prevail”). Others, by contrast, argue that אֻכָל derives from the root כלה (“to be used up, spent”) (Paul Franklyn, “The Sayings of Agur in Proverbs 30: Piety or Scepticism?,” *ZAW* 95 [1983]: 243–44; Clifford, *Proverbs*, 260; Fox, *Proverbs 10–31*, 854). The former reading is preferred, since the defective form of the root יכל occurs several times in the Old Testament (Josh 7:12; Ps 18:39[38]; Jer 20:11) and the verb is used without an object in several instances. Plöger, *Sprüche Salomos*, 354; Murphy, *Proverbs*, 226; Waltke, *Proverbs: Chapters 15–31*, 468n102; *BHQ*. Cf. Alexander T. Kirk, “Toward a Reading of Proverbs 30:1b: Tracing the Life of the Text in the Versions,” *VT* (2022): 1–19.

40. Fox, *Proverbs 10–31*, 853.

41. Waltke, *Proverbs: Chapters 15–31*, 467–68.

42. Yoder, *Proverbs*, 279; Brown, “Rebuke, Complaint, Lament,” 72.

43. In contrast to the asseverative function of כִּי (Franklyn, “The Sayings of Agur,” 244; Waltke, *Proverbs: Chapters 15–31*, 456n11, 468), others contend that the conjunction opens a subordinate causal clause (“for”) dependent on v. 1c or a subordinate concessive clause (“even though”) dependent on v. 3b. Both readings are possible, but they encounter potential problems. If כִּי opens an extended causal clause (vv. 2–3), it modifies the conjectural reading in v. 1c. And if כִּי opens a concessive clause, the main clause in v. 3b is forced to adopt two minority interpretations: the clause’s initial *waw* is disjunctive, and the force of the negation in v. 3a does not infiltrate v. 3b. Clifford, *Proverbs*, 259; Fox, *Proverbs 10–31*, 850; Kirk, “Moral Animals,” 9–10n10, 11.

44. Kirk, “Moral Animals,” 5–13.

v. 2a; cf. 12:1; Pss 73:22; 92:7[6]). And this ontological status carries epistemological implications. These implications are delineated in vv. 2b–3a. The former clarifies Agur's subhuman ontology in terms of his lack of "*human* understanding" (בִּינַת אָדָם, v. 2b). This lack of human understanding is developed in v. 3a, where Agur asserts "I have not learned wisdom" (לֹא־לָמַדְתִּי חָכְמָה, v. 3a). To learn is to be taught;[45] and it appears that the foreign sage has not been taught wisdom. As an animal, Agur has failed to acquire human knowledge and wisdom mediated by a human teacher. This does not mean, however, that the foreign sage is the epitome of ignorance. To the contrary, he epitomizes one who acknowledges and accepts his ontological status as a creature and his epistemological limits. Agur may not possess human knowledge, but according to v. 3b, he will acquire "knowledge of the Holy One" (דַעַת קְדֹשִׁים, v. 3b).[46] In accord with his opening words, he will overcome (v. 1c). The expression "knowledge of the Holy One" is mentioned elsewhere only in Prov 9:10, where it stands in interlinear relationship with the "fear of YHWH" (יִרְאַת יְהוָה) and expresses relational knowledge of God and God's transcendence. It appears that the foreign sage will overcome because he has profound self-knowledge, a clear understanding of who he is and what he knows in relation to God. He assumes the humble posture and the perspectival knowledge of the fearer of YHWH. This engenders confidence. And this humble confidence is not surprising, for Agur's self-knowledge and knowledge of the Holy One are expressed through the barrage of rhetorical questions that pervade 30:4.

The string of rhetorical questions represents the second part of Agur's lament. They move from four "who" (מִי, vv. 4a–d) questions to two "what" (מַה, v. 4e) questions and culminate in direct address (v. 4f), challenging the reader to respond. The "who" questions highlight the severe limits intrinsic to human finitude. The first employs the conventional motif of heavenly ascent/descent to map the yawning gulf that separates creatures from the realm of the divine (v. 4a).[47] This gulf entails not only that the heavens are inaccessible to mortals but also that the prerogatives of the divine are beyond human reach.[48] Power is among these divine prerogatives. And the limits of human power are the focus of attention in the remaining "who" questions. Inasmuch as humans lack the capacity to gather the wind in their hands (v. 4b; cf. Amos 4:13; Ps 135:7; Job 38:24), swaddle the waters (Prov 30:4c; cf. Isa 40:12; Job 26:8; 38:25–27), and establish the boundaries of the earth (Prov 30:4d; cf. 3:19; 8:29; Job 28:23–24), they are also incapable of exercising their power so as to manage the cosmos. The "who" questions cover the vertical and horizonal extremities of the cosmos. They bear witness to the harsh realities of human finitude. And their intertextual affinities with other biblical texts suggests that Agur redeploys terms and expressions reserved to describe God's power to mark off the limits of human power.

The same is true of the "what" questions (Prov 30:4e), which gesture to texts pertaining to YHWH to rule out any pretentions that humans can transcend their ontological and epistemological limits. The first "what" question mirrors Moses's question

45. Despite its concern with pedagogy, this is the only occurrence of the verb למד ("to learn [*qal*], teach [*piel*]") within Proverbs (cf. 5:13).

46. While many argue that the negative in v. 3a is implied in v. 3b, the placement of the verb at the end of v. 3b and the imprecise parallelism between "wisdom" and "knowledge of the Holy One" suggest that the negative is not implied in the line. LXX; Waltke, *Proverbs: Chapters 15–31*, 470.

47. Raymond Van Leeuwen, "The Background to Proverbs 30:4aα," in Barré, *Wisdom, You Are My Sister*, 102–21.

48. Raymond Van Leeuwen, "The Background to Proverbs 30:4aα," 121.

in Exod 3:13: "What is his name?" (מַה־שְּׁמוֹ, Prov 30:4e). The second extends the thought of the first through a natural corollary, "What is the name of his son?" (מַה־שֶּׁם־בְּנוֹ, v. 4e). Those who answer the "who" questions as well as the first "what" question (vv. 4a–d) as "YHWH" attempt to identify the "son" (v. 4e) in varying ways. Much ink has been spilt on the matter[49] but this ink misses the rhetorical point of Agur's questions. While the inner-biblical echoes produced by Agur's rhetorical questions give the impression that YHWH is in view, human limits remain the focus of attention.[50] No human can ascend to heaven, gather the wind, swaddle the waters, or establish the boundaries of the earth. The "what" questions force one to confess this reality and set the stage for the culmination of Agur's lament, where he challenges the reader to respond by declaring, "Surely, you know!" (כִּי תֵדָע, v. 4f). If one is humble and honest, the answer is clear: "No, I do not know such a human." And through this answer the reader articulates the ontological and epistemological limits of humanity expressed by Agur in vv. 2–3.

b. Agur's Dependence: The Relational Resolution to the Epistemological Limits of Humans (30:5–6)

Having forced the reader to confess his confession (v. 4e–f), the foreign sage ventures a resolution to the severe limits of creaturehood. This resolution is delineated in vv. 5–6. And this resolution is relational.[51] Far from inducing despair, a recognition of the severe limits of creaturehood nurtures dependence on the divine. To be specific, these limits create a consciousness of one's reliance on God through his revealed word. This relational reliance is expressed through the language of 2 Sam 22:31 (= Ps 18:31) and Deut 4:2 (cf. 13:1). Agur modifies the former in Prov 30:5 to foreground the reliability of divine revelation.[52] The initial line traffics in the metaphorical concept of MORAL PURITY (v. 5a): every word of God is "refined" (צְרוּפָה, v. 5a)—pure and true, like precious metals cleansed of their dross. The second line extends the thought of the first through asymmetrical parallelism.[53] It moves from every word of God to God himself and from the concept of purity to the promise of protection (v. 5b). God is depicted as a "shield" (מָגֵן, v. 5b); and as a shield, he protects those who recognize their dependence upon him through his revealed words (cf. 2:7). These revealed words are the focus of the prohibition in 30:6a, which mirrors the language of Deut 4:2 (cf. 13:1).[54] To add to God's revealed words would be tantamount to desecrating their purity. And the severe punishment for this act of sacrilege is sounded in the negative purpose clause (פֶּן, "lest," v. 6b), which prompts one to imagine the many ways in which God may reprove and expose one as a liar.

49. Proposals for the identity of the "son" range from members of the divine council (Pss 29:1; 89:7[6]) to Israel as the covenant people of God (Exod 4:22; Deut 14:1; Hos 11:1). Franklyn, "The Sayings of Agur," 247–48; Meinhold, *Die Sprüche*, 2:498; Waltke, *Proverbs: Chapters 15–31*, 473–74.

50. Whybray, *Proverbs*, 409; Clifford, *Proverbs*, 262; Fox, *Proverbs 10–31*, 856–57.

51. Jerry V. Pauls, "Proverbs 30:1–6: 'The Words of Agur' as Epistemological Statement" (Th.M. thesis, Regent College, 1998), 124, cited in Waltke, *Proverbs: Chapters 15–31*, 475.

52. Agur modifies 2 Sam 22:31 in three ways: (1) he omits the introductory phrase "as for God, his way is perfect" (הָאֵל תָּמִים דַּרְכּוֹ) to focus attention on God's revelation; (2) he transposes "all" (כָּל) from 2 Sam 22:31c to the second line to emphasize the extent of God's reliable words; and (3) he replaces the Tetragrammaton with "God" (אֱלוֹהַּ).

53. Waltke, *Proverbs: Chapters 15–31*, 476–77.

54. For some, Agur's use of 2 Sam 22:31 (= Ps 18:31) and Deut 4:2 (cf. 13:1) bears witness to either tradition-historical debates or to a canonical conversation regarding the relationship between wisdom and torah in general and among the Torah (Deut 4:1), Prophets (2 Sam 22:31), and the "wisdom tradition" (Prov 30:5–6) in particular. For discussion, see McKane, *Proverbs*, 648; Moore, "A Home for the Alien," 102–6; Meinhold, *Die Sprüche*, 2:496; Schipper, "When Wisdom Is Not Enough!," 55–79.

Taken together, the composite quotations in vv. 5–6 venture a resolution to the reality of human limits. This resolution does not involve humans transcending their ontological and epistemological limits. Instead, it involves a relationship. The reality of human limits engenders humility and dependence on the divine through his revealed word. This humility and dependence are motivated by the promise of safety (v. 5b) and the warning of chastisement (v. 6). As mentioned above, Agur prescribes a harsh pill. Humans will always and forever be created creatures. They may possess human understanding and wisdom, but that human understanding and wisdom is a divine gift (2:1–6). In the same way, every word of God is a gift. It is revealed. It graciously comes from the eternal transcendent to the finite imminent. Against the backdrop of the presumed optimism regarding the acquisition of wisdom in Proverbs, Agur focuses the reader's attention on whom you know, not what you know. This is genuine wisdom. This is what it means to fear YHWH.

c. Agur's Prayer: The Embodiment of Humble Dependence (30:7–9)

Refusing to leave the relational resolution to human limits in the abstract, the foreign sage embodies relational dependence on the divine through a humble practice in vv. 7–9: prayer. This is the only prayer within Proverbs. The prayer opens with a formal introduction, which captures the urgency of Agur's requests (v. 7). The use of the perfect in the initial line suggests that these requests have been Agur's recurrent prayer.[55] He has asked them (v. 7a). And he asks them again, weary and in the twilight of his life (v. 7b; cf. v. 1c). The two things for which Agur prays are delineated in v. 8: mirroring the purity of God's words (v. 5a), he asks to be kept from deceit (v. 8a);[56] and aware of the dangers posed by poverty and wealth, he asks for a life of moderation (v. 8c), burdened by neither lack nor abundance (v. 8b).[57] The theological rationale for these requests is expressed through a pair of negative purpose clauses (פֶּן, "lest," vv. 9a, 9c). The first considers the conditions created by abundance (vv. 9a–b), which foster self-sufficiency and erode any sense of humble dependence on YHWH. The second considers the conditions created by poverty (vv. 9c–d). More than moving one to take the property of another, the act of theft desecrates the name of God. When read together, these negative purpose clauses indicate that Agur's requests share a common theme. The foreign sage is concerned that deceit as well as the excesses of poverty and wealth will drive him to misrepresent YHWH, his personal God. Again, the foreign sage exhibits wisdom through profound self-awareness (v. 9a, c). Agur knows himself, and he knows himself because he knows YHWH.[58]

The closing lines of Agur's prayer constitute the denouement of his burden. The foreign sage opened with an address to "God" (אֵל, vv. 1c), expressed confidence in acquiring "knowledge of the Holy One" (דַעַת קְדֹשִׁים, v. 3b), and affirmed the purity of "every word of God" (כָּל־אִמְרַת אֱלוֹהַּ, v. 5a). He closes his burden by identifying this

55. Franklyn, "The Sayings of Agur," 249.

56. Davis, *Proverbs*, 140.

57. Within the complex socioeconomic discourse of Proverbs, Agur's *via media* position is unique; it promotes virtue over material resources and relationship with YHWH over economic status. Brown, "The Pedagogy of Proverbs 10:1–31:9," 178; Sandoval, *The Discourse of Wealth and Poverty*, 209.

58. This hermeneutical circle is captured by Calvin: "Nearly all the wisdom we possess, that is to say, true and sound wisdom, consists of two parts: the knowledge of God and of ourselves." John Calvin, *Institutes of the Christian Religion*, ed. J. T. McNeill, trans. F. L. Battles (Louisville: Westminster John Knox, 1960), 1.1.1.

God as "YHWH" (יְהוָה, v. 9b), "my God" (אֱלֹהָי, v. 9d).[59] In the same way, Agur's burden incorporates language and concepts redolent of several other Old Testament texts,[60] and it closes with requests reminiscent of certain regulations in the Decalogue (vv. 8a, 9).[61] As an animal with a clear understanding of the severe limits of creaturehood, Agur may not have human understanding. But he embodies a humble ontology that is inextricably linked to his relationship with and knowledge of YHWH through his revealed will. His burden is heavy. This is not surprising, for the load of this burden is designed to form the meta-skill of the wise: humility.

3. Placing the Burden on the Reader (30:10–33)

The same is true of the second half of Agur's discourse, which consists of admonitions and epigrams intended to cultivate humility through the wonder and boundaries of God's good creation. The foreign sage blurs the ontological boundaries between humans and animals. And he incorporates various forms that form the reader's perception of life within the created order. In so doing, he places his weighty message on the reader. This weighty message includes admonitions (vv. 10, 32–33), aphorisms (v. 15a, 17), numerical sayings (vv. 15b–16, 18–20, 21–23, 24–28, 29–31), and thematic epigrams (vv. 11–14), each of which deserves specific comment.

a. Defending the Defenseless (30:10)

Similar to the syntax of v. 6 (cf. v. 4e), v. 10 returns to direct address, placing the reader in an ambiguous relationship with a servant and his master. In light of the servant's vulnerability, the admonition prohibits slandering or criticizing a subordinate before his social superior.[62] Irrespective of whether the report is true or false, it is deemed inappropriate, for it endangers the defenseless. The admonition seeks to rein in the potential abuse of servants; and it accomplishes this through a negative purpose clause (פֶּן, "lest," v. 10b). By virtue of his vulnerability, the servant resorts to his only defense: a curse. And this curse proves to be efficacious, for it exposes one's culpability, presumably before God. The use of the second-person singular across the admonition places the reader in this precarious act and consequence. In so doing, it not only cultivates sympathy for a fellow creature; it also inspires this sympathy through one's desire for safety.

b. A Devouring Generation (30:11–14)

While the extended profile of a generation in vv. 11–14 is cast in the third person, the illocutionary force of the unit corresponds with the illocutionary force of v. 10. Similar to the previous admonition, the unit denounces particular forms of behavior.[63] It is linked to the previous admonition by the catchword "curse(s)" (קלל, vv. 10b, 11a); and it is bound together by anaphora (i.e., דּוֹר, "a generation," vv. 11a, 12a, 13a, 14a). This rhetorical

59. Moore, "A Home for the Alien," 100n12.

60. In addition to the texts noted in the discussion above, see Franklyn, "The Sayings of Agur," 238–52; Clifford, *Proverbs*, 258.

61. These regulations include the prohibitions against falsehood (Prov 30:8a; cf. Deut 5:20), misrepresenting YHWH's name (Prov 30:9b, 9d; cf. Deut 5:11), and theft (Prov 30:9c; cf. Deut 5:19). Meinhold, *Die Sprüche*, 2:500; Schipper, "When Wisdom Is Not Enough!," 70–71.

62. The verb "slander" (תַּלְשֵׁן, v. 10a; cf. Ps 101:5) derives from the noun "tongue" (לָשׁוֹן) and conveys the manner in which one reveals information, not necessarily the truthfulness or falsity of the information. Fox, *Proverbs 10–31*, 864.

63. McKane, *Proverbs*, 651; Van Leeuwen, "The Book of Proverbs," *NIB* 5:253; Davis, *Proverbs*, 143.

device indicates that a single generation is in view. The character of this generation is described in a manner comparable to the things that YHWH loathes (6:16–19). And the character of this type of generation is constructed through both interlinear and translinear parallelism.

At both the interlinear and translinear levels, the anaphoric poem renders the character of a generation though a sequence of noun phrases. The first focuses on a generation's disposition toward the hierarchical structure of the moral order: it curses its parents, subverting the moral order of the household by deriding God's authorized authorities (v. 11; cf. 20:20). The remaining noun phrases offer variations on this theme through their consideration of the distorted perception and immoral anatomy of a type of generation (30:12–14). The distorted perception of the generation is captured in v. 12. Like one "wise in his own eyes" (חָכָם בְּעֵינָיו), this generation engages in that "fatal act of self-perception."[64] It considers itself as the epitome of moral purity, when the reality is that its moral garments are covered in filth (v. 12; cf. 16:2; 20:9). This distorted self-perception is developed in v. 13, which also attends to the "eyes" (עֵינָיו) of the generation. The noun phrases traffic in the metaphorical concept ARROGANCE IS BEING HIGH,[65] indicating that the generation's distorted sight is due to its inflated sense of self. This inflated sense of self is the product of an immoral ontology. And this immoral ontology is the focus of attention in v. 14. The generation is depicted as a ravenous animal with sharp "fangs" (מְתַלְּעֹתָי, v. 14b),[66] whose bite is as bad as its bark. This is expressed through the final purpose clause (vv. 14c–d). The subhuman generation feeds on the poor, devouring the powerless as a ferocious predator. Taken as a whole, the impressionistic portrait of a type of generation is shocking. This portrait not only condemns the immoral characteristics of the generation, but also awakens the moral emotions of the reader and invites one to consider whether one sees one's reflection in this poetic picture.

c. A Devouring Animal (30:15a)

The subhuman nature and animalistic appetite of the generation is recast in v. 15a through the nature and appetite of a particular animal. The leech is the embodiment of insatiability, and its two suckers are personified as two daughters, each of whom either cry or are named "Give, Give" (הַב הַב, v. 15a). The appetite of the leech matches its ontology: it is a parasitic bloodsucker. The same is true of the type of generation in vv. 11–14: its animal appetite matches its subhuman ontology. Neither finds satisfaction, and this motif is developed in vv. 15b–16.

d. Devouring Things that are Never Satisfied (30:15b–16)

The graded numerical saying extends the insatiability of the leech and her daughters through a catalogue of four elements from the cosmic and human worlds. These elements share an essential quality: they are "never satisfied" (לֹא תִשְׂבַּעְנָה, v. 15b), that is, they "never say, 'Enough'" (לֹא־אָמְרוּ הוֹן, v. 15c). Sheol has a voracious appetite for death, whereas the barren womb has an insatiable desire for life (v. 16a).[67] In the same way, the earth "is not quenched with water" (לֹא־שָׂבְעָה מַּיִם, v. 16b), which nourishes the ground so as to sustain human life. And fire is never satiated with the produce

64. Van Leeuwen, *Context and Meaning*, 105.

65. Tilford, *Sensing World, Sensing Wisdom*, 162–64.

66. The noun occurs elsewhere only in Joel 1:6, Job 29:17, and Ps 58:7[6], where it describes the fangs of a lion and/or the wicked.

67. Cf. Fox, *Proverbs 10-31*, 868.

of the earth: "it never says, 'Enough!'" (לֹא־אָמְרָה הוֹן, v. 16c). The expressions "never satisfied" and "never say, 'Enough'" frame the numerical saying, providing a lens through which to contemplate its elements. In different ways, the saying explores the power and insatiability of desire through phenomena that yearn for either life or death.[68] In so doing, it offers the reader a mirror, for humans are also desiring creatures that are never satisfied. The saying does not consider whether satisfaction can be found; rather, it stimulates the moral imagination by asking whether one's desire is directed toward objects that promote life or death.

e. Animals Devouring an Immoral Animal (30:17)

The concept of consumption also funds the aphorism in v. 17. The saying recalls a type of generation's treatment of parents (v. 11), its immoral anatomy (עַיִן, "eye," vv. 12a, 13), and its desire to "devour" others (אכל, vv. 14c, 17d). In contrast to the description of a type of generation, however, the aphorism delivers an explicit punishment. As the window into one's inner self, the eye serves as the signpost of one's desires.[69] An eye that expresses contempt for one's parents not only subverts the moral order and spurns moral authority; it also betrays one's immoral ontology and desire. This ontology, desire, and posture are subhuman. Accordingly, the punishment is subhuman. Unclean animals consume the eye of a subhuman corpse that has not received a proper burial (vv. 17c–d; cf. Lev 11:13–19). Similar to the description of a type of generation, the aphorism engenders horror. And in so doing, it inspires obedience to one's moral authorities.

f. The Wonder of Ways (30:18–20)

Horror is transformed into "awe-filled and awful" astonishment occasioned by the way of four things within the created order as well as the way of an adulteress (vv. 18–19, 20).[70] The four things are framed by a heading, which identifies the number of phenomena and their common denominator (v. 18). The trait shared by these diverse phenomena is expressed through a first-person confession: they are "too wonderful" (נִפְלְאוּ מִמֶּ-, v. 18a), beyond human understanding. The repetition of the term "way" (דֶּרֶךְ, v. 19) indicates that their inexplicable wonder is manifested through their irrecoverable course.[71] The ways of these things are wondrous because their tracks elude human comprehension. The trajectory of an eagle soaring through the sky, the movement of a serpent gliding on a rock, and the precise course of a ship slicing through the deep elude human calculation. The same is true of the climactic element: the way of a man with "a maiden" (עַלְמָה, v. 19d; cf. Gen 24:43; Exod 2:8; Song 1:3; Isa 7:14). The mysterious forces that lead to the union of a man and a young woman as one flesh evoke wonder at the beauty of this distinct human relationship.[72]

The wonder of this union serves as the backdrop to Prov 30:20, which moves from the awe-filled nature of erotic love to the awful way of an adulteress (cf. 5:1–6; 6:20–35; 7:1–27). The way of the adulteress is rendered in shocking terms: she eats, wipes her mouth, and claims that she has done

68. Waltke, *Proverbs: Chapters 15–31*, 488; Fox, *Proverbs 10–31*, 868.

69. Waltke, *Proverbs: Chapters 15–31*, 489; Fox, *Proverbs 10–31*, 870.

70. Brown, *Wisdom's Wonder*, 20.

71. Murphy, *Proverbs*, 235. Cf. Fox, *Proverbs 10–31*, 871–72, who, with others, argues that "tracelessness" represents the unifying element among these things.

72. Murphy, *Proverbs*, 235.

no wrong (30:20b–c). That is, she appeases her sexual appetite in the same way that one satisfies one's stomach (cf. Prov 5:19; Song 5:1). For the adulteress, sex is not a divine gift enjoyed in the confines of a covenant relationship; it is a casual meal consumed without commitment and outside of the sanctioned boundaries of the moral order. The awful way of the adulteress stands in sharp contrast to the wondrous ways in Prov 30:19, especially the way of a man with a young woman. Taken together, these ways stimulate one's moral imagination, nurture one's moral emotions, and help one to perceive the world anew.

g. The "World Upside Down" (30:21–23)

The adulteress's transgression of sanctioned sexual boundaries sets the stage for vv. 21–23, which catalogue "inverted social relations."[73] Like many other sayings in the book, the epigram assumes the concept of a moral order, according to which society operates under a hierarchical structure.[74] This assumed hierarchical structure coincides with the stable, literary structure of the numerical saying. Each verse opens with the preposition "under" (תַּחַת, vv. 21a, 22a, 23a); and each line ends with a temporal clause marked by "when" (כִּי, vv. 22, 23). This stable structure, however, stands in sharp contrast to the inverted relations that cause the earth to quake to the extent that it is unable to bear the weight of the disorder (v. 21). The destabilization engendered by these inverted relations represents the unifying element of the epigram. And this destabilization is due to the fact that the inverted social relations are unfitting. Royal rule does not befit the nature of "a servant" (עֶבֶד, v. 22a).[75] Satisfaction does not befit the moral character of "a fool" (נָבָל, v. 22b; cf. 12:11; 19:10), who is sustained by the resources of an order that he undermines.[76] Authority over the household does not befit an unloved or "a scorned woman" (שְׂנוּאָה, v. 23a), who uses her favored position to tyrannize others.[77] The position of "mistress" (גְּבִרְתּ, v. 23b)—an honorific title for the queen mother (Prov 30:23; 1 Kgs 11:19; 15:13; Isa 47:5, 7; Jer 13:18; 29:2; 2 Chron 15:16)—does not befit a maidservant who usurps the woman of the household. While these social inversions may convey a hint of humor, the intimate link between the stability of the earth and the stability of society suggests that the epigram underscores the importance of preserving the moral order and, by implication, the moral responsibilities associated with one's place in this order.[78]

h. Success through Limits (30:24–28)[79]

Social order remains in view within vv. 24–28,[80] but this order is constructed through a catalogue of four creatures. According to the heading, these creatures share two things in common: they are

73. Van Leeuwen, "Proverbs 30:21–23," 601.

74. Lakoff and Johnson, *Philosophy in the Flesh*, 303–4; Van Leeuwen, "Proverbs 30:21–23," 599–610.

75. Here "servant" (עֶבֶד) appears to function as a designation for a royal official. This is reinforced by the notion that a government official could more readily usurp the throne than a domestic servant. Van Leeuwen, "The Book of Proverbs," *NIB* 5:254–55; Waltke, *Proverbs: Chapters 15–31*, 493.

76. This term for "fool" (נָבָל) is associated with actions contrary to law and order and may be rendered as "outlaw" or social outcast (cf. 12:9; 17:7). Wolfgang M. W. Roth, "*NBL*," *VT* 10 (1960): 401–4; Van Leeuwen, "Proverbs 30:21–23," 607.

77. While the expression "scorned/hated woman" (שְׂנוּאָה) occurs in Pentateuchal texts pertaining to divorce (Deut 21:14–17; 24:1–4), divorce does not appear to be the issue in this inversion. Instead, a scorned or an unloved wife who obtains a favored position within a polygamous household appears to be in view. Van Leeuwen, "Proverbs 30:21–23," 608–9; Yoder, *Proverbs*, 285. Cf. Fox, *Proverbs 10–31*, 876–77.

78. Van Leeuwen, "Proverbs 30:21–23," 608–10; Lakoff and Johnson, *Philosophy in the Flesh*, 303. For a satirical reading of the epigram, see Toy, *Proverbs*, 532; McKane, *Proverbs*, 659–60; Clifford, *Proverbs*, 266.

79. Kirk, "Moral Animals," 18.

80. Forti, *Animal Imagery in the Book of Proverbs*, 117–18.

"smallest on earth" (קְטַנֵּי־אָרֶץ, v. 24a), and they are "inherently wise" (חֲכָמִים מְחֻכָּמִים, v. 24b).[81] The human attribute of wisdom is mapped onto the actions and organization of each creature.[82] Each creature is depicted in terms of human actions or social organizations, that is, as a "people" (עַם, vv. 25a, 26a), an orderly army (v. 27), and a resident of royal palaces (v. 28b).[83] And each creature achieves success through its limits.[84] These limits do not hinder success; rather, they serve as the concrete reality within which wisdom is manifested. Ants work in accord with the rhythm of creation, demonstrating industry and foresight in securing provisions (v. 25; cf. 6:8). Badgers evince technological ingenuity through their construction of impenetrable fortresses (30:26). Locusts march as a cohesive, integrated group, despite their lack of a leader (v. 27).[85] And lizards live in royal palaces (v. 28).[86] In contrast to the other creatures, the description of lizards culminates in an implicit reward: social mobility. As models of human behavior and social organization, these creatures epitomize inherent wisdom. They act in accord with their nature.[87] The same is true of the wise person. The wise act in accord with their nature as limited creatures. And like these animals in general and lizards in particular, they achieve success through their limits rather than by transcending the limits intrinsic to creaturehood.[88]

i. Stride and Self-Exaltation (30:29–31)

Whereas the creatures in vv. 24–28 manifest their innate wisdom through limits, the things catalogued in vv. 29–31 manifest their power through their stride. The heading identifies the "stride" (צָעַד, v. 29a) or "gait" (לָכֶת, v. 29b) of these things as their shared quality; and the repetition of the participle "stately" (מֵיטִיבֵי, vv. 29) implies that their gait is majestic. The description of the first thing, however, qualifies the nature of the stately stride of these creatures. The lion is depicted as a paragon of power that manifests its invulnerability through its gait: it "never retreats before anything" (לֹא־יָשׁוּב מִפְּנֵי־כֹל, v. 30b). Among the things catalogued in the epigram, the description of the lion is not only the clearest; it is also the most detailed. This detailed description orients one to the remaining things, many of which are obscure. The "זַרְזִיר of loins" has been construed in several ways, ranging from a cock, a greyhound, and a warhorse to a specific bird within the raven family (v. 31a).[89] In light of the ancient versions, "strutting rooster" or "cock (girt) of loins" may be the best reading.[90] In this case, the expression highlights the way in which the rooster's reddish legs give the impression that it is poised for battle.[91] This ambiguous animal is linked to a "he-goat" (תַיִשׁ, v. 31a) by the unexpected conjunction "or" (אוֹ, v. 31a). Its stately

---

81. Kirk, "Moral Animals," 20. While some render the phrase as a superlative, the use of the participle with an adjective from the same root amplifies the quality in view (Exod 12:9; Isa 28:16; cf. Pss 58:6[5]; 64:7[6]). In light of this construction, the adjective "wise" (חֲכָמִים) + the rare *pual* participle "being made wise" (מְחֻכָּמִים) seem to identify the inherent wisdom of these creatures. For an excellent discussion of the construction, see Kirk, "Moral Animals," 18–20. Also see Delitzsch, "Book of Proverbs," 6:464 (2:301); Waltke, *Proverbs: Chapters 15–31*, 461n66; Fox, *Proverbs 10–31*, 879.

82. Kirk, "Moral Animals," 20.

83. Kirk, "Moral Animals," 13–14.

84. Kirk, "Moral Animals," 18.

85. Forti, *Animal Imagery in the Book of Proverbs*, 117.

86. The noun שְׂמָמִית is a *hapax legomenon*, which may be construed as either "lizard" or "spider." For discussion, see Clifford, *Proverbs*, 267; Fox, *Proverbs 10–31*, 879.

87. Kirk, "Moral Animals," 20.

88. Kirk, "Moral Animals," 20.

89. b. B. Qam. 92b; b. Ḥul. 65a; Gen. Rab. 65:75; McKane, *Proverbs*, 663–64; Forti, *Animal Imagery in the Book of Proverbs*, 119.

90. Waltke, *Proverbs: Chapters 15–31*, 499–500; Fox, *Proverbs 10–31*, 880.

91. Fox, *Proverbs 10–31*, 880.

stride is uncertain, but if one follows the LXX, the manner by which the he-goat leads the herd may be assumed.

The final creature within the list is surprising, for it resides in the human realm. The king is included among the animals. While the king is compared to a lion elsewhere in the anthology (Prov 19:12; 20:2), here he represents the climactic creature with a stately gait. Like the strutting rooster and the he-goat, however, the nature of his gait is open. Various proposals offer possible explanations for the final phrase of the epigram, which remains uncertain.[92] Among these proposals, dividing אַלְקוּם into אַל קוּם yields the best reading. Similar to the stride of the lion, "no one can resist" or "rise up against" (אַל קוּם, v. 31b) the king.[93] Taken together, the gait of these creatures may be construed positively or negatively. If the epigram offers a positive evaluation of the manner by which these creatures manifest power in their respective spheres, it commends the courage and confidence by which they establish and inspire orderly rule. If, on the other hand, the epigram offers a negative evaluation of power manifested through self-exaltation, then it serves as a critique of arrogance.[94] Both readings are possible. But when the epigram is heard within the broader context of Agur's discourse, it appears to depict animals who fail to recognize that they are animals. Agur knows that he is an animal (v. 2); and this ontological state represents the requisite posture for the acquisition of knowledge of the Holy One. These creatures, by contrast, do not embody this posture. They may be paragons of power, but they are not exemplars of humility.[95]

j. Silencing the Arrogance of Self-Exaltation (30:32–33)

If vv. 29–31 censure arrogance expressed through self-exaltation, vv. 32–33 seek to cultivate humility by silencing arrogant expressions of self-exaltation. Similar to v. 10, the initial line delivers an admonition. This admonition is elliptical; and it serves as the apodosis of a conditional clause. The protasis includes two conditions: acting like a fool, which is clarified by the gerundive use of the infinitive construct, "by exalting yourself" (בְהִתְנַשֵּׂא, v. 32a); and scheming. The admonition condemns these expressions of arrogance by commending a particular posture, namely, "hand over your mouth!" (יָד לְפֶה, v. 32c; cf. Judg 18:19; Mic 7:16; Job 21:5). Silence replaces self-exaltation and scheming. The rationale for this silent posture is expressed through an extended causal clause (v. 33). Following the conjunction "for" (כִּי, v. 33a), each line opens with the noun "pressing" (מִיץ, vv. 33a–c) and includes the verb "produces" (יוֹצִיא, vv. 33a–c). And the terms used across the causal clause exhibit wordplay. The noun "curds" (חֶמְאָה, v. 33a) sounds like the Hebrew word for "wrath" (חֵמָה).[96] What is more, the noun "nose" (אַף, v. 33b) also means "anger," while the dual "anger" (אַפַּיִם, v. 33c) also means "nose/nostrils."[97] These literary techniques combine to form a powerful motivation against arrogant self-exaltation. Just as the churning of milk produces curds and the pinching of the nose produces blood, so also anger produces strife when it is pressed beyond proper limits. Together, the admonition and motivation reiterate and recast the principal theme of the collection.[98] They promote the meta-skill of the wise: humility.

92. For discussion of these proposals, see Waltke, *Proverbs: Chapters 15–31*, 462n79; Fox, *Proverbs 10–31*, 881; Fox, *Proverbs: An Eclectic Edition*, 387.

93. Waltke, *Proverbs: Chapters 15–31*, 462n79; Fox, *Proverbs 10–31*, 881.

94. Kirk, "Moral Animals," 20–21.

95. Kirk, "Moral Animals," 21–22.

96. Schökel, *A Manual of Hebrew Poetics*, 29.

97. Schökel, *A Manual of Hebrew Poetics*, 29.

98. Sauer, *Die Sprüche Agurs*, 111.

Canonical and Theological Significance

From a literary perspective, the formal diversity of the words of Agur may suggest that his discourse consists of a cacophony of "clanging symbols."[99] But from a rhetorical and theological perspective, Agur's discourse sounds like a continuous burst of clanging cymbals. His words are jarring. Within the broader context of the anthology, they provide the reader with a pedagogical wake-up call. This wake-up call alerts one to the harsh reality that humans never arrive in the life of wisdom. The quest for wisdom is never complete, for humans will never fully possess wisdom. These clanging cymbals are hard on the ears. While Agur's words may strike a discordant note in Proverbs, they play an invaluable role in the anthology's recital of the wise and virtuous life. Among other things, Agur's performance demonstrates that a wise and virtuous life embraces finitude and responds to this reality with a posture of humility.

Finitude is "constitutive of human being."[100] Put differently, to be human is to be a finite creature. This means that humans are limited, and it means that humans are dependent beings. Neither are bad. To the contrary, they are good. Finitude is not the product of sin; it is the product of creaturehood grounded in God's good creation. As David Kelsey notes, it is "precisely *in* their finitude, fragility, and vulnerability" that humans "are deemed by God to be good."[101] Everything points to humanity's finitude, fragility, and vulnerability: the air they breathe, the food and drink they consume, the rest they receive. The intimate relationship between creaturely finitude and dependence is captured by John Webster, who writes:

> [T]he manner in which creatures 'have' being and life can only be explained by extensive description of the will and work of God. Creatureliness means absolute dependence upon that will and work across the entire span of creaturely being. To be a creature, therefore, is not simply to be a self-standing product of an initial cause; it is to be and to live—without restriction—*ex nihilo* and therefore *ab extra*.[102]

Embracing one's finitude and absolute dependence on God is fundamental to a life of wisdom and virtue. This may explain why Calvin opened his *Institutes* with the observation that "Nearly all the wisdom we possess, that is to say, true and sound wisdom, consists of two parts: the knowledge of God and of ourselves."[103] Agur exemplifies this wisdom through his confession (vv. 1c–4), his resolution (vv. 5–6), and

99. Crenshaw, "Clanging Symbols," 51–64.
100. Young, *God's Presence*, 136.
101. David H. Kelsey, *Eccentric Existence: A Theological Anthropology*, 2 vols. (Louisville: Westminster John Knox, 2009), 1:308.
102. John Webster, "The Dignity of Creatures," in *God without Measure: Working Papers in Christian Theology, Volume II: Virtue and Intellect* (London: T&T Clark, 2018), 34.
103. Calvin, *Institutes of the Christian Religion*, 1.1.1.

his prayer (vv. 7–9). This wisdom, however, is unwelcomed in the modern world. To be specific, the acceptance of humanity's limits, vulnerability, and dependence is concealed by what Ephraim Radner calls "the Great Transition."[104] Aspects of this "Transition" are sketched by Francis Young:

> In the Modern Western world, people forget the limitations and vulnerability of human life. The success of medical science has done so much to ensure that our ills are cured, our brokenness repaired and the expectation of life prolonged, that most people live as if everything should be perfect. Suffering and death, disfigurement and disability seem uncomfortable. The cult of sport exposes perfect bodies and encourages their development through training—aiming to be the gold and silver vessels rather than clay pots, we might say. Women are seduced into emulating the exposed perfect bodies of those ideal models whose images are all around us in the media.[105]

This is just the tip of the iceberg. People live longer. Infant mortality rates are low. Retirement is now a season within the span of one's life. And human bodies can be refashioned. Any sense of human limits, vulnerability, and dependence is easily forgotten.

Agur refuses to allow readers to forget these realities of creaturehood. Like Gregory of Nyssa, he argues that, inasmuch as humans are unable to understand and control the intricacies of the natural world, they are unable to understand wisdom and manage the cosmos (v. 4).[106] With Alasdair MacIntyre, Agur fesses up to the fact that humans are animals in desperate need of "the virtues of acknowledged dependence (vv. 2, 14)."[107] Agur defines these virtues as dependence on God through his revealed word (vv. 5–6) as well as dependence on God for daily provision through personal prayer (vv. 7–9). Dependence dominates Agur's discourse. This is not surprising since, according to the foreign sage, "acknowledging dependence is the key to independence."[108]

Agur's account of human finitude and its implications reinforces and extends many admonitions and aphorisms in Proverbs (e.g., 3:5–6, 7–8; 16:1–9). What's more, Agur's attention to the severe limits of creaturehood complements the treatment of finitude in Job and Ecclesiastes.[109] Across the Joban dialogue, the friends

104. Ephraim Radner, *A Time to Keep: Theology, Mortality, and the Shape of a Human Life* (Waco, TX: Baylor University Press, 2016), 23–35.

105. Young, *God's Presence*, 141.

106. Stephen Pardue, "On Faithfully Knowing an Infinite God: Humility as an Intellectual Virtue in Gregory of Nyssa's *Contra Eunomium* II," *IJST* 13 (2011): 62–76.

107. Alasdair MacIntyre, *Dependent Rational Animals: Why Human Beings Need the Virtues* (Open Court: Chicago, 1999), 8–9.

108. MacIntyre, *Dependent Rational Animals*, 85.

109. Some of the following reflections on Job and Ecclesiastes were published in a chapter contribution. Christopher B. Ansberry, "Sin in the Writings," in *T&T Clark Companion to the Doctrine of Sin*, ed. Keith L. Johnson and David Lauber (London: T&T Clark, 2016), 45–60.

appeal to divine inscrutability in an attempt to move Job to recognize his intellectual limitations (Job 11:7–9; 15:7–8; cf. 36:26–29; 37:5). The wisdom hymn indicates that, despite their power and ingenuity, humans are unable to find wisdom, for their capacities are limited (Job 28:1–28). And the barrage of rhetorical questions as well as the wild and wondrous world projected in the divine speeches help Job to recognize this reality: his wisdom and power are limited (Job 38:1–41:34). Job acknowledges these limits in his climactic confession (Job 42:2–6); he concedes that he overreached or transgressed intellectual boundaries: he declared things he did not understand, things too wonderful, which he did not know (Job 42:3).

Finitude is also foregrounded in Ecclesiastes. In fact, Qoheleth's recognition of fundamental frustration in every human endeavor is inextricably linked to his conception of human limits.[110] Qoheleth observes that human memory is shortsighted and faulty (Eccl 1:9–11; 6:10). Human activity is transient (2:18–19). Human life is ephemeral (1:4; 7:15). Human power and planning are deficient (3:14; 8:8; 9:11–12), human wisdom is finite (7:14, 23–24; 8:17; 11:5), and the human appetite is insatiable (Eccl 4:8; 5:10; 6:7). In view of these observations, it is not surprising that Qoheleth restricts the verdict *hebel* to human activities and aspirations. Qoheleth accentuates the severe limitations inherent within and placed upon humans. These limits are not bad. The problem is that humans refuse to acknowledge their creatureliness and live within their limits. Put differently, humans fail to accept their lot and embrace life's limited possibilities within God's inscrutable design.[111] Ecclesiastes seeks to recalibrate the expectations of humans by identifying the boundaries of human ability and the space within which humans should live.[112]

The reality and implications of finitude reverberate across the canon. Job and Ecclesiastes offer distinct responses to how creatures should respond to their finitude. The same is true of Agur. In the face of creaturehood, limits, vulnerability, and dependence, Agur commends humility. This virtue is mentioned elsewhere in the anthology (Prov 11:2; 15:33; 22:4). While humility is not attributed to one of Proverbs's moral prototypes (e.g., the wise or righteous),[113] it is exemplified by Agur. And while humility as a social virtue is absent from the Old Testament,[114] humility as a theological virtue is common in the Old Testament (e.g., Prov 15:33; 22:4; 28:12). This quality of character makes sense only in relationship with God: it flows from

110. Mark R. Sneed, *The Politics of Pessimism in Ecclesiastes: A Social-Science Perspective*, AIL 12 (Atlanta: SBL Press, 2012), 162.

111. Michael V. Fox, *A Time to Tear Down and A Time to Build Up: A Rereading of Ecclesiastes* (Grand Rapids: Eerdmans, 1999; repr. Eugene, OR: Wipf & Stock, 2010), 11.

112. Sneed, *The Politics of Pessimism*, 162, 240–52. For a superb discussion of the intersection of finitude, Ecclesiastes, and a theology of education, see Daniel J. Treier, "The Gift of Finitude: Wisdom from Ecclesiastes for a Theology of Education," *CSR* 48 (2019): 371–90.

113. Arthur Jan Keefer, *The Book of Proverbs and Virtue Ethics: Integrating the Biblical and Philosophical Traditions* (Cambridge: Cambridge University Press, 2021), 209–10.

114. John P. Dickson and Brian S. Rosner, "Humility as a Social Virtue in the Hebrew Bible?," *VT* 54 (2004): 459–79.

that relationship, ordering human "passions in accord with the truth about human beings compared with and related to God."[115] Or, as Kelly Kapic contends, "humility consists in a recognition of (and rejoicing in) the good limitations that God has given us."[116] Agur recognizes his ontological and epistemological limits (vv. 2–4). He does not deny that humans can possess wisdom; rather, he models a modest approach to human knowing. He situates knowing in relationship with God through his revealed word. And he expresses humble dependence on God through prayer (vv. 7–9).

If Agur exemplifies humility, Jesus epitomizes humility. Humility marks a life of human flourishing in the kingdom of heaven (Matt 5:3). The rationale for this paradoxical form of life is found in the life of the incarnate Son. Jesus is humble of heart (11:28–29). Although he was in the form of God, he did not consider divine equality as something to be used for his own advantage. Instead, he emptied himself by taking the form of a servant and humbled himself by becoming obedient to the point of death (Phil 2:6–8). In light of this model of humility, Christians are not only called to humble dependence upon God; they are also called to something more radical: a humility that regards others as better than themselves (2:3). As an exemplar of humility, Agur commends a theological virtue: humble dependence on God. As the paragon of humility, Jesus combines and commends both a theological and a social virtue: humble dependence on God and humble regard for others, whether or not they are one's social equals. In so doing, Jesus amplifies the ontological, epistemological, and ethical meta-skill of the wise: humility.

115. Mary M. Keys, "Aquinas and the Challenge of Aristotelian Magnanimity," *History of Political Thought* 24 (2003): 37–65, esp. 56.

116. Kelly M. Kapic, *You're Only Human: How Your Limits Reflect God's Design and Why That's Good News* (Grand Rapids: Brazos, 2022), 103.

37

CHAPTER

Proverbs 31:1–31

B. The Embodiment of Wisdom and Virtue:

WISDOM IS THE EXERCISE OF POWER FOR THE BENEFIT OF THE OTHER

Main Idea of the Passage

The discourses within the final collection portray wisdom as a skilled practice in particular spheres of life, where one embodies and exercises one's knowledge and power for the benefit of the other.

Literary Context

According to the burden of Agur, humility is the meta-skill of the wise (30:1–33). This meta-skill serves as an appropriate backdrop to the burden taught to Lemuel. If humility is the requisite posture for receiving wisdom, how does one embody and exercise this wisdom in particular spheres of life? The discourses in Prov 31 answer this question through the overarching conceptual metaphor WISDOM IS THE EXERCISE OF POWER FOR THE BENEFIT OF THE OTHER. Their vision of wisdom and power is a far cry from the animalistic arrogance and self-exaltation profiled in ch. 30. It is a vision that is fully human, marked by the fear of YHWH, and oriented to the flourishing of others; and it is a vision that, in different ways, is taught and instantiated in the respective discourses that close the anthology.

These concluding discourses are intimately related to the materials in the central collections in general and Prov 1–9 in particular. Each "puts flesh and a face on" virtues delineated throughout the anthology.[1] The words of Lemuel provide a paradigm

1. Ellen F. Davis, *Scripture, Culture, and Agriculture: An Agrarian Reading of the Bible* (New York: Cambridge University Press, 2009), 151.

of royal rule, according to which the king exercises his power by establishing justice for the marginalized (31:1–9; cf. 16:10–15; 20:8, 26; 29:4, 14). This power is expressed through verbal advocacy, that is, by serving as a voice for the voiceless (31:8–9). And this expression of power on behalf of the powerless illuminates aspects of continuity as well as development within Proverbs. The anthology concludes by returning to the pedagogical setting within which it began: the home (vv. 1–2; 1:8). The voiceless mother mentioned in Prov 1–9 speaks (31:1; 1:8; 6:20). And the silent, receptive son in Prov 1–9 is replaced by a royal son, who is enjoined to speak for the silent.[2]

Whereas Lemuel's mother "puts flesh and a face on" responsible rule, the valiant woman "puts flesh and a face on" various virtues in Proverbs (vv. 10–31).[3] She is a composite portrait of the wise person in female dress. Like the wise, the valiant woman is strong and confident (31:10, 11b, 15b, 17, 21, 25, 29; 14:21; 24:5; 28:1). She is diligent and generous (31:13, 15a, 18b, 19, 27; 12:27; 13:4; 21:5; 22:9). She is skilled and indispensable to her household and community (31:10b, 11a, 13, 16, 18, 19, 24; 11:26; 22:29; 28:12). She speaks wisdom (31:26; 10:11, 31; 15:2). She fears YHWH (31:20b; 14:2; 19:23; 22:4). She is among a class of women who build their homes (31:11, 12, 15, 21, 23, 27; 14:1; 24:3–4). She is good to her husband (31:12; 18:22). She cares for the poor (31:20; 14:21, 31; 19:17). And she is honored (31:28–31; 11:16). The valiant woman embodies the virtues that characterize the wise and the righteous throughout the anthology. The episodic snapshots of virtuous character across the central collections are combined to form a coherent montage of moral character instantiated in a new, female figure: the valiant woman (31:10a; cf. Ruth 3:11).

The designation of this woman may be new within Proverbs, but many have noted that she bears a striking resemblance to Lady Wisdom. In fact, the valiant woman is described through terms and expressions that are used elsewhere only for Lady Wisdom. Like Lady Wisdom, the valiant woman is difficult to obtain (Prov 31:10a; 1:28; 8:17). She is more precious than corals (31:10b; 3:15 [*qere*]; 8:11). She is the proprietress of a substantial household (31:15, 21, 27; 9:1, 3). She is a source of security (31:11; 1:33). And she fears YHWH (31:30; 1:29; 8:13).[4] In light of the family resemblance between these figures, some have maintained that the valiant woman is a symbol or an allegory of wisdom.[5] Others have pushed back, demonstrating that the valiant woman embodies the activities of real women in particular periods of Israel's history.[6] And still others have contended that the impressionistic portrait of

2. For an excellent discussion of this development, see Catherine Petrany, "Fathers, Mothers, Sons, and Silence: Rhetorical Reconfiguration in Proverbs," *BTB* 50 (2020): 154–60.

3. Fox, *Proverbs 10–31*, 912, 916–17.

4. McCreesh, "Wisdom as Wife," 25–46; Camp, *Wisdom and the Feminine*, 186–208; Yoder, *Wisdom as a Woman of Substance*, 91–93; Fox, *Proverbs 10–31*, 908–9.

5. McCreesh, "Wisdom as Wife," 25–46; Hausmann, "Beobachtungen zu Spr 31,10–31," 265–66.

6. Yoder, *Wisdom as a Woman of Substance*, 41–90; Davis, *Scripture, Culture, and Agriculture*, 147–54.

the valiant woman projects an impossible ideal.[7] The truth, it seems, is somewhere in between. The valiant woman resembles Lady Wisdom. But she is neither a symbol nor an allegory. The realism of her activities is not dependent on a particular period of Israelite history. And these activities are not an impossible ideal. When the predominance of perfect verbs is rendered rightly in this depiction of the "perfect woman," the poem may be understood as the activities and achievements of a real type of woman who embodied and practiced these activities across her life.[8] It is a poem that praises her "lifetime achievement," "not her daily planner."[9] She was and is a real type of woman. As a real type of woman, she serves as the positive counterpart to another type of woman, viz., the "strange woman" (2:16; 5:3; 6:24; 7:5).[10]

7. Joseph Blenkinsopp, *Sage, Priest, Prophet: Religious and Intellectual Leadership in Ancient Israel* (Louisville: Westminster John Knox, 1995), 35; Murphy, *Proverbs*, 245.

8. Brian L. Webster, "The Perfect Verb and the Perfect Woman in Proverbs," in *Windows to the Ancient World of the Hebrew Bible: Essays in Honor of Samuel Greengus*, ed. Bill T. Arnold, Nancy L. Erickson, and John H. Walton (Winona Lake, IN: Eisenbrauns, 2014), 263–74. Also see, Max Rogland, *Alleged Non-Past Uses of Qatal in Classical Hebrew* (Assen: Van Gorcum, 2003), 15–51.

9. Webster, "The Perfect Verb," 274.

10. In addition to the valiant woman, Lemuel's mother also serves as a positive counterpart to the strange woman. Like the strange woman, Lemuel's mother is "foreign." And like

And as a real type of woman, she instantiates the moral character of the wise and righteous as well as the power and value of Lady Wisdom.

The shared setting, imagery, and language between the discourses in chs. 1–9 and ch. 31 indicate that these collections function as a literary framework for the canonical form of the anthology.[11] The implied, ideal reader who has accepted Lady Wisdom's invitation (9:4–6), ingested the varied courses of her "curricular cuisine" (10:1–29:27),[12] and eaten Agur's humble pie (30:1–33) is installed as a king (31:1–9).[13] And yet, this subject position does not eliminate the need for instruction. The king remains a student. And the description of the valiant woman's "lifetime achievement" intimates that the embodied practice of wisdom is a lifelong practice (31:10–31). The discourses within ch. 31 may bring the anthology to a fitting close, but they also remind the reader of the beginning and recall the truth that the pursuit of wisdom is perpetual.[14]

Translation and Exegetical Outline

(See pages 639–41.)

Structure and Literary Form

In contrast to the words of Agur (30:1–33), the literary architecture of the words of Lemuel is clear. These words consist of two discourses, each of which are cast in discrete literary forms (31:1–9, 10–31). The first bears a faint family resemblance to royal instructions from the ancient world (vv. 1–9).[15] Like the Egyptian instructions of Hardjedef, Merikare, and Amenemhet, a royal persona distills advice for the benefit of their son and successor (v. 1).[16] With the exception of this general performance context, Prov 31:2–9 share little in common with these Egyptian instructions. These instructions are performed by a king, not a queen mother. The Instruction of Hardjedef focuses on the importance of establishing a house and making proper mortuary preparations.

the strange woman, Lemuel's mother offers "vows" (נְדָרָי; 7:14; 31:2); but in contrast to the strange woman, these vows bring life, not death. For this antithesis, see Hatton, *Contradiction in the Book of Proverbs*, 73–77.

11. Camp, *Wisdom and the Feminine*, 179–208; McCreesh, "Wisdom as Wife," 25–46; Meinhold, *Die Sprüche*, 2:522; Van Leeuwen, "The Book of Proverbs," *NIB* 5:257; Yoder, *Wisdom as a Woman of Substance*, 75, 93. Cf. Fox, *Proverbs 10–31*, 915–16.

12. Brown, "The Didactic Power of Metaphor," 138.

13. Brown, *Wisdom's Wonder*, 64–66.

14. Yoder, *Proverbs*, 297.

15. For the concept of "family resemblance" (*Familienähnlichkeit*), see Ludwig Wittgenstein, *Philosophische Untersuchungen = Philosophical Investigations*, rev. 4th ed. (Oxford: Wiley-Blackwell, 2009), 35–38.

16. "The Instruction of Prince Hardjedef" (*AEL* 1:58–59); "The Instruction Addressed to King Merikare" (*AEL* 1:97–109); "The Instruction of King Amenhemet I for His Son Sesostris I" (*AEL* 1:135–39).

Proverbs 31:1–31

			B. The Embodiment of Wisdom and Virtue: Wisdom is the Exercise of Power for the Benefit of the Other (31:1–31)
			1. The Words of Lemuel (31:1–31)
1a	דִּבְרֵי לְמוּאֵל מֶלֶךְ	The words of Lemuel, a king;	a. The Title (31:1)
1b	מַשָּׂא אֲשֶׁר־יִסְּרַתּוּ אִמּוֹ	a burden which his mother taught him:	
2a	מַה־בְּרִי וּמַה־בַּר־בִּטְנִי	"What, my son? What, son of my womb?	b. The Clamor for Attention (31:2)
2b	וּמֶה בַּר־נְדָרָי	What, son of my vows?	
			c. Admonitions regarding the Exercise of Power (31:3–9)
3a	אַל־תִּתֵּן לַנָּשִׁים חֵילֶךָ	Do not give your strength to women,	(1) Self-Interested Satisfaction: Sex (31:3)
3b	וּדְרָכֶיךָ לַמְחוֹת מְלָכִין	nor your ways to those who destroy kings.	
4a	אַל לַמְלָכִים לְמוֹאֵל	Not for kings, Lemuel,	(2) Self-Interested Satisfaction: Drink (31:4–5)
4b	אַל לַמְלָכִים שְׁתוֹ־יָיִן	not for kings to drink wine,	
4c	וּלְרוֹזְנִים אוֹ שֵׁכָר	nor for rulers strong drink;	
5a	↑ פֶּן־יִשְׁתֶּה וְיִשְׁכַּח מְחֻקָּק	↑ lest he drink and forget what has been decreed,	
5b	וִישַׁנֶּה דִּין כָּל־בְּנֵי־עֹנִי	and change the verdict of any of the afflicted.	
6a	תְּנוּ־שֵׁכָר לְאוֹבֵד	Give strong drink to one who is perishing,	(3) Alleviating the Other through Drink (31:6–7)
6b	וְיַיִן לְמָרֵי נָפֶשׁ	and wine to the bitter of spirit,	
7a	↑ יִשְׁתֶּה וְיִשְׁכַּח רִישׁוֹ	↑ so that he may drink and forget his poverty,	
7b	וַעֲמָלוֹ לֹא יִזְכָּר־עוֹד	and no longer remember his misery.	
8a	פְּתַח־פִּיךָ לְאִלֵּם	Open your mouth for the mute,	(4) Exercising Power for the Benefit of the Other (31:8–9)
8b	↑ אֶל־דִּין כָּל־בְּנֵי חֲלוֹף	↑ for the rights of those passing away.	
9a	פְּתַח־פִּיךָ שְׁפָט־צֶדֶק	Open your mouth, judge righteously,	
9b	וְדִין עָנִי וְאֶבְיוֹן	and defend the rights of the poor and needy."	
			2. The Poem of the Valiant Woman (31:10–31)
10a	אֵשֶׁת־חַיִל מִי יִמְצָא	A valiant woman, who can find?	a. The Exercise of Power for the Benefit of the Household (31:10–18)
10b	וְרָחֹק מִפְּנִינִים מִכְרָהּ	Her value is beyond corals.	
11a	בָּטַח בָּהּ לֵב בַּעְלָהּ	The heart of her husband trusted in her	
11b	וְשָׁלָל לֹא יֶחְסָר	and he had no lack of plunder.	

Continued on next page.

Continued from previous page.

12a	גְּמָלַתְהוּ טוֹב וְלֹא־רָע	She showed him good and not evil	
12b	↑ כֹּל יְמֵי חַיֶּיהָ	↑ all the days of her life.	
13a	דָּרְשָׁה צֶמֶר וּפִשְׁתִּים	She sought out wool and flax,	a. The Exercise of Power for the Benefit of the Household (31:10–18) *cont.*
13b	וַתַּעַשׂ בְּחֵפֶץ כַּפֶּיהָ	and she worked with delight with her hands.	
14a	הָיְתָה כָּאֳנִיּוֹת סוֹחֵר	She was like merchant ships;	
14b	מִמֶּרְחָק תָּבִיא לַחְמָהּ	she would bring her food from afar;	
15a	וַתָּקָם בְּעוֹד לַיְלָה	and she rose while it was still night,	
15b	וַתִּתֵּן טֶרֶף לְבֵיתָהּ	and gave prey to her household,	
15c	↑ וְחֹק לְנַעֲרֹתֶיהָ	↑ and a portion to her maids.	
16a	זָמְמָה שָׂדֶה וַתִּקָּחֵהוּ	She considered a field and took it,	
16b	מִפְּרִי כַפֶּיהָ נָטְעָה כָּרֶם	from the fruit of her hands she planted a vineyard.	
17a	חָגְרָה בְעוֹז מָתְנֶיהָ	She girded her loins with strength,	
17b	וַתְּאַמֵּץ זְרֹעוֹתֶיהָ	and made strong her arms.	
18a	טָעֲמָה כִּי־טוֹב סַחְרָהּ	She tasted that her wares were good;	
18b	לֹא־יִכְבֶּה בַלַּיְלָה נֵרָהּ	her lamp did not go out at night.	
19a	יָדֶיהָ שִׁלְּחָה בַכִּישׁוֹר	She stretched out her hands to the double spindle,	b. The Exercise of Power for the Benefit of the Household and the Poor (31:19–20)
19b	וְכַפֶּיהָ תָּמְכוּ פָלֶךְ	and her palms grasped the spindle.	
20a	כַּפָּהּ פָּרְשָׂה לֶעָנִי	She opened her palm to the poor,	
20b	וְיָדֶיהָ שִׁלְּחָה לָאֶבְיוֹן	and stretched out her hands to the needy.	
21a	לֹא־תִירָא לְבֵיתָהּ מִשָּׁלֶג	She did not fear for her household because of snow,	c. The Exercise of Power for the Benefit of the Household and the Community (31:21–29)
21b	כִּי כָל־בֵּיתָהּ לָבֻשׁ שָׁנִים	for all her household were clothed in scarlet.	
22a	מַרְבַדִּים עָשְׂתָה־לָּהּ	She made for herself coverings,	
22b	שֵׁשׁ וְאַרְגָּמָן לְבוּשָׁהּ	linen and purple, her clothing.	
23a	נוֹדָע בַּשְּׁעָרִים בַּעְלָהּ	Her husband was known in the gates,	
23b	↑ בְּשִׁבְתּוֹ עִם־זִקְנֵי־אָרֶץ	↑ when he sat with the elders of the land.	

24a	סָדִין עָשְׂתָה וַתִּמְכֹּר	She made a linen garment and sold it,	
24b	וַחֲגוֹר נָתְנָה לַכְּנַעֲנִי	and provided girdles to the merchant.	
25a	עֹז־וְהָדָר לְבוּשָׁהּ	Strength and majesty, her clothing;	
25b	וַתִּשְׂחַק לְיוֹם אַחֲרוֹן	and she laughed at the future.	
26a	פִּיהָ פָּתְחָה בְחָכְמָה	She opened her mouth in wisdom,	
26b	וְתוֹרַת־חֶסֶד עַל־לְשׁוֹנָהּ	and loyal instruction was on her tongue.	
27a	צוֹפִיָּה הֲלִיכוֹת בֵּיתָהּ	She watched over the ways of her household,	
27b	וְלֶחֶם עַצְלוּת לֹא תֹאכֵל	and the bread of idleness she did not eat.	
28a	קָמוּ בָנֶיהָ וַיְאַשְּׁרוּהָ	Her children rose up and blessed her;	
28b	בַּעְלָהּ וַיְהַלְלָהּ	her husband praised her:	
29a	רַבּוֹת בָּנוֹת עָשׂוּ חָיִל	"Many daughters have done valiantly,	
29b	וְאַתְּ עָלִית עַל־כֻּלָּנָה	but you have surpassed them all."	
30a	שֶׁקֶר הַחֵן וְהֶבֶל הַיֹּפִי	Charm, deceitful—and beauty, fleeting,	d. True Beauty and its Recognition (31:30–31)
30b	אִשָּׁה יִרְאַת־יְהוָה הִיא תִתְהַלָּל	a woman who fears YHWH, she is to be praised.	
31a	תְּנוּ־לָהּ מִפְּרִי יָדֶיהָ	Give to her from the fruit of her hands,	
31b	↑ וִיהַלְלוּהָ בַשְּׁעָרִים מַעֲשֶׂיהָ	↑ so that her works praise her in the gates.	

The Instruction of Merikare sketches the political responsibilities and diplomatic prerogatives of the monarchy. And the Instruction of Amenemhet is an extended warning concerning the threats posed by royal advisors. The content of these self-interested royal testaments stands in sharp contrast to the content of Prov 31:2–9, which censure self-indulgence and abuse of power to encourage verbal advocacy for the powerless. Among comparable ancient Near Eastern texts, the content of Prov 31:2–9 is closer to the Akkadian Advice to a Prince, which focuses on royal abuse of power.[17] While the form of the Akkadian text differs from the form of Prov 31:2–9, both serve as warnings regarding the misuse of royal power. If vv. 1–9 bear any family resemblance to royal instructions from the ancient world, it is their performance context in general and their illocutionary force as instruction or warning in particular. And if the MT's reading of v. 1 is retained, the specific form of this instruction comes into focus. Similar to the words of Agur (30:1b), the instruction is a "burden," that is, "a weighty message."[18]

The second discourse unit is cast in the form of an alphabetic acrostic, which projects a "totalizing," "impressionistic" portrait of the valiant woman.[19] Many have followed Al Wolters and designated the acrostic poem as a brand of heroic poetry;[20] it renders the valiant woman in terms and images redolent of military prowess, subverting conventional descriptions of women that focus exclusively on their external appearance.[21] The acrostic poem possesses a heroic flavor. But in light of the predominance of perfect verbs as well as the concluding call to praise, it appears the piece is a type of encomium, one that praises the character, accomplishments, and enduring faithfulness of a particular type of woman.[22] This generic classification does not diminish the encomium's use of images of power; rather, it reframes them as the embodiment and performance of a praiseworthy type of woman across her life. The poem eulogizes the deeds of the valiant woman and moves one to praise, for these deeds are an instantiation of the fear of YHWH (v. 30).

While the discourses within ch. 31 differ on formal grounds, they share several similarities.[23] Both are concerned with women and care for the poor (vv. 3, 8, 9, 10, 20). Each unit employs the noun "strength/valiant" (חַיִל, vv. 3a, 10a, 29a) as well as the expression "open one's mouth" (פתח פִּי, vv. 8a, 9a, 26a). And these units attend to the use of power. To be specific, they traffic in the overarching conceptual metaphor

17. "Advice to a Prince" (Benjamin R. Foster, *Before the Muses: An Anthology of Akkadian Literature*, 3rd ed. [Bethesda, MD: CDL, 2005], 867–69).

18. See Kirk, "The Burden of the Sages," 1 et passim, with reference to Prov 30:1b. Also see Sneed, "Inspired Sages," 21–23. For discussion of the reading "burden" rather than "Massa," see the Explanation of the Text below.

19. Jacqueline Vayntrub, "Beauty, Wisdom, and Handiwork in Proverbs 31:10–31," *HTR* 113 (2020): 45–62; Yoder, *Proverbs*, 290.

20. Al Wolters, "Proverbs XXXI 10–31 as Heroic Hymn: A Form-Critical Analysis," *VT* 4 (1988): 446–57.

21. Wolters, "Proverbs XXXI 10–31," 455–57. Also see Vayntrub, "Beauty," 45–62.

22. Fox, *Proverbs 10–31*, 902–5; Webster, "The Perfect Verb," 273–74.

23. Murray H. Lichtenstein, "Chiasm and Symmetry in Proverbs 31," *CBQ* 44 (1982): 202–3.

WISDOM IS THE EXERCISE OF POWER FOR THE BENEFIT OF THE OTHER. In addition to these thematic similarities, some argue that the discourse units exhibit structural symmetry through their use of chiasm (vv. 4–7, 19–20).[24] These chiasms illuminate the symmetrical components of each unit. Lemuel's mother juxtaposes a prohibition + negative result clause (vv. 4–5) with an exhortation + result clause (vv. 6–7), and the chiastic verbal repetition across this sequence is mirrored by the verbal repetition in the conclusion of the instruction (vv. 8–9). Similar signs of symmetry are evident in the acrostic poem (vv. 10–31). The conclusion of the acrostic delineates the boundaries of its main body (vv. 30–31). These boundaries are substantiated by the use of a double *inclusio*. Together, "valiant/valiantly" (חַיִל, vv. 10a, 29a) and "her husband" (בַּעְלָהּ, vv. 11a, 28b) frame the main body of piece. And the chiasm in vv. 19–20 serves as the hinge of the poem, dividing the piece into two constituent parts (vv. 10–18, 21–29).[25] The comparable subject matter within these parts, combined with the frame around the main body and the chiasm within the center of the poem, evince deliberate design. If nothing else, the shared thematic and structural features between the discourse units suggest that their juxtaposition was far from haphazard.[26]

Explanation of the Text

1. The Words of Lemuel (31:1–9)

The words of Lemuel sketch a vision of responsible leadership, according to which WISDOM IS THE EXERCISE OF POWER FOR THE BENEFIT OF THE OTHER. Following the title (v. 1), the instruction moves from a call to attention (v. 2) to a sequence of admonitions (vv. 3–7) to a pair of concluding exhortations (vv. 8–9).

a. The Title (31:1)

Similar to the "words of the wise" (22:17) and the "words of Agur" (30:1), the expression "words of Lemuel" (דִּבְרֵי לְמוּאֵל, 31:1a) introduces a new discourse unit. While Lemuel is an unknown figure, he is designated as "a king" (מֶלֶךְ, v. 1a). The placement of the disjunctive accent under "king" produces a construction that has engendered different readings. In light of the fact that "king" lacks

24. These signs of structural symmetry are taken from Lichtenstein, "Chiasm and Symmetry," 203–11.

25. Lichtenstein, "Chiasm and Symmetry," 205–9. Hurowitz extends Lichtenstein's proposal, identifying intricate connections within and across the discourse units (Victor A. Hurowitz, "The Seventh Pillar–Reconsidering the Literary Structure and Unity of Proverbs 31," *ZAW* 113 [2001]: 209–18). Many follow the general contours of Lichtenstein's argument (e.g., Clifford, *Proverbs*, 273; Waltke, *Proverbs: Chapters 15–31*, 515). Garrett, by contrast, perceives the entire acrostic as a coherent chiasm that revolves around v. 23. This proposal is less than convincing, for it overlooks the contribution of vv. 19–20 within the unit and places vv. 13–19 in chiastic relationship with v. 27. Garrett, *Proverbs*, 248.

26. Lichtenstein, "Chiasm and Symmetry," 210–11.

the definite article, many relocate the disjunctive accent under "Lemuel," separating his words from what follows. And since the pattern "words of" + personal name/designation + "king" + place name is woven into other titles (1:1; Eccl 1:1), many read Prov 31:1a as "the words of Lemuel, king of Massa."[27] Others, by contrast, retain the placement of the disjunctive accent and construe the indefinite noun "king" as an appositive that specifies the office of Lemuel.[28] This construal suggests that מַשָּׂא is not a place name; rather, like in 30:1, it is a "burden" or "weighty" instruction.[29] The weight of this instruction is conveyed through a relative clause (v. 1b). The burden was placed on Lemuel by his mother; she "taught him" (יִסְּרַתּוּ, v. 1b), that is, she delivered "disciplinary instruction."[30] This is no light matter; and this is confirmed by the content of the words of Lemuel.

The words of Lemuel memorialize his mother's instruction. Like the father's reiteration of his own father's words in 4:3–9, Lemuel bears witness to his own mother's words. And like the performance frame of the lectures in chs. 1–9, 31:1 establishes the performance context of the discourse.[31] Lemuel's mother is unnamed, but her words live on through the memory and speech of her son.

b. The Clamor for Attention (31:2)

This weighty speech opens with an arresting string of clauses, each of which is foregrounded by the interrogative pronoun "what" (מַה, vv. 2a, 2b). The pronoun has been rendered in different ways. Whether it functions as a negative ("No!"), as a cognate equivalent to the Arabic injunction "listen," or as an elliptical expression that calls attention to the object ("what are you doing?"), the terse directives clamor for Lemuel's attention.[32] These startling calls for attention are balanced by terms of warmth and endearment. Lemuel's mother does not commence her instruction by placing her addressee in the subject position of king. She begins by placing her addressee in the relational subject position of son. The repetition of the Aramaic noun "son" (בַּר, vv. 2a, 2b, 2c), combined with the use of the first-person singular pronominal suffix, imbues the instruction with a sense of intimacy. And this relational intimacy extends from the present to the past. Lemuel's mother moves from his present state as "my son" (בְּרִי, v. 2a) back to his gestation and her multiple vows (v. 2a), yearning for his conception (v. 2b). Her disciplinary tone is tinged with affection. This rhetorical combination not only awakens Lemuel's attention; it also presses him into a posture of relational receptivity.

c. Admonitions regarding the Exercise of Power (31:3–7)

Having cultivated a receptive posture, Lemuel's mother shifts the subject position of her addressee from son to king. The moral authority of this office entails moral responsibilities. These responsibilities are expressed through a pair of admonitions (vv. 3, 4–5) and an exhortation (vv. 6–7).

(1) Self-Interested Satisfaction: Sex (31:3)

The initial admonition prohibits Lemuel from expending his "strength" (חַיִל, v. 3a) on women. The term "strength" denotes power in general and

27. McKane, *Proverbs*, 407–8; Murphy, *Proverbs*, 239; Clifford, *Proverbs*, 268–69; Fox, *Proverbs 10–31*, 884.

28. Waltke, *Proverbs: Chapters 15–31*, 501nn1–2; *IBHS* §12.3e.

29. Kirk, "The Burden of the Sages," 1 et passim; Vayntrub, *Beyond Orality*, 134; Sneed, "Inspired Sages," 21–23.

30. Fox, *Proverbs 10–31*, 884.

31. Vayntrub, *Beyond Orality*, 202–4.

32. For these respective proposals, see Fox, *Proverbs 10–31*, 884; Waltke, *Proverbs: Chapters 15–31*, 503–4n14; Clifford, *Proverbs*, 269. While מַה is used with the ל of advantage to focus attention on the object (e.g., Jonah 1:6; Ps 50:16), it appears the vocative can function in a comparable way.

its manifestation in economic holdings, competence, and character in particular (1 Sam 2:4; Job 20:18; Exod 18:21; Ruth 2:1). While some restrict the sense of the term to sexual virility,[33] the parallel expression "your ways" (דְּרָכֶיךָ, v. 3b) appears to encapsulate the varied semantic shades of strength.[34] When read in light of the root metaphor that pervades chs. 1–9 (i.e., LIFE IS A PATH), the way gestures to the manner and orientation of one's life. If Lemuel gives his strength to a class of women who "destroy kings" (לַמְחוֹת מְלָכִין, 31:3b),[35] then he jeopardizes his legitimacy, wealth, effectiveness, and moral character. Position and power are not designed for the self-interested satisfaction of one's desires. Position and power require moral responsibility for the benefit of the other.

(2) Self-Interested Satisfaction: Drink (31:4–5)

This conception of power and moral responsibility is explicit in the second admonition, which prohibits Lemuel from overindulging in alcohol. By means of the vocative, Lemuel's mother renews her direct address to her son (v. 4a). And building on her opening prohibition, she proscribes intemperance, which is inappropriate for those in positions of power (vv. 4b–c; cf. 20:1; 21:17; 23:20, 29–35).[36] The rationale for this prohibition is expressed through a negative result clause (31:5). Intoxication impairs the cognitive faculties necessary for fulfilling the kings' moral responsibilities; it erases the memory of what has been decreed (v. 5a), creating the conditions for the king to render a fallacious verdict against the afflicted (v. 5b). The admonition assumes that kings and rulers are granted power to administer justice in general and to protect the powerless in particular;[37] it forbids the exercise of power for personal satisfaction by attending to the cognitive and judicial implications of royal intemperance.

(3) Alleviating the Other through Drink (31:6–7)

The admonition against overindulging in alcohol is balanced by an exhortation regarding its distribution for the benefit of the other. In contrast to the previous admonitions, the exhortation is cast in the second-personal plural.[38] Whatever the explanation for this shift in address, the call to palliate the plight of the dying and despondent through the provision of drink has struck many readers as out of keeping with wisdom. While this may be true from a modern perspective, it appears anachronistic for an underdeveloped pharmaceutical society. Kings are not to drink wine or strong drink in order to fulfill their moral responsibilities as those in positions of judicial authority (v. 4). The dying and destitute, by contrast, neither occupy this position of moral authority nor share its moral responsibilities. Strong drink and wine, therefore, may be given to the dying and despondent (v. 6). The rationale for this exhortation is delineated

33. Fox, *Proverbs 10–31*, 885–86.

34. In light of its asymmetrical relationship with "strength," some render the expression "your ways" as "dominion, power" in accord with the Ugaritic term *drkt* (e.g., Murphy, *Proverbs*, 240–41; Waltke, *Proverbs: Chapters 15–31*, 504n18). Since asymmetrical parallelism is common in Proverbs and "your ways" makes good sense, the appeal to the Ugaritic term is unnecessary.

35. Following *BHS* and many others, לַמְחוֹת should be revocalized as the plural participle לְמֹחוֹת.

36. The rendering "nor" follows *qere* (אֵי), repointing the consonants as the negative particle אִי (cf. 1 Sam 4:21). While several emendations have been proposed, none of these proposals alter the general sense of the line. For discussion of these proposals, see Waltke, *Proverbs: Chapters 15–31*, 504–5n24; Fox, *Proverbs 10–31*, 886–87.

37. James L. Crenshaw, "A Mother's Instruction to Her Son (Proverbs 31:1–9)," in *Perspectives on the Hebrew Bible*, ed. J. L. Crenshaw (Macon, GA: Mercer University Press, 1988), 17.

38. According to Fox, the plural form of address may indicate that Lemuel's mother is quoting a popular saying (*Proverbs 10–31*, 887).

through a result clause (v. 7). Whereas the king must not drink and forget (v. 5a), the dying and despondent may drink so as to forget their poverty and misery (v. 7). The provision of drink to the destitute is intended neither to anesthetize them from their harsh lot nor to place them "permanently in a drunken stupor."[39] Rather, the provision of alcohol is intended to alleviate the suffering of the dying and despondent (cf. Ps 104:15; Eccl 10:19);[40] it is an act of care and compassion, not an attempt to numb the powerless.

d. Exercising Power for the Benefit of the Other (31:8–9)

The closing exhortations extend the moral responsibilities of the king. In addition to alleviating the suffering of the dying and despondent, Lemuel must serve as a voice for the voiceless. That is, he must exercise his power for the benefit of the powerless. The repetition of the command "open your mouth" (פְּתַח־פִּיךָ, vv. 8a, 9a), combined with the noun "rights" (דִּין, vv. 8b, 9b), captures the thrust of the Lemuel's mother's weighty instruction. Whereas the son within Prov 1–9 remained silent under parental instruction, Lemuel's mother concludes her instruction with the expectation that her son will speak for the silent.[41] Instead of opening his mouth to satisfy his personal desires, Lemuel must open his mouth to judge and defend the mute, poor, and needy—those whose voice remains unheard in the court and society. It is important to note, however, that the expectation of Lemuel's mother remains unrealized. He does not speak as a verbal advocate for the speechless. His voice remains silent within the text. This silence may be intentional. Lemuel's lack of speech invites the reader to fill the void and to "heed the Queen Mother's urgent commands" by speaking up for the speechless.[42] In so doing, one not only obeys the weighty instruction of Lemuel's mother; one also embodies wisdom, for WISDOM IS THE EXERCISE OF POWER FOR THE BENEFIT OF THE OTHER.

2. The Poem of the Valiant Woman (31:10–31)

This embodiment of wisdom is also reflected in the acrostic poem devoted to the valiant woman (vv. 10–31). By virtue of its acrostic structure and focus on a single subject, the poem exhibits a remarkable unity. Despite its literary and thematic unity, however, the poem may be divided into four parts (vv. 10–18, 19–20, 21–29, 30–31). As noted above, the opening verses of the first and the concluding verses of the third mark off the main body by means of a double *inclusio* (vv. 10, 11, 28, 29). The chiasm represented in the second part functions as the hinge of the poem (vv. 19–20). And the shift in address within the final section brings both the poem and the book of Proverbs to a close (vv. 30–31).

a. The Exercise of Power for the Benefit of the Household (31:10–18)

The acrostic poem opens with a rhetorical question that introduces its central subject: "a valiant woman" (אֵשֶׁת־חַיִל, v. 10a). Similar to its use in v. 3a ("strength"), חַיִל denotes power in general and its manifestation in economic holdings, competence, and character in particular (1 Sam 2:4; Job 20:18; Exod 18:21; Ruth 2:1). In light of the content of the poem, this type of women embodies the full

39. Waltke, *Proverbs: Chapters 15–31*, 509.

40. McKane, *Proverbs*, 410; Murphy, *Proverbs*, 241; Clifford, *Proverbs*, 270; Fox, *Proverbs 10–31*, 887.

41. Petrany, "Fathers, Mothers, Sons, and Silence," 154–60.

42. Petrany, "Fathers, Mothers, Sons, and Silence," 160.

semantic range of the term. And in light of the semantics of the poem as well as its attention to certain body parts, the power of this type of woman predominates.[43] The term חַיִל, combined with the military expressions that punctuate the piece, creates a heroic portrait of this type of woman.[44] Her heroic power does not consist of her innate or external beauty, which the poem resists.[45] Nor does her heroic power consist of exploits performed for the sake of personal praise, though that is what this type of woman deserves; rather, her heroic power is embodied in a form of life, where WISDOM IS THE EXERCISE OF POWER FOR THE BENEFIT OF THE OTHER.

As the rhetorical question intimates, this type of woman is rare. The question "Who can find?" (מִי יִמְצָא, v. 10a) recalls the search-and-find motif woven into the discourses of chs. 1–9 (1:28; 2:4–5; 3:13; 8:17, 35). It does not imply that such a woman is an unattainable fantasy;[46] rather, it indicates that such a woman is inestimably precious.[47] Like Lady Wisdom, her worth is beyond "corals" (פְּנִינִים, 31:10b; cf. 3:15; 8:11): just as it cannot be weighed, so she cannot be bought.[48] The rationale for this striking assessment is supplied in 31:11–18. Across this woman's life, her husband "trusted in her" (בָּטַח בָּהּ, v. 11a). Elsewhere in the anthology, trust serves as the relational bond between a person and YHWH (3:5; 16:20; 28:25; 29:25). Here it binds the marital relationship. Far from a mere feeling of confidence and security, this trust materialized in the woman's concrete provision for her husband. He had no lack of "plunder" (שָׁלָל, 31:11b)—a term used elsewhere for the spoil taken in war (Josh 7:21; 2 Sam 3:22; 8:12; 2 Kgs 3:23). This term from the semantic field of warfare suggests that the valiant woman secured her plunder by means of her power and she exercised this power for the benefit of her husband. What is more, in response to her husband's trust, the woman showed him good every day of her life (Prov 31:12). In the words of 18:22, she was a good and favorable gift from YHWH, and she manifested this goodness by the good that she displayed to her husband.

The power and goodness of this type of woman, however, extended well beyond the confines of her marriage. According to 31:13, she sought raw materials for weaving, and she worked "with delight with her hands" (בְּחֵפֶץ כַּפֶּיהָ, v. 13b). That is, she embodied the cognitive, physical, and aesthetic dimensions of lived wisdom. Her pursuit of goods was by no means restricted to the local shop. The woman herself was like a merchant ship, one who brought her household assorted foods from afar (v. 14). And her provisions fed a substantial household. In addition to the nuclear family, the woman had a retinue of maids (v. 15 b–c; cf. 9:3; 27:23–27). She would rise early to provide each with "prey" (טֶרֶף, 31:15b)—food hunted and caught by her boldness and power. Whereas the language of v. 15 portrays the woman as a fierce predator, the language of v. 16 paints the woman as a calculated conqueror.[49] She evaluated a field, perceived its productiveness, and "took it" (תִּקָּחֵהוּ, v. 16a; cf. Deut 3:14). Having acquired the property, she transformed it into a vineyard, financing the arduous project "from the fruit of her hands" (מִפְּרִי כַפֶּיהָ, Prov 31:16b). Not content to merely oversee

43. M. Beth Szlos, "Body Parts as Metaphor and the Value of a Cognitive Approach: A Study of the Female Figures in Proverbs via Metaphor," in *Metaphor in the Hebrew Bible*, ed. P. van Hecke, BETL 187 (Leuven: Leuven University Press, 2005), 185–95.

44. Wolters, "Proverbs XXXI 10–31," 446–57.

45. Vayntrub, "Beauty," 45–62.

46. Hausmann, "Beobachtungen zu Spr 31,10–31," 262–63.

47. Fox, *Proverbs 10–31*, 891.

48. For 31:10b as a reference to the literal bride-price of the woman, see Yoder, *Wisdom as a Woman of Substance*, 77–78.

49. Van Leeuwen, "The Book of Proverbs," *NIB* 5:261.

projects, she "girded her loins with strength" (חָגְרָה בְעוֹז מָתְנֶיהָ, v. 17a) and "made strong her arms" (תְּאַמֵּץ זְרֹעוֹתֶיהָ, v. 17b). These expressions of physical power are reserved for men elsewhere in the Old Testament.[50] Here they refer to the intellectual preparations and physical power of the valiant woman. Both capture her battle readiness for the tasks at hand. And this readiness was manifested through the concrete way in which the woman tucked in her skirt and bound her sleeves to free her legs and arms for work.[51] These physical descriptions of the woman's power coincide with v. 18 and its depiction of the woman's aesthetic power. By virtue of her discernment, she "tasted" (טָעֲמָה, v. 18a) that her merchandise was good. And these powers of judgment were not dulled by seasons of long work (v. 18b).

Overall, the first half of the poem employs various terms, images, and expressions to paint a vivid portrait of the valiant woman's power. Her power encompasses the intellectual, physical, and aesthetic dimensions of embodied practice; and her power is exercised for the sake of the other.

b. The Exercise of Power for the Benefit of the Household and the Poor (31:19–20)

This conception of power for the benefit of the other is distilled in vv. 19–20, which are cast in the form of a chiasm. The chiasm functions as the hinge of the acrostic poem. The expression "stretched out her hands" (יָדֶיהָ שִׁלְּחָה, vv. 19a, 20b) frames the phrases "her palms" (כַפֶּיהָ, v. 19b) and "her palm" (כַּפָּהּ, v. 20a).[52] These "body parts of power" illuminate the physical strength of the valiant woman.[53] She wove textiles, spun on a "double spindle" (כִּישׁוֹר, v. 19a) that was grasped by both hands.[54] And these body parts of power provided for the poor. More than using her palms to support the household economy, the valiant woman opened her palm to the marginalized members of her community (v. 20). She harnessed her creative handiwork and physical power for the benefit of the powerless.

c. The Exercise of Power for the Benefit of the Household and the Community (31:21–29)

These acts of power for the benefit of the household and the community are developed in the third section of the poem (vv. 21–29). The valiant woman epitomized foresight and emotional strength. She did not fear the cold, for her household was clothed in quality garments of "scarlet" (שָׁנִים, v. 21b)—a palatial dye that exuded wealth and status.[55] These luxurious garments corresponded with the linens and clothing of the valiant woman. She lined her bed with "coverings" (מַרְבַדִּים, v. 22a) to enhance the status of her household rather than to entice prospective sexual partners (7:16). She wore imported Egyptian linen and purple dyed wool (31:22b), fabrics and colors that reflected her noble character.[56] As the crown that adorns her husband's head (12:4), she endowed him with repute when-

50. Szlos, "Body Parts as Metaphor," 188–89.

51. Yoder, *Proverbs*, 295; Tzvi Novick, "'She Binds Her Arms': Rereading Proverbs 31:17," *JBL* 128 (2009): 107–13.

52. Lichtenstein, "Chiasm and Symmetry," 207.

53. Szlos, "Body Parts as Metaphor," 187.

54. For discussion of the "double spindle" or "grasped spindle" and its role in the art of spinning, see Al Wolters, "The Meaning of *Kîšôr* (Prov. 31:19)," *HUCA* 65 (1994): 91–104.

55. Some scholars follow the LXX and read "double" (שְׁנַיִם) rather than "scarlet" (שָׁנִים), since the latter term is a rare plural (Murphy, *Proverbs*, 244; Clifford, *Proverbs*, 276). But the rendering of the MT should be retained for two reasons: (1) the plural form שָׁנִים is attested in Isa 1:18, where it is parallel to "snow" (שֶׁלֶג); and (2) based on the parallel "purple" (אַרְגָּמָן) in Prov 31:22b, it seems the issue in the present text is the quality rather than the quantity of garments. Yoder, *Wisdom as a Woman of Substance*, 84n55; Waltke, *Proverbs: Chapters 15–31*, 512n85.

56. Yoder, *Wisdom as a Woman of Substance*, 85.

ever he sat with the leaders of the community at the center of public life (31:23).[57] She produced an excess of fine clothing, both outer garments and sashes, which she sold to merchants (v. 24). The dress of her household, her clothing, and her merchandise bespoke her moral and emotional power: she wore "strength and majesty" (עֹז־וְהָדָר, v. 25a; cf. Pss 93:1; 104:1) as the qualities that clothed her character; and she approached the future without any sense of foreboding (v. 25). What is more, she manifested her moral essence through her moral actions. She fulfilled the desire of Lemuel's mother (vv. 8–9), opening her mouth in wisdom and dispensing "loyal instruction" (תּוֹרַת־חֶסֶד, v. 26b).[58] She presided over her household's manner of life (v. 27a),[59] and she displayed her moral identity through the food that she ate (v. 27b).[60]

In light of the valiant woman's actions, clothing, attitudes, and moral identity, each of which supported her household and enhanced its reputation in the community, it is not surprising that her household responded to her lifetime achievements on its behalf with praise. As a gesture of admiration, the woman's children and husband rose and praised her (v. 28). The content of their praise consisted of a comparison. While many daughters "have done valiantly" (עָשׂוּ חָיִל, v. 29a), that is, have accomplished great things (cf. Ruth 4:11), these daughters and their deeds pale in comparison with the character, strength, and accomplishments of the valiant woman. Her valiance (v. 10a), in other words, placed her in a class of her own. She embodied wisdom and the virtues of Proverbs across her life and her power, combined with the outward-looking orientation of her life, epitomized an instantiation of wisdom, according to which WISDOM IS THE EXERCISE OF POWER FOR THE BENEFIT OF THE OTHER.

d. True Beauty and Its Recognition (31:30–31)

The valiant woman's exercise of power for the benefit of the other serves as the backdrop to the poem's conclusion, where the community is called upon to add their praise to that of the woman's household. This climactic invitation is preceded by a striking critique of physical beauty (v. 30). The innate traits of charm and beauty are deemed misleading and ephemeral. This assessment explains why the acrostic poem resists any description of the valiant woman's physical appearance.[61] Instead, it focuses on her power expressed through her moral identity and moral actions. Whereas the discourses devoted to the strange woman focus on her "palate" (חֵךְ; 5:3), "lips" (שְׂפָתֵי; 5:2; 7:21), "tongue" (לָשׁוֹן; 6:24), and "eyelashes" (עַפְעַפֵּי-; 6:25) so as to foreground her slippery, seductive rhetoric, the poem of the valiant woman focuses of her "hands" (יָדֵי-, 30:19a, 20b), "palms" (כַּפֵּי-, vv. 13b, 16b, 19b, 20a), "loins" (מָתְנֵי-, v. 17a), and "arms" (מָתְנֵי-, v. 17b) so as to foreground her physical strength and moral character.[62] The portrait of the strange woman, in other words, does not contain body parts of power, while the portrait of the valiant woman, by contrast, avoids body parts of sexual seduction. External or innate beauty is not true beauty according to the acrostic poem. Rather, a woman "who fears

57. Yoder, *Wisdom as a Woman of Substance*, 89.

58. While the construct is rendered as an attributive genitive ("loyal instruction"), it may also be construed as an objective genitive ("instruction about kindness/covenant commitment").

59. According to Wolters, the participle צוֹפִיָּה ("watched over") is a play on the Greek term σοφία (Al Wolters, "*Sôpiyyâ* (Prov 31:27) as Hymnic Participle and Play on *Sophia*," *JBL* 104 [1985]: 577–87). For a critique of this reading, see Fox, *Proverbs 10–31*, 897.

60. For the conceptual metaphor MORAL IDENTITY IS FOOD EATEN, see Tilford, *Sensing World, Sensing Wisdom*, 206.

61. Vayntrub, "Beauty," 45–62.

62. Szlos, "Body Parts as Metaphor," 186–95, esp. 193.

YHWH" (יִרְאַת־יְהוָה, v. 30b) embodies true inner beauty. This sort of beauty is delineated across the acrostic poem through the person and activities of the valiant woman; and this sort of beauty deserves praise.

The poem, therefore, concludes with an exhortation to commend the works of this type of woman. This commendation moves from the material to the verbal.[63] The former is delineated in the opening line, which commands the audience in general and readers in particular to "give to her from the fruit of her hands" (תְּנוּ־לָהּ מִפְּרִי יָדֶיהָ, v. 31a), that is, to return to the valiant woman a portion of her earnings. In light of the unusual nature of the command and the desire to create so-called synonymous parallelism between the contiguous lines, many repoint the imperative to read "extol."[64] But when the command is read in light of the valiant woman's exercise of power for the benefit of *others* and with a recognition of the phenomenon of imprecise parallelism, the reading of the MT may stand.[65] Far from exercising her power for self-interest, the valiant woman has exerted her energy for the sake of her household and community. The community is called to reciprocate and to express their appreciation for the woman's activities by giving her what she deserves.[66] The result of this act is that the woman's deeds serve as instruments of praise in the center of public life (v. 31b). The reciprocal relationship between the valiant woman's provision for the community and the community's recompense for her other-person-centered service culminates in the abiding praise and memory of her works—works that proclaim WISDOM IS THE EXERCISE OF POWER FOR THE BENEFIT OF THE OTHER.

Canonical and Theological Significance

The book of Proverbs concludes in dramatic fashion with two discourses that, in their own ways, indicate WISDOM IS THE EXERCISE OF POWER FOR THE BENEFIT OF THE OTHER. Wisdom and power are familiar bedfellows (Prov 24:5). But the exercise of power in relation to others is a complex and fraught subject.[67] Might does not make right, even *if* "the essence of life" is "its *will to power*."[68] The exercise of power in relation to others is unavoidable. Viewed from an immanent perspective, "a society without power relations can only be an abstraction."[69] Viewed from a theological perspective, power and authority are a natural corollary of the divinely established orders of creation: marriage and family, covenant community and society. Power and authority are always exercised in relation. Social and political theorists conceptualize this power-in-relation through two ideal models: superordination or power-over

63. Fox, *Proverbs 10–31*, 899.

64. That is, many identify the root as תנה rather than נתן. Murphy, *Proverbs*, 245; Clifford, *Proverbs*, 278.

65. Delitzsch, "Book of Proverbs," 6:490 (2:341–42); Fox, *Proverbs 10–31*, 899.

66. McKane, *Proverbs*, 670; Fox, *Proverbs 10–31*, 899.

67. For discussion of the nature and complexities of power in relation to others, see Michel Foucault, "The Subject and Power," *Critical Inquiry* 8 (1982): 777–95.

68. Friedrich Nietzsche, *On the Genealogy of Morals*, trans. Douglas Smith (Oxford: Oxford University Press, 1996), 56, italics original.

69. Foucault, "The Subject and Power," 791.

and effective capacity or power-to.[70] These models serve as a useful heuristic guide through which to explore God's exercise of power as well as the exercise of power across Prov 31. Moreover, they provide a backdrop against which to consider why the exercise of power in the discourses of ch. 31 is an expression of wisdom.

As Christine Firer Hinze notes, the two models of power-in-relation paint different pictures: "power-over involves any agent's capacity to significantly affect others, especially by eliciting their cooperation, obedience, or acquiescence in furthering ends determined by that agent."[71] Power-to, by contrast, "focuses on power's efficacy as emerging *with* or *because of* others."[72] These respective pictures of power orient one to the depiction of God's power across Scripture. As the creator of all things, the triune God exercises power-over all things; he is king and judge (Gen 18:25; 1 Sam 2:10; Pss 10:16; 96:10, 13). As sustainer of all things, the triune God exercises power-to all things; they exist by his gracious, sovereign will (Heb 1:3; Rev 4:11).[73] In the same way, Jesus exercises these models of power. As the one through whom all things were created (John 1:1–3; Col 1:16–17), he exercises power-over creation and its creatures: he stills storms (Mark 4:35–41), heals diseases (Mark 1:21–34, 40–45), forgives sins (Mark 2:1–12), and triumphs over sin and death through his resurrection. And as the one who came to serve (Mark 10:45), he reveals the triune God's power-to, that is, "God's posture towards and intentions for humanity."[74] Bruce Ashford and Craig Bartholomew capture the coalescence of these models of power. Reflecting on the doctrine of creation through the concept of hospitality, they write:

> This [hospitality], after all, is a major theme in Genesis 1–2. Unlike the gods in other creation accounts, God directs his power lovingly toward creating a good creation and the perfect home for human beings. *God exercises his power in an other-centered way.* He brings into being and creates the space apart from himself for the creation and in particular for the human person, who has the freedom to respond to God as a covenant partner or not.[75]

God exercises his power in an other-centered way. God's power-over all things is inextricably linked to his power-to all things. They are not mutually exclusive. The same is true of the discourses in Prov 31.

70. Christine Firer Hinze, *Comprehending Power in Christian Social Ethics*, AARAS 93 (Atlanta: Scholars Press, 1995), 4–5.

71. Hinze, *Comprehending Power*, 5.

72. Hinze, *Comprehending Power*, 6, italics original.

73. Bavinck, *Reformed Dogmatics*, 2:246–47.

74. Hinze, *Comprehending Power*, 274.

75. Ashford and Bartholomew, *The Doctrine of Creation*, 126, emphasis mine. Also see James K. A. Smith, *Awaiting the King: Reforming Public Theology* (Grand Rapids: Baker Academic, 2017), 67. Smith contends that "God's rule is not an antinatural tyranny but more like the authority of the gardener who husbands creation to its fullness."

Taken together, the words of Lemuel and the eulogy of the valiant woman traffic in power-over and power-to models, respectively. Lemuel's mother addresses her son as king, as one in a position of power-over others. This position of moral authority involves moral responsibilities. Lemuel's mother operates under the assumption that power holders face a particular temptation: they are prone to use their position and power-over others in an irresponsible and self-interested fashion.[76] To curb this temptation, Lemuel's mother prescribes a form of power-over others that privileges the interests, rights, and flourishing of others. Instead of using his power and position to feed his self-interested desires (vv. 3–5), Lemuel must use his power over others to extend empathy to the perishing, to advocate for the voiceless, and to defend the rights of the poor (vv. 6–9). When read in conjunction with Prov 30:10–31, it appears that this form of power-over others creates the conditions for the valiant woman's exercise of power-to others. This woman is a model of effective capacity. She uses her power in collaboration with others to effect particular ends. And these ends are for the benefit of others: the woman's household (vv. 10–18), the poor (v. 20), and her community (vv. 21–29). Just as the triune God exercises power-over as well as power-to others in a beneficent and legitimate fashion, so also the words of Lemuel and the eulogy of the valiant woman commend and embody power-over as well as power-to others in a beneficent and legitimate fashion.

The discourses in Prov 31 sketch models of power that mirror God's exercise of power. These models, like their conceptualization in social and political theory, are *ideal*. But they are not unique in the canon of Scripture. In addition to the triune God's power-over and power-to others, these ideal forms of power are reflected in the law of the king (Deut 17:14–20),[77] Boaz's treatment of Ruth (Ruth 2:5–16; 3:10–13; 4:1–10), and David's care for Mephibosheth (2 Sam 9:3–13), just to name a few (cf. Job 31:13–23, 31–32, 38–40). Across these texts, ideal forms of power in relation to others are actualized. More often than not, however, these ideal forms of power in relation to others are neither reflected nor embodied in reality. Power is used in self-interest to exploit, control, and abuse others. This reality is not only acknowledged in Scripture (e.g., Exod 1:15–16, 22; Judg 19; 2 Sam 13; Amos 1:3–2:16), it is all too apparent in our contemporary world, from totalitarian regimes and the mass incarceration of people groups to human trafficking, to the MeToo movement, to sexual and spiritual abuse within the church. Power is an inevitable reality. And, as Lord Acton recognized, power has the potential to corrupt power holders and to corrode the relational infrastructure of society and the church.

The ideal vision of power-over and power-to others in the discourses of Prov 31 serves as a counterpoint to the reality of the abuse of power. But this vision is

76. Hinze, *Comprehending Power*, 275.

77. Daniel I. Block, "The Burden of Leadership: The Mosaic Paradigm of Kingship (Deut. 17:14–20)," *BSac* 162 (2005): 259–78.

more than ideal; it is also wise. At bottom, wisdom is an embodied skill, or better, a skilled practice;[78] it is "cognitive *and* emotional *and* aesthetic."[79] The words of Lemuel commend a form of leadership grounded on responsibility, care, advocacy, and justice for the other. The eulogy of the valiant woman portrays the incarnation of the fear of YHWH. As "the most extended description of the regular activity of an ordinary person" in the canon of Scripture,[80] this woman performs "the art of the locality."[81] This art is a skilled practice in a particular environment and for the benefit of both the family and the community. Like the models of power-in-relation, the discourses in Prov 31 paint different portraits of power-in-relation. These portraits, however, share a common telos. Whether power-over or power-to, power is exercised for the benefit of the other. This telos renders these portraits of power wise. They are portraits that one is to animate and imitate, for **WISDOM IS THE EXERCISE OF POWER FOR THE BENEFIT OF THE OTHER.**

78. Matthew Crawford, *Shop Class as Soulcraft: An Inquiry into the Value of Work* (New York: Penguin, 2010); idem, *The World Beyond Your Head: How to Flourish in an Age of Distraction* (New York: Penguin, 2016).

79. Fox, "The Epistemology of the Book of Proverbs," 684, author's emphasis.

80. Davis, *Scripture, Culture, and Agriculture*, 148.

81. The phrase is taken from Henri Mendras, *The Vanishing Peasant: Innovation and Change in French Agriculture*, trans. Jean Lerner (Cambridge: Cambridge University Press, 1970), cited in Davis, *Scripture, Culture, and Agriculture*, 151.

Appendixes

Appendix 1

List of Key Terms/Concepts in Proverbs

Key Terms	English Gloss	Representative Texts
אָדָם־, אִישׁ־בְּלִיַּעַל	Scoundrel	6:12–15; 16:27
אֱוִיל	Fool	1:7; 27:22
אַכְזָרִי	Ruthless	5:9
אֹרַח	Path, way	1:19; 2:13; 8:20; 10:17; 12:28; 22:25
בִּינָה	Understanding	3:5; 4:1, 5, 7; 7:4; 23:23
דֶּרֶךְ	Path, way	1:15, 31; 2:12; 3:23; 4:26; 12:15; 16:2
זָרָה	Strange	2:16; 5:3, 20; 7:5; 22:14
חַי	Life	3:22; 8:35; 9:11; 10:16; 12:28; 16:22
חָכָם	Wise	9:8; 10:8, 14; 12:15; 14:16; 16:21
חָכָם בְּעֵינָיו	Wise in his own eyes	26:5, 12
חָכְמָה	Wisdom	1:2; 2:6; 3:19; 8:1–36; 14:6, 33; 24:3
חֲסַר־לֵב	Senseless, lacks sense	7:7; 9:4; 10:13, 21
יִרְאַת יְהוָה	Fear of YHWH	1:7; 2:5; 8:13; 9:10; 15:33; 22:4
יָשָׁר, יְשָׁרִים	Upright	2:21; 12:6; 14:2; 16:17
כְּסִיל	Fool	10:1, 26:1–12
לֵץ	Scoffer	1:22; 9:7–8; 14:6
לֶקַח	Instruction, learning	1:5; 4:2; 7:21; 9:9; 16:21, 23
מוּסָר	Instruction, discipline	1:2; 3:11; 5:12; 12:1; 22:15
מְזִמָּה	Discretion, scheme	1:4; 2:11; 3:21; 8:12; 12:2; 14:17; 24:8
מְסִלָּה	highway	16:17
מַעְגָּל	Path, way	2:9; 4:11; 5:21
מַשְׂכִּיל	Perceptive, prudent	10:5, 19; 14:35; 16:20
מִשְׁפָּט	justice	2:9;

Key Terms	English Gloss	Representative Texts
נָבוֹן	Discerning	1:5; 10:13; 14:33; 15:14; 19:25
נָכְרִיָּה	Outsider, adulteress	2:16; 5:20; 7:5; 23:27
נְתִיבָה	Path, way	1:15; 3:17; 7:25; 8:20; 12:28
עָצֵל	Sluggard	6:6–11; 10:26; 26:13–16
עִקְּשׁוּת	Crooked	4:24; 6:12
עָרוּם	Shrewd	12:16, 23; 14:8, 15, 18
עָרְמָה	Shrewdness	1:4; 8:5, 12
פֶּתִי	Uncommitted, simple	1:4, 22; 9:4; 14:15, 18; 19:25; 21:11
צֶדֶק	Righteousness	1:3; 2:9; 16:13; 25:5; 31:9
צַדִּיק	Righteous	2:20; 9:9; 10:11, 16, 21; 12:12; 29:7
רָשָׁע	Wicked	4:14–19; 10:6, 32; 12:5, 10
שֶׂכֶל	Intelligence, good sense	12:8; 16:22; 19:11
תְּבוּנָה	Understanding	2:6; 14:29; 20:5; 24:3
תַּהְפֻּכוֹת	Perversity, perversely	2:12
תַּחְבֻּלוֹת	Guidance	1:5
תּוֹרָה	Instruction, teaching	1:8; 3:1; 4:2; 7:2; 29:18; 31:26
תּוּשִׁיָּה	Resourcefulness	3:27–30

Appendix 2

Glossary of Key Terms/Concepts in Proverbs

Crooked

עִקְּשׁוּת. n. fem., abstract pl. **crooked.** A term for uneven terrain that aligns with the path metaphor of Proverbs and is used metaphorically to connote the twisted nature of certain character types and their speech. Prov 4:24; 6:12 (For treatment in the commentary, see pp. 235, 263, 269.)

Cruel

אַכְזָרִי. adj. **ruthless.** A term that describes the cruel or merciless nature of one's character and their inhuman treatment of others. Prov 5:9. (For treatment in the commentary, see pp. 250, 387.)

Discerning

נָבוֹן. part. masc. **discerning**. As an exemplar of "understanding" (בין), the discerning manifest their understanding through their pursuit of knowledge, their intimate relationship with wisdom, their speech, and their acceptance of rebuke. Prov 1:5; 10:13; 14:33; 15:14; 19:25. (For treatment in the commentary, see pp. 114, 367, 415.)

Discretion, Scheme

מְזִמָּה. n. fem. **discretion, scheme**. A term that denotes one's internal plans or intentions. In the light of the purpose of these plans or intentions, the term is construed positively or negatively in Proverbs. From a positive perspective, מְזִמָּה is associated with wisdom, understanding, and knowledge; it is an instrumental virtue that conveys prudent planning. From a negative perspective, מְזִמָּה connotes malicious scheming. Prov 1:4; 2:11; 3:21; 8:12; 12:2; 14:17; 24:8. (For treatment in the commentary, see pp. 113, 171, 310, 537.)

Fear of YHWH

יִרְאַת יְהוָה. **fear of YHWH**. A mode of being that serves as the fundamental prerequisite for the acquisition of wisdom and virtue in Proverbs. This posture is formed in relationship with YHWH and through knowledge of his will. It is a perspectival posture that recognizes one's creaturehood, contingency, and dependence on YHWH. This mode of being represents first principle of wisdom *and* the first fruit of wisdom *and* instruction in wisdom. In the light of its dynamic description across Proverbs, it is not surprising that one can grow in one's understanding of the fear of YHWH. And it is not surprising that the fear of YHWH is bound up with humility. Prov 1:7; 2:5; 8:13; 9:10; 15:33; 22:4. (For treatment in the commentary, see pp. 115–16, 310, 339.)

Fool

אֱוִיל. n. masc. **fool**. This species of fool is unmalleable and morally obstinate. As a figure who despises instruction, this type of fool is unable to learn. While a rod of discipline may remove folly (אִוֶּלֶת; Prov 22:15) from a youth's heart, even the most severe forms of discipline prove ineffective in extracting folly (אִוֶּלֶת; Prov 27:22) from this species of fool. Prov 1:7; 27:22. (For treatment in the commentary, see p. 565.)

כְּסִיל. n. masc. **fool**. Whereas the אֱוִיל is morally obstinate, the כְּסִיל is thoughtless, insensitive, and incompetent. The problem with this species of fool is neither the intellect nor a lack of propositional knowledge. The problem with this type of fool is their lack of perspectival knowledge. They fail to see themselves and the world in relationship with YHWH. Accordingly, the fool is self-centered, bent on evil, and inclined to immoderation because of their inability to assess situations. Prov 10:1, 26:1–12. (For treatment in the commentary, see p. 569.)

See also Intelligence, Good Sense, Lacking Sense, Uncommitted/Simple.

Guidance

תַּחְבֻּלוֹת. n. fem., abstract pl. **guidance**. A term pertaining to nautical expertise that Proverbs deploys in a moral sense to connote the ability to navigate the discrete circumstances of life. Prov 1:5. (For treatment in the commentary, see pp. 114–15).

Instruction, Discipline

מוּסָר. n. masc. **instruction, discipline**. The book of Proverbs traffics in instruction. This instruction is cast in a variety of different forms, ranging from exhortation and motivation to warning and rebuke. And it includes both verbal instruction as well as physical discipline, each of which are designed to cultivate wisdom and virtue through guidance and correction. Prov 1:2; 3:11; 5:12; 12:1; 22:15. (For treatment in the commentary, see pp. 111–12.)

Instruction, Learning

לֶקַח. n. masc. **instruction, learning**. A term that describes the verbal quality of teaching or instruction, rather than its content. The term is used as a cipher for the teaching of Proverbs in general as well as the instruction of the parents in particular. And it is used in specific instances to convey the power or persuasiveness of verbal instruction. Prov 1:5; 4:2; 7:21; 9:9; 16:21, 23. (For treatment in the commentary, see pp. 213, 293.)

Instruction, Teaching

תּוֹרָה. n. fem. **instruction, teaching**. A shorthand designation for the guidance of the parents, the teaching of the wise, or norms the govern the life of both the individual and the community. While the covenantal connotations of the term are not foregrounded in Proverbs, it is important to note that the teaching of the parents and the wise as well as the norms of the community are consonant with the form of life outlined in Israel's covenantal tradition. Prov 1:8; 3:1; 4:2; 7:2; 29:18; 31:26. (For treatment in the commentary, see p. 132.)

Intelligence, Good Sense

שֵׂכֶל. n. masc. **intelligence, good sense.** As a virtue intimately related to the perceptive, intelligence or good sense captures the discernment of the prudent, who interpret people and circumstances as well as acts and consequences in an insightful fashion. Prov 12:8; 16:22; 19:11. (For treatment in the commentary, see pp. 445–64.)

See also Fool, Senseless.

Life

חַי. n. masc. **life.** Life constitutes the quintessential reward for one who is wise and virtuous. Proverbs defines this reward as a life of personal flourishing in relation to God and members of the community. In accord with the underdeveloped eschatology of the Old Testament's witness, Proverbs does not construe life in terms of eternal life or immorality. But it is important to note that some sayings are patient with an eschatological understanding of life (e.g., Prov 12:28; 15:24). Prov 3:22; 8:35; 9:11; 10:16; 12:28; 16:22. (For treatment in the commentary, see p. 368.)

Outsider, Adulteress

נָכְרִיָּה. adj. fem. **outsider, adulteress.** A term used to the describe the seductive woman in Proverbs, especially in Proverbs 1–9. Together with the designation "strange" (see below), the term tends to function as a social designation, denoting foreignness. Like the adjective "strange," the descriptive term is used to portray the woman as "other," that is, as outside the boundaries of what is socially, legally, or sexually appropriate. Prov 2:16; 5:20; 7:5; 23:27. (For treatment in the commentary, see p. 172.)

Also see "strange."

Path, Way

אֹרַח. n. **path, way.** A term that specifies the nature and shape of one's way of life, rather particular behaviors that manifest a way of life. Prov 1:19; 2:13; 8:20; 10:17; 12:28; 22:25.

דֶּרֶךְ. n. **path, way.** A general term that connotes the manner of one's life manifest in particular actions. Prov 1:15, 31; 2:12; 3:23; 4:26; 12:15; 16:2. (For discussion in the commentary, see on 4:10–19; Structure and Form, p. 220; Canonical and Theological Significance, pp. 227–28.)

מְסִלָּה. n. fem. **highway, way**. A term for a highway or main road that is even and free of obstacles. Proverbs foregrounds the metaphorical sense of the term to describe the orientation, stature, and security of moral character types. Prov 16:17. (For treatment in the commentary, see p. 444.)

מַעְגָּל. n. masc. **path, way**. A term that leverages the phenomena of cart tracks on a path to convey the impression and results of one's way of life. Prov 2:9; 4:11; 5:21.

נְתִיבָה. n. fem. **path, way**. A term that connotes one's lifestyle and course of life. Prov 1:15; 3:17; 7:25; 8:20; 12:28.

Taken together, these discrete terms fund the root metaphor of the book of Proverbs: life is a path. Proverbs maximizes the metaphorical entailments of the way or path to describe one's character, movements, orientation, course of life, and the consequences associated with one's behavior. (For treatment in the commentary, see pp. 84–87, 121, 229.)

Perceptive, Prudent

מַשְׂכִּיל. part. masc. **perceptive, prudent**. This species of the wise is characterized by perception and discernment. The prudent are competent characters, who possess the ability to read people and situations so as to act in the right way at the right time. Prov 10:5, 19; 14:35; 16:20. (For treatment in the commentary, see p. 364.)

Resourcefulness

תֻּשִׁיָּה. n. fem. **resourcefulness**. The ability to think clearly, especially in the exercise of power. Prov 3:27–30. (For treatment in the commentary, see p. 200).

Righteousness, Righteous

צֶדֶק. n. masc. **righteousness**. A moral virtue that denotes right or virtuous being and behavior in accord with some standard. While this standard is implicit in Proverbs, it appears that the norm for righteousness is God's being and actions. Prov 1:3; 2:9; 16:13; 25:5; 31:9. (For treatment in the commentary, see pp. 321–23.)

צַדִּיק. adj. masc. **righteous**. The righteous person is Proverbs' moral exemplar, the character type who epitomizes moral virtue and human flourishing. In accord with their characterization, the righteous participate in and imitate God's righteousness. This figure exhibits a form of life that is desirable. In so doing, the righteous induce and direct desire to a life of wisdom and virtue. The righteous tend to be depicted in relation to others. Among other things, they are characterized by justice, loyalty, generosity, mercy, and honesty. They nourish the community and serve as a path to life. Prov 2:20; 9:9; 10:11, 16, 21; 12:12; 29:7. (For treatment in the commentary, see Canonical and Theological Significance, pp. 424–28.)

Scoffer

לֵץ. n. masc. **scoffer**. This character is the embodiment of hubris in Proverbs. The scoffer refuses to listen to rebuke and, by implication, fails to receive correction from others. Prov 1:22; 9:7–8; 14:6. (For treatment in the commentary, see p. 338.)

Scoundrel

אָדָם־, אִישׁ־בְּלִיַּעַל. **scoundrel**. The attitudes and actions of this character type epitomize those attitudes and actions that YHWH despises. As a person devoid of moral character and prone to all forms of depravity, this figure is classified among idolaters, rapists, murders, slanderers, and those who distort justice elsewhere in the Old Testament. Prov 6:12–15; 16:27. (For treatment in the commentary, see pp. 269–70.)

Senseless, Lacks Sense

חֲסַר־לֵב. **senseless, lacks sense**. As the characterization suggests, the senseless is one who lacks a heart or mind. That is, this figure possesses an impoverished moral and intellectual essence. Accordingly, this character type is marked by rashness and vain pursuits. Prov 7:7; 10:13, 21. (For treatment in the commentary, see pp. 289–90, 337n25.)

Shrewd, Shrewdness

עָרוּם. adj. masc. **shrewd**. A character type marked by perception and discretion. This figure perceives the nature of actions, understands their consequences, and discerns the appropriate form of action. Prov 12:16, 23; 14:8, 15, 18. (For treatment in the commentary, see pp. 408–9.)

עָרְמָה. n. fem. **shrewdness**. A faculty of judgment that enables a person to craft plans or devise practices to achieve a particular outcome. While shrewdness carries negative connotations related to craftiness or deception elsewhere in the Old Testament, it is used in a positive sense in Proverbs. Prov 1:4; 8:5, 12. (For treatment in the commentary, see p. 113.)

Sluggard

עָצֵל. adj. masc. **sluggard**. As a figure who epitomizes the vice of sloth, the sluggard fails to live in accord with the grain of creation. This failure to live in accord with the rhythm of reality has deleterious effects for both the sluggard as well as members of the community. Prov 6:6–11; 10:26; 26:13–16. (For treatment in the commentary, see pp. 266–68.)

Strange

זָרָה. adj. fem. **strange**. A term used to the describe the seductive woman in Proverbs, especially in Proverbs 1–9. While the term is used elsewhere in the Old Testament to designate Israelites outside the nuclear family as well as to describe ethnic foreignness and apostasy with foreign women, across Proverbs it is used to portray the woman as "other," that is, as outside the boundaries of what is socially, legally, or sexually appropriate. Prov 2:16; 5:3, 20; 7:5; 22:14. (For treatment in the commentary, see pp. 172–73.)

Also see "outsider."

נָכְרִיָּה. adj. fem. **outsider**. A social designation that tends to denote ethnic or national foreignness. Prov 2:16–19. (For treatment in the commentary, see pp. 172–73.)

Uncommitted, Simple

פֶּתִי. n. masc. **uncommitted, simple**. As one of the principal addressees of Proverbs, the uncommitted occupy a liminal moral state. This figure is neither wise nor foolish, neither righteous nor wicked. The uncommitted are inexperienced, prone to folly, and easily seduced; but this character type is also malleable and capable of being shaped in accord with a life of wisdom and virtue. Prov 1:4, 22; 9:4; 14:15, 18; 19:25; 21:11. (For treatment in the commentary, see pp. 148, 337n25.)

Understanding

בִּינָה. n. fem. **understanding**. Understanding is intimately related to both wisdom (חָכְמָה) and a synonymous Hebrew term for understanding (תְּבוּנָה). Following Michael Fox, בִּינָה denotes mental thoughts and interpretations as well as their communication and application through speech and comprehension (Fox, *Proverbs 1–9*, 30, 37–38). Prov 3:5; 4:1, 5, 7; 7:4; 23:23. (For treatment in the commentary, see p. 215.)

תְּבוּנָה. n. fem. **understanding**. As noted above, this term is intimately related to both wisdom (חָכְמָה) and a synonymous Hebrew term for understanding (בִּינָה). Following Michael Fox, תְּבוּנָה lives in the realm of *action* rather than conceptual thought; it refers to the application of thought in specific circumstances, that is, a "know-how" as opposed to a "knowing-that" (Fox, *Proverbs 1–9*, 37–38). Prov 2:6; 14:29; 20:5; 24:3. (For treatment in the commentary, see p. 536.)

Upright

יָשָׁר. adj. masc. **upright**. An ethical designation that denotes one's moral posture and strength. The upright are marked by a strong, physically straight posture, which exemplifies their moral fortitude. This vertically straight posture evinces the upright's vertical relationship with YHWH. Prov 2:21; 12:6; 14:2. (For treatment in the commentary, see pp. 406–7.)

Wicked

רָשָׁע. adj. masc. **wicked**. As the moral antithesis to the righteous, the wicked tend to be depicted in relation to others. Among other things, this figure is marked by greed, violence, deceit, and perverse speech that destroys members of the community. Prov 4:14–19; 10:6, 32; 12:5, 10. (For treatment in the commentary, see pp. 224–26.)

Wisdom

חָכְמָה. n. fem. **wisdom**. While wisdom involves a cognitive or intellectual grasp of knowledge pertaining to the good life, the witness of Proverbs indicates that wisdom is much more than this. Wisdom is a skilled practice; it involves knowing the good, loving the good, and doing the good. This holistic sense of wisdom is sketched across Proverbs' characterization of the wise person. And this holistic sense of wisdom is embodied in the figures of Lady Wisdom and the valiant women. Lady Wisdom epitomizes all that is desirable. She possesses all the virtues Proverbs seeks to inculcate within readers; and as a personified figure, Lady Wisdom indicates that wisdom is acquired in interpersonal relationship. The valiant woman is the concrete embodiment of wisdom across a life. Her portrait evinces that wisdom is the exercise of power for the benefit of the other. Whether wisdom is profiled through the wise person, Lady Wisdom, or the valiant woman, Proverbs suggests that genuine wisdom imitates and enacts God's wisdom. Prov 1:2; 2:6; 3:19; 8:1–36; 14:6, 33; 24:3. (For treatment in the commentary, see pp. 301–20.)

Wise

חָכָם. adj. masc. **wise**. The wise person epitomizes intellectual virtue across Proverbs. This character type is teachable. The wise receive correction and internalize knowledge. And the wise exemplify perception and discretion. They possess the intellectual ability to interpret people, evaluate specific circumstances, consider the consequences associated with actions, and act in accord with wisdom. Prov 9:8; 10:8, 14; 12:15; 14:16; 16:21. (For treatment in the commentary, see pp. 338, 365.)

Wise in His Own Eyes

חָכָם בְּעֵינָיו. **wise in his own eyes**. This characterization is among the most fatal in Proverbs. One wise in one's own eyes engages self-deception through self-evaluation. This person is unable to see and know themselves before the face of the Other. And they are unable to learn from others. No wonder this figure is unable to gain wisdom; it is not surprising that there is more hope than a fool than for this personage. Prov 26:5, 12. (For treatment in the commentary, see p. 565.)

Scripture and Extrabiblical Index

Old Testament

Genesis

Exodus

Leviticus

Numbers

1 Samuel

2 Samuel

1 Kings

2 Kings

1 Chronicles

2 Chronicles

Ezra

Nehemiah

Esther

Job

Psalms

Proverbs

Subject Index

Author Index